FROM A "RACE OF MASTERS" TO A "MASTER RACE": 1948 to 1848
Eugenics Anthology - Vol. #1
Copyright © A.E. Samaan with Library Without Walls, LLC - 2020

Cover design concept by A.E. Samaan with with Mariana Garcia Pizá.
Interior graphics, design, and images by A.E. Samaan.
All rights reserved.

ISBN-13: 978-1-954249-06-6 (Deluxe Format)
ISBN-10: 1954249063
ISBN (Kindle): 978-0-9964163-7-5
ISBN (ePub): 978-0-9964163-4-4
Library of Congress: 2020920428

First circulated as a preliminary Advanced Readers Copy through CreateSpace.com by A.E. Samaan on Jan. 2013: ISBN-13: 978-0615747880, ISBN-10: 0615747884, ISBN (Digital Edition): 978-1-62660-000-3, and Library of Congress: 2012924377

Samaan, A.E., 1968 -
From a "Race of Masters" to a "Master Race": 1948 to 1848

Library Without Walls, LLC., 2020.
Knoxville, TN – Nov. 9th, 2020

~~~~~~

1. The Holocaust - History – Eugenics. 2. Nazi Era - History - 20th century. 3. Hitler, Adolf, 1889-1945 - World War II. 4. Sceintific racism – Utopian Studies. 5. National Socialism - philosophy. 6. race laws - anti-miscegenation - segregation. 7. Slavery - History - civil rights legislation. 8. Darwin, Charles, 1809-1882 -Evolutionary theory – Population Control – Nuremberg Trials.

CENTER FOR MEDICINE AFTER THE HOLOCAUST:

Although German violations of basic medical ethics are well documented, they are virtually unknown by today's students in the health sciences. It's rarely discussed that American eugenicists played a critical role in the development of German "racial hygiene" policies. Although healthcare in Western democracies is arguably the best in the world today, we should pause and reflect upon the similarities to German medicine ethics in the 1930s. There is a resurgence of interest in eugenics and biological determinism following the success of the Human Genome Project, violating medical ethics. Controversy persists regarding abortion, pre-implantation genetic diagnosis, embryonic stem cell research, assisted suicide, and euthanasia. The original Hippocratic Oath is in disrepute. Healthcare ethics is being formulated at a centralized, national level.

The mission of the Center for Medicine after the Holocaust (CMATH) is to challenge doctors, nurses, and bio-scientists to personally confront the medical ethics of the Holocaust and apply that knowledge to contemporary practice and research, being mindful of the Hippocratic Oath with every step. CMATH is concerned that healthcare personnel, like all human beings, have the capacity to believe they are doing good when they are actually doing harm.

By studying the past, we hope to provide knowledge for today that will prevent the repetition of previous errors and lead to wisdom in future doctors, nurses, bio-scientists, and healthcare policymakers. If the best physicians, nurses, and scientists of the early 20th century could sacrifice their patients for utopian goals, can we be certain that we will not do the same?

EVOLUTION OF THE COVER ART:

The original 2013 A.R.C. publishing of this book took 10 to 15 years to research. Of all the original research conducted, one memory stands out; the bone-chilling experience of first seeing actual Nazi paraphernalia. It is not an experience many Americans have, as you typically have to travel to Belgium or the Alsace border between France and Germany to see the exceptionally large quantity of artifacts left behind. Seeing, and more importantly actually being able to touch and feel, makes the horrid history of Hitler's regime palpable and real.

I wanted to share that experience, admittedly in a limited scope, with the reader. I believe that history can only be 'denied' if it becomes too fictionalized and distant. The picture of the Nazi armband that was utilized as the background to the 2013 cover is a photo of an authentic Nazi armband. A donation was made to the museum for their kindness. (www.GeneralPattonMuseum.com)

A.E. Samaan is a CMATH Champion. For more information, visit AESamaan.com

> "There is nothing new in the world
> but the history you do not know"
> ~ Harry S. Truman ~

My pen name is a tribute to my paternal grandfather.
Both of my grandfathers are deserving of recognition.
They are two men whom lived a moral life
amidst a reign of chaos and corruption.
~ December 21, 2012 ~

From a "Race of Masters"

c. 1948 «» c. 1848

to a "Master Race"

WRITTEN BY: A.E. Samaan
www.RaceOfMasters.com

Vol. #1
Eugenics Anthology
www.EugenicsAnthology.com

Table of Contents

Author's Note on Methods and Standards 4
Prologue is Past 7

Chap. 1: From the Doctors' Trial to 1941 11

- Sec. 1 - With the Embers Still Burning: 11
- Sec. 2 - A Conflict of Interests: 14
- Sec. 3 - A Legal Quagmire: 25
- Sec. 4 - The "Silence of Decades": 38
- Sec. 5 - "Mens Rea": 46
- Sec. 6 - Sterilizing the "Greatest Generation": 53
- Sec. 7 - Merchants of Light: 57
- Sec. 8 - Medicine Gone Mad? 68
- Sec. 9 - From "Agony of Living" to "Lives Not Worth Living": 72

Chap. 2: 1940 to 1936 76

- Sec. 1 - From War to the Final Solution (or Vise Versa): 76
- Sec. 2 - Lothrop Stoddard's "Into the Darkness": 81
- Sec. 3 - Julian Huxley's "Eugenics Manifesto": 88
- Sec. 4 - Margaret Sanger's "Negro Project": 94
- Sec. 5 - From *Kristallnacht* to "Man of the Year": 100
- Sec. 6 - From "Baby Knauer" to the T4 Euthanasia Program: 103
- Sec. 7 - Hitler's Exhibition of "Degenerate Art": 112
- Sec. 8 - "Erbkrank": 119
- Sec. 9 - Pandora's Book: 122

Chap. 3: 1935 to 1931 134

- Sec. 1 - Edward Bellamy, "The Great American Prophet": 134
- Sec. 2 - The Unknown Man: 145
- Sec. 3 - The Book is the Thing That Reveals the ...: 151
- Sec. 4 - "Nazi War on Cancer": 164
- Sec. 5 - Nazi Origins of the "Precautionary Principle": 170
- Sec. 6 - Controlling Culture or the Culture of Control? 180
- Sec. 7 - From the Enabling Act to *"Führerprinzip"*: 186
- Sec. 8 - Who Voted for Hitler? 193
- Sec. 9 - From "American Adonis" to Hitler's "Aryan Man": 204
- Sec. 10 - Was It Julian Huxley's "Brave New World"? 208

Chap. 4: 1930 to 1926 217

- Sec. 1 - "Central Planning" to Nationalized "Socialism": 217
- Sec. 2 - Ernst Rüdin, "Merchant of Light": 225
- Sec. 3 - From Welfare to Subordination: 232
- Sec. 4 - Three Generations, One Supreme Imbecile: 237
- Sec. 5 - From Homosapien to Hominoidea: 249
- Sec. 6 - Was Leonard Darwin Complicit in "Eugenocide"? 254

Chap. 5: 1925 to 1921 268

- Sec. 1 - From "Looking Backwards" to "Mein Kampf": 268
- Sec. 2 - The A.C.L.U.'s Circus Monkey: 291
- Sec. 3 - From Revolutionary to Statesman: 297
- Sec. 4 - One-World Immigration Controls: 301
- Sec. 5 - From Oppressed to Oppressor: 317
- Sec. 6 - From "Control" of Births to "Control" of People: 331

Chap. 6: 1920 to 1916 343

- Sec. 1 - Nietzsche's "Merchants of Light": 343
- Sec. 2 - Where Was the A.C.L.U. in the Era of Eugenics? 359
- Sec. 3 - From the Palmer Raids to Immigration Controls: 362
- Sec. 4 - Who Was J.F. Lehmann? 366
- Sec. 5 - German Eugenics in Dissaray: 371
- Sec. 6 - The "Racialist" vs. the "Racist": 375
- Sec. 7 - From Darwin to American Eugenics: 381
- Sec. 8 - Goethe's "Federation" of Racialist Institutions: 387

Chap. 7: 1915 to 1911 396

- SEC. 1 - UNION, DISUNION, & THE GREAT WAR: 396
- SEC. 3 - "THE BLACK STORK": 403
- SEC. 4 - NATIONALIZED MEDICINE & EUGENIC SUBORDINATION: 412
- SEC. 5 - GENETICS; THE LEGITIMATE SCIENCE OF HEREDITY: 421
- SEC. 6 - ALL IN THE FAMILY: 426
- SEC. 7 - FROM "THE WILL-TO-LIVE" TO "THE WILL-TO-POWER": 435
- SEC. 8 - FRANCIS GALTON'S "KANTSAYWHERE": 440

Chap. 8: 1910 to 1906 450

- SEC. 1 - TOWARDS A COLLECTIVE GUILT??? 450
- SEC. 2 - EUGEN FISCHER'S "REHOBOTH BASTARDS": 453
- SEC. 3 - "HARD" VS. "SOFT" SCIENCE: 457
- SEC. 4 - ADOLF HITLER'S "IDEAL STATE": 461

Chap. 9: 1905 to 1901 474

- SEC. 1 - "IN THAT HOUR IT BEGAN...": 474
- SEC. 2 - FROM "MITTGART" TO "LEBENSRAUM": 478
- SEC. 4 - MEIN BÜCHER: 484

Chap. 10: 1900 501

- SEC. 1 - FROM GOOD PUPIL TO FAITHFUL APOSTLE: 501
- SEC. 2 - WHERE WAS THE HOLOCAUST BY THE "FASCISTS"? 514
- SEC. 3 - A CONSPICUOUS REVERSAL OF ROLES: 528

Chap. 11: 1899 to 1895 540

- SEC. 1 - THE "*ÜBER ETHIK*": 540
- SEC. 2 - WHERE WAS THE N.A.A.C.P. DURING THE EUGENICS ERA? 552
- SEC. 3 - WILHELM SCHALLMAYER'S COLLECTIVIST UTOPIAS: 557
- SEC. 4 - "SEPARATE BUT EQUAL": 564
- SEC. 5 - FROM "COMMUNISME" TO "RASSENHYGIENE": 571

Chap. 12: 1894 to 1890 584

- SEC. 1 - FASHIONING THE NOOSE THAT THEY WILL HANG YOU BY: 584
- SEC. 2 - THOMAS HENRY HUXLEY'S "*PROLEGOMENA*": 592
- SEC. 4 - HARVARD'S CHARLES B. DAVENPORT 599

Chap. 13: 1889 to 1885 612

- SEC. 1 - GIVING BIRTH TO THE 20TH CENTURY: 612
- SEC. 2 - BELLAMY'S "LOOKING BACKWARD" IS PUBLISHED: 615
- SEC. 3 - "FORGOTTEN FATHERLAND": 622

Chap. 14: 1884 to 1880 628

- SEC. 1 - PACE V. ALABAMA: 628
- SEC. 2 - WEISMANN'S "GERM-PLASM": 634

Chap. 15: 1879 to 1875 639

- SEC. 1 - FROM "STIRPICULTURE" TO "EUGENICS": 639
- SEC. 2 - "HUMAN ZOOS" – EVOLUTION ON DISPLAY: 648
- SEC. 3 - THE "SAVAGE DEBATE": 656
- SEC. 4 - FROM "ATAVISM" TO "DEGENERATION": 662

Chap. 16: 1874 to 1870 666

- SEC. 1 - FROM RESERVATION TO CONCENTRATION CAMP: 666
- SEC. 2 - FROM "SCIENTISM," TO "RACIALISM," TO "RACISM": 675
- SEC. 3 - FROM "AQUIRED" TO "UNIT" CHARCTERISTICS: 689

Chap. 17: 1869 to 1865 697

- SEC. 1 - INHERITED LEGITIMACY: 697
- SEC. 2 - THE ESSENCE OF ZEALOTRY: 703

Chap. 18: 1864 to 1860 715

- SEC. 1 - MAKING THE "THEORY" THE ONLY THEORY: 715
- SEC. 2 - KARL MARX ON DARWINISM & EUGENIC SUBORDINATION: 723

Chap. 19: 1859 to 1848 731

- SEC. 1 - FROM A "MASTER RACE" TO A "RACE OF MASTERS": 731
- SEC. 3 - DE-EVOLUTION, DEGENERATION, AND LIBERATION: 738

Past is Prologue 752
Bibliography & Notes 768

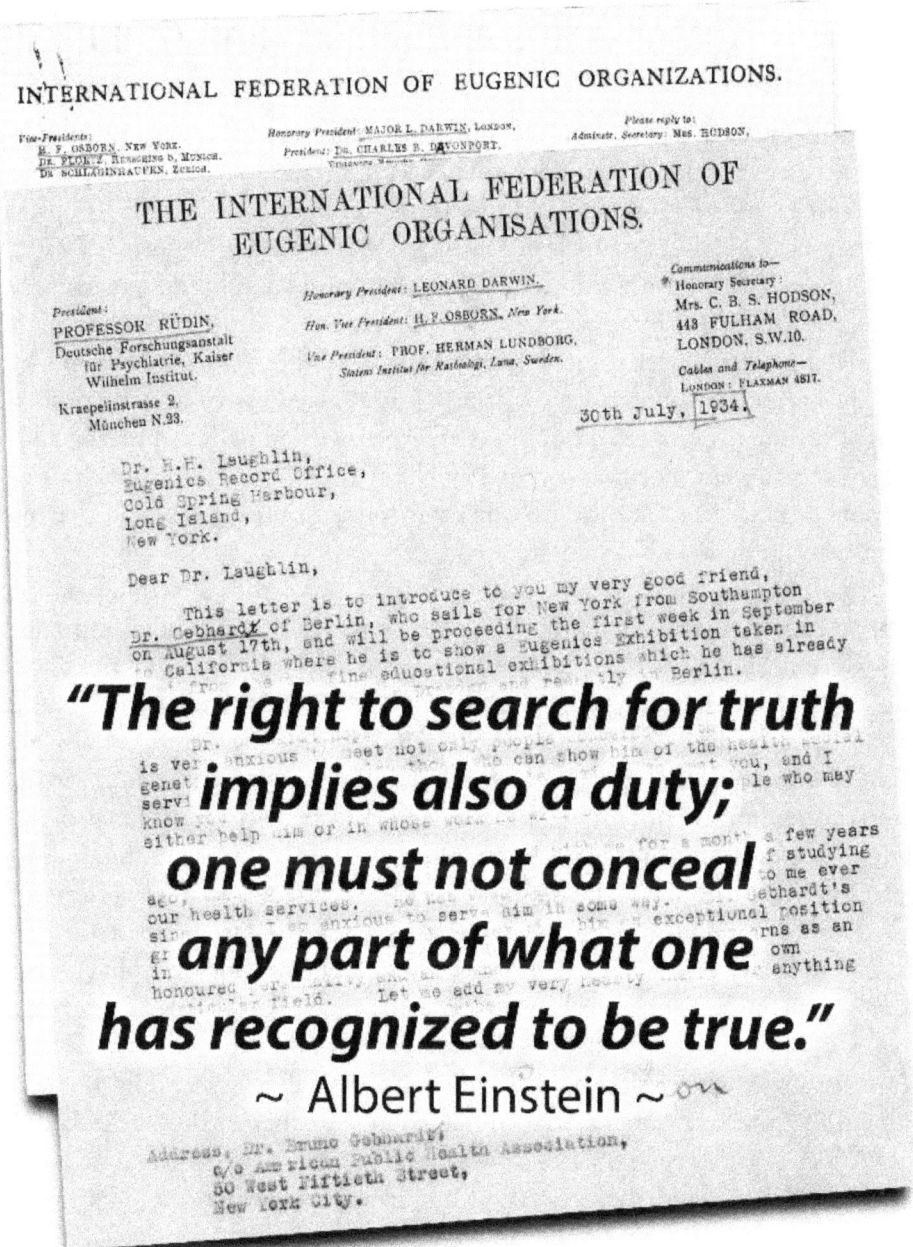

FIGURE 1: CORRESPONDENCE BETWEEN THE AMERICAN, BRITISH, AND THE GERMAN EUGENICISTS IN CHARGE OF HITLER'S RACIAL POLICIES, WRITTEN ON THE LETTERHEAD OF THE INTERNATIONAL FEDERATION OF EUGENIC ORGANIZATIONS. THE ORGANIZATION'S LEADERSHIP AS PRESENTED ON ITS LETTERHEAD INCLUDES LEONARD DARWIN, CHARLES B. DAVENPORT, HARRY H. LAUGHLIN, ERNST RÜDIN, HENRY FAIRFIELD OSBORN, AND ALFRED PLOETZ. (HEREIN PUBLISHED AND PRINTED FOR THE FIRST TIME WITH PERMISSION OF THE SPECIAL COLLECTIONS DEPARTMENT AT TRUMAN UNIVERSITY. — JULY 30TH, 1934 LETTER FROM CORA HODSON TO H.H. LAUGHLIN — BOX-C-4-4:7)

Author's Note on Methods and Standards:

ON METHODS: I have employed a peculiar approach. It is a result of my life-long experience in the paper manufacturing and publishing industry. I am part of a generation that was born into age-old publishing technology, which had improved in efficiency, but not substantially changed since the Industrial Revolution. I had the opportunity of working with old Heidelberg letterpresses and binding machinery. I had the pleasure of typesetting pages letter by letter, a process that I did not sufficiently appreciate at the time. I learned how to publish a tome with physical printing plates and the annoyance of printing inks. Needless to say, the process I was taught for the printing of a book was an expensive and tedious process, and in many ways, more than a skill and probably closer to an art. Naturally, I was that much more astonished to see the first direct-to-press printing press and delighted when on-demand digital publishing first emerged.

Technology has upended an entire industry. Today, the only thing standing between an author's manuscript and a bound tome is a click of a mouse. The author can easily create all the graphics, book cover design, and formatting of the book; a process that used to span several industries and professions. Paperback books are now very easy to make. What used to be a ceremonious event, is now not any more ceremonious than ordering underpants from an online service. As such, it seems to me that the traditional publishing process needs to be reversed. The paperback should go first, and the hardbound book after, once all the quirks of first editions are corrected. The hardbound should be reserved for the final edition, perfected for all posterity. This realization came to me when I wrote the first draft of this book in 2012. I realized I had enough research to write not one, not two, but maybe as many as seven books on this subject. I decided to release an A.R.C. (Advanced Readers' Copy) of "Race of Masters" to preserve the work, and as a way of reaching out to interested parties, knowing full well that the final version would be heavily edited and that much of the material contained in the A.R.C. would be pulled and distributed amongst several volumes of a series.

In 20/20 hindsight, the process accomplished its purpose. I published the 2013 A.R.C. version of this book and immediately started working on "H.H. Laughlin: American Scientist. American Progressive. Nazi Collaborator." Much to my pleasant surprise, the two initial printings garnered the attention of several figures in academia, namely Professor Ken Gemes of Birkbeck University of London, Garland Allen of Washington University of St. Louis, and Sheldon Rubenfeld, M.D. of Medicine After the Holocaust. I am eternally thankful for their support and encouragement. It is largely because of them that I find the motivation to persist upon the path of completing this series, groping for the puzzle pieces without the benefit of the final image in sight. Printing a temporary paperback as each milestone is reached provides a much-needed sense of accomplishment along the path of this decades-long project, as well as allowing me to share the findings with colleagues as I go along.

ON STANDARDS: I am not part of academia, and many of my accomplishments are a result of questioning prevailing wisdom and standards. The methodology described here is but one aspect of how this affects my writing. That said, this book can be described as a book on the history of history. We are quickly coming up on the 100th anniversary of World War II and The Holocaust. Our understanding, our interpretation of these catastrophes still shape the direction of the future. This knowledge was formed by the books, journals, speeches, movies and newspaper articles that attempted to come to terms with the unprecedented nature of the "crimes against humanity." These post-WWII attempts at clarity are as important to this analysis as the documentation leading up to and during these catastrophic events. As such, books written decades ago are now part of history themselves and will generally be treated no differently than other primary sources.

Everything in Holocaust history began to crumble with the Berlin Wall, and Germany united. The once accepted narrative of Holocaust history forever changed once the USSR fell, and the rest of the world had access to what amounted to more than half the documentary evidence and historical sites. Furthermore, the fall of the Berlin Wall and the Iron Curtain seems to coincide with a time when the World War II generation in Germany was dying away, and sources and evidence once closely guarded became available to the archives and researchers.

Technology has also radically changed academic research just as drastically as it changed the paper and publishing industry. This is another concept that is difficult to explain to the younger generations. What was once scarcely accessible to the general public through the archives and journals, is now available to everyone. The clear majority of people that will come across this book will do so through search engines, not libraries, journals, or even a physical copy of the book itself. More often than not, the researcher of the 21st Century will see only the page that results from a Google Books query, and not have ready or even manageable access to the index or citation pages at the end of a physical copy of the book. It is for this reason that I have documented sources in-line or in footnotes on the same page whenever possible; for the ease of the online researcher and casual internet query. I have endeavored to be careful not to disrupt continuity and readability, if at all possible while employing this method of source documentation.

The world has changed, and drastically so as I write this on my 50th birthday. This was made wonderfully clear when I first uploaded the A.R.C. copy of this book in January of 2013 to Amazon.com, only to notice fifteen minutes later that someone had bought it in Germany. English is not my first language. So, the fact that technology empowers me to research archives throughout the world, books long forgotten, and write, publish, and sell an 800-page book all through my laptop still fascinates and inspires me.

A.E. Samaan, San Diego, CA. – November 30th, 2018

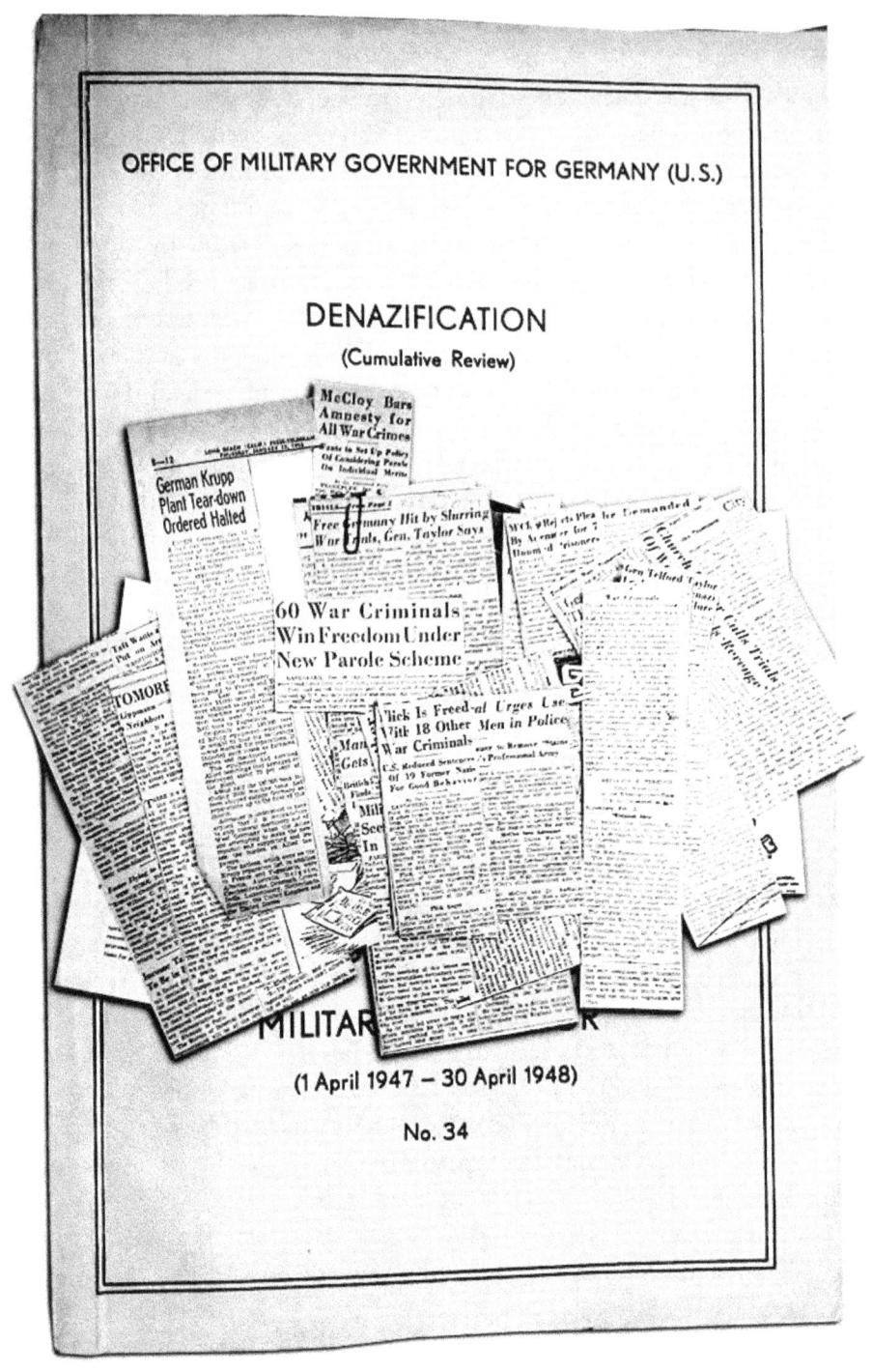

FIGURE 2: Brig. Gen., Telford Taylor's press clippings on Nazi war criminals being set free pictured here along with his copy of the official memorandum on Denazification policy. (Telford Taylor Papers, Colombia Univ.- SERIES XIX)

Prologue is Past

Both Japan and Germany had just surrendered, as the Vietnam War and Israeli-Palestinian conflicts commenced. The collective psyche of the world had suffered successive jolts in 1945, first with the visual evidence of Hitler's concentration camps publicly revealed in April and May, and then with the nuclear annihilation of Hiroshima and Nagasaki in August of 1945. World War II was the deadliest military conflict in history. More than 60 million people had perished during the war. It seemed as if antiquity had ripped itself apart to give birth to an emerging modern era. This modernity had been born of unimaginable carnage and unprecedented horrors. Humanity grasped for answers and explanations. President Truman's radio address of August 9, 1945, reminded its audience what World War II had essentially been about.

> Our victory in Europe was more than a victory of arms. It was a victory of one way of life over another. It was a victory of an ideal founded on the rights of the common man, on the dignity of the human being, on the conception of the State as the servant — and not the master — of its people. (trumanlibrary.org - 97. Radio Report to the American People on the Potsdam Conference)

War is incidental to ideology. Yet, this struggle between "master" and "servant" had neither begun nor ended with World War II. As President Truman uttered these words, a significant portion of the globe was descending into darkness behind the Iron Curtain, further prolonging the contentious debate about the proper role of government and the governed. Antiquity clashed with modernity in World War II. The 100 years leading up to World War II saw wars of antiquated brutality increasingly employing modern armaments to answer this age-old contention between "master" and "servant." The world contemplated the series of events and gasped for explanations, and President Truman warned that victorious ideologies can be lost in the wake of victory:

> Any man who sees Europe now must realize that victory in a great war is not something you win once and for all, like victory in a ball game. Victory in a great war is something that must be won and kept won. It can be lost after you have won it — if you are careless or negligent or indifferent. (trumanlibrary.org - 97. Radio Report to the American People on the Potsdam Conference)

By this measure, can it be said that World War II adequately addressed and answered for all of posterity the proper relationship between the governed and the government, between "master" and "slave"? Have we, as President Truman stated, settled the question of the "dignity of the human being"? Our armies won militarily over the nation that proclaimed itself to be the "master race," and the Nuremberg Trials were supposed to have exposed for all posterity the erroneous ways of its barbaric ideology. Yet, the quintessential questions surrounding The Holocaust persist in our collective conscience. We persist in asking how the most educated nation in the world could have been enticed upon the path of mass murder and genocide. We still wonder where any responsible or sober minds were when Germany seemed to dispose of its humanity. Despite the many other wars of significance since the end of World War II, humanity remains fixated and perplexed by this one pivotal conflict, and answers to the questions sound more and more unconvincing as the passage of time allows us a broader perspective. We still cannot give an authoritative answer to that question posed so long ago: Why the "land of poets and thinkers," the most cultured nation of the era, was able to sustain such a formidable campaign of horrific barbarity.

Questions not properly answered linger. Those of us that grew up during the Cold War were living within the fog of war. Half, or even most, of World War II history was locked behind the Iron Curtain. However, a deluge of historical information has recently become available to Western scholars with the uniting of East and West Germany, the fall of the secretive USSR, and the release of previously classified documents in the United States and Britain. The end of the Cold War has produced a fresh perspective, whereas we were previously confined to one side of the Iron Curtain. The drastic polarity of the Cold War polemic has been largely relaxed, allowing introspection and reflection.

Most embarrassingly, we still buy into the excuse given by Hitler's henchmen at the Nuremberg Trials; we still operate on the myth of Adolf Hitler as the supernatural boogie man, the anti-Christ, the magician who was able to convince millions of otherwise sophisticated and cultured Germans into committing the most unspeakable crimes. The history we are told is more like the plot of some comic book, where a super-villain is spewed out of the depths of hell to use his supernatural powers to wreak havoc upon defenseless humanity. Ironically enough, it is the bombastic nature of this myth that has prepared a fertile ground for Holocaust denier. The idea that The Holocaust was an unanticipated outcome of a single man's will remains a fraudulent view of history, which has served only to cover up a more horrid reality and allow for the most ludicrous speculation to pass off as actual history.

With the fall of the Berlin Wall, German historians, especially, have been privy to a renaissance of evidence and documentation previously unavailable, and our view of World War II and Holocaust history is changing. One of these historians is Christian Pross. Pross has documented that catalyst in the recent surge in Holocaust history is that the generation that grew up in Hitler's Germany is dying, and documentation has become available that was not before:

> The system of silence, lies, half-truths, excuses, and angry denials of the last four decades is in retreat. The open debate about the Nazi past has raised the consciousness of many German doctors and of parts of the German public toward contemporary medical abuses. It has shaken the German doctors' self-image of infallibility, of a profession that stands above political and social forces and that presumably has always had a clean shirt and has acted out of noble, altruistic motives. (Pg. 47, Chap.: 3, "The Nazi Doctors and the Nuremberg Code: Human Rights in Human Experimentation", Oxford Univ. Press, 1992)

As a proximate result, the standard excuse given by Hitler's henchmen, that they were just following orders, is simply no longer tenable. The revelation is much more disconcerting, and more and more historians are coming to terms with the "rationality" of evil and discarding past notions of "irrational" mob behavior as the culprit. The depth and breadth of complicity by allegedly sober-minded professionals in Hitler's genocidal policies have resulted in a reformulation of our understanding of the forces that lead up to The Holocaust. Christian Pross clarifies:

> Anti-Semitism and racism can no longer be identified as the sole driving forces behind Nazi politics, nor can the Nazi power elite be viewed as a small group of deviant monsters who misled a supposedly passive constituency. (Pg. 32, "The Nazi Doctors and the Nuremberg Code: Human Rights in Human Experimentation", Oxford Univ. Press, 1992)

For the English-speaking world, the consequence of uncovering all these previously unavailable documents is the revelation of whom in England and the United States was in direct communication with the doctors and scientists of Hitler's Third Reich. Several generations have been told that the world was simply unaware of what was going on inside Hitler's Third Reich. Introspection is in order. This newly acquired clarity provided insight into just how indispensable many respected British and American institutions were to the creation of Hitler's eugenic state. The complicity pulls up the roots of The Holocaust. The mass murders commonly recognized as The Holocaust occupy only three to four years of Hitler's reign, yet the history of events that contributed to that final outcome occupies a 100-year trajectory. Adolf Hitler had not even been born when the movement intent on removing entire swaths of humanity began gathering momentum, and he was nothing but a brat when this movement had rooted itself in the most respected scientific, legal, legislative and medical institutions in the United States, England, and Germany. Adolf Hitler is long gone. These institutions remain, and they do so with a similar taint in their thinking. The most important of historical inquiries remain unanswered, seemingly intentionally, as these relationships remain politically inconvenient even today.

To make sense of the recent flow of documentation, we must trace our steps backward, beginning with the end, beginning with the explanations provided for all posterity at the Nuremberg Trials. We trace the origins of the ideology that fueled Nazism, not unlike tracing the path from a leaf down to the roots.

"Human kind cannot bear very much reality."
T.S. Eliot – 1935 – Murder in the Cathedral

Chap. 1: From the Doctors' Trial to 1941

POLITICS: THE LEAGUE OF NATIONS DISBANDS ITSELF AND TRANSFERS ITS MISSION TO THE UNITED NATIONS. • FRANKLIN D. ROOSEVELT IS INAUGURATED TO AN UNPRECEDENTED FOURTH TERM. AVIATOR CHARLES LINDBERGH TESTIFIES BEFORE THE US CONGRESS AND RECOMMENDS THAT THE UNITED STATES NEGOTIATE A NEUTRALITY PACT WITH ADOLF HITLER. • **EUROPEAN FRONT:** ADOLF HITLER AND HIS WIFE OF ONE DAY COMMIT SUICIDE AS THE RED ARMY APPROACHES. • **PACIFIC FRONT:** HO CHI MINH IS ELECTED PRESIDENT OF NORTH VIETNAM AND HIS FORCES BEGIN A WAR AGAINST THE OCCUPYING FRENCH FORCES. • **SCIENCE & TECHNOLOGY:** BONAMPAK IS FIRST VISITED BY NON-MAYANS. •THE ENIAC, THE FIRST COMPUTER BECOMES OPERATIONAL. ROCKET SCIENTIST WERNHER VON BRAUN AND 120 MEMBERS OF HIS TEAM SURRENDER TO US FORCES. – ARTHUR C. CLARKE PUTS FORWARD THE IDEA OF A COMMUNICATIONS SATELLITE. STEPHEN HAWKING IS BORN. NIKOLA TESLA DIES. ALBERT HOFMANN SELF ADMINISTERS THE DRUG LSD FOR THE FIRST TIME. • **LIFE:** ANIMAL FARM BY GEORGE ORWELL IS PUBLISHED. – GEORGE W. BUSH AND BILL CLINTON ARE BORN. EDVARD MUNCH AND WASSILY KANDINSKY DIE. DISNEY'S BAMBI AND DUMBO PREMIERE.

Sec. I - WITH THE EMBERS STILL BURNING:

The scientific community has done a pronounced amount of handwringing about its involvement in the atomic bomb's creation, and a disproportionately absent amount of soul-searching with respects to its creation of the science of eugenics. The 450,000 deaths due to the bomb are relatively small in the shadow of the many millions of dead as a result of National Socialism's eugenic campaign. The casualties of The Holocaust are the casualties of the science of eugenics, which so many scientists had actively campaigned for leading up to World War II. Yet, the scientific community has confronted its complicity in the "crimes against humanity" with collective silence and sometimes outright censorship.

The creation of the United Nations was the direct response to the collective shock the world experienced as the extreme violence reached its crescendo during the last years of the war. By the time the bomb was dropped on Hiroshima, Germany had already lost more than 5 million military personnel to the war, and about 2 million civilians. The USSR had lost approximately 9 million military personnel and 13 million civilians. The United States had already lost approximately 350,000 soldiers in the European Front, and another 100,000 in the Pacific Front. Humanity had outdone itself, and it grasped and groped for answers amidst these darkest of hours. A United Nations Conference was held in San Francisco in April–June 1945 for the establishment of an educational and cultural organization (ECO/CONF), which was convened in London from November 1st to the 16th, 1945 where 37 nations signed the Constitution of UNESCO. The first General Conference for UNESCO took place from November 19 to December 10, 1946, and elected Julian Huxley to Director-General.

Julian Huxley came from the distinguished Huxley family. His brother was the writer Aldous Huxley, and his paternal grandfather was Thomas Henry Huxley, otherwise known as "Darwin's Bulldog" for his controversial propagandizing of Darwin's Theory. Julian Huxley followed and extended the family's work. He was a proponent of natural selection and a devout Internationalist. He was a man of unparalleled elitist credentials. He was Secretary of the Zoological Society of London and a founding member of the World Wildlife Fund. Huxley would be recognized with a Special Award of the Lasker Foundation in the category Planned Parenthood – World Population in 1959, and was a prominent member of the British Eugenics Society and its president from 1959 to 1962.

Huxley's eugenic ideology is of importance. The whitewash of eugenics' role in the "crimes against humanity" was made readily apparent by Julian Huxley's 1946 statement as the first director of UNESCO. Julian Huxley spent a fortnight penning the 60-page document titled "UNESCO Its Purpose and Philosophy," where Huxley began by stating: "Biological inequality is, of course, the bedrock fact on which all of eugenics is predicated." Huxley continued:

> While there may be dispute over certain qualities, there can be none over a number of the most important, such as a healthy constitution, a high innate general intelligence, or a special aptitude such as that for mathematics or music. (unesco.org, Pg. 19, "UNESCO Its Purpose & Philosophy: A Preparatory Commission of UNESCO", Cat. No. 68197)

These were the justifications that Huxley and the eugenics movement used to organize humanity into an evolutionary hierarchy, and in turn to justify drastic intrusions into individual freedom and bodily integrity such as sterilization, segregation and ultimately euthanasia:

> At the moment, it is probable that the indirect effect of civilization is dysgenic instead of eugenic; and in any case it seems likely that the dead weight of genetic stupidity, physical weakness, mental instability, and disease-proneness, which already exist in the human species, will prove too great a burden for real progress to be achieved. Thus, even though it is quite a burden for real progress to be achieved. Thus, even though it is quite true that any radical eugenic policy will be for many years politically and psychologically impossible, it will be important for UNESCO to see that the eugenic problem is examined with the greatest care, and that the public mind is informed of the issues at stake so that much that now is unthinkable may at least become thinkable. (unesco.org, Pg. 19, "UNESCO Its Purpose & Philosophy", Cat. No. 68197)

At minimum, this statement underscores the danger of scientific movements too drunk on their zealotry to understand the magnitude of the events transpiring at the human level. The embers of The Holocaust were still burning in the ovens at Auschwitz, and one of the scientific elite sitting at a leadership position at the United Nations was regurgitating the same scientific premises for which the doctors, scientists, legislators, and jurists were on trial for at Nuremberg. Huxley's statement was mainstream eugenics at its worst, as expressed in the many books, laws, and propaganda of Hitler's National Socialism. Yet, here was the ideology rearing its ugly head out of the ashes and embers.

Julian Huxley's published opinions on eugenics prior to World War II certainly supported the drastic policies that would later lead to barbarous "crimes against humanity." No honest person can read his pre-WWII publications and not find disturbing parallels. Prior to The Holocaust, Huxley obviously didn't regard these opinions as unreasonable or unconscionable, and plenty of eugenicists close to Huxley openly applauded the connection to Nazi science in the early days of Hitler's reign.

Huxley's term of office, originally intended for six years, was cut to only two years, lasting from 1946 to 1948. He was dismissed at the behest of the United States delegation. The exact reasons for his dismissal are not known, though curiously enough, UNESCO subsequently revised Huxley's statements by releasing a series of official statements on the topic of "race," all of which were intended to differentiate from the traditional eugenic definition. The first of these was titled "The Race Question." The typical semantic shell game that is common from Progressive political circles is evident in point #6 of the "The Race Question." This statement suggests the term "race" should be substituted by "ethnic group":

> National, religious, geographic, linguistic and cultural groups do not necessarily coincide with racial groups: and the cultural traits of such groups have no demonstrated genetic connection with racial traits. Because serious errors of this kind are habitually committed when the term 'race' is used in popular parlance, it would be better when speaking of human races to drop the term 'race' altogether and speak of 'ethnic groups'. (unesdoc.unesco.org, Pg. 6, "UNESCO and its Programme: The Race Question", 1950)

This was the shell-game that the scientific industry played; pretending that playing word games tempered the totalitarian nature of eugenic legislation. Huxley and his devoted followers have since done a significant amount of historical revisionism, as has the rest of the scientific and medical community. Interestingly enough, Julian Huxley's two-volume autobiography makes no mention of his vast involvement in the science of eugenics. The subject, now considered taboo, was omitted from many obituaries and biographies. Case in point, Huxley, like many of his colleagues, eventually distanced himself from the eugenics of the Third Reich by qualifying himself as not being concerned with "race." This was a disingenuous position. The truth is that Huxley, through the international eugenic groups he belonged to, possessed enough contacts with insider knowledge of the Third Reich's eugenic policies to know that these policies were applicable regardless of "race." Huxley knew perfectly well that "racism" was not a prerequisite to the Third Reich's policies, and that eugenics was equally as dangerous with or without overt racism.

More to the point, Huxley is singled out here because of his prominence in the international eugenics movement as well as his position at UNESCO. That one of the appointed leaders of the United Nations, the very institution explicitly created to prevent a repeat of The Holocaust would author and distribute a eugenic tract with the compromising title "UNESCO Its Purpose & Philosophy" certainly goes a long way to evidence the failure of the Nuremberg Trials. Humanity was in collective shock. The film reels and photos coming from the extermination camps begged to be addressed. For a sitting director of the United Nations to regurgitate the very ideology that kept the fires burning at Auschwitz, Sobibor and Treblinka as official UN policy was by itself evidence of the collective failure of humanity to make sense of the horrid history.

Sec. 2 - A CONFLICT OF INTERESTS:

The "Nuremberg Code" is touted as the resulting victory of the Nuremberg Trials, as the product of the valiant efforts by the Allies to ensure that the criminal "human experimentation" conducted by Hitler's doctors and scientists would not repeat itself in history again. We are told that the "Nuremberg Code" established for all time thereafter a guideline by which experimentation on humans can be conducted in a humane fashion. The "Nuremberg Code" had largely been the work of Andrew C. Ivy during his tenure at the Nuremberg Trials. [1]

Yet, similar codes existed in the United States and Britain, and were in effect in Germany at the time when scientists and doctors under Hitler's reign willingly conducted these horrid experiments. In fact, it was largely due to the new eugenic worldview propagated by Julian Huxley and company that the old codes and old ethics were intentionally supplanted by the German doctors and scientists. German medicine was otherwise legally bound to respect individual rights. It was this eugenic mindset that subordinated the individual to the needs of the state, and thus provided the justification for these doctors, scientists, lawyers and legislators to discard the established codes. Just a few decades prior, the German Supreme Court had held in a landmark case in 1894 that surgical and life-threatening procedures required consent by law. The physician Albert Neisser had been charged with violating the principle of obtaining said consent in a very public case in 1900. At the end of the 1920s a series of unethical experiments that resulted in fatalities of children caused a public uproar in Germany. In response, the Reich Ministry of the Interior issued the "Regulations Concerning New Therapy and Human Experimentation" in February 1931, just a year or two before the change of power to Hitler's government: "The directives were among the most comprehensive research rules by any contemporary standards and some elements were even more elaborate than the principles of the Nuremberg Code." [2] Thus, the actual evidence weighs strongly against the notion that medical or scientific codes of ethics were lacking in Germany. More precisely, the evidence stands strong against that notion that more codes could prevent the medical extremes of German doctors, or that going forward they would be the bulwark against a repeat of the "crimes against humanity." These codes were either ignored or altered in order to reflect the *"Über Ethik,"* this new "progressive" ethic which placed society above individual rights.

In retrospect, one must also question why the Allied prosecution at Nuremberg focused so much attention at the "human experimentation" in the first place, as opposed to the other eugenic policies which claimed millions upon millions of victims. The Nuremberg Trials focused an inordinate amount of time on the military experiments on human subjects. Yet, the scale of the murders resulting from human experimentation are significantly limited to the few hundred victims in comparison to the many millions whom were murdered under the Third Reich's eugenic policies. More to the point, the amount of time expended by the Nuremberg prosecution team on human experimentation took the focus away from the nature, intent, and

---

[1] Pg. 135 - "The Birth of Bioethics", Albert R. Johnson, Oxford University Press; 1st edition (1998), 2003.
[2] Pg. 12 - "Justice at Nuremberg: Leo Alexander and the Nazi Doctors' Trial", Ulf Schmidt, Palgrave Macmillan UK, 2004.

justification for the clear majority of the murders we now recognize as The Holocaust. However horrid the few hundred military experiments may have been, they pale in comparison to the millions euthanized in the death camps. Arthur L. Caplan provides an opinion of how skewed the Nuremberg Trials were in respect to reality:

> Whereas it is known that some German physicians and scientists tortured and killed innocent persons, many histories of the Nazi era concentrate on the direct involvement in killing of a relatively small number of biomedical scientists and thus ignore or downplay the broad complicity of German medicine and science with Nazism. Ironically, even the post-war legal proceedings against war criminals tended to lend weight to the view that relatively few doctors or scientists killed, tortured or murdered in the name of the Nazi state. (Pg. 62, "When Medicine Went Mad: Bioethics and the Holocaust", Humana Press, 1992 – Chapter: "How Did Medicine Go So Wrong?")

In fact, one could easily argue that if Hitler's doctors and scientists had limited themselves to conducting several hundred ethically questionable experiments with war prisoners, and not set about exterminating entire swaths of the population, then no Nuremberg Trials would ever have been conducted. The facilities would have been limited to one or two German labs, instead of the industrial scale of the extermination camps, and the hundreds of thousands of bodies piled up and buried would not have been so exorbitantly numerous as to attract the attention of the Allied generals and admirals. The experiments would certainly have taken a back seat to events like the infamous Malmedy Massacre, which was dominating the headlines until the photos and film reels of the extermination camps were brought front and center by General Eisenhower. The massacre of 84 defenseless American soldiers had been discovered in January 1945, and General Eisenhower insisted upon documenting the system of extermination and concentration camps the following May. The images in those newsreels demanded attention. It was the unimaginable scale of the industrialized execution machine that forced Americans to look away from the crimes against their own soldiers and forever be haunted by crimes against the citizens within enemy nations.

The lawyers defending the Germans at the Nuremberg Doctors' Trials were certainly prepared to aggressively defend their clients. They would cite the parallels between US and British human experimentation, and namely, immigration policies, coerced sterilization, euthanasia, and the segregation laws in place in the United States. To be fully honest, the nature of the military experiments by the German military was uncomfortably like the infamous 1932 Tuskegee Experiments, where 600 African Americans were used for research into syphilis. Of specific importance was the fact that ethically questionable experimentation in the United States was already a topic for the headlines leading up to the Nuremberg Trials. In 1945, The Lancet, the major British medical journal, published "Sterilization of the insane in the USA." According to this article, which was based on information in the Journal of the American Medical Association, more than 42,000 people were sterilized in the United States in the three-year period of 1940-1943. California led all other states with more than 10,000.

The appointment of Andrew Ivy perfectly illustrates the embarrassing and potentially catastrophic conundrum the American prosecution faced at Nuremberg. Andrew Ivy not only authored the Nuremberg Code, but was also the man who shaped the strategy for the Doctors' Trial. By the end of World War II, Ivy was probably the most famous doctor in the United States, otherwise known as the "conscience of US science." [3] He was president of the American Physiological Society. He was also a member of the National Research Council, the operating agency of the National Academy of Sciences. As such, the Allied prosecution presented Ivy to the Tribunal as an expert in "medical ethics." According to the prosecution, Ivy had headed up the "Green Report," a study on "human experimentation" which had supposedly been conducted inside the United States, but which in actuality had never been written, nor any committee convened. Ivy had intentionally misled the court about the "Green Report" in order to strengthen the prosecution's case. The "tactics" used by this renowned scientist were intended to mislead not just the court, but the worldwide audience of the Trials. [4] Ivy had written the report alone after testifying of its existence. The report was later published in JAMA and was used as a basis in subsequent decades to justify medical research the US had conducted on its prison population. [5]

The British had their own skeletons in their medical closet as they had supported Robert Alexander McCance, a doctor who had carried out experiments on infants suffering from *spina bifida*. [6] All of this created a serious problem for Telford Taylor, the head of the Allied prosecution team. Clearly, this juxtaposition compromised the Allied prosecution:

> These cases raised the question whether American and perhaps British researchers were likewise guilty of professional misconduct, and if not, why not. The evidence suggests that neither the prosecution nor the judges, nor anyone else involved in establishing the trial, had a clear idea at this point what the main legal and ethical issues were that the trial needed to address. 'If we had been able to do it over again three years later', Taylor mused in 1976, 'we would have done it in a much more sophisticated way...with greater awareness of the implication of the positions we were taking.' Upon his arrival in Germany, Ivy found that the prosecution appeared to be 'somewhat confused' about the legal, ethical and indeed scientific dimensions in the forthcoming trial. Taylor put it more diplomatically: **'We were educated in large part by our opponents.'"** (emphasis mine, Pg. 135, "Justice at Nuremberg: Leo Alexander and the Nazi Doctors' Trial", Ulf Schmidt, Palgrave Macmillan UK, 2004)

In historical hindsight, the prosecution's position became increasingly suspect

---

[3] Pg. 134 - "Justice at Nuremberg: Leo Alexander and the Nazi Doctors' Trial", Ulf Schmidt, Palgrave Macmillan UK, 2004.
[4] "Historian Examines US Ethics in Nuremberg Medical Trial Tactics", Larry Bernard, Cornell Chronicle, Sept. 17, 2006.
[5] Ibid.
[6] Pg. 77 – "History and Theory of Human Experimentation: The Declaration of Helsinki and Modern Medical Ethics", Ulf Schmidt and Andreas Frewer, Steiner, 2007.

after the war when Andrew C. Ivy was found guilty of medical fraud. On October 28, 1964, Ivy and his partners at the Krebiozen Research Foundation were indicted for introducing mislabeled drugs into interstate commerce in violation of the Food, Drug and Cosmetic Act. The drug that Ivy had used to tout his reputation was found to be completely ineffectual by a series of independent experiments. Ivy had claimed that of 22 treated patients, 14 were alive and none had died of cancer. In a repeat of the fraudulent claims made when called to the stand at Nuremberg, Ivy was aware that the facts he presented were far from reality; 10 of the treated patients had died, and all from cancer by the time Ivy made the claims in a 1951 press conference. Even worse, the Food and Drug Administration inspections found that the drugs being distributed by Ivy's company had no active ingredients. Ivy, the Allied Prosecution's expert on medical ethics turned out to be a textbook snake-oil salesman.

However, this book was not written to expose Andrew Ivy, but to document the many inconvenient relationships he intended to cover up. Ivy had a significant conflict of interest as a member of the National Research Council. The National Research Council was populated with American eugenicists, whom were in no place to criticize the German counterparts they had corresponded and collaborated with in order to create the international eugenics movement. The National Research Council had, after all, conducted the tests on the US Army recruits during World War I, which so many of the statistical claims of the American eugenics movement were based upon. One of the most egregious examples was the infamous 1926 "Committee on the Negro," organized by the American Association of Physical Anthropology and the National Research Council. Among those appointed to the Committee on the Negro were prominent eugenicists like Earnest Hooton and Charles B. Davenport. The committee endorsed a comparison of African babies with young apes. Ten years later, the group published findings in the American Journal of Physical Anthropology to "prove that the negro race is phylogenetically a closer approach to primitive man than the white race." [7] Work by prominent scientists such as this evidenced that racially charged eugenic thinking was firmly entrenched in American science. More to the point, Andrew C. Ivy, as a prominent US doctor and member of the American Medical Association and the National Research Council, knew this all too well.

When Telford Taylor observed that his prosecution team was "educated in large part by our opponents," he meant that the defendants were submitting as evidence examples of United States and British laws, statutes, and medical examples which revealed for all the world the extent to which eugenic policies were practiced by the Allies. It seemed as if the German defendants knew more about American medicine and the eugenic laws passed in the United States than did the American prosecutors, and the trajectory and strategy of the Doctors' Trial were significantly altered upon this revelation. There really was no excuse for this deficiency in the American prosecution. They had the staff in hand to preempt this legal malpractice. One of

---

[7] Pgs. 105-113 - "Two faces of earnest A. Hooton", Eugene Giles, Volume 149, Issue S55 Supplement: Yearbook of Physical Anthropology, 2012.

the key figures chosen to conduct interviews of the German defendants and as a medical expert was the German-born scientist and medical expert, Leo Alexander. The complexities and contradictions abounded, and Leo Alexander knew them well. Leo Alexander's story is a tragic one. Alexander was a German Jewish scientist who had dedicated the first part of his career towards tirelessly researching and advancing the science of eugenics in the very same institutions that would later be used to exterminate his family and Jewish brethren. Alexander would pay personal consequences for his eugenic mindset, as the parents of the young German woman he proposed to marry ultimately rejected him upon explicitly eugenic notions. Alexander would also be kicked out of the institutions he helped build due to his Jewish religion, again, as a consequence of the eugenic standards implemented by the Third Reich as part of the April 1933 "Law for the Restoration of the Professional Civil Service." Most revealing is that Leo Alexander's career in eugenics had largely been funded by the Rockefeller Institution both before and after escaping Germany. Leo Alexander had literally helped fashion the weapon that would later be used against him and his loved ones, but in the process, had been fully funded by a formidable American institution. Alexander escaped Hitler's Germany and emigrated to the United States. As such, his past made him uniquely qualified to become the American consultant to the legal team at the Nuremberg Doctors' Trial. Leo Alexander literally and figuratively knew where all the bones were buried.

Alexander's work had flourished in the Kaiser Wilhelm Institute even during the hardest years of the Great Depression. Alexander had been responsible for the extensive genealogical studies of families with hereditary and mental diseases, and his work had been leveraged by key figures in the Third Reich's eugenics such as Ernst Rüdin. These genealogies enhanced Alexander's reputation, as well as provide Alexander a working relationship with the attending scientists that would run the murder factories such as Hadamar, Eichberg, and Herborn. Like the Nazi defendants interrogated by Alexander, it is more likely than not that Alexander also failed to obtain consent from the individuals that were the subjects of his experiments; "and not unlike Julius Hallervorden, whom he later interrogated about his involvement in the 'euthanasia' program, Alexander made sure that he could use as many brains and body parts as possible in his neuropathological studies." [8]

While still a student at the University of Frankfurt am Main, Leo Alexander had studied and worked under Professor Karl Kleist on various eugenic studies and the production of medical films about racial purity and eugenics which would later be used to propagandize the Third Reich's eugenic legislation. Of note is that Professor Kleist was also one of the individuals who sat on the eugenic courts of hereditary health, or *Erbgesundheitsgerichte* in German. Professor Kleist, like many of Alexander's past colleagues, ended up being one of the witnesses and defendants interviewed by then 'Major' Alexander. Alexander interviewed Kleist on August 19, 1945. Clearly, a eugenic-minded scientist whom failed to follow the dictates of standing ethical codes in his own work, as well as used questionably acquired body

---

[8] Pg. 32, "Justice at Nuremberg: Leo Alexander and the Nazi Doctors' Trial", Ulf Schmidt, Palgrave Macmillan UK, 2004.

parts for his research, was in no position to sit in judgment of the German scientists accused of doing precisely the same thing, regardless of how repentant Alexander may have been as a reaction to his own personal suffering. It must also be clarified that Alexander was no foot soldier of the prosecution. Leo Alexander did most of the essential background work for the Doctors' Trial, interrogating the defendants before and during the trial, studying their mentalities and rationale for participating in the crimes, as well as writing dozens of memoranda needed to prepare the Allied prosecution team. In other words, Leo Alexander was one of the leaders of Telford Taylor's legal team and one of the architects of the prosecution's strategy.

Further blurring the demarcation between acceptable and unacceptable medical ethics was the fact that Leo Alexander had personally recommended Dr. Hubertus Strughold for Project Paperclip. This project brought a small army of German doctors and scientists to the United States to the great benefit of the US Air Force and the US space program that ultimately landed American astronauts on the moon. Strughold ultimately became known as "The Father of Space Medicine" for his work at NASA. However, prior to working for NASA, Dr. Hubertus Strughold had served as chief of Aeromedical Research for Hitler's Luftwaffe, conducting the very experiments at the Dachau concentration camp which the Doctors' Trial deemed criminal. Among other scientists who conducted the infamous high-altitude experiments at Dachau, and which were subsequently employed by the US military, were Hermann Becker-Freysing, Konrad Schäfer, and Siegfried Ruff. Their sadistic experiments had come to the attention of both the Nuremberg prosecution and the US military through Leo Alexander's report titled "The Treatment of Shock from Prolonged Exposure to Cold, Especially in Water." The Nuremberg prosecution used the information to condemn German scientists and doctors. Yet, the US military later treated it as valid science.

Another eugenic-minded member of the Allied prosecution team was John M. Woolsey, Jr. He was an American jurist who graduated from Yale College and Yale Law School. During World War II, Woolsey served in the Office of Naval Intelligence in Washington. As hostilities ceased in Europe, Woolsey was assigned to the staff of Justice Robert H. Jackson to assist in Nuremberg. He would receive the Order of the White Lion from the Czechoslovakian Government for his work at the Nuremberg Trials, and was a lifelong conservationist who was awarded the Allen Morgan Prize by the Massachusetts Audubon Society in 1997. However, of particular interest is his post-war position as director of the Pioneer Fund, one of the most notorious eugenic-minded institutions which had been funding the international eugenics movement since 1937. Previous presidents of the Pioneer Fund include the most prominent eugenicists in history, including Wickliffe Draper, Harry H. Laughlin, Karl Pearson, and Fredrick Henry Osborn. Of note is that the racial laws implemented by the Third Reich had been written by Laughlin.

Consider the importance of these relevations. While many conspiracy theorists and historians alike dig up even the most tangential connections between major American industry and banking institutions, the uncomfortably close relationship between American and German intellectual and governmental institutions is largely treated as inconsequential even though these relationships were indispensable in the development of eugenics as a mainline science leading up to The Holocaust. The relationships were hardly superficial. This book will document and prove that:

- The US Supreme Court had legalized the very three-panel eugenic courts that Hitler's government would implement. Hitler himself attested to educating himself in the various eugenic laws upheld by American jurisprudence.
- At least two American Presidents had not only condoned but actively participated in the legislative efforts to implement eugenic policies in the United States.
- British prime ministers had led the way to pass eugenic legislation like that which would later be implemented by the Third Reich.
- The most elite universities in both the United States and Britain were educating the future leaders of the international eugenics movement.
- The leaders of prominent Civil Rights organizations subscribed to the eugenic-minded value systems, and thus were both silent and complicit in the advance of the eugenics movement inside the United States
- Cultural leaders in both the United States and Britain were using the media and the arts to propagandize the eugenic cause with the tactics that would later be utilized by Hitler's own propaganda minister.
- The most influential charities in the United States and Britain were funding projects of a distinct eugenic nature in Germany and back home. These institutions would become the epicenters of the Third Reich's eugenic crimes.
- Leading scientists and doctors from the United States and Britain worked tirelessly to help implement eugenic legislation in Germany and openly collaborate and trade information with their German counterparts.
- American scientists whom had once worked in the top laboratories, funded by the most prestigious institutions, would ultimately collaborate as scientific staff in the Third Reich's extermination camps.
- Prominent American and British scientists had been ceremoniously awarded medals and honorary degrees by Hitler's government for their work in eugenics.
- The leading German scientists that headed up the eugenic legislative efforts in Hitler's Germany were regularly invited or paid to contribute to several key medical journals in the United States and Britain well into Hitler's reign.

All in all, the world-wide campaign and international collaboration was publicized well enough that the connections between the eugenics of the Allies and the eugenics of the Third Reich were unquestionably the products of the same movement. About the only dispute that may have separated them is the level to which anti-Semitism played a role in the German movement, but this type of "racism" played a significant role across the entire international eugenic movement, and not in any way confined to Germany, as the likes of Julian Huxley would have liked to characterize it. British and American eugenicists were just as "racially" motivated as scientists inside the Third Reich, if not more. The Holocaust historian Robert Proctor's provided perspective of precisely how American science and jurisprudence was regarded just prior to Hitler coming to power:

> In 1932, Bavarian Health Inspector Walter Schultze noted that the US must be regarded as a nation where "racial policy and thinking has become much more popular than in other countries." Schultze was referring not just to sterilization laws, but to American immigration restriction laws – especially the 1924 Immigration Restriction Act. (Pg. 33, "When Medicine Went Mad: Bioethics and the Holocaust", Humana Press, 1992)

In short, no honest person can read the decades upon decades of American and British eugenic publications and not see the parallels and overlap with the eugenic publications of the Third Reich. Many American and British proponents of eugenics would live long enough to have to confront this reality when the photographs and film reels of the extermination camps started coming back from the front in 1945. Charles Lindberg and H.G. Wells would be haunted by the images, as they knew perfectly well that the "crimes" were the product of the campaign they personally had helped flourish and expand across the world. American and British eugenic institutions would change their names and expel staff if they felt they too much betrayed their eugenic pasts. This was the "education" that Telford Taylor refers to when stating that the German defendants knew enough about American and British sciences to potentially compromise the outcome of the Doctors' Trial at Nuremberg. Not only were the German doctors and scientists right in stating that American and British doctors and scientists had been instrumental in creating the eugenic institutions they utilized to conduct the "crimes," but among the ranks of the Allied prosecution team were individuals who had an active role in creating the international eugenics movement. The behind the scenes leadership in the United States, Britain, and the USSR – the top brass and highest offices of these nations – were figureheads of the international eugenics movement, imposing the very trials that deemed the product of eugenics "criminal."

This is not to say that the public or even the rest of the leadership of either the United States or Britain condoned or supported eugenics. There was a drastic and pronounced divide within both nations, and those that supported the eugenic cause were able to do so only by leveraging their elite positions. Whatever divide existed in Germany before Hitler was stamped out and silenced by the monolithic one-party system. In the United States and Britain, eugenics was an outright revolution against the traditional values, both legislative and moral, and very much so a part of the era's allure to anything perceived as "progressive." The eugenic-minded elites responsible for the expansion of the movement explicitly set out to dethrone traditional morals and the conservative legislative traditions that stood in the way of radical eugenic proposals. Thus, the eugenics movement, like any other movement, was the cause of political posturing and bitter debates. There were high political stakes as a consequence of telling "the whole truth, and nothing but the truth" at the Nuremberg Doctors' Trial. While we would like to revere our leaders and historical icons, politicians did what politicians are known to do when politically sensitive situations arise and political stakes are too costly to trust to blind justice.

In hindsight, the positions of the different Allied leaders are revealing. Not everyone wanted to hold a trial, as it was unprecedented in world history, and everyone remembered how a young Adolf Hitler had used the German courts as a pulpit. Joseph Stalin, whom had once commissioned his scientists to create a superior industrial military by leveraging the science of eugenics, was for holding some sort of trial, albeit the style of trial that had "purged" the innocent and guilty alike in Bolshevik Russia. Winston Churchill, the man whom had initiated and headed up the legislative effort to pass the 1913 Mental Deficiency Act, Britain's landmark eugenic legislation, coincidentally did not want any kind of a trial, and vigorously lobbied for summary execution for the entirety of the National Socialist leadership. The American political scene was openly and vigorously divided on the issue of having trials for Hitler's men. Some were vigorously opposed to holding trials if the trials were not sincerely committed to the finding of truth, and if necessary, finding that some of the Germans were not guilty. Others discerned that this had been a war like no others, and that Hitler's policies demanded some sort of closure and vindication for the victims beyond that of military victory. Yet, lurking in the ranks of the slew of political advisors and interest groups behind the President of the United States were influential voices whom had a distinct stake in deciding how the history of eugenics would be written, especially if the eugenic cause would survive the taint of the Third Reich's "war crimes" and endure into the future as a viable science.

Obviously, if the US government wanted to prosecute those that either "aided," "abetted" or "gave aid and comfort" to the enemy, they certainly had the legal precedent leading up to the 1945 Nuremberg Trials. In 1944, the Supreme Court upheld the constitutionality of the Roosevelt administration "exclusion orders" that were utilized to restrict or intern thousands upon thousands of Japanese American citizens or immigrants of Japanese descent. More than 4,000 Latin Americans of German ancestry had their livelihoods destroyed and were held in concentration camps in Crystal City, Texas, for allegedly collaborating with Hitler's government.[9] Thousands of other Latin Americans were blacklisted from conducting business in the United States upon nothing more than suspicion or conjecture. Most importantly, in 1942 the US Congress had initiated the Senate Patents Committee, the Truman Committee, and the Antitrust Division of the Department of Justice had begun separate inquiries into overt or clandestine transactions between Americans and Germans. More to the point, Law No. 10, which the Nuremberg Trials were based on, recognized "initiating," "ordering," and "abetting" as part "crimes against humanity." This opened legal avenues to pursue, which the American

---

[9] See Generally: "Nazis and Good Neighbors", Max Paul Friedman, Cambridge Univ. Press, 2003.

team left unexplored. Thought, essentially, the Nuremberg Trials were a series of trials for the charge of "conspiracy," which in the American legal tradition, direct involvement amongst the disparate conspirators need not be proven. Yet, even after finding that German doctors and scientists had been complicit in "crime against humanity," no inquiries or committees were formed to investigate into the relationship between these Germans and the Americans that assisted them in transforming Germany into a eugenic state. Adolf Hitler was a third-rate intellect, at best, and incapable of contributing anything beyond vague notions gleaned from the works of actual eugenic-minded scientific and legal minds. Even Karl Brandt, the primary defendant at the Doctors' Trial, lacked the sophistication and experience necessary to erect the eugenic state that was the Third Reich. Vulgar racism only gets a mob so far. The scope and scale of the crimes committed by Hitler's Third Reich were the product of a sustained, rational and sophisticated infrastructure:

> Racism and sexism are necessary components of a repressive eugenics policy, but they are not sufficient. In Germany, it took not only a racist ideology, but a totalitarian state with the will and ability to impose this ideology ruthlessly and murderously on its people. (Pg. 302, "When Medicine Went Mad: Bioethics and the Holocaust", Humana Press, 1992 – See George J. Annas Chapter: "The Human Genome Project in Perspective: Confronting our Past to Protect our Future")

These eugenic laws and statutes in question were policies refined by the combined efforts of the top minds in the United States, Britain, and Germany and tempered and forged in the United States, Britain, and Scandinavia decades prior to the Third Reich. The eugenic policies of the Third Reich were created by a brain trust that had access to and longstanding connections with internationally renowned eugenic experts. Conspicuously enough, many of these elite German doctors and scientists were captured by the Allied forces and then released, never to pay the price for masterminding these "crimes against humanity." Arthur L. Caplan provides a perspective of just how toxic this is to our understanding of the crimes:

> Placing all of the physicians, health professionals, and scientists who took part in the crimes of the Holocaust on the periphery of medicine and science allows another myth to flourish – that medicine and science went mad when Adolf Hitler took control of Germany. Those physicians and public health officials who staffed the camps, murdered the demented, and advanced theories of racial hygiene were, according to this myth, simply lunatics, charlatans and quacks. The myth of madness disguises all those who carried out crimes in the camps as incorrigible fiends, such as Josef Mengele, or suffering from pathological personality disorders, such as Sigmund Rascher. Competent and responsible physicians and scientist could not willingly have had anything to do with such evil deeds. However, the actions as well as the beliefs of German physicians and scientists under Nazism stand in glaring contrast to this myth. (Pg. 56, "When Medicine Went Mad: Bioethics and the Holocaust", Humana Press, 1992)

This book also seeks to shed light on why historians have taken so long to document this insidious history. This retrospective analysis of the nature of the crimes of The Holocaust is increasingly becoming understood by historians that these scientists and doctors were not part of the "periphery"; that they were not aberrations or cranks:

> **A great deal of the literature on the eugenics movement is based on a myth.** The myth is comforting because it pits the forces of evil and power (bigotry, racism, privileged classes) against the forces of innocence and vulnerability. (the poor, the retarded, the insane, the downtrodden) **The myth is wrong and dangerous.** (emphasis mine, Pgs. 351-352, "The Unfit: A History of a Bad Idea", Elof Axel Carlson Cold Spring Harbor Lab. Press, 2001)

To the contrary: these scientists were part of the emerging mainstream, whose beliefs were in vogue around the world. The Allied prosecution team at Nuremberg should have been and probably was keenly aware of the complicity that "civilian," or rather non-military, institutions played in the crimes. The British prosecutor, Lord Elwyn-Jones, dug up documentation of a "Jewish Skeleton Collection" that had been compiled by the Reich University of Strasbourg, and Leo Alexander himself was keenly aware of the relationship between the other universities, the Kaiser Wilhelm Institute, and the broader eugenic efforts of the Third Reich. It was clear that the non-military institutions were instructing the extermination camp staff to harvest body parts for further research and study. To be precise, Josef Mengele was the subordinate of and working for the scientists at the Kaiser Wilhelm Institute, and not the other way around. The infamous Dr. Mengele was a foot soldier in the greater crime. Yet, Mengele was brought to justice. The leadership he answered to was not.

The strategic decision to allow many non-military scientists and doctors to go free was explained away as necessary to keep some semblance of order and medical infrastructure in the aftermath of the war. The other explanation given was that the population would lose confidence and begin to distrust the medical sciences if the trial exposed the actual scale and scope of the complicity in the crimes. This may be the most honest explanation, and it likely was not a concern about the German populace, as the trials themselves were intended for a worldwide audience. Revealing the relationship between the extermination camps and the non-military institutions, the civilian doctors, nurses, lawyers, and judges would document the very close relationship between American and British elites and the German criminals. The political stakes were too high to allow that to happen.

Sec. 3 - A LEGAL QUAGMIRE:

The Nuremberg Trials were essentially trials for the "conspiracy" to commit "murder," and differentiating between deaths during the war and civilians killed with murderous intent. As is with any other "murder trial," the main goal was to document and expose the "intent" of the murderers, as "intent" is what differentiates between "murder" and "manslaughter." This was the stated purpose of the unprecedented world tribunal, created under the auspices of the newly founded United Nations; to expose to the world the nature of the atrocities in hopes of preventing them in the future. The film reels and photos emerging from the concentration and extermination camps begged for this distinction, and the Nuremberg Trials were the attempt at exposing the nature of the unprecedented crimes. Telford Taylor said as much in his opening statement; that this was "no mere murder trial," because the defendants were physicians who had sworn to "do no harm" and to abide by the Hippocratic Oath. Taylor told the judges at this Doctor's Trial that the people of the world needed to know "with conspicuous clarity" the ideas and motives that moved these doctors "to treat their fellow human beings as less than beasts," and that "brought about such savageries" so that they could be "cut out and exposed before they become a spreading cancer in the breast of humanity." [10]

We must recall that the task of prosecuting crimes on an international scale implied major obstacles and issues. From the onset, the effort was liable to be regarded as nothing more than the victor's vengeance. It was unprecedented for an international tribunal to stand in judgment of a sovereign nation in order to pass judgment on crimes committed within the borders of that sovereign nation, against its own people, and under the laws of that nation by popularly elected legislatures. Yet, if one was to adequately expose the unprecedented nature of the crimes of The Holocaust, the tribunal needed to address that civilians were killed outside of the line of fire and within the jurisdiction of German sovereignty.

"Jurisdiction" is the all-important term in jurisprudence, and it is said that without "jurisdiction" a tribunal has no authority to act. While the victors had authority to dictate the terms of the peace and surrender, they possessed no clear jurisdiction over anything that may have transpired among civilians in a sovereign nation, especially if the alleged crimes had been committed prior to the declaration of war with the prosecuting nation, and outside of the field of battle which the prosecuting nation was engaged in. This was especially the case between Germany and the American prosecution: Many of the murders were committed by Germans against German citizens, and many much prior to the declaration of war between the United States and Germany. Furthermore, most were conducted in a geographical location that had nothing to do with the battlefields the United States engaged in. This complication became only more exacerbated as the Iron Curtain fell, and the Cold War tensions ripped the Allies apart in the middle of the Nuremberg Trials. Once the USSR departed from the trials, the question of "jurisdiction" by a military tribunal became much more complicated, and the Allies"

---

[10] nuremberg.law.harvard.edu – "Opening Statement for the United States of America", Dec. 9, 1946, HLSL Item No.: 565.

claim to "jurisdiction" that much more tenuous. The geographical location where the criminal acts were committed was a central deciding factor in the creation of an international tribunal. The leaders of the smaller nations vanquished and brutalized by Hitler's henchmen were clamoring for the leadership of the Third Reich to be turned over to them. However, as the responsibility for the crimes climbed up the hierarchy in Hitler's government, the geographical and jurisdictional distinctions became increasingly unclear:

> It was one thing to agree to hold a trial in 1945, quite another to decide who should be arraigned before it. From the moment when war crimes began to be discussed in detail, in the summer of 1942, a distinction was made between those guilty of local war crimes in a particular theater of war and those major war criminals 'whose notorious offences,' as Churchill put it, 'have no special geographical location'." (Pg. 28, "Interrogations: The Nazi Elite in Allied Hands, 1945", Richard Overy, Allen Lane, 2001)

Oddly enough, the American team found itself agreeing with the Joseph Stalin, and on the opposing side of the British, whom under Winston Churchill were insisting that the National Socialist leadership be shot "within 6 hours" of being captured. [11] There was no question as to why Stalin wanted highly publicized trials; Stalin and his Bolsheviks had made a career out of show trials, and thus welcomed the opportunity for a show trial with a world-wide audience. What was then, and still remains a mystery, is why the British lobbied so vigorously for summary execution. American officials were struck by the evident hypocrisy by the British whom, after all, were "the ones in whom the concept of trial before punishment" was "fundamental." [12] Winston Churchill and his Foreign Secretary, Anthony Eden, pushed for summary execution and argued against a trial in all of the major and minor conferences between the Allies from 1943 until 1945, when the British delegation to the United Nation's opening conference in San Francisco finally capitulated. Of note, this date coincides in the turning of the guard when the British people voted Winston Churchill out of office:

> It was Churchill's earnest wish, which he expressed repeatedly in the months running up to the end of the European war in May 1945, that captured German leaders, whether party bosses, soldiers, or ministers, should be identified positively on the say of any local army officer with the rank of major-general or above, and then shot within six hours. (Pg. 6, "Interrogations: The Nazi Elite in Allied Hands, 1945", Richard Overy, Allen Lane, 2001)

This is not to say that there weren't legitimate doubts about the prospects of a trial. Adolf Hitler's use of the courtroom for propagandizing and soliloquy during his trial for the Beer Hall Putsch was well known, and no one wanted to give him a venue by which to reargue the case for the theories expounded in "Mein Kampf." Ironically the British public clamored for "British Justice" against the wishes of their

---

[11] Pg. 6 - "Interrogations: The Nazi Elite in Allied Hands, 1945", Richard Overy, Allen Lane, 2001.
[12] Pg. 11 – Ibid.

leadership, while the American public feared acquittal resulting from a trial consistent with the American Bill of Rights. The appointed Chief Counsel of the American prosecution team, Supreme Court Justice Robert Jackson, learned in a not-so-subtle way how the American public demanded "justice." The editor of Fortune magazine sent Justice Jackson a preview of an article he intended to publish, detailing a strong rebuttal to the legal basis of the Tribunal. The article condemned the notion that Nazi war criminals could potentially be acquitted; what the Fortune editor deemed "would be the greatest crime of the age." [13]

It was not until Vice-President Harry S. Truman ascended to the Presidency after Roosevelt's untimely death that the United States took a stern stance against the British preference for summary judgment, and decidedly for a War Crimes Tribunal. President Truman instructed his top advisor on war crimes, Judge Samuel Rosenman, to accompany the American delegation to the United Nation's founding conference in San Francisco to make Truman's position clearly known to the British. However, even after the British capitulated to President Truman's insistence, they brought a paltry showing to the effort itself, assigning less than 34 staff members to the trials, in comparison to the more than 200 people working under Justice Robert Jackson.

By the time the Nuremberg trials began, the Allies had already begun to split Germany into spheres of influence, and the prediction by Joseph Goebbels, which Winston Churchill is often wrongly credited for, that an Iron Curtain would descend over Europe was now the new reality for the "free-world" to contend with. The big wigs of National Socialism were tried in the first Nuremberg Trial with the Allies collaborating. The star witness was Hermann Göring, as Hitler and Goebbels had committed suicide before surrendering. As such, the first Nuremberg trial was the last collective effort by the Allies. The USSR withdrew after the main Nuremberg Trial, and the United States proceeded with the exacerbated complication of "jurisdictional" legitimacy. The United States decided to continue using the methods and procedures of American jurisprudence, and the German defendants could not have been more relieved; the German defendants were quite familiar with American law and the concept of "innocent before proven guilty." They were intimately familiar with American jurisprudence, as this had been an important topic of investigation for the eugenic-minded policymakers of the Third Reich.

The twelve trials that the United States conducted became known as the Subsequent Nuremberg Trials. The judges in all these trials were American, and so were the prosecutors; the Chief of Counsel for the Prosecution was Brigadier General Telford Taylor. The twelve US trials by the Nuremberg Military Tribunals (NMT) took place from December 9, 1946, to April 13, 1949:

1.) The Doctors' Trial (December 9, 1946 - August 20, 1947)
2.) The Milch Trial (January 2, 1947 - April 14, 1947)
3.) The Judges' Trial (March 5, 1947 - December 4, 1947)
4.) The Pohl Trial (April 8, 1947 - November 3, 1947)
5.) The Flick Trial (April 19, 1947 - December 22, 1947)

---

[13] Pg. 6 - "Interrogations: The Nazi Elite in Allied Hands, 1945", Richard Overy, Allen Lane, 2001.

6.) The IG Farben Trial (August 27, 1947 - July 30, 1948)
7.) The Hostages Trial (July 8, 1947 – February 19, 1948)
8.) The RuSHA Trial (October 20, 1947 - March 10, 1948)
9.) The Einsatzgruppen Trial (September 29, 1947 - April 10, 1948)
10.) The Krupp Trial (December 8, 1947 - July 31, 1948)
11.) The Ministries Trial (January 6, 1948 - April 13, 1949)
12.) The High Command Trial (December 30, 1947 - October 28, 1948)

Any historian who knows anything about the Third Reich is cognizant of just how pervasive the science of eugenics was in the laws of the Third Reich. Everything within the boundaries of Hitler's government was seen from a eugenic perspective. Hitler's "total state" took great pains to insert and inject itself into every aspect of German life, and all state policy was in one way or another eugenic policy. This should have been an important clarification for the Trials to document for all posterity. Instead, the process of dissection between justifiable "war casualties," "war crimes," and the "criminal" human experimentation began. One of the ways in which this dissection was made was by defining what an act of "genocide" comprised of. The term "genocide" was then relatively new, and in retrospect somewhat inappropriate to what makes The Holocaust unique and different from other "genocidal" acts by other governments throughout world history.

The term "genocide" was coined by a Polish-Jewish legal scholar named Raphael Lemkin. The term joins the Greek root "*génos*" meaning birth, race, stock, kind, with the Latin "*cidium*," meaning cutting or killing" via the French ending "*cide*." Lemkin had first proposed the legal concept in 1933 to the Legal Council of the League of Nations in his "crime of barbarity." The concept originated in his youth when he first heard of the Ottoman government's mass killings of its Armenian-Christian population during the First World War. Lemkin's own life experience informed his proposal, as his Polish birth home was the frequent scene of pogroms. When Hitler invaded Poland, Lemkin fled, but he was unable to convince his parents, his neighbors, or his fellow refugees of the gravity of the National Socialist threat. Although he managed to escape to the United States, Lemkin lost 49 relatives in the Holocaust. After arriving in the United States, Lemkin joined the law faculty at Duke University in North Carolina. While the League of Nations had not adopted his initial proposal, the Carnegie Endowment for International Peace published Lemkin's "Axis Rule in Occupied Europe," where a preliminary version of his more fully developed and formulated concept of "genocide" first appeared. "Axis Rule" included an extensive legal analysis of German rule in countries occupied by Hitler's troops, along with the definition of the term genocide, "the destruction of a nation or of an ethnic group." Lemkin defined "genocide" as such:

> Generally speaking, genocide does not necessarily mean the immediate destruction of a nation, except when accomplished by mass killings of all members of a nation. It is intended rather to signify a coordinated plan of different actions aiming at the destruction of essential foundations of the life of national groups, with the aim of annihilating the groups themselves. The

objectives of such a plan would be the disintegration of the political and social institutions, of culture, language, national feelings, religion, and the economic existence of national groups, and the destruction of the personal security, liberty, health, dignity, and even the lives of the individuals belonging to such groups. (Pg. 79, "Axis Rule in Occupied Europe: Laws of Occupation, Analysis of Government, Proposals for Redress", The Lawbook Exchange, Ltd., 2005)

Lemkin was appointed consultant to the US Board of Economic Warfare and Foreign Economic Administration in 1943 and later became a special adviser on foreign affairs to the War Department because of his work and experience. Lemkin served as an advisor to the Supreme Court of the United States Justice and Nuremberg Trial chief counsel Robert H. Jackson from 1945 to 1946, and through Lemkin's participation, "genocide" became one of the legal bases of the Nuremberg Trials. Count #3 of the indictment of the 24 German defendants in the first Nuremberg Trial specifies that the defendants "conducted deliberate and systematic genocide."

However, the Nuremberg definition is different than that originally drafted by Lemkin as it defines the term beyond the limited scope of "nationalities" and expanded it to include "the extermination of racial" groups as part of the definition of the crime. This was key, as clearly the original reading would fail to describe what had transpired in the extermination camps. Clearly, any definition of the crime that didn't include the plight of the German-born Jews would be a tragic failure, thus the expansion beyond the limitations of the term "nationalities" was key in order to address the nature and intent of the crimes. Yet, herein lay the "jurisdictional" conundrum posed by the time and geography in which the alleged crimes were committed.

One could argue that the term "genocide" failed to accurately describe what transpired in The Holocaust, as even the updated definition ignores the unique aspect of it as a crime of scope beyond what modern scholars have come to call "ethnic cleansing." We must remember that the first half-million victims of Hitler's eugenic euthanasia were "Aryans." The victims of the T4 Euthanasia program, which perfected the murderous technology that would literally be transferred along with its medical staff to the extermination camps, targeted Germans that suffered from birth defects, alcoholism, undesirable social behavior, skin conditions as mild as acne, and even war veterans too crippled to work or to support themselves. The limited or literal reading of Lemkin's term thus fell short of capturing the nature, "intent," or "motive" behind the deliberate acts of murder.

More to the point, Hitler's showboating and propagandizing left no shortage of knowledge as to what exactly was the motive and intent. We know the "intention" behind the murders of the Third Reich was to make the German state "applied biology" or a "racial state." The Third Reich could not have advertised their "eugenic" intentions more clearly prior to and through the duration of the regime. This was done so in the movies, public awareness posters, political platforms, in the classroom, and in just about every policy speech given by Hitler himself. The truth is that the only term that could accurately grasp the scope of the crime as well as its "intent," and include all of its victims from ethnic Germans to German Jews to foreign nationals was "eugenics." Lemkin himself documented this aspect of National Socialism in the "Political Indoctrination" section of "Axis Rule":

> Members of the police, particularly of the Gestapo, are, practically speaking, the most active fighters for National Socialism. Therefore, they are trained carefully in its doctrines. Such matters as racial theories, geopolitics, history of German ideas of hegemony, **eugenics**, the Jewish problem, Catholicism and a political problem, Communism, relations with the Anglo-Saxon world, colonial questions, economic and political penetration – to cite only some of them – are basic subjects in the program for indoctrination the police, especially the Gestapo. (emphasis mine, Pg. 18, "Axis Rule in Occupied Europe: Laws of Occupation, Analysis of Government, Proposals for Redress", The Lawbook Exchange, Ltd., 2005)

Furthermore, the Germans on trial made it abundantly clear what they were trying to accomplish in spilling so much blood. Dr. Karl Brandt was the key target of the Doctor's Trial, which was officially titled <u>United States of America v. Karl Brandt et al</u>. A key piece of evidence against Brandt was a letter signed by Adolf Hitler to Philip Bouhler charging Bouhler and Brandt with the task of "mercy killing" not for the murder of "ethnic," "racial," or "nationalities," but against "Aryan" Germans that had been deemed "life unworthy of living" or "useless eaters." This was the letter characterized by the prosecution as the evidence that Hitler authorized the murders and placed Brandt personally in charge.

More specifically and of greater consequence, these German doctors and jurists submitted all of the eugenic laws and texts produced by American and British doctors and lawmakers as their source of eugenic knowledge. The infamous "eugenic" laws enacted by the Third Reich were verbatim translations of the "Model Eugenical Sterilization Law" used by countless state legislatures in the United States to enact similar laws decades before Adolf Hitler. The German defense lawyers asserted that "civilized" nations such as France, the Netherlands, Britain, and the United States had performed dangerous medical experiments on prisoners, often without their consent. They called to the stand witnesses that testified as much, and this created "major unanticipated problems for the prosecution." It also significantly altered the prosecution's strategy by forcing it to sidetrack in order to define when risky human experimentation was ethically permissible. [14] As such, the scope and reach of the American prosecution in the Doctor's Trial was ultimately defined by the German defense. Leo Alexander knew very well that neither the experiments nor the euthanasia could be taken out of their eugenic context. To say that The Holocaust was merely a case of ethical violations in a relative handful of medical experiments ignores the millions upon millions of deaths that happened outside the scope of experimentation. To deny the integral and central role of eugenics in the

---

[14] nejm.org, "Fifty Years Later: The Significance of the Nuremberg Code", Evelyne Shuster, Ph.D., New England Journal of Medicine, November 13, 1997.

crimes of Third Reich was an abortion of justice and logic. Leo Alexander admitted as much:

> I believe that we do not contribute to our understanding of historical events if we simply 'question' whether these experiments had been carried out when they seem incredible to us. Instead we must face the facts, ascribing them to the power which social and political forces have upon the practical aspects of scientific and medical endeavor. (Pgs. 9-10, "Justice at Nuremberg: Leo Alexander and the Nazi Doctors' Trial", Ulf Schmidt, Palgrave Macmillan UK, 2004)

Yet, this is exactly what happened. The more the German doctors and lawyers insisted that their laws were derived from American eugenic laws, the more the American prosecutors avoided uttering the term "eugenics." Conspicuously so, this is the one term that went unspoken during the Doctor's Trial. The term "eugenics" was never used to accurately describe and document for all posterity the intent behind the crimes. In fact, neither "genocide" nor "eugenics" was utilized in any significant way throughout these extensive proceedings. [15] Instead, prosecutor Jackson chose the term "thanatology" for his opening statement of December 9, 1946. Leo Alexander claimed to have coined the terms "thanatology," defined as the study of death, and "ktenology," the science of killing. [16] These terms may have been appropriate for understanding a very limited amount of the human experiments conducted in the concentration camps. However, they detract from the legal requirement in a criminal case to accurately define the intent behind the overall murders. Their use is also evidence of just how limited the prosecution's argument became due to the pigeonhole the German defense cornered them into. Neither of these terms accurately or completely described the full scope of the "crimes against humanity." Even if the prosecution wanted to limit itself to only the experiments conducted in the concentration camps, there were a whole series of horrid human experiments that were in line with Hitler's dream of perfecting a "master race," and which had nothing to do with a fascination with how humans die, as the term "thanatology" suggests. Clearly, one cannot attribute to a curiosity with death the experiments which injected chemicals into the eyes of the victims to see if they could change the color from brown to the desirable "Aryan" blue. Yet, the portion of the indictment classified under Crimes Committed in the Guise of Scientific Research defined the work of these scientists not as "eugenics," but as "thanatology":

> Mankind has not heretofore felt the need of a word to denominate the science of how most rapidly to kill prisoners and subjugated people in large numbers. This case and these defendants have created this gruesome question for the lexicographer. For the moment, we will christen this macabre science **'thanatology,'** the science of producing death. The thanatological knowledge, derived in part from these experiments, supplied the techniques for genocide, a policy of the Third Reich exemplified in the "euthanasia" program and in the

---

[15] See Trial Transcripts: "Trials of War Criminals Before the Nuernberg Military Tribunals", Vol. 1. "The Medical Case", Superintendent of Documents, U.S. Government Printing Office.

[16] See: "War Crimes and Their Motivation: The Socio Psychological Structure of the SS and the Criminalization of a Society", Leo Alexander, Journal of Criminal Law and Criminology, 39 (3): 326, 1948.

widespread slaughter of Jews, gypsies, Poles and Russians. This policy of mass extermination could not have been so effectively carried out without the active participation of German medical scientists. (emphasis mine, ushmm.org, "Crimes Committed in the Guise of Scientific Research: From the Opening Statement by Telford Taylor", United States Holocaust Memorial – Citing "Trials of War Criminals Before the Nuremberg Military Tribunals Under Control Council Law No. 10, Nuremberg, October 1946 – April 1949", US G.P.O, 1949–1953)

Furthermore, the term was not invented in 1947, as Leo Alexander claimed. The term was used by scientists at least as far back as 1886. A medical dictionary from 1886 details the term, and the Online Etymology Dictionary dates the term as far back as 1842. [17] Yet another fraudulent claim by the American prosecution. The National Socialists went to great lengths to document the efforts they put towards purifying their "race." Yet, there was no evidence that there was a pathological or cultural fascination with the way humans die. Death was a means to an end, and not the end itself as the term "thanatology" erroneously indicates. To the contrary, what is truly disconcerting is the callous indifference there was with the death toll resulting from the leadership's policies.

This limitation of scope had its consequences, and what is truly gut-wrenching was the obvious disinterest with the large piles of cadavers and body parts traded amongst the various German institutions. More specifically, it is the civilian medical and scientific community that insisted on "learning" from what was transpiring in the camps, and it is the German academic community that was interested in the details of the experimentation, as well as in the harvest of body parts and medical data. By contrast, it is the indifference of the high-ranking policymakers of the Third Reich to the conditions of their victims that resonates to this day. Everything points to the fact that the mass murders, were just a means to an end no different than deportation, segregation, or sterilization of the unwanted.

The term "thanatology" has since been mentioned only in reference to Leo Alexander's claim to the term, and it has largely gone unnoticed even by Holocaust historians even though the American prosecution made the concept central to their opening statements at the Trial. In fact, the glaring omission of the role of "eugenics" now seems like a sleight of hand, a shell game on the part of the American prosecutors at Nuremberg. Why replace the otherwise verbose ideological propaganda of the National Socialists with term or a concept that was completely unknown to the criminals themselves? This decision certainly goes against the purposes of shedding light on the nature of the crimes, as any prosecution team should aspire to do in documenting the "intent" behind a series of murders. This certainly is a disservice to the effort to present compelling evidence, penned by the hands of the accused. Was this admission by omission on the part of the American prosecutors? Was it a tacit admission that they recognized the text of the laws passed

---

[17] Pg. 723 - "Complete Pronouncing Medical Dictionary: Terminology of Medicine and the Kindred Sciences with their Signification, Etymology, and Pronunciation", 1886.

by the Third Reich originated with the American legal and medical community? At the very least, it can be said that prosecutor Jackson's depiction was a grossly inaccurate definition of what these criminals were up to, and thus lacking as a valid legal strategy.

Most importantly, this conceptual detour is in large part to be blamed for the post-war amnesia with the central role eugenics played in the crime of The Holocaust. It is also a significant part of the reason why the medical and scientific community emerging from World War II were unable or unwilling to hold accountable the doctors and scientists that had obviously been complicit or criminally complacent. This is precisely what the Nuremberg Trials were meant to prevent, and Julian Huxley's UNESCO statement evidences the extent to which the global eugenics movement escaped culpability. We are still living under the fog of the American prosecution's limited depiction and description of the crime. Case in point, the fact that eugenic sterilizations continued to be legally practiced within the United States until the late 1970s evidence how lacking the prosecution's effort was in clearly documenting the nature of the crimes. This limited description of the crimes to this day diminishes the deeds of National Socialism to a common form of guttural racism by petty street thugs and whitewashed the broader role of the doctors, scientists, judges, legislators, and lawyers in the crime.

In retrospect, it has taken historians 50 to 60 years to lift this fog, unearth the facts, and understand National Socialism's true "eugenic" aspirations. Arthur L. Caplan touches upon the necessity to accurately describe the "nature of the wrong-doing," whether it be criminal human experimentation, genocide, "thanatology," or outright murder:

> But murder and genocide are not the same as intentionally causing someone to suffer and die to fulfill a scientific goal. Killing for scientific purposes, while certainly as evil as murder in the service of racial hygiene, is, nonetheless, morally different. The torture and killing that were at the core of Nazi medical experiments involves not only torture and murder but also the exploitation of human beings to serve the goals of science. To describe what happened in language other than that... blurs the nature of the wrong-doing. (Pg. 65, "When Medicine Went Mad: Bioethics and the Holocaust", Humana Press, 1992)

What Caplan calls for was, after all, the entire justification for holding a trial, as opposed to summary executions as Winston Churchill desired. Any deviation from this goal served only to hijack history and pervert any understanding of the crimes by future generations. Arguably, this is precisely what has happened. Any "blurring" of the "nature of the wrong-doing" severely undermined the effectiveness of the Nuremberg Trials and left a vacuum for Holocaust denial theories to fill. The Holocaust is commonly understood as the product of vulgar racism and irrational behavior, and it has taken nearly half a century to simply begin to uncover the serious amount of complicity from the scientific and medical fields. Richard John Neuhaus's observation has become iconic of the focus of 21st Century Holocaust study: "We think of the Holocaust as a rampage of irrationality, but as we tend to overlook the banality of evil so also we overlook the rationality of evil." [18] Sara Seiler Vigorito, one of the unfortunate twins that Dr. Mengele experimented on, provides clarity:

> It is most important to realize that these Nazi physicians or scientists were not monsters or madmen. The Nazi doctor did not have any physical or immediately recognizable distinction that would set him apart from our family doctor. After my sister and I were selected by Mengele for his experiments on twins and diseases, we had almost daily contact with him. He was extremely intelligent and although his victims feared him, he was never thought of as a monster. Rather, it was the depth of his intellect twisted into a science of human destruction that we, even the youngest of his victims, feared most. (Pg. 11, "When Medicine Went Mad: Bioethics and the Holocaust", Humana Press, 1992)

John Foster Dulles's appointment to Secretary of State during the Nuremberg Trials may be a clue as to why the American prosecution avoided the obvious "eugenic" subject-matter. As the Secretary of State, the foreign affairs arm of American government, John Foster Dulles would have a significant influence on the trials. John Foster Dulles was a Rockefeller man. The Kaiser Wilhelm Institute for Eugenics, Anthropology and Human Heredity was run by Ernst Rüdin, Hitler's foremost "racial hygienist," and financing for entire wings of the institute came from Rockefeller. The Rockefeller Foundation was also a financial spearhead for eugenics in the United State with John Foster Dulles, not just as the lawyer for Rockefeller's Standard Oil, but as an active participant when the Eugenics Record Office was erected on Dulles's estate. The Eugenics Record Office at Cold Spring Harbor was the epicenter of American eugenics under the leadership of Harvard's Charles Benedict Davenport and his cohort Harry H. Laughlin. Laughlin not only wrote the eugenic laws that were copied verbatim by Hitler's jurists and legislators, but had been the "Expert Eugenicist" for the United States Congress and had appeared as an expert witness before the US Supreme Court in the landmark case that made eugenic sterilization legal in the United States. The Cold Spring Harbor Laboratory was built on the estates of John Foster and Allen Dulles in 1904, and both Dulles brothers openly professed John D. Rockefeller's racial hygiene and human perfectibility doctrines. John Foster Dulles has been quoted as saying that a purer race could be created by eliminating "the weakest members of the population." [19]

John Foster Dulles served as the Chairman of the Board at the Rockefeller Foundation, which was the organization through which Rockefeller embarked on recreating the medical industry in the United States. For example, William Welch was the president of the Board of Directors of the Rockefeller Institute of Medicine, trustee of the Carnegie Institute, and president of the American Medical Association. [20] He was also a founding member of various eugenics organizations in the United States. Beyond that, before becoming Eisenhower's Secretary of State, John Foster Dulles was an OSS spy during the war, director of the CIA, and part of

---

[18] Pg. 226, "When Medicine Went Mad: Bioethics and the Holocaust", Humana Press, 1992.
[19] Pg. 20 - "Abraham Flexner: A Flawed American Icon," Michael Nevins, iUniverse, 2010.
[20] "Time for another revolution? The Flexner Report in Historic Context, Reflections on our Profession", Michael R. Mindrum, Coronary Artery Disease Journal, 2006 Ed.

the American delegation that decided US policy in occupied Germany. Dulles, his brother, his famously wealthy former clients, and former employers, all had an active role in the American eugenics organization that had drafted the laws that the Germans defense would submit as evidence in the Doctor's Trial.

Needless to say, there was no way John Foster Dulles was unaware of the central role "eugenics" played in the Third Reich, and it would hardly be believable to contend that he was unaware of just how influential the eugenic-minded community was inside the United States. Could Secretary Dulles condone an international tribunal that criminalized and demonized the very science that was being carried out in his family's estate with the funding of his most famous and lucrative client? The political stakes were high, and the political class acted accordingly.

Researchers will come across a seemingly innocuous, but altogether revealing series of letters when one peruses General Telford Taylor's papers at Columbia University. The Columbia University archives have a folder with a series of letters between Telford Taylor, Dr. Olga Lang, and the Carnegie and Rockefeller institutions. Dr. Lang was an accomplished Russian born sociologist who had previously published on Chinese family structures and, more importantly, had been a "chief research analyst" for the Subsequent Trials, namely the first Doctors' Trial and the RuSHA trials. [21] She had access to all of the evidence for the Subsequent Trials as she was in charge of preparing the evidence for those trials, and more so, had been sponsored by Rafael Lemkin and the Institute of European Affairs of Columbia University to use her time at Nuremberg for research. A March 15th, 1949 letter from Dr. Lang requests Telford Taylor's help in acquiring a grant from either the Carnegie or Rockefeller institutions so she could complete and publish a book to be titled "Master Race and Genocide." [22] The letter states her intentions to publish "much of the material which was not used as evidence," namely the part concerning "Nazi eugenics." The most interesting item in this archival folder is Dr. Lang's six-page outline that was included in a June 9th, 1949 letter to Telford Taylor, and which was later copied to the heads of the Carnegie and Rockefeller institutions. That six-page summary of Dr. Lang's proposed book offers a far more lucid and comprehensive explanation for the "crimes" and Nazism's "race hygiene" policies than the voluminous presentations by both Telford Taylor and Justice Jackson during the various trials. It elucidates the connection between "positive" and "negative" eugenics, Nietzsche and Gobineau as predecessors of eugenics and "race hygiene," National Socialist marriage laws, "Lebensraum" expansionist policy, Nordicism, Aryanism, the kidnapping of "Nordic" children from conquered nations, "cultural and moral genocide," the creation of a "racial elite" in the ranks of the SS, and most importantly, the annihilation of "inferior races" and "useless eaters" through eugenic "sterilization" and eugenic "euthanasia." Dr. Lang clearly understood the evidence to point to an all-encompassing eugenic program with no demarcations between civilian and military.

---

[21] BOX 46 – Folder No. 5-3-2-11 – Telford Taylor Papers, Columbia Univ., Rare Book & Manuscript Library, Call No.: MS#1647 (All letters mentioned in this paragraph are contained in the same folder).
[22] Ibid.

To Telford Taylor's credit, a March 17th, 1949 letter to the Director of Social Sciences at the Rockefeller Foundation even pinpoints the very paragraphs of the memorandum of the Carnegie Endowment for International Peace which mandate the utilization of the Nuremberg Trial materials for publications precisely like the one proposed by Dr. Lang. [23] Yet, curiously enough, both Rockefeller and Carnegie denied her. A March 24th, 1949 letter from Dr. James T. Shotwell of the Carnegie Endowment for International Peace shares the letter of denial with Telford Taylor, seemingly hoping for approval on how he handled the matters. Incidentally, Dr. Shotwell was not only one of the heads of Carnegie, but a founding member of UNESCO along with Julian Huxley.

As a "chief research analyst" with unimpeded access to all the evidence lockers, Dr. Lang clearly had a handle on the evidence available to the American prosecution. Why was all this evidence on "Nazi eugenics" not utilized? Did a lowly research analyst have a better understanding of Nazism, its policies and laws, than the top jurists, justices, and attorneys from the United States appointed to the task of precisely defining the nature of the "crimes"? However sophisticated Dr. Lang was, the proposition that she knew something that a Supreme Court Justice and the Chief Counsel for the Prosecution didn't is silly, to put it kindly.

Thus, it begs to question: Was the American prosecution team cornered into a limited exposition of the criminal complicity of the medical and scientific community in Germany, or were they pigeonholed from the onset out of recognition of the deep entanglement between the American and German medical and legal communities? This isn't a question emerging from conspiracy theories. We must recognize that this is real politics in a world where wealth and political position steer the course of historical events. Just about every major player involved was compromised by a history with the "science" of eugenics including Churchill, Dulles, the US Supreme Court, as well as the German-speaking medical experts pulled in for the Doctor's Trial. The fact that the chief expert, Ivy, was nothing short of a conman willing to mislead not just the court, but the entire world despite the deep and sensitive wounds certainly doesn't speak well of the ethics of the American prosecution.

It is also important to mention that one of the American judges appointed to preside over the Subsequent Trials, Judge Charles F. Wennerstrum of the Iowa Supreme Court, felt that the Trials had been administered unjustly. The correspondence between Judge Wennestrum and other members of the International Military Tribunal is revealing. In a June 21st, 1948 letter Judge Wennerstrum complains to Gorge M. Read, a Secretary-General of the Courts in Nuremberg, that Telford Taylor used his position as General to intercept the contents of the contentious interview with the Chicago Tribune before it being published. [24] Taylor responded by calling Judge Wennerstrum "warped" and "psychopathic" in a response

---

[23] BOX 46 – Folder No. 5-3-2-11 – Telford Taylor Papers, Columbia Univ., Rare Book & Manuscript Library, Call No.: MS#1647 (All letters mentioned in this paragraph are contained in the same folder).
[24] Correspondence 4.001-4.006 – Judge Wennestrum Papers, State Historical Society of Iowa.

Taylor had published prior to Wennerstrum's original interview. [25] Of note is that Judge Wennerstrum is remembered as a "strict law judge, fair in his decisions, and not a publicity seeker," and that certainly comes through in reading his personal correspondence. [26] Telford Taylor tried to escalate the spat into a public battle, but Wennestrum seems to have taken the level headed approach of making his arguments and complaints in speeches and intentionally leave it to history to be the judge of the issues he raised. More to the point, Wennerstrum is important to the subject of this book because his speeches and personal correspondence provide the first-person testimony of one of the Nuremberg Trial judges as to the legal aberrations and questionable tactics of the American Military Tribunals. A whole book could be written deliberating his legal analysis of the Trials, but the more salient and relevant points reveal serious improprieties, namely having the Office of the Chief Counsel of the Prosecution enjoy administrative power over the court, a position used to exert questionable controls by toying with the Rules of Evidence; an observation that goes a long way to explain how evidence and issues central to the grander questions at trial went unaddressed. [27] The judge could not have been far off the mark, as a Writ of Habeas Corpus was brought before the United States Supreme Court complaining of the tactics and aberrant practices employed at the Nuremberg Trials, and the Court delivered a 4-to-4 divided opinion, hardly a resounding endorsement or bill of good health. [28] The ninth deciding vote would have been Justice Robert Jackson, who recused himself for obvious reasons.

The proximate consequence of Nuremberg was that German top doctors and scientists central to the crimes of the Third Reich not only escaped punishment but went on to finish their careers unscathed and uninterrupted. They were captured, then allowed to walk free despite their central role in the crimes. Case in point, the World Medical Association, which was established during World War II, has been accused of undermining the Nuremberg Trials in order to distance physicians from the medical crimes. [29] The election of a former National Socialist physician and SS member, Hans-Joachim Sewering, to the presidency of that organization in 1992 added credibility to that accusation. Many of the decisions made by the American prosecution are to blame for the artificial line of demarcation that punished some doctors and scientists and absolved their equally complicit counterparts. It has certainly contributed to the relative impunity the eugenic-minded scientific and medical community has enjoyed. Many of the international organizations that aided and abetted, or in a wartime sense gave "aid and comfort to the enemy," were spared the scorn of history and continue to operate with impunity to this day. Some have changed their names, and others simply coined different medical terms for the same eugenic concepts.

---

[25] uipress.llib.uiowa.edu - Wennerstrum, Charles Fredrick – The Biographical Dictionary of Iowa, Univ. of Iowa Digital Edition.

[26] Ibid.

[27] Speeches 5.001-5.008 – Judge Wennestrum Papers, State Historical Society of Iowa, "Joint Luncheon Meeting of Section of International & Comparative Law and Junior Bar Conference at the Annual Meeting of the American Bar Association, Sept. 7th, 1948".

[28] See: Everett v. Truman, 1948, 334 U.S. 824, 68 S.Ct. 1081.

[29] "Fifty Years Later", Dr. Evelyne Shuster, New England Journal of Medicine, Nov. 13, 1997.

The history of The Holocaust has proven for all eternity that questions improperly answered will linger in our collective conscience. How do you get a highly educated and cultured population, the "land of poets and thinkers," to commit mass murder? The answer to this lingering question was within the grasp of the American prosecution at Nuremberg. It was these very German "thinkers" that should have been on trial. The subsequent trials for the German doctors, scientists, lawyers, and judges was the opportunity to provide answers to this very poignant question: Where were all the educated men of sober mind when Adolf Hitler called for an eradication of significant swaths of German society?

Sec. 4 – THE "SILENCE OF DECADES":

A smattering of the "Nazi atrocities" had appeared throughout newspapers in the United States during the war. Early on, it was difficult for the public to distinguish them from the atrocities of World War I, the Russian famines, and many pro-German Americans were claiming such events were just propaganda. There is certainly something to be said for raw images and film footage, as no amount of reports made any impact until the public saw actual film footage and photography of the extermination camps.

On April 11, 1945, the American Third Army liberated the Buchenwald concentration camp near Weimar, Germany. Young American soldiers came face to face with Hitler's atrocities for the first time, and thereafter, a ghastly realism came to replace what had once been the topic of scant reports and rumors. The following month, the American public was shocked by film footage of the "Nazi atrocities." General Eisenhower made it a point to document the ghastly sights his army had seen with its own eyes. Pictures are in fact worth a thousand words, and these pictures would forever separate the long line of injustices and genocidal acts of antiquity with the acts Eisenhower's filmmakers captured. In fact, it would be years before the world would come to know the exact scope and number of victims documented by the photography and film, yet the images communicated the unprecedented nature of the crimes. The specific knowledge of the industrialization and methodology of the murders was also a realization that would come after the photos and film reels, but the images of the piles of bodies communicated the methodological aspect of the murders.

Holocaust history has become a topic of history itself. The history of the history evidence that this brief period of awareness following the initial shock was followed by decades of silence both in the Gentile and Jewish circles. Historians since have grappled with understanding this seemingly inexplicable silence in the aftermath of such barbarity. Cited here are some of these historians, as their precise words are worth documenting for posterity, and are in of themselves now part of the historical account of Holocaust history. Among the works important for this specific section are:

- "The Holocaust and American Public Memory, 1945-1960," an in-depth study of post-war Holocaust studies and coverage by Lawrence Baron. Baron is an Abraham Nasatir Professor of Modern Jewish History and Director of the Lipinsky Institute for Judaic Studies at San Diego State University.
- Sean Warsch's "A 'holocaust' becomes 'the Holocaust'" for the October 2006 Jewish Magazine.
- Lastly is the indispensable 2004 documentary by Daniel Anker titled "Imaginary Witness: Hollywood and the Holocaust. The documentary interviews key Hollywood and media players of the past and present to gather authoritative opinions on the role the media played in the decades of silence and then the subsequent onslaught of recent Holocaust awareness.

As the "Imaginary Witness" documentary aptly points out, it is not until May 1945 that the newsreels aired for movie-going audiences that the American public was shaken out of its state of incredulity and denial. According to the documentary, record audiences crowded into theaters to see the "Nazi atrocities" for themselves. General Eisenhower made personally sure that both German and American public would be made aware of the harsh realities. The story of him forcing Germans to clean up the concentration camps is well documented by World War II historians. Anker's documentary adds to this history by telling the story of how Eisenhower personally made sure that key American filmmakers were flown in to document the horrors.

The resulting shock was unprecedented, and the Allies were literally forced to respond to world-wide indignation with the Nuremberg Trials. It is the educated guess of this author that the Allies would not have done so if it not for General Eisenhower's deliberate efforts. Without those film reels, the Holocaust may very well have remained a rumor, as history proves that despite the preponderance of evidence, many still question whether the Holocaust ever happened. While no one questions if the Spanish Inquisition or the Cambodian Killing Fields ever happened, the Holocaust uncomfortably shares persistent conspiracy theories and denials, as if it were a UFO sighting. This difference in historical treatment, by itself, is worth exploring, and this book delves into the various possible reasons for this phenomenon. One thing is for sure: factual inconsistencies and disingenuous untruth harbor conspiracy theories like filth harbor disease, and the highly questionable approach of the Allies in the Nuremberg Trials must be blamed for leaving a legacy of doubt and unanswered questions. The crimes of The Holocaust did not need building up, yet it is the Allied prosecution that is responsible for creating an aura of "otherness" for the crimes. It is the Allied prosecution at Nuremberg that is responsible for the illusion that the crimes sprouted seemingly out of one dictator's mind, and that they had no root in history prior. Much of this was obviously done to hide any of the relevant connections between German eugenics and American and

British eugenic organizations. The Russians, under Stalin's rule, had their own skeletons to hide and disingenuously stood in judgment of the Germans after having annihilated tens of millions of their own citizens.

It is also the educated guess of this author that the silent decades that followed made denial easier, as the catalog of evidence demonstrates how The Holocaust initially disappeared as a topic, only to resurface with renewed interest decades after. This inexplicable gap and subsequent resurgence are of interest, historically speaking. The American public was shocked up through the main Nuremberg Trial, and then it seems as if all of General Eisenhower's efforts were blown away with the blinding flash of Hiroshima. From Hiroshima on, the public was mesmerized and focused by the very reality of having the Cold War turn into thermo-nuclear war, and the world remained in this state of fear for decades to follow. For the contentious decades of the Cold War the history of World War II was mostly limited to military and political topics, and there seemed to be no serious recognition of the greatest murders in history – not Hitler's, not Lenin's, not Stalin's or Mao's mega-murders received the recognition that these events demanded.

This was the reality of Holocaust studies up until the very recent past. Up until the late 1970's and early 1980's, the focus of World War II history had been a military one, focusing on the headlines and sound bites of the major battles and political events, mostly treating World War II as if it was any other war, and The Holocaust just any other among many war crimes. Very little was written about the link between the eugenics movement and the Holocaust, and even through the revelation of "Nazi atrocities" and the subsequent Nuremberg Trials, the link was largely ignored. The link between the American eugenic organizations and their German counterparts was seldom explored thereafter. Evidence to this was how eugenic groups in the United States emerged completely unscathed and were able to continue for decades sterilizing tens of thousands of victims against their will much in the way the Nazis had. Much less did the American public learn of an even more disturbing connection; that the boys and girls that we now recognize as being part of "The Greatest Generation" were the target of these American eugenic organizations, and that many of the soldiers that liberated Europe from Hitler's eugenic Holocaust, were themselves sterilized against their will. [30] These were the sons and daughters of the "unfit" and the undesired populations of immigrants and poorly educated rural Americans. They were the Italian, Irish and African Americans who would be asked to return to the countries of their immediate ancestry and liberate worlds their fathers and grandfathers had left behind. That this "Greatest Generation" was the target of the very same American eugenicists that also helped Hitler create his eugenic state is a topic that historians have only recently begun to document.

Several milestones in history contributed to this relative silence about The Holocaust. First, one must realize that one of the main reasons for not properly documenting or addressing such a critical historical event was the result of the

---

[30] "The Greatest Generation" term was coined and popularized by Tom Brokaw's 1998 book by that title.

practical and political realities of the Cold War. An entire portion of the world was behind the "Iron Curtain," along with half of the historical records. Individuals that remember living in the Cold War remember the great obscurity there was about anything that transpired behind the Iron Curtain. The West simply had very little knowledge of what daily life was like inside the USSR, and much less access to the historical records of anything that transpired inside the territories that fell into Stalin's hands. This territory of obscurity represented not only half of Germany but most of the Eastern European nations where the Jewish populations were decimated. Until then, it can easily be said that Western historians had at best access to only half of the facts and half of the evidence. As Christian Pross opined, many of the participating individuals and institutions, those people and organizations which were entangled with German eugenics, were for their own reasons not forthcoming about their relationships. Doctors and scientists who had inconvenient connections with Hitler's policies kept this information closely guarded and reportedly engaged in the outright destruction and concealment of the remaining documentation.

One would have to have grown up during the Cold War to remember the persistent fear of world-destruction through a nuclear holocaust. Experiencing how the Cold War escalated first the Korean War, then Vietnam, along with the various incidents in Latin America, including the Cuban Revolution and subsequent Missile Crisis, is the only way to understand how the fear of a nuclear "holocaust" would go a long way to obscuring or at least postponing, the memory of The Holocaust:

> Despite disagreements over what sparked the 1960s and 1970s interest in the Holocaust, scholars seem to agree upon why the memory of the Jewish catastrophe was either forgotten or repressed between the end of World War II and the Eichmann trial. Following Allied victory, the destruction of European Jewry was widely subsumed under the generic category of war casualties and crimes. The mushroom clouds over Hiroshima and Nagasaki appeared to many as ominous as the smoke rising from the crematoria of Auschwitz. (Pgs. 62-88, "The Holocaust and American Public Memory, 1945–1960", Holocaust and Genocide Studies, Vol. 17, Issue 1, Jan. 1, 2003)

Furthermore, the bitter partisanship and propaganda of the Cold War within the West only made the fog of this war that much denser. One simply could not count on getting the unfiltered facts from supposedly reputable sources. Even the most reputable of academic institutions or publications were deeply partisan. The university classroom suffered from partisan taint as much as the formal journals, news outlets, and publications. Major outlets simply whitewashed, downplayed, or altogether dismissed the genocidal acts of the USSR even after Khrushchev denounced the excesses of Stalin. This is precisely where the perversion of the definitions of terms such as "right" and "left," "liberal" or "conservative," "democracy" and "freedom" became subject to the manipulations of Cold War propaganda. This is where they lost their usefulness as formal terms for historical accuracy and were otherwise twisted into tools for partisan propaganda. Clarity was simply not forthcoming until decades after the fall of the Berlin Wall, and the boom in Holocaust studies followed.

Germany had been splintered into sections, and the Cold War was in full sway before troops could be drawn down and reconstruction of Europe begin. One must remember that this was the time at the end of the war when General Patton was clamoring to keep advancing toward Moscow in order to eradicate Stalin before he became a bigger problem, and that the British, in tacit support of Patton's suggestion, kept the confiscated German armaments and munitions intact in the places where they were conquered, as opposed to removing them as the orders called for them to do. Tensions in occupied Germany as to the propriety and impartiality of the Nuremberg Trials were a significant issue for the Americans to contend with as well, and this ran counter to the efforts of creating a free and democratic Germany that would be immune to the enticements of Marxist advancement. The notion that all Germans shared in a "collective guilt" conspired to potentially keep German "hearts and minds" as dedicated enemies, instead of friends. This would turn out to be another reason for limiting the scope of the conspirators at Nuremberg, specifically not to include the various civilian research institutions and German universities known at the time of the Nuremberg Doctors' Trial to be complicit.

The artificial limitation of the Nuremberg Trials accomplished its goal: the crimes were cleanly cordoned off and erroneously defined as a peculiarity specific to bigotry allegedly ingrained in German culture. The Nuremberg Trials contained the potential political catastrophe to American and British science, and thus the inconvenient connections remained in obscurity preventing any further discussion beyond Nuremberg. "Imaginary Witness" discusses the decades-long silence that spanned entire generations about a topic so central to our humanity. The documentary features interviews with some of Hollywood's present and past greats, including substantial input from filmmaker Steven Spielberg discussing the task of capturing the essence of such a traumatizing and ground-shaking event such as the Holocaust. The very first images of The Holocaust came through these news reels that were played before main features, and that it was the newsreels, not the main feature that the American public was lining up to see in droves. [31] As "Imaginary Witness" recalls, this serves to illustrate just how limited and focused the channels of information were in that era. Satellite TV, streaming Internet video, and the many venues that have dedicated themselves to history and documentaries, have made history more readily available to the public than it was during the days of local TV and the paltry number of channels one received through rabbit-ear antennas. The Internet has allowed first-hand information about history to become easily accessible by the public, along with a seemingly infinite amount of scholarly and non-scholarly historical analysis that simply was previously the realm of the professional. Before then, one could easily argue that the typical person's knowledge of the Holocaust came from the infrequent Hollywood or made-for-TV dramas about World War II. Thus, recent generations, as well as those of us who have forgotten our disconnected and analog lives, may find it hard to comprehend the relative hush about The

---

[31] "The Holocaust in the Movies", Tova Stulman, Jewish Press review of "Imaginary Witness", January 9, 2008.

Holocaust up until the very late 20th and early 21st centuries. The aptly titled "A 'holocaust' becomes 'The Holocaust'," by Sean Warsch, makes several important points:

> If one looked in the dictionary, he/she would see that the definition of the word holocaust reads along the line of "complete destruction, usually by fire." Some dictionaries also include in their definition references to a sacrifice and/or loss of life. However, when the term holocaust is used today, one immediately thinks of the systematic killing of millions of European Jews at the hands of the Nazis. When news of these atrocities first reached the United States, reactions to this news ranged from horror to sadness to complete disbelief. Only after seeing firsthand the physical proof (pictures of those interred at the concentration camps, proof that gas chambers, whose sole purpose of killing human beings, had been erected) of this massacre did people come to accept what had occurred. (jewishmag.com, "A 'holocaust' becomes 'The Holocaust'," Jewish Magazine, Oct. 2006)

Warsch reminds us that it was decades after World War II that the "crimes against humanity" came to encompass and define the term "holocaust" as "The" Holocaust:

> "Starting in the 1940s, when the majority of the killings took place, some people described the massacre as "the Hitler holocaust" or "the Nazi holocaust." However, only much later, when full accounts of what had happened came to light, were fully accepted in society, and frequently talked about, did people start using the term "the Holocaust," Holocaust being capitalized and being proceeded by the word "the." (jewishmag.com, "A 'holocaust' becomes 'The Holocaust'," Jewish Magazine, Oct. 2006)

Zev Garber researched the slow appearance of The Holocaust as a topic of scholarly interest by researching the number of doctoral dissertations with the word "Holocaust" in the title. Sean Warsch documents Garber's findings and reports that there were none before 1970, 21 between 1970 and 1975, 97 between 1976 and 1980, and 274 between 1981 and 1985. In other words, scholarly interest in The Holocaust did not begin until forty years after Eisenhower forced the images upon the public.

This book documents why Winston Churchill never wanted to shine too much light on the link between pre-war eugenics and Hitler's henchmen. The following quote is attributed to Richard Lynn, Professor Emeritus, University of Ulster, contributor to Mankind Quarterly, president of the Pioneer Fund, and one of the sources cited in the infamous book, "The Bell Curve"; all infamous names that the reader will become familiar with. Lynn was labeled a Holocaust-denier, and more importantly, this quote has fueled vile anti-Semites and white supremacists to double-down on their denial claims:

> I've checked out Churchill's Second World War and the statement is quite correct not a single mention of Nazi 'gas chambers,' a 'genocide' of the Jews, or of 'six million' Jewish victims of the war. This is astonishing. How can it be

explained? Eisenhower's Crusade in Europe is a book of 559 pages; the six volumes of Churchill's Second World War total 4,448 pages; and de Gaulle's three-volume Memoires de guerre is 2,054 pages. In this mass of writing, which altogether totals 7,061 pages (not including the introductory parts), published from 1948 to 1959, one will find no mention either of Nazi 'gas chambers,' a 'genocide' of the Jews, or of 'six million' Jewish victims of the war. (Richard Lynn, December 5, 2005)

The above quote is more indicative of Churchill's motivations than it is of Lynn's for all the reasons extrapolated throughout this book. This book was conceived upon the observation that the seeds of Holocaust denial take root in misinformation. Clarity and transparency are imperative, as they leave no room for denial theories that would deprive the victims of justice or rob the living of a reliable history from which to chart the future.

Why is it that Churchill omitted any mention of the Holocaust in the 4,448 pages he wrote about WWII? The public still is fascinated by World War II and The Holocaust, and arguably more so than with more recent wars such as Vietnam, Korea, and the Middle East wars. However, the scholars did stop documenting it for nearly half a century, as the evidence demonstrates. Obviously, this vacuum of information provided ample room for Holocaust denial;

> Abstract: Until the 1960s, many scholars assert, most Americans' awareness of the Holocaust was based upon vague, trivial, or inaccurate representations. Between the end of the war and the 1960s, as anyone who has lived through those years can testify, the Holocaust made scarcely any appearance in American public discourse, and hardly more in Jewish public discourse - especially discourse directed to gentiles. (Pgs. 62-88, "The Holocaust and American Public Memory, 1945–1960", Lawrence Baron, Holocaust and Genocide Studies, Vol. 17, Issue I, Jan. 1, 2003)

If we return to Buchenwald in April 1945, the camp whose atrocities first inspired Eisenhower to document the crimes with film and photography, we are reminded of one of the many reasons why revealing too much about the medical and scientific complicity in the "crimes against humanity" were politically inconvenient. Buchenwald is just the start of how this politically inconvenient link quickly begins to unravel. Dr. Edwin Katzen-Ellenbogen, the Harvard-educated doctor from New Jersey had originally served as a translator and expert during the Nuremberg Doctors Trial but was ultimately singled out as a collaborator and perpetrator. [32] Dr. Katzen-Ellenbogen was a particularly difficult defendant for the International Military Tribunal to pin with guilt, as he was fluent in English and knew enough about the American origins of the eugenics movement to dance circles around the prosecution. He certainly understood how eugenic policies were at the center of many of the activities at Buchenwald:

---

[32] "The Story of the New Jersey Doctor Who Helped Kill Prisoners at Buchenwald in the Name of Eugenics", Edwin Black, waragainsttheweak.com, Nov. 10, 2003.

Eugenics was always an undercurrent at Buchenwald. One block was known as the *Ahnenforschung* barrack, or ancestral research barrack. It was worked by a small detachment known as *Kommando 22a*, mainly Czech prisoners, researching and assembling family trees of SS officers. SS officers were required to document pure Aryan heredity. In addition, the SS Race and Settlement Office was systematically sweeping through Poland looking for *Volksdeutsche*, that is, persons of any German ancestry. When this agency discovered Polish children eugenically certified to have Aryan blood, the youngsters were kidnapped and raised in "Germanized" Nazi environments. As a skilled and doctrinaire eugenicist, Katzen-Ellenbogen was assigned to perform eugenic examinations of Polish prisoners, seeking those fit for Germanization. Eugenic certification saved them from extermination. (waragainsttheweak.com, "The Story of the New Jersey Doctor Who Helped Kill Prisoners at Buchenwald in the Name of Eugenics", Edwin Black, Nov. 10, 2003)

Katzen-Ellenbogen was Catholic with Jewish ancestry and thus was sent to the concentration camps when captured in Paris, despite his collaboration with the Gestapo. The Buchenwald administrators learned through the prisoner grapevine about Katzen-Ellenbogen's helpfulness to the Gestapo in France. He quickly became a trusted prisoner to the camp's medical staff and its SS officers, namely the camp doctor, Gerhard Schiedlausky. Dr. Katzen-Ellenbogen made it known that he was an American doctor, and the German doctors found him not only useful because of his ability to speak several languages but because he was sympathetic to their cause. He ultimately became one of doctors and scientists at Buchenwald that conducted the horrifying series of medical experiments.

Interestingly enough, Katzen-Ellenbogen was both a founding member of the prestigious Carnegie Institution as well as the chief eugenicist of New Jersey under Woodrow Wilson when Wilson was governor of the state. Under Woodrow Wilson's governorship, Dr. Katzen-Ellenbogen was asked to become scientific director of the State Village for Epileptics at Skillman, New Jersey. It was there that he would develop his eugenic interests, and when he was asked by Wilson to draft New Jersey's law to sterilize epileptics and defectives forcibly. In 1913, Katzen-Ellenbogen became charter member #14 of the Eugenics Research Association at Cold Spring Harbor at the Rockefeller and Carnegie funded facility located on the Dulles family estate. Yet, despite his leadership role in the murders and tortures in one of the main extermination camps, Dr. Katzen-Ellenbogen was not made to answer for his complicity in the "conspiracy" to commit "murder" at the Nuremberg Doctors' Trial, nor was he dealt with in American courts for any charges of treason or aiding and abetting the enemy. Clearly, the revelation of a prestigious American doctor, connected to a US President and the most prestigious financial and civic institutions was but the beginning of an uncomfortable silence which endured for decades after American soldiers liberated the first concentration camp.

In a broader sense, the crimes committed at Buchenwald are connected to two different presidents, and these two relationships evidence the political divergence that persists within the United States. Eisenhower's eagerness to permanently document the atrocities indicates either a commendable honesty or an obliviousness to the political implications. The deputy in charge of Wilson's eugenic policies as was central to the eugenic barbarism of Buchenwald. Eisenhower represents an America oblivious to and traditionally educated against the elitist aspirations of dogmas like that of eugenics. Eugenics cannot be anything but elitism at its worst, in its arrogant claim to place in the hands of so very few the decision of who dies and who lives to contribute to society. It is a creed that is at odds with a traditional anti-elitist American ethic that put an end to rule by an elite aristocracy or monarchy. It is therefore of crucial importance to understand precisely how the science of eugenics came to gain such a strong foothold within the United States, the very place where it should have been vehemently banished. Revealing the reasons is one of the purposes of this book, as in doing so we gain an accurate understanding of the crimes and a reasoning for the silence that followed General Eisenhower exposing them.

Sec. 5 - "MENS REA":

On January 16, 1944, the US Secretary of the Treasury, Henry Morgenthau, Jr., and one of his deputies, Randolph Paul, visited President Franklin D. Roosevelt to coerce him to finally act and do something to help refugees escaping The Holocaust. More diplomatic efforts had failed, so Morgenthau's approach strengthened. The report delivered to the President reads as a desperate and necessary act to coerce a response from an administration that was systematically and overtly preventing both private and official help for the victims escaping Hitler. The report documents a pattern of attempts by the State Department to obstruct various rescue opportunities and block the flow of Holocaust information to the United States. Morgenthau warned that the refugee issue had become "a boiling pot on [Capitol] Hill," and Congress was likely to pass the rescue resolution if faced with a White House unwilling to act. Roosevelt understood the deep political implications of inaction and pre-empted "The Hill" by establishing the War Refugee Board. The result was "Executive Order 9417" issued on January 22, 1944.

The report Morgenthau and Paul delivered was titled "Report to the Secretary on the Acquiescence of this Government in the Murder of the Jews." Josiah DuBois wrote the report for Morgenthau and Paul, and it was an all-out indictment of the US State Department's diplomatic, military and immigration policies. The Jewish Virtual Library website by the American-Israeli Cooperative Enterprise has a copy of the report posted, reprinted here at length, as it is useful in depicting the severity of the situation:

> I am convinced on the basis of the information which is available to me that certain officials in our State Department, which – have been guilty not only of

gross procrastination and willful failure to act, but even of willful attempts to prevent action from being taken to rescue Jews from Hitler.

CONTINUES...

Unless remedial steps of a drastic nature are taken, and taken immediately, I am certain that no effective action will be taken by this government to prevent the complete extermination of the Jews in German controlled Europe, and that this Government will have to share for all time responsibility for this extermination. (jewishvirtuallibrary.org, January 13, 1944, "Report to the Secretary on the Acquiescence of this Government in the Murder of the Jews")

The catalyst for the report was an incident involving 70,000 Jews whose evacuation from Romania could have been procured with a relatively meager $170,000 bribe. The Foreign Funds Control unit of the US Treasury, which was within Randolph Paul's jurisdiction, had already authorized the payment of the funds. From mid-July 1943, when the proposal was made, and Treasury approved, through December 1943, a combination of the State Department's bureaucracy and the British Ministry of Economic Warfare interposed various obstacles. In a broader context, the report enumerates a larger pattern and practice of obstructionist policies intended to prevent the immigration of Jewish refugees into the United States:

(1) They have not only failed to use the Governmental machinery at their disposal to rescue Jews from Hitler, but have even gone so far as to use this Government machinery to prevent the rescue of these Jews.
(2) They have not only failed to cooperate with private organizations in the efforts of these organizations to work out individual programs of their own, but have taken steps designed to prevent these programs from being put into effect.
(3) They not only have failed to facilitate the obtaining of information concerning Hitler's plans to exterminate the Jews of Europe but in their official capacity have gone so far as to surreptitiously attempt to stop the obtaining of information concerning the murder of the Jewish population of Europe.
(jewishvirtuallibrary.org, January 13, 1944, "Report to the Secretary on the Acquiescence of this Government in the Murder of the Jews")

The report accused the heads of the US State Department under President Roosevelt as actively trying to "cover up their guilt by" acts of "concealment and misrepresentation," the "giving of false and misleading explanations" for their "failures to act," as well as their willful "attempts to prevent action." While the implications were clearly detrimental to Secretary of State, Cordell Hull, the President was liable to pay the ultimate political price for inaction and the politically adept Roosevelt knew it.

Cordell Hull's political history reveals potential reasons or ideological justifications for his persistent connivance against any attempt to bring Jewish refugees to American shores. Hull is recognized as the "Father of the United Nations." Hull and his staff drafted the original charter in 1943, and as Julian

Huxley's work at UNESCO evidence, the U.N. was in the business of population control from its onset. In order to comprehend how so many Europeans, Jewish and non-Jewish alike, were turned away by the US State Department one must first understand that the level of micro-management employed by Hull's State Department was not possible before 1924. While the State Department has always overseen immigration and naturalization in some capacity, the Secretary of State is not consulted on a case by case basis on the entry of foreign individuals into the country. The office of Secretary of State is part of the President's inner circle, and otherwise too important, especially during a world war, to preoccupy itself with the job otherwise relegated to lower-level immigration officials at the various ports of entry. Secretary of State Cordell Hull was given this inordinate amount of power to accept or reject refugees precisely because the acceptance of Jews, along with many other ethnicities, was made illegal by the Johnson-Reed Immigration Restriction Act. The 1924 Act would be systematically and consistently cited by Hull's State Department to prevent the rescuing of Jews escaping Hitler's henchmen, and on various occasions, send them back into the hands of the enemy.

In effect, what Morgenthau was asking Cordell Hull's State Department to do was to waive the 1924 Act in the face of an unprecedented emergency. More to the point, any competent politician or legislator in the United States at the time knew perfectly well that the Immigration Restriction Act was wholeheartedly the product of eugenic racial policies. The 1924 Act was created under the consultation of the very same internationally renowned eugenics experts that Hitler's government would use to create its own racial restrictions and exclusionary laws; both Madison Grant and Harry Laughlin were the experts consulted by the House Committee in 1924 to pass the Act.

Case in point, Laughlin would be honored by Hitler's Third Reich for the work that was so instrumental in creating the "racial state" that was Hitler's Germany. In 1936, Harry Laughlin received an invitation from Carl Schneider, a professor of racial hygiene to attend the 550-year Jubilee at Heidelberg University and receive an honorary Doctor of Medicine degree. Laughlin, who had been the "scientific expert" on immigration for the US Congress the years preceding the passing of the Johnson-Reed Act, was asked to attend the be an honored guest of the celebrations by Hitler's government on June 27-30, 1936. Laughlin was invited to personally receive the honorary degree in recognition for his substantial influence on the Third Reich's own legislative efforts. The date of the event had ideological connotations as it was the anniversary of Hitler's 1934 purge of the Jewish faculty at Heidelberg University. [33] Furthermore, the German press announced that the invitations would provide a "foreign endorsement" to the regime. The implications could not be clearer, as the invitation letter ended with a list of Laughlin's publications:

- → A decade of progress in Eugenics, 1934.
- → Laughlin, A Report of the Special Committee on Immigration, 1934.

---

[33] Pg. 212 - "Three Generations No Imbeciles: Eugenics, the Supreme Court, and Buck v. Bell", Paul Lombardo, JHU Press, 2008.

- The Legal Status of Eugenical Sterilization, Eugenical Sterilization in the US, 1922.
- Europe as an Immigrant-Exporting Cont., 1924.
- Analysis of (the) America's Mod. Melting Pot, 1923.
- Biological Aspects of Immigration, 1927.
- Eugenical Aspects of Deportation, 1928.
- Am. History in Terms of Human Migration, 1928

(BOX: E-1-3:8 – Laughlin Collection, Truman University – Special Collections)

Historians have documented how Hitler and Goebbels micro-managed precisely this type of propaganda event for the international audience. The list given by Hitler's government in Laughlin's invitation is important as two or three of the items on the list were the very reports commissioned by the US House Committee on Immigration and Naturalization for the passage of the Immigration Restriction Act of 1924, namely Laughlin's "Melting Pot" report, which was used to give "scientific" legitimacy to the "race" fears expounded by Madison Grant and his Immigration Restriction League. We know this because the Congressional reports that document the repealing and replacing the Immigration Restriction Act in 1952 make specific mention of the veil of legitimacy provided by Laughlin's "science," and thus the importance of Laughlin's work for the passage of the 1924 Act. [34] None of these observations should be regarded by historians as the product of hindsight, as it was Cordell Hull's own State Department which acted to prevent Harry H. Laughlin to travel to Germany to accept the honors. Laughlin was told by the State Department not to go to Germany to pick it up and he instead received his honor at the German embassy in Rockefeller Center in New York. [35] Clearly, the State Department was aware of the uncomfortable commonalities between the Third Reich's legislative efforts with the 1924 Immigration Restriction Act. After all, Laughlin's "Model Eugenical Sterilization Law" had been the basis for the infamous 1933 Nuremberg racial laws, and Laughlin had also been an expert witness for the US Supreme Court, when the "highest court in the land" was used to uphold the eugenic laws Laughlin drafted for various States in the Union. Clearly, the media coverage of America's "expert eugenicists" being honored by Hitler's Germany was not a juxtaposition Cordell Hull's State Department was willing to contend with.

Historians have given disparate accounts of what has otherwise been presented as a series of unconnected and unfortunate events regarding the boatloads of Jewish refugees that never reached the safety of US shores. The reality is that it is impossible not to see a pattern and practice on the part of the Roosevelt Administration when all the relevant evidence is considered. In 1939, Hull advised President Roosevelt to reject the SS St. Louis carrying 936 Jews seeking asylum. He did so on the basis of

---

[34] See Generally: "Hearings Before the Presidential Commission on Immigration and Naturalization – Appendix: Special Studies Memorandum by Oscar Handlin – I. Basic Assumptions of the National-Origins Quota", 82nd Congress, 2nd Session, 1952.

[35] Pg. 67 - "Davenport's Dream: 21st Century Reflections on Heredity and Eugenics", Jan A. Witkowski, CSHL Press, 2008.

the 1924 Immigration Restriction Act. [36] The Coast Guard posted an article to explain what happened when the ships filled with Jewish refugees escaping Hitler's Germany were turned back:

> To wit, there were two conversations on the subject between (Secretary of the Treasury) Morgenthau and Secretary of State Cordell Hull. In the first, 3:17 PM on 5 June 1939, Hull made it clear to Morgenthau that the passengers could not legally be issued US tourist visas as they had no return addresses. ("What Was the Coast Guard's Role in the SS St. Louis Affair?", history.uscg.mil, US Coast Guard's Historian's Office, Dept. of Homeland Security)

The "Voyage of the Damned," as the event came to be known, was hardly a unique event as a similar turn of events occurred with a ship named the Quanza attempting to dock in New York Harbor. In September 1940, First Lady Eleanor Roosevelt maneuvered with another State Department official to bypass Hull's refusal to allow Jewish refugees to disembark. Mrs. Roosevelt's efforts allowed the Jewish refugees to disembark on September 11, 1940. [37]

The reaction of the British government sheds light on just how important the quotas of the 1924 Act truly were. The British government reacted when the fate of the Jews became clear. In the week following *Kristallnacht*, in November 1938, the British government stated that it would be willing to give up the major part of the quota of 65,000 British citizens that could emigrate to the United States so that this portion of the 1924 Immigration Restriction Act quota could be used by Jews fleeing Hitler instead. Cordell Hull's Under-Secretary, Sumner Welles, rejected the offer:

> I reminded the Ambassador that the President stated there was no intention on the part of his government to increase the quota for German nationals. I added that it was my strong impression that the responsible leaders among American Jews would be the first to urge that no change in the present quota for German Jews be made. (Pg. 128, "Heroes, Antiheroes, and the Holocaust: American Jewry and Historical Choice", David Morrison, Geffen, 1995)

Another similar incident occurred where the State Department intentionally stalled or rejected plans to accommodate Jewish refugees. [38] In 1938, during the aftermath of the *Kristallnacht*, some members of Roosevelt's cabinet began to consider ways that the strict 1924 Immigration Restriction Act could be circumvented. Secretary of the Interior Harold Ickes suggested the possibility of resettling European refugees in the undeveloped tracts of federal government land in Alaska. Ickes's officers at the Interior Department drafted a proposal that outlined the economic and social effects of allowing several thousand European refugees to settle Alaska. The recommendations of the investigation were very positive. The committee's final report provided Ickes with a strong economic case for the feasibility

---

[37] "Fleeing Hitler and Meeting at Reluctant Miss Liberty", Cara Buckley, New York Times, July 8, 2007.
[38] "Anti-Semitism and American Refugee Immigration Policy during the Holocaust: A Reassessment", Sikeli Neil Ratu, Dissertation for the University of Sydney, 2006.

of the proposal, especially the committee's findings that the Alaskan territory contained "more than sufficient…unexploited natural resources" that would sustain the development of industry fueled by immigrant labor. The committee's report argued that the quota system established by the 1924 Immigration Restriction Act had hindered the natural growth of the Alaskan economy. The report demonstrated the reluctance of American citizens to relocate to Alaska. Ickes immediately asked President Roosevelt to consider the proposal, only to have President Roosevelt place it in the hands of Cordell Hull's State Department. The State Department's response was drafted by Under Secretary Sumner Welles, who cited concern that acting on the proposal would create a precedent and weaken the Immigration Restriction Act provisions. In other words, the explicitly eugenic Immigration Restriction Act was the primary tool and justification for not helping the victims of the ensuing holocaust.

All this political stonewalling would inevitably come to a head. In July 1942, a German industrialist living near Auschwitz-Birkenau, Dr. Eduard Schulte, learned of the camp's existence through friends and contacts with National Socialist commanders. Through his contacts, Schulte learned of the "Final Solution." Understanding the prospects of this unprecedented catastrophe, Schulte traveled to neutral Switzerland to alert the leaders of the Western democracies. In Geneva, Schulte relayed the information through an intermediary to Dr. Gerhardt Reigner, an official of the World Jewish Congress in Switzerland. Dr. Reigner, in turn, relayed the intelligence report to the American consulate in Geneva and to the British Foreign Ministry. Dr. Reigner specifically requested the State Department forward the information to Rabbi Stephen Wise, president of the World Jewish Congress in New York. When Dr. Reigner's telegram reached the State Department in Washington, officials described its contents as "fantastic allegations" and refused to pass on the information to Rabbi Wise. The State Department refused to publish the information contained in the Dr. Reigner telegram, for three months, despite having previous intelligence that corroborated the claims. Instead, the State Department instructed the American consulate in Switzerland to stop transmitting information about the destruction of the Jews because "it would expose us to increased pressure to do something more specific to aid these people." [39] Morgenthau's report made direct reference to these events:

> As early as August 1942, a message from the Secretary of the World Jewish Congress in Switzerland (Riegner), transmitted through the British Foreign Office, reported that Hitler had under consideration a plan to exterminate all Jews in German controlled Europe. By November 1942 sufficient evidence had been received, including substantial documentary evidence transmitted through our Legation in Switzerland, to confirm that Hitler had actually adopted and was carrying out his plan to exterminate the Jews. (jewishvirtuallibrary.org, January 13, 1944, "Report to the Secretary on the Acquiescence of this Government in the Murder of the Jews")

---

[39] Pg. 264 – "Breaking the Silence", Walter Laqueur, Richard Breitman, Simon & Schuster, Mar 1, 1987.

The Morgenthau report goes into detail of the actions by Cordell Hull's State Department to delay action, withhold information, and suppress knowledge:

> The highlights relating to the efforts of State Department officials to prevent this proposal from being put into effect are the following:
> (a) On March 13, 1942, a cable was received from the World Jewish Congress representatives in London stating that information reaching London indicated the possibility of rescuing Jews provided funds were put at the disposal of the world Jewish Congress representation in Switzerland.
> (b) On April 10, 1943, Sumner Welles cabled our Legation in Bern and requested them to get in touch with the World Jewish Congress representative in Switzerland, whom Welles had been informed was in possession of important information regarding the situation of the Jews.
> (c) On April 20, 1943, a cable was received from Bern relating to the proposed financial arrangements in connection with the evacuation of the Jews from Rumania and France.
> (d) On May 25, 1943, State Department cabled for a clarification of these proposed financial arrangements. This matter was not called to the attention of the Treasury Department at this time.
> (e) This whole question of financing the evacuation of the Jews from Rumania and France was first called to the attention of the Treasury Department on June 25, 1943.
> (f) A conference was held with the State Department relating to this matter on July 15, 1943.
> (g) One day after this conference, on July 16, 1943, the Treasury Department advised the State Department that it was prepared to issue in this matter.
> (h) The license was not issued until December 13, 1943.
> (jewishvirtuallibrary.org, January 13, 1944, "Report to the Secretary on the Acquiescence of this Government in the Murder of the Jews")

The final tip that shook Cordell Hull's State Department out of silence came from Polish underground courier Jan Karski. He entered both the Warsaw Ghetto and the Belzec death camp to witness the Final Solution's destruction policies first-hand. Karski traveled to the United States to provide first-hand witness testimony that verified all that had been known by high-ranking officials in Roosevelt's administration. It became impossible for the State Department to keep a lid on the story, so finally, on November 24, 1942, Sumner Welles admitted to Rabbi Wise, "I regret to tell you, Dr. Wise, that these (documents) confirm and justify your deepest fears" about the annihilation of European Jewry. [40] Rabbi Wise gave a press conference the day that he received official confirmation from Sumner Wells and the State Department. In this press conference of November 24, 1942, Wise detailed the destruction of the Jews in Europe citing the State Department's confirmation. The New York Times published an article covering Wise's press conference the following day. Yet, it would not be until 1944, as a reaction to Morgenthau's coercion

---

[40] Pg. 123 – "The Jews Should Keep Quiet: Franklin D. Roosevelt, Rabbi Stephen S. Wise, and the Holocaust", Rafael Medoff, Univ. of Nebraska Press, 2019.

of President Roosevelt, that the State Department would ultimately act.

One of the purposes of this book is to bestow upon these events their true meaning by placing them within the context of a timeline. Historians have poorly documented just how late the Roosevelt Administration was to act, and more precisely, that the outright and systematic blockade on victims trying to escape Hitler's grasp did not end until President Roosevelt was coerced to do so in 1944 by Morgenthau and Paul. The largest amount of murders in the Holocaust occurred well within the time when the Roosevelt Administration had received confirmation of Hitler's extermination policies, and 1944 when the administration finally acted. The horrific *Kristallnacht* had occurred a full six years before 1944, which by itself should have made the various threats by Hitler and Goebbels palpable and real. While other authors have dedicated entire books to fully extrapolating the Roosevelt Administration's complicity, the purpose of documenting these facts in this book is to evidence the mindset of the very State Department officials who would at the end of the war have formidable influence over the Nuremberg Trials.

Sec. 6 - STERILIZING THE "GREATEST GENERATION":

Operation Overlord was the code name the Allies gave the Battle of Normandy. We have come to know this day as D-Day. Operation Overlord involved an unprecedented 12,000-plane airborne assault and an amphibious assault of almost 7,000 vessels. Nearly 160,000 troops crossed the English Channel on June 6, 1944, and because of their efforts, more than 3 million Allied troops were in France by the end of August. The landings took place along a 50-mile stretch of the Normandy coast divided into five sectors: Utah, Omaha, Gold, Juno and Sword as so many movies and documentaries have depicted. We look back on D-Day and reminisce on the courage and sacrifice of this "Greatest Generation."

One of the men embarking on that "great crusade" was young Raymond Hudlow. He was part of the Omaha Beach landings, or what would later be aptly called "Bloody Omaha." Omaha was the most heavily fortified beach, with high bluffs defended by funneled mortars, machine guns, and artillery. American casualties at Omaha on D-Day numbered around 5,000 out of 50,000 men, most in the first few hours. To put this into a contemporary perspective, the fatalities in the first eight years of the Iraq war totaled 4,483 US soldiers.

Raymond Hudlow then served in General Patton's army, which rumbled in to liberate Bastogne in the historic Battle of the Bulge in Ardennes forest in Belgium. Hudlow also served in Holland, where shrapnel wrecked his left knee. German soldiers captured him, beat him, and nearly starved him to death while captured. Yet, according to Raymond Hudlow, none of these instances were as painful as the sterilization that the Commonwealth of Virginia performed on him against his will at the age of 16, just two years prior to landing on "Bloody Omaha." Recalling the story at age 79, Hudlow claimed that the 30 days recovering from the surgery was the most pain he remembers ever feeling. [41] Raymond Hudlow had been one of more than 8,000 individuals who were forcibly sterilized by the Commonwealth of Virginia because of the eugenic legislation adopted by that state. The truth is that it is highly improbable that Raymond Hudlow was the only American World War II veteran who had suffered such a fate, considering the great number of youths like Raymond serving in the US Armed Forces, and the tens of thousands of sterilizations forced on youths prior to D-Day and World War II. The numbers sterilized is unknown, namely because sterilizations of African-Americans and Native-Americans were not officially recorded. To make matters worse, many doctors performed them without notice or record prior to the laws being passed and feeling protected by US Supreme Court decisions after 1927. Beyond that, a sizeable amount of the sterilizations were done without the knowledge or consent of the victim, and many did not find out about their condition until visiting doctors decades later after futile attempts to have children. The numbers are reported as low as 60,000 sterilizations in the United States. The number is very likely closer to 80,000 based on known records. The true figure is impossible to know as many states refuse to release the records. In fact, many of those sterilized in the 20th century did not find out until the 21st century when a number of these states were forced to issue apologies. The official apology to Raymond Hudlow reads in part:

> Commending Raymond W. Hudlow. -- Agreed to by the Senate, January 17, 2002 -- Agreed to by the House of Delegates, January 25, 2002
>
> WHEREAS, the now-discredited pseudo-science of eugenics was based on theories first propounded in England by Francis Galton, the cousin and disciple of famed biologist Charles Darwin; and
>
> WHEREAS, in 1924, Virginia passed two eugenics-related laws, the second of which permitted involuntary sterilization, the most egregious outcome of the lamentable eugenics movement in the Commonwealth; and
>
> WHEREAS, under this act, those labeled "feebleminded," including the "insane, idiotic, imbecile, feebleminded or epileptic" could be involuntarily sterilized, so that they would not produce similarly disabled offspring; and
>
> WHEREAS, in 1941, Raymond Hudlow, a 16-year-old boy who repeatedly ran away from home to escape an abusive father, was committed to the Virginia Colony for Epileptics and Feebleminded near Lynchburg; and
>
> WHEREAS, on June 17, 1942, an Amherst County Circuit Court judge granted the Virginia Colony's request that Raymond Hudlow be sterilized; and
>
> WHEREAS, in October of 1943, Raymond Hudlow was released from the Virginia Colony, was drafted into the United States Army two months later, and in August 1944, was at Omaha Beach in France two months after D-Day; and
>
> WHEREAS, Raymond Hudlow saw combat in France, Belgium, and Holland, was wounded in the left knee and captured by the Germans, was in various prison camps for seven months before being liberated by the Russians, and was awarded

---

[41] "Human Weeds", Stephen Buckley, St. Petersburg Times, Nov. 11, 2001.

the Bronze Star for Valor, the Purple Heart, and the Prisoner of War Medal; –
(2002 SESSION - SENATE JOINT RESOLUTION NO. 79)

The ACLU helped Raymond Hudlow sue the Commonwealth of Virginia in 1985. Surprisingly enough, all Raymond received was the above apology and a lot of resistance from politicians nervous about further litigation. The Federal judge pointed to the fact that Raymond had been sterilized according to the law; a law that had been deemed "constitutional" by the US Supreme Court in the 1927 case of Buck v. Bell. While most historians mistakenly think that Buck v. Bell was repealed by Skinner v. Oklahoma, Raymond Hudlow's 1985 Federal lawsuit incontrovertibly reveals quite the opposite.[42] Buck v. Bell is still what lawyers and judges call "valid controlling precedent." Eugenic laws, along with the right of the US Government to enact mass-sterilizations and mass-segregation in the name of the greater good to society, are still valid per the 1927 Buck v. Bell decision. Most, if not all, of the States, have repealed their sterilization laws. However, the hierarchy of the judicial branch makes the US Supreme Court decision controlling law, which means that any of these States can today reinstate their eugenic laws and be fully within "constitutionality" per the Buck v. Bell opinion.

More to the point, Raymond Hudlow risked life and limb on various occasions during World War II. He landed on "Bloody Omaha," fought under General Patton in the decisive battles in Belgium and endured being a prisoner of war, all to rid the Earth of the threat of Adolf Hitler and his xenophobic National Socialists. Historians tell us that Raymond Hudlow was part of the "Greatest Generation" for risking life and limb for this "great crusade." He fought to rid the planet of what generally is accepted as the greatest evil in history. It is important to clarify that we consider Hitler to be that greatest evil precisely because their actions went beyond what is typical to war; Hitler and his cohorts embarked on the most notorious campaign of "ethnic cleansing" in history. It is because of individuals like Raymond Hudlow, this "greatest of generations," that the Allies were able to deliver Hitler's henchmen to the 1947 Nuremberg Doctor's Trial. It was those simple-living farm boys, those descendants of the slave population, the displaced Native Americans, and first and second-generation immigrants from Europe, that ironically made up this "Greatest Generation," and which were precisely the target of the eugenic laws in the United States. General Eisenhower's film reels displayed for the entire world the barbarity of Hitler's doctors and scientists. Yet, the same law that the German National Socialists held up in their defense in the Nuremberg Doctor's Trial is still valid law in the United States.

None of this takes away from the valiant sacrifice made by Raymond Hudlow or any of the other members of the US Armed Forces. None of this takes away from their leaders such as General Patton or General Eisenhower. This was very much so "The Greatest Generation" and they were cognizant of the principles that the United States represented, and they were willing to give up life and limb for these

---

[42] Pg. 254 - "Three Generations No Imbeciles: Eugenics, the Supreme Court, and Buck v. Bell", Paul Lombardo, JHU, 2008.

principles. Nor does this mean that there is a moral equivalency between the eugenic campaigns in the United States and those enacted by Hitler's henchmen, as it is because the United States was founded upon the principles of individual liberty that the scale and scope of the atrocities did not reach the proportions it did in Germany. The disgrace surrounding the 1924 Racial Integrity Law, along with all its equivalent laws across a dozen other States, can be pinpointed to a group of individuals and their corresponding organizations. Historians have as of late claimed that eugenics appealed to a broad spectrum of political preferences. This notion that the eugenics movement was spread across many political ideologies is a farce. We know exactly who the leading members and the institutions responsible for the passing of these laws were. Furthermore, these individuals were well organized and arrogant enough to boast about the products of their efforts in the various books and publications. While there may have been many foot soldiers involved in the effort to make the United States into a "eugenic" or "racial" state, the names of the individuals leading the eugenic cause in the United States are documented frequently and often in the very large paper trail they left behind, and the group is elite and select, largely to the exclusion of inconsequential others. Historians know exactly who these self-proclaimed elites were, and it is fraudulent to claim that the movement was too broad to be traced back to its source.

The truth is that we have as much evidence to pinpoint the leadership of the American eugenics movement as we did to convict the German scientists, doctors, judges and National Socialist leadership in the Nuremberg Trials. The evidence goes far beyond the "aid and comfort to the enemy" standard and is much more direct and overt than the evidence used to convict other collaborators. The consequences of the American eugenicist's actions were much more serious than those of the American industrialists that were hauled in front of Congressional hearings for charges of profiteering. The correspondence between these Americans and their German counterparts is there for anyone to see. We know who these people and institutions were, so any judgment that would cast blanket culpability on the Raymond Hudlow's of America is fraudulent and disingenuous. The consequences of the eugenics movement in the United States and its collaboration with Adolf Hitler's government is the fault of a very elite and select group of people, and the names of those individuals and institutions will be frequently repeated in this book, as the length of this book is representative of the mountain of evidence left behind by these zealots.

Sec. 7 - MERCHANTS OF LIGHT:

Francis Bacon, in his 1626 Utopian vision "The New Atlantis," described the role that the international intellectual elite played in the formation of his utopia:

> For the several employments and offices of our fellows, we have twelve that sail into foreign countries under the names of other nations (for our own we conceal), who bring us the books and abstracts, and patterns of experiments of all other parts. These we call merchants of light. (Pg. 269, Francis Bacon/Basil Montagu, "The Works of Francis Bacon, Lord Chancellor of England: With a Life of the Author", Carey and Hart, Vol. I, 1844)

These "merchants of light" provided that most ephemeral, but crucial ingredient, indispensable to the creation of utopias; these "merchants" traded in ideas. As utopias, by their very nature failed or survived on the sustenance of ideas, the "merchants of light" in the 20th century too peddled in the currency of ideas. This was especially true for a Germany trying to lift itself out of the devastation caused by World War I and the subsequent Great Depression. Historians have adequately documented the street-level violence that broke out among the different factions in the absence of direction or order. Historians have explained that this vacancy, this destitution in a decimated economy, led some to desire the heavy hand of the totalitarian state to provide what individuals could not provide on their own in those circumstances. It can be said that the market was ripe for utopian schemes, where the public could be enticed to "escape" from the "burdens of freedom," as one propagandizing Austrian would preach to them. Through propaganda and showmanship, they would sell the false virtues of surrendering to a statist utopia, to a "total state" that would lead them away from "degeneracy" and into world domination, to their status as the alleged superior "race," to be the "masters" of European civilization.

These 20th Century "merchants of light" injected the masses with precise dosages of the utopian ideal through propaganda. In 20/20 hindsight the differences between the Fascist "total state," the Bolshevik "total state," or the National Socialist "total state," may be academic, but to the "merchants of light," as it is with any good merchant, the minuscule differences between them were magnified beyond reason.

These "merchants" of elusive utopian ideas, these elitist intellectuals were there, ready to share all the advances made in the United States and Britain had made in eugenic science and law with Germans that were still struggling with basic survival in the wake of World War I and The Great Depression. Eugenics had been a British creation by their proudest and most celebrated scientists. Through the international eugenic organizations run by Leonard Darwin, Karl Pearson, and Francis Galton, British eugenic organizations became a beacon guiding anyone in the market for eugenic utopian solutions to significant social problems. This is how Germany became the proving ground, the blank slate, for all the eugenic goals that could or would not be adopted by the democratic governments of the United States or Britain. This is what drove the American eugenicists, Joseph DeJarnette, to utter that now-infamous comment to the Richmond Times-Dispatch about the strides that Adolf Hitler's Germany was making with eugenics: "<u>The Germans are beating us at our own game and are more progressive than we are</u>." [43]

Leonard Darwin of the British Eugenics Society and son of Charles Darwin was the beacon who summoned eugenic-minded scientists and policymakers to England. The stated goal of his organization was to inform, educate and disseminate the gospel of eugenics, or more precisely the "religion" of eugenics, as Francis Galton thought of his creation. It was founded in 1907 as the Eugenics Education Society, becoming the Eugenics Society in 1926, and was popularly referred to as the British Eugenics Society as to distinguish it from the other eugenic societies. The organization quietly and conveniently changed its name to the Galton Institute in 1989, removing the overt reference to "eugenics" in the wake of The Holocaust.

This book will document the many and varied ways in which key members of the international eugenics community networked and collaborated in forwarding their cause. Figures such as Margaret Sanger, Ernst Rüdin, Harry H. Laughlin, C.M. Goethe, and Charles B. Davenport excelled in the exchange of information and the collaborative refinement of policies. Evidence of this still exists in the correspondence between the various members on various continents. The Cold Spring Harbor archives still have a letter dated November 11, 1922, from the American, Charles B. Davenport to the Briton, Leonard Darwin, discussing the increased collaboration with the German and Austrian scientists, namely their fellow British Eugenics Society member and subsequent Hitler supporter, Alfred Ploetz. [44] The relationship between the high-ranking members of the British Eugenics Society and Alfred Ploetz is not inconsequential. Alfred Ploetz's and Ernst Rüdin's relationship with Leonard Darwin, Charles B. Davenport, Harry H. Laughlin, and Margaret Sanger is historically critical when you realize that Ploetz and Rüdin were given the job of drafting National Socialism's eugenic and racial policies by Hitler.

The "International Commission of Eugenics" was one of the major networking organizations that spanned the globe to bring the eugenicists together despite lingering animosities against the Germans after WWI. A November 1922 edition of the "Eugenical News" reports on a key meeting of the "International Commission of Eugenics": The report documents that this international organization "voted unanimously to invite German delegates to the Commission", thus commencing the relationship between American, British, and German eugenicists. [45] The intention to include the Germans in the "International Commission of Eugenics" was clearly successful as the subsequent correspondence reveals. Communication across borders and oceans was a monthly, and sometimes weekly in frequency, with members taking every opportunity to meet with each other casually or formally. The members made it a point to send carbon copies of their conversations to players that would prove to be indispensable to the Adolf Hitler's

---

[43] "1933: American donates $1,000,000 to Kaiser-Wilhelm; "400,000 Germans to be sterilized", Alliance for Human Research Protection website: ahrp.org.

[44] Item ID: 10435 - dnalc.cshl.edu, November 11, 1922 letter from Charles B. Davenport to Leonard Darwin, DNA Learning Center online archives.

[45] Pg. 117 – "Eugenical News", American Eugenics Society, Volume No. 7, No. 11, Nov. 1922.

eugenic program. A June 28, 1925 letter from Leonard Darwin to Harry H. Laughlin housed at Truman University's Special Collections Department was written in the "International Commission of Eugenics" letterhead. [46] The letterhead displays three offices with Leonard Darwin for London, H.F. Osborn for New York, and Dr. A. Govaerts for Brussels. The group seemed to have gelled into the "International Federation of Eugenic Organizations" as a May 30, 1928 letter from C. Hodson to Harry H. Laughlin demonstrates Alfred Ploetz, the father of German "race hygiene" as Vice President along with H.F. Osborn, and Leonard Darwin as Honorary President, and Davenport as acting President. [47]

Subsequent correspondence displays a similar format, but under the letterhead of "The International Federation of Eugenic Organizations" with Professor Ernst Rüdin in Munich as President, H.F. Osborn as Vice President in New York, and Leonard Darwin as Honorary President in London. [48] The correspondence continues way into the late 1930s and long after Hitler made his convictions clear through barbarous acts. The International Federation of Eugenic Organizations was officially founded in 1925. The Harvard professor, Charles Davenport, head of the Eugenic Records Office housed in the Dulles estate, was its first president, and frequent and substantial collaboration between German and American eugenicists followed.

Stefan Kühl's "The Nazi Connection" documents that the collaboration goes back as far as the 1912 International Congress where over 300 eugenicists attended, including Davenport, and Winston Churchill:

> The Congress succeeded in fulfilling its stated goals, particularly regarding the mission of international organization. The London Congress strengthened existing informal contacts between eugenicists of different countries and led to the creation of the Permanent International Commission of Eugenics. – American eugenicists enjoyed a strong standing among their foreign colleagues. European eugenicists admired the success of their American counterparts in influencing eugenics legislation and gaining extensive financial support for the American eugenics movement. The German racial hygiene movement followed the development of the American eugenics movement closely. During World War I, the Society for Racial Hygiene in Berlin distributed a public flyer extolling "the dedication with which Americans sponsor research in the field of racial hygiene and with which they translate theoretical knowledge into practice." The Flyer referred to a donation of several million dollars by a widow of a railway magnate in support of the eugenics laboratory in Cold Spring Harbor. (Pgs. 14-15, "The Nazi Connection: Eugenics, American Racism, and German National Socialism", Oxford Univ. Press, 1994)

The widow mentioned above was the wife of E.H. Harriman, and the Battle Creek institution was that of the Kellogg brothers, the famous breakfast cereal family

---

[46] BOX: C-2-5:6 – Harry H. Laughlin Papers, Truman University Archives, Special Collections, Pickler Memorial Library.
[47] Ibid.
[48] BOX: C-4-4:7 - Harry H. Laughlin Papers, Truman University Archives, Special Collections, Pickler Memorial Library.

which would later become chief sponsors of Davenport's and Laughlin's Cold Spring Harbor laboratory.

Some of this has to be attributed to the California State at Sacramento President and leader of the California environmentalist movement, C.M. Goethe, which from the onset corresponded with religious consistency with Harry H. Laughlin in order to create the "Goethe Fund" for the Cold Spring Harbor's Eugenic Records Office to study immigration restrictions, and more importantly, in an effort to confederate the eugenics movement across the United States and the world. C.M. Goethe's correspondence with Harry H. Laughlin reveals the effort to include the "Rotary Clubs," the "Human Betterment Foundation," and the "Federal Council of Churches." Goethe consistently called for the "federation" of eugenics societies in the United States and the World, and consistently suggested ideas and potential connections on how to accomplish this goal. Leonard Darwin chimes in on a June 18, 1925 letter under the "International Commission of Eugenics" letterhead to suggest cooperation with the "Red Cross Societies" and other "Health organizations." [49] Among the institutions named or copied in the correspondence include the presidents of Columbia and Princeton universities as well as the Carnegie and Rockefeller institutions.

These institutions overlapped with like-minded organizations, namely Margaret Sanger's American Birth Control. Margaret Sanger personally invited Harry H. Laughlin to join a "round-table" between eugenicists and "birth control" advocates at her "Sixth International Neo-Malthusian and Birth Control Conference" of March 25-31, 1925. [50] Harry H. Laughlin dutifully agreed and the roster of attendants reveals the overlap in the institutions, including Havelock Ellis, Julian Huxley, John Maynard Keynes, Raymond Pearl, Lothrop Stoddard, and H.G. Wells, all devoted eugenicists.

Stefan Kühl documents how the participation and acceptance into the International Federation of Eugenic Organizations were subsequently used by German eugenicists to justify the Third Reich's eugenic policies when confronted by international criticism of the policies:

> In the summer of 1934, one and a half years after the Nazis came to power in Germany, the International Federation of Eugenic Organizations, meeting in Zurich, passed a resolution to which Nazi propaganda frequently referred in order to illustrate the international acceptance of their race policies. In this unanimously passed resolution, sent to the prime ministers of all the major Western powers, the IFEO stated that, despite all differences in political and social outlooks, the organization was "united by the deep conviction that eugenic research and practice is of the highest and most urgent importance for the existence of all civilized countries." It recommended that all governments "make themselves acquainted with the problems of heredity, population studies, and eugenics." It stated that eugenic principles should be adopted as state policies "for the good of their nations . . . with suitable regional modifications. German

---

[49] BOX: C-2-5:6 - Laughlin Papers, Truman Univ., Special Collections.
[50] BOX: E-1-1:1 – Ibid. – See Illustration.

racial hygienists and Nazi race politicians viewed this resolution as confirmation of German and American dominance in the eugenics movement and as international approval of the 1933 German sterilization law. Although the resolution did not refer directly to Germany, its adoption was seen as an achievement for national Socialists in gaining international acceptance of their policies. (Pgs. 26-27, "The Nazi Connection: Eugenics, American Racism, and German National Socialism", Oxford Univ. Press, 1994)

Again, the rosters in the letterhead of these societies demonstrate the level of support they had. The American Eugenics Society, Inc. letterhead has Dr. John Harvey Kellogg and Dr. Vernon Kellogg as its "Advisory Council" for 1927, with Harry H. Laughlin as President, Henry Pratt Fairchild as Secretary, and Leon F. Whitney, the direct descendant of the inventor of the cotton gin, as its Executive Secretary. The "Advisory Council" lists Dr. Arthur Eastabrook, one of the parties at the infamous 1927 US Supreme Court case of <u>Buck v. Bell</u> which made eugenic sterilization legal, Dr. David Fairchild, Dr. Earnest A. Hooton, David Star Jordan whom was president of Stanford University, Lothrop Stoddard, Paul Popenoe, Lewis Terman, and Robert Yerkes.

A listing of the members of the British Eugenics Society helps illustrate just how far and wide their influence reached. The two most recognizable members were Neville Chamberlain, the British prime minister between 1937 and 1940, and John Maynard Keynes, the Progressive economist whose policies influenced governments across several centuries. Keynes was the director of the British Eugenics Society between 1937-1944 and then vice president in 1937. Beyond that:

- **LEONARD DARWIN**: Son of Charles Darwin, was a Liberal Unionist Member of Parliament. He was the dominant force in the British eugenics movement after his father and uncle, Francis Galton, passed away.
- **JULIAN HUXLEY**: Huxley was president of the British Eugenics Society from 1959 to 1962, vice-president between 1937 and 1944, and then president again between 1959 and 1962.
- **CHARLES GALTON DARWIN**: An English physicist, the grandson of Charles Darwin. The family entanglements multiplied their British lineage when his sister married into the John Maynard Keynes's family.
- **RICHARD TITMUSS**: Held the founding chair in the subject at the London School of Economics, where Fabian Socialism blossomed. His books and articles of the 1950s helped to define the characteristics of Britain's post World War II welfare state and of a universal welfare society.
- **WILLIAM BEVERIDGE**: First Baron Beveridge was a British economist and social reformer. He is best known for his 1942 report "Social Insurance and Allied Services," otherwise known as the Beveridge Report, which served as the basis for the post- World War II welfare state put in place by the Labour government elected in 1945.
- **DR. LEONARD JOHN HENRY ARTHUR**: A British doctor tried in 1981 for the attempted murder of John Pearson, a newborn child with

Down's Syndrome.
- **HENRY HAVELOCK ELLIS**: A British physician and psychologist, writer, and social reformer. He was a co-author of the first medical textbook in English on homosexuality in 1897 and published works on a variety of sexual practices and inclinations, including transgender psychology.
- **SIR RONALD AYLMER FISHER**: An English statistician, evolutionary biologist, eugenicist and geneticist. Among other things, Fisher is well known for his contributions to statistics by creating Fisher's exact test and Fisher's equation.
- **FRANZ JOSEF KALLMANN**: A German-born American psychiatrist, was one of the pioneers in the study of the genetic basis of psychiatric disorders. He developed the use of twin studies in the assessment of the relative roles of heredity and the environment in the pathogenesis of psychiatric disease. As a Jew, he fled Germany in 1936 for the United States. He had been a student of Ernst Rüdin. In a speech delivered in 1935, and several years after Hitler consolidating power, he advocated the examination of relatives of schizophrenia patients with the aim to find and sterilize the "unaffected carriers" of the supposed recessive gene responsible for the condition.
- **KARL PEARSON**: In 1911, he founded the world's first university statistics department at University College London. He was Sir Francis Galton's protégé and his biographer. Pearson was vocally supportive of the Third Reich and its eugenic policies, a fact that is only underscored by his brother, Roger Pearson, the anthropologist and conservationist, whom after World War II was the founder of the Neo-Nazi organization called The Northern League.
- **MARGARET AMY PYKE**: A founding member of the British National Birth Control Committee.
- **MARIE CARMICHAEL STOPES**: A British author, paleobotanist, campaigner for women's rights, and pioneer in the field of birth control.

The founding and managing members from the United States were a mirror image of the intellectual and political elitism of the British Eugenics Society.
- **CHARLES B. DAVENPORT**: Largely due to his Harvard education and networking, Davenport was arguably the undisputed leader of the American eugenics movement. He was regarded as America's top scientist of the era.
- **CHARLES M. GOETHE**: Founder of California State University in Sacramento, an entrepreneur, land developer, philanthropist, conservationist, founder of the Eugenics Society of Northern California. His philanthropy work included the Save the Redwoods Foundation and the Sierra Club.
- **EZRA GOSNEY**: An American philanthropist. In 1928 he founded the Human Betterment Foundation in California. In 1934 Charles Goethe wrote to Gosney from Germany to congratulate him that Gosney's work "has

played a powerful part in shaping the opinions of the group of intellectuals who are behind Hitler in this epoch-making program."

- **JOHN HARVEY KELLOG**: The American medical doctor from Battle Creek, Michigan, best known for the invention of the Corn Flakes breakfast cereal. He ran a sanitarium using holistic methods, with a focus on nutrition, enemas and exercise. Kellogg was outspoken on his beliefs on race and segregation, although he adopted several black children. In 1906, together with Irving Fisher and Charles Davenport, Kellogg founded the Race Betterment Foundation, which became a major center of the new eugenics movement in America.
- **MADISON GRANT**: An American lawyer, historian and physical anthropologist, and conservationist. Grant is most famous for authoring "The Passing of the Great Race" in 1916, which is known to be referred to as "his Bible" by Adolf Hitler. At the Doctor's Trial in Nuremberg, Grant's "Passing of the Great Race" was one of the pieces of evidence introduced by the defense to demonstrate the parallels between American and German eugenic policies.
- **MARGARET HIGGINS SANGER:** An American sex educator, nurse, and birth control activist given credit for coining the term "birth control." Sanger opened the first birth control clinic in the United States and established Planned Parenthood.
- **DAVID STARR JORDAN**: He was president of Indiana University and Stanford University. He was a leading peace activist who worked closely with Ezra Gosney, Paul Popenoe, and Charles M. Goethe to create the eugenic policies in California that would later influence Hitler's legislators and policymakers.
- **HENRY FAIRFIELD OSBORN**: President of the American Museum of Natural History for 25 years and a constant force in the promotion of the cause of eugenics in the United States. His brother, Major General Frederick Henry Osborn, was an American philanthropist, military leader, and eugenicist.
- **PAUL BEECHER BLANSHARD**: Assistant editor of The Nation magazine, a lawyer, a socialist, a secular humanist, and from 1949 an outspoken critic of Catholicism. Blanshard and his wife he met at Harvard and became close friends with both Helen Keller and Margaret Sanger.

The American Eugenics Society started by promoting racial betterment, eugenic health, and genetic education through public lectures, exhibits at county fairs and world exhibitions, but after World War II and the negative publicity by the awareness of the role of eugenics in The Holocaust, the American Eugenics Society changed both its name and its focus under the direction of Frederick Osborn. The Society placed greater emphasis on issues of population control, genetics and, later, medical genetics, and was reorganized and renamed "The Society for the Study of Social Biology" as its uncomfortable past was deemed politically inconvenient in the wake of the US Supreme Court's decision on Roe v. Wade. Osborn was pleased with the direction of birth control as a eugenic measure and did not want to hinder its progress by any immediate relationship between eugenics and birth control. Osborn claimed that the change in name was "because it became evident that changes of a eugenic nature would be made for reasons other than eugenics, and that tying a eugenic label on them would more often hinder than help their adoption. Birth control and abortion are turning out to be great eugenic advances of our time." [51] His fears were justified. The Roe v. Wade opinion directly cites Buck v. Bell, the 1927 US Supreme Court case that made eugenics "constitutional" in the United States.

To illustrate the pervasiveness of eugenics among the American elite, it is useful to document the other eugenic organizations in operation at the time when Hitler's "merchants of light" set out to source the knowledge of eugenic utopianism. The Human Betterment Foundation was an American eugenics organization established in Pasadena, California, in 1928 by E.S. Gosney and C.M. Goethe. It primarily served to compile and distribute information about compulsory sterilization legislation in the United States. Through the Human Betterment Foundation, C.M. Goethe lobbied the state to restrict immigration from Mexico and carry out involuntary sterilizations of mostly poor women, defined as "feeble-minded" or "socially inadequate" by medical authorities between 1909 and the 1960s. Around 20,000 patients in California state psychiatric hospitals were sterilized with minimal or non-existent consent between 1909 and 1950 when the law went into general disuse before its repeal in the 1960s. The initial board of trustees were C.M. Goethe, the founder of Cal State Sacramento, David Starr Jordan, the chancellor of Stanford University, Justin Miller, Stanford graduate and dean of the University of Southern California Law, Otis Castle, a Los Angeles attorney from Stanford, and Paul Popenoe, the famous biologist from Stanford. Later members included William B. Munro, a Harvard professor of political science, Herbert M. Evans, U.C. Berkeley anatomy professor, Samuel J. Holmes, U.C. Berkley zoologist. A member of particular importance was Lewis Terman, the Stanford psychologist best known for creating the Stanford-Binet IQ test, which is used to this day to test the intelligence of children. Terman was a pioneer in educational psychology in the early 20th century at the Stanford University School of Education. In 1916 Terman published the Stanford Revision of the Binet-Simon, based on previous work by Alfred Binet and Theodore Simon of France. Terman promoted his test as an aid for the classification of developmentally disabled children. The first mass administration of IQ testing was done with 1.7 million soldiers during World War I when Terman served in the US military while conducting psychological tests. The results of this skewed test were later regurgitated repeatedly by eugenicists to propagate fear that the population of the United States was "degenerating" because of immigration.

More specific to the purpose of this book, E.S. Gosney and Paul B. Popenoe published a report touting the results of the sterilizations in California. This would

---

[51] Pgs. 3, 65 – "Organized Eugenics", American Eugenics Society, Inc., Jan. 1931.

culminate in several works, most prominently their joint-authored "Sterilization for Human Betterment: A Summary of Results of 6,000 Operations in California, 1909-1929." This specific report was cited by the German defendants at the Doctor's Trial in Nuremberg as evidence that the programs adopted by Hitler's government were no different than those adopted by other Western nations.

The Human Betterment Foundation had an East Coast equivalent: The Human Betterment League. The East Coast version was founded by James G. Hanes in 1947 and Dr. Clarence Gamble, an heir to the Procter and Gamble fortune. [52] Closely aligned with the Human Betterment Foundation, the Human Betterment League of North Carolina used mass media and advertisements to propagandize and peddle their eugenic views. The media campaign was intended to convince the public that sterilizations were necessary measures. The public was informed that most of the "unfit" did not live in mental institutions but were in the community and "breeding," according to the literature, with normal people. An equally disturbing period of mass sterilizations occurred in North Carolina as a result of these propaganda campaigns. The campaign began with the passage of the North Carolina Sterilization Act in 1929. While many states dismantled their sterilization programs after World War II due to fears that their eugenics efforts might be compared to those of Hitler's Germany, North Carolina only redoubled their effort sterilization campaign and are regarded as responsible for a vast swath of the post-war eugenic sterilizations in the United States.

Dr. Gamble also spearheaded the movement to gain acceptance for birth control in the United States along with Margaret Sanger. Dr. Gamble urged the unification of Margaret Sanger's Clinical Birth Control Research Bureau with the competing American Birth Control League. In 1939, the two organizations became the Birth Control Federation of America. Dr. Gamble had started his work to disseminate the gospel of "birth control" through the Pathfinder Fund in 1929 when he gave $5,000 to open a maternal health clinic in Cincinnati, Ohio. Clarence Gamble would always call the drive to make birth control available world-wide the "Great Cause." The Human Betterment Foundation went out of existence in 1988, but before this, it changed its focus from sterilization to that of promoting "birth control." During the early 1970s, the League stopped promoting eugenic sterilizations and started producing educational material regarding birth control and genetic counseling. The League's name changed to The Human Genetics League as part of this transformation.

In summary, the above list is a veritable who's who of influence and progressive-minded elitism, even when leaving out some of its lesser-known but wealthiest members. For the sake of brevity, what honest historian could claim that the Allied prosecution at Nuremberg was oblivious to the decades of work and philanthropy of these internationally recognized individuals?

To be more precise, when Adolf Hitler finally reached his goal of assuming unchecked power, he created a committee to delve deeper into the specifics of how

---

[52] "The Human Betterment League", Maggie Ghallager, National Review, December 12, 2011.

to create the "racial state" he had vaguely described in "Mein Kampf." In 1933, Reich Interior Minister Wilhelm Frick established an "expert advisory committee for population and racial policy," which included Ploetz, Fritz Lenz, Ernst Rüdin and Hans F.K. Günther. This expert advisory committee had the task of advising Hitler's government on the implementation and enforcement of legislation regarding racial and eugenic issues. In fact, it can be said that Hitler was quite correctly sourcing from the recognized original authority on "race." Alfred Ploetz was not just the vice-president of the British Eugenics Society in 1916. Ploetz was the German physician known for coining the term "racial hygiene," or *Rassenhygiene*. Hitler was copying the work of Ploetz and his eugenic colleagues when writing "Mein Kampf," and not the other way around. Hitler was following the lead of the prominent international eugenicists, as opposed to leading in that direction as history has credited him. Ploetz voiced this very sentiment when in April 1933 he wrote that he believed Hitler would bring racial hygiene from its previous marginality into the mainstream. [53] Hitler was providing these scientists and doctors the opportunity that the governments in the United States and the United Kingdom were prevented from fully implementing due to their nation's libertarian legal traditions.

To understand just how crucial these international relationships were, one only need to recognize that the laws that Hitler's government implemented were verbatim translations from the "Model Eugenical Sterilization Law" that had been written by Harry H. Laughlin. Laughlin had distilled his "Model Eugenical Sterilization Law" after almost a decade of helping draft the laws of more than 30 States and sourcing the expert opinion of the most prominent lawyers, judges, and legislators in the United States. Through the International Federation of Eugenic Organizations, Adolf Hitler was given access to tried and true law that had taken the best minds of the legislatures and courts of the United States various decades to mature. This was no small gesture, as "racial hygiene" was beyond policy in Third Reich law; it was its guiding principle.

Furthermore, when one puts this into the context of the timeline, one notices this transfer of knowledge was utilized at the fortuitous moment just after the Reichstag fire and Hitler's consolidation of power with the passing of the Enabling Act of 1933. The perfecting of a "Model Eugenical Sterilization Law" had consumed a lot of Rockefeller, Carnegie, Kellogg, Goethe, and Merriman money along with the sizeable staff these institutions employed in Cold Spring Harbor and London to arrive at this work product. Through Ploetz and Rüdin, Hitler was given fully matured and proven legal mechanisms and bestowed the luxury of not having to start from scratch.

The United States and Britain had enjoyed the luxury of developing these eugenic measures at the time when Germans could simply not aspire to do so because of the devastation following World War I and the Great Depression. This allowed the Hitler government to erase the decades which Germany had fallen behind in the science of eugenics. One only needs to gauge the numbers murdered per month by

---

[53] Pg. 507 - "The Third Reich in Power", Richard J. Evans, Penguin Books, 2006.

Hitler's henchmen to put a price on the true value of the time saved by being able to source a ready-made and fully designed "racial state" from the United States and Britain. Most importantly, Adolf Hitler got what he wanted most: international legitimacy and the ability to claim that his racial laws were no different than those already adopted by the United States and Britain. Hitler certainly was thankful. Adolf Hitler recognized his indebtedness to Ploetz in 1936 by appointing him to a professorship. Ploetz reciprocated by officially joining the National Socialist party in 1937. The German institutes of higher education during Hitler's reign, in turn, awarded Harry H. Laughlin and Karl Pearson with honors. International recognition and press coverage followed. According to the Nobel Prize nomination database, the Scandinavian eugenic-minded Erling Bjørnson and Alf Mjøen of the Norwegian Parliament nominated Ploetz for the Nobel Peace Prize in 1936 for his work on eugenics. [54]

As late as August 12, 1939, just two weeks before Hitler's Germany would invade Poland and a full year after the intensification of aggression against the Jewish population commenced with *Kristallnacht*, Harry H. Laughlin was still corresponding with Ernst Rüdin to coordinate the Fourth International Congress for Eugenics, scheduled to take place in Vienna during 1940. Laughlin had been the Secretary of the Third International Congress and was writing to Rüdin, who had been named president of the Fourth International Congress to "evaluate the technique of practical population-control" and to "exchange experiences and plans among leaders in the biological betterment of mankind." [55]

Mark Lilla, author of "The Reckless Mind" addresses the fixation the intellectual and political elite have with utopian schemes. Lilla reminds us that the love for a pristine idea is "maddening" and potentially intoxicating, just like a physical passion:

> What has philosophy to do with love? If Plato is to be believed, everything. While all lovers are not philosophers, philosophers are the only true lovers, since they alone understand what love blindly seeks. Love evokes in us all an unconscious memory of the beauty of the Ideas, and this memory maddens us; we feel possessed by a frenzied yearning to couple and to "beget in the beautiful." (Pg. 3, "The Reckless Mind: Intellectuals in Politics", Review Books, 2006)

With social stature comes the danger of overestimating one's opinion on social matters, and thus society's most prominent members often suffer from this "reckless passion" for controlling, molding or ordering society. Mark Lilla points to Plato's "philosopher kings" in his famous "Republic" as being the prototypical cultural elitist, enamored with their vision of the world as being the only correct vision, and the goal for which all else should be sacrificed. In the end, the eugenic ideal is largely driven by an aesthetic ideal about an ordered and predictable society, free from disease and unpleasantness. The popularity of utopian novels by H.G. Wells and the allure of the socialist perfectionism, despite their obvious dangers and pitfalls, only

---

[54] nobelprize.org, Nomination Database, Nominee: Alfred Ploetz, Number: 29-1.
[55] BOX: C-2-5:3, Letter dated: Aug. 12, 1939, Laughlin to Rüdin, Truman Univ., Laughlin Collection.

serves to evidence the addictive nature of the utopian vision. These visions, by their very nature, failed or survived on the sustenance of ideas. These "merchants of light," provided that most ephemeral but crucial ingredient indispensable to the creation of utopias: the idea, refined and ready for implementation by willing "philosopher kings," or führers, whatever the difference may be.

Sec. 8 - MEDICINE GONE MAD?

Auschwitz was a network of both concentration and extermination camps built and operated by the National Socialists in Polish areas annexed during World War II. It was the largest of the camps at 40 square kilometers of land. Auschwitz consisted of the Auschwitz I base camp, the Auschwitz II–Birkenau extermination camp, the Auschwitz III–Monowitz labor camp, and 45 satellite camps. Auschwitz I served as the administrative center for the whole complex. Construction on Auschwitz II-Birkenau, the extermination camp, began in October 1941 to ease congestion at the main camp. From early 1942 until late 1944, transport trains delivered Jews to the camp's gas chambers from all over Nazi-occupied Europe. We must contextualize and differentiate between a concentration camp and an extermination camp. Just about everything that Hitler's National Socialists had done to minorities and ethnic groups was distasteful but not unheard of. Segregating undesirables and war prisoners into concentration camps had been done before. The decision to exterminate *en masse* entire sectors of the population made Auschwitz what it was, and what came to characterize and separate Nazism from the typical barbarism of humanity.

Auschwitz is also a prime example of how the regime's grand eugenic program bridged between military and civilian. Unfortunately, the American prosecutors at the Nuremberg Doctor's Trials employed the questionable demarcation of focusing on the medical research conducted for the war effort. They intentionally tried to separate the horrid human experimentation conducted for the war effort from that done by the regime allegedly in a lawful manner in observance of German law, regardless if the National Socialists themselves did not make that arbitrary distinction. Joseph Mengele is the best example of how useless this arbitrary demarcation was. Mengele, a combat field doctor in the *Waffen-SS*, transferred to Auschwitz in 1943 after being wounded in combat and has since become the most notorious member of the multitude of medical doctors and scientists which staffed Auschwitz. Joseph Mengele headed up experiments that can be labeled either of military or purely civilian scientific value. However, Mengele made no such distinction among the varied types of experiments he conducted on inmates.

The arbitrary distinction quickly falls apart upon closer inspection. German doctors performed a wide variety of experiments on prisoners at Auschwitz. SS doctors tested the efficacy of X-rays as a sterilization device by administering large doses to female prisoners. Prof. Dr. Carl Clauberg injected chemicals into women's uteruses to glue them shut. The most infamous experiments were Mengele's research on identical twins. Mengele performed cruel experiments on them, such as inducing diseases in one twin and killing the other when the first died to perform comparative autopsies. He also took a special interest in dwarfs. Clearly, none of these experiments can be said to have been conducted for the war effort. To be more precise, much of the experimental data and biological material harvested at Auschwitz went toward the direct benefit of civilian research operations in universities and civilian medical laboratories, namely the Kaiser Wilhelm Institute in Berlin. They were, as the National Socialists considered them, part of the larger scope of creating a "racial state" by a National Socialist ideology that prided itself in being "applied biology."[56]

Gisela Konopka was a survivor. She clarifies why she was made to suffer at the hands of Hitler's henchmen. Her observation helps contextualize what transpired at Auschwitz and differentiates it from previous atrocities:

> Nazi persecution of the Jews was not a religious persecution, it was a racial persecution, racism in its worst form. ---- Centuries ago, persecution of Jews was based on religion. This was definitely not the case under the Nazis. They persecuted Jews because of their so-called "racial inferiority". (Pg. 15-16, "When Medicine Went Mad: Bioethics and the Holocaust", Humana Press, 1992 – Chapter: "The Meaning of the Holocaust for Bioethics")

In other words, the murders and scientific experiments conducted at Auschwitz were substantially different than the Russian pogroms or the Spanish Inquisition. To the contrary, Adolf Hitler and most of the top National Socialists held a contemptuous admiration for traditional Judaism in its effort to keep their "blood" and culture "pure" per the dictates of the religion. The murders and experiments conducted at Auschwitz were part of the core ideology of National Socialism and were more accurately part of the eugenic goals central to the Reich, along with the T4 Euthanasia Program, Himmler's *Lebensborn* program, and the Nuremberg Laws.

More precisely, Adolf Hitler used the word "socialism" to describe his racial utopia because he believed in a society that cooperated and operated in solidarity towards a common destiny, as opposed to a capitalistic and individualistic society. Hitler had nothing but contempt for "Jewish capitalism," "democracy," and what he regarded as outmoded, sentimental, and antiquated respect for the individual. As such, Hitler's concept of society was not conducive to the divisions and demarcations the American prosecution at Nuremberg devised, and thus one must look to these divisions and demarcations with suspicion as valid legal strategies to document the perpetrator's "intent" behind the murders:

---

[56] "Applied Biology" was a phrase popular with the Nazi ranks to describe the nature of their regime. It was first coined by Fritz Lenz in 1931: "National Socialism is nothing but applied biology" – See: Pg. 36 - "The Nazi Connection: Eugenics, American Racism, and German National Socialism", Stefan Kühl, Oxford, 1994.

Fritz Lenz, for example, praised Hitler in 1930 as "the first politician of truly great import who has taken racial hygiene as a serious element of state policy." Hitler himself was lauded as the "great doctor of the German people"; he once called his revolution "the final step in the overcoming of historicism and the recognition of purely biological values." (Pg. 26, "When Medicine Went Mad: Bioethics and the Holocaust", Humana Press, 1992 – Chapter: "Nazi Biomedical Policies")

Without the National Socialist state's backing, racial hygiene would have been an impotent scientific movement. This is certainly true when one realizes that "racial hygiene" was not of any consequence in Mussolini's Italy or Franco's Spain, the other two "fascist" regimes of the Axis Powers. Scientists approached Mussolini after the 1929 International Congress for Eugenics, but that Il Duce was simply not interested. [57] This "applied biology" ethos was central to Nazism alone, and not a part of Fascism in general.

The relationship between Auschwitz and the civilian Kaiser Wilhelm Institute is made gruesomely clear when one realizes that Dr. Mengele was the "appointed assistant" to Otmar von Verschuer at the Frankfurt Institute for Racial Hygiene and that his job was to provide the Institute with eyes, blood and body parts harvested from the Auschwitz inmates. [58] This, of course, clarifies the hierarchy of the relationship, and the American Prosecution team knew this to be the case. Yet, the American Prosecution at the Doctors' Trial did not place the Kaiser Wilhelm Institute in the various charts and graphs explaining the chain of command dictating the activities at the camps. [59] Medical doctors were not coerced or conscripted to work at Auschwitz; Auschwitz was conscripted to work for the civilian doctors and scientists. Hans Hefelmann's testimony at a 1964 trial provides an answer to this lingering issue:

> Among physicians, there were as many volunteers as victims: no one had to force physicians to support the regime. Hefelmann testified to this effect in the euthanasia trial at Limburg in 1964: "No doctor was ever ordered to participate in the euthanasia program; they came of their own volition." (Pg. 41, "When Medicine Went Mad: Bioethics and the Holocaust", Humana Press, 1992)

The realization of this fact devastates the pedestrian myth of the coerced German doctor. "Racial hygiene" was the creation of German medical science and not the National Socialists as the popular history of the regime otherwise insinuates:

> One often hears that National Socialists distorted science, that doctors perhaps cooperated more with the Nazi regime than they should have, but that by 1933, as one émigré said, it was too late, and scientists had no alternative but to cooperate or flee. There is certainly some truth in this, but I think it misses the

---

[57] Pg. 45 - "When Medicine Went Mad: Bioethics and the Holocaust", Arthur L. Caplan, Humana Press, 1992
[58] Pg. 28 – Ibid.
[59] Pgs. 27-74 – Opening Statement of the Prosecution by Brigadier General Telford Taylor, 9 December 1946, "Trials of War Criminals Before the Nuernberg Military Tribunals Under Control Council Law No. 10", Vol. 1, "The Medical Case", Superintendent of Documents, U.S. Government Printing Office.

more important point that medical scientists were the ones who invented racial hygiene in the first place. (Pg. 27, "When Medicine Went Mad: Bioethics and the Holocaust", Humana Press, 1992)

The famous historian of eugenics, Robert Proctor aptly points out that "physicians, in other words, were not simply "pawns" in the hands of Nazi officials - not pawns, but pioneers." [60] Mengele's work was funded by the *Deutsche Forschungsgemeinschaft* (German Research Council), further blurring the line between public and private, military and civilian. [61] Racial hygiene was recognized as the primary research goal of two separate institutes under the Kaiser Wilhelm Gesellschaft. The Kaiser Wilhelm Institute for Anthropology in Berlin was directed by Eugen Fischer, and the Kaiser Wilhelm Institute for Genealogy in Munich was directed by psychiatrist Ernst Rüdin. Note the extent of cooperation between the "civilian" and "military" branches of National Socialist medicine:

> German doctors plundered the remains of murdered individuals for university institutes of anatomy and pathology as well as prestigious research institutes. Requests for tissues and specimens came from anatomy and pathology departments in leading German universities and scientific institution in Heidelberg, Berlin, Berlin Charité Hospital, Tübingen, Vienna, Humboldt, Kaiser Wilhelm Institute (now Max Planck Institute), Graz, Jena, Reichsunversität Posen, Strassburg, and the Vienna Museum of Natural History's anthropology section. (Pg. 71, "Murderous Medicine: Nazi Doctors, Human Experimentation, and Typhus", Naomi Baumslag, Praeger Publishers, 2005)

To reiterate the central theme of this book, here is the crux of the matter; here is the proximate consequence of the relative failure of the Nuremberg Doctor's Trial:

> Despite the glaring evidence of gross negligence and unethical conduct, most of the guilty doctors were never held accountable for their actions. There is no complete list of doctors who were involved. Most were never found or tried, and only a few of the doctors charged with criminal acts were sentenced. (Pg. 73-75, "Murderous Medicine: Nazi Doctors, Human Experimentation, and Typhus", Praeger Publishers, 2005)

Even the detestable Dr. Mengele escaped the dragnet. Mengele was listed on the Allies' list of war criminals as early as 1944. His name was mentioned in the Nuremberg trials several times, but Allied forces were convinced that Mengele was dead, but the fact that Mengele escaped justice is just one of the many failures of Nuremberg. Mengele's relationship to civilian laboratories and hospitals stands as proof that the imaginary demarcation line drawn by the American prosecution team at the Nuremberg Doctor's Trial was questionable at best and fraudulent at worst.

---

[60] Pg. 410 – Opening Statement of the Prosecution by Brigadier General Telford Taylor, 9 December 1946, "Trials of War Criminals Before the Nuernberg Military Tribunals Under Control Council Law No. 10", Vol. I, "The Medical Case", Superintendent of Documents, U.S. Government Printing Office.

[61] Pg. 410 - "Nazi Medical Ethics: Ordinary Doctors?", Robert Proctor, Military Medical Ethics, Vol. 2, 2003.

Even the slightest scrutiny would arrive at the conclusion that Dr. Mengele's experiments were not done for the benefit of the German armed forces or as research for the war effort. The American prosecutors allowed many doctors and scientists to go free from prosecution under the notion that they were civilian doctors working under the rule of law in civilian operations, and that it was only the human experimentation and murders conducted with the goal of waging war which was to be constituted as crimes. This assumption falls apart with one quick survey of Dr. Mengele's experiments at Auschwitz. There was no military need or justification for conducting tests on eye color or infant twins. Yet, it would be preposterous to claim that Dr. Mengele's activities were not an integral port of the "crimes against humanity."

Sec. 9 - FROM "AGONY OF LIVING" TO "LIVES NOT WORTH LIVING":

In May of 1941, the very same year the National Socialists were meeting in Wannsee to determine the "Final Solution," US psychiatrist Foster Kennedy addressed the 97th annual meeting of the American Psychiatric Association and he explicitly advocated the killing of "retarded" children and the "utterly unfit" to relieve them "the agony of living" and to spare their parents expense and anguish.[62]

Foster Kennedy became a professor of neurology at Cornell University and in 1940 was elected president of the "American Neurological Association." Kennedy's speech was published the following year by the American Psychiatric Association's journal. In the article, Kennedy stated that "We have too many feebleminded people among us." The journal printed an editorial following Kennedy's article, endorsing Kennedy's approach and emphasizing the important role that all psychiatrists could play in letting parents know that euthanizing severely disabled children was humane and that it was kind to put an end to what Kennedy had termed "nature's mistakes." Clearly, Kennedy advocated the solution endorsed by many in the eugenics movement up to that time. More poignantly, the endorsement by the association's journal proved that his views were hardly extreme and were perfectly in line within the medical ethic of the T4 Euthanasia program for which Karl Brandt was found guilty at the Nuremberg Doctors' Trial.

As this book will evidence, Kennedy was hardly alone amongst Americans and Britons. Referring to the destruction of life as "humane" was popular amongst eugenic circles. It was thus that Charles Francis Potter was able to announce euthanasia as a "humanist cause" before the First Humanist Society of New York in 1936, well within the shadow of Nazi Germany, by touting it as "mercy killing" and

---

[62] Pgs. 13-16 - "The Problem of Social Control of the Congenital Defective: Education, Sterilization, Euthanasia", American Journal of Psychiatry, July 1942, vol. 99.

a "triumph over the flesh." Not only was it touted as the "humane" thing to do, but according to the devout "humanists" like Potter, it served a social purpose. Potter called for the incurably insane and mentally retarded to be "mercifully executed by the lethal chamber," stating that "it is simply our social cowardice that keeps [imbeciles and idiot infants and 'monsters' alive." [63] Potter was joined by Inez Celia Philbrick, a physician and faculty member of the University of Nebraska in their disdain for Catholicism and traditional morals. Both were Unitarians, and Philbrick supported women's suffrage, birth control, eugenic sterilization, and world peace. Interestingly enough, Philbrick was bitterly opposed to professional medicine's "rigid adherence to the Hippocratic Oath," which prohibited doctors from administering lethal doses.

However much the pro-euthanasia groups of today try to distance themselves from the eugenics of World War II, the bottom line that throughout the United States and Britain the pro-euthanasia groups overlapped and shared a following with the eugenics groups. Incidentally, Hitler's government honored John Foster Kennedy. In turn, William W. Peter of the US government's Public Health Service praised the German sterilization program in an article of the "American Journal of Public Health" in 1934. [64] The Voluntary Euthanasia Legislation Society was founded by a retired Unitarian physician C. Killick Millard. "Millard championed temperance, eugenics, cremation, and birth control. He was convinced that when public health was at stake, nothing was taboo." [65] Of note is that the Society's ranks included Havelock Ellis, H.G. Wells, and Julian Huxley, Max Eastman, Fannie Hurst, and Robert Frost, to name a few of the mainstream and vocal "merchants of light" for the eugenic cause.

Furthermore, as later chapters will elucidate, American doctors were killing off those "lives unworthy of lives" decades before the Nazi doctors. The fact that the American scientific and medical community were active participants in the wanton destruction of "lives unworthy of living" brings serious concerns about the Nuremberg Doctors' Trial, or as it is otherwise known, the Medical Case. Recall the case of Judge Charles F. Wennerstrum and his vocal complaints about the tactics and format of the Subsequent Trials. He was deeply troubled by practices "not in keeping with our generally accepted concept of proper administration of justice." [66] One of his main concerns was what jurists know as the "clean hands doctrine." This bedrock concept of law dictates that those that are guilty of the same offenses should not stand in judgment of others if they are either complicit in the wrongdoing or guilty of the same transgressions or crimes. He pointed to the biblical concept of "judge not that ye be not judged." [67] Judge Wennerstrum was mostly directing this

---

[63] Pg. 43, "A Merciful End: The Euthanasia Movement in Modern America", Oxford Univ. Press, 2003.
[64] Pgs. 135-136 - "The Last Gasp: The Rise and Fall of the American Gas Chamber", Scott Christianson, Univ. of Cal. Press, 2010.
[65] Pgs. 135-136 – Ibid.
[66] Speeches 5.001-5.008 – "Paper by Charles F. Wennerstrum Presented at Joint Luncheon Meeting of Section of International & Comparative Law and Junior Bar Conference at the Annual Meeting of the American Bar Association", Sept., 7, 1948, Judge Wennerstrum Papers, State Historical Society of Iowa.
[67] From Mathew 7:1-3, King James Version – As cited by Judge Wennerstrum, Speeches 5.001-5.008, Judge Wennerstrum Papers, State Historical Society of Iowa.

criticism at the inclusion of the USSR in a trial for mass murder, but it is widely applicable to any court deemed "*iudex inhabilis*" by conflicting associations, acts, or relationships. Judge Wennerstrum's solution to the various fatal problems he saw was to have jurists from nations that didn't participate in WWII both administer and conduct the trials. No wonder Telford Taylor reacted in such a visceral fashion to Wennerstrum's criticism. In 20/20 hindsight, Judge Wennerstrum's suggestion makes absolute sense. Politically speaking, allowing the defense the ability to bring forth all the evidence of American and British complicity in the international eugenics movement would have been more than devastating; it would have been catastrophic to a significant number of American and British institutions, political parties, political movements, and political figures, not to mention the effect it would have had on the Allied occupation of Germany after the war.

What knows the laws
That thieves to pass on thieves?[68]

---

[68] William Shakespeare, "Measure for Measure", Act 2, Scene I – As cited by Wennerstrum.

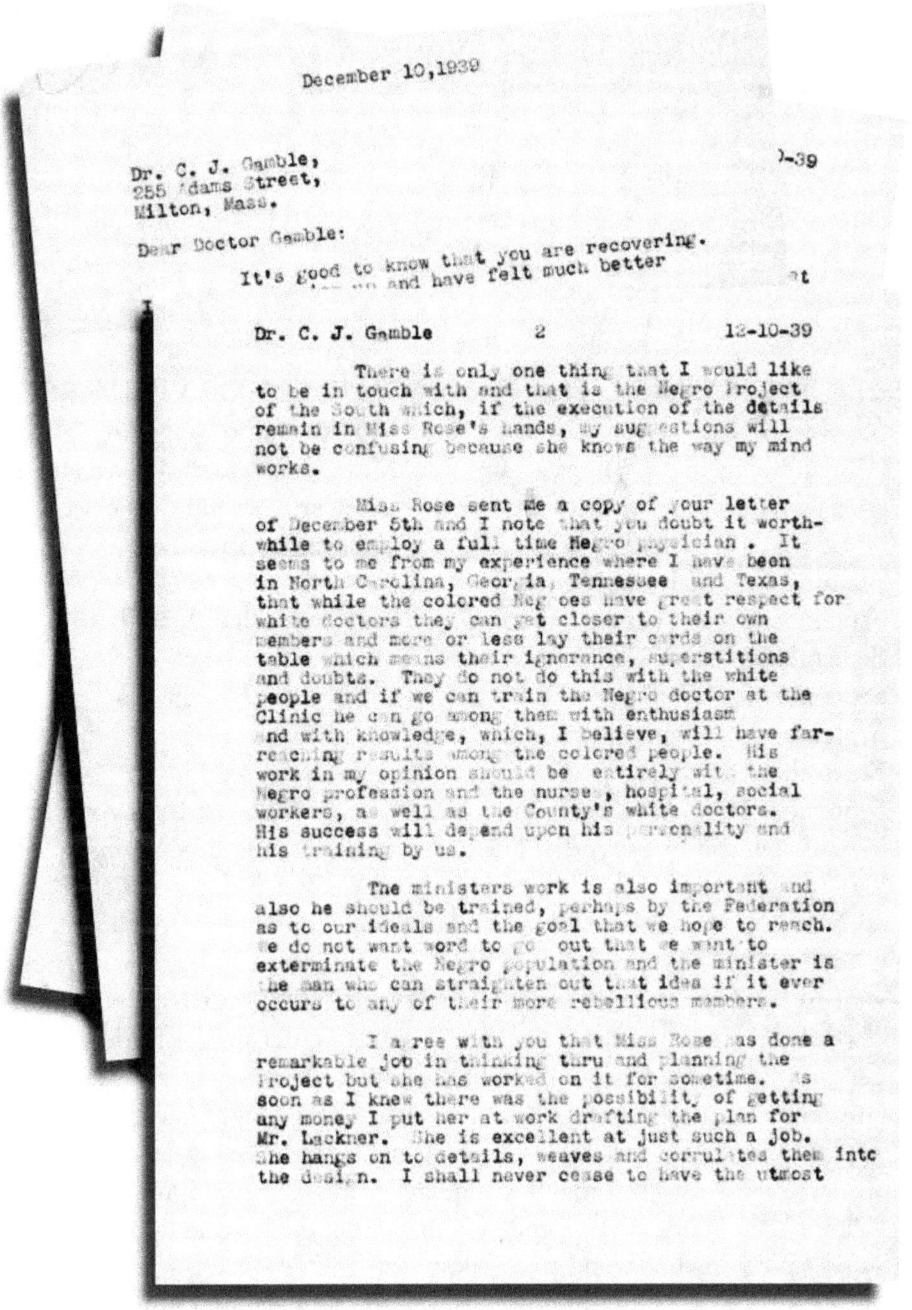

December 10, 1939

Dr. C. J. Gamble,
255 Adams Street,
Milton, Mass.

Dear Doctor Gamble:

It's good to know that you are recovering.

Dr. C. J. Gamble   2   12-10-39

There is only one thing that I would like to be in touch with and that is the Negro Project of the South which, if the execution of the details remain in Miss Rose's hands, my suggestions will not be confusing because she knows the way my mind works.

Miss Rose sent me a copy of your letter of December 5th and I note that you doubt it worthwhile to employ a full time Negro physician. It seems to me from my experience where I have been in North Carolina, Georgia, Tennessee and Texas, that while the colored Negroes have great respect for white doctors they can get closer to their own members and more or less lay their cards on the table which means their ignorance, superstitions and doubts. They do not do this with the white people and if we can train the Negro doctor at the Clinic he can go among them with enthusiasm and with knowledge, which, I believe, will have far-reaching results among the colored people. His work in my opinion should be entirely with the Negro profession and the nurse, hospital, social workers, as well as the County's white doctors. His success will depend upon his personality and his training by us.

The ministers work is also important and also he should be trained, perhaps by the Federation as to our ideals and the goal that we hope to reach. We do not want word to go out that we want to exterminate the Negro population and the minister is the man who can straighten out that idea if it ever occurs to any of their more rebellious members.

I agree with you that Miss Rose has done a remarkable job in thinking thru and planning the Project but she has worked on it for sometime. As soon as I knew there was the possibility of getting any money I put her at work drafting the plan for Mr. Lackner. She is excellent at just such a job. She hangs on to details, weaves and correlates them into the design. I shall never cease to have the utmost

---

FIGURE 3: CORRESPONDENCE FROM MARGARET SANGER TO DR. CLARENCE GAMBLE DISCUSSING THE "NEGRO PROJECT". THE THIRD PARAGRAPH DOWN DETAILS THE NEED TO EMPLOY MINISTERS IN ORDER TO "STRAIGHTEN OUT" THE "MORE REBELLIOUS MEMBERS" OF THE BLACK COMMUNITY. (IMAGE PROVIDED BY THE SOPHIA SMITH COLLECTION ARCHIVISTS AT SMITH COLLEGE.)

Chap. 2: 1940 to 1936

EUROPEAN FRONT: WINSTON CHURCHILL TELLS THE HOUSE OF COMMONS, "I HAVE NOTHING TO OFFER YOU BUT BLOOD, TOIL, TEARS, AND SWEAT." FRANKLIN D. ROOSEVELT DECLARES THAT THE UNITED STATES MUST BECOME "THE GREAT ARSENAL OF DEMOCRACY." NEVILLE CHAMBERLAIN RETURNS TO BRITAIN AND DECLARES "PEACE FOR OUR TIME". • **SCIENCE & TECHNOLOGY:** IN LASCAUX, FRANCE, 17,000-YEAR-OLD CAVE PAINTINGS ARE DISCOVERED. THE HEWLETT-PACKARD COMPANY IS FOUNDED. PRESIDENT FRANKLIN D. ROOSEVELT IS PRESENTED A LETTER SIGNED BY ALBERT EINSTEIN, URGING THE UNITED STATES TO RAPIDLY DEVELOP THE ATOMIC BOMB. HINDENBURG DISASTER: IN THE UNITED STATES, – AMELIA EARHART DISAPPEARS. – EXCAVATIONS BEGIN AT THE NEOLITHIC SITE OF HYRAX HILL, KENYA, BY MARY LEAKEY. - THE GOLDEN GATE BRIDGE IS OPENED. • **POLITICS:** THE SOVIET UNION EXECUTES 31 PEOPLE FOR ALLEGED TROTSKYISM. WITHIN THE FOLLOWING YEAR, AT LEAST 724,000 PEOPLE ARE PURGED. • **LIFE:** MCDONALD'S RESTAURANT OPENS IN SAN BERNARDINO, CALIFORNIA. – AL CAPONE IS RELEASED FROM ALCATRAZ. ORSON WELLES'S THE WAR OF THE WORLDS IS BROADCAST. – PICASSO COMPLETES GUERNICA. – ABRAHAM LINCOLN'S HEAD IS DEDICATED AT MOUNT RUSHMORE. LIFE MAGAZINE IS FIRST PUBLISHED. MAXIM GORKY DIES.

Sec. I - FROM WAR TO THE FINAL SOLUTION (OR VISE VERSA):

July 23 –Mahatma Gandhi writes a letter to Hitler addressing him "My friend," requesting that he prevent any war. Meanwhile, Adolf Hitler and Joseph Stalin negotiate to divide Europe between Germany and the Soviet Union in the agreement known as the Molotov-Ribbentrop Pact.

August 24 – The Royal Navy is put on a war footing.

September 1 – A German battleship bombards a Polish military base.

September 3 – The U.K., France, New Zealand, and Australia declare war.

September 5 – The United States declares its neutrality in the war.

September 6 – South Africa declares war on Germany.

September 10 – Canada declares war on Germany.

September 15 – Diverse elements of the German Wehrmacht surround Warsaw and demand its surrender. The Poles refuse, and the siege begins.

War is incidental to ideology, and this was certainly true for the war instigated by Adolf Hitler. Historians have aptly documented that Hitler knew he needed the fog of war and a radicalized population to enact his most extreme policies. The war allowed Hitler both the cover and justification to enact the T4 Euthanasia program designed to eradicate those lives deemed "not worth living" by pointing to the costs of maintaining those "useless eaters" during a time of war. It allowed license for Karl Brandt to "clear hospital beds" in the name of the war effort. In turn, the war's conquered territory also brought conquered populations and increased the number of "unfit" and "undesired" population, including the Jewish population of Eastern Europe. The methods and technology of the T4 Euthanasia program were transferred from the German hospitals to the extermination camps, doctors, nurses, equipment, and all. This transfer and repurposing of medical resources was allegedly decided in the infamous Wannsee Conference, which we now believe was the beginning of the Final Solution: "The aim of all this was to cleanse German living space of Jews in a **legal manner**." [69]

Reinhard Heydrich, the man appointed to head up "The Final Solution of the

---

[69] Pgs. 18 – 32, "Nuremberg Trials: The Holocaust: Selected Documents in Eighteen Volumes", Vol. 11: The Wannsee Protocol, Translation by John Mendelsohn for the 1944 Report on Auschwitz by the OSS, New York: Garland, 1982.

Jewish Question," sent invitations for a meeting to be held at Wannsee, on the western edge of Berlin. He enclosed a copy of Göring's letter of July 31st, 1941, to indicate his authority in the matter. [70] This was a meeting of administrators to discuss the implementation of a policy already decided at the executive level based on a July 31st, 1941 letter, so those invited were mostly chief administrative officers of government ministries. The meeting was originally scheduled for December 1941. The Japanese attack on Pearl Harbor and the Soviet counter-offensive delayed the meeting as some invitees were thus indisposed. In early January 1942, Heydrich sent new invitations to a meeting to be held on January 20, 1942.

The "solution" to the "Jewish question" aspired to be the "final" one to a series of other proposals, namely allowing the German Jews to emigrate elsewhere. The "Madagascar Plan" was but one of the suggested "solutions" with its proposal to relocate the Jewish population of Europe to the island. Britain had also limited the number of people allowed into Palestine, what is now Israel. As history evidences, the United States had closed its borders due to the eugenic immigration acts drafted up by Ivy League eugenicists, specifically the 1924 Immigration Restriction Act.

The rapid German advances in the opening weeks of the invasion of the Soviet Union made finding an answer to the so-called "Jewish question" seem even more urgent with the growing likelihood that the 4 million Jews of the western Soviet Union would fall under German control. The land needed to be cleared of its population to fulfill Hitler's dream of an enlarged geography for "Aryan" Germans, in what is otherwise known as the regime's *"Lebensraum"* policy. Like many of the other policies, *"Lebensraum"* had been conceived much prior to Hitler by like-minded zealots. The purpose of the July 31, 1941 letter was to document Hitler's earlier meeting with Reichsmarschall Hermann Göring of July 16, 1941, at which Hitler said that Soviet territories west of the Urals were to become a "German Garden of Eden." Göring would later testify at Nuremberg that he took this comment in the context of other dictates and policies as authority to proceed with the physical removal of all Jews from Germany, as had been discussed at length by the leadership for a decade before Wannsee. The July 31, 1941 document provided Göring authorization for Heydrich to "make all necessary preparations" for a "total solution of the Jewish question" in all the territories under German influence which would coordinate all aspects of the National Socialist government as the scope and scale of the operation required, and to submit a "comprehensive draft" of a plan for the "final solution of the Jewish question."

Because of his organizational talents and ideological reliability, Adolf Eichmann was charged by Reinhard Heydrich with the task of facilitating and managing the logistics of mass deportation of Jews to ghettos and extermination camps in German-occupied Eastern Europe. In preparation for the conference, Eichmann drafted a list of the numbers of Jews in the various European countries. The list totaled to approximately 11 million people.

Context is everything, and the proclamations and goals of the Wannsee

---

[70] jewishvirtuallibrary.org, "Göring Commission to Heydrich".

Conference must be put into historical context in order to comprehend it as an event with both a past and a present. By the time Hitler's deputies met at Wannsee, Vladimir Lenin and Joseph Stalin had already murdered more than 20 million of their own people by transporting them *en masse* to forced labor agricultural camps and intentional starvation. It must also be noted that Hitler had a particular fixation with the wars of antiquity and was enamored by the theatrical violence. In other words, Hitler had an "artistic" appetite for destruction, if such an appetite for war can be defined as such. Adolf Hitler was, after all, obsessed with the aesthetic physicality of Germany. His dictatorial imposition on the way the "New Aryan Man" was to be displayed by his chosen artists and sculptors shows a definite and precise aesthetic vision, which inversely was intentionally made to be thought of as the diametric opposite of Jewish stereotypes through propagandistic venues. The image of the stereotypical Jew was to be removed from the sphere of German life, and this was meant both literally and artistically.

It is also critical to understand that Hitler did not regard the eradication of unwanted humanity as a one-time effort or even as a single project. The eradication of unwanted humanity was seen by Hitler as the ongoing policy of an eugenic utopia; his Aryan Garden of Eden. While historians have pointed to Hitler's lack of hands-on participation in the Wannsee Conference, it is important to note that it did not require so much of his direct leadership as it required his insistence that it be part of the day-to-day mechanisms of the National Socialist state. The National Socialist state was already engaged in the perpetual business of creating and maintaining its racial stock.

This last point is of some importance. Looking back at Wannsee, we are aghast at the business-like and matter-of-fact approach to mass murder. Historians generally agree that the reason that the Wannsee Conference was carried out without fanfare or celebration was that it was just another business meeting penned onto several bureaucrats' busy calendars. To come to terms with it, we must realize that this was not a lynching at a Ku Klux Klan rally but a policy meeting that involved several mid-level agents of the German National Socialist government. The peculiar lack of fanfare in a conference pertaining to the regime's major goals can only be explained by the fact that the conference was nothing more than part of a continuing policy in creating and maintaining the "racial state." These mid-level bureaucrats were simply deliberating on how to most efficiently carry out the goals of the "Final Solution" pertaining to the "Jewish Problem." Even this seemingly ominous phrase was only another use for the "final solution" of the various social problems that National Socialism's utopian government claimed it could stamp out with the help of science, efficiency, and solidarity. The "problem solving rhetoric" of the regime framed its various campaigns for the "final solution" to the "bread question," the "tobacco question." [71]

> ... about finding "radical," "final," or "permanent" solutions to Germany's problems — especially in the early war years, when plans for the radical

---

[71] Pg. 8 - "Nazi War on Cancer", Robert Proctor, Princeton Univ. Press, 2000.

transformation of German society reached a fever pitch. The Final Solution (*Endlösung*) to the Jewish Question is the best known and most ghastly, but similar expressions were used for countless other problems. (Pg. 47-48, "Nazi War on Cancer", Robert Proctor, Princeton Univ. Press, 2000)

There was a "millenarian," or turn-of-the-century expectation that a "New World Order" could be imposed via "radical" solutions. [72] The "Final Solution to the Jewish Problem" was by far the most important of programs under Hitler's leadership, but his utopian technocrats and bureaucrats could not have accomplished its scope or scale if this was not the common thread running through all facets of the National Socialist government. The roster of attendees at Wannsee evidences this. Even the most remote departments were necessary for carrying out the gargantuan task of eliminating the 11 million people. These were the best of Germany's professional class. No less than eight of the fifteen participants held a doctorate. [73]

More precisely, the Wannsee Conference was about the mundane planning of logistics and methodology. The Wannsee Conference was not concerned with debating "if" the Final Solution would happen, only "how" it would be brought about. It was the head of the "one-party" system of government sending his directives down the chain of command and having every aspect of government do their part to make the decisions of the party happen. Thus, the Wannsee Conference was a meeting of all the relevant scientific, jurisprudence, executive, and military authorities having a formal policy meeting. This is an all-important distinction. Plain bigotry lynches men one by one. "Scientific racism," armed with all the power of an "industrial army," murders at industrial scales, in the millions.

Let's place Wannsee in the timeline: January 20th, 1942, was the very beginning, or rather end, of this very long history of genocide. In just three, quick-paced, and manic years, Adolf Hitler would be dead. Hitler had amassed total control over Germany eight years earlier in 1933, at which point his eugenic and euthanasia plans begun in earnest. The killing on a mass scale started in October 1939 with the T4 Euthanasia Program, which put into practice the National Socialist government's "mercy killing" ideology. The Wannsee Conference was nothing more but the meeting that decided how to scale up the "mercy killing" technology developed by the T4 doctors. The ramp-up demanded the killing in the millions, instead of the hundreds of thousands, and trainloads instead of busloads. The Wannsee Conference bureaucrats determined that bullets were too expensive for the task and that soldiers, ironically those trained specifically to kill, were not adequate for the task at hand due to the traditional morality of the soldier, which regarded themselves as the protectors of the people and not its executioners. The task of killing millions of defenseless civilians needed to be handed off to the more willing hands of the scientists and doctors, whom toward the turn-of-the-century had adopted a "new

---

[72] Pg. 47-48 – Ibid.
[73] Pg. 411 - "The Origins of The Final Solution: The Evolution of Nazi Jewish Policy, September 1939-March 1942", Christopher R. Browning/Jürgen Matthäus, Random House, 2004.

ethic," an *"Über Ethik,"* which was not constrained by traditional morality as was the German military.

War is incidental to ideology, and battles are the backdrop to the daily lives of the victims. Civilians experience the polemic of war through the media and are subject to the ideologically motivated whims of those in power. War offers cover by realigning priorities and limiting resources. It crowds out the individual voices with the social polemic. This is the peculiar reversal of life that takes place during wartime: War becomes the news, as the news of daily human lives recedes from the headlines. The unfolding melodrama discards individual rights. Modern warfare inspires a sense of solidarity, if not a survivalist ethos. This is the reason why "propaganda" was invented, why it became a technology to be wielded by those in power: The populous now must be convinced, must be manipulated and controlled at a time of war.

The above point is crucial towards an understanding of the era. At no point prior to the 20th century did kings or queens require the approbation or support of the civilian to wage war. Adolf Hitler knew this to be an impediment. The theory that the German troops had been "stabbed in the back" and betrayed by those who stayed in the home front was a real issue for Hitler, who had world conquest in his plans. Hitler was keen on the fact that war forces solidarity and a collectivist spirit on a nation, if for nothing other than a sense of survival. Historians have documented that Hitler knew there were just some projects that had to wait until the German population was "nationalized." In 1935 Hitler told Gerhard Wagner, a prominent German physician, that "if war should break out, he would take up the euthanasia question and implement it . . . because the Führer was of the opinion that such a problem would be easier and smoother to carry out in wartime" and because "the public resistance which one would expect from the churches would not play such a prominent role amidst the events of wartime as it otherwise would." [74] It is important to understand that the "euthanasia" program that Hitler and Wagner were talking about were not the Jews or the Gypsies but were people that were otherwise "Aryans" with birth defects and even things as minor as alcoholism and bad acne. Hitler understood that in order for the German public to passively accept, or even collaborate with a program that did away with the "useless eaters," their national solidarity and unity of purpose had to be tweaked and leveraged; their sense of national survival had to be threatened.

This is where the eugenic propaganda became entangled with wartime propaganda. This is why Hitler and his henchmen forever referred to the T4 Euthanasia program along with The Final Solution as one and the same struggle and war as that with actual military enemies. Hitler needed the war to enhance the "solidarity" that only the feeling of being on a sinking ship could inspire in a population, or more precisely, the life and death proposals of a "total war" as the one the Germans had come to know in World War I. The steady beat of the war drums provided Hitler with a "nationalized" and "socialized" consciousness.

---

[74] Pg. 97 - "Death and Deliverance: 'Euthanasia' in Germany, C.1900 to 1945", Michael Burleigh, CUP Archive, Oct. 27, 1994.

Sec. 2 - LOTHROP STODDARD'S "INTO THE DARKNESS":

Lothrop Stoddard is an indispensable figure in the effort to understand the nature of National Socialism and eugenics. Stoddard was born in Brookline, Massachusetts, and received a Ph.D. in History from Harvard University in 1914. Stoddard is mostly remembered for his 1920 book, "The Rising Tide of Color against White World-Supremacy." Margaret Sanger partnered with him the following year to create the American Birth Control League, the forerunner to Planned Parenthood. The infamous Madison Grant wrote the introduction to Stoddard's book, and together with Grant and Harry H. Laughlin, Stoddard was integral in the effort to pass the 1924 Immigration Restriction Act which Cordell Hull would use to keep out so many victims of The Holocaust from reaching the safety of US shores. Yet, he is almost altogether forgotten despite these pivotal contributions to world history.

Stoddard's "racialist" fame opened doors to the Third Reich. Stoddard enjoyed unimpeded access to Adolf Hitler's "racial state." In fact, Stoddard enjoyed more access than would have been given to a European journalist, and certainly more freedom than a writer/journalist under Goebbels' Propaganda Ministry. Stoddard had earned his "white supremacist" and eugenic credentials with the publication of his "racialist" books, and these books earned Stoddard notoriety around the world, and Hitler deeply coveted the propaganda value of having a famous American reporter write a piece about National Socialism's eugenic policies from the American eugenic viewpoint. Hitler personally made sure Stoddard's visit into the institutions of National Socialism would be unimpeded and that the most important figures in the National Socialist state would be his hosts. Stoddard's inspection resulted in his 1940 publication of the book "Into the Darkness." In it Stoddard makes an interesting observation about his December 19, 1939 interview with Hitler:

> Whatever he may be to his friends and intimates, I came away feeling that, however interested Hitler may be in people collectively, he is not interested in the average individual, as such. (Pgs. 201-202, Chp. XVII, I See Hitler, "Into the Darkness: A Sympathetic Report from Hitler's Wartime Reich")

The extent and the depth of the access Lothrop Stoddard enjoyed was probably best described by Theodore J. O'Keefe's book review for the Institute for Historical Review. It documents the depth and breadth of Stoddard's visit:

> He was able not merely to get access to Joseph Goebbels, Heinrich Himmler, Robert Ley, Wilhelm Frick, Walter Darré, Gertrud Scholz-Klink and many other leaders, but to talk directly and knowledgeably with them about their achievements, problems, and goals. Stoddard then went off to observe what the Nazis were doing ---- on the farm, in the workplace, with the Labor Service, through the Winterhilfe aid campaign, and in the eugenics court. (Before visiting the last, he talked with such figures of the Reich's racial and genetics programs as Eugen Fischer, Fritz Lenz, and Hans F. K. Günther.) What Party officials and government ministers wouldn't tell him, he was often able to learn from taxi drivers, letter carriers, and cleaning women. ("Veteran American Journalist

Provides Valuable Inside Look at Third Reich Germany", Journal of Historical Review, Vol. 19, 2000, No. 2)

O'Keefe goes on to quote Stoddard's description of National Socialist Germany. Stoddard accurately thought of it as the "New Sparta with its cult of ruthless efficiency." This is, of course, if you see something redeeming in the way the Spartans ran their social lives. Stoddard's enemies had something to say about that, and in 1940 TIME magazine sniped at Stoddard as "persona grata to Nazis." This was obviously true. Stoddard clearly achieved a chummy and cozy relationship with the subjects of his study. This is probably also a tribute to his skills as an interviewer and investigative journalist. However, "Into the Darkness" is only that much more chilling for it. Stoddard claims that he was told by an interview subject in charge of the tuberculosis section of the public health service headquarters that:

> The treatment given a tuberculosis patient is partly determined by his social worth. If he is a valuable citizen and his case is curable no expense is spared. If he is adjudged incurable he is kept comfortable of course but no special effort is made to prolong slightly an existence which will benefit neither the community nor himself. Germany can nourish only a certain amount of human life at a given time. We National Socialists are in duty bound to foster individuals of social and biological value. (Pg. 179, "Into the Darkness: Nazi Germany Today", Duell, Sloan & Pearce, Inc., 1940)

Stoddard was apparently impressed by the "health measures" implemented by Hitler's National Socialist government and later in his book recounts his participation in the sessions of the Upper Court for Hereditary Health in Berlin-Charlottenburg. This is of incredible importance. Stoddard, the American eugenicist, was given access to the eugenic courts that sealed the fate of so many Europeans. As this book documents, these infamous eugenic courts were copied from the "Model Eugenical Sterilization Law" which Harry H. Laughlin drafted years prior to it being adopted by the Third Reich. At the Hereditary Health Supreme Court in Charlottenburg, Berlin, he joined two regular Nazi judges, a psychopathologist, and a criminal psychologist. Stoddard reported on four cases that he reviewed in order to illustrate the urgency of sterilizations:

- An "apelike" man with a receding forehead and flaring nostrils who had a history of homosexuality and was married to a "Jewess" by whom he had three "ne'er-do-well children.
- An obvious manic-depressive, of whom Stoddard wrote that "there was no doubt that he should be sterilized."
- An eighteen-year-old deaf-mute girl with several "unfortunate" hereditary factors in her family.
- A seventeen-year-old mentally retarded girl employed as a helper in an inexpensive restaurant. (Pgs. 62-63, Stefan Kühl, "Nazi Connection"/ Pgs. 193-195, "Into the Darkness")

One must seriously question why American historians have missed this jaw-dropping event in world history. One of the founders of the most prominent American political organizations dedicated to reproductive rights sat in as a judge in Hitler's infamous eugenic courts, and by his participation helped paint them with a veil of legitimacy. Stoddard's lack of sympathy for the defenseless and weak comes through just as clear as the ease with which he depicts his elbow-rubbing with Hitler's henchmen. Yet, the historical significance of his trip is largely forgotten or ignored. Here was Harry H. Laughlin's "Model Eugenical Sterilization Law" in practice, with an American eugenic expert sitting in judgment of defenseless minors in precisely the three-panel courts that the US Supreme Court had found to be constitutional in the 1927 landmark case of <u>Buck v. Bell</u>. These eugenic courts have rightfully earned the contempt of historians. Unfortunately, they have not documented that prominent Americans approved of how Hitler's henchmen implemented them. Of more importance is the matter-of-fact way in which Stoddard treated the "Jewish Question." Note the date:

> He viewed racialism, on the other hand, as a "passing phenomenon." Stoddard claimed **in 1940** that the "Jews problem" is already settled in principle and soon to be settled in fact by the physical elimination of the Jews themselves from the Third Reich. (emphasis mine, Pg. 62, "Nazi Connection"/ Pg. 189, "Into the Darkness")

As planned, Stoddard got access to those in charge of Hitler's eugenic programs. This included official spokesmen such as Frick and Darré and leading scientists Eugen Fischer, Fritz Lenz, Hans Günther, and others. It had been through their recommendations that he was able to sit beside the judges during a session of the Eugenic High Court of Appeals. Stoddard quoted Professor Günther:

> The Nordic ideal becomes for us an ideal of unity. That which is common to all divisions of the German people is the Nordic strain. The question is not so much whether we men now living are more or less Nordic; the question put to us is whether we have the courage to make ready for future generations a world cleansing itself racially and eugenically. (Pgs. 189-190, "Into the Darkness: Nazi Germany Today", Duell, Sloan & Pearce, Inc., 1940)

If historians, or more poignantly, the Allied prosecution at the Nuremberg Trials had forgotten the true nature of National Socialism's policies, Stoddard accurately documented them for all posterity:

> Without attempting to appraise this highly controversial racial doctrine (regarding the Jews), it is fair to say that Nazi Germany's eugenic program is the most ambitious and far-reaching experiment in eugenics ever attempted by any nation. (Pg. 190, "Into the Darkness: Nazi Germany Today", Duell, Sloan & Pearce, Inc., 1940)

After having observed several trials at the three-panel tribunals, Stoddard stated that the eugenic legislation of National Socialist Germany "was weeding out the worst strains in the Germanic stock in a scientific and truly humanitarian way."

Stoddard went on to document how the public consensus was built up and maintained in support of the eugenic efforts. The National Socialists were aware that ideology had to be mobilized, so the German people were systematically conditioned for the creation of what may be described as racial and eugenic consciousness through propaganda.

Stoddard's interview of Heinrich Himmler makes one uncomfortable in more ways than one. First, Stoddard's jovial conversation with the man history now recognizes as a mass murderer is disconcerting, to say the least. Secondly, Himmler's answers are way too reminiscent of the answers many other powerful figures would give in defense of their actions:

> "Perhaps you know that, in America, we hear rather terrible things about the Gestapo. Indeed," I added with a smile, "it is sometimes compared to the Russian Cheka, with you yourself, Excellency, as a second Dzherzhinski!" ---- Himmler took this in good part. He laughed easily. ---- "Frankly, we believe that habitual offenders should not be at large to plague society, so we keep them locked up. ---- Ever seen one of our concentration-camps?" (Pg. 256, "Into the Darkness: Nazi Germany Today", Duell, Sloan & Pearce, Inc., 1940)

Himmler's invite to see a concentration camp is interesting, as history has otherwise recorded these camps were off-limits to outsiders. To invite the most prominent foreign journalists to visit them is clearly noteworthy. Himmler's reception indicates that he did not think his policies were those to be ashamed of, or the impulsive byproducts of racial bigotry, but rather the means and methods of a scientific and efficient social order.

During the Himmler interview, Stoddard did his best as a journalist to inquire about the issues that his American readership would want to know about, namely the political persecution that they were hearing about, namely that of Pastor Niemöller, who by this time was known around the world:

> I felt that ought to bring some reaction, because the Pastor is poison-ivy to most Nazis. Only a few days before, one fairly prominent member of the Party had grown red in the face at the mention of Niemöller's name and had hissed: "The dirty traitor! If I had my way, I'd order him put up against a wall and shot!" ---- Himmler took it more calmly. He merely raised a deprecating hand, replying: "Please understand, it was a political controversy which got him into trouble. We never interfere with matters of religious dogma." (Pg. 257, "Into the Darkness: Nazi Germany Today", Duell, Sloan & Pearce, Inc., 1940)

From Himmler's secular point-of-view, these factions were interfering with the Third Reich's health policies. This would be the characterization that Stoddard and other American eugenicists would report back to their fellow countrymen, that the Third Reich's eugenic policies were of a scientific nature. Stoddard also inquired into the nature of the SS, and received the following answer:

> "The Schutzstaffel," answered Himmler blandly, "represents the best and soundest young manhood of our race. It is founded on the ideals of self-sacrifice, loyalty, discipline, and all-round excellence. Besides being soldiers, the S.S. has

many cultural sides. For instance, we have our own porcelain factory, make our own furniture, and do much scholarly research." (Pg. 250, "Into the Darkness: Nazi Germany Today", Duell, Sloan & Pearce, Inc., 1940)

Himmler certainly makes the S.S. sound like a quaint Boy Scout squad. The jarring thing is that he wasn't lying. Himmler was what one would describe as an "earthy" type in the 21st century. He fully believed in the communal experience of self-sacrifice and solidarity, and furthermore ran the single largest organic farm in the world on the grounds of the concentration camps. Stoddard provides a disturbing glimpse into the mind of this fiend, and it is uncomfortable as it evidences a kind of evil that is much more dangerous than simple bigotry. There is no reason why Himmler's statements would have seemed extreme to someone like Stoddard. After all, Stoddard had been personally hired by Margaret Sanger as director of the American Birth Control League. Racially charged language was commonplace in Sanger's publications. Sanger's Birth Control Review of December 1921 masthead could have been written by a Third Reich eugenicist: "Birth control to create a race of thoroughbreds." Her famous book, "Pivot of Civilization," is replete with racially charged statements. Therefore, Stoddard was hardly outside of his comfort level when he interviewed all of those "race hygiene" scientists and demagogues. He was, after all, a product of the Harvard eugenic crowd.

In fact, Sanger probably hired him due to the eugenic credentials he earned by publishing his book "The Rising Tide of Color Against White World-Supremacy," in which Stoddard fleshed out his "Pan-Aryan" views of a united Aryan people, which was certainly a view shared by his National Socialist interviewees. "The Rising Tide" was one of the two or three pivotal books in American legislative history. It was instrumental in forming the various immigration laws of the era. In "The Revolt Against Civilization," which he published in 1922, Stoddard put forward the theory that civilization places a growing burden on individuals, leading to a growing underclass of individuals who cannot keep up, and a "ground-swell of revolt." Stoddard advocated immigration restriction and birth control legislation to reduce the numbers of the underclass while promoting the growth of the middle and upper classes. He believed social progress was impossible unless it was guided by a "neo-aristocracy" made up of the most capable individuals and reconciled with the findings of science rather than based on abstract idealism and egalitarianism; again, views central to the "racial state" prescribed by Hitler himself, and not at all foreign to what British Fabian Socialists like H.G. Wells were clamoring for, and as Sanger's endorsement evidences, well within the political aspirations of his American Progressive brethren of the era.

Aside from Stoddard, three other important Americans were permitted to survey the Third Reich's eugenic program. The most prominent of these was C.M. Goethe, the founder of Cal State Sacramento University and the Save the Redwoods foundation. Goethe reported back to the Eugenics Research Association in Cold Spring Harbor and the Human Betterment Foundation. His letter to Gosney is but one of many proclamations by leading American eugenicists that the policies of

Hitler's Germany were mimicking and copied from the work of American and British eugenicists:

> You will be interested to know that your work has played a powerful part in shaping the opinions of the group of intellectuals who are behind Hitler in this epoch-making program. Everywhere I sensed that their opinions have been tremendously stimulated by American thought, and particularly by the work of the Human Betterment Foundation. I want you, my dear friend, to carry this thought with you for the rest of your life, that you have really jolted into action a great government of 60,000,000 people. (Pg. 58, "The Nazi Connection: Eugenics, American Racism, and German National Socialism", Stefan Kühl, Oxford Univ. Press, 1994)

Another prominent American eugenicist was Marion S. Norton, the Princeton educated eugenicist who visited Germany in 1938. Norton was a product of Woodrow Wilson's eugenic efforts in New Jersey. The reader will recall the story of Dr. Edwin Katzen-Ellenbogen, the Harvard lecturer and New Jersey's chief eugenic legal advisers under Governor Wilson who ended up actively collaborating in the murders and tortures in the Buchenwald camp. Norton was received with welcome arms because of the similarities between the policies she wrote about in her publications and the eugenic policies of the Third Reich. Furthermore, Norton actively collaborated by helping the Third Reich compose the English translation of their sterilization propaganda, namely of the film "The Fatal Chain of Hereditary Disease." Of note are the 1937 "Selective Sterilization in Primer Form" and the 1935 "Sterilization and the Organized Opposition," where she openly names Pope Pius XI as a prime enemy of the eugenic cause:

> She countered claims that sterilization in Germany was used to eliminate Jews, and complained that such rumors stemmed from the "cunning effort on the part of Catholics to emotionally stampede people, who otherwise would support a measure for social health." She criticized the "strangulating power" of Pope Pius XI's opposition to all forms of population control that he reiterated in his Encyclical Casti Connubii. (Pgs. 58-59, "The Nazi Connection: Eugenics, American Racism, and German National Socialism", Stefan Kühl, Oxford Univ. Press, 1994)

Marion S. Norton also published under Marion S. Olden and in collaboration with the American Eugenics Society, namely the 1946 "Present Status of Sterilization Legislation in the United States." She would publish her first-hand observation of Hitler's eugenic policies, namely the now-infamous Nuremberg laws, in her 1938 "Major Provisions for Population Control Abroad." Norton was an active member of the League of Women Voters and lobbied for several pieces of eugenic legislation. Even with the hindsight of decades, at eighty-eight years old, Mrs. Olden was "unrepentant," and "proudly recalled her support for Nazi race policies." [75]

---

[75] Pg. 47 - "A Tale of Two Villages: Vineland and Skillman, Nj", Michael Nevins, iUniverse, 2009.

The third prominent American to personally survey the Nazi eugenic infrastructure was the geneticist T.U.H. Ellinger. Ellinger visited Hitler's Germany between 1939 and 1940. Ellinger would return to report in the "Journal of Heredity" that the treatment of the Jews in Germany had nothing to do with religious persecution, but more precisely "a large-scale breeding project, with the purpose of eliminating from the nation the hereditary attributes of the Semitic race." [76] In this, he was unquestionably correct. Hitler's henchmen were not persecuting the Jews for their religion, but for their allegedly inferior hereditary value. Case in point, Jewish converts to Christianity were still persecuted as Jews, and Jews could not negotiate away their fate through conversion as they had during the Spanish Inquisition:

> ...the year that witnessed the installation of the gas chambers in Auschwitz, Ellinger argued that if the cruelties were accomplished, the Jewish problem would solve itself in a generation, but it would have been a great deal more merciful to kill the unfortunate outright. (Pg. 60 - "The Nazi Connection: Eugenics, American Racism, and German National Socialism", Stefan Kühl, Oxford Univ. Press, 1994)

These American scientists and professionals were all well-respected and well-connected. Their first-hand surveys went a long way to provide "expert" opinions on what precisely was transpiring inside Hitler's Germany at the crucial time when the world's public was trying to discern if the rumors of the atrocities were true. Stoddard's mere participation in the eugenic courts was specifically beneficial, as taking part in sending the defenseless to either their deaths or bodily mutilation went a long way to legitimizing those courts. Stoddard's relationship with Margaret Sanger was, after all, that of a founding member of the most recognizable reproductive rights organizations in world history. Most importantly, this approbation gave Hitler's henchmen the veil of legitimacy they needed to continue with the policies that would ultimately result in The Holocaust. Historically speaking, these visits provide unimpeachable refutation of the commonly held notion that the "responsible" and "sober" minds were not aware of what was transpiring inside Hitler's Germany. The elite members of the scientific community knew perfectly well what was going on and did its best to support the regime's efforts. Leading American minds were not only allowed to witness but to participate in the very eugenic courts historians would later condemn.

---

[76] Pg. 60 - "The Nazi Connection: Eugenics, American Racism, and German National Socialism", Stefan Kühl, Oxford, 1994.

Sec. 3 - JULIAN HUXLEY'S "EUGENICS MANIFESTO":

Julian Huxley's "Eugenic Manifesto" appeared in Nature, September 16, 1939, was a joint statement issued by America's and Britain's most prominent biologists. The manifesto was a response to a request from the Science Service of Washington, D.C., for a reply to the question "How could the world's population be improved most effectively genetically?" Two of the principal signatories and authors were Hermann J. Muller and Julian Huxley. Julian Huxley, as this book documents, was the founding director of UNESCO from the famous Huxley family. Muller was an American geneticist, educator, and Nobel laureate best known for his work on the physiological and genetic effects of radiation. Put into the context of the timeline, this document was published 15 years after "Mein Kampf" and a year after the highly publicized violence of *Kristallnacht*. In other words, there is no way either Muller or Huxley was unaware at the moment of publication of the historical implications of eugenic agendas.

Muller's family had come to the United States in 1848, escaping from the revolutions that sparked all over Europe that year. Like Huxley, Muller's scientific work was entangled with and inseparable from his socialist political beliefs. Muller's "Biographical Memoir" at the National Academy of Sciences documents how Muller's "early enthusiasm for socialism and communism cost him dearly later in life." [77] Muller openly voiced the view that only a socialist economic system would be able to deliver on the promise of eugenics without the inaccurate prejudices of racism, a view that gained the attention of The New York Times and the media as it was delivered at an international eugenics conference in New York as part of Muller's "The Dominance of Economics over Eugenics." Muller had the opportunity to expand on these ideas between 1932 and 1936 when he set up a laboratory inside of the Soviet Union to conduct tests on biological twins to prove his eugenic theories. The findings were presented to the Soviet leadership as far up as Stalin. As a result, Muller was investigated by the FBI for his cozy relationship with the Soviet.

The timing of this presentation to Uncle Joe should have awakened Muller, as he presented his radical views at the height of the purges when many scientists with views that Stalin found distasteful were either murdered or permanently ostracized. The dangerous similarities between National Socialism and Bolshevik Socialism should have been most apparent in 1939, the year of the "Manifesto's" publication. The timing of "The Eugenics Manifesto" could not be more compromising of the "Manifesto's" overt socialist embellishment, as it was published in the same year that Stalin and Hitler announced their pact. Neither Muller nor Huxley could have claimed ignorance in this aspect, as both traveled to and had intimate contact with Stalinist Russia. Huxley would come to Muller's rescue after he defected to France, escaping Stalin's rage against radical influences in his Soviet state. But, alas, Muller did not learn from his catastrophic flirtation with totalitarian governments.

With Huxley's timely assistance, Muller would be able to persist in his belief

---

[77] Pg. 4 - "Herman J. Muller: A Biographical Memoir", Elof Axel Carlson, nasonline.org, 2009.

that an elite could be bred like rabbits by an all-powerful state. The Muller-Huxley friendship was likely based on ideology. In 1931, Huxley also visited the USSR at the invitation of Intourist, where initially, he admired the results of social and economic planning on a grand scale. Later, back in the United Kingdom, he became a founding member of Political and Economic Planning. The P.E.P. was inspired by Edward Max Nicholson's publication of Nicholson's 1931 essay "A National Plan for Britain." Edward Max Nicholson was a pioneering environmentalist, ornithologist, and Internationalist, as well as a founder of the World Wildlife Fund. Nicholson had definite ideas about how a country should be run and wrote "The System." Nicholson's socio-political views were fundamental to Huxley's and Muller's eugenic proposal, as the proposal called for a central planned eugenic "college" with power to subordinate individual rights to the eugenic goals of the society.

As such, Huxley's "Eugenics Manifesto" is hardly unique in arriving at the conclusion that individual rights needed to be subordinated to an all-powerful state. Huxley's and Muller's eugenic colleagues made similar proposals, some in the form of novels and others in the form of actual proposals for a government. H.G. Wells made several fictional and non-fictional proposals for a "eugenic state," and George Orwell and Aldous Huxley, Julian's brother, made their counter-proposals by warning society what these eugenic utopias would look like. As this book will document, some of the most committed eugenic zealots even ventured into penning their own proposals for global governments, as did Harry H. Laughlin while working in the Eugenics Records Office at the Dulles Cold Spring Harbor estate. All these eugenic utopias subordinated the rights of the individual to the right of the government to mold society as it saw fit. They also held in common a fascination for a one-world government as a necessary condition for a successful eugenic policy. "The Eugenics Manifesto" was wholly based on this socio-economic premise by stating that the eugenic goal "requires some effective sort of federation of the whole world." For the signatories, there needed to be fundamental and transformative change, for the "genetic improvement of mankind is dependent upon major changes in social conditions, and correlative changes in human attitudes." The proposal called for "conscious selection," a term meant to invoke Darwin's "natural selection" but carried out by a scientific and planned society:

> Sixthly, conscious selection requires, in addition, an agreed direction or directions for selection to take, and these directions cannot be social ones, that is, for the good of mankind at large, unless social motives predominate in society. This in turn implies its socialized organization. ("The Eugenics Manifesto", published as "Social Biology and Population Improvement", Nature, No. 144, Sept. 16, 1939, Pgs. 521–522)

Statist utopias cannot withstand a diversity of thought or beliefs, as they presume a pre-determined direction from which there can be no divergence if the utopian ideal is to be sustained. Therefore, among the "prerequisites" was education, or propaganda, depending on how you view utopian schemes. If you are a socialist, this process of persuading individuals to surrender their individuality is called "education." This form of "education" was deemed not just necessary, but it is clear that the authors and signatories of the "Manifesto" understood that the compulsory, and thus unsavory, aspect of this highly-collectivized humanity was somehow ameliorated by making their victims think like themselves:

> Along with all this the development of social consciousness and responsibility in regard to the production of children is required, and this cannot be expected to be operative unless the above-mentioned economic and social conditions for its fulfillment are present, and unless the superstitious attitude towards sex and reproduction now prevalent has been replaced by a scientific and social attitude. ("The Eugenics Manifesto", published as "Social Biology and Population Improvement", Nature, No. 144, Sept. 16, 1939, Pgs. 521–522)

Traditional views were deemed "superstitious" and by implication, inferior to the educated and scientific elite. The authors of the manifesto considered "education" as somehow softening the compulsion the manifesto proposes. Despite the highly intrusive nature of the procedures, they ask the public to subject themselves to "permanent sterilization, contraception, abortion, control of fertility and the sexual cycle, artificial insemination, etc." Needless to say, "conscious guidance" and "agreed direction" by an elite group that regards their world view as superior to others, without even the most minimal presence of humility, is a recipe for catastrophe precisely as George Orwell and Aldous Huxley predicted. In fact, Julian Huxley made the very same proposals for such centralized control over human reproduction that would otherwise appear in the various works of eugenic utopias. Julian Huxley called for a "Ministry of Eugenics" in 1928, and Huxley's proposal enticed John Charles Lucas Fitzpatrick, a politician, and journalist, to react to by stating that "so many strange and fanatical ideas are being propounded just now that one hardly knows whether to treat them seriously." [78]

Huxley's proto-Nazi proposal for a "Ministry of Eugenics" was perfectly in line with his fellow members of the British Eugenics Education Society. The Society voiced chagrin over the fact that the Australian government was giving tax breaks to that "lower strata." Note, Leonard Darwin's, reaction to the Eldridge's "endowment of Motherhood" proposal, stated at the Second International Eugenics Congress held in London, England:

> It follows that to increase the taxation on the more fit in order to ease the strain of family life among the less fit would do a double dose of harm; that is by decreasing the output of children where it should be increased and by increasing it where it should be diminished. (Pg. 194, "Striving for National Fitness: Eugenics in Australia, 1910s to the 1930s", Doctoral Thesis, 1996)

Julian Huxley's and Leonard Darwin's eugenic views shared significant commonalities because together were the devoted leaders of the Eugenics Education

---

[78] Pg. 194, "Striving for National Fitness: Eugenics in Australia, 1910s to the 1930s", ses.library.usyd.edu.au, Diana H. Wyndham, Doctoral Thesis, 1996.

Society in Britain, and not passive acquaintances. One would think that this supposedly well-read, intellectual and worldly group in 1939 Europe, the year of the manifesto's publication as well as some of the most violent years of both the Stalin and Hitler governments, would have made the intellectual leap that all-powerful governments would abuse the powers given to them. While the reign of Adolf Hitler may seem like a flash to us in hindsight, Hitler's government dominated the headlines and public discourse for 15 to 20 years of contemporaries like Huxley, Darwin, and Muller. Furthermore, Julian Huxley and Leonard Darwin certainly had the benefit from the experiences of the other leading members of the Eugenics Education Society who visited Hitler's Germany and were guest participants of Hitler's versions of a "Ministry of Eugenics," namely David Star Jordan and C.M. Goethe, whom they corresponded with regularly. Yet, these scientists clamored for more controls, not less. Note the choice of term "selection," as in natural and unnatural selection:

> Under modern civilized conditions such selection is far less likely to be automatic than under primitive conditions, hence some kind of conscious guidance of selection is called for to make this possible, however, the population must first appreciate the force of the above principles, and the social value which a wisely guided selection would have. ("The Eugenics Manifesto", published as "Social Biology and Population Improvement", Nature, No. 144, Sept. 16, 1939, Pgs. 521–522)

Despite having a front-row seat to totalitarian catastrophes, the trajectory of Julian Huxley's eugenic thinking only seemed to become increasingly aggressive:

> The lowest strata are reproducing too fast. Therefore...they must not have too easy access to relief or hospital treatment lest the removal of the last check on natural selection should make it too easy for children to be produced or to survive; long unemployment should be a ground for sterilization. ("Eugenics and Society", The Galton Lecture given to the Eugenics Society, Julian S. Huxley, Eugenics Review, Vol. 28:1/13, Doc. ID 11751, dnalc.org)

Anyone that has studied the history of eugenics knows that similar statements as the one depicted above were regurgitated over and over again by the Third Reich's propaganda films, publications, and political speeches. The fear of the "lower strata reproducing too fast" was the underlying theme of the Third Reich's eugenic propaganda film, *Erbkrank*. Elitists like Julian Huxley and Herman J. Muller were able to talk themselves out of these uncomfortable and obvious parallels by convincing themselves that theirs was eugenics pure and free from "racism." They were smart enough intellectually to understand that classifying entire swaths of humanity as "lowest strata" was highly suspect, to say the least, but apparently their political and cultural zealotry prevented them from seeing their own prejudices. Muller's "Biographical Memoir" documents that Muller was:

> ...both a critic and advocate of eugenics, denouncing the American eugenics movement for its racism, spurious elitism, sexism, and mistaken assumptions on both the transmission of behavioral traits and the belief that many social traits were primarily innate. (Pg. 3 - "Biographical Memoir Hermann Joseph Muller.

1890-1967", Elof Axel Carlson, Biographical Memoirs, National Academies Press, Vol. 91, Nov. 2009)

Yet, Muller believed that "those with beneficial genes should have opportunities to transmit them." In other words, Muller was supportive of a type of eugenics that would allow an elite to make qualitative and culturally subjective "selections" among the human lot, and literally decide who lived and died, who reproduced and whom was sterilized, whom was free and whom was segregated, as long as these compulsory restrictions did not come with the "racial" slurs typical of his American colleagues. This was the weak excuse that the supporters of eugenics made in 1939 as the result of the Third Reich's eugenic laws became crystal clear, and this is the superficial excuse used by sympathetic scientists use to this day in the apologetics that ensues from the realization that their most lauded figureheads inspired and even collaborated with Hitler's genocidal acts. It was the "happy fascism" that Aldous Huxley warned us about in his "Brave New World." It was a high-browed form of eugenic dehumanization.

Upon returning to the United States, Muller was generously supported by the Rockefeller Foundation. The "Biographical Memoir" also documents that despite having insider knowledge of the workings of the Soviet Union since 1936, Muller didn't betray his socialist partisanship or go public on the Lysenko affair until after 1948. Muller was not only pursued by the FBI because of his Bolshevik sympathies; he was called to testify before the House Un-American Activities Committee. That testimony was still immune from access as of the writing of the memoir, and Muller and his wife burned thousands of items they had accumulated in his travels, including correspondence with known communists or communist sympathizers. [79] Muller's naivete did not go unnoticed:

> He felt the abuses of Nazi eugenics and the American eugenics movement were historical accidents not likely to be repeated in democratic societies. ---- He was criticized in editorials as being ignorant of the Holocaust and the excesses humans are cable of applying against humanity. Many thought he was trying to revive the old-line eugenics he had condemned. (Pg. 211, "Biographical Memoir Hermann Joseph Muller. 1890-1967", Biographical Memoirs, National Academies Press, Vol. 91, Nov. 2009)

As we know, Julian Huxley's views hardly evolved away from its elitist barbarism. The 60-page pamphlet he authored for UNESCO only underscores the eugenic views proclaimed in the immediate aftermath of the Nuremberg Trials:

> At the moment, it is probable that the indirect effect of civilization is dysgenic instead of eugenic; and in any case it seems likely that the dead weight of genetic stupidity, physical weakness, mental instability, and disease-proneness, which already exist in the human species, will prove too great a burden for real progress to be achieved. (unesco.org, Pg. 19, "UNESCO Its Purpose & Philosophy", Cat. No. 68197)

---

[79] Pg. 25 - "The Unfit: A History of a Bad Idea", Elof Axel Carlson, Cold Spring Harbor Laboratory Press, 2001.

Julian Huxley, like his colleague Muller and the countless other politically sympathetic scientists, sidestepped culpability by raising their noses to overt "racist" comments, and thus, playing semantic shell-games. It is no coincidence that Julian Huxley is also known and credited by the scientific community for coining certain phrases, namely by swapping the term "race" with "ethnic group," incidentally as part of penning "UNESCO and its Programme - The Race Question." Interestingly enough, Julian Huxley is also credited with coining and popularizing the concept of "transhumanism." "Transhumanism" is an international movement that affirms the possibility and desirability of fundamentally transforming humanity by leveraging technologies that would eliminate aging, and enhance human intellectual, physical and psychological capacities. They predict that human beings may eventually be able to transform themselves into beings with such greatly expanded abilities as to merit the label "posthuman." More specifically, Huxley saw eugenics as the means to achieving his "posthuman," and you would have to split hairs to argue a difference with Adolf Hitler's desire to leverage the science of eugenics in order to create a "master race."

> In his influential essay on liberal eugenics, Habermas talks about some freaky intellectuals who reject what they see as the illusion of equality and try to develop a very German naturalistic ideology. This seriously considers the potential for employing human biotechnology in the service of Nietzschean breeding fantasies. (Pg. 4, Stefan Lorenz Sorgner quoting Babette Babich in "Zarathustra 2.0 and Beyond: Further Remarks on the Complex Relationship between Nietzsche and Transhumanism")

These semantic shell games are still used to conceal the origins of one of the most dangerous aspects of the Third Reich and are mainly at fault for the myths and mischaracterizations about the Third Reich's eugenic policies. This myth that Hitler was dangerous only because he was a "racist" begins with the semantic manipulation that eugenic-minded scientists like Julian Huxley and H.J. Muller propagandized during and after The Holocaust. There are many "racists" still in the world, making judgments about their fellow humans as they go about their daily lives. There is a distinct difference between those that have "racist" thoughts and those that dedicate their entire lives to the eradication of a sizeable number of humans they deem undesirable, in some ill-conceived desire to create a "race of masters." Julian Huxley desired a polite and happy eugenics, where the unfit were discarded without insult. Julian Huxley wanted a world where the "inferior stocks" passively submitted to the guidance of the scientific elite; a world much like the one his brother, Aldous, accurately portrayed for him in "Brave New World."

Sec. 4 - MARGARET SANGER'S "NEGRO PROJECT":

> ...I have set before you life and death,
> blessing and cursing' therefore choose life,
> that both you and your descendants may live.
> (Deuteronomy 30:19)

The above quote was aptly chosen by Tanya L. Green, author of the article that was posted at www.BlackGenocide.org titled, "The Negro Project: Margaret Sanger's Eugenic Plan for Black America." BlackGenocide.org is the website of Life, Education and Resource Network (LEARN), the largest black pro-life organization. They target Sanger, founder of Planned Parenthood, because of quotes such as this one:

> Before eugenists and others who are laboring for racial betterment can succeed, they must first clear the way for Birth Control. Like the advocates of Birth Control, the eugenists, for instance, are seeking to assist the race toward the **elimination of the unfit**. (emphasis mine, "Birth Control and Racial Betterment," Feb 1919. Birth Control Review, Library of Congress Microfilm 131:0099B)

One can scour through Margaret Sanger's speeches and books and read comparatively little about "choice," yet come across a stunning amount of ink dedicated towards the complete opposite end; towards the goal of social control, lack of choice, lack of individual rights, and lack of empathy for ethnic minorities. The Birth Control movement and the mainline eugenicists did not agree on everything, but they did agree on one thing: the reproduction of the undesired peoples had to be curtailed. This opinion was held in common with The Klan. While the Ivy League eugenicists saw themselves as above and apart from petty bigots, Sanger found nothing wrong with seeking funding and support from the Ku Klux Klan. Page 366 to 367 of Sanger's "Autobiography" describes how she personally addressed the Women's Chapter of the KKK:

> I accepted an invitation to talk to the women's branch of the Ku Klux Klan. . . .In the end, through simple illustrations I believed I had accomplished my purpose. A dozen invitations to speak to similar groups were proffered. (Pg. 366, "An Autobiography", Margaret Sanger, Dover Publications, 1971)

Tanya L. Green and her associates are right to find Sanger's work disturbing. Sanger delineated the strategy for her "Negro Project" in a December 10, 1939; letter to Dr. Clarence Gamble. [80] Dr. Clarence J. Gamble would later use the Proctor & Gamble fortune to create the eugenic organization, the Pathfinder Fund, in 1957. However, his efforts to make birth control available began some 28 years earlier, in 1929, when Dr. Gamble gave $5,000 to fund a maternal health clinic in Cincinnati, Ohio. He set up the Pathfinder Fund to fund American Birth Control, the previous name of Margaret Sanger's Planned Parenthood before it was changed to disassociate

---

[80] Sanger manuscripts, Sophia Smith Collection, Smith College, North Hampton, Massachusetts. New York: Grossman Publishers, 1976. - See Illustration.

Planned Parenthood from the organization's eugenic past. He would also set up a sister organization to the Human Betterment Foundation, the Human Betterment League, in 1947 after all the horrors of the Holocaust had become common knowledge.

As the December 10, 1939 letter evidences, Sanger and Gamble's intent was to recruit black America's crème-de-la-crème, the most prominent, well-educated and well-to-do—into African-American to minimize scrutiny of their "Negro Project." The exchange between Gamble and Sanger recognized that "black leaders might regard birth control as an extermination plot." Thus, they turned to sympathetic black leaders and placed them in positions where it would appear they were in charge:

> I note that you doubt it worthwhile to employ a full-time Negro physician. It seems to me from my experience ... that, while the colored Negroes have great respect for white doctors, they can get closer to their own members and more or less lay their cards on the table, which means their ignorance, superstitions and doubts. They do not do this with white people and if we can train the Negro doctor at the clinic, he can go among them with enthusiasm and ... knowledge, which ... will have far-reaching results among the colored people. (Sanger manuscripts, Sophia Smith Collection, Smith College, North Hampton, Massachusetts. New York: Grossman Publishers, 1976. -- Note: There is a different date circulated, e.g. Oct. 19, 1939; but Dec. 10 is the correct date of Mrs. Sanger's letter to Mr. Gamble.)

The correspondence continues along these lines:
> [We propose to] hire three or four colored ministers, preferably with social-service backgrounds, and with engaging personalities. --- And we do not want word to go out that we want to exterminate the Negro population, and the minister is the man who can straighten out that idea if it ever occurs to any of their more rebellious members. (Sanger manuscripts, Sophia Smith Collection, Smith College, North Hampton, Massachusetts. New York: Grossman Publishers, 1976 – See Illustration)

However, it would be an error to try to understand the Birth Control movement as solely part of mainline eugenics. Sanger's movement is easily categorized as part of the feminist movement, whose ideals overlapped with those of the mainline eugenicists, but who diverge in their fundamental strategy. Despite the many commonalities, Sanger's reputation as an activist was undesirable to eugenic kingpins such as Charles B. Davenport, who were specifically laboring towards having eugenics accepted as a mainline scientific movement, as opposed to a revolutionary movement like Sanger's "Birth Control." This is not to say that the two movements didn't share core concepts. Early 20th Century feminism employed blatantly white-supremacist arguments to advance women's suffrage, pointing out that white women would add to the white vote since they were more likely to vote than minority women. [81] The

---

[81] "Freedom, Feminism, and the State", Wendy McElroy, Independent Institute, Jan. 1, 1991 – Citing Alan P. Grimes, "The Puritan Ethic and Woman Suffrage", Oxford University Press, 1967.

feminist's xenophobic argument was adapted to counter the fear of enfranchising immigrant women and their foreign values and religious practices. The feminists argued that millions of American-born women were more likely to vote than foreigners, thus softening the impact of foreign morals, namely those of the Catholic mores being imported by the Irish and Italians. For similar reasons, the feminists called for a limited suffrage. Even the former abolitionist, Elizabeth Cady Stanton, supported literacy tests as a prerequisite for the vote. Consider this now infamous Susan B. Anthony quote:

> …the worst elements have been put into the ballot-box and the best elements kept out. This fatal mistake is even now beginning to dawn upon the minds of those who have cherished an ideal of the grandeur of a republic, and they dimly see that in woman lies the highest promise of its fulfillment. Those who fear the foreign vote will learn eventually that there are more American-born women in the United States than foreign born men and women; and those who dread the ignorant vote will study the statistics and see that the percentage of illiteracy is much smaller among women than among men. (google.com, "HISTORY OF WOMEN'S SUFFRAGE – Part 2: The Trailblazing Documentation on Women's Enfranchisement in USA, Great Britain & Other Parts of the World", Susan B. Anthony/Ida H. Harper)

Eugenics was regarded as a social purity reform by the feminists, and social purity issues became staples of the women's suffrage movement and mainstream feminism in the early 20th Century. Aside from, and in contrast to, mainline eugenics, the social purity campaigns included raising the age of consent, the reformation of prostitutes, censorship of obscenity, and the advocacy of birth control. By contrast, the eugenicists regarded a prostitute, for example, as someone to be sterilized or eradicated, not reformed or supported. Eugenicists also were opposed to birth control for the "fit" or desired portion of the populace either.

Although social purity was a goal of abolitionist feminists, the crucial difference began with the feminism following the Civil War with their willingness to enforce morality through the coercive power of the state. While the abolitionist feminists, who were largely Quakers believed that the individual must be free to find salvation and perfect the soul, later feminists wished to take choice out of moral issues. Many of the Reconstruction and turn-of-the-century feminists held distinctly anti-immigrant and white-supremacist views, and Sanger clearly shared these views. The book she published to explain the ideology behind Birth Control, her "Pivot of Civilization," cites and quotes eugenicists with a distinct white-supremacist view as a means to demonstrate the alleged scientific legitimacy of her cause. The fact that she started her Birth Control organization with Lothrop Stoddard and advanced the cause by speaking before the K.K.K. further cements her movement as part of white-supremacist eugenics. One can easily argue that the ideological bedrock of Sanger's Birth Control was not just eugenics, but eugenics at its white-supremacist extreme.

One crucial overlap between Sanger and mainline eugenics is her Nietzschean disdain for any measure of charity that would allow defective strains to pollute the genetic pool. This is a fundamental and inalienable part of eugenics, without which the philosophy falls apart. This also was a fundamental part of many of Sanger's writing and public speaking. Anyone reading Sanger's "Pivot of Civilization" will be struck by her statements:

> Organized charity itself is the symptom of a malignant social disease. Those vast, complex, interrelated organizations aiming to control and to diminish the spread of misery and destitution and all the menacing evils that spring out of this sinisterly fertile soil, are the surest sign that our civilization has bred, is breeding and perpetuating constantly increasing numbers of defectives, delinquents and dependents. (Pg. 109)

Case in point, the "Negro Project" evidences the eugenic nature of Margaret Sanger's efforts. Clearly, singling out and targeting entire chunks of the population is where Birth Control starts to step outside of its claim of individual "choice," and into the realm of a eugenics population control campaign:

> It [charity] encourages the healthier and more normal sections of the world to shoulder the burden of unthinking and indiscriminate fecundity of others; which brings with it, as I think the reader must agree, a dead weight of human waste. Instead of decreasing and aiming to eliminate the stocks that are most detrimental to the future of the race and the world, it tends to render them to a menacing degree dominant. (Pg. 116, "Pivot of Civilization", Brentano's Publishers, 1922)

Sanger's "Negro Project" had truly begun in earnest in 1929, a decade before Sanger concluded that it needed to be a grander project beyond that of a single clinic. Sanger's first clinic, and effectively the prototype for the "Negro Project," was installed in Harlem at the peak of the Great Depression, and at a time of terrible suffering for its segregated population. Blacks faced harsher conditions of desperation and privation because of widespread racial prejudice and discrimination during this difficult era. Harlem was the ideal place for this "experimental clinic," which officially opened on November 21, 1930. Many blacks looked to escape their adverse circumstances and therefore, did not recognize the eugenic undercurrent of the clinic. In addition to being thought of as "inferior" by Sanger, the predominantly black Harlem population disproportionately represented the "dependent" and "unfit" underclass. The Harlem Clinic's files explain their efforts in this light. Harlem was:

- Segregated in an over-populated area (224,760 of 330,000 of greater New York's population lived in Harlem during the late 1920s and 1930s)
- Comprised 12 percent of New York City's population but accounted for 18.4 percent of New York City's unemployment;
- Had an infant mortality rate of 101 per 1000 births, compared to 56 among whites
- Had a death rate from tuberculosis–237 per 100,000–that was highest in all of New York City

(Pg. 106-107, Tarik Saeed, "What Is Wrong with Black People \\\White People?", Feb 20, 2013, google.com ebook)

Margaret Sanger could not have embarked on a venture of the nature of the "Negro Project" without the assistance, cooperation, and blessing of the "three or four colored ministers" she hand-picked. This has been the history of the "Negro Project," which endures to this day and is mostly responsible for the fact that minorities account for 57 percent of the abortions in the United States. The "intent" behind the projects was made aptly clear by Sanger time and time again, yet it is an aspect of Planned Parenthood that has conveniently been swept under the rug, just as her relationship with Lothrop Stoddard, the American journalist that sat in the three-panel eugenics courts in Hitler's Germany seems to have been conveniently forgotten.

Although the clinic served whites as well as blacks, it "was established for the benefit of the colored people," according to Sanger. Sanger expressed this sentiment in a letter to Dr. W. E. B. DuBois, one of the day's most influential blacks. DuBois, a sociologist, and author, helped found the National Association for the Advancement of Colored People (NAACP) in 1909. He was also a devoted eugenicist. Author Daylanne English dedicates an entire chapter to DuBois's own personal brand of eugenics in her book "Unnatural Selections." [82] Both Sanger, and apparently DuBois himself, identified DuBois as one of those crème-de-la-crème, well educated, and elite well-to-do African-Americans.

The June 1932 edition of Sanger's The Birth Control Review, entitled "The Negro Number," featured a series of articles written by blacks on the "virtues" of birth control. DuBois, in his contributing piece, "Black Folk and Birth Control" noted the "inevitable clash of ideals between those Negroes who were striving to improve their economic position and those whose religious faith made the limitation of children a sin." He criticized the "mass of ignorant Negroes" who bred "carelessly and disastrously so that the increase among [them] ... is from that part of the population least intelligent and fit, and least able to rear their children properly." DuBois' statement could easily have been confused with those from mainline eugenicists such as Charles Davenport, Leonard Darwin, or Francis Galton.

Dr. Aveda King, grand-niece of Martin Luther King, Jr., often cites the grim statistic that still today, 78 percent of abortion clinics are in neighborhoods where minorities live, and that black women account for over a third of all abortions, even though the black population represents less than 13 percent of the United States. [83] The US Census statistics certainly justify Dr. Alveda King's concerns. It is important to note that the US Census reports that the black population in the United States started close to 20 percent in 1790, and plummeted as low as 9 percent after 1900, at the peak of the eugenics movement, and never returned to higher than 11 percent

---

[82] Pgs. 35-64 – "Unnatural Selections: Eugenics in American Modernism and the Harlem Renaissance", Daylanne K. English, Univ. of North Carolina Press, 2004.
[83] See Also – "Policy Report: The Effects of Abortion on the Black Community", Center for Uban Renewal and Education, June 2015, urgancure.org.

until after the late 1970s, coincidentally, as most states were repealing their eugenically-minded laws.

Another revealing relationship in Sanger's eugenic history is her enduring relationship with Hans Harmsen. Sabdste Schleiermacher of the *Universitätskrankenhaus Eppendorf, Institut für Medizinsoziologie* documented the long-standing relationship between Harmsen and Sanger.

> The co-founder of the International Planned Parenthood Federation (IPPF) and president, for many years, of its daughter organization in the Federal Republic of Germany, *Pro Familia* (the Germany Society for Sexual Counselling and Family Planning), Hans Harmsen developed a concept for a population policy at the peak of the world economic crisis (1928–1932) that was the foundation for the systematic execution of the racial policy in National Socialist Germany. ("Racial Hygiene and Deliberate Parenthood: Two Sides of Demographer Hans Harmsen's Population Policy", Sabdste Schleiermacher, Reproductive and Genetic Engineering: Journal of International Feminist Analysis Vol. 3, Nov. 3, 1990)

Sabdste Schleiermacher recalls that Harmsen was part of International Planned Parenthood until the 1980s and that the reasons given by the organization for his involvement were "on the basis of numerous scientific contributions to German demography, to birth control, eugenics and planned parenthood." Clearly, the organization was aware of his eugenic past. However, International Planned Parenthood did not distance themselves from Harmsen until 1984, when his past finally became a political liability. The Federal Board of *Pro Familia* published a statement explaining Harmsen's resignation:

> The cause was criticism of his publication and activities as demographer and social hygiene specialist in the years 1920 to 1945 . . . Apparently Harmsen represented positions at the time which are today condemned by the Association. ("Harmsen No Longer Honorary President", *Pro Familia Magazin*, 1984, p. 21; Kaupen-Haas, 1984, p. 41)

Nor can it be said that Harmsen's Nazi credentials had not been highly publicized before being hired by Sanger. Hans Harmsen "demonstrated his power and prestige in Nazi Germany by hosting the World Population Congress" held in Berlin in 1935. [84] The TIME article titled "Praise for Nazis" covered this 1935 congress. The article depicts the link between population control, birth control, and the "Nazi eugenists plans for breeding Germans like prize cattle."

> Sore from the slings and arrows of foreign criticism, Germans heard gratefully last week a warm, approving speech from Dr. Clarence Gordon Campbell, president of the American Eugenics Research Association, delivered before the World Population Congress in Berlin. (Pgs. 20-21, "Praise for Nazis", TIME Mag., Sept. 9, 1935)

---

[84] Pg. 209 - "Reforming Sex: The German Movement for Birth Control and Abortion Reform", Atina Grossmann, Oxford Univ. Press, 1995.

Dr. Clarence Gordon Campbell, the president of the American Eugenics Research Association, revealed his sympathies during the 1935 congress:

> Dr. Campbell sat down last week, Chief Arthur Giitt of the German Public Health Department bluntly told the Congress: "Our penal code will shortly make compulsory a health examination for all marrying persons. The purpose of this is first to dissuade bodily or mental inferiors from marrying and especially from procreation. Second, to prevent marriages between hereditarily tainted persons, the same as a marriage between an Aryan and a non-Aryan. Third, to influence the choice of life partners from a health as well as a racial viewpoint." (Pgs. 20-21, "Praise for Nazis", TIME Mag., Sept. 9, 1935)

TIME provides a quote from Dr. Campbell that should repulse every American: The difference between the Jew and the Aryan is as insurmountable as that between black and white . . . Germany has set a pattern which other nations must follow. (Pgs. 20-21, "Praise for Nazis", TIME Mag., Sept. 9, 1935)

In other words, Dr. Campbell believed Hitler's policies towards the Jews should be applied to American blacks. Any honest reading of the multitude of articles or books by the eugenic elite would indicate that Dr. Campbell's 'solution' for American blacks was hardly an extreme one amongst his peers. Considered together with Harmsen's leadership roll in Margaret Sanger's movement, the "Negro Project" should make every American shudder. TIME Magazine describes the toast given at the closing banquet by Dr. Campbell while dawning a stiff-arm salute: **"To that great leader, Adolf Hitler!"**

Sec. 5 - FROM *Kristallnacht* TO "MAN OF THE YEAR":

The world has not forgotten that TIME Magazine named Adolf Hitler "Man of the Year" for 1938. TIME Magazine released the issue on January 2, 1939. Only two months prior, on November 9, 1938, Hitler's henchmen were unleashed on the German Jewish community in what historians now recognize the commencement of aggression in The Holocaust. The horrific event called *Kristallnacht,* also referred to as the Night of Broken Glass, claimed the lives of at least 91 Jews in the attacks, and a further 30,000 arrested and sent to concentration camps. Jewish homes, hospitals, and schools were ransacked. Over 1,000 synagogues were burned, and over 7,000 Jewish businesses destroyed or damaged. The gravity of this event is emphasized to illustrate that there is no way the editors of TIME were unaware of these events. Sir Martin Gilbert, the Oxford biographer of Winston Churchill, wrote that no event in the history of German Jews between 1933 and 1945 was so widely reported as it was happening, and the accounts from the foreign journalists working in Germany sent shock waves around the world. [85] An article that appeared in The Times of London put the event into perspective:

> No foreign propagandist bent upon blackening Germany before the world could outdo the tale of burnings and beatings, of blackguardly assaults on defenseless and innocent people, which disgraced that country yesterday. ("A Black Day for Germany," The Times of London, November 11, 1938)

Fifty years later, a November 9, 1988, New York Times article, "In 1938, The World Knew," documents the media coverage this atrocity garnered. The opinion article in The New York Times claims that until then, "the wishful could argue that Adolf Hitler's ravings were worse than his bite. Then came *Kristallnacht*, the night of broken glass. Instantly, the world grasped the horror, recognized that the Nazi orgy of hate was plunging into savagery a country known for its learning and literacy." The New York Times article quotes Otto Tolischus, author of The Times of London 1938 article:

> A wave of destruction, looting and incendiarism unparalleled in Germany since the Thirty Years War and in Europe generally since the Bolshevist Revolution, swept over Great Germany today as National Socialist cohorts took vengeance on Jewish shops, offices and synagogues for the murder by a young Polish Jew of Ernst vom Rath, third secretary of the Germany Embassy in Paris. (N.Y.T. quoting O. Tolischus, Nov. 9, 1988, "In 1938, The World Knew")

While the general public is keen on the historical trivia that Hitler was once named TIME Magazine's "Man of the Year," the world has forgotten what the article actually said. The piece represents the type of frankness that was later made impossible by the FDR administration's tight controls over the free press, or with a media that no longer criticized socialism or communism.

> Rant as he might against the machinations of international Communism and international Jewry, or rave as he would that he was just a Pan-German trying to get all the Germans back in one nation, Führer Hitler had himself become the world's No. 1 International Revolutionist—so much so that if the oft-predicted struggle between Fascism and Communism now takes place it will be only because two revolutionist dictators, Hitler and Stalin, are too big to let each other live in the same world. (time.com, "Adolf Hitler: Man of the Year, 1938", Jan. 2, 1939)

The tone and wording of the infamous TIME article made it plain that Hitler and Stalin were considered two sides of the same coin. The only thing that would change this honest appraisal of Communism was President Roosevelt's censorship of the press about Stalin when Roosevelt made him an ally.

A generation ago western civilization had apparently outgrown the major evils of barbarism except for war between nations. The Russian Communist

---

[85] theyeshivaworld.com - "Tonight – 80th Yartzheit: Kristallnacht – the Night of Broken Glass", posted 24 October 2018.

Revolution promoted the evil of class war. Hitler topped it by another, race war. Fascism and Communism both resurrected religious war. These multiple forms of barbarism gave shape in 1938 to an issue over which men may again, perhaps soon, shed blood: the issue of civilized liberty v. barbaric authoritarianism. (time.com, "Adolf Hitler: Man of the Year, 1938", Jan. 02, 1939)

Another contrast between then and now is that the press coverage contemporary to the era recognized Pope Pius XI and the Catholic Church as the most persistent enemy of the National Socialist regime, as opposed to the story of complicity that has been built since then.

In religion, the two outstanding figures of 1938 were in sharp contrast save for their opposition to Adolf Hitler. One of them, Pope Pius XI, 81, spoke with "bitter sadness" of Italy's anti-Semitic laws, the harrying of Italian Catholic Action groups, the reception Mussolini gave Hitler last May, declared sadly: "We have offered our now old life for the peace and prosperity of peoples. We offer it anew." By spending most of the year in a concentration camp, Protestant Pastor Martin Niemöller gave courageous witness to his faith. (time.com, "Adolf Hitler: Man of the Year, 1938", Jan. 02, 1939)

The press coverage of the era understood that National Socialism was pitted against democracy and *laissez-faire* economics and that Adolf Hitler was not a tool of the leading industrialists but a man with total control over his sphere of influence. The TIME Magazine article makes clear that Hitler did not share power or bow to anyone, no matter how powerful financially or politically:

The situation which gave rise to this demagogic, ignorant, desperate movement was inherent in the German Republic's birth and in the craving of large sections of the politically immature German people for strong, masterful leadership. Democracy in Germany was conceived in the womb of military defeat. (time.com, "Adolf Hitler: Man of the Year, 1938", Jan. 02, 1939)

Most importantly, the TIME article recognized that National Socialism was in large part a "socialist" movement; a revelation that you could not get the politicized journalists of today to admit under any circumstance:

The **"socialist"** part of National Socialism might be scoffed at by hard-&-fast Marxists, but the Nazi movement nevertheless had a mass basis. The 1,500 miles of magnificent highways built, schemes for cheap cars and simple workers' benefits, grandiose plans for rebuilding German cities made Germans burst with pride. (emphasis mine, time.com, "Adolf Hitler: Man of the Year, 1938", Jan. 02, 1939)

All these characterizations of National Socialism were largely smudged and clouded in the subsequent 50 years of journalism. National Socialism was divested of its "socialist" underpinning and erroneously posed as the flip side of Communism, even though any contemporary understood National Socialism to be Bolshevism's fraternal twin. The secularist antipathy towards the Catholic Church engendered many works which framed the Church as collaborating with Hitler, even though anyone during the era would have recognized the Church as the most persistent and consistent enemy of the Third Reich's policies. Most notably, Fascism and National Socialism were bundled into one movement, despite the fact that Fascist Spain and Italy did more to rescue Jews from Hitler than did the Roosevelt administration. All of this was the consequence of the fog of war, which was only extended and intensified by the Cold War that immediately followed.

Sec. 6 - FROM "BABY KNAUER" TO THE T4 EUTHANASIA PROGRAM:

In 1938, the case of a newborn with severe birth defects would become the legal precedent and the tragic beginning to the heartless slaughter of hundreds of thousands of handicapped Germans. The incident has become known as the case of Baby Knauer, and it is probably the last case where Adolf Hitler's direct involvement with the murderous policies is documented by physical evidence.

The Baby Knauer case provided the opportunity to usher in euthanasia as National Socialist policy. The story we know is that the parents personally petitioned Hitler to have the infant child killed after the child was born blind and with some physical deformities. The infant's real name was Gerhard Herbert Kretschmar. He was born on February 29, 1939, in a village called *Pomβen*. He was blind, and "lacked one leg and part of an arm." Some doctors speculated that he was "feeble-minded," but realistically, they probably couldn't have known this at his age. His parents, Richard Gerhardt Kretschmar and Lina Sonja Kretschmar believed strongly in National Socialist ideology, and his father wanted his son dead. Richard Kretschmar took Gerhardt to the Leipzig Children's Clinic in the spring of 1939 when Gerhardt was just one or two months old and had him institutionalized there. Werner Catel, the head of the clinic, later testified that Herr Kretschmar had wanted him to kill Gerhardt right then, but Catel refused because of legal concerns. [86] When Catel would not euthanize Gerhardt, Herr Kretschmar petitioned Hitler directly. Hitler responded by sending Karl Brandt to examine the child with orders to decide whether the child should live or die. After confirming that Gerhard was blind and physically disabled, Brandt authorized the clinic staff to kill the baby, and Gerhard was murdered on July 25, 1939. He was five months old. This is what Karl Brandt had to say about the incident before the Nuremberg Tribunal:

> **BRANDT:** The father of a deformed child approached the Führer and asked that this **child or creature** should be killed. Hitler turned this matter over to me and told me to go to Leipzig immediately . . . to confirm the fact on the spot. It

---

[86] Catel later took part in the T4 Euthanasia program, so when he refused to kill Gerhardt he didn't have any moral objections to infanticide, he was just concerned about going to jail.

was a child, who had been born blind, and an idiot—at least it seemed to be an idiot—and it lacked one leg and part of an arm.

QUESTION: Witness, you were speaking about the Leipzig affair, about this deformed child. What did Hitler order you to do?

BRANDT: He ordered me to talk to the physicians who were looking after the child to find out whether the statements of the father were true. If they were correct, then I was to inform the physicians in his name that they could carry out the euthanasia. The important thing was that the parents should not feel themselves incriminated at some later date as a result of this euthanasia that the parents should not have the impression that they themselves were responsible for the death of the child. I was further ordered to state that if these physicians should become involved in some legal proceedings because of this measure, these proceedings would be quashed by order of Hitler.

QUESTION: What did the doctors who were involved say?

BRANDT: The doctors were of the opinion that there was no justification for keeping such a child alive.

(emphasis mine, Pgs. 94-96, "Death and Deliverance: 'Euthanasia' in Germany, C.1900 to 1945", Michael Burleigh, CUP Archive, Oct. 27, 1994)

The Baby Knauer incident provided the legal precedent for subsequent reforms. Dr. Leonardo Conti, Philipp Bouhler, and Karl Brandt formed the May 1939 formation of the Committee for the Scientific Treatment of Severe, Genetically Determined Illness paved the way for the secret euthanizing of infants. The resulting secret order to register ill children was drafted on August 18, 1939, three weeks after the murder of Baby Knauer. Hitler signed the letter in October but backdated and made official on September 1st, 1939 stated:

> Reichsleiter Bouhler and Dr. Brandt, M.D., are charged with the responsibility of enlarging the authority of certain physicians to be designated by name in such a manner that persons who, according to human judgement, are incurable can, upon a most careful diagnosis of their condition of sickness, be accorded a mercy death. – Adolf Hitler (Pg. 64, "Trials of War Criminals Before the Nuernberg Military Tribunals Under Control Council Law No. 10", Vol. I, "The Medical Case", Superintendent of Documents, US Government Printing Office)

The above excerpt is taken from the Euthanasia section of Telford Taylor's opening statement at the Doctors' Trial on December 9th, 1946. Telford Taylor preceded by describing how this letter was the legal basis for all of the efforts by the "criminals" to erect the necessary infrastructure dedicated to the extermination conducted at the camps, with Buchenwald being specifically mentioned by Taylor. Herein lay the fallacy that the American Prosecution team could not avoid stepping into. The entire eugenic euthanasia enterprise was the direct result of the civilian case of Baby Knauer. Hitler's September 1st, 1939 letter was presented by the American Prosecution as the only piece of physical evidence tying Adolf Hitler to the murders, and historians have treated it as such ever since. More so, the laws implemented by the regime upon this precedent were lifted from the American laws

and statutes intended for civilian courts:
> In August 1939, a circular issued by the Reich Interior Ministry mandated a "duty to report deformed births." All newborn infants "suspected of suffering from the following congenital defects" were to be registered: (1) Idiocy and Mongolism (particularly cases that involved blindness and deafness); (2) Microcephalia; (3) Hydrocephalus of a serious or progressive nature; (4) Deformities of every kind, in particular, the absence of limbs, spina bifida, and so on; (5) Paralysis, including Little's disease. (Pg. 184, "When Medicine Went Mad", 1992, Article: "Which Way Down the Slippery Slope: Nazi Medical Killing and Euthanasia Today", Ruth Macklin)

The reader will note, as is the case throughout the history of the eugenics movement, that the definitions used by Hitler's doctors and scientists were translations of those drafted in Britain and the United States. Rüdin, Lenz, Ploetz, and Fischer worked lock-step with Leonard Darwin, Karl Pearson, Charles B. Davenport, and Harry H. Laughlin. The movement not only organized itself around the International Federation of Eugenics Organizations, but their *modus operandi* was that of a monolithic movement, regardless of borders or language differences. One of the obstacles the eugenics movement faced was compliance. Thus, it is interesting to note that the method of coercing conformity that was used in the United States would later be used by the doctors working under Hitler's National Socialism: the patients were threatened to have their welfare benefits taken away if they did not agree to the procedure. [87] This threat to withdraw the medical help provided by the state was a practice that went on in the United States with ethnic minorities dependent on the state's help, and was often employed in the infamous "Appalachian Appendectomies," where the state would agree to provide hospitalization for childbirth only if the mother agreed to be sterilized, often already under the influence of medication necessary for childbirth.

All these coercive legal mechanisms utilized by the eugenic creed were ironically, documented by the Carnegie organization. A 1936 book commissioned by the Carnegie Foundation remains one of the most significant refutations of eugenics. "Eugenical Sterilization," became one of the most cogent refutations of eugenics, though largely forgotten to history now. The book touches on this coercive aspect of the movement:
> …the word *voluntary* is frequently a mere subterfuge, in that it is often a condition of discharge from the institution that the patient be sterilized, and consequently the individual involved is in the position of being confined or confinable until the gives his consent for sterilization, which hardly makes the bargain free and equal and nullifies the real meaning of the word voluntary. (Pg. 7, "Eugenic Sterilization: A Reorientation of the Problem", American Neurological Association, Committee for the Investigation of Eugenical Sterilization", Macmillan, 1936)

---

[87] Pgs. 185-186 - "When Medicine Went Mad: Bioethics and the Holocaust", Humana Press, 1992.

Incidentally, Brandt recalled a meeting with Hitler at *Obersalzberg* after the conclusion of the Polish campaign at which Hitler stated that he "wanted to bring about a definite solution in the euthanasia question." Brandt recalled during his sworn testimony that Hitler provided him "general directives on how he imagined it, and the fundamentals were that insane persons who were in such a condition that they could no longer take any conscious part in life were to be given relief through death. General instructions followed." [88] Though, Hitler's speeches provide evidence that these ideas were already in place a decade before the Third Reich taking power:

> The right of personal freedom recedes before the duty to preserve the race. There must be no half measures. It is a half measure to let incurably sick people steadily contaminate the remaining healthy ones. This is in keeping with the humanitarianism which, to avoid hurting one individual, lets a hundred others perish. If necessary, the incurably sick will be pitilessly segregated—a barbaric measure for the unfortunate who is struck by it, but a blessing for his fellow men and posterity. (Pg. 25, Citing Hitler's speech in 1923, "Hitler's Ideology: Embodied Metaphor, Fantasy and History", Richard A. Konigsberg, IAP, Dec. 1, 2007)

To harp on previously made observations, pay close attention to the above date: this 1923 speech occurred a full two decades prior to The Holocaust. Clearly the history of the eugenics movements proves that the elimination of the unfit had been contemplated for decades. The work of Ernst Rüdin and Alfred Ploetz by itself devastates the erroneous belief that eugenics was a product of the Nazi state warping the medical profession. The truth is that medicine helped create Nazism, and not the other way around.

In a broader sense, the idea of enforcing "racial hygiene" had been an essential element of Hitler's ideology from the "Mein Kampf" onwards, and thereafter never presented separately from the "Jewish question." The extermination of the Jews and "racial hygiene" were one and the same for Hitler once he had been educated on eugenics by his publisher, J.F. Lehmann. Paul Popenoe, one of the world-renowned American eugenicists of the era, cited Hitler:

> He who is bodily and mentally not sound and deserving may not perpetuate this misfortune in the bodies of his children. The völkisch [people's] state has to perform the most gigantic rearing-task here. One day, however, it will appear as a deed greater than the most victorious wars of our present bourgeois era. (dnalc.org Doc. ID 12208, "The German Sterilization Law," Paul Popenoe, "Journal of Heredity", Vol. 25, Jan. 1, 1934)

The transition from idea to fully matured methodology transpired in the infamous T4 facilities. The name T4 was an abbreviation of *"Tiergartenstraße 4,"* the address of a villa in the Berlin borough of Tiergarten that was the headquarters of the *Gemeinnützige Stiftung für Heil- und Anstaltspflege*, bearing the Orwellian

---

[88] Pg. 97 - "Death and Deliverance: 'Euthanasia' in Germany, C.1900 to 1945", Michael Burleigh, CUP Archive, Oct. 27, 1994.

name literally translating into "Charitable Foundation for Cure and Institutional Care." The "Action T4" program officially ran from September 1939 until August 1941, but it continued unofficially until the end of the war. During the official stage of Action T4, around 70,273 people were put to death, but the Nuremberg Trials found evidence that German and Austrian physicians continued the murder of patients after October 1941 and that about 275,000 people were killed under T4. The operation was officially under the direction of Philipp Bouhler, the head of Hitler's private chancellery, and Dr. Karl Brandt. The "euthanasia decree" that set all of this in motion was written on Adolf Hitler's personal stationery and backdated September 1, 1939, translates into English as follows:

> Reich Leader Bouhler and Dr. Brandt are charged with the responsibility for expanding the authority of physicians, to be designated by name, to the end that patients considered incurable according to the best available human judgment [menschlichem Ermessen] of their state of health, can be granted a mercy death [Gnadentod]. (Translation by L. Scott Lissner, "The Holocaust Began With People With Disabilities", 2009, incl.ca / See also Dr. Robert Jay Lifton's 1986 book: "The Nazi Doctors: Medical Killing and the Psychology of Genocide")

It is important to remember that these eugenic sterilizations in the United States and Germany were carried out for social "defects" such as alcoholism, pauperism, prostitution, and even masturbation. The carriers of cancer and epilepsy were also consistent targets of the eugenic legislation. These alleged "defects" had been the target of eugenic "sterilization," "segregation," and ultimate "elimination" since the 1870s when Francis Galton began to popularize the idea that humanity had to take charge of Darwin's "natural selection" and replace it with a "rational selection." The infamous T4 Program originated from the belief that the German people needed to be "cleansed" of "racially unsound" elements. Eugenics and euthanasia were indistinguishable and inseparable policies originating from the concept of *Volkskörper*, or body politic, which regarded a doctor's duty to the race and nation as prioritized over the doctor's duty to any individual:

> Like 'surgeons of the Volk', as Karl Brandt stressed, Nazi physicians believed that they were 'cutting out' the 'infected' and 'unhealthy' elements of social organism. After the war, one Nazi doctor said that German physicians wanted to 'eliminate sickness by eliminating the sick.' In the world view of Brandt and other Nazi physicians, the murder of tens of thousands was a medical operation. At the same time, they genuinely believed that their actions could be justified on the basis of what they perceived as their noble motivation. In 1947, Brandt stated that the introduction of the 'euthanasia' programme had been 'dictated by purely human considerations.' (Pg. 43, "Karl Brandt: Medicine and Power in the Third Reich", Ulf Schmidt, Bloomsbury Academic, 2007)

According to this view, the euthanasia program represents an evolution in policy toward the later Holocaust of the Jews of Europe. Jews, along with other cultures and ethnicities had been defined by the various racial anthropologists and evolutionary scientists, namely Ernst Haeckel, as lesser evolved and thus a danger to the Nordic racial stock. In this way, euthanasia and the marriage restriction laws evolved from this same concept of preventing "degeneration" by "race-mixing" with allegedly lesser evolved people. It is an idea that was scientifically bolstered after Haeckel by Erwin Fischer's work on the "bastard" sons of Africans and Germans. It is why German eugenicists embraced the broader concept of "race hygiene," which targeted any hereditary and environmental threats to the race. The Canadian medical officer, John W.R. Thompson, challenged Brandt on this conception during the Nuremberg Trials in 1947:

> To help another person requires the existence of a person, who should be helped, but in the same moment where the "help" of euthanasia is apparently being received, the alleged recipient ceases to exist. (Pg. 7, "Karl Brandt: Medicine and Power in the Third Reich", Ulf Schmidt, Bloomsbury Academic, 2007)

Brandt felt that Thompson had "missed the point" and whose comments were "too ridiculous" to warrant a response. In turn, Brandt's response to Thompson's biting criticism reveals that the policies were irreconcilable because of the secular socialist understanding of the individual's standing in society. The individual was only of "biological value" to statist scientists like Brandt. Brandt's generation of doctors intentionally discarded the traditional Hippocratic Oath's mandate to "do no harm" due to a belief that it was outdated and inconsistent with the solidarity and unity of purpose inherent in the collectivist concept of *Volkskörper*. For Brandt, "all the actions of a doctor needed to be directed towards improving and safeguarding the biological quality of the community." [89]

Historians like to paint Nazism as street-level mob mentality. In hindsight, the evidence proves that the scientific community was fully engaged and ready for these eugenic measures. To the contrary, it was the layman, the German public that needed convincing. The National Socialists put their propaganda machine toward building consensus support from the public. The National Socialist Racial and Political Office (NSRPA) produced leaflets, posters, and short films to be shown in cinemas, pointing out to everyday Germans the cost of maintaining asylums for the incurably ill and insane. These films included "The Inheritance" (*Das Erbe*, 1935), "The Victim of the Past" (*Opfer der Vergangenheit*, 1937), which was given a major premiere in Berlin and was shown in all German cinemas, and "I Accuse" (*Ich klage an*, 1941), which was based on a novel by Dr. Helmut Unger, a consultant for the child euthanasia program.

We also know that the euthanasia program was not in any way informally arrived at as historical research has proven that the National Socialists had researched the full history of eugenics before implementing T4. In the summer of 1939, Hitler's physician, Theo Morell, reviewed everything that had been written since the 19th century on the subject of euthanasia. Morell then used those materials to write a lengthy memorandum about the need for a law authorizing the "Destruction of Life Unworthy of Life." [90] Among other measures, Morell proposed killing people

---

[89] Pg. 7, "Karl Brandt: Medicine and Power in the Third Reich", Ulf Schmidt, Bloomsbury Academic, 2007.
[90] Pg. 98 – "Death and Deliverance: 'Euthanasia' in Germany, C.1900 to 1945", Michael Burleigh, CUP Archive, Oct 27,

who suffered from congenital mental or physical "malformations" because such "creatures" required costly long-term care, aroused "horror" in other people, and represented the "the lowest animal level."

The laws that were passed in August 18, 1939 called for the compulsory registration of all "malformed" newborn children provided for a small payment to the German doctors and midwives which were obliged to report all children under their care who had been born with Down's syndrome, microcephaly, hydrocephaly, paralysis, congenital deafness, blindness, and other physical and neurological disorders. These reports were to be returned to the Reich Committee central offices in Berlin where they would be reviewed by a panel of three "medical experts." Note that these "three-panel courts" were the direct product of Harry H. Laughlin's "Model Eugenical Sterilization Law," and which Lothrop Stoddard participated in when visiting Hitler's eugenic infrastructure. T4 was but one of the measures which were "*Geheime Reichssache*," or in English, "Secret Reich Matters," and those involved were bound by silence. One of the ways silence was enforced was by threatening to send the assigned personnel to the front lines of the war. Many of the uncooperative were assigned to the Yugoslav front, where Tito's partisans had a reputation for never taking prisoners, and a great many of them died there.

Let's recall that at this juncture, only civilians were being killed, and herein lay the murky waters the American prosecution at Nuremberg stepped into when attempting to construct imaginary demarcations within the Third Reich's eugenic cleansing programs. The "Project T4" or "Action T4" was fully integrated into the organizational structure of the Reich and fell under section IIb.-"Mercy-death" of the Chancellery of the Führer [KdF]. "Action T4" was pivotal to the dubious distinction that the American prosecutors at Nuremberg made between the supposedly "legal" euthanasia and eugenics program headed by Ernst Rüdin at the Kaiser-Wilhelm Institute, and the "crimes" supposedly done with the intent of forwarding the war effort. As we have documented, Dr. Rüdin and Dr. von Verschuer were released under this justification. This was and continues to be, the conception by which Ploetz, Rüdin, Verschuer, and others like Julian Huxley and Leonard Darwin are exonerated under; that their support for euthanasia and eugenics was not tainted by the anti-Semitism of Rosenberg and Hitler, and thus should be regarded as separate and even benign. This was also Karl Brandt's strategy at Nuremberg:

> His main concern was how to disconnect the murder of millions of Jews from 'euthanasia' programme. **'How shall I now separate this from the honest euthanasia?'** he noted in his diary. (emphasis mine, Pg. 2, "Karl Brandt: Medicine and Power in the Third Reich", Ulf Schmidt, Bloomsbury Academic, 2007)

Historians should be careful to note that Brandt's "good Nazi" routine was not wholly a fabrication either. Neither Brandt or Albert Speer, Hitler's friend and personal architect, indulged in the racial insults and vulgar anti-Semitism typical of

---

1994. – Citing National Archives – Captured Records of Private Individuals and Enterprises, NAW T-253, Roll 44, Morell Files.

Rosenberg, Goebbels, and Hitler. Posterity needs to pay special attention to the fact that technically speaking, the Third Reich's sterilization law was drafted free from "religious bias." It actually was the polite and refined form of eugenics that Julian Huxley and Muller called for. Leon Whitney made this crucial observation that the German sterilization law was free from "religious bias" and leveraged it to forward the cause:

> The main reason why the Law on Preventing Hereditarily Ill Progeny gained nearly unanimous support among American eugenicists was due to the fact that the law did not sanction sterilization based on ethnic or religious background. Leon F. Whitney assumed that "American Jewry is naturally suspecting that the German chancellor had the law enacted for the specific purpose of sterilizing the German Jews." He claimed that the German law provided for sterilization of hereditary defectives only, and that it stated that "the measure is solely eugenic in its purpose, and were it not for its compulsory character, it would probably meet with the approval of all who are free from religious bias." (Pgs. 51-52, "The Nazi Connection: Eugenics, American Racism, and German National Socialism", Stefan Kühl, Oxford Univ. Press, 1994)

Brandt certainly played the part of the "Good Nazi." He was no Rosenberg or poorly educated Hitler. By all accounts, namely those of the German Catholic priests that confronted Brandt about the euthanasia program, Brandt was an educated man of good upbringing. He was known to give blood and take an active role in helping others in dire situations. This is an aspect of Brandt that his biographer makes amply clear:

> Brandt's biography sits uncomfortably with the image of the drunken, ruthless Nazi hordes, who vented their pent-up aggressions, as well as social and professional frustrations, on Jews and political opponents in the aftermath of the Nazi takeover of power, or burned and vandalized hundreds of synagogues in the wake of the 'Crystal Night' (*Reichskristallnacht*), or with some of the fanatical ideologues, *SS-Einstzgruppen* in the eastern territories, or indeed with most of the medical and administrative personnel involved in the planning and execution of the 'euthanasia' programme. Brandt was neither a party ideologue who, like Himmler and Rosenberg, called for the annihilation of an entire people and the expansion of German 'living space' (*Lebensraum*), nor did he represent the kind of technocratic 'desk perpetrator' (*Schreibtishtäter*) who, like Eichmann, planned and organized an efficient deportation system which ferried hundreds of thousands of Jews and others to the death camps. (Pg. 3, "Karl Brandt: Medicine and Power in the Third Reich", Ulf Schmidt, Bloomsbury Academic, 2007)

To the contrary, Brandt's name was totally absent from any of the paperwork directing the extermination camps, and was about to be set free by the Allied prosecution, as had been Rüdin and Verschuer, until a Belgian representative of the U.N. War Crimes Commission, M. de Baer, stepped in to point out the grave mistake that was being made. [91] Brandt was too high in the officer in the Nazi ranks to claim obliviousness to the nature of the regime's eugenic policy.

The most notable of protests for the regime's eugenic policies came from the Church and were addressed directly to the Ministry of Justice. The Bishop of Limburg is typically credited with creating enough publicity that a change was forced. It was at this point in about December 1941 that a change in procedure occurred. However, early historians of the T4 program were mistaken in reporting that the killing stopped because of the ever-increasing protests. To the contrary, the gassing facilities at T4 were put in the service of the concentration camps as they themselves made changes to become extermination camps. T4 was expanded under the code 14f13. This was the turning point from euthanasia of the deformed and helplessly ill, to the final goal of eliminating anyone deemed undesirable either because of politics, religion, race or health issues.

The directive to go further under the radar, however, was primarily due to the very public opposition mounted by the German Catholic Church. The starting date for the operation of 14f13 appears to have been some time in December 1941. Special commissions composed of doctors reporting to the Berlin staff of T4 were reassigned to the concentration camps to clear the medical bays of the ill and undesirables. At Auschwitz, around this time, about 800 patients in the infectious block were sent to death chambers. Testimony was given at Nuremberg by the S.S. camp doctor at Dachau that in 1941, a group of four doctors under the leadership of Professor Dr. Werner Heyde, *SS Standartenführer* rid the camp of those deemed too sick to work. The evidence was presented at Nuremberg was in the form of correspondence sent by the T4 doctors from the extermination camps back to their families, thus proving their whereabouts, along with brief descriptions of what they were up to.

To further blur the fictitious differentiation between "civilian" and "military" facilities, Hartheim also served as a safety valve when executions taking place in nearby concentration camps such as Mauthausen and Dachau became more than the staff could manage. Victims were sent to Hartheim and "dispatched" there. Later, towards the end of the war, Hartheim became just another place for extermination, its staff, and personnel having been assigned to other duties. The dubious separation between the civilian eugenics program and the war effort gets even thinner with the realization that the "civilian" T4 doctors were sent to the Eastern front to euthanize injured soldiers. [92] While historians do not link back to the justification given by the American prosecutors at Nuremberg for releasing the staff of the Kaiser-Wilhelm Institute from prosecution, there can be no other understanding of these facts. The T4 civilian eugenics program clearly took part in the concentration camps, extermination camps, and the Eastern front activities that Nuremberg would deem "criminal." If the T4 activities were "criminal," then by definition, so were the

---

[91] Pg. 133 - "Justice at Nuremberg: Leo Alexander and the Nazi Doctors' Trial", Ulf Schmidt, Palgrave Macmillan UK, 2004.

[92] This is confirmed by several authors, including Ulf Schmidt in "Karl Brandt," Michael Burleigh in "Surveys of Developments in the Social History of Medicine," and by Dr. Robert J. Lifton in "The Nazi Doctors: Medical Killing and the Psychology of Genocide."

activities at the Kaiser-Wilhelm Institute. Any distinction to the contrary is a fabricated notion with no footing on reality. That the Allied prosecution at Nuremberg fabricated this arbitrary demarcation justifies a reexamination of the work done at Nuremberg.

Sec. 7 - HITLER'S EXHIBITION OF "DEGENERATE ART":

Adolf Hitler is where the line demarcating construction and destruction blurs. Despite the gargantuan amount of time, effort and national resources he devoted to his new civic Germany, it is difficult to tell whether Adolf Hitler was in the business of creation or destruction. Alas, art has always necessitated both construction as well as destruction. In some of the arts, one must destroy in order to reveal that which only the visionary could imagine. In Hitler's warped mind, he was doing no different. He was primarily an artist. He called it his "true calling," and saw world domination and wars as just another hurdle in the path to this end. What made Hitler's artistic vision more dangerous and sinister is that he saw all of humanity as his canvas, his block of stone, and Hitler felt no more pity for the shards of humanity he discarded than the sculptor feels for the broken pieces of travertine that fall by the wayside as he hammers away to reveal his vision.

Hitler also had the aspirations of an architect and city planner. Hitler's unified Germanic Reich was intended to be everything that architects like Frank Lloyd Wright and Le Corbusier designed into their imaginary urban proposals along with every aspect of the utopian aspirations. The difference was that Hitler didn't just propose one city or even a model city. Hitler embarked on not just remaking every major city and town in his Pan-German dream, but to extend and connect them under one Reich. The geographic scale of Hitler's Pan-German utopia was too grand to be expressed in a single drawing, as Wright's and Corbu's. The scale of Hitler's plans was very literally the map of Europe.

Hitler, like any other artist, was driven and obsessed with communicating his vision. It was not enough to be a dictator in a totalitarian state. Hitler needed the public to be in awe of his creation, and to do so they had to understand Hitler's new Germany. This was Josef Goebbels's task as propaganda minister. The dream and ideals of National Socialism had to inspire the German people and entice them to embrace their roles as the humans sitting at top of the evolutionary ladder. This was crucial to both the war effort, to the rebuilding of Germany along National Socialist lines, and for the discarding of any part of German society that threatened to detract from this grand vision. The task of elevating Germany to these new aspirations necessitated the task of purifying it and purging it from the elements "unfit" to belong. This was the task of propaganda, the new art of communication.

A cartoon contemporary to the era documents that Germans were aware that they had been drawn into a bizarre artistic endeavor. *Kladderadatch* was a leading German satirical weekly journal that was an early supporter of National Socialism. A 1933 cartoon signed by cartoonist "O. Gravens" titled "Germany's Sculptor" depicted Hitler destroying an *avant-garde* artist's modern sculpture of a pile of cadavers and later sculpting a German colossus out of the resulting mound of clay. [93] The message was clear: Hitler's "New Aryan Man" and his new "Aryan Nation" was an aesthetic venture like that of any other artistic venture; and like any other sculpture, it required the destruction of the base material in order to shape it into something new. The method of how this new vision for Germany would be achieved was not left to interpretation.

Adolf Ziegler was Hitler's favorite painter. His painting The Four Elements hung in Hitler's living room, and he was awarded the Gold Badge, the highest party member recognition of Hitler's National Socialist German Workers' Party. He was president of the Reich Chamber of the Visual Arts under Josef Goebbels. Ziegler was also given the honor and responsibility of organizing the 1937 Exhibition of Degenerate Art in Munich. In all, the *Aktion Entartete Kunst* confiscated over 16,000 works of art from over 32 German museums and public collections. Six hundred and fifty of these (by 112 artists) were earmarked for the *Entarte Kunst*. Opening in the *Hofgarten* arcades of Munich's *Residenz* on July 18, 1937, the exhibition traveled to eleven sites throughout Germany and Austria over a four-year period and was seen by a record-breaking 3 million viewers. The exhibition was to display, in no uncertain terms, precisely what the regime discarded as not worthy of being called German.

More importantly, the exhibition was to be contrasted by what Hitler did regard as accurate depictions of his pure German vision. The "Degenerate Art" exhibition was strategically opened on the day after and across the street to the grand German Art Exhibition at the recently completed House of German Art (*Grosse Deutsche Kunstausstellung*). It was the first of eight annual exhibitions that showcased what the National Socialists regarded as Germany's finest. Hitler had appointed Ziegler to select the works for this grand exhibition, but in disgust over Ziegler's selections, Hitler undertook the task of selecting the works himself. Hitler, in addition, delivered six speeches on the topic of art, and these were distributed as pamphlets. Prior to this, Hitler had also written about the crucial role art played in the people's community, and thus the danger he perceived in having it controlled or influenced by cultural forces he considered to be "degenerate." Hitler, for example, made his views on Jewish influence on the arts known in "Mein Kampf":

> Culturally his activity consists in bowdlerizing art, literature and the theatre, holding the expressions of national sentiment up to scorn, overturning all concepts of the sublime and beautiful, the worthy and the good finally dragging the people to the level of his own low mentality. (gutenberg.net.au, Pg. 281 book version, "Mein Kampf", James Murphy translation)

---

[93] Pg. 97 - "Hitler and the Power of Aesthetics," Frederic Spotts, Overlook Press, 2018.

At the groundbreaking ceremony in October 1933, Hitler declared The House of German Art a "temple to house a new German art." The three days preceding the grand opening, Munich was draped in banners and flags, in celebration of German Art Day in the extravagant pageantry choreographed by Joseph Goebbels. The Propaganda Minister spared no expense for these spectacular ceremonies. The parades consisted of monumental gilded paper-mache heads of classical statuary, costumed Rhine maidens, and warriors of the Teutonburg forest. The three-day festivities culminated in a parade of a thousand marching soldiers enshrining "Two Thousand Years of German Culture."

Nor was Hitler alone in his devotion to aesthetic visions. Hitler was not the only frustrated artists amongst the National Socialist leadership. Joseph Goebbels was a poet, a Ph. D., and had a refined taste for the arts. He saw his role as Reich Minister of Public Enlightenment and Propaganda as key towards a total "synchronization" (*Gleichschaltung*) of all aspects of society with art, and art with all aspects of society. This, after all, was an inherent task of sculpting the "total state." In fact, one curious and revealing aspect of this topic of "Degenerate Art" is that, at first, Goebbels embraced the Modern Art of the Bauhaus, and in one way or another tried to *politik* Modern Art into the realm of National Socialism. The early days of National Socialism had Goebbels dealing and scheming to squeeze Modern Art into the vocabulary of National Socialism. He would have succeeded in making Modern Art the visual depiction of National Socialism if it were not for the fact that his Führer was so ardently opposed to it as an artist that clearly understood the political undercurrent of Modernism.

> Politics, too, is an art . . . and we who shape modern German policy feel ourselves in this to be artists who have been given the responsible task of forming, out of the raw material of the mass, the firm concrete structure of a people . . . it is [the artists'] task to form, to give shape, to remove the diseased and create freedom for the healthy. ("TIME Magazine", Mar. 22, 1937 citing Goebbels in 1933)

Unfortunately for the fashionable Goebbels, Hitler understood that controlling art was part of the larger effort of controlling society in a "total state":

> This process of cleansing our 'Kultur' will have to be applied in practically all spheres. The stage, art, literature, the cinema, the Press and advertisement posters, all must have the stains of pollution removed and be placed in the service of a national and cultural idea. (gutenberg.net.au, Pg. 220 book version, "Mein Kampf", James Murphy translation)

To be precise, Adolf Hitler regarded the remaking of Germany in the same terms he approached the creation of art, as the *Kladderadatch* cartoon depicted. Grand civic works were an integral part of his vision, if not the one Hitler was the most passionate about. Hitler had embarked on the most ambitious building projects in history. "The New Aryan" man and its embodiment, the Third Reich, needed a civic architecture to exemplify its greatness to all the world and to all generations to come. He commissioned for the rebuilding of all of Germany in 1937, and Hitler appointed the young architect, Albert Speer, to accomplish this task of theatrical proportions. This task of rebuilding all of Germany would consume an unprecedented amount of resources and technology. Speer was promoted to a position second only to Hitler himself, a position best described as a parallel military force with Speer as the highest-ranking admiral under the commander in chief, able to drop in and commandeer the resources of other agencies as needed to accomplish Hitler's vision. His new title was General Building Inspector for the Reich Capital with the rank of undersecretary of state in the Reich government. The position carried with it extraordinary powers over the regular ranks of government. Clearly, this was no routine architectural commission.

The position enjoyed the privileges of being the preferred member of Hitler's "inner circle." Hitler would confide in Albert Speer, as he was the closest thing the dictator had to a friend. Both shared a passion for architecture, and Hitler deferred to the master architects with a docile reverence that was shown to no others, as Hitler otherwise had a pronounced disdain for "experts." Just compare how Hitler treated his military officers, even though the many high-ranking officers of his armed forces had a vast amount of experience over him. Hitler consistently insulted and humiliated them. This was not so with his architects:

> Hitler, normally arrogant and argumentative was never less than humble and deferential – timid even – before the towering professorial figure of Troost, and transformed himself, before the astonished Speer, from the iron-willed chancellor of the German Reich into an eager, ever-respectful student of architecture. (Pg. 198, "Architects of Fortune: Mies Van Der Rohe and the Third Reich", Elaine S. Hochman, Fromm International Pub. Corp., 1989)

Speer recalls in his memoirs that Adolf Hitler, the man who mercilessly sent millions upon millions to their deaths, cried openly when his first architect died. [94] Speer had replaced Fritz Todt. But Speer was more approachable than Todt and the other master architects, as Speer was much younger than Hitler. Thus, Hitler had a unique relationship, often sharing both lunch and dinner most of the days of the week with Speer:

> "Architecture relaxes me, Speer. --- Before going to bed I spend some time on architecture. I look at pictures . . . Otherwise I wouldn't be able to sleep." He was silent for a moment, his eyes held by the plans in front of them, then turned to the young architect. "I tell you, Speer, these buildings are more important than anything else. You must do everything you can to complete them in my lifetime." (Pg. 195, "Architects of Fortune: Mies Van Der Rohe and the Third Reich", Fromm International Pub. Corp., 1989)

The most ambitious part of their overall project was the rebuilding of Berlin. The city was to be the capital of the new Europe, the new world organized around Aryan supremacy. The design had to live up to its purpose. New Berlin's civic center ran north-south along a three-mile-long grand boulevard, which culminated with a

---

[94] Pg. 199 - "Inside the Third Reich: Memoirs of Albert Speer", Albert Speer, Avon, 1971.

colossal 700-foot-high dome that would dwarf Rome's Pantheon and the dome of the Florence Cathedral. The interior space of the dome was high enough to accommodate the Eiffel Tower. It would seat more than 180,000 spectators, a volume two or three times the seating of late 20th Century football or baseball stadiums. Speer had to devise a technology we now call "closed-circuit TV" to be able to project the image of the speaker onto large screens, as the speaker would be dwarfed to insignificance when the dome was occupied with the 180,000 participants. Speer and Hitler called it the *Volkshalle*. The north-south boulevard Speer called the *Prachtstrasse*, or Street of Magnificence. At the southern end of the avenue would be a huge triumphal arch. This arch would be almost 400 feet high, and able to fit the French *Arc de Triomphe* inside its opening. The design of the arch was based on a sketch that Hitler had drawn while an aspiring architect in Vienna. The plan of this city center was intended to function as a permanent World's Fair, with hotels to accommodate visitors and permanent exhibition halls to display the products of German industry. It was also to be Germany's cultural center with an opera halls of a matching megalomaniac scope and scale.

The same rigorous approach was implemented in smaller towns as well. Wolfsburg was the best example of several planned cities. It was erected around the village of Fallersleben specifically to develop the *"Volkswagen"* project and was intended to operate as an industrial colony to house workers at the VW production facility. The city was founded on July 1, 1938, as *Stadt des KdF-Wagens bei Fallersleben*, or in English "City of the KdF Car at Fallersleben." The city planning was the work of architect Peter Koller, and it was not until 1945 that the city was renamed Wolfsburg after the castle located there.

The Volkswagen project itself should also be regarded as part of Hitler's grand artistic vision. The Volkswagen project was originally founded in 1937 by the National Socialist trade union, the German Labour Front, or *"Deutsche Arbeitsfront."* Up until the early 1930s, the German auto industry was dedicated to one-off luxury models, built with tradition machine shop tools. The cost of what would be considered hand-crafting by today's standard resulted in unaffordable automobiles for the vast majority of the population. Cars at the time were items of extreme luxury. That changed with the production line process created by Hitler's idol, Henry Ford, and Hitler was blatantly copying Henry Ford's Model-T when he created the Volkswagen project.

Hitler wanted a "people's car," hence the marrying of the terms *"volks"* and *"wagen."* This was in line with the ideals of the German Labour Front's (KdF) "Strength Through Joy" program, which sought to enforce a clean industry and healthy workers. Thus, the original VW Beetle was christened with the unwieldy name of "City of the Strength Through Joy Car." Hitler commissioned a basic vehicle capable of transporting two adults and three children at 100 km/h (62 mph). The car that later became known as the "People's Car" would be available to citizens of the Third Reich through a savings scheme at 990 *Reichsmark*, about the price of a motorcycle. The intention was that ordinary Germans would buy the car by means of a savings scheme (*"Fünf Mark die Woche musst Du sparen, willst*

Du im eigenen Wagen fahren" — "Five Marks a week you must put aside, if in your own car you want to ride"), which around 336,000 people eventually paid into.

In the spirit of National Socialism, the "Volkswagen" project would be a state-owned venture. The engineer chosen for the task was FDr. Ferdinand Porsche. By then an already famed engineer, Porsche was the designer of the Mercedes 170H. Like the Model-T Ford, the car had to be easily repairable with interchangeable parts. Erwin Komenda, the longstanding Auto Union chief designer, developed the car body of the prototype, which was recognizably the VW Beetle known today. The car was one of the first to be engineered with the aid of a wind tunnel. The construction of the new factory started May 26, 1938, and the first Type I Cabriolet was presented to Hitler on April 20Th, 1938, as a birthday present.

The "People's Car," the "New Aryan Man," and all of the projects prefaced with "*Volks*" were part of the grander socialist utopia being crafted by Hitler. Nazi Germany, in fact, should be understood as a gargantuan "art installation," the term artists of the early 21st Century use for a living or participatory work of art. Case in point, one of Hitler's first official decisions was the approval of the Autobahn construction project. Hitler appointed Fritz Todt as the Inspector General of German Road Construction and assigned him over 100,000 laborers for construction sites all over Germany. It was the most ambitious road network to date, and the Autobahn project was in many ways an artistic endeavor:

> Officially sponsored art could simultaneously channel money to artists and produce art celebrating the accomplishments of the regime. In November 1936, for example, public agencies spent almost RM 75,000 on art at the Berlin exhibition with the theme, "The Roads of Adolf Hitler in Art." In 1938 the chief of the Autobahn project, Fritz Todt, commissioned several dozen paintings to celebrate the progress attained on the highway system. (Pg. 77, "Art, Ideology, & Economics in Nazi Germany", Alan E. Steinweiss, Univ. of North Carolina Press, 1993)

The Autobahn intentionally invoked the classical grandeur of Rome. The dirt roads of the day connecting the European cities simply would not do. Hitler's army needed to harness the speed of the German automotive industry. It was the speed of technology that Hitler sought to harness in his *Blitzkrieg* style warfare. The project provided Hitler a propaganda piece that embodied his plans for Europe. The Autobahn was necessary to unite the geography under one Pan-German aspiration.

Aesthetic utopianism goes hand-in-hand with eugenic utopianism. Wolfgang Voigt's article titled "The Garden City as Eugenic Utopia," documents that the intertwined relationship between city planning and eugenics predated Adolf Hitler by several generations, going back to the eugenicists that were initially inspired by H.G. Wells and Edward Bellamy's utopian fictions. In fact, German eugenicists belonged to both city planning and eugenic political lobbies, many of which sprung from the "*Lebensreform*" movement, which was a naturalist movement which promoted the "garden city" as an aesthetic and health measure:

> In the year 1903, the author Heinrich Driesmans, an ardent admirer of Francis

Galton, held the earliest meeting of Galton's Eugenics and the German *Reformbaukultur*. Driesman's Forum was the *Deutscher Bund fur Bodenreform* (German Land Reform League) which was the most energetic supporter of the doctrines of Henry George outside the United States in the decade after 1900. In the political economics seminar conducted every year by the German land reformers in Berlin, Driesman called for the synthesis of eugenics and land reform. (Pg. 295-312, W. Voigt, "Garden City as Eugenic Utopia", Planning Perspectives, Vol. 4, Issue 31989, 1989)

According to Voigt, leading German eugenicists were included in the board of the German City Association (*Deutsche Gartenstadt-Gesellschaft DGG*) which was founded in 1902. Voigt documents that two key eugenicists were on the board of the German City Association: Alfred Ploetz and the Alfred Grotjahn. Recall that Ploetz was the pivotal scientist who coined the term "racial hygiene." The Social Democrat Grotjahn drafted the Socialist Party's health platform while as its representative in the Reichstag from 1921. Grotjahn proved himself a devotee of "rational selection" and regularly published concepts for identifying and registering "degenerated" individuals.

Historically speaking, one could argue that it was via Albert Speer that all of Hitler's destructive ability was refocused into a constructive force. Hitler's Pan-German dream was a "planned community" in the grandest of scales. Albert Speer certainly understood it as such, and often reflected on this aspect of Hitler's megalomania while in his jail cell. Speer had become increasingly estranged from his father, who was also an architect as had been Speer's grandfather. Speer's father was a "liberal" in the old sense of the word and did not share the desire for a "Total State" with the megalomania expressed through ridiculously oversized civic architecture. Albert Speer recalls his father's reaction to Hitler and the models of the city designs which the young Speer had brought his father to see:

> When my father—still erect and self-controlled in spite of his seventy-five years—was introduced to Hitler, he was overcome by a violent quivering such as I had never seen him exhibit before, nor ever did again. He turned pale, did not respond to Hitler's lavish praise of his son, and then took his leave in silence. (Pg. 133, "Inside the Third Reich: Memoirs of Albert Speer", Avon, 1971)

Speer recalls what his father told him when he had a moment alone with the young Speer: "You've all gone completely crazy." Reminiscing in his post-war jail cell, Speer was able to appreciate how deeply Hitler's politics influenced his designs: "Designs of such scale naturally indicate a kind of chronic megalomania, which is reason enough to dwell on these grandiose plans." [95] To further underscore the mania of the artistic effort, Speer also recalls Hitler sending the comedian Werner Fink to a concentration camp for making fun of Hitler's megalomaniac city plans. [96]

As mentioned earlier, these city plans drew the jealousy and chagrin of Speer's

---

[95] Pg. 138 - "Inside the Third Reich: Memoirs of Albert Speer", Albert Speer, Avon, 1971
[96] Pg. 139 – Ibid.

colleagues, who saw vital and scarce resources going to artistic endeavors even at the peak of the war. This questionable prioritization evidences the motivations of the architect of the Third Reich, Adolf Hitler, as well as his personal motivations. Like the "The Final Solution," the megalomaniac city-planning aspirations sucked precious resources away from what a conventional leader would regard as the priority during a world war. That both of these goals were pursued mercilessly to the bitter end documents that Hitler's aspirations were that of a master builder and sculptor, intent on redesigning not just a building or a city, but an entire people and geography, in its totality. Speer would recall Hitler's reaction to his suggestion, then as armaments minister, that any peacetime civic projects be abandoned until the war ended:

> My proposals that we cease peacetime building continued to be disregarded even when the outlines of the disaster of the winter of 1941 in Russia began to be apparent. On November 29, 1941, Hitler told me bluntly: "The building must begin even while this war is still going on. I am not going to let the war keep me from accomplishing my plans." (Pg. 181, "Inside the Third Reich", Avon, 1971)

Hitler was competing, not with his contemporaries, but with the Greeks and the Romans, and many of the designs were Speer's tribute to Hitler's designs. Under his instructions, Speer would build the architectural wonders Hitler dreamed of as a starving artist in Vienna. The new German cities were to represent Aryan rule for all ages to come. Case in point, Hitler and Speer intentionally designed their structures to deteriorate with the picturesque quality of the ancient ruins of Greece and Rome. Speer's set of plans included views into the distant future with the buildings partially crumbled as if the backdrop to a fresco or oil painting. Hitler delighted in this. Speer recalls the importance of these works for Hitler, even as Nazi Germany crumbled:

> In the final hours of his life, with Russian tanks at the doorstep of Berlin and his plans for the thousand-year Reich crumbling in fetid ruin, a withered and red-eyed Führer sat silent within his bunker before the tiny models of his "new" Linz. (Pg. 178, "Architects of Fortune: Mies Van Der Rohe and the Third Reich", Elaine Hochman, Fromm International Pub. Corp., 1989)

Sec. 8 - "ERBKRANK":

Hitler's vision was certainly a participatory art installation, and the participation of "willing executioners" was required to chisel away at the raw marble block to ultimately reveal the Fuhrer's vision. As such, propaganda was the most important tool in Hitler's disposal, as an entire nation had to be conscripted to create National Socialism's eugenic utopia. Of all the propaganda schemes available to the regime, film making was a tool of choice.

The most notorious of these propaganda films was *Erbkrank*. [97] *Erbkrank* was Laughlin's "Model Eugenical Sterilization Law" translated into cinematographic drama. Laughlin had followed Hitler's career prior to him becoming a figure of international notoriety. One of the newspaper clippings in Laughlin's Hitler file at the Truman University collection has a margin note that says, "Hitler should be made an honorary member of the E.R.A.!!!" [98] Laughlin was referring to one of the many eugenic bodies he belonged to, the Eugenics Research Association. Adolf Hitler's government returned the sentiment. The Nazis considered Laughlin's work on the segregation and sterilization of the "unfit" as his greatest accomplishment, and *Erbkrank* was one of the various ways they demonstrated this. The infamous 1933 eugenic laws, otherwise known as the Nuremberg Laws, were largely a verbatim copy of Laughlin's "Model Sterilization Law," specifically the 1933 "Law for the Prevention of Hereditarily Diseased Offspring," and *Erbkrank* was the regime's way of having the German public accept these extreme eugenic measures.

Erbkrank or in English "The Hereditary Defectives," was directed by Herbert Gerdes. It was one of six propagandistic movies produced by National Socialism's *"Reichsleitung, Rassenpolitisches Amt"* or the "Office of Racial Policy," to sell the idea to the German public that the "unfit" were liable to cause a serious social catastrophe if left to reproduce their kind. Of note is also the film's portrayal of "the idiotic black bastard from the Rhineland," which is surely input from Eugen Fischer's study of the "Rehoboth bastards," the children of German colonists with African wives. As was typical of Laughlin and other eugenic zealots, *Erbkrank* made unrealistic apocalyptic predictions about what would happen to humanity if extreme eugenic measures were not taken. These apocalyptic predictions were made personal to the audience in a convincing manner. The film utilized grotesque images of actual patients living in relatively luxurious hospitals juxtaposed against poor German families living in comparatively meager conditions. This was surely a sentiment Hitler held with some conviction, as Hitler spent many months in the luxurious, but drastically overcrowded Beelitz-Heilstätten sanatorium when he was injured in World War I. *Erbkrank* magnified these sentiments. The German public was made keenly aware of the dire situation of German hospitals. The goal of the movie was to gain public support for the various 1933 Nuremberg decrees, and in this respect, the project was substantially successful.

Harry Laughlin brought *Erbkrank* over to the United States to be shown to the Carnegie Institution, one of the major funders of Cold Spring Harbor. [99] Laughlin edited the film for his own purposes and distributed it in the United States under the title "Eugenics in Germany." The film was distributed to American schools, churches, and colleges with the financial help of millionaire Wickliffe Draper of the Pioneer Fund. Draper's Pioneer Fund also facilitated the printing of 3,000 flyers

---

[97] Pg. 138 - "The Black Stork: Eugenics and the Death of "Defective" Babies in American Medicine and Motion Pictures since 1915", Martin S. Pernick, Oxford Univ. Press, 1996.

[98] Box: E-1-4:2, "Harry H. Laughlin Papers", Truman Univ. Archives, Special Collections.

[99] Pg. 49 - "The Nazi Connection: Eugenics, American Racism, and German National Socialism", Stefan Kühl, Oxford Univ. Press, 1994.

advertising the film to biology teachers across the United States in order to generate demand. [100]

Most importantly, the reception of the film in the United States was used to bolster eugenics back in Germany. A leading National Socialist newspaper reported on the "exceptionally strong impression" the film had made on American eugenicists in an article titled *"Rassenpolitische Aufklärung nach deutschem Vorbild: Grosse Beachtung durch die amerikanische Wissenschaft,"* or "Racial Political Propaganda on German Model Receives Great Attention among American Eugenicists." [101] As this book will continually document, Adolf Hitler's government always had their ear on the ground to gauge interest and response to German internal affairs. Policy was written and revised around international reactions; thus the enthusiasm from the Carnegie and Rockefeller Institutions and high-profile individuals such as Charles B. Davenport, Harry H. Laughlin, C.M. Goethe, and Wickliffe Draper were welcome bolsters to the public image Hitler tirelessly cultivated through extensive propaganda efforts.

The New Jersey Sterilization League, a eugenic advocacy group from Woodrow Wilson's days as governor, also translated a National Socialist propaganda film and released it under the title "The Fatal Chain of Hereditary Disease" in 1938. In fact, Hitler's propaganda machine released an onslaught of other films promoting National Socialism as a "eugenic state" depicting the Nuremberg Laws as nothing more than "applied biology." The National Socialist government followed up with a full-length film *"Opfer der Vergangenheit: Die Sünde wider Blut und Rasse,"* or "Victims of the Past: The Sin against Blood and Race." These were but the most successful in a long list of other eugenic film productions that were authored by Hitler's National Socialist government:

1935 – *"Was du erebt"* (What You Inherit)
1937 – *"Opfer der Vergangenheit"* (Victims of the Past)
1939 – *"Geisteskrank"* (Mentally Ill)
1939 – *"Dasein ohne Leben"* (Existence without Life)
1940 – *"Alles Leben ist Kampf"* (All Life is Struggle)
1940 – *"Das Erbe"* (The Inheritance)
1941 – *"Ich Klage An"* (I Accuse) [102]

Was Adolf Hitler a pioneer in the use of propaganda to motivate the masses to both accept and act on eugenics? Not at all. This book will provide further examples of mainstream eugenic propaganda. It is of note, for the purposes of this book, to remind the reader that one of Leo Alexander's job functions while working for the German eugenic institutions prior to emigrating to the United States was to use film to document the work of the eugenicists. The reader will recall the pivotal

---

[100] For more on this topic see: 1937 – Erbkrank chapter in "H.H. Laughlin: American Progressive, American Scientist, Nazi Collaborator", A.E. Samaan.
[101] Pg. 50 – "The Nazi Connection: Eugenics, American Racism, and German National Socialism", Stefan Kühl, Oxford Univ. Press, 1994.
[102] Pg. 164-165 - "The Black Stork: Eugenics and the Death of "Defective" Babies in American Medicine and Motion Pictures since 1915", Martin S. Pernick, Oxford Univ. Press, 1996 - Summarized list of movies more broadly detailed by Pernick.

role Leo Alexander played as an expert for the Allied prosecution team at Nuremberg. The use of footage taken of the actual patients residing across the various mental hospitals controlled and administered by the eugenic institutions in Germany only becomes that much more uncomfortable when one realizes that one of the leaders of the American prosecution at the Nuremberg had participated in creating such films.

Sec. 9 - PANDORA'S BOOK:

Adolf Hitler's government continually had their ear on the ground to gauge interest and response to Nazi domestic policy, and books would play an equally influential role in exposing the commonalities and collaboration between eugenicists in the United States and Hitler's Germany. This did not always serve Hitler's cause. Several key books conspired to unravel the inconvenient political connections between the eugenic schemes of the two nations.

"*Das Rassenrecht in Den Vereinigten Staaten*" was published by Heinrich Krieger in 1936. The title literally translates to "The Race Law in the United States." Hitler's regarded it a success. The "*Grossdeutscher Pressedienst*" applauded the book by stating:

> [F]or us Germans it is especially important to known and to see how one of the biggest states in the world with Nordic stock already has race legislation which is quite comparable to that of the German Reich. (Pg. 99, "The Nazi Connection: Eugenics, American Racism, and German National Socialism", Stefan Kühl, Oxford Univ. Press, 1994)

Back in the United States, the "Living Age" did a book review of Heinrich Krieger's work in an article titled "Heil Lincoln!" Littell's "Living Age" was a magazine mostly consisting of selections from various English and American magazines and newspapers. It was published weekly from 1844 to 1941. It documented that "*Die Tat*," the monthly publication of National Socialism used Krieger's work in juxtaposing American race laws to those of the Third Reich, and in the process, made some controversial claims that must have raised eyebrows across the United States:

> Kreiger states that Lincoln was 'far removed from the sentimental idea of equality with which his name has time and again been falsely coupled', and 'often and vigorously supported the expulsion of the Negroes from the United States. (Pg. 257, "Heil Lincoln!", Littell's Living Age, March-August 1936)

The article goes on to blame the "crushing burden of ideology" as standing in the way of America's "racial salvation":

> Visitors to the United States whose instincts have not been adultered are stirred and deeply revolted by the form which racial co-existence has taken, especially in the great cities of the East. (Pg. 257, "Heil Lincoln!", Littell's Living Age, March-August 1936)

The article goes on to make some poignant recommendations in order to achieve the "racial salvation" it desires for the "Nordic" and "Germanic" Americans:

> First and most important: the ideology of racial equality must be relinquished. In particular there must never be, not even in theory, legal equality between Nordics and Negroes. ---- Second: The Fourteenth and Fifteenth Amendments to the Constitution must be repealed. This would lead to the disenfranchisement of the Negroes and do away with all enforcement legislation. – Third: Lincoln's plans for expulsion should be taken up again and gradually realized. The promising manner in which Germany is attempting broadly and finally to liquidate centuries of racial mixture undoubtedly will in due time attract notice in America. (Pg. 257, "Heil Lincoln!", Littell's Living Age, March-August 1936)

The article goes on to allude to the fact that some in the United States agreed with the stated goals of "racial salvation," and pinpointed the culprit for the alleged resistance:

> It is understandable that the underminers of the American Nation's Germanic character are fanatically at work inculculating into Americans the paralyzing ideology of racial equality. The Jews, with an exemplary instinct for their own welfare, here, too, are in the van. --- As racial comrades we Germans hope and wish that Germanic America will increasingly find its way back to the principles of its great statesmen, Washington, Jefferson and Lincoln, who were worlds removed from the liberalistic idea of racial equality. (Pg. 258, "Heil Lincoln!", Littell's Living Age, March-August 1936)

However ridiculous the interpretation of American history, the article was undoubtedly correct in documenting the aspirations of the leading American eugenicists. The correspondence between C.M. Goethe, Madison Grant, Harry H. Laughlin, Charles B. Davenport, and their colleagues consistently referred to "Nordic," "Aryan," and "Germanic" heritage of the "American race." [103] As we know, this point-of-view made its way into the 1924 Johnson-Reed Immigration Restriction Act, which was the direct product of Grant's, Goethe's, and Laughlin's work. Thus, any German that studied American immigration laws, namely the German eugenicists that actively corresponded with Goethe, Davenport, and Laughlin, would have had knowledge of the efforts within the United States to restrict the population to a "Nordic" stock.

---

[103] Impressions from reading Harry H. Laughlin's, Madison Grant's, C.M. Goethe's and Charles B. Davenport's personal correspondence held at the Harry H. Laughlin Papers in Truman Univ., and the papers of the Eugenics Records Office held at the Carnegie Institution of Washington, D.C. and the American Philosophical Society.

Of specific importance is the fact that Krieger's book also caught the attention of key policy-making bodies back in the United States. The Council of Foreign Relations reviewed Heinrich Krieger's 1936 book in "Foreign Affairs":

> The Nazis point to American racial discrimination in support of their laws against ethnic minorities. The present work is a description of the legal disabilities enforced against Negroes and Indians in the United States. ("Foreign Affairs", Council of Foreign Relations, July 1937)

Catching the attention of Foreign Affairs was no small accomplishment. Since its founding in 1922, Foreign Affairs has been the leading forum for serious discussion of American foreign policy and global affairs. It is published by the Council on Foreign Relations (CFR), a non-profit and nonpartisan membership organization dedicated to improving the understanding of US foreign policy and international affairs through the free exchange of ideas. It convenes meetings at which government officials, global leaders and prominent members of the foreign policy community discuss major international issues. Its think tank, the David Rockefeller Studies Program, is composed of about 50 adjunct and full-time scholars, as well as 10 in-resident recipients of year-long fellowships, who cover the major regions and significant issues shaping international agenda. These scholars contribute to the foreign policy debate by making recommendations to the presidential administration, testifying before Congress, serving as a resource to the diplomatic community, interacting with the media, authoring books, reports, articles, and op-eds on foreign policy issues.

If you are familiar with the history of eugenics, this David Rockefeller Studies Program raises eyebrows. The name Rockefeller keeps popping up whenever researching the topic of population control and eugenic organizations. In the 1920's Raymond B. Fosdick, an important official of the Rockefeller Foundation was a member of the American Eugenics Society Advisory council. Margaret Sanger's first birth control clinic, the Clinical Research Bureau (CRB), was started with the help of the Rockefellers in 1923. As this book documents, the all-important Eugenics Records Office in Cold Spring Harbor was also funded by Rockefeller.

Heinrich Krieger's 1936 book clearly raised eyebrows, and the unavoidable and uncomfortable relationship between German National Socialist eugenic policies and the substantial help Hitler's scientists and legislators received from individuals in the United States threatened to be a source of severe political embarrassment. The Rockefellers were at the same time funding the Kaiser-Wilhelm Institute in Berlin, the German counterpart to Cold Spring Harbor. The fact that the Council of Foreign Relations and its "Foreign Affairs" bi-monthly publication was also a Rockefeller creation evidence that this uncomfortable tangle had begun to be an issue for the high and mighty in the United States a full decade before the 1946 Nuremberg Doctors Trials. That the Rockefeller Standard Oil and chemical interests were also uncomfortably intertwined with Hitler's government and under investigation by the authorities suggests that care would have been taken to avoid another round of Congressional hearings and public scrutiny.

Shockwaves must have resonated through both the Rockefeller and Carnegie foundations, as one of the first answers to this growing concern over the obvious commonalities between American and German eugenics came from the Carnegie Foundation itself. What transpired next is telling of the heightened sensitivity to the "Nazi Connection." The Carnegie Foundation conducted a detailed audit of Laughlin's work in 1935:

> They described the records collected at the ERO as a "vast and inert accumulation," "unsatisfactory for the scientific study of human genetics" and judged the "system of recording . . . unsound." The auditors recommended a new direction for Laughlin's program to insure that it was "divorced from all forms of propaganda and the urging or sponsoring of programs for social reform or race betterment such as sterilization, birth-control, inculcation of race (sic) or national consciousness, restriction of immigration, etc." A change to the name of the Eugenical News was recommended to avoid the negative connotations of the word "eugenics," which the auditors suggested was "not a science." (Pgs. 1125-1143, "Pioneer's Big Lie", Paul Lombardo, Albany Law Review, Vol. 66. No. 4, Summer 2003)

Paul Lombardo further documents that A.V. Kidder chaired the Carnegie evaluation committee, and described Laughlin as having "a messiah attitude toward eugenics." Kidder corresponded with George Streeter of Johns Hopkins University, stating that Laughlin was more of a propagandist, and was out of place in a scientific institution. John C. Merriam, the head of the Carnegie Institution, accepted the committee's report and agreed with the premise that there needed to be a separation between "fundamental research and propaganda." L.C. Dunn, a prominent geneticist of the era, wrote to the Carnegie leadership after visiting Nazi Germany around this time, and his observations sealed Laughlin's fate:

> Eugenical research was not always activated by purely disinterested scientific motives. – Eugenics has come to mean an effort to foster a program of social improvement rather than an effort to discover facts. (Pgs. 1125-1143, "Pioneer's Big Lie", Paul Lombardo, Albany Law Review, Vol. 66. No. 4, Summer 2003)

More to the purposes of this book, Dunn expanded his comments to clarify the consequences of the commonality between German and American eugenics:

> I have just observed in Germany some of the consequences of reversing the order as between [social] program and discovery. The incomplete knowledge of today, much of it based on a theory of the state which has been influenced by the racial, class and religious prejudices of the group in power, has been embalmed in law . . . The genealogical [sic] record offices have become powerful agencies of the state, and medical judgments even when possible, appear to be subservient to political purposes. (Pgs. 1125-1143, "Pioneer's Big Lie", Paul Lombardo, Albany Law Review, Vol. 66. No. 4, Summer 2003)

L.C. Dunn depicted the clear and unmistakable parallels between the most virulent American eugenics propaganda and Nazi abuses in the name of science. [104] The revelation by Dunn documents the serious reservations, and likely evidence the intent to whitewash on the part of the Allied prosecution at the Nuremberg Doctors' Trial of any reference to the term "eugenics" by the high-profile individuals and institutions that had significant influence over the post-war tribunal. Posterity must also take note of the fact that Dunn's comments reveal an aspect of eugenics that is not sufficiently discussed by history books. Despite calling itself a "science," the allegedly respectable "scientists" of eugenics, such as Francis Galton and Julian Huxley, spent an inordinate amount of time mapping out proposals for legislative, legal and governmental initiatives, as opposed to spending this time on actual scientific experimentation. This book juxtaposes the fictional utopias of Edward Bellamy and H.G. Wells with the actual proposals by Harry H. Laughlin and Francis Galton precisely to demonstrate how there was hardly a difference between the proposals of fiction writers and that published by the alleged "scientists," with the most poignant juxtaposition being the one between Julian Huxley's "Eugenic Manifesto" and Aldous Huxley's "Brave New World." It becomes impossible to distinguish between H.G. Wells' fictional eugenic utopias from that of Harry H. Laughlin's proposal for a one-world government. This interplay between the fictional and utopian notions of Francis Galton's eugenics was pointed out early on by T.H. Huxley in his 1894 "Prolegomena." As T.H. Huxley explained in his 1894 work, the amount of control one needed to exert over a population for eugenic ends was that of a tyrannical overseer. Francis Galton himself was uncomfortable enough upon writing his "Kantsaywhere" utopian work that he asked that it never be published. Eugenic utopias are socialist and collectivist utopias as by necessity they are totalitarian states with power over the populace like a farmer enjoys over livestock. Anyone of sober mind understood this upon witnessing what was transpiring in Hitler's eugenic utopia, and this is what L.C. Dunn's letter made uncomfortably clear.

Laughlin was forced to defend the continuation of the eugenics work at the Cold Spring Harbor facilities. Laughlin answered the concerns at the Carnegie Foundation with his "Proposed Clinic of Human Heredity," addressed to Vannevar Bush. [105] C.M. Goethe stepped in to support Laughlin in a letter to James G. Eddy of the Carnegie Foundation in an October 27, 1937, letter. C.M. Goethe expressed concern that the Germans would steal the credit away from the American eugenicists, precisely the very juxtaposition that the Carnegie Foundation now sought to avoid:

> The Germans are forging far ahead of us in this matter of accumulated data. They say they have already 4 Nobel prizes to 1 of ours, population considered, and that if we do not accept their methods, they will run away from us with world leaders. (Item No.: 1035, "Eugenics Records Office Papers," Carnegie Inst. of Washington D.C. / See also Box: E-2-1:4, "Harry H. Laughlin Papers", Truman University Archives, Special Collections.)

---

[104] Pgs. 1125-1143, "Pioneer's Big Lie", Paul Lombardo, Albany Law Review, Vol. 66. No. 4, Summer 2003.
[105] Item Id.: 11710 / Box 5: Eugenics Records Office Papers, Carnegie Institution of Wash. D.C. / See also Box E-2-2:18, Harry Laughlin Papers, Truman University Archives, Special Collections.

Another Carnegie initiative is of critical importance to the understanding of the institutions distancing from its previous support for the eugenics movement. In May of 1934, the Carnegie Foundation appointed a committee made up of Abraham Myerson, M.D., James B. Ayer, M.D. Tracy J. Putnam, M.D., Clyde E. Keeler, ScD, and most notably Leo Alexander, M.D., the "expert" at the Nuremberg Doctors' Trial. The choice of Myerson and Alexander are revealing. As previously discussed, the parents of the young German woman he proposed to marry ultimately rejected him upon eugenic notions, and Alexander would also be kicked out of the institutions he helped build due to his Jewish religion. More to the point, Leo Alexander's career in eugenics had largely been funded by the Rockefeller Institution both before and after escaping Germany. The choice of Meyerson, by itself, reveals the intentions of the prestigious American Neurological Association. They were looking for a strong voice to create a gulf between the Association and the science of eugenics, and Meyerson filled that requirement. Abraham Meyerson openly attacked the leading proponents of eugenics, namely Harvard's Davenport and his minion Laughlin, as being "anti-democratic"; an accusation transparent in its juxtaposition to Hitler's dictatorship:

> Meyerson enjoyed attacking 'harebrained' eugenic ideas that called for the sterilization of all 'potential parents of socially inadequate offspring'. Future eugenicists, he argued, would need to be clairvoyants with supernatural powers to detect whether someone fulfilled the criteria. He felt that the proposal to sterilize people on the assumption that their future offspring might be socially inadequate was 'naïve beyond [the] ... powers of expression'. 'Imagine the graft, the blackmail and the generally muddled and corrupt social reactions involved in this proposal!', he told his audience. (Pg. 56, "Justice at Nuremberg: Leo Alexander and the Nazi Doctors' Trial", Ulf Schmidt, Palgrave UK, 2004)

The introduction of Hitler's compulsory sterilization law of January of 1934 gave enough people at the American Neurological Association reason to begin distancing themselves from previous eugenic beliefs, and that is why they looked to Meyerson and Alexander to investigate and report on the effectiveness of sterilization laws. It was Leo Alexander, feeling pronounced regrets for his support of eugenics as well, that contacted Meyerson to assist with the inquiry. [106] They set off to review and document the work of the international eugenics movement, and all the major publications it had produced. The resulting report would be the 1935 "Eugenical Sterilization," and it became known as one of the most sophisticated and comprehensive rebuttals of the claims made by the proponents of eugenics. The book conclusively demonstrated that "the concept of eugenics was riddled with methodological errors and it lacked scientific support from modern genetic studies." [107] The committee published a preliminary report, and Carnegie funded the publication of a book-length version. The introductory statement sets the tone:

> The most primitive form of sterilization is undoubtedly castration. The impulse

---

[106] Pg. 55 - "Justice at Nuremberg: Leo Alexander and the Nazi Doctors' Trial", Ulf Schmidt, Palgrave Macmillan UK, 2004.
[107] Pg. 57 – Ibid.

to inflict injury upon an enemy's genitalia as a measure of punishment and insult is a deeply rooted one in the human race, which finds expression at times among the most civilized modern nations, as well as among savages. ---- The suspicion of a sadistic motive must always arise when genitalectomy is advocated for any group of physically healthy people. . . (Intro, "Eugenic Sterilization: A Reorientation of the Problem", American Neurological Association, Committee for the Investigation of Eugenical Sterilization", Macmillan, 1936)

The observation was spot on: Emasculation is the type of sadistic control that those obsessed with power inflict on their subjects. Eugenic emasculation was certainly a political form of sadism. It should not be understood as a purely "scientific" affair. More to the point, the Carnegie book continues its introduction by pointing to the fact that eugenics has lagged behind the science of genetics, which began with Gregor Mendel's work:

> Many an eloquent voice has been raised against the pollution of the race which might be feared as a result. The term "eugenics" originated with Galton, who based his social doctrines upon what was then known of heredity, a field of study in which he was a pioneer. Enormous strides have since been made in the field of genetics. It may, however, be seriously questioned whether many of the eugenic proposals now current take into account the newer genetic data; and further, whether the data upon which some are based – derived from experiments upon plants and lower animals – are applicable also to man. (Pg. 2. "Eugenic Sterilization: A Reorientation of the Problem", American Neurological Association, Committee for the Investigation of Eugenical Sterilization", Macmillan, 1936)

"Eugenical Sterilization" aptly pointed to Francis Galton as the "father of eugenics." Speaking diplomatically, the Darwinists had pushed so hard to animalize humanity and remove any notion of differentiation between man and animal that his devoted followers, starting with Galton, had persisted along these lines. This notion began with the conversation between Galton and Darwin, where Darwin incorporated Galton's work into his "Descent of Man," and proposed that humanity may gain if its reproduction was tended to much like breeders control the breeding of livestock. However, between the publication of Darwin's "Descent of Man" and the 1930s, eugenics had done little to mature its empirical studies. It remained stuck in the comparative anthropology and phrenology of the 19th century. As such, the Carnegie book was right to criticize the gulf between Mendelian genetics and eugenics as the difference between a "hard" and a "soft" science:

> On the whole, eugenics receives scant support on any scientific basis from genetics. Genetics has largely concerned itself in the past twenty-five years with those experimental procedures by which, in lower animals especially, the genes have been discovered and their laws of appearance and combination have been formulated. (Pg. 69, "Eugenic Sterilization: A Reorientation of the Problem", American Neurological Association, Committee for the Investigation of Eugenical Sterilization", Macmillan, 1936)

The committee made it clear that, regardless of the claims of the eugenicists, the inability to clearly and scientifically define the characteristics of the allegedly hereditary phenomenon makes these phenomena impossible to study with the rigor which Mendelian science provides:

> It is true that many men have set up the hypothesis of Mendelian recessiveness of one type or another in the case of the conditions we are studying. But nothing like proof has been adduced. The leading geneticists, at least of America and England, have been very cautious in their pronunciamentos concerning eugenics, and it is apparent from their writings that they look with disfavor upon the sweeping statements made popularly and, to some extent, in the scientific literature concerning eugenic measures. (Pg. 70)

CONTINUES...

> ...we discuss the heredity of schizophrenia, manic-depressive psychosis, feeblemindedness, epilepsy, and crime, more or less as if these were definable entities, and thus that it is possible to study them statistically and scientifically. No psychiatrist of first rank believes this to be the case; for him the term dementia praecox, for example, represents the best we can do in the way of classifying what is obviously a group of conditions which is very likely of heterogeneous composition. (Pg. 81, Abraham Myerson, "Eugenic Sterilization: A Reorientation of the Problem", American Neurological Association, Committee for the Investigation of Eugenical Sterilization, Macmillan, 1936)

To illustrate, the committee called the eugenicists to task for their unscientific use of the term "Mendelian," claiming that their use of the term had been carelessly used for any and all "deviation from normality," and, more importantly, that Mendel's "precise method of studying heredity" has never been utilized in actual experimentation despite their use of the terminology. [108] Of note is that the committee treated the claims of the eugenicists as one monolithic international movement, as this is how the movement presented itself to the world, as well as how it operated through the various international eugenic organizations it convened:

> Such men as Rüdin, and Whitney, stress the fact that insanity is increasing at a terrific rate and imply quite definitely that the biological unfitness is thus threatening two swamp the race. Joseph Mayer quotes this change in the statistics of the cultural countries as alarming. The writings of Laughlin, Baur, Fischer, Lenz, Mjoen and, practically speaking, all the important books echo these statements and stress eugenic measures as the only possible protection society has against further deterioration. (Pg. 25, Abraham Myerson, "Eugenic Sterilization: A Reorientation of the Problem", American Neurological Association, Committee for the Investigation of Eugenical Sterilization", Macmillan, 1936)

---

[108] Pg. 101 - "Eugenic Sterilization: A Reorientation of the Problem", Abraham Myerson, American Neurological Association, Committee for the Investigation of Eugenical Sterilization", Macmillan, 1936.

Of importance is that the committee recognized that the eugenic measures being implemented by Hitler's government predated Hitler by various decades, and furthermore, that these laws followed the legislative recommendations of the prominent international eugenicists of the time:

> It is fair to state that it is not a product of the Hitler regime, in that its main tenets were proposed and considered several years before the Nazi regime took possession of Germany. – It will be seen that this law is very precise and, as appears later, conforms closely with the present knowledge of medical eugenics. (Pg. 22, "Eugenic Sterilization: A Reorientation of the Problem", American Neurological Association, Committee for the Investigation of Eugenical Sterilization", Macmillan, 1936)

"Eugenic Sterilization" reminds us that this group was claiming that cases of degeneracy had increased as much as 400 percent in the United States alone. It is important to remember that these were the claims made in the infamous propaganda films used by the Third Reich and that these films, namely *Erbkrank,* were distributed in the United States by those American eugenicists that kept close ties with their German counterparts. The claims made by the Germans explicitly cited their American counterparts and vice versa. Each side pointed across the ocean to leverage the reputations of their respective institutions to bolster their claims, and certainly brandishing names like Harvard, Darwin, Galton, Princeton, Stanford, and Kaiser Wilhelm Institute helped bolster the credibility of the eugenicists on either side of the borders.

The Carnegie book continues with an analysis of the various claims of the eugenic movement on a case by case basis. The committee offers is its scientific dissection of the various works, illuminating just how deficient the studies were from the perspective of rigorous and empirical science. One of their most important observations was to deflate the claims made by the genealogical studies of the various "cacogenic" families, such as the Jukes, the Nams, and the dozens of other allegedly scientific studies on heredity conducted by various eugenicists. The committee explains that for the studies to arrive at scientifically sound empirical data, the studies would have to include samples upwards of 15 million to 25 million individuals, as opposed to the paltry thousands of these infamous studies. The committee goes into detail and further explains the deficiency of the staff utilized to conduct these studies, the lack of trustworthy data, and the amount of data arrived at by assumption, prejudice, and deduction as opposed to empirical observation.

Interestingly enough, the scientists in this committee also documented where the opposition to the eugenics movement came from and singled out the Catholic Church as one of the "leading forces" offering resistance to the movement. It quoted the Pope's encyclical at length:

> Finally, that pernicious practice must be condemned which closely touches upon the natural right of man to enter matrimony but affects also in a real way the welfare of the offspring. For there are some who over-solicitous for the cause of

eugenics, not only give salutary counsel for more certainly procuring the strength and health of the future child – which, indeed, is not contrary to right reason – but put eugenics before aims of a higher order, and by public authority wish to prevent from marrying all those whom, even though naturally fit for marriage, they consider, according to the norms and conjectures of their investigations, would, through hereditary transmission, bring forth defective offspring. And more, they wish to legislate to deprive these of that natural faculty by medical action despite their unwillingness; and this they do not propose as an infliction of grave punishment under the authority of the state for a crime committed, nor to prevent future crimes by guilty persons, but against every right and good they wish the civil authority to arrogate to itself a power over a faculty which it never had and can never legitimately possess. (Pgs. 60-61, "Eugenic Sterilization: A Reorientation of the Problem", American Neurological Association, Committee for the Investigation of Eugenical Sterilization", Macmillan, 1936)

Consider the above quote; this extract from the proclamations of the Roman Catholic Pope hardly reads like liturgy or appeals to a religious sensibility, but rather reads like the declarations of "inalienable rights" proclaimed by the Founding Fathers of the American Revolution. The citation continued along this secular tone:
Public magistrates have no direct power over the bodies of their subjects; therefore, where no crime has taken place and there is no cause present for grave punishment, they can never directly harm, or tamper with the integrity of the body, either for the reasons of eugenics or for any other reason. (Pg. 61, "Eugenic Sterilization: A Reorientation of the Problem", American Neurological Association, Committee for the Investigation of Eugenical Sterilization", Macmillan, 1936)

For the purposes of this book it is important to point out that the committee also referred to the dangers of establishing a tyrannical utopia, as eugenics was inevitably a "social religion" as was intended by Francis Galton himself. The committee quoted the warnings of Charles A. Ellwood:
It is a counsel of perfection, which modern science has given us in the doctrines of eugenics; but like all such counsels it is socially valuable and is obviously closely allied with idealistic social religion. If eugenics were ever made the basis of a code of minute legislative prescriptions regarding marriage and reproduction, doubtless it would become an **intolerable tyranny**. (emphasis mine, Pg. 64, "Eugenic Sterilization: A Reorientation of the Problem", American Neurological Association, Committee for the Investigation of Eugenical Sterilization", Macmillan, 1936)

The above observation turned out to be prophetic. Eugenics was applied at a "minute legislative" level by Hitler's Third Reich, and as history evidences, the effect was an "intolerable tyranny." The committee, funded by the Carnegie Foundation, concluded its study by recommending a retreat from eugenic sterilization. The committee was clear in its discomfort with the impending doom of any governmental policy that implemented the recommendations of the international eugenics movement, as the Third Reich had already begun to do at this point in history. The book anticipated the problem posed by the commonalities between American eugenics and the policies of Hitler's government. The study is clearly one of the various steps the Carnegie Institution took to distance itself from the Third Reich.

For the purposes of this book, it is crucial to note that the top consultants at the Carnegie institution proposed that any relationship with the term "eugenics" be dropped, that its research facilities be closed, and that the names of publications be changed as damage control. In retrospect, these were the first recommendations that American institutions cease and desist from any mention of "eugenics," as it would inevitably and forever connect them to Hitler's henchmen. The closing of the Eugenics Records Office at Cold Spring Harbor, the forced retirement of Laughlin, and the publication and commissioning of studies retreating from the work the Carnegie Foundation had funded for decades prior, evidence the state of mind and a palpable sense of impending doom by these prestigious American institutions.

In hindsight, one could question why the Carnegie institution confined its reactions to the publishing of a book, which would mostly be read only by the scientific insiders. This was their *modus operandi*, and after all, up until the early 20th century, eugenics existed only in the realm of ideas. But alas, the ideas were already being applied in day to day reality. The tone of the Carnegie funded book is forceful as if they were desperately trying to close Pandora's Box. The Carnegie funded group of experts seemed to want to squash the ill-conceived idea by claiming the high ground in the battleground of ideas. However, as history evidences, the effort was too little and way too late to combat eugenics as still existing only in the realm of the theoretical. By this point, eugenics had been enshrined as law and put into day-to-day practice. More importantly, it had been introduced into the mind of Adolf Hitler by the eugenicists who saw in Hitler a man with the will to create the eugenic utopia of their dreams. By the time the book was published, the time to intellectually quash the eugenics movement had long since passed.

Unfortunately, the story neither begins nor ends with providing proof that the Allied prosecution strategy at Nuremberg was intended to whitewash the complicity of American and British science. As of the writing of this book, the US Supreme Court precedent still sanctions the eugenic sterilization that the Carnegie study recommended be abandoned. Hitler is long gone, but much of the eugenic legal precedent remains in place at a time when the American public contemplates handing the US government power over all medical considerations through a "nationalized" health care initiative. This is the danger created by the whitewashing of science's complicity in the crimes of The Holocaust. The public in general attributes The Holocaust to the irrational impulses of racism, and is ill-informed about the very rational, calculating, systematic, and scientific aspect of the crimes. The public in general remains oblivious to the key role that otherwise trusted institutions such as Harvard, Stanford, Yale, and Johns Hopkins played in creating the eugenic measures the Carnegie study recommended be abandoned.

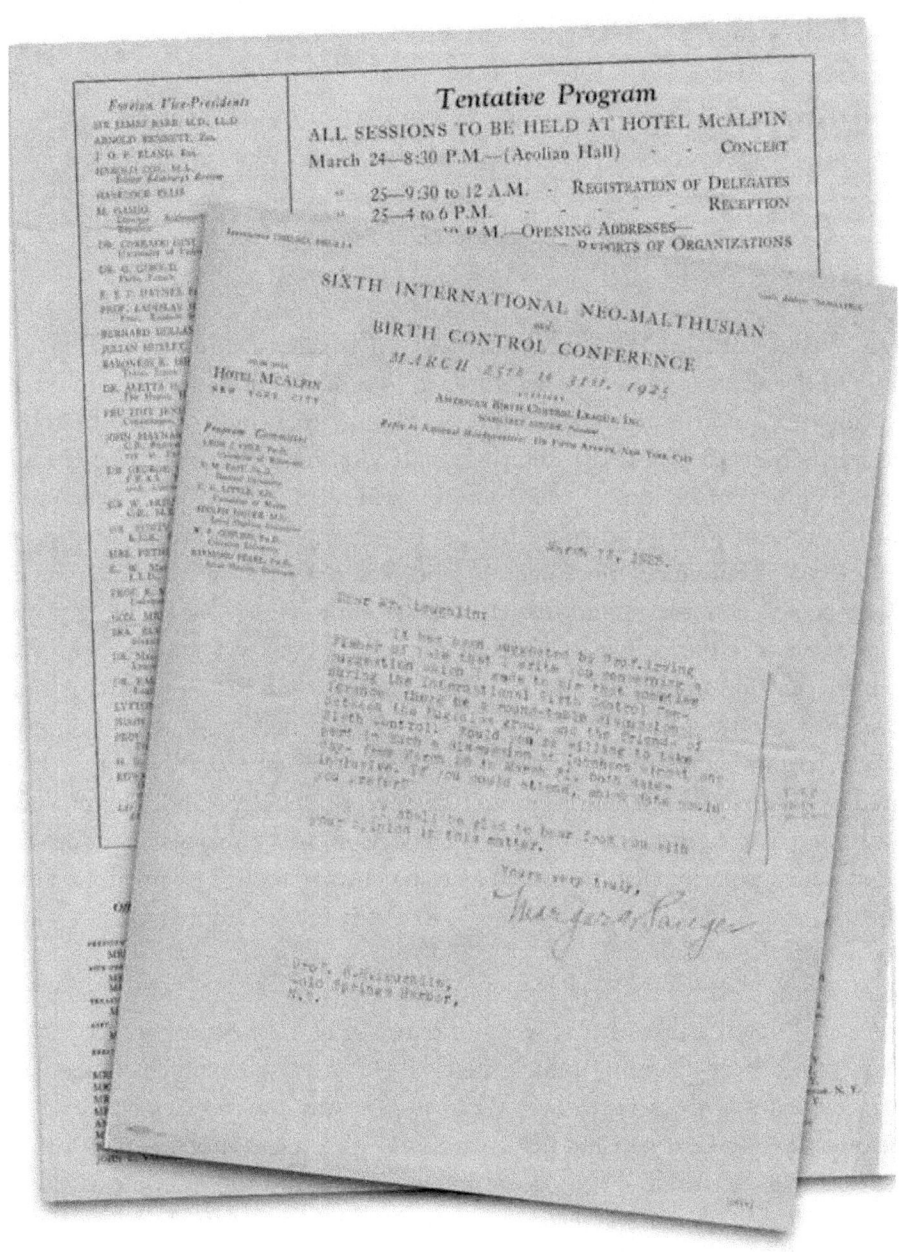

FIGURE 4: CORRESPONDENCE FROM MARGARET SANGER TO HARRY H. LAUGHLIN IN PREPARATION FOR THE NEO-MALTHUSIAN BIRTH CONTROL CONFERENCE, WHICH WOULD INCLUDE JULIAN HUXLEY, JOHN MAYNARD KEYNES, HAVELOCK ELLIS, AND OTHER PROMINENT EUGENICISTS. (HEREIN PUBLISHED AND PRINTED FOR THE FIRST TIME WITH PERMISSION OF THE SPECIAL COLLECTIONS DEPARTMENT AT TRUMAN UNIVERSITY — BOX E-1-1:1- HARRY H. LAUGHLIN PAPERS)

Chap. 3: 1935 to 1931

EUROPEAN FRONT: THE SOVIET UNION JOINS THE LEAGUE OF NATIONS. THE CREDITANSTALT, AUSTRIA'S LARGEST BANK, GOES BANKRUPT, BEGINNING THE BANKING COLLAPSE IN CENTRAL EUROPE. • **AMERICAN FRONT:** UNITED STATES PRESIDENT FRANKLIN ROOSEVELT SIGNS THE SOCIAL SECURITY ACT INTO LAW. THE 21ST AMENDMENT TO THE US CONSTITUTION IS PASSED, REPEALING PROHIBITION. THE DOW JONES INDUSTRIAL AVERAGE REACHES ITS LOWEST LEVEL OF THE GREAT DEPRESSION, BOTTOMING OUT AT 41.22. • **SCIENCE & TECHNOLOGY:** AMELIA EARHART BECOMES THE FIRST PERSON TO FLY SOLO FROM HAWAII TO CALIFORNIA. – HOWARD HUGHES, FLYING THE HUGHES H-1 RACER, SETS AN AIRSPEED RECORD OF 352 MPH (566 KM/H). – US PRESIDENT FRANKLIN D. ROOSEVELT DEDICATES HOOVER DAM. – LEÓ SZILÁRD CONCEIVES THE IDEA OF THE NUCLEAR CHAIN REACTION. – ALBERT EINSTEIN ARRIVES IN THE UNITED STATES. THOMAS EDISON SUBMITS HIS LAST PATENT APPLICATION. GEORGE EASTMAN, FOUNDER OF KODAK, COMMITS SUICIDE. • **LIFE:** JOHN DILLINGER ESCAPES FROM JAIL IN CROWN POINT, INDIANA, USING A WOODEN PISTOL. ALCATRAZ BECOMES A PRISON. EUGENE CERNAN, AMERICAN ASTRONAUT IS BORN. CHARLES MANSON, AMERICAN CRIMINAL IS BORN. – TARZAN THE APE MAN OPENS IN MOVIE THEATERS. THE EMPIRE STATE BUILDING IS COMPLETED. – AL CAPONE IS SENTENCED TO 11 YEARS IN PRISON. – RELEASE OF FRANKENSTEIN. – MIKHAIL GORBACHEV IS BORN•

Sec. I - EDWARD BELLAMY, "THE GREAT AMERICAN PROPHET":

Adolf Hitler was not always reviled. In fact, at first, Adolf Hitler was admired by many Americans. Hitler exemplified the world-wide movement to find a "third way" between the extremes of International Communism and *laissez-faire* democracy. Significant portions of humanity was still reeling from World War I and the Great Depression. To this generation, the surrendering of national autonomy to an International Communist movement or the return to the lack of control in *laissez-faire* socio-economic policy were equally undesirable. Many movements sprung up from this desire for a "third way," and Hitler's version of National Socialism was but one among Fabian Socialism, Fascism, and Progressivism. All of them combined a national pride with the belief that a centrally planned economy was the way to prevent a repeat of the recurring boom and bust cycle that had culminated in the Great Depression. The recurring economic depressions along with the radical effects of industrialization and urbanization, had on society produced a long line of social experiments that aimed at restructuring society to ameliorate the onslaught of rapid and drastic changes. Governments attempted "third-way" solutions around the world.

For Americans, the most recognizable of these efforts was President Franklin D. Roosevelt's "New Deal" policies, which attempted to fold American economic activity under a central-planning body run by the Federal government. President Roosevelt believed that the severity of the Depression was due to excessive business competition that lowered wages and prices, and his "New Deal" policies were based upon the idea that a centrally-planned economy would avoid these problems. New Deal economists argued that cut-throat competition had hurt many businesses and that with prices having fallen 20 percent, "deflation" exacerbated the burden of debt and would delay recovery. The supposed remedy was the NIRA and the WPA, which included centrally planned cooperation with big business to reduce the perceived harmful competition. The measures sought to raise prices of consumer goods at the same time as giving more bargaining power for unions. At the center of the NIRA was the National Recovery Administration (NRA), which imposed a stopgap "blanket code" on every business in the nation.

To mobilize political support for the NRA, the Roosevelt administration launched the "NRA Blue Eagle" campaign to boost what he called "industrial self-government." This was propaganda conscripting the masses in the collectivized efforts of the central planning visionaries. The NRA brought together leaders in each industry to design specific sets of codes and regulations for each respective industry. The most important provision to the codes and regulations were anti-deflationary regulations that prohibited companies from competing by lowering prices or wages, and agreements on maintaining employment and production. Hugh Samuel Johnson, the head of the NRA warned: "May God have mercy on the man or group of men who attempt to trifle with this bird." He continued his dire warning by framing the "New Deal" and the "Blue Eagle" in the nationalistic and socialist terminology:

> Those who are not with us are against us, and the way to show that you are a part of this great army of the New Deal is to insist on this symbol of solidarity ---- This campaign is a frank dependence on the power and the willingness of the American people to act together as one person in an hour of great danger. (Pg. 114, "The Coming of the New Deal, 1933-1935", Arthur Meier Schlesinger, Houghton Mifflin Harcourt, 2003)

The head of the NRA persisted along the same collectivist terms which would become typical of "third-way" proposals around the globe, some of which were called "Fascism," others which were called "Progressivism," but all which adopted the views of the vastly famous utopian socialist, Edward Bellamy. Bellamy had written his internationally renowned book "Looking Backward: 2000-1887" which depicted a centrally-planned eugenic utopia in which all citizens were part of an "industrial army." The masterminds behind Roosevelt's "New Deal" were enamored with Bellamy's vision, and like many other American Progressives, desired that Bellamy's vision be translated into reality:

> There is no choice presented to American business between intelligently planned and uncontrolled industrial operations and a return to the gold-plated anarchy that masqueraded as "rugged individualism" ... Unless industry is sufficiently socialized by its private owners and managers so that great essential industries are operated under public obligation appropriate to the public interest in them, the advance of political control over private industry is inevitable. (Pgs. 114-115, "The Coming of the New Deal, 1933-1935", Arthur Meier Schlesinger, Houghton Mifflin Harcourt, 2003)

Franklin D. Roosevelt's "New Deal" policies, namely that of the Tennessee Valley Authority (TVA), were directly credited to Edward Bellamy by Roosevelt's own "brain trust." The public school system in the United States along with the Pledge of Allegiance that school children recite every morning were the creations of Edward and Francis Bellamy. Such a contribution to history should have gained Edward Bellamy recognition as one of the single most influential individuals in United States and world history. Many Americans will recognize the names of Eugene V. Debbs, John Dewey, and others from the heyday of popular socialism in turn-of-the-century United States. Yet, even the most informed segments of the public have never heard of Bellamy. He has been conveniently, and likely intentionally erased from the public conscience as Bellamy was the first to marry the terms "national" and "socialism." The uncomfortable parallels between Bellamy's "socialistic" form of "nationalism" and Adolf Hitler's "National Socialist" policies go much further than a similarity in names, and this uncomfortable relationship is likely the cause for the fact that Bellamy does not get the credit he deserves for being the father of Progressivism, Fascism, and Fabian Socialism as well. Yet, prior to World War II and The Holocaust, Edward Bellamy's place in history was undisputed and unquestioned:

> The worth of Bellamy's books in effecting a translation of the ideas of democracy into economic terms is incalculable. What 'Uncle Tom's Cabin' was to the anti-slavery movement, Bellamy's books may well be to the shaping of popular opinion for a new social order. (Pg. 106, "The Later Works of John Dewey, 1925-1953: Essays, Reviews, Miscellany, and a Common Faith 1933-1934", SIU Press, 2008 - first published in Common Sense, April 1934)

Nor can Bellamy's international importance during the era be questioned. Arthur Kelly, author of the 1947 book, "The Descent of Darwin," studied the sociological surveys, statistical reports, and questionnaires filled out by German factory workers taking evening courses to determine what the reading habits were by this group targeted by socialist propaganda during the turn-of-the-century. The study placed Bellamy at the top along with Darwin and Zola. [109] Arthur Kelly further documents that even though these German workers and producers were the target of European socialist ideologies: "Worker's memoirs rarely mention Marx or the possibility of revolution; more frequently they pay tribute to Bellamy's influence." [110] In fact, it is truly difficult to overstate the influence of Edward Bellamy's 1888 book, "Looking Backward" as it is to accept that a book of such influence is now largely forgotten. The once ubiquitous "Looking Backward" has mostly disappeared from the American zeitgeist. Yet, as late as 1936, three years into Hitler's reign of power and a decade following "Mein Kampf," Edward Bellamy's followers were still flaunting his "third-way" marriage of "nationalism" and "socialism" as a desirable political direction.

Edward Bellamy had started a world-wide movement of "Nationalist" clubs all dedicated to the "nationalization" of major industry and the "solidarity" of a collectivized society. In 1888, Cyrus Field Willard, a Boston newspaperman, proposed to Bellamy "that it would be a good idea to organize an association to spread the ideas contained in your book." [111] Bellamy responded to Willard on Independence Day in 1888 with the proposal to promote national socialism in "Nationalist Clubs." More than 165 "Bellamy" or "Nationalist" clubs sprouted up. They were endorsed by both the Knights of Labor, Industrial Workers of the World

---

[109] Pg. 129, "The Descent of Darwin: The Popularization of Darwinism in Germany, 1860-1914", UNC, 1947.
[110] Pg. 137 – Ibid.
[111] historycooperative.org – "Looking Backward at Edward Bellamy's Influence in Oregon, 1888–1936", James J. Kopp, History Cooperative, No date given. – Accessed Sept. 13, 2019.

and the American Federation of Labor. The main purpose of the clubs was to create and promote the practical realization of Bellamy's utopian vision. The creation of the "Nationalist Clubs" was followed by an effort to create the Nationalist Party and work within the People's Party and the Populist Party. Members became involved with other reform political groups and the Nationalists were represented at the 1891 Populist Party convention.

Edward Bellamy's fame and influence were largely crafted by the dedication his family had for "third way" utopian vision. Frederick Bellamy, Charles Bellamy, and Edward Bellamy were brothers who all shared a passion for "socialism," "nationalism," "solidarity" and "the brotherhood of man." All of them contributed volumes of text in support of their political theories, and the family kept the flame alive through the hundreds of "Nationalist" clubs that popped up all around the world. Bellamy's daughter, Marion, was still lecturing to "Nationalist" clubs as late as 1936. Consider the context; political elite in 1936, three years into Hitler's reign, propagandizing the ideas of "nationalism" and "socialism" with not just impunity, but the adulation of the audience. The reason Marion Bellamy could stand proud before a crowd and lecture about "nationalist" and "socialist" political programs was because in 1936 Theodore Roosevelt's and Franklin D. Roosevelt's Progressivism was largely based upon it:

> It seems to be pretty well agreed upon by thoughtful men and women the world over that the change from this initial stage of exploitation to one of cooperation is inevitable if we are to survive as a nation. The question which faces us is – how shall such a change be effected? Must it be accomplished by force, disruption, and chaos or can we bring it about by gradual, wisely ordered progression? (Pg. 4, "Edward Bellamy Today: A Lecture", Peerage Press, 1936)

Marion Bellamy outlined in terminology still used by 21st century Progressives, that society must guaranty "economic equality" from the "cradle to the grave." [112] She recognized that Americans had enjoyed a "political equality" but interpreted the founding documents as guaranteeing beyond mere "opportunity" and ensuring actual results. To accomplish this, the Bellamys proposed that society be organized scientifically, and the reference to "Fordism" and "Taylorism" was overt, just as it was in Hitler's version of "national socialism." Most importantly, it justified these measures with the rhetoric of class warfare, guaranteeing "economic equality" as the cornerstone of the cooperative measures:

> ...to rear our new world, of which economic equality will be the corner stone. This is a plan which guarantees to every citizen his maintenance, liberty and security on a basis of economic equality corresponding to an supplementing his political equality. (Pg. 8, "Edward Bellamy Today: A Lecture", Peerage Press, 1936)

Today, it has become taboo to insinuate that Franklin Delano Roosevelt's "New Deal" policies were influenced by the same type of "third-way" thinking that the

---

[112] Pg. 9 - "Edward Bellamy Today: A Lecture", Marion Bellamy, Peerage Press, 1936.

German "National Socialists" of the time were practicing under Adolf Hitler. Yet, the F.D.R. administration certainly felt a debt to the Bellamy family. Bellamy's son, Paul, had ridden his father's tailcoats to some of the most influential positions in the United States. Paul ultimately became editor-in-chief of the Cleveland Plain-Dealer, president of the American Society of Newspaper Editors in 1933, and subsequently the director of the Associated Press for 18 years. He was a Democrat and knew President Franklin D. Roosevelt personally. More specifically, Paul Bellamy was one of the various members of Roosevelt's staff which openly cited Edward Bellamy as their inspiration for the radical policies the administration enacted. Case in point, Paul helped write the National Recovery Administration (NRA) code for newspapers even though many rightfully saw the National Industrial Recovery Act (NIRA) code as an attempt to destroy freedom of the press. In 1943 Paul Bellamy saw the light and became critical of the Roosevelt administration's excessive wartime censorship. The Democratic Plain Dealer jumped ship and endorsed Wendell Willkie in 1940 under Paul's leadership. Nonetheless, Roosevelt made Bellamy head of a wartime committee formulating policies governing occupational draft deferments for federal employees.

Paul Bellamy was not the only direct link between the "New Deal" and Edward Bellamy's version of "nationalism" and "socialism." Arthur Ernest Morgan was a civil engineer, US administrator, and educator. Morgan directed the building of dams and nationalized energy as president of Roosevelt's Tennessee Valley Authority. [113] Morgan advanced a wide variety of cooperative enterprises and cottage industries and created a series of planned towns that followed the English garden city model for the TVA. Heavily influenced by Edward Bellamy's "Looking Backwards," Morgan gained a reputation as a utopian dreamer. Inspired by the Bellamy brother's activism in progressive education, he sent his kids to pioneering boarding schools, and later he established his own experimental schools. Morgan became the first president of The Association for the Advancement of Progressive Education, later renamed in 1931 as Progressive Education Association (PEA). Morgan's community organizing continued in the postwar period. He founded the Celo Community, which still exists today. Although Celo does not require members to accept any religious creed or ideology, it is built on cooperation between members and care for the natural environment.

To further underscore Morgan's debt to Bellamy, it is important to note that Arthur E. Morgan was also an Edward Bellamy biographer. Arthur E. Morgan's 1944 book titled "Edward Bellamy" is a work of "hero study." [114] Here, Morgan detailed the fact that the "New Deal" was directly inspired by Edward Bellamy's brand of "national socialism." Morgan himself clarified that some of the men directly responsible for New Deal legislation were a "direct line of descent from the First National Club of Boston, or received their first social stimulus from Looking

---

[113] Pgs. 162-165 - "The Quest for Utopia in 20 Century America. Volume I: 1900-1960", Timothy Miller, Syracuse Univ. Press, 1998.
[114] "Great Reformers: Edward Bellamy", MANAS, Vol. II, No. 33, Aug. 17, 1949.

Backward." [115] The parallels in policy are certainly relevant. Like its Nazi counterpart, the NRA was famous for its overwhelming bureaucracy. It was estimated that between 4,000 and 5,000 business practices were prohibited by NRA orders, all of which carried the force of law. The NRA included a multitude of regulations imposing the pricing and production standards for all sorts of goods and services. The stringent regulations on what Americans deemed a free market inevitably led to violations of the NRA codes. Individuals were arrested for non-compliance. Jack Madid, a New Jersey tailor was arrested, convicted, and jailed for committing the crime of pressing a suit for 35 rather than NRA-required 40 cents. In hindsight, the consequences of such a micro-managed society should have been predictable:

> The NRA was discovering it could not enforce its rules. Black markets grew up. **Only the most violent police methods could procure enforcement.** In Sidney Hillman's garment industry the code authority employed enforcement police. They roamed through the garment district like storm troopers. They could enter a man's factory, send him out, line up his employees, subject them to minute interrogation, take over his books on the instant. Night work was forbidden. Flying squadrons of these private coat-and-suit police went through the district at night, battering down doors with axes looking for men who were committing the crime of sewing together a pair of pants at night. But without these harsh methods many code authorities said there could be no compliance because the public was not back of it. (emphasis mine, Pg. 45, "The Roosevelt Myth", John T. Flynn, Devin-Adair Company, 1944)

The centralized micro-management of the daily lives and transactions of individual citizens was counter to the promises of the founding documents of the American nation, and bitter opposition came from all sides. Even the radical Populist governor of Louisiana, Huey Long, was quoted as saying: "I raise my hand in reverence to the Supreme Court that saved this nation from fascism." [116] Clarence Darrow, someone who can hardly be considered a conservative icon, also attacked the New Deal:

> I see today that the spirit of human freedom has vanished from the peoples of this world especially from America! We have forgotten it. We care nothing about. If we can make money by compelling people to do certain things by law, or if some fool reformers think they can save the souls of men by passing laws, we say: let them do it. We would not fight for liberty today; we have forgotten it. (Originally From: Pg. 24 – "The Darrow-Kennedy Debate", Garrick Theater, Maclaskey & Maclaskey Court Reporters, John F. Higgins Printers, Chicago, IL, March 23, 1919 – See Also: encyclopedia.com, video clip of later interview, Clarence Darrow, 1933 – See Also: BBC Motion Gallery, video clip)

Darrow's vocal opposition caught the ear of President Roosevelt. On March 7,

---

[115] "Great Reformers: Edward Bellamy", MANAS, Vol. II, No. 33, Aug. 17, 1949.
[116] Pg. 284 - "The Politics of Upheaval: 1935-1936, the Age of Roosevelt", Arthur Meier Schlesinger, Jr., Volume III, Houghton Mifflin Books, 2003.

1934, Roosevelt issued an executive order creating a National Recovery Review Board to investigate the widely reported ill-effects of the codes on small business and labor unions. Clearly, neither Clarence Darrow nor Huey Long can be considered pro-business conservatives, and their opposition exemplifies just how intrusive a centrally planned economy was on the individual lives of ordinary people, and it was the intrusion on ordinary people that ultimately brought down Roosevelt's attempt at centrally-planned socio-economic solidarity.

On May 27, 1935, the NRA was found to be unconstitutional by a unanimous decision of the US Supreme Court in the case of <u>Schechter Poultry Corp. v. United States</u>, 295 US 495 (1935). The decision invalidated regulations of the poultry industry according to the non-delegation doctrine and deemed an invalid use of Congress' power under the commerce clause. The regulations at issue in this landmark Supreme Court case were the price and wage-fixing provisions of the NRA, as well as requirements regarding the sale of whole chickens, including unhealthy ones. The Schechter brothers were Jewish immigrants running a kosher poultry business in Brooklyn, New York. The US Government had thrown down a jaw-dropping 60 charges against Schechter Poultry, which were reduced to 18 charges plus charges of conspiracy by the time the case was appealed to the U. S. Supreme Court. This is where the parallels between the Third Reich, Edward Bellamy's "nationalism," and President Roosevelt's New Deal policies become clear. The Third Reich set out to implement a law for every activity under the sun, injecting itself between individuals in their daily transactions. Of course, in order to "centrally plan" an economy, all aspects of the economy had to be regulated, and this was at the crux of the <u>Schechter Poultry Corp. v. United States</u>, 295 US 495 (1935). A New Deal version of David v. Goliath ensued:

> ... they had neither a legal education nor corporate money behind them. Unlike Insull, they were unknown and unable to purchase city officials. Unlike the wealthy East Siders of their city, they had no social status to fall back on. Unlike their opponents in the Justice Department, the Schecters were inconsistent, almost comically ambivalent, about their case. These were not board members, nor stock market players, but rather slaughterhouse men who served a market as humble as they were. Their English was laughable. (Pgs. 214-215, "The Forgotten Man: A New History of the Great Depression", Amity Shlaes, Harper Collins, 2007)

Amity Shlaes clarifies that "Schechter" translates to "ritual butcher" in Yiddish, as it is derived from the Hebrew word for "*schochet*." Both terms were used to describe those qualified to perform ritual slaughter of the animals as required under Jewish dietary law. In fact, David, the father of the three brothers qualified his profession as "Rabbi" because he was the head of a religious household and business. It was clear from the onset that the value in their product was that it conformed to Jewish dietary law, and thus was of religious importance to the brothers and their customers. If the Schechters would have had access to a savvy Civil Rights attorney, then they would have had a solid First Amendment case against the New Deal policies that intruded not just in their economic but in the religious lives of the community they catered to. The Schechter case is a prime example of how Progressives and Fabians fundamentally misunderstand capitalism as they do not understand that trade, more often than not, results from individual expression and personal prerogative. Curtailing and controlling trade amongst individuals inevitably tramples on their fundamental rights, namely their rights to express themselves or practice their beliefs. All of this illustrates that governments based on Edward Bellamy's "centrally planned" utopia inevitably intrude, not just into the dealings of the big industrialists, but into the details of the daily lives of everyone. The Schechter brothers were about as far from robber barons as you can get, and if you asked Rabbi David Schechter, he would probably say their Jewish faith superseded their need to turn a profit.

In a similar fashion, Hitler's policy regulated even when choir boys could perform at church, all in the name of the economic necessity of the trade unions that represented performing artists. Hitler, of course, would have objected to the Schechters because their "Jewishness" was regarded as an intrusion on German culture. This only serves to underscore the ridiculousness of the "collectivist" mindset and how injurious it is at the street level of society. The only way Hitler could even begin to make such a claim is by first subrogating the rights of the individual to that of the society, as had American eugenicists like Harry H. Laughlin done much prior to Hitler in proposing "protective" immigration policies banning races deemed undesirable to the greater society.

Chief Justice Hughes wrote for a unanimous Court in invalidating the industrial "codes of fair competition." The Court held that the codes violated the constitutional separation of powers as an impermissible delegation of legislative power to the Executive Branch. Justice Cardozo's concurred. Cardozo felt that in this case, Schechter was simply too small a player to be relevant to interstate commerce. From the US Supreme Court's published opinion:

> The further point is urged that the national crisis demanded a broad and intensive cooperative effort by those engaged in trade and industry, and that this necessary cooperation was sought to be fostered by permitting them to initiate the adoption of codes. But the statutory plan is not simply one for voluntary effort. It does not seek merely to endow voluntary trade or industrial associations or groups with privileges or immunities. It involves the coercive exercise of the law-making power. The codes of fair competition which the statute attempts to authorize are codes of laws. If valid, they place all persons within their reach under the obligation of positive law, binding equally those who assent and those who do not assent. Violations of the provisions of the codes are punishable as crimes.

CONTINUES...

If the codes have standing as penal statutes, this must be due to the effect of the executive action. But Congress cannot delegate legislative power to the President to exercise an unfettered discretion to make whatever laws he thinks may be needed or advisable for the rehabilitation and expansion of trade or industry. Schechter Poultry Corp. v. United States, 295 US 495 (1935)

The Supreme Court was telling President Roosevelt that he could not unite the powers of the Executive branch with the powers of the Legislative branch. To compare by juxtaposition, the President was forbidden to amass the powers vested in the "chancellorship" and "presidency" as Adolf Hitler had done, precisely to prevent what Adolf Hitler was in the process accomplishing in Germany. James Madison explained in Federalist No. 47 that power amassed in the "same hands" was a clear and present danger to humanity: "The accumulation of all power, legislative, executive, and judiciary, in the same hands, whether of one, a few, or many, and whether hereditary, self-appointed, or elective, may justly be pronounced the very definition of tyranny." Justice Brandeis was more obtuse and direct. He sent a clear message to President Roosevelt through Harry Hopkins, one of the President's closest advisors and an author of the New Deal policies. An April 3, 1939 entry in "Harry Hopkins Papers" quotes Justice Brandeis:

> This is the end of this business of centralization, and I want you to go back and tell the president that we're not going to let this government centralize everything. (The Never-Ending "Business of Centralization", Reason.org, Dec. 22, 2010)

Roosevelt, in all his capacity for humility and deference to the wisdom of the Founding Fathers, then drafted a response to Justice Brandeis. This was the infamous Judicial Procedures Reform Bill of 1937, more commonly referred to as the court-packing plan, which sought to forcibly infuse the Supreme Court with Justices with opinions sympathetic to President Roosevelt by increasing the number of justices. This scheme, too, was ultimately rejected by the population at large as well. Comically enough, Adolf Hitler made it a point to applaud President Roosevelt's overt circumventing of constitutional and republican forms of government. Hitler explained his version of "centralization" in a July 10, 1933 interview with The New York Times correspondent Anne O'Hare McCormick,:

> Parties were in the way of such a programme. They have disappeared. Parliament has obstructed my reforms. It has disappeared also. In Germany and elsewhere parliaments have proved themselves utterly incapable of dealing with the preposterous developments of the last ten years. ---- I have sympathy with President Roosevelt because he marches straight to his objective over Congress, over lobbies, over stubborn bureaucracies. (Pg. 428, "Speeches of Adolf Hitler: April 1922-August 1939", Oxford Univ. Press along with the Royal Institute of International Affairs in England, 1942)

All-in-all, the NRA and the New Deal were textbook "third-way" socio-economic politics intended to fold all activity under a centrally-planned economy that traded free-market competition for cooperative solidarity, or as the Nazis termed it, *"Gleischschaltung."* This "third-way" Progressivism was largely inspired by the utopian vision of that young American who traveled to study in Germany between 1868 and 1869 when Karl Marx's work was reaching its pinnacle. Bellamy's 1887 book, "Looking Backward" sparked a socio-economic movement based on a eugenic solidarity, where society avoided the boom-and-bust capitalistic cycle by centrally planning all aspects of human existence. Bellamy alike believed he had found a superior method of governing than that put in place by the Founding Fathers, which slowly evolved out of the *laissez-faire* policies of the American Constitution into a system of solidarity and united purpose actively directed by a central planning governmental body. From the start, Arthur E. Morgan's TVA had a utopian feel to it. Morgan used the opportunity opened to him by the TVA to create model communities, namely Cove Creek. [117] The TVA project was an attempt at a Bellamyte form of a "total state." David Lilienthal, the other Bellamyte director of the TVA saw the project in the spirit of Bellamy's "nationalization" of industry:

> I have a very strong feeling that if we cannot control our basic industries, and certainly nothing is more basic than the utilities industry, then we have no government in fact, merely a pathetic fiction of government. (Pg. 178, "The Forgotten Man: A New History of the Great Depression", Amity Shlaes, Harper Collins, 2007)

Lilienthal was correct; no centrally-planned utopia can afford to be a half measure. Therefore, this drive for the "nationalization" of "basic industry" was a desire common to utopian proponents of eugenics as well. Karl Pearson was a supporter of "national socialism" well into Hitler's reign, and Leonard Darwin, Charles's son, was a strong proponent and author of several books on "municipalization" and "nationalization" of all the major components of society. The control of basic industry was key to the control of man, and controlling men was key to creating a utopia. Morgan had practically lifted his ideas for the administration of all details of the TVA from Edward Bellamy's idea of an "industrial army" and the hopes for planned green cities. The flooding of the Tennessee Valley created a blank slate from which utopian towns would be erected from scratch. Morgan went even further:

> The TVA management hired thousands of people. By the middle of 1934, there would be more than 9,000 employees at TVA. ---- Arthur Morris, who at first ran the whole project – especially the details at Norris – recognized that it was the greatest opportunity to build a community he would have in his lifetime. He and his wife, Lucy, poured energy into each detail of Norris. – The soul of the TVA worker also concerned Morgan. . . . Morgan roughed out a moral code for the staff of the Tennessee Valley Authority. (Pgs. 179-180, "The Forgotten Man: A New History of the Great Depression", Amity Shlaes, Harper Collins, 2007)

The similarities between Edward Bellamy's "industrial army" and Adolf Hitler's "National Socialist German Workers Party" are far from academic either. In fact, Hitler's proudly documented his "industrial army" in the one propaganda piece the

---

[117] Pg. 177 - "The Forgotten Man: A New History of the Great Depression", Amity Shlaes, Harper Collins, 2007.

Third Reich is best known for. The infamous 1934 film "Triumph of the Will," directed by Leni Riefenstahl, shows the National Socialist workers parading its "industrial army." The foot soldiers in Riefenstahl's choreographed parades are filmed carrying farming implements. Hitler's speech in the movie echoes Edward Bellamy as Hitler's monologue frequents the themes of the "epitome of altruism" and the various supporting speakers refer to each other as "comrades" who will cause a "revolution of the people and workers" to end "class struggle" and create "egalitarianism." These are the unmistakeable battle cries of utopian socialism and cannot be understood as anything else considering their historical context. More to the point, Riefenstahl's film depicts the different sectors of the National Socialist economy presenting themselves before their leader display their pickaxes, shovels, and rakes precisely in the way a regular army would rifles and armaments. The labor leaders ceremoniously present their ranks to Hitler: "My Führer! I report 52,000 Labor Services men for review."

Hitler's speech in "Triumph of the Will" is evidence to the fact that this tour-de-force of National Socialist propaganda was about "nationalizing" labor for "socialist" political ends, as the name of the National Socialist German Workers' Party otherwise illustrates. Hitler's opening remarks to the entire Nuremberg rally attendance were: "Hail, my Labor Service men!" After an extended review of individual youths presenting their shovels in military fashion, Hitler continues:

> Men of the Labor Service! For the first time you appear before me for review and therefore the entire German nation. You represent a great idea, and we know for millions of our fellow followers the concept of labor will no longer be a dividing factor but one of unification and that no longer will there be anybody in Germany who will regard manual labor less highly than any other form of work. The whole nation will have to go through your school. A time will come when no German will be able to join the community of this nation unless he has first been a member of yours first. (From "Triumph of the Will" subtitles)

The German Labor Corps, or the *Reichs Arbeits Dienst,* was the compulsory labor service Hitler described in his monologue. Formed in July 1934 as the official state labor service, the RAD was an amalgamation of many labor organizations. Many civilian labor forces had cropped up in many countries in response to the Great Depression, but what makes Bellamy's and Hitler's organizations similar is that they were compulsory and a part of a larger movement to "nationalize" labor with "socialist" goals as their justification. Every young German male was required to serve as of June 26, 1935. The Reich Labor Service Law among other measures created a centralized, national and compulsory system in which all males between the ages 18 and 25 would first enter labor service and upon completion, enter service for two years in one of the branches of the *Wehrmacht,* the German Armed Forces. With the passing of the Reich's Labor Service Law, the RAD ceased to be a party organization and was made a Supreme Reich Authority and full-fledged state organization equal to the other Reich ministries.

The leader of National Socialism's "industrial army," Konstantin Hierl, was an associate of Adolf Hitler much before he came to power. In fact, Hierl can be said to be the one to command Hitler down a path that would ultimately sway him away from his desire to be an artist and toward his ambition to be a political leader. As a major in the *Reichswehr's* Political Department in Munich at the end of World War I, it was Hierl who ordered the ex-soldier Hitler to attend a meeting of the German Workers' Party, which Hitler would later convert to the National Socialist German Workers Party.

Similar to the "industrial army" envisioned by Edward Bellamy, the German National Socialist "industrial army" was also organized and administered along military lines. It was divided into separate sections for males and for females. Before World War II began in 1939, the RAD took part in labor projects such as the reclamation of marshland for cultivation, the construction of dikes, drainage improvement work, and the construction of roads, much like its American counterpart at the Tennessee Valley Authority. Throughout World War II, the RAD continued to serve its originally established duty of training young men prior to their service in the *Wehrmacht* by providing construction and agricultural work for the nation.

Historians mistakenly attribute the industrial nature of "Triumph of the Will" as a way to secretly practice military formations while complying with the ban on German rearmament per the Versailles Treaty. This view simply forgets that by this time in history Hitler had long since done away with any pretense of compliance. Adolf Hitler withdrew Germany from the League of Nations and the Geneva Disarmament Conference a full year prior to the release of "Triumph of the Will" in 1933. Thus, the "Triumph of the Will" is a genuine propaganda effort geared towards the "nationalization" of the German public, dedicated to the idea of an "industrial army" of a planned economy, and at the same time, an overt homage for the American "national socialists" by Germany's "National Socialists."

Sec. 2 – THE UNKNOWN MAN:

By now, the reader can discern that there was a template from which these utopian aspirations were molded. Whether consciously or serendipitously, the fact is that these utopian visions all share a template and a list of prerequisites. More importantly, they also shared a methodology. In 1935, Dr. Alexis Carrel, a French-American Nobel Prize winner, published "Man, The Unknown" in which he advocated killing the "mentally ill and criminals" in "euthanasia" institutions. The book was highly influential. It was also timely as it bolstered National Socialism's eugenic aspirations just as the 1933-1935 Nuremberg Laws were put into place. It gave Adolf Hitler exactly what he needed and when he needed it: a Nobel Prize winner and highly respected physician telling the world that society needed to be re-engineered along the lines that Adolf Hitler was proposing.

Carrel's mix of holistic mysticism with the racist eugenic theories was typical of the many utopian socialist proposals. In hindsight, Dr. Carrel's book is one of many in a long line of socio-economic proposals that eugenic-minded doctors, scientists, artists, writers, and lawmakers made across several decades spanning the time between 1848 and 1948, with most of them blatant regurgitations of Edward Bellamy's "Looking Backward." Carrel applied the themes typical to these works. His utopian society:

- Entrusted the leadership of society in the hands of a select number of scientific elite.
- A better human would be accomplished by scientific human breeding.
- Society would be engineered by compulsory eugenic measures.
- Unwanted elements, such as criminals or the born defective, would be eradicated.
- Crime, illness, and idleness would be eliminated by applied eugenic measures.
- Marriage among thoroughbred mates would be rationally and scientifically decided.
- Marriage among the unfit would be scientifically and legislatively prevented.
- Children would be separated from the parents so they can be properly 'educated.'
- Exchanges among the civilians would no longer be along capitalistic lines.
- Capitalism would be replaced with a better social order.
- Technology would only be applied for 'useful' measures.
- 'Wasteful' technology or use of resources would be forbidden.
- Art and artists would occupy a higher place in society.
- Order would be the product of a society along militaristic lines.
- The industrial city would be remade into a garden city.
- Religion would be a thing of the past to be discarded as mere superstition.

The consistency with which the decades upon decades of utopian-socialist proposals follow this cookie-cutter formula becomes nauseating when one reads enough of them in a short span of time. Yet, amazingly enough, each time one of these utopian proposals cropped up, a good portion of the public and its author reveled in its alleged originality and brilliance. Realistically speaking, the last intellectual that was able to claim originality for creating a socialist utopia was Plato, when he wrote "The Republic" in 360 B.C. Yet, what is truly incredible is how many of those individuals, whose intellects are otherwise admired, suffer from such amnesia and myopic thinking that they would regurgitate one work of zealotry after the other, never thinking to look back to learn from the failures of others. The consistency of this century-long line of utopian models based on "scientific" and "rational" lines is inexplicably redundant; each time, the author believed he had solved the problems of humanity with the stroke of their pen and imagination. Yet, somehow, inexplicably, incredibly every attempt thereafter, from Fourier, Saint-Simon, and Owen onto Marx and Engels is still praised for their allegedly brilliant originality. To be truthful, one could easily construct a cookie-cutter recipe for a totalitarian state by mapping out the distinct patterns of utopian socialism. Alas, the recipe for utopia is unsurprisingly similar to that commonly utilized to justify a totalitarian dictatorship:

- Formulate a set of ideals and orthodoxy.
- Define and delineate the collective.
- Identify the excluded others.
- Classify disagreement with orthodoxy as a threat to the collective.
- Identify the enemies of orthodoxy living within the collective.
- Consecrate devotion to orthodoxy as the highest possible virtue.
- Fabricate a crisis.
- Demand obedience and compliance with orthodoxy as a means to preserve the collective.

All of the above points can be found to a large extent throughout utopian works, and they certainly apply to the totalitarian regimes of Germany and Russia. Of specific importance to this book are those "scientifically" organized utopias that begun to spring up at the beginning of the 1800s and ran rampant as alternatives to the Industrial Revolution. It is the "scientific socialism" between the 1840s and 1940s, which, despite failure after failure, persisted in the desire of re-engineering humanity in projects of ever-increasing grandeur and ever-widening catastrophic consequences. These "scientific utopias" snowballed as they picked up the steam of "scientific racism," and as such, became indistinguishable and inseparable from the topic of eugenics. Eugenic novelists were busy writing about their dream society during the era, clamoring and politicking for it in their spare time, while eugenic scientists were developing the science and laws of eugenics during the day and writing eugenic novels at night. The decades-long exchange between the two culminated in an orgy of delusion where fiction and fact became indistinguishable for a good portion of the politically zealous populous.

Born in Sainte-Foy-lès-Lyon, Rhône, Alexis Carrel was raised in a devout Catholic family and was educated by Jesuits, though he no longer practiced his religion when he entered the university. He received his medical degree from Université de Lyon and practiced in France and the United States at the University of Chicago and the Rockefeller Institute for Medical Research. Alexis Carrel was also a member of learned societies in the United States, Spain, Russia, Sweden, the Netherlands, Belgium, France, Vatican City, Germany, Italy, and Greece and received honorary doctorates from Queen's University of Belfast, Princeton University, California, New York, Brown and Columbia Universities.

Carrel's 1935 *"L'Homme, cet inconnu"* (Man, The Unknown) was a bestseller. The book discussed "the nature of society in light of discoveries in biology, physics, and medicine," but integral was Carrel's own version of a eugenic utopia, advocating that an elite group of intellectuals guide and rule mankind. Carrel, like the British Fabian Socialists and the American Progressives, claimed the existence of a "hereditary biological aristocracy" and argued that "deviant" human types should be suppressed:

> **A euthanasia establishment, equipped with a suitable gas**, would allow the humanitarian and economic disposal of those who have killed, committed armed robbery, kidnapped children, robbed the poor or seriously betrayed public confidence. (emphasis mine - translated quote from: Pg. 51, Milton W. Taylor, "Viruses and Man: A History of Interactions", Springer, Jul 21, 2014)

None of these observations are mere academic hindsight. Carrel's praise and collaboration were instrumental in implementing National Socialism's goals in the occupation Vichy government in France. Carrel's preface to his 1936 German edition of "*L'Homme, cet Inconnu*," praised the eugenics policies of the Third Reich:

> The German government has taken energetic measures against the propagation of the defective, the mentally diseased, and the criminal. The ideal solution would be the suppression of each of these individuals as soon as he has proven himself to be dangerous. (Pg. 71, "God's Eugenicist: Alexis Carrel and the Sociobiology of Decline", Translation by: Andrés Horacio Reggiani, Berghahn Books, 2007)

Sadly enough, Carrel is one of those scientists that escaped having his "aid and comfort to the enemy" scrutinized at the end of the war. Consider the severity of his views in the context of 1935 Europe:

> There remains the unsolved problem of the immense number of defectives and criminals. They are an enormous burden for the part of the population that has remained normal.... Why do we preserve these useless and harmful beings?... Why should society not dispose of the criminals and the insane in a more economical manner?.... in Germany, the Government has taken energetic measures against the multiplication of inferior types, the insane and criminals.... Perhaps prisons should be abolished. They could be replaced by smaller and less expensive institutions. -- should be humanely and economically disposed of in small euthanasia institutions supplied with proper gases. (Translation by: Thomas Stephen Szasz, "The Theology of Medicine: The Political-philosophical Foundations of Medical Ethics", Syracuse University Press, 1988, Pg. 11)

In an eerie foreshadowing, Carrel speaks of humanity and the world in terms that would have been endearing to Adolf Hitler:

> To progress again, man must remake himself. And he cannot remake himself without suffering. For he is both the marble and the sculptor. In order to uncover his true visage, he must shatter his own substance with heavy blows of his hammer. (Translation by Eric Michaud and Janet Lloyd, "The Cult of Art in Nazi Germany", Stanford University Press, 2004, Pg. 125)

Here was an internationally prominent French scientist cheering on the Nazis as they murdered millions in the name of "racial hygiene." Here was a politically connected Frenchman, demanding for a *Führer* in the thick of the occupation. In the final chapter in his book, titled "The Remaking of Man," Carrel oscillates between his elitist eugenic views and humanitarian compassion. His book is not unlike that of Leonard Darwin's two books on eugenics, which flip-flop from making the harshest of eugenic remarks to an apologetic humanitarian tone. Clearly, Carrel understood the limits of specialized professionalism but was willing to give doctors unlimited powers over the lives of others. He regarded all other professions to be "ignorant of man" and not to be "trusted beyond the limits of their own field." [118] Carrel felt the scientist and the doctor had the knowledge to lead all others, and their position and rank set at the top of humanity, above government, and above all limiting factors:

> Modern society should be given an intellectual focus, an immortal brain, capable of conceiving and planning its future, and of promoting and pushing forward fundamental researches, in spite of the death of the individual researchers, or the bankruptcy of the research institutes. Such an organization would be the salvation of the white races in their staggering advance toward civilization. This thinking center would consist, as does the Supreme Court of the United States, of a few individuals; the latter being trained in the knowledge of man by many years of study. It should perpetuate itself automatically, in such a manner as to radiate ever young ideas. Democratic rulers, as well as dictators, could receive from this source of scientific truth the information that they need in order to develop a civilization really suitable to man. (Pg. 291, "Man the Unknown", Health Research Books, 2004)

This is where the line between fictional utopia and scientific proposal became blurred. These works became indistinguishable from the scientific proposals that read like the various descriptions of fictional worlds:

> The members of this high council would be free from research and teaching. They would deliver no addresses. They would dedicate their lives to the contemplation of the economic, sociological, psychological, physiological, and pathological phenomena manifested by the civilized nations and their constitutive individuals. ---- Their importance would, in truth, be much greater than that of the jurists who watch over the Constitution. For they would be the defenders of the body and the soul of a great race in its tragic struggle against the blind sciences of matter.
>
> CONTINUES...
>
> A group, although very small, is capable of eluding the harmful influence of the society of its epoch by imposing upon its members rules of conduct modeled on

---

[118] Translation by: Sami Daoud Ibrahim, Book Review for: "Man the Unknown", Harper Brothers 1935 edition.

military or monastic discipline. (Pg. 292, "Man the Unknown", Health Research Books, 2004)

As was the case with a long line of other eugenic-minded utopians, Carrel's goal was to create a "super-human," a "master race," born to lead:

> The free practice of eugenics could lead not only to the development of stronger individuals, but also of strains endowed with more endurance, intelligence, and courage. These strains should **constitute an aristocracy**, from which great men would probably appear. (emphasis mine, Pg. 302, "Man the Unknown", Health Research Books, 2004)

The story of Alexis Carrel becomes even more relevant when one recalls his collaboration with Charles Lindbergh. Their story serves as a microcosm of the 100-year trajectory of eugenics. Aside from their collaboration on eugenics, Carrel and the famed pilot co-authored "The Culture of Organs." They also collaborated in the mid-30s to create the "perfusion pump," which allowed organs to survive outside of the body during surgery. Lindbergh, a mechanical wizard, had innovated some ideas for fixing his sister-in-law's damaged heart valves, and due to his international fame, was introduced the Nobel Prize-winning Carrel. His heart valve ideas proved impractical, but the friendship persisted. They were philosophic soulmates, both interested in eugenics and the perfection of humanity. They were utopian zealots emblematic of the "Jekyll, Hyde and Frankenstein" type of "scientific brilliance and moral idiocy" that so often thrives side by side. [119]

Lindbergh has been castigated by historians for being on the wrong side of history because of his support of the anti-war America First movement as well as for his public adulation for Nazi Germany. Lindbergh had visited Hitler's Germany in its early days and returned to the United States to openly praise it. As such, the relationship between National Socialist Germany and Charles Lindbergh would be closer than what his admirers would like to admit. Most embarrassingly, Lindbergh received the Commander Cross of the Order of the German Eagle from Hitler himself and refused to give it back even after the events of *Kristallnacht* brought controversy on the award. Interestingly enough, the kidnapping of Lindbergh's child spurred the Hitler government to make kidnapping punishable by death. [120]

Lindbergh would live to see the horrid product of his eugenic zealotry. On May 7, 1945, Lindbergh was on a naval technical mission when he arrived at Nordhausen. His survey of Nordhausen also brought him to Camp Dora, where Lindbergh reportedly came face to face with the product of his eugenic convictions. A New York Times article provides Lindbergh's account:

> It was here that he faced for the first time the horrifying remains of the Nazi death factories, about which he wrote in his wartime journals: 'Here was a place where men and life and death had reached the lowest form of degradation. How

---

[119] nyt.com, "Collaborators in a Quest for Human Perfection", M.D. Abigail Zuger, Aug. 28, 2007.
[120] Pg. 134 - "The Last Gasp: The Rise and Fall of the American Gas Chamber", Scott Christiansen, Univ. of California, 2010.

could any reward in national progress even faintly justify the establishment and operation of such a place?' 'It seemed impossible that men - civilized men - could degenerate to such a level.' (archive.nytimes.com, Herber Mitgang, "Lindbergh Said to Regret Misperceptions over Jews", April 20, 1980)

There is some disagreement on the topic of Lindbergh's repentance. His children do not recall their father ever saying any anti-Semitic comments while in their presence, but Henry Ford historians claim that Ford and Lindbergh would discuss their anti-Semitic views while in private. Lindbergh's wife obviously had reason to want to believe that her husband had repented and regretted his anti-Semitic and pro-Hitler stance. Unfortunately, the evidence in the archives betrays these claims. The American Philosophical Society has in its eugenics collection a slew of letters from Lindbergh donating and corresponding to eugenic organizations. These letters were written long after The Holocaust.

History has castigated Henry Ford and Charles Lindbergh for their support of Hitler, and rightfully so. It is fair to note that Henry Ford apologized publicly to American Jews for his comments and publications, and even more important to note that several prominent eugenicists, including C.M. Goethe, Harry H. Laughlin, and Leon Whitney tried unsuccessfully to gain Ford's support for eugenics.[121] Lindbergh vocally supported eugenics before the war and financially supported it long after The Holocaust.[122] He knew that no matter how veiled in "science" his and Carrel's eugenics may have been, the eugenic rhetoric was indistinguishable from that which the scientists in Hitler's Germany practiced. Lindbergh knew them to be one and the same and came face to face with the product of his prejudices at Nordhausen. Lindbergh never again spoke publicly about eugenics, but apparently kept funding it in private.

Sec. 3 - THE BOOK IS THE THING THAT REVEALS THE...:

The Law for the Prevention of Genetically Diseased Offspring in National Socialist Germany was enacted on July 14, 1933. The law allowed for the compulsory sterilization of any citizen who in the opinion of a "Genetic Health Court," or *Gr. Erbgesundheitsgericht*, suffered from a list of disorders thought to be hereditary. Many were not hereditary or genetic in nature and had been proven so by the time sterilization laws were enacted in the United States and Germany. The law was largely the work of Ernst Rüdin, Arthur Gütt and the lawyer Falk Ruttke,

---

[121] BOX C-4-1:2 – Letter from C.M. Goethe to Leon Whitney – Copy to H.H. Laughlin 5/3/1926 – Harry H. Laughlin Papers, Truman Univ. Special Collections Dept., Pickler Memorial Library.

[122] BOX 16 – Various letters accompanying donations – American Philosophical Society, American Eugenics Society Records, Mss.575.06.Am3.

but the list of alleged disorders and the text of the law had been the cumulative product of several decades of work by eugenicists around the world. The law also enforced sterilization on the so-called "Rhineland bastards," a term used by the eugenicist, Eugen Fischer, to describe the children of mixed German and African parentage in his 1908 study conducted with Charles B. Davenport, the director of the Eugenics Records Office in Cold Spring Harbor, NY.

The "Genetic Health Courts" created by the 1933 law consisted of a judge, a medical officer, and medical practitioner, as they were copied from Harry H. Laughlin's "Model Eugenical Sterilization Law." More precisely, these three-panel eugenic courts operated in the same way which the US Supreme Court found to be sufficiently observant of "due process" in the 1927 case of Buck v. Bell. In Germany there were three amendments by 1935, the most significant of which allowed the Higher Court to renounce a patient's right to appeal, and to fine physicians who did not report patients who they knew would qualify for sterilization under the law; yet another aspect adopted from Laughlin's original version. [123]

These eugenic courts were given a veil of legitimacy when famous individuals reported back to the world their participation in the courts and their approbation of the system. Leon F. Whitney's 1934 book, "The Case for Sterilization," gave open praise for Hitler's sterilization policies. Leon F. Whitney was a prominent eugenicist who had a significant hand in molding eugenic sterilization policies in the United States. He was the direct descendant of the famous inventor of the cotton gin, Eli Whitney, and had a familial relationship with Wickliffe Draper, the wealthy eugenicists and founder of the Human Betterment Foundation and the infamous Pioneer Fund. Whitney openly praised the Third Reich in his book:

> Many far-sighted men and women in both England and America have long been working earnestly toward something very like what Hitler has now made compulsory. (Pg. 36, "The Nazi Connection: Eugenics, American Racism, and German National Socialism", Oxford Univ. Press, 1994)

Whitney was the executive secretary of the American Eugenics Society and collaborated in the International Federation of Eugenics Organizations with Davenport, Laughlin, and Leonard Darwin. Whitney's above statement about "far-sighted men and women" from England and America would not have been controversial in the pre-Holocaust era. England and the United States were recognized as the leaders in eugenics and racially-based laws, especially in the wake of the devastation which World War I left Germany reeling. In fact, Leon Whitney's eugenic goals were much more ambitious than even the horrific results of The Holocaust, and most leading American eugenicists agreed with the scope and scale of Whitney's eugenic aspirations. Leon Whitney proposed sterilizing 10 percent of the entire population of the United States, which at the time would have been around 10 million "hereditary defectives," and was openly jealous of the power the

---

[123] See Section 21. Punishment of Responsible Head of Institution for Dereliction, "Eugenical Sterilization in the United States", Harry H. Laughlin, Psychopathic Laboratory, 1922. – For an in-depth analysis see chapter 1922 – Model Eugenical Law of "H.H. Laughlin: American Progressive, American Scientist, Nazi Collaborator", A.E. Samaan.

Third Reich wielded towards this effect. [124] Curiously enough, Whitney's book begins by paying homage to Oliver Wendell Holmes, son and father, for their contribution to United States eugenic laws. Justice Oliver Wendell Holmes had written the 1927 <u>Buck v. Bell</u> opinion:

> "Choose good grandparents." – Dr. Oliver Wendell Holmes
> "Three generations of imbeciles are enough." – Oliver Wendell Holmes, Jr. [125]

The famous Holocaust historian, Edwin Black quotes Leon Whitney, "While we were pussy-footing around…the Germans were calling a spade a spade." [126] This was hardly the most lavish praise Whitney would lavish upon Hitler's regime. Whitney's book makes repeated and laudatory references to the laws passed by the Third Reich. Whitney proclaims, in part:

> If Herr Hitler deserves any approbation at all it must be for his services in making John Citizen think about sterilization. Eugenics is being taught now in three-quarters of our five hundred colleges and universities, and in many high and preparatory schools. (archive.org digitized version, Leon Whitney, CHAPTER XVIII: Holding the Bear by the Tail, "The Case for Sterilization", Leon Whitney, Frederick A. Stokes Company, 1934 - Sourced From: archive.org)

If Whitney is right that eugenics was being taught in "three quarters" of the universities in the United States in 1934, then this only serves as further proof to this book's claim that it was disingenuous, if not fraudulent, for the Allied prosecution at Nuremberg to exclude the topic from the proceedings. But Whitney was right; the topic of eugenics appeared consistently and often in newspapers and books of the era. It would have been as disingenuous to claim ignorance about the topic of eugenics back then, as it would be for anyone to claim ignorance of the contentious topic of Global Warming today. A lot has been written about how these sterilizations and euthanasia efforts within Germany were kept secret from the German public. While Hitler's government took certain steps to keep the euthanasia part secret, historical accounts document how everyday people were aware of the campaign, especially in the residential areas surrounding the euthanasia clinics. Hitler's government sterilized an average of 165,000 Germans of both sexes per year, at the astonishing rate of 450 forced sterilizations per day. [127] At war's end, it was revealed by the German Central Association of Sterilized Persons that a grand total of about two million human beings had been ruled "unfit" and sterilized against their will during the twelve years by the three-panel eugenic courts modelled per the specifications delineated in Laughlin's "Eugenical Sterilization Law." While many eugenicists were feigning ignorance on the connection between eugenics and the extermination camps, Whitney outright admitted to knowing the connection between eugenic sterilization and plans for eugenic euthanasia:

---

[124] Pg. 59 - "The Case for Sterilization", Leon Whitney, archive.org digitized version.
[125] digitized version, Dedication, "The Case for Sterilization", Leon Whitney, Frederick A. Stokes Company, 1934 - Sourced From: archive.org
[126] "The Horrifying American Roots of Nazi Eugenics", History News Network website, George Mason Univ., Nov. 25, 2003.
[127] Pg. 135 - "Legacy of Malthus: The Social Costs of the New Scientific Racism", Allan Chase, 1975.

Will sterilization laws lead straight to legislation establishing the practice of "euthanasia"? That idea has not been without its advocates among estimable members of society. (archive.org digitized version, Leon Whitney, CHAPTER I: Sterilization, A Burning Issue To-Day, "The Case for Sterilization", Leon Whitney, Frederick A. Stokes Company, 1934 - Sourced From: archive.org)

Whitney clearly knew something about these institutions as the first paragraph in his book makes a direct reference to the National Socialist's sterilization project:

Since the year 1934 opened there has been a startling increase in the attention given to the subject of sterilization, an increase which among American newspaper-readers is probably due largely to the news from Germany that Hitler has undertaken to have some four hundred thousand Germans sterilized – nearly a hundredth part of the population. Whether this order is or is not directed exclusively at the Jews, it is so grave a decision as to justify fully the recent discussion of it among thousands of persons in our own country who may never before have taken any real interest in the subject. (archive.org digitized version, Leon Whitney, CHAPTER I: Sterilization, A Burning Issue To-Day, "The Case for Sterilization", Leon Whitney, Frederick A. Stokes Company, 1934)

Whitney's book went on to ask for an "enlightened understanding" of sterilization, free from the typical "uneducated" notions and objections from the "religious," and free from the "abuse the supporters of sterilization" receive from these sectors of the concerned public. However, he is clear on the point that eugenics was synonymous with "social planning."

No one can deny that our present trend is toward a planned society – planned biologically as well as economically; and no planned social order is attainable without careful consideration of the kind of people we want to have forming the race of the future. ---- I believe that sterilization is but a part of the general discipline that we call social planning, and it is from this point of view that I shall discuss it. (archive.org digitized version, CHAPTER I: Sterilization, A Burning Issue To-Day, "The Case for Sterilization", Leon Whitney, Frederick A. Stokes Company, 1934 - Sourced From: archive.org)

Herein lays the truth, brazen and arrogant. Whitney states the obvious: Society is to be planned, and the members of this planned society are to be selected by the upper echelon of society, among which he undoubtedly included himself. Whitney's position is equally honest about the dramatic change in course that these scientists saw for themselves, no longer as the detached truth-seeker, but as part of the social planning and political activist leadership:

My position is not that of the scientist of earlier days, who was supposed only to collect facts and was not expected to publish the views he had derived from them except through learned scientific monographs that could hardly reach the people. (emphasis mine, archive.org digitized version, Chpt: The Case for Sterilization, "The Case for Sterilization", Leon Whitney, Frederick A. Stokes Company, 1934 - Sourced From: archive.org)

Rather, Whitney applauds the practical application of his science by openly stating that "Many thousands of men and women have been sterilized under the laws of the United States, and thousands others have been sterilized privately." Referring to the work of Paul Popenoe and E.S. Gosney of Pasadena, California, "Sterilization for Human Betterment: A Summary of 6000 Operations in California, 1909–1929," Whitney asserts that he reviewed the public records, but also "interviewed in person a considerable number of the people" and argued that there was enough data to ascertain the results were predominantly beneficial. Whitney deemed his justification as "therapeutic reasons" for sterilization, at the same time recognizing the high likelihood and possibility of abuse:

> We live in an age of social control, and here – in eugenics – lies our most glorious opportunity of controlling the quality of our children and our children's children. ---- **The doctors, too, may sometimes exceed their duties.** I know of one young woman who was told by the surgeon after she came out from an appendectomy, "Now, my dear, there is one burden that you have off your mind forever. **While I was taking out your appendix I tied off your tubes, and you'll never have to worry for fear you'll have babies. Isn't that nice**?" (emphasis mine, archive.org digitized version, Chpt: Does Sterilization Work Satisfactorily, "The Case for Sterilization", Leon Whitney, Frederick A. Stokes Company, 1934 - Sourced From: archive.org)

The above incident was more common than Whitney admits, as is evidenced by the case of Raymond Hudlow, the World War II vet that was sterilized. Whitney wasn't bothered by the abuses because he did not see the victims as his equals. Here is Whitney qualifying the social status and financial ability the "rural" families who were the object of his obsession:

> Indeed, there are many families on rundown farms all over the land who are one and all feeble-minded and who go on reproducing their kind generation after generation, supported by the community through jobs requiring little or no intelligence. (archive.org digitized version, Leon Whitney, Chpt: Does Sterilization Work Satisfactorily, "The Case for Sterilization", Leon Whitney, Frederick A. Stokes Company, 1934 - Sourced From: archive.org)

Whitney goes on to state that sexual perversion was one of the justifications for sterilization. Like Hitler and other eugenicists, he blamed the influence of modernity as the cause for sexual perversion by stating that "not a little sex perversion is developed by our overcivilization." This was an aspect of the eugenic thinking that was either hypocritical or self-contradictory. While most eugenicists point to the pace of modernity and urbanization to be one of the primary reasons for "degeneration," it is the "rural" population which became the largest target of their efforts:

> These are all low-grade persons, nearly always too stupid or too insane to apply voluntarily for the operation. Those among the low-grade class who are so imbecile or so insane that they will always remain incarcerated do not enter our

present consideration, since in their case there is no need for sterilization. It is the border-line cases — those who can be given partial or entire freedom at times or even permanently — that fall into this class. (archive.org digitized version, Leon Whitney, Chpt: Does Sterilization Work Satisfactorily, "The Case for Sterilization", Leon Whitney, Frederick A. Stokes Company, 1934 - Sourced From: archive.org)

Whitney tells the story of the old New England town of Cellarholes, whose prosperity caught the eye of the British, who soon started letting just about anyone who wanted to emigrate to leave Britain.

The news that came from the young colony was presently so good, bearing promise of such certain security, that the British Government began to encourage emigration and colonization. But did that government try to select the best of its families and urge them to emigrate to Massachusetts? No. Instead, it allowed those to go who wanted to, and every once in a while exported a shipload of prostitutes and misfits of the same kind as were being sent to Georgia. (archive.org digitized version, Leon Whitney, Chp. VI: Importing Trouble, "The Case for Sterilization", Leon Whitney, Frederick A. Stokes Company, 1934 - Sourced From: archive.org)

This disdain for rural populations was a consistent theme for eugenicists. Despite spewing a constant stream of derision against industrialization, capitalism and modern urbanity, the eugenicists had a pronounced disdain for simple living people. Francis Darwin, Charles Darwin's third son and a botanist, gave the first "Galton Lecture" where he recalled how Francis Galton, the father of eugenics and his uncle, shared this elitist view of rural life:

Later he defines mediocrity in a way not very flattering to those, who, like myself, live in the country. Mediocrity then "defines the intellectual power found in most provincial gatherings, because the attractions of a more stirring life in the metropolis and elsewhere are apt to draw away the abler classes of men, and the silly and imbecile do not take a part in the gatherings. (Francis Darwin, "Galton Lecture", Eugenics Education Society, Feb. 16, 1914, Printed in Eugenics Review, 1914)

Allan Chase observed the same trend of thinking in Galton:
Better-class of Englishmen, Galton wrote, "prefer to live in the high intellectual and moral atmosphere of the more intelligent circles of English society, to a self-banishment among people of altogether lower grades of mind and interest." As a result, Galton added: "England has certainly got rid of a great deal of refuse, through means of emigration." --- The emigration of the human refuse who, Galton wrote in Hereditary Genius, were "not wanted in old civilizations" to lands of lower grades of mind and interest — such as America, Canada, and Australia — saw England become "disembarrassed of a vast number of turbulent radicals and the like, men who are decidedly able but by no means eminent, and whose zeal, self-confidence, and irreverence far outbalance their other qualities.

(Pg. 104, "Legacy of Malthus: The Social Costs of the New Scientific Racism", 1975)

Whitney certainly held the rural populations with some disdain, and this disrespect for his fellow humans was arguably reinforced by his belief in Darwin. In Chapter VI, titled "Importing Trouble," Whitney makes his Darwinistic and biohistorical case for eugenic sterilization:

> We have no way of knowing just how much feeble-mindedness and insanity there was in the United States in the early days, but we do know that at the very first there was practically none, because the environment was too harsh to allow a degenerate to live. — There is no place for the misfits in the upward scheme of evolution. Indeed, if we can learn anything from that lesson, it is that Nature certainly does not want weaklings. In every species, we find that the inferior individual is soon exterminated and the superior allowed to survive. (archive.org digitized version, Leon Whitney, Chp. VI: Importing Trouble, "The Case for Sterilization", Leon Whitney, Frederick A. Stokes Company, 1934 - Sourced From: archive.org)

This elitist undercurrent must be checked against the pecking order from hard to soft sciences. Posterity must note that Whitney and company, while certain in their convictions, were at the same time fully aware that their scientific abilities were extremely limited, if not primitive. All their brutal assessments must, therefore, be weighed against Whitney's knowledge that he was unsuccessful in identifying just what portion of the population carried the ailments he was supposedly curing. Whitney fully recognized that his methods would fail to identify the alleged carriers he supposedly was trying to eradicate; that sterilization of any individual that demonstrated symptoms of a hereditary defect or predisposition for illness did nothing to address those that were "carriers" that showed no signs of affliction whatsoever. [128] In other words, Whitney failed to arrive at the same scientific conclusion that eugenicists like Raymond Pearl arrived at looking at the same work by the same scientist, H.S. Jennings. The obvious jumped out of the pages for Pearl; that recessive genes make unlikely that any eugenic measure can succeed, as the "carriers" are more often than not healthy individuals with no sign that they are carrying a genetic disorder that may or may not appear generations later. Whitney like Galton, Laughlin, Leonard Darwin and Pearson relied wholly on "statistical" methods for identifying "carriers." However, these "statistical" methods that Whitney refers to are the same statistical results that Pearl would later prove to be undisciplined and tainted with false assumptions. Note just how reliant their methods were on informal documentation and even a practice as antiquated as phrenology:

> …human beings have very obligingly (if unconsciously) done the mating themselves, and have left records. Often there are three generations of the same

---

[128] archive.org digitized version, Leon Whitney, Chp. V: The Relation of Mendelism to Sterilization, "The Case for Sterilization", Leon Whitney, Frederick A. Stokes Company, 1934 - Sourced From: archive.org.

family living, so that the geneticist may go forth with his measuring instruments and his pencil and paper and reach valid conclusions. (archive.org, digitized version, Leon Whitney, Chp. V: The Relation of Mendelism to Sterilization, "The Case for Sterilization", Leon Whitney, Frederick A. Stokes Company, 1934 - Sourced From: archive.org)

Whitney also co-authored "The Builders of America" with Prof. Ellsworth Huntington, who also wrote "The Decline of American Capitalism." Whitney frequently collaborated with Laughlin, who was crucial in distributing Hitler's eugenic propaganda film *Erbkrank* in the United States. It is no surprise that Whitney makes the same claims of an impending catastrophe as Hitler's propaganda made in its movies, books, and magazine articles. "Capitalism," along with "modernity," were regarded as some of the leading causes of "degeneration":

> Our final consideration is the rate at which the subnormal group is reproducing. If as a group the feeble-minded are having more than 3.5 children to a family, they are increasing; if less, they are decreasing. One American figure and one English may serve to answer this question. In my New Haven study I found the average to be 7.1 children, which means that the group is practically doubling with each generation. (archive.org digitized version, Leon Whitney, Ch.: Degeneracy in the Making, "The Case for Sterilization")

Whitney proudly claims that "more than 16,000 persons have been sterilized in our public institutions since the practice first became authorized by law," and credited the "Superintendent of the Eugenics Record Office, Dr. Harry H. Laughlin," as having been of the "greatest assistance to the legislators of many States." Whitney documented that all the States that enacted sterilization laws had gone to Laughlin for help and information and that the correspondence between Laughlin and State legislators was "voluminous"; a fact this author can attest to after rummaging through the Laughlin Papers held at Truman University archives. [129]

This famous descendant of an eternally famous inventor made it a point to announce to the world his intimate relationship with Hitler's Third Reich, a fact that has been forgotten along with Whitney despite his family's persisting fame:

> Under the dictatorship of Adolph Hitler, a compulsory law has been passed with his approval. I have had considerable correspondence with certain German scientists who ever since the War have been enthusiastic advocates of sterilization. (archive.org digitized version, Leon Whitney, Chp.: A Page of History, "The Case for Sterilization")

Of specific importance, historically speaking, is that Whitney was fully cognizant of the scale and scope of the Third Reich's eugenic efforts. This is important, as this book documents just how the history of American eugenics has been systematically divorced from the history of The Holocaust. It is also of historical importance as it debunks the notion that the scale and scope of The

---

[129] archive.org digitized version, Chp.: A Page of History, "The Case for Sterilization", Leon Whitney, Frederick A. Stokes Company, 1934.

Holocaust were unknown until after the war. Upon reading Whitney's book, it becomes clear that the political relationships were discoverable and that the Third Reich's aspirations were well known in eugenic circles:

> The 400,000 known defectives in Germany who become subject of the new law are about equally divided into men and women ---- **And this represents but a small beginning, we are told!** Though not all of us, probably, will approve of the compulsory character of this law – as it applies, for instance, to the sterilizing of drunkards – we cannot but admire the foresight revealed by the plan in general. (emphasis mine, archive.org digitized version, Chp.: A Page of History, "The Case for Sterilization", Leon Whitney, Frederick A. Stokes Company, 1934 - Sourced From: archive.org)

It is thus essential to note how Whitney described what was going on inside Hitler's Germany. Whitney engages in the sleight-of-hand that was employed by other prominent American eugenicists, which surveyed the Third Reich's eugenic policies, namely that of Marion S. Olsen and Lothrop Stoddard. Whitney portrayed the law as having no "religious bias," as he knew this was important to Americans who valued as "separation of church and state" and freedom from religious prosecution:

> American Jewry is naturally suspecting that the German chancellor had the law enacted for the specific purpose of sterilizing the German Jews, but I believe nothing to be further from the truth. The German law provides for the sterilization of hereditary defectives only. It safeguards the rights of every individual, and where it sterilizes it will not maim. The measure is solely eugenic in its purpose and were it not for its compulsory character it would probably meet with the approval of all who are free from religious bias. (archive.org digitized version, Chp.: The Case for Sterilization, "The Case for Sterilization", Leon Whitney, Frederick A. Stokes Company, 1934 - Sourced From: archive.org)

In this sense, he was technically right. The law as written did not specifically target "religions." It targeted biological groups as categorized by eugenicists who saw certain ethnic minorities, namely Jews, as being biologically inferior and detrimental to the gene pool. In a broader sense, Whitney, Olson, and Stoddard knew they were omitting the focus and priority that the Nazis gave to eradicating the Jewish population. Whitney's correspondence with Harry H. Laughlin and C.M. Goethe reveal just how disingenuous this characterization of the Third Reich's eugenic policies was. Clearly, Whitney himself was not the objective scientist, free of racial prejudices that he claimed to be. Whitney provides an answer to this question as just who was the intended target:

> The Negroes in New Haven furnished six times as many subnormals as did the native-born whites, and the Negro population of that city is probably no less intelligent than the rest of the Negro population all over the country; if anything, it may be higher, since some students hold that a Negro has to have more intelligence and gumption to migrate from his Southland than he needs to stay

in it. (archive.org digitized version, Chp.: The Case for Sterilization, "The Case for Sterilization", Leon Whitney, Frederick A. Stokes Company, 1934 - Sourced From: archive.org)

Leon Whitney, following in the footsteps of Margaret Sanger, Nietzsche, and H.G. Wells, treated the moral dilemma with a flippant attitude towards "compassion":

> It is for this reason that I am somewhat in sympathy with those who ask: Suppose in a few cases we do sterilize some person who is not likely to pass dysgenic traits on? Suppose we do make a mistake occasionally and sterilize somebody whose subnormality is due to accident and not to heredity? What's the difference? Whether we believe that the subnormality is traceable to heredity or to environment, what we want is good children in good homes. Degenerate parents cannot bring children up properly. What harm if they become sterile? (archive.org digitized version, Chp.: How Many Ought to be Sterilized, "The Case for Sterilization")

Was this an aberration for the United States? The country which disavowed titles of nobility and privileges by heredity had many of its intellectual leaders willing to destroy a life based solely on hereditary criteria. The United States is the one country where laws based on the assumptions of hereditary value should have been outright banished. Yet, that was obviously not the case. More specifically, Whitney's understanding of the law was one of betrayal to the US Constitution. His notions would have been untenable to the Founding Fathers as they explicitly abolished the notion that an individual's status before the law was dictated by their family lineage. Ironically enough, Whitney did not find opposition among the secular leadership of the United States. Whitney goes into detail as to just how instrumental the Catholic Church was in blocking the aspirations of the eugenic elite. This is of historical importance, as we are often told quite the opposite:

> The main, and most seriously taken objection comes, as would naturally be expected, from the Roman Catholic Church. Its head, Pope Pius XI, has decreed against sterilization, notably in the encyclical *Casti Connubii* issue in January 1931. That document is, in general, the expression of an ideal that cannot but appeal strongly to any who are eager for race betterment. (archive.org digitized version, Chap. XII: The Objections Most Often Urged, "The Case for Sterilization")

Historians must take note that Whitney, just like all the most prominent supporters and detractors of the eugenics movement, recognized that the Catholic Church was the movement's greatest enemy:

> Up until 1931 the movement was promoted by public-spirited men and women of all religious faiths; but in that year an encyclical of the Pope arrayed the Roman Catholic Church against it. This attitude is of course regretted by all those who are advocating the benefits that sterilization will bring to society; yet they know that the cause is a noble one, supported by the soundest scientific

principles as well as by the highest ethical considerations and they believe that when it is correctly understood it cannot fail to appeal to every intelligent, sensible, and forward-looking person in the community. (archive.org digitized version, Chap. XII: The Objections Most Often Urged, "The Case for Sterilization")

Whitney's argument is inescapably one of a Progressive, fully convinced of the modernity of his beliefs. However, it may be pointed out that the Pope's dictum was hardly one of the Catholic faith either. The Pope was making more of a legal statement as the just interpretation of laws composed by decent men, and not a religious prohibition. Whitney retorted that the debate should not be one over "ethical" criteria, but scientific considerations alone. [130] Yet, what can be said of a man that proposes a law that does not take "ethical" considerations into account? What can be said of an American that knows less of the founding principles of his own country than does an Old World religious leader?

The family is paramount? With this we may agree. The family's claims are higher than the states? With this we need not agree. (archive.org digitized version, Chap. XII: The Objections Most Often Urged, "The Case for Sterilization")

Herein lay the pivot upon which eugenics tips towards socialism, collectivism, or as Whitney would describe it, "a planned society." Per Whitney's above statement, the "state" had superior rights to its inhabitants. Of note is that Whitney adopts the same parable like the one originally posed by Darwin and later adopted by Galton:

The family is not paramount. It is an integral part of the great unit which we call the state. Just as the agriculturist works his farm, so the state or family-culturist must cultivate its families by seeing that the better type of individuals are served. – Here is a high testing cow. She must be preserved. - Here is an outstandingly obnoxious weed. It must be destroyed. – There are figs and thistles, grapes and thorns, wheat and tares in human society and the state must practice family culture. (archive.org digitized version, Chap. XII: The Objections Most Often Urged, "The Case for Sterilization")

Clearly, Whitney saw himself and his cohorts as the state's "family-culturist," claiming a "superior" position what was to become of those beneath him. This is the fundamental precondition of a "planned society," that there are those that simply know better, and must be given the power to impose their ideals on those deemed to be lesser. Where was Whitney's intellectual prowess when Stalin was enacting his "social consciousness" in order to eradicate tens of millions of the population Stalin deemed to be superfluous? It would be wonderful to know what people like Whitney, Leonard Darwin, Harry H. Laughlin, Charles B. Davenport, and the other zealots thought or said as the realities of Hitler's reign became part of public knowledge.

---

[130] archive.org digitized version, "The Case for Sterilization", Leon Whitney, Frederick A. Stokes Company, 1934 - Chap. XII: The Objections Most Often Urged.

Unfortunately, history gave these individuals a pass, and allowed them to be forgotten for decades, never making the obvious connection between them and the "crimes against humanity." Whitney's description of his ideal society is an accurate description of Hitler's National Socialist policies, where births of those deemed desirable to the state were encouraged while the births of the unwanted are actively prevented:

> To-day's discussion of our need for "a planned Society" usually emphasizes aspects of our economic structure. As yet, current talk has not touched on a far more important need of contemporary life, the foundation on which any new economic structure must be built, if it is to stay firm. I mean a eugenic program. – A planned society must imply the regulation of births. But its birth-control program must be threefold: birth-*liberation* for those best endowed by Nature; birth-*maintenance* for the great average; birth-*reduction* for the lowest social elements. (archive.org digitized version, Chap. XVII: A Planned Society, "The Case for Sterilization")

Posterity must also note that Leon Whitney did much more than just give aid and comfort to Hitler's regime. Leon Whitney put his ideas into practice. Leon Whitney is one of those "scientists" that scoured the rural areas of the United States intent on sterilizing its youth against their will, and as this book has documented, often without their knowledge. Leon Whitney should be counted among those "scientists" who embarked on sterilizing and violating the human rights of the boys, which we would later come to know as "The Greatest Generation." In 1928, Whitney and his Boston metropolitan elites took a gaze at the rural population just outside of their city and sterilized boys as young as 14 allegedly for their "poor moral condition." It was a campaign by Harvard and the New England higher education institutions to cut this population out of history, no different than the Nazi campaign to erase European Jewry from memory: It is essential to place the Shutesbury incident into the timeline of history:

> In fact, the Northampton man behind the Shutesbury study was corresponding with German scientists, whose sterilization policies he called "courageous" and "admirable." And that man, Leon Whitney a thin, bespectacled dog breeder whose book, The Case for Sterilization, won him an admiring personal letter from Adolf Hitler was no crackpot loner. There was a whole movement behind him, legitimized by scientists, academics, and influential policymakers. And Massachusetts was one of its epicenters, beginning at a time when Hitler was an aimless Austrian barely in his teens. ("The Master Race", Welling Savo, Boston Mag., Dec. 2002)

The above statement hits the nail on the head. The veil of legitimacy provided by prestigious names like Darwin, Galton, and Whitney to the "science" of eugenics is precisely the reason why governmental bodies acted in ways that would by any other measure be considered inhumane and unconstitutional. It is this veil of scientific legitimacy that was explicitly referenced by the 1924 House Committee on Immigration and Naturalization to pass the Immigration Restriction Act, which would ultimately deny millions of refugees from Hitler's Europe from entering the safety of the United States. It is this veil of scientific legitimacy that allowed Leon Whitney to put his views into actual practice in rural towns like Shutesbury. It is the "scientific expert" status that Laughlin qualified himself as for his deposition submitted for 1927 <u>Buck v. Bell</u> case; that "these people belong to the shiftless, ignorant, and worthless class of anti-social whites of the South." [131]

The correspondence held at the Harry H. Laughlin Papers at Truman University evidence that Leon Whitney was one of those "Merchants of Light," which dedicated such an inordinate amount of their time towards propaganda as opposed to work in an actual laboratory. As Executive Secretary of the American Eugenics Society and as a key member of the International Federation of Eugenic Organizations, Whitney corresponded frequently with Charles B. Davenport, Harry H. Laughlin, and C.M. Goethe. Truman University has Laughlin's papers in its Special Collections, and this book publishes portions of them for the first time. Whitney shares with Laughlin the "prospectus" for the creation of the "Galton Publishing Company" in a May 14, 1929 letter from Whitney to Laughlin. [132] In a June 16, 1926 letter from C.M. Goethe to Whitney, and copied to Laughlin, they discuss the employment of Protestant "Federal Council of Churches" for the cause of eugenics, a wish that would come true through various rural programs such as the infamous "Fitter Family" contests. [133] It is because of "scientists" like Whitney that is has become impossible to tell the difference between eugenicists and lawmakers or propaganda and utopian fiction. Whitney's influence on the history of eugenics is confirmed by Adolf Hitler's personal recognition:

> In 1934, one of Hitler's staff members wrote to Leon Whitney of the American Eugenics Society and asked in the name of the Führer for a copy of Whitney's recently published book, The Case for Sterilization. Whitney complied immediately, and shortly thereafter received a personal letter of thanks from Adolf Hitler. In his unpublished autobiography, Whitney reported a conversation he had with Madison Grant about the letter from the Führer. Because he thought that Grant might be interested in Hitler's letter he showed it to him during their next meeting. Grant only smiled, reached for a folder on his desk, and gave Whitney a letter from Hitler to read. In this, Hitler thanked Grant for writing The Passing of the Great Race and said that "the book was his Bible." Whitney concluded that, following Hitler's actions, one could believe it. (Pg. 85, "The Nazi Connection: Eugenics, American Racism, and German National Socialism", Stefan Kühl, Oxford Univ. Press, 1994)

---

[131] Harry H. Laughlin, "Expert Analysis," Buck v. Bell, 1927 – "Eugenic Sterilization Laws", Paul Lombardo, eugenicsarchive.org.
[132] Box: C-2-4:2 – "Harry Laughlin Papers", Truman Univ., Special Collections.
[133] Box: C-4-1:2 – Ibid.

Sec. 4 – "NAZI WAR ON CANCER":

The Third Reich was what Hitler and his colleagues called a "Total State," which very literally meant that every single aspect of life would be under the government's jurisdiction and prerogative. This was the essence of "totalitarianism," which is used mindlessly today to refer to dictatorships, often forgetting it refers to the "cradle-to-grave" aspect of socialist dictatorships by making a direct reference to their "total" control. The prerogative of the "Total State" reached into the most private and intimate details of a person's life, and there was no line of demarcation where the government stopped, and the individual's autonomy was respected. Although "total" control over aspects of the individual's life has rightfully come to be recognized as oppressive, this aspect of the Third Reich was a very much welcome idea in an era where "individualism" was deemed a cancer by Progressives and Socialists alike. The Nazis fully concurred on this measure. Case in point, Joseph Goebbels proclaimed in 1933: "The dethroning of the individual [is] the most essential principle of our now victoriously conquering movement." [134] As extrapolated in the previous section, Progressives like Leon Whitney and Harry H. Laughlin clearly shared in this disdain for the rights of the individual. Juxtapose this view of government against the intended scope of the US Government. Thomas Jefferson warned posterity of politicians that lust after the role of paternalistic caretaker. This now-famous quote is from a Thomas Jefferson to Thomas Cooper letter dated November 29, 1802 resonates:

> If we can but prevent the government from wasting the labours of the people, under the pretence of taking care of them, they must become happy. (The Thomas Jefferson Papers Series 1. General Correspondence. 1651-1827)

Another portion of this letter is equally revealing of exactly where Jefferson stood on the subject of limited government and the intrusion on the personal finances of the citizenry under the guise of good causes:

> The path we have to pursue is so quiet that we have nothing scarcely to propose to our Legislature. A noiseless course, not meddling with the affairs of others, unattractive of notice, is a mark that society is going on in happiness. (The Thomas Jefferson Papers Series 1. General Correspondence. 1651-1827)

Contrasts are instrumental in defining opposites. Robert Proctor, author of "The Nazi War on Cancer" documents that the motto *"Gesundheit über Alles,"* which he translates to mean "duty to be healthy" was crafted by the German National Socialists to engender the ideals of bodily purity. [135] The notion that a person's body was the property, or at least within the jurisdiction of the state, is crucial towards an understanding of what National Socialism was at its core. It is a concept that is diametrically opposed to individual liberty, and about as far away from a *laissez-faire* government as you can get. Understanding this notion where an individual has a duty to society to stay healthy goes a long way towards understanding

---
[134] Pg. 316, "Architects of Fortune: Mies Van Der Rohe and the Third Reich", Fromm International Pub. Corp., 1989.
[135] Pg. 222 - "Nazi War on Cancer", Robert Proctor, Princeton Univ. Press, 2000.

how or why doctors under National Socialism were able to turn the Hippocratic Oath's command to "do no harm" on its head. Per the sworn testimony given by Karl Brandt during the Nuremberg trials, the National Socialist doctors perceived their duty to be owed to maintaining the health of the society, the state, and the nation. They did not adhere to the traditional doctor-patient relationship where the doctor's primary duty was to cure the individual patient. This is precisely how individual lives became expendable: individual lives were to be eradicated or segregated from society if they were deemed to be a health risk or a negative influence on the race, no different than if they were cancerous tissue or a pathogen on the body of the state:

> Along with the homeless, the beggars, the inmates of insane asylums, and the Jews of the East Europeans ghettos, the German authorities eliminated the visible poor, nonproductive people who caused the state expenses during their lifetime. Their mistreatment and liquidation provided housing, employment, assets, and old-age pensions for others. In this sense, the National Socialist *Volksgemeinschaft* (community of the people) really existed. Health policy in Nazi Germany – scientifically labeled as "hereditary and race hygiene" – **was a concept of rule.** It unified German population, economic, and social policies to achieve one goal: the final solution of the social question. On the whole, the functionaries of the Nazi state were extraordinarily young, and they consciously relied on the results of scientific research. This elite did away with rusty old structures and started to put their political utopias – such as the concept of a common *Gesundeheitspflicht* (obligation for health) – into practice. (emphasis mine, Pgs. 32-33, Chap.: 3, "The Nazi Doctors and the Nuremberg Code", 1992 - Christian Pross's contributing chapter)

This shift in the political thinking of the doctors inevitably meant a shift in medical practice. No one had to coerce doctors to switch from their focus on the individual to the collectivized body as the patient. No one had to force the doctors or the scientists, as they were leading the way. This change in focus went along with the change from curative medicine to preventative medicine intertwined with socialist political convictions. Doctors under National Socialism believed that the lifestyle of the individuals was behind the increase in cancer rates, and thus changes in lifestyle would reverse the trend, even if those changes in lifestyle had to be coerced or forced onto the individual. The scientific and medical community were the most devoted and energetic members of the National Socialist movement; with physicians joining the party in large numbers, with 60 percent of all biologists and 80 percent of all professors of anthropology joining the party. [136] Here is an illuminating quote from Robert Hofstätter, a German anti-tobacco activist:

> We have the duty, if necessary, to die for the Fatherland; why should we not also have the duty to be healthy? Has the Führer not explicitly demanded this? [137]

---

[136] Pg. 15 - "The Nazi War on Cancer", Robert Proctor, Princeton Univ. Press, 2000.
[137] Pg. 58 – Ibid.

Most "racial hygiene" legislation was enacted in 1933. However, the regime redoubled its efforts to combat cancer in the 1940s parallel with the onset of war. The timing of these efforts is noteworthy and go a long way to reveal the priorities within the minds of the National Socialist state. The effort was a major focus for the German Research Council and the Kaiser Wilhelm Institute. The Reich Institute for Cancer Research was established in Nesselstedt in 1942. There is some dispute as to the nature of the extensive investments in the Reich Institute for Cancer Research. The Institute may have been, at least in part, a camouflaged operation for the development of biological warfare. One of its directors, Kurt Blome, who was known to be part of Hitler's biowarfare effort worked for the Institute. However, the explanation of a cover-story does not begin to explain the extent of the National Socialist's government expenditure in anti-smoking legislation and propaganda. It certainly doesn't explain just how central and pervasive the anti-smoking and anti-cancer rhetoric was during the full tenure of the National Socialist government. National Socialist anti-tobacco propaganda was heavily intertwined with its "racial hygiene" message, which in turn was central to the National Socialist ethos and jurisprudence. Robert Proctor documents that the National Socialists framed their opposition to tobacco products as opposition to "diseases of civilization" which were "relics of a liberal lifestyle." [138] According to Robert Proctor, "smoking was associated with swing dancing, with rebellion, with Africa, with degenerate blacks, Jews, and Gypsies." [139] Proctor also documents that the term "Damen-Zigarette," German for "ladies' cigarette" was henceforth banned and prohibited from use in packaging or advertisement along with the use of sexual or female-centered imagery. These efforts must be considered in conjunction with the "Maternal Protection Law" of 1942, or "*Mutterschutzgesetz*," which barred pregnant women from employment that endangered either the mother or the child. Both efforts were intended toward protecting the nation's Aryan gene pool. The anti-smoking December 17, 1941, restrictions of the Advertising Council read:

The Content of Tobacco Advertising:

- Tobacco advertisements should be reserved and tasteful in both images and text. They must not run counter to efforts to maintain and promote public health, and must not violate the following principles:
- Smoking may not be portrayed as health-promoting or as harmless.
- Images that create the impression that smoking is a sign of masculinity are barred, as are images depicting men engaged in activities attractive to youthful males (athletes or pilots, for example).
- Advocates of tobacco abstinence or temperance must not be mocked.
- Tobacco advertising may not be directed as sportsmen or automobile drivers, and may not depict such activities.
- Attention may not be drawn to the low nicotine content of a tobacco product if suggesting that the smoker may thereby safely increase his

---

[138] Pg. 179 – "The Nazi War on Cancer", Robert Proctor, Princeton Univ. Press, 2000.
[139] Pgs. 218-219 – Ibid.

tobacco use.

Advertising for tobacco products may not be conducted:
- In films.
- Using billboards or posters, especially on gables but also along railway lines, in rural areas, at sports fields and racetracks.
- On posters in post offices.
- On billboards in or on public or private transportation, at bus stops or similar facilities.
- On posters on walls, fences, at sports arenas or racetracks, or by removable tags on commercial products or adhesive posters on storefronts and doors of shops.
- By loudspeaker (on top of cars, for example).
- By mail.
- By ads in the text sections of journals and newspapers.[140]

The above is quoted at length so the reader can grasp the nature of a government set on enforcing good health as a matter of law and compare these measures to contemporary proposals. The proposals by the Nazis seemed legitimate to the German public as they had heard doctors and scientists make their eugenic arguments for decades before Hitler. Doctors and scientists were at the forefront of the National Socialist movement and were deemed part of the Führer hierarchy as *Gesundheitsführung* (health leadership), which placed the primacy of the public good over individual liberties. Precisely as Leon Whitney proposed in his book, "The Case for Sterilization," the individual owed to the state a "duty to be healthy" or *"Gesundheitspflicht."* Consider this popular Nazi slogan:

Your body belongs to the nation!
Your body belongs to the Führer!
You have the duty to be healthy!
Food is not a private matter![141]

While the German National Socialists never enacted a total ban on cigarettes, as the Americans did on alcohol, that is not to say that the movement was any less injurious to the public's autonomy and freedom. The German National Socialists just went about their laws in the way that fell in line with their broader "racial hygiene" goals. They were regarded as preventive medicine, for the body of the nation, and only indirectly for the individual patient. For example, the "1933 Sterilization Laws (were) for the sterilization of a broad class of genetic defectives, and familiar cancers were sometimes categorized as falling under the rubric of the law." [142] Those deemed to have a predisposition to cancer were liable to be sterilized under the law.

---

[140] Pgs. 204-206, "The Nazi War on Cancer", Robert Proctor, Princeton Univ. Press, 2000.
[141] Pg. 120 – Ibid.
[142] Pg. 68 – Ibid.

Interestingly enough, the only significant backlash against the National Socialist anti-tobacco movement came from within the party. Ernst Röhm's *Sturmabteilung*, or "brown shirts" as historians have come to refer to them, funded their organization via the production and sale of "Storm Cigarettes." [143] Sales ending in 1934 coincided with the Knight of the Long Knives in July 1934, when quarreling among factions inside of the National Socialist party came to a violent end. Resistance henceforth came in a passive form, from young people smoking while listening to jazz or dancing "swing" in clandestine parties after the "Negro" music had been banned. The Nazis otherwise tempered their heavy hand with tobacco legislation and did not enact the total ban they desired as they were keenly aware of the backlash that had occurred in the United States as a reaction to the Prohibition Era total ban on alcohol. [144] Prohibition in the United States was repealed in 1933, the same year that the German National Socialists were amid enacting the many pieces of legislation intended as social controls. The puritanical and paternalistic movements on either side of the Atlantic were aware of each other. For example, the "Scientific Temperance Journal," an anti-alcohol journal, applauded the election of Adolf Hitler in a spring 1933 article titled "Hitler's Attitude Toward Alcohol." [145] The Nazis, however, passed a veritable onslaught of laws ranging from advertisement laws to sterilization laws that were enacted as part of the greater "racial hygiene" movement.

> We Germans stand at an important turning point: new men are shaping the destiny of our fatherland, new laws are being created, new measures put into place, new forces awakened. The struggle touches on everything that has been and is unclean. (quoting Prof. Dr. Immanuel Gosner, leading anti-tobacco activist in 1933 - Pg. 35, "The Nazi War on Cancer")

While a concern for good health may be desirable by some, the reader should understand that *Gesundheit über Alles* is the type of policy of biological collectivism feasible only in socialist utopias where any notion of personal autonomy was deemed to be an injurious concept. It was the health concerns of the society pitted against individual "indulgence" and greed of "capitalism." Robert Proctor reprinted a 1941 propaganda poster titled "*Tabak-Kapital*" which depicted the devil distributing tobacco products and laying waste to "purchasing power," "racial goals," "health" and "labor power." [146] The propaganda clearly alluded to the state's interest in the health and efficiency of its industrial army, as the state recognized no difference between civilian and military goals.

However, the best way to understand just how ingrained and intertwined the anti-tobacco movement was within National Socialism is to understand just how deeply personal it was to its Führer. Most historians agree that the death of Klara Hitler was a pivotal moment for her son. Hitler would leave behind the provincial life after his mother's death and throw himself into the depths of urban Vienna. If

---

[143] Pg. 234 – "The Nazi War on Cancer", Robert Proctor, Princeton Univ. Press, 2000.
[144] Pg. 231 – Ibid.
[145] Pg. 18 - "Hitler's Attitude toward Alcohol", Scientific Temperance Journal, Spring 1933.
[146] Pg. 233 - "Nazi War on Cancer", Robert Proctor, Princeton Univ. Press, 2000.

the scale and scope of The Holocaust are a measure to Adolf Hitler's pathological hatred for the Jews, then the special treatment and protection he gave his mother's Jewish doctor is an equal measure of just how deeply her death affected him. Klara Hitler was treated for her cancer by the Jewish physician Dr. Edward Bloch, and by all accounts, Adolf Hitler was eternally thankful. One of the most bizarre and inexplicably overlooked aspects of Holocaust history is the fact that Hitler protected Bloch from his henchmen and his own government until the very end.

Yet, as extrapolated earlier, those extreme coercive measures cannot be attributed to the will of a single dictator. The impetus for eugenic and racial hygienic measures existed much prior to Adolf Hitler coming to power, and the medical and scientific community in Germany applauded that much louder when a politician surfaced clamoring for the wide-spread health measures they had been requesting for decades. Hitler adopted scientific and medical views that had been adopted by leading scientific minds several generations before him. Dr. Devra Davis puts it another way:

> Germany did not adopt these broad eugenics policies based merely on the rantings of a solitary, insane, grief-maddened politician. If Hitler had not existed, given the tremendous and widespread enthusiasm for protecting the Aryan race and elites, someone else – quite possibly a physician – would have spearheaded the effort for racial hygiene. (Pg. 57, "The Secret History of the War on Cancer", Basic Books, 2009)

The impulse to reject everything related to German National Socialism inevitably caused us to collectively forget the nature of the regime. This is part of the wake of World War II and The Holocaust, which still, to this day, influences us greatly. Our repugnance with the regime largely prevents us from inspecting it too closely, especially when our acts come too close to National Socialism for us to withstand:

> Rather than see Nazi biomedicine as morally bad, the field of bioethics has generally accepted the myths that Nazi biomedicine was either inept, mad, or coerced. By subscribing to these myths, bioethics has been able to avoid a painful confrontation with the fact that many who committed the crimes of the Holocaust were competent physicians and health care professionals acting from their moral convictions. Not one of the doctors or public health officials on trial at Nuremberg pleaded for mercy on the grounds of insanity. A few claimed they were merely following legitimate orders, but no one alleged coercion. (Pg. 58-59, "When Medicine Went Mad: Bioethics and the Holocaust", Arthur L. Caplan, Humana Press, 1992)

Robert Proctor captures the intent of these laws succinctly; most of their highly intrusive health initiatives of the National Socialist regime were enacted with the "goal of creating a secure and sanitary utopia." [147] Adolf Hitler did not have the intellectual capacity or education to produce an original scientific thought, or even coherent legal text. Hitler was a plagiarist, and "Mein Kampf" evidences that he was

---

[147] Pg. 71 - "Nazi War on Cancer", Robert Proctor, Princeton Univ. Press, 2000.

an incoherent and rambling one at that:

> When called to account for their actions, Nazi doctors, scientists, and public health officials were surprisingly forthright about their reasons for their conduct. The same cannot be said for the ethical evaluations offered in Germany and in the West for their crimes. A fog of excuses, lies, and exculpation has been laid over the crematoria and laboratories of the concentration camps. (Pg. 59, "When Medicine Went Mad: Bioethics and the Holocaust", Arthur L. Caplan, Humana Press, 1992)

Our desire to eradicate the disease of cancer or the vices which cause it, entices us to go down a path that should inspire caution, yet we insist on keeping our eyes turned away. This is how we learn to forget. We depersonalize those unpalpable historic figures that participated in creating our history by convincing ourselves that we share nothing with them. We pigeonhole them into whatever category is convenient to our preferred politics and box away their memory into small coffins called books.

Sec. 5 - NAZI ORIGINS OF THE "PRECAUTIONARY PRINCIPLE":

The sheer quantity of laws speaks to the zealotry of the National Socialist movement and illustrates for all posterity that more laws are not in any way an indication of better government: "The number of regulating decrees was estimated to have amounted to more than a thousand a week." [148] National Socialism can be described as "a vast hygienic experiment designed to bring about an exclusionist sanitary utopia." [149] This is as good of a summation of Hitler's National Socialism as any other. Though barely any of National Socialism's aggressive legislation can be understood without first coming to terms with the fact that theirs was a scientific, aesthetic, medical, and biological type of racism. The 1933 legislative efforts were geared towards achieving a "master race" that was superior aesthetically and medically. The muscular figures depicted in the propaganda's posters, films, and sculptures were not stylized fiction; this racial aesthetic was the stated goal of National Socialism, and medicine and science were just the means to this end. None of these ideas originated with National Socialism. Any honest reading of historical evidence says otherwise. Hitler was but a focusing lens for well-entrenched wishes and desires:

> Nazi nutritionist stressed the importance of a diet free of petrochemical dyes

---

[148] Pg. 302 - "Architects of Fortune: Mies Van Der Rohe and the Third Reich", Elaine S. Hochman, Fromm International Pub. Corp., 1989.
[149] Pg. 71 - "Nazi War on Cancer", Robert Proctor, Princeton Univ. Press, 2000.

and preservatives; Nazi health activists stressed the virtues of whole-grain bread and foods high in vitamins and fiber. Many Nazis were environmentalists; many were vegetarians. Species protection was a going concern, as was animal welfare. Nazi doctors worried about overmedication and the overzealous use of X-rays; Nazi doctors cautioned against an unhealthy workplace and the failure of physicians to be honest with their patients. (Pg. 5, "Nazi War on Cancer", Robert Proctor, Princeton Univ. Press, 2000)

Soybeans came to be known as "Nazi beans" during the era as their use originated from the recommendation of the German medical community. [150] "Holistic medicine" was "embraced by many Nazi leaders – medical men like Kurt Klare, Karl Kötschau, Walter Schultze, and Ernst Günther Schenk, but also high-placed politicos like Heinrich Himmler, Julius Streicher, Rudolf Hess, and even Hitler himself." [151] However, the naturalist bent in National Socialism was not in any way restricted to the quacks or the zealots. Even the party members regarded as level-headed were tuned into the naturalist movement. Albert Speer, once known as the "good Nazi," wrote in his memoirs:

> Many of our generation sought such contact with nature. This was not merely a romantic protest against the narrowness of middle-class life. We were also escaping from the demands of a world growing increasingly complicated. We felt that the world around us was out of balance. (Pg. 10, "Inside the Third Reich", Avon, 1971)

The National Socialists were devout believers in the theory of "degeneration" coined by Morel but, ironically, popularized by the famous Viennese Zionist, Max Nordau. The Nazis were convinced that a race could "degenerate" by both poor breeding and by cultural and social pollutants. "Racial hygiene" thus demanded that the state intervene to control the "blood," or heredity, and prohibit by whatever means possible the consumption of pollutants that could taint the racial pool such as alcohol, tobacco, artificial dyes, and modern urban lifestyle in general. Specifically, the rise in cancer rates was directly attributed as a symptom of the general "degeneration," and apocalyptic and catastrophic predictions from the activist medical community abounded. According to Robert Proctor, "if lifestyle degradations were behind the increase, then lifestyle changes could reverse the trend. What was needed was a reorientation of medicine from cure and care to prevention." [152] Prevention, namely the preventing "degeneration" of the Aryan breeding stock, was the goal, and this was a multi-faceted front involving control over reproduction and consumption. This is the reason why the *Völkisch* movement was so integral to National Socialism. Germany had a strong "back to nature," or *Lebensreform* movement that diagnosed cancer as the proximate result of humans distancing themselves from nature. [153] Albert Speer documents Hitler's view on the

---

[150] Pg. 4 – "The Nazi War on Cancer", Robert Proctor, Princeton Univ. Press, 2000.
[151] Pg. 22 – Ibid.
[152] Pg. 25 – Ibid.
[153] Pg. 20 – Ibid.

matter: "Hitler cried out against the erosion of morals in the big cities. He warned against the ill effects of civilization which, he said, damaged the biological substance of the people." [154]

Were all these health measures based on solid research and empirical evidence? Clearly, the German eugenicists were making a huge leap in causality. Their diagnosis was preliminary, at best, and they knew it. However, zealots typically are convinced their assumptions are right before empirical proof justifies drastic actions. The reliance on "prevention" as the goal behind all of the compulsory health laws during Hitler's National Socialism has strong parallels with the "precautionary principle" of today's environmentalists. In fact, the term *"Vorsorgeprinzip"* or "precautionary principle," originated in Germany during the National Socialist era:

> The precautionary principle emerged out of the German socio-legal tradition in the 1930's and implies that in the face of scientific uncertainty, action to prevent potential harm is favored over non-action. (Pgs. 137-176, Stephanie Joan Mead, "The Precautionary Principle: A Discussion on the Principles Meaning & Status in an Attempt to Further Define and Understand the Principle," New Zealand journal of Environment, Vol. 8, 2004)

A report prepared for the January 1998 Wingspread Conference in Budapest, Hungary also states that the "precautionary principle" can be traced back to German legislation of the 1930s:

> When an activity raises threat of harm to the environment or human health, precautionary measures should be taken even if some cause and effect relationships are not fully established scientifically.

The paper gives an alternative definition:
> When the health of humans and the environment is at stake, it may not be necessary to wait for the scientific certainty to take protective action. (Pg. 429, P. Crabbè, "Implementing Ecological Integrity: Restoring Regional and Global Environmental and Human Health", Scientific Affairs Division of the North Atlantic Treaty Organization (NATO), Conference Proceedings, June 2000)

In other words, zealotry does not wait for empirical evidence to confirm its radical assumptions. An apt example is the Nazi propaganda film *Erbkrank,* that faithfully communicated the "precautionary principle" through and through by warning of the catastrophic consequences of allowing the "unfit" to propagate at will. This is the underlying and persistent dogma that this insidious film communicated so successfully; it made everyday Germans fearful and therefore willing to act ruthlessly under the influence of its apocalyptic message.

As was the case with most things Nazi, prominent Americans and Britons had proposed such ideas much prior to Hitler. The most prominent of eugenicists, Leonard Darwin, utilized the "precautionary principle" concept to urge legislative action before having all the scientific facts. In fact, Leonard Darwin was lobbying

---

[154] Pg. 15 - "Inside the Third Reich", Albert Speer, Avon, 1971.

heavily for adopting the principle as early as 1924 or 1926. Leonard Darwin's 1926 book, "The Need for Eugenic Reform" frequently addresses the need to take precautionary action or "condemn our own nation to disaster" and those that followed Leonard Darwin's lead in the eugenic community adopted this stance:

> **Our admitted ignorance concerning the ways of nature affords no excuse for altogether neglecting to promote eugenic reform**, because inaction may leave us at the mercy of unperceived retrograde tendencies, and because evolution is not always progressive. Risks must be run; for to wait for perfect knowledge would be to wait forever. A purely conservative policy on the part of the wise may place the steering of the ship in the hands of the foolish. (emphasis mine, Pg. 10, "The Need for Eugenic Reform", D. Appleton & Co., 1926)

Vorsorgeprinzip then, as it remains to this day, was meant as the legalistic justification for taking drastic action prior to a full accounting of the facts could be attained, and employed, much as it is today, the propaganda of impending doom and catastrophe. The catastrophic and apocalyptic predictions of the "race hygienists" demanded that precautions be taken even if there was no consensus on the truth of their predictions. This was the political motivation for a group of scientists that spent just as much time drafting proposals for utopian governments as they did practice actual science. The ideology of prevention was by necessity a social and political control measure. In order to care for the breeding stock of Aryan society, a society governed by "racial hygiene" philosophy demanded that individual freedoms, namely the freedom to reproduce and consume, be subordinated to the need to preserve the society and prevent it from "degenerating," and that this subordination happen sooner than later:

> The ideology of prevention merged with the ideology of "one for all and all for one" (*Gemeinnutz geht vor Eigennutz*) that was yet another hallmark of Nazi thought: as one anti-tobacco activist put it, nicotine damages not just the individual but the population as a whole. (Pg. 26, "Nazi War on Cancer", Robert Proctor, Princeton Univ. Press, 2000)

This was a medical type of collectivism, which could not occur or survive in a constitutional democracy, that protects individual rights and the right to "life, liberty, and the pursuit of happiness" from undue government intrusion or intervention. The subordination of the individual is indispensable in the making of people expendable for a nation-wide eugenic strategy. This is exactly why Hitler and his cohorts were so critical of "democracy" or *laissez-faire* forms of government. They had fully bought into the apocalyptic warnings of the eugenicists, and thus took extreme measures to prevent the cultural, physical, and aesthetic "degeneration" brought by foreign cultures, peoples, and substances. This paranoia based on the apocalyptic predictions of the scientific community was the basis for the "emergency measures" put in place by Hitler's regime, and the scientific and medical community was not only supportive of the coerced health-measures but drafted the laws which made "race hygiene" state policy. Robert Proctor beautifully summarizes when he

writes:
> Efforts to eliminate illness turned into efforts to eliminate sick workers from the factory, from the hospital, and in certain cases from life itself. The war on disease turned into a war on the diseased. As one prominent Nazi doctor put it after the war, Nazi physicians wanted "to eliminate sickness by eliminating the sick." (Pg. 114, "Nazi War on Cancer", Robert Proctor, Princeton, 2000)

Those that were deemed undesirable health-wise to the community and race were just as liable to be sterilized, segregated, and exterminated as the gypsies and the Jews, and no measure seemed too drastic when framed with the apocalyptic predictions of the propaganda:
> The goal of occupational medicine likewise became a worker who would remain productive until retirement and then pass away shortly thereafter. As Hermann Hebestreit of the German Labor Front put the matter, the aim was to reduce the difference between the age of retirement and the age of death – ideally zero. Werner Bockhacker, chief of the DAF's health office, put forward pretty much the same idea – as did Hellmut Haubold, who characterized the elderly as people "no longer useful to the community." In the idealized Nazi scheme of things, workers would work long and hard and then die – saving for the *Volksgemeinschaft* the financial burdens of the elderly and "unproductive" infirm. (Pg. 119, "Nazi War on Cancer", Robert Proctor, Princeton, 2000)

This was all part of National Socialist's objection to "useless eaters" consuming the resources of an "industrial army" like the one idealized and depicted in Leni Riefenstahl's "Triumph of the Will." The right to life became a meaningless concept in the highly socialized and collectivized National Socialist state. In this way, vegetarianism was an integral part of the "personal habits" which National Socialism sought to change through coercion. Hitler Youth members were instructed against the inclusion of too much meat in their diet, according to the Hitler Youth manual "Health through Proper Eating." [155] Both Hitler and Himmler were hostile to "flesh-eating," and the propaganda against meat-eating was framed as part of the campaign against bourgeois consumerism, gluttony, and overindulgence. The leading German medical journal of the era, the *Deutsches Ärzteblatt* framed this concept with all the melodrama typical of health and science zealots:
> The person who, in his greed for food, eats - or rather gobbles – more meat and fats than he needs for the maintenance of his health and working capacity, robs other racial comrades of these foods; he is a debauchee and a traitor to his land and his country. (Pg. 132, "Nazi War on Cancer", Robert Proctor, Princeton Univ. Press, 2000)

This sentiment, which identified socialism as a cure for "degenerate" gluttony, overindulgence, and bourgeois capitalism, is captured by Albert Speer in his memoirs:

---

[155] Pg. 127 - "Nazi War on Cancer", Robert Proctor, Princeton Univ. Press, 2000.

> Spengler's *Decline of the West* had convinced me that we were living in a period of decay strongly similar to the late Roman Empire: inflation, decline of morals, impotence of the German Reich. His essay "Prussianism and Socialism" excited me especially because of the contempt for luxury and comfort it expressed. (Pg. 12, "Inside the Third Reich", Avon, 1971)

A lot of ink has been wasted trying to psychoanalyze Adolf Hitler. In that effort, a bitter debate over his sexual and social habits has erupted as of late, namely questions about his homosexuality and vegetarianism. The debate is being fought in the context of 21st Century politics, and not historical accuracy. A politician's personal life typically should not be included in the discussion of public policy, except when that politician endorses and pushes onto his constituency personal lifestyle choices as part of a paternalistic philosophy. This is certainly the case with Adolf Hitler and the paternalistic policies of National Socialism. As we have seen, National Socialism demanded total control over even the most private matters and claimed ownership of the individual's physicality in its misguided and twisted paternalism. As we have seen, many of these policies are rooted in the personal lifestyle preferences of the leadership; thus Hitler's vegetarianism comes front and center as it was of consequence to the regime's "racial hygiene" laws that resulted. While many baselessly cast doubt over Hitler's vegetarianism because of the political implications to 21st Century vegetarianism, the facts leave no reasonable doubt. Hitler's vegetarianism is a matter of historical fact, as Hitler's daily regimen was faithfully recorded. [156] More to the point, the vegetarian ideals of a totalitarian dictator bent on forcing a new diet on an entire nation are clearly of historical relevance. Yet, the historical facts about Hitler's vegetarianism have been so vehemently denied that clarification is in order. Beyond official records, we have the contemporary accounts of Hitler's closest friends and associates. The recollections of those close to Hitler are documented at length here as they are firsthand accounts of his vegetarianism. Albert Speer admitted in Nuremberg to being the closest thing to a friend that Hitler had within the staff, and that they shared meals as a matter of daily routine in order to discuss architecture:

> Hitler was served his vegetarian food, drank Fachinger mineral water, and those of his guests who wished could imitate him. But few did. It was Hitler himself who insisted on this simplicity. He could count on its being talked about in Germany. Once, when the Helgoland fishermen presented him with a gigantic lobster, this delicacy was served at table, much to the satisfaction of the guests, but Hitler made disapproving remarks about the human error of consuming such ugly monstrosities. Moreover, he wanted to have such luxuries forbidden, he declared. (Pg. 119, "Inside the Third Reich", Avon, 1971)

Hitler's lack of manners can be added to his list of unappealing features, as he made it a point to shame his guests into a vegetarian diet:

> He was highly pleased with his diet cook and praised her skill at vegetarian

---

[156] Pg. 135 - "Nazi War on Cancer", Robert Proctor, Princeton Univ. Press, 2000.

cuisine. If a dish seemed to him especially good, he asked me to taste of it. ----
If there were a meat broth I could depend on him speaking of "corpse tea"; in
connection with crayfish he brought out his story of a deceased grandmother
where relations had thrown her body into the brook to lure the crustaceans. (Pg.
301, "Inside the Third Reich", Avon, 1971)

Hitler was vocal about how he felt about "flesh eaters" and most often so while at the dinner table:
> In the 1920s, for example, on a romantic date, the future Führer scolded his female companion for having ordered *Wienerschnitzel*. Clearly bothered by his reaction, she asked if she had done something wrong, to which he replied: "No, go ahead and have it, but I don't understand why you want it. I didn't think you wanted to devour a corpse. . . the flesh of dead animals. Cadavers!" (Pg. 135, "Nazi War on Cancer", Robert Proctor, Princeton Univ. Press, 2000)

Apparently, stately guests were not the only ones who were annoyed by the Fuehrer's insistence on a vegetarian diet, as Albert Speer documents:
> I avoided, as did any reasonably prudent visitor to Hitler, arousing any feelings of friendship in the dog. That was not often easy, especially when at meals the dog laid his head on my knee and in this position attentively studied the pieces of meat, which he evidently preferred to his master's vegetarian dishes. When Hitler noticed such disloyalty, he irritably called the dog back. (Pg. 302, "Inside the Third Reich", Avon, 1971)

Interestingly enough, Joseph Goebbels attributed Hitler's vegetarianism to his belief that humans were animals, and that humanity denied its animal nature to its own demise:
> The Führer is deeply religious, though completely anti-Christian. He views Christianity as a symptom of decay. Rightly so. It is a branch of the Jewish race. . . Both [Judaism and Christianity] have no point of contact to the animal element, and thus, in the end, they will be destroyed. The Führer is a convinced vegetarian, on principle. His arguments cannot be refuted on any serious basis. They are totally unanswerable. (Pg. 136, "Nazi War on Cancer", Robert Proctor, Princeton Univ. Press, 2000)

And as explained, Hitler's personal lifestyle preferences significantly influenced public policy in the National Socialist government:
> Shortly after taking office, for example, he arranged a meeting with an eighty-year old woman from Bad Godesberg ("known up and down the Rhine as the *Seniorin* of vegetarianism, cold-water cures, and herbal healing") to discuss the benefits of a vegetarian diet. That same day, when his Gestapo chief tried to broach with him the need to simplify the party's complicated bureaucratic structure, Hitler responded that there were "far more important things than politics – reforming the human lifestyle, for example. What this old woman told me this morning is far more important than anything I can do in my life". (Pgs.

134-135, "Nazi War on Cancer", Princeton Univ. Press, 2000)

Several institutions of a "naturopathic" ethos that exemplified the National Socialist back-to-nature outlook were created in 1933. The most ambitious project was the *Rudolf Hess Krankenhaus* in Dresden. Hess had always lobbied to make "natural healing" command the importance and political respect that "academic medicine" enjoyed, and many of the leaders of the natural health movement, namely Reich Physician's Führer, Gerhard Wagner, owed much of their political success within the party to Hess' patronage and support:

> Rudolf Hess was another fussy eater. Like Himmler, Hitler's deputy and successor was fond of herbal remedies and homeopathy, and took great care in foods he ate. He used to bring his own vegetarian food to meetings at the Chancellery, which he would then warm up for dinner. This annoyed Hitler, who complained to Hess, "I have an excellent dietician/cook here. If your doctor has prescribed something special for you, she could certainly prepare it. You cannot bring your own food in here." Hess countered that his food had to contain certain biodynamic ingredients, prompting Hitler to suggest that he (Hess) might prefer to eat at home. Hess was apparently less often invited to lunch with the Führer after that episode. (Pg. 139, "Nazi War on Cancer", Robert Proctor, Princeton Univ. Press, 2000)

As with all other things Hitler, the influence from composer Richard Wagner becomes central to the personality profile. Hitler was a devout follower of Wagner, and his vegetarianism was but one way for Adolf Hitler to mimic and pay homage to his idol. Wagner's political writings were gospel to Hitler, and the pomposity of Wagner's style influenced Hitler whose education was otherwise, incomplete, to say the least. It was precisely in Richard Wagner that Hitler found the "granite foundations" for his views of the world. Wagner wrote at length about the benefits of vegetarianism, in his 1880 "The Highest Motive for Vegetarianism," which is part of Wagner's essays from "Religion and Art." Robert Proctor documents this aspect of Hitler's life:

> In an 1881 essay, Wagner had claimed that the human race had become contaminated and impure through racial mixing and the eating of animal flesh; a new kind of socialism was needed to purify Germany of these twin evils, calling upon "true and hearty fellowship with the vegetarians, the protectors of animals, and the friends of temperance" to save the German people from Jewish aggression. Wagner claimed that abstaining from a fleshy diet would allow a human moral redemption – possibly even for the Jews. (Pg. 136, "Nazi War on Cancer", Robert Proctor, Princeton Univ. Press, 2000)

Hitler himself addressed the inspiration for his vegetarianism: "I don't touch meat largely because of what Wagner says on the subject." [157] Yet, despite the overwhelming first-hand evidence, some second-hand accounts of Hitler's lack of

---

[157] Pg. 136 - "Nazi War on Cancer", Robert Proctor, Princeton Univ. Press, 2000.

consistency with vegetarianism have been the basis of much of what has been written to debate first-hand accounts of Hitler's vegetarianism. There are reports of the fact that Hitler would make an exception when his very close friend and potential lover, Heinrich Hoffman, prepared dumplings for the Führer. These reports are tangled with the equally contentious subject of Hitler's homosexuality.

However, Hitler was far from being the only fussy eater within the regime's top ranks. Another important way to gauge the persistent influence of "naturopathic" influence within National Socialism would be to weigh Heinrich Himmler's importance within the party. Himmler's personal "naturopathic" project was carried out in the various concentration camps that were directly under his jurisdiction and political control. This is another aspect of Holocaust history that seems to have been conveniently forgotten for the sake of contemporary political posturing. Dachau was the first concentration camp opened in Hitler's Germany, located on the grounds of an abandoned munitions factory near the medieval town of Dachau, northwest of Munich in the state of Bavaria. Dachau opened March 22, 1933, just 51 days after Hitler took power, and according to various sources, Dachau had the most ambitious organic garden in the world:

> The Dachau concentration camp had several greenhouses in which various herbs and medicinal plants were grown both for experiments and for large-scale production. Himmler remained enthusiastic about homeopathy, mesmerism, and the holistic traditions that went under the name of *Biochemie*. (Pg. 56, "Nazi War on Cancer", Robert Proctor, Princeton Univ. Press, 2000)

The famous German organic guru Alwin Seifert used the gardens of Dachau as research grounds and to his personal benefit. Seifert went on to become a best-selling author and well-regarded scholar of organic farming. Seifert's career took off during Hitler's regime as the landscape architect for the Autobahn project. In 1933 Seifert was the Commissioner for highway construction under Fritz Todt, Hitler's architect prior to Speer. In May 1940, Seifert was also "Reich Landscape attorney." The Times reported on this embarrassing aspect of Seifert's past. The article reports that Seifert oversaw the 211 hectares that Himmler dedicated to organic gardening:[158]

> "The question has to be how much of the information that flowed into his book derived from the research being done in Dachau," says the Munich-based cultural historian Daniella Seidl - "He was a regular visitor, maintained a correspondence with the head gardener Franz Lippert, and even arranged for a couple from the camp to work in his own household." Some of the ideas being tried out in the Dachau gardens were certainly adopted by Seifert for use in his own garden in the Tyrol. (thetimes.co.uk, Article No.: 6831453, "German Organic Gardening Guru Alwin Seifert Took Tips from Dachau Experiments", The Times, 2009)

Seifert used the Dachau complex to conduct research experiments meant to improve organic gardening techniques, such as why potatoes had become so

---

[158] See also: *"Zwischen Himmel Und Hölle-Das Kommando 'Plantage' Des Konzentrationslagers Dachau"* or in English, "Between Heaven and Hell: The Command 'Plantation' at the Dachau Concentration Camp", Daniella Seidl, 2009.

vulnerable to pests and early decay. According to The Times, the facility was supposed to provide a scientific basis for an alternative "biological-dynamic lifestyle." This meant growing herbs for use as medicine and extracting vitamins. One of the aims was to assist in Hitler's call for making Germany independent of food imports and self-sustaining. Work was done on making a German pepper. Fermented blackberry and raspberry leaves were used to create a German tea. Gladioli were grown in vast quantities to milk them for their vitamin-C. The leaves were dried and pulverized in the camp garden complex and then mixed with a mixture of spices, beef fat, and cooking salt to make a food supplement for SS troopers.

The Nazi camps were also utilized in a more sinister form of "holistic" medicine. There is a gruesome relationship between Himmler's belief in natural cures and the "freezing" experiments, which were later determined to be "war crimes":

> His belief that "vital heat" of the human body was fundamentally different from ordinary mechanical heat led him to support the notorious experiments to determine whether pilots downed in the icy waters of the North Sea might be more rapidly warmed by human flesh than by conventional methods. At Dachau, naked women were forced to embrace the frozen, near-dead victims of hypothermia experiments, the theory being that their "organic" heat would prove more effective than, say, submersion in a bath of warm water. (Pg. 56, "Nazi War on Cancer", Princeton Univ. Press, 2000)

Seifert was not the only National Socialist to subsequently earn notoriety during the upsurge in "environmentalism" in the 1970s. Dr. Wilhelm Hueper, the chief pathologist at the University of Pennsylvania's Cancer Research Laboratory, wrote to a letter to Hitler's government on September 28, 1933, requesting a position at a university or hospital. Hueper had left Germany in 1923, was familiar with the National Socialist movement, and wanted to return to participate. The letter was enthusiastically signed "Heil Hitler!" Dr. Wilhelm Hueper would go on to earn fame and honors upon returning to the United States and working on occupational and environmental cancer. Hueper was the first director of the Environmental Cancer Section of the National Cancer Institute, holding that post from 1938 to 1964. However, his most recognizable project was the work he did with Rachel Carson, the environmentalist icon who wrote the famous book "Silent Sprint." Carson's practice of framing her argument in apocalyptic and catastrophic terms likely was gleaned from Hueper's guidance. [159]

All of this was common knowledge to National Socialism's contemporaries, but current political ideologies refuse to allow us to remember the "environmentalist" and "natural living" side to Hitler's National Socialism. It is unwise to stop consulting history due to political inconvenience, especially when we may be going down similar paths of government coercion seeking to achieve allegedly positive goals. Our natural impulse with all things Hitler is repulsion and revulsion. Our impulse to reject inevitably led us to forget historically valuable lessons learned from National Socialism.

---

[159] Pgs. 13-15 - "The Nazi War on Cancer", Robert Proctor, Princeton Univ. Press, 2000.

Sec. 6 - CONTROLLING CULTURE OR THE CULTURE OF CONTROL?

The stereotype of the independent artist has led to erroneous assumptions of the role artists played in Hitler's Germany. As was the case with the Russian Constructivists, German artists were among the most enthusiastic zealots to welcome in the new socialist regime. This was no small political victory for Hitler; "the number of Germans officially designated as artists or entertainers exceeded the combined figures for those designated as doctors and lawyers." [160]

> Artists had been profoundly affected by the unionization and professionalization trends of the Imperial and Weimar periods. In the nineteenth century, artists had begun to recognize the value of occupational associations as vehicles for influencing legislators, state regulators, and employers. Moreover, only in combination with occupational colleagues could most individual artists find, or afford, the specialized kinds of job counseling, legal representation, and social welfare programs required for a secure economic existence. The pressures of war, economic difficulties during the immediate postwar period, and the Weimar Republic's legislative promotion of institutionalized collective bargaining all accelerated the process of interest group formation. (Pg. 8, "Art, Ideology, & Economics in Nazi Germany", Alan E. Steinweis, Univ. of North Carolina Press, 1993)

Hitler converted an incomplete existing and somewhat dissatisfactory system of union representation into a means for cultural regulation and regimentation. The *Kulturkammer* was created by the Reich Cabinet in September of 1933. Its stated goal was to "promote German culture on behalf of the German Volk and Reich" and to "regulate the economic and social affairs of the culture professions." The *Kulturkammer* was subdivided into separate divisions for music, theater, the visual arts, literature, film, radio, and the press, and thus it leveraged control over several hundred thousand professional and any amateur performer from church choirs to people who just happened to express themselves artistically in any public venue. The *Kulturkammer* was an initiative close to Adolf Hitler's heart, as he intended to improve the living conditions of starving artists as he had once endured. It was also intended to curtail the creation of any art he disdained as an artist himself.

The pressure to collectivize was not just a political one, but a cultural one too. The newly invented forms of modern transportation brought unwelcome and unprecedented competition from foreign artists. Equally devastating was the modern technology in the form of "mechanical music" and "moving pictures" which also brought competition for the performing artists. The invention of the phonograph cut deep into the pockets of musicians that would otherwise perform in coffee shops and restaurants to make ends meet between more serious gigs, and more importantly, it brought the issue of copyright protection to the forefront. It created a political rift between the "*schaffende*," or creative musicians, and those that only performed, the "*nachschaffende*," who were seen as unjustly profiting from the composers.

To make matters worse, the less structured and stratified society of the 20th

---

[160] Pg. 7 - "Art, Ideology, & Economics in Nazi Germany", Alan E. Steinweis, Univ. of North Carolina Press, 1993.

Century produced plenty of amateur artists, which also cut into the full-time artist's economic opportunity. Thus, the political moves designed to marginalize and exclude the amateur artists was an effort that begun with the Weimar era collective organizations and was only exacerbated as a result of the total power and total control which the National Socialist government provided the organizations it rolled under its wing. The German Musicians' Association, the *DeMuV*, founded in 1872, had become a socialist-oriented trade union after World War I. Its intended purpose was to protect the "*ernste*," or serious, musicians from the encroachments into the profession:

> Neocorporatism represented a non-Marxist alternative to a failing liberal social and economic order. It envisaged a society divided into self-regulating estates (Stände), each composed of members of the same profession or occupation. The estates would establish qualifications for professional practice and safeguard market monopolies for their own members. Such regulatory powers would be constitutionally and legally recognized. ---- Neocorporatist thinking among artistic and cultural professionals manifested itself primarily in the form of calls for the creation of officially recognized professional chambers, which would replace the fragmented, messy system of unions and professional associations. (Pg. 17, "Art, Ideology, & Economics in Nazi Germany", Univ. of North Carolina Press, 1993)

In hindsight, it would seem as if Adolf Hitler was able to capitalize on pre-existing prejudices. However, it would be more correct to state that Hitler's world view was a product of these realities. He had known hunger and homelessness because of these cultural and political realities. The trend to control and restrict the arts was not a product of the totalitarian National Socialist scheme, but rather the other way around. Artists had only become "more vocal in their demands for de-liberalization and official restrictions on access to the art market" due to the increased hardships resulting from the Great Depression. [161] Figures no less influential than Richard Wagner, Arthur de Gobineau, Julius Langbehn, and Houston Stewart Chamberlain had all publicly voiced their views of the politics of art, or in German, *Kunstpolitik*. As was the case with all things Hitler, the elements of the contentious issue did not originate with him, but with his those he idolized or absorbed through one medium or another. [162]

These collective bargaining organizations, once imbued with complete and total power of the National Socialist state, became the legal method upon which to exclude undesired participation. However, these labor unions could create the illusory economic balance only if they could centrally plan professional education and participation. To this end, the Music and Visual Arts Chambers took control of the schools so they could prevent overcrowding of the professions. [163] This political protectionism easily translated into cultural xenophobia when these "*völkisch*" cultural leaders begun to resent the heavy influence of Jews and Marxists,

---

[161] Pg. 19 - "Art, Ideology, & Economics in Nazi Germany", Alan E. Steinweis, Univ. of North Carolina Press, 1993.
[162] Pg. 21 – Ibid.
[163] Pg. 66 – Ibid.

often seen as one, into the cultural arts. The art of the modern era, and its urban reality, was received as a culturally contaminated and a detraction and decay of the traditional German culture. The avant-garde fashion and new modernist aesthetics were deemed alien. More importantly, the artistic depictions of the world by modernist artists easily played into the narrative that they were decadent, and more precisely, "degenerate" world views. They did not represent or accurately depict as much as they seemed to distort and detract from the proud cultural traditions. As such, they were seen as an affront and explicit danger to the Aryan "purity." It was "settled science" that cultural intrusions by "inferior" races meant racial and cultural "degeneration." German cultural accomplishments were pointed to as irrefutable proof of Aryan or Nordic racial superiority. Germany was, after all, the "land of poets and thinkers." Thus, any cultural affront or intrusion from foreign elements was perceived as a direct attack on the cultural value of the German people, or *volk*:

> During the Nazi "era of struggle" before 1933, Hitler's speeches often stressed the necessity of a new national *Kunstpolitik*. In Mein Kampf (1924-25) Hitler elaborated on his conception of the relationship between art and a *völkisch* state. "It is the business of the state," he wrote, "to prevent a people from being driven into the arms of spiritual madness" and to guarantee "the preservation of those original racial elements which bestow culture and create beauty and dignity of a higher mankind." (Pg. 22, Alan E. Steinweis, "Art, Ideology, & Economics in Nazi Germany", Univ. of North Carolina Press, 1993)

In 20/20 hindsight, the modernists came up with what was arguably the most threatening phrase to identify the new art in this eugenic-minded cultural atmosphere. "The International Style" was the term coined by Walter Gropius, the German architect and founder of the Bauhaus. Not only was Gropius intentionally referencing his Marxist tendencies in creating this label, but nothing could have been a more poignant affront to those obsessed with preserving the purity of "national" identity. Eugenics is the antithesis of inclusiveness. No one obsessed with a xenophobic fear of including lesser cultures wanted anything to do with the watering-down and degeneration implied by "internationalism." This is precisely why the Bauhaus, the famous architecture and design school, became the epicenter for this struggle for the German soul. [164] Gropius, unable to cope with the political war he so epically misjudged, ultimately shoved the problem off to his successor Mies Van Der Rohe, the architect known for stating that "God is in the details" and "less is more," but most popularly known in popular culture for designing the Barcelona Chair.

To add to the fog of this conflict, instead of swaying to the opposite side of artistic independence and autonomy, the allegedly opposing Communist faction within the Bauhaus created its own group to represent the Marxist "revolutionary class struggle." They injected a Marxist methodology into the creation of their art. For example, the German Association of Revolutionary Visual Artists rejected the

---

[164] See generally – "Architects of Fortune: Mies van der Roheand the Third Reich", Elaine S. Hochman, Fromm Intl. Publishing, 1990.

notion of "art for art's sake" and stated that art only existed for the expression of "the revolution."

As this book documents, aesthetics and propaganda were central to the National Socialist ethos and political aspirations. Hitler's eugenic vision had very specific aesthetic aspirations beyond the fancy uniforms and flags and was deeply rooted in an aesthetic preference for Aryan bodily features and Nordic culture. Despite this deeply rooted artistic bent to the political movement, Hitler was able to keep his artistic prejudices close to his chest for a long time. Both Alan E. Steinweis and Elaine S. Hochman comment on the fact that even those predisposed to the avant-garde, namely Joseph Goebbels, were unaware of the bitter hatred Adolf Hitler had for modern art and architecture for the first five to 10 years of the regime. Alfred Rosenberg made clear his hatred for modern architecture often enough in the National Socialist newspaper the *Völkischer Beobachter*. However, figures closer to Hitler, such as Joseph Goebbels and Ebhard Hanfstaengl, the Harvard educated art dealer who had been an early contributor to Hitler's political cause, had a distinct taste for modernism. Meanwhile, Hitler pretty much kept his discussions on art and architecture limited to those whose opinions he respected, mainly his fellow architect, Albert Speer, and not anyone else. Thus, the various factions of subordinates misjudged the importance of the arts for their leader and made the mistake of thinking that architecture and art were not much more than a hobby for Adolf Hitler. Nothing could have been further from the truth. According to Erich Fromm, "Architecture was the only field in which Hitler had a real interest in something outside of himself, the only area in which he was alive." [165] Nothing illustrates this aspect of Adolf Hitler better than the fact that in the final hours of his life, with the Russian tanks at the doorstep of Berlin, the defeated and decimated Adolf Hitler sat silently in his bunker looking at the scale models of the architectural plans for his "new" Linz. Nor can it be said that this artistic ethos was particular to Adolf Hitler. For Hitler, Gropius, and Mies alike, architecture was an expression of the central spirit of an era, far beyond the utilitarian or ceremonial. However, for some reason yet unknown to this author, Hitler did not make his architectural preferences clearly known until 1934, and not state policy until the exposition of "Degenerate Art." For a brief window of time, it seems as either classicism or modernism could be the adopted aesthetic of the Third Reich. The very existence of the Bauhaus precariously persisted and dangled upon this uncertainty for years. Mies was caught in the middle of the bitter uprisings within and without the Bauhaus, which Gropius was unable to contend with, and which ultimately resulted in Van Der Rohe's inevitable emigration out of his beloved Germany.

More in keeping with the central theme of this book, posterity must take note that Hitler's desire to monopolize control over the arts and cultural life went much deeper than artistic preferences. Hitler's National Socialism was after all a proposal for a "total state," where the state exerted control over every aspect of life, and thus needed the ability to steer public opinion:

---

[165] Pg. 177 - "Architects of Fortune: Mies Van Der Rohe and the Third Reich", Elaine S. Hochman, Fromm Intl. Pub., 1989.

The "implementation and administration of all tasks of popular enlightenment" required the leadership of a "single will" embodied in the Propaganda Ministry. By "popular enlightenment," Hitler and Goebbels meant far more than propaganda in the narrow sense. The ministry, they asserted, would establish control over "organizations in the fields of radio, the press, film, theater, music, and other areas of propaganda, enlightenment, and advertising." (Pg. 34, "Art, Ideology, & Economics in Nazi Germany", Alan E. Steinweis, Univ. of North Carolina, 1993)

This was an integral part of the state that sought to subordinate the individual to the needs of the society. Goebbels explicitly articulated the differences between art in a National Socialist state and a "liberal" state as *Volksgemeinschaft*, or people's community, taking precedence over the rights of the individual artist. Interestingly enough, Goebbels echoes the sentiments of the Bolshevik elements within the Bauhaus:

> The "liberal" notion of "art for art's sake" was therefore inconsistent with the tenets of National Socialism. As Goebbels explained, "we have replaced individuality with *Volk* and individual people with *Volksgemeinschaft*." The state had not only the right but also the obligation to advance art in the interests of the *Volksgemeinschaft*. (Pg. 22, "Art, Ideology, & Economics in Nazi Germany", Univ. of North Carolina Press, 1993)

Architecture, like the Munich Olympics after, was communicating the Nazi ideal within and abroad in the frequent world expositions, who have lost their importance today, but were events of significant importance in a world before television and satellite communications. World exhibitions and international symposiums was how the talent and technology of the era was marketed and presented to colleagues around the world, specifically Mies Van Der Rohe's 1929 Barcelona Pavilion, arguably one of the most important pieces of architecture ever, had been both a source a pride for Germany and a source of tension between Mies and the National Socialists. Mies refused to place the German eagle insignia on the pavilion. Thus, Hitler saw to it to start judging the expositions himself, and it is in the 1934 competition for the Brussels Pavilion which Hitler made his preference known, in no uncertain terms. When it came time to judge the various proposals Hitler kept returning to Mies Van Der Rohe's entry while pacing around the various presentations made in scale model form:

> Hitler's reaction to the pavilion entries is unknown. However, the state in which they were found — lying in a heap behind his desk — suggests that his response was violent. "Hitler had sealed his decision with his foot," recalled Serigius Ruegenberg. (Pg. 228, "Architects of Fortune: Mies Van Der Rohe and the Third Reich", Elaine S. Hochman, Fromm International Pub. Corp., 1989)

From 1934 onwards, Hitler no longer stayed above the fray in discussions about the aesthetics appropriate to his "total state." The conversation was no longer left for the Rosenberg and Goebbels camps to debate, with Goebbels winning politically but silenced aesthetically and made to purge any modernist strains within the artistic community Goebbels had previously supported. In the Cultural Address of September 1935, Hitler referred to modernism as "criminals of the world," "destroyers of art," and "imbecile degenerates interested in the destruction of the nation." [166] The proximate product of Hitler's convictions was the exhibition of "Degenerate Art," whose collection was displayed alongside photographs of mental and criminal institution patients and inmates. This aspect of the exhibit illustrated just how entangled Hitler's aesthetic vision was to his eugenic goals.

So, why were allegedly "liberal" artists then attracted to totalitarian forms of government? Because they believed in collectivism then, much as artists do today. For collectivism to work, whether justified under the empty claims of "class struggle" or "nationalism," it must be made compulsory and enforced with the iron fist of the state. More to the point, compulsory collectivism was an alluring proposition for the starving artist as it remains so today. Most artists emerging out of the Great Depression were without unemployment insurance coverage, yet Bismarck's state system offered it to government employees and thus made the folding of the arts into an all-encompassing state-controlled venture a prospect attractive to the financially unstable artists:

> With low earning power and little job security, artists presented a poor insurance risk even under normal circumstances; during the depression their lack of insurance protection had become especially distressing. To overcome the problem, the chambers had to achieve two vital preconditions. First, a general improvement in the economic fortunes of artists was needed to provide the necessary actuarial foundation for a workable insurance scheme. Second, an insurance framework could be effective only if subscription to the insurance were made compulsory. (Pgs. 98-99, "Art, Ideology, & Economics in Nazi Germany", Alan E. Steinweis, Univ. of North Carolina Press, 1993)

Thus, the coerced collectivism of National Socialism was largely welcomed by the artists who felt helpless and without control under a "liberal" economic system. Hitler promised to reverse that and most German artists, far from being a resistance force, were willing collaborators. These disturbing facts go a long way to answering the lingering question of where all the sober minds and responsible people were when the threat of National Socialism arrived. Contemporary historians like Alan E. Steinweis concludes that much of the responsibility for what ultimately resulted in the atrocities of the Third Reich lay at the feet of German artist's conscious choice to support a system of exclusion and collectivization. He documents that artists who spoke up in defense of their Jewish colleagues were far outnumbered by those who passively accepted, actively participated, and directly benefited from the consolidation and centralization of political power:

> …artists bestowed a certain cultural legitimacy on the movement. After the Nazi seizure of power, the illusion of professional autonomy wooed many more artists into collaboration with the regime. Again, what the regime most needed from

---

[166] Pg. 222 - "Architects of Fortune: Mies Van Der Rohe and the Third Reich", E.S. Hochman, Fromm Int, 1989.

them ---- especially during the early, often tumultuous, period of consolidation – was a stamp of legitimacy. ---- Whether working for their own sakes, for the sake of the Volk, or purely for the sake of art, German artists reassured their countrymen that the land of Hitler could indeed still be the land of Goethe, Schiller, and Beethoven. (Pg. 176, "Art, Ideology, & Economics in Nazi Germany", Alan E. Steinweis, Univ. of North Carolina Press, 1993)

Sec. 7 - FROM THE ENABLING ACT TO *"FÜHRERPRINZIP":*

As the reader traces backward, from leaf down to the root, the topic of the *Führerprinzip* increases in importance. How did Adolf Hitler amass all-encompassing power? This catastrophic tumble into dictatorial totalitarianism begins with the passing of the Enabling Act. The Enabling Act was passed by Germany's Reichstag and signed by Hindenburg on March 23, 1933. It was the second major step, after the Reichstag Fire Decree, through which Chancellor Adolf Hitler legally obtained plenary powers and established his dictatorship. The act stated that it was to last for four years unless renewed by the Reichstag. However, once power was surrendered, there was no turning back. Once fully immersed in Hitler's reign the Reichstag renewed the Enabling Act twice and would have likely renewed it indefinitely if Hitler's reign had not been brought to an abrupt end by the Allied Forces.

The formal name of the Enabling Act was *"Gesetz zur Behebung der Not von Volk und Reich,"* which interestingly enough, translates as the "Law to Remedy the Distress of People and Reich." The laws of socialist states are never given names that betray their truly intrusive nature. Historians really should teach the history of the Third Reich governmental activity using the full name of the Act, as its full name is indicative of its true nature; Hitler sought to relieve the German people of the burden of self-government and replace it with his "Leader Principle." Evidence of this can be seen in the early speeches where Hitler gives an accurate description of what National Socialism precisely meant as a system of government and directly attacks "self-government" and "parliamentary democracy" as "Jewish inventions." It would be of service for historians to accurately document that the political rhetoric propagandizing the Act was not framed in the predictable language of dictatorship. In a December 11, 1933, speech, Hitler played the part of the humble servant, claiming that he would once more "appeal to the people" once the four-year measure had expired. [167] How Adolf Hitler proposed to take an accurate account of the "voice of the people" after doing away with "democracy," he, of course, does not explain. He viewed himself as the embodiment of the "will of the people," even

---

[167] Pg. 431 - "Speeches of Adolf Hitler: April 1922-August 1939", Oxford Univ. Press along with the Royal Institute of International Affairs in England, 1942.

recognizing that some would disagree, and viewed them as being dragged onward and forward. The convictions that the governing elite know best, and the masses must be dragged along despite reservations, is a conviction that persist to this day among Progressive circles. The "People's will" in National Socialism was not as much defined by popular vote or parliamentary procedure, as it was sensed or ordained by the ruling elite, whose wisdom was to be trusted:

> The people on a basis of common blood creates a community and as such possess a spirit – a *Volksgeist*—which is no mere opinion of the moment but is rooted in national history and national character. That spirit of the people may indeed be falsified and misled—to it "public opinion" may at any given time be no safe guide: it remains, however, anchored in the subconsciousness of the people until the time when a Leader arises who is profoundly inspired by a realization of the uncorrupted *Volksgeist* which he can then evoke once more from the people's subconciousness, and by this power of evocation demonstrates his autonomous immediate title to Leadership. That title is not conferred upon him by any human authority: "he is his own best evidence, his witness is within." Through his own personality he awakes the unquestioning absolute loyalty of the people as his followers. He is no representative to whom the people has given a mandate: he is the incarnation of the Spirit of the people. (Pg. 414, "Speeches of Adolf Hitler: April 1922-August 1939", Oxford Univ. Press along with the Royal Institute of International Affairs in England, 1942)

In his speech at the Harvest Festival on the Bückeberg on October 3, 1937, Hitler summarized some of the "fundamental principles" that made National Socialism the "Revolution" of the "People" by the total submission of this very same populace to the "will" of the leader:

> Above all we have worked out in Germany a single will. Without such a single will, a Four Year Plan could not be carried into execution. ---- The individual has no knowledge of what is necessary for the survival of all. ---- So long as the German nation in every walk of life subjects itself to a single will, so long can all problems be solved. (Pg. 435, "Speeches of Adolf Hitler: April 1922-August 1939", Oxford Univ. Press along with the Royal Institute of International Affairs in England, 1942)

This subservience was an explicit doctrine of National Socialism under Hitler's "*Führerprinzip*" or "Leaders Principle." For the purposes of this book, it must be noted that the goals of the eugenicists could not exist without this pyramidal social structure that Hitler described. Individual rights or aspirations could not be allowed to impede the collectivized needs of the social body, lest the will of the "unfit" be allowed to infect this social body. The eugenic doctrine necessitated that the legal stature and political voice of those deemed "unfit" be eternally subordinated to the will of the governing elite tasked with the responsibility of sifting through and choosing those deemed "fit" and "unfit." Both Hitler's "*Führerprinzip*" and the eugenic creed are by necessity elitist. In fact, the philosophies are one and the same and can hardly be separated, as the utopian eugenic vision could not survive any other form of governmental structure. National Socialism demanded "faith" in its leadership, and Hitler and his cohorts described it as such. Furthermore, this eugenic vision could not sustain itself if it had to contend with competition from a higher faith or a higher calling. As has previously been evidenced, all eugenicists saw the Catholic Church as their greatest obstacle:

> "Naturally, practical politics demands that, for the time being at least, we must avoid any appearance of a campaign against the Church." He was careful to emphasize again that he was a Politiker, with no ambition to become a prophet. But National Socialism, he said, was a Weltanschauung and in fact a religion which was now building itself up and disseminating itself. ---- "Yes, National Socialism is a form of conversion, a new faith, but we don't need to raise that issue – it will come of itself. "I insist on the certainty that sooner or later, once we hold the power, Christianity will be overcome and the 'Deutsche Kirche' established. Yes, the German Church, without a Pope and without the Bible - and Luther, if he could be with us, would give us his blessing. "Hitler was ablaze now, and I could see the ideas of Rosenberg's Mythus working in him. He shouted with passionate energy: 'Of course, I myself am a heathen to the core!' . . . "No, Ludecke, we don't need to declare this fight openly. It would be political stupidity to show the masses." (Pg. 369, "Speeches of Adolf Hitler: April 1922-August 1939", Oxford Univ. Press along with the Royal Institute of International Affairs in England, 1942)

Hitler explained this aspect of his movement early on as a *"Politiker."* Norman H. Baynes, who collected Hitler's speeches in the early 1940s, explains that Hitler considered the entirety of government to be an expression of the leader's will:

> The aim of the whole legal profession is "to serve the people and to serve the Führer." The source of German legislation are "statutes, the former customary law, the order of the Führer, the word of the Führer." "The law and the will of the Führer are one." Previously one spoke of Justice and Injustice, but now a judge before giving his decision must ask himself: "What would the Führer say to this?" (Pg. 518, "Speeches of Adolf Hitler: April 1922-August 1939", Oxford Univ. Press along with the Royal Institute of International Affairs in England, 1942)

These were the founding principles of a movement that clearly identified itself as "Socialist," and which pretended to or at least aspired to act under "one will," as stated by Hitler himself. The Minister of the Interior, William Frick, reiterated how this concept applied to the law:

> If the Englishman with sound political sense has coined the phrase 'Right or Wrong, my Country' so we National Socialist go beyond that and say '*Recht* is what benefits the German People and *Unrecht* is that which harms the German People.' This principle which governs all our legislative action is identical with the other **National Socialist maxim 'Common Interest goes before Private Interest'**. These guiding principles must dominate our whole people." (emphasis mine, Pg. 515, "Speeches of Adolf Hitler: April 1922-August 1939", Oxford

Univ. Press along with the Royal Institute of International Affairs in England, 1942)

What happened to the German constitution and the rights of Germans? Baynes reminds us that the Weimar Constitution was never formally abrogated. In fact, it was through the procedures of the Weimar Constitution that the Nazis came to power. However, Hitler was clear that the assumption to power of his Third Reich was no mere change of government but a "Revolution" and a triumph of the "*Weltanschauung*," or the popular will, which had clear legislative implications. At the center of this proclamation was the eternal and enduring argument about "positive" and "negative" rights in the "social contracts" we call "constitutions":

> Just as the Weimar Constitution fully reflected the principles of the Liberalistic period with its insistence on Parliamentarism, on the "fundamental rights" of the individual which could be asserted against the State, with its "objectivity" permitting freedom of expression to differing political parties representing varying political standpoints; so the new Constitution must mirror the sole supremacy of an essentially intolerant Weltanschauung which fanatically denies the values of the Liberalistic age. The individual can no longer assert his "fundamental rights": he must be reminded that his duties to the community of the people are paramount; for other political parties than the National Socialist Movement there can be no place: Parliamentarism, together with its principle of authority coming from below, must be superseded by a principle of personal responsibility with authority coming from above. Government through the decisions of majorities is incompatible with the new Weltanschauung: in its stead the principle of Leadership must prevail. (Pgs. 413-414, "Speeches of Adolf Hitler: April 1922-August 1939", Oxford Univ. Press along with the Royal Institute of International Affairs in England, 1942)

Hitler was crystal clear on the fact that it was not an "ideal" which they were following, but the "will" of a "Leader," which allegedly was the embodiment, conscious or subconscious, of the "unity of purpose" and "single mind" of the "People." In a conversation between Hitler and Otto Strasser on May 21, 1930, Strasser made the mistake of stating that "Ideas are eternal" and that the "Leaders are servants of the idea." Hitler reprimanded Strasser by stating, in part:

> This is all bombastic nonsense:... it boils down to this, that you would give to every member of the Party the right to decide on the idea—even to decide whether the Leader is true to the so-called idea or not. That is democracy at its worst and there is no place with us for any such view. With us the Leader and the idea are one, and every member of the Party has to do what the Leader orders. The Leader incorporates the idea and alone knows its ultimate goal. (Pg. 460, "Speeches of Adolf Hitler: April 1922-August 1939", Oxford Univ. Press along with the Royal Institute of International Affairs in England, 1942)

This was paternalism at its worst, with the "Leader" being the arbiter of what constitutes the "purpose" upon which the "People" are united as a "single mind" or

"Gleischschaltung." This disdain for popular sovereignty was rooted in a belief that individual liberty was a distraction from the "progress" that can only be accomplished if everyone acted with the "solidarity" of a "single mind." Where did such paternalistic ideas originate? Where they a lingering leftover from the monarchical powers? Where these a desire to return to the guiding hand of a paternalistic monarchy? It is more likely that they are the inevitable structure of a utopian ethos, convinced of its ethical superiority.

Much of this *"Über Ethik"* originates with Karl Marx and Edward Bellamy, and it was the foundation of National Socialism. It is the very root of a "national" form of "socialism," which Edward Bellamy described in his utopian novels "Looking Backward" and "Equality." In "Equality," the sequel to "Looking Backward," Bellamy continues the fictional conversations between the time traveler, the doctor, and his beautiful daughter in a futuristic Boston of the year 2000. Chapter II of "Equality" is titled "Why the Revolution Did Not Come Earlier," and it depicts the time-traveling protagonist describing to the future utopians his theory of why the transformative change towards their "socialist utopia" did not come sooner, even though the founding documents of the United States seemingly promised "equality." Bellamy's time-traveler explains that the flaw existed in the way the Founding Documents defined liberty as a "negative liberty" that guaranteed what government could "not do to you," and therefore was limited in its ability to actively enforce the promise "equality":

> We divide the history of the evolution of the democratic idea into two broadly contrasted phases. The first of these we call the phase of negative democracy. -- -- This first phase of the evolution of democracy, during which it was conceived of solely as a substitute for royalty, includes all the so-called republican experiments up to the beginning of the 20 century, of which, of course, the American Republic was the most important. During this period the democratic idea remained a mere protest against a previous form of government, absolutely without any new positive or vital principle of its own.---- The second phase in the evolution of the democratic idea began with the awakening of the people to the perception that the deposing of kings, instead of being the main end and mission of democracy, was merely preliminary to its real programme, which was the use of the collective social machinery for the indefinite promotion of the welfare of the people at large. ---- During the negative phase of democracy it had been considered as differing from monarchy only as two machines might differ, the general use and purpose of which were the same. With the evolution of the democratic idea into the second or positive phase, it was recognized that the transfer of the supreme power from king and nobles to people meant not merely a change in the forms of government, but a fundamental revolution in the whole idea of government, its motives, purposes, and functions--a revolution equivalent to a reversal of polarity of the entire social system. (Pg. 30, "Equality", Cosimo, Inc. printing, 2008)

What Bellamy was specifically describing and complaining about was the fact that the Declaration of Independence and the US Constitution guarantee by "contract" that the power of Kings, namely those of the likes of King George, will never again be awarded to government. Furthermore, these founding documents delineate what "the people as rulers ought not to do," regardless of their elitist titles of nobility or perceived wisdom. Bellamy's futuristic utopia is framed as the last phase in the "evolution" of democracies where the "negative liberties" imposed on government are discarded, and the work of the creation of the Founding Fathers is described as "pseudo-republics," or as mere "steps in the evolution of society from pure monarchy to pure democracy." [168] In Bellamy's futurism, "the democracy of the second or positive phase triumphed in the great Revolution and has since been the only form of government known in the world." Bellamy points to the various socialist revolutions as "the rise of positive democracy in the 20th century." This link between Edward Bellamy and Adolf Hitler was lost due to Cold War propaganda, which sold the public on a simplistic dualistic view of political movements, and desperately tried to erase the "socialism" aspect of "National Socialism." The fact that Hitler's form of government enshrined in the Fuhrer the power of kings to enforce their prerogative on their subjects has been lost to history. Hitler was slotted as part of the "Right" and Stalin was slotted to the "Left," despite their overwhelming similarities. All the discussion in the 1920s and 1930s about a "third way" were swept under the rug, and Progressivism was rebranded as "liberalism" so as to discard any connection between the "Progressives" and the "third-way" movements they once proudly and vocally admired, namely Fascism. However, those that lived in the decades up to World War II recognized that Edward Bellamy had been the precursor to this "third-way" form of government. M. G. Kemperink and Willemien H.S. Roenhorst agree with this assessment, and provide an example of the general disillusionment with the teachings of "Looking Backwards":

> By the 1940s popular interest in Looking Backward had run its course. - in a move that Bellamy never anticipated, his prophecy of centralized control of the economy and society was being grotesquely fulfilled in fascist or communist regimes that subjected their peoples to totalitarian rule under various forms of 'National Socialism'. In the post-World War II era, Looking Backward fell under the dark shadow cast by Mussolini, Hitler, Stalin, and it began to be interpreted as their precursor. The American critic Lewis Mumford, who in the early 20th century had absorbed Bellamy's ideas through the town planning movement, later declared that Bellamy's novel 'turns out to the first authentic picture of National Socialism (German-style), or State Capitalism (Russian-style), in its most insidiously corrupting form', bribing the masses to accept dictatorship by promising them material comfort. As the wheel of history turned, one generation's utopia became another's nightmare. (Pg. 29, "Visualizing Utopia", M. G. Kemperink and Willemien H.S. Roenhorst, WHS Roenhorst Peeters Publishers, 2007)

However, this is not to say that the core concepts in Bellamy's form of "Nationalism" did not endure. To the contrary, they only found direct expression

---

[168] Pg. 31, "Equality", Edward Bellamy, Cosimo, Inc. printing, 2008.

through American Progressivism and British Fabian Socialism, which persist to this day to insist that the government should do away with the "constraints" that keep the leaders from "acting on the people's behalf." The American Constitution is a contract. To be more precise, it is a "Social Contract" that binds the government to a non-interference policy with respects to the individual's "life, liberty, and the pursuit of happiness." It explicitly prohibits the government from defining what "happiness" any individual may see fit to pursue as long as that pursuit does not infringe on the personal pursuit of others. More to the point, it explicitly prohibits the government from acting as a "single mind" or *"Gleischschaltung."* For Bellamy, who saw a need to organize and orchestrate the efforts of society, "negative democracy" and its "negative liberties" were a significant hurdle as they directly imply that the elite are forever banned from naming themselves the conductors of a "nation" based upon "socialist" solidarity. In this respect, there is barely any difference between Bellamy's "national" form of "socialism" and Hitler's "National Socialism." To overcome this obstacle, the "socialists" since Bellamy have contended that the Founding documents are not a "social contract" but a "living document," which must be changed in order to lift restrictions that would otherwise get in their way. As seen above, this is basically the essence of the law in the Third Reich. The law under Hitler was not guaranteed by statute or by contract. It was forever changing and evolving according to the "will of the leader" which its deputies perceived and acted upon.

It must also be remembered that at the core of the "single party" system which fused the "Party" with the central government are the notions of *"Volksgeist,"* "solidarity," "single mind," and "unity of purpose." This is a hallmark of all "socialist" governments throughout history, and Hitler's "National Socialism" was no exception. The National Socialists, just like any other socialists before and after them, had the explicit goal of uniting party and government to form a one-party governmental system and to supposedly end the alleged disunity in society. Henry David Thoreau wrote in 1849 that "government is best which governs least." One would think that by removing the Reichstag from the equation, the main legislative body of a nation that legislation would cease, or at the very least slow down. The dilettantes of the Third Reich would pat themselves on the back for doing precisely the opposite. They would claim fame for enacting a dizzying amount of laws and statutes in a relatively short span of time, as this was their measure for effective leadership. With all restraints removed, the Nazi government enacted laws like an addict unable to control his impulses. The National Socialist state would organize a veritable orgy of regulations and oversight administrations. There were "eight citizens per civil servant" and that "30 to 35 per cent of the people's income of sixty million was paid out to officialdom." [169] 21st Century readers may chuckle at a 30% tax rate, as contemporary Progressive and Fabian minded governments have far surpassed those figures.

Unfortunately, it has become cliché for Holocaust historians to proclaim that

---

[169] Pg. 80 - "The Speeches of Adolf Hitler", Norman H. Baynes, Oxford University Press in the United States and the Royal Institute of International Affairs in Britain, 1942.

understanding The Holocaust is crucial to preventing history from repeating itself. This is precisely the point of this chapter. The first order of business in preventing a government from ever being as intrusive as Hitler's National Socialism is to prevent the government from ever acquiring the powers that Nazism acquired. Towards this effort, it is crucial to remember that Hitler failed as a violent revolutionary; the so-called Beer Hall Putsch failed, and Hitler went to jail as a result. Hitler spent his time in Landsberg prison reevaluating his political strategy and came out convinced that National Socialism had to leverage propaganda and reinvest itself in its populist message in order to gain power through "legal means."

Sec. 8 - WHO VOTED FOR HITLER?

The story of how Hitler became a dictator is documented in the famous book, "The Rise and Fall of the Third Reich," by William Shirer. In the presidential election held on March 13, 1932, there were four candidates: the incumbent, Field Marshall Paul von Hindenburg, Hitler, and two minor candidates, Ernst Thaelmann and Theodore Duesterberg. The results were:

- Hindenburg 49.6%
- Hitler 30.1%
- Thaelmann 13.2%
- Duesterberg 6.8%

Nearly 70 percent of the German people voted against Hitler. Since Hindenburg had not received a majority of the vote, however, a runoff election had to be held among the top three vote-getters. On April 19, 1932, the runoff results were not much different with Hindenburg's tally at 53%, Thaelmann 10.2%, and Hitler increasing only slightly and earning 36.8%. Even though Hitler's share of the vote had risen, the majority of Germans had rejected him. Thus, it begs to question: Exactly who did vote for Adolf Hitler?

Even though Hitler had badly lost the presidential election, he was drawing ever-larger crowds during the congressional election. As Shirer points out, Hitler spoke to sizeable crowds between 60,000 and 120,000 people. These were crowds to rival even the largest of stadiums of today. The July 31, 1932 election, however, did produce a significant victory for Hitler's National Socialist Party. The party won 230 seats in the Reichstag, making it Germany's largest political party, yet still falling far short of a majority in the 608-member body. Emboldened by that victory, Hitler demanded that President Hindenburg appoint him chancellor and place him in complete control of the state. Hindenburg initially denied Hitler this amount of power as he knew him to be dangerous. However, political deadlocks in the Reichstag soon brought a new election on November 6, 1932. The National Socialist party lost 2 million votes and 34 seats, even further reversing their actual claim to power but remaining the largest party in a highly divided and confused nation. In a horribly misguided attempt to remedy the chaos, Hindenburg fired Papen and appointed Kurt von Schleicher as the new German chancellor. Unable to secure a majority coalition in the Reichstag, Schleicher presented Hindenburg his resignation a mere 57 days after he had been appointed. This led to Hindenburg's capitulation. On January 30, 1933, President Hindenburg appointed Adolf Hitler chancellor of Germany, giving the latter a formidable amount of political power, even though the National Socialists never captured more than 37 percent of the national vote, and possessed fewer than 50 percent of the seats in the Reichstag once in the chancellorship.

The infamous and controversial Reichstag fire is said to have changed the trajectory of history and given Hitler the excuse to amass power. Hitler had set out to acquire power through legitimate and legal means after the failed Beer Hall Putsch, and events had been consistently in Hitler's favor because of the grander chaos and identity crisis Germany suffered at the time. The day after the fire, Hitler persuaded President Hindenburg to issue the decree entitled, "For the Protection of the People and the State." The decree was justified as a "defensive measure against Communist acts of violence endangering the state," as communists had been apprehended at the fire and were the primary suspects. Hitler requested the Reichstag temporarily delegate its powers to him so that he could adequately deal with the crisis. When the vote was taken, the result was 441 for and 84 against, giving Hitler the two-thirds majority needed to suspend the German constitution. The infamous "Enabling Act" was ratified on March 23, 1933.

Yet, the question persists to be relevant. The vast amount of Germans did not vote for Adolf Hitler. So, it begs to question who his supporters in the general populace actually were. Despite the modern journalist's attempts to link Adolf Hitler to his mother's Catholicism, most German Catholics did not vote for Hitler. To the contrary, Catholic votes for the National Socialist party were atypical:

> Although Hitler's political career began in Munich, in the elections of 1928 to November 1932 the NSDAP won a higher share of the vote in Protestant than in Catholic Germany. In the Catholic Rhineland and Bavaria (apart from Protestant Franconia) it polled disproportionately badly. In fact in July 1932 the Nazi share of the vote was almost twice as high in Protestant as in Catholic areas. The inability, of Nazis to attract the Catholic vote was demonstrated by the stable support for the Catholic Centre Party, which regularly gained between 11.8 and 12.5 per cent between 1928, and November 1932; and by that of its sister confessional party, the Bavarian People's Party (BVP), which stayed firm at around 3 per cent in those same elections. ("Who Voted for the Nazis? Electoral History of the National Socialist German Workers Party", Dick Geary, History Today, October 1998)

This above reality makes sense when one links these facts to the relevant timeline and cultural history. Germany was, after all, the epicenter of the Protestant

Reformation. The Ninety-Five Theses were famously delivered upon the Holy Roman Empire by Martin Luther on the gates of the Castle Church in Wittenberg, Germany. Martin Luther's antagonism towards the Catholic Church remained a driving force. The enmity between Catholics and Protestants did not begin to die down in Germany until they recognized secularism as a common enemy, well into the late 20th Century. Until then, German Christians were as divided as they were in the United States, with Protestant eugenic "racialists" proclaiming an equal antipathy to Catholic immigrants as to blacks and Jews. The infamous "niggers, Jews, Orientals, and Papists" was the racist line of demarcation by the KKK, both from North and South, with "Papists" directly referring to the Roman Catholic Pope. It must be remembered that in the United States, antipathy towards Catholic immigrants, whether Irish, Italian or Hispanic, did not begin to die down until after President John F. Kennedy was assassinated. Kennedy's candidacy was otherwise highly contentious as he was the first Catholic candidate for the presidency that had a high probability of winning, as he ultimately did, and that anti-Catholic contention only diffused in part because of Kennedy's martyrdom. Before then, eugenicists like Madison Grant, Charles B. Davenport, C.M. Goethe, and Harry H. Laughlin associated Italians and Irish immigrants with the surge of criminality due to the infamous mafias and gangs of the era. Catholics, or "Papists," were just as undesirable to them as Eastern European Jews, Chinese, or Japanese immigrants, and the 1924 Immigration Restriction Act was explicitly intended to keep them out. Previously unpublished correspondence currently held at Truman University's Laughlin Collection provide evidence to these assertions. A January 1929, letter from Goethe as president of the Immigration Study Commission to Laughlin regarding his testimony before Congress clarifies this point:

> Gangster rule in our great cities is only one phase of America's increasing urban problem. Gangster influence at Washington is powerful in a way few citizens understand. Their methods, being those of Mediterranean Europe, are basically un-American. (BOX C-4-I:2, Goethe to Laughlin, Jan. 26th, 1929, Special Coll. – Truman Univ.)

The term "Mediterranean Europe" was a clear reference to Italian immigrants. In a similar letter of October 22, 1928, C.M. Goethe proclaims Italian Catholics as a danger to the United States to be remedied with the Immigration Restriction Act, curiously enough deemed "dangerous" because of their similarities to "Caucasians," as opposed to their differences:

> The danger to our American wage standard is not in the immigration from the Orient. The color difference there is so great that Americans react vigorously to such coolie immigration. The real menace to our living standards lies in countries like Italy. With a heavy excess of births over deaths, Italian wages are low compared with the United States. If America wishes to hold its present living standard, it must vigorously protest against the present beginnings of a movement to amend to death the Johnson Immigration Restriction Act. (BOX C-4-I:2, Goethe to Laughlin, Oct. 22nd, 1928, Special Coll. – Truman Univ.)

C.M. Goethe, Harry H. Laughlin, and Madison Grant would correspond at length about immigration restrictions based on racial definitions and sought out legalistic and authoritative definitions of what constituted being "Mexican" or part of an alleged "American Race." The difficulty in vague terms such as "white," as detailed above, posed a problem for the eugenic-minded lobbyists. A July 22, 1936, letter from Madison Grant to Harry H. Laughlin illustrates this:

> It seems clear that a categorical definition of the American Race should be available for legal use when an opportunity arises. Doubtless the time will again return when the Senate and the House Committees on Immigration will desire data on and analyses of the racial make-up of the American people, in their anticipated efforts to conserve and improve our foundation racial stocks. --- I have followed your advice by using the term "Caucasian" instead of "White" throughout because of the definite legal meaning which the word Caucasian has already acquired in this country. (BOX C-2-2:15, Grant to Laughlin, July 22nd, 1936, Special Coll. – Truman Univ.)

A July 28, 1936, letter from Madison Grant to Harry H. Laughlin continues along these lines asking that immigration restrictions be delineated along "thoroughly Nordic" racial lines, where "Scandinavians," "Dutch," "English Scotch," and specifically "North Irish" and "North Germans" be among the unrestricted and preferred populations:

> I entirely agree with you, of course, that the use of the word "Caucasian" is better than that of "White." The Jews can and do claim that they are White, but they can hardly claim that they are "Caucasian," although, perhaps, they do claim it. We should say that all ancestors of true American should be born in the thirteen colonies or the territory East of the Mississippi prior to Independence, namely 1783. I had suggested a later date, namely 1800, before the Louisiana Purchase, but I think perhaps your date is to be preferred as it equally well leaves out the New Orleans French. (Item No.: 072836, H.H. Laughlin Papers, Truman University, Special Collections)

Furthermore, Protestants were much more receptive to "hygiene" movements like eugenics. The link between Protestant Christianity and "clean living" progressive reform movements is clear:

> Native-born white Protestant Americans of Anglo-Saxon stock feared the Roman Catholic "alien menace" from Ireland and southern and eastern Europe. These Nativists blamed immigrants for many diseases, crime, and other social problems. There was a belief that drunkenness, tuberculosis, and poverty could be passed down to succeeding generation, leading to more poverty and disease among these "undesirables" due to inheritance of acquired characteristics (Lamarckian theory). The desire for healthy offspring and for keeping the "race from being polluted" led to eugenic reforms. (Pg. 14, "Clean Living Movements: American Cycles of Health Reform", Ruth C. Engs, Greenwood Publishing Group, 2001)

In the United States, this uncomfortable relationship between Protestantism and eugenics was recognized by the Methodist Church with their 2008 resolution:
> Ironically, as the Eugenics movement came to the United States, the churches, especially the Methodists, the Presbyterians, and the Episcopalians, embraced it. Methodist churches around the country promoted the American Eugenics Society "Fitter Family Contests" wherein the fittest families were invariably fair skinned and well off. Methodist bishops endorsed one of the first books circulated to the US churches promoting eugenics. -- Methodists were active on the planning committees of the Race Betterment Conferences held in 1914, and 1915. In the 1910s, Methodist Churches hosted forums in their churches to discuss eugenics. In the 1920s, many Methodist preachers submitted their eugenics sermons to contests hosted by the American Eugenics Society. (umc.org, "An Apology for Support of Eugenics", Petition 81175, 81175-C2-R9999, March 30, 2008)

In Germany, the originators of the National Socialist movement, namely Rosenberg and Ludendorff, were bitterly anti-clerical and anti-Catholic, and the persecution in Poland of the Catholic clergy was as extreme as it was for the Jews. Ernst Hanfstaengl identified General Ludendorff, one of Hitler's earliest allies from within the ranks of the German army, as part of the "*Kulturkampf*" movement in Germany that went back to the days of Otton Von Bismark's prosecution of the Catholic Church from 1871 to 1878. Bismark wanted to reduce the political influence of the 36 percent of the German population that was Catholic, and the resulting backlash was the creation of the Catholic Center Party, which endured as a major party during the political campaigns Hitler participated in.
> The danger for Ludendorff was clear: If nothing were done to reverse the process then Protestants would flock to the Catholic fold, making the entire nation once again Catholic. However, Ludendorff overstated the degree of Protestant indifference toward the Catholic threat. Many Protestants, especially those in the Protestant League, saw the Catholic danger in much the same way as he. As we have seen, they even depicted Ludendorff as a Protestant warrior fighting Catholicism's supposedly ongoing counterreformation. (Pg. 90, Richard Steigmann-Gall, "The Holy Reich: Nazi Conceptions of Christianity, 1919-1945", Cambridge University Press, 2003)

In fact, Ernst Hanfstaengl believed that the anti-Catholic aspect of National Socialism played a decisive part in the failed Beer-Hall Putsch. Recall that Hitler fled to and hid in Hanfstaengl's home when the Beer Hall Putsch failed, and Hitler became a fugitive of the law:
> What was to prove an even more decisive factor was Hitler's disregard of the need to placate Catholic opinion. Ludendorff and a considerable portion of the North German nationalist malcontents who had found refuge in Bavaria were either Protestants or violently anti-Church and specifically anti-Catholic. The mistake was to assume the Putsch would succeed with their help alone. General

von Epp, himself a Roman Catholic, had been so grossly offended by Rosenberg that he became indifferent to any Putsch led by Hitler or Ludendorff. Von Epp's action in ordering a Mass and TeDeum of thanksgiving to be held in Munich's largest square at the liberation in 1919, had led Rosenberg to refer to him repeatedly in sarcastic articles in the Beobachter as the 'Mutter-gottes-General'. This so alienated von Epp that he would have little further to do with the Nazis. Yet he had a personal following of some 25,000 Life Guard reservists and his influence on Hitler's side might have tipped the scales. (Pg. 94, "Hitler: The Memoir of the Nazi Insider Who Turned Against the Fuhrer", Republished by Arcade Pub., 2011)

However, this is not to say that Ludendorff's influence as a Protestant had any kind of a lasting influence on the National Socialists, if any at all, beyond the tense alliance with Hitler leading up to the Beer Hall Putsch. Shortly after the failed Putsch, Ludendorff went in his own direction as the leader of a competing political party. In 1925, Ludendorff ran for president against his former colleague, Paul von Hindenburg, who he claimed had taken credit for Ludendorff's victories against Russia, and from 1924 to 1928 he represented the German Völkisch Freedom Party in the German Parliament. Ludendorff also grew disillusioned with Hitler, actually believing him to be too moderate, too political, and not militant enough.

Meanwhile, the National Socialist party adopted Rosenberg's animosity towards the Catholic Church and Christianity in general along with Himmler's and Hess's allure to the occult. Whatever scant pretense to respect Christianity Hitler had played in his early campaign speeches fell by the wayside once Hitler made all other political parties illegal. More to the point, traditional Christian compassion became a prime obstacle for a regime that wanted its citizens to carry out the most brutal and inhumane acts. As thoroughly documented by eugenicists and their enemies alike, the Roman Catholic Church was the one persistent obstacle for the eugenics movement wherever it arose, thus it was a natural enemy for Hitler's eugenic state. The Third Reich was thus bitterly opposed to any traditional values, namely that of traditional Christianity, which they believed to be "Jew-tainted" due to its Judeo-Christian values of "compassion" and "sympathy."

It would also be entirely incorrect to attribute National Socialism to Protestantism, as clearly Hitler never received more than 36 percent of the German vote. Whatever votes came from the various Christian faith were from the reactionary wings of Christianity. There were then, as there are now, radicalized Christians that equally profess Christian fundamentalist views as well as a disdain for the traditional institutions of society. This is just as true of Catholicism as it is of Protestantism. The Jesuit order has for all its history, entangled itself with the most radical of movements, where it has become difficult to discern where the Jesuits begin and its revolutionary aspects end. Hitler's Germany was no exception for the Jesuits. Despite the emphatic admonitions of any "birth control," "sterilization" or "eugenic" policies by the Vatican and the Catholic Church in general, some German Jesuits embarked on their own volition to support the eugenics movement. The German-

Jesuit priests, Hermann Muckermann and Joseph Mayer, both supported eugenics. Hermann Muckermann, S.J. was the only prominent Catholic scholar possessing both the scientific and theological qualifications to have an authoritative voice in the eugenics movement. He was ordained into the Society of Jesus in 1896 but was released from his duties in the Order in 1927. The incompatibility of the Society's principles with Muckermann's (specifically, his desire for a comfortable home with a wine cellar) apparently led to the separation. Muckermann originally received his training in cell biology at the University of Louvain, where he was inspired by the Catholic opponents of the evolutionary monist, Ernst Haeckel. From 1916 Muckermann became a tireless crusader for family welfare. By 1919 he had become intellectually opposed to eugenics, since he disapproved of the concept of biological degeneracy. Increasingly, however, he came to accept the importance of eugenics for social welfare, and by 1922 had thoroughly removed his prior opposition to the eugenics movement. (Pg. 578, "Catholic Eugenics in Germany, 1920-1945: Hermann Muckermann, S.J. and Joseph Mayer," "Catholic Eugenics", Donald J. Dietrich, Journal of Church and State, Vol. 34, No. 3 (1992), pp. 575-600)

In 1927, Muckermann was invited to accept a position as professor and director of the Eugenics Section in the recently founded Kaiser Wilhelm Institute in Berlin but was dismissed from this post in 1933 due to subsequent conflicts over his lack of support for biological racism. Muckermann was adamant, despite the 1930 proclamation, "*Casti Connubii*" by Pope Pius and the subsequent clarification by church authorities, that he could support sterilization as well as positive eugenics as a Catholic. Muckermann insisted that no conflict need arise between racial hygiene and Catholicism as long as racial hygiene was applied to the human species as a whole. Muckermann only retreated after the Catholic Church put pressure on him to do so in the face of the euthanasia policies the German Church was contesting. To create a gulf of distance between himself and the pagan eugenics, Muckermann preached against the heathendom of prominent National Socialists, namely in his 1933 stance against Alfred Rosenberg's "*Mythus*."

Mayer had supported eugenics since the 1920s. Unconvinced by "*Casti Connubii,*" Mayer continued to defend not only sterilization but abortion as well. Even in 1933, in the heat of the Third Reich's eugenic legislation, Mayer persisted on supporting eugenics, and was a source of serious confusion for the faithful who looked to the Catholic Church for guidance during those trying years. His views were aligned with the National Socialist regime, likely because of his collectivist aspirations. He seemed obsessed with what was allegedly "good" for society in general, and disdainful of individual rights, as were his Nazi contemporaries. [170] Yet, Muckermann and Meyer maintained their support for an allegedly non-racist form of eugenics as late as 1952, forever claiming, as did Julian Huxley and Karl Brandt; that their eugenics was free from the racist overtones of Hitler and Rosenberg.

---

[170] Pg. 588 - "Catholic Eugenics in Germany, 1920-1945: Hermann Muckermann, S.J. and Joseph Mayer," "Catholic Eugenics", Journal of Church and State, Vol. 34, No. 3 (SUMMER 1992), pp. 575-600.

Posterity must also note that German Protestants were also a force for the National Socialists to contend with. The most famous Protestant to initially support, and then bitterly regret supporting Hitler was Friedrich Gustav Emil Martin Niemöller. Niemöller was a German theologian and Lutheran. He is best known as the author of the poem "First They Came." The statement was published in a 1955 book by Milton Mayer, "They Thought They Were Free," based on interviews he had conducted in Germany years earlier. Its exact origin is unclear, and some historians have incorrectly suggested that the text arose after Niemöller's death. The research traces the text to several speeches given by Niemöller in 1946:

First they came for the Jews, and I didn't speak out because I wasn't a Jew.
Then they came for the trade unionists,
and I didn't speak out because I wasn't a trade unionist.
Then they came for the communists, and I didn't speak out because I wasn't a communist.
Then they came for me, and there was no one left to speak out for me.

With his writings, Martin Niemöller has become the stereotypical thinking and repentant German. He drew the line when Hitler enacted state control over the German Protestant churches. Niemöller was imprisoned in Sachsenhausen and Dachau concentration camps from 1937 to 1945. Niemöller's former Sachsenhausen cellmate, Leo Stein, wrote an article about Niemöller for "The National Jewish Monthly" issue of May 1941. In it, Stein tells Niemöller's answer to why he supported the National Socialists:

I find myself wondering about that too. I wonder about it as much as I regret it. Still, it is true that Hitler betrayed me. I had an audience with him, as a representative of the Protestant Church, shortly before he became Chancellor, in 1932. Hitler promised me on his word of honor, to protect the Church, and not to issue any anti-Church laws. He also agreed not to allow pogroms against the Jews, assuring me as follows: "There will be restrictions against the Jews, but there will be no ghettos, no pogroms, in Germany."

CONTINUES . . .

I really believed, given the widespread anti-Semitism in Germany, at that time — that Jews should avoid aspiring to Government positions or seats in the Reichstag. There were many Jews, especially among the Zionists, who took a similar stand. Hitler's assurance satisfied me at the time. On the other hand, I hated the growing atheistic movement, which was fostered and promoted by the Social Democrats and the Communists. Their hostility toward the Church made me pin my hopes on Hitler for a while.

CONTINUES . . .

I am paying for that mistake now; and not me alone, but thousands of other persons like me. (Pgs. 284–5, 301–2, "NIEMOELLER speaks!", The National Jewish Monthly, May 1941 – Sourced From: history.ucsb.edu, Prof. Harold Marcuse)

So, how did Hitler silence these two sizeable Christian voting blocs? Hitler had asked Pastor Niemöller and other Protestant Pastors the same that he had asked of the Catholic Church: to be silent and stay out of secular governmental matters with a promise that those that followed their faith would not be persecuted. As extrapolated earlier, every eugenicist in the United States, Britain, and Germany had identified the Catholic Church as their most persistent enemy, namely because of the Vatican's *"Casti Connubii"* of December 31, 1930. This doctrine had become a problem for Hitler as the vast majority of Catholic priests in Germany were preaching to their followers to not vote for Hitler and vote according to the dictates of their Catholic faith. In this respect, Hitler's very actions serve to confirm the voting statistics documented above. Furthermore, this thorn on Hitler's side persisted as the German Catholic bishops were instructing the Catholic Center Party members of the Reichstag to vote against the Enabling Act. [171] Yet, the sequence of events in 1933 must be retraced. Pinchas Lapide, the Israeli consul in Milan that interviewed Italian Holocaust survivors, claimed in his 1967 book "Three Popes and the Jews," that it was Hitler which approached the Vatican to reach the now-infamous July 20, 1933, *Reichskonkordat* agreement. [172] In a move to gain international respectability and to quash opposition by the Catholic Center Party, Hitler dispatched his vice-chancellor Franz von Papen, a Catholic nobleman and former member of the Centre Party, to the Vatican to resurrect negotiations that had stalled with previous administrations. [173]

Ironically enough, it is the very *Reichskonkordat* that has been used by the enemies of the Catholic Church to portray a history of complicity with the Third Reich. This version turns history on its head, as it unfairly forgets that it was the Catholic Church's principled stance that brought Hitler's diplomats to the door of the Vatican. Secondly, it forgets that the Catholic Church's proclamations in the 1930 *"Casti Connubii"* were dutifully followed by German Catholics, as the overwhelming majority of them voted their conscience and not for Hitler. If Germans of the various Christian faiths made a mistake, it was in actually complying with what the enemies of their faith continue to demand of Christians today, that they stay out of secular matters. Whether their temporary acquiescence or Hindenburg's capitulation is to blame for Hitler's ascension to power is arguable and worth further analysis.

So, who voted for Hitler then? Dick Geary's focused study on these matters points to the fact that allegedly it was the *Mittelstand*, the middle-class, white-collar electorate, so commonly identified as Hitler's base, that was the typical National Socialist supporter. However, Geary points out that civil servants were more likely to register higher levels of support for Hitler than their counterparts within the private sector. This certainly is in line with the trend of eugenics in the United States and Britain, where the most ardent supporters of eugenic politics were the civil

---

[171] Pg. 36 – "The Hitler Myth", Ian Kershaw, Oxford, reissued 2001.
[172] newworldencyclopedia.org, Pope Pius XII entry.
[173] Ibid.

workers in charge of public health clinics, mental health hospitals, homes for the elderly or unemployed, and criminologists, along with medical professionals:

> Considerable attention has been devoted to the appeal of Nazism to many in the professions such as doctors and engineers, as well as civil servants, leading some to claim that anti-modernism provides the key to Hitler's triumph. A vast literature has also been devoted to the relationship between the Nazis and big business. It is fairly clear that big business was less likely to support the NSDAP than small business; that the party allegiances of individual industrialists varied; and that Fritz Thyssen's membership of and donations to the Nazi Party were a typical of the business community as a whole. The Nazi Party was largely self-financing, and industrial money was most likely to find its way into the coffers of the DNVP and DVP, though some concerns (such as Flick) did spread their donations over virtually all bourgeois parties, including the NSDAP, as a kind of political insurance. (Dick Geary, "Who Voted for the Nazis? Electoral History of the National Socialist German Workers Party", History Today, October 1998)

Furthermore, it is essential to remember that a significant portion of the early National Socialists, namely the members of the Brown Shirts, were ex-communists, which had vocal hostility towards traditional Christianity, capitalism, international banking, and big industry. While far from attracting the mass of the German Communist vote, Hitler was able to appeal to many ex-Marxists whom, like the Italian Fascist, Mussolini, was not keen to support the "international" aspect of the socialism of the day, or in any way subsume Germany under foreign rule by Bolshevik Russians, as the Marxists proposed:

> Recent research has revised the impression of working-class immunity to Nazism: around 55 per cent of SA Stormtroopers came from working-class backgrounds and the Nazis made substantial gains from working-class communities in parts of Saxony, especially around Chemnitz. Around 40 per cent of members of the Party seem to have been of working-class origins; similarly 40 per cent of the Nazi vote came from workers and one worker in every four voted for Hitler in July 1932. ("Who Voted for the Nazis? Electoral History of the National Socialist German Workers Party", Dick Geary, History Today, October 1998)

Some historians write off any memoirs by Nazi party members, but Hanfstaengl's accounts on this topic triangulate with other accounts. Ernst Hanfstaengl's memoirs serve to document the observation that National Socialism was a "working class" movement. Hanfstaengl often advised Hitler against wearing expensive clothing that may make him look like an aristocrat. Hanfstaengl gave this advice to other members of the National Socialist Party, and in hindsight, this falls in line with the populist aspirations of the party:

> I remember rebuking Göring once at one of the Munich cafes for screwing a monocle into his eye and then looking round with the stupid air of superiority that the wearers of such objects usually affect. "Mein Lieber Hermann," I told

him, "this is supposed to be a working-class party and if you go round looking like a Junker we shall never attract their support." Whereupon he looked rather deflated and sheepish and stuffed it in his pocket. (Pg. 72, "Hitler: The Memoir of the Nazi Insider Who Turned Against the Fuhrer", Republished by Arcade Pub., 2011)

Of note also is Geary's observation that the National Socialist party was a youth movement, even more so than the socialist or communist parties. This would be in line with the observations by Alan E. Steinweiss, author of "Art, Ideology, & Economics in Nazi Germany," which documents the disproportional support German artists and musicians gave Hitler. Elaine S. Hochman's book "Architects of Fortune," makes similar claims and documents that the Bauhaus, the revolutionary school of modernism, was bitterly divided between supporters for Hitler and Marxism, and that this bitter divide conspired to make the school dysfunctional to the point where Walter Gropius gave up and handed off its reigns to Mies Van Der Rohe.

> The Nazi Party has often been portrayed as a dynamic inspirer of youth and contrasted with the sclerosis of the traditional Right. This youthful image of the NSDAP (and more rightly of the SA) certainly has some foundation. NSDAP membership was younger than that of other parties; the average age of those joining between 1925 and 1932 was slightly under twenty-nine. It rose slightly, to an average of thirty-two in 1932. ---- Firstly, youth support for the NSDAP cannot be divorced from issues of class and confession. Of the new members, 47 per cent were workers (under-representing them as a percentage of the population as a whole), whereas white-collar employees at 20 per cent were overrepresented and the old middle class of the self-employed at 27 per cent more so. ("Who Voted for the Nazis? Electoral History of the National Socialist German Workers Party", Dick Geary, History Today, October 1998)

Donald M. Douglas, Assistant Professor of History at Wichita State University, conducted a statistical study of the early recruits of the German Workers Party and its subsequent iteration as the National Socialist Party. [174] Douglas wanted to gauge precisely how Hitler's speech-giving affected party membership. Douglas input the membership statistics collected and related the age, gender, occupation, and other relevant attributes of each member to the dates when speeches were given and when membership was enrolled. Douglas wanted to know how many of the 2,548 members accounted for in the party's records had likely joined because of hearing Adolf Hitler speak, and more importantly, establish some demographic data of those who signed up because of Hitler as opposed to those that signed up because of the dozen or so other speakers that represented the party at this juncture. The result of this statistical approach was his 1974 article, "The Evangelist's Apprenticeship: Hitler's Effectiveness as a Public Speaker, 1919-1921." Hitler's

---

[174] "The Evangelist's Apprenticeship: Hitler's Effectiveness as a Public Speaker, 1919-1921", Donald M. Douglas, Wichita State University Bulletin, Feb. 1974.

followers amounted to 15.5 percent of the party membership, the largest portion among the dozen or so party leaders. More important were the demographical data Douglas's statistical analysis revealed. Among all of Hitler's devoted followers, blue-collar workers such as craftsmen, artisans, and mechanics amounted to 20.6 percent of those he was able to attract, in comparison to the surprisingly low 2.2 percent who were soldiers. This certainly flies in the face of any notion of Hitler attracting militant conservatives as "right-wing" movements are traditionally understood to attract. Students amounted to 9.7 percent and civil servants amounted to 6.9 percent of those brought into the party due to Hitler's allure. Ernst Hanfstaengl's recollection of whom attended these early speeches, namely the one in the Kindlkeller beer-hall, corroborates Donald M. Douglas's statistics:

> There seemed to be a lot of people of the concierge or small shopkeeper class, a sprinkling of the former officer and minor civil servant type, a tremendous number of young people, and the rest artisans, with a high proportion of the spectators in Bavarian national costume. (Pg. 33, "Hitler: The Memoir of the Nazi Insider Who Turned Against the Fuhrer", Republished by Arcade Pub., 2011)

As Donald M. Douglas documents, Hitler was able to leverage the fact that he drew in a disproportionate number of followers in comparison to the other party representatives to coerce the party to make him its undisputed leader. This observation also tumbles the notion that The Holocaust was the product of some inherent German militancy or racism from simpletons and typical bigots. Rather, the numbers and the history evidence the indispensable involvement of scientists and doctors with utopian socialist aspirations points to an altogether different type of "dictatorship" than what is expected from the traditional militant conservatives, namely Spanish Fascist, Franco.

Sec. 9 - FROM "AMERICAN ADONIS" TO HITLER'S "ARYAN MAN":

The 2006 book by Susan Currell, "Popular Eugenics: National Efficiency and American Mass Culture in the 1930s" documents the sculpture that was commissioned by Charles B. Davenport, the head of the Cold Spring Harbor Eugenics Records Office. The statue was not "art for art's sake," but a propaganda piece specifically crafted to entice a political reaction. This "Average Man" was first rendered in three dimensions when Jane Davenport, daughter of Charles, sculpted a 22-inch plaster composite of 100,000 veterans. The sculpture was based on her father's research for the Surgeon General's Office of the War Department during World War I, which had been disseminated through Carl Brigham's "A Study of

American Intelligence" in 1923. When the sculpture was first unveiled, it was displayed next to a similar work but made from the composite measurements of a Harvard University athletes in order to show the "degeneration" from the Nordic type. As an image of the national body, the "American Adonis" cast the nation in decidedly white and masculine form, but in a degraded state of nature rather than an elevated state of culture.

The reception of the sculpture depended less on its aesthetic properties than on the venue of its display. It was displayed at the 1932 Third International Congress of Eugenics, held at the American Museum of Natural History. The sculpture had been exhibited once before in the exhibitions accompanying the Second International Congress of Eugenics in 1921, also held at the Museum. In 1932, however, the "Adonis" was presented as a representation of the degenerating Caucasian body: the "Average American." The 1932 display reflected the changing agenda of eugenicists. Between 1921 and 1932, eugenicists shifted their attention from the problem of immigration to the question of domestic reproduction. The new target of eugenics was not the dysgenic body of the immigrant, but the perfection of the white population.

Davenport and the American eugenicists were hardly alone in the utilization of art to convey their eugenic message. This was a pattern-in-practice for the eugenics movement. The "American Adonis" had its binary parallels, the "New Woman" and the "Mother of Tomorrow," which stood as eugenic examples of womanhood and racial betterment at the Pacific International Exposition of 1915 in San Francisco. [175] However, the purchase of the "The Discobolus of Myron" by Hitler is instrumental in defining this aspect of the movement. Otherwise known as the "Discus Thrower," the iconic Greek sculpture of an Olympian in motion, the sculpture was purchased by Adolf Hitler in 1938. Adolf Hitler acquired the work when Galeazzo Ciano, Minister of Foreign Affairs, sold it to him for 5 million lire. Like the "American Adonis," the "Discuss Thrower" was displayed in juxtaposition to "degenerate" works of art and was explicitly intended to communicate the aesthetic ideals of a eugenic-minded National Socialism.

The 1991 documentary by Peter Cohen, "The Architecture of Doom," does an excellent job of highlighting the ties between National Socialism and the arts. The documentary is indispensable. One of the topics it documents is Hitler's purchase of Myron's "Discuss Thrower." For Hitler, the sculpture was the perfect expression of Aryan aesthetics, and its significance to National Socialism was inseparable from its eugenic value. Cubist and Modernist depictions of the human figure were intentionally contorted and distorted in order to depict various perspectives in a single view. The National Socialists understood the warping of the human figure as a Jewish and "degenerate" mindset, no different than the contorted bodies of those born defective. The Classical sculptures of the Greeks, on the other hand, represented purity and ideal Aryan bodily proportions as eugenic biometrics demanded, and therein lay the value of this iconic Greek sculpture.

---

[175] Pg. 7-8 – "The Anthropology of World's Fairs: San Francisco's Panama Pacific International Exposition of 1915", Burton Benedict and Robert H. Lowie Museum of Anthropology, Scholar Press, 1983.

In art, Hitler found the medium necessary to express that his eugenic ideals were aesthetic ideals as well. The artist Michael Cahier passed away just as the ARC version of this book was being written, but his work had been left posted up until 2013. However, this author finds his observations relevant and worth preserving for posterity. Cahier posted on his personal website:

> In sculpture, Hitler had one passion, the Greeks and his favorite sculpture was the Discus Thrower by Myron that he eventually managed to purchase for the astronomical sum of $327,000 in order to complete his Linz museum collection. His views about sculpture were once more neo-classical and some talented sculptors literally threw themselves to his feet to enter the private cenacle of his providers. The most famous was Arno Breker, an extremely talented artist who prostituted his talent to the Fuhrer and became a rabid Nazi, going to such extremes as tipping off Hitler about non-Nazis artistic activities or exhibitions. ---- To please his master, Breker produced caricatures of virility: his works owed to size and exaggeration, shoulders too broad, hips too narrow, muscles outrageously pronounced... The whole thing reeked of some sort of homoerotic scent that raised questions about the Nazi ideals of comradeship. ---- So by exalting virile virtues and Nazi comradeship, in the end Hitler and his henchmen obtained - as said once Trotsky - an atmosphere of military barracks homosexuality. ("The Artistic Ambitions of Prometheus: with the tastes of an autodidactic petit-bourgeois", defunct website)

Cahier, a French artist, understood Hitler's intentions as an artist, and Cahier apparently devoted a significant amount of his time toward reconciling the positive and negative sides of art:

> The reality is that Hitler was a mix of Prometheus and of a Demiurge pretending to shape everything cultural or artistic in Nazi Germany and to this end enrolled army of artists, architects and painters who jumped on the bandwagon with the appetite of their devouring ambitions.

Cahier warned against teaching a simplistic version of Hitler that would deny the sophistication that his propaganda employed, as this leaves future youth exposed to the same vulnerabilities. Cahier is entirely correct, as it was the credulousness and naiveté of the German youth that allowed them to be so easily seduced into serving Hitler:

> Millions of little French kids have never been told anything about Hitler's artistic views and achievements except that he was a miserable "*peintre en bâtiment*" (building painter) not far from being a complete "clochard" (bum). That such an ordinary and mediocre man would elevate himself to the position of Germany's Fuhrer should be a subject of puzzlement for smart little French but in fact the lies or the omissions of the victors have been swallowed all along without questioning since the glorious Liberation of Paris by Gaullist troops. As far as propaganda was concerned, European nations especially the "collaborative" ones – stepped in Goebbels boots with flamboyant panache.

Cahier is hardly exaggerating, as history proves that it was the younger elements of National Socialism that were the most zealous and prone to violence. Mies Van Der Rohe's life story reveals that there were just as many pro-Hitler elements in the Bauhaus as there were anti-Hitler elements, and to make things worse, their disagreement only lay in 'which' totalitarian state these young artists wished to usher in. The activist world of artists was seduced by the radicalism of both the "Nazis" and the "Commies," and the only person in the Bauhaus asking for moderation was Mies. Mies was apolitical in a politically charged era and suffered greatly in trying to do "art for art's sake" in an era when radicals demanded that art be the voice of revolutions.

Seventy years later, the message conveyed by the art of the eugenic movements still resonates. Christoph Stölzl, historian and vice-president of Berlin's city council, wrote an article for the *Deutsche Welle* website which explained the pervasiveness of this use of sculpture in both the United States and Europe during the era:

> The connection between idealization of the body and racism is very complicated, because there were both right and left wing variations on the body cult, ---- The art of the 20 century was often wrapped up in dictatorships. ---- The style was in step with the zeitgeist. ---- The Neoclassical sculptures made in the United States at the time of the New Deal look just like the sculptures produced in Germany in the 1930s, in the Soviet Union, Italy, or at the Palais Chaillot in Paris. article titled (dw.com, Christoph Stölzl, "Nazi Sculptures at World Cup Venue Spark Protest", *Deutsche Welle*, June 2, 2006)

Christoph Stölzl is correct in pointing out that much of the art in Europe and the United States of the era was inspired by, or even commissioned for, the purposes of communicating the social hygiene and eugenic movements. Where Christoph Stölzl may have been mistaken in his defense of keeping the statues put up by Albert Speer and Adolf Hitler for the 1936 Berlin Games is that, like Davenport's sculpture, these statues had a very direct and political purpose. Their authors certainly didn't see them as "art for art's sake." To the contrary, these sculptures served a purpose no different than the political posters and eugenic films distributed by the Third Reich. Displaying them out of the context of their message is just as awkward as airing "Triumph of the Will" with no further explanation or contextualization.

Sec. 10 - WAS IT JULIAN HUXLEY'S "BRAVE NEW WORLD"?

Aldous Huxley was an outstanding novelist, and one of the most prominent members of the Huxley family. His brother was the head of UNESCO that prescribed a continuation of eugenic policies in the immediate aftermath of The Holocaust. Aldous Huxley's main works include the 1921 "Crome Yellow" and the 1923 "Antic Hay." Huxley is probably most famous for his 1954 "The Doors of Perception," whose title was taken from a poem by William Blake, and in turn, inspired poet/singer Jim Morrison to name his 1960s rock band The Doors.

Aldous and Julian were born into a close-knit scientific community that orbited around Charles Darwin, Francis Galton, and T.H. Huxley. Julian Huxley would recall how his famous brother would often take part in the discussions with Julian's circle of eugenic-minded friends. Aldous Huxley came away from those gatherings severely questioning the alleged benevolence of Fabian Socialism. Incidentally, Aldous Huxley's most memorable work was his 1932 dystopian novel "Brave New World." The initial idea for the novel was a parody of "Men Like Gods" by Fabian Socialist H.G. Wells, and a criticism of the eugenic beliefs H.G. Wells and Julian Huxley held. "Brave New World" turns Well's optimistic utopias on their head and exposes the dire consequences of their paternalistic collectivism.

The young H.G. Wells had studied under Julian's and Aldus's grandfather, Thomas Henry Huxley. Wells would become a devoted Darwinist and proponent of eugenics, likely because of the Huxley family's influence. He also found himself collaborating towards the effort of eugenics and Fabian Socialism with the Huxley family. In 1931, "The Science of Life" became one of the bestselling books on popular science in the early 20th century. "The Science of Life" itself, was a collaborative effort between Julian Huxley, H.G. Wells, and his eldest son, George Phillip Wells. "The Science of Life" paints a picture of the continued urgency to find some form of directed evolution, or what they call an "ethical evolution." They refer the reader to Carr-Saunder's "Eugenics" or Karl Pearson's "Grammar of Science" to learn more about the "science." Eugenics would always be a topic consistently woven into the many futuristic utopias written by H.G. Wells. It seems that while Julian Huxley was making real-world proposals for eugenic-minded legislation, H.G. Wells was dreaming up eugenic states in order to paint a picture of what these eugenic utopias would look like once these laws had their intended effect:

> Perhaps in years to come our descendants will look with intelligence over their pedigree, and if there is a probability of recessive genius in a family and no reason to suspect a grave recessive taint they will deliberately encourage inbreeding. A rather grim Utopia might be devised in which for some generations [...] inbreeding would be made compulsory, with a prompt resort to the lethal chamber for any undesirable results. A grim Utopia, no doubt, but in that manner our race might be purged of its evil recessives forever. (Pg. 503, "Science of Life", Doubleday, Doran, Incorporated, 1931)

Reading Aldous' "Brave New World" along with Julian's "Eugenic Manifesto" reveals exactly who Aldous' target audience was, as "Brave New World" reads like a principled rebuttal to Julian's work. "Brave New World" was a warning. Aldous Huxley's political life before writing "Brave New World" is that of flirtation with socialist and collectivist schemes. However, it seems that along the way Aldous became acutely aware that utopian writers from Plato to H.G. Wells have believed that reform, or what they called "progress," required their ideal governments to pay some attention to breeding. They set out to supply society with improved men, instead of providing men with an improved society. "Planning was the key word of the 1930s," wrote A. J. P. Taylor, "planned economy, plan for peace, planned families, plan for holidays. The standard was Utopia." Planning was also Huxley's personal shibboleth during the composition of "Brave New World." [176] Huxley began writing "Brave New World" in April 1931 while struggling with his political convictions.

Huxley's matured opinion of a planned society is made clear in "Brave New World." Mustapha Mond is one of the central planning elite in "Brave New World," one of ten "World Controllers" in Huxley's fictional account. The character's job as one of the "World Controllers" was to censor scientific discoveries and exile people for unorthodox beliefs. Mond is portrayed as speaking up with passion and resolution for "stability": "No civilization without social stability. No social stability without individual stability . . . Stability. The primal and the ultimate need." The caricature of a statesman desperately trying to maintain the illusory utopian stasis is clear.

Aldous was undoubtedly familiar with the work of the leading figures of the eugenics movement, and there exists evidence that the Nazi shadow had begun to weigh heavily on the eugenic insiders. "Brave New World" seems to be at least in part a product of the departure of a previously sympathetic mind. He was after all Julian Huxley's brother and the grandson of Thomas H. Huxley. Huxley was also friends with C. P. Blacker, general secretary of the Eugenics Society from 1931 until 1952, and the principal architect of reform eugenics. The Eugenics Society had begun a campaign to legalize voluntary sterilization at this time, and mainly as a retreat from the harsher stance of compulsory sterilization. A letter to Huxley from Blacker provides proof:

> The adoption of a drastic eugenic policy by the Nazis has had the not unnatural effect of still further antagonizing persons of Labour persuasion against eugenics. (independent.co.uk, "BOOKS / Planning for a Brave New World", David Bradshaw, Jan. 23, 1994)

Thus, "Brave New World" seems to serve as Aldous Huxley's announcement that he was now skeptical about what his friends and family were proposing. The man once convinced by fabian planning began to turn into a reclusive humanist, and Huxley utilized "Brave New World" to satirize the utopian dreams of the era as well as its obsession with efficiency and progress. Henry Ford was the object of Aldous Huxley's disgust, as Ford was the undisputed icon of efficiency of the era. Fordism was used to depict a society based upon an orderly cycle of production and

---

[176] independent.co.uk, "BOOKS / Planning for a Brave New World", David Bradshaw, January 23, 1994.

consumption. It also seems that Ford's real-world disdain for scholarly knowledge amused Huxley. Huxley appears to mock the well-worn propaganda practice of reducing dogma into sound bites:

"You all remember, I suppose, that beautiful and inspired saying of Our Ford's: History is bunk." (Ch. 3)
"Cleanliness is next to Fordliness."
"Yes, and civilization is sterilization." ("Brave New World," Ch. 7)

As was the case with any utopian proposal, the political structure of Huxley's dystopia subordinated the individual to the state and society. Huxley's vivid depiction of a "planned" society through forced "stability" leaves no doubt as to the necessary role of government in maintaining a utopian stasis. No eugenic proposal is functional if individual rights are allowed to supersede the dictates of the central planners:

The greater a man's talents, the greater his power to lead astray. It is better that [only] one should suffer than that many should be corrupted. Consider the matter dispassionately, Mr. Foster, and you will see that no offense is so heinous as unorthodoxy of behavior. Murder kills only the individual-and, after all, what is an individual? ("Brave New World," Ch. 10)

Huxley found a sympathetic ear in George Orwell. Huxley's position is made clear in his interviews and personal correspondence. On October 21, 1949, Huxley wrote to George Orwell, author of the utopian/dystopian "Nineteen Eighty-Four," congratulating him on "how fine and how profoundly important the book is." In his letter to Orwell, he predicted:

Within the next generation I believe that the world's leaders will discover that infant conditioning and narco-hypnosis are more efficient, as instruments of government, than clubs and prisons, and that the lust for power can be just as completely satisfied by suggesting people into loving their servitude as by flogging them and kicking them into obedience. (theatlantic.com, Shaun Usher, "Aldous Huxley to George Orwell: My Dystopia Is Better Than Yours", Jan./Feb. 2017 – From Usher's book, "Letters of Note: Vol. 2", 2016)

Orwell himself had departed from socialism's utopian delusion. George Orwell also vented his frustration with his counterparts, except in a more direct and less subtle way. On August 1941, with World War II and the consequences of Stalinism and Hitlerism fully apparent, Orwell penned an article in Horizon Magazine of London. The article was titled "Wells, Hitler and the World State," and it was a direct shot at H.G. Wells and his naïve and slavish devotion to socialism and all its predictable traps. Like many of the International Socialists of the era, Wells was busy defending Stalin while ridiculing Hitler, propagandizing for Bolshevik totalitarianism, while criticizing Hitler's National Socialism. "What has Wells to set against the 'screaming little defective in Berlin'? The usual rigmarole about a World

State," Orwell sniped. [177] More along the lines of the central theme of this book, it is important to note that Orwell pointed out that what H.G. Wells had been peddling for his entire career was no different than what the "screaming little defective" from Berlin was selling:

> Much of what Wells has imagined and worked for is physically there in Nazi Germany. The order, the planning, the State encouragement of science, the steel, the concrete, the aeroplanes, are all there, but all in there. ("Wells, Hitler and the World State", George Orwell, Horizon Mag., Aug. 1941)

As extrapolated earlier, the recipe for utopian socialism is revealed as substantially similar to the recipe for totalitarian collectivism. What makes "Brave New World" unique is that it predicts that modern utopias would be achieved through propaganda and that its rulers would maintain order through persuasion, and not necessarily with an "iron fist" as dictatorships are typically understood. In this sense, Aldous Huxley fully predicted the hold that Adolf Hitler and Joseph Goebbels would have over the unsuspecting German public. "Brave New World" addresses this notion that future leaders of society would have to gain the acceptance of their totalitarian policies by feeding the people's pleasures. The utopian government depicted in "Brave New World" turns to mandatory drugging of the populace in order to make them more amenable to the totalitarian realities of their existence. In "Brave New World," order is maintained by the governing elite by the distribution of the drug "soma." "Soma" kept the populace docile and receptive to their rule, and eternally deferring to the "central planners" for the life-choices autonomous individuals otherwise make for themselves. "Brave New World" depicts a eugenically organized society whose totalitarian government is rendered palatable by the consistent drugging of the populace, and a centrally planned society controlled using technological advancements and planned sexuality.

> There's always soma to calm your anger, to reconcile you to your enemies, to make you patient and long-suffering. In the past you could only accomplish these things by making a great effort and after years of hard moral training. Now, you swallow two or three half-gramme tablets, and there you are. Anybody can be virtuous now. You can carry at least half your morality about in a bottle. Christianity without tears-that's what soma is. (Pg. 228, James E. Gunn, "The Road to Science Fiction: From Wells to Heinlein ," Scarecrow Press, 2002)

None of this is speculative. Huxley confirms the juxtaposition observed herein in his personal correspondence and in interviews. Huxley gave his best description during an interview with Mike Wallace. Mike Wallace interviewed Huxley on May 18th, 1958, where Huxley gave a vivid explanation, if not justification, for his change of heart with the radical "progressive" policies he once espoused. The interview gave insight into what Huxley was thinking in 1931 when he wrote "Brave New World" in the midst of the totalitarian era, just after the Bolshevik Revolution, and just at

---

[177] "Wells, Hitler and the World State", George Orwell, Horizon Mag., Aug. 1941, Sourced from www.Orwell.ru – Reprinted in "Critical Essays", George Orwell, Secker & Warburg, 1946.

the beginning of National Socialism. Huxley began the interview by explaining how the drive for efficiency was slowly but surely eroding our humanity and our individual autonomy:

> **WALLACE**: Another force that is diminishing our freedoms?
>
> **HUXLEY**: Well, another force which I think is very strongly operative in this country is the force of what may be called over-organization. ...As technology becomes more and more complicated, it becomes necessary to have more and more elaborate organizations, more hierarchical organizations, and incidentally the advance of technology is being accompanied by an advance in the science of organization. It's now possible to make organizations on a larger scale than it was ever possible before, and so that you have more and more people living their lives out as subordinates in these hierarchical systems controlled by bureaucracies, either the bureaucracies of big business or the bureaucracies of big government. (Box: 8, Call number: 85472 Aa 2, Huxley, Aldous, Mike Wallace papers: 1956-1963, Univ. of Michigan, Bentley Historical Archive)

The interview proceeds with Aldous Huxley explaining how the totalitarian states of the future will be the sort of "happy fascism," where the individuals willingly give up their freedoms and autonomy through the persuasion of propaganda and the complacency sustained by artificial bliss:

> **WALLACE**: Mr. Huxley, in your new essays you state that these various enemies of freedom are pushing us to a real-life Brave New World, and you say that it's awaiting us just around the corner. First of all, can you detail for us, what life in this Brave New World that you would fear so much, or what life might be like?
>
> **HUXLEY**: Well, to start with, I think this kind of dictatorship of the future, I think will be very unlike the dictatorships which we've been familiar with in the immediate past. I mean, take another book prophesying the future, which was a very remarkable book, George Orwell's "1984." Well this book was written at the height of the Stalinist regime, and just after the Hitler regime, and there he foresaw a dictatorship using entirely the methods of terror, the methods of physical violence. Now, I think what is going to happen in the future is that dictators will find, as the old saying goes, that you can do everything with bayonets except sit on them! That if you want to preserve your power indefinitely, you have to get the consent of the ruled, and this they will do partly by drugs as I foresaw in "Brave New World," partly by these new techniques of propaganda. They will do it by bypassing the sort of rational side of man and appealing to his subconscious and his deeper emotions, and his physiology even, and so making him actually love his slavery. I mean, I think, this is the danger that actually people may be, in some ways, happy under the new regime, but that they will be happy in situations where they oughtn't to be happy. (Box: 8, Call number: 85472 Aa 2, Huxley, Aldous, Mike Wallace papers: 1956-1963, Univ. of Michigan, Bentley Historical Archive)

Aldous Huxley was not alone in predicting the "political spin" that would allow Fascism to be welcome into the United States with open arms and enthusiastic adulation. Huey Long once responded to the question of whether Fascism would come to America, to which Long aptly replied: "Yes, but it will be called antifascism." [178] These predictions have proven to be prophetic, as the most invasive and intrusive legislative measures to be implemented in the United States have come under the guise of "liberalism." Personal liberty and individual autonomy in the United States has indeed been significantly eroded by those who proclaim to espouse "liberal" values, and the alleged liberating effect of modern technology. Huxley and Wallace continued by explaining the role of technology in maintaining the consensus to be subordinated and controlled:

> **WALLACE**: The question, of course, that keeps coming back to my mind is this: obviously politics in themselves are not evil, television is not in itself evil, atomic energy is not evil, and yet you seem to fear that it will be used in an evil way. Why is it that the right people will not, in your estimation, use them? Why is it that the wrong people will use these various devices and for the wrong motives?
>
> **HUXLEY**: Well, I think one of the reasons is that these are all instruments for obtaining power, and obviously the passion for power is one of the most moving passions that exists in man; and after all, all democracies are based on the proposition that power is very dangerous and that it is extremely important not to let any one man or any one small group have too much power for too long a time. After all, what are the British and American Constitutions except devices for limiting power, and all these new devices are extremely efficient instruments for the imposition of power by small groups over larger masses. (Box: 8, Call number: 85472 Aa 2, Huxley, Aldous, Mike Wallace papers: 1956-1963, Univ. of Michigan, Bentley Historical Archive)

Huxley's disdain for an overarching "total state" is clearly communicated in this interview with Wallace. It seems as if Hitler's Nazism and Stalin's Bolshevism were enough to prove to Huxley that his fears were well-founded. Here we see Huxley as the champion of a decentralized civilization, the complete antithesis to the "centrally planned" economies of the American Progressives, the British Fabian Socialists, the German National Socialism, and International Communism.

> **WALLACE**: You're a prophet of decentralization?
>
> **HUXLEY**: Well, the…yes…if it…it's feasible. It's one of these tragedies it seems to be. I mean, many people have been talking about the importance of decentralization in order to give back to the voter a sense of direct power. I mean…the voter in an enormous electorate feels quite impotent, and his vote seems to count for nothing which is not true where the electorate is small, and where he is dealing with a…group which he can manage and understand…and if one can, as Jefferson after all suggested, break up the units into smaller and smaller units and so, get a real, self-governing democracy. (Box: 8, Call number: 85472 Aa 2, Huxley, Aldous, Mike Wallace papers: 1956-1963, Univ. of Michigan, Bentley Historical Archive)

---

[178] Pg. 114 - "The Nazi Connection: Eugenics, American Racism, and German National Socialism", Stefan Kühl, Oxford, 1994.

The connections to American Progressivism are further underscored when one realizes that H.G. Wells practically plagiarized Edward Bellamy's plot in "Looking Backward." H.G. Wells' "Men Like Gods" is the story of a group of 20th century Englishmen accidentally transported into an alternate dimension of peaceful and servile utopians who uncritically accept subservience of their individual autonomy to their scientifically organized collectivist state. In Wells' "Men Like Gods," the citizens of this socialist utopia explain to the time travelers that through eugenics and technology they were able to breed out "the primordial fierce combativeness of the ancestral man-ape." The society had achieved a cooperative state with "no parliament, no politics, no private wealth, no business competition, no police nor prisons, no lunatics, no defectives nor cripples." Aldous Huxley thought this vision preposterous. The socio-economic recipe of "Men Like Gods" was clearly familiar to Aldous Huxley, whose brother, Julian peddled and lobbied for an almost identical idea. Julian Huxley proposed that through eugenics, the leveraging of genetic technology, education and a collectivist governmental structure, man could transcend his primitive animal self. Julian Huxley coined the term "transhumanism" to describe this eugenic ideal. Aldous Huxley had to have seen the parallels to his brother's utopian ideals upon reading "Men Like Gods," specifically when reading the motto of Wells' utopian state: "Our education is our government," which echoes the core concept of Julian's "Eugenic Manifesto." It is "Men Like Gods" that Huxley specifically points to as the inspiration for a "negative utopia" for his "Brave New World":

> Get rid of priests and kings, make Aeschylus and the differential calculus available to all, and the world will become a paradise . . . "Men Like Gods" "annoyed me to the point of planning a parody, but when I started writing I found the idea of a negative Utopia so interesting that I forgot about Wells and launched into "Brave New World." (Pg. 205, Bernfried Nugel/Jerome Meckier "Aldous Huxley Annual", *LIT Verlag Münster*, Dec. 28, 2009)

"Brave New World" had a mostly chilly reception upon its initial publication. Most reviewers were upset with what they saw as unjustified alarmism on the part of Aldous Huxley. H. G. Wells felt personally offended, stating that "a writer of the standing of Aldous Huxley has no right to betray the future as he did in that book." [179] The harshest criticism came from Julian's colleagues. Wells' friend and fellow writer Wyndham Lewis called it "an unforgivable offense to Progress." [180] In other words, Aldous Huxley hit the target smack in the center.

Huxley had told a friend in 1931 that he was "writing a novel about the future - on the horror of the Wellsian Utopia and a revolt against it." [181] H.G. Wells, as George Orwell correctly sniped, was the one person within the Huxley social circle that had been prolific in authoring depictions of eugenic and socialist utopias based

---

[179] Pgs. 41-54 - "Brave New World at 75", Caitrin Keiper, Number 16, Spring 2007.
[180] Ibid.
[181] Ibid.

upon the convictions of the British Fabian Socialists. "Brave New World" certainly does read like a personal insult, or at the very least, a stern rebuttal of everything H.G. Wells and Julian Huxley stood for. Nor is this author the first to notice this connection. The eugenic faithful took notice of Huxley's blasphemous depiction of their "religion." The December 1999 issue of the Galton Institute's newsletter has an article, "Portraits of the Pioneers: Sir Julian Huxley, FRS, Evolution and Eugenics," where author John Timson opines that it was likely that Julian and his eugenic counterparts were the inspiration for the characters of "Brave New World." Timson points to the Foreword to the 1955 Penguin edition of "Brave New World" where Aldous refers to a "foolproof system of eugenics" as an essential part of his plot. Julian Huxley certainly felt the heat of the spotlight shinned on him by Aldous, as Julian explicitly disavowed any notion that he had contributed to "Brave New World," claiming that Aldous Huxley's ideas were already fully formed when Aldous first discussed the book with him. [182] What may be a totally unconnected quote from Aldous seems applicable: **"God deliver us from such criminal imbecility."** [183]

The Mike Wallace interview concludes with recognizing that Aldous Huxley's warning to the world was prophetic at the time of its writing, and continued to be dangerously relevant as humanity had yet to learn its lesson:

> **WALLACE**: Aldous Huxley finds himself these days in a peculiar and disturbing position; a quarter of a century after prophesying an authoritarian state in which people were reduced to ciphers, he can point at Soviet Russia and say **"I told you so!"** The crucial question, as he sees it now, is whether the so-called Free World is shortly going to give Mr. Huxley the further dubious satisfaction of saying the same thing about us. (emphasis mine, Box: 8, Call number: 85472 Aa 2, Huxley, Aldous, Mike Wallace papers: 1956-1963, Univ. of Michigan, Bentley Historical Archive)

---

[182] Pgs. 41-54 - "Brave New World at 75", Caitrin Keiper, Number 16, Spring 2007.
[183] "Ends and Means: An Inquiry into the Nature of Ideals", Aldous Huxley, Routledge, Sep. 2017.

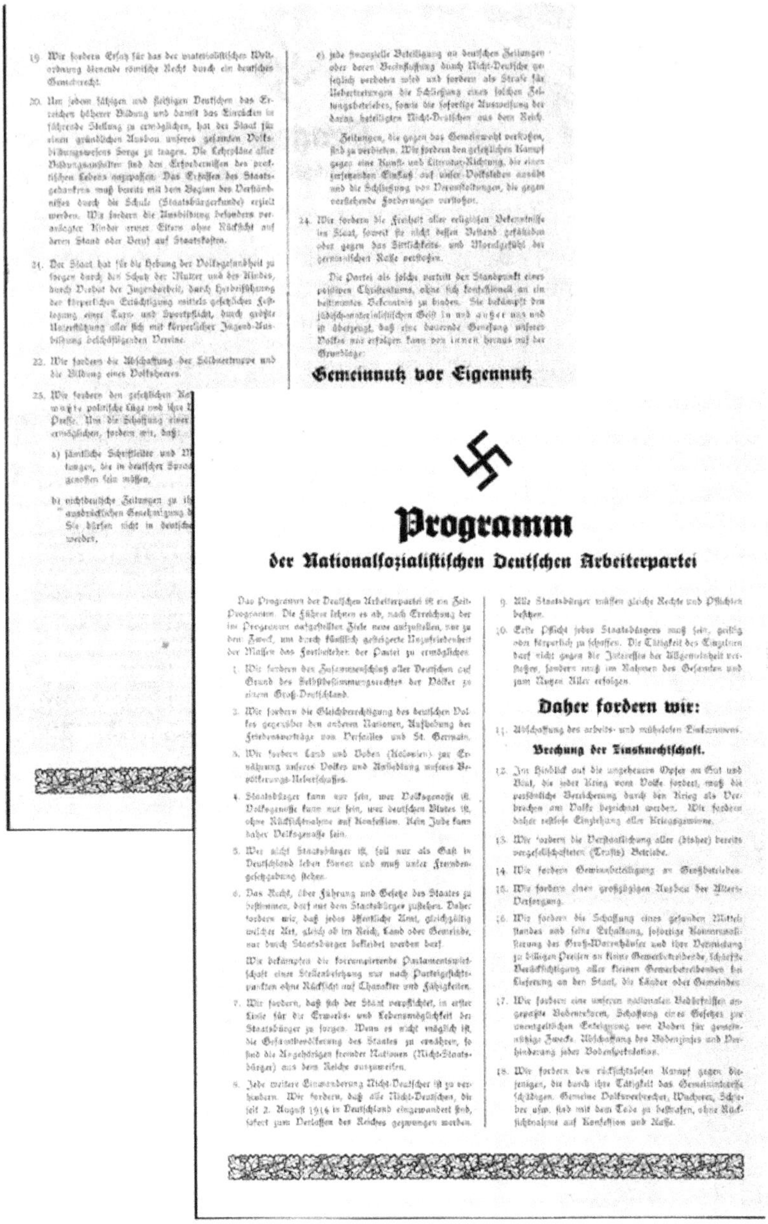

Gemeinnutz vor Eigennutz

Programm

der Nationalsozialistischen Deutschen Arbeiterpartei

Daher fordern wir:

Brechung der Zinsknechtschaft.

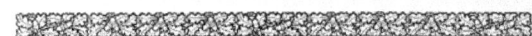

FIGURE 5: THE "NATIONAL SOCIALIST PROGRAMME" - OTHERWISE KNOWN AS THE "25-POINT PROGRAMME" OR THE "25-POINT PLAN", WAS FIRST THE POLITICAL FORMULATION OF THE NATIONAL SOCIALIST PARTY. THE "NATIONAL SOCIALIST PROGRAMME" ORIGINATED AT A DAP CONGRESS IN VIENNA. ADOLF HITLER PUBLICLY ANNOUNCED THE "25-POINT PROGRAM" IN MUNICH, ON FEBRUARY 24, 1920, WHEN THE PARTY WAS STILL KNOWN AS THE GERMAN WORKERS PARTY. HITLER RETAINED THE "25-POINT PROGRAMME" UPON RENAMING THE PARTY AS THE NATIONAL SOCIALIST GERMAN WORKERS PARTY IN APRIL 1920.

Chap. 4: 1930 to 1926

EUROPEAN FRONT: THE YOUNG PLAN, WHICH SET THE TOTAL WORLD WAR I REPARATIONS OWED BY GERMANY AT US$26,350,000,000 TO BE PAID OVER A PERIOD OF 58½ YEARS, IS FINALIZED. TROTSKY IS EXILED TO ALMA ATA. **AMERICAN FRONT:** WALL STREET CRASH OF 1929: THREE MULTI-DIGIT PERCENTAGE DROPS WIPE OUT MORE THAN $30 BILLION FROM THE NEW YORK STOCK EXCHANGE (10 TIMES GREATER THAN THE ANNUAL BUDGET OF THE FEDERAL GOVERNMENT). **MIDDLE EAST:** THE 1929 PALESTINE RIOTS BREAKS OUT BETWEEN PALESTINIANS AND JEWS. THE BRITISH WHITE PAPER DEMANDS RESTRICTIONS ON JEWISH IMMIGRATION INTO PALESTINE. **SCIENCE & TECHNOLOGY:** AVIATOR AMELIA EARHART STARTS HER FLIGHT. THE GALVIN MANUFACTURING CORPORATION NOW KNOWN AS MOTOROLA IS INCORPORATED. – ALEXANDER FLEMING DISCOVERS PENICILLIN. ROBERT GODDARD LAUNCHES THE FIRST ROCKET. **LIFE:** ST. VALENTINE'S DAY MASSACRE. – MARTIN LUTHER KING JR. IS BORN. – WYATT EARP, AMERICAN GUNFIGHTER DIES. - KARL BENZ, GERMAN AUTOMOTIVE PIONEER DIES. – HERMAN HOLLERITH, FATHER OF THE COMPUTER DIES. MICHAEL COLLINS, ASTRONAUT, IS BORN. – EDWARD WHITE, ASTRONAUT IS BORN. – ELIE WIESEL IS BORN. - ANDY WARHOL IS BORN. – VILLA SAVOYE BY LE CORBUSIER IS COMPLETED. - JACK KEVORKIAN, RIGHT-TO-DIE ADVOCATE IS BORN. – ANTONI GAUDÍ DIES. EUGENE V. DEBS, POLITICAL LEADER DIES. CLAUDE MONET DIES. - JOHN MOSES BROWNING, INVENTOR OF VARIOUS FIREARMS DIES.

Sec. I - "CENTRAL PLANNING" TO NATIONALIZED "SOCIALISM":

So, what exactly was "Nazism"? The first thing to realize is that the term "Nazi" was generally not utilized by Hitler's government. It was mostly a term used by their opponents. At all times, Hitler's party referred to themselves as "National Socialists," short for "National Socialist German Workers Party" or *Nationalsozialistische Deutsche Arbeiterpartei* in German. Abbreviated NSDAP, it was the offspring of the German Workers' Party (DAP), which existed from 1919 to 1920. Interestingly enough, the Nazis also used the socialist term "comrade" to refer to each other.

To understand the importance of the long form of the Nazi party name, one must understand just how obsessed Adolf Hitler was with propaganda and presentation. There are many things that can be said about Hitler's shortcomings. It cannot be said that Hitler lacked skills in the art of propaganda. He was an expert speaker and propagandist. When he took over the German Workers' Party and chose to marry the terms "nationalism" and "socialism," it can be assumed that he knew exactly what message this would convey and that these terms were carefully and precisely chosen.

Hitler understood better than anyone that to enact his plans he first had to establish a form of government that subordinated individual rights to the goals of the society or state. This is precisely what he meant by "socialism": a "unity of purpose" with every aspect of society subordinated towards the ultimate goal of a "racial state" or a "master race." There was no room for democracy within the scope of Hitler's goals. More to the point, Hitler blamed democracy and egalitarianism for the "racial decay" which allegedly lead to Germany's downfall. This is precisely the eugenic notion that Hitler described to Hermann Göring in the formative years of National Socialism, and which Göring recounted as part of his sworn testimony during the Nuremberg Trials on March 13, 1946:

> **GÖRING:** The second point which impressed me very strongly at the time and which I felt very deeply and really considered to be a basic condition, was the

fact that he explained to me at length that it was not possible under the conditions then prevailing to bring about, in co-operation with only that element which at that time considered itself national -- whether it be the political so-called nationalist parties or those which still called themselves national, or the then existing clubs, fighter organizations, the Free Corps, et cetera -- with these people alone it was not possible to bring about a reconstruction with the aim of creating a strong national will among the German people, as long as the masses of German labor opposed this idea. One could only rebuild Germany again if one could enlist the masses of German labor. This could be achieved only if the will to become free from the unbearable shackles of the Treaty of Versailles were really felt by the broad masses of the people, and that would be possible only by combining the national conception with a social goal.

CONTINUES...

He gave me on that occasion for the first time a very wonderful and profound explanation of the concept of National Socialism; the unity of the two concepts of nationalism on the one hand and socialism on the other, which should prove themselves the absolute supporters of nationalism as well as of socialism -- the nationalism, if I may say so, of the bourgeois world and the socialism of the Marxist world. We must clarify these concepts again and through this union of the two ideas create a new vehicle for these new thoughts. (trial transcripts available online at nizkor.org, "The Trial of German Major War Criminals: Nuremberg, Germany, March 12-22, 1946")

This is also what Hitler communicated to an American spy posing as a member of the press during the early days of his reign. The archives of the US Office of Strategic Services, the predecessor to the modern-day Central Intelligence Agency and the Federal Bureau of Investigation, document this meeting. The report reads in part:

> He sees the world as a clash of opposing forces, and genius in man as the power to synthesize these opposing forces for the purpose of evolving a third and more powerful force. His personality is a synthesis of Austria and Prussia, of Marxian materialism and metaphysics. National Socialism, he was always proud of describing as a synthesis of Nationalism and Socialism. His appeal to the German people based on this synthesis. (Office of Strategic Services – Hitler Source Book – Recollections of Adolf Hitler – Memorandum To: Professor Crane Brinton, From: Edward Deuss. -- Recollections of Adolf Hitler Gained from personal contact, interviews and on airplane campaign tours with Hitler from September 1931 – May 1933)

Hitler gave this explanation of Nazism to other contemporaries. Hermann Rauschning was a German revolutionary who briefly joined the Nazis. Rauschning is known for "Conversations with Hitler," which was published in Britain under the titles "The Voice of Destruction" and "Hitler Speaks," both which allegedly document conversations with Hitler. The following quote is included, despite the reservations of other historians to quote Rauschning, because verifiable sources of Hitler, Goebbels, and Goering describing National Socialism in such terms exist, and thus corroborate Rauschnig's definition. "Hitler Speaks" documents Hitler's understanding of Nazism in relation to Soviet-style socialism:

> Besides, there is more that binds us to Bolshevism than separates us from it. There is, above all, genuine, revolutionary feeling, which is alive everywhere in Russia except where there are Jewish Marxists. I have always made allowance for this circumstance, and given orders that former Communists are to be admitted to the party at once. The petit bourgeois Social-Democrat and the trade-union boss will never make a National Socialist, but the Communist always will. (Pg. 131, "Hitler Speaks: A Series of Political Conversations with Adolf Hitler on his Real Aims", Thornton Butterworth, Ltd., 1939)

Yet, despite the plethora of first-hand accounts, these definitions go counter to the pedestrian understanding of what "Nazism" was. Why? The history of National Socialism was politicized and skewed by the Cold War. We still operate under the fog of the Cold War whenever we utilize the fictitious existence of a political "Left" or "Right." In this fictional and polarized account of world history, there are but two options, and Hitler's government is conveniently and inaccurately placed as part of the "conservative right" due to its supposed patriotic "nationalism." This is a misinterpretation of what "conservatism" and supposedly "rightist" policies meant for Hitler's generation. In 1939 Rauschning also wrote, "The Revolution of Nihilism: Warning to the West," in which he reveals the opposition of true German "conservatives" to the National Socialists. Rauschning was a monarchist, who was an early supporter of Hitler until he came to understand that Hitler was a "revolutionary" and not a "conservative." This was a reality of *fin-de-siècle* Germany that needs no verification. To be a conservative in Hitler's generation was to be loyal to the Habsburg Monarchy, and there was no aspect of Adolf Hitler which sought to restore the power of the monarchy. In "The Revolution of Nihilism," Rauschning wrote that "the National Socialism that came to power in 1933 was no longer a nationalist but a revolutionary movement." [184] As such, Rauschning believed that the only alternative to "Nazism" was the restoration of the monarchy. [185]

That said, Rauschning's confusion is understandable. In Nazism, the total subordination of the individual to the state was structured in a pyramidal scheme culminating in Hitler himself as if he were a monarch. The *Führerprinzip,* or "leader principle," prescribed the fundamental basis of political authority in the governmental structures of the Third Reich. This principle was understood to mean that "the Fuehrer's word is above all written law" and that all governmental policies, decisions, and offices worked toward the realization of this end. Yet, this role of a *Führer* must be differentiated from that of a monarch. The political use and meaning

---

[184] Pg. 16 - "The Revolution of Nihilism, Warning to the West", Hermann Rauschning, Translated by E. W. Dickes, Longmans-Green, 1939.
[185] Pgs. 170-172 – Ibid.

of *Führer* climbs down the pyramidal scheme and utilized to structure all aspects of the Third Reich around the principle of blind trust and obedience to its leaders. For example, Heinrich Himmler's title and rank in the SS was "*Reichsführer-SS,*" and the heads of the other organizations within Hitler's National Socialist government shared similar tiles of *"Führer."* Thus, National Socialism was in practice a pyramidal governing structure by the central planning elite, where the elitist credentials were based upon eugenic dogma.

More precisely, most of the leadership of Hitler's National Socialist government considered themselves "socialists" and as historians have noted, a sizeable portion of the early Brown Shirts were recruited from the German communist party. Gregor Strasser and Joseph Goebbels were two devout socialists, for example. Guenter Reimann knew this better than anyone as part of the Communist resistance to Hitler's government. Reimann wrote the "Vampire Economy: Doing Business under Fascism" in 1939. It is a rare and detailed account of how the National Socialist government crushed the private sector and hamstrung the economy with vast regulations, violations of property rights, inflation, price controls, and taxes. As a devout communist, Reimann understood the centrally planned economy, and as a member of the resistance he had a first-row seat of Hitler's policies as they were being put in place. Reimann points to Hitler's 25-point Programme as National Socialism's party platform as one piece of evidence qualifying Nazism as a socialist movement. The "National Socialist Programme," otherwise known as the "25-point Programme" or the "25-point Plan," was first the political platform of the party. Adolf Hitler publicly announced the "25-point Program" in Munich, on February 24, 1920, when the party was still known as the German Workers Party. Hitler retained the "25-Point Programme" upon renaming the party as the National Socialist German Workers Party in April 1920. It is quoted here in its entirety so the reader can understand how the Nazis viewed movement:

- We demand the union of all Germans in a Great Germany on the basis of the principle of self-determination of all peoples.
- We demand that the German people have rights equal to those of other nations; and that the Peace Treaties of Versailles and St. Germain shall be abrogated.
- We demand land and territory (colonies) for the maintenance of our people and the settlement of our surplus population.
- Only those who are our fellow countrymen can become citizens. Only those who have German blood, regardless of creed, can be our countrymen. Hence no Jew can be a countryman.
- Those who are not citizens must live in Germany as foreigners and must be subject to the law of aliens.
- The right to choose the government and determine the laws of the State shall belong only to citizens. We therefore demand that no public office, of whatever nature, whether in the central government, the province, or the municipality, shall be held by anyone who is not a citizen. We wage

war against the corrupt parliamentary administration whereby men are appointed to posts by favor of the party without regard to character and fitness.

- **We demand that the State shall above all undertake to ensure that every citizen shall have the possibility of living decently and earning a livelihood.** If it should not be possible to feed the whole population, then aliens (non-citizens) must be expelled from the Reich.
- Any further immigration of non-Germans must be prevented. We demand that all non-Germans who have entered Germany since August 2, 1914, shall be compelled to leave the Reich immediately.
- All citizens must possess equal rights and duties.
- The first duty of every citizen must be to work mentally or physically. **No individual shall do any work that offends against the interest of the community to the benefit of all.**
- Therefore we demand:
- **That all unearned income, and all income that does not arise from work, be abolished.**
- Since every war imposes on the people fearful sacrifices in blood and treasure, all personal profit arising from the war must be regarded as treason to the people. We therefore demand the **total confiscation of all war profits**.
- We demand the **nationalization of all trusts.**
- We demand **profit-sharing in large industries.**
- We demand a generous increase in old-age pensions.
- We demand the creation and maintenance of a sound middle class, the immediate **communalization of large stores** which will be rented cheaply to small trades people, and the strongest consideration must be given to ensure that small traders shall deliver the supplies needed by the State, the provinces and municipalities.
- We demand an agrarian reform in accordance with our national requirements, and the enactment of a law to **expropriate the owners without compensation of any land needed for the common purpose.** The abolition of ground rents, and the prohibition of all speculation in land.
- We demand that ruthless war be waged against those who work to the injury of the common welfare. Traitors, usurers, profiteers, etc., are to be punished with death, regardless of creed or race.
- We demand that Roman law, which serves a materialist ordering of the world, be replaced by German common law.
- In order to make it possible for every capable and industrious German to obtain higher education, and thus the opportunity to reach into positions of leadership, **the State must assume the responsibility of organizing thoroughly the entire cultural system of the people.** The curricula of all educational establishments shall be adapted to practical life. The

conception of the State Idea (science of citizenship) must be taught in the schools from the very beginning. We demand that specially talented children of poor parents, whatever their station or occupation, be educated at the expense of the State.

- The State has the duty to help raise the standard of national health by providing maternity welfare centers, by prohibiting juvenile labor, by increasing physical fitness through the introduction of compulsory games and gymnastics, and by the greatest possible encouragement of associations concerned with the physical education of the young.
- We demand the abolition of the regular army and the creation of a national (folk) army.
- **We demand that there be a legal campaign against those who propagate deliberate political lies and disseminate them through the press.** In order to make possible the creation of a German press, we demand: (a) All editors and their assistants on newspapers published in the German language shall be German citizens. (b) Non-German newspapers shall only be published with the express permission of the State. They must not be published in the German language. (c) All financial interests in or in any way affecting German newspapers shall be forbidden to non-Germans by law, and we demand that the punishment for transgressing this law be the immediate suppression of the newspaper and the expulsion of the non-Germans from the Reich. **Newspapers transgressing against the common welfare shall be suppressed.** We demand legal action against those tendencies in art and literature that have a disruptive influence upon the life of our folk, and that any organizations that offend against the foregoing demands shall be dissolved.
- We demand freedom for all religious faiths in the state, insofar as they do not endanger its existence or offend the moral and ethical sense of the Germanic race. The party as such represents the point of view of a positive Christianity without binding itself to any one particular confession. It fights against the Jewish materialist spirit within and without, and is convinced that a lasting recovery of our folk can only come about from within on the principle: **COMMON GOOD BEFORE INDIVIDUAL GOOD**
- In order to carry out this program **we demand: the creation of a strong central authority in the State, the unconditional authority by the political central parliament of the whole State and all its organizations.** The formation of professional committees and of committees representing the several estates of the realm, to ensure that the laws promulgated by the central authority shall be carried out by the federal states. The leaders of the party undertake to promote the execution of the foregoing points at all costs, if necessary at the sacrifice of their own lives. (emphasis mine, Published by: Central Publishing House of the N.S.D.A.P., Translation 1708-PS, Available at Yale Law School, The Avalon Project, "Nazi

Conspiracy and Aggression: Volume IV, Document No. 1708-PS", avalon.law.yale.edu)

Clearly, the above platform delineates a collectivist policy. Case in point, the "25-Points of National Socialism" are eerily similar to the "Twenty-one Conditions," officially the "Conditions of Admission to the Communist International" given by Vladimir Lenin to the adhesion of the socialists to the Third International (Comintern), formally adopted by the Second Congress of the Comintern in 1920. The truth is that one could substitute the word "Communist" with the term "National Socialist," and the rules and regulations are interchangeable. They are the very nature of "totalitarian" governments, seeking a "total state," with control over every aspect of society, and demanding absolute obedience and uniformity of opinion. The points are a prime example of the language of domination and subjection, master and subject. It is a pyramidal scheme in structure, and it is by no coincidence that the term "soviet" implies a pyramidal scheme as demanded and depicted in the National Socialist *Führerprinzip*." "Soviet" is defined by Webster's Collegiate Dictionary as "a governmental council, being part of a hierarchy of councils at various levels of government, culminating in the Supreme Soviet." Take note of Lenin's implementation of this "soviet" style pyramidal government structure:

> The guiding organizational principle of the party was "democratic centralism." According to Lenin, this concept meant choosing leaders (in a pyramidal system of indirect elections) by the rank and file, followed by binding decisions from above. Between elections, the party leaders were supreme, and any effort to agitate or combine against their decisions was treason to the party. Similarly, party policies might be debated openly (in the appropriate party meetings or committees) before decisions were made; after that no opposition was permitted. (Pg. 36, "Ideology, Politics, and Government in the Soviet Union", John Alexander Armstrong, Praeger, 1978)

Lenin's "democratic centralism" was still the guiding principle of the Communist Party and the Soviet state according to the 1977 version of the Soviet Constitution. While Marxist intellectuals bemoan the "terror" of the Soviet system under Stalin, the reality is that Stalin delivered on the promise of the Soviet constitution and its "democratic centralism." The horrible history under both Stalin and Lenin evidence just how overrated the right to vote is without a "balance of power." The Russian people received their health care, education, rest, leisure, cultural benefits, and housing – along with their right to vote for the leaders they would be bound to blindly follow as Vladimir Lenin proposed, and Hitler put into practice. Yet, would any reasonable person contend that the Soviet political pyramid was any less totalitarian than Hitler's *Führerprinzip?*

Totalitarianism is totalitarianism, and the idea that one flavor of it is more palatable than another is the dribble of minions. The real-world differences between *Führerprinzip* and the realities under "democratic centralism" under "Soviet" rule quickly become futile exercises in splitting hairs. Both theories were about control – control over every aspect of the economy, and most importantly, control over the population. Both were utopian schemes that set a specific ideal for society, and the governmental structure as a means to that end, with one justifying the monopoly on power on "class consciousness" and the other on "racial consciousness."

More importantly, both flavors of totalitarianism trend towards genocide. Both knew that their Achilles heel was the uncontrollable common denominator which conspires to upturn any scheme for an ideal society: the population. Uncontrolled and unplanned population growth is the nightmare of any "central planner." Marx and Engels knew this all too well. Friedrich Engels wrote to Kautsky on February 1, 1881, to elaborate on this specific topic:

> If at some stage communist society finds itself obliged to regulate the production of human beings, just as it has already come to regulate the production of things, it will be precisely this society, and this society alone, which can carry this out without difficulty. (Pg. 120, "Marx and Engels on the Population Bomb: Selections from the Writings of Marx and Engels Dealing with the Theories of Thomas Robert Malthus", Ronald L. Meek, Ramparts Press, 1971)

Opposites help us define and understand. This is the reason this book will continually refer back to the Founding Fathers of the American Revolution. In a sense, the Founding Fathers did not seek to create a recipe for the ideal state. To the contrary, they sought to take away the power of anyone to impose themselves over others precisely by dismantling the traditional pyramidal scheme of political power. The political scheme designed by the Founding Fathers does the exact opposite of "centralism." It intentionally disburses power among three branches of government and further distributes it by limiting the power of the Federal (central) government and establishes that all powers not "enumerated" in the Federal Constitution are reserved to the States and the people. This is what was called *"imperium in imperio,"* or empire within an empire, and it is the diametric opposite of the pyramidal schemes under a Soviet or *Führerprinzip* governing principles.

So, what was the well-propagandized hatred between the "Communists" and the "Fascists" if in practice their schemes were so similar? None of it had to do with disagreement on how to organize a society or a government. Stalin certainly believed he saw eye to eye with Adolf Hitler as it is well documented that Stalin refused to accept his friend had betrayed their pact for the first 24 hours of Operation Barbarossa, while Hitler's army consumed significant portions of the USSR. During hose critical 24 hours, Stalin refused to believe his generals that his friend had betrayed him. Stalin failed to realize that Adolf Hitler truly believed what he frequently said about "Slavs." Hitler meant it when he characterized Eastern Europeans as inferior to his beloved "Aryans" and certainly would not submit to having his German public under the rule of "International Socialism" by people he deemed inferior. Hitler, as he described to Göring, was opposed to "international" socialism, but not at all opposed to a "national" socialism organized around "race consciousness." This is, after all, what Hitler truly meant when he deemed his

Germanic people the "master race" – that they were at the top of the hierarchy and not to be lost among lesser people in some scheme focused on "class" as opposed to "race."

Sec. 2 - ERNST RÜDIN, "MERCHANT OF LIGHT":

The Third International Eugenics Congress is important for many reasons, one of which is the point upon which Leonard Darwin stepped down from leadership in order to pass the baton onto Ernst Rüdin. Ernst Rüdin was unanimously elected president of the International Federation of Eugenics Societies at this third congress, and as this book documents, would go on to make immediate use of the information exchanged at the congress.

Influenced in racial hygiene and Social Darwinism by his brother-in-law Alfred Ploetz, Rüdin started his career as a psychiatrist. Rüdin was the director of the Genealogical-Demographic Department at the German Institute for Psychiatric Research in Munich from 1917 to 1945. More importantly, he directed the Kaiser Wilhelm Institute. In 1933, just one year after this critical meeting of the top international eugenic minds, Ernst Rüdin and Alfred Ploetz, also a key member of the British Eugenics Society and International Federation of Eugenic Organizations, were brought together to form the Expert Committee on Questions of Population and Racial Policy under Reich Interior Minister Wilhelm Frick. The committee's work product would literally become the racial policy of Hitler's Germany. The "Law for the Prevention of Genetically Diseased Offspring" was passed by the German government on January 1, 1934.

Evidence to the importance of the Third International Eugenics Congress is the fact that critical parts of these statutes were copied from the "Model Eugenical Sterilization Law" drafted by Harry H. Laughlin. Rüdin put this collaborative effort immediately to use. As Leonard Darwin described in his address to the congress, this was no small measure. Laughlin's research was the compilation of decades of legislative and judicial work across 30 states in the Union. His proposal for the "Model Eugenical Sterilization Law" included the expert opinion of the top legal minds, scientists, and legislators in the United States. Hitler's government had just amassed power through the Enabling Act and the death of President Hindenburg. Having a ready-made policy guaranteed that Hitler could immediately enact the racial policies without "growing pains." Leonard Darwin had seen poorly drafted eugenic legislation fail when the influence and lobbying efforts by himself and his family members were insufficient to pass the eugenic passages of the Mental Deficiency Act of 1913 in Britain. Leonard Darwin would allude to this in his book "Modern Eugenics and Human Behavior":

> In reply to all that has been said in favour of sterilization, it may be urged that, in such a serious matter, mere theoretical considerations are an insufficient guide, and that reform can only be safely based on actual experiences gained in the past. But how are such experiences to be gained if no one will make a move? Luckily, there is one place in the world, though only one place, to which we can look when seeking for practical information in regard to sterilization; and that, is the State of California in the United States. (Pgs. 34-35, "Modern Eugenics and Human Behavior", Metropolitan Publishing Co., 1900, scanned copy available at archive.org)

When Adolf Hitler came to power in Germany, Ernst Rüdin praised Hitler stating that "the dream we have cherished for more than thirty years of seeing racial hygiene converted into action has become reality." [186] The scope and scale of the laws subsequently enacted reveal the substantial similarities to Harry H. Laughlin's "Model Eugenical Sterilization Law":

> By 1939, in accordance with the regulations set forth in the sterilization law, at least 300,000 people had been sterilized who had "hereditary feeblemindedness" (angeborener Schwachsinn), "schizophrenia," "circular (manic-depressive) insanity" (zirkulares [manischdepressives] Irresein), "hereditary epilepsy" (erbliche Fallsucht), "hereditary Huntington's chorea" (erblicher Veitstanz), "hereditary blindness" (erbliche Blindheit), "hereditary deafness" (erbliche Taubheit), a "severe hereditary physical malformation" (schwere erbliche korperliche Mipbildung), or "severe alcoholism." ("Ernst Rüdin, 1874-1952: A German Psychiatrist and Geneticist", Matthias M. Weber, American Journal of Medical Genetics (Neuropsychiatric Genetics) 67 (1996): 343–346)

Rüdin's contacts and access to information in the United States, Britain and Scandinavia flourished at this critical time when the National Socialists were ramping up and feverishly restructuring the entire German government. One of the various prestigious relationships that Rüdin fostered during this time is with Margaret Sanger, and the product of the relationship was that Rüdin would be published in Sanger's Birth Control Review and allow him to maintain a reputation of respect all the while he was ramping up the extermination of all undesired people in Germany. In hindsight, the political connections harnessed during Rüdin's visit to the United States in 1930 likely decided his fate, whether he would live as a free man or be put to death as a criminal by the Allied prosecution at Nuremberg.

So how did this pivotal German achieve such prestigious connections across the Atlantic? Ernst Rüdin sought help from Charles B. Davenport of the Eugenics Record Office as early as 1910. He was on the advisory board of Eugenical News, the publication of the American Eugenics Society. Davenport put Ernst Rüdin in touch with his colleague Harry H. Laughlin, and the international eugenics organizations and Davenport's contact lists were used to share information across borders between German and American eugenicists. Thus, it is by no mistake or

---

[186] Pg. 31 - "The Origins of the Holocaust", Michael R. Marrus, Walter de Gruyter, Jan. 1989.

coincidence that the 1933 "Law for the Prevention of Hereditary Disease in Posterity" passed in Nuremberg was a verbatim copy of Harry H. Laughlin's "Model Law."

However, it would be a mistake to say that the collaboration ended with a carbon copy of Laughlin's law. "Rüdin saw the rights of the individual as a stumbling block on the path to the ideal eugenic society." [187] This is where Laughlin's model law excels. If nothing else, Harry H. Laughlin can be credited for becoming an expert in circumventing civil rights through legislative acrobatics. For a German looking to overcome the civil rights hurdle, help from the expert who personally crafted the law that circumvented all the American civil rights protections was priceless. The Germans set up a whole legal system that mirrored Laughlin's recommendations for State-run facilities. Courts for the prevention of hereditary illnesses called *Erbgesundheitsgerichte*, or Hereditary Health Courts, were instituted and attached to the existing district courts as well as the Higher Courts. These were three-panel tribunals with one judge and two doctors, just as Laughlin had recommended for the state-run eugenic panels, and precisely like the one Lothrop Stoddard took part in during his visit to Nazi Germany. As in the United States, the pretense of "due process" and "scientific impartiality" provided these courts with a veil of legal legitimacy. Rüdin didn't complete his work of transforming German law into the laws of a "racial state" until 1935:

> Prior to 1933 anti-Jewish acts by the Nazis had no legal basis under the Constitution. After the seizure of power a stream of anti-Jewish legislation commenced. ---- The first, the Reich Law of Citizenship, divided the German nation into classes of citizens, those who were merely subjects of the State and those who possessed full citizenship including political rights. ---- The law "For the Protection of German Blood and German Honour" [the second of the Nuremberg laws and called the "Blood Protection Law" for short] was intended to ensure the racial purity of the nation for all time. Fundamentally it made criminal any sexual intercourse between both these new groups the "Reich Citizens" and the "Subjects" but it was aimed specifically at the Jews. (digital scan and translation, "The Men Behind Hitler: A German Warning to the World", Bernhard Schreiber, H. R. Martindale translation as permitted by Schreiber, provided by Liz Toolan of toolan.com - From Chapter Four: The Secret Seizure of Power: The Nuremberg Laws)

The observation that prominent Americans likely had a hand in setting criminals like Rüdin free is hardly academic. This is *realpolitik* at the ground level of an international catastrophe with sensitive international relationships. Doris Kaufmann's study was published in German with a title that translates to: "History of the Kaiser Wilhelm Society under National Socialism: Inventory and Perspectives of Research." In it, Kaufmann explains precisely that the Nuremberg Tribunal made a political and logistical decision to allow a very large part of the guilty German

---

[187] "Ernst Rüdin, 1874-1952: A German Psychiatrist and Geneticist", Matthias M. Weber, American Journal of Medical Genetics (Neuropsychiatric Genetics) 67 (1996): 343–346.

doctors to go without prosecution. Somehow it was deemed that "further investigation of hospitals and universities was undesirable" because it may have resulted in stripping "German medicine of large number of highly qualified men at a time when their services are most needed." [188]

None of these observations are 20/20 hindsight. All of this was understood by the vast number of legal experts and eugenicists that were connected to or somehow entangled with the international eugenics movement as Ernst Rüdin was. Furthermore, one must remember that Lothrop Stoddard and several other prominent American scientists traveled to National Socialist Germany to witness and inspect the application of sterilization laws, courts, and facilities in detail. Ernst Rüdin was a participating member of those tribunals – the same tribunals which the Nuremberg prosecutors sentenced several German Judges for their participation and collaboration. Yet, Rüdin was released and allowed to walk free.

Doris Kaufmann's research points to a tactical and political decision by the heads of the prosecution at the Nuremberg Trial, which likely is the origins of the myth of the oppressed and coerced German scientist under National Socialism. German doctors, like Rüdin, who are more accurately classified as instigators and inspiration for the crimes of The Holocaust, were painted as one of the victims in order to preserve public confidence in the medical field at a point where the Allies were trying to keep post-war Germany from sliding into chaos:

"Publicizing German medical atrocities could undermine wholesale public confidence in clinical science." To avoid the appearance that the entire medical community could no longer be trusted, the Nuremberg Medical Trial political appointees."... presented medical researchers as having been 'perverted' by the manipulative control of the SS and as poisoned by Nazism..." (Pg. 638, "*Geschichte Der Kaiser-Wilhelm-Gesellschaft im Nationalsozialismus. Bestandsaufnahme und Perspektiven der Forschung. 2 Bde, Göttingen*", Doris Kaufmann, Wallstein, 2000.)

We tempt fate by prolonging this myth of the coerced doctor and victimized scientist. We also commit fraud by persisting in claiming that the Allied prosecution was oblivious to these uncomfortable relationships between the death camps and the civilian scientific institutions, civilian hospitals, and universities. Doris Kaufmann documents that the prosecution at Nuremberg was perfectly aware of the relationship between camps like Auschwitz and German research institutes and universities. We know that Karin Magnussen was but one of the researchers at the Kaiser Wilhelm Institute during Germany's Third Reich who routinely used iris specimens from Auschwitz concentration camp victims who were supplied by Joseph Mengele. She documents that the prosecution's expert, Leo Alexander, had collected medical evidence in 1946 before the Doctors' Trial, and noted the relationship in his personal correspondence:

---

[188] Pg. 642, "Geschichte Der Kaiser-Wilhelm-Gesellschaft im Nationalsozialismus. Bestandsaufnahme und Perspektiven der Forschung. 2 Bde, Göttingen" Wallstein, 2000, ISBN 3-89244-423-4, Translation provided by enacademic.com, Section: Otmar Freiherr von Verschuer.

Some new evidence has come in where two doctors in Berlin, one a man and the other a woman, collected eyes of different color. It seems that the concentration camps were combed for people who had slightly differently-colored eyes. That means that people whose one eye had a slightly different color than the other. Whoever was unlucky enough to possess such a pair of slightly unequal eyes had them cut out and was killed, the eyes being sent to Berlin. ---The grim part of the story is that Drs. Von Verschuer and Magnussen in Berlin prefer children and particularly twins. (Pg. 635, *"Geschichte Der Kaiser-Wilhelm-Gesellschaft im Nationalsozialismus. Bestandsaufnahme und Perspektiven der Forschung. 2 Bde, Göttingen"*, Wallstein, 2000.)

How can history justify holding contempt for the likes of Mengele but not his superiors, or more specifically those that directed him to conduct his horrific studies? Verschuer was Mengele's superior, so why does posterity revile with mention of Mengele's name but not Verschuer's? Verschuer and Rüdin ran the Kaiser-Wilhelm Institute. If Mengele was culpable, then by definition so were his superiors. What about those that "aided and abetted the enemy" on the Allied side? American courts were hardly shy about convicting American citizens that conducted commerce with the enemy, so why not those that traded in the ideas and ideologically supported those that conducted the "crimes against humanity"? Historians need to look at the Rüdin case and question exactly just how much his Davenport, Carnegie and Rockefeller connections came into play when he was released in 1946. Rüdin's staff nicknamed him "the beggar of millions" in recognition for his fundraising talents. Rüdin had a generous staff of 48 secretaries and 12 dedicated to his own department at the Institute. [189] It would be logical to presume that the prosecutors saw the strong ties as a potential threat to their efforts, as most of the German doctors and scientists being held for trial were equally adamant about the very close cooperation between American and German eugenicists and lawmakers. Finding Rüdin's actions to be criminal would have been tantamount to finding all the eugenic efforts of the Carnegies, the Rockefellers, and the long list of Harvard, Yale, Colombia, and Stanford scientists and lawmakers guilty of the same crimes. Or, even worse, a finding that similar acts had been deemed legal by the US Supreme Court would have meant that the Nuremberg Tribunal would have had to concede legality of a significant portion of the deeds otherwise deemed criminal. At the very minimum, they would have had to significantly question the funds the Kaiser-Wilhelm institute and Ernst Rüdin received from the Carnegies and Rockefellers.

This is where the questionable demarcation between "civilian" and "military" crafted by the Allied prosecution in Nuremberg comes into play. The research that was done by the 1999 Max-Planck commission revealed a significant relationship between the German scientific institutes and universities and the experiments conducted in the camps. Paul Lombardo documents that since the American prosecutors at the Military Tribunals in Nuremberg "limited the criminal charges

---

[189] "Ernst Rüdin, 1874-1952: A German Psychiatrist and Geneticist", Matthias M. Weber, American Journal of Medical Genetics (Neuropsychiatric Genetics) 67 (1996): 343-346.

against the Nazi doctors to illegal acts taken in furtherance of the war effort, the trials largely ignored the hundreds of thousands of involuntary sterilizations carried out on German citizens under German law." [190] Lombardo explains that Rüdin, while captured and facing criminal prosecution, widely cited the sterilization programs in the United States to bolster his claim that his efforts had been conducted according to legitimate German laws. Apparently, this was enough to set Rüdin free, and the incongruity of it is an embarrassment in the eyes of history. We would otherwise have to believe that Rüdin was set free due to vast number of political and financial connections with prestigious Americans. The decision to set Rüdin free is highly questionable no matter what the official justification was.

As we know, Karl Brandt tried the same approach but was less successful. Brandt hung for his crimes. What, if any, was the difference between Brandt and Rüdin? Rockefeller money? Harvard connections? The prosecution at Nuremberg decided to qualify the scope of the "crimes" by limiting the extension of the definition of "crime" to only include the sterilizations that were conducted in the concentration and death camps, labeling them as "Crimes Committed in the Guise of Scientific Research." Clearly, this description applied to the sterilizations conducted as part of the ramp-up toward the Final Solution, and the distinction between "Germans" and "Jews" was a specious one, as many of the Jews were legitimate Germans. Any further differentiation between Germans of Jewish or "Aryan" descent would only concede legality to the decrees deemed criminal by the same prosecution.

As stated above, the hair-splitting of this definition of the crimes leaves much to be desired. In 20/20 hindsight, the connection between concentration camps and civilian sterilization should have been evident to anyone even vaguely familiar with the eugenic laws in the United States, and certainly obvious to any attorney that spent any amount of time reading the work of the National Socialist scientists. The connection with the civilian institutions was obviously apparent to the prosecution's expert, as Leo Alexander's discovery of where all those eyeballs were being sent from the concentration camps makes amply clear.

Needless to say, Ernst Rüdin was not the only high-ranking scientist under National Socialism to escape being tried as a criminal. German scientists and business leaders were funneled out of Germany after the war by the hundreds. This book previously documented the story of Hans Harmsen, the other scientist who had a prolonged political relationship with Margaret Sanger and the various prominent financial backers for International Planned Parenthood. However, what makes the case of Ernst Rüdin specifically frustrating is that he was instrumental in paving the way to the Holocaust. Ernst Rüdin was by no means a foot soldier or a detached scientist working in isolation of what transpired in Adolf Hitler's Germany. Adolf Hitler would be the first to disagree on this count, as Rüdin was vocally proud of his contributions to Hitler's Germany. Any honest reading of history would be hard-pressed to make the case that Ernst Rüdin was any less

---

[190] Pg. 237 - "Three Generations No Imbeciles: Eugenics, the Supreme Court, and Buck v. Bell", Paul Lombardo, JHU, 2008.

valuable to Hitler in the effort to eradicate significant portions of Europe's population than Karl Brandt, whom the Allies executed for his participation in the organizing and planning of the crimes. Rüdin was at the level of Brandt in the scheme of things, and definitely of more value to Hitler than Dr. Josef Mengele, later known as Auschwitz's "Angel of Death." To the contrary, Mengele had studied under Rüdin, who instilled into his students the concept that some lives were not worth living, and doctors were responsible for destroying such lives and thus ensuring the security of the general population. Mengele was hired by the Kaiser-Wilhelm Institute that was run by Rüdin and which sponsored, controlled and funded the infamous "twin studies" where very young children were exposed to unimaginable experiments.

To be more precise, the very wealthy contacts Rüdin made during his travels to the United States made an initial grant of $2.5 million in 1925 to the Kaiser-Wilhelm Institute and gave it $325,000 for a new building in 1928. Rüdin's wealthy friends also funded a 1930-35 anthropological survey of the eugenically worthwhile population by Nazi eugenicists Rüdin, Verschuer, Eugen Fischer, and others. The prosecutors representing the United States in the Nuremberg Doctors Trials jailed and sentenced to death dozens of lesser scientists, doctors, lawyers and judges for participating in the infrastructure Rüdin had been instrumental in creating. Karl Brandt became the focus and primary defendant in the Nuremberg Doctors Trial, while Rüdin was immediately freed. Dr. Mengele was rightfully hunted down like the animal that he was, but Rüdin was never bothered again. Back in the United States, many German-Americans and international businessmen were summoned to appear before Congress to investigate even the most tangential of business relations with Germany. In fact, the United States used its power and clout to shut down, confiscate, and then extradite thousands of Latin American businessmen from Mexico down to the tip of Argentina for doing business with Hitler. Even Jews that had escaped Germany after the National Socialists had burned their businesses down, and started again in Latin America, were extradited to a concentration camp in the United States to be held for years alongside devoted Nazis. Texas had three of these camps, located at Seagoville, Kenedy, and Crystal City. [191]

Rüdin died a free man in 1952. Astonishingly enough, Rüdin saw himself as an "apolitical scientist" and remained an "unrelenting defender of doctrines on racial hygiene and psychiatric genetics that centered on a concept of collective health at the expense of the individual, on conservative ideals relating to social order, and on utopian-biological models of society." [192] The American prosecution at Nuremberg allowed Rüdin this luxury of waxing philosophical about his criminal ideas, while his subordinates hung for implementing them.

The whitewashing of history has direct and dire consequences. The inseparable link between the international eugenics movement and The Holocaust was effectively whitewashed through its exclusion from the Nuremberg Trials, and as a direct result,

---

[191] See Generally – "Nazis and Good Neighbors", Max Paul Friedman, Cambridge Univ. Press, 2003.
[192] Matthias M. Weber, "Ernst Rüdin, 1874-1952: A German Psychiatrist and Geneticist American", Journal of Medical Genetics (Neuropsychiatric Genetics) 67:323-331, 996, available at docme.ru

tens of thousands of Americans would continue to be sterilized against their wishes, and mostly without their knowledge until the late 1970s, using the identical laws that the National Socialists had used to make the Holocaust legal under German law.

Sec. 3 - FROM WELFARE TO SUBORDINATION:

Studying the surge of the eugenics movement in Scandinavia helps us understand precisely the volatile ingredients that were brought together to cause the human-made catastrophe of The Holocaust. Historians have recently begun to uncover just how expansive the eugenics movement was in Scandinavia. Yet, missing from the Scandinavian formula are the typical culprits that historians point to in Germany's eugenics program. These Scandinavian countries were free from imperialist or militant aspirations. Missing were the pervasive levels of thuggish bigotry attributed to the American South or post-World War I Germany. Missing were the economic factors as found in post-World War I Germany. None of the typical culprits were present, yet these Scandinavian countries embarked on a systematic campaign to "racially cleanse" their populace. This seemingly peculiar surge of eugenic-thinking in countries allegedly unhampered by vulgar bigotry was documented by authors Gunnar Broberg and Nils Roll-Hansen:

> The preconditions that have been postulated for the development of the eugenics movement – ethnic antagonism, social unrest, conservative opposition to social relief – seem to have been absent, or only weakly represented in Denmark. Yet Denmark was the first European state to introduce national legislation concerning eugenic sterilization in 1929. (Pg. 10, "Eugenics and the Welfare State: Norway, Sweden, Denmark, and Finland", Michigan State Univ. Press, 1996)

This observation is supported by Jacqueline Bollmann who opines that by the first decades of the 20th century, Denmark, like Britain and the United States, was an industrialized nation governed by two-chamber parliaments contending with increased migration to the towns, rapid growth of urban slum areas, and the formation of an urban proletariat.

> Imperial concerns did not exist. ---- The absence of violent confrontations between the Social Democrats and other parties, and comparably peaceful labour relationships were characteristic for this country at this time. In this political climate of consensus, the medical and psychological professionals of the institutions for the mentally ill drew the attention of politicians and the public to the country's social problems. (Jacqueline Bollmann, "Influence of Eugenics

on the Social Welfare Legislation of Britain and Denmark in 1913 and 1929", June 15, 2009, link defunct as of 2018)

In order to make sense of this seeming conundrum, we must also note that the peak of the American eugenics movement coincided with the era of the welfare state. The eugenics movement in the United States emerged with the Progressive welfare state, took strength with President Roosevelt's New Deal, and persisted through President Lyndon B. Johnson's Great Society in the 1960s. The more the leaders of society, including its jurists, legislators, and executives considered themselves the caretakers of the populace, above and distinct from the masses, the more formidable the political strength of the eugenics movement. Again, here we see communication and collaboration that spanned across both national borders and oceans. Broberg and Roll-Hansen document that Scandinavia countries were beginning to implement the "third-way" Progressive measures, and that at least in one case, the Scandinavian countries were the example to be followed:

> That other countries took an interest in Scandinavia is apparent. For instance, Sweden: The Middle Way (1935), by the American journalist Marquis Childs, had some influence on Roosevelt's New Deal, with its praise of Swedish welfare policies. A country with rational, organized education, light veneer or steel furniture, kindergartens, cleanliness, and order – that is how Sweden looked, at least from a distance. (Pg. 5, "Eugenics and the Welfare State: Norway, Sweden, Denmark, and Finland", Michigan State Univ. Press, 1996)

More to the point, Jacqueline Bollmann points to the important historical fact, that the drive for eugenic legislation in Scandinavia was almost entirely the product of doctors, scientists, and professionals in charge of institutions. Thus, historians must regard this as more than just a coincidence but rather a prerequisite for the eugenic movements and dispense with the notion that the crimes resulting from eugenics start with the vulgar bigot or militant dictator. To do otherwise is to buy into Karl Brandt's arguments made at Nuremberg and ignore the direct link between Brandt's non-racist euthanasia program and the gas chambers. In fact, the Danish professionals in charge of hospitals and institutions subscribed to the similar scientific dogmas as their British and American counterparts, and actively translated the works of British and American eugenicists into Danish to support their cause. The correspondence between Davenport and Scandinavian eugenicists evidences this. This Scandinavian-American collaboration was done in concert with Leonard Darwin in Britain, where everyone was kept in the loop in the correspondence, with the United States and England as the hubs of the movement.

> Danish Sterilization Law of 1929, the high-grade mentally deficient "feeble-minded" seemed to pose the gravest danger to society. To determine the individual degree of the mental defects, IQ-tests were used in both countries. -- -- In Denmark too, there was a reform of the social welfare legislation. During the 1920s and 1930s, a whole body of social legislation was gradually being introduced, marking the beginnings of the Danish welfare state. The lengthy

debate about a Sterilization Law went on from 1921 until 1928 under differing governments of the left (*Socialdemokraterne*) and the right (*Venstre*). ---- Thus, both Acts must be considered as parts of the respective welfare reforms in Denmark and Britain. ("Influence of Eugenics on the Social Welfare Legislation of Britain and Denmark in 1913 and 1929", Jacqueline Bollmann, June 15, 2009, link defunct as of 2018)

While historians have uncovered the words and deeds of some vulgar racists within the Scandinavian leadership, these findings must be weighed against the larger scope and scale of the movement. This handful of vulgar bigots neither passed the laws nor ran the programs on their own. In order to achieve the scope and scale of the Scandinavian eugenics program, there had to have been the cooperation of the supposedly sober-minded scientists, doctors, and bureaucrats, as extensive as we have found to be the case in National Socialist Germany.

In following the example of American sterilization campaigns, the Scandinavians did not need "racial antagonism." To enact these measures, which are now largely regarded as criminal by Scandinavians, what was needed was a "subordination" of the otherwise autonomous individual to the "paternalism" of the governing elite. The review essay by David Gems, which incidentally was written for the Galton Laboratory of University College London, dispenses with the argument that the Scandinavian laws were "humane" despite the alleged "good faith" intent:

> An insidious element of the Nordic sterilization laws was that sterilization was ostensibly never compulsory (apart from in Finland), leaving the false impression that these programmes were humane. They were not, for several reasons. Firstly, many of the mentally ill and retarded were incapable of giving or withholding consent; as legal incompetents, decisions were taken on their behalf by relatives. Secondly, sterilization was often a condition for teenagers to be released from schools for children with learning difficulties. For example, between 1937 and 1956, 36 percent of all girls leaving Swedish special schools were sterilized. Similarly, sterilization was sometimes specified as a prerequisite for obtaining an abortion, or permission to marry. Sterilization orders requiring consent are potentially unethical even where good faith is shown by the authorities with regard to understanding the wishes of confused or not very intelligent subjects. ("Politically Correct Eugenics", David Gems, Theoretical Medicine and Bioethics, April 1999, Pgs. 201-213)

The description of the "prerequisites" tied to welfare benefits described above certainly brings to mind the practice of "Appalachian Appendectomies" that used similar forms of coercion in the United States. The observation that the laws were "inhumane" is not only correct but also places the laws in the historical context in which they occurred. The eugenic activists in Scandinavia were part of the era's purity movement. The *Lebensreform* movement sprung up in 19-century and early 20-century Germany and Switzerland. The movement propagated a back-to-nature lifestyle, emphasizing among others, health food, raw food, organic food, nudism, sexual liberation, alternative medicine, and religious reform and at the same time abstention from alcohol, tobacco, drugs, and vaccines. The movement had its icons and flashpoints. The most famous of these was the Fraternitas lodge, Monte Veritá, which was established in the Swiss village of Ascona by Frantz Hartmann and Madame Blavatsky, the spiritual leader of Theosophy that would, in turn, inspire the Thule Society from which the German Worker's Party would emerge:

> The feminism, pacifism and psychoanalysis we now know too form in part from the work of those who trekked to Ascona at this time. Perhaps the anarchist leader Mickhail Bakunin, who settled nearby in 1869, opened the door to an international set of well-connected dissenters against Western civilization, but Hartmann was among the first to establish himself at this mecca for discontent. Hartmann's collaborators in Fraternitas included Blavatsky's close friend, the Swedish countess Constance Wachtmeister, and Alfred Pioda, as member of the Swiss parliament. Rudolf Steiner, Vladimir Lenin, Carl Jung, and Hermann Hesse would at one time or another call Ascona home. (Pg. 15, "Hammer of the Gods: The Thule Society and the Birth of Nazism," David Luhrssen, Potomac Books, Inc., 2012)

Furthermore, Hartmann, like Alfred Ploetz after him, would begin his journey into alternative and radical lifestyles by visiting American radicals. Hartmann came to the United States in 1865 as a ship's doctor after studying medicine at the University of Munich, and "after discovering Blavatsky's writings," in 1883, "he joined the Theosophical Society in Colorado." [193] Hartmann would then travel the world with Madame Blavatsky before creating the pseudo-monastery in Ascona, which would ultimately be the ideological source for the *Lebensraum* expansionist policy Hitler adopted from the movement. All of this is crucial to the history of the movement and an honest understanding of why cosmopolitan populations like that of Germany and Scandinavian welcomed eugenics. It is essential to answer that lingering question as to how the land of "poets and thinkers" could perpetrate the most heinous atrocity in human history. To understand this phenomenon, we must realize that the movement which started as a "lifestyle choice" transformed itself into "coercion" when its proponents achieved political power. This is why even German National Socialism never shed its "lifestyle" aspects, with its campaigns against any and all substances deemed to be "race poisons"; the compulsory health aspects of National Socialism are rooted in the same *Lebensreform* movement which was used to justify Scandinavian eugenics legislation.

Broberg and Roll-Hanson make an interesting observation. They document this phenomenon and attribute the departure from the eugenic campaigns in the 1970s to the distaste society grew to have with coercive health measures. Broberg and Roll-Hansen cite at least four different studies concerning the decline of the eugenics movement in Scandinavia, and every study attributed the end of the movement to

---

[193] Pg. 14 - "Hammer of the Gods: The Thule Society and the Birth of Nazism," David Luhrssen, Potomac Books, Inc., 2012.

this distaste for coercive health measures:

STUDY #1: "*Racehygiejne I Danmark 1920-56*" by Lene Koch – "Koch discusses . . . the problematic and changing balance between free choice and coercion. The paternalist moralism that still reigned in the 1930s and '70s produced new sterilization laws and quite different practices." (Pg. xi, "Eugenics and the Welfare State")

STUDY #2: "*Steriliseringar I folkhemmer*" (Sterilization in the people's home) by Maya Runcis – "Runcis also argues that there was a strong connection between the rise of the Swedish welfare model, on one hand, and the sterilization program, on the other." (Pg. xi, "Eugenics and the Welfare State")

STUDY #3: "*Från politik till praktik. De svenska steriliseringslagarna 1935-1975*" (From politics to practice: The Swedish sterilization laws, 1935-1975" By Mattias Tydén) – "Tydén claims there was a gradual change in attitude starting in the 1950s. A widespread culture of paternalistic coercion gave way to free individual choice, and motives shifted from eugenic and biological to individual and social: "sterilizations in the interests of society were replaced by sterilizations in the interest of the individual." (Pg. xii, "Eugenics and the Welfare State")

STUDY #4: "*Sterilisering av tatere 1934-1977*" (Sterilization of traveling people, 1934-1977) by Per Haave – "Per Haave presents a corresponding description and analysis of Norwegian law-making and sterilization practice that contains a similar story of change from sterilization as a means of social control to sterilization as a means of individual freedom." (Pg. xi, "Eugenics and the Welfare State")

Other recurring themes surfaced: The opposition came mainly from the Scandinavian Catholic Church, as was also the case in other countries due to the monolithic structure of the Church's beliefs. Some of the main resistance and calls for restraint came from the non-politicized scientists, namely from geneticists who felt that the science was too much in its infancy to allow for such drastic legislative measures to be enacted as a response. The coerced enactment of a "single-party system" in Germany cleared the path for Hitler's henchmen to act with impunity and largely without restraint until the devout Christian community in Germany spoke up. Parallels can be drawn with Bolshevik Russia, and its "single party" structure, and the lack of political opposition and debate in the face of the planned famines. Elof Axel Carlson of the current Cold Spring Harbor laboratory staff provides perspective on the history of eugenics: "What characterized eugenic thinking in early 20-century intellectual thought in almost every country was the belief that the state had higher interests and rights than the individual." [194]

It was paternalism run amok, and in the end, it was the Scandinavian public's

---

[194] Pg. 276, "The Unfit: A History of a Bad Idea", Cold Spring Harbor Laboratory Press, 2001.

reaction to the experience of "paternalism" and "moralistic coercion," which ultimately unraveled the legislative measures. The Scandinavian states had subordinated individual rights to the perceived needs of society, and in the process instituted coercive measures to force the policies upon those that resisted. Policies that sounded attractive in theory were exposed in their actual practice when individuals struggled to maintain their bodily integrity and autonomy in the face of the state's coercive powers. All the policies had begun as alternatives to the mainstream, and as "reform" lifestyle choices. It is this cycle from voluntary reform movement, to mainstream dogma, to a political movement, to institutionalized reform, to coerced reform, to oversaturation and overreaching that makes the history of eugenics relevant to this day. Parliamentary bodies persist to this day to implement coercive measures intended to make the populace adopt the lifestyles the elite deem as healthy and beneficial. The disbalance in legal standing between the individual and society follows this intentional or unintended subordination. The history of this fundamental change in legal standing is a history stained by blood and unspeakable catastrophes; human-caused and fully preventable catastrophes.

Sec. 4 - THREE GENERATIONS, ONE SUPREME IMBECILE:

Oliver Wendell Holmes, Jr. was an American jurist who served as an Associate Justice of the Supreme Court of the United States from 1902 to 1932. Holmes retired from the Court at the age of 90, making him the oldest Justice in the Supreme Court's history. He also served as an Associate Justice and as Chief Justice on the Massachusetts Supreme Judicial Court and was Weld Professor of Law at the Harvard Law School, of which he was an alumnus. Holmes helped move American legal thinking away from "formalism" and towards legal "realism," as summed up in his maxim: "The life of the law has not been logic; it has been experience." Holmes espoused a form of moral skepticism and opposed the doctrine of natural law, marking a significant shift in American jurisprudence. As he wrote in one of his most famous decisions, his dissent in Abrams v. United States (1919), he regarded the US Constitution as "an experiment," a hallmark of American Progressive ideology.

However, this shift in American jurisprudence became palpable and historically relevant in 1927. Justice Oliver Wendell Holmes, Jr. has an important place in the history of The Holocaust and the international eugenics movement. He wrote the opinion of the Court for the 1927 case of Buck v. Bell in which Harry H. Laughlin's "Model Eugenical Sterilization Law" was deemed "constitutional":

> The case comes here upon the contention that the statute authorizing the judgment is void under the Fourteenth Amendment as denying to the plaintiff in error due process of law and the equal protection of the laws. (Buck v. Bell,

SUPERINTENDENT. No. 292. Supreme Court of United States. -- Argued April 22, 1927. Decided May 2, 1927)

As the opening statement in this landmark Supreme Court opinion clarified, the entire decision hinged upon "due process," and eight of the nine justices believed that the three-panel eugenic courts recommended by Laughlin satisfied the Constitutional requirement of "due process" before the forcible deprivation of reproductive capacity. Not surprisingly, the Court's opinion ends with a justification of the State's prerogative over an individual's right to bodily integrity. The opinion is quoted here at length, so its logic can be clearly understood:

> The attack is not upon the procedure but upon the substantive law. It seems to be contended that in no circumstances could such an order be justified. It certainly is contended that the order cannot be justified upon the existing grounds. The judgment finds the facts that have been recited and that **Carrie Buck "is the probable potential parent of socially inadequate offspring, likewise afflicted, that she may be sexually sterilized without detriment to her general health and that her welfare and that of society will be promoted by her sterilization,"** and thereupon makes the order. In view of the general declarations of the legislature and the specific findings of the Court, obviously we cannot say as matter of law that the grounds do not exist, and if they exist they justify the result. We have seen more than once that the public welfare may call upon the best citizens for their lives. It would be strange if it could not call upon those who already sap the strength of the State for these lesser sacrifices, often not felt to be such by those concerned, in order to prevent our being swamped with incompetence. It is better for all the world, if instead of waiting to execute degenerate offspring for crime, or to let them starve for their imbecility, society can prevent those who are manifestly unfit from continuing their kind. The principle that sustains compulsory vaccination is broad enough to cover cutting the Fallopian tubes. Jacobson v. Massachusetts, 197 US 11. **Three generations of imbeciles are enough**. (Buck v. Bell, SUPERINTENDENT. No. 292. Supreme Court of United States. -- Argued April 22, 1927. Decided May 2, 1927, emphasis mine)

Depending on where a historian falls in the highly polarized political atmosphere in the United States, Justice Oliver Wendell Holmes, Jr. is either remembered as a champion of the people or as a symbol of a government abusing its powers. If the recollection comes from the later, the portion of the opinion that claims "three generations of imbeciles are enough" has come to exemplify the extreme arrogance of the Supreme Court Justice. Case in point, it is an opinion that resonated around the world with eugenic-minded legislators, and which the German defendants at Nuremberg used in their defense. How could it be possible that the Supreme Court of the United States, the one body of government that should have been the shining beacon of individual rights, came to be aligned with the minds behind the eugenic laws of the Third Reich? The Justice's belief system is worth analyzing.

In the 1919 case of Schenck v. United States, Holmes declared that the First Amendment would not protect a person "falsely shouting fire in a theatre and causing a panic." The following year, however, in Abrams v. United States, Holmes, influenced by Zechariah Chafee's article "Freedom of Speech in War Time," delivered a strongly worded dissent in which he criticized the majority's use of the clear and present danger test, arguing that protests by political dissidents posed no actual risk of interfering with war effort. Most poignantly, Holmes famously proclaimed that "certitude is not the test of certainty. We have been cocksure of many things that were not so." [195] This now-famous legal analysis is interesting as it poses an incongruity with the "precautionary" aspect of the opinion he would write for the Buck v. Bell case. Holmes justified the "precautionary" posture of Buck v. Bell by citing the precedent of the 1905 case which upheld forcible vaccination as constitutional:

> It is better for all the world, if instead of waiting to execute degenerate offspring for crime, or to let them starve for their imbecility, society can prevent those who are manifestly unfit from continuing their kind. The principle that sustains compulsory vaccination is broad enough to cover cutting the Fallopian tubes. (Jacobson v. Massachusetts, 197 US 11, 25 S.Ct. 358, 49 L.Ed. 643, 3 Ann.Cas. 765. . . .)

Even worse, the collectivist logic in the infamous Buck v. Bell opinion, even though severely tainted by the fact that Hitler's henchmen usurped it in order to justify their crimes, continues to be used by courts around the country and the United States Supreme Court itself to justify other governmental actions. For example, the Nebraska Supreme Court Case of In the Matter of the Sterilization of Gloria Cavitt of 1968 referred to it, as did countless other opinions which in turn referenced the opinions by the various State courts:

> It can hardly be disputed that the right of a woman to bear and the right of a man to beget children is a natural and constitutional right, nor can it be successfully disputed that no citizen has any rights that are superior to the common welfare. Acting for the public good, the state, in the exercise of its police power, may impose reasonable restrictions upon the natural and constitutional rights of its citizens. Measured by its injurious effect upon society, **the state may limit a class of citizens in its right to bear or beget children** with an inherited tendency to mental deficiency, including feeblemindedness, idiocy, or imbecility. It is the function of the Legislature, and its duty as well, to enact appropriate legislation to protect the public and preserve the race from the known effects of the procreation of mentally deficient children by the mentally deficient... (emphasis mine) In re Cavitt, 182 Neb. 712, 157 N.W.2d 171 (1968)

Court precedents open paths to scenarios unimaginable at the moment of their passing. More often than not, court opinions are the proverbial "slippery slope" upon which civilization descends. It must be understood that American jurists

---

[195] "Natural Law", Oliver Wendell Holmes, Harvard Law Review, Volume 32, 1918.

interpret the logic behind precedent in ways sometimes only tangentially related to the core issue of the cited reference. It is in this way that Justice Holmes used the 1905 Jacobson decision on compulsory vaccination, which was but a mild attack on an individual's bodily integrity, to justify compulsory sterilization which permanently removed an individual's reproductive capabilities, and even stretched to apply to the right to public education of minorities. Even unrelated issues come into play as they did in the case of In San Antonio Independent School Dist. v. Rodriguez, 411 US 1 - Supreme Court 1973, a suit attacking the system of financing public education:

> Thus, in Buck v. Bell, 274 U. S. 200 (1927), the Court refused to recognize a substantive constitutional guarantee of the right to procreate. Nevertheless, in Skinner v. Oklahoma, supra, at 541, the Court, without impugning the continuing validity of Buck v. Bell, held that "strict scrutiny" of state discrimination affecting procreation "is essential," for "[m]arriage and procreation are fundamental to the very existence and survival of the race."

It is because of the above paragraph that historians typically state that the Buck v. Bell decision was reversed by the Skinner v. Oklahoma decision. This is not so if you carefully read the opinion provided above. Skinner and Bell are parallel decisions that do not cancel each other out. [196] The Skinner decision pertained only to the rights of a criminal, and that is how it has been cited as precedent. The Buck decision has influenced Supreme Court outcomes all the way up to the passing of the Americans Disabilities Act of 1990. Most notably, it was cited by the landmark abortion decision of Roe v. Wade:

> In fact, it is not clear to us that the claim asserted by some amici that one has an unlimited right to do with one's body as one pleases bears a close relationship to the right of privacy previously articulated in the Court's decisions. The Court has refused to recognize an unlimited right of this kind in the past. Jacobson v. Massachusetts, 197 U. S. 11 (1905) (vaccination); Buck v. Bell, 274 US 200 (1927) (sterilization). We, therefore, conclude that the right of personal privacy includes the abortion decision, but that this right is not unqualified and must be considered against important state interests in regulation. Roe v. Wade, 407 US 113 (US Supreme Court 1973)

The eugenic taint upon the Roe v. Wade decision and Sanger's extensive writing on the subject was undoubtedly apparent to eugenic insiders, and political maneuvering resulted. The American Eugenics Society was intentionally reorganized and renamed The Society for the Study of Social Biology directly after the Roe v. Wade opinion was released in 1973. The "Eugenic Journal" had already changed its name in 1968 to "Social Biology." Here is the reasoning of the famous eugenicists Frederick Henry Osborn:

> The name was changed because it became evident that changes of a eugenic

---

[196] Pg. 232 – "Three Generations, No Imbeciles: Eugenics, the Supreme Court, and Buck v. Bell", Paul A. Lombardo, Johns Hopkins Univ. Press, 2008.

nature would be made for reasons other than eugenics, and that tying a eugenic label on them would more often hinder than help their adoption. Birth control and abortion are turning out to be great eugenic advances of our time. ("The Long Road of Eugenics: From Rockefeller to Roe v. Wade", Rebecca Messall, Human Life Review, Fall 2004, Pgs. 33-74 – See Also: Pg. 7, Transcript of July 10, 1974 interview, Oral History, Columbia University)

As this book will document, these eugenic institutions repeatedly changed their names to avoid the negative taint of The Holocaust and eugenics. The politically connected and politically powerful take concrete actions to avoid any embarrassment that would deteriorate their political power. The "British Annals of Eugenics" was renamed "Annals of Human Genetics" in 1954, and in 1969, "Eugenics Quarterly" was changed to "Journal of Social Biology." [197]

Time passed, and tens of thousands of Americans were sterilized against their will and often without their knowledge. The last recorded eugenic sterilization in the United States was in 1973. The State courts revisited the Buck v. Bell opinion decades later in the 1981 Federal Court case of Poe v. Lynchburg; the main issue being that of following "due process":

> In 1924, the Commonwealth enacted legislation providing for the sexual sterilization of "mental defectives" in certain cases. ---- the statute specifically prescribed certain preliminary procedural steps including **notification to the individual**, or his or her parent, guardian, or committee as might be appropriate. (emphasis mine, Poe v. Lynchburg Training School and Hospital, 518 F. Supp. 789 - Dist. Court, WD Virginia 1981)

The State court threw out and dismissed part of the claim based mainly on the view that the doctors had acted according to a valid law and that the "highest court in the land," the United States Supreme Court, had upheld their decision in 1927:

> Regardless of whatever philosophical and sociological valuation may be made regarding involuntary sterilizations in terms of current mores and social thought, the fact remains that the general practice and procedure under the old Virginia statute were upheld by the highest court in the land in Buck v. Bell, supra. (Poe v. Lynchburg Training School and Hospital, 518 F. Supp. 789 - Dist. Court, WD Virginia 1981)

Herein lay the conundrum which highlights the difficulties faced by the Allied prosecution at Nuremberg. By the logic of the Supreme Court of the State of Virginia, the acts of the various doctors were to be protected because, at the time, the doctors acted to deprive individuals of their bodily integrity, the "highest court in the land" deemed these forcible and compulsory acts as legal. Clearly, the various German doctors could and did claim they were acting within the laws passed by their legally elected legislature. Does this make all those violations upon civilians by

---

[197] Pg. 249 - "Racism and Sexual Oppression in Anglo-America: A Genealogy", Ladelle McWhorter, Indiana Univ. Press, 2009.

civilian doctors legal, and not "crimes against humanity"? This makes no sense, of course. It can only make sense in the convoluted nature of a lawyer's logic. If the harm brought by the abuses and excess of government were a "crime" in Germany, then clearly the same logic applies back in the United States. The fact that the government can be deemed to act lawfully in wantonly mutilating the bodies of its citizens is a warning to any citizenry that would trust too much in government.

Unfortunately, the Virginia case turned on the technical aspect of "notice," and not the grander principles at issue. Note that in Poe v. Lynchburg, the Virginia court deemed the whole process to be valid because the patients were "properly noticed" of the horrid process the State had in mind for them. Judges and Justices have repeatedly stated that the definition of "due process" can only be said to be grounded in the premise of "basic fairness" and "decency," and that it is otherwise a difficult concept to pin down. Each State has its own practices and procedures. In essence, what the court was explaining in the case was that the victims had been given "notification" and an opportunity to appeal the decision of the panel, as prescribed by the law, and therefore they were acting in comport with "due process." People outside of the legal profession probably have a hard time reconciling this reasoning. In the convoluted lawyer logic, it is perfectly fine to mutilate someone's genitals against their will; its just not ok to do so without notifying the victim of your intentions beforehand.

From a pedestrian standpoint, the notion that an option for appeal ameliorates the injustice is hard to understand. The cruel implications that any appeal to a governing elite, drunk with power and believing in their own infallibility, is a reasonable recourse for the weakest amongst us is preposterous. Carrie Buck was undoubtedly a person that can be said to be one of the weaker members of society in dire need of protection from the overwhelming power of the state:

> The court recognizes that in making these arguments, and in attempting to distinguish Buck v. Bell, supra, plaintiffs have relied primarily on what they perceive as a constitutional deficiency in the procedural aspects of the old Virginia statute. The court also recognizes that Buck dealt with an attack to the statute's substance rather than its procedure. Nevertheless, in delivering the court's opinion in Buck, Justice Holmes specifically noted that ". . . there is no doubt that . . . plaintiff in error has had due process of law." 274 US at 207, 47 S.Ct. at 584. (Poe v. Lynchburg Training School and Hospital, 518 F. Supp. 789 - Dist. Court, WD Virginia 1981)

Jurisdiction had also been a potential Achilles' heel for the Allies' prosecution at Nuremberg. The legalism that "proper notice" perfects "jurisdiction" was the governing issue, if the various opinions by the courts can be taken at face value. The only way that the National Socialist government officials could be put on trial by a foreign body was if the National Socialist government was found to be illegal. Otherwise, the United States had no jurisdiction over many of the defendants and much less their co-conspirators. They could not be deemed to be "conspirators" if they were acting lawfully. That is exactly the point the Federal Court made in Poe v.

Lynchburg; the fact that our morals have allegedly evolved do not render the decision taken in 1927 void.

While the crassness of Justice Oliver Wendell Holmes, Jr's pronouncement that "three generations of imbeciles are enough" has rightfully earned him scorn, we must remember that only one Justice voted against him. In hindsight, this crass proclamation along with the fact that Hitler's henchmen used the Buck v. Bell opinion to defend themselves, is embarrassing enough. However, the comparison goes beyond that of an interesting quote or factoid. Historians must engage in serious introspection as to what exactly was the United Supreme Court was truly deliberating. Can it be said that the three-panel eugenic courts of the States were any better than the three-panel eugenic courts in Hitler's Germany? The United States Supreme Court proclaimed these to be constitutional since the procedure of proper notification was followed, which along with the opportunity for appealing to a higher court, gave the appearance of due process. This begs to question the worth of these formalities when the victim was prejudged because of their heredity? If the two preceding "generations" were "enough" to convince Justice Oliver Wendell Holmes, Jr. and his fellow Justices that Carrie Buck should be forcibly sterilized, then of what use was the pretense of observing procedure? Carrie had been condemned before she ever entered the court, or for that matter, before she was ever even born, because of her mother's and grandmother's alleged eugenical worth. This was, after all, the scientific determination behind the three-panel court's decision. This practice of predetermining worth, and by extension the results within the courtroom, is too similar to the predetermined legal outcomes of Hitler's sham court system to ignore. While it would be unfair to state that the entire history of the US Supreme Court is that of sham pretense, it is certainly correct to state that these are the murky waters the Court and the various State congresses stepped into when they began to entertain eugenic legislation. Any law that predetermines rights by virtue of heredity are by their very nature the playthings of dictators and totalitarian states. More to the point, the fact that the US Supreme Court, the one institution that is held up to the world as the bastion of freedom and liberty, entertained such anti-democratic notions went a long way to bolster the claims made by Hitler's henchmen at Nuremberg.

As actions speak louder than words, one must take Hitler's carefully calculated actions as evidence towards this question. Hitler was an impulsive and impatient man, to say the least. The fact that he carefully, patiently, and deliberately made it a point to follow practices and procedures in his ascension to the position of Chancellor indicates that Hitler himself placed a high value on legally legitimizing his reign of power. Furthermore, the concerted effort to make the eugenic aspirations of the Third Rich observe internationally respected legal measures is indicative of the importance Hitler placed upon the image of legality. Otto Wagner, head of the Nazi Economic Policy Office, quoted Hitler as stating:

> I have studied with great interest the laws of several American states concerning the prevention of reproduction by people whose progeny would, in all probability, be of no value or be injurious to the racial stock. (Pg. 116, "The

Right to Reproduce: A History of Coercive Sterilization", Stephen Trombley, Weidenfeld and Nicolson, 1988 – Also quoted by Stefan Kühl, Pgs. 37-39, "The Nazi Connection")

In a broader sense, historians must also take note of the fact that Adolf Hitler's government wrote their eugenic laws in the eugenical language that was conspicuously devoid of the racial overtones which he was known for. This is of note when one considers the lengths to which Hitler and the National Socialist regime went to give the appearance of legality. It is also important towards an understanding of the T4 Euthanasia program, which targeted otherwise ethnic "Aryans" for their hereditary defects, and not their racial background. In the following passage from "Mein Kampf" Hitler was employing the language of the eugenicists:

> If for a period of only 600 years those individuals would be sterilized who are physically degenerate or mentally diseased, humanity would not only be delivered from an immense misfortune but also restored to a state of general health such as we at present can hardly imagine. If the fecundity of the healthy portion of the nation should be made a practical matter in a conscientious and methodical way, we should have at least the beginnings of a race from which all those germs would be eliminated which are to-day the cause of our moral and physical decadence. (gutenberg.net.au, "Mein Kampf", Chapter II: The State - Book Pg. 227)

The fact that Hitler refers to "several American states" is an indication of the eugenic laws and practices which Laughlin eagerly passed on to his German counterparts, namely Alfred Ploetz, Ernst Rüdin, and Erwin Baur, who had translated Harry H. Laughlin's work into German. Clearly, Hitler was referring to the laws passed at the State level within the United States. The question if the State of Indiana's actions were lawful is what the Supreme Court answered in 1927, but a survey of the variation from state to state is precisely what Harry H. Laughlin provided through the International eugenic organizations and likely what Hitler was referring to. It was Harry Laughlin's "Model Eugenical Sterilization Law" that was tested by the Buck v. Bell case, and it was this "Model Eugenical Sterilization Law" that Hitler's henchmen copied verbatim to implement it in the Third Reich's policies. The Third Reich allegedly complied with "due process" and "rule of law" by creating the three-panel eugenic courts per Laughlin's recommendation. Most importantly, these recommendations were not adopted necessarily because a prominent American eugenicist was recommending that they be adopted, but because by 1933, six years after the Buck v. Bell case, the most respected of all courts of law had deemed them "constitutional."

Portions of Laughlin's "Law" evidence that totalitarian tendencies were written into its original English language version. Who was liable to fall under the "Law" for compulsory sterilization in Germany? Who was to sacrifice their "fallopian tubes" when "called upon" to do so by the Führer? Anyone deemed a threat to the social body by their poor hereditary traits as specified by Laughlin's "Law":

> **Persons Subject.** All persons in the State who, because of degenerate or defective hereditary qualities are potential parents of socially inadequate offspring, regardless of whether such persons be in the population at large or inmates of custodial institutions, regardless also of the personality, sex, age, marital condition, race, or possessions of such person. Standards established and terms defined by the statute. (Pg. 446, Chap. 15, "Eugenical Sterilization in the United States", Psychopathic Laboratory of the Municipal Court of Chicago, Dec. 1922)

Laughlin proposed that a government official, a "State Eugenicist," would "devote his entire time" with the help of "an ample corps of assistants," to providing the service of making the legal determinations of an individual's eugenic worth to the society:

> **Basis of Selection: Procedure.** 1. Investigation by State Eugenicist upon his own initiative or upon complaints lodged or information given by an official, an organization or a citizen. 2. Opinion concerning a particular individual in reference to "potential parenthood of socially inadequate offspring" rendered after scientific investigation, by State Eugenicist to Court of Record. 3. Early date set by court for hearing case. 4. Court to notify and summon interested parties. 5. Due provision for legal counsel for the defendant and for trial by jury. 6. Judgment: Order for eugenical sterilization if the contention of the State Eugenicist is upheld 7. Execution of the order under the supervision and responsibility of the State Eugenicist. 8. In case of inmates of institutions, execution of order may be suspended until inmate is about to be released, allowing ample time for convalescence. 9. Provision for the study of mental, moral, physiological, social and economic effects of different types of sterilization. (Pg. 446, Chpt. 15, "Eugenical Sterilization in the United States", Psychopathic Laboratory of the Municipal Court of Chicago, Dec. 1922)

Point number 4 is precisely where the United States Supreme Court attached itself as having "due process" met. This is precisely the analysis provided in hindsight by the Virginia Supreme Court. The provisions for notification of the legal procedure to "perfect jurisdiction" over the subject, the provision of legal counsel, a trial by jury, and appellate court are the token niceties that the US Supreme Court clung to as proof that the person in question was afforded the Constitutional guarantee of "due process" before the State deprived them of "life, liberty," or "property."

The types of individuals included in Laughlin's legal definition of people dangerous to the future prosperity of the State perfectly explain why Germany's doctors made that all-important and fundamental change from curing patients, to curing the state by riding it of unhealthy patients. They are highlighted here and quoted at length to demonstrate that the medical officials of the Third Reich, who are rightfully portrayed as monsters for their lack of sympathy toward children with congenital disabilities, were following the distinctions made by an American "scientist":

(a) A socially inadequate person is one who by his or her own effort, regardless of etiology or prognosis, fails chronically in comparison with normal persons, to maintain himself or herself as a useful member of the organized social life of the state; provided that the term socially inadequate shall not be applied to any person whose individual or social ineffectiveness is due to the normally expected exigencies of youth, old age, curable injuries, or temporary physical or mental illness, in case such ineffectiveness is adequately taken care of by the particular family in which it occurs.

(b) The socially inadequate classes, regardless of etiology or prognosis, are the following: (1) **Feeble-minded**; (2) Insane, (including the psychopathic); (3) **Criminalistic** (including the delinquent and wayward); (4) **Epileptic**; (5) **Inebriate** (including drug-habitués); (6) Diseased (including the tuberculosis, the syphilitic, the leprous, and others with chronic, infectious and legally segregable diseases); (7) **Blind** (including those with seriously impaired vision); (8) **Deaf** (including those with seriously impaired hearing); (9) Deformed (including the crippled); and (10) **Dependent (including orphans, ne'er-do-wells, the homeless, tramps and paupers).** (emphasis mine, Pgs. 446-447, Chpt. 15, "Eugenical Sterilization in the United States", Psychopathic Laboratory of the Municipal Court of Chicago, Dec. 1922)

The inclusion of terms such as "feeble-minded," "criminalistic," and "dependent" is historically important as their broad scope and vagueness as legal terminology provided wiggle room for state officials to do as they pleased in both the United States and Germany. Furthermore, it is important to note that the individual need not fall into any of the above-mentioned categories as was the case of Carrie Buck. It was enough to be deemed to be a "carrier" of potential defects through heredity to fall under the grasp of this compulsory sterilization law:

(c) **Heredity** in the human species is the transmission, through spermatozoön and ovum, of physical, physiological and psychological qualities, from parents to offspring; by extension it shall be interpreted in this Act to include also the transmission post-conceptionally and ante-natally of physiological weakness, poisons or infections from parent or parents to offspring.

(d) A potential parent is a person who now, or in the future course of development, may reasonably be expected to be able to procreate offspring.

(e) To procreate means to beget or to conceive offspring, and applies equally to males and females.

(f) A potential parent of socially inadequate offspring is a person who, regardless of his or her own physical, physiological or psychological personality, and of the nature of the germ-plasm of such person's co-parent, is a potential parent at least one-fourth of whose possible offspring, because of the certain inheritance from said parent of one or more inferior or degenerate physical, physiological or psychological qualities would, on the average, according to the demonstrated laws of heredity, most probably function as socially inadequate persons; or at least one-half of whose possible offspring would receive from said parent, and would carry in the germ-plasm but would not necessarily show in the personality, the genes or genes-complex for one or more inferior or degenerate physical, physiological or psychological qualities, the appearance of which quality or qualities in the personality would cause the possessor thereof to function as a socially inadequate person, under the normal environment of the state.

(g) The term cacogenic person, as herein used, is a purely legal expression, and shall be applied only to persons declared, under the legal procedure provided by this Act, to be potential parents of socially inadequate offspring. (Pg. 447, Chpt. 15, "Eugenical Sterilization in the United States", Psychopathic Laboratory of the Municipal Court of Chicago, Dec. 1922)

The section goes on to define all "inmates" as qualifying by the very nature of their status as "criminals" to fall within the scope of the law. One other crucial element, deemed to be the most important aspect of the "Model Eugenical Sterilization Law" by eugenicists in the United States and Europe, was to make the State representatives immune from any legal consequences of their actions. Recall that this aspect of the law was upheld up until the 1981 Poe v. Lynchberg case:

Section 19. Liability. Neither the State Eugenicist, nor any other person legally participating in the execution of the provisions of this Act, shall be liable either civilly or criminally on account of said participation. (Pg. 450, Chpt. 15, "Eugenical Sterilization in the United States", Psychopathic Laboratory of the Municipal Court of Chicago, Dec. 1922)

The mechanisms of totalitarianism were already written into the American version of the law. Laughlin's version of the "Law" makes State functionary liable for not performing their duties and releasing of anyone who has been slotted for compulsory sterilization by the process; a bludgeon that would later be utilized by Hitler's police state to ensure enforcement of its otherwise unpalatable eugenic measures:

Section 21. Punishment of Responsible Head of Institution for Dereliction. The responsible head of any public or private custodial institution in the State who shall discharge, release or parole from his or her custody or care any inmate who has been duly ordered by a court of this State to be eugenically sterilized, before due consummation of such order as herein contemplated, unless, as herein provided, such particular inmate be discharged, released or paroled into the custody of the State Eugenicist, shall be guilty of a misdemeanor, and shall be punished by not less than — months imprisonment or — dollars fine, or both; or by not more than — months imprisonment or — dollars fine, or both. (Pg. 450, Chpt. 15, "Eugenical Sterilization in the United States", Psychopathic Laboratory of the Municipal Court of Chicago, Dec. 1922)

The coercive aspect of the "Model Law" should come as no surprise. Clearly, Laughlin and his eugenic counterparts had a pronounced disdain for any form of democratic government that would allow anyone to stray from the dictates of the central planning body. In Laughlin's case, it is interesting to see him leverage the "supremacy clause" of the Federal Constitution as a bulwark against the independent States.

> **Section 22. Supremacy of this Act.** All statutes or portions of statutes of this State contrary to this Act are hereby repealed. (Pg. 451, Chpt. 15, "Eugenical Sterilization in the United States", Psychopathic Laboratory of the Municipal Court of Chicago, Dec. 1922)

The US Supreme Court's upholding of the lower court's decision was a crucial step for Laughlin and company, as they knew this was a significant bulwark against any future attacks on the "Model Eugenical Sterilization Law" as implemented in the various States. The need for eugenic measures at a Federal level was important for other reasons as well. The section "Principles Suggested for a Federal Statute" extend the legislation to individuals that fall outside of a strict reading of an individual state's jurisdiction, namely immigrants and Native Americans living in reservations, as well as "soldiers and sailors" living within Federal jurisdiction, and suggests that the "Model Eugenical Sterilization Law" become a Federal law to allow the "segregation," "sterilization" or "otherwise rendering non-productive" those that the Federal government deemed a danger to the eugenic future of the Nation:

> **Persons Subject.** 1. Immigrants who are personally eligible to admission but who by the standards recommended in the model state law are potential parents of socially inadequate offspring. 2. All persons below the standards of parenthood set in the model state law who are beyond the jurisdiction of state laws, including the inhabitants of the District of Columbia, unorganized and outlying territories, Indian reservations, inmates of federal institutions, and soldiers and sailors.

CONTINUES . . .

> Up to the present time, the Federal Government has not enacted any legislation bearing either directly or indirectly upon eugenical sterilization. The matter of segregating, sterilizing, or otherwise rendering non-reproductive the degenerate human strains in America is, in accordance with the spirit of our institutions, fundamentally a matter for each state to decide for itself. There is, however, a specialized field in which the Federal Government must cooperate with the several states, if the human breeding stock in our population is to be purged of its defective parenthood. (Pg. 451, Chpt. 15, "Eugenical Sterilization in the United States", Psychopathic Laboratory of the Municipal Court of Chicago, Dec. 1922)

Laughlin knew what was at stake. His very close friends and associates made sure to have representation on both sides of the Buck v. Bell trial. This is where Paul A. Lombardo's 2008 book "Three Generations No Imbeciles" becomes so important for all posterity to reference, as Lombardo proves that the Buck v. Bell case was heavily tainted with fraud and severe conflicts of interests. Professor Lombardo shows that the lawyer supposedly protecting Carrie's interests was also being paid by the opposing side. As such, one can justifiably claim that the Buck v.

Bell case was wholeheartedly manufactured. Professor Lombardo provides irrefutable evidence that all the players, on either side of the case, were sympathetic to the cause of eugenics, and more accurately described as part of the movement's leadership. Carrie Buck never stood a chance. Carrie Buck's defense team was literally paid by her persecutors, and the defense of Carrie Buck was designed to help decide against her favor and help establish the legality of eugenic sterilization in the United States. [198] As such, the history of the Buck v. Bell case reads as the concerted effort to legitimize a dubious law by controlling all parties involved. This Supreme Court opinion was not just an act of fraud to deprive an innocent woman of her bodily integrity; it would also prove a powerful precedent that was held up by the German eugenicists as proof that their policies were perfectly legal.

Every US citizen must look upon the Supreme Court's Buck v. Bell decision and realize that it is the product of a government drunk with power. The Harvard Law professor, Justice Oliver Wendell Holmes, Jr. had taught the world how to deprive citizens of their rights under the "color of law." Paul Lombardo documents the pleasure Oliver Wendell Holmes took in writing the Buck v. Bell opinion:

> One decision that I wrote gave me pleasure, establishing the constitutionality of a law permitting the sterilization of imbeciles. (emphasis mine, Pg. 173, "Three Generations No Imbeciles: Eugenics, the Supreme Court, and Buck v. Bell", JHU Press, 2008)

Sec. 5 - FROM HOMOSAPIEN TO HOMINOIDEA:

There are certain astounding and jaw-dropping episodes in scientific history that reveal the mindset of a particular era. Some are barely believable. Soviet dictator Joseph Stalin embarked on such a project. He tried to rebuild the Red Army in the mid-1920s by crossing humans with apes. In February 1926, Ilia Ivanov, one of Russia's most respected biologists, set out for Guinea in French West Africa, where he planned to perform the experiments. When details of the project emerged in the 1990s from the newly opened Russian archives, they prompted a rash of lurid headlines. Ivanov became known as the "Red Frankenstein." This episode in Soviet history is so bizarre, even for the Soviet, that this author felt compelled to track down the scholarly origins of the otherwise sensational sounding online blogs. Thus, this section relies on the peer-reviewed papers of Jerry Bergman, Ph.D. and Alexander Etkind. Bergman authored the article "Human-Ape Hybridization: A Failed Attempt to Prove Darwinism." [199] Bergman is an Adjunct Associate Professor at the University of Toledo Medical School in Ohio. Alexander Etkind is a Soviet-born specialist in Russian history now part of the University of Cambridge staff. Etkind documented this bizarre episode in Soviet history in his "Beyond Eugenics: the

---

[198] Pg. 155 - "Three Generations No Imbeciles: Eugenics, the Supreme Court, and Buck v. Bell", Paul Lombardo, JHU, 2008.
[199] "Human-Ape Hybridization: A Failed Attempt to Prove Darwinism", Jerry Bergman, Ph.D., Acts and Facts, Vol. 38, 2009.

forgotten scandal of hybridizing humans and apes" paper. [200] Their credentials are recounted herein because of the implausible and barely believable aspect of this episode in history. Incredibly enough though, this X-File of a story actually occurred, and the general details are instrumental in revealing the era's irrational obsession with Darwin's Theory.

According to Dr. Bergman, Ilja Ivanov had achieved considerable success in the field of artificial insemination. Ivanov graduated from Kharkov University in 1896 and became a professor of zoology in 1907, and had used artificial insemination to produce various hybrids, including that of a zebra and a donkey, a rat and a mouse, a mouse and a guinea pig, and an antelope and a cow. His most radical experiment, though, would be his attempt to produce a human-ape hybrid. Ivanov felt that this ambitious feat was possible as he had already been successful in his other animal hybridization experiments. More so, Darwinian biologists of the era regarded apes and humans to be just a few steps separated in a common evolutionary ladder, so doubts were shelved. His trip to Africa cost millions of 1920s money, yet the Bolshevik government was willing to foot the bill, indicating that his argument was persuasive to his superiors.

The project's origins go back to 1910 when Ivanov gave a presentation at the World Congress of Zoologists in Graz, Austria, on the possibility of creating a human-ape hybrid. In 1924, he obtained permission from the Pasteur Institute in Paris to use its experimental primate station in Kindia, French Guinea, for such an experiment. He sought backing for this from the Soviet Government. Stalin is quoted as saying: "I want a new invincible human being, insensitive to pain, resistant and indifferent about the quality of food they eat." [201] Finally, in 1925 he obtained US$10,000 from the Academy of Sciences for his experiments in Africa. In 1926, the Politburo in Moscow approved this request to build a 'living war machine' and sent Ivanov to West Africa. Facilities were also set up in the Soviet province of Georgia, Stalin's birthplace, for the 'apes' to be raised.

Ivanov's project was a sensation at the time. Fully formed, healthy offspring, if they resulted, would not be regarded as "missing links," but as living proof that apes and men are species as closely allied as horses and asses which can be hybridized to produce mules or hinnies. More to the point, it was regarded as an experiment in Darwinian evolution. If an ape-man or man-ape hybrid should prove fecund, the relationship of the two-parent species would be proved even closer than supposed. If no offspring resulted, evolution would by no means fail; the distance of apes and men from a parent stock would merely be demonstrated to be greater than estimated.

The experiments were supported by some of the most respected biologists of the day. Because Ivanov was then an internationally respected scientist, he was able to obtain prominent sponsors for his project, including the polymath Otto Schmidt, editor of the Great Soviet Encyclopedia, and Nikolai Gorbunov, a chemical engineer and close friend of Lenin. After Professor Ivanov detailed the rationale behind his

---

[200] Pgs. 205-210 - "Beyond Eugenics: the forgotten scandal of hybridizing humans and apes", Alexander Etkind, Studies in History and Philosophy of Biological and Biomedical Sciences, Vol. 39, Issue 2, June 2008.
[201] "Blasts from the past: The Soviet ape-man scandal", Stephanie Pain, New Scientist online, Aug. 23, 2008.

idea, the British government also promised to help raise money for the project. Several prominent American patrons of science were also very supportive of the project. Charles Lee Smith wrote in a June 17, 1926, article in The New York Times titled "Soviet Backs Plan to Test Evolution" that the objective of Ivanov's experiments was to achieve "artificial insemination of the human and anthropoid species, to support the doctrine of evolution, by establishing close kinship between man and the higher apes." Etkind reports that the project was supported by The American Association for the Advancement of Atheism because it was regarded as "proof of human evolution and therefore of atheism." Ivanov concurred. When applying to the Soviet government for funds, Ivanov emphasized the importance of his research for anti-religious propaganda.

In February 1926, Ivanov set off for Africa. His first stop was Paris, where he also won the enthusiastic support of the directors of the Pasteur Institute and the promise of access to the chimps at its new primate center in Guinea, then part of French West Africa. Ivanov passed the summer in Paris, where he spent some of his time at the Pasteur Institute working on ways to capture and subdue chimps. Ivanov also spent some of his time in Paris working with the celebrated surgeon Serge Voronoff, inventor of an increasingly fashionable "rejuvenation therapy." Voronoff grafted slices of ape testes into those of rich and aging men hoping to regain their youthful manhood. That summer, he and Ivanov made headlines by transplanting a woman's ovary into a chimp called Nora and then inseminating her with human sperm.

Ivanov reached Guinea in late March only to discover none of the chimps were mature enough to breed, so he obtained permission from French Guinea's colonial governor to work at the botanical gardens in Conakry. Here Ivanov artificially inseminated three chimpanzees. All three failed to become pregnant. He returned to the Soviet Union, where further planned experiments also failed. In November, Ivanov returned to Guinea, captured more chimps, and tried again to inseminate three of them. By now, he had a second experiment in mind: to inseminate women with chimp sperm. Knowing that no local woman would agree, he planned to do this under the pretext of a medical examination, but the French governor forbade it. The French governor was a little more particular about the moral implications, while Ivanov saw no ethical dilemma. He angrily reported to his sponsors in the Kremlin about the primitive fears of the blacks and the bourgeois prejudices of the French.

All of Ivanov's experiments eventually failed. Disappointed, Ivanov headed home with 20 chimps to stock a new ape nursery in the subtropical Soviet republic of Abkhazia. He knew now that his only remaining chance of creating his hybrid was to find Soviet women willing to carry half-ape babies in the interests of science. In the event, only four chimps made it to Abkhazia, and while the nursery set about acquiring more apes, Ivanov looked for human volunteers. Five women volunteered. However, by the time Ivanov was ready to proceed, the only adult male left was Tarzan, a 26-year-old orangutan. Ivanov pressed on until fate dealt his project a fatal blow: Tarzan, the orangutan had a brain hemorrhage before his family jewels could be used to create an ape-man.

It is of note that Ivanov never attempted to use his own sperm while in French-Africa. Neither did he try to use that of his son, who was his aide throughout the experiments. Instead, Ivanov used the sperm of local French-African natives and sought African women to inseminate. Ivanov was a devout Darwinist. Thus, it is very likely that this choice to use African blacks was due to the Darwinian racial hierarchy that estimates Africans to be more closely related to apes than to Anglo men. This is evidenced by the requests of the scientific advisors assigned to Ivanov's project. According to an August 16, 1926, article in TIME Magazine titled "Ape-Child?" the scientist advisors wanted the field researchers to use orangutans, chimpanzees, gorillas, and possibly gibbons in the experiments. The suggestions of the researchers were revealing. The researchers believed that orangutans should be crossed with humans of the "yellow race," gorillas with humans of the "black race," chimpanzees with the "white race," and gibbons with "the more brachycephalic peoples of Europe."

Ivanov's failure only earned him embarrassment and frustration. One problem is humans have 46 chromosomes, while apes have 48, and this is an impediment for the chromosomes to pair up properly even if a zygote is formed. Another problem is a conservatively estimated 40 million base pair differences exist between humans and our putative closest evolutionary relatives, the chimps. Whatever the cause or reason, Ivanov was now disgraced and discredited. Apparently, Ivanov's failures and delays irked Stalin. In 1930, Ivanov came under "political criticism" during the Great Purge and was arrested. Ivanov was sentenced to five years in jail for his million-dollar failure, but the sentence was commuted to five years' exile in Alma Ata, Kazakh S.S.R., now known as Kazakhstan. Ivanov spent his last days working for the Kazakh Veterinary-Zoology Institute until his death on March 20, 1932, at age 61.

Due to longstanding animosities between Russia and Germany, the scientists on either side were not aware that they were not alone in performing or proposing such ghastly experiments. When the Kaiser Wilhelm Institute for Anthropology, Human Heredity, and Eugenics was founded in 1927, the new institute inherited the skull collection amassed by Rudolf Virchow and Felix von Luschan when created in 1927. [202] Hans Weinert was appointed as the custodian of the famous skull collection at the Institute. Weinert was also responsible for paleoanthropology and blood group research at the Institute. Studying the blood-group analyses of apes, Weinert was able to establish the same blood groups as for humans, O, A, B, and AB, while the findings for other kinds of monkeys clearly deviated from this classification. Weinert used his work with blood groups of apes and humans to further the longstanding desire of Darwin's followers to prove the connection between apes and man. Like Ivanov, Weinert was interested in the question of whether the problem of the missing link could be clarified by crossing humans and apes. Weinert also considered inseminating a female chimpanzee with the sperm of an "African negro, probably best by a jungle pygmy." [203]

---

[202] Pg. 83 - "The Kaiser Wilhelm Institute for Anthropology, Human heredity and Eugenics, 1927-1945" Hans-Walter Schmuhl, Boston Studies in the Philosophy of Science, Vol. 259, 2008.
[203] Pg. 83 – Ibid.

Why is this gut-wrenching episode important towards an in-depth understanding of eugenics? As this book will further elucidate, the logic behind eugenics is in more ways than one an extrapolation of the evolutionary ladder Charles Darwin proposed in his book, "The Descent of Man," where Darwin extrapolates his hierarchy of the "races of man" and their ape origins. Explicit in Darwin's hierarchy is the notion that the "races" at the lower rungs of the evolutionary ladder were closer to apes than to the white man. Darwin was explicit in his observation that evolution could work backward towards a more ape-like state through sexual selection of the lesser types. This is the eugenic notion that Darwin incorporated into his "Theory," extensively citing Francis Galton and Ernst Haeckel in support.

This book traces the steps between Darwin-Galton-Haeckel theory of degenerating evolution and the eugenics movement that it sparked. It was this degenerating aspect of Darwinian evolutionary theory, which was at the very core of eugenics at the turn of the century, and the justification for all the institutes, journals, and legislation that followed. As with all things eugenic, famous Harvard Darwinists exemplify this aspect of the movement. Professor Earnest A. Hooten organized a study for the National Research Council called the "Committee on the American Negro." Hooton was a US physical anthropologist known for his work on racial classification and his popular writings such as the book "Up from the Ape." Hooton was hired by Harvard University, where he taught and became Curator at the Peabody Museum of Archaeology and Ethnology. Hooton peddled popular books extrapolating his ape-human eugenic theories with curiously telling titles such as "You are Normal," and "Apes, Men, and Morons."

Hooton used comparative anatomy to divide humanity into different "primary races" and the various "subtypes." As such, the 1926 Committee on the Negro focused on the anatomy of blacks, and in 1927, the committee endorsed a comparison of African babies with young apes. Ten years later, the group published findings in the American Journal of Physical Anthropology explicitly to "prove that the negro race is phylogenetically a closer approach to primitive man than the white race."

Hooton was also a pioneer of criminology, the science that linked criminal behavior to biological determinism. Hooton dominated the field between 1930 and 1940. [204] During the phase spanning from 1926 through 1940, he focused on large-scale surveys of living populations and produced works on race, evolution, and eugenics. During the final stage of Hooton's work, from 1940 through 1954, he attempted to correlate different body types with different personality types and traits, a methodology fully leveraged by the Nazi race hygienists.

Hooton considered eugenics the most salient social issue of his time, a hallmark of eugenical thinking of the era. According to Hooton, criminals belong to a "class of hereditary degenerates" who ruin society and needed to be brought under control through "sterilization, euthanasia, and cutbacks in welfare." It was these "rank-order

---

[204] Pgs. 735-771 - "Earnest A. Hooton and the Biological Tradition in American Criminology", Nicole Rafter, Journal Criminology, Vol. 42, Issue 3 of 4, Aug. 2004.

hierarchies" which were at the core of the eugenics movement's horrid history. [205] The Darwinian evolutionary ladder and the desire to eradicate its lower elements were at the core of the movement. Case in point, the 1937 TIME review, titled "Hooton's Horrors," provides a quote as to precisely why this ape-human hierarchy is crucial towards an understanding of eugenics and The Holocaust: "I think that a biological purge is the essential prerequisite for a social and spiritual salvation."

Sec. 6 - WAS LEONARD DARWIN COMPLICIT IN "EUGENOCIDE"?

Before Darwin and Nietzsche, the belief in the sanctity of human life dominated European thought and law. Judeo-Christian ethics proscribed the killing of innocent human beings, and the Christian churches explicitly forbade murder, infanticide, abortion, and suicide. The "sanctity" of human life became enshrined in classical liberal human rights ideology as "the right to life," which according to John Locke and the Declaration of Independence, was one of the "inalienable" rights of every individual. This "natural" right was reflected in European legal codes. Obviously, these traditional values were not always observed or respected. However, as the *fin-de-siecle* approached society's leadership began to overturn and contradict the concept of the "right to life" in the new secular ethic that resulted from Darwin's and Nietzsche's formidable influence. The significance of this turning point in history cannot be overstated. Richard Weikart, the author of the infamous book, "From Darwin to Hitler," wrote an article for "Touchstone" magazine which discusses this very point:

> Immediately after explaining that each organism "has to struggle for life, and to suffer great destruction," he closed his chapter on "The Struggle for Existence" in On the Origin of Species on a more comforting note: "When we reflect on this struggle, we may console ourselves with the full belief, that the war of nature is not incessant, that no fear is felt, that death is generally prompt, and that the vigorous, the healthy, and the happy survive and multiply." This put a rather positive spin on the struggle for existence, the law, as he put it, "leading to the advancement of all organic beings, namely, multiply, vary, let the strongest live and the weakest die." Even while overtly denying any purpose or goal for evolution, Darwin could not resist the mid-Victorian cult of progress. ("EUGENOCIDE: Darwinism & the Rise of German Eugenics", Touchstone, July/August 2004)

As Weikart points out, Charles Darwin was a "progressive," and he framed even the destructive and violent aspects of nature in a positive progression. Despite

---

[205] See Generally – "The Misuse of Biological Hierarchies: The American Eugenics Movement, 1900-1940", Garland E. Allen, History and Philosophy of the Life Sciences, Vol. 5, No. 2, 1983, Pgs. 105-128.

Darwin's positive spin on the violence in nature, the underlying message could not have been more frightening to the other progressives, as Darwin's theory also explained in scientific terms how life and culture could "regress." The possibility of regression back to antiquated and lesser evolved life was the epitome and sum of all fears for the progressives. This was no small matter. Darwin's Theory of Evolution with respect to mankind was driven by his theory of "sexual selection" and the pronouncement that humans were animals like any others. Thus, humanity was subject to the consequences of "sexual selection" with the "fit" as well as with the "unfit." It could "progress" as easily as it could "regress."

History gives his cousin, Francis Galton, credit for dreaming up the science of eugenics, but the truth is that the underlying theory of eugenics was inalienably interwoven into the Theory of Evolution. Darwin's theory of "sexual selection" would simply fall apart without the aspect of "regression" or "progression" explicitly written into it. In a speech in 1909 honoring Darwin's hundredth birthday, a famous professor at the University of Munich expressed exactly this point. Max von Gruber opened his speech by countering the common characterization of nature as peaceful, harmonious, or balanced; Darwin had discovered a rationale behind all this seemingly meaningless upheaval and violence in nature:

> The never-ceasing struggle is, according to him [Darwin], not useless. It constantly clears away the malformed, the weak, and the inferior among the generations and thus secures the future for the fit. Thus only through the inexorable extermination of the negative variants does it provide living space for the strong and its strong offspring, and it keeps the species healthy, strong, and able to live. (Cited by Weikart, July/August 2004, "Touchstone")

The reader should take note of von Gruber's reference to "living space," as this concept would resonate with Darwinists of the era, and ultimately be translated by participants of the *Lebensreform* back-to-nature movement into the infamous concept of *Lebensraum*, which Hitler used to justify his expansionist policy. Ernst Haeckel, the German Darwinist that became influential among the early National Socialists, remarked in his 1904 book, "The Wonders of Life" that "the value of our human life appears to us today, on the firm foundation of evolutionary theory, in an entirely different light than it did fifty years ago." [206] Haeckel, like the National Socialists that found such fascination in his work, did not think human life particularly valuable in itself, nor did they think that all people had the same evolutionary value. Weikart quotes Haeckel in an 1864 letter to his devout Christian father:

> I share essentially your view of life, dear father, only I value human life and humans themselves much less than you . . . The individual with his personal existence appears to me only a temporary member in this large chain, as a rapidly vanishing vapor . . . Personal individual existence appears to me so horribly miserable, petty, and worthless, that I see it as intended for nothing but for

---

[206] Pg. 76 – "From Darwin to Hitler: Evolutionary Ethics, Eugenics and Racism in Germany", Richard Weikart, Springer, 2016.

destruction. (Pg. 76, "From Darwin to Hitler: Evolutionary Ethics, Eugenics and Racism in Germany", Palgrave Macmillan US, 2004)

So how do you make that critical turn from theory to practice? How do you make the leap from "destruction" in theory, as posed by Haeckel above, to "destruction" in practice? This thin red line was crossed when theory started being enshrined into law when the previously held notions of the "sanctity of life" and "right to life" became systematically replaced with the devaluation of the individual. If we are to ask when or how Francis Galton's and Charles Darwin's theories became potentially dangerous, we must ask by whom and when were their theories converted into public policy and legal concepts. This effort clearly started with the eugenicists, which all seemed to spend an inordinate amount of time drafting proposals for laws, instead of spending their time and energy on actual science. This effort began with Francis Galton and his various proposals but did not become a coherent international movement until after his passing. It was the subsequent generation that was led by Darwin's son, Leonard Darwin, which were responsible for translating this new ethic into a law where the all-powerful state would systematically and continually intervene in the process which Darwin called evolution, with the explicit intent of preventing atavism, or more precisely, "regression" or "degeneration." Again, this is no insignificant shift, as it is the power of the state that separates a random lynching from the mass-murder of the scope of The Holocaust. Mass murder was the "law of the land" during the Third Reich, as its laws commanded that the state continually and systematically eradicate those "useless eaters" and "life unworthy of life."

Leonard Darwin was an active lobbyist in British socio-economic policy, and he obviously leveraged his father's fame to advance the cause of eugenics, as he had none of his own to otherwise leverage. Leonard Darwin proposed that British society become increasingly collectivized along the lines which Edward Bellamy's "nationalistic" form of "socialism" prescribed, precisely so its evolutionary trajectory could be "centrally planned." Like the champions of "centrally planned" economists of Fabian Socialist persuasion, the young Darwin insisted that all major industries be "municipally owned," or how it is more commonly understood, "nationalized." But most specifically, Leonard Darwin became the spearhead of the eugenic movement that demanded that all of society be collectivized where the individual rights became subordinated to the society's need to weed out the "unfit." Leonard Darwin wasn't suggesting half-measures. Leonard Darwin was actively lobbying for the "widespread" application of "eugenic reform." His 1926 book, "The Need for Eugenic Reform," called for a total restructuring of society along eugenic ideology. A May 1926 TIME Magazine book review addressed this aspect of Leonard Darwin's work:

> Londoners of a Victorian cast of mind peeped cautiously last week into a new book, The Need for Eugenic Reform, by Major Leonard Darwin. They had not yet recovered from The Origin of Species by the Major's late father, Charles Darwin. Their horridest fears were stirred when they discovered that the "eugenic

reform" demanded by the major is a law penalizing individuals who bring into the world a greater number of children than their income will permit them to support decently. Stouter-hearted readers pondered well Major Darwin's proposals: All couples receiving public assistance, relief from the state, unemployment doles, or free feeding of children, shall be warned that they must have not more than two children. Upon the birth of a third child, all public assistance shall cease immediately. Should subsequent investigation (to be made in all cases) show that the children are not being reared under decent conditions, then the father and mother shall be segregated from each other until such time as they may possess the means to rear their children adequately. (May 3, 1926, "British Commonwealth of Nations: Young Darwin", TIME)

The review continues to shed light on just how drastic Leonard Darwin's proposals truly were:
The proposed deterrent should be known by all to be certain to follow immediately on any disregard of a warning given, and it should be sufficiently drastic to strike the imagination of even the dull witted. If it became known that all this would be the inevitable result of parenthood under these conditions, a fall would take place in the birth rate of all this section of the less fit, with great beneficial results, both immediate and racial. (May 3, 1926, "British Commonwealth of Nations: Young Darwin", TIME)

The journal Nature also ran a book review of Leonard Darwin's "Need for Eugenic Reform" in July of the same year and it was hardly more kind:
The word "Eugenics" signifying "the study of the agencies under human control by which the human stock can be improved" was coined by Galton, as most people know. Most are also aware that it was associated in the public mind with a number of fantastic projects for the compulsory mating of specially selected specimens of opposite sexes in order to improve the race. For this conception of the subject Galton is directly responsible; it has led to eugenists being regarded as a collection of faddists, and has drawn on to the whole subject the sharpest shafts of ridicule and sarcasm. G. K. Chesterton has said of eugenic reform that it could be imposed only on slaves and cowards, and it is, no doubt, of "Galtonian" reforms that he was thinking when he made this statement. (July 10, 1926, "Nature")

However, the ridicule that Nature and TIME Magazine unleashed upon Leonard Darwin would not endure for long. The ethos in vogue throughout the metropolitan world was changing, and largely due to Leonard's father. Leonard Darwin was, after all, leveraging his father's science, and thus eugenics gained strength as his father's "theory" achieved the status of scientific gospel. Julian Huxley's review of Leonard's book in "The Sociological Review" exemplifies this change. Julian Huxley's point-of-view represented the new ethos, that *"Über Ethik"* emerging from scientific and legislative minds:
Major Leonard Darwin's book (The Need for Eugenic Reform, J. Murray,

London: 1921: pp. xvii.—529) is without question the most important single contribution to Eugenics that has been made since Galton first coined the word. ("The Sociological Review," Volume 18, Issue 4)

But we need not rely on book reviews to discern just how radical Leonard's proposals were. Upon reading Leonard Darwin's various books, it becomes clear that Leonard Darwin was keenly aware of just how extreme his proposals were, and how they departed from the widely accepted concept of what a "humanitarian" was expected to believe. Anyone that reads Leonard Darwin's "Need for Eugenic Reform" will be confronted with a semantic tightrope walk where Darwin vacillates between making the most extreme proposals and equivocating with moral platitudes. Like Julian Huxley after him, Leonard Darwin attempted to make his version of eugenics more socially palatable by sidestepping the overt racist commentary that his eugenic brethren had become known for. In "The Need for Eugenic Reform," Leonard Darwin equivocates from decrying the intrusion of "racial" considerations into eugenics all in one page:

> The advocates of the English Mental Deficiency Act and of the American sterilization laws certainly were influenced by racial considerations; but these were but the exceptions which proved the rule. (Pg. 41, "The Need for Eugenic Reform", D. Appleton & Co., 1926)

Leonard's condemnation of "racial considerations" would fine, but then he turns around and justifies his demands upon a "racial" basis, repeatedly using charged terms such as "inferior races" and "leading civilized nations" [207]:

> But in the past we have relied mainly on our intellectual superiority in our dealings with coloured races, and on all accounts military and civil, it would be a fatal blunder now to neglect any steps tending to maintain or enhance that superiority. (Pg. 308, "The Need for Eugenic Reform", D. Appleton & Co., 1926)

Not only was Leonard Darwin's eugenics the work of a white-supremacist, but it was also replete with class bias. Leonard Darwin, in keeping with the elitist convictions of his uncle, Francis Galton, believed earning capacity to be linked with eugenic worth. Thus, he proposed that eugenic laws also be guided by economic contribution instead of just racial considerations:

> Again, if the families of the rich were to become bigger and the families of the poor smaller, wealth would in consequence come to be more uniformly divided at each generation. Lastly, the eugenist is bound to suggest, against his inclinations, that the incomes earned by wage-earners and their natural capacities must be to some extent correlated; and, if this be the case, the inborn qualities of future generations would inevitably be improved as the result of any better adjustment of birth rate to incomes. (Pg. 164, "The Need for Eugenic Reform", D. Appleton & Co., 1926)

---

[207] Pg. 61 - "The Need for Eugenic Reform", Leonard Darwin, D. Appleton & Co., 1926.

This was elitism at its worst. In Chapter VI, titled "Racial Poisons," Leonard maps out the broad scope of a eugenic-minded state structure:

> ...the term 'germ plasm' is here intended to indicate the thing, whatever it may be, by means of which the natural qualities of parents are transmitted to their offspring, or the physical link which binds succeeding generation one to another. Looking only to beneficial results, every method by means of which we may hope to affect the well-being of our nation in the future may be included under one of the following five headings:
>
> <u>Environmental Inheritance</u>; or the passing on to future generations both of good traditions by speech and by writing and of enduring physical improvements.
>
> Pre-natal environment; or the safeguarding of children before birth from infections, poisons and improper nourishment.
>
> <u>Racial poisons</u>; or the guarding against any directly injurious effect on the germ plasm which might result from the presence of certain substances or organisms in the body of the parent.
>
> <u>The inheritance of acquired differences</u>; or the beneficial effects which the good surroundings, mental or physical, of existing potential parents may have on their germ plasms and consequently on their descendants.
>
> <u>Selection</u>; or the relative increase in the numbers of persons to be born in the future of good stock and therefore likely to be endowed with good inborn qualities. (Pgs. 73-74, "The Need for Eugenic Reform", D. Appleton & Co., 1926)

Clearly, points 1, 3, and 4 indicate broad reaching societal controls, as they would later be applied in the United States during Prohibition and in Hitler's Germany with respect to bans on food substances and cigarette smoke in the case of the Third Reich's war on cancer. Point number 1 certainly implies a cultural and educational regimen, as was later seen in the Third Reich's ban on Jazz music or any behavior that was deemed "poisonous" to the development of the nation or race. Leonard Darwin himself identifies alcohol and tobacco as a "racial poison" in later chapters. Darwin makes it clear that his proposal for "eugenics reform" goes far beyond the prevention of hereditary diseases, and into the directing of society itself:

> In passing it may here be worth noting that if in scientific discussions the survival of the fittest means little more than the survival of those who do in fact survive, yet when we come to discuss eugenic reforms, we are apt to attach somewhat different meaning to the word 'fittest.' The aim of eugenists is to alter human surroundings in such a way as to increase the chance of 'survival' of those types which are held to be most desirable; and consequently in eugenic discussions the 'fittest' is a term sometimes used to indicate those who *ought* to 'survive' in the evolutionary sense — that is to help to people the earth — rather than those who actually do survive. Natural selection seems to take no thought as to what is 'good,' whilst in eugenic problems the moral qualities of man should be the primary consideration. (Pgs. 114-115, "The Need for Eugenic Reform", D. Appleton & Co., 1926)

It is here again that Leonard Darwin equivocates and pays lip-service to some nebulous morality he later decries and discards as past superstitions and religious mores. This was the proverbial genie that Darwinists, namely the son, Leonard, could not put back in the bottle; Leonard Darwin champions his father's success at proving the "animal origins of man" throughout his book, but then provides a weak attempt to refute that man should act like an animal, or more precisely, that his proposed program of eugenics reform should be carried out with the harshness of natural selection:

> Nature shows no concern for the sufferings she causes by her methods of eliminating the less fit; and, if natural selection were our guide, our duties would include the getting rid of all inferior human beings no matter how. Natural selection points to no kindness being shown by man to inferior animals, or to other tribes ---- nothing is to be learnt from biology as to the ultimate aims of our existence, and but little as to the exact ways in which the evolutionary method should be utilized in eugenic reform. (Pgs. 124-125, "The Need for Eugenic Reform", D. Appleton & Co., 1926)

Largely because of Leonard's urging, the rest of the eugenic-minded community was poised to do exactly what he decried, and Leonard knew this perfectly well as the correspondence in the archives proves. More specifically, it was by no coincidence that the SS and Hitler Youth officers taught that "compassion" or "sentimentality" was a weakness, as theirs was precisely intended to instill a cold "survivalist" mentality towards the elimination of "inferior animals, or to other tribes." Leonard Darwin called for a similarly cold and "rational" selection:

> Our aim should be to substitute for the blind, cruel and often retrograde methods of natural selection some form of conscious selection which will make all men in future more able than at present to follow in the footsteps of the noblest human beings now on earth. (Pg. 130, "The Need for Eugenic Reform", D. Appleton & Co., 1926)

Should we understand the above passage as an example of Leonard Darwin calling for the creation of a "master race"? As Karl Brandt and the rest of the German defendants at Nuremberg would repeatedly testify, it is precisely this "rational selection" which the scientists and doctors of the Third Reich enacted.

Leonard Darwin includes a telling parable in the chapter titled "The Lessons of the Stockyard." In it he tells a quick and short story, which interestingly enough, predates George Orwell's "Animal Farm" by about 20 years. In Leonard Darwin's short version, he tells of a post-human society of sheep. The sheep were deeply concerned about how the "black sheep" darkened the color of their wool and made it spotty and blotted. "The Council" was convened to inquire how the humans had addressed this problem, and it was dutifully recalled that the human masters exterminated tainted stock:

> ...and when they studied the ancient books they found that men, when they were our shepherds, would only allow the pure white sheep to take each other in

marriage. Here they found the secret they had been seeking, a secret which they took to heart, and ruled themselves accordingly. Soon a great change came over them, and now our flocks are whiter even than when men drove us into pens with dogs. Thus it was that we learnt how to spend our days so that now never a black sheep appears in our midst. (Pg. 132, "The Need for Eugenic Reform", D. Appleton & Co., 1926)

It would be interesting to know if George Orwell's "Animal Farm" was in any way inspired by Leonard Darwin's work, just as Aldous Huxley's "Brave New World" was a mirror held up against Julian Huxley's eugenic and socio-economic proposals. In Leonard Darwin's equivocation, we see the happy totalitarianism that Aldous Huxley so eloquently satirizes in "Brave New World." As Leonard Darwin states, "we want the lessons but not the methods of the stockyard." In other words, he wanted to eradicate the "black sheep" without the messy guilt or suffering that would come about if we were not first conditioned to think of it as a good instead of evil:

> When the farmer sees signs of deterioration in the breed of his cattle he knows that it is due to his own carelessness in regard to the hereditary qualities of the animals selected for breeding purposes. Can the politician and the social reformer be made to acquire a similar firm belief in the power of inheritance? Can they be induced to consider which are the best hereditary types that our nation now contains, or who would make the most desirable ancestors for posterity? If not, probably our nation will decline in quality like the stocks of the foolish farmer. (Pg. 138, "The Need for Eugenic Reform", D. Appleton & Co., 1926)

Leonard Darwin's belief system, like Earnest Hooton and all the eugenicists from Francis Galton onwards, was based on the Darwinian belief that evolution could work both forward and backward, or more precisely, "progress" as well as "regress." The section titled "Evolution May Be Retrograde" makes this amply clear with its reference to the Darwinian "ape-human metaphor" which Hooton and Stalin's scientists extrapolated to ludicrous ends:

> …the march of evolution has not infrequently been backwards and not forwards. Judging by this analogy there would be nothing surprising in the human race, whilst possibly becoming far more numerous, at the same time becoming more ape-like. (Pg. 7, "The Need for Eugenic Reform", D. Appleton & Co., 1926)

For both Charles and Leonard Darwin, the intermarriage with what they deemed "inferior races" meant "deterioration" or an atavistic regression back towards the "ape-origin" of man. What Leonard Darwin called "deterioration" or "degradation" was what other eugenic-minded zealots called "degeneration," and just as was in the case of Leonard Darwin, they did so with a "nationalist" mindset, repeatedly warning of the consequences to the "nation":

> On the other hand there are now many students of racial problems who regard the signs of the times as clearly pointing to a slow and progressive deterioration in many of the most important innate qualities of all civilized peoples; that is to a **national** degradation which it will only be possible to arrest by **national** efforts

covering a wide field of endeavor. (emphasis mine, Pg. 146, "The Need for Eugenic Reform", D. Appleton & Co., 1926)

Clearly, Leonard Darwin meant to enlist the full might of the government in order to make eugenics a "religion" as his uncle Francis Galton had explicitly intended; to make it the underlying and overriding principle of society as it became under the Nazis. By "eugenic reform" Leonard Darwin meant a government dedicated to and organized under eugenic principles, precisely as would be the Third Reich. How did Leonard justify such extreme measures? Much like the eugenic propaganda films of Hitler's Germany, Leonard Darwin pointed to an "end of days" catastrophic scenario to justify the extreme legislative steps he was prescribing. In the section titled "Dangers of Inaction," Leonard Darwin extrapolates the type of logic the Third Reich played with eugenic films like *Erbkrank*:

>...to be careless about the future may be to condemn our own nation to disaster. For a long time it will be impossible to remove all doubts concerning the workings of the laws of nature, especially as to the way in which living things have been slowly modified in the process of time; and we can indeed hardly even imagine a time when a theory of evolution will be so firmly established as to defy all criticism. We cannot wait till all doubts are removed, because that would probably mean postponing all eugenic reform forever. The reformer, whatever be his objects, must own to some doubts and accept some risks. (Pgs. 7-8, "The Need for Eugenic Reform", D. Appleton & Co., 1926)

Above, Leonard Darwin was utilizing to what is now called the "Precautionary Principle," which asks that the most extreme reforms be accepted in recognition that they may be staving off the most extreme catastrophes, even if the proof isn't yet conclusive:

>A reform must not, therefore, be condemned merely because it produces some injurious effects: for it is the balance between its good and evil consequences which should always be held in view. Unfortunately, certain reforms, which are demanded on behalf of posterity and which would unquestionably benefit future generations, would be harmful to the present generation; for many restrictions and restraints which would slowly tend to improve the breed of the race would be immediately galling or harmful. (Pg. 37, "The Need for Eugenic Reform", D. Appleton & Co., 1926)

In a proposal that eerily foreshadows the Jewish ghettos of Hitler's Germany, Leonard Darwin calls for us to consider the creation of "Eugenic Communities" by segregating the superior as well as restricting the reproduction of the inferior in order to create a "eugenic superior caste" [208]:

>It is no doubt true that if any group of selected individuals were to be kept quite apart from the rest of the nation as a eugenic community, a certain average superiority would be permanently maintained, at all events after the first

---

[208] Pg. 155 - "The Need for Eugenic Reform", Leonard Darwin, D. Appleton & Co., 1926.

generation after their selection. Moreover, the formation of such a community of the more fit would produce certain advantages which would be reaped to a large extent by the whole nation; for one result of the separation of the more intelligent individuals from the rest of the community would be that a large proportion of men of high intellect would make their appearance in future generations, with a consequent more rapid advancement in material welfare and possible in morals also. The segregation of the more fit would also necessarily result to some extent in a corresponding segregation of the less fit; consequently, the number of individuals whose qualities were sufficiently inferior to justify the prohibition or discouragement of parenthood would thus be increased; and in this way more of the seed of inferiority might be eliminated at each generation. (Pg. 154, "The Need for Eugenic Reform", D. Appleton & Co., 1926)

What Leonard Darwin was proposing to create a "eugenic superior caste" was exactly the means that would later be employed in order to create a "master race." Interestingly enough, Leonard Darwin knew that the alleged gains would be "negligible" in proportion with the scope of the endeavor. He writes that to have effect, the endeavor must employ "mass selection":

But as long as the eugenic caste comprised but a small fraction of the whole community, this last-mentioned beneficial effect of its creation would be so small as to be negligible for a very long period of time. (Pg. 154, "The Need for Eugenic Reform", D. Appleton & Co., 1926)

Leonard Darwin then touches upon the possibility of such an endeavor, again, sounding disturbingly like the means later employed by Heinrich Himmler in the now-infamous *"Lebensborn"* project that created camps facilitating the mating of SS ranks with young German girls without the hindrance of marriage or even courtship:

A widespread campaign directed towards increasing the rate of multiplication of the great mass of those who are decidedly above the average in qualities held to be desirable, or of diminishing the fertility of all the possessors of qualities distinctly undesirable, is likely, therefore, to have a considerably greater beneficial effect in regard to the average qualities of the nation in the future than could result from any attempt to focus attention in regard to parenthood on the rare or more exceptional individuals at either end of the scale of merit. (Pg. 162, "The Need for Eugenic Reform", D. Appleton & Co., 1926)

It should also be clear that Leonard Darwin was perfectly willing to make cold calculations as to who would be deemed "inferior" and who would be deemed "superior" while admitting there were no such clear demarcations. This is made clear in the chapter disturbingly titled "Methods of Elimination":

On this account it is generally impossible to draw a clear line separating those who should be regarded as possessing a defect dependent on many factors from those who should be classed as free from it; yet when a defect makes an individual a danger to society, such a line often has to be drawn in order to decide who shall com within the arm of the law and who shall escape. For example, there is every grade of insanity, and yet it is necessary for legal authorities to declare one man to be insane whilst holding another man, nearly as abnormal, not to be so. Legal decisions have also to be made as to who is a criminal, a mentally defective person, a vagabond or a drunkard; though in all such cases the decisions are more the less arbitrary. (Pg. 169, "The Need for Eugenic Reform", D. Appleton & Co., 1926)

You do not need to read much eugenic propaganda released by the Third Reich to recognize the similarity of regarding an individual a "danger to society" for simply existing with inborn traits. Darwin clearly means to treat certain "undesirable" humans as a contagious disease, as did his German counterparts. In the subsection titled "Segregation," Leonard Darwin makes it clear that individual rights must be subordinated to the society, especially when "racial defects" are the perceived danger:
> No doubt we all dislike any interference with liberty; but liberty implies a certain degree of equality, and as equality between aments and the normal population does not and cannot exist, mental defectives can under no circumstances enjoy true liberty. (Pgs. 198-199)

CONTINUES ...

The popular belief in the innate equality of all men is, however, slowly but surely disappearing in the face of irrefutable facts, and it will not be long before it is generally recognized that there does exist a large class of human being shoes fertility should as far as possible be diminished for the sake of posterity. (Pgs. 206-207, "The Need for Eugenic Reform", D. Appleton & Co., 1926)

One aspect of Leonard Darwin's eugenic proposals that must also be underscored is his proposal for "special tribunals" to be set up to "search into the family history" of those who came under the definition of undesirable or unfit. These clearly follow the proposals for eugenic tribunals in Harry H. Laughlin's 1922 "Model Eugenical Sterilization Law" as well as their implementation in Hitler's Germany in 1935.

Let us not misjudge the importance of Leonard Darwin because of his current day obscurity. Leonard Darwin did much more than write an unsavory book. Leonard Darwin leveraged his father's fame in order to unite like-minded individuals from the United States, Britain, Scandinavia, and namely Germany in an international eugenics movement. Let us not misjudge the extent to which Charles Darwin's work was ingrained in Leonard's. In "The Need for Eugenic Reform," he cites Charles B. Davenport, Harry H. Laughlin, Karl Pearson, Francis Galton, and most importantly, his father, Charles Darwin. The book's dedication is particularly important and telling, to the extent that his father's theory played a part in Francis Galton's creation of the science of eugenics, and in turn the work of all of Charles Darwin's followers as cited in Leonard's book:

DEDICATED TO THE MEMORY OF MY FATHER FOR IF I HAD NOT BELIEVED

THAT HE WOULD HAVE WISHED ME TO GIVE SUCH HELP AS I COULD TOWARDS MAKING HIS LIFE'S WORK OF SERVICE TO MANKIND, I SHOULD NEVER HAVE BEEN LED TO WRITE THIS BOOK.

The debate over how much, or even if, Charles Darwin's Theory of Evolution had a direct influence on The Holocaust is an enduring controversy. The zealotry evident in protecting Charles Darwin's work from any negative taint is formidable. This zealotry is a significant source for the misinformation of precisely what forces were at play in the crimes of The Holocaust. First, it must be noted that Leonard Darwin knew his father better than any of the contemporary Darwinist apologists and zealots can claim. If Leonard Darwin claimed that Charles Darwin would have approved of the eugenic measures outlined in "The Need for Eugenic Reform," then his word is worth more than that of those who would counter for political posturing.

More to the point, Leonard Darwin can be said to have been parroting the claims which Charles Darwin made in the introduction to "The Descent of Man," where Charles lavishes significant praise upon Francis Galton and Ernst Haeckel. Furthermore, the history of the British Eugenics Society and the many publications such as "The Need for Eugenic Reform" settles the controversy. Leonard Darwin's proposals, and more importantly his pivotal role in the International Federation of Eugenic Organizations, was the venue by which all that crucial eugenic legislative work was delivered to the hands of Hitler's top "racial hygienists." The name Darwin not only gave "racial hygiene" and eugenics a veil of legitimacy, but also the clout necessary for the Kaiser-Wilhelm Institute, the Human Betterment Foundation, and Cold Spring Harbor to secure funds for their work. You would have to be a real partisan to contest the obvious parallels and plagiarisms. Alfred Ploetz's and Ernst Rüdin's role in the implementation of the 1933 eugenic laws cannot be contested any more than can their membership in the British Eugenics Society, and thus their relationship with Leonard Darwin, Harry H. Laughlin, and Charles B. Davenport.

Richard Weikart's highly controversial book, "From Darwin to Hitler" points to a dizzying amount of connections between Darwin and Hitler. With all due respect for Mr. Weikart, the path is not as serpentine as he makes it. The relationships are direct and linear. Darwin proclaimed that evolution could work backward, and that humanity could "degenerate" to an inferior type, closer to man's "ape-origins," and this fear-fueled the development of eugenics. Charles Darwin's fame also provided a cloak of scientific legitimacy to eugenics, which it would not have enjoyed if it were not fully based on his Theory of Evolution. The Darwinist zealots then and now, strike at anyone who dares question Darwin, and the science of eugenics was a direct beneficiary of this zealous closing of the ranks. Proposals that were morally suspect went uncontested and unchallenged, allowing them to survive and later to thrive under Hitler.

It must also be emphatically underscored that Leonard Darwin was not a man operating in a vacuum when he wrote "The Need for Eugenic Reform" in 1926. His proposals were obviously dangerous, and Leonard Darwin's frequent equivocation throughout his book evidences that he was keenly aware of the legal and moral deficiencies in his proposal. Most importantly, it must be noted that the Mental Deficiency Act of 1913, which he often refers to in the book and which will be documented in later chapters, came to meet significant opposition by a prominent member of the Darwin-Galton-Wedgwood family. The debates over this Act were too highly publicized and too bitterly contested for him to have been unaware of the objections to his proposals. In other words, there were plenty of people pointing to the obvious dangers in Leonard Darwin's eugenic proposals. Leonard Darwin simply chose to dismiss these objections and persist in the pursuit of his eugenic utopia and his "superior eugenic caste."

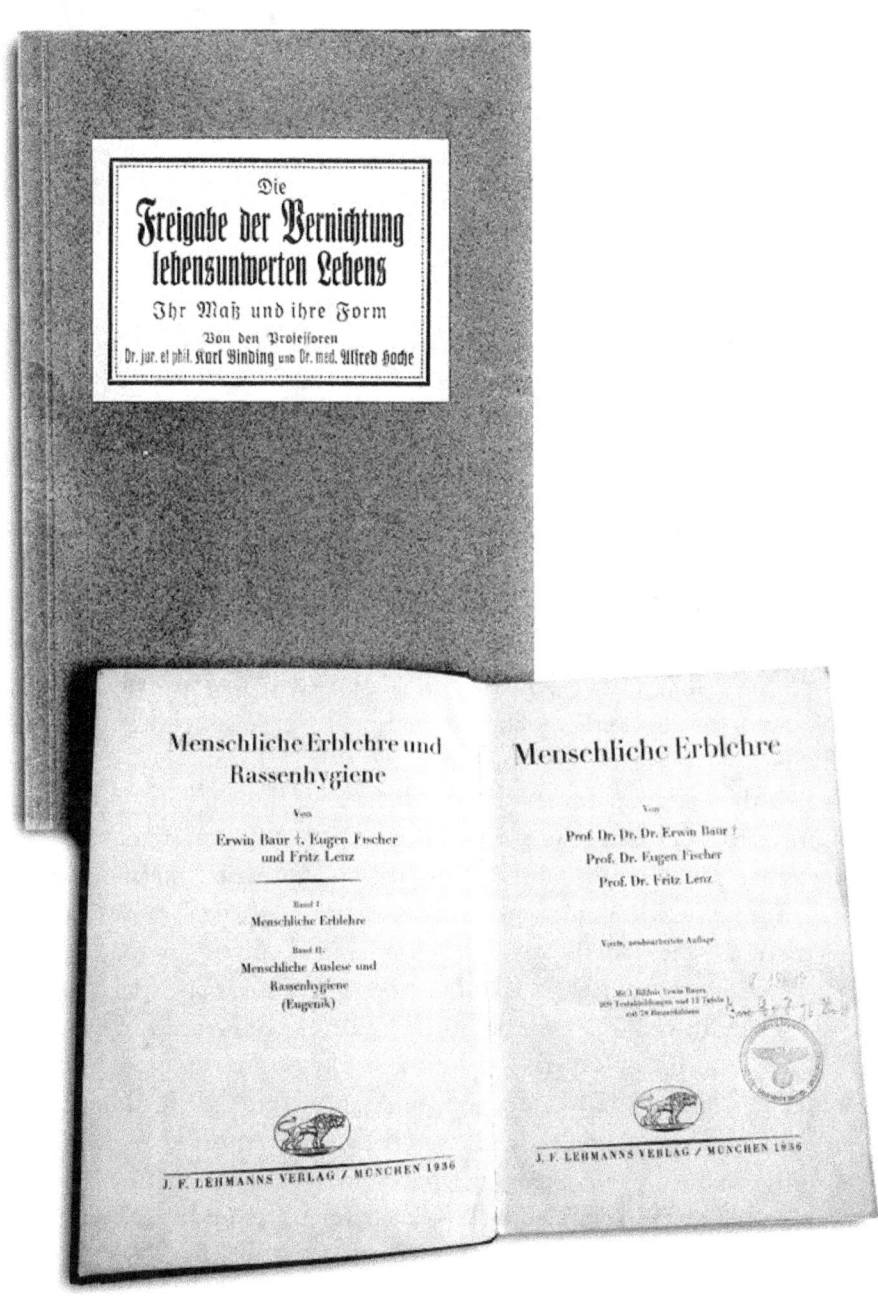

FIGURE 6: THE 1920 BOOK BY ALFRED HOCHE AND KARL BINDING *"DIE FREIGABE DER VERNICHTUNG LEBENSUNWERTEM LEBENS,"* OR IN ENGLISH, "ANNIHILATION OF LIFE UNWORTHY OF BEING LIVED," PICTURED HERE ALONG WITH THE 1923 *"GRUNDRISS DER MENSCHLICHEN ERBLICHKEITSLEHRE UND RASSENHYGIENE,"* OR IN ENGLISH THE "PRINCIPLES OF HUMAN HEREDITY AND RACIAL HYGIENE," BY EUGEN FISCHER, FRITZ LENZ AND ERWIN BAUR.

Chap. 5: 1925 to 1921

SCIENCE & TECHNOLOGY: Astronomer Edwin Hubble announces that Andromeda, previously believed to be a nebula, is actually another galaxy, and that the Milky Way is only one of many such galaxies in the universe. In Egypt, British archaeologist Howard Carter and his men find the entrance to Pharaoh Tutankhamun's tomb. Peking Man Site at Zhoukoudian, China is first excavated. **EUROPEAN FRONT**: Benito Mussolini announces he is taking dictatorial powers over Italy. The United Kingdom recognizes the Soviet Union. Vladimir Lenin suffers his third stroke. **AMERICAN FRONT**: The Ku Klux Klan demonstrate their popularity by holding a parade in Washington DC; as many as 40,000 male and female members of the Klan march down Pennsylvania Avenue. **LIFE**: F. Scott Fitzgerald publishes The Great Gatsby. – Pol Pot, Cambodian Khmer Rouge leader is born. In Washington, D.C., the Lincoln Memorial is dedicated.

Sec. I – FROM "LOOKING BACKWARDS" TO "MEIN KAMPF":

The German words "Mein Kampf" translate into "My Struggle" or "My Battle." The book itself is a combination of autobiographical elements along with an introduction to Hitler's socio-political ideals. Volume 1 of "Mein Kampf" was published in 1925 and Volume 2 in 1926. Most importantly, "Mein Kampf" goes a long way to clarify what type of collectivism he subscribed to and why. Neither "Mein Kampf" nor Hitler's National Socialism can be understood without first comprehending Hitler's understanding of Bolshevism as being an "international" form of "Communism." It is not the "socialist," "communist," or "collectivist" form of government that Hitler was allegedly opposed to. As is evidenced by "Mein Kampf" and the domestic policy of National Socialism, Hitler believed in the "solidarity" of "socialism" and the "collective spirit" if it was utilized to bolster and strengthen the "nation." Hitler did not believe in the solidarity of "class" as the Internationalists did. Hitler's idea of the collective was a community based on racial qualifications, and this is what the term "nation" ultimately meant to him.

That said, Hitler's idea of what Germany entailed must also be clearly understood. Despite all the political activity and all the propaganda claims to Germanic heritage, Adolf Hitler did not become a German citizen until February 25, 1932, literally only one year before being elected to power. Hitler renounced his Austrian citizenship on April 7, 1925, just after being released from Landsberg prison in December 1924, and upon publications of "Mein Kampf." For almost seven years, Hitler was stateless and faced the risk of deportation. This ambivalence towards the country of his birth has gone conveniently ignored by those historians who would like to characterize Hitler as a creature of the political "Right" and of a traditional patriotic "nationalism." Hitler was undoubtedly a xenophobe, but his antipathies were not born out of the "God and country" type of patriotism as typically understood. There is nothing about Adolf Hitler's "nationalism" that originated in the pedestrian definition of "national pride" based on monarchs, flags, constitutions, or geographic borders. Case in point, Hitler discarded the traditional German flag, the anthem, and the uniforms, and replaced them with his highly stylized designs. There was very little about monarchs, flags, constitutions, or geographic borders that remained from the Hapsburg reign that Hitler cared to "conserve" or devote any patriotic duty towards. In fact, Hitler defined the borders of his "Nordic" Germany in a very different way than would those that considered themselves "conservatives" or German patriots of his time. Contrast Hitler's definition of "patriotism" with Theodore Roosevelt's. You could make some comparison between Roosevelt's "manifest destiny" with Hitler's "*Lebensraum*," and Hitler's "racism" with Roosevelt's "racialist" world-view. You could, in fact, compare their socio-economic policy as being along the lines of Progressivism. However, they had a very different idea of what comprised a "nation":

> Patriotism means to stand by the country. It does not mean to stand by the president or any other public official. (Theodore Roosevelt, "The Great Adventure: Present-Day Studies in American Nationalism", Essay #7 Lincoln and Free Speech)

Clearly, Roosevelt's idea of patriotic "nationalism" is the mirror opposite of Hitler's *Führerprinzip*, which asked that any loyalty to country, flag, and nation become subservient, or even irrelevant, to make the loyalty he demanded from all under his "Leadership Principle." Furthermore, Hitler's national boundaries were drawn along ethnic lines. While Roosevelt had some clearly defined "racial" prejudices, his patriotism towards the American ideal required of Roosevelt to accept people of all backgrounds and ethnicities:

> I am among those Americans whose ancestors include men and women from many different European countries. The proportion of Americans of this type will steadily increase. I do not believe in hyphenated Americans. I do not believe in German-Americans or Irish-Americans; and I believe just as little in English-Americans. (Theodore Roosevelt, theodoreroosevelt.org)

One thing is clear: Adolf Hitler did not proclaim himself to be a "nationalist" until after he had deeply rooted convictions to be the catalyst of a "socialist" revolution. Hitler's German citizenship was a requirement for the political campaigns, not an aspiration to become part of Germany as it stood before he amassed power. If put in the context of the timeline, it is easy to understand that Hitler's acquiescence to citizenship was also one of the consequences of the failed attempt at "violent revolution." Hitler had tried "revolution" by force in the Beer-Hall Putsch, only to resurface from his stint in jail with the manuscript for "Mein Kampf" and a fully restructured political strategy. Hitler had clearly learned his lesson, and from then on, the strategy was to ascend to power within the confines of legality. It is Hitler's desire to reach power through legality as opposed to brute force that explains his desire to acquire German citizenship, not love or patriotism for the traditional German nation.

The German city of Braunschweig, unfortunately, bears the stigma of having been responsible for handing this most infamous Austrian a German citizenship. By 1930, the National Socialists were already politically influential in the Braunschweig Free State. For Hitler, an appointment to a government office in Braunschweig was the only opportunity to get German citizenship since the Free State was the only state in the Weimar Republic with members of the National Socialist party with positions in the government. The State Minister for the Interior and Education and NSDAP member Dietrich Klagges got Adolf Hitler fast-tracked by giving Hitler the government job of *Regierungsrat* at the Braunschweig State Culture and Surveying Office, which granted Hitler German citizenship. Joseph Goebbels reportedly planned to get Hitler appointed as an associate professor. Klagges first tried to procure for Hitler an associate professorship in the made-up position of "Politics and Organic Sociology" at the Braunschweig Technical College. This original plan soon leaked out to the public and thus had to be scrapped. Thus followed the subsequent and successful attempt to get Hitler a government job, this time by Dr. Wessels, a German People's Party (DVP) Member of the Reichstag. Dr. Wessels suggested that a post be procured for Hitler in the Braunschweig Legation at the Reichsrat in Berlin.

Once a German, Hitler had an open door to German rule, and by this time, the admixture of "nationalism" and "socialism" was a frequently discussed scheme. Hitler was hardly the first socialist to follow Bellamy in combining collectivism with a Darwinian nationalism. However, if one is to look for a source of Hitler's political convictions, and thus the source of his "nationalism" and "socialism," Hitler's time in Vienna is decidedly the time and place where his political convictions would largely be formed. We know with reasonable certainty that the first time that Adolf Hitler heard the political title of "national socialism" was during his frequent visits to the Vienna parliament. Brigitte Hamann documents how the young Hitler regularly sat in and watched speeches and deliberations in the Vienna Reichsrat as if it were some sort of sporting event. [209] One of the political parties was the Czech National Socialist Party, and their obstructionist and radical methods made them all but impossible for the young Hitler to have been unaware of them in the two years he religiously attended the parliamentary sessions. The Czech National Social Party was a socialist political party with distinctly nationalist undertones, which stressed Czech independence from Austria–Hungary. This observation would also be consistent with Hitler's nature as a plagiarist. Hitler's National Socialist party platform was in many cases a copy of the Czech one. [210] It is impossible to understand the emergence of nationalistic collectivism before World War I without noting the paradigm change that took place at the end of the 19th Century. Consistent with the pattern-in-practice, all of these national-socialist concepts were a byproduct of Darwinism's influence in politics. [211] Proposals for a national-socialist state first appeared at the end of the 19th Century, and shortly afterward "nationalsocial," "national-socialist," or "socialist-nationalist" groups popped up in England, France, Germany, Italy, and Austria:

> Social Darwinism has dealt a deadly blow not only to Christian creationism but also to the idea, dominant since the enlightenment, that history would find its

---

[209] Pgs. 175-177 – "Hitler's Vienna: A Dictator's Apprenticeship", Brigitte Hamann, Oxford Univ. Press, 1999 – Translated by Thomas Thorton.

[210] Pgs. 145-146 - "Leftism Revisited: From de Sade and Marx to Hitler and Pol Pot", Erik von Kuehnelt-Leddihn, Regnery Gateway, 1990.

[211] Pg. 259 - "The Epoch of National Socialism", Karlheinz Weissmann, The Journal of Libertarian Studies, Fall 1996.

fulfillment in an all-encompassing humanization of man. Darwin, still convinced of the intelligibility of the world and the idea of human progress, unwittingly created the precondition for a dramatic change in the intellectual atmosphere from his death in 1882 to the outbreak of World War I. (Pg. 259, "The Epoch of National Socialism", Karlheinz Weissmann, The Journal of Libertarian Studies, Fall 1996)

Karlheinz Weismann points out that Hitler's "National Socialist" state was certainly understood to be in line with the eugenic nationalism of the Fabian Socialists. It was perceived as a model of a new order between liberal capitalism and communism, not only by many Germans but also by the many small national-socialist movements in Europe. That was certainly the case with the "nationalist" movement that Marion Bellamy spearheaded in the Americas. In the chapter aptly titled "Socialist Nationalism – National Socialism," Karlheinz Weissmann explains:

> What Corradini, Naumann, or the Fabians meant by socialism had little to do with what the political left had meant by the term. Cosmopolitism and the idea of absolute equality appeared unscientific to them. In this, they could invoke not only Darwinism, which seemed to make an elitist concept of politics necessary, but also the new realist sociology, which was represented around the turn of the century by men such as Max Weber, Robert Michels, Gaetano Mosca, Vilfredo Pareto, and Georges Sorel. Socialism for Corradini, Naumann, and the Fabians was a synonym for increased and intensified organizational integration of the entire nation. They were not concerned with ending the exploitation of men by men, but with preventing social disintegration as a consequence of the process of modernization, so as to strengthen the state for the process of international competition. For them, socialism was to serve and promote nationalism. (Pgs. 268, "The Epoch of National Socialism", Karlheinz Weissmann, The Journal of Libertarian Studies, Fall 1996)

Clearly, the marriage of "nationalism" and "socialism" was a world-wide movement long before Hitler, and the movement can largely be credited to Edward Bellamy. Edward Bellamy's form of "nationalistic solidarity" went hand-in-hand with the Darwinian "struggle for existence." As explained by the above quote, Bellamite socialism was a way to enroll an entire people in the struggle between the races. Eugen Dühring, the socialist and Marxist of the early "German-Darwinian left," was an ardent defender of the "descendence-theory," a special type of "socialism of the Aryan people" and the simultaneous "restriction, concentration, and exclusion" of the Jews. Ludwig Woltmann, a physician, and private scholar, had begun as a traditional socialist, but also evolved into this Darwinistic form of Nationalistic socialism:

> In its final development, the capitalist mode of production will become an obstacle for the social selection of natural talents and indeed become antiselectionist. Hence, we are convinced that the future will bring great economic upheavals which will have a constitutional-collectivist character. (Ludwig Woltmann, "*Politische Anthropologie: Eine Untersuchung über den*

Einfluss der Descendenz-theorie auf die Lehre von der politischen Entwicklung der Völker", 1903 – Translation from Karlheinz Weissmann, "The Epoch of National Socialism", Pg. 262)

This was the prevailing political thought of a large portion of the intellectual class. In the 1880s and 1890s, Georges Vacher de Lapouge wrote for various journals of the French socialists and ran repeatedly as a candidate for the *Parti socialiste ouvrier*. He liked the fatalistic view of the Marxists but advocated a socialist order because only socialism could assure that each individual's racially based abilities could be determined independently of his class. In an article published in 1896, Vacher de Lapouge referred to a type of socialism of distinct Darwinist and eugenic creed by proclaiming that "socialism will be selectionist or it will not be at all." La Pouge's assertions could easily be confused with a passage ripped out of the pages of "Mein Kampf":

> The individual is dominated by his race and is nothing. The race, the nation is everything. Every man is related to all other men and all living beings. There is no such thing as human rights, no more than there are rights of the armadillo or the Gibbons syndactylus, of the horse which is harnessed or the ox which one eats. As soon as man loses the privilege of being a special being created in God's image, he possesses no more rights than any other mammal. The idea of justice is an illusion. There exists nothing but force. Rights are only agreements—contracts between equal or unequal powers. (Georges Vacher de Lapouge, L'Aryen, son rôle sociale. Cours libre de science politique: Professé a l'Universite de Montpellier (1889–1890) (Paris, 1899), pp. 511f)

In fact, there were numerous groups who considered class struggle and race struggle as one and the same, especially with reference to the Jews, who were regarded as the embodiment of capitalism and German–Marxist internationalism. Karl Popper, the Jewish born Fabian economist from Vienna turned Lutheran and Marxist, was a follower of Edward Bellamy's "national" form of "socialism" from early on. Popper read Edward Bellamy's "Looking Backward" around 1914, and "socialism and nationalism would remain Popper's preoccupation throughout his life." [212]

The politically radical scientists behind the eugenics movement certainly believed in a marriage between xenophobia and socialism. Karl Pearson, the Fabian mathematician and first chair of the eugenics department at the University of London was born Carl but changed his name to Karl after becoming a devoted Marxist. Pearson is identified by historians for his devotion to Francis Galton. Like many other Darwinists, Pearson took the next step in applying Darwinism and eugenics to social planning. Pearson belonged to the Fabian Socialist circle of radical intellectuals assembling around Eleanor Marx, Havelock Ellis, George Bernhard Shaw, and Sidney and Beatrice Webb. Pearson too defined his Darwinism as applying to entire nations and saw "war" against "inferior races" as a logical implication of

---

[212] Pgs. 67-68 - "Karl Popper: The Formative Years, 1902-1945," Malachi Haim Hacohen, Cambridge Univ. Press, 2002.

his science.

> My view — and I think it may be called the scientific view of a nation . . . is that of an organized whole, kept up to a high pitch of internal efficiency by insuring that its numbers are substantially recruited from the better stocks, and kept up to a high pitch of external efficiency by contest, chiefly by way of war with inferior races. (Pgs. 43 – 44, "National Life from the Standpoint of Science", 1901, as quoted by "Biometrics: Bodies, Technologies, Biopolitics" by Joseph Pugliese, Pg. 46)

Pearson was a "rather jingoistic patriot" who "embraced an authoritarian 'national socialism'." [213] Pearson's 1888 "Ethic of Free Thought" and his 1889 "Natural Inheritance" proposed a racial war of the scope that Hitler would later carry out:

> ...was warlike at the macro level. Socialists were acting in accordance with biological law by regulating internal conflict within their society, because by doing so they conferred advantage upon themselves in the wider struggle being constantly waged between societies for markets, living space, power and racial domination. There would be at least two types of selection under socialism. There would be 'physical selection', the struggle of the group against its physical environment, against disease and climate. Then there would be the selection caused by 'the struggle of superior with inferior races, especially of civilized with uncivilized man' (Pg. 88, "Darwinism, War, and History: The Debate over the Biology of War from the 'Origin of species' to the First World War", David Paul Cook, Cambridge Univ. Press, 1994)

In 1900, Pearson gave a lecture titled "National Life from the Standpoint of Science" and further expounded his views of a state based on racial principles and eugenics in a fashion that could easily have been lifted from National Socialist propaganda:

> History shows me one way, and one way only, in which a high state of civilization has been produced, namely, the struggle of race with race, and the survival of the physically and mentally fitter race. If you want to know whether the lower races of man can evolve a higher type, I fear the only course is to leave them to fight it out among themselves, and even then the struggle for existence between individual and individual, between tribe and tribe, may not be supported by that physical selection due to a particular climate on which probably so much of the Aryan's success depended... (wright.edu, "Karl Pearson: National Life from the Standpoint of Science")

This list *Nationalistische* predecessors to Hitler would be immeasurably longer if the criteria of being a "nationalist" was taken in consideration apart from being a "socialist." There are plenty of "nationalists" whose impetus is an enhanced form of patriotism, but whom otherwise do not practice or preach any form of "racialist,"

---

[213] Pg. 87 - "Darwinism, War, and History: The Debate over the Biology of War from the 'Origin of species' to the First World War", David Paul Cook, Cambridge Univ. Press, 1994.

"racist," "eugenic," or other forms of segregation, or the desire to sterilize or exterminate portions of the population. That was certainly the case with the Italian and Spanish Fascists who never made any discernible effort towards ethnic cleansing. Clearly, the one source for a "nationalized" form of "socialism" that was a commonly held inspiration around the world was that of Edward Bellamy. Traditional nationalists, as such, cannot be considered as the precursors to Hitler's flavor of "nationalist-socialism." Verifiable history weighs heavily against this claim.

Furthermore, the leading eugenicists had espoused the economic policies now commonly attributed to National Socialism. "The Accountant" edition of 1903 editorialized on this link between Henry George's "municipalization" and Edward Bellamy's "nationalization." [214] Using government to confiscate significant sectors of industry and subsequently make the services or industries government-run were ideas central to Henry George in Britain and Edward Bellamy in the United States. "The Accountant" documents that in Britain, the movement went under the flags of "Municipal Trading," "Municipal Enterprise," "The Socialist Idea," and "Municipal Socialism." The article in "The Accountant" answers several other contemporary articles in The Times on the topic of deficit spending to fund or erect the "municipally" owned enterprises and pointed out their similarity to Edward Bellamy's "nationalization," a book the author felt most everyone at the time had read.

More to the point, "Municipalization," was extensively written and lectured about by Leonard Darwin. The 1907 book "Municipal Ownership" by Leonard Darwin was based on four lectures he delivered at Harvard. It gives insight on where Leonard Darwin stood in the British political map. Leonard Darwin, as can be expected from his utopian eugenic views, was a "central planner." He believed there to be an aristocratic or scientific elite that had the right and/or ability to plan humanity. What he calls for in "Municipal Ownership" is in essence "control" by the state of a planned economy where major industry is brought under "national" or "municipal" control:

> This enquiry concerning private industry is a necessary preliminary to a study of municipal ownership; because, in cases where municipal ownership would now be an improvement on private industry, it would not necessarily be so if private industry were better controlled. (Pg. 8, "Municipal Ownership: Four Lectures Delivered at Harvard University 1907")

What Leonard Darwin is describing by "Municipal Ownership" or "Municipal Trade" is what Edward Bellamy and Adolf Hitler understood as "nationalization." Among the pros and cons in Leonard Darwin's analysis is the question of where the benefit will land, and how the investment in nationalized industry will serve the "socialistic" ends of "distributed wealth," a political notion that remains a staple of the Progressive, Fabian, and Socialist "Left."

Still, Hitler's "nationalism" has consistently been confused with "conservatism." Why? Any policies geared toward engendering a "*Völkisch*" attitude in Germany was

---

[214] Pg. 127 - The Accountant, Jan. 24, 1903.

a policy of "racial conscience" and more in line with Darwinian theory than any middle-class or bourgeois religious values of the era. More importantly, any lip service Hitler played towards "family" or "middle class" was hardly a sentiment towards the values Hitler himself held. Hitler was an artist and would never have lowered himself to participate in the bourgeois lifestyle he claimed to protect. That he saw the quaint Germanic lifestyle as worth protecting is more indicative of his self-appointed role of master planner than of any indication that Hitler himself identified with the lifestyle. Hitler's friend and roommate, August Kubizek attested to the pains which Hitler avoided contact with the very "people" he was supposedly fond of. Hitler was the stereotypical artist type that ranted and raved endlessly about the plight of the masses but would never be caught dead mingling among them. Kubizek states this in no uncertain terms. Hitler never sought out the people of the "Imperial City," mostly because he voiced a pronounced disdain for the common Viennese. [215] Hitler no more belonged to the typical German people than he did to its ruling elements. Hitler was an artist and political radical. Ernst Hanfstaengl is explicit about Hitler's peculiar nature in his 1957 book. Hanfstaengl, who described himself as a supporter of the liberal German monarchy, defined Hitler's nationalism and socialism:

> When I talked of National-Socialism I meant it in the old Friedrich Naumann sense, a fusion of all that was best in the traditional and socialist elements of the community. Hitler was not thinking along the lines of a patriotic confederation of this sort at all. When he talked of National-Socialism what he really meant was military-Socialism, Socialism within a framework of military discipline or, in civilian terms, police-Socialism. At what point along the line his mind took the final shape it did I do not know, but the germ was always there. (Pgs. 70-71, "I Iitler: The Memoir of the Nazi Insider Who Turned Against the Fuhrer", 1957, Republished by Arcade Pub., 2011)

Göring, Speer, Goebbels, and Hitler would all provide this definition of "National Socialism," and it was along the "militaristic" lines that Edward Bellamy would otherwise characterize as an "industrial army" of civilians, all marching lock-step towards a unified goal. As Hanfstaengl clarifies, Hitler certainly did not subscribe to the "international" socialism, as was traditionally understood by the Communists and Bolsheviks of the era. Hitler would never allow his Nordic culture to be subsumed under an "international" structure, which blurred cultural or racial lines and treated Nordics and Aryans on an equal footing with Slavs and Frenchmen. Neither would have the French or British Fabians for that matter. It is of note that Edward Bellamy's "nationalized" brand of "socialism" also worked along eugenic demarcations.

As far as the commonplace conspiracy theories that Hitler was supported by big-money "conservatives," "industrialists," and that National Socialism was a political move of the "Right," Ernst Hanfstaengl's testimony would indicate otherwise. Hanfstaengl spent many years trying to get Hitler to appeal to the wealthy

---

[215] Pg. 163, "The Young Hitler I Knew: The Memoirs of Hitler's Childhood Friend", August Kubizek, 1955.

monarchists and traditional business leaders like himself but reports only frustration and little success. The industrialists that supported Hitler financially and politically are J.F. Lehmann, the devoted publicist for all eugenic and racial hygiene ideas, and Krupp, the amateur biologist who gave the money for the Krupp Competition that asked eugenicists how they would make Darwinism applicable to socio-economic policies.

Most revealing is that Hitler had no ambition for personal wealth as can be said about Hermann Göring, and thus, no need for financial sponsors to whom he would be indebted or beholden. In this aspect, all that were close to Hitler agreed. Aside from his art collection, which Hitler was amassing only to put it in a museum of his design in his town of Linz, Hitler was immune to the allure of money. Hitler had a desire for power, but not the spoils of power. Hitler wanted power for the sake of what power could accomplish: the remaking of the world to his liking. All of Hitler's biggest delights came from either an architectural or artistic remaking of Germany, none of which were projects intended to increase his personal wealth.

As far as Hitler's "conservatism," it must also be understood that there is no scenario where Hitler would have shared power with the "conservative" seats of power of the era like the Church, the monarchy, or the capitalists in any way, shape, or form. All of these were his sworn enemies, which in his twisted logic, were the products of a "Jewified" modernity. Ernst Hanfstaengl testifies as much:

> But when they made veiled suggestions about a political alliance, Hitler shied away. "I know these people," he told me, "their own meetings are empty and they want me to come along and fill the hall for them and then split the proceeds. We National-Socialist have our own programme and they can join up with us if they like, but I will not come in as a subordinate ally." (Pg. 42, "Hitler: The Memoir of the Nazi Insider Who Turned Against the Fuhrer", 1957, Republished by Arcade Pub., 2011)

If anyone in Hitler's inner circle had the means and ability to create an alliance between wealthy American and German businessmen, it was Ernst Hanfstaengl. Hanfstaengl was a Harvard graduate with all the friendships and connections it implied. His family owned an art gallery in New York's Fifth Avenue, where figures no less famous than T.S. Eliot, Walter Lippmann, and John Reed were among his clients. He was a member of the Harvard Club in New York and as part of it had friendships with Franklin D. Roosevelt and his son, prior to the presidency. Hanfstaengl's lawyer was none other than Senator Elihu Root, who became Theodore Roosevelt's Secretary of State. He had married Helene Niemeyer, the daughter of a wealthy German-American industrialist, and Hanfstaengl's mother was from the famous New England family descending from General John Sedgwick, one of President Lincoln's generals during the American Civil War and a famous West Point graduate. His grandfather, William Heine, was another famous Civil War general whose parents were personal friends of Mark Twain. Needless to say, Hanfstaengl had all the traditional political and capitalist connections any aspiring politician would need, if they actually wanted them, which as Hanfstaengl documents, Hitler did not.

Hitler's political aspirations, along with his definition of "nationalism," are self-explanatory when understood in the context of his eugenic and racial policies. According to the accounts of August Kubizek, Hitler's childhood friend, Hitler was a Pan-German from his early childhood. It must also be remembered that Adolf Hitler was by all accounts the typical miscreant artist, whose intellectual zealotry made him hostile towards people and ideas he considered lesser to himself. Hitler's xenophobia was intellectual zealotry based fully on the works of philosophers and scientists of the 19th century who had divided humanity up into racial rivalries and deemed them "natural" enemies. Hitler's "Germania" included "Nordics" living within the boundaries of Poland, the Czech Republic, Austria, the French side of Alsace Loraine, and just about all of Scandinavia, Britain, and the United States, and if his "Thousand Year Reich" would have endured, the map of the region would likely have been redrawn along the definition of "Germany" that is in actuality more like the definition of "Nordic" geography. Some light may also be shed by remembering that Hitler thought of German Jews as a "nation within a nation." Despite their loyal service during World War I, Hitler did not consider German Jews his compatriots. They were not part of his "nation." Hitler's "nation" was a Pan-German "Aryan nation."

So why did Hitler so adamantly pursue a "socialist" domestic policy under National Socialism? If Hitler was sympathetic to "socialism" and desired to implement a totalitarian and centrally planned governmental scheme, as found in the USSR, then why his outspoken animosity towards "Communism." To understand this aspect of Hitler, one must first understand that Hitler was clear that his hostility was towards "international" socialism, or "international" communism, or "international" Bolshevism, and not the governmental structure itself. It goes without saying that Hitler would have been against anything that would engulf his Aryan and Teutonic people into an "international" one-world government with no racial or national distinctions.

Recall that Hitler's understanding of how the world's economy worked was gleaned from Henry Ford's proclamations against the "International Jew." Below are excerpts from Hitler's "Mein Kampf" that describe his conception of how Bolshevism, Communism, Socialism and even Capitalism are all "internationalist" movements meant to serve an "international" Jewish conspiracy. One could argue that these conceptions are a depraved reality. However, it is this reality that drove both Hitler and his many followers to adopt a "Nationalist" form of solidarity. It is this "*volk*" or folk solidarity which Hitler defined as the "Socialist" component of National Socialism. "Nationalism" was not enough for Hitler. The "*volk*" solidarity is what made all "nationalist" aspirations viable:

> The **internationalization** of our German economic system, that is to say, the transference of our productive forces to the control of Jewish international finance, can be completely carried out only in a State that has been politically Bolshevized. (emphasis mine, gutenberg.net.au, Pg. 523 book version, "Mein Kampf", James Murphy translation)

For Hitler, "nationalization" was a way to encircle and define a "racial" group, regardless of where borders were drawn at the moment, and to differentiate them from races of people that were deemed to be of lesser biological worth. "Nationalism," for Hitler was a racial idea well within Darwinian ideological boundaries, and not the "God and country" type of patriotism as is commonly understood. Hitler's call to arms was a pagan-naturalistic "blood and soil," with the "blood" being a direct allusion to race. Below are quotes from "Mein Kampf" that help clarify Hitler's definition of "Marxism," "Bolshevism," and "Internationalism":

> The nationalization of the masses can be successfully achieved only if, in the positive struggle to win the soul of the people, those who spread the **international** poison among them are exterminated. (emphasis mine, Pg. 292)

CONTINUES . . .

> The assumption that all races are alike leads to the assumption that nations and individuals are equal to one another. And **international Marxism** is nothing but the application – effected by the Jew, Karl Marx – of a general conception of life to a definite profession of political faith. (emphasis mine, gutenberg.net.au, Pg. 328 book version, "Mein Kampf", James Murphy translation)

Henry Ford's influence was therefore significant. One can read "Mein Kampf" and "The International Jew" and easily confuse one for the other, again evidencing Hitler's inclination towards plagiarism. More to the point, Hitler's definition of the "Jewish" and "international" likely originated with or was highly influenced by Ford, the only American to be mentioned by name in "Mein Kampf":

> The real organizer of the Revolution and the actual wire-puller behind it, the **international** Jew, had sized up the situation correctly. The German people were not yet ripe to be drawn into the blood swamp of Bolshevism. (emphasis mine, Pg. 442, "Mein Kampf", James Murphy translation)

An effective way to define what National Socialism was is to also define what it was not. National Socialism was a collectivist form of centrally planned government. To state otherwise would be to entertain the ridiculous, as it is obvious that Hitler would not share power as in a *laissez-faire* type economy. To the contrary, Hitler continually and consistently railed against capitalism as being Jewish, and *laissez-faire* democracy as being "degenerate." Here are excerpts from Hitler's "Mein Kampf" defining the boundaries of his concept of "nationalism" and its relation to "socialism":

> The National Socialist Trades Union is not an instrument for class warfare, but a representative organ of the various occupations and callings. The National Socialist State recognizes no "classes." (Pg. 504, "Mein Kampf", James Murphy translation)

Hitler's National Socialism was a populist party geared towards benefiting the "people," not the moneyed interests. This is evidenced by the Third Reich's obsession with naming everything as *Volk*, including the "people's drink," the "people's art," and the *Volkswagen*, the "people's car":

> The National Socialist Movement, which aims at establishing the National Socialist People's State, must always bear steadfastly in mind the principle that every future institution under that State must be rooted in the movement itself. (Pg. 503, "Mein Kampf", James Murphy translation)

Thus, it was a hallmark of National Socialist domestic policy to do everything to win over the masses and to win their support and approval, not by coercion and fear, as is commonly thought, but by winning their hearts and minds. The general support by the German population evidences this. The history is clear that Germans that were dedicated to Hitler, were so not out of fear, but out of admiration and appreciation for the improvements he had made within Germany and for the German people. Passages from "Mein Kampf" indicate that this was intentional:

> As early as 1919 we were convinced that the nationalization of the masses would have to constitute the first and paramount aim of the new movement. ---- The nationalization of the broad masses can never be achieved by half-measures – that is to say, by feebly insisting on what is called the objective side of the question – but only by a ruthless and devoted insistence on the one aim which must be achieved. This means that a people cannot be made "national" according to the signification attached to that word by our **bourgeois** class to-day – that is to say, nationalism with many reservations – but national in the vehement and extreme sense. (emphasis mine, gutenberg.net.au, Pgs. 290-292 book version, "Mein Kampf", James Murphy translation)

Clearly, Hitler regarded the pedestrian definition of "nationalism" as "bourgeois," a term that need not be qualified as socialist in origin. Furthermore, as was the case with any socialist system, including the American Progressives beginning with Edward Bellamy's "nationalized" form of "socialism," a unified and coordinated educational system was indispensable:

> Such conduct is not the manifestation of a malicious intent, nor is it the outcome of orders given from 'above', as we say; but such a lack of national grit and determination is due to defects in our educational system. ---- The education which makes them the devotees of such abstract notions as 'Democracy', **'International Socialism'**, 'Pacifism', etc., is so hard-and-fast and exclusive and, operating as it does from within outwards, is so purely subjective that in forming their general picture of outside life as a whole they are fundamentally influenced by these a priori notions. (emphasis mine, gutenberg.net.au, Pg. 105 book version, "Mein Kampf", James Murphy translation)

The "revulsion" and "reactionary" attitude towards traditional monarchies are explained in "Mein Kampf" as well, and this serves as a significant line of demarcation between Hitler's National Socialism and Franco's and Mussolini's Fascism. Both Franco and Mussolini not only maintained the traditional monarchies of Spain and Italy into their governments but respected the supreme power of the Catholic Church in both of those cultures. A "conservative" in Hitler's time was a monarchist loyal to the preservation of the monarchy and clergy. Clearly, preserving any monarchy directly implied destroying the dreams of the Pan-German nationalists. Thus, Hitler's "nationalism" is not evidence of his "conservatism" but rather his "radicalism":

> After the great war of 1870-71 the House of Habsburg set to work with all its determination to exterminate the dangerous German element – about whose inner feelings and attitude there could be no doubt – slowly but deliberately. I use the word exterminate, because that alone expresses what must have been the final result of the Slavophile policy. Then it was that the fire of rebellion blazed up among the people whose extermination had been decreed. – For the first time nationalists and patriots were transformed into rebels. ---- for the first time in modern history the traditional dynastic patriotism and national love of fatherland and people were in open conflict. It was to the merit of the Pan-German movement in Austria during the closing decade of the last century that it pointed out clearly and unequivocally that a Stat is entitled to demand respect and protection for its authority only when such authority is administered in accordance with the interests of the nation, or at least not in a manner detrimental to those interests. – Generally speaking, we must not forget that the highest aim of human existence is not the maintenance of a State of Government but rather the conservation of the race. (gutenberg.net.au, Pgs. 90-91 book version, "Mein Kampf", James Murphy translation)

As mentioned above, one can easily confuse what was written in "The International Jew" with what Hitler would later incorporate into "Mein Kampf" and into his usual speeches. In consideration of the profound impact "The International Jew" had on Adolf Hitler, we must look at Ford's definition of similar concepts. Below are excerpts from Henry Ford's "The International Jew," which define the boundaries of what is meant by "national" and "international," as well as their respective racial connotations:

> Whatever else may be national, no one today believes that finance is national. Finance is international. Nobody today believes that international finance is in any way competitive. These are some independent banking houses, but few strong independent ones. The great masters, the few whose minds see clearly the entire play of the plan. (Pg. 20)

CONTINUES...

> The main source of the sickness of the German national body is charged to be the influence of the Jews, and although this was apparent to acute minds years ago, it is now said to have gone so far as to be apparent to the least observing. ----- It is the belief of all classes of the German people that the collapse which has come since the armistice, and the revolution from which they are being prevented a recovery, are the result of Jewish intrigue and purpose. ---- The Jew in Germany

is regarded as only a guest of the people; he has offended by trying to turn himself into the host. (Pg. 23)

CONTINUES . . .

In modern times, however, the Jew has found a means of knocking down the walls and throwing the whole national house into confusion, and in the darkness and riot that follows, seize the place he has long coveted. When Russia broke, who came first to light? Kerensky, who is a Jew. But his plans were not radical enough, and then came Trotsky, another Jew. Trotsky found the system too strong for him to break in America – he broke through the weak spot in Russia and would extend that weakness round the world. Every commissar in Russia today is a Jew. (archive.org, Pg. 29, Chap.: Germany's Reaction Against the Jew, "The International Jew", Dearborn Publishing Company – Dearborn Independent, 1920-1922)

Adolf Hitler could have claimed authorship of the above extract from the "Dearborn Independent" and no historian would be the wiser. The commonalities are more than coincidental. Hitler adopted from Henry Ford the idea that Jews were in control of all critical capital, journalism, and propaganda as an international Jewish conspiracy:
> The name which is given in Germany to this State which circulates among all the states is "All-Judeaan. The means of power of the State of All-Judaan are capital and journalism, or money and propaganda. – All-Judaan is the only State that exercises world government; all the other States can and may exercise national government only. (archive.org, Pg. 30, "The International Jew", Dearborn Publishing Company – Dearborn Independent, 1920-1922)

Hitler's notion that it was the Jews that manipulated the world into WWI and which pulled the strings to pit Germans against the Allies, despite their racial commonalities, was also directly the influence of Henry Ford:
> It is the whole truth that Jewish finance in all the countries was interested in Bolshevism as an All-Jewish investment. For the whole period of the war, the Jewish World Program was cloaked under this or that national name – the blame being laid on the Germans by the Allies, and on the Allies by the Germans, and the people kept in ignorance of who the real personages were. (archive.org, Pg. 228, Chap.: Jewish Testimony in Favor of Bolshevism, "The International Jew", Dearborn Publishing Company – Dearborn Independent, 1920-1922)

Here are excerpts from "The International Jew" on the meaning of "socialism" as juxtaposed to "Bolshevism," and that it was "international socialism" which was a Jewish enterprise, and not "socialism" of a Gentile flavoring:
> There is, of course, the evidence brought to light by our own United States Senate and printed in a Report of the Committee on the Judiciary. ---- William Chapin Huntington, who was commercial attaché of the United States Embassy

at Petrograd, testified: "The leaders of the movement, I should say, are about two-thirds Russian Jews. The **Bolsheviks are internationalists**, and they were not interested in the particular national ideals of Russia." (emphasis mine, Pg. 218)

CONTINUES . . .

Bolshevism aims for the overthrow of existing society and the establishment of an **international** brotherhood of men who work with their hands as rulers of the world. The second movement aims for the establishment of a new racial domination of the world. So far as the British, French and our own department's inquiry have been able to trace, the moving spirits in the second scheme are Jewish radicals. (archive.org, Pg. 99, "The International Jew", Dearborn Publishing Company – Dearborn Independent, 1920-1922)

The emphasis on "international" should by now be clear. That which was Bolshevik and Jewish was deemed "international," and Hitler's counter-revolution would be a "national" one.

The denial of the Jewish character of Bolshevism is made to the Gentile; but in the confidence and secrecy of Jewish communication, or buried in the Yiddish dialect, or obscurely hidden in the Jewish national press, we find the proud assertion made – to their own people! – that Bolshevism is Jewish. (Pg. 214, Chptr.: The All-Jewish Mark on "Red Russia", "The International Jew", Dearborn Publishing Company – Dearborn Independent, 1920-1922)

However, Ford is significantly different than Hitler in his capacity for sober-minded thought. Henry Ford claimed to have Jewish friends, and he was not lying. Henry Ford documents why he associated Jews with "internationalism," even though the definition did not apply to powerless Jews:

Now, this **international** type of Jew, this grasper after world-control, this actual possessor and wielder of world-control is a very unfortunate connection for his race to have. The most unfortunate thing about the **international** Jew, from the standpoint of the ordinary Jew, is that the **international** type is also a Jew. And the significance of this is that the type does not grow anywhere else than on a Jewish stem. There is no other racial nor national type which puts forth this kind of person. It is not merely that there are a few Jews among **international** financial controllers; it is that these world controllers are exclusively Jews. ---- This brings another difficulty: in discussing this group of world-controllers under the name of Jews (and they are Jews), it is not always possible to stop and distinguish the group of Jews that is meant. The candid reader can usually determine that, but the Jew who is in a state of mind to be injured is sometimes pained by reading as a charge against himself what was intended for the upper group. "Then why not discuss the upper group as financiers and not as Jews?" may be asked. Because they are Jews. It is not to the point to insist that in any list of rich men there are more Gentiles than Jews; we are not talking about merely rich men who have, many of them, gained their riches by serving a System, we are talking about those who Control ---- The **international** Jew, as already defined, rules not because he is rich, but because in a most marked degree he possesses the commercial and masterful genius of his race, and avails himself of a racial loyalty and solidarity the like of which exists in no other human group. (emphasis mine, archive.org, Pg. 47, "The International Jew", Dearborn Publishing Company – Dearborn Independent, 1920-1922)

Thus, one thing must be clarified for posterity. However, much Henry Ford's anti-Semitism may be insulting, abrasive and even fanatical, Hitler did not get his genocidal policies from Henry Ford. In retrospect, the eugenic policies woven into "Mein Kampf" are vague in comparison to the very specific calls for segregation, extermination, euthanasia, and sterilization explicitly mapped out and described by writers such as H.G. Wells, Leonard Darwin, Karl Pearson, Julian Huxley, Charles B. Davenport, and Harry H. Laughlin. In fact, the correspondence between Leon Whitney, C.M. Goethe, and Harry H. Laughlin document precisely this point. The American eugenicists tried and repeatedly failed to recruit Henry Ford to their eugenic campaigns. A letter from C.M. Goethe to Leon Whitney, copied to Laughlin, says as much:

> Regarding Mr. Ford, may I say very confidentially, that my judgment is his ideals are directed more toward giving employment to as many men as possible than toward contributing to such work as ours. I served on a national board with him once. I have no recollection of his ever having contributed to its work. I think he lacks the vision of Mr. Eastman and both Mr. Rockefeller and his father in this matter. (Box: C-4-1:2 - C.M. Goethe to L. Whitney, 5/3/1926, Harry Laughlin Papers, Truman Univ. Archives, Special Collections)

When it comes to the eugenic aspects of "Mein Kampf" one can find stronger parallels in the works of H.G. Wells than Henry Ford. Much in the same way that the anti-Semitic musings written into "The International Jew" are interchangeable with the anti-Marxist, anti-Internationalist, and anti-Semitic passages of "Mein Kampf," the same can be said about the eugenic mindset that H.G. Wells writes into his "Modern Utopia" and "Anticipations." Both are not only violently anti-Semitic but go the extra step to explicitly encourage euthanasia and all the eugenic immigration, segregation and sterilization policies to an extent that even "Mein Kampf" does not delve into. This is not to say that Hitler got his eugenic theories from H.G. Wells, but that both Wells and Hitler got them from a common source.

So, if not by Henry Ford, who did Hitler learn his eugenics from? A chronological reading of Hitler's speeches indicates that eugenic notions made it into Hitler's repertoire around the time he was in jail, writing "Mein Kampf." Hitler's business manager, Max Amman, had been the one to propose that Hitler spend his time in prison writing his autobiography. Hitler, who had never fully mastered writing, was not keen on the idea at first. However, he agreed when it was suggested that he should dictate his thoughts to a ghostwriter. The prison authorities at Landsberg agreed to allow Hitler's chauffeur, Emile Maurice, to live in the prison in order to take dictation. Maurice, whose main talent was as a street fighter, was a poor writer and the job was eventually taken over by Rudolf Hess. Hess made a valiant attempt at turning Hitler's spoken ideas into prose. The result was predictably repetitive, confused and meandering. Hitler's rants did not transfer well to text, hence "Mein Kampf" reads as exactly what it is: a crude plagiarism of the disparate sources Hitler had consumed since his teenage years, influenced by and lifted from Henry Ford's publications, but further radicalized by the various eugenic books J.F. Lehmann had delivered to Hitler's jail cell.

The heavily edited and final version of the book was generally regarded as unreadable, and as a cacophony of rants and disparate thoughts. Historians like to quote the Italian Fascist dictator, Mussolini, as saying that the book was "a boring tome that I have never been able to read" and that it was "little more than commonplace clichés." [216] This criticism was valid, and it probably extends to most, if not all, of Hitler's socio-political and cultural views. Nothing Hitler stated in "Mein Kampf" can be considered to have been new to the readers of his era, and this is probably why Hitler's readers, even his most ardent followers, generally found the book to be intolerable. The more one studies the scientific racism of the era leading up to "Mein Kampf," the more one comes to terms with the fact that Hitler was an unoriginal plagiarist, and that the most likely reason "Mein Kampf" did not arouse moral indignation was because the same thoughts and policies had been previously extrapolated in the writings of respected social and scientific thinkers.

Winston Churchill's opinion of "Mein Kampf" is instrumental in understanding this last point. In his book "The Second World War," Winston Churchill felt no other book deserved more intensive scrutiny than "Mein Kampf." The hypocrisy in this statement has rarely, if at all, been called to question. Churchill was an avid supporter of eugenics in England. Author Sir Martin Gilbert is an honorary member and trustee of The Churchill Centre and is the official biographer of Sir Winston Churchill. Gilbert posted an article in the official Winston Churchill website in 2009. In this article, Gilbert documents that when Churchill was Home Secretary between February 1910 and October 1911, Churchill was in favor of segregation and sterilization of a class of persons contemporarily described as the "feeble-minded." One of the main pieces of evidence provided by Gilbert is the letter Churchill wrote to Prime Minister, H.H. Asquith, in December 1910:

> The unnatural and increasingly rapid growth of the Feeble-Minded and Insane classes, coupled as it is with a steady restriction among all the thrifty, energetic and superior stocks, constitutes a national and race danger which it is impossible to exaggerate. (theguardian.com, "The Churchill You Didn't Know", Nov. 27, 2007)

The above statement by itself could easily have been lifted from the pages of

---

[216] Pg. 4 – Introduction – "Hitler: Personal Recollections: Memoirs of Hitler From Those Who Knew Him", Heinz A. Heinz, Pen and Sword, 2014.

"Mein Kampf," but the uncomfortable reality is that the statement came from Winston Churchill, and it preceded Hitler by nearly 15 years. This was no passing notion for Churchill either. Churchill maintained his commitment to eugenics on through his appointment as vice president of the International Eugenics Conference of 1912, until to the culmination of his life's "aim" with the passing of the British Mental Deficiency Act in 1913.

This begs to question, what precisely did Winston Churchill think would change if more people had read "Mein Kampf"? The 1912 Eugenics Conference had provided Churchill with all the details of the eugenicist's plans for a pure Anglo-Saxon and Protestant race. What was the reason for Churchill's indignation then? Was the famous Briton only offended by Hitler's call for territorial expansion? Martin Gilbert documents that by 1910 Churchill was already making his transformation from conservative to liberal. Did "Mein Kampf's" call for the nationalization of industry, the abolition of private property in land ownership, or centrally planned economy worry the recently converted Fabian? Churchill fell under the influence of Beatrice and Sidney Webb, the leaders of the Fabian Society right around this time. [217] At one of her famous strategic dinner parties, Beatrice Webb introduced Churchill to a young protégé, William Beveridge, the economist who would ultimately implement many of John Maynard Keynes' Fabian economic policies once Churchill brought him into the Board of Trade. All these Britons were devoted eugenicists. There was clearly very little in "Mein Kampf's" eugenics, economic, or expansionist views that can honestly be said to come as a surprise to the Prime Minister, especially after one reads the extensive efforts Churchill made towards enacting eugenic policies in the United Kingdom.

Despite the uncomfortable parallels, Churchill's comment about "Mein Kampf" has been propagated by many historians, yet few of them elaborate on exactly who should have been appalled by "Mein Kampf's" ranting, or for what reason. All the Fabian supporters of England's Labour or Liberal Party were avid supporters of eugenics at the time that "Mein Kampf" was written. Exactly one decade before "Mein Kampf" was published, famous figures such as Helen Keller had made very public pronouncements in support of euthanizing babies born with serious congenital disabilities. [218] President Woodrow Wilson had enacted eugenic legislation while as Governor of New Jersey. President Theodore Roosevelt had been making eugenic remarks in the various books he published in the late 1880s and early 1890s. Charles Darwin had been anointed the second coming of scientific genius by then, and Francis Galton's eugenics had been accepted as fact by Darwinists throughout the modern world. Harvard, Yale, Princeton, Brown, and Columbia had professors regularly lecturing on eugenics as the science derived from Darwinian evolution. Roosevelt's New Deal policies mimicked those of the National Socialists, and nearly half of the states had eugenic legislation in the books, as had England and the various Scandinavian countries. Henry Ford's anti-Semitic publications were just as explicit as Hitler's but preceded Hitler by decades. So exactly who would have

---

[217] Mises.org, "Rethinking Churchill - Churchill and the New Liberalism", Ralph Raico, Nov. 14, 2008.
[218] "Physicians' juries for defective babies", Helen Keller, The New 3 Republic, December 18, 1915, pp. 173-74.

been outraged or forewarned by what was written in the pages of "Mein Kampf"?

The Jewish community in the United States protested both Hitler and Ford, with very little success, and with the unfortunate result of enraging Hitler at the expense of German Jews, both for boycotting German products and for boycotting his idol, Ford. More telling, the world had stood silent as both Lenin and Stalin manufactured famines to rid themselves of excess and undesired population. Genocide was hardly new to the world, thus any indications toward genocide by Hitler in "Mein Kampf" can hardly be said to have aroused suspicions. More precisely, it can be said that genocidal acts were commonplace in antiquity and that it is not until the world was forced to confront it through the advent of modern photography and filmmaking that these acts became deplorable to the collective conscience. The history of The Holocaust certainly points to the fact that without the photographs and film reels which General Eisenhower insisted upon, the collective revulsion at Hitler's policies may never have emerged. The eugenicists in the United States, Britain, and Scandinavia, were all openly speaking about eradicating anywhere between 5 percent and 15 percent of the population for eugenic purposes, as the writings of Leonard Darwin, Leon Whitney, and Harry H. Laughlin evidence. These "scientific" musings did not become unpopular until after the photographs and film reels of the extermination camps were screened for all to contemplate the stark realities of such policies. Thus, people could have read what Hitler wrote in "Mein Kampf" and have not shown more alarm than they did when reading the works of Francis Galton, Charles B. Davenport, Margaret Sanger, H.G. Wells, and George Bernard Shaw.

Furthermore, it must be remembered that the most respected philosophers and political thinkers of the era had a well-documented contempt for "compassion" and the traditional sentimentality of religion. The moral hardening that "Mein Kampf" called for was in vogue. Professor Gunnar Heinsohn wrote an article for the Journal of Genocide Research where he claims that Hitler also read Friedrich Nietzsche while in Landsberg prison in 1923. While many of Nietzsche's works have been criticized as being proto-Nazi, Nietzsche's followers aptly point to the oversimplification of Nietzsche's "overman" in comparison to Hitler's "master race." This oversimplification does not release Nietzsche from fault. It is Nietzsche's pronounced derision towards the traditional values of human compassion and the sentimentality that were ultimately crucial and indispensable towards committing genocide. The bottom line is that if one desires to enlist a population in participating in a protracted and methodical genocidal campaign, the first order of business is to harden their hearts and nullify their sentimentality. By the time Hitler wrote "Mein Kampf," this aspect of Nietzsche's thinking had pervaded and been accepted by the German intellectual elite. Heinsohn provides this 1882 Nietzsche quote in support:

> Sin is a Jewish feeling and a Jewish invention, and in view of this background to all Christian morality, Christianity was in fact out to "Jewify" the entire world. (Pg. 12, "What Makes the Holocaust a Uniquely Unique Genocide?", Gunnar Heinsohn, Journal of Genocide Research, 2000, 411–430)

Hitler's address at the 1929 party convention mirrors this disdain for human compassion that had been a part of mainline eugenics for decades before Hitler. Hitler explicitly claimed that "Jewish train of thought" was dysgenic at this rally:

> If one million children were born in Germany per year and 700,000 to 800,000 of the weakest eliminated, the énal result might possibly even be an increase of strength. The worst danger is that we are interrupting the natural selection process ourselves (by caring for the sick and weak). … The most far-sighted racial state of history, Sparta, systematically implemented these racial laws. (Pg. 416, "What Makes the Holocaust a Uniquely Unique Genocide?", Gunnar Heinsohn, Journal of Genocide Research, 2000, 2(3), 411–430)

Gunnar Heinsohn further quotes the first edition of Volume I of "Mein Kampf," where Hitler writes about destruction as ultimately being natural. Note the similarities to Charles Darwin's claims:

> A stronger race will banish the weaker ones, for in the end the instinct to survive will always break the ridiculous bonds of a so-called humanity of the individual, allowing the humanity of nature to take its place, a humanity which destroys the weak to provide space for the strong. (Pg. 416, "What Makes the Holocaust a Uniquely Unique Genocide?", Gunnar Heinsohn, Journal of Genocide Research, 2000, 2(3), 411–430)

It was human compassion that stood in the way of enacting a eugenic plan, and Hitler had very little convincing to do to sell this concept to his "Mein Kampf" readership. Professor Heinsohn details the concepts that Hitler was selling through "Mein Kampf." Note the intentional discarding of the "sanctity of life" concept:

> *Der neue Glaube* ("The new belief"), for example, replaced "Thou shalt not kill" with neo-archaic commandments concerning the "eternal struggle": The supposedly unanswerable question as to the content of Hitler's own anti-Semitism is answered by this author by pointing to Hitler's deadly animosity to the very core of the Jewish faith—the sanctity of life. Hitler wanted to reintroduce the archaic rights to (1) infanticide—to strengthen Germany internally by killing the handicapped including the newborn and to (2) genocide—to give Germany strategic superiority externally by annihilating the monotheistic people of the Ten Commandments whom—as distinct from the Ancient Israelites—he regarded as the first abolishers of these archaic practices. To Hitler the sanctity of life was the ultimate Jewish *"Weltanschauung"* which could be eliminated like any other ideology—e.g. the communism of the commissars in the Red Army—by exterminating its "carriers. (Pgs. 425 - 426, "What Makes the Holocaust a Uniquely Unique Genocide?", Gunnar Heinsohn, Journal of Genocide Research, 2000, 2(3), 411–430)

On July 25, 1933, just five days after becoming Chancellor and, more importantly, just days after signing the infamous Concordat with the Vatican, Hitler's Nazi youth leader, Baldur von Schirach, disbanded the Catholic Youth

League and forced its membership into the Hitler Youth. [219] Parents were pressured to take their children out of religious schools. This was all part of the regime's campaign to dislodge Christianity from German life, otherwise known as the *Kirchenkampf*, which ultimately led Martin Niemoller to create the Pastors' Emergency League that later transformed into the Confessing Church. However, the focus on youth was of paramount importance to Hitler. These were measures to remove the youth from the influence of "Jewification." Case in point, this Hitler Youth chant expresses precisely this anti-religious sentiment:

> *We follow not Christ, but Horst Wessel,*
> *Away with incense and Holy Water,*
> *The Church can go hang for all we care,*
> *The Swastika brings salvation on Earth.*[220]

Professor Heinsohn asks why the Holocaust was "a uniquely unique genocide?" Professor Heinsohn's conclusion is on point:

> Conclusion: The Holocaust was "uniquely unique"—this author claims—because it was a genocide for the purpose of reinstalling the right to genocide. Hitler was not unprecedented in ruthlessly and massively breaking the commandment "Thou shalt not kill!"; he was irreducibly distinct from other megamurderers by abrogating it. (Pgs. 424–425, "What Makes the Holocaust a Uniquely Unique Genocide?", Gunnar Heinsohn, Journal of Genocide Research, 2000, 2(3), 411–430)

On December 4, 1940, on or around the time when the killing of the handicapped accelerated, the High Consistory of Stuttgart, Reinhold Sautter, begged of Eugen Staehle to stop the transgression of divine law. Staehle was Hitler's official in charge of the gassing facilities in Grafeneck, Wuerttemberg. Staehle reprimanded Sautter by telling him that "'Thou shalt not kill,' is not a commandment of God at all but a Jewish invention." [221] Staehle dismissed Sautter as being a "*verjudet*," a victim of "Jewifcation." This was the core message of "Mein Kampf." This is what Adolf Hitler saw as the most significant obstacle to its eugenic program. It was a Nietzschean rejection of Judeo-Christian compassion and Enlightenment egalitarianism, which all mainline eugenicists shared. Professor Heinsohn quotes from "Mein Kampf":

> From time to time magazines call the attention of the bourgeoisie to another case of the first Negro ever to have become a lawyer, teacher, even a pastor or star tenor or the like. While the feeble-minded bourgeoisie marvels at this miraculous feat of trained performance, full of respect for this fabulous result of present-day pedagogy, the Jew slyly takes advantage of the opportunity to construct new proof of the correctness of his theory of the equality of human beings which it is his mission to hammer into the heads of the nations. It does not dawn on the

---

[219] Pgs. 234-235 – "The Rise and Fall of the Third Reich", William L. Shirer, Secker & Warburg, London; 1960.
[220] Pg. 251 - "The Third Reich in Power", Richard Evans, Penguin Books, 2006.
[221] Pg. 413 - "What Makes the Holocaust a Uniquely Unique Genocide?", Gunnar Heinsohn, Journal of Genocide Research, 2000, 2(3), 411–430.

degenerate bourgeois world that in truth what we have here is an offense against all reason, that it is outrageous lunacy to keep drilling a native anthropoid until one is convinced of having made a lawyer of him. (Pg. 413, "What Makes the Holocaust a Uniquely Unique Genocide?", Gunnar Heinsohn, Journal of Genocide Research, 2000, 2(3), 411–430)

Heinsohn cites a letter from Adolf Hitler to Martin Bormann dated February 3, 1945. Here, Heinsohn relies on Hugh Trevor-Roper and André Francois-Poncet:
> We use the term Jewish race merely for reasons of linguistic convenience, for in the real sense of the word, and from a genetic point of view there is no Jewish race. Present circumstances force upon us this characterization of the group of common race and intellect, to which all the Jews of the world profess their loyalty, regardless of the nationality identified in the passport of each individual. This group of persons we designate as the Jewish race. ---- The Jewish race is above all a community of the spirit. ---- Spiritual race is of a more solid and more durable kind than natural race. Wherever he goes, the Jew remains a Jew ---- presenting sad proof of the superiority of the 'spirit' over the flesh. (Pg. 412, "What Makes the Holocaust a Uniquely Unique Genocide?", Gunnar Heinsohn, Journal of Genocide Research, 2000, 2(3), 411–430 – Citing *"Hitlers Politisches Testament. Die Bormann Diktate vom Februar und April 1945", Albrecht Knaus*, 1981, Pgs. 66-69)

A lot of ink has been expended trying to decipher Hitler's racism. The above excerpt should be understood in the context of the timeline, as Adolf Hitler transitioned from a pedestrian type of racial prejudice as found in beer halls, towards a scientific racism, as found in the halls of Harvard and Oxford universities of the era. This is the point Heinsohn conclusively illustrates in his paper. Heinsohn quotes many Holocaust and Hitler historians in their praise for Brigitte Hamann's 1996 book "Hitler's Vienna." The book came as a shock to many researchers because the period of Hitler's life in Austria from 1889 to 1913, long regarded as the time when Hitler learned to be an anti-Semite, Hamann's book provides substantial evidence to the contrary. This was summarized by one of those scholars, Gordon A. Craig, in his review of the English translation of Hamann's book:
> Hamann tells us of a stormy discussion in 1910 about Empress Elizabeth's veneration for Heinrich Heine, in which Hitler defended the [German-Jewish] poet and regretted that there were no statues to him in Germany. In other discussions in the men's hostel, he was reported to have praised Maria Theresia's great reforming minister Joseph von Sonnenfels and Jewish musicians like Mendelssohn and Offenbach. He had Jewish friends with whom he discussed religious questions and the future of the Zionist movement and upon whom he could rely for loans and other help in his worst times. He always preferred to sell his watercolors to Jewish dealers, because he thought that they were more honest and gave him better prices. No reliable source has reported Hitler making any anti-Semitic remarks in his Vienna period; on the contrary, he was known to have expressed admiration for the courage with which the Jews had withstood a

long history of persecution. (Pg. 414, "What Makes the Holocaust a Uniquely Unique Genocide?", Gunnar Heinsohn, Journal of Genocide Research, 2000, 2(3), 411–430)

Heinsohn compels us to conclude that that Hitler's racism cannot be categorized as what could be called "guttural racism" and what Hitler would call *Radau-Antisemitismus* or "rowdy anti-Semitism." An analysis that paints in broad strokes and generalities is the wrong approach to such an important question. The question is not what type of racist Hitler was. A question formulated in such general terms is not precise enough for an in-depth historical analysis. There have always been, and always will be a sizeable number of racists in humanity, the majority of which never acts to physically harm another. Asking if someone was a racist serves little purpose when attempting to understand the impetus behind the "crimes against humanity." The more precise question is when Hitler turned genocidal. Hopefully, this book will help to answer that question by chronologically organizing the various influences and events that contextualize Hitler's genocidal intentions.

Furthermore, a personality profile of Hitler would demonstrate an almost effeminate temperament, that of an artist, someone who considers himself learned, and, most importantly, above pedestrian and commonplace. Hitler saw himself as better than someone who would engage in "rowdy anti-Semitism." Hitler's racism was that of an elitist, rooted in an artist's sentiment for the aesthetic, with pretensions of being rational and scientific. This is the picture that is painted by Albert Speer in his memoirs, as well as by his best friend August Kubizek. Kubizek's description of his opera-going partner is that of an effeminate artistic misfit, too weakly to do manual work, and too lazy and arrogant to maintain the routine of a regimented work schedule. This personality profile is also consistent with the reports from the WWII spy, Bella Fromm, as detailed in the "Office of Strategic Services, Adolf Hitler Source Book & Psychological Profile." [222]

In short, Hitler may have leveraged the typical street thug in the Brown Shirts, but he was not one himself. Hitler may have enjoyed arousing the guttural racism in the members of these groups, but he saw himself as above that. Hitler's racism was a plagiarized from Richard Wagner, Nietzsche, Henry Ford, H.G. Wells, Lothrop Stoddard, and Madison Grant. More importantly, Hitler's racism turned genocidal when J.F. Lehmann brought him the work of highly-respected eugenicists including Ernst Haeckel, Alfred Ploetz, Erwin Baur, Eugen Fischer, Fritz Lenz, Charles B. Davenport, Harry H. Laughlin, and Francis Galton, all of which indicated to Hitler that his elitist views about the supreme German man were scientifically justified, and worse, widely accepted by the leading minds around the world.

All in all, "Mein Kampf" was a work of plagiarism, and it is doubtful that its contents would have aroused much indignation at the time it was published, as the genocidal policies it espoused were those championed by the most prestigious scientists from the most prestigious institutions around the world. Its bitter hatred

---

[222] "Office of Strategic Services, Adolf Hitler Source Book & Psychological Profile", Available at nizkor.org.

for Jews had been popularized by world-famous individuals, namely Henry Ford and H.G. Wells. The anti-Semitism in "Mein Kampf" presented nothing new that had not been already been said publicly by both Henry Ford and H.G. Wells in equally explicit ways. "Mein Kampf" represents Hitler's dedication to the ideas he considered to be revolutionary and worth finally coalescing into a form of government, which although highly digested by the era's respected intellects, had never been implemented. One can look at H.G. Wells's various eugenic and socialist utopias and find too many commonalities with National Socialism to ignore. One can look at the Fabian Socialist politics, namely those extrapolated by eugenicist Leonard Darwin, and see the Third Reich's "nationalization" of industry. Most importantly, the "nationalized" form of "socialism" had already been made a popular goal by Edward Bellamy, and implemented by Franklin D. Roosevelt in his New Deal policies. The leaders of the Allied countries, namely Winston Churchill and Woodrow Wilson, had both been intensely involved in legalizing the eugenics that called for the segregation, sterilization, and eradication of entire swaths of the population. Their thoughts were backed up by prestigious institutions such as Harvard, Yale, and Stanford in the United States, and several generations of the famous Darwin-Galton family had dedicated their life's work towards the enacting of eugenics in the United Kingdom. In retrospect, "Mein Kampf" is useful only in preserving for all posterity precisely how entangled Hitler's policies are with the scientific and political concepts that survive to this day.

Sec. 2 - THE A.C.L.U's CIRCUS MONKEY:

The Scopes "Monkey Trials," which so many intellectuals do gratuitous chest-pounding over, was nothing more than a publicity stunt. Mr. Scopes' involvement in the so-called Monkey Trial came about after the American Civil Liberties Union (ACLU) announced that it would finance a test case challenging the constitutionality of the Butler Act if they could find a Tennessee teacher willing to be a defendant. The law officially known as Tenn. HB 185, 1925 specifically prohibited "any teacher" in any of the "Universities, Normals and all other public schools of the State" supported in whole or in part by the public school funds of the State," to teach "any theory" that denied the "Story of the Divine Creation of man as taught in the Bible, and to teach instead that man has descended from a lower order of animals." [223] A group of businessmen in Dayton, Tennessee, led by a New York transplant George Rappleyea, saw this as an opportunity to get publicity for the tiny town and approached one of the small town's teachers, Mr. Scopes. Rappleyea pointed out that while the Butler Act prohibited the teaching of human evolution, the state required teachers to use the assigned textbook, "Hunter's Civic Biology,"

---

[223] todayinsci.org, Public Acts of the State of Tennessee Passed by the Sixty - Fourth General Assembly, 1925, Chapter No. 27. House Bill No. 185.

which explicitly extrapolated the Darwinian evolution of man. Rappleyea correctly argued that teachers were essentially required to break the law. When asked about the test case, Scopes was initially reluctant to get involved, but after some discussion, he decided to cooperate as a defendant. As such, one can only conclude that the outrage surrounding this famous case was manufactured: Rappleyea both instigated the controversy and then filed the official complaint as "prosecutor." [224] Rappleyea stayed on top of his circus act, often sitting with the defense team during the trial though he was not an attorney, and hosted defense lawyers and expert witnesses at his home. [225] The duplicity by those allegedly on the side of academic freedom was exposed by the *quid pro quo*: Before leaving town, one of the defense's scientific experts asked Scopes if he was interested in attending graduate school. Scopes replied positively, especially if the opportunity were to study geology at the University of Chicago. A committee was organized to raise funds, headed by former Stanford University president and member of the eugenics movement, David Starr Jordan. However, the offer of free graduate school came with a condition; that Scopes would "adhere to the spirit of the evolution law." Scopes declined, ironically, not wanting to give up his academic freedom.

Despite celebrating this fabricated controversy for over 100 years, what historians have failed to mention is how "A Civic Biology: Presented in Problems," the textbook at issue, wholeheartedly propagated the views of the international eugenics movement. The chapter of the textbook that covered humanity had been penned by none other than Charles Benedict Davenport, the head of the Cold Spring Harbor Eugenic Records Office, and mentor to Harry H. Laughlin. While historians have feigned outrage over the alleged disservice of attempting to keep evolution out of the classrooms, they have equally forgotten the one chapter that everyone should have been paying attention to:

The Races of Man. -- At the present time there exist upon the earth five races or varieties of man, each very different from the other in instincts, social customs, and, to an extent, in structure. These are the Ethiopian or negro type, originating in Africa; the Malay or brown race, from the islands of the Pacific; The American Indian; the Mongolian or yellow race, including the natives of China, Japan, and the Eskimos; and finally, **the highest type of all, the Caucasians,** represented by the civilized white inhabitants of Europe and America. ...

Improvement of Man. - If the stock of domesticated animals can be improved, it is not unfair to ask if the health and vigor of the future generations of men and women on the earth might not be improved by applying to them the laws of selection. This improvement of the future race has a number of factors in which we as individuals may play a part. These are personal hygiene, selection of healthy mates, and the betterment of the environment.

Eugenics. - When people marry there are certain things that the individual as well as the race should demand. The most important of these is freedom from germ diseases which might be handed down to the offspring. Tuberculosis,

---

[224] "Evolution Case a Civil War of Thought Evolution", Philip Kinsley, Chicago Daily Tribune, May 31st, 1925, Pg. 12.
[225] moses.law.umn.edu - "George Washinton Rappleyea", The Clarence Darrow Digital Collection, Univ. of Minnesota.

syphilis, that dread disease which cripples and kills hundreds of thousands of innocent children, epilepsy, and feeble-mindedness are handicaps which it is not only unfair but criminal to hand down to posterity. The science of being well born is called eugenics. (emphasis mine, Pg. 261, Ch.: Heredity and Variations, "A Civic Biology: Presented in Problems", American Book Company, 1914)

By now, the reader will recognize the eugenic template, as well as its dire implications. The schoolhouse textbook mapped out the typical eugenic proposals that were the template of the movement:

Parasitism and its Cost to Society. -- Hundreds of families such as those described above exist today, spreading disease, immorality, and crime to all parts of this country. The cost to society of such families is very severe. Just as certain animals or plants become parasitic on other plants or animals, these families have become parasitic on society. They not only do harm to others by corrupting, stealing, or spreading disease, but they are actually protected and cared for by the state out of public money. Largely for them the poorhouse and the asylum exist. They take from society, but they give nothing in return. They are true parasites.

The Remedy. - If such people were lower animals, we would probably kill them off to prevent them from spreading. Humanity will not allow this, but we do have the remedy of separating the sexes in asylums or other places and in various ways preventing intermarriage and the possibilities of perpetuating such a low and degenerate race. Remedies of this sort have been tried successfully in Europe and are now meeting with some success in this country.

Blood Tells. - Eugenics shows us, on the other hand, in a study of the families in which are brilliant men and women, the fact that the descendants have received the good inheritance from their ancestors. The following, taken from Davenport's Heredity in Relationship to Eugenics, illustrates how one family has been famous in American History. (Pg. 263, Ch.: Heredity and Variations, "A Civic Biology: Presented in Problems", American Book Company, 1914)

Consider the above excerpt. Here was the textbook which would be used by American public-schools for several generations expounding the virtues of adopting precisely the central guiding principle of Hitler's National Socialism. Somehow, this aspect of the Scopes' Monkey Trial rarely, if ever, is told as part of this contentious event in American history. Never is it cited as a possible explanation for the all-too-common accusations of American racism or the causes behind 20th Century racial tensions. More so, the Scopes trial helps reveal a pattern in all of these so-called "test trials," like the one that decided the future of Carrie Buck in the infamous 1927 Buck v. Bell Supreme Court case. As was the case in the Nuremberg Doctors' Trial, the word "eugenics" was never used throughout these trials, despite being a central and unavoidable part of the evidence presented. This curious aspect of the case can be explained by the fact that both attorneys subscribed to the eugenic creed despite advertising themselves as representing diametrically opposed sides of the core argument, just like in the Buck v. Bell case.

Both Clarence Darrow and William Jennings Bryan had at some point vocally supported eugenics or had direct ties to the movement's organizations. Recall that Darrow had vocally supported Dr. Haiselden in his eugenic euthanasia campaign. Darrow sidestepped the issue during the Scopes Trial, only to write two scathing pieces that would appear in H.L. Mencken's magazine shortly after the end of the trial. [226] The very short amount of time separating the end of the Scopes Trial and the publication of the articles proves that Clarence Darrow held these views while the Scopes Trial elapsed. Scathing as Darrow's 1926 "The Eugenics Cult" was, Darrow never betrayed the ACLU by exposing the insidious nature of indoctrinating America's youth into the white-supremacist dogmas of said eugenics "cult."

Far from being the representative of anti-science fundamentalism, William Jennings Bryan was distinctly sympathetic to the cause of science, and not at all opposed to it as the mythos of the Scopes Trial suggests. Williams Jennings Bryan joined the American Association for the Advancement of Science in 1924. [227] The American Association for the Advancement of Science is a non-profit organization with the stated goals of promoting cooperation among scientists, defending scientific freedom, encouraging scientific responsibility, and supporting scientific education and science outreach for the betterment of all humanity. It is the world's largest general scientific society and is the publisher of the well-known scientific journal "Science." James Gilbert documents this curious aspect of Scopes Monkey Trial in the chapter entitled "William Jennings Bryan, Scientist":

> But the larger question is, why did Bryan join the AAAS in 1924? What was his motivation in pledging membership to the largest and most reputable scientific organization in the United States and one known, incidentally, for its vocal support of evolution theory? Quite clearly the answer has nothing to do with a run-up to the Scopes trial. The Tennessee antievolution law that created the case did not pass until the spring of 1925, well after he secured his membership. Neither the American Civil Liberties Union nor John Scopes had yet imagined initiating a test case for Darwinism. The explanation lies instead in taking seriously Bryan's assumption that he was, on his own terms at least, a scientist. Doing so reveals the sort of science to which he committed his soul and how, perhaps, millions of other Americans understood science.

CONTINUES...

> One of the most pointed of his testimonies came when he addressed the state legislature of West Virginia on 13 April 1923 as an expert witness on evolution theory and modern science. He repaid the attentive legislators with an extended lesson in chemistry. For his text Bryan took an interpretation of the second law of thermodynamics that appeared to nullify any possible natural evolution toward more complex life forms. (Pg. 27, "Redeeming Culture: American Religion in an Age of Science", University of Chicago Press, 2008)

As such, contrary to Scopes Monkey mythos, Bryan was not nearly as much of

---

[226] "The Eugenics Cult", Clarence Darrow, The American Mercury, V8, No. 30, June, 1926.
[227] Pg. 13 - "The Creationists: From Scientific Creationism to Intelligent Design," Ronald L. Numbers, Univ. of Ca., 2006.

a fundamentalist as many modern-day creationists, and was more accurately described as a "day-age creationist": "William Jennings Bryan, the much misunderstood leader of the post–World War I antievolution crusade, not only read the Mosaic "days" as geological "ages" but allowed for the possibility of organic evolution - so long as it did not impinge on the supernatural origin of Adam and Eve." [228] Needless to say, this is not the position of a fundamentalist or literal interpretation of Christian theology.

More to the point, Bryan served as Secretary of State under the Progressive and pro-eugenics radical, Woodrow Wilson. [229] Both Wilson's and Bryan's wives were part of the leadership of the National Society for the Promotion of Practical Eugenics. [230] William Jennings Bryan was also a devout Methodist during an era when the Methodist Church was intertwined with the American eugenics movement. If the architects of the Scopes Trial wanted to find someone to represent the Fundamentalist Christian view, or more precisely, defend the law that nothing else other than the "Story of the Divine Creation of man as taught in the Bible," as the law explicitly stipulated, then Bryan was not the best choice. The fact that he never once attacked the insidious eugenic views expounded in "Hunter's Civic Biology" proves that he was not opposed to the teaching of Darwinian theories of sexual selection and evolutionary hierarchies or Darwin's Theory as it specifically applied to mankind; the core argument as was advertised by the show trial's promoters.

Consider the consequences of teaching several generations of children the eugenic ideals extrapolated in "Hunter's Civic Biology." Ideas have consequences, especially when they are dogmatic ideals indoctrinated into the minds of generation after generation of impressionable youths. An article in "Science News," the child publication of the Washington D.C. Science Service, now the Society for Science and the Public, provides an open admission of the prejudice with which the publication has treated the role of science in politically sensitive topics. The March 1997 article admits fault in the fact that the biased coverage of the Scopes Trial lead the way for its uncritical coverage of eugenics later:

> In its early days, Science Service did not always display the objectivity so prized in journalism today. The service clearly breached the objectivity barrier in 1925 during the trial of John Scopes, who challenged a Tennessee law that forbade the teaching of evolution. Science Service staffers Davis and Frank Thone went to Tennessee to cover the trial that summer, filing dispatches that went into daily newspapers and SCIENCE NEWS LETTER. At the same time, Science Service was helping Clarence Darrow's defense team gather expert witnesses to testify on Scopes' behalf. After Scopes lost, Science Service raised funds for tuition so the teacher could continue his education. ----Throughout the 1920s, SCIENCE NEWS LETTER included extensive and uncritical coverage of eugenics, a favorite topic of many scientists and journalists at the time, including Davis, who

---

[228] Pg. 13 - "The Creationists: From Scientific Creationism to Intelligent Design," Ronald L. Numbers, Univ. of Ca., 2006.
[229] history.com - "The 'Trial of the Century' Draw National Attention", A&E Television Networks, Nov. 13th, 2009. – See Also: Pg. 13 - "The Creationists: From Scientific Creationism to Intelligent Design," Ronald L. Numbers, Univ. of Ca., 2006.
[230] Pg. 46 – "Three Generations no Imbeciles: Eugenics, the Supreme Court, and Buck v. Bell", Paul A. Lombardo, Johns Hopkins Univ. Press, 2008.

was a member of the board of the American Eugenics Society. The Jan. 19, 1924, issue described a report of the Eugenics Committee of the United States that favored the immigration of northwestern over southeastern Europeans. "Will Blending of Races Produce Super-men?" dominated the Nov. 26, 1927, issue. Based on the comments of a geneticist at the Carnegie Institution of Washington, the article discussed, most often in negative terms, offspring of various mixed ancestries. Slosson wrote that the public needed to understood that "the fate of the nation depends . . . on how they combine their chromosomes. (Pg. S10, Anna Maria Gillis, "From News Wire to Newsweekly: 75 years of Science Service", Science News, March 1, 1997)

"A Civic Biology" was used by American public-schools for several generations, despite the fact that it expounded the very dogma central to Hitler's National Socialism. In 1926, the year after the trial, a revised edition of Hunter's book appeared without the use of the word "evolution." However, the revised edition expanded its section on eugenics, albeit with some telling changes. The section "The Remedy" no longer included the sentence "If such people were lower animals, we would probably kill them off to prevent them from spreading. Humanity will not allow this," but, the explanation of the Jukes and Kallikak eugenic family studies was enlarged. It also seems that the Cold Spring Harbor studies by Harry H. Laughlin made their way into the text as the section titled "Parasitism and its Cost to Society" added the sentence "It is estimated that between 25% and 50% of all prisoners in penal institutions are feeble-minded." The section "The Races of Man" remained with the claim about "Caucasians" being "the highest type of all" was removed. This was obviously a case of admission by deletion. Clearly, the authors of "A Civic Biology" understood that the contentious dispute over evolution inescapably linked the Theory to its eugenic extrapolation.

The Darwin family certainly knew what was at play in the Scopes' Trial. It is interesting to note, that Leonard Darwin, the devoted eugenicist, wrote to John Scopes to offer emotional support. Leonard Darwin wrote to John Scopes: "May the son of Charles Darwin send you one word of warm encouragement. To state that which is true cannot be irreligious." [231]

---

[231] Pg. 7 - "Evolution in the Courtroom: A Reference Guide", Randy Moore, ABC-CLIO, 2002.

Sec. 3 - FROM REVOLUTIONARY TO STATESMAN:

In the early 20th century, hundreds or even thousands of Germans gathered together in beer halls often to engage in political or social debate. Political rallies in Germany are still commonly held at the local beer halls. One of the largest beer halls in Munich was the "*Bürgerbräukeller*," where the National Socialists decided to make their first attempt at taking over the German government. What we now refer to as the "Beer Hall Putsch," but Germans call the "Hitler-Ludendorff Putsch," was Hitler's failed attempt at revolution through violence.

On the evening of November 8, 1923, Adolf Hitler, Erich Ludendorff, and others unsuccessfully tried to seize power in Germany. Two days after the putsch, Hitler was arrested and charged with high treason in the special People's Court. His trial began on February 26th, 1924 and would last until April 1, 1924. Hitler was called to the stand and questioned about the intended violence and the nature of the National Socialist movement. Hitler personally paid for the failure of the putsch, and it was clear to Hitler that not only had violent revolution failed but that its failure exposed the limitations of the Strasser brothers and their militant thugs, the Brownshirts. Hitler defined their usefulness in his testimony, and it seems that by the time the trial rolled around, Hitler probably understood that the S.A. was necessary to keep the "Reds" from disrupting his public speaking gigs, but for not much else. Hitler would ultimately murder one of the Strasser brothers and disband the S.A. in 1934 in what became known as the "Night of the Long Knives." It is noteworthy that two of the opponents that had successfully stopped the Beer Hall Putsch were murdered along with Strasser in the Night of the Long Knives, thus exposing at least part of the motivation for the 1934 purge. While some historians would like to attribute this to the "leftists" being purged by the "rightists," the murder of Chancellor Kurt von Schleicher and Gustav Ritter von Kahr indicated otherwise. Furthermore, party insiders like Ernst Hanfstaengl, the Harvard educated New York art dealer, attributed Hitler's anger for their attempt to take power while he was in Landsberg. Hanfstaengl recalls in his 1957 book "Hitler" that while the trial made Hitler a nationally recognized figure, the typical animosities and political maneuvering increased inside the party because of Hitler's imprisonment:

> They called Hitler a dictator and a *prima donna* and proclaimed that he must be brought under greater control if the Party was ever to be built up again. He was generally blamed for the failure of the Putsch, which in retrospect they regarded as an over-hasty and ill-organized attempt to seize power. More dangerous still was the determination of Ludendorff to centre the control of the nationalist groups in his own hands and take advantage of Hitler's absence to neutralize him permanently. To achieve this and bring the banned but still functioning Nazi Party under his wing he called in Gregor Strasser to act as political leader and organizer. (Pg. 117, "Hitler: The Memoir of a Nazi Insider Who Turned against the Fuhrer", 1957, Republished by Arcade Pub., 2011)

Hitler and Hess were both sentenced to five years imprisonment for the crime of treason. Hitler spent 264 days in Landsberg, a jail that was designated a

Festungshaft prison. *Festungshaft* facilities were like a modern protective custody unit. Prisoners were excluded from forced labor and had reasonably comfortable cells. Despite the catastrophic failure of the putsch to achieve its initial goal, Hitler's subsequent testimony at trial succeeded brilliantly at capturing the hearts and minds of the German public. Every word he spoke was reported in the newspaper the following day. The event provided the National Socialists their first major and continued exposure to a national audience. The crowd in the room became loud enough that the judge had to warn Hitler that he would not allow a political speech. Yet, it quickly became an opportunity for Hitler to sound the basic premises of National Socialism. Notably, Hitler clarified that it was pitted against "Internationalism," "Democracy" and "Capitalism." He did not use the terms "Communist." Hitler only used "Marxist," and "Internationalist" when referencing Bolshevik style socialism. More interestingly, he claimed that his efforts were to compete "against the Fascists," obviously making a distinction between his movement and the then established Mussolini regime:

> There are in general three phenomena which always reappear at such times, when the country is declining and which have slowly disintegrated the German people also. The non-utilization of our own national strength brought about by the general international attitude. – The second factor is the setting aside of all authority and the third the pacifist spirit, the pandering to corrupt influences and the international feeling in general. It is obvious that the only kind of movement which could rise above this debacle is the one which makes a determined stand against these aspects. (Hitler's Testimony, Translation of Document No. 2512-PS. FRANKDURTER ZEITUNG, September 26, 1931, Translated November 1945)

Most importantly, Hitler's testimony marked the beginning of a change from violent revolutionary to a politician keenly observant of legality. Hitler's conversion towards respecting the law and achieving political power through legal means is noteworthy, as this is precisely what the National Socialists would accomplish through systematic and patient strategy. Most of the exchanges between Hitler and the judge (President), as documented by the official transcripts, were spent deliberating if the National Socialists intended to take power by "legal" or "illegal" means. Political calculation, manipulation, and propaganda were Adolf Hitler's strengths. Hitler may have outdone Machiavelli, but he certainly could not impose himself physically. While the failed Beer Hall Putsch made Hitler realize the limits of violent uprisings and of Strasser's SA, the brilliant success of his testimony at trial must have revealed the strength of propaganda. He basically said as much in his testimony, and anyone listening could have guessed at the direction National Socialism would take then afterward:

> Naturally a movement will always represent an uprising, but it does not need to prepare it by illegal means. If we were to have two or three elections today, the National Socialist movement would have the majority in the Reichstag and would prepare the National Socialist revolution then. ---- Our opponents are interested in representing our movement as anti-state, because they know our

goal is to be attained by legal means. – We honor the memory of the old German Empire, we have fought for it. But this State had an inner weakness from the very beginning. Out of it came the present Germany. It is the embodiment of Democracy and Internationalism. (lawcollections.library.cornell.edu, Donovan Nuremberg Trial Collection, Hitler's Testimony Before the Court for High Treason from Frankfurter Zeitung - 1st Morning Edition, 26 September 1931, Translation of Extract of Document 2512-PS / Office of US Chief of Counsel)

While many historians document the opportunity for grandstanding that this trial offered Hitler, few extrapolate what his message was. Even though Adolf Hitler and the judge (President) had already spent a significant amount of time deliberating on the intent to act "legally" or "illegally," the testimony ended with this exchange as if to highlight Hitler's strategy:

> **PRESIDENT:** How do you imagine the setting up of a Third Reich?
> **HITLER:** This term only describes the basis of the struggle but not the objective. We will enter the legal organizations and will make our Party a decisive factor in this way. But when we do possess constitutional rights then we will form the State in the manner which we consider to be the right one.
> **PRESIDENT:** This too by constitutional means?
> HITLER: Yes.

(lawcollections.library.cornell.edu, Donovan Nuremberg Trial Collection, Hitler's Testimony Before the Court for High Treason from Frankfurter Zeitung - 1st Morning Edition, 26 September 1931, Translation of Extract of Document 2512-PS / Office of US Chief of Counsel)

In retrospect, Hitler's grandstanding at the trial served the purpose of a modern-day "focus group." Hitler's appeal to achieving social change through legal venues played well with the German audience. Hitler often joked about how the German people and the German government was paying for his education while at Landsberg. Hitler's assessment is an accurate appraisal of the situation. History proves how focused and distilled Hitler's political goals became during his stay at Landsberg where he spent a significant amount of time reading and researching the topics that would ultimately fill the pages of "Mein Kampf." The political success resulting from the trial was palpable. Ernst Hanfstaengl documents the outpouring of respect and appreciation Hitler received while at Landsberg prison:

> The ascendancy he gained over the officials and guards at Landsberg was quite extraordinary. The gaolers even used to say *Heil Hitler* when they came into his cell. This was partly due to the extraordinary magnetism of his personality, and to his political martyrdom, which found a wide acclaim across many varied sections of the community. He received favored treatment, which included freedom to accept gifts of food from outside, and this again gave him a further hold over his warders. It was very easy to say 'take this box of chocolates home to your wife' when he had almost unlimited quantities available. He and Hess had not so much cells as a small suite of rooms forming an apartment. The place looked like a delicatessen store. You could have opened up a flower and fruit

and a wine shop with all the stuff stacked there. (Pg. 114, "Hitler: The Memoir of a Nazi Insider Who Turned against the Fuhrer", 1957, Republished by Arcade Pub. 2011)

This was undoubtedly a huge turn around for the defeated revolutionary. Ernst Hanfstaengl describes Hitler's physical appearance on the night of the Beer Hall Putsch, and provides insight into the power of Hitler's oratory skills, which would be on full display while taking the stand to testify before the German court:

> He could not have looked less like a revolutionary; he was more like a collector of taxes in his Sunday best. This was the extraordinary thing about him, he still looked utterly mediocre in repose. A certain quality in his eyes and a certain reserve in his manner were all that made you look twice. He was still distinctly subservient in his attitude, except, of course, when he began to speak, as he had just shown. Then he rose into something superhuman. It was the only element in which he felt himself totally at home. It was like the difference between a Stradivarius lying in its case, just a few bits of wood and lengths of catgut, and the same violin being played by a master. (Pg. 100, "Hitler: The Memoir of a Nazi Insider Who Turned against the Fuhrer", 1957, Republished by Arcade Pub., 2011)

In other words, Hitler entered Landsberg as an ill-groomed, barely known, provincial political agitator and emerged a political icon, with a new book to match his nation-wide notoriety. The failed Beer Hall Putsch and the stay at Landsberg distilled Adolf Hitler into the figure we outsiders recognize. The most important aspect of Hitler's stay at Landsberg is that this "free education" ultimately changed his views on the desirability of violent revolution. This lesson would stay with Hitler, as every change he made to German social life from then on was either based on existing law, or new laws were created to provide the appearance of legality. As a proximate result, the party itself was transformed along with Hitler. The National Socialist party that planned and embarked on the Beer Hall Putsch was largely indistinguishable from the various other reformist and revolutionary movements. The National Socialist party that emerged from prison was different and vastly more dangerous. This is the party that learned to create consensus through propaganda as no other political party had done so before them. For however much the National Socialists were prone to violence, it is unlikely they would have accomplished what they did without that patience and political positioning that ultimately handed them unbridled power. A National Socialist party that would have persisted in violence may have been stalled or forever entertained in its petty street fighting. In many ways, Hitler was most dangerous when he acted with patience and weakest when he moved with haste.

Sec. 4 - ONE-WORLD IMMIGRATION CONTROLS:

The Immigration Act of 1924, including the National Origins Act, and Asian Exclusion Act, were United States federal laws that limited the annual number of immigrants who could be admitted from any country to 2 percent of the number of people from that country who were already living in the United States in 1890. The 1924 Immigration Restriction Act replaced the 1921 Emergency Quota Act. The Immigration Restriction Act made permanent the basic limitations on immigration into the United States established in 1921 and modified the National Origins Formula down from the 3 percent cap set by the Emergency Quota Act of 1921, according to the Census of 1890. In conjunction with the Immigration Act of 1917, the 1924 Act governed American immigration policy until the passage of the Immigration and Nationality Act of 1952, which revised it completely. Most notably, The 1924 Act was the instrument Cordell Hull utilized in repeated occasions to keep Jewish refugees from reaching the safety of US shores.

Albert Johnson, the sponsor of the bill, had become "increasingly influenced by eugenics and consulted frequently with Madison Grant," the author of the infamously successful book, "The Passing of the Great Race." [232] The idea of quotas based on the national origins of the entire population in 1920 was conceived by Sen. David Reed of Pennsylvania, chair of the Senate immigration committee, and John Trevor, a colleague of Madison Grant. Madison Grant was part of a New York society of Progressive-minded politicians, and a member of their clubs, namely the Boone and Crocket Club of New York, whose president was fellow eugenicist and Ivy League graduate, Theodore Roosevelt. Madison Grant himself had been part of the Yale University class of 1887 and subsequently received a law degree from Columbia. Trevor had attended Columbia Law School and Harvard, and his wife was "one of Eleanor Roosevelt's oldest and most cherished friends." [233] These Ivy League friendships were the basis of the lobbying organization that was the impetus behind the 1924 Act. In 1894, Davenport's classmate at Harvard, Prescott Hall, and Robert deCourcy Ward founded the Immigration Restriction League. The League never had more than 30 members, and its membership was a close-knit group from New York high-society or Ivy League contacts, mostly members of the Harvard class of 1889. In other words, this was hardly a populist movement that was the impetus behind the 1924 Immigration Restriction Act. It was very much a product of the top echelon of American elitist academic institutions. The ranks of the League were made up mostly of university presidents and professors, namely the presidents of Harvard, Bodoin, Stanford, Western Reserve, Georgia Tech, and the Wharton School of Finance of the University of Pennsylvania. [234]

The Immigration Restriction League elitists set out to find minions to do their bidding in Congress. They found Albert Johnson and recruited him to be the sponsor of the bill. Johnson had risen from his position as editor of the Daily

---

[232] Pg. 112 - "The Changing Nature of Racial and Ethnic Conflict in United States History: 1492 To the Present", Leslie Vincent Tischauser, University Press of America, 2002.
[233] Pg. 290 - "Legacy of Malthus: the social costs of the new scientific racism", Allan Chase, Knopf: distributed by Random House, 1977.
[234] Pg. 113 – Ibid.

Washingtonian to become one of the most powerful congressional leaders in the United States. Representative Johnson was "a high-school dropout and semiliterate" who owed his job to the lobbying of "the Immigration Restriction League's paid full-time Washington lobbyist, James H. Patten." [235] The fact that Johnson was both malleable and beholden meant that the Immigration Restriction League controlled the congressman in charge of House Committee tasked with passing the 1924 Act. This would prove crucial, as Johnson's bully tactics ensured that Harry H. Laughlin's testimony overshadowed all others.

The 2% aspect of the quota was also elitist and racialist in origins. Trevor's and Reed's 2 percent-National-Origin quota was intentionally based on the 1890 Census, as opposed to the latest and greatest census of the time which was the 1920 Census. The quota was portrayed as being based on existing US population, but the eugenic-minded racialists did not want that starting point to include the millions of immigrants that had come to the United States at the turn-of-the-century and during World War I. Furthermore, the Jewish population that existed in the United States prior to 1890 were the refuges of the European Revolutions of 1848, and had been around long enough that Trevor counted them not as immigrants for the quota percentages but as American born. This formulation effectively reduced to nothing the number of Jewish immigrants allowed by the quota.

The underlying assumptions of the 1924 Act would be severely questioned in the effort to repeal it. Before having the Immigration and Nationality Act of 1952 replace and repeal the 1924 Act, the House of Representatives held hearings to evaluate the Act along with all its fallacies. The resulting report documented the hearings held between September and October 1952. The US House of Representatives printed the report for the use of the Judiciary Committee, and the report recalls precisely how influential Harry H. Laughlin and Madison Grant were in the passing of 1924 Act. The section titled "II. ORIGINS OF THE NEW-OLD IMMIGRATION DISTINCTION" quoted directly from Madison Grant's now infamous book, "The Passing of the Great Race":

> The conception of a new immigration inferior to the old began to take form in the writings of some sociologists and social thinkers in the 1890's. At root, this conception rested on racist notions that the peoples of the Mediterranean region were biologically different from those of Northern and Western Europe. ---- These new immigrants were no longer exclusively members of the Nordic race as were the earlier ones-The new immigration - contained a large and increasing number of the weak, the drunken, and the mentally crippled of all races drawn from the lowest stratum of the Mediterranean basin and the Balkans, together with hordes of the wretched, submerged populations of the Polish ghettos. Our jails, insane asylums, and almshouses are filled with this human flotsam and the whole tone of American life, social, moral, and political has been lowered and vulgarized by them. (Pgs. 1840-1841, 82nd Congress, "Hearings before the President's Commission on Immigration and Naturalization", US Gov. Printing

---

[235] Pg. 289 - "Legacy of Malthus: the social costs of the new scientific racism", Allan Chase, Knopf: distributed by Random House, 1977.

Office, Sept. 30 and Oct. 29, 1952 – Available at catalog.hathitrust.org, No.: 100671453)

The connection to Madison Grant was part of the justification given in by the Congress in 1952 for repealing the 1924 Act. The 1952 Congressional report is explicit in pointing to Madison Grant and his eugenic minded colleagues as the ultimate source and inspiration of the 1924 Act. The report's subsection entitled "I. BASIC ASSUMPTIONS OF NATIONAL-ORIGINS QUOTA" documents just how skewed and prejudiced the law had been made by the politically connected eugenicists:

> That assumption, embodied in the national-origins quota, is that the national origins of immigrants is a reliable indication of their capacity for Americanization. Generally, this assumption takes the form of an assertion that some people by their racial or national constitution are more capable of becoming Americanized than others. This is usually coupled with the assertion that the immigrants who came to the United States before 1880, the old immigrants, were drawn from the superior stocks of Northern and Western Europe, while those who came after that date were drawn from the inferior breeds of Southern and Eastern Europe. (Pg. 1839, 82nd Congress, "Hearings before the President's Commission on Immigration and Naturalization", US Gov. Printing Office, Sept. 30 and Oct. 29, 1952 – Available at catalog.hathitrust.org, No.: 100671453)

Literacy tests had been used by immigration officials before. However, the "science" of eugenics and the highly influential political forces behind it gave these literacy tests importance they did not have before. Oscar Handlin's summary in the Congressional report recalls that the literacy test initially adopted in previous Congressional acts alone proved insufficient to prevent most of the immigrants undesired by the eugenic-minded commission that created previous legislation, thus the push for tighter restrictions in the 1920s. The revised Act aimed at further restricting the Southern and Eastern Europeans, mainly Jews fleeing persecution in Poland and Russia. The 1924 Act also sought to prohibit the immigration of "Middle Easterners," "East Asians" and "Asian Indians." According to the US Department of State Office of the Historian, "In all its parts, the most basic purpose of the 1924 Immigration Act was to preserve the ideal of American homogeneity." [236] However, the definition of "American homogeneity" was explicitly eugenic, as the expert used by the House Committee in order to arrive at the definition of "American Homogeneity" was Harry H. Laughlin.

Scientists who espouse and support the type of mental testing that eugenicists created and developed have tried to downplay the central role these tests played. The article "Rewriting Mental Testing History" was a critique of Mark Snyderman's and Richard J. Herrnstein's article, "Intelligence Tests and the Immigration Act of

---

[236] 2001-2009.state.gov, US Department of State Archive, The Immigration Act of 1924 (The Johnson-Reed Act)

1924." [237] Snyderman and Herrnstein argue that the "testing community did not generally view its findings as favoring restrictive immigration policies like those of the 1924 Act, and Congress took virtually no notice of intelligence testing, as far as one can ascertain from the records and publications of the time." [238] The official documentation of the US Congress evidences otherwise. The 1952 report by Congress admits as much. The history proves that the eugenics movement not only had undue influence with the "semiliterate" congressmen in charge of the 1924 Act but placed them there through the elitist friendships and political connections:

> The eugenics movement had a strong congressional advocate in Representative Albert Johnson, powerfully positioned as Chairman of the House Committee on Immigration and Naturalization. Johnson had been elected to Congress in 1912 from the state of Washington on a platform of opposition to immigration and to radical union organizing (for which he believed immigrants were responsible). He was a close personal friend of both Laughlin and Madison Grant, and in 1924 was elected President of the Eugenics Research Association, a select group of the most influential and committed eugenicists. (ferris.edu, "Rewriting Mental Testing History: The View from the American Psychologist", Sage Race Relations Abstracts 11 #2, May 1986 - Posted in the online archives of Ferris University's Institute for the Study of Academic Racism)

Furthermore, Grant's and Davenport's Immigration Restriction League operatives had Laughlin appointed as the scientific expert advising the House Committee on Immigration and Naturalization that informed the decision of the Immigration Restriction Act. On or around 1922, Laughlin was designated as the "Expert Eugenics Agent" to the Committee chaired by Congressman Albert Johnson. Between 1920 and 1924, he testified three times before the House Committee on Immigration and Naturalization, declaring that a disproportionate number of inmates in mental institutions were from Southern and Eastern Europe, even though his own data showed a high proportion were German and Irish.

> In the 1922 testimony, Laughlin plastered the Committee room with charts and graphs showing ethnic differences in rates of institutionalization for various degenerative conditions, and verbally presented a barrage of data about the mental and physical inferiority of recent immigrant groups. These data included a "rogue's gallery" of photographs of "defectives" taken at Ellis Island, which purported to show "Carriers of the Germ Plasm of the Future American Population." Laughlin was a good showman, and effectively combined statistics and visual aids to create a strong fear of the feeble-minded in his listeners. ("Rewriting Mental Testing History," online version, www.ferris.edu)

The 1952 Congressional report explains that the House Committee made its decision largely relying on the "science" presented by Laughlin. It cites the "Report

---

[237] Pgs. 18-31 - "Rewriting Mental Testing History: The View from the American Psychologist," Steven A. Gelb, Garland E. Allen, Andrew Futterman, and Barry A. Mehler, Sage Race Relations Abstracts 11 #2, May 1986 - Posted in the online archives of Ferris University's Institute for the Study of Academic Racism.

[238] Pgs. 986-995 - "Intelligence Tests and the Immigration Act of 1924," Mark Snyderman's and Richard J. Herrnstein, American Psychologist, No.: 38, Sept. 1983.

of the Immigration Commission" of the Congressional Record, and provides an estimation of the importance of Laughlin's input upon the final decision to pass the 1924 Act, as Grant's input by itself was insufficient as his infamous book was prose, not science:

> These theories were bitterly and inconclusively debated through the early years of this century. The decisive turn in the argument came when they seemed to receive validation from the reports of two governmental investigations. The first was the detailed study of the Immigration Commission under the chairmanship of Senator Dillingham. The second was a report by Dr. Harry H. Laughlin of the Carnegie Institution, expert eugenics agent of the House Committee on Immigration and Naturalization. ---- These reports had a direct impact upon subsequent legislation, for they supplied what had formerly been theoretical opinions privately held with a validation that was official and presumably scientific.

CONTINUES...

> In the same way, the Laughlin report presented in 1922 and printed in 1923, laid the groundwork for the legislation of 1924. The report was widely quoted in quasi-scientific articles and entered prominently into the debate as a result of which the act of 1924 was enacted." It therefore becomes a matter of prime importance to investigate the nature of those reports and the soundness of their conclusions. (Pgs. 1840-1841, LXI, 558 - 73d Cong., 3d Sess., Hearings before the Committee on Immigration and Naturalization. House of Representatives, November 21, 1922. Serial 7-C0)

Harry H. Laughlin also produced the statistical data upon which the Act was based upon. His "Analysis of America's Melting Pot," produced for the Sixty-Seventh Congress, was one of the key documents upon which the Congressmen crafted the definition of "American homogeneity." [239] The section titled "V. THE LAUGHLIN REPORT" of the 1952 report documents that "Dr. Harry Laughlin's Analysis of America's Modern Melting Pot was designed to correct the inability of the Dillingham Commission report to demonstrate conclusively the social inferiority of the "new" immigrants." The 1952 Congressional report recalls just how instrumental Laughlin's "Melting Pot" document truly was:

> Laughlin's report was presented to the committee in November 1922. The Honorable Albert Johnson, chairman of the committee, examined the report and certified: "I have examined Dr. Laughlin's data and charts and find that they are both biologically and statistically thorough, and apparently sound." ---- Whatever the chairman's competence to pass upon these matters, he was satisfied that the investigation had proved the inferiority of the new immigrants. The opinions that were before long to be reflected in legislation were summarized by

---

[239] "Analysis of America's Melting Pot Hearings Before the Committee on Immigration and Naturalization House of Representatives" Sixty-Seventh Congress, Third Session of Nov. 21, 1922, (Serial 7-C Washington Government Printing Office 1923)

Dr. Laughlin: "The outstanding conclusion is that, making all logical allowances for environmental conditions, which may be unfavorable to the immigrant, the recent immigrants as a whole, present a higher percentage of inborn socially inadequate qualities than do the older stocks." (82nd Congress, "Hearings before the President's Commission on Immigration and Naturalization", US Gov. Printing Office, Sept. 30 and Oct. 29, 1952 – Available at catalog.hathitrust.org, No.: 100671453)

The reader will recall that these reports and publications were specifically listed in the invitation the Third Reich sent Laughlin for the honorary degree they bestowed upon him. Posterity should take note that Hitler's regime found Laughlin's work as an "expert eugenicist" for the United States Congress worthy of praise. Astonishingly enough, these "scientific" papers directly attacked the founding concepts upon which the Congress was consecrated:

Before advancing to an examination of those data, it will however, be worth making note of Dr. Laughlin's own sentiments as he explicitly stated them to the committee: "We in this country have been so imbued with the idea of democracy, or the equality of all men, that we have left out of consideration the matter of blood or natural inborn hereditary mental and moral differences. No man who breeds pedigreed plants and animals can afford to neglect this thing." (Pgs. 1853-1854, 82nd Congress, "Hearings before the President's Commission on Immigration and Naturalization", US Gov. Printing Office, Sept. 30 and Oct. 29, 1952 – Available at catalog.hathitrust.org, No.: 100671453)

Here was the United States Congress entertaining the core concepts from which Nazism would later be woven. The 1952 report documents the above comment without fanfare. However, considered together with the honorary degree the Nazis bestowed upon Laughlin, his contempt for the founding principles of the American government qualifies the insidiousness of the above statement.

According to the authors of the "Rewriting Mental Testing History" article, the uncritical acceptance of Laughlin's "science" by Johnson did not go completely uncontested. Rep. Celler's criticized the Immigration Committee, complaining to congressman Johnson that Laughlin's undue influence on the committee had been so great that:

He [Laughlin] has hoodwinked the Immigration Committee into believing his conclusions. ---- Celler forced Johnson to call in another geneticist to respond to Laughlin's allegations. Herbert Spencer Jennings of Johns Hopkins University was invited to Washington, DC on the last day of the hearing, but given only a few minutes to testify. As Celler complained, Johnson stacked the hearings to favor the hereditarian eugenic position. Johnson had even gone further; with Laughlin and Henry Fairfield Osborn he had had the large exhibit on the inheritance of mental, moral and physical traits from the Second International Congress of Eugenics (held in New York in September 1921), shipped to and displayed in the Capitol Building in Washington, DC. There it remained for three years, providing the representatives and senators with "daily exposure to...exhibits on the heredity of criminality, idiocy, musical talent, epilepsy and other physical and mental traits." So successful were his efforts that Johnson could boast that before the debate on the floor of Congress ever began, "the biological questions of immigration. . . [had] already been settled in the minds of the members of the House and Senate." (ferris.edu, "Rewriting Mental Testing History")

First, Rep. Celler's accounts testify to the fact that the semi-literate legislative muscle, Rep. Johnson, used his position to stamp out opinions contradictory to those of the Immigration Restriction League. Secondly, this episode in American legislative history reveals the uncomfortable truth of how several generations of Progressives have been fully willing to defer critical decisions to those allegedly intellectual elites. This had always been part of the Progressive template, beginning with the fictional utopias and enduring through actual legislative efforts. This is the belief system that they held in common with the British Fabian Socialists, and which had sprouted from the minds of utopian socialists like Edward Bellamy, which looked to society to evolve under the guidance of the experts, namely scientists. This generation of Progressive-minded legislators was willing to take Harry H. Laughlin's Princeton degree and Madison Grant's Yale undergraduate and Columbia law degree as proof that their views were "scientific," and as such, a higher guidance than the founding principles of the nation:

> ... the Commission's report was neither impartial nor scientific, and that confidence in it was not altogether justified. No public hearings were held, no witnesses cross-examined by the members of the Commission. Largely the study was conducted by experts who each compiled their voluminous reports which were not printed until after the Commission had reached its conclusions. It is doubtful whether the Senators and Congressmen on the Commission ever had the time to examine the voluminous reports in manuscript. It is most likely they were compelled to rest their judgment upon the two-volume summary prepared for it by its body of experts. The final report was "adopted within a half hour of the time when, under the law, it must be filed." The identity of the experts must therefore become of some significance. (Pg. 1841, 82nd Congress, "Hearings before the President's Commission on Immigration and Naturalization", US Gov. Printing Office, Sept. 30 and Oct. 29, 1952 – Available at catalog.hathitrust.org, No.: 100671453)

A decade after the passing of the 1924 Act, a May 9, 1932 letter from Johnson to Harry H. Laughlin documents the persistence with which the Act was supported. This letter requests demographic information on criminals imprisoned in the United States. [240] To put the following letters into historical context, one must remember that the 1920s and 1930s were the golden age of the Italian Mafia and the Irish gangs, and the allusions to criminality were a direct reference to immigration from Irish and Italian Catholics at an era of the United States when Protestant animosity

---

[240] Item #1042 – Cold Spring Harbor Lab., Online Eugenics Archive, DNALC Learning Center.

towards Catholics was still very pronounced. Thus, whatever may have been stated officially, this private correspondence reveals the true intentions and racial prejudices that were the impetus behind the 1924 Act.

Fieldworkers traveled abroad to gather information for C.M. Goethe's Immigration Study Commission and reported back to Goethe with a copy to Harry H. Laughlin. These fieldworkers reported back from Haifa, Palestine, Smyrna, and Florence, Italy. Note the letter from Haifa, on March 15, 1926, where the fieldworker reported to Goethe and Laughlin that:

> These men are usually illiterates. – The Johnson Immigration Act is a powerful strainer, at the very spot where such a strainer is needed. (BOX: C-4-I:2, Laughlin Papers, Truman Univ.)

From Smyrna on April 1926, the fieldworker reported to Charles M. Goethe and Laughlin in part:

> Their accompanying children constitute an interesting example of race hybridization. Some showed inherited characteristics so mixes as to be tragic. One felt that here, in human shape, were examples of the trite proverb. "One cannot unscramble eggs." American sociologists declare that in just such hybridization were the seeds of the decay of Egypt, Greece, Rome. They say, hopefully, however that, while the causes of such decay are in operation today, that we now have the knowledge and can organize the will to prevent similar destruction of our civilization. (BOX: C-4-I:2H.H. Laughlin Papers, Truman University, Special Collections)

The vast correspondence between Goethe and Laughlin documents their desire to pin down a legal definition of an "American Race," which explicitly stipulated "Caucasian" as opposed to "White" precisely because Irish and Italian Catholics, as well as Jews, could claim to be "White." In support of this, the letter sent from the "famous old Baptistery in Florence" states in part:

> This high excess of Italian births not only constitutes Italy's chief problem, but is also a world problem, causing concern even in al European countries with high standards of living. England and Germany, both weighted down with unemployment problems, are discussing barring aliens from nearby low-wage areas. Switzerland is worried over Fascist threats from Italian immigrants in her Italian-speaking canton. France complains that not only Tunis, but certain parts of southern France, are becoming Italianized. – Against such population pressure, America's only dyke is the Johnson Immigration Restriction Act. Should this weaken, the Chinafication of our country will have begun. (BOX: C-4-I:2, H.H. Laughlin Papers, Truman University, Special Collections)

The C.M. Goethe correspondence also evidences how the international eugenics movement took extra steps to keep every eugenic-minded expert around the world well-informed and in the loop. The correspondence was pervasively carbon copied and distributed to all interested parties to an impressive consistency even by modern-day computerized communication standards. Harry H. Laughlin employed the same practices. Aside from C.M. Goethe, Harry H. Laughlin kept Madison Grant, Charles B. Davenport, H.F. Osborn, E.S. Gosney, Paul Popenoe, and Wickliffe Draper as well as foreign eugenicists such as Dr. Mjøen of Norway, Leonard Darwin and Irving Fischer of the United Kingdom, and Alfred Ploetz, Ernst Rüdin, and Alfred Dr. Verschuer of the Kaiser-Wilhelm Institute appraised of events and news important to the eugenicists. As we know, Hitler was educated on American eugenics via the vast amount of information the International Federation of Eugenic Organization made available to its German members. It is therefore by no surprise that the greatest and most historically important praise for the Johnson-Reed Immigration Restriction Act would come from Hitler himself, in "Mein Kampf." Recall that Hitler's publisher, J.F. Lehmann brought Hitler these eugenic tracts while he was in jail writing "Mein Kampf":

> There is today one state in which at least weak beginnings toward a better conception are noticeable. Of course, it is not our model German Republic, but the American Union, in which an effort is made to consult reason at least partially. By refusing immigration on principle to elements in poor health, by simply excluding certain races from naturalization, it professes in slow beginnings a view which is peculiar to the *folkish* state concept. ---- The *folkish* state divides its inhabitants into three classes: citizens, subjects, and foreigners. (Pg. 439, "Mein Kampf", Vol. 2, Ch. 3 – Subjects and Citizens, 1925)

It is at this juncture that the reader must recall that these were scientists, not legislators. What is truly astonishing about the contents of their personal files is how little amount of "science" was the topic of the extensive correspondence among the international eugenic think-tanks. Most of the correspondence among these "scientists," or those non-scientists espousing a concern over the "science of heredity," covered legalistic and governmental topics. This fact comes front and center when researching the historical importance of the enacting of eugenic legislation. All effort was focused, not on proving or developing the "science of eugenics," but on drafting, reporting and maturing the laws, statutes, and codes by which a eugenic mindset would be applied to government. An inordinate amount of time was expended at creating a eugenic utopia by using the various parliaments, legislatures, and court systems to establish laws about sterilization, euthanasia, segregation and immigration policies. While this surely proves some measure of disingenuous intent from these eugenicists, more importantly, it proves just how dependent eugenics was upon governmental structures. Eugenics can be nothing else but political, as no eugenic measures can be put into effect without extreme governmental intervention into the lives of otherwise autonomous individuals. This is also the reason all the top eugenicists spent so much of their time either dreaming up fictional worlds or why so many fictional authors, namely H.G. Wells, wrote so many fictional accounts about ideal governments. The father of eugenics, Francis Galton, would write "Kantsaywhere" in order to create a palpable vision of the eugenic world he envisioned, and before him, T.H. Huxley would write "Prolegomena" to postulate the implications of Darwin's and Galton's eugenics.

Both Wilhelm Schallmayer and Alfred Ploetz, two German eugenicists indispensable to the Third Reich's "racial hygiene" policies, were devout followers of Edward Bellamy, who had written a eugenic utopian vision of what a eugenic United States would look like. Ploetz himself traveled to the United States explicitly to study Bellamy and the various utopian colonies that had sprung up during the era.

The most telling, and most historically valuable of this long list of utopian proposals came from Laughlin, who would spend a formidable amount of time while at Cold Spring Harbor drafting a constitution for a one-world government. Laughlin's one-world eugenic utopia project spanned about a decade. There are several drafts held at Truman University's Laughlin collection. This proposal has been altogether ignored by historians, and portions are printed here for the first time. Laughlin's correspondence document that Laughlin presented this one-world utopian government to Scribner's Publishers in 1932 with the help of Madison Grant. [241] To understand Laughlin's intentions of creating a one-world government, one must go back to the correspondence between him and C.M. Goethe about foreign immigration, and the Immigration Restriction Act as the bulwark and "strainer" stopping immigration at the source of the problem. While Laughlin employs the politically correct catchwords like "freedom," "peace," and "democracy," the actual application of the government policies betray the true purpose of the effort. In fact, one just needs to refer to the related correspondence to get an explanation of what the purpose of the utopian effort was. A June 13, 1932, letter from Laughlin to Grant provides an explanation for "The Fundamental Instrument for the Common Government of the World":

> The reason most of us have for condemning the so-called internationalist is primarily because he strives to break down national barriers instead of coordinating sovereign nations. In this book I have gone over the unusual formula for world government and have changed it to call for organization, not by breaking down national and racial boundaries but by providing for the development of each race and culture independently. Instead of breaking down immigration bars my draft gives international sanction to control absolutely its own immigration policy. It also enjoins upon each nation the moral obligation to control its own population numbers and to direct its own racial evolution in accordance with its own ideals. Migration control is, of course, the one thing which makes such a long time international program possible. Consequently migration control on the basis which we have many times discussed, should constitute a cornerstone of future international polity. Incidentally my proposed draft calls for complete control over deportation of aliens by the host country, and for the abolition of dual citizenship. (BOX: B-5-2-B:6, H.H. Laughlin Papers, Truman University, Special Collections)

The section of the one-world government proposal labeled "Race Betterment" describes the eugenic nature of the one-world government, which resonates with the proposal made by Julian Huxley while serving as the director at the UNESCO:

---

[241] Box: D-2-1:5 – Laughlin Papers, Truman Univ. Archives, Special Collections.

Modern social biology has demonstrated that a nation can, if it so chooses, direct its own future racial evolution, and control the number and distribution of its own future population. Such control means that each of the more capable nations of mankind will guide its own emigration and immigration, will limit mate-selection among its own people, and will foster family fertility differentially in favor of its better stocks to the end that, with each passing generation those natural endowments which are sounder in body, more capable in mind and more virtuous in spirit than their present inborn counterparts will appear with increased frequency among the particular people. Sound and honest World Government and biological race-betterment by each of the several nations would interact to strengthen each other. (Boxes: D-2-1:3, E-2-5:4, E-2-5:14, Laughlin Papers, Truman University)

Laughlin proposed in this one-world constitution that the world government be broken down to six continents with a "federated" structure mimicking that of the US federal government and its independent state governments. While the document text itself provides extensive lip-service to the politically correct notions of a one-world government, the actual numbers of a "federation" of nations betray precisely where the power lies. Laughlin's June 13, 1932, letter to Madison Grant explains:

...the allotment of voices in World Council, based on the following formula: Area counts 5 percent, wealth 10 percent, total population 15 percent, literate population 35 percent, and world commerce 35 percent. This works out, for example, by making the representation value of one man in the United States equal to more than 25 times the representation value of one man in India. This seems sound and fair. (BOX: B-5-2B:6, Laughlin Papers, Truman University, Special Collections)

The letter goes on to explain precisely how Laughlin's version of "internationalism" was intended as a target to the traditional Communist or Socialist version of "internationalism." Adolf Hitler would concur on this point, as this was precisely Hitler's opposition to Bolshevik style Communism, that it broke down racial and ethnic barriers and put the power in the hands of Slavs in Russia, which he considered to be lesser humans than the ethnic "Nordics" and "Aryans":

This book is an invasion of the territory of the internationalists and hits what I believe to constitute their weakest part – their tendency to abolish migration barriers on the theory that the whole earth belongs to all of its inhabitants in common and that all men are created equal. (BOX: B-5-2B:6, June 13th, 1932, Laughlin to Grant, Laughlin Papers, Truman University, Special Collections)

This last line mocking the text of the Declaration of Independence, written from one American to the other, explains exactly where eugenics stood in opposition to the traditional values of the form of government established by the Founding Fathers. While Laughlin may have mimicked the "federal" model of the US Constitution in his proposal, he certainly held it with bitter disdain, as did his fellow eugenicists. Clearly, neither Laughlin nor Grant believed "all men" to be "created equal" as enshrined in the Declaration of Independence, and they were in open and direct opposition to the traditional egalitarian values which their nation was founded upon. Hitler's eugenicists certainly saw eye-to-eye with Laughlin and Grant on the obstacle the Founding Documents of the American Revolutions were to the eugenics movement. On page 75 of the training manual for the "Law for the Protection of German Blood and German Honor," the German translation of Laughlin's "Model Eugenic Law," the manual states:

> With this law a final line is drawn beneath a fateful development, which found its first historically documented expression in the famous American **Declaration of Independence in 1776**, which contains the lapidary sentence: **'We hold these truths to be self-evident, that all men are created equal.'** The cast of mind emanating from this proclamation flowed into the various populations through the French Revolution of 1789 with its thesis of the alleged **'equality, liberty, fraternity of all men,'** and during a century and a half deranged the thinking of even the cleverest minds; it was, as is well known, used in the most adroit way **by the Jewish race** to gnaw away at the foundations of state, culture, and the Volk in the most dangerous way and to undermine them. National Socialism was the first to show the German people **the colossal** lie that is contained in this delusion of equality. (emphasis in the original, american_almanac.tripod.com, "Eugenics and Population Control: The 1935 Nazi World Population Conference, and the 1994 U.N. Cairo Population Conference", Gabriele Liebig, The American Almanac, 1994 – Republished: The New Federalist Newspaper)

One of the curiously titled drafts, "America and The Common Government of the World: A draft of a World Constitution in Accordance with Unhampered American Ideals," throws around the catchwords of American values, but subsequently betrays them by defining the terms and conditions upon which the one-world government would operate. Laughlin describes his proposal as a "federal form of government" for "a group of free states" under a "democratic world government" only to qualify these initiatives with the paternalistic views of a person that subscribes to ethnic and cultural superiority:

> A strong world government would not issue territorial mandates but would administer at first hand the government of its backwards and its immature nations, and would educate them in sanitation, self-government and modern learning. (BOX: B-5-3B:1, Laughlin Papers, Truman University, Special Collections)

True to its Progressive notions, Harry Laughlin postulates that his proposal is necessary as a bulwark to "international injustice, which we call oppression" and as a method to prevent "national murder which we now call war." Here, Laughlin employs the well-worn Progressive argument for creating a one-world government:

> The principle of arming the state and disarming the constituent individual is perhaps the only plan which will make for the destruction of militarism and competitive armament. – The fact that a world government would have no coordinate competitor would relive it of the necessity of arming competitively,

the people of Wars cannot yet get at us to do military violence. (BOX: B-5-3B:1, Laughlin Papers, Truman University, Special Collections)

The belief that war was deleterious to racial concerns was a view shared by all eugenicists, namely David Starr Jordan, Leonard Darwin, Leon Whitney, and later Adolf Hitler. The concern of the dysgenic effects of war was consistent in their statements as if it were a baton being handed off from one generation of eugenicists to the next. David Starr Jordan, Ph.D., LL.D., was a leading eugenicist, ichthyologist, educator, and peace activist. He was president of Indiana University and Stanford University. One of Jordan's favorite topics was how war affected the gene pool, a notion that Adolf Hitler would regurgitate to voice his displeasure in waging war on England, whom he considered being the racial equals to Germans. Jordan popularized this notion by writing about the American Civil War and World War I. "Only the man who survives is followed by his kind. The man who is left determines the future," wrote Jordan, who would address the effects of the impending World War in the introduction to his book. [242]

This commonality of subject-matter is delved into here as it represents more than just a curious factoid: it evidences a continuum of subject-matter that proves a shared knowledge base and more specifically, a discernible origin for Adolf Hitler's eugenic mindset. Leonard Darwin, Leon Whitney, and more importantly, Adolf Hitler would make almost identical observations about the dysgenic effects of World War I. Jordan and Darwin wrote and publicly spoke on the subject too often to dismiss the probability that their thoughts were absorbed by Hitler's plagiarist mind. Hitler would mourn the loss of Europe's best racial stock being pitted against each other, while the less developed civilizations endured without loss, and the allegedly least valuable citizens remained home to and betray the nationalist causes, or as he more generally put it, "stabbed them in the back." When Hitler held a meeting on August 20, 1942, to appoint Otto-Georg Thierack as Reich Justice Minister and Roland Freisler as President of the People's Court, he entered into one of his infamous tirades about the dysgenic effects of war, which left only the poorest stock to breed for the future. Hitler raged about the need to reconstruct the criminal justice system in order to rebalance the equation by killing off the "negative" elements of the population. Below is a newspaper article covering Leaonard Drawing. Note the continuum in thought process:

> Major Leonard Darwin, in his presidential address on "Eugenics During and After the War" to the Eugenics Education Society at the Grafton Galleries yesterday, said that our military system seemed to be devised with the object of insuring that all who were defective should be exempt from risks, whilst the strong, courageous, and patriotic should be endangered. Men with noble qualities were being destroyed, whilst the unfit remained at home to become fathers of families, and this must deteriorate the natural qualities of the coming generations. ("War and Racial Progress", Morning Post of London, July 2, 1915)

---

[242] archive.org, Intro., David Starr Jordan / Harvey Ernest Jordan, "War's aftermath; a preliminary study of the eugenics of war as illustrated by the civil war of the United States and the late wars in the Balkans", Houghton Mifflin, 1914.

This anti-war stance is also but one of the ways how the "progressive" minded eugenicists passed off their otherwise sinister science as benevolent and in the interests of world peace. Notably, Laughlin's proposal was intent on "disarming" all "individuals," a topic continuously revisited in his proposal, and another clear indication of the fact that these xenophobes had very little in common with any notion of American "conservatism." Instead of the 2nd Amendment of the US Constitution, Laughlin proposes a court system to resolve all disputes among individuals and nations. An "armed police force" would enforce the mandates of these courts as a replacement for the right to bear arms. Hitler surely would have smiled upon this opinion. Comically enough, Laughlin frames his proposal as "dedicated to individual liberty, to national patriotism" in all the drafts he created.

The section labeled "Empire vs. Federal Democracy" also provides insight into the movement's continuum with the thought process. Laughlin aptly points out that "all empires have been and are motivated primarily by desire for mastery and gain." His analysis of earlier versions of one-world structures, such as that of the Romans or the Spaniards, certainly underscores his pseudo-Marxist opinion that all of world history was dictated by the desire for "mastery and gain." That said, Laughlin's proposal may not have been about "gain," but it certainly was about "mastery": control over the outcome of immigration and emigration at large, and in detail, control over human reproduction. To acquire and maintain such a coercive control over humanity, Laughlin understood that he had to disarm the individual, lest these individuals rebel against the controls imposed on them by the World Courts of Laughlin's utopian imagination. At the individual level, Laughlin envisioned his one-world proposal would "forbid human slavery" and "abolish the death penalty for crime," and even prohibit "cruel and unusual punishment" for its "duly qualified" citizens. All these sound like constitutional niceties until one reads the section that defines suffrage. "Section 6" of the "Common Government of the World," defines precisely the requirements for a citizen to have the right to vote:

> The right to vote shall not be denied or abridged by the World, or by any of its political subdivisions of any degree, on account of race, sex, belief, or station; but throughout the World the right to vote shall be vouchsafed and limited in each political unit to citizens thereof who have attained the age of personal responsibility, who are intelligent, literate, sane, patriotic, and obedient to law, who have visible means of support, and who have duly qualified as voters, according to the just and equal standards and tests legalized for the particular unit. (BOX: B-5-3B:I, Laughlin Papers, Truman Univ., Special Collections)

In other words, to be a "duly qualified citizen" in Laughlin's utopian government, one had to pass the tests that eugenicists used to determine "fitness." One could not be a "useless eater" as the German "racial hygienists" would later define. This citizenship test is yet another idea shared by the various generations of eugenicists from Bellamy to Galton and onto Hitler himself.

Here again we can employ an analysis of opposites in order to define the nature of this eugenic creed. Laughlin's proposal can be said to be the mirror opposite of the founding documents of the American Revolution. Nowhere is the healthy fear of an overwhelmingly powerful government, or the notion of "limited government" present. To the contrary, Laughlin intentionally disarms the "individual constituent" under the premise that it is the "militant individuals" who are responsible for war among nations. Laughlin was not stupid enough to believe this notion, that an "individual" who is in possession of one or two guns is the cause of world wars. Clearly, he understood that an all-powerful government could maintain power only if it removed the rights and protections so painfully gained by the Founding Fathers. Clearly, Laughlin understood what happened to despots that abused the populace, as he certainly intended to do. The Founding Fathers of the American Revolution had a justified fear of all-powerful governments, namely the British Empire under King George, and thus enshrined the "right to bear arms" into the Second Amendment of the US Constitution. The Founding Fathers were not trying to prevent future wars between nations but further incursions on their individual liberties by their own government. The founding concepts of a "balance" and a "separation" of powers were explicitly written into the founding documents of both the state and federal government to create a "limited government" incapable of precisely the over-arching and abusive powers that Progressives and Fabian Socialists desired; namely to have the power to enact their "race betterment," "racial hygiene," "population control" and other "eugenic" policies. The Founding Fathers created their government proposal to enable the individual to "self-govern," as opposed to having bureaucrats and elites like Leonard Darwin, H.G. Wells, C.M. Goethe, Madison Grant, Alfred Ploetz, and Ernst Rüdin impose their views on them. The Second Amendment can be said to be the most important aspect of the founding documents that creates a "balance" and a "separation" of powers. It distributes and balances power between the government and its constituents by respecting the right of the individual to defend themselves against an over-zealous government. This is a concept that would certainly come front and center as eugenicists like Laughlin and Leon Whitney scoured the countryside to sterilize young boys and girls that they deemed "inferior" or "unfit." These eugenicists sterilized the individuals we now call "The Greatest Generation," the recently arrived immigrants from Eastern Europe, Italy, and Ireland, as well as perfectly healthy, but culturally unsophisticated American-born boys and girls against their will.

Eugenicists in Europe were also keen on the fact that their belief system was at odds with the egalitarian values of the new democracies popping up around the world. Francis Galton gripped about it in his article "Hereditary Improvement," which appeared in a January 1873 edition of "Fraser's Magazine":

> As regards the democratic feelings, its assertion of equality is deserving of the highest admiration so far as it demands equal consideration for the feelings of all, just as in the same way as their rights are equally maintained by the law. But it goes farther than this, for it asserts that men are of equal value as social units, equally capable of voting, and the rest. This feeling is undeniably wrong, and cannot last. (As quoted by A. Chase, Pg. 85, "Legacy of Malthus", 1975)

To what do we attribute this violent swing away from egalitarianism? Maybe the best way to explain such a perverse disdain for one's fellow humans is their admission that eugenics was a "religion." Francis Darwin was Charles Darwin's third son and a botanist like his father. Francis Darwin gave the first "Galton Lecture" before the Eugenics Education Society on February 16, 1914. In it, Darwin's son recants Galton's postulate that eugenics should be regarded a "religion," alluding to the fact that he felt its dictate should govern all aspects of life as traditional religious morality did. We should therefore not be surprised that eugenicists from Galton onwards recant the dogma of their "religion" as the faithful recite scripture; with the salient passages told and retold *ad nauseam*.

> Galton sums up the stages in the development of eugenics. (I) "It must be made familiar as an academic question." (II) As a practical subject worthy of serious consideration. (III) It must be "introduced into the national conscience, like a new religion." He recapitulates in an eloquent phrase: "It has, indeed, strong claims to become an orthodox religious tenet of the future, for Eugenics co-operates with the workings of Nature by securing that humanity shall be represented by the fittest races. What Nature does blindly, slowly, and ruthlessly, man may do providently, quickly, and kindly. ("Galton Lecture", Francis Darwin, Eugenics Education Society, Feb. 16, 1914, Printed in Eugenics Review, 1914)

Considering the above devotion, it is no surprise that eugenicists from Galton onwards were set on the remaking of society, and his devoted followers, like Harry H. Laughlin, would spend an inordinate amount of time on legislation as opposed to scientific endeavors. Case in point, Laughlin was working on this one-world constitution while he was serving as the Congressional expert on immigration for the Immigration Restriction Act, as a February 19, 1921 letter to H.G. Wells documents the fact that Laughlin sent Wells an early copy of the utopian proposal. [243] Most notably, a September 19, 1933, letter from the Under Secretary at the Secretary of State's office documents that Laughlin sent off copies to President F.D. Roosevelt and Secretary of State Cordell Hull. [244] Laughlin made sure that his proposal was not received blindly, as the September 9, 1933, letter to Secretary of State Cordell Hull reminds the Secretary that Laughlin had been an expert advisor to the Committee on Immigration and Naturalization between 1922 and 1924 for the creation of the 1924 Act. Laughlin can hardly be said to have been aiming high by delivering this proposal to the President and the Secretary of State, as the influence he wielded over key pieces of legislation proved he certainly had more than just a foot in the door.

---

[243] BOX: B-5-4B:11 – Harry H. Laughlin Papers, Truman Univ. Special Collections, Pickler Memorial Library.
[244] BOX: D-2-1:1 – Ibid.

Sec. 5 - FROM OPPRESSED TO OPPRESSOR:

The Beer Hall Putsch, Hitler's attempt at violent revolution was inspired by Benito Mussolini's successful March on Rome. As this book has earlier opined, Hitler's experience at trial and later stay in jail were critical and important learning experiences for the evolving dictator. This transformation from failed thug to informed political figure was critical to the evolution of National Socialism, as historians have also noted that thereafter Hitler insisted in gaining, amassing, and achieving power only through legal means, or at least means that gave the appearance of legality. This is no small turn of events, and it must be noted that this *modus operandi* only became more pervasive after Hitler had consolidated political power.

While in Landsberg, Hitler read a lot of books. Hitler would describe his spell in prison as "free education at the state's expense." Of critical importance is the book hand-delivered by J.F. Lehmann, Hitler's publisher, financier, and sympathizer. *"Grundriss der Menschlichen Erblichkeitslehre und Rassenhygiene,"* or in English the "Principles of Human Heredity and Racial Hygiene" was written by Eugen Fischer, Fritz Lenz, and Erwin Baur. It comprehensively detailed the "science" of eugenics. The book was first published by J.f. Lehmann in 1923, and it is quite literally the "scientific" blueprint for Hitler's racial policies. The book has come to be known by historians as the "Baur-Fischer-Lenz" book or as "Human Heredity," the title given to the English edition. The "Human Heredity" edition was translated in 1931 by Eden & Cedar Paul.

Hitler is also quoted by historians as stating that he had "studied with great interest the laws of several American states concerning prevention of reproduction by people whose progeny would, in all probability, be of no value or be injurious to the racial stock." [245] The "Baur-Fischer-Lenz" book was the primary source of that study. While some historians of the eugenics movement make a direct reference to the "Baur-Fischer-Lenz" book as influencing Hitler's views of eugenics, the actual contents of the book have not been adequately documented by American historians. The book is replete with references to the anti-miscegenation laws of the United States and the eugenic laws of Britain:

> For the sake of completeness we must glance at the Negroes outside Africa, and above all in the United States. In the American Union we find a peculiar intermediate type which has been produced by the indiscriminate crossing of all sorts of Negroid stocks, so that individual characters are chaotically intermingled without the formation of a genuinely new race. The American Negroes have, however, retained the typical Negroid characters, the mental ones not excepted. Where they have been left pretty much to themselves (as, for instance, in Jamaica), isolated groups have relapsed into states of primitive culture (fetish, voodoo, etc.), and have become what are sometimes termed "Bush Negroes." (Pg. 206, Description of Races of Man chapter, "Human Heredity," English version: Eden & Ceder Paul, 1931)

---

[245] Pg. 37 – "The Nazi Connection: Eugenics, American Racism, and German National Socialism", Stefan Kuhl, Oxford Univ. Press, 2002.

"Human Heredity" juxtaposes Charles B. Davenport's studies of black-white intermixing with Eugen Fischer's study of the Hottentots interracial children from German colonies, or the "Rehobother Bastards" as labeled by Fischer:

> F.L. Hoffmann reports that in his experience the individuals who in the southern States of the American Union enter into mixed marriages or illegal relationships between white and coloured, are far below the average of the two races. (Pg. 691, Chap.: Racial Psychology, "Human Heredity," citing "Race Traits and Tendencies of the American Negro, New York, 1896; Negro-White Intermixture and Intermarriage, in Eugenics in Race and State, Baltimore, 1923)

The book references Francis Galton's work at least 11 times and Galton's book "Hereditary Genius" five times. The authors give Francis Galton credit for being the father, not just of "eugenics" but its German iteration, "racial hygiene"; a pretty big crown to be awarded by the intellectual leaders of Hitler's infamous Nuremberg Laws, as well as proof that Hitler's top scientists recognized that their "racial hygiene" policies originated from Anglo "eugenics," precisely the distinction the Allied prosecution at Nuremberg evaded:

> Galton was the founder of racial hygiene. In the domain of genetics, indeed, he had clearer notions than had his cousin Darwin, and he can be placed beside Mendel as a pioneer in the modern study of heredity. (Pgs. 575-576, Chap.: The Inheritance of Talents, "Human Heredity," English version: Eden & Ceder Paul, 1931)

The book references Charles B. Davenport on 18 separate instances, more than Darwin and Galton themselves. The Cold Spring Harbor Eugenic Records Office is referenced 8 times. Harry H. Laughlin's work is referenced at least 3 times, namely his 1922 book "Eugenic Sterilization in the United States," where Laughlin's "Model Eugenical Sterilization Law" was first published. It specifically refers to Davenport's work in biometrics of all US Army men enrolled in World War II which was published in 1921. [246] In fact, the book relies substantially on the pedigree studies of families specifically ones produced by Charles B. Davenport and Harry H. Laughlin. One of the works cited for inherited feeble-mindedness comes from Davenport's Eugenic Record Office publication of 1912 titled "Hill Folk," which included mention of the infamous "Kallikak" and "Jukes" dysgenic family studies. Of specific importance to a study of the Holocaust and the infamous "twin studies" conducted by Dr. Mengele at Auschwitz is the fact that much of the book's inquiry into twins came from Davenport's "Influence of the Male in the Production of Human Twins," which had previously been published in "American Naturalist," Vol. XXXIV in 1920. The Morbific Heredity Factors chapter of "Human Heredity" address twins and especially those with birth defects.

The admiration Adolf Hitler had for Henry Ford has also been widely documented by historians and here again, the "Baur-Fischer-Lenz" book serves as a likely source where this admiration was bolstered as rational and scientific. Henry

---

[246] Pg. 198 - "Human Heredity," Eugen Fischer, Fritz Lenz, Erwin Baur, English version: Eden & Ceder Paul, 1931.

Ford and "The International Jew" is quoted by the "Baur-Fischer-Lenz" book on 3 separate occasions, insultingly enough as an authority on the psychology of Jews:
> The theaters are for the most part in the hands of Jews; in the United States exclusively so, according to Henry Ford. The same is true of the movies. A large proportion of daily newspapers and other periodicals are issued by Jews, edited by Jews, and provided with articles by Jewish journalists. The legal profession would almost seem to have been created especially for Jews. (Pg. 668)

CONTINUES...

> Where the Jews form only a small minority, the economic position is as a rule an extremely good one. Their influence and their power will be found to be much greater than is proportional to their numbers. Salaman shows this as regards England, and Ford as regards the United States. (Pg. 670, "Human Heredity," chapter: Racial Psychology, English version: Eden & Ceder Paul, 1931)

Of note is that Nietzsche is quoted and referenced on 9 separate instances, largely as an example of the genius mentality, but also as a philosophical reference.
> "The cultivation of suffering, of great suffering – do you know that this and nothing but this has hitherto led to all the advancement of mankind?"- Thus writes Nietzsche. (Pg. 618, "Human Heredity," chapter: Talent and Psychopathy, English version: Eden & Ceder Paul, 1931)

Why is the "Baur-Fischer-Lenz" book important in the timeline leading up to The Holocaust? With the "Baur-Fischer-Lenz" book J.F. Lehmann succeeded in transforming Adolf Hitler from the racism of a typical uneducated foot soldier, who felt victimized and "stabbed-in-the-back" by powerful Jewish forces, to a Hitler which now saw himself as part of the elite, justified by science in his racism and desire for a racially pure society. J.F. Lehmann made Adolf Hitler a eugenicist and a scientific racist by delivering the "Baur-Fischer-Lenz" book on the precise moment when Hitler was reconciling all his views into "Mein Kampf." J.F. Lehmann provided Hitler a book about eugenic legalisms precisely at the juncture when Hitler was rethinking his revolutionary strategy from a violent to a legal one. Ernst Hanfstaengl, the Harvard educated Foreign Secretary noticed a change in Hitler's anti-Semitism at this critical juncture, although he attributed it to influence by Hitler's cellmates at Landsberg:
> He seemed to have come out of Landsberg with all his worst prejudices reinforced. I am sure that this is the point at which his latent radical tendencies started to crystallize, although there were still years to go before he became the unteachable, unreasonable and unapproachable fanatic whom the world knows from his days of power. The year he spent in Landsberg, instead of giving him time to sit back and take a broader view of political problems, had only given those imprisoned with him an opportunity to narrow his mind within their own confined limits. His anti-Semitism had acquired even more specific racial undertones. Between them, they had filled his mind with fury about the French

use of Senegalese troops in the Ruhr during the occupation, and I am not at all sure that this was not the starting-point of the racial purity laws which the Nazis finally evolved. They would pick these ideas up and embroider on them and, to bolster their arguments, even quote such respected sources as Bernard Shaw, who was not averse to advocating the necessity of breeding human beings according to the standards we have developed in the domestic animal world. (Pgs. 120-121, "Hitler: The Memoir of the Nazi Insider Who Turned Against the Fuhrer", 1957, Republished by Arcade Pub., 2011)

If Hanfstaengl is right, then Hitler gleaned the idea of "breeding human beings" as a result of his prison education. This is no small revelation. It is a critical observation to make if one is to understand when and where Hitler made the all-important conversion from street-level bigotry to genocidal despot. In turn, it is important to ask where Baur, Fischer, or Lenz obtained such detailed information about American and British eugenic policies? Paul Lombardo provides the answer:

In late 1920, Erwin Baur wrote to the ERO for information on US sterilization practices that he could distribute to "his committee of eugenic advisors for the German government. Davenport referred the inquiry to Harry Laughlin, a recognized expert on sterilization who had just completed an article on national eugenics in Germany that would appear in the London-based Eugenics Review. There Laughlin praised the "Teutonic stock" and its instincts for self-preservation memorialized in a new constitution. He believed the time was "ripe for the development of a [German] national eugenical policy" and told Davenport that he would be "especially interested in the success that Dr. Baur's committee has in developing eugenical interest in Germany." Laughlin's correspondents eventually included a virtual who's who of German eugenics. In addition to Baur, Ploetz, and Rüdin, he knew Fritz Lenz, a coauthor of the influential eugenics text. Lenz wrote to Laughlin in 1928, asking permission to reprint a Laughlin paper on sterilization in a German eugenics journal. Eugen Fischer was the third coauthor of that volume, and he developed a particularly collegial relationship with Laughlin. More than once, Fischer and Laughlin had each other's articles translated for publication in both Germany and the United States. (Pg. 200, "Three Generations No Imbeciles: Eugenics, the Supreme Court, and Buck v. Bell", Johns Hopkins University Press, 2008)

Hitler was fed the knowledge that had been the longstanding project of people like Davenport, Laughlin, Galton, Pearson, and Darwin, and the result was a fundamental shift in Hitler's revolution. The revolutionary that entered the jail cell was best known for leveraging the "stabbed-in-the-back" myth, which painted a picture of a German people allegedly victimized by "International Jewry." The Hitler that emerged was a prophet of Aryan superiority. Ponder upon the drastic differences in these two conceptions. These are two drastically different and diametrical opposite views of the German people; superiority and victim status cannot be reconciled.

Historians must take note of this fundamental change, which can only be attributed to Hitler's "indoctrination" into the eugenics creed. Aside from Hansftaengl's observation, one can verify this shift in Hitler's mindset by tracking it in his speeches. Hitler relied heavily on speeches in order to attain power, so the changing themes in these speeches are the best way to chart a shift in his thinking. According to Norman H. Baynes', the editor of 1942 book, "The Speeches of Adolf Hitler," Hitler's first speech was on April 12, 1922. In these early speeches, Hitler adopted themes of "interest slavery," and the "November criminals," which was a direct reference to the "stabbed-in-the-back" myth that alluded that German Jews of a Bolshevik political taint betrayed the German soldiers in World War I:

> "Christian capitalism" is already as good as destroyed, the international Jewish Stock Exchange capital gains in proportion as the other loses ground. It is only the international Stock Exchange and loan-capital, the so-called "supra-state (*überstaaliche*) capital," which has profited from the collapse of our economic life, "the capital which receives its character from the single supra-state nation which is itself national to the core, which fancies itself to be above all other nations, which places itself above other nations and which already rules over them. (Pg. 7, "Speeches of Adolf Hitler: April 1922-August 1939", Oxford Univ. Press along with the Royal Institute of International Affairs in England, 1942)

On September 18, 1922, Hitler carried on with the theme of "The Stock Exchange Revolution of 1918," illustrating that local economics was of secondary concern to the greater conflict he saw at play at a world stage; the Jewish influence of democratic egalitarianism and equality. Note again the emphasis on "international":

> Internationalization to-day means only Judaization. We in Germany have come to this: that a sixty-million people sees its destiny to lie at the will of a few dozen Jewish bankers. This was possible only because our civilization had first been Judaized. The undermining of the German conception of personality by catchwords had begun long before. Ideas such as 'Democracy', 'Majority', 'Conscience of the World', 'World-solidarity', 'World-peace', 'Internationality of Art', &c. disintegrate our race-consciousness, breed cowardice, and so to-day we are bound to say that the simple Turk is no more man than we are. – No salvation is possible until the bearer of disunion, the Jew, has been rendered powerless to harm. (Pg. 42, "Speeches of Adolf Hitler: April 1922-August 1939", Oxford Univ. Press along with the Royal Institute of International Affairs in England, 1942)

From very early on, Hitler makes plain that he was neither a man of the "Left," which he identifies as beholden to either "International" Communism or "International" capital nor was he a man of the "Right," which he claimed was exploitative of the working class. He held equal condemnation for them, and blamed them both for helping the Jews oppress people like himself:

> There were Jews who in politics took the side of the Right: they were there to see to it that people did not have their eyes opened their eyes. . . . This was their

only object for joining the Right; for the most part they acted as "leaders of the proletariat" for the working classes. ---- The guilt of the Jews lies in the fact that they have "agitated" the masses into this November madness. When we look at the parties we son on the Left lying and deceit on the part of the leaders, blind faith on the part of the led and all alike in the service of a single aim: to destroy this State, to rob this people of its freedom, to enslave its labour-strength. On the Right we see that the masses in part recognize the true position, but among the leaders there is limitless incapacity. There are but two alternatives: either "remain quiet and become slaves," or Resistance. And if you decide for resistance who will lead you? "the Left? First: it does not wish to do so; and secondly, it cannot dos so. For your leaders of the Left are still the same as those who scourged you into this misery . . The same Jew who, whether as majority Socialist or Independent, led you then leads you still: whether as Independent or as Communist, whatever he calls himself, he is still the same.." (Pgs. 8-9, "Speeches of Adolf Hitler: April 1922-August 1939", Oxford Univ. Press along with the Royal Institute of International Affairs in England, 1942)

Hitler makes it clear through his public speaking that he identifies the Jew with Bolshevism or "International" Communism:

While now in Soviet Russia the millions are ruined and are dying, Chicherin – and with him a staff of over 200 Soviet Jews – travels by express train through Europe, visits the cabarets, watches naked dancers perform for his pleasure, lives in the finest hotels, and does himself better than the millions whom once you thought you must fight as 'Bourgeois'. The 400 Soviet Commissars of Jewish nationality – they do not suffer, the thousands upon thousands of Sub-Commissars – they do not suffer. No! all the treasures which the 'Proletarian' in his madness took from the 'Bourgeoisie' in order to fight so-called capitalism – they have all gone into their hands. --- But the bread is in the hands of the State Central Organization and this is in the hands of the Jews: so everything, everything that the common man thought that he was winning for himself, flows back again to his seducers. (Pgs. 9-10, "Speeches of Adolf Hitler: April 1922-August 1939", Oxford Univ. Press along with the Royal Institute of International Affairs in England, 1942)

Hitler opined that the interests of the "International" Jewish community were to maintain an ongoing and never-ending Communist Revolution, in order to keep reaping the profits he describes above. Hitler characterizes the Soviet "Revolution" with the "land of milk and honey," which is the promise-land according to Old Testament scripture:

And now, my dear fellow-country men, do you believe that these men, who with us are going the same way, will end the Revolution? They do not wish the end of the Revolution, for they do not need it. For them the Revolution is milk and honey. (Pgs. 9-10, "Speeches of Adolf Hitler: April 1922-August 1939", Oxford Univ. Press along with the Royal Institute of International Affairs in England, 1942)

From very early on in these first speeches, Hitler makes it clear that the "Right" was confused and held back by clinging to what Hitler regarded as outdated and outmoded conservative and traditional political models:

> And there is another fundamental error: they have never got it clear in their own minds that there is a difference on how a great a difference there is between the conception of 'National' and the word 'dynastic' or 'monarchistic.' They do not understand that to-day it is more than ever necessary in our thought as Nationalists to avoid anything which might perhaps cause the individual to think that the National Idea was identical with petty everyday political views. (Pg. 12, "Speeches of Adolf Hitler: April 1922-August 1939", Oxford Univ. Press along with the Royal Institute of International Affairs in England, 1942)

Hitler also detested the tendency of the conservative "Right" to depend on "Jewish democracy" to rule. Hitler announced his hatred of "democracy" in his speech by immediately instituting the "Leadership Principle" and abandoning any sort of parliamentary system of committees and majority voting within the Party:

> And the Right has further completely forgotten that Democracy is fundamentally not German: it is Jewish. It has completely forgotten that this Jewish democracy with its majority decisions has always been without exception only a means towards the destruction of any existing Aryan leadership. (Pg. 13, "Speeches of Adolf Hitler: April 1922-August 1939", Oxford Univ. Press along with the Royal Institute of International Affairs in England, 1942)

It is also in these early speeches that Hitler qualified the collectivist and socialist aspect of his movement. In his speech delivered on April 27, 1923, on "The Paradise of the Jew or the State of the German People," Hitler drummed up the hardline Socialist theme of attacking private property. Clearly, this was a message intended to warn the "Right" as to the economic intentions of the National Socialists to confiscate private property:

> And land (*Grund und Boden*), we must insist, cannot be made an object for speculation. Private property can be only that which a man has gained for himself, has won through his work. A natural product is not private property, that is national property. Land is thus no object for bargaining. – Further, there must be a reform in our law. Our present law regards only the rights of the individual. It does not regard the protection of the race, the protection of the community of the people. It permits the befouling of the nation's honour and of the greatness of the nation. A law which is so far removed from the conception of the community of the people is in need of reform. (Pg. 65, "Speeches of Adolf Hitler: April 1922-August 1939", Oxford Univ. Press along with the Royal Institute of International Affairs in England, 1942)

The early speeches also help to clarify other core concepts of Hitlerism. Hitler's claim that he is both against "capitalism" and "communism" has been a real source of confusion for historians, for it's a seeming contradiction if understood in the polarized politics of today. First, this is a simplistic understanding that is mostly the product of the polarized Cold War two-party system in the United States, which sees left vs. right as "capitalism" vs. "communism." It forgets that "National Socialism" as created by Edward Bellamy, and then followed by British Fabians and American Progressives was meant as a "third way." Hitler understood "nation" to be one and the same with "race," and that any cooperation or socialist coordination was most natural when it occurred amongst people of a shared ethnic background, as opposed to the economic class distinctions of the Marxists. Hitler's position is explained in these early speeches:

> Every truly national idea is in the last resort social, i.e. he who is prepared so completely to adopt the cause of his people that he really knows no higher ideal than the prosperity of this – his own – people, he who has so taken to hear the meaning of our great song 'Deutschland, Deutschland über alles', that nothing in this world stands for him higher than this Germany, people and land, land and people, **he is a Socialist!** (emphasis mine, Pg. 35)

And again:
> And one can see constantly how wonderfully the Stock Exchange Jew and the leader of the workers, how the Stock Exchange Jew organ and the journal of the workers, co-operate. They both pursue one common policy and a single aim. Moses Kohn on the one side encourages his association to refuse the workers' demands, while his brother Isaac in the factory incites the masses and shouts, 'Look at them! They only want to oppress you! Shake off your fetters . . ' His brother takes care that the fetters are well and truly forged. (Pg. 29, "Speeches of Adolf Hitler: April 1922-August 1939", Oxford Univ. Press along with the Royal Institute of International Affairs in England, 1942)

To further underscore the socialist aspect of "National Socialism," Hitler delivered a speech on May Day Festival, May 1st, 1923, in which he promised that May Day, a socialist holiday, would be a yearly festival in the Third Reich:

> So on the 1st of May can be only a glorification of the national creative will over against the conception international disintegration, of the liberation of the nation's spirit and of its economic outlook from the infection of internationalism. – Our will is to be National Socialists – not National in the current sense of the word—not National by halves. We are National Socialist fanatics, not dancers on the tight-rope of moderation! (Pg. 68, "Speeches of Adolf Hitler: April 1922-August 1939", Oxford Univ. Press along with the Royal Institute of International Affairs in England, 1942)

For Hitler, the State was the "essential character of the people." Economics was secondary, as long as the State was the "fusing together" of those who "have still a German heart and a love for their people in the fight against the common hereditary foe of the Aryans." [247] None of this meant that Hitler's "third way" was in any way,

---

[247] Pg. 12 - "Speeches of Adolf Hitler: April 1922-August 1939", Oxford Univ. Press along with the Royal Institute of International Affairs in England, 1942.

shape or form the party of the independents or the party of the middle compromise. The "socialism" that Hitler describes was radicalized by its racialism. He clearly intended to usurp the "socialist" forms and radicalize them along "nationalistic" boundaries that were drawn upon ethnicity. Hitler proposes the alternative to the Soviet Bolshevism and the ineptitude and corruption of the conservatives precisely by proposing a socialism radicalized by a racial nationalism, prophesizing that it would be "a sorry day for them when this Socialist idea is grasped by a Movement which unites it with the highest Nationalist pride, with Nationalist defiance." [248]

In fact, that first speech of April 12th, 1922 in which Adolf Hitler gives his most coherent explanation of what precisely was the concept of National Socialism:

1. 'National' and 'social' are two identical conceptions. It was only the Jew who succeeded, thought falsifying the social idea and turning it into Marxism, not only in divorcing the social idea from the national, but in actually representing them as utterly contradictory. That aim he has in fact achieved. --- We said to ourselves that to be 'national' means above everything to act with boundless and all-embracing love for the people and, if necessary, even to die for it. And similarly to be 'social' means so to build up the State and the community of the people that every individual acts in the interest of the community of the people and must be to such an extent convinced of the goodness, of the honourable straightforwardness of this community of the people as to be ready to die for it. (Pg. 14)

2. And then we said to ourselves: there are no such things as classes: they cannot be. Class means caste and caste means race. If there are castes in India, well and good; there it is possible, for there there were formerly Aryans and dark aborigines. So it was in Egypt and in Rome. But with us in Germany where everyone who is a German at all has the same blood, has the same eyes and speaks the same language, here there can be no class, here there can be only a single people and beyond that nothing else… (Pgs. 15-16)

3. And in the third place it was clear to us that this particular view is based on an impulse which springs from our race and from our blood. We said to ourselves that race differs from race and, further, that each race in accordance with its fundamental demands shows externally certain specific tendencies, and these tendencies can perhaps be most clearly traced in their relation to the conception of work. The Aryan regards work as the foundation for the maintenance of the community of the people among its members, the Jew regards work as the means to the exploitation of other peoples. (Pgs. 16-17)

4. And fourthly we were further persuaded that economic prosperity is inseparable from political freedom and that therefore that house of lies, 'Internationalism', must immediately collapse. (Pgs. 17-18, "Speeches of Adolf Hitler: April 1922-August 1939", Oxford Univ. Press along with the Royal Institute of International Affairs in England, 1942)

---

[248] Pg. 11 – Ibid.

Hitler closes by identifying the "International Jew" as the "November criminals" or, in other words, the ones responsible for "stabbing" the German soldier in the back:
> And finally we were also the first to point the people on any large scale to a danger which insinuated itself into our midst – a danger which millions failed to realize and which will none the less lead us all into ruin – the Jewish danger. (Pg. 19, "Speeches of Adolf Hitler: April 1922-August 1939", Oxford Univ. Press along with the Royal Institute of International Affairs in England, 1942)

Taken as a whole, Hitler's first speech presents a well-formed conception of what "National Socialism" would become, and as this is how Göring and Brandt defined the Party when interrogated in the Nuremberg Trials. It was also the description of the movement by those that survived it to recount it in retrospect, as Albert Speer did when he wrote his memoirs. This is also the conception of the movement that Joseph Goebbels describes in his diary, and the description of the movement which American OSS intelligence reports depict.

The evidence found in the memoirs of his close associates also points to Hitler's indoctrination into the eugenics. Hitler had been jailed before. There was an unproductive four-week imprisonment two years earlier in 1922 between Hitler's first and second speech. Hitler dedicated himself to the researching and the writing of "Mein Kampf" during his second jail sentence, while at Landsberg prison. The 1924 imprisonment at Landsberg, which produced "Mein Kampf," must be compared to the unproductive 1922 imprisonment, as the absence of policy developments are important toward an understanding of exactly when and where these policies were adopted. Analyzing the contents of these early speeches is crucial in answering the question of when Hitler became genocidal. Case in point, Hitler emerged from that first four-week imprisonment to give a speech on July 28, 1922, with any policy of genocide or mass murder conspicuously absent:
> Everywhere—in Russia, in Italy, in France, and in England – he saw a vast battle in progress between the ideals of the nationalist and those of the supra-State International. "It is a battle which began nearly 120 years ago, at the moment when the Jew was granted citizen rights in the European States. The political emancipation of the Jews was the beginning of an attack of delirium. For thereby there were given full citizen rights and equality to a people which was much more clearly and definitely a race apart than all others, that has always formed and will form a State within the State. (Pg. 21, "Speeches of Adolf Hitler: April 1922-August 1939", Oxford Univ. Press along with the Royal Institute of International Affairs in England, 1942)

Hitler tied his imagined debacle of civilization with the emigration from rural to urban, where the Jewish influence was felt in "moneyfication" of the nation:
> Especially in England crowds of farm labourers, sons of farmers, or even ruined farmers themselves streamed into the towns and there formed a new fourth estate (Stand). But here one fact is of more importance than we are accustomed to

admit: this England, like France, had relatively few Jews. And the consequence of that was that the great masses, concentrated in towns, did not come into immediate contact with this alien nation. (Pgs. 22-23)

Hitler continued this early speech with his disdain for "self-government" and "democracy":

As everyone knows, this system is given some such name as 'Self-Government of a People'. Besides this we always find two great catchwords, 'Freedom' and 'Democracy', used, I might say, as signboards. 'Freedom': under that term is understood, at least among those in authority who in fact carry on the Government, the possibility of an unchecked plundering of the masses of the people to which no resistance can be offered. The masses themselves naturally believe that under the term 'freedom' they possess the right to a quite peculiar freedom of motion – freedom to move the tongue and to say what they choose, freedom to move about the streets. A bitter deception! – And the same is true of democracy. (Pg. 24, "Speeches of Adolf Hitler: April 1922-August 1939", Oxford Univ. Press along with the Royal Institute of International Affairs in England, 1942)

Hitler spares no effort to advance the concepts popularized by Henry Ford through the "Protocols of Zion" and the "International Jew." The themes are plagiaristic and unoriginal. Pregnant as they were with the most acidic Jew-hating rhetoric, it is important to note that these speeches only identified why and how Jews had come to be regarded by Hitler as the enduring enemies of his beloved "Aryans." They pretend to prophesize a great collision between "Internationalism" in the form of "Jewish capitalism," "Bolshevik Communism," and his "National Socialism." However, these speeches lean towards a defensive stance, if not to overtly demonize the "International Jew" as the alleged aggressor, and the Aryan, not as "master," but as a victim:

On one point there should be no doubt: we will not let the Jews slit our gullets and not defend ourselves. To-day in Berlin they may already be arranging their festival-dinners with the Jewish hangmen of Soviet-Russia – they will never do that here. (Pg. 39, "Speeches of Adolf Hitler: April 1922-August 1939", Oxford Univ. Press along with the Royal Institute of International Affairs in England, 1942)

The Versailles war reparations that the Allies placed on the Germans were based upon "war guilt," or in other words, who was responsible for instigating World War I. Hitler gave his opinion on whom had instigated and profited from the war on April 17, 1923:

"Who," he asked "were the real rulers of Germany in 1914 to whom war guilt might be attributed: not the Kaiser, not the Pan-Germans, but Messrs. Ballin, Bleichröder, Mendelssohn, &c., a whole brood of Hebrews who formed the unofficial Government. And in 1914 the real ruler of the Reich was Her Bethmann-Hollweg, "a descendant of a Jewish family of Frankfurt—the genuine article, and in his every act the Yiddish philosopher all over. (Pgs. 54-54, "Speeches of Adolf Hitler: April 1922-August 1939", Oxford Univ. Press along with the Royal Institute of International Affairs in England, 1942)

On April 20th, 1923, Hitler spoke on "Politics and Race: why are we Anti-Semites?" paralleling what Americans of this era propagandized as the "Yellow Peril" of Chinese immigration, and belittling those concerns against the German's "Jewish Peril":

> The German people was once clear thinking and simple: why has it lost these characteristics? Any inner renewal is possible only if one realizes that this is a question of race: America forbids the yellow peoples to settle there, but this is a lesser peril than that which stretches out its hand over the entire world—the Jewish peril. Many hold that the Jews are not a race, but is there a second people anywhere in the wide world which is so determined to maintain its race? (Pg. 59, "Speeches of Adolf Hitler: April 1922-August 1939", Oxford Univ. Press with the Royal Institute of Intl. Affairs in England, 1942)

More to the point, about the closest Hitler ever came to eugenic or genocidal concepts in the early speeches was in calling for the cultural exclusion of the Jews, but does so explicitly claiming that the influential Jews would no longer drown out the German voices if they were segregated:

> Clear away the Jews! Our own people has genius enough—we need no Hebrews. If we were to put in their place intelligences drawn from the great body of our people, then we should have recovered the bridge which leads to the community of the people. – Finally we need a reform in the sphere of art, literature, and the theater. The Government must see to it that its people is not poisoned. There is a higher right which is based on the recognition of that which harms a people, and that which harms a people must be done away with. (Pg. 66, "Speeches of Adolf Hitler: April 1922-August 1939", Royal Institute of International Affairs in England, 1942)

We have a backward view of history, analyzing it by coloring that the latest developments give historical events. This is our viewpoint: a white-supremacist Hitler who regarded Jews as lower than humans, and barely as formidable as a pestilent species. When one reads the speeches given between 1920 and 1924 one is struck by the recurring theme of German victimhood and Jewish aggression and cunning, which is the diametric opposite of the white-supremacist views Hitler would later propagandize. This is an all-important distinction to understand if one is to comprehend the roots of the genocidal acts that would follow. Conspicuous enough is the absence of a policy of annihilation of the Jews or any elements Hitler and his henchmen would later identify as undesirable to their "National Socialist" community. Historians quibble as to when Hitler's racism appeared during his lifespan, and as opined earlier, this is the wrong question to ask. There have always been and always be "racists." The more important question is when Adolf Hitler turned petty racism into a plan of annihilation and genocide. The identification of the "International Jew" as the enemy was clearly present in his first speech, but there is no mention or allusion as to how to address the advances of this alleged enemy. This is why the more appropriate question is when Hitler's policies became murderous, and when his "Ideal State" became the mechanism and engine of the destruction of entire portions of both Aryans and Jews.

If we are to adequately answer this poignant question, it is crucial to note that the most important shift in strategy is the immeasurably important shift from characterizing the Aryans as the oppressed and defeated nation of humble laborers by a cunning and formidable onslaught of the "International Jew," to that of Germans as a superior race whose biological and cultural superiority could only be diminished by inclusion of the allegedly inferior, pestilent, downtrodden and disease-ridden Jew. This is a shift that can only be attributed to the white-supremacy inherent in the eugenic creed and the "science" and law documented in the "Baur-Fischer-Lenz" book that was delivered to Hitler while imprisoned at Landsberg in 1924. This shift from the defeated and vanquished German to an arrogant white-supremacy is an all-important one, as it is the "scientific" justification for the Nuremberg laws that were implemented in 1933 and 1935. This was the justification for the T4 Euthanasia program that annihilated half-a-million "Aryans" and whose technology and personnel were later transferred to the extermination camps to carry out the Final Solution. It was these laws that deemed marriage with allegedly inferior biological stock or degenerated races as an imminent danger to the German gene pool. More to the point, none of these laws could have implemented with force or authority if they would have attempted to prevent marriage or procreation among cultures deemed equal, or worse, the marriage between the victorious Jew and the oppressed and humble German laborer, as Hitler characterized the conflict before studying eugenics. The "International Jew" had to be subordinated and demoted for those laws to make any sense at all.

The white-supremacy gleaned from American jurisprudence and Ivy League "science" was also a necessary precondition for enlisting an entire nation to commit the crimes of The Holocaust. Historians must note that this was not the brutish bigotry of the Southern states, but rather the intellectual elite of the United States. In fact, Alfred Ploetz said so explicitly in a famously bitter debate between Ploetz and Max Weber. Ploetz illustrated just what he absorbed from race relations in the United States during the afternoon of October 21, 1910, at the first meeting in Frankfurt of the German Sociological Society. The contentious debate was over the paper presented by Ploetz on "The Concepts of Race and Society." Ploetz had spent more than four years in the United States, and it was the "scholars" and the elite "Yankees," which according to Ploetz, prevented blacks from entering American universities and mixing with the white race. [249] Ploetz understood this to mean that this was the opinion of educated men and that therefore their reasons must have been justified by logic and facts.

Ploetz was correct in one respect. It actually was the heads of Harvard, Yale,

---

[249] Pgs. 311-312 – "Max Weber, Dr. Alfred Ploetz, and W.E.B. DuBois: Max Weber on Race and Society II", Sociological Analysis, Vol. 34, No. 4, Winter 1973, Pgs. 308-312.

Stanford, Johns Hopkins, and Cal. State which were the leaders of any eugenic segregation in the United States, and it was this elite crowd that would actively correspond and collaborate with the heads of German eugenics such as Ploetz and Rüdin. It was the icons of American Progressivism which made them their partners. It was the prestigious Rockefellers and Carnegies who were eager to fund a movement that enjoyed the reputation as a serious "science" peddling on Charles Darwin's reputation.

Clearly, a Jewish "dictatorship" is very different from the portrayal of Jews as the inferior, rodent-like, poor of the slums and ghettoes, as the eugenic propaganda films of the Third Reich would later portray. Historians must take note at the absence of any eugenic or genocidal policies in Hitler's diatribe when he took the stand for his trial in 1923, and contrast it to their sudden emergence after his stint in jail. There is a shift in thinking that can only be attributed to the influence of the eugenicists, and an honest historical perspective would reveal that Hitler was true to the policies that had already been developed and matured by Alfred Ploetz, Leonard Darwin, Harry H. Laughlin, and Charles B. Davenport. Science wasn't perverted, as is popular to claim. Any honest reading of the works of the eugenicists proves that Hitler was faithful to the goals and desires that the scientific elite had been clamoring for decades prior.

Upon these revelations, we can state with some conviction that historians have awarded way too much importance to the Wannsee Conference of 1942 as the turning point into the "Final Solution" and The Holocaust. We like our historical events grand and punctuated, and the anti-climatic occurrence of a publisher delivering something as seemingly innocuous as a book to an inmate at a jail may seem unimportant against a conference of the middle ranks of the Third Reich held in a luxurious estate. Yet, the facts evidence that the Final Solution was the product of that seemingly innocuous transfer of knowledge from publisher to imprisoned author. Historians must reconsider the importance of Wannsee against the absorption of the "Baur-Fischer-Lenz" policies into "Mein Kampf" and National Socialist policy. They have given way too much importance to Adolf Eichmann, and way too little to Fritz Lenz, Ernst Rüdin, Eugen Fischer, Erwin Baur, Alfred Ploetz, and Wilhelm Schallmayer. Compared to these intellectual leaders, Adolf Eichmann is nothing but a pencil pusher and an administrator. Important as he may have been to the day to day logistics, the entire program, the Final Solution had been digested, formalized, matured, and enshrined into German law by the time Eichmann and the Wannsee Conference came to pass. Realistically speaking, Adolf Eichmann was a minion to the eugenic masters in Ploetz, Rüdin, Lenz, Verschuer, Fischer, and Baur. In fact, Eichmann's contribution pales in comparison to that of foreigners such as Harry H. Laughlin, Charles B. Davenport, Julian Huxley, and Leonard Darwin. Ironically, the best way to characterize Eichmann's contribution is to recognize that all he actually did was to "follow orders."

Sec. 6 – FROM "CONTROL" OF BIRTHS TO "CONTROL" OF PEOPLE:

Margaret Sanger is one of those annoyingly polarizing figures in the battlefield of ideas. Ironically enough, her ideas are typically defended by people who are ignorant about her beliefs and whose beliefs are supposedly considered repugnant by those who otherwise support her. This is a recurring phenomenon for which modern-day Progressives suffer from collective amnesia. This phenomenon is duplicated by the countless Marxists that have never read Marx, and Darwinists who have never read Darwin, many of which overlap with Sanger's base of supporters. Case in point, her organization, International Planned Parenthood, has become the spearhead in the pro-abortion movement, even though Sanger personally found the practice repulsive. All in all, Sanger was the quintessential "third way" Progressive, who openly voiced annoyance with the Marxists of her day but was equally distrustful of traditional values. History has passed judgment on Sanger's life and work, whether her modern-day supporters want to recognize this or not. History passed judgment upon her and her eugenic counterparts by providing Martin Luther King, Jr. as a moral compass:

The worth of an individual does not lie in the measure of his intellect, his racial origin, or his social position.[250]

Per the standard set by this universally accepted measuring stick, Margaret Sanger fails on all three counts; Sanger sought to control the births of those she found unproductive, racially tainted or undereducated. This is not an opinion or a criticism, but rather a fact-based summary of her 1922 *magnum opus*, "The Pivot of Civilization." Sanger's book is a proposal for a "racial state" where enfranchisement is determined by the governing elite, precisely upon the criterion that Martin Luther King, Jr. warns us about in the above quote.

Before Dr. King, history had provided its own measuring stick for those who would base civilization upon a racial and hereditary criterion by regurgitating Adolf Hitler into existence. Humanity lost patience with individuals like Sanger upon learning of the product of the Third Reich's racial policies, and upon this revelation the whitewashing of Sanger's history begun in earnest. Evidence of this is that most pro-abortion zealots today are clueless as to the race-based utopia that Sanger called for in "The Pivot of Civilization" and erroneously believe that Sanger's mission was just about freedom of choice. Sanger's "Pivot of Civilization" is replete with eugenic terminology of a racial and nationalist bent such as "biological and racial mistakes," "a race of genius," "racial health" and she saw alleged racial taints as the "greatest peril" poised to "undermine the vigor and efficiency of an entire nation and an entire race." [251] To be clear, this cannot be said to be a message of inclusion or diversity by any stretch of the imagination. One must only remember that one of Sanger's most important actions towards the attainment of her racial goals was the infamous "Negro Project," which explicitly sought to reduce the number of Americans of

---

[250] Martin Luther King, Jr., "Man in a Revolutionary World", Sermon at the United Church of Christ in Chicago, July 6, 1965.
[251] Pgs. 274, 267, 262, 176 respectively - "The Pivot of Civilization", Margaret Sanger, Brentano's Publishers, 1922.

African descent. Sanger explains in "Pivot of Civilization" that she is referring to the large families of the poor and ethnic minorities when she talks of "fertile stocks," and it is these "fertile stocks," which she deems as the greatest peril to the "race" and "nation." This is the same apocalyptic premise popularized by the Third Reich film, *Erbkrank*, which claimed that the masses of the "unfit" were also the most fertile:

> The danger of recruiting our numbers from the most "fertile stocks" is further emphasized when we recall that in a democracy like that of the United States every man and woman is permitted a vote in the government, and that it is the representatives of this grade of intelligence who may destroy our liberties, and who may thus be the most far-reaching peril to the future of civilization. (Pg. 177, "The Pivot of Civilization", Brentano's Publishers, 1922)

Sanger wasn't simply seeking to relieve society of an unfit few. Like her elitist counterparts, Sanger thought the greatest threat came from the general masses:

> As a matter of fact, there is sufficient evidence to lead us to believe that the so-called "borderline cases" are a greater menace than the out-ant-out "defective delinquents" who can be supervised, controlled and prevented from procreating their kind. (Pg. 91, "The Pivot of Civilization", Brentano's Publishers, 1922)

"Restriction of output" is the solution Sanger proposes, and this is her best illustration of the "Control" component in her "Birth Control" movement. [252] The utopian component to Sanger's goals was to "maintain civilization at its present level." [253] In other words, she saw unchecked and unregulated population as an affront to her "earthly paradise"; she sought the same stasis necessary for the "socialist utopias" depicted by her comrade, H.G. Wells. More to the point, Sanger fully admitted that the "Birth Control" movement was a proposal to mold and shape society, and not just personal choice, as it is commonly described:

> As a social program, Birth Control is not merely concerned with population questions. In this respect, it is a distinct step in advance of earlier Malthusian doctrines, which concerned themselves chiefly with economics and population. (Pg. 16, "The Pivot of Civilization", Brentano's Publishers, 1922)

Sanger, however, was not part of the eugenics movement per se, though this was not by choice. Historians of the movement have recorded that she was intentionally kept at a distance and outside of the mainline movement by leaders like Charles Davenport, as she was too controversial for their political and legislative aspirations. Davenport was fully aware that the eugenics movement already had an uphill battle with institutions like the Supreme Court, and eugenic leaders like Davenport took great pains to make sure that their Ivy League credentials were not tainted by the street-level activism of Sanger. In turn, Sanger voiced a view that the eugenics movement was limited and insensitive to the revelation of sexuality as a "force of nature" to be harnessed in a spiritual sense, and criticized the movement's disdain

---

[252] Pg. 79 – "The Pivot of Civilization", Margaret Sanger, Brentano's Publishers, 1922.
[253] Pg. 23 – Ibid.

for "environmental" components in the "nature v. nurture" argument:

> Our debt to the science of Eugenics is great in that it directs our attention to the biological nature of humanity. Yet there is too great a tendency among the thinkers of this school, to restrict their ideas of sex to its expression as a purely procreative function. (Pg. 186, "The Pivot of Civilization", Brentano's Publishers, 1922)

The relationship between Margaret Sanger's movement and the prominent eugenicists such as Madison Grant and Charles B. Davenport was tempered by perception and academic respectability:

> In 1923, Margaret Sanger told Madison Grant that it would give her "great pleasure" if he would deliver a paper at the Birth Control Conference held in Chicago. Sanger invited many other eugenicists, for as she explained to Harry H. Laughlin: "I believe that this conference is going to do much to unite the Eugenic Movement and the Birth Control movement, for after all they should be and are the right and left had of one body." Because of illness Grant could not travel to Chicago, but it is doubtful that he would have attended the conference if healthy. Like Henry Fairfield Osborn and Charles Benedict Davenport, Grant was one of the old-guard eugenicists who never felt comfortable with Sanger's radical origins, and he definitely feared that an alliance with her organization would discredit his own movement. Davenport pointed out that while agitators like Margaret Sanger actually gloried in being arrested, "no police have closed the doors of a eugenics meeting yet." And Grant himself explained to Leon F. Whitney that although he had "nothing but cordial sympathy for the birth control movement, especially if it can be applied to undesirable strains and races," he thought it wise to "keep clear" of the ABCL, as it was "a feminist movement and would bring us a lot of unnecessary enemies. --- Besides, the movement is hardly respectable and can only injure the scientific standing of the American Eugenics Society."

CONTINUES…

> Grant's instincts were correct. In the 1920's, after all, the former Wobbly Margaret Sanger needed respected conservationist Madison Grant much more than he needed her, and Grant had little to gain by going to Chicago and sitting on a dais with the likes of Sanger, Jane Addams, and Harold Ickes. Nonetheless, Sanger never stopped pressing for closer ties with the American Eugenics Society; she repeatedly proposed, for example, that the American Birth Control League and the AES merge their journals. But Madison Grant was "definitely opposed" to any connection between the AES and Sanger, and the union never occurred. (Pg. 194, "Defending the Master Race: Conservation, Eugenics, and the Legacy of Madison Grant", Jonathan Peter Spiro, UPNE, 2008)

This is not to say that Sanger didn't understand the value of Ivy League credentials and its eugenic elite. Whatever amount of posturing existed between

Davenport and Sanger, just about every chapter and concept Sanger otherwise delineates in "Pivot" is supported with citations of the major eugenicists including Karl Pearson, George Bernard Shaw, Francis Galton, Havelock Ellis, Davenport himself, and of course H.G. Wells, who wrote the introduction to "Pivot of Civilization." She also cited the various centers of the eugenics movement, namely the Fabian Society, the Eugenics Education Society, the Eugenics Laboratory, and the Galton Society. Her devotion to the eugenic tenets of Darwinism are apparent in "Pivot" where she, as Charles Darwin had done, compares humanity to the livestock in a farm:

> Would any corporation for one moment conduct for one moment conduct its affairs as we conduct the infinitely more important affairs of our civilization? Would any modern stockbreeder permit the deterioration of his livestock. (Pg. 262, "The Pivot of Civilization", Brentano's Publishers, 1922)

While the more refined and elitist Ivy League eugenicists like Harvard's Davenport and Yale's Grant did not desire too close of a relationship with Margaret Sanger, other leading eugenicists of less prestigious pedigrees welcomed the association. Sanger still sought out and acquired the support and collaboration of other leading eugenicists. Leon Whitney's unpublished autobiography describes how Sanger repeatedly requested that he and Laughlin appear as her expert witnesses. [254] Truman University's Harry H. Laughlin Papers contain the correspondence between Laughlin and Sanger. The back and forth correspondence between March 13 and March 26, 1925, documents how Sanger invited Laughlin to participate in a "round table" that would be held as part of Sanger's Sixth International Neo-Malthusian and Birth Control Conference. [255] The correspondence lists the other prominent eugenicists that would be attending. The list includes Irving Fischer, Lothrop Stoddard, Raymond Pearl, Havelock Ellis, H.G. Wells, Julian Huxley, and John Maynard Keynes, the Fabian Socialist economist. The tentative program lists topics such as "Differential Birth Rate," "Hygiene – Social Diseases," and "Eugenical and Biological Sterilization."

It may also come as a surprise to contemporary supporters of Sanger that she was harshly critical of Marxism. She criticized it as a "religion" that calls upon the "conversion" and "docile acceptance" of the "doctrines of the Master" as it was "interpreted by the popes and bishops" of the "new church." [256] She claimed that the Marxist "nurture" solutions to the "nature v. nurture" problems of civilization were founded upon a false premise:

> Discontented workers may rally to Marxism because it places the blame for their misery outside of themselves and depicts their conditions as the result of a capitalistic conspiracy, thereby satisfying that innate tendency of every human being to shift the blame to some living person outside himself . . . No true solution is possible . . . until the worker is awakened to the realization that the

---

[254] Leon Fradley Whitney, Unpublished Autobiography 1971, American Philosophical Society, American Eugenics Society Papers, Vol. 1, 50 pgs., Mss.B.W613b.
[255] Box: E-I-I:I – Laughlin Collection, Truman Univ., Special Collections.
[256] Pg. 162 - "The Pivot of Civilization", Margaret Sanger, Brentano's Publishers, 1922.

roots of his malady lie deep in his own nature, his own organism, his own habits. To blame everything upon the capitalists and the environment produced by capitalism is to focus attention upon merely one of the elements of the problem. – Capitalism has not created the lamentable state of affairs in which the world now finds itself. (Pgs. 162 - 164, "The Pivot of Civilization", Brentano's Publishers, 1922)

Sanger undoubtedly was correct about Marxism. This was somewhat of a curious complaint for her to make, though. "Pivot" is clear that Sanger is calling for "human control" over these "primordial forces of nature." [257] Like her fellow eugenicists, she understood that the greatest threat to this ideal society was the uncontrolled component of a fluctuating population. Without control over ther population, the ideal could not be achieved or maintained. It is curious then that the fix she proposed for Marxism was more control, not less:

> In pointing out the limitations and fallacies of the orthodox Marxian opinion, my purpose is not to depreciate the efforts of the Socialists aiming to create a new society, but rather to emphasize what seems to me the greatest and most neglected truth of our day: -- Unless sexual science is incorporated as an integral part of world-statesmanship and the pivotal importance of Birth Control is recognized in any program of reconstruction, all efforts to create a new world and a new civilization are foredoomed to failure. (Pg. 140, "The Pivot of Civilization", Brentano's Publishers, 1922)

One of the issues that may have caused a rift between Davenport and Sanger was Sanger's religious views. Sanger was too deeply influenced by occultist views of sexuality for her to pass as a representative of the sciences:

> Through sex, mankind may attain the great spiritual illumination which will transform the world, which will light up the only path to an earthly paradise. (Pg. 271, "The Pivot of Civilization", Brentano's Publishers, 1922)

We do know that this view of sexuality as a "force of nature to be wielded," instead of repressed, is at least in part influenced by Sanger's ties to Theosophy. Theosophists such as Helen Keller, Mme. Curie, Emma Goldman, and most importantly Annie Besant, the true mother of "Birth Control" saw sexual liberation through a spiritual lens, as opposed to it being purely a movement for individual liberty. "The Selected Papers of Margaret Sanger, Volume I" by Margaret Sanger herself as the author, contains a February 23, 1919, letter documenting the day she visited the Isis Theatre in San Diego, California to hear Mrs. Tingley speak. Katherine Augusta Tingley was a spiritual medium, who in 1897 founded the Theosophical Society's international headquarters at Point Loma, an expansive campus that included the Theosophical University, a home for orphans, and a Greek theater. Margaret Sanger recalls in her autobiography how she felt about Annie Besant:

---

[257] Pg. 218 – "The Pivot of Civilization", Margaret Sanger, Brentano's Publishers, 1922.

Since I was no more than an hour by motor from Adyar, the former home of Annie Besant, who had been such an influence in the movement, I made a pilgrimage there. As I walked down winding pathways under huge banyans, cocoanuts, and bananas, ever and again glimpsing the lovely water of the Bay in the distance, I imagined I caught an echo of her words reaching across the decade since I had hear her explain the philosophy of reincarnation: the more you have evolved here on earth, the less certain it is that you will have to return to undo your mistakes – best clear them up as you go along.

CONTINUES…

Annie Besant, as soon as she had become a Theosophist, had withdrawn her books on population. I was interested to find out the attitude of present Theosophists towards birth control, and discovered that those at Adyar were persuaded of its importance. Among their beliefs was that great soul did not reincarnate unless the bodies of parents, their vehicles for birth, were perfect. If they were to perform their missions, they must wait for purity in their physical vestures. (Pgs. 484 -485, "The Autobiography of Margaret Sanger", Dover Pub., 1938)

Sanger also dedicates an entire chapter of her autobiography to occultist and eugenicist Havelock Ellis. Sanger's relationship to Ellis as well as her religion of choice is covered here because of the commonalities to Adolf Hitler and a racialist-eugenic worldview. Both Hitler and Sanger were devoted followers of Madame Blavatsky. Havelock Ellis was also an admirer of Madame Blavatsky, and women with a strong masculine personality, for that matter. More specifically, the occultist influence on Sanger's eugenic and "racialist" world-view is of consequence, as explicit in Madame Blavatsky's Theosophy is the belief in a superior "Aryan" race. One of Blavatsky's many publications was the "Aryan Path Magazine." The term 'Root Race' was first used by Blavatsky in A.P. Sinnett's 1883 book "Esoteric Buddhism." Explicit to Blavatsky's Theosophy is a belief in "seven root races," where the "god-like" Aryan race lived on Atlantis and lost their god-like status by intermarrying with the "semi-human" Jews. Of note is that Blavatsky also believed that the intermarrying with Jews caused the Aryans to devolve.

Blavatsky and many of her accomplices were exposed as frauds and snake-oil salesmen during her time, yet her Theosophy survives today, and was a deep influence on famous eugenicists like Helen Keller, Margaret Sanger, and most notably the early iterations of "Aryan" occultism in Austria and Germany which would influence the highest-ranking members of Hitler's Third Reich. The *Reichsführer* of the *SS*, Heinrich Himmler, told his personal masseur Felix Kersten that he always carried with him a copy of the Theosophical bible, the "Bhagavad Gita," because it relieved him of guilt about what he was doing. [258] Himmler felt that like the warrior Arjuna; he was simply doing his duty without attachment to his actions. Gautama Buddha's

---

[258] Pg. 402 – "Himmler: Reichsführer-SS", Peter Padfield, MacMillan, 1990.

original name for the religion we now call Buddhism was The Aryan Path. Himmler embarked on all those archeological projects searching for the origins of the "Aryans" because he fully believed in this alternative history. Himmler sent a German expedition to Tibet in 1939 as part of his research into "Aryan" origins, and Himmler was hardly alone within the National Socialists as an occultist. It is well documented that Hitler's subordinates were more devout to Theosophy and its German offshoots than even Hitler, who seems to have been marginally skeptical of them per the opinions he voiced.

None of this is intended to confuse Sanger with Himmler. There is certainly a sizeable chasm between Heinrich Himmler and Margaret Sanger. Sanger was not just opposed to the violence of abortion but also outright condemned the use of the "lethal chamber" in "Pivot of Civilization." Yet, Himmler's and Sanger's ideology not only shared an ideological wellspring but more importantly, a willingness to act on their prejudices. Their commonalities are more than mere coincidence, and their methodology evidence this. Sanger shares with the National Socialists, and namely Himmler's SS officers, a disdain for "sentimentality," "charity," and "benevolence." Both saw "sentimentality" as a dangerous hurdle to be overcome in order to enact their eugenic policies. The "Pivot of Civilization" repeatedly attacks the church for its "crimes of charity." Or to put it another way, the Nazis, the Theosophists, and Sanger shared admiration of Nietzsche's disdain for traditional morality:

> Organized charity itself is the symptom of a malignant social disease. Those vast, complex, interrelated organizations aiming to control and to diminish the spread of misery and destitution and all the menacing evils that spring out of this sinisterly fertile soil, are the surest sign that our civilization has bred, is breeding and is perpetuating constantly increasing numbers of defectives, delinquents and dependents. My criticism, therefore, is not directed at the "failure" of philanthropy, but rather at its successes. These dangers inherent in the very idea of humanitarianism and altruism, dangers which to-day produced their full harvest of human waste. (Pgs. 108-109, "The Pivot of Civilization", Brentano's Publishers, 1922)

Nietzsche is likely the wellspring in common. The "Margaret Sanger Papers" published a draft of a Sanger article titled "Frederick Nietzsche" dated November 1914. No final version was found, but the short paper expounds precisely what Sanger found tantalizing about Nietzsche:

> Nietzsche philosophy not only calls in question the moral law itself it challenges & attacks the foundation of all moral law. Before this almost all schools of philosophy had been agreed upon the fact that a universal moral law exists. (Margaret Sanger Papers, Library of Congress, LCM 130:356, "Frederick Nietzsche")

Notably, Sanger also credits Thomas H. Huxley for this concept of the "crimes of charity." [259] Sanger credits this view on Huxley's attack on the Salvation Army's

---

[259] Pg. 109 - "The Pivot of Civilization", Margaret Sanger, Brentano's Publishers, 1922.

condemnation of the "debauch of sentimentalism." Here again, Sanger finds Thomas H. Huxley's political view of Darwinism appealing, and a kindred spirit in Nietzsche:

> He applied the principle of evolution to the extant system of morals. -- Nietzsche sees the world becoming peopled with a ludicrous species--a tame, obliging sickly, mediocre kind of gently--grunting domestic animal. (Margaret Sanger Papers, Library of Congress, LCM 130:356, "Frederick Nietzsche")

If Sanger is guilty of a willful disregard for the consequences of her actions, it is because she shares with SS officers a willful repression of empathy and sentimentality, claiming that "benevolence" was "not merely ineffectual," but "positively injurious to the community and the future of the race." [260] The reader will come to recognize just how central this concept was to Nazism. Let us not forget what Himmler's proud SS officer, *Untersturmführer* Hans Stark, the head of the admissions detail at Auschwitz concentration camp had as a motto hanging in his office: "Compassion is weakness." This was hardly an aberration or coincidence. It was the running theme throughout the ranks of German National Socialism as entries in Joseph Goebbels's personal diary evidence:

> Aim—drive the Jews out of Berlin, and without any sentimentality. (Joseph Goebbels, Diary entry, June 1938, www.HolocaustResearchProject.org)

Goebbels voiced a similar disdain for "sentimentalism" four years later at the peak of the Final Solution on March of 1942:

> With regard to the Jewish Question, the Führer is determined to make a clean sweep of it. He prophesied that, if they brought about another World War, they would experience their annihilation. The annihilation of Jewry must be the necessary consequence. The question is to be viewed without any sentimentality. (Joseph Goebbels, Diary entry, March 1942, HolocaustResearchProject.org)

If there is such a thing as evil, it is in the absence of an empathic analysis of your actions, and the belief that your goals are worth the suffering of those who are affected. This sort of evil is magnified exponentially with power, and more pronounced when the victims are weak and defenseless:

> *What is good?*
> *all that elevates the feeling of power.*
> *What is bad?*
> *All that proceeds from weakness.*[261]

Should Margaret Sanger be judged as harshly as the leadership of National Socialism? There are miscalculations and unintended consequences in all human affairs. The answer to this question is best answered by asking if it is fair to label Margaret Sanger a genocidal racist? Her collaboration with the "race hygienists"

---

[260] Pg. 113 – "The Pivot of Civilization", Margaret Sanger, Brentano's Publishers, 1922.
[261] Margaret Sanger Papers, Library of Congress, LCM 130:356, "Frederick Nietzsche".

from Hitler's Third Reich makes this an important question in the grander analysis of population control. As this book documents, prominent members of Hitler's Third Reich, namely Ernst Rüdin and Hans Harmsen, contributed to or were part of Sanger's organizations after The Holocaust. Hans Harmsen was a "leading racial hygienist during the Third Reich and supporter of compulsory sterilization." [262] In the Evangelical Conference of Eugenics of May 18, 1931, Harmsen is documented as claiming that the state has the right to destroy human lives, namely that of war criminals, thus the state had the right to destroy the lives of those with lives not worth living. Historians like Pross document that Harmsen never dropped the eugenic views even after World War II. After 1945, he became a professor at the University of Hamburg and was one of those ex-Nazis given the luxury of escaping prosecution.

This chapter relies on Sabdste Schleiermacher's article titled "Racial Hygiene and Deliberate Parenthood." [263] Hans Harmsen had developed a population policy for German institutions as a response to the Great Depression, which was "the foundation for the systematic execution of the racial policy in National Socialist Germany." The policy called for "eugenically worthy" children, and it was a concept that was applied to Harmsen's post-war family planning work, "not only in the Family Planning Campaign in the Federal Republic of Germany but also in countries of the Third World." Sabdste Schleiermacher documents that the Federal Board of *Pro Familia,* the European wing of Sanger's organization, did not distance itself from Harmsen until 1984. This only evidences the selective amnesia or outright obliviousness of Sanger's apologists. How else can one explain having one of Hitler's henchmen as the head of a prominent international institution for the full forty years immediately following The Holocaust:

> The cause was criticism of his publication and activities as demographer and social hygiene specialist in the years 1920 to 1945 . . . . Apparently Harmsen represented positions at the time which are **today** condemned by the Association. (emphasis mine, "Racial Hygiene and Deliberate Parenthood: Two Sides of Demographer Hans Harmsen's Population Policy", Sabdste Schleiermacher, Reproductive and Genetic Engineering: Journal of International FeministAnalysis, 1990;3(3):201-10, quoting Pg. 21, *Pro Familia Magazin,* Kaupen-Haas, Pg. 41, 1984)

Most importantly, Sabdste Schleiermacher documents that Harmsen worked with Margaret Sanger before World War II. As Sabdste Schleiermacher points out, Harmsen's views were still acceptable to *Pro Familia* as of 1981; thus the distancing from its co-founder must be called into question. Margaret Sanger knew him from the early 1920s and had openly voiced his views in international journals, many of which he helped set up himself. Schleiermacher quotes Gunnar Heinsohn that after

---

[262] Pg. 46 - "The Nazi Doctors and the Nuremberg Code: Human Rights in Human Experimentation", Oxford Univ. Press, 1992 – Christian Pross chapter: Nazi Doctors, German Medicine, and Historical Truth.

[263] "Racial Hygiene and Deliberate Parenthood: Two Sides of Demographer Hans Harmsen's Population Policy", Sabdste Schleiermacher, Reproductive and Genetic Engineering: Journal of International FeministAnalysis, 1990;3(3):201-10, quoting Pg. 21, Pro Familia Magazin, Kaupen-Haas, Pg. 41, 1984.

1945, "the leading Nazi racial hygiene specialist H. Harmsen – carried on working as a respected social hygiene expert in the Federal Republic." It was in 1952, well within the memory of The Holocaust, that along with Anne Marie Durand-Wever and Margaret Sanger, Harmsen founded *Pro Familia* and later consolidated it with International Planned Parenthood. Harmsen was chosen as president of *Pro Familia*, "on the basis of numerous scientific contributions to German demography, to birth control, eugenics and planned parenthood." In other words, Harmsen was recognized by and honored with a position of leadership by International Planned Parenthood precisely because of his work in eugenics. Thus, to state that his work came as a post-war revelation to *Pro Familia* in the late 1980s is disingenuous at best.

Sanger has been accused of being a "racist" because of her various statements and historically inconvenient relationships. However, saying that Sanger was a "racist," as would be said about any common bigot, misses the point of her life's work. It is important to note that a mere "racist" is just someone who applies a "racial hierarchy" to their world view. Margaret Sanger went much beyond inappropriate words and inconvenient political relationships. Sanger's "Negro Project" and her speeches at Ku Klux Klan rallies evidence precisely what "race" she was obsessed with diminishing, and her "Pivot of Civilization" makes it clear that her goals are political and governmental in their intended application. The business of picking who is "fit" implies a subordination of entire swaths of humanity beneath those that Sanger deems "racially" worthwhile, and her observations on Nietzsche betray the thin vale of altruism she hides behind:

> There is a morality of Master & a Morality of Slaves-- Moral values have been determined either by a **race of masters**, conscious & proud of the distance that separates them from the ruled race-or by a crowd of subjugated ones, slaves, inferiors of all kinds. (emphasis mine, Margaret Sanger Papers, Library of Congress, LCM 130:356, "Frederick Nietzsche")

However much Sanger may have paid lip-service to the liberty of the individual, she always circled back to explaining her mission as within the jurisdiction and powers of the state and the statesmen. Thus, at all times her propositions assumed control over the individual by a central planning and all-powerful governmental body. The "Birth Control" canvas was painted with an uncompromising application of compulsory segregation and sterilization of large swaths of the population.

Still, there is an even more important lesson to be gleaned from Margaret Sanger's history. Her relationship with Ernst Rüdin and Hans Harmsen is indicative of the great danger and the severe damage resulting directly from an unclear or misleading Holocaust history. The fact that *Pro Familia* did not come around to distancing itself from Harmsen until the 1980s and sought out a relationship with Harmsen in the decades immediately following World War II, is indicative of the failure of the Nuremberg Doctors' Trial to accurately document for all posterity precisely how and why those "crimes against humanity" were committed. Clearly, International Planned Parenthood knew about Harmsen's "racial hygiene" past, yet they were able to exist and thrive politically with Harmsen as its co-founder and president for 40 years after The Holocaust. That Harmsen kept spewing the same eugenic filth and passing it off as "science" with complete impunity is a fact that can be used to measure the success of the Nuremberg Trials. The inability or reluctance to connect the "science" of eugenics to the crimes of The Holocaust can only be said to have been the reason that culprits like Harmsen were able to continue propagating the message of eugenics afterward. That these important historical facts remain obscure to this day is a tacit admission by omission by these institutions and their intellectual supporters at the bastions of education and journalism. History is liable to repeat itself precisely because the powerful and elite are keenly aware of the fact that those that control the past, control the future, and that those that control births, control the humanity.

FIGURE 7: "A Civic Biology: Presented in Problems", the textbook at issue in the Scopes' Monkey Trial, fully propagated the views of the international eugenics movement. The chapter of the textbook that covered humanity had been written by Charles Benedict Davenport, head of the Cold Spring Harbor Eugenics Records Office.

Chap. 6: 1920 to 1916

NEW WORLD: The 18 Amendment to the US Constitution, authorizing Prohibition, is ratified. – The United States Congress refuses to ratify the Treaty of Versailles. – The Nineteenth Amendment to the US Constitution is passed, guaranteeing women's suffrage. **SCIENCE & TECHNOLOGY:** The first domestic radio sets come to stores in the United States; a Westinghouse radio costs $10. Einstein's theory of general relativity is tested/confirmed by Arthur Eddington's observation of a total solar eclipse in Principe, and by Andrew Crommelin in Sobral, Ceará, Brazil **OLD WORLD:** The Second Congress of the Communist International takes place in Saint Petersburg and Moscow. In Geneva, the first assembly of the League of Nations is held. By order of the Bolshevik Party and carried out by the Cheka, Emperor Nicholas II of Russia, his wife Alexandra Feodorovna, their children, Olga, Tatiana, Maria, Anastasia, and Alexei, and retainers are executed at the Ipatiev House in Ekaterinburg, Russia. **LIFE:** The Bauhaus architectural movement is founded in Weimar, Germany. John F. Kennedy, 35th President of the United States is born. – The 2 millionth Ford Model T rolls off the line.

Sec. I - NIETZSCHE'S "MERCHANTS OF LIGHT":

There are several books that should be forever linked with the crimes of The Holocaust. As previously illustrated in this book, Hitler's "Mein Kampf" was, in reality, a collage of poorly plagiarized ideas repackaged as political propaganda. This list of books would contain the 1921 "Baur-Fischer-Lenz" volume delivered to Hitler while he was writing "Mein Kampf" in Landsberg prison. The list would certainly be incomplete without Harry H. Laughlin's 1922 documentation of all the sterilization laws in the United States, the "Eugenical Sterilization in the United States," which provided the "Model Eugenical Sterilization Law." The fourth book to join the ranks of "Mein Kampf" unquestionably has to be the 1920 book by Alfred Hoche and Karl Binding *"Die Freigabe der Vernichtung Lebensunwertem Lebens,"* whose title has been translated as the "Allowing the Destruction of Life Unworthy of Living," and the "Annihilation of Life Unworthy of Being Lived," as well as the "Permission to Destroy Life Unworthy of Life." Binding and Hoche paraphrased Plato in creating the concept of *"lebensunwertes Leben,"* or in English, "that life which being born is now unworthy of living." The book provided the legal and philosophical foundation for the Third Reich's eugenic euthanasia policies. The book also outlines the philosophy that would later be distilled down to the various propaganda posters, propaganda films, and newspaper articles released by the Third Reich to gain public support for its eugenic policies. The book was translated into English in 1975 by Robert I. Sassone. Consider a passage that illustrates the tone of the book:

> ...All the institutions for mentally sick persons... the tremendous care that these creatures receive; creatures of no value at all... incurable idiots... have no will for life or for death. They give no definite consent to the euthanasia.... Their life is completely useless, but they don't consider it unbearable. For the idiots... the continuation of life for society as well as for the person himself has no value. ("The Release of the Destruction of Life Devoid of Value, Its Measure and Its Form", Felix Meiner in Leipzig, 1920 – Pgs. 20-21 in the English language translation by Robert L. Sassone, 1975)

While the scope initially included only those born with defects or hereditary illnesses, the National Socialists expanded it to broader terms that would mirror the social "unfit" as defined by Laughlin's "Law." These would include those prone to "prostitution," "alcoholism," "pauperism," and other conditions deemed to be "degenerate," or more precisely, debilitating and detrimental to the health of the societal body. The policy went through several modifications:

> Of the five identifiable steps by which the Nazis carried out the principle of "life unworthy of life," coercive sterilization was the first. There followed the killing of "impaired" children in hospitals; and then the killing of "impaired" adults, mostly collected from mental hospitals, in centers especially equipped with carbon monoxide gas. This project was extended (in the same killing centers) to "impaired" inmates of concentration and extermination camps and, finally, to mass killings in the extermination camps themselves. (Pg. 21, "The Nazi Doctors: Medical Killing and the Psychology of Genocide", Robert Jay Lifton, Basic Books, 1986)

After the publication of the Binding-Hoche book, the statements of both authors raised broad opposition, mainly by Ewald Meltzer, a German director of an asylum in Saxony. According to Michael Burleigh, Meltzer hotly disputed the claim that people with mental handicaps had lost the last vestiges of human personality, stressing instead their capacity and will to enjoy life. In Meltzer's 1925 rebuttal titled *"Das Problem der Abkürzung 'lebensunwerten' Lebens,"* Meltzer wrote that it was "far more heroic to accept these beings to the best of one's abilities, to bring sunshine into their lives, and therewith to serve humanity." [264] He claimed asylums for handicapped people were not only valuable centers of scientific research but also tangible manifestations of Christian charity. Meltzer's work had the opposite of its intended effect:

> In an attempt to support his belief, Meltzer surveyed the parents of his patients to ascertain their perceptions of disability and euthanasia. To Meltzer's astonishment, the survey results showed a widely held contradiction among the parents that although they had strong emotional ties to their children, they simultaneously expressed, with varying degrees of qualification, a 'positive' attitude toward killing them. In fact, only a handful of respondents completely rejected all notions of euthanasia. (Pgs. 155-168, "Useless Eaters: Disability as Genocidal Marker in Nazi Germany", Mark Mostert, The Journal of Special Education, Vol. 36, Issue 3, Nov. 1, 2002)

Meltzer's survey was later used as justification for the killing of thousands of people with disabilities under the National Socialists' program otherwise known as "Action T4." "Special treatment" as part of the T4 program meant either being injected with a lethal dose of medicine or simply starved to death. [265] Meltzer was speaking for traditional medicine, and his reference to "Christian charity" identifies

---

[264] Pg. 21 - "Death and Deliverance: Euthanasia in Germany 1900-45," Michael Burleigh, CUP Archive, 1994.
[265] Pgs. 134-135 - "Racial Hygiene: Medicine under the Nazis", Robert Proctor, Harvard Univ. Press, 1988.

him as part of the legacy of German doctors and scientists in the tradition of Rudolf Virchow, Albert Schweitzer, and Alexander von Humboldt. Recall that the Hippocratic Oath dictates "first do no harm." The Hippocratic Oath is perhaps the most widely known of Greek medical texts. The Oath requires a new physician to swear upon several healing gods that he will uphold a number of professional ethical standards. The original oath has been adopted throughout the centuries and almost all adaptations contain the promise from doctor to patient "I will do no harm or injustice to them." The oath also provides a direct prohibition on abortion or euthanasia, stating in part:

> I will not give a lethal drug to anyone if I am asked, nor will I advise such a plan; and similarly I will not give a woman a pessary to cause an abortion. (nlm.nih.gov, "The Greek Oath", Translated by Michael North, National Library of Medicine, 2002)

Thus, it begs to question: If the ancient Greeks disapproved of euthanasia in the Hippocratic Oath and medical doctors have adopted its general premise as their oath and creed, why did so many German doctors support the eugenic euthanasia leading up to and through the Third Reich? The answer to this question lay in the 1920 book by Binding and Hoche, which lay down the legal and philosophical foundations of this "new ethos," this *"Über Ethik,"* and literally called for the discarding of the Hippocratic Oath in order to allow eugenics and euthanasia. While Binding and Hoche are its official authors, the generously repeated references to Nietzsche's influence on Binding, and Hoche practically justify Nietzsche as its third author. Nietzsche had previously made his support of euthanasia absolutely clear in "Twilight of the Idols." Karl Binding and Friedrich Nietzsche were good friends. [266]

Nietzsche's apologists vehemently reject the notion that Nietzsche had any part in the policies enacted by Hitler's henchmen. In doing so, they make atypically superficial arguments for a readership otherwise known for deep thinking. Nietzsche's apologists typically claim that references to a "master race" are not enough to justify their connection to Hitler's mass-murders, as Nietzsche himself was not anti-Semitic. In one sense they are right; a juxtaposition of Nietzsche's "over-man" with Hitler's "master race" is too superficial of a connection to indict Nietzsche. However, the connection between Nietzsche and The Holocaust is embodied in the Binding-Hoche book. If Nietzsche can be said to be fully culpable in the crimes of The Holocaust, it is because he was significantly responsible for instigating the destruction of the traditional moral values of sympathy, compassion, and the sanctity of life. The Binding-Hoche book represents the departure from the humanitarian values of internationally renowned German doctors and scientists such as Virchow, Schweitzer, and von Humboldt, and the adoption of the "new ethic." This "new philosophy" was made culturally respectable by the lauded philosopher, and it is doubtful either Binding or Hoche had the clout to make it as influential as it ultimately was. This was precisely the philosophy taught to the Hitler Youth and

---

[266] Pg. 21 - "The Curse of 1920", Gary D. Naler, Self-Publish, 1994.

the ranks of the SS, namely those put in charge of the concentration camps. More to the point, this hardening of the heart and ridiculing of the emotions of sympathy and compassion was precisely what a demagogue like Hitler needed to enlist the masses to engage in a protracted and systematic campaign of mass murder.

Furthermore, Nietzsche rejected without exception theories affirming the equality and comparability of all human beings. The "new philosophers," as he calls the "free spirits" who shared this view, "desire precisely the opposite of an assimilation, an equalization." [267] The main task of Nietzsche's "new philosophy" was to strengthen life continually in a eugenic sense, and as it was dictated by those devoted eugenicists, this goal could not be accomplished without simultaneously excluding life that "does not deserve to be lived," the precise words of Karl Binding would use as a rationale in his 1920 book with Alfred Hoche:

> The increasing dwarfing of man is precisely the driving force that brings to mind the breeding of a stronger race--a race that would be excessive precisely where the dwarfed species was weak and growing weaker (in will, responsibility, self-assurance, ability to posit goals for oneself). (Friedrich Nietzsche, Book IV, Chap.: Discipline and Breeding, Sec.: The Strong and the Weak, "The Will to Power")

Friedrich Nietzsche was anti-democracy, anti-Christianity, anti-Judaism, anti-socialist, and self-acclaimed Anti-Christ. He expressed his belief in a master race and the coming of a superman in many of his works. He certainly was not subtle about his belief in the destruction of life:

> The sick are the great danger of man, not the evil, not the 'beasts of prey.' They who are from the outset botched, oppressed, broken those are they, the weakest are they, who most undermine the life beneath the feet of man, who instill the most dangerous venom and skepticism into our trust in life, in man, in ourselves...Here teem the worms of revenge and vindictiveness; here the air reeks of things secret and unmentionable; here is ever spun the net of the most malignant conspiracy – the conspiracy of the sufferers against the sound and the victorious; here is the sight of the victorious hated. (Pg. 14, Essay III, What is the meaning of ascetic ideals? "Genealogy of Morals", Translation by Horace B. Samuel, M.A., Boni & Liveright, 1921)

This devaluation of sympathy and compassion for the sick and needy was a theme that Adolf Hitler directly picked up from Nietzsche, his lifetime hero. Here again Hitler is, if not directly plagiarizing, then at the very least unknowingly parroting the disdain for sentimentalism written into the theories of all the prominent eugenicists. This is further evidence of Hitler transitioning from a rabble-rousing malcontent spewing common *fin-de-siècle* racial prejudices, towards a concrete eugenic and genocidal political platform. This book postulates that this concrete eugenic outlook became the guiding principle of National Socialism was injected by his exposure to eugenic literature; specifically, the academic literature

---

[267] Pg. 57 – "Nietzsche and Legal Theory: Half-Written Laws", Peter Goodrich, Mariana Valverde, Routledge, Aug 21, 2013.

brought to him by his publisher, J.F. Lehmann. Consider the content of Hitler's pre-Landsberg speeches vs the content of his later speeches. While addressing the Nuremberg rally of in August 1929, Adolf Hitler defined and justified Nazi eugenic policy in the terms utilized by the eugenic academia. Here is a passage from a post-Landsberg speech where Nietzschean disdain of sentimentalism is proposed as an integral part of a coherent eugenic thesis, utilizing the language of the prominent eugenicists:

> If Germany was to get a million children a year and was to remove 700,000–800,000 of the weakest people, then the final result might even be an increase in strength. The most dangerous thing is for us to cut off the **natural process of selection** and thereby gradually rob ourselves of the possibility of acquiring able people ... As a result of our **modern sentimental humanitarianism** we are trying to maintain the weak at the expense of the healthy. It goes so far that a **sense of charity**, which calls itself socially responsible, is concerned to ensure that even cretins are able to procreate while more healthy people refrain from doing so, and all that is considered perfectly understandable. Criminals have the opportunity of procreating, **degenerates** are raised artificially and with difficulty. And in this way we are gradually breeding the weak and killing off the strong. (emphasis mine, Pg. 72, Susan Benedict and Linda Shields, "Nurses and Midwives in Nazi Germany: The 'Euthanasia Programs'", Routledge, 2014, - citing translation by Jeremy Noakes, "Nazism: 1919-1945", 1983, Pg. 1002)

The above passage could have been pulled from any of the leading eugenic tracts by Charles B. Davenport, Harry H. Laughlin, H.G. Wells, Julian Huxley, or Francis Galton. In "The Genealogy of Morals," Nietzsche described the state of European civilization utilizing the pedestrian terms of racial selection, "blood-poisoning," a term used by layman eugenicists precisely like Hitler:

> The 'masters' have been done away with; the morality of the vulgar man has triumphed. This triumph may also be called a blood-poisoning (it has mutually fused the races)...Everything is obviously becoming Judaised, or Christianised, or vulgarized... (Pg. 18, "The Genealogy of Morals", Courier Corporation, 2012)

It would be silly to argue that Nietzsche was not the impetus for that emerging ethos that all prominent racial philosophers of the era would subscribe to. To deny this would be to pretend that Nietzsche was not as consequential to his followers as he truly was; an indefensible position to postulate. Nietzsche prophesied that a new morality would harness the human "will to power," and that the resulting human would be the "overman," or "superman" as most commonly translated. In "Will to Power," Nietzsche justified terror with the belief that it would bring a higher state for mankind:

> Man is beast and superbeast; the higher human is inhuman and superhuman: these belong together. (Pg. 101, Weaver Santaniello, "Nietzsche, God, and the Jews: His Critique of Judeo-Christianity in Relation to the Nazi Myth", SUNY Press, 2012)

The extended version of the above Nietzsche quote is followed by the sentence: "With every increase of greatness and height in man, there is also an increase in depth and terribleness." Clearly, Nietzsche believed that man became harsher and more calculating as he evolved away from "beast" and towards a "master" of domains. Nietzsche believed that the "overman" would rule as a "master," and WWII historians have never let go of this overlap between Hitler and Nietzsche:

> The strong men, the masters, regain the pure conscience of a beast of prey; monsters filled with joy, they can return from a fearful succession of murder…when a man is capable of commanding, when he is by nature a 'master,' when he is violent in act and gesture … to judge morality properly, it must be replaced by two concepts borrowed from zoology: the taming of a beast and the breeding of a specific species. (Pg. 111, William L. Shirer, "The Rise and Fall of the Third Reich: A History of Nazi Germany", Simon and Schuster, 2011)

Yet, this commonality of terminology between Hitler and Nietzsche, this overplay of the "overman" and "superhuman" phraseology, is insufficient to explain how the most educated populace of the 20th century was conscripted to carry out a sustained program of ethnic cleansing. One can easily arouse violent outbursts by appealing to the base instincts of a population. To sustain a systematic and industrial campaign of murder, one must do much more than incite riots or violence; one must make true believers of those conscripted to annihilate. This is where Nietzsche's new ethos comes front and center. This hardening of the heart; this discarding of the Hippocratic Oath; this *modus operandi* had direct application in the crimes of The Holocaust. For those that would deny the Nietzsche-Nazi link, it is important to remember that Hans Stark, the *SS-Untersturmführer* at Auschwitz-II Birkenau of Auschwitz concentration camp, had a plaque hanging over his desk that read "compassion is weakness," or in German, *Mitleid ist Schwäche*. [268]

Furthermore, Nietzsche attacked the hard-fought and desperately earned values that rejected the stratification of men. The "equality before the law" which had been gained by the Enlightenment and the various revolutions in Europe and America, was for Nietzsche an impediment to those he considered as "superior." Recall that this too was a theme of Hitler's speeches which can be found in Nietzsche's work. Hitler can't be credited with this line of thinking. Hitler was a plagiarist of concepts exactly like this one:

> Here the concept of the "equal value of men before God" is extraordinarily harmful; one forbade actions and attitudes that were in themselves among the prerogatives of the strongly constituted--as if they were in themselves unworthy of men. One brought the entire tendency of the strong into disrepute when one erected the protective measures of the weakest (those who were weakest also when confronting themselves) as a norm of value. (Book IV, Chap.: Discipline and Breeding, Sec.: The Strong and the Weak, "The Will to Power")

---

[268] Pg. 282 - "People in Auschwitz", Hermann Langbein, Published with The US Holocaust Memorial Museum, Univ. of North Carolina Press, 2004.

In other words, Nietzsche's concept of a "master" and "slave" race is deeply rooted in this stratification of humanity. Nietzsche believed that some were destined to be subservient and others "masters," and more importantly, that some conscious measure should be taken so that Europeans be bred for this inborn trait to rule as "masters." As Garland Allen has explained, these "rank-order hierarchies" were a central and indispensable part of the ideological foundations of eugenics [269]:

> The homogenizing of European man is the great process that cannot be obstructed: one should even hasten it. The necessity to create a gulf, distance, **order of rank**, is given eo ipso--not the necessity to retard the process. — As soon as it is established, this homogenizing species requires a justification: it lies in serving a higher sovereign species that stands upon the former and can raise itself to its task only by doing this. Not merely a master race whose sole task is to rule, but a race with its own sphere of life, with an excess of strength for beauty, bravery, culture, manners to the highest peak of the spirit; an affirming race that may grant itself every great luxury--strong enough to have no need of the tyranny of the virtue-imperative, rich enough to have no need of thrift and pedantry, beyond good and evil; a hothouse for strange and choice plants. (emphasis mine, Book IV, Chap.: Discipline and Breeding, Sec.: The Strong and the Weak, "The Will to Power")

These concepts are central and indispensable to both Nietzsche's work and the work of National Socialist core eugenic philosophy. To postulate otherwise is to entertain the ridiculous. The notion that Nietzsche's philosophy was misapplied or misinterpreted by Hitler's henchmen is outright rejected by authors Robert Baker and Laurence McCullough. Baker and McCullough provide proof of the very direct link between Nietzsche and the work of the National Socialist doctors that were directly inspired by Hoche and Binding's book:

> Nietzsche's and Plato's intent in penning their words is thus irrelevant. Hoche wanted to challenge a received medical morality grounded in Christian ideals sanctifying all forms of human life and in the Gregorian ideal of the humanely sympathetic physician. He knew that the received German medical discourse with its celebration of humanity and sympathy would never countenance the killing of the mentally disabled. So he turned to discourse from Nietzsche and Plato to offer a medical discourse that extolled "hardness" as a virtue, that derided sympathy, and that conceptualized the mentally disabled as *lebensunwertes Leben*. (Pg. 18, Robert Baker and Laurence McCullough, "Medical Ethics' Appropriation of Moral Philosophy: The Case of the Sympathetic and the Unsympathetic Physician", Kennedy Institute of Ethics Journal, March 2007)

Baker and McCullough also document just how pervasive Nietzsche's philosophy was in the Hoche and Binding book. Hoche opens his section of the

---

[269] "The Misuse of Biological Hierarchies: The American Eugenics Movement, 1900-1940", Garland E. Allen, History and Philosophy of the Life Sciences, Vol. 5, No. 2, 1983, pp. 105-128.

book by stating that the Hippocratic Oath was "no longer binding." [270] In keeping with the values prescribed by Nietzsche, Hoche extrapolates this new Nietzschean ethics in the context of the destruction of "life devoid of value"- i.e., the mentally disabled, or as they phrased it, "ballast persons." [271]

> Par. 226. The question of whether we should spend all of this money on ballast type persons of no value was not important in previous years because the state had sufficient money. Now conditions are different. . . .
> Par. 227. Opposed to our task is the modern effort to keep alive all sorts of weaklings and to care for all those who are perhaps not mentally retarded but are still large burdens. . . .
> Par. 228. The granting of death with dignity to life devoid of value to affect the release of the burden will for a long time be met with resistance for mostly sentimental reasons. . . .
> Par. 229. In order to attain the necessary results, we must investigate . . . the possibility and conditions for euthanasia.
> 233. . . . one of these days . . . we will come to the conclusion that the elimination of the mentally dead is no crime, nor an immoral act, and no unfeeling cruelty, but a permissible and necessary act.
> The [era] in which we are still living during which the support of every [form of] existence—no matter how worthless—has become the highest moral norm. A new time will come when we no longer . . . carry out this demand, which has its origins in an exaggerated ideal of humanity. The present morality places too much value on mere continued existence and asks too high a sacrifice. (Pg. 15, Robert Baker and Laurence McCullough, "Medical Ethics' Appropriation of Moral Philosophy: The Case of the Sympathetic and the Unsympathetic Physician", Kennedy Institute of Ethics Journal, March 2007)

Baker and McCullough correctly point to the fact that Hoche refers to these less valuable members of society as *Ballastexistenzen* or "ballast people" or "dead weight" and that this characterization echoes Nietzsche labeling the less fortunate as having "the character of a parasite...on modern society." [272] Hoche gave Nietzsche's words a biological twist:

> ...there is no doubt that in trying to preserve life without dignity by all means, exaggeration has occurred . . . We doctors know that in the interest of the whole human organism, single, less valuable members have to be abandoned and pushed out. (Par. 231, Binding and Hoche [1920] 1975, p. 37 – As cited by Robert Baker and Laurence McCullough, "Medical Ethics' Appropriation of Moral Philosophy: The Case of the Sympathetic and the Unsympathetic Physician", Kennedy Institute of Ethics Journal, March 2007)

Baker and McCullough aptly point out that the entire notion that Nietzsche's

---

[270] Par: 203 – Karl Binding and Hoche, Pg. 37 [1920] 1975 - As cited by Robert Baker and Laurence McCullough, "Medical Ethics' Appropriation of Moral Philosophy: The Case of the Sympathetic and the Unsympathetic Physician", Kennedy Institute of Ethics Journal, March 2007.
[271] Par: 230 – Ibid.
[272] Par: 234 – Ibid.

philosophy was misapplied or misinterpreted by German doctors by documenting the origins of the translation from philosophy to practical application back to Nietzsche himself. Hoche recalls that Nietzsche had explicitly meant his philosophy for doctors:

> A moral for doctors. —The sick man is a parasite of society. In certain cases it is indecent to go on living. To continue to vegetate in a cowardly dependence on doctors and special treatments, once the meaning of life, the right to life, has been lost, ought to be regarded with the greatest of contempt by society. . . A new responsibility should be created for the doctor—the responsibility of ruthlessly suppressing and eliminating degenerate life, in all cases in which the highest interests of life itself, of ascending life, demand such a course. . . One should die proudly when it is no longer possible to live proudly. (Pg. 15, Robert Baker and Laurence McCullough, "Medical Ethics' Appropriation of Moral Philosophy: The Case of the Sympathetic and the Unsympathetic Physician", Kennedy Institute of Ethics Journal, March 2007)

More so, it must be recognized that Nietzsche is sufficiently specific as to what his call for artificial selection meant. Nietzsche dictated that a "doctrine is needed powerful enough to work as a breeding agent." [273] Though the musings below are not as defined and purposed as those of the scientific breeders of men, what must be gleaned from this passage is that Nietzsche clearly meant that a force above the populace must be imbued with the power to make such decisions; the decisions a breeder makes over his livestock:

> The annihilation of the decaying races. Decay of Europe. — The annihilation of slavish evaluations. -- Dominion over the earth as a means of producing a higher type. -- The annihilation of the tartuffery called "morality" (Christianity as a hysterical kind of honesty in this: Augustine, Bunyan). -- The annihilation of suffrage universal; i. e., the system through which the lowest natures prescribe themselves as laws for the higher. (Book IV, Chap.: Discipline and Breeding, Sec.: The Strong and the Weak, "The Will to Power")

The values lifted from Nietzsche by Binding and Hoche, and wholeheartedly adopted by a political movement equally hostile to traditional ethics evidence just how far departed Hitler's regime was from any notion of what it meant to be "conservative." This view is only further bolstered by the sector of German society which put up the only real opposition to the regime's euthanasia program. This book documents that the most successful and persistent pushback on the euthanasia campaign came from the German Catholic Church. Dr. Hilfrich, Bishop of Limburg wrote a protest on behalf of the Roman Catholic Church on August 13, 1941. Below is the text of the petition of Dr. Hilfrich, Bishop of Limburg, to the Reich Minister of Justice concerning the killing of patients at the State Hospital for the Mentally Ill at Hadamar. While this incident has been largely covered by historians,

---

[273] Pg. 179 – "Biology and the Foundation of Ethics", Jane Maienschein, Michael Ruse, Cambridge Univ. Press, 1999. – Citing "Will to Power", IV, 862 and IV, 1055.

it is important to note that the bishop makes direct reference to the philosophy of Binding, Hoche, and Nietzsche. The Bishop of Limburg wrote on Aug 13, 1941:

> Regarding the report submitted on July 16 (Sub IV, pp 6-7) by the Chairman of the Fulda Bishops' Conference, Cardinal Dr. Bertram, I consider it my duty to present the following as a concrete illustration of destruction of so-called **"useless life."** ---- About 8 kilometers from Limburg, in the little town of Hadamar, on a hill overlooking the town, there is an institution which had formerly served various purposes and of late had been used as a nursing home; this institution was renovated and furnished as a place in which, by consensus of opinion, the above mentioned euthanasia has been systematically practiced for months-approximately since February 1941. The fact has become known beyond the administrative district of Wiesbaden, because death certificates from a Registry Hadamar-Moenchberg are sent to the home communities. (emphasis mine, Pg. 449, Vol. III, Doc.: 615-PS "Nazi Conspiracy and Aggression", USGPO, 1946,)

On August 3, 1941, Bishop Clemens Graf von Galen from Munster held a sermon preaching against "euthanasia" in the Lambertikirche in Munster; its written reproduction had a large-scale distribution. Von Galen called the "euthanasia programme" "pure murder" and declared he would bring a charge against those responsible for this crime on the grounds of an offense against section 211 (murder) of the German Penal Code. He ended the sermon with the words: "Do you, do I have the right to live only as long as we are productive, as long as others acknowledge that we are productive?" Clearly, the bishop was making a rebutal to the Binding-Hoche concept of "life unworthy of life."

Needless to say, the bishop's sermon did not come without consequences. Owing to Von Galen's reputation, he was allowed to go on exercising his function as bishop, but only under constant observation of the Gestapo. Notwithstanding, the bishop's words deeply impacted the German youth, which felt their freedoms slipping from them. The German youth activists known as the "White Rose" were awakened by the bishop's sermon. The regime's push for expanding the euthanasia program was temporarily stopped by the bishop's push back. The euthanasia campaign was broken up and dispersed across several institutions, likely to make it less conspicuous. The actual doctors, nurses, and technological infrastructure were transferred to death camps like Auschwitz, and the directives to euthanize "useless eaters" were then transferred from the secret facilities under the T4 Euthanasia program to regular hospitals under "Aktion Brandt."

The White Rose were not the only protests originating from the Church faithful. Historians have also documented Bishop of Fulda's refusal to co-operate in the "extermination of life unworthy of life." The Bishop also had presented a petition on the former transfers to the Reich Minister of the Interior. On August 11, 1940, the Bishop's Conference of Fulda sent correspondence to the Reich Chancellery, protesting the killing of mentally sick individuals, "unworthy of life," and the life-threatening experiments on new therapies involving other sick people.

It is also of historical importance to note that there is a direct link between Karl Brandt, the head of the T4 program, and Alfred Hoche. Brandt had taken his medical exams under Hoche in *Freiburg im Brisgau*. [274] They became lifelong friends as both Hoche and Brandt were from Alsace-Loraine, and both saw eye to eye on the legality and ethics behind euthanasia. Baker and McCullough shed light on other links between the Hoche and Binding book and Hitler's euthanasia policies by documenting that the director of the *Eglfinger-Haar* asylum, Herman Pfannmüller, was also an admirer of Hoche and Binding. Baker and McCullough document that Herman Pfannmüller gave tours of the eugenic-euthanasia program to young physicians and framed the euthanasia work done in the facilities in the terms established by Nietzsche, Hoche, and Binding:

> Since I had studied psychology in 1934/1935 as part of my professional training ... I took part in a conducted tour ... The asylum director ... Pfannmüller, led us into a children's ward ... [He] explained ... "As a National Socialist, these creatures ... naturally only represent to me a burden upon the healthy body of our nation. We don't kill (he may have used a more circumlocutory expression...) with poison, injections, etc., since that would only give the foreign press and certain gentlemen in Switzerland new hate propaganda material. No: as you see, our method is simpler and even more natural." With these words, and assisted by a nurse ... he pulled one of the children out of the bed. As he displayed the child around like a dead hare, he pointed out, with a knowing look and a cynical grin, "This one will last another two or three days." The image of this fat, grinning man, with the whimpering skeleton in his fleshy hand is still clear before my eyes ... A lady who also took part in our tour asked, with an outrage she had difficulty suppressing, whether a quick death aided by injections would not be more merciful. (Baker and McCullough citing Pgs. 45–46, Michael Burleigh, "Death and Deliverance: 'Euthanasia' in Germany 1900-1945", Cambridge University Press, 1994)

Here again, the influence of Binding-Hoche-Nietzsche is too pronounced to be denied. Baker and McCullough point to the fact that historians who have examined the intellectual background of Pfannmüller and other German physicians found that Hoche and Binding had a profound influence on the physicians responsible for the daily euthanasia operations in Hitler's Germany:

> From the program's co-director Karl Brandt (1904–1948) and administrators such as Viktor Brack (1904–1948) to the pediatricians who selected infants for "euthanasia," Werner Catel (1894–1981) and Ernst Wentzler (1891–1973)— inventor of an incubator for premature babies—all had read Hoche or been his students. Their discourse was studded with Hoche's language, especially *lebensunwerten Lebens*, the idea that certain people lived a life unworthy of being lived—a phrase from Plato that Hoche had appropriated as the title of his book (Lifton 1986, p. 107). Most had accepted Hoche's views before joining the program (Burleigh 1994, pp. 100, 273–74). Some, like Werner Heyde (1902–1964), had attended Hoche's lectures (Lifton 1986, p. 117). Others report that Hoche's ideas

---

[274] Pg. 33 - "Karl Brandt: Medicine and Power in the Third Reich", Ulf Schmidt, Bloomsbury Academic, 2007.

were used to recruit them into the program (Lifton 1986, p. 104). – (Pgs. 13-14, Robert Baker and Laurence McCullough, "Medical Ethics' Appropriation of Moral Philosophy: The Case of the Sympathetic and the Unsympathetic Physician", Kennedy Institute of Ethics Journal, March 2007)

Baker and McCullough point to another parallel that is consistent with the core concepts of this book. They point to the fact that Binding, Hoche, and Nietzsche had all consciously borrowed from Plato's utopian novel, the "Republic." As this book establishes, euthanasia and eugenics are consistent components of the "Ideal States," which were either fiction or attempts at utopia throughout history. Hoche addresses this aspect of Plato by stating that this view of ethics was "first raised by Plato, how to deal with 'sick person[s] who [are] a parasite on society'." The concept of *lebensunwerten Lebens* is from an argument in Plato's "Republic":

> If a man had a sickly constitution and intemperate habits, his life was worth nothing to himself or anyone else; medicine was not meant for such people and they should not be treated, though they be richer than Midas. (Plato, "Republic")

Baker and McCullough document that Plato goes on to state that physicians should "put to death those who are incurably corrupt in mind," and that Plato does so on a collectivized frame of reference by justifying that the act of euthanizing the suffering "will be the best thing for them as well as for the community." This is the core concept of Francis Galton's eugenic religion, and the logic only makes sense if understood in the frame of mind that thinks of the "nation's" or "race's" need to weed out lives that are "ballast" or dead-weight in the pursuit of a predetermined social goal. It is a concept that is directly antagonistic to the notion that all individuals are free to pursue happiness and establish their own goals apart from those of the state or society. A handicapped life only becomes a financial negative if the collectivized resources of the state are compromised by the mere existence of an individual. The fact that Plato, and every other utopian thinker thereafter, made euthanasia and eugenics a central concept of their idealized state evidence just how integral these concepts are to those who would attempt to erect a utopia on earth. It also evidences that the typical pedestrian "racism" is unnecessary in repeating another Holocaust. The philosophical, legal, and ethical policies of an all-encompassing state are the main ingredients of genocide and not the guttural, pedestrian, brutish type of racism. Nietzsche zealots would only validate this observation by pointing to the fact that Nietzsche himself was not anti-Semitic and that he condemned his sister's and brother-in-law's anti-Semitism.

Yet, it is clear how indispensable Nietzsche's views were to the practical execution of the Third Reich's murderous laws and policies. It is also clear that Nietzsche's call for a "master" and "subservient" races, framed in the context of his dehumanizing euthanasia and eugenic views, fully endorsed the enslavement of those he deemed inferior for the direct benefit of his "race of masters." You would have to be somewhat of a blind zealot to claim that an intellect like that of Nietzsche's would have been oblivious to the implications of making such a statement in the century in which abolition and slavery were the enduring controversies. Nietzsche was calling for this stratification of humanity on the heels of the Reconstruction Era that followed the American Civil War. Unfortunately, neither Nietzsche or his friend Karl Biding would live to see the horrifying application of their philosophy. Karl Binding died just after the publication of *"Die Freigabe der Vernichtung Lebensunwertem Lebens."*

Alfred Hoche would suffer the fate of Leo Alexander, the medical expert for the American prosecution at Nuremberg. Alfred Hoche would live to be personally affected by Hitler's policies as Hoche's wife was Jewish. Clearly, Hoche was not anti-Semitic, only further proves that anti-Semitism was not a necessary component for the policies which Hoche drafted. The policies would be used to legalize the murder half-a-million disabled Germans in the T4 Euthanasia program. The T4 doctors, nurses, and equipment were then physically relocated and transferred to Auschwitz and other death camps. All that was needed was a general scientific consensus that Jews were inferior as a "race," and that their marriage or mixing with the "Aryan" gene-pool was detrimental and "degenerative" to the race in order to justify the murder of the Jews along the same legal and philosophical lines drafted by Hoche and Binding.

In turn, it was Charles Darwin, also likely not anti-Semitic himself, which provided this hierarchical view of humanity. The view that there were different levels of evolution within humanity was indispensable for Darwin's theory. A monolithic progression of humanity was contrary to Darwin's theory of gradual mutations through "sexual selection." "Atavisms" or a "regression" or "degeneration" backward in the evolutionary tree were one of the core concepts of Darwin's evolutionary theory, and thus was the justification for his cousin's creation of the science of eugenics. The fame and zealotry with which Darwin's theory was supported by the scientific community provided the veil of scientific legitimacy to the eugenic-minded leadership of the Third Reich. Nietzsche provided philosophical clout.

Dr. S. D. Stein of the University of West England in Bristol points out that those that were put to death in the euthanasia program and in the extermination camps were killed for the same justification, or one may say, under the same "intent" as described in the German Penal Code:

> The fact that the enveloping conceptual framework was medico-demographic rather than xenophobic-racist, as it was respecting the Jews, should not obscure the fact that both derived sustenance from the same source, a desire to be rid of unacceptable others, a socially induced drive that was given free reign in a political framework that placed no limitations on goal attainment, and where those classified as being outside the framework of moral consideration were considered unworthy of being treated as anything other than expendable and replaceable objects. This same environment permitted medical experiments on individuals with no consideration as to the impact that these might have on their wellbeing or longevity. (archive.org, "'Life Unworthy of Life' and other Medical Killing Programmes", Dr. S.D. Stein, Jan. 29, 2007)

The very dangerous myth that the crimes of The Holocaust were just a product of racism is a misleading notion that was the source of injustice at Nuremberg, and precisely the myth that has been utilized by the eugenicists who strove to have their movement endure The Holocaust. This was also the argument Albert Speer and Karl Brandt would voice in their defense at the Nuremberg Trial, with albeit different degrees of success. Albert Speer rightfully claimed that he did not partake in any of the overt anti-Semitism of the Third Reich, and that he had been oblivious to the death camps. Speer was for 70 years deemed as "the good Nazi," and he received a relatively light sentence at Nuremberg by distancing himself from the "racist" aspects of the regime in the main trial at Nuremberg. Historians would decades later prove that many of the concentration camps were built and erected under Speer's orders and leadership and that Speer was directly enriched by the confiscated property of murdered Jews. Speer's best friend and director of the T4 Euthanasia program, Karl Brandt, would defend himself in the Nuremberg Doctors' Trial by also claiming that his was a purely scientific involvement, and that he didn't participate in any of the anti-Semitic policies of the regime. Brandt studied and took his medical exams under Alfred Hoche between 1926 and 1928, and well after Hoche had become a recognized authority on euthanasia. [275] The fact that Karl Brandt was the top doctor in charge of the very euthanasia measures that were used to murder sickly "Aryans" and Jews alike, makes the Hoche-Binding work the direct precursor to the crimes of The Holocaust. Brandt was rightfully sentenced to hang by the Nuremberg Tribunal as his attempt at exoneration, technically correct as it may have been, hardly relieved him of culpability in the crimes of The Holocaust.

Remember that this was also Julian Huxley's excuse and the defense of all eugenic-minded scientists who lived through and survived The Holocaust without consequence. Huxley, like many of the American and British eugenic organizations that survived through World War II simply disassociated themselves from the "racist" aspect of Hitler's Germany, and proceeded to change the names of their institutions and intentionally change the language utilized in their various publications.

We must come to grips with the fact that the entire legal, ethical, scientific, and philosophical structure necessary for The Holocaust was refined and in place prior to Hitler coming to power. Hitler's "Mein Kampf" was actually a step backward, eugenically speaking, as most historians would agree that "Mein Kampf" was a muddle-headed, meandering, and imprecise work undeserving of any credit in the development of the eugenic "science." A list of books necessary for the writing of "Mein Kampf" or the criminality of The Holocaust would probably look like this, and possibly be in this order:
- The "Baur-Fischer-Lenz," which was a compendium of racial and eugenic policies from around the world.
- Harry H. Laughlin's 1922 "Model Eugenical Sterilization Law."

---

[275] Pg. 33 - "Karl Brandt: Medicine and Power in the Third Reich", Ulf Schmidt, Bloomsbury Academic, 2007.

- Hoche's and Binding's 1920 "Die Freigabe der Vernichtung Lebensunwertem Lebens."
- Leonard Darwin's "The Need for Eugenic Reform" not so much for the success of the book, but for the success of its author in establishing the various International eugenic organizations through which the top three books on this list were matured and distributed.
- Nietzsche's "The Will to Power" provided the philosophical clout to the notion that traditional morality could or should be ignored when making socio-economic or medical policies.
- Henry Ford's "The International Jew," which solidified in Hitler's mind the notion of a world-wide Jewish conspiracy.
- Francis Galton's "Hereditary Genius," which took the step Charles Darwin would not take himself and gave a scientific patina to an idea otherwise voiced by cranks.
- Charles Darwin's "The Descent of Man" provided the scientific basis for the stratification of humanity into "rank-order hierarchies."
- Max Nordau's "Degeneration," which thoroughly popularized Morel's and Lombroso's notion that evolutionary "regressions" or "atavisms" were directly reflected in the cultural advancements and viability of a "nation" or a "race."
- Edward Bellamy's "Looking Backward" for popularizing throughout the world the concept of a eugenic form of "nationalized" socialism.
- Madison Grant's "The Passing of the Great Race," which Adolf Hitler called his "bible."
- Leon F. Whitney's "The Case for Sterilization," which Adolf Hitler personally requested.
- Cesar Lombroso's "Criminal Man, According to the Classification of Cesare Lombroso."
- Alexis Carrel's "Man, The Unknown"
- Ernst Haeckel's "The Evolution of Man."
- Bénédict Augustin Morel's "Traité des Dégénérescences Physiques."
- The Human Betterment Foundation's "Collected Papers On Eugenic Sterilization in California: A Critical Study Of Results In 6000 Cases."

Trace back up this timeline to the previous section on "Baby Knauer," the infant with birth defects that the Hitler regime used as a legal precedent to enact euthanasia legislation: Werner Catel, the doctor the infant had been brought to by the parents, was a respected neurologist. Catel had refused the parent's request because of the legal liability of putting the infant to death but was otherwise sympathetic ideologically as Catel himself would later write on the subject. His 1962 book *"Grenzsituation des Lebens,"* which translates to "Extreme Life Situations," defined deformed children as "such monsters...that they are nothing but *massa carnis*," the term Martin Luther used to describe flesh without a soul. [276] Karl Brandt provided Catel's subordinate, Dr. Kohl, with assurances of legal protections, and he carried out the murderous process while Catel was on vacation. Theo Morell, Hitler's personal physician, was then tasked with researching the subject of euthanasia. That summer of 1939, Morell drafted a lengthy memo with the curiously similar title, "Life Unworthy of Life." [277] Morell expanded the scope from infants to all people with "malformations," justified by claiming that such "creatures" of the "lowest animal level" aroused "horror" and were an undue burden on society:

> 5,000 idiots costing 2,000 RMs [reichsmarks] each per annum = 100 million a year. With interest at 5% that corresponds to a capital reserve of 200 million. That should even mean something to those whose concept of figures has gone awry since the period of inflation. In addition one must separately take into account the release of domestic foddstuffs and the lessening of demand for certain imports. (Pg. 25, "Forgotten Crimes: The Holocaust and People with Disabilities", Suzanne E. Evans, Ivan R. Dee, 2004.)

Trace back up this timeline to the section on *"Erbkrank,"* the movie on hereditary defectives, and this mathematical justification will fall into context: the propaganda machine churned into action upon the ideological justification provided by the academics, scientists, and jurists. Morell's expansion of the scope of the killings was instrumental, as the Ministry of Justice Commission on the Reform of Criminal Code translated these ideals into an actual law sanctioning the "mercy killing" of all people suffering from incurable diseases. Upon this basis, the Reich Committee for the Scientific Registration of Severe Hereditary Ailments issued a decree on August 18th, 1939, that made reporting and registering all "malformed" infants compulsory. [278] Recall that a mandate making doctors liable to the state for withholding information was written into Harry H. Laughlin's "Model Law," and that Ernst Rüdin and Alfred Ploetz had provided German legislators that work of American jurisprudence. Laughlin's "Model Law" was clearly on the minds of the Germans drafting the "mercy killing" mandate, as they also copied the tell-tale three-panel eugenic courts of "medical experts" that Laughlin had prescribed in his "Model Law," and more importantly which the Supreme Court of the United States had deemed "constitutional" in the 1927 Buck v. Bell case. These mandates were brutally enforced by the Nazi regime, as all involved were forced to sign a loyalty oath vowing never to speak on the subject. Those that did were reported to the Gestapo and often paid for it with their lives.

This is how an idea that gained respectability with Nietzsche's "Merchants of Light" bounced around academic circles, and ultimately translated into medical and legal texts, which in turn, provided intellectual precedent to what would otherwise be characterized as illegal, or at least barbaric policy by a regime unmoved by

---

[276] Pg. 131 - "NeuroTribes: The Legacy of Autism and the Future of Neurodiversity", Steve Silberman, Penguin, 2016.
[277] Pg. 24 – "Forgotten Crimes: The Holocaust and People with Disabilities", Suzanne E. Evans, Ivan R. Dee, 2004. – See Also: Michael Burleigh, "Death and Deliverance", Pg. 98, citing National Archives, Captured Records of Private Individuals and Enterprises, NAW T-253, Roll 44, Morell Files.
[278] Pg. 27 – Ibid.

"sentimentality." The 1921 "Baur-Fischer-Lenz book," Harry H. Laughlin's 1922 "Model Eugenical Sterilization Law," and Hoche's and Binding's 1920 "*Die Freigabe der Vernichtung Lebensunwertem Lebens*," had matured and refined the legal, ethical, scientific and philosophical concepts necessary for The Holocaust. These would occupy the top three spots of this book list as they transformed a vague notion and concept into practical reality, ready for implementation by Hitler's many minions. However, it must be stressed that without Nietzsche's clout as a philosopher, Karl Binding's and Alfred Hoche's work would never have received the respect that it did. Without Charles Darwin, neither Francis Galton nor Leonard Darwin would have been able to accomplish what they did, and American eugenicists like Harry H. Laughlin and Charles Davenport would not have been able to establish their views with the help of institutions like Harvard, Stanford or California State universities, or with the backing of the Rockefellers or Carnegies.

The injection of Henry Ford's anti-Semitic views into Hitler's "Mein Kampf" provided a clear impetus to the movement but was inconsequential for the erection of an entire governmental structure based on actual science and philosophy. Case in point: anti-Semitism as allegedly documented by "The Protocols" was a force to reckon with much prior to Adolf Hitler and survives as a force to be reckoned with to this day; The Holocaust has come to occupy the unique use of the term "holocaust" as it is a singular occurrence in world history. It is precisely this gargantuan governmental structure, whose every law responded to the concepts of eugenics that made The Holocaust logistically and legally feasible. It is the gargantuan infrastructure and undertaking called National Socialism that separates previous plights of the Jewish people such as the Russian pogroms from the unique event we call The Holocaust.

Sec. 2 - WHERE WAS THE A.C.L.U. IN THE ERA OF EUGENICS?

This book documents how many of the boys, which we would ultimately honor as the "Greatest Generation" were systematically sterilized against their will, and often without their knowledge. With the civil rights of thousands of Americans being violated *en masse*, it begs to question: Where was the American Civil Liberties Union while 30 State governments in the Union were violating the civil liberties of Americans?

The American Civil Liberties Union was founded in 1920 under the claim of being a "nonpartisan" and "non-profit organization" whose stated mission was "to defend and preserve the individual rights and liberties guaranteed to every person in this country by the Constitution and laws of the United States." Whether the ACLU was a positive or negative influence on the lives of Americans is a highly debated and politicized issue. For the purposes of this book, the lingering question is where the

ACLU stood on the question of eugenics and its self-imposed duty to "defend and preserve individual rights"? Where was the ACLU when the most poignant of controversies concerning personal bodily integrity and individual autonomy came front and center?

The answer to the above question is at least in part answered with a brief history of the ACLU's founding members and its early activity. The ACLU was founded primarily by Crystal Eastman, Roger Baldwin, and Walter Nelles. Historians typically give a longer list including Helen Keller, A.J. Muste, Elizabeth Flynn Gurley, Harry F. Ward, and Norman Thomas. Legal action is the ACLU's largest megaphone and its preferred choice of initiating social change it deems as desirable. This was true from the onset, as a lawsuit was how the ACLU made itself known as a force to be contended with. In 1925, the initial five years of the ACLU were a disappointment. That changed in 1925 when the ACLU engineered a court battle suited to its mission. H.L. Mencken brought the suit to the attention of the ACLU by persuading Clarence Darrow to take on the case. H.L. Mencken was an early version of a "shock-jock," who reveled in and was famous for his outrageous remarks. The ACLU persuaded John T. Scopes to defy Tennessee's anti-evolution law in the infamous Scopes Monkey Trial. Despite losing the actual legal battle, the Scopes trial was a phenomenal public relations success for the ACLU. The ACLU became well known across America, and the case led to the first endorsement of the ACLU by a major US newspaper.

First, it must be remembered that "A Civic Biology" dedicated an entire chapter to eugenics. That the question of eugenics was not touched upon at the Monkey Trial only begs to question why such a controversial topic would be sidestepped. Historians have documented that Clarence Darrow had vocally supported the practice of the infamous Dr. Haiselden, the "Black Stork" of the euthanasia movement and that William Jennings Bryan's wife was an active supporter of the eugenics movement. Thus, both sides of the trial probably agreed to table the issue of eugenics for the Scopes Monkey Trial.

Second in this leader by leader analysis of the ACLU, it must be remembered that Helen Keller, a founding member of the ACLU, also vocally supported Dr. Haiselden in his propagandistic campaign to gain acceptance for euthanasia and eugenics. Helen Keller likely supported Dr. Haiselden because of her political convictions, as her justifications read like a Progressive Party commentary on eugenics and the right of society to curtail elements it deemed unfit to live.

Norman Mattoon Thomas was another early member of the ACLU with sympathies for the eugenics movement. Thomas was a leading American socialist, pacifist and six-time presidential candidate for the Socialist Party of America. He was one of the founders of the National Civil Liberties Bureau, the precursor of the ACLU. Thomas was also an early proponent of birth control. Margaret Sanger recruited him to write "Some Objections to Birth Control Considered" in Religious and Ethical Aspects of Birth Control, edited and published by Sanger in 1926.

Roger Nash Baldwin was the Harvard educated executive director of the ACLU from its founding until 1950. Many of the ACLU's original landmark cases took place under his direction, namely the Scopes Trial. Originally, Baldwin was noted for saying, "Communism, of course, is the goal" of the ACLU. [279] Baldwin had been greatly influenced by the radical social movement of the anarchist Emma Goldman and had joined the Industrial Workers of the World. This changed in 1927 because of what he witnessed during his visit to the Soviet Union. Baldwin wrote "Liberty Under the Soviets" documenting his revised opinion based on what he had seen Communism was first hand, ultimately calling Soviet-style Communism as "the new slavery." [280] As a result of his drastic change of heart, Baldwin led the campaign to purge the ACLU of Communist Party members during the 1940s, yet, Baldwin saw eye-to-eye with the Progressives and Socialists on the issue of eugenics. Baldwin and his wife were supporters of birth control and eugenics through their friendship with Margaret Sanger. [281] In 1929, under Baldwin's direction, the ACLU defended Sanger in her legal battle over the dissemination of birth control literature.

Crystal Eastman cofounded the National Civil Liberties Bureau, the predecessor to the ACLU. A socialist, antimilitarist, pacifist and feminist, Eastman worked with Emma Goldman to promote birth control and legalize prostitution. Emma Goldman was a vocal supporter and promoter of the eugenics movement and lectured and taught eugenics. Crystal Eastman was also a follower of Leta Anna Stetter Hollingworth, a radical feminist supporter of the eugenics movement. [282]

Elizabeth Gurley Flynn was a labor leader, activist, and feminist who played a leading role in the Industrial Workers of the World. As a founding member of the ACLU, Flynn was a visible proponent of women's rights, birth control, and women's suffrage. She joined the American Communist Party in 1936 and late in life, in 1961, became its chairwoman. She died during a visit to the Soviet Union, where she was accorded a state funeral. She was also involved with Margaret Sanger and Emma Goldman, landing in jail for her activism.

Harry F. Ward was an American Methodist minister and left-wing activist. He was the first chairman of the ACLU, leading the group from its creation in 1920 until 1940. He received a bachelor's degree from Northwestern University in 1897 and a master's degree from Harvard in 1868. As this book documents, the United Methodist Church passed petition 81175 in 2008, which expresses an apology for the support of eugenics. Ward was a founder of the Methodist Federation for Social Service and a contributor to "Eugenics," the magazine of the American Eugenics Society. In "Eugenics," Harry F. Ward proposed that Christianity and Eugenics were compatible because both pursued the "challenge of removing the causes that produce the weak." He was not alone as the 2008 apology clarified. Methodists were active on the planning committees of the Race Betterment Conferences held in 1914 and 1915. In the 1910s, Methodist Churches hosted forums in their churches to discuss eugenics. In the 1920s, many Methodist preachers submitted their eugenics sermons

---

[279] "Guide to the American Civil Liberties Union Illinois Division Records 1920-1982", Historical Note, Univ. of Chicago Library, 2013.
[280] See also: "A New Slavery: Forced Labor: The Communist Betrayal of Human Rights," Roger Baldwin, 1953.
[281] Pg. 60 - "A Nation Under God?: The ACLU and Religion in American Politics", Thomas L. Krannawitter. Daniel C. Palm, Rowman & Littlefield, 2005.
[282] Pg. 300 - "The American New Woman Revisited," Martha H. Patterson, Rutgers Univ. Press, 2008.

to contests hosted by the American Eugenics Society. By 1927, when the American Eugenics Society formed its Committee on the Cooperation with Clergymen, Bishop Francis McConnell, President of the Methodist Federation for Social Service served on the committee. In 1936, he would chair the roundtable discussion on Religion and Eugenics at the American Eugenics Society Meeting. The laity of the Methodist church also took up the cause of eugenics. In 1929, the Methodist Review published the sermon "Eugenics: A Lay Sermon" by George Huntington Donaldson. In the sermon, Donaldson argues, "the strongest and the best are selected for the task of propagating the likeness of God and carrying on his work of improving the race."

All in all, the ACLU leadership, representative of a mix of socialists, Marxists, Progressives, and Methodists, were a tangle of intertwined interests, most of which supported eugenics directly. This is unquestionably the reason why the ACLU, the one organization that should have spoken out against the obvious civil rights intrusions of eugenic legislation, chose to stay quiet and on the sidelines on an issue that fell within their mission to protect "individual rights" and "civil liberties." It is core Marxist doctrine, after all, that even science and medicine bend to the needs of the party and the revolution. [283]

Sec. 3 - FROM THE PALMER RAIDS TO IMMIGRATION CONTROLS:

The Palmer Raids are typically known as the episode when the United States Department of Justice arrested and deport radical socialists and anarchists from the United States. On May 1, 1919, on May Day, postal officials discovered 20 bombs in the mail of prominent Americans, including John D. Rockefeller and J.P. Morgan, Jr., and Supreme Court Justice Oliver Wendell Holmes, Jr. A month later, bombs exploded in eight American cities. The raids and arrests occurred in November 1919 and January 1920 under the leadership of Attorney General A. Mitchell Palmer. What would become infamously known as the "Russian Ark" was also the culmination of the Palmer Raids. The US government deported 249 people, including Margaret Sanger's eugenic-minded idol, Emma Goldman, to Russia on the *USAT Buford*.

It is noteworthy that the targets of the initial bombings turned out to be some of the most prominent figures in the American eugenics movement, which was inseparably tied to the anti-immigration efforts that followed. As discussed earlier, both John D. Rockefeller and John D. Rockefeller Jr. were members of the American Eugenics Society. Furthermore, in the 1920s, Raymond Fosdick, an important

---

[283] "NOTAS: On the Marxist's Rejection of the Distinction Between Pure and Applied Science, and its Consequences for Marxist Science Policy", Gerard Radinitzky, Revista Portuguesa de Filosofia, T. 41, Fasc. I (Jan. - Mar., 1985), Pgs. 95-99.

official of the Rockefeller Foundation, was a member of the American Eugenics Society Advisory council. Margaret Sanger's first birth control clinic, the Clinical Research Bureau (CRB), was started with the help of the Rockefellers in 1923. We don't know to what extent the bombing attempts affected John D. Rockefeller's and Oliver Wendell Holmes's views on immigration, but their support for the eugenics movement that fueled and informed immigration reform is well documented. American opposition to open immigration became an issue of national security, and immigration reform would follow soon after.

The Palmer Raids were also the culmination of socialist, anarchist, and communist agitation that had been postponed in the United States due to the Civil War. Karl Marx and Friedrich Engels were publishing their radical tracts in Europe while the American Civil War was just erupting. Karl Marx covered the American Civil War as a war correspondent and did not believe his revolution would ever catch on in the United States. Thus, the United States avoided the first 50 years of communist agitation. Communism trickled into the United States as European radicals arrived in American shores, and thus the movement inevitably came to be identified as a foreign ideology unnaturally transplanted onto the American political scene. This perception was justified. Of the 24,000 due-paying members of the Communist Party of America, roughly 22,000 were immigrant aliens who did not speak English and which organized under the stated policy of overthrowing the government by force. [284] In fact, the bombings were hardly random events of political violence. They had clearly identifiable ethnic undertones. They were more akin to the ritualistic killings of modern-day gangs and terrorists, who saw the taking of an infidel's life as part of their mode of operation. For example, the Italian branch of the movement taught its members the propaganda value of "the insurrectionary deed" of assassinating heads of state as a way of weakening the structure of the sitting government. [285]

The bombings, 30 in all, were predictable as the propaganda leaflets of the movement called for it. A February 1919 leaflet reacted to the deportations with the headline "Go–Head! Deport us! We will dynamite you." [286] This is exactly what Leon Czolgosz was up to when he shot President William McKinley on September 6, 1901, and precisely the reason why Congress tightened immigration shortly thereafter, specifically prohibiting the immigration of "anarchists or persons who believe in or advocate the overthrow by force of the government of the United States, or the assassination of public officials." [287] The Emergency Quota Act of 1921, the precursor to the more extensive Immigration Restriction Act of 1924, was the predictable reaction to the terrorist activities of anarchists, socialists, and communists of the immigrant population.

From this perspective, the Palmer Raids are inseparable from the anti-immigration history of the United States. Harry H. Laughlin's eugenics, largely

---

[284] Pg. 86 - "Reds: McCarthyism in 20th Century America," Ted Morgan, Random House, 2003.
[285] Pg. 56 – Ibid.
[286] Pg. 69 – Ibid.
[287] Pg. 57 – Ibid.

funded by the Rockefellers and Carnegies, was used as the "science" to justify the more extensive immigration restrictions in 1924. For the purposes of this specific conversation, it is important to document that aversion to the political beliefs of immigrants had been present prior to the American Civil War. There were longstanding ties to immigration restriction and the Rockefellers. The historical arc tying the Know-Nothing anti-immigration group of the Civil War era to turn-of-the-century Progressivism was funded by Rockefeller. The National League for the Protection of American Institutions (NLPAI), Junior Order United American Mechanics, American Protective Association, and the Scottish Rite Masons were anti-Catholic nativist organizations formed in response to the surge of Irish Catholic immigration following the famines of the 1840s. [288] The NLPAI sought to unite Protestant anti-Catholic prejudice by appealing to the similarities between the various Protestant groups in the United States. The NLPAI prestigious membership included John D. Rockefeller, Cornelius Vanderbilt, J. Pierpont Morgan, and publishers such as George Putnam and Charles Scribner. An 1890 New York Times article also recites the membership and support of the NLPAI as including eugenicist Wickliffe Draper. The organization largely confined itself to leveraging the strength of its members to put high-level pressure on Congress to limit Catholic power. Its main objective was to complete the "separation of Church and State in the management of schools." [289] The New York Times article also reported that the first goal of the Law Committee of the NLPAI was the passage of an amendment to the Constitution of the United States, a sixteenth amendment, which would block state funds for Catholic schools, a goal shared by members of Edward Bellamy's family. The article points to pledges signed by both Republicans and Democrats in an 1875 attempt to pass a similar amendment to the Constitution. The pledge declared that Americans wanted "no foreign schools with doctrines, ideas, and methods at variance with our constitutional principles" seeking to pervert "the infant mind of America" and vowed "to free the elementary schools from partisan or denominational control." [290]

By now, the reader should understand just how integral names like Rockefeller, Carnegie, and Draper were to the anti-immigration and eugenics movements. More so, Rockefeller cannot be understood as a random target for the anarchist's bombing campaign. The anarchists had his murder in mind because of the Ludlow Massacre. On April 20, 1914, on the behest of John D. Rockefeller, National Guardsmen entered the tent cities of striking miners in Ludlow, Colorado. The Guardsmen attacked the miners then set fire to their tents. The targeted group was almost entirely made up of recently arrived immigrants. Reports state that as many as 24 languages were being spoken among the miners. The violent crackdown left 11 children and two women dead. Following this, three individuals, including a strike leader, were beaten and killed. The massacre set off a series of protests across the nation. These

---

[288] Pg. 178, William J. Phalen, "American Evangelical Protestantism and European Immigrants, 1800-1924", McFarland, 2011.
[289] "To Save Our Institutions: The Object of a Powerful League Recently Formed", New York Times, May 16, 1890.
[290] Ibid.

demonstrations directed their anger at John D. Rockefeller Jr. for being the one responsible for calling out the Guardsmen. Organizers held their demonstrations at the front gate of Rockefeller's mansion in Tarrytown, New York, and the radical immigrant element began to plot revenge against Rockefeller.

To make matters worse, these bombings occurred with WWI as the backdrop, and at this time, the tensions against immigrants and ethnic groups in United States were erupting nationwide due to the perception that these immigrants harbored divided loyalties at the time of war. Germans with sympathies for their homeland and Irish whose countrymen were in revolt against America's ally, Great Britain, were the common target of these animosities.

As discussed earlier, Germans paid close attention to American legislation and legislative affairs. Recall that Heinrich Kreiger's book ultimately caught the eye of the Rockefeller run Council of Foreign Relations. German authorities were closely paying attention to the American legal system, namely during the formative years of the FBI, while J. Edgar Hoover was creating the criminal investigation infrastructure necessary to combat organized crime and deport anarchists. The famous victims of the anti-radical campaigns, Sacco and Vanzetti, were among the targets for anarchist activities by J. Edgar Hoover's FBI agency:

> The Germans had been closely following developments in the US criminal justice system for years. In Weimar days, many leading German jurists had expressed shock over such high-profile cases as Sacco and Vanzetti, in part because of the protracted delay between the time of their trial and their execution, which many saw as an inexplicable flaw in American judicial methods. Under Nazi influence, the Germans had also closely examined such American criminal justice issues as the "third degree" (the use of police brutality and torture to extract confessions), corruption, the "war on crime," intelligence-gathering and crime-fighting approaches by the Federal Bureau of Investigation, criminal identification techniques, centralized police operations, sentencing policies, and racial laws. American policies of racial exclusion, for example, were approvingly detailed in Heinrich Krieger's book Das *Rassenrecht in den Vereinigten Staaten*, published in Berlin in 1936. (Pgs. 133–134, "The Last Gasp: The Rise and Fall of The American Gas Chamber", Scott Christianson, Univ. of Cal. Press, 2010)

An interesting irony is that John D. Rockefeller, Jr. apparently empathized with Sacco and Vanzetti. Their trial was billed as the "trial of the century" prior to the Scopes Monkey Trial took the crown. People had stopped going to work and an entire industry and publication had been set up because of the highly controversial trial. The defense committee set up to free Sacco and Vanzetti continued its monthly bulletin after the trial while a new Sacco-Vanzetti National League arranged publication of the prisoners' letters and the trial transcript. The publication and compilation of the two-volume set which included affidavits, appeal briefs, and the judicial opinions were funded by John D. Rockefeller, Jr. [291] It is largely through "The Letters of Sacco and Vanzetti" that the entire mythos of the two defendants

---

[291] Ep. - "Sacco and Vanzetti: The Men, the Murders, and the Judgment of Mankind", Bruce Watson, Penguin, 2008.

has been built upon. Thus, the empathy historians have built around the history of their case, ironically, is largely due to anti-immigration John D. Rockefeller, Jr.

Sec. 4 - WHO WAS J.F. LEHMANN?

This book postulates that Adolf Hitler made a subtle, but all-important shift from proselytizing the myth of Germans as the oppressed victims of an "International Jewish conspiracy" to that of the superior race and oppressor. It is not until after J.F. Lehmann brought Hitler the infamous "Baur-Fischer-Lenz" book on eugenics that Hitler's speeches shifted from the stab-in-the-back myth, or the *"Dolchstoßlegende,"* with Germans as the oppressed victims of betrayal, to the eugenic propaganda of Germans as the pinnacle of white-supremacy. Weakness and superiority are incompatible attributes, and J.F. Lehmann is responsible for Hitler's shift away from this concept of weakness inherent in victimhood towards a radical belief in racial superiority. Thus, it begs to question, who was this pivotal figure in Adolf Hitler's life, and why are his name and history not part of the commonly digested history of The Holocaust? Nothing of The Holocaust or World War II can be understood without documenting who was Julius Friedrich Lehmann. Yet, J.F. Lehmann barely makes it onto the radar of even the most thorough books on the subject, and then only to name him as Adolf Hitler's publisher.

Lehmann was indispensable to the early organization of the National Socialist party, its paramilitary and insurrectionist activities, its propaganda, and the formation of its radical program, aside from providing its funding and the locations that served as its planning epicenter and safe houses. [292] In fact, the infamous Beer-Hall Putsch that landed Hitler in prison was staged from Lehmann's home. More importantly, in 1909, J. F. Lehmann published the first of many books on the controversial topics of "race hygiene," eugenics, and *"lebensraum."* His company would distribute the books as part of the goal to substantially transform German culture and society. Clearly, Lehmann was much more than the person who happened to publish Hitler's "Mein Kampf."

> Who is familiar with the role played by J. F. Lehmann and his publishing house in the emergence of social psychiatry during German fascism and its further development in today's psychiatric system? What kind of ideology did this man stand for? Who were his friends? Which ideologies are still at work today? Many readers will not understand the significance of these questions. This is largely due to the work of most medical historians ---- normal historians placed the responsibility for the social-psychiatric horrors in Germany primarily in the lap

---

[292] "Deutsche Rassepolitik und die Erziehung zu nationalem Ehrgefühl", Eberhard Meinhold, J.F. Lehmann, 1908.

of Adolf Hitler and his Nazis. In doing so they contributed little to expose the origins of social psychiatry and its catalytic effect and perhaps decisive precondition of the possibility for the Holocaust. (Pgs. 37-49, "Progressive Psychiatry: Publisher J. F. Lehmann as Promoter of Social Psychiatry under Fascism", Peter Lehmann, Changes: An International Journal of Psychology and Psychotherapy, Vol. 12, No. 1, 1994, translation by Peter Stastny)

Lehmann was in a unique position to merge the desires of eugenic-minded scientists with the aspirations of the militant right. Lehmann's publishing company specialized in scientific books and journals, and it literally made the careers of many scientists and doctors by patronizing their work, commissioning new studies, publishing their papers, and popularizing them through advertising and propaganda. Therefore, it must be remembered that Lehmann was viewed by the scientific and medical community as holding the keys to recognition. These intellectual professions were then, as they are now, professions obsessed with publishing their findings. "Publish or perish" was just as true for the medical sciences then as it is now, and Lehmann was the leading publisher of medical and scientific texts for German-speaking Europe. Doctors were thus politically inclined to sympathize with the politics of the purse holder and publishing house of the German sciences:

> Lehmann... launched the popular journal, *Volk and Rasse* in 1926. It was in competition with the state-supported journal *Eugenik* of the League for Regeneration, which Lehmann loathed. Lehmann's journal achieved a circulation of 1,000. It linked the fragmented Nordic groups and provided a channel of communication to academics in the racial hygiene movement. Lehmann offered cash prizes for photographs of Nordic racial types, for compiling pictorial family trees to show the inheritance of facial features, and for essays on German customs. He involved organizations such as the Nordic Ring and the Young Nordic League. Subscriptions to the journal involved membership of a *Werkbund* for Germanic *Volk* Character and Racial Research. The aim of this association was to link scientific and popular racial research. (Pg. 472, "Health, Race and German Politics Between National Unification and Nazism, 1870-1945", Paul Weindling, Cambridge Univ. Press, 1993)

Needless to say, Lehmann was personally and politically invested in the cause, and thus reinvested his personal wealth in the political campaigns that he deemed as friendly to his ideals. This made him a dangerous combination of wealth and idealism, without which pathetic sociopaths like Adolf Hitler would never have succeeded. If National Socialism can be said to have succeeded with the support of "industrialists," then Lehmann is that key idealistic and committed "industrialist," which so many historians blame. His aims were a "racial hygiene programme, a dictatorship, anti-Semitic and anti-Catholic discrimination, and racial Germanic culture." [293] Peter Lehmann's "Progressive Psychiatry" seconds this observation:

---

[293] Pgs. 472-473 - "Health, Race and German Politics Between National Unification and Nazism, 1870-1945", Paul Weindling, Cambridge Univ. Press, 1993.

However, the name J. F. Lehmann keeps coming up among the promoters of social psychiatric interests throughout its early years. ---- J. F. Lehmann made sure that the unwritten rule of the MMW was observed that "no Jew could be admitted to the editorial board" (J. F. Lehmanns Verlag, 1940, p. 43). ---- Not only did J. F. Lehmann consider his publications as "in the trenches", he also participated actively in the political struggle. He worked on and publicised several racist nationalistic organisations: The Thule Society, Society for Eugenics, Evangelic Association, German People's Protection and Resistance Troop, Free-corps von Epp and, finally, the National Socialist German Workers' Party (NSDAP). In a 1976 study, Professor Gary D. Stark from Arlington, Texas, finds that J. F. Lehmann was in the unique position to "co-ordinate the press and his personal influence within organisations with maximal impact—that is to connect personal, publicist and group—activities in a manner that no other racist ideologue could." (Stark, 1976, column 314). (Pgs. 37-49, "Progressive Psychiatry: Publisher J. F. Lehmann as Promoter of Social Psychiatry under Fascism", Peter Lehmann, Changes: An International Journal of Psychology and Psychotherapy, Vol. 12, No. 1, 1994, translation by Peter Stastny)

Lehmann was instrumental in bringing together disparate political parties in the service of the greater ideology of racial purity. Lehmann would bring together nationalists like Max von Gruber, secretary of the Bavarian *Vaterlandspartei*, Dietrich Eckart, the occultist members of the Thule Society where Hitler would eventually meet his mentor and the socialists like Ploetz and Schallmayer. Lehmann took it upon himself to organize *völkisch* radicals from the ranks of the Thule Society and the Pan-German League to create a "Committee of National Defence." This had been a reaction to a November 7, 1918 coup, lead by Jewish-born German Bolshevik, Kurt Eisner, as Eisner had coerced Chancellor, Prince Max of Baden, to transfer power to the Soviet SPD party. As the Munich government passed from being a "democratic council" to a "communist soviet," Lehmann and like-minded Germans intensified the counter-revolutionary efforts. Lehmann escaped only to join General Epp's militant *Freikorps*, and took a leading role in the Munich counter-revolution that occurred between April and May 1919. He allowed Rudolf Hessused to use his villa to abduct reigning Bavarian ministers. [294] He participated in organizing the *Deutsch-völkische Schutz-und Trutz-Bund*, or in English the "League for the Defence of German Honour and Ethics," to instigate in the public an anti-Semitic stance based on racial nationalism. He put the resources of his publishing house at the League's disposal and redoubled his efforts in recruiting racial hygienists to publish. In March 1919, Lehmann tried to persuade Ploetz to publish a series of anti-Semitic articles blaming the German defeat in World War I on the Jews. The anti-Semitic campaign was aimed at Ernst Niekisch member of the National Bolshevist party, the playwright Ernst Toller of the Bavarian Soviet

---

[294] Pgs. 37-49 - "Progressive Psychiatry: Publisher J. F. Lehmann as Promoter of Social Psychiatry under Fascism", Peter Lehmann, Changes: An International Journal of Psychology and Psychotherapy, Vol. 12, No. 1, 1994, translation by Peter Stastny.

Republic, the communist anarchist Gustav Landauer, and the poet Erich Mühsam of the Bavarian Soviet Republic. He supported the murders of politicians such as Walther Rathenau. He put his printing presses to work, publicly criticizing "the Weimar Republic as a compromise of Jewish capitalism with Catholic and Masonic internationalism." [295] The *Bund Oberland* together with the Thule Society planned to overthrow Eisner's Soviet, and weapons were stored on Lehmann's premises. [296]

All of the above insurrectionist activity culminated with the assassination of Kurt Eisner by a member of the Thule group, and in the aftermath, Lehmann was arrested in February 1919. J.F. Lehmann's dedication to the cause is proven by this fact: He was imprisoned twice for his political maneuvering and likely for his participation in political assassinations. Neither of the two stints in prison dissuaded his radical revolutionary tendencies, as he would later allow Hitler to make use of his mansion to stage further acts of insurrection. Not surprisingly, Lehmann was there when Hitler began climbing the ranks as a newcomer to the groups, which had existed and survived under Lehmann's zeal and dedication. Lehmann was at the *Bürgerbräu* beer hall for the 1923 Beer Hall Putsch. Lehmann's home was utilized to imprison captured members of the government. As we know, all of this landed Hitler in prison, but Lehmann campaigned on his behalf in the meantime, namely by distributing to Hitler's writings. [297] While it is true that J.F. Lehmann reaped the financial benefits of the politically charged publications, it is more accurate to state that he actively sought out and recruited scientists and doctors to publish the ideals he wholeheartedly subscribed to. His enthusiastic marketing skills directly contributed to the success of Binding's and Hoche's "*Die Freigabe der Vernichtung lebensunwerten Lebens,*" or "The Legalization of Destroying Unworthy Lives." [298]

Lehmann's eugenic activism and political impetus clearly pre-dated Hitler and the National Socialist party by many decades. In 1935, J.F. Lehmann's widow, Melanie Lehmann, recalled in the biography that in the years 1908 to 1911 her husband spent time in the Swiss spa Davos reading and devouring eugenics, an interest which ultimately coalesced as a business venture printing the works of Gruber, Kraepelin, Rüdin and Ploetz, Lenz, Baur, and Fischer. [299] J.F. Lehmann's former associate and son-in-law, Otto Spatz, stated in 1940 in the 50 anniversary issue the "*Archiv für Rassen und Gesellschaftsbiologie,*" which was published five years after Lehmann's death, that J.F. Lehmann's close circle of friends included Ploetz, Gruber, Kraepelin, Rüdin, Fischer, Baur, Lenz, and Hitler's future Secretary of the Interior, Arthur Gütt. [300] Thus, it is correct to state that this pivotal figure was a radical eugenicist much prior to the prospects of WWI or WWII becoming a possibility, and that J.F. Lehmann and his circle of friends navigated and

---

[295] Pg. 310 - "Health, Race and German Politics Between National Unification and Nazism, 1870-1945", Paul Weindling, Cambridge Univ. Press, 1993.
[296] Pgs. 307-308 – "Health, Race and German Politics Between National Unification and Nazism, 1870-1945", Paul Weindling, Cambridge Univ. Press, 1993.
[297] Pg. 311 – Ibid.
[298] Pgs. 37-49, "Progressive Psychiatry: Publisher J. F. Lehmann as Promoter of Social Psychiatry under Fascism", Peter Lehmann, Changes: An International Journal of Psychology and Psychotherapy, Vol. 12, No. 1, 1994, translation by Peter Stastny.
[299] Ibid – Citing M. Lehmann, 1935, p. 36.
[300] Ibid.

endeavored to change the trajectory of history much prior to Hitler and Nazism.

So, what instigated this pivotal figure to light the fire under future racial instigators? Paul Weindling documents that J.F. Lehmann's eugenic ideals changed from personal interests to political goals somewhere in the trajectory of WWI. The Great War transformed the eugenics and racial hygiene movement in Germany. First, the war resurrected the traditional observation that war served to kill off the "fittest" in and allowed the "degenerate" to survive, as David Starr Jordan, Leon Whitney, Leonard Darwin, and Adolf Hitler would later postulate. Secondly, population policy was given prominence in public opinion, and the various reformist organizations each had their proposal. Most importantly, WWI exposed animosities between eugenicists politically sympathetic to International Socialism and those whose eugenic views prohibited them from any international venture organized upon "economic class" instead of "racial" distinctions. As a result, the German Racial Hygiene Society was transformed from an "international" to a "national" society much at the insistence of Lehmann and was reconstituted in July 1916 as a result. The surviving members agreed that "Internationalism" hampered recruitment of the target membership, and that the Society needed to focus its efforts on propaganda and dissemination of its ideals. Of course, this only reinforced Lehmann's pivotal importance to the group as both declarations played into his personal strengths. The new iteration of the German Racial Hygiene Society was registered in Munich on April 7, 1917, and one of the first decisions of the reintegrated Society was the publication of a journal, again cementing Lehmann's central role in the group which would reinvent German society around eugenic values.

Here was the all-important divide between "national" and "international," "race" and "class," manifest in the financial and ideological leader that preceded Hitler by decades. The history of this pivotal persona also serves to answer the question which the Nuremberg tribunal grappled with: Were the German doctors and scientists the victims of Hitler's militaristic state? Or, was the National Socialist state implementing the ideals of the German doctors and scientists? Questions not adequately answered linger in the public mind, and this question was never properly addressed, and if anything, the truth was intentionally blurred and suppressed in order to evade the counter-accusations that much of what they practiced and preached was learned from the American and British medical community. J.F. Lehmann's story documents the sizeable portion of Hitler's rhetoric that had been in circulation decades prior to the creation of Hitler's National Socialist Party, or even its predecessor, the German Workers Party. Hitler's "Mein Kampf" was nothing but a muddle-headed plagiarism of the ideas and concepts that Lehmann and his intellectual cohorts had been disseminating for decades prior, much of it while Adolf Hitler was nothing more than a snot-nosed teenage artist in Vienna:

> Lehman advocated depopulation of the inferior Slavs to make way for German settlers. He was ferociously anti-Jewish. In 1915 Ploetz had to calm Lehmann down in a dispute with the editor of a medical journal (Sarason of the *Zeitschrift für ärztliche Fortbildung*), when Lehmann attacked 'the international Jewish world conspiracy'. In April 1917 – just when the Berlin eugenicists were

proposing a journal – Lehmann launched a Pan-German journal, *Deutschlands Erneuerung*, calling for national regeneration and territorial acquisitions. It accused the establishment of cultural decadence and with allowing alien and inferior racial elements to sap the vigour of the nation. (Pg. 302, "Health, Race and German Politics Between National Unification and Nazism, 1870-1945", Paul Weindling, Cambridge Univ. Press, 1993)

This is not to detract from Hitler's culpability, as he provided the momentum that had been missing. This is what made this otherwise socially awkward sociopath attractive to J.H. Lehmann and Dietrich Eckart. Hitler had an unusual talent for communication and propaganda. He was the ideal megaphone for ideas already firmly entrenched, and thus already deemed acceptable by the intellectual elite, the very people that should have served as a bulwark to erroneous doctrines and dogmas. There is certainly a significant and palpable turn in Hitler's rhetoric after J.H. Lehmann delivered the infamous "Baur-Fischer-Lenz" eugenic tract while Hitler was imprisoned at Landsberg. As this book documents, Hitler's speeches take a decisive turn away from the theme of Germans as the oppressed victims of Jewish and Bolshevik cunning, to that of a messianic vision to eradicate the subsequently "inferior" Jewish "parasites" and "degenerates" from the superior "Aryan" blood. This is a subtle but significant conversion from the cries of betrayal and victimhood, to prophesying the institutionalization of segregation and eradication. It is the necessary turn from the "stabbed-in-the-back" protestations of the oppressed to the proclamations and propagandizing as the oppressor. This is the indispensable ideological precursor to the recruitment of countless ranks of willing executioners tasked with a deed that could only be committed with absolute faith and belief in its correctness.

Sec. 5 - GERMAN EUGENICS IN DISSARAY:

Paul Weindling's "Health, Race and German Politics" documents how the German eugenicists found themselves disbanded and in complete disarray in the aftermath of World War I. Uncovering the forces that enabled them to rally together and survive to heavily influence world history thereafter go a long way towards revealing just how indispensable the transatlantic political relationships truly were to the movement. American scientists, many of whom were educated in Germany, regarded German medicine as being of vital significance, so the Rockefeller Foundation came to the rescue in 1922.

The post-war destitution certainly hit key eugenicists like Ploetz, who retreated from the Racial Hygiene Society and used this time to develop the *"Archiv für Rassen und Gesellschaftsbiologie"* in collaboration with J.F. Lehmann. However, the post-war situation also drove Ploetz into isolation and Lehmann into militant insurrection:

> Depressed by the worsening situation in October 1918, Ploetz found consolation in Nordic ideals. He kept closely in touch with Lehmann and Gruber, with whom he intensively discussed the Nordic race. On 9 November 1918 he reacted to the armistice with the decision to form an armed militia against 'plunderers'. He retreated to his country house, Schloss Reid, at Herrsching on the Ammersee. He fortified this with machine guns and armed a local militia. He lived in terror expecting the Munich Soviet to storm his nationalist enclave. On a visit to Munich, Ploetz narrowly escaped arrest by hiding in the mental hospital of the psychiatrist Kraeplin. (Pg. 313, "Health, Race and German Politics Between National Unification and Nazism, 1870-1945", Cambridge Univ. Press, 1993)

The above characterization of Ploetz was hardly atypical. At this critical moment in history, German "racial hygienists" began their swerve towards the militancy that would ultimately marry them with insurrectionist, counter-revolutionary, and ethnic nationalism. Ploetz's Nordic Archery Club survived the war. Its twenty-five members included Lehmann and Lenz. While Lehmann was plotting coups and insurrection, Ploetz transformed this Archery Club into a Nordic group called the *Widar Bund*. Members met to discuss politics, biology, and race. Lehmann lectured on the crippling effect of the Versailles Treaty, a topic we know Hitler later harped on.[301] To put this into context, all this activity occurred while Hitler was still groping around, trying to find his footing after serving in WWI. This otherwise obscure piece of history proves that the volatile admixture of militancy, eugenics, and occultism was forming with or without Adolf Hitler. Hitler would rise to prominence only because individuals like Lehmann and Eckhart recognized his abilities as a megaphone for the movement. The need for an individual like Hitler preceded the miscreant; Adolf filled a vacuum.

More to the point, it is equally accurate to state that key German eugenicists like Ploetz and Lenz would only survive to propagate their eugenic racial ideas because of help directly from their American friends. Abraham Flexner found that German science was on the brink of collapse. Flexner was an American educator most famous for his "Flexner Report," published in 1910, which was the basis for medical educational reform in the United States. He was the younger brother of the medical researcher Simon Flexner, who was employed by the Rockefeller Institute for Medical Research from 1901 to 1935. Flexner graduated from Johns Hopkins University at age 19, then he completed graduate studies at Harvard University and then at University of Berlin. Flexner's German education is important. Flexner was an admirer of German *Kultur* and was instrumental in modeling the United States scientific and medical institutions after the German example. He understood one could not practice medicine in continental Europe without having undergone an

---

[301] Pg. 313 - "Health, Race and German Politics Between National Unification and Nazism, 1870-1945", Paul Weindling, Cambridge Univ. Press, 1993.

extensive specialized university education. Flexner soon conducted a related study of medical education in Europe. With funding from the Rockefeller Foundation, he worked toward restructuring America's medical schools. In effect, Flexner was demanding that American medical education conform to prevailing practice in continental Europe, and more specifically, Germany.

The "Flexner Report" was also funded by the Carnegie Foundation, and thus is also referred to as the "Carnegie Foundation Bulletin Number Four." The report called on American medical schools to enact higher admission and graduation standards and to adhere strictly to the protocols of mainstream science in their teaching and research. Many American medical schools fell short of the standard advocated in the report, and after its publication, nearly half of such schools merged or were closed outright. The report also concluded that there were too many medical schools in the United States and that too many doctors were being trained. Flexner's report would be pivotal in consolidating American science and medicine under the Rockefeller and Carnegie influence. In turn, Flexner would be there for the German medical community's time of need. It was Emil Abderhalden, the prominent psychologist, that tipped Flexner off that German researchers were not only being deprived of research materials but were literally starving. [302]

Clearly, making it possible for German eugenicists to continue their work would ultimately have dire consequences. This decision was not taken blindly of the potential consequences, as it was well known back then that much of the "survival of the fittest" rhetoric that fueled the Great War came directly from scientists like Ernst Haeckel and his scientific following. The Rockefeller Foundation's New York office warned precisely of such consequences, pointing out that universities had nurtured the nationalism that had caused WWI and that the younger generation of scientists and doctors were even more nationalistic than the older generation of liberal monarchist professors. [303] This would certainly prove to be true, as Hitler's National Socialism was a rebellion and revolution against the traditional German monarchy and values. Rockefeller's New York office decided to fund individual scientists instead of universities. They chose Professor Heinrich Poll to manage the assistance channeled through various Rockefeller programs as Flexner had established a close friendship with him in previous visits to Germany. [304] Incidentally, Poll was a founding member of the Kaiser Wilhelm Institute for Anthropology, Human Heredity, and Eugenics and focused on twin studies, the subject Verschuer and Mengele would later extrapolate on for the Institute during the Nazi era.

As postulated earlier, the politically powerful react and overreact when their power is threatened. Their actions are deliberate and their reactions to the political fallout from their ties to Hitler's scientists were no exception. Poll, like Leo Alexander, was not only a product of the eugenic-minded German universities and

---

[302] Pg. 325 – "Health, Race and German Politics Between National Unification and Nazism, 1870-1945", Paul Weindling, Cambridge Univ. Press, 1993.
[303] Pg. 325 – Ibid.
[304] Pg. 36 - "Abraham Flexner: A Flawed American Icon", Michael Nevins, iUniverse, 2010.

institutions, but also its ultimate victim. Poll was born Jewish but converted to Protestantism and ultimately was rejected by the very eugenic policies he helped formulate. Flexner would attempt to bring Poll to the United States but was not able to secure his stay. However tragic Poll's story may have been, he was yet another thread in the tangled web that was the American, British, and German eugenics movement.

Yet, all these relationships between powerful American institutions and influential German eugenicists were documented and easily discoverable. For example, Flexner's relationship with Rockefeller Jr. and his deputy, John Foster Dulles, was instrumental in Rockefeller's seemingly unyielding support for the eugenics movement. Rockefeller, Jr. was so impressed with Flexner's report on medical education that he engaged the young reformer to study the nature of modern prostitution in Europe in order to apply the findings in the United States. In it Flexner's conclusions were that the best way to eliminate prostitution was by preventing it from originating in the first place, through educational and eugenic means. [305] Rockefeller, Jr. even wrote the introduction to this highly publicized work of eugenics, only further cementing Rockefeller's feet in the foundations of the eugenics movement.

The relationship between American and German eugenics was a tangled one. They operated with the same mentality, and their funds sourced from the same fountains, the Rockefellers and Carnegies. German medicine helped form the professional and educational infrastructure of American medicine, and American science repaid the favor by being there to rescue German sciences at a critical juncture in the wake of World War I. The immediate effect was the prolonging and propagation of German eugenics, as well as nurturing the close ties between the Rockefeller and Carnegie funded eugenics ventures in Germany with their American eugenic ventures. This is an aspect that the Allied prosecution at the Nuremberg Doctors' Trial tried to sidestep, as at the head of this prosecution team were individual's whose history was closely tied to the Rockefeller and Carnegie foundations, as well as the National Research Council and Council for Foreign Relations. Leo Alexander was a Rockefeller man as well as a product of the eugenic-minded German institutions that Rockefeller and Flexner sought to rescue after World War I. Andrew C. Ivy, the scientist ultimately convicted of scientific fraud whose testimony on American medical ethics was taken as gospel during the Nuremberg Doctors' Trials, was part of the National Research Council, yet another Rockefeller funded project. The top echelon of American science was inescapably tied and entangled with the German scientific community that would be put on trial by the very men that created the tangled relationship in the first place; a relationship that could not be untangled or compartmentalized when the time for reckoning arrived with the Nuremberg Doctors' Trial.

---

[305] Pg. 20 – "Abraham Flexner: A Flawed American Icon", Michael Nevins, iUniverse, 2010.

Sec. 6 - THE "RACIALIST" VS. THE "RACIST":

"The Birth of a Nation" was a silent film co-directed by D. W. Griffith and the author of the original novel, Thomas Dixon, Jr. It was originally released as "The Clansmen." According to "Variety" magazine, "The Birth of a Nation" was the highest-grossing film of the silent film era, with earnings of approximately $10 million in 1915 dollars. It is credited with several technical innovations in filmmaking, but most importantly, the release of the film is credited with inspiring the formation of the "second era" Ku Klux Klan at Stone Mountain, Georgia, and a renewed era of violence that would last up until the Civil Rights era. In a 1980 interview, Karl Brown, the assistant cameraman in the filming of "The Birth of a Nation," recounts that during the filming of "The Birth of a Nation" someone had mentioned to Griffith that if the film were ever shown in Atlanta the result would be a race riot. To this Griffith prophetically replied, "I hope to God they do." [306]

In fact, "The Birth of a Nation" incited riots in most of the Northern cities that it was shown. The NAACP and others attempted to seek either a complete ban of the film or to force the editing-out of the most egregious racist scenes. A multitude of hearings were held before mayors, state legislatures, city councils, state, and city censorship boards across the country. These hearings became platforms for the pro-Griffith lobby to pronounce the alleged virtues of anti-miscegenation laws. In New York City, Griffith's lawyer Martin W. Littleton told Mayor Mitchell that the film was a "protest against the mongrel mixture of black and white." [307] A New York Globe article from April 10, 1915, quotes Griffith as saying, "The attack of the organized opponents to the picture is centered upon that feature of it which they deem might become an influence against intermarriage of blacks and whites."

The other highly influential work of fiction of the era was Madison Grant's 1916 book "The Passing of the Great Race." Both Griffith's film and Grant's book are typically bundled into the same category of works of racism. However much this may be true, there is an important distinction that has hereto been left undocumented by historians. "The Clansman" was a work that captured the lingering animosities of the once Confederate South. "The Passing" is a work of the elitist North and altogether the product of their self-centered convictions. Grant's work was informed by a scientist whom at that point in history was regarded second only to Albert Einstein: Henry Fairfield Osborn, like Madison Grant, was the product of elite Ivy League education, and he not only educated Grant on the Darwinian interpretation of human history that is extrapolated in "The Passing of the Great Race," but wrote its preface. More precisely, the "Clansman" and "Passing" worldviews were not just opposing, but hostile to each other. These animosities between the North and South linger to this day.

Griffith was born in Crestwood, Kentucky, to Mary Perkins and Jacob "Roaring Jake" Griffith. His father served as a colonel in the Confederate Army and was

---

[306] "Hollywood", Thames Television documentary. – Book version: "Hollywood: The Pioneers", Kevin Brownlow, Knopf, 1979.
[307] "D. W. Griffith and 'The Birth of a Monster' How the Confederacy Revived The KKK and Created Hollywood", Mark Calney, The American Almanac, January 11, 1993.

elected as a Kentucky state legislator. Griffith was raised as a Methodist and attended a one-room schoolhouse where he was taught by his older sister. After his father died, the family struggled with poverty.

Thomas Dixon, Jr's life story also serves to underscore the North-South animosities that were the original inspiration for the film. Dixon grew up during Reconstruction following the Civil War. The government confiscation of farmland, the corruption of local politicians, and particularly the vengefulness of Federal troops formed in young Dixon's mind. He referred to the American Civil Wr as one of history's greatest tragedies. Among Dixon's earliest memories was that of a widow of a Confederate soldier who had served under Dixon's uncle Col. Leroy McAfee pleading for his family's help. The widow claimed that a black man had raped her daughter. In retribution, the local Ku Klux Klan hung and repeatedly shot the alleged rapist in the town square. Dixon's mother commented to him that night that "[The Klan are] our people – they're guarding us from harm." [308] Dixon's father, Thomas, Sr., and his uncle Leroy McAfee, both joined the Ku Klux Klan, and Col. McAfee even attained the rank of Chief of the Klan of the Piedmont area of North Carolina. This experience created the political opinions that would be etched into posterity with the writing of "The Clansman." Dixon felt that the Klan's actions were justified and that desperate times called for extreme measures.

Needless to say, both Dixon's and Griffith's upbringing were a far cry from Madison Grant's or Henry Fairfield Osborn's Ivy League pedigree. Grant was an Ivy League educated lawyer, historian, and physical anthropologist, known primarily for his work as a eugenicist and conservationist. He had close relationships with the other Ivy League elites that resided in New York at the time. These friendships included Theodore Roosevelt and Elihu Root.

As this book documents, Grant collaborated closely with Harry H. Laughlin and Congressman Johnson in the passing of the 1924 Johnson-Reed Immigration Restriction Act. Grant's 1916 book "The Passing of the Great Race" was presented as evidence in the Congressional hearings that led up to the 1924 Act. The book was embraced by the National Socialists. The book was also the first non-German book ordered to be reprinted by the National Socialists when they took power, and Adolf Hitler personally wrote to Grant to tell him: "The book is my Bible." [309]

Historians have tried to pigeonhole Grant as a "conservative," citing his relationship to Hitler as proof. However, any honest reading of "The Passing of the Great Race" reveals where Grant's philosophical and political views truly lay. Grant, like Hitler, would write about the "falsehood" of the "dogmas" upon which *laissez-faire* democracy was created. For Grant, Hitler, and for that matter, every leading eugenicist of utopian-socialist sentiments, *laissez-faire* democracy was the culprit working against a "racial hygiene" or a "racial consciousness," as excerpts from the book evidence:

---

[308] Pg. 34 – "White Robes and Burning Crosses: A History of the Ku Klux Klan from 1866", Michael Newton, McFarland, 2014.

[309] Pg. 357 - Defending the Master Race: Conservation, Eugenics, and the Legacy of Madison Grant", Jonathan Peter Spiro, UPNE, 2009. – NOTE: This is a popular quote with many historians.

Democratic theories of government in their modern form are based on dogmas of equality formulated some hundred and fifty years ago, and rest upon the assumption that environment and not heredity is the controlling factor in human development. Philanthropy and noble purpose dictated the doctrine expressed in the Declaration of Independence, the document which to-day constitutes the actual basis of American institutions. The men who wrote the words, "we hold these truths to be self-evident, that all men are created equal," were themselves the owners of slaves, and despised Indians as something less than human. Equality in their minds meant merely that they were just as good Englishmen as their brothers across the sea. (Pg. xvi, "The Passing of the Great Race or the Racial Basis of European History", Charles Scribner's Sons, 1916)

Consider the above passage. In what world do the above concepts pass off as American style "conservatism"? Grant was intent in propagating a perverted version of the governmental traditions handed down by the Founding Fathers of the American Revolution, a version far departed from any "conservative" reading of the founding documents:

The words "that all men are created equal" have since been subtly falsified by adding the word "free," although no such expression is found in the original document, and the teachings based on these altered words in the American public schools of to-day would startle and amaze the men who formulated the Declaration. (Pg. xvi, "The Passing of the Great Race or the Racial Basis of European History", Charles Scribner's Sons, 1916)

More to the point, Madison Grant's version of "natural law" was based not upon Locke or the Enlightenment, but upon his belief in Charles Darwin's Theory of Evolution. Grant's political views had very little semblance to the "natural law" as defined by the Founding Fathers of the American Revolution:

Aboriginal populations from time immemorial have been again and again swamped under floods of newcomers and have disappeared for a time from historic view. In the course of centuries, however, these primitive elements have slowly reasserted their physical type and have gradually bred out their conquerors, so that the racial history of Europe has been in the past, and is to-day a story of the repression and resurgence of ancient races. (Pg. xxii, "The Passing of the Great Race or the Racial Basis of European History", Charles Scribner's Sons, 1916)

CONTINUES…

The laws of nature operate with the same relentless and unchanging force in human affairs as in the phenomena of inanimate nature, and the basis of the government of man is now and always has been, and always will be, force and not sentiment, a truth demonstrated anew by the present world conflagration. (Pg. xx, "The Passing of the Great Race or the Racial Basis of European History", Charles Scribner's Sons, 1916)

Grant's book repeatedly reiterates his derision for the *laissez-faire* democracy of the Founding Fathers, continually questioning the wisdom of doctrines that proclaim that "all men are created equal" and blaming the American Revolution for destroying the notion of a natural aristocracy, where one group was biologically predetermined to rule over others. No genuine American "conservative" would, least of all make appeals to notions of monarchies, aristocracies, or blind acceptance of Darwinist theory as the replacement for traditional religion. More poignantly, these views are explained in the terms that eugenic-minded socialists like H.G. Wells, Edward Bellamy, and Francis Galton would identify with:

> In the democratic forms of government the operation of universal suffrage tends toward the selection of the average man for public office rather than the man qualified by birth, education, and integrity. How this scheme of administration will ultimately work out remains to be seen, but from a racial point of view, it will inevitably increase the preponderance of the lower types and cause a corresponding loss of efficiency in the community as a whole. (Pg. 5, "The Passing of the Great Race or the Racial Basis of European History", Charles Scribner's Sons, 1916)

In the chapter titled "Race and Democracy," the radical anti-clerical and anti-Biblical view of history with eugenicists from American to Germany is also a concept that Madison Grant adopted. Note that Grant's view is more in line with the Darwinian side of the Scopes' Monkey Trial:

> The question of race has been further complicated by the effort of old-fashioned theologians to cramp all mankind into the scant six thousand years of Hebrew chronology, as expounded by Archbishop Ussher. Religious teachers have also maintained the proposition not only that man is something fundamentally distinct from other living creatures, but that there are no inherited differences in humanity that cannot be obliterated by education and environment. (Pg. 4, "The Passing of the Great Race or the Racial Basis of European History", Charles Scribner's Sons, 1916)

In Chapter 2, aptly entitled "The Physical Basis of the Race," Grant further expounds on the Darwinist underpinnings of his racial theories:

> It must be borne in mind that the specializations which characterize the **higher races** are of relatively recent development, are highly unstable and when mixed with generalized or primitive characters, tend to disappear. Whether we like to admit it or not, the result of the mixture of two races, in the long run, gives us a race reverting to the more ancient, generalized and lower type. The cross between a white man and an Indian is an Indian; the cross between a white man and a negro is a negro; the cross between a white man and a Hindu is a Hindu; and the cross between any of the three European races and a Jew is a Jew. (emphasis mine, Pg. 17, "The Passing of the Great Race or the Racial Basis of European History", Charles Scribner's Sons, 1916)

Chapter 4, "The Competition of the Races," is unmistakably derived from Charles Darwin's and Francis Galton's work. The reference to "breeders" in the caretaking of the human species is distinctly that expounded by Leonard Darwin, Francis Galton, and Darwin's devoted American eugenicists:

> Under existing conditions the most practical and hopeful method of race improvement is through the elimination of the least desirable elements in the nation by depriving them of the power to contribute to future generations. It is well known to stock breeders that the color of a herd of cattle can be modified by continuous elimination of worthless shades, and of course this is true of other characters. Black sheep, for instance, have been practically destroyed by cutting out generation after generation all animals that show this color phase, until in carefully maintained flocks a black individual only appears as a rare sport. (Pg. 53, "The Passing of the Great Race or the Racial Basis of European History", Charles Scribner's Sons, 1916)

Recall that Charles Darwin gave Francis Galton full credit for the parts of "Descent of Man" that incorporated eugenics into his theory of "sexual selection." Grant's book is clearly influenced by this admixture of Darwin's and Galton's work:

> Man has the choice of two methods of race improvement. He can breed from the best, or he can eliminate the worst by segregation or sterilization. The first method was adopted by the Spartans, who had for their national ideals, military efficiency and the virtues of self control, and along these lines the results were completely successful. Under modern social conditions it would be extremely difficult in the first instance to determine which were the most desirable types, except in the most general way, and even if a satisfactory selection were finally made, it would be, in a democracy, a virtual impossibility to limit by law the right to breed to a privileged and chosen few. (Pg. 51, "The Passing of the Great Race or the Racial Basis of European History", Charles Scribner's Sons, 1916)

Like Francis Galton before him and Leonard Darwin after, Grant recommends segregating "unfavorable" races in ghettos by installing civil organizations through the public health system to establish quasi-dictatorships in their particular fields. "The Passing of the Great Race" was unmistakably a "racial" and "eugenic" interpretation of history, placing racial concerns and "sexual selection" as the driving force of civilization. Note the Nietzschean appeals to "misguided sentimentalism":

> A rigid system of selection through the elimination of those who are weak or unfit—in other words social failures—would solve the whole question in one hundred years, as well as enable us to get rid of the undesirables who crowd our jails, hospitals, and insane asylums. The individual himself can be nourished, educated and protected by the community during his lifetime, but the state through sterilization must see to it that his line stops with him, or else future generations will be cursed with an ever increasing load of **misguided sentimentalism**. This is a practical, merciful, and inevitable solution of the whole problem, and can be applied to an ever widening circle of social discards, beginning always with the criminal, the diseased, and the insane, and extending

gradually to types which may be called weaklings rather than defectives, and perhaps ultimately to worthless race types. (emphasis mine, Pg. 50, "The Passing of the Great Race or the Racial Basis of European History", Charles Scribner's Sons, 1916)

Beyond that, historians have desperately tried to forget Grant's work as a naturalist and environmentalist. Grant was a close friend of Theodore Roosevelt and an avid conservationist. Madison Grant, the extravagant racist, is credited with saving many natural species from extinction and co-founded the Save-the-Redwoods League with fellow eugenicists C.M. Goethe, Frederick Russell Burnham, John C. Merriam, and Henry Fairfield Osborn. Grant is also credited with helping develop the first deer hunting laws in New York state, legislation which spread to other states as well over time. He was also the creator of wildlife management and original founders of the Bronx Zoo, organizer of the American Bison Society, and helped to create Glacier National Park and Denali National Park. He was awarded the gold medal of the Society of Arts and Sciences in 1929. In 1931, the world's largest tree was dedicated to Grant, Merriam, and Osborn by the California State Board of Parks in recognition of their environmental efforts. A species of caribou was named after Grant as well. He was head of the New York Zoological Society from 1925 until his death. All of this has been conveniently forgotten as historians desperately try to create a gulf of distance between Darwin and Grant, and Grant and quintessential Progressive causes. Bottom line is that there are more commonalities between Madison Grant and the darling of the socialists, Julian Huxley, than Grant has with any podunk ex-Confederate.

J.F. Lehmann looked to the United States for the sort of racial propaganda that had been so successful in creating a racial consciousness. J.F. Lehmann had personal contact with Grant and Lothrop Stoddard. Lehmann wanted a German version of Madison Grant. So, Lehmann went on to recruit the school teacher, Hans F.K. Günther, to mold him into Germany's version of Grant:

> Lehmann invited Günther to join him on an Alpine walk, when on a high mountain ridge they surveyed the issues determining the fate of Germany. Lehmann transformed Günther from a heroic and chivalrous-spirited nationalist into a biological racist. This metamorphosis encapsulated the transition to a new type of scientific racism. Lehmann persuaded Günther to write a piece on racial biological identity. He arranged for Günther to visit Lenz and Ploetz. Günther made revisions armed with an article by Lenz on 'The Nordic Race and the Blood-Mixture of our Eastern Neighbours'. Lenz, Ploetz and Lehmann all approved of the resulting work, and Lehmann invited Günther to write a racial study of the Germans. Lehmann supported Günther's research with money and such scientific materials as photographs of racial types, and encouraged him to acquire the skill of a practicing anthropologist. (Pg. 312, "Health, Race and German Politics Between National Unification and Nazism, 1870-1945", Cambridge Univ. Press, 1993)

Günther's 1922 "Racial Lore of the German Volk" followed Madison Grant's lead and became an instant success. Lehmann printed and sold over 30,000 copies by 1932. Lehmann then leveraged the contents of the book to justify his political endeavors. He used the contents to justify the idea that people of "Nordic" ethnicity had a superior right to lead the nation and had the right to protect German "blood." Lehmann would perpetuate this by publishing a steady stream of Günther's books. Stefan Kühl, author of "The Nazi Connection" quotes Günther praising Grant:

> In February 1934, Hans F. K. Günther, race anthropologist and a special protégé of the Nazis, explained to his audience in a crowded hall at the University of Munich that it was remarkable that "American immigration laws were accepted by the overwhelming majority, although the United States appeared the most liberal country of the world." He referred to Grant and Stoddard as the "spiritual fathers" of immigration legislation and proposed that the laws serve as a model for Germany. (Pgs. 37-38, "The Nazi Connection: Eugenics, American Racism, and German National Socialism", Oxford Univ. Press, 1994)

J.F. Lehman was also the publisher for both of Hitler's and Grant's books. By feeding Adolf a dose of Günther's and Grant's "racial lore," J.F. Lehmann became the direct link between Madison Grant and Adolf Hitler. J.F. Lehmann was one of a handful of critical conduits, uniting eugenicists from various continents and nations into one coherent movement.

A critical distinction must be made here. Scientific minds like that of Lehmann, Ploetz, and Lenz were not looking to connect with the podunk left-overs from the rural Confederacy. They were looking to network with the high and mighty Ivy League protégés in order to glean legitimacy from their reputations. The Nazi eugenicists from the vaunted Kaiser-Wilhelm Institute were not looking to connect with the likes of Dixon, but rather with the elites, namely Grant, Davenport, and Henry Fairfield Osborn.

Sec. 7 – FROM DARWIN TO AMERICAN EUGENICS:

To understand just how Darwinism was ingrained in Madison Grant's "Passing of the Great Race" was in Darwinism, we must recall that most, if not all of the scientific claims in "Passing" were due to Henry Fairfield Osborn's influence and friendship with Grant. An honest history of American eugenics cannot be written without Henry Fairfield Osborn, and in turn, you cannot write an honest history of Henry Fairfield Osborn without documenting his extensive Darwinist credentials. Henry Fairfield Osborn has been sanitized of his "racialist" and eugenicist credentials and is more often than not remembered as a respected president of the American Association for the Advancement of Science. Osborn was in his day "second only to Albert Einstein as the most popular and well-known scientist in America," and his eugenic past has been an inconvenience for those that would like to remember him in a positive light. [310]

Like Grant, much of Osborn's elitist and racialist outlook was due to his privileged pedigree. Osborn's uncle was the famous financier, J.P. Morgan, and his boyhood friends included the future president of the United States, Theodore Roosevelt. Osborn "began writing evolutionary articles in the late 1880s." [311] Osborn graduated from the College of New Jersey, which later became the Ivy League powerhouse, Princeton University. In 1891 Osborn left Princeton to accept two jobs in New York; the first at Columbia University, where he was to set up a new biology department, and the second at the American Museum of Natural History.

In 1894 Osborn and Madison Grant's shared enthusiasm for zoology inspired them in the creation of the New York Zoological Society Park, now more commonly known as the Bronx Zoo, with the help of Theodore Roosevelt, Elihu Root, and the grand old man of New York politics, Andrew H. Green, whom incidentally was a longtime friend of Osborn's father William Henry. In 1918, Grant and Osborn would leverage their relationship with John C. Merriam, the president of the Carnegie Institution, to co-found the Save the Redwoods League. Osborn would go on to become President of the American Museum of Natural History and cement his Darwinist credentials when he was awarded the Darwin Medal by the Royal Society in 1918. The Royal Society created the Darwin Medal in 1890 for "work of acknowledged distinction in the broad area of biology in which Charles Darwin worked."

However, Osborn's most historically important effort was advancing the cause of eugenics through his collaboration with Madison Grant and Harry H. Laughlin. As was the case with other Ivy League Darwinists, Osborn's racism was integral and inseparable to his views on evolution. [312] Osborn would successfully leverage his Ivy League pedigree. He was a member of the Boone and Crockett Club in New York, and his contacts and friendships among the Northeastern elite would serve eugenics well. While historians would like to either forget or distance Osborn from this pivotal episode, it must also be remembered that Osborn used the relationship to present himself as an expert before the House Committee which was responsible for creating the Johnson-Reed Immigration Restriction Act of 1924, which Secretary of State Cordell Hull would later utilize to prevent Jewish victims of The Holocaust from seeking refuge within the United States. It is because Madison Grant is vilified by history that it is important to remember that Osborn inspired much of Grant's work and should be remembered in the same light. Grant and Osborn worked closely together on the Bronx Zoo project, and it is then that Osborn's science informed Grant's political theories. Osborn's Central Asia hypothesis was Grant's starting point for his history of the Nordics, and by extension, the main thesis of "The

---

[310] swans.com, "The Life and Controversies of Henry Fairfield Osborn: Part I of II", Michael Barker, Feb. 13, 2010.
[311] Ibid.
[312] Ibid.

Passing of the Great Race." [313]

Osborn's hypothesis applied Darwinism's evolutionary history to human history and would pave the way for what is now termed "Biohistory." The movement "has its roots in the late nineteenth century with the evolutionary biology theories of Charles Darwin." [314] Prior to Darwin, the primary focus of history was to study the lives and events of important people including kings and generals. For example, in 1901, the president of the American Historical Association, Charles Francis Adams Jr., stated that Darwinian Theory "was the dividing line between us [contemporary historians] and the historians of the old school." [315] The Preface to "The Passing of the Great Race," which Osborn wrote, clearly evidences the "biohistorical" aspects of Madison Grant's theories, and more precisely, that Grant's work was rooted in Darwin's work, through Osborn, Galton and knowingly or unknowingly, through Weismann:

> European history has been written in terms of nationality and of language, but never before in terms of race; yet race has played a far larger part than either language or nationality in molding the destinies of men; race implies heredity and heredity implies all the moral, social and intellectual characteristics and traits which are the springs of politics and government. Quite independently and unconsciously the author, never before a historian, has turned this historical sketch into the current of a great biological movement, which may be traced back to the teachings of Galton and Weismann. (Preface, "The Passing of the Great Race or the Racial Basis of European History", Charles Scribner's Sons, 1916)

One of the first contributors to what can be deemed "biohistory" was Yale geographer and one president of the American Eugenics Society, Ellsworth Huntington. Although a geographer by study, Huntington believed a correlation between the climate, geography, and culture. In his 1915 book, "Climate and Civilization," Huntington claimed that there is a positive correlation between the amount of energy exerted based on climate regions and the perceived areas of civilization. Both Osborn and Grant would be influenced by Huntington's work. "The Passing of the Great Race" followed Huntington's 1915 book and was published a year after Huntington's book. Note Osborn elaborating the preface of Grant's infamous work along a "biohistorical" line of thinking:

> Thus the racial history of Europe, which forms the author's main outline and subject and which is wholly original in treatment, might be paraphrased as the heredity history of Europe. It is history as influenced by the hereditary impulses, predispositions and tendencies which, as highly distinctive racial traits, date back many thousands of years and were originally formed when man was still in the tribal state, long before the advent of civilization. (Preface, "The Passing of the Great Race or the Racial Basis of European History", Charles Scribner's Sons, 1916)

---

[313] swans.com, "The Life and Controversies of Henry Fairfield Osborn: Part I of II", Michael Barker, Feb. 13, 2010.
[314] "Biohistory", Eric Paulson, Occidental Quarterly Online Journal, May 26, 2010.
[315] Ibid.

The "biohistorical" aspect of American eugenics would have far-reaching consequences through the various institutions that it would engender. In 1918, Osborn, Grant, and Charles B. Davenport formed the Galton Society "to study human anthropology, evolution, and eugenics." The formation of this Society was undertaken in large measure to present an organized challenge to the threat posed by scientists like Franz Boas, who had embarked on an all-out assault on the claims of the international eugenics movement. The founding members of the Galton Society would include the leading American eugenicists Raymond Pearl, Earnest Hooton, Edwin Conklin, E.L. Thorndike, and notably John C. Merriam, the president of the Carnegie Institution of Washington DC. Osborn was also a founding member of the controversial Pioneer Fund, along with fellow eugenicists Wickliffe Draper and Harry H. Laughlin. Osborn would become president of the Pioneer Fund, and fund Laughlin's work after the Carnegie Institution forced him to retire.

Osborn would also write the preface to Grant's second book "Conquest of a Continent." Grant had this second book sent to Eugen Fischer and Fritz Lenz, the authors of the infamous "Baur-Fischer-Lenz" book. Copies also went to Alfred Rosenberg, Hitler's racialist megaphone and editor of the infamous newspaper of Hitler's party, the "*Völkischer Beobachter*":

> In 1937 the book appeared in a full German translation. In a foreword to the translated version, Eugen Fischer stressed that Grant was "no stranger to German readers of writing on race and eugenics" and added that, in a time when the racial idea has become one of the chief foundations of the National Social State's policies, "no one has as much reason to note the work of this man with the keenest of attention as does a German of today. (Pg. 74, "The Nazi Connection: Eugenics, American Racism, and German National Socialism", Stefan Kühl, Oxford Univ. Press, 1994)

"The Eugenic Review" lauded "Conquest of a Continent" in the July 1934 edition as "devoting nearly half a century to the study of human evolution." As such, eugenicists like Harry H. Laughlin fully expected "Conquest" would be a significant success and serve as a "reference" for generations to come. However, by the time it was published in 1934 the American public had begun to sour on eugenics to the confusion of Grant, Laughlin, and Osborn. Grant had spent a fortune preparing the manuscript but earned a miniscule return in royalties. Grant was devastated and threw a prolonged temper tantrum spending a significant amount of time writing bitter letters to bookstores and book reviewers. [316]

The stark difference in popularity between "The Passing of the Great Race" and "Conquest of a Continent" is a testament to how Adolf Hitler's eugenic rants affected the public's perception of the eugenic movement. Both books were supposedly the works of "science" and prestigious scientists like Osborn and Laughlin certainly thought so. The environmentalist and conservationist extraordinaire, C.M. Goethe, was "so profoundly stirred" by the book that he stayed

---

[316] Pg. 346 - "Defending the Master Race: Conservation, Eugenics, and the Legacy of Madison Grant", Jonathan Peter Spiro, UPNE, 2008.

up an entire night to read it cover to cover. Grant revealed the sentiment behind his expectations by eagerly predicting that "Conquest" would be denounced "by those who, like the Jews" were "egalitarians." [317] Considering his *modus operandi*, it is probable that Grant desired a vocal opposition, so he could instigate controversy and derision towards the traditional "egalitarian" American values, much in the same way "Passing" had set up the immigration debate. However, by this time, the world had started to know the reality of what eugenics looked like when implemented by a government. Grant and Laughlin could not see this, as their work evidenced their preference for a "total state," and chalked up the criticism on "Conquest," and Hitler's regime for that matter, as nothing more than Jewish propaganda.

Osborn, along with "biohistorian" Ellsworth Huntington, started to distance themselves from the overt racial overtones of German eugenics, despite serving as presidents of the American Eugenics Society. [318] This was a thinly veiled effort. Osborn persisted with his eugenic work. In 1937 Osborn praised National Socialism's eugenic legislation as the "most important experiment which has ever been tried." Osborn lamented that the public was becoming opposed to "the excellent sterilization program in Germany because of its Nazi origin" before the Annual Meeting of the American Eugenics Society in 1938." [319] He saw the Mexican and Native American population in the United States as a "problem" of "differential fertility." "Differential fertility" is the scientific term used by eugenicists to fan the flames of fear, much through propaganda films like *Erbkrank*, that the "genetically inferior" tended to reproduce faster than allegedly healthy people. "Differential fertility" was the Global Warming fear-mongering of the racial biologists. [320]

Truthfully, historians don't know how to handle Henry Fairfield Osborn, and this has to be largely attributed to the fact that it is hard to hide his racialist credentials. Osborn is rumored to have been the inspiration for the character of Indiana Jones that appeared in the famous Steven Spielberg movies of the 1980s and 1990s. Aside from the prestigious Darwin Medal by the Royal Society, Osborn was also elected a Fellow of the American Academy of Arts and Sciences in 1901. Osborn is credited for describing and naming Ornitholestes in 1903, Tyrannosaurus Rex in 1905, Pentaceratops in 1923, and Velociraptor in 1924. In 1929 Osborn was awarded the Daniel Giraud Elliot Medal from the National Academy of Sciences, and the Academy wrote a laudatory biographical memoir which was presented to the Autumn Meeting of the Academy in 1937. Yet, a truthful history of the eugenics movement cannot be written without Osborn, and in turn, Osborn's history cannot be written honestly and faithfully without taking note of his extensive Darwinist credentials. Like other leaders of the eugenics movement, namely H.G. Wells, Osborn studied comparative anatomy at the Royal College of Science under

---

[317] Pg. 345 – "Defending the Master Race: Conservation, Eugenics, and the Legacy of Madison Grant", Jonathan Peter Spiro, UPNE, 2008.
[318] Pg. 74 - "The Nazi Connection: Eugenics, American Racism, and German National Socialism", Stefan Kühl, Oxford Univ. Press, 1994.
[319] Pgs. 75-76 – Ibid.
[320] Pg. 75 – Ibid.

Professor T. H. Huxley, the scientist remembered as "Darwin's Bulldog":

> And we can well imagine how deeply the sensitive young Osborn must have been moved when Professor Huxley, conducting Charles Darwin through the laboratory of comparative anatomy in London, stopped and presented the young American to that incomparably great and gentle man. On this and succeeding periods in England he not only formed friendships of great value, with Professor Huxley, with Francis Galton, Edward B. Poulton, Leonard Darwin, and many others, but also acquired an abiding interest in the grand problems of evolution. (nasonline.org, "Biographical Memoir of Henry Fairfield Osborn, 1857-1935", by William K. Gregory, Vol. XIX, Third Memoir, Nat. Academy of Sciences, 1937)

In other words, Osborn's connection to Darwinism was no academic or tangential connection. Osborn's Darwinist worldview came from the original source. Osborn's Darwinism was born of a firsthand tutelage from one of the masters, T.H. Huxley. Despite the direct connection, some historians have also tried to distance Osborn from Darwinism by documenting that Osborn was critical of Darwin's work. Osborn mostly agreed with Darwin, and his Royal Society's Darwin Medal underscores this better than any tit-for-tat argument. Osborn only differed with Darwin in claiming that the common ancestor between man and ape was more human than ape, a subtle disagreement on the particulars of the Theory of Evolution, if it can be called a genuine disagreement at all. Due to this small distinction, Creationists wrongfully leaned on Osborn's work, and this in turn, greatly frustrated Osborn. Osborn was no Creationist, and to mischaracterize him as such just to shield Darwin from the taint of eugenics is equally questionable, to say the least.

More to the point, the National Academy's memoir lavishes praise on Osborn for extending his work beyond mere fact-finding. It diminishes the work of "many most useful and even eminent naturalists" for spending "their entire lives" as the "drawers of water and hewers of wood." The memoir criticizes the dry fact-finding efforts of other scientists for apparently taking "no interest in generalization for the drawing of inductions." It praises Osborn's work as in the tradition of Charles Darwin, describing Darwin as a "true naturalist" that was "not content with merely assembling facts." The memoir quotes Darwin:

> I have myself always found the mere assemblage of facts an extremely painful and self-denying process and I have always been animated by the hope that such dry work would finally be rewarded by an interpretation or the discovery of a new principle. (nasonline.org, "Biographical Memoir of Henry Fairfield Osborn, 1857-1935", by William K. Gregory, Vol. XIX, Third Memoir, Nat. Academy of Sciences, 1937)

Arriving at generalizations and new principles Henry Fairfield Osborn did, and did so very much so in the tradition of his mentors; Charles Darwin, Francis Galton, and T.H. Huxley. As their student, Henry Fairfield Osborn arrived at the same generalizations and conclusions that Julian Huxley, H.G. Wells and Leonard Darwin did. No honest reading of his eugenic "inductions" and "generalizations" can be claimed to have been a "misinterpretation" or "misapplication" of Darwin's work, as his supporters often claim. Osborn's generalizations and conclusions not only expanded but were perfectly in line with Galton's eugenics, and this only serves to further cement Osborn as a devoted Darwinist. Osborn's most consequential contribution to history would undoubtedly be his eugenics, and this has thrown the historians for a tailspin. They do not know how to praise Osborn for his work while distancing him from the inescapable and entangled relationship with German eugenicists and the "biohistorians" who saw all human history through a racial lens.

Sec. 8 - GOETHE'S "FEDERATION" OF RACIALIST INSTITUTIONS:

There is one question about Holocaust history that has gone unanswered: How do you convince the most educated and sophisticated society in the world to commit mass murder? The answer is not as ephemeral as historians have made it out to be. If you want the educated elite to carry out the task of eliminating millions, all you need to do is appeal to their vanity and intellect. You appeal to their belief in reason, logic, and belittle traditional morality as the relic of superstitious belief systems. You frame the task of genocide as grounded in "settled science" and stoke the fires of urgency with propaganda, precisely as Hitler's and Goebbels's propaganda did in films such as "*Erbkrank.*"

This book documents how Hitler's henchmen plagiarized the eugenic laws from intellectuals educated in Cambridge, Oxford, and the American Ivy League universities. The flip side to this disturbing fact is that it is also the well-educated, well-traveled, and most prominent American "progressives" who lauded Hitler for his eugenic policies. This is undoubtedly true about the earliest and most prominent pioneers of American environmentalism such as Madison Grant, but it is underscored with the story of early environmentalists and presidents of prestigious universities such as the founders of Stanford and California State in Sacramento.

C.M. Goethe persistently sought out association with the East Coast Ivy League eugenicist, Charles Davenport, and his sidekick, Harry H. Laughlin. Charles M. Goethe was a wealthy land developer, philanthropist, conservationist, and lifelong resident of Sacramento, California. [321] Goethe is best known for being the founder of California State University, Sacramento, then known as Sacramento State College. The university has recognized Goethe as its founding father since it appointed him chairman of the University's advisory board. The university would receive the largest share of Goethe's $24 million estate.

Goethe's Progressive credentials are as pronounced as Henry Fairfield Osborn's.

---

[321] "Advertising Eugenics: Charles M. Goethe's Campaign to Improve the Race", William Schoenl and Danielle Peck, Endeavour Journal, Vol.34 No.2.

Goethe was an environmentalist who wrote admiringly of California's Forty-Niners, the State's giant redwood trees. He became a member of the American Association for the Advancement of Science in 1913. He founded the Nature Study League of California in 1918. According to the timeline of Goethe's life posted in the Cal. State website, he was appointed Regional Head of the Sierra Club in 1921. Goethe used his substantial wealth to establish several memorial groves in Northern California through the Save-the-Redwoods Foundation. Goethe and his wife have been called the "The father and mother of the Nature Guide Movement." The couple was inspired by the back-to-nature movements they saw as part of their travels to Europe. The couple traveled to Florida to attend an Audubon Society meeting called for the creation of the Everglades National Park in 1946. Cal. State Sacramento dedicated the Goethe Arboretum to commemorate his ecologist credentials in 1961. It also organized an elaborate gala to mark his 90th birthday in 1965, when he received letters of appreciation, most notably from other environmentalists such as the president of the Nature Conservancy, Edmund G. Brown, and prominent Democrats such as President Lyndon Johnson.

Like many of his eugenic brethren, Goethe had a taste for city planning and a highly landscaped urbanity. According to the timeline of Goethe's life posted in the Cal State University website, Goethe was appointed to the Committee of City Planning in Sacramento in 1912 and had a special appointment by California's Governor Wallace as a "special commissioner" in charge of investigating and studying children's playgrounds around the world for future incorporation into the cityscape. As part of this "special commission," Goethe traveled to Japan, Korea, Burma, India, China, Italy, France, and Germany in 1912 to study playgrounds and green space.

Goethe sought out association with the Eugenics Record Office as early January 1924. In August 15, 1925, Goethe wrote to Laughlin and Davenport to inform them that he had been successful at gaining the cooperation of the Commonwealth Club to create a Section on Eugenics. The club's membership already included many prominent intellectuals and eugenicists, including Lewis Terman and David Starr Jordan of Stanford University. Goethe had for a long time been a member of their Section on Immigration and had observed the group's impact upon Congress. According to the Cal State Goethe exhibit, he petitioned the club's Board of Governors to further the work of the Immigration Section with a Section on Eugenics, which was finally established in 1924 by Goethe and UC Berkeley professor Samuel J. Holmes.

The Commonwealth Club was much more than some local charity. The Commonwealth Club of California describes itself as "the nation's oldest and largest public affairs forum." According to the 2012 version of the club's website, its mission is to be "the leading national forum open to all for the impartial discussion of public issues important to the membership, community, and nation." The club's focus on immigration in the 1930's evidence just how pervasive the topic was on the

West Coast of the United States. [322] The immigration section of the club had dedicated the majority of its biweekly meetings to the topic of registration and deportation. One of its members, M.A. Goldstone, spoke for imposing immigration quotas on India, China, and Japan. One of his speeches, "Race Mixture and Selective Immigration in Their Relation to a Quota for Japan," argued for immigration restrictions that selected only "above-average" and "exceptionally endowed Asiatics." Likewise, according to the Cal. State online Goethe exhibit, Goethe personally championed the cause of systematically excluding Mexicans. In fact, Charles M. Goethe founded the Immigration Study specifically to investigate the influx of "low-powers" to California, especially Mexicans and Southern Europeans, whom he alleged were endangering the state's pioneer heritage. Alarmed by the apparent "over-breeding" of "Mexican peons," who "multiply like rabbits," and the "under-breeding" of "old American-Nordic" families, Goethe publicly railed against the dangers of "race suicide," a term later popular with Hitler's National Socialists. Likewise, Goethe was inspired by his National Socialist counterparts, and vocally so. Goethe wrote to a eugenicist in Hitler's Germany in early 1938, that he was "telling our people here, who are only too often poisoned by anti-German propaganda, of the marvelous progress you and your German associates are making." [323] In 1938, following *Kristallnacht,* Goethe again wrote to his German colleague. "I regret that my fellow countrymen are so blinded by propaganda just at present that they are not reasoning out regarding the very fine work which the splendid eugenists of Germany are doing." [324] The timing is important as it indicates that American eugenicists regarded the street violence against the Jews as a legitimate part of a eugenic campaign. Goethe also praised Hitler's eugenic policies publicly in a speech to the Sacramento Twenty-Third Club, stating in part that: "Germany in a few months outdistanced California's sterilization world record of a quarter-century. We must study Germany's methods." [325]

Yet, Goethe didn't believe himself a racist. This distancing from guttural and pedestrian racism comes as no surprise. According to Professor Tony Platt of Cal. State Sacramento, Goethe believed in the scientific need for a master race of "high-powereds" and based his beliefs about human breeding upon his study of plants and animals. A December 18, 1933 lecture given by fellow eugenicist and member of California's Commonwealth Club is instrumental in illustrating the way in which well-traveled elitists such as C.M. Goethe, Harry H. Laughlin, and Charles Davenport rationalized their "racialist" views. All of them believed themselves to be men of science, standing on the shoulders of scientists no less reputable than Charles Darwin and Francis Galton. A copy of the lecture titled "Race Prejudices" was kept by Harry Laughlin and is still available at the Special Collections Department at the Truman State library which houses Laughlin's papers. It qualifies racial "preferences"

---

[322] Pg. 156 - "Japanese Pride, American Prejudice: Modifying the Exclusion Clause of the 1924 Immigration Act," Izumi Hirobe, Stanford Univ. Press, 2001.
[323] "Darkness on the Edge of Campus: University's Philanthropic 'Godfather' Was Mad About Eugenics", Chrisanne Beckner, Sacramento News and Review, Feb. 19, 2004– Now posted at newsreview.com
[324] Ibid.
[325] Ibid.

on Darwinist terms. In fact, the lecture qualifies as a "racialist" interpretation of Darwin's "sexual selection":

> Selection is almost synonymous with discrimination. We may define it as the act of choosing or picking out; as a preference for persons or things. Selection is a causative factor in the process of evolution. It operates as an aversion to dissimilar organisms; it contributes to the law of survival of the fittest and to the creation of new species. The organism that fails to respond to the primary instincts of fear, pugnacity and sex leaves no successors. Hence, the axiom dislike for the unlike, has a biological affinity and may be traced back to the impulse of fear which is linked to the instinct of self-preservation. (Box: E-I-4:2, "Race Prejudices, a paper read before the Immigration Section of the Commonwealth Club", by M. A. Goldsone, Harry H. Laughlin Papers, Special Collections, Truman Univ.)

The lecture by the Commonwealth Club's member, M.A. Goldstone, was delivered to the immigration section of the club, and it furthered Darwin's idea that aesthetics play a part in "sexual selection." The lecture extrapolates this to the idea that "selection" is "discerning" and "preference" no different than that "applied to music, art, or a keen appreciation of the beautiful." In other words, "discrimination" in an aesthetic and Darwinian sense is "distinction" and a method for "preservation." Goldstone quotes psychologists and sociologists, and differentiates between guttural "prejudice" and "preference" in order to distance the selectiveness of the educated to the base acts of uneducated bigots:

> Prejudice we will define as a decision in advance, as a prepossession formed without due examination of the facts: as a leaning adverse to anything – the result of hasty or unfair judgment. For example, Baptists dislike Unitarians, Germans dislike Jews, Mohammedans hate Christians, conservatives dislike radicals. Prejudice clearly appear to approach instinctive behavior implying the absence of a rational balanced judgment. (Box: E-I-4:2, "Race Prejudices, a paper read before the Immigration Section of the Commonwealth Club", by M. A. Goldsone, Harry H. Laughlin Papers, Special Collections, Truman Univ.)

Goldstone proceeds along Darwinian line of thinking where an instinct for "preference" for "like for like" is inherited from our simian ancestors:

> Hankins in his book, "the Caveman's Legacy" states that despite the usual good nature of chimpanzees they ill-treat strangers and he therefore assumes that our ancestors inherited the stranger-hating instinct from the apes. The impulse is still strongly marked among the Australian aborigines. (Box: E-I-4:2, "Race Prejudices, a paper read before the Immigration Section of the Commonwealth Club", by M. A. Goldsone, Harry H. Laughlin Papers, Special Collections, Truman Univ.)

Goldstone rejects the "nurture" justification for racial prejudices, instead claiming that these "preferences" were inherited:

> The stock argument of those who reject the innateness of race antipathies is that

children are less prone to it and play together promiscuously. But actually it becomes manifest and intensified with the approach of puberty and adolescence, thus indicating that it has been merely delayed and latent just as the sex instinct is delayed though latent. We do have, however, many cases of two year old white children becoming seized with terror at the first sight of a black face, denoting the involuntary dread of the unaccustomed or strange. (Box: E-I-4:2, "Race Prejudices, a paper read before the Immigration Section of the Commonwealth Club", by M. A. Goldsone, Harry H. Laughlin Papers, Special Collections, Truman Univ.)

Interestingly enough, Goldstone addressed the racial prejudices erupting in Germany at the time, and reiterates the overplayed German excuse that Jews were a minority in control of a majority, blaming the victim instead of the victimizer:

> In that outburst there is exemplified the interaction, or a complex of many different forces. The personality, the pride of a people is affected; certain traditions are revived; political motives and economic stress are present; the fear, real or imaginary, of a minority group dominating a majority is aroused and an explosion takes place. – The only safeguard against such eruptions is for the minority to conduct itself with such uprightness, reserve and loyalty, with such exemplary behavior, as to remove suspicion and to replace it with esteem if not affection. (Box: E-I-4:2, "Race Prejudices, a paper read before the Immigration Section of the Commonwealth Club", by M. A. Goldsone, Harry H. Laughlin Papers, Special Collections, Truman Univ.)

The Commonwealth Club lecture concludes by paying lip-service to the platitudes of hoping that education and social interaction may ultimately help overcome what humanity inherited from evolution, but circles around to further underscore that eventually removing the inherited prejudice, breeding for better individual traits in humans and eugenics are the answer.

Goethe's life story serves as a cookie-cutter template for the prototypical educated and Progressive eugenicist. Like his eugenic brethren, Francis Galton, H.G. Wells, T.H. Huxley, Alexis Carrel, and Edward Bellamy, Goethe took to authoring a eugenic fiction which taught his eugenic message through parable. "Sierran Cabin…From Skyscraper" mixes botany, geology, eugenics, biology, history, and folklore with Mother Nature as the narrator. Note the allusions to a "master race" or a "race of masters":

> It seemed wise to reduce gradually, and with due caution, the number of congenitally unfit, such as criminals, sex-perverts, the insane, the blind. HOWEVER, THE GRAND AIM MUST BE TO INCREASE THE PROPORTION OF THE TALENTED. (Pg. 16, C.M. Goethe, "Sierran Cabin…from Skyscraper: A Tale from the Sierran Piedmont", 1943)

Goethe, like his brethren, hungered for an actual application of his eugenic beliefs. To this end, Goethe would create the Eugenics Society of Northern California, and worked with Ezra S. Gosney of the Human Betterment Foundation in Pasadena, California. Through these organizations, Goethe lobbied the State to restrict immigration from Mexico, but the most enduring legacy of these organizations was California's policy of performing involuntary and coerced sterilizations on poor, uneducated, or foreign-born women. The Cal. State Goethe exhibition documents that upon returning from a trip to Hitler's Germany in 1934, Goethe told fellow eugenicist E.S. Gosney:

> You will be interested to know that your work has played a powerful part in shaping the opinions of the group of intellectuals who are behind Hitler in this epoch-making program. Everywhere I sensed that their opinions have been tremendously stimulated by American thought...I want you, my dear friend, to carry this thought with you for the rest of your life, that you have really jolted into action a great government of 60 million people. (digital.lib.csus.edu - Sourced 2013. No longer active as of July 2018)

Ponder the historical weight of the above statement. Dr. Alexandra Minna Stern of the Center for the History of Medicine documented the legacy of the work done by Goethe and his colleagues. Dr. Stern documents that although States like Virginia ultimately caught up to California in sterilizations, up until the 1940s California was performing nearly 60 percent of all eugenic sterilizations in the United States. [326] Paul Popenoe, another leading eugenicist from California, documented that the foreign-born constituted 39 percent of men and 31 percent of women sterilized. Consequently, according to Dr. Stern, it was first the Southern Europeans who were the target, and then the Mexicans, which confirms Goethe's deep influence on the program.

Most importantly, Dr. Stern demonstrates that increases in the number of sterilizations were linked to political and social movements, explaining that sterilizations increased in the Southeast United States in the 1950s and 1960s where it was aimed at African American and poor women, and in the 1960s and 1970s in California when the popularity of "zero population growth." [327] This fact only helps underscore the link between Progressive political goals and eugenic central planning. The sterilizations in the 1960s and 1970s were funded by the allegedly benign Federal government's War on Poverty, which rolled family planning into its strategy and targeted the "destructive overbreeders." The racial stereotype made poor Mexican women the target of sterilizations whose consent was attained by threatening to take away welfare help or simply never requested at all. Dr. Stern documents that the Dr. Bernard Rosenfeld of the Los Angeles County General Hospital coauthored a report on these abuses, detailing that in a period between 1968 and 1970 there was a 742 percent increase in hysterectomies, a 470 percent increase in elective tubal ligations, and a 151 percent increase in post-delivery tubal ligations. Karen Benker, a medical student at the hospital testified in support of Dr. Rosenfeld's findings at the ensuing trial, and reported that the heads of Gynecology

---

[326] Pg. 1131 - "Sterilized in the Name of Public Health: Race, Immigration, and Reproductive Control in Modern California", Dr. Alexandra Minna Stern, American Journal of Public Health, V.95(7), July 2005.
[327] Pg. 1132 – Ibid.

at County General had stated that "poor minority women in L.A. County were having too many babies; that it was a strain on society; and that it was good that they be sterilized." [328] This is consistent with the anti-immigration and population control views of the movement. It can hardly be a coincidence that the "zero population growth" upsurge in sterilizations of ethnic minorities in the 1970s in California coincided with the 1968 publication of the highly popular book "The Population Bomb" by Paul Ehrlich. The entire movement in California was started by environmentalists and Darwinists such as David Star Jordan and C.M. Goethe. It was funded and fueled by President Lyndon Johnson's War on Poverty and Federally funded family planning programs. It was sold to the public as a positive health measure by Goethe's onslaught of Orwellian propaganda selling it as protective measures. An equally disturbing fact is that California eugenicists spoke of the "Mexican problem" in an eerie mirror of the German eugenicist's "Jewish problem." Dr. Stern quotes a pamphlet distributed by the Human Betterment Foundation during the 1940s, well into the years when the world became aware of the eugenic activity in Hitler's Germany, which was titled "Effects of Eugenic Sterilization as Practiced in California" which billed the sterilization campaign in Orwellian terms:

> It is a protection, not a punishment; therefore carries no stigma or humiliation. Patients and their families are among the best friends of sterilization. They know by experience what its protection means. (Pg. 1129, "Sterilized in the Name of Public Health," A.J.P.H. Vol. 95, No. 7)

California performed by far the highest number of sterilizations in the United States at nearly one-third of all sterilizations nationwide between the 1900s and the 1970s. Estimates as to the total number can't be confirmed because of the privacy laws. Rough estimates suggest that as many as 20,000 Californians were sterilized up until the 1960s. This was the legacy of the Eugenics section of the Commonwealth Club, the Human Betterment Foundation, and the Eugenics Society of Northern California, which was then continued by a succeeding generation of naturalists and environmentalists after a small lull between the 1940s and the late 1960s. Gov. Gray Davis issued an apology on March of 2003, stating:

> To the victims and their families of this past injustice, the people of California are deeply sorry for the suffering you endured over the years. Our hearts are heavy for the pain caused by eugenics. (mn.gov, "Davis Apologizes for 20,000 Sterilized", Dave Reynolds, Inclusion Daily Express, March 12, 2003)

Professor Platt of Cal State Sacramento claims that Goethe never issued any kind of condemnation of Hitler's policies against the Jews and others. There is little known about Goethe's response when he heard that Hitler's scientists not only sterilized non-Aryans, but also murdered them. Yet, his actions speak volumes: According to the timeline of Goethe's life posted in the Cal State Sacramento website, Goethe was actively lobbying the US Congress to restrict immigration based

---

[328] Pg. 1135 – "Sterilized in the Name of Public Health: Race, Immigration, and Reproductive Control in Modern California", Dr. Alexandra Minna Stern, American Journal of Public Health, V.95(7), July 2005.

on race in the 1950s; with the images of the Hitler's extermination camps still searing in the collective mind of humanity. The following passage from Goethe's 1949 book indicates that he still believed in eugenics even in the immediate aftermath of The Holocaust:

> One continually is amazed at the appalling and tragic ignorance of the average American in matters biological. Have we not a responsibility to end biological illiteracy? If once we raise a generation trained in biology, we will have different kind of law-making. (Pg. 28, Charles M. Goethe, "Seeking to Serve", Keystone Press, 1949)

It is of note that none of his eugenic propagandizing affected Goethe's stature. Goethe's public praise for Hitler's eugenic policies certainly didn't prevent President Johnson or the founder of the Nature Conservancy from lavishing praise upon him long after the consequence of these policies became known after The Holocaust. The conspicuous silence about the uncomfortable tangle between Hitler's eugenic policies and prestigious groups such as Stanford University, Cal State Sacramento, the Sierra Club, and the Save-the-Redwoods Foundation is palpable. Sympathetic political circles persist in the denial of this aspect of their history as like-minded 21st Century environmentalists call for literally cutting the Earth's population in half.

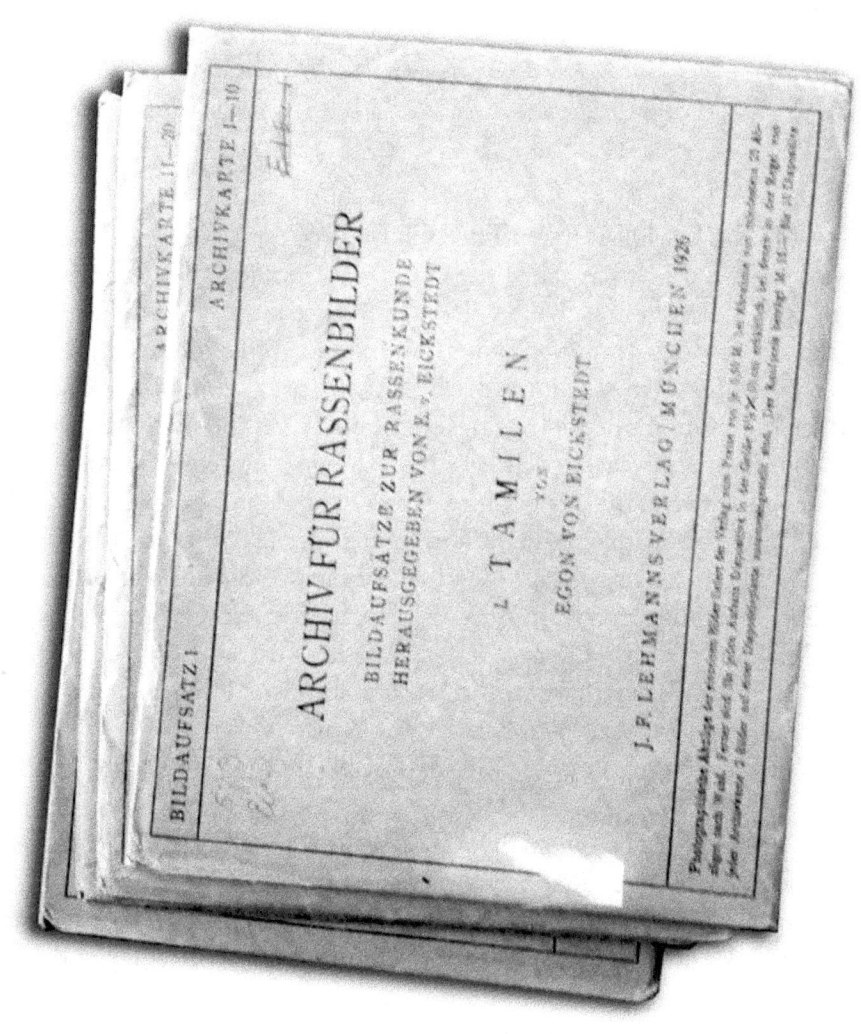

FIGURE 8: "Race Hygiene" flash cards from the Charles B. Davenport and Harry H. Laughlin eugenic collection still held at the Eugenics Records Office's collection at Cold Spring Harbor, N.Y. Note that these flashcards are a J.F. Lehmann product.

Chap. 7: 1915 to 1911

EUROPEAN FRONT: THE FIRST PROTOTYPE TANK IS TESTED FOR THE BRITISH ARMY. • SCIENCE & TECHNOLOGY: PLUTO IS PHOTOGRAPHED FOR THE FIRST TIME BUT WAS NOT RECOGNIZED AS A PLANET. FRENCH PHYSICIST GEORGES SAGNAC SHOWS THAT THE SPEED OF LIGHT DEPENDS ON THE SPEED OF A ROTATING PLATFORM. - THE MODERN ZIPPER IS INVENTED. • LIFE: THE FIRST STONE OF THE LINCOLN MEMORIAL IS PUT INTO PLACE. - THE FIRST STOP SIGN APPEARS IN DETROIT, MICHIGAN. – THE UNITED STATES HOUSE OF REPRESENTATIVES REJECTS A PROPOSAL TO GIVE WOMEN THE RIGHT TO VOTE. CHARLES CHAPLIN MAKES HIS FILM DEBUT IN THE COMEDY SHORT MAKING A LIVING – THE FORD MOTOR COMPANY ANNOUNCES AN EIGHT-HOUR WORKDAY AND A MINIMUM WAGE OF $5 FOR A DAY'S LABOR. THE BRITISH OCEAN LINER RMS TITANIC LEAVES SOUTHAMPTON, ENGLAND ON HER MAIDEN VOYAGE FOR NEW YORK CITY AND SUBSEQUENTLY STRIKES AN ICEBERG IN THE NORTHERN ATLANTIC OCEAN. – WILBUR WRIGHT, AMERICAN AVIATION PIONEER IS BORN.

Sec. I - UNION, DISUNION, & THE GREAT WAR:

World War I, which was called the Great War from its onset until the outbreak of World War II, began on July 28th, 1914, and lasted until November 11th, 1918. Ultimately, more than 70 million military personnel were mobilized. More than 9 million combatants were killed, mainly because of great technological advances in firepower resulting from the Industrial Revolution. It was the sixth deadliest conflict in world history, but it may as well have been the first battle of World War II. The conflict began between the Austro-Hungarian Empire and Serbia, and world war avalanched into fruition due to the various mutual-defense agreements and alliances:

June 28, 1914: Assassination of Archduke Franz Ferdinand of Austria.
July 23: July Ultimatum from Austria-Hungary to Serbia.
July 24: Germany officially declares support for Austria's position.
July 25: Serbia mobilizes its army; responds to Austro-Hungarian démarche.
July 28: Austria-Hungary declares war on Serbia.
July 29: Sir Edward Grey of England appeals to Germany to intervene to maintain peace.
July 30: Russian general mobilization.
July 31: Austrian general mobilization.
July 31: Germany sends an ultimatum to Russia.
August 1 (3 a.m.): The King of Great Britain personally telegraphs the Tsar of Russia.
August 1: French general mobilization.
August 1: German general mobilization.
August 1: Germany declares war against Russia.
August 2: Germany and the Ottoman Empire sign a secret treaty.
August 3: Germany, after France declines neutrality, declares war on France.
August 3: Britain, expecting German naval attack on the northern French coast, states that Britain would give "…all the protection in its powers."
August 4: Germany invades Belgium.
August 4: Britain declares war on Germany.
August 6: Austria-Hungary declares war on Russia.
August 23: Japan declares war on Germany.

War is instigated by idealism. In this sense, the "nationalistic" and "imperialistic" battle cries replete with Darwinist overtones have long been recognized as the spark that both lit and fueled the fires of World War I. The assassination of Archduke Franz Ferdinand of Austria on June 28, 1914, the heir to the throne of Austria-Hungary, by a Yugoslav nationalist was the proximate trigger of the war, but this event had its origins and inspiration harkening back to the Revolutions of 1848, which grappled with the union or disunion of cultural hegemonies. It was ethnic nationalism, the desire for union with culturally similar populations, and the equal disunion from dissimilar peoples that pulled the trigger, which killed the Archduke.

Gavrilo Princip, the man attributed with the assassination of Austrian Archduke, sought to rally Yugoslavs against Austro-Hungarian imperial domination and in support of an independent Yugoslavia by his acts. "Yugoslavism" refers to nationalism of the Yugoslav, or "South Slav" peoples who populate the territories of Southeastern Europe. "Yugoslavism" as a nationalistic movement has historically advocated the union of all Yugoslav populated territories now composing Bosnia and Herzegovina, Bulgaria, Croatia, Montenegro, Serbia and the presently disputed region of Kosovo, Slovenia, and Vardar Macedonia. Gavrilo Princip was a Yugoslav nationalist associated with the movement "*Mlada Bosna*," which translates to "Young Bosnia" that predominantly consisted of Serbs, Bosnians, and Croats. Princip's ties implicated several members of the Serbian military, which in turn lead Austria-Hungary to react with an ultimatum to Serbia known as the July Ultimatum. This ultimatum triggered various mutual-defense and alliance treaties which dragged the major powers into the fight.

These nationalistic movements originated in the Hapsburg Austrian Empire during the Revolutions of 1848. All these movements pushing towards union and disunion became an issue to be reckoned with in 1867, when the Austrian Empire fundamentally changed its governmental structure, becoming the Dual Monarchy of Austria-Hungary with the Austro-Hungarian Compromise. The Compromise re-established the sovereignty of the Kingdom of Hungary, separate from and no longer subject to the Austrian Empire. The Compromise made the Magyar elite in Hungary almost equal partners in the government of Austria-Hungary. For hundreds of years, the empire had been run in an essentially feudal manner with a German-speaking aristocracy at its head. However, with the threat represented by an emerging nationalism, some elements, including Emperor Franz Joseph, decided that a compromise was required to preserve the power of the German aristocracy. Vienna was the natural choice for the capital and imperial residence of the Austro-Hungarian Dual Monarchy. Under the national constitution of 1867, "All ethnic groups in the nation have equal rights, and each ethnic group has an inalienable right to preserve and cultivate its nationality and language." Furthermore, Emperor Franz Josef personally guaranteed strict adherence to this law. [329] Yet, this Austro-Hungarian Compromise fostered a tremendous degree of angst and bitterness

---

[329] Pg. 91 - "Hitler's Vienna: A Dictator's Apprenticeship", Brigitte Hamann, Oxford, 1999.

among the various nationalistic factions, all vying for power and representation within the parliament in Vienna. As the ironic twists and turns of history would prove, it was this clumsy attempt at parliamentary democracy that created in the mind of a young Adolf Hitler a disdain and disrespect for democracy and parliamentary government. August Kubizek, Hitler's roommate during his years in Vienna, wrote in his memoir that Adolf would attend these parliamentary sessions as if they were theater dramas or sporting events:

> Looking down from the gallery, one had a very good view of the imposing semicircle which the great assembly chamber formed. Its classic beauty would have provided a fitting background for any artistic performance – a concert, a choir singing hymns, or even with some adjustments, an opera. (Pg. 242, "The Young Hitler I Knew: The Memoirs of Hitler's Childhood Friend", 1955)

The daily arguments among dignitaries representing no less than 10 different languages and cultures were supposed to compromise and govern, but in reality, they practiced filibustering and intentionally disruptive tactics. These tactics many times were intended to worsen an already tenuous parliamentary situation, with the inciting of disunion as its goal. Hitler was not alone finding entertainment in the daily drama:

> An observer from Berlin noticed with astonishment that attending parliament was very popular with the Viennese. As far as he was concerned, the large number of parties represented in the Cisleithanian parliament made any serious work impossible anyway, and visits to the Reichsrat were "amusing" to the "natives": "There they can. . . attend an entertainment for free. The representatives personally 'jumping on' each other compensates the Viennese entirely for theater performances, which they would have to pay for after all if they wanted some entertainment. In Parliament they can have a grand time, 'by the grace of the representatives,' and what they get out of it also gives them enough material to amuse their good friends for many an evening in the tavern. (Pg. 119, "Hitler's Vienna: A Dictator's Apprenticeship", Brigitte Hamann, Oxford Univ. Press, 1999)

In many ways, the Viennese Parliament served as a sort of schooling for the young Adolf Hitler, and it fed his insatiable appetite for Wagnerian style conflict and drama. Many of Hitler's most enduring political convictions were cemented during this time in Vienna, where he studied and read as if he were an actual student, and wandered without focus among the architectural, musical and political subject-matter that interested him. Kubizek reminds us why Hitler's form of "nationalism" was in no way a patriotism for the traditional boundaries of the Austrian or German states:

> This, too, was one of his oft-repeated phrases: "German Vienna," but Adolf pronounced it with a bitter undertone. Was this Vienna, into which streamed from all sides Czechs, Magyars, Croats, Poles, Italians, Slovaks, Ruthenians, and above all Galician Jews, still indeed a Germany City? In the state of affairs in Vienna my friend saw a symbol of the struggle of the Germans in the Hapsburg

Empire. He hated the babel in the streets of Vienna, this "incest incarnate" as he called it later. He hated this State, which ruined Germanism, and the pillars that supported this State: the reigning house, the Church, the nobility, the capitalists and the Jews. – This Hapsburg State, he felt, must fall, and the sooner the better, for every moment of its continued existence cost the Germans honour, property and their very life. (Pgs. 248 – 249, "The Young Hitler I Knew: The Memoirs of Hitler's Childhood Friend", 1955)

Kubizek recalled young Adolf's emotional reaction during one of the visits to the Parliament hall in Vienna:

…and in the middle of this dreadful spectacle, German, Czech, Italian, and Polish curses – God knows how many languages there were – were flitting across the hall. I looked at Adolf. Was this not the ideal moment to leave? But what had happened to my friend? He had jumped up, his fingers clenched to fists, and his face was burning with excitement. (Pg. 121, "Hitler's Vienna: A Dictator's Apprenticeship", Brigitte Hamann, Oxford Univ. Press, 1999)

Hitler recalled this spectacle years later while reminiscing as to his ideological beginnings:

From now on, whenever time offered me the slightest opportunity, I went back and, with silence and attention, viewed whatever picture presented itself, listened to the speeches in so far as they were intelligible, studied the more or less intelligent faces of those chosen by the peoples of this woebegone state – and little by little formed my own ideas. (Pg. 120, "Hitler's Vienna: A Dictator's Apprenticeship", Brigitte Hamann, Oxford Univ. Press, 1999)

This is the demarcation point from which one can conclusively state that Adolf Hitler was never a "conservative." A "conservative" at the time of Adolf Hitler was a monarchist, and there was nothing in either the young or the old Adolf Hitler that ever desired to "conserve" the "Babel" or the "incest incarnate" that he regarded the monarchy to represent. Hitler believed the Slav to be a "sub-human," and this disdain was fueled by his experience in Vienna. Much of this was attributed not just to young Adolf's experience within the Parliamentary hall, but outside in the overcrowded metropolis that Vienna had become. There was a vast discrepancy in wealth and education among the various nationalities represented in Vienna at the time when Hitler called it his home: "the illiteracy rate among the Ruthenians, Serbo-Croats, and Romanians was more than 60 percent, but among the Germans only 3.12, and among the Czechs no more than 2.38 percent." [330]

The encounter with so many representatives of the "underdeveloped," "barbaric" peoples in the extremely elegant capital and imperial residence took place at a time that was deeply influenced by Darwin's theories and that believed in humankind's development from primitive ancient times to the "noble man" of the future as in a natural law. The different stages of development as determined

---

[330] Pg. 101 - "Hitler's Vienna: A Dictator's Apprenticeship", Brigitte Hamann, Oxford Univ. Press, 1999.

by appearances, conduct, language, and cleanliness, resulted in the belief in man's inequality: "civilized" people considered themselves superior to "primitive" ones. In Vienna it was the Germans who looked upon themselves as the "noble people" as opposed to the "inferior" peoples of the monarchy. (Pg. 102, "Hitler's Vienna: A Dictator's Apprenticeship", Brigitte Hamann, Oxford Univ. Press, 1999)

Many pointed to the Compromise of 1867 as a calamity because it often frustrated their intentions in the governance of Austria-Hungary. For example, it was extremely difficult for Austria-Hungary to form a coherent foreign policy that suited the interests of both the German and Magyar elite. Throughout the 50 years from 1867 to 1914, adequate political compromises in the governance of Austria-Hungary were increasingly difficult to reach, leading many to search for non-diplomatic solutions. The forces of union and disunion molded the Pan-German movement as a movement convinced it had to unite the disparate German-speaking people and disassociate itself from the "slave people" or the less-evolved cultures. [331] In this sense, World War I was but the first battle in a war of unresolved conflicts dating back to the Revolutions of 1848. The evolutionary and eugenic overtones were present when Adolf Hitler was but a mere teenager and spectator to the underlying tectonic shifts that would soon shake the world. War is incidental to ideology, and Germany's imperialistic impulses to control resources for its survival did not arise out of a vacuum. The fires of World War I and World War II were products of the same fuel and flame: ethnic nationalism and a Darwinist racial hierarchy. World War I was but one of the three major eugenic-minded wars to decimate humanity. Germany's imperialistic impulses were a direct descendant of its belief in a Darwinist view of humanity, and for most Germans, Darwin came the way of the man called Haeckel.

Ernst Heinrich Philipp August Haeckel was a prominent comparative anatomist and active lecturer in the late 19th and early 20 centuries. He is most well known for his descriptions of phylogenetic trees, studies of radiolarians, and illustrations of vertebrate embryos to support his biogenetic law and Darwin's work with evolution. By the end of WWI, Ernst Haeckel's most famous work, "The Riddle of the Universe" had sold nearly 100,000 copies. Ernst Haeckel was also a prominent driving force of German nationalism based on a biological superiority justified along Darwinian lines. Haeckel's German nationalism was "chauvinistic" and "expansionist." [332] More to the point, Haeckel was a founding member of the Pan-German League, a heavily influential organization which clamored for the unity of the European Germanic populations. Haeckel died in 1919, but his legacy and influence only grew. "The Riddle of the Universe" was translated into 25 languages and had sold nearly half a million copies by 1933, when the National Socialists fulfilled his calling for a state-created around the biological laws of eugenics, an expansionist foreign policy, unity of purpose, and a "blood and soil" reverence of

---

[331] Pg. 127 – "Hitler's Vienna: A Dictator's Apprenticeship", Brigitte Hamann, Oxford Univ. Press, 1999.
[332] Pg. 4 - "Scientific Origins of National Socialism", Daniel Gasman, Transaction Publishers, 2007.

"fatherland" and the German "*Volk.*"

As such, the well-documented imperialism and expansionism that most historians attribute to Germans as the cause of WWI was largely the product of Ernst Haeckel and his devoted followers. Haeckel traveled to Algeria in 1890 and after witnessing the French occupation of North Africa came to the "overwhelming conviction" that Germany was obligated, for its own security, to acquire new territories. Haeckel thus popularized the infamous concept later to be known as *Lebensraum,* though the German practice of expanding territorially when demographics required dates back to the Middle Ages. Through the Middle Ages, German population pressures resulted in the settlement of Eastern Europe, a practice termed *Ostsiedlung.* The modern adaptation of *Ostsiedlung* was *Lebensraum,* a term that was coined by Friedrich Ratzel, a student of Haeckel's, in 1901. Ratzel, like Haeckel before him, meant the concept to refer to the unification of the country into one ethnic unity and the acquisition of colonies to compete with the English and French and to mimic the westward expansion of the United States. Ratzel's 1901 book titled *"Lebensraum"* was replete with Haeckel's influence. Ratzel's proposal was predicated on a belief that the development of a people was primarily influenced by their geographical situation and that a people that successfully adapted to one location would proceed naturally to another. Ratzel followed Haeckel and Darwin in his university studies of zoology and the study of adaptation in Jena, where Haeckel taught and dominated the philosophical landscape. The territorial expansion, Ratzel claimed as Haeckel had done before him, was a natural and necessary feature of any healthy species.

Specifically, Ratzel called for overseas colonies to which Germans ought to migrate. Later, Karl Haushofer and General Friedrich von Bernhardi were credited for the Eastern European *Lebensraum* that became infamous under Adolf Hitler's reign. In von Bernhardi's 1912 book "Germany and the Next War," Bernhardi explicitly identified Eastern Europe as a source of new space. Poignantly enough, the concept persisted as a zoological construct of distinct Haeckelian influence. According to Bernhardi, war with the express purpose of achieving *Lebensraum* was a distinct "biological necessity," and he targeted the Slavic races as "inferior or decaying races" ripe for displacement by a superior race as Darwinism taught. [333] Like Haeckel and Ratzel before him, Bernhardi framed the need for "living space" as a necessity for reversing the trend of eugenic "degeneration."

It is important to mention that Haeckel was much more to Germans than just an intellectual. Haeckel was a prominent enough figure in turn-of-the-century Germany that his political might was enough to drive movements. Thus, *"Lebensraum"* became the driving force for the Pan-German League for which Haeckel was one of the founding members. Daniel Gasman, a Haeckel biographer, describes the Pan-German League as "Germany's most militant imperialistic, nationalistic and anti-Semitic organization." Gasman continues:

The Pan-German League wished for nothing less than the creation of an

---

[333] Pg. 35 - "The Coming of the Third Reich", Richard J. Evans, Penguin, 2004.

enormous world-wide German community which would be bound politically and culturally to an enlarged Germany on the continent. It was clearly the underlying assumption of the League that an expanded Germany would have the right and the obligation to rule the world. And, although its membership was comparatively small, consisting for the most part of individuals representing the German academic community, the League was able to exercise enormous influence on both the governmental and private level in the years before and during the First World War. In the words of the famous socialist Kurt Eisner, the Pan-German League 'attained a greater influence on the direction of policy than even the powerful associations of landlords and capitalists... From the first naval measure to the last army bill, all the armaments plans originated in the circles of the Pan-Germans. (Pg. 129, "Scientific Origins of National Socialism", Transaction Publishers, 2007)

Haeckel would also develop the philosophy of Monism. Monism was based on Darwin's work and preached a creed formulated upon scientific knowledge. In Monism, all organic and inorganic things, whether mind or matter, were ruled by materialistic scientific laws. Monism was an all-encompassing movement that had political, ethical, and scientific implications. Here is Haeckel's description:

There can be but one answer in the present advanced stage of natural and human history: No. The fate of those branches of the human family, those nations and races which struggle for existence and progress for thousands of years, is determined by the same "eternal laws of iron" as the history of the whole organic would which has peopled the earth for millions of years. (Pg. xxii, "Scientific Origins of National Socialism", Transaction Publishers, 2007)

Haeckel's Monism was an all-encompassing "religion" as Francis Galton had intended eugenics to be. As such, the influence of this emerging creed cannot be underestimated. Daniel Gasman explains that "in no other country of Europe, or for that matter even in the United States, did the ideas of Darwinism develop as seriously as a total explanation of the world as in Germany." [334] Haeckel was a devoted Darwinist who interpreted Darwin's work to have real-world implications, much in the same way as Galton and T.H. Huxley did in England.

Haeckel also became a member of the *Thule Gesellschaft* in 1918, some of whose members later became members of the early German Workers Party, the forerunner of Hitler's National Socialist German Workers Party. Haeckel died shortly thereafter. However, his life spanned from the time of Bismarck to the demise of the German Empire at Versailles in 1919. Like-minded German technocrats and radicals such as Haeckel championed Bismarck. Haeckel, like many of the "National Liberals" like him, tended to seek authoritarian solutions to Germany's problems, thus their admiration for Bismarck. As Gasman reminds us, the Enlightenment was brought to Germany by the conquering Napoleonic French, and therefore the Enlightenment view that the human community superseded the nation

---

[334] Pg. xxxvii - "Scientific Origins of National Socialism", Daniel Gasman, Transaction Publishers, 2007.

was an unwelcomed concept. For Germans, the exact opposite was true: the nation, the *"volk,"* which were ultimately amalgamated to mean the "race," reigned supreme. The "struggle for existence," as Haeckel translated Darwin for the German-speaking public, was an unavoidable conflict between the "races" of the world. To secure survival, control over natural resources was a vital priority. This was, after all, the inherent Malthusian element about Darwin's work as well as the rallying cry of WWI. As such, Haeckel remained vocally committed to the achievement of a full military victory for Germany through to the bitter end of WWI. As late as September 1917, he still clamored continuously against the notion of a peace compromise. Haeckel gave his support to the *Vaterlandpartei,* which more or less translates to Fatherland Party. This political entity was opposed to any peaceful termination of the war. Many of the members of this anti-peace party would later become members of the National Socialist party. Like the National Socialists, this Fatherland Party saw the war in biological and eugenic terms; thus, the violent reaction to the Versailles Treaty. Haeckel certainly saw it this way:

> I fear that the greatly longed for peace will result in a full reversal of modern culture. Our laughing heirs will apparently be the yellow Mongolians. (Pg. 25, "Scientific Origins of National Socialism", Transaction Publishers, 2007)

Sec. 2 - "THE BLACK STORK":

On November 12, 1915, a full two decades prior to the "Baby Knauer" incident in Hitler's Germany, a now largely forgotten but then famous case catapulted eugenics into the American polemic. In Chicago's German-American Hospital, a severely deformed baby boy was born to the Bollinger family. The surgeon who headed the hospital staff, Dr. Harry J. Haiselden, convinced the mother not to treat the child but to let it die. Haiselden revealed that he had let several "defectives" die during the preceding decade and that he would continue to do so.

Like many leading American eugenicists, Dr. Haiselden had been tuned into the eugenic movement by reading the work of Dudley Sargent, the director of the Hemenway Gymnasium at Harvard. Haiselden's actions won editorial endorsement from the Chicago Herald, the Tribune, the New York American, the Detroit News and Free Press, the Baltimore American, the Philadelphia Ledger, the Washington Herald, and namely the New Republic. According to Martin S. Pernick, author of "The Black Stork," Dr. Haiselden "vigorously publicized" the event with absolutely no respect for doctor-patient confidentiality. Haiselden displayed the dying infants to reporters and allowed the press to interview the mothers while they were still hospitalized. It was an all-out propaganda campaign designed from the start to create awareness for Dr. Haiselden's euthanasia and eugenics.

In fact, the story made the front page across the country and even managed to push news about World War I aside. In collaboration with Hearst newspaper, the Chicago American, Haiselden wrote a six-week-long series of articles, delivered public lectures, and appeared in movie newsreels. Subsequently, Hearst and Haiselden produced a movie in which Haiselden starred. In the film entitled "The Black Stork," Haiselden advocated the protection of society from "defectives." It was a kind of morality play based on the dangers of allowing mentally or physically defective children to live because of the likely possibility that they might become criminals. Despite the objections of many film regulators and censors, "The Black Stork" was shown from 1916 on through to the 1920s in movie theaters across the United States. The movie also showed under the title "Are You Fit to Marry?" in 1918 and was slightly revised and rereleased in 1927. It then enjoyed an underground afterlife showing in small theaters and in traveling road shows up until 1942.

Doctor Haiselden insisted that he let the malformed infants die "because he loved them." On the other hand, he also emphasized the need to protect society from what he termed "lives of no value," a concept that would be used and reused by eugenicists on through to those in Germany, namely Karl Binding and Alfred Hoche. He maintained that "by the weeding out of our undesirables, we decrease their burden and ours." [335] Clearly, the "love" he felt for them was more 'pity' like that for a dying animal, than the 'empathy' shared between humans. As we have seen, the leading intellectuals of the time believed that scientific methods provided an objective basis for both emotions and ethics, allegedly superior to otherwise questionable sentimentality. Allowing baby Bollinger to die was not a victory of cold logic over love, Haiselden insisted, but a victory of objective love over sentimental love. "Kindness took the highest form," triumphing over "false sentiment, false manhood, false humanity," he claimed. The Philadelphia Ledger called his decision "the highest benefaction." [336] Martin S. Pernick forwards the analysis that Haiselden's view was part of a larger movement that had constructed a "new ethic" from the certainty of science:

> Haiselden successfully argued that such subjective and emotional disputes could be eliminated by science. He appealed to a faith common among turn-of-the-century Americans who considered themselves "progressive" – the belief that science constituted an objective method for resolving social and ethical questions, such as the quality-of-life decisions eugenics and euthanasia required. His backers could even simultaneously love and loathe those that they labeled unfit, without acknowledging much emotional conflict, because they believe their attitudes were products of an objective method that had resolved such ethical and emotional contradictions. Haiselden and his supporters did not consider their decisions to be value free, but they insisted that their choice of values was derived from and proven by objective methods. (Pg. 15, "The Black Stork:

---

[335] "JURY OF SURGEONS STUDIES BABE'S CASE; Holds Second Examination and Finds More Defects in Chicago Child", New York Times, Nov. 19th, 1915.
[336] Pg. 98 - "The Black Stork: Eugenics and the Death of "Defective" Babies in American Medicine and Motion Pictures since 1915", Martin S. Pernick, Oxford Univ. Press, 1996.

Eugenics and the Death of "Defective" Babies in American Medicine and Motion Pictures since 1915", Martin S. Pernick, Oxford Univ. Press, 1996)

Medicine in this era began to develop enormous power. The New York Times, for example, strongly urged that non-treatment decisions should be "kept strictly within professional circles, without the horrified exclamations of unenlightened sentimentality." [337] A Chicago realtor called for "legislation creating a commission authorized to put to death painlessly hopelessly imbecile children." [338] Clarence Darrow, the darling of the Scope's Monkey Trial, proposed that society should "Chloroform unfit children. Show them the same mercy that is shown beasts that are no longer fit to live." [339] Haiselden postulated that: "Cold hard logic...cannot be overturned by false and sickly sentiment." [340] Other famous figures interested in "The Black Stork's" eugenic value spoke in support including eugenicists Charles B. Davenport, Raymond Pearl, and Irving Fischer.

The very public debate also prompted support from perplexing sources, namely that of the famous deaf-mute, Helen Keller. Naturally, everyone expected Keller to be on the side of the handicapped. She was not. Keller's call for special juries to decide upon life and death issues was typical of mainstream eugenics:

> Eugenicists like Haiselden not only believed their decisions to be objective; they considered objectivity itself to be an ethical imperative of almost mystical power. Science not only banished outdated traditional moral beliefs, it provided a new and better set of social and moral duties. (Pg. 16, "The Black Stork: Eugenics and the Death of "Defective" Babies in American Medicine and Motion Pictures since 1915", Martin S. Pernick, Oxford Univ. Press, 1996)

Keller was initially silent on the matters. Jane Addams called Keller out, and Keller was forced out of her silence. She responded in an article in The New Republic. The letter titled "Physicians' Juries for Defective Babies" was published on December 18, 1915. As Helen Keller put it, "Our puny sentimentalism has caused us to forget that human life is sacred only when it may be of some use to itself and to the world." Note the Nietzschean disdain for compassion.

While it is true that Helen Keller was at other times an advocate of the handicapped, she also had two other passions which clue us into why she may have sided with Dr. Haiselden. First, Helen Keller, like Dr. Haiselden, was a socialist. Her call for government control over life and death decisions through death panels was not some off-the-cuff remark. Helen Keller was quoting from accepted Fabian and socialist tracts. The 1912 article written by Helen Keller for "New York Call" magazine provides a clue. Helen Keller had campaigned for Eugene V. Debbs and became a socialist the way many of her contemporaries became socialists; by reading H.G. Wells: "The first book I read was Wells' 'New Worlds for Old'," a book that

---

[337] Pg. 103 - "The Black Stork: Eugenics and the Death of "Defective" Babies in American Medicine and Motion Pictures since 1915", Martin S. Pernick, Oxford Univ. Press, 1996.
[338] Pg. 103 – Ibid.
[339] Pg. 96 – Ibid.
[340] Pg. 96 – Ibid.

explained why H.G. Wells had become a socialist himself. [341] Helen Keller's 1912 article goes on to explain how her favorite articles were from a publication with the curious name of the "National Socialist." This journal was published much prior to Adolf Hitler's "National Socialist German Workers Party," as the publication Keller refers to was published a decade prior to Hitler's political career beginning. However, it is important to remember that the admixture of "nationalism" and "socialism" was not Adolf Hitler's original creation. The move to "nationalize" in America or "municipalize" in Britain was a political agenda that emerged from the many "Nationalist Clubs" that Edward Bellamy's work inspired. Keller read "German bimonthly Socialist periodicals printed in Braille" by her "German comrades," with the periodical which she "most often requested" was the curiously titled "National Socialist." [342]

The other aspect of Helen Keller that would link her to iterations of early "nationalist" and "socialist" agendas was Keller's devotion to the religion of "Theosophy." Theosophy was a religion that would typically be labeled as part of the occult, and which was popular with British and American feminists. It was popularized by Madame Blavatsky and was one of the sources for early German "race" theories about "Aryans" and their alleged superiority. Helen Keller's 1927 book "Light in My Darkness," which was later re-titled as "My Religion" is a book on Theosophy through and through. Furthermore, Helen Keller was also a close friend and strong admirer of Sanger, the founder of Planned Parenthood and a supporter of eugenics and Theosophy alike. As such, Helen Keller shared in theories about "race," and a "socialist" form of "nationalism," along with socialism's issue of the era, eugenics, and control over births.

Contextualize all of this by placing it in the timeline, and it becomes clear that "The Black Stork" was a direct product of a political movement radicalized by the realization that Darwinian evolution could both "progress" and "regress." This was the phenomenon labeled as "degeneration" which, as we know, put apocalyptic fears of regression into Darwin's devoted followers. The convergence of eugenics and euthanasia had begun as early as 1868:

> From the first, impaired newborns were singled out as prime targets for selective elimination. German zoologist Ernst Haeckel, whose philosophy of monism attempted to apply Darwinism to society, first suggested killing impaired infants in 1868. The proposal was amplified by his disciple Adolf Jost and by pioneer race hygienist Alfred Ploetz in 1895. – Writing in German, Hungarian child-welfare pioneer Sigmund Engel appealed to the "joint outlook of Socialism and Darwinism" to demand that "cripples, high-grade cretins, idiots, and children with gross deformities" "should be quickly and painlessly destroyed," a process he termed "euthanasia." "For the present we may leave the question open whether the consent of the parents should first be obtained," because "the interest of the species is more important than that of a few individuals useless to society. (Pg. 22–23, "The Black Stork: Eugenics and the Death of "Defective"

---

[341] "How I Became a Socialist", Helen Keller, New York Call, Nov. 3, 1912.
[342] Ibid.

Babies in American Medicine and Motion Pictures since 1915", Oxford Univ. Press, 1996)

This was equally the case with the American "progressives" and German "socialists" and "Monists" as Martin Pernick points out. It was certainly the consensus among British Fabians such as George B. Shaw, Leonard Darwin, and Karl Pearson, the devoted follower of Francis Galton.

Early British eugenicists Dr. Robert Rentoul favored selective infanticide in 1906. A prominent British health official, Dr. Charles E. Goddard, proposed killing idiots, imbeciles, and monstrosities. That doctors already routinely practiced selective infanticide was assumed by Swedish inventor and chronic invalid Alfred Nobel, who reportedly described himself around 1887 as a "pitiful creature" who "ought to have been suffocated by a humane physician when he made his howling entrance into life." (Pg. 23, "The Black Stork: Eugenics and the Death of "Defective" Babies in American Medicine and Motion Pictures since 1915", Oxford Univ. Press, 1996)

Martin S. Pernick concurs that the belief in "degeneracy" was a by-product of the belief in Darwin's evolution. Through "sexual selection," hereditary traits were successively and inevitably passed on from one generation to the next. Undesirable hereditary traits compounded with the reproduction of the unfit. The apocalyptic predictions only worsened as scientists at the turn-of-the-century came to believe that changing an individual's inherited traits through education or therapy was a futile effort, if not altogether impossible. August Weismann preached that treating individuals with inherited diseases would in no way ameliorate the continuation of the inherited factors in the offspring of the hereditarily diseased. According to Weismann, no amount of improvements in education or environment would help, only selective control of reproduction would improve heredity. [343]

This was precisely the apocalyptic message in National Socialism's *"Erbkrank"* film, which mirrored the apocalyptic predictions of "The Black Stork." This was the underlying message that multi-faceted propaganda blitz of the National Socialists intended to sell to the German public: Killing the unfit and the undesirable was a measure of self-defense, and a matter of national defense. This is how Hitler's henchmen blurred the line between the actual enemy across the battle lines and the imagined enemies such as the Jews, the Gypsies, the infirmed, and the undesirable. In fact, there is no reason to believe that the National Socialists didn't fully believe this theory themselves. All evidence points to the fact that they were part of the larger movement, convinced of the moral superiority of objective medicine, and intent on using the power of the state to forcibly turn the tide on "degeneracy." As Pernick aptly opines, the racial hierarchies delineated by Charles Darwin inevitably lead to the "racialist" application of the "science." It was not the invention of virulent bigots in Hitler's Germany:

---

[343] Pg. 45 - "The Black Stork: Eugenics and the Death of "Defective" Babies in American Medicine and Motion Pictures since 1915", Oxford Univ. Press, 1996.

Race played a key role in many early eugenic constructions of the unfit. An article on "The Race Problem" by Chicago doctor Charles S. Bacon in a mainstream medical journal of 1903 noted that "the tendency to negro degeneracy and eventual elimination is I believe apparent." The author predicted that "The 'Black Belt' will be defined by the government as a negro reservation similar to Indian reservations," this being "the plan. . . that has worked so well in its treatment of the Indian question until it has practically eliminated the question with the race." As early as 1888, one Boston physician reportedly advocated extending the same "solution" to "the problem of the feeble-minded" that has been applied" practically to the Indian question." "I would stamp out and kill the whole brood."

CONTINUES. . .

Motion pictures invoked Darwinian competition to explain the impending extinction of the Native Americans, both in fictional features like *The Vanishing American* (Paramount 1925) and in educational films like *A Vanishing Race* (Edison 1917) or *The Vanishing Indian* (Sioux ca. 1920). – Dr. J. G. Wilson, a US Public Health Service doctor in charge of examining immigrants on Ellis Island in New York, wrote in *Popular Science Monthly*, "If the science of eugenics deserves any practical application at all, it should insist upon a careful study of the . . . Jews," because "the Jews are a highly inbred and psychopathically inclined race," whose defects are "almost entirely due to heredity. (Pgs. 55–56, "The Black Stork: Eugenics and the Death of "Defective" Babies in American Medicine and Motion Pictures since 1915", Oxford, 1996)

A New York Times article of November 18th, 1915, provides the testimony Dr. Haiselden gave at his trial. Dr. Haiselden basically dictates Charles Darwin's views, which saw the world through the eyes of a "breeder":

> Farmers select the best stock for reproduction; the best seed, without rust or other disease for sowing. Poor humans rely only upon chance. -- So let us be sensible. Let us approve the sterilization of the insane and the defective, and of the children of the habitual drunkards, when both father and mother are so. Let us reproduce ourselves in 100 per cent fashion, so that by the weeding out of our undesirables we decrease their burden and ours and lay the foundation for a normal race, which would result four generations from now. Let us venerate a standard with soul and sense, instead of desecrating it with crumbling tradition and mindless sentimentality. ("Jury of Surgeons Studies Babe's Case", NYT, Nov. 18, 1915.)

Martin S. Pernick further reinforces this aspect of Dr. Haiselden's view that the Bollinger baby was an "atavism," a "throwback" to an earlier stage of evolution. Pernick cites Haiselden as concluding that X-Rays of the baby showed "the skeleton of a monkey . . . an animal lower than man." [344]

---

[344] Pg. 72 - "The Black Stork: Eugenics and the Death of "Defective" Babies in American Medicine and Motion Pictures

To further cement the socialist underpinning of eugenic euthanasia, Pernick documents Haiselden's "propaganda of the deed," a time-honored socialist tactic. Haiselden, like any good socialist agitator then and now fully subscribed to the notion that shocking acts would awaken the consciousness. Haiselden believed eugenics and euthanasia would sanitize; "Death is the Great and Lasting Disinfectant" was the motto Dr. Haiselden provided for his vast audience:

> Until 1915 most prominent eugenicists carefully distinguished preventive eugenics from euthanasia. Yet when Haiselden's actions move the issue from theory to practice, the distinction virtually collapsed. Many of the same leaders who only a few years earlier had vigorously denied seeking the deaths of defectives now trumpeted the Bollinger case as a major breakthrough in eugenics. ---- Irving Fischer now wrote to "emphatically approve" Haiselden's action: "I hope the time may come when it will be a commonplace" that "defective babies be allowed to die." Likewise Charles Davenport abandoned his previous position. If surgery were used for "the artificial preservation of those whom the operation of natural agencies tended to eliminate," he warned, "it may conceivably destroy the race." (Pg. 84, "The Black Stork: Eugenics and the Death of "Defective" Babies in American Medicine and Motion Pictures since 1915", Oxford Univ. Press, 1996)

Haiselden, like a multitude of medical doctors and scientists following him, had intentionally turned the Hippocratic Oath on its head. In their eyes, they were ridding society of illness by getting rid of the ill. Haiselden saw his first obligation to the "society," and like other like-minded individuals, the "society" was confined to the "race" or the "nation." While Haiselden arrogantly found refuge in the ancient Greek practice of infanticide to paint his actions as cultured and justified, he was quick with derision upon the equally ancient Hippocratic Oath as being "2000 years behind the times." [345]

As Pernick opines, Haiselden's Black Stork propaganda blitz did not cause The Holocaust. Neither did Helen Keller for that matter. They just sprout from the same soil. They share a philosophical common ground. There are too many parallels between "The Black Stork" and Hitler's penchant for propaganda to ignore. Martin S. Pernick sees a strong and undeniable pattern between "The Black Stork" and the 1934 film *"Erbkrank."* Both films propose that they were justified in their cruelty by juxtaposing the way poor people lived and the supposedly luxurious way "defectives" were accommodated in the institutions they resided in. Pernick provides quotes from both movies:

> Our defectives are housed in palaces costing fortunes while our unfortunate normal children live like maggots in filthy hovels where the death rate is high. (Pg. 95, "The Black Stork: Eugenics and the Death of "Defective" Babies in American Medicine and Motion Pictures since 1915", Oxford Univ. Press, 1996)

---

since 1915", Oxford Univ. Press, 1996.
[345] Pg. 105 – "The Black Stork: Eugenics and the Death of "Defective" Babies in American Medicine and Motion Pictures since 1915", Oxford Univ. Press, 1996.

Compare the above quote from Dr. Haiselden to this excerpt from the infamous National Socialist propaganda movie:

> Where palaces are built for the offspring of drunkards, criminals, and imbeciles, while the worker and peasant must put up with miserable huts, such a nation approaches its end with giant steps . . . [under old order] healthy families were housed in half-fallen-down huts and cramped back houses. But for lunatics who were totally indifferent to their surroundings, palaces were built. (*"Erbkrank"*, Transcribed from subtitles)

Martin S. Pernick admits to not being able to find any direct link between Hitler's National Socialist government and "The Black Stork" film but provides the observation that the use of propaganda and catch-phrases such as "lives of no value" by Dr. Haiselden in "The Black Stork" certainly raise eyebrows. Martin S. Pernick did not delve into the similarities between the Baby Knauer case in Germany and the Bollinger baby in "The Black Stork," but the parallels only serve to underscore Pernick's observations. Pernick provides the opinion that the Bollinger baby and Haiselden's story was "intentionally erased" from history and that we forget them at our own peril:

> Almost no one today remembers that Americans ever died in the name of eugenics, much less that such deaths were highly publicized and broadly supported. Yet in the wake of Haiselden's campaign, death became a widely discussed and often advocated measure for dealing with the unfit. To overlook the support for eugenic euthanasia in the late 1910s is to seriously skew the dimensions of both movements. (Pg. 15, "The Black Stork: Eugenics and the Death of "Defective" Babies in American Medicine and Motion Pictures since 1915", Oxford Univ. Press, 1996)

Pernick is right. The many commonalities between Haiselden and the Nazi doctors are intriguing and undeniable. The ideological leaders and masterminds of the Third Reich's eugenic policies thought of eugenics and euthanasia interchangeably, and as two different tools towards the achievement of the same goals. The common histories that span oceans abound as do the patterns in practice. Consider the story of Gerhart Hauptmann, a German dramatist and novelist who received the Nobel Prize in Literature in 1912. Brothers Carl and Gerhart Hauptmann were among the very close circle of friends with the "racial hygienist," Alfred Ploetz, who helped author the Third Reich's eugenic policies. The Hauptmann brothers and Ploetz swore to create a racially pure utopian colony called "Pacific" in 1883. They planned a "community on friendly, socialist and maybe also pan-Germanic basis," decades prior to Hitler attempting the same goal for Germany. This circle enthusiastically read the works of Ernst Haeckel and Charles Darwin. Carl Hauptmann was a student of Ernst Haeckel, and Gerhart Hauptmann and Ploetz attended some of his lectures. The group was in close contact with Haeckel even after Hauptmann graduated, and as late as 1884 as they were "enthused over evolution as a basis for social reform." [346]

Hauptmann's first drama, "*Vor Sonnenaufgang*" or in English "Before Dawn" is credited with inaugurating the "naturalistic" movement in modern German literature, whose aims were to portray a palpable realism upon the stage. Hauptmann's play was first performed in Berlin by the naturalist Free Stage company on October 20, 1889. More to the point, the storyline of Hauptmann's "Before Dawn" is incredibly similar to Dr. Harry J. Haiselden's 1917 movie "The Black Stork." Both works propagandized infanticide for eugenic purposes. The public uproar that followed was no less dramatic twenty-eight years earlier. An outraged physician by the name of Isidor Kastan flung a pair of obstetric forceps onto the stage. Eugenic historian, Paul Weindling characterizes *Vor Sonnenaufgang* as the first major public statement in Germany on racial biology: "It exposed the moral, emotional and social dilemmas arising from the use of the laws of heredity as a means of governing human behavior." [347]

Dr. Haiselden pulled from real-life occurrences as had Hauptmann. Hauptmann's play dealt with the conflict between personal emotions and the laws of heredity, and in order to do so, the main character was a mimic of the real-life drama surrounding Alfred Ploetz's love life. The protagonist, Alfred Loth, fell in love with Helene, the daughter of a peasant drunkard whose hereditary value was called into question by her lineage. Helene was also likely modeled after Pauline Rüdin, Alfred Ploetz's first wife and sister to fellow eugenicist Ernst Rüdin. The protagonist, Loth, valued "racial purity," and had vowed to abstain from alcohol and marry only into a healthy family. Loth, like Ploetz, had organized a colonization society of which doctors and engineers were its leaders, as was the case in Ploetz's "Pacific" colony. The aim of Loth's colony was the "propagation of a race sound in mind and body." [348] Hauptmann's plot, like Dr. Haiselden's after, circled the difficulties created for the love affair when the village doctor diagnosed Helene's family as inflicted with "nothing but drunkenness, gluttony, inbreeding and, in consequence, degeneration along the whole line." [349] The play culminated with illicit sex, hysteria, and ultimately a suicide.

Paul Weindling documents that Alfred Ploetz saw the play at the German theater in New York and was touched by the love scene. The website Ancestry.com has a passenger list for Dr. Alfred Ploetz showing a departure from Hamburg, Germany, and arriving in New York City on November 17th, 1890, coinciding with the dates that historians claim Ploetz traveled to the United States with the explicit purpose of further studying utopian colonies. Dr. Harry J. Haiselden graduated from the College of Medicine at the University of Illinois in 1893. While there is no evidence that directly proves that Haiselden's inspiration was Hauptmann, a case can certainly be made that they circled the same eugenic-minded intellectuals. Both dramatic works took advantage of the very explicit emotions that inevitably surfaced

---

[346] Pg. 68 – "Health, Race and German Politics Between National Unification and Nazism, 1870-1945", Paul Weindling, Cambridge Univ. Press, 1993.
[347] Pg. 89 – Ibid..
[348] Pg. 88 – Ibid.
[349] Pg. 88 – Ibid.

when an audience is confronted with the moral dilemmas inherent in eugenics, and both works aroused public outrage as a result.

Keller's support was likely nothing more than a display of her radical political opinions, recanting the general philosophy of the Progressive Eugenics movement." [350] Helen Keller either lost interest or distanced herself from the eugenics movement soon thereafter, likely because of her collaboration with Henry Ford and the efforts to stop World War I with the now-infamous "peace ship." It is of note that Keller's 1929 book "Midstream," which deals with her activities and opinion of the era, does not mention the subject despite the national coverage it received.

Dr. Haiselden left for Cuba shortly after the Bollinger baby case came to fruition. The reason Dr. Haiselden gave for his departure was that his research allegedly could not be done without interference in the United States. This is a crucial fact to note. In other words, the laws of the United States in 1915 were still prohibitive to the goals of the eugenicists prior to the intense amount of work done by Charles B. Davenport, Harry H. Laughlin, and the Carnegie and Rockefeller funded Eugenics Record Office in Cold Spring Harbor. Haiselden died of a stroke in Cuba in 1919, and his participation ended there. However, Haiselden's propaganda blitz was a tacit admission that its intentions were more political than medical, as eugenics would continue to be thereafter.

Sec. 3 - NATIONALIZED MEDICINE & EUGENIC SUBORDINATION:

Dr. Haiselden's highly publicized campaign coincided with a period of transformation in professional attitudes toward government and public welfare. Martin S. Pernick documents that in 1915, at the height of the Bollinger baby controversy, the American Medical Association was beginning to form an opposition to the increasingly collectivist tendencies of the medical profession. By 1920 the dogmatic insistence that government intrude in medical matters was broadly identified as an afront to individual rights. [351] The reactions of the scientific and medical world to Haiselden's collectivist agenda exposed the goal to "socialize" and "nationalize" medicine. As Pernick aptly points out, this effort to "nationalize" medicine was hardly limited to medicine alone:

> ...neither Haiselden backers nor his critics confined the word "socialism" to the doctrines of a specific political movement. The term included any actions that subordinated the interests of individuals to the good of society. This kind of

---

[350] "Disability and Euthanasia: The Case of Helen Keller and the Bollinger Baby", Joan Gerdtz, Life and Learning, No. XVI, Pgs. 491-500, 2006.
[351] Pg. 92 - "The Black Stork: Eugenics and the Death of "Defective" Babies in American Medicine and Motion Pictures since 1915", Oxford Univ. Press, 1996.

"socialism" was not limited to the collective ownership of the means of production, but included any collectivist utilitarianism, especially if the greatest good for the greatest number was defined by the state. (Pg. 93, "The Black Stork: Eugenics and the Death of "Defective" Babies in American Medicine and Motion Pictures since 1915", Oxford Univ. Press, 1996)

Haiselden's supporters were calling for a National Health Bureau that would reorganize the medical industry into a centrally planned and "nationalized" monolithic organization. Their biggest and most well-funded opponent was the National League for Medical Freedom. The battle was fought in the press, and in popular media such as movies and books. Pernick documents the barrage of newspaper articles, and the volley of political accusations and counteraccusations that erupted:

> The socialists quoted on the issue strongly supported not treating impaired infants. The Call, New York's leading socialist newspaper, commissioned front-page articles by Haiselden and Mrs. Bollinger and printed them more prominently than news of execution of radical I.W.W. union organizer Joe Hill. Socialist physician William J. Robinson and his son Frederic, founding secretary of the Voluntary Parenthood League, portrayed Haiselden's actions as supporting their efforts to legalize birth control, while Anita Black, editor of the Call's women's page, backed Haiselden in stridently eugenic terms. In a series of essays, poems and cartoons, other socialist writers linked his actions to pacifism and class conflict. (Pg. 33, "The Black Stork: Eugenics and the Death of "Defective" Babies in American Medicine and Motion Pictures since 1915", Oxford Univ. Press, 1996)

The New York Times was quick to take the side of the Progressives and oppose and ridicule the National League for Medical Freedom. The May 1910 article makes it clear that the intention of the various medical associations was to "consolidate the agencies of public health at Washington into one efficient department or bureau." In other words, the National League of Medical Freedom was correct in fearing an overly powerful and centralized medical industry that would be "nationalized" under the auspices of "control," "coordination" and namely, the drive for "strength and purity":

> In the various departments and bureaus of the Federal Government are lodged powers that cannot be wielded effectively until they shall be co-ordinated under one head. Once united, they can be used in a great propaganda for educating the people --- and for the establishment of standards of purity and strength that would be copied by the States and cities of the Nation. ("Medical Freedom", NYT, May 18, 1910)

Note that the goals of centralization are presented as one and the same as the eugenic goal of creating a "pure" and "strong" populace. Case in point, the New York Times article identifies the leading eugenicist from Davenport's Eugenic Records Office, Irvin Fisher, as the leader of the political movement to bring the "entire Nation's" medical industry under Federal control. Under Irving Fisher's guidance, the movement was clearly tied to his eugenic zealotry, as he like all the other progressive-minded eugenicists understood a "eugenic state" was simply out of reach without the central control and coercive powers of the Federal government. Medicine had to be "nationalized" as a pre-requisite to controlling the "breeding" of the population.

Lyman Abbott responded to the May 18 article in a June 6, 1910 letter to the editor. Lyman Abbott entered into the accusations typical of socialist agitators, accusing the National League for Medical Freedom as being the puppets of capitalist interests. Abbott was secretary of the American Freedmen's Bureau, and editor-in-chief of "The Outlook." Theodore Roosevelt was an associate editor for "The Outlook," and Abbott was a constant advocate of social reform and was an advocate of Theodore Roosevelt's progressivism for almost 20 years. He was also a pronounced Darwinist. Abbott's New York Times letter to the editor was the classic "big business" vs. "social" interest argument, lauding the benefits of a centrally planned effort. Abbott's zealotry was evident. Abbott completely ignored the need for autonomy in the most private aspect of an individual's life and revealingly compares the medical industry to the forest industry. People may as well have been fixed to the ground in a rank and file formation, unable to uproot themselves from the collective as far as Lyman Abbott and Irving Fisher were concerned. They absolutely needed the populous to fall into formation as an "industrial army" of a single purpose and single will. Eugenic laws simply could not allow otherwise. They also insisted on curtailing the physician's autonomy; enforcing ideological obedience would be a requirement for acquiring a license to practice medicine. No measure was too extreme in the pursuit of their eugenic utopia.

Under the circumstances, the League had ample reason to be concerned about a move to make the medical industry a monolithic organization. Eugenicists like Irving Fisher were not shy about lobbying for massive eugenic reforms. The Eugenics Record Office and the various international sister organizations that Irving Fisher was part of frequently published plans to sterilize, segregate, or eradicate as much as 10 percent to 20 percent of the population. A military-style professional hierarchy and board with the power to enforce its will was absolutely necessary for these goals, no different than Edward Bellamy's "industrial army" was necessary to micro-manage the productive assets that each individual citizen represented. This is precisely the complaint of the National League for Medical Freedom: "…monopoly legislation would take from the citizens the right and power to employ the practitioners of their choice if those practitioners did not belong to the law-protected or privileged class." [352]

Furthermore, many key professions were targeted for annihilation by the socialist-minded doctors. One of the professions that were not desired and deemed as competition by the elite in the medical industry was that of the midwife. By 1910 at least 50 percent of all births in the United States were conducted by midwives.

---

[352] Pg. 114 - "The National League of Medical Freedom: Its Aim and Its Contention", National Magazine, Vol. 39, April-Sept. 1912.

The profession had been around for millennia, and its modern competitor of obstetrics had only been around for a few decades. The professional obstetricians were part of the American Medical Association. The midwives were mostly ethnic European immigrants and African-American women providing services to their own, namely when language was an issue. The customer-midwife relationship was typically defined by race, nationality, and language, and thus was seen in the negative context of undesirable immigration or the migration of rural blacks escaping the South. Midwifery was "all but eradicated by the 1940s." [353] Thus, we can assume that midwifery was a casualty of the efforts to fold all of medicine under the emerging specialization.

A September 1912 "National Magazine" article documents the accusations and responses of this debate extensively. It was an answer to Abbott's accusation that the National League was controlled by "capitalists." The representative for the National League for Medical Freedom is quoted as stating that they were willing to open the full financial documents of the League to any of the leading members of the opposition to prove, based on facts, exactly whom financed the League and whose interests it represented provided that such a committee would make public its findings. Interestingly enough, neither Abbott nor Fisher took them up on their offer. They were content to continue making baseless accusations about the League. The representative went on to be perfectly clear about their objection to "nationalized" medicine:

> The people have a right to be protected from adulterated or impure foods, but this protection should be secured in a constitutional manner and in accordance with the democratic theory of government, and not by the Russian bureaucratic system. Their protection should be secured by laws, the execution of which should be given to the executive department of government, with the judiciary left free to pass on the judicial aspects. Only in this way can we preserve freedom and justice for all the people. To give to a bureau what is in reality legislative and judicial as well as executive power, is to pattern after despotic Russia. Such action is incompatible with free institutions and must sooner or later result in injustice, despotism and the overthrow of popular rule. (Pg. 115)

CONTINUES…

> Our League is opposed to anything that points toward state medicine, exactly as we are opposed to state religion. State medicine, as the Rev. Reynold E. Blight well observed in a recent address, 'means tyranny of a most obnoxious character. Let any clique of physicians of any school get control of the government, and entrench themselves behind legislation, and they will impose their theories and methods of treatment upon all citizens, without respect for the individual opinions or conscientious scruples of such citizens. (Pg. 115)

CONTINUES…

---

[353] Pgs. 108-109 – "Unnatural Selections: Eugenics in American Modernism and the Harlem Renaissance", Daylanne K. English, Univ. of North Carolina Press, 2004.

The aim and purpose of this League is, as our prospectus points out, the maintenance of 'the rights of the American people against unnecessary, unjust, oppressive, paternal and un-American laws, ostensibly related to the subject of health. (Pg. 115, "The National League of Medical Freedom: Its Aim and Its Contention", National Magazine, Vol. 39, April-Sept. 1912)

The representative of the National League for Medical Freedom addresses the question of why so much money from private hands and private industry was invested in their campaign against "nationalized" medicine, and his answer fell right in line with many of the underlying themes of this book:

> But behind and beyond all of this, there is a great vital, moral principle involved; and history teaches no fact more clearly than the great and really powerful movements which have shaped the course of civilization have been dominated by moral conviction or ethical principles. Men who are wholly dominated by the spirit of commercial greed, who are ever seeking to secure special legislation that would enable them to enjoy power and revenue at the expense of the rights and wishes of the people, cannot understand how our fathers in 1776 risked their lives and poured out their fortunes like water in support of a great fundamental, but more or less abstract moral principle voiced in the Declaration of Independence. (Pg. 116, "The National League of Medical Freedom: Its Aim and Its Contention", National Magazine, Vol. 39, April-Sept. 1912)

This went to the heart of the matter and explained that the League's stance was taking the higher ground by rooting itself in the principles of the Founding Fathers. The interviewer recognized how deep the scalpel was cutting:

> Stop right there! – You assume that such legislation would result in an attempt at compulsory medication, while jeopardizing the right of the general citizen freely to select the practitioner of his choice. Now, on what do you base these assumptions? (Pg. 119)

Compulsory medication was very much the goal of nationalized medicine controlled by a eugenic elite. The representative for the National League for Medical Freedom answered:

> I could give you any amount of authoritative medical utterances from the master spirits among those who are working for this legislation, which prove beyond the shadow of a doubt the clear-cut, definite purpose of the American Medical Association to be precisely what the League contends. (Pg. 119, "The National League of Medical Freedom: Its Aim and Its Contention", National Magazine, Vol. 39, April-Sept. 1912)

The representative of the National League for Medical Freedom went on to quote Dr. Samuel G. Dixon's statements made for JAMA:

> The law we must have. These laws must reach into all the relations of life . . . Compulsion, not persuasion, is the keynote of state medicine. (Pg. 119, "The

National League of Medical Freedom: Its Aim and Its Contention", National Magazine, Vol. 39, April-Sept. 1912)

Obviously, "compulsion" and not "persuasion" was the medical ethic practiced by eugenicists around the world. Clearly, the representative of the National League of Medical Freedom was spot on when accusing those in favor of a National Health Bureau of trying to destroy Constitutional principles upon which the country was established. Fisher had made clear the link between "eugenics" and "nationalized medicine" in an article supporting the creation of the National Health Bureau:

> Men and women are waking to their responsibility to the race. Eugenics will be a watchword of the future. To squander our natural resources is ignoble indeed, but far worse is it to squander our vital resources. The most sacred obligation of each generation is to bequeath its life capital unimpaired to the generation which comes after. – Marriage laws and customs must be adjusted so as to discourage or forbid procreation by the unfit. All these and other hygienic and eugenic reforms will be realized as fast as public sentiment becomes educated to the solemn responsibilities and higher valuation of human life. The noblest task, therefore, which I conceive for any man is to aid in erecting true ideals of perfect manhood and womanhood. (Pg. 48, "July 19 – Measure Number Three: Creation of a National Health Bureaus – Scriptural Basis", The Homiletic Review, Funk & Wagnalls Co., Vol. LXVIII, July-Dec. 1914)

Irving Fisher continued with an observation that would have made Adolf Hitler proud referencing Spartan eugenics of ancient Greece:

> Our ideals, tho improving, are not yet worthy to be compared with those of Japan or Sweden, and the ideals even these countries have not yet reached the level of those of ancient Greece still imaged for us in imperishable marble. (Pg. 49, "July 19 – Measure Number Three: Creation of a National Health Bureaus – Scriptural Basis", The Homiletic Review, Funk & Wagnalls Co., Vol. LXVIII, July-Dec. 1914)

The most revealing aspect of this battle between the scientific elite and the everyday doctor was the fact that the drive to "nationalize" medicine was headed not by a doctor or a scientist but by an economist. Irving Fisher was a professor of economics at Yale and an advisor to President Theodore Roosevelt. Fisher was also an inventor. Fisher produced various inventions during his lifetime, the most notable of which was an "index visible filing system" which later became popularized as the now-famous "Rolodex." Not surprisingly, he was also an active campaigner and an advocate of vegetarianism and Prohibition, in addition to his pro-eugenic political efforts. His views parallel that of another respected economist, John Maynard Keynes, who too was a member of the various British eugenic organizations and a champion of "nationalized" and "socialized" economies. As we know, Irving Fisher was one of the most vocal supporters of Dr. Haiselden drive to euthanize newborns born with birth defects. Fisher was quoted as stating that "The chief significance (of the Bollinger case) is the eugenic question." Dr. Haiselden seconded Fisher's observation by commenting: "Eugenics? Of course it's eugenics." Fisher would later write to Haiselden voicing his "hope that the time may come when it will be commonplace [that] defective babies be allowed to die." [354]

Interestingly enough, Martin S. Pernick points to Aldous Huxley's assessment of the amount of "control" that would be necessary to enact the Progressive ideals to society. Even a well-intentioned attempt to eradicate pain and suffering would require the all-powerful and all-encompassing state depicted by Huxley's "Brave New World" dystopian fiction. [355] Total control inevitably results in the "total state," and it is no coincidence that these are the very words Adolf Hitler used to describe German National Socialism. Pernick quotes an article that confirmed the fears of the National League for Medical Freedom: "individualism and socialism have grappled in a life and death struggle, and socialism appears to be the victor." [356]

Clearly, the motivations for the campaign to "nationalize" medicine went far beyond quality of care or bedside manners. This was a political campaign intended to remake society to the likings of the elite. The protections for individual liberty and autonomy that were inherent in the Declaration of Independence and the US Constitution were a clear obstacle to the goal of remaking the United States into a "eugenic state," as Haiselden made perfectly clear upon justifying his emigration to Cuba. The successes and failures of the National Health Bureau and the Eugenics Records Office, both of which Irving Fisher was a leader would depend greatly on overcoming these obstacles.

Can there be any doubt about what Irving Fisher and his cohorts would have wanted to accomplish if they had the luxury of unchecked political power? Their successes include the Race Betterment Law of 1924 in Virginia, which was ultimately upheld by the US Supreme Court in Buck v. Bell. The difference between a fully "nationalized" society in Adolf Hitler's Germany and the United States were the many protections the Founding Fathers intentionally placed in the way, and at least part of the American public opposed these elites by standing on the principles enshrined in the Founding documents. This is what had prompted Dr. Haiselden to leave for Cuba in 1919, as he was right that at that time his research "could not be done without the interference of the United States." Ultimately, this was the difference that kept the equally zealous American eugenicists from achieving what their German counterparts did. This is what kept the numbers of the mass-sterilizations in the United States down in comparison to those achieved by the German National Socialists in their T4 Euthanasia program and The Holocaust.

Posterity must clearly understand that the "nationalization" of medicine has always gone hand in hand with eugenics and euthanasia. Eugenicists began clamoring for a "nationalization" of health care as far back as 1892 with the esteemed Henry Havelock Ellis, the English essayist, psychologist, a pioneer in sexology, and an illustrious member of the eugenics creed. Ellis was integral to the eugenics

---

[354] Pg. 41 and 84 - "The Black Stork: Eugenics and the Death of "Defective" Babies in American Medicine and Motion Pictures since 1915", Martin S. Pernick, Oxford Univ. Press, 1996.
[355] Pg. 94 – Ibid.
[356] Pg. 92 – Ibid.

movement. In 1912 Ellis published "The Task of Social Hygiene" where he supported "the science and art of Good Breeding in the human race," further stating:

> Eventually, it seems evident, a general system, whether private or public, whereby all personal facts, biological and mental, normal and morbid, are duly and systematically registered, must become inevitable if we are to have a real guide as to those persons who are most fit, or most unfit to carry on the race. Unless they are full and frank such records are useless. (Pg. 200, Havelock Ellis, "The Task of Social Hygiene", Houghton Mifflin Co., 1912)

Havelock Ellis had preceded the German National Socialist obsession with social hygiene by several decades. He had called for a "gigantic system of healthy living" in his 1892 book titled the "Nationalisation of Health." While Ellis's "Nationalisation" was much less detailed and coherent than the thousands of laws erected by the National Socialists in the 1930s, the basic concept was the same: Society could not afford to allow either the individual patient nor the individual doctor to maintain their *laissez-faire* relationship. The entire state needed to be organized around medicine with an overarching government structure:

> An organism badly born and badly bred, always placed under unwholesome conditions and slowly saturated with disease, finally breaks down and is brought to the doctor to be drugged into health: it is a sorry task for medical science, and, what is of much more consequence, it involves fearful expense, not merely to the individual, but to all those with whom he comes in contact, expense of money, expense of happiness, expense of life. The key-word of our modern methods is not cure but prevention, and while this task is more complex it is also far easier. It is to a gigantic system of healthy living, and by a perpetual avoidance of the very beginning of evil, that our medical science is now leading us. (Pg. 18, "Nationalisation of Health", T. Fisher Unwin, 1892)

Like his German counterparts, Ellis saw "competition" and *laissez-faire* democracy as the culprit. Thus, individual rights and economic interests needed to succumb to the needs of the society. Ellis fully subscribed to the view that the social body was the patient and regarded unhealthy individuals as malignant tissue threatening the health of the greater society. He also shared a commonality of political maneuvers. Like his American and German counterparts, Ellis saw propaganda value in the "panic" caused by epidemics, and thus was willing to leverage epidemics to enact social change as Americans would later use influenza to justify their nation-wide compulsory vaccination laws:

> It was not, however, until more than a hundred years later, in 1831, under the influence of the terror of cholera, that this first step was taken; so that, as it has been well said and often since proved, "panic is the parent of sanitation." In 1842 Sir Edwin Chadwick issued his report on 'The Sanitary Condition of the Laboring Population of Great Britain." This report produced marked effect, and may truly be said to have inaugurated the new era of collective action, embodying itself in legislation directed to the preservation of national health. (Pg. 28, "Nationalisation of Health", T. Fisher Unwin, 1892)

Not surprisingly, Ellis was part of the Fabian Socialists in Britain, along with fellow eugenicists George Bernard Shaw, Sydney Webb, H.G. Wells, and Leonard Darwin. Ellis served as president of the Galton Institute and vice-president of the Eugenics Education Society. Ellis was inspired by Edward Carpenter's poem *Towards Democracy*, about the march of humanity toward socialism. As a devout Fabian, Ellis saw the "nationalization" of healthcare as part of the greater movement to "nationalize" or "municipalize" all other aspects of society, as had Leonard Darwin and other like-minded eugenicists. Ellis pointed to the nationalization of education as the model for the nationalization of medicine. [357] He believed that the public would come to accept it once implemented, well, much as present-day Progressive strategists believe to this day.

Ellis's 1892 "Nationalization of Health" by itself is deceptively benign. Any honest appreciation of Ellis's demand for a "gigantic" and overarching state infrastructure must be evaluated in the context of his work in eugenics. Clearly, no eugenic program can get very far without the coercive power of government. Hitler's "eugenic state" proved this. When Adolf Hitler's National Socialist policies aroused criticism around the world, Ellis defended the German legislation stating in volume 6 of his 1937 "Studies in the Psychology of Sex" that the law had "no relation to 'Aryan' aspirations" if "properly administered." [358]

The drive for the "nationalization" of "healthcare" is a topic that has never gone away. The lack of historical perspective has to be attributed to the selective amnesia about the medical industry's complicity in The Holocaust. Even in Germany, where the population should be the most sensitive to medical abuses, has recently had its share of avoidable abuses at the hand of "socialized" medicine:

> In contemporary Germany, the official dramatic rhetoric about the "cost explosion" in health care and the continuous cuts in spending have produced new prophets of euthanasia. In a prepared television show, surgeon Julius Hackethal handed a cancer patient potassium cyanide and advocated active euthanasia. A growing number of court cases are being reported in which nurses have intentionally killed old and chronically ill patients in nursing homes and intensive care units. (Pg. 40, "The Nazi Doctors and the Nuremberg Code: Human Rights in Human Experimentation", Paul Weindling, Oxford, 1992)

This is the persistent danger that can only be attributed to the failure of the Nuremberg Doctors' Trial. The failure to accurately document for all posterity the "scientific" and "socio-economic" policies that lead up to the T4 Euthanasia program and The Holocaust allow contemporary doctors and scientists to operate in a historical vacuum. The prosecution at Nuremberg left that door wide open by sparing the vast number of scientists, doctors, and nurses that participated in the non-military public sector crimes. These doctors and scientists deserved disdain and

---

[357] Pg. 288 - "Nationalisation of Health", Havelock Ellis, T. Fisher Unwin, 1892.
[358] Pg. 370 - "Sex in Relation to Society: Studies in The Psychology of Sex", Volume 6, 1937, Havelock Ellis, reprinted by Butterworth-Heinemann, 2013.

mistrust. Only in the persisting ignorance about the complicity of German medicine can modern-day doctors and nurses entertain the euthanasia measures described above.

Sec. 4 – GENETICS; THE LEGITIMATE SCIENCE OF HEREDITY:

In 1900 three scientists, Carl Correns, Erich von Tschermak, and Hugo De Vries rediscovered the work of Gregor Mendel, and with it, the foundation of genetics. Then in 1915, Thomas Hunt Morgan co-authored the seminal book "The Mechanism of Mendelian Heredity" with Calvin Bridges and H.J. Muller. In the years following "Mechanism of Mendelian Heredity," most biologists came to accept the Mendelian-chromosome theory. The scientific concepts in this book would do more to discredit eugenics than what has been typically attributed to it. It accomplished the task of discrediting eugenics from within the scientific community, which for one reason or another, had cowered from confronting the eugenically minded scientists at the top echelons of the community. Eugenics, once the musings of cranks and radical agitators like John Humphrey Noyes and Victoria Woodhull, became enshrined into the sciences when Francis Galton piggybacked his cousin's "Origin of the Species" in 1865. Eugenics emerged as the "applied" version of the Theory of Evolution when Charles Darwin incorporated it into his second book, "The Descent of Man." The Science of genetics was not officially born until 1900 or 1915 when Mendel's work was rediscovered, and its truer adherence to the scientific method eventually exposed the "science" of eugenics as a pretender, an alchemist's attempt at modernity.

In 1908, Morgan started working on the fruit fly *Drosophila melanogaster* and encouraging students to do so as well. He mutated *Drosophila* through physical, chemical, and radiational means, and began crossbreeding experiments to find heritable mutations. Morgan and his students became successful at finding mutations in flies; they counted the mutant characteristics of thousands of fruit flies and studied their inheritance. As they accumulated multiple mutants, they combined them to study more complex inheritance patterns.

The more Morgan found evidence to prove his theories, the more he became a strong critic of the eugenics movement. Even in its day, many people saw that eugenics was a dubious discipline, riddled with inconsistencies, but it was championed by a very prominent and respected biologist, Charles Davenport, and various members of the Darwin-Galton family. Furthermore, the work of the eugenicists told many people what they wanted to hear: that certain "racial stock" was superior to others in such traits as intelligence, hard work, cleanliness, and so on. Furthermore, the "nurture" side of the argument was also gaining ground. Behaviorism was introduced in 1913, and its impetus helped modern genetics and the work of Thomas Hunt Morgan to become known through the 1910s. As the weight of the scientific community shifted toward behaviorism and true genetics, popular opinion followed. By the late 1920s, the implications of the work on chromosomal inheritance by Thomas Hunt Morgan and his students at Columbia University made it clear that human intelligence and morality were far too complex to be understood in simple terms, and certainly not describable by the simplistic concepts of "unit characters" as the eugenicists claimed, or the "gemmules" of Charles Darwin's imagination.

Morgan's work exposed several key deficiencies in eugenics. [359] Morgan personally thought eugenics was a "vulgar" science. Other scientists may not have agreed with Madison Grant, Charles Davenport, or the illustrious Britons, but certainly didn't disagree with them publicly. As such, the story of Thomas Hunt Morgan and eugenics is a story of the dangers of a monolithic and self-interested industry, where its members are discouraged or afraid to criticize or expose the corruption of others. During the heyday of the eugenics movement, virtually every geneticist of note served below Grant and Davenport on the Advisory Board of the American Eugenics Society. Morgan published some polite reservations about eugenics in the mid-1920s, but not confrontational enough to allow people to invoke his prestige to repudiate the movement. In the mid-1920s the only critics of eugenics were non-scientists or soft scientists, like Franz Boas. Curiously enough, Morgan worked in the same building as Boas.

Morgan's work was instrumental in exposing that traits such as eye color, stature, and blood group are relatively easy to define and measure. Eugenicists, however, were mostly interested in mental and behavioral traits, intelligence, feeblemindedness, alcoholism, and criminality. Not only are such traits highly complex, but they were also subjectively defined. This problem was recognized by Thomas Hunt Morgan, who wrote in 1932 that "the main difficulty is one of definition... Accurate work in heredity can only be obtained when the diagnosis of the elements [trait]...is known." [360] In a diplomatic manner, Charles Darwin's third son alluded as much in the first "Galton Lecture" before the Eugenics Education Society on February 16, 1914:

> The contrast between Galtonism and Mendelism may be illustrated by an example which if not a strict analogy has in it something illuminating, especially for those who do not know too much of the subject. **Galton seems to me like a medieval chemist while Mendel is a modern one.** Galton can observe, or can follow the changes that occur when two compounds are mixed. But the Mendelian is like a modern chemist who calls the chemical elements to his aid, and is able to express the result of the experiment in terms of these elements. This is an enormous advantage, and if my analogy is to be trusted it would seem as though a progressive study of heredity must necessarily be on Mendelian lines. (emphasis mine, Francis Darwin, "Galton Lecture", Eugenics Education Society, Feb. 16, 1914, Printed in Eugenics Review, 1914)

---

[359] eugenicsarchive.org, "Flaws in Eugenics Research: Social Origins of Eugenicson", Garland E. Allen, March 2, 2004.
[360] Ibid.

In short, Francis Darwin honored Mendel's work as "hard science" born of empirical methods, and Francis Galton's eugenics as desperately outdated. Humorously enough, Francis Darwin also admitted in this same lecture that his father fully incorporated and gave eugenics the impetus it would not have enjoyed if his father had not incorporated it in the "sexual selection" component of his "Theory of Evolution," an observation most of Darwin's apologists would vehemently deny.

Most importantly, Morgan's observations must be regarded as part of the instigation behind the Carnegie foundation's sudden withdrawing of support for the Cold Spring Harbor facility. Eugenics research came under increasing scrutiny, and independent analysis revealed that most eugenic data was useless. A committee of the American Neurological Association reported that "[The definitional problem] invalidates, we believe, the earlier work which comes from Davenport, Rosanoff and the American Eugenics School with its headquarters at Cold Spring Harbor." [361] The American Neurological Association criticism, among other factors, prompted the Carnegie Institution to withdraw its funding and permanently close the ERO in December 1939. According to an external visiting committee assembled by the Carnegie Institution:

> Some traits such as 'personality' or 'character' lack precise definition or quantitative methods of measurement; some traits such as 'sense of humor,' 'self respect,' 'loyalty' or 'holding a grudge' could seldom be known outside an individual's close friends and associates…Even more objective characteristics, such as hair form or eye color, become relatively worthless items of genetic data when recorded by an untrained observer. (eugenicsarchive.org, "Flaws in Eugenics Research: Social Origins of Eugenics", Garland E. Allen, March 2, 2004)

Another scientist to reject eugenics on the basis of Mendelism is Wilhelm Johannsen. Wilhelm Johannsen, the leading Danish geneticist, had also become internationally recognized for rediscovering Gregor Mendel's work. [362] Johannsen voiced his doubts about the claims of the eugenicists, and his rejection became a matter of contention among eugenicists around the world. Johannsen was opposed to propagating the "ideal members of humanity" concept because he found the defining criteria too vague, though he disapproved of the reproduction of individuals with birth defects.

In fact, the birth of modern genetics must be at least in part attributed to a rejection of eugenics by those rediscovering the long-forgotten Mendel. The word "genetics" was coined in 1905 by William Bateson, a half-hearted believer in eugenics who became famous for questioning Karl Pearson, the duly appointed successor to Francis Galton. Bateson suggested the term "genetics" describe the study

---

[361] eugenicsarchive.org, "Flaws in Eugenics Research: Social Origins of Eugenicson", Garland E. Allen, March 2, 2004.
[362] "The Influence of Eugenics on the Social Welfare Legislation of Britain and Denmark in 1913 and 1929", Jacqueline Bollmann, 2009.

of inheritance and the science of variation in a personal letter to Adam Sedgwick, dated April 18, 1905, though Bateson first used the term "genetics" in public at the Third International Conference on Plant Hybridization in London in 1906. Bateson was not familiar with Mendel's work but became a staunch supporter of Mendel's work once he was made aware of it. Bateson gave a lecture to the Royal Horticultural Society in July 1899, which was attended by Hugo de Vries, in which he describes his investigations into discontinuous variation, his experimental crosses, and the significance of such studies for the understanding of heredity. In this lecture, de Vries urged his colleagues to conduct large-scale, well-designed and statistically analyzed experiments of the sort that, although he did not know it, Mendel had already conducted, and which would be "rediscovered" by de Vries and Correns just six months later.

Karl Pearson, Francis Galton's protégé and the editor of the eugenic journal "Biometrika," was specifically bothered by the implications of Mendel's work on the future of eugenics. When Gregor Mendel's long-overlooked paper of 1866 was resurrected in 1900, the particulate nature of Mendel's theory of "dominance" and "segregation" was clearly in keeping with Bateson's views; he became a committed Mendelist, taking it upon himself to convert all English biologists into disciples of Mendel. Meanwhile, Pearson had become deeply committed to Galton's law of ancestral heredity, to which Bateson was antipathetic. There followed a heated controversy between the "ancestrians," led by Pearson, and the "Mendelians," led by Bateson. Historians seem to disagree on exactly how opposed Karl Pearson was to Mendelism, but the correspondence points to someone who was deeply opposed to, or more correctly, took it deeply personal and had a bitter reaction to Mendelism. Specifically, Bateson's and Pearson's views clashed over saltationism versus gradualism. In Pearson's eyes, evolution proceeds, not, as Bateson thought, by leaps and bounds, but continuous variations as Darwin had believed.

Galton too had an alarmist reaction to Mendelism. In May 28, 1904, Bateson had written to Francis Galton on the subject of "eugenics." Galton's letter of June 12th, 1904, was an alarmist response, stating that an in-depth knowledge of the science of heredity would not help in the quest for a more eugenic society. Apparently, the science did not matter as much as the utopian goal:

> I quite understand now (I think) your point, and to a great extent agree with it. But what are we humans to do, if any 'eugenic' progress is attempted? We can't mate men and women as we please, like cocks and hens, but we could I think gradually evolve some plan by which there would be a steady, though slow amelioration of the human breed. The aim being to increase the contributions of the more valuable classes of the population and to diminish the converse. We now want better criteria than we have of which is which. --- Do what we can (within reasonable limits as regards mankind), fraternal variability will never be much lessened; but I do think that the fraternal means might on the whole be raised. (eugenicsarchive.org, Item ID 12106, Cold Spring Harbor's Laboratory, The DNA Learning Center)

But the quest for a eugenic utopia was precisely what Baetson was against. The New York Times covered a conference on heredity in Melbourne, Australia, in 1914. The article quotes Bateson criticizing American eugenic legislation, and prophetically predicting a nation that would fully dedicate itself to the enterprise of achieving a "master race." Note Bateson's concern for individual autonomy:

> The remedies proposed in America, so far as they aim at the eugenic regulation of marriage on a comprehensive scale . . . devised without regard to the needs either of the individuals or a modern state. ---- It will be very surprising indeed if some nation does not make trial of this new power. They may make awful mistakes, but I think they will try. (Pg. 325, "Science", John Michels, The Science Press, New Series Vol. XL, July-Dec. 1914)

The debate succeeded in cracking the foundations of the otherwise monolithic leadership of the International eugenics movement. Davenport certainly didn't take kindly to anyone dictating the direction of his research:

> Dear Pearson: Your letter of June 16 reached me at Cold Spring Harbor & I waited until I have returned to Chicago where I could reread my paper and your letter before replying. Now that I have done so I find myself still at a loss to understand your refusal to publish the "General Conclusions." From you first letter I gather that you think I am defending [underscore]deVries[end underscore]. Yet my aim was quite the opposite. --The differences seemed to me also to belong to Darwin's category (Orig. of Species, Chap. IV, par. I) "neither useful nor injurious" and as such "not affected by natural Selection." It seemed to me, in any case, that they were due to the "direct" action of "the conditions of life", in the sense of Darwin, Chap. I, "Causes of Var." [paragraph sign]2. (See also Chap V, [paragraph sign]. 2. "definite action"). All this is heresy for the ultra mutationists - and I was aiming a blow at them. I have never been more surprised that to find that I was interpreted as supporting deVries and Bateson. I did not find any evidence [underscore]against[end underscore] "spats"[?] (1901-10, Unive. College London, Pearson Papers, The University of Chicago) (dnalc.org, Item No.: 12034, "Charles Davenport letter to Karl Pearson, emphasizing his break with Bateson and De Vries on environmentally induced mutations - 7,7, 1903", DNA Learning Center, Cold Spring Harbor Lab.)

It is telling that Pearson abolished the board when in 1910 Davenport proposed to publish a pro-Mendel paper. Even more revealing is the fact that in 1910, Raymond Pearl was fired by Karl Pearson from the editors' board of "Biometrika" as a result of one of Pearson's various temper tantrums over Mendelism. Here is Raymond Pearl's February 15, 1910 response to Pearson:

> I am exceedingly sorry that you feel obliged to remove my name from the list of editors of Biometrika for the reasons which you give in your letter. --- but it is rather a blow to be told that I am removed because I am "opposed to the principles for which Biometrika was founded". (dnalc.org, Item No.: 12037, "Raymond Pearl letter to Karl Pearson", DNA Learning Center, Cold Spring Harbor Lab.)

Medical history now records that Morgan's work on genetics not only helped discredit eugenics within the ranks of science but kicked off a scientific reinvigoration and revolution. During his distinguished career, Morgan wrote 22 books and 370 scientific papers. His discoveries formed the basis of the modern science of genetics. He was awarded the 1933 Nobel Prize in Physiology or Medicine for his work in genetics. Ironically enough, this one historical figure responsible for dismantling the eugenics movement from the inside was the descendant of a prestigious family of the Confederacy in the Civil War. Morgan was born in Lexington, Kentucky, to Charlton Hunt Morgan and Ellen Key Howard Morgan. Morgan was a nephew of Confederate General John Hunt Morgan, and part of a long line of Southern aristocracy on his father's side. Through his mother, he was the great-grandson of Francis Scott Key, the composer of "The Star-Spangled Banner." Morgan's family fell on hard times due to their support of the Confederacy through Civil War. The loss of civil and property rights all but insured financial difficulty for the Morgans in addition to his father's difficulty finding work due to his political ties. As such, Thomas Hunt Morgan, the person who did as much as anyone else to discredit eugenics, was one generation removed from fighting to maintaining an institution based on the view that some races were inferior, or altogether subordinate types of humans, precisely because of their heredity.

Sec. 5 - ALL IN THE FAMILY:

Leonard Darwin was born in 1850 in Down House in Kent, England, and was the last of Charles Darwin's immediate offspring to die. In 1900 he married a first cousin Charlotte Mildred Massingberd, as had his father before him. She was the daughter of Edmund Langton and Charlotte Wedgwood. Their shared ancestor was their maternal grandfather Josiah Wedgwood II. Since Charles Darwin and Emma Wedgwood were also cousins, Charlotte Mildred Massingberd was also a second cousin on his father's side. After leaving the British Army with the rank of major in 1895, Leonard was elected as a Liberal Unionist Member of Parliament (MP) for Lichfield constituency in Staffordshire. His grandfather Josiah Wedgwood II had also been a Liberal MP, and as history has failed to note, a bitter opponent of the eugenic policies forwarded by Leonard Darwin and Francis Galton.

The debates over the Mental Deficiency Act of 1913 were heavily publicized throughout England, and in retrospect, they were the showdown between the Darwin-Galton and the Wedgwood side of the famous family. Francis Galton had passed away, but Leonard Darwin had become the leader of the eugenics movement with his passing. Much of the policies which would have been enshrined into law by the Mental Deficiency Act of 1913 were the work product of Leonard Darwin, who had been proposing government restructure its policies to make a eugenic mindset its guiding principle:

> Finally, we advocate economic forces being brought to bear in certain directions; as for instance, in making taxation, and also the pay of employees in all public services, vary somewhat with the size of the family to be maintained, and in administering the poor law so as not to encourage reproduction on the part of degenerate paupers. ("Babes of the Future; Major Leonard Darwin Tells True Purposes of Eugenics", Leonard Darwin, NYT, Dec. 21, 1912)

The cascade of events towards the 1913 Mental Deficiency Act is illuminating. The Royal Commission "On the Care and Control of the Feeble-Minded" had convened in 1908 under the Liberal Government of 1905. This began the official legislative push for a eugenic utopia in Britain. As this book previously documents, Winston Churchill took up the political cause. Churchill had read a booklet by an Indiana doctor, H.C. Sharp, "The Sterilization of Degenerates" while he was Home Secretary in 1910. In September 1910, Churchill wrote to his Home Office officials asking them to investigate putting into practice the "Indiana Law," which prescribed sterilization, and the prevention of the marriage of the "Feeble-Minded." In October 1910, a deputation to the Government called for the implementation of the Royal Commission's recommendations "without delay." To reinforce his sense of urgency, Churchill circulated to his Cabinet colleagues the text of a 1909 lecture by Dr. A.F. Treadgold, one of the expert advisers to the Royal Commission. It was entitled "The Feeble-Minded-A Social Danger." In 1912, a Mental Deficiency Bill was brought into the Commons by Winston Churchill as the Home Secretary. Churchill spoke in the House of Commons in February of 1911 about the need to introduce compulsory labor camps for "mental defectives." Churchill's efforts were significantly bolstered by the First International Eugenics Congress, which was held in London just a month prior to the Second Reading of the Mental Deficiency Bill in Parliament in July 1912. Incidentally, Leonard Darwin had been the person in charge of the 1912 congress. Churchill was the Vice-President of the Congress.

On October 1911, Churchill was appointed First Lord of the Admiralty, in charge of the Royal Navy, with new concerns and new responsibilities. On May 17, 1912, while he was at the Admiralty, a Private Members' Bill was introduced in the House of Commons, entitled the "Feeble-Minded Control Bill." This called for the implementation of the Royal Commission's conclusions. Hundreds of petitions were sent to Parliament in support of the legislation. The Committee to further the Bill was headed by the two Anglican primates, the Archbishops of Canterbury and York. As one would expect, H.G. Wells and his fellow Fabian Socialists were vocal supporters of the Bill. Yet, when all was said and done, the British public was able to avoid the mass sterilizations, marriage prohibitions, and mass segregations of their population. This blessing can be attributed largely to the work of one man struggling against forces much more powerful than he: Colonel Josiah Clement Wedgwood.

Colonel Josiah Clement Wedgwood was born on March 16, 1872. He belonged to the well-known family of potters, and of humanitarian politicians. He was a member of the House of Commons from 1906 to 1941, when he was made a Baron and entered the House of Lords. He began his political career as a Liberal but later changed to the Labour Party. He was the great-grandson of Josiah Wedgwood I, Liberal M.P. for Newcastle-under-Lyme from 1906 to 1919, then Labour M.P. for the same constituency from 1919 to 1942.

Josiah Wedgwood became the leading voice against the implementation of eugenic policies in Britain as proposed by his Galton and Darwin family members. Wedgwood led a vocal, principled, and widely publicized campaign against the passage of the Mental Deficiency Bill. Although Wedgwood ultimately failed in preventing the bill from passing, he certainly was instrumental in watering it down enough to the point where the British public was spared the mass-sterilizations that tens of thousands of Americans were subjected to as a result of the Oliver Wendell Holmes, Jr., Harry H. Laughlin, Charles Davenport, and their wealthy supporters such as the Carnegies and the Rockefellers. More importantly, Wedgewood stands as vivid proof that there was a higher road to be taken for those who would excuse the rest of the Darwin-Galton family for their unrelenting support for eugenics, segregation, sterilization, and euthanasia.

Thwarting the Darwin-Galton side of his family was no small accomplishment. Josiah Wedgwood not only had to fight all of Parliament, all of the Darwin-Galton side of the family, but also the very powerful and vocal Fabian Socialists in his effort to block Britain from becoming a eugenic state. There was a very powerful social network that supported eugenics in the United Kingdom. Virginia Woolf and her various friends in the Fabian political circle worked tirelessly to make Britain a eugenic state. Virginia Woolf's circle of Fabian friends included the Beatrice Webb, John Maynard Keynes, H.G. Wells, George Bernard Shaw, and Leonard Darwin. [363] Virginia Woolf became an outspoken proponent and visible public figure supporting eugenics at the behest of her Fabian friends. Exemplifying the Fabian point of view, Woolf was cited as saying: "I am right, and Wedgwood is wrong: they should certainly be killed." [364]

Wedgwood fought his battle in the court of public opinion. Wedgwood had the help of "individualists" such as Hilaire Belloc and the Chesterton brothers. He was also able to leverage a split in opinion between the Liberal MPs and the Liberal press, with publications such as "The Nation" warning of the "totalitarian implications of such legislation." Wedgwood was outnumbered in its first-round; the vote count was 242 for and only 19 against. However, the bill was dropped when it became clear exactly just how big and expensive a bureaucracy it would take to run a eugenic state; one of the defects Wedgwood successfully shed light on was the fact that no one could really pin down how many Britons would fall under the definition

---

[363] Pg. 27 – "Modernism and Eugenics: Woolf, Eliot, Yeats, and the Culture of Degeneration", Donald J. Childs, Cambridge Univ. Press, 2001.
[364] Pg. 38 - "Political Life of Josiah C. Wedgwood: Land, Liberty and Empire, 1872-1943", Paul Mulvey, Boydell & Brewer, 2010.

of "unfit," "feebleminded" or any other nebulous concept that had otherwise been presented as the terminology of an exact and disciplined science. Wedgwood was able to muster concern about the eugenic overtones by exposing just how inexact and arbitrary the "science" of Galton's eugenics really was, and thus how uncontrollably costly it would be in both money and personal liberty.

A watered-down version of the bill was reintroduced later that year. Wedgwood dug his heels in and mounted unprecedented "obstructionist" measures in Parliament, or what in the US Congress would be called a filibuster. Wedgwood singlehandedly spent two straight days and nights, from July 28 to 29, 1913, proposing an endless amount of amendments, winning over much support and admiration from the press and public for his principled stand. Outnumbered as he was, this was a true showing of what President John F. Kennedy called "political courage"; to do the right thing no matter how unpopular. The bill finally passed with a vote of 180 to 3, but heavily watered down and debilitated.

Many historians remember Josiah Wedgwood's measures as courageous and grounded in the principles of "classical liberalism," yet they overlook the most important facet of Wedgwood's attack; Wedgwood exposed the dangers by extrapolating the logical outcome of passing such a measure. In 20/20 hindsight his observations seem prophetic. Wedgwood clearly mapped out the path from legislation to the proximate outcome as would later develop in the United States, or worse in Germany. This was three decades of foresight on Wedgwood's part, but placed in historical context, one cannot escape the observation that his principles were those of the Enlightenment or the American Revolution. There was nothing novel or unique about Wedgwood's observations. A more accurate depiction would be to realize that the "liberal" camp had undergone a transformation, and Wedgwood's compatriots no longer stood for the values that would have labeled them "liberals" in the decades prior to "Progressivism." A "New Ethic" reigned, and Wedgwood was defending a definition of "liberty" that had otherwise been forgotten. The constitutional theorist A.V. Dicey, described Wedgewood's plight as highlighting the tension between democracy and collectivism, the former which he defined as "government for the people by the people, and the later as government for the people by the experts." [365]

Wedgwood's distrust of so-called "experts" stands out in the transcripts of those two memorable days in Parliament. Galton's eugenics was not the precise and objective "science" it was billed to be, and Wedgwood exposed it for what it was. Wedgwood showed the so-called "experts" could not even define the crucial legal term "feebleminded." It was clear that Fabian zealots like Virginia Woolf were putting way too much trust in the opinions of their friend Leonard Darwin, likely because of their adulation for his father, and Leonard's representation that his father fully endorsed his work. Understanding the dangers of such legislative measures necessitates defining exactly who was targeted by such legislative acts. The definition of "defectives" used by the British Parliament, and given a veil of scientific legitimacy

---

[365] Pg. 40 - "Political Life of Josiah C. Wedgwood: Land, Liberty and Empire, 1872-1943", Paul Mulvey, Boydell & Brewer, 2010.

as it was the work-product of prestigious scientists such as the Darwins and Galtons, is documented by "Clause I" of the proposed Act:

> **CLAUSE I. – (Definition of Defectives):** "The following classes of persons who are mentally defective shall be deemed to be defectives within the meaning of this Act:—
>
> (a) Idiots; that is to say, persons so deeply defective in mind from birth or from an early age as to be unable to guard themselves against common physical dangers;
>
> (b) Imbeciles; that is to say, persons in whose case there exists from birth or from an early age mental defectiveness not amounting to idiocy, yet so pronounced that they are incapable of managing themselves or their affairs, or, in the case of children, of being taught to do so;
>
> (c) Feeble-minded persons; that is to say, persons in whose case there exists from birth or from an early age mental defectiveness not amounting to imbecility, yet so pronounced that they require care, supervision, and control for their own protection or for the protection of others, or, in the case of children, are incapable of receiving proper benefit from the instruction in ordinary schools;
>
> (d) Moral imbeciles; that is to say, persons who from an early age display some permanent mental defect coupled with strong vicious or criminal propensities on which punishment has little or no deterrent effect."
>
> (House of Commons, July 28, 1913 - vol. 56 cc82-15382)

In retrospect, Josiah Wedgwood made much more sense in those two days in Parliament than his family members Charles Darwin, Francis Galton, Leonard Darwin, and the dozens of other Darwin-Galton foot soldiers ever did in the various decades they dedicated to the eugenic cause. Josiah Wedgwood's scalpel was not that sharp. His analysis was not as sophisticated as it was humorous and relentless. Josiah Wedgwood's observations were just firmly grounded in an honest appraisal of humanity and a true version of "liberal" values. Note the ludicrous tangle that was eugenic legislation:

> **§Mr. WEDGWOOD:** I beg to move to leave out paragraph (c). We are not asking to leave out paragraphs (a) and (b) because they deal with imbeciles who are pretty easily distinguishable. There is not much difficulty in discovering whether a person is an idiot or an imbecile. It is only when we come to the definition of what constitutes feebleminded persons that we come to the real difficulty so far as definition is concerned. We want the House to understand what feeble-minded persons are; that is to say, persons in whose case there exists from birth or from an early age, defective-ness not amounting to imbecility. If it does not amount to imbecility, you have to refer to the previous definition of what constitutes an imbecile. These are persons in whose case there exists from birth or early age mental defectiveness not amounting to idiocy, which renders them incapable of managing themselves or their affairs; but feeble-minded persons are people who are not so defective that they are incapable of managing themselves or their own affairs, or in other words, they are persons who are capable of managing themselves and their own affairs. Does this House really

mean to say that they want to have the power given to the Home Secretary or the Courts of Justice to lock up for life people who are capable of managing themselves or their own affairs?

CONTINUES...

Member for Stirlingshire (Dr. Chapple) is always so anxious to drive home, the thin edge of the wedge of the Eugenic theory. What is, or what is not, for the protection of others? According to the hon. Member for Stirlingshire, it is for the protection of other people, that people who are bad breeders should not be allowed to breed, that they should have operations performed on them so that they should not be able to breed. (api.parliament.uk, 28 July 1913, Commons Sitting, MENTAL DEFICIENCY BILL)

Wedgwood also pointed out that drafting such vague language allowed for the segregation of children whom do not do well in school and need a teacher to keep them in line, but whom otherwise make for good citizens. Dr. Chapple took issue with this interpretation, but as history would prove, this very definition of "feebleminded" was used in the United States and in Germany precisely to the ill-effects that Wedgwood predicted. As this book has documented, many of the boys we would ultimately define as part of the "Greatest Generation" were sterilized against their will exactly as Wedgwood warned. If it not for Wedgwood, many unfortunate British children would have suffered the same fate.

§**Mr. WEDGWOOD:** Are you content that all those children should be severed from their families and sent to these special schools during their school age, and thereafter sent to the feeble-minded institutions? Let hon. Members think what these feeble-minded institutions are. They are full of people who are horrible to see, mentally defective persons, idiots, and imbeciles, people it would be the severest possible penalty to have to live in company with, and to these institutions you are condemning children in this country who are normal in all respects except in so far as their work is concerned, children who are merely a little bit lazy and backward, and they are to be sent to these hells upon earth, to these institutions from which they will never emerge! (api.parliament.uk, 28 July 1913, Commons Sitting, MENTAL DEFICIENCY BILL)

A fellow member of Parliament, Mr. John Ward, seconded Wedgwood's concerns, and added the observation that the legislation as it read as a tool to be used against the working class, whose children may not be as well behaved or with access to the quality of education as the upper class:

§**Mr. JOHN WARD:** This is really legislation for the working-class children, and let us make no error about that. The hon. Member for Stirlingshire shakes his head, but there is no doubt about it. A person who is fairly well off has a governess at home and instructs his children at home, and up to a certain point of their age they do not come under the cognisance of regulations of this description.

CONTINUES...

I submit that that is much too big a risk to allow the people of this country to run. At the present time, as this Bill stands, any child who goes to a special school or class runs very grave risk of being incarcerated for life. In a large part of the country where there are no special schools or classes I am afraid you have an even wider area of danger for the children of the working classes. Where there is no special school or class there will only be one weeding-out process. -- That is a very grave danger. (api.parliament.uk, 28 July 1913, Commons Sitting, MENTAL DEFICIENCY BILL)

The debate then turns back to the overt eugenic connotations of the legislation and to question if the Act was meant to create a superior race, as opposed to protecting the weak as its proponents claimed it did:

§**Mr. WEDGWOOD:** Will the right hon. Gentleman say what the Legislature does mean by the words? Do the Government mean to protect other people from physical danger, or to protect the community from the production of an inferior race? (api.parliament.uk, 28 July 1913, Commons Sitting, MENTAL DEFICIENCY BILL)

In this portion of the transcripts, Josiah Wedgwood basically predicts the dilemma that the US legal system was faced within the landmark case of Buck v. Bell, which would decide the fates of tens of thousands of Americans, and condemn them to the exact horrid fate that Josiah Wedgwood prophesized. As documented in this book, Carrie Buck, and many other boys and girls like her had their lives destroyed precisely in the way described by Josiah Wedgwood. She was accused of "moral delinquency," among other things, to justify her "feeblemindedness." The Dobbses, her foster parents, had enlisted the help of the eugenic-minded doctors in an effort to get rid of Carrie after their nephew had raped Carrie and gotten her pregnant. A slew of "experts" from the Eugenic Records Office, namely Harry H. Laughlin, was brought in to get Carrie institutionalized and then sterilized. The attorney that was hand-picked to represent Carrie's interests was literally paid by both sides and employed by sister institutions. [366] Josiah Wedgwood saw right through the arrogance and irresponsibility of the legislative measures proposed in the Mental Deficiency Act, while supposed bastions of liberty such as Oliver Wendell Holmes, Jr. and seven other Supreme Court justices of the United States completely whiffed on this aspect of the eugenic-minded law under consideration in Buck v. Bell:

Mr. WEDGWOOD: It seems to me rather serious if you are going to make it easy for certain evilly disposed guardians or parents to get rid of their children by locking them up in these feeble-minded institutions. There have been cases

---

[366] See Generally – "Three Generations, No Imbeciles: Eugenics, the Supreme Court, and Buck v. Bell", Paul Lombardo, Johns Hopkins Univ. Press, 2008.

of evilly-disposed parents or guardians getting their children consigned to lunatic asylums. The difficulties in the way of such parents or guardians are considerable. The doctors who sign the certificates have to be satisfied that there are certain definite symptoms of insanity. The cases under subheads (c) and (d)—moral imbeciles and feeble-minded persons—are border-line cases, in which it is less the business of the medical man to decide whether the persons ought to be sent to these institutions, than that of the educators of children or those who have practical experience of children. I am against giving greater powers to evilly-disposed parents to put their offspring into these homes. (api.parliament.uk, 28 July 1913, Commons Sitting, MENTAL DEFICIENCY BILL)

Josiah Wedgwood had effectively extrapolated what transpired in the United States where the poor, rural, simple folk would be the ultimate targets of eugenic-minded legislations, or what would sarcastically be termed the "Appalachian Appendectomy" were poorly educated rural people were asexualized without their knowledge or consent. Paul Lombardo, author of the book that exposes the <u>Buck v. Bell</u> trial, documents what was written in the "medical" profile of Carrie Buck provided to the court: "These people belong to the shiftless, ignorant, and worthless class of antisocial whites of the South." [367]

It is of note that the text of the Act hardly differed from its American and German counterparts, but that in England, someone like Wedgwood was around to point to the obvious concerns where his American and German counterparts failed. Wedgwood proved himself prophetic where otherwise lauded legal minds, namely that of Justice, Oliver Wendell Holmes, Jr., betrayed of the principles they supposedly stood for:

> **Mr. WEDGWOOD:** Does the right hon. Gentleman pretend that a child without visible means of support is committing a crime. As a Radical I have always protested against sending a tramp to prison; but in that case the term is only a fortnight, whereas here it is for life. People so poor as to be without visible means of support are to be deprived of their privileges as citizens, and treated as though they were persons who had committed a crime sufficiently heavy to warrant their being taken away.

The circumstances described above are precisely what transpired in the mass-roundups like the one conducted in 1928 by Leon Whitney in the small rural town of Shutesbury, Boston. [368] As documented, these efforts were done without notice, without press publication, and many times without the knowledge of both the parents and the children that were taken away during school hours. Tens of thousands of Americans were sterilized against their will, and largely against their knowledge, as many were sterilized at a very young age under false pretenses. The laws passed allowed the "experts" to make the decision instead of the parents.

There are many who would defend the Darwins, Galton, the justices of the US

---

[367] Pg. 134 - "Three Generations, No Imbeciles: Eugenics, the Supreme Court, and Buck v. Bell", Paul Lombardo, JHU Press, 2008.
[368] "The Master Race", Welling Savo, Boston Mag., May 15, 2006.

Supreme Court, or Fabians like Virginia Woolf and John Maynard Keynes by stating that they did not have the benefit of Holocaust history to help them understand the dangers of legislation like the Mental Deficiency Act. Josiah Wedgwood is evidence of the exact opposite: that the Darwins, Galton, the Fabians, and the Supreme Court justices lacked common sense foresight. From 1906 until 1943, "Josh" Wedgwood was one of Britain's most outspoken Radical politicians, serving in three wars and fighting in both the Liberal and Labour parties to uphold individual freedom and limit the power of the state. As opposed to the collectivism of the socialists, Wedgwood advocated a radical vision of Victorian individualism as the solution to the problems that Britain faced in the first half of the 20th Century. He defended individual rights against the state, and he argued for the creation of a new type of empire, based on democratic rather than racial values.

On the flip side, we have the Darwin-Galton side of the family influencing or instigating the murder or mutilation of millions. Even historians who recognize that eugenics was Francis Galton's contribution often excuse his cousin Charles Darwin by explaining that Darwin's ideas were misunderstood and misapplied. Charles Darwin's own words betray this, as he incorporated the eugenics into his second book, "Descent of Man." This version of history also ignores the laudatory praise Charles Darwin gave Galton in its introductory pages. Most importantly, this version of history fraudulently ignores that Darwin's son, Leonard, picked up where Francis Galton left off and proudly forwarded the cause of eugenics, and played such a crucial role in its popularization and acceptance internationally, all with his father's approbation and blessing. Francis Darwin, Charles's third son, gave the first "Galton Lecture" before the Eugenics Education Society on February 16, 1914. In it, Francis Darwin supports his brother Leonard's claim that father Charles fully supported the work of the eugenicists. [369] Francis Darwin documents that it was Charles Darwin's approval that gave Galton the encouragement to keep going with the cause of eugenics. Most importantly, Francis Darwin documents that it was Charles Darwin who gave Galton's work the greatest impetus by incorporating and citing Galton's work into his:

> But if *Natural Inheritance*, and *Hereditary Genius* had not been written; if the papers on eugenics had not appeared, and especially if he had not convinced the world of his seriousness by creating a eugenic foundation at University College, where his friend Professor Karl Pearson carries on the Galtonian traditions – why then the paper in *Macmillan* would have counted for very little. But it was not quite unnoticed. By my father it is referred to in the *Variation of Animals and Plants under Domestication*. Galton was encouraged and reassured by Darwin's appreciation of his work: his words in *Hereditary Genius* are "I feel assured that, inasmuch as what I then wrote was sufficient to earn the acceptance of Mr. Darwin". ("Galton Lecture", Francis Darwin, Eugenics Education Society, Feb. 16, 1914, Printed in Eugenics Review, 1914)

Richard Weikart's infamous book, "From Darwin to Hitler" points to a

---

[369] "Galton Lecture", Francis Darwin, Eugenics Education Society, Feb. 16, 1914, Eugenics Review, 1914.

dizzying amount of connections between Charles Darwin and Hitler. Replete with evidence as Weikart's work may be, the connection is not as convoluted or obscure as Weikart depicts. The relationships are direct and linear, starting with Darwin's theory of racial hierarchies in humanity, which he presented in the qualitative terms which Galton and his son Leonard later adopted. These "racialists" certainly knew who the first apostle of their "religion" was. Consider the implications of this letter from Charles B. Davenport, the king-pin of American eugenics, to Francis Galton on October 26, 1910: "There has been started here a Record Office in Eugenics; so you see the seed sown by you is still sprouting in distant countries." [370] It seems like everyone except Darwin-Galton historians are clear on exactly whom was the main impetus for the International eugenics lobby.

Most importantly, it must be noted that Leonard and Francis Darwin knew their father better than any of the Darwinist apologists and zealots can claim. If Leonard Darwin claimed that his father approved of the eugenic measures, his firsthand knowledge is worth more than that of those who would counter for political posturing. Leonard Darwin was not the only one of the Darwin-Galton family to acknowledge that Charles Darwin's Theory of Evolution was heavily influenced by Francis Galton's eugenics. Francis Darwin stated it succinctly and accurately in his lecture before the Eugenics Education Society: **"Origin was the fuse."** [371]

Sec. 6 - FROM "THE WILL-TO-LIVE" TO "THE WILL-TO-POWER":

The story of Albert Schweitzer's life serves to clarify the choice, that very conscious choice to depart from the humanistic traditions in German medicine that had been exemplified by the likes of Alexander Von Humboldt and Rudolf Virchow prior to Ernst Haeckel and Friedrich Nietzsche. Schweitzer is the textbook example of the compassionate German, and he was recognized as such by the 1952 Nobel Prize for his work upholding the sanctity of life.

Schweitzer has been called the greatest Christian of his time largely due to his "Reverence for Life" philosophy. Schweitzer was born in Alsace-Lorraine like Karl Brandt, Hitler's appointed head of the T4 Euthanasia program and the primary defendant at the Nuremberg Doctors' Trial. Albert Schweitzer departed for Africa to provide help for the needy at a time when fellow Germans were colonizing and brutalizing the continent. Ironically, Brandt seriously considered working under Schweitzer after receiving his medical license. [372] Instead, Brandt followed in the footsteps of Alfred Hoche, the pro-euthanasia Nietzsche admirer who popularized the notion of "life not worth living," which would be used to justify countless

---

[370] Pg. 111 - "Legacy of Malthus: The Social Costs of the New Scientific Racism", Allan Chase, Knopf, 1975.
[371] Francis Darwin, "Galton Lecture", Eugenics Education Society, Feb. 16, 1914.
[372] Pg. 42 - "Karl Brandt: Medicine and Power in the Third Reich", Ulf Schmidt, Bloomsbury Academic, 2007.

murders by Hitler's regime.

The choice made by Brandt is emblematic of the choice his generation of German scientists and doctors made to completely redefine medical ethics. This choice between a "Reverence for Life" and the notion that there are "lives unworthy living" were mirror opposites and the proverbial fork-in-the-road where German medicine took a turn away from empathy and distinctly towards a distinctly Nietzschean derision for "compassion." Albert Schweitzer pointed to this crossroad in history in his 1936 article titled "The Ethics of Reverence for Life," which was originally published in the periodical "Christendom":

> As a result of the failure to find ethics reflected in the natural order, the disillusioned cry has been raised that ethics can therefore have no ultimate validity. In the world of human thought and action today, humanitarianism is definitely on the wane. Brutality and trust in force are in the ascendant. What, then, is to become of that vigorous ethics which we inherited from our fathers? (Pgs. 180-194, Henry B. Clark, "The Ethical Mysticism of Albert Schweitzer", Beacon Press, 1962)

Schweitzer does not make direct references to eugenics, racial hygiene, or his German colleagues, which were proclaiming that some "life" was "unworthy" of being preserved. Schweitzer was clearly answering their attestations. "Reverence for Life" is an answer to eugenic and "therapeutic" euthanasia:

> Instinct, thought, the capacity for divination, all these are fused with the will-to-live. And when it reflects upon itself, what path does it follow? When my will-to-live begins to think, it sees life as a mystery in which I remain by thought. I cling to life because of my reverence for life. For, when it begins to think, the will-to-live realizes that it is free. It is free to leave life. It is free to choose whether or not to live. This fact is of particular significance for us in this modern age, when there are abundant possibilities for abandoning life, painlessly and without agony. (Pgs. 180-194, Henry B. Clark, "The Ethical Mysticism of Albert Schweitzer", Beacon Press, 1962)

Schweitzer spent his childhood in the village of Gunsbach, Alsace, and was the eldest son of the local Lutheran-Evangelical pastor. Schweitzer studied philosophy and theology at the University of Strasbourg, where he received a doctor's degree in philosophy in 1899. At that time, he also served as a lecturer in philosophy and a preacher at St. Nicholas' Church in Strasbourg. Two years later he obtained a doctorate in theology, and within the next two years was appointed principal of St. Thomas College in Strasbourg, Curate at St. Nicholas, and to the faculty in both theology and philosophy at the University of Strasbourg. While some historians have fully pushed Albert Schweitzer to the side of theology and Christianity, it must be noted that "The Ethics of Reverence for Life" is not in any way a theological tract. Like the *Casti Connubii* by Pope Pius XI, "The Ethics of Reverence" extrapolates the duty from one human to the other with secular language which made it valid beyond Christian circles. In it, Schweitzer considers and digests the musings of Kant and Descartes. More poignantly, it must be noted that Schweitzer was in no way a strict Creationist by the Biblical sense, and that "Reverence for Life" reads like a philosophical, and not theological, answer to the popular German philosophers of his time:

> Indeed, when we consider the immensity of the universe, we must confess that man is insignificant. The world began, as it were, yesterday. It may end tomorrow. Life has existed in the universe but a brief second. And certainly man's life can hardly be considered the goal of the universe. Its margin of existence is always precarious. Study of the geologic periods shows that. So does the battle against disease. (Pgs. 180-194, "The Ethical Mysticism of Albert Schweitzer", Henry B. Clark, Beacon Press, 1962)

In fact, an accurate depiction of Schweitzer's life evidences his choice to depart from the ministry. In 1904 he chanced upon an article in the Paris Missionary Society's publication indicating their urgent need for physicians in the French colony of Gabon. He was greatly affected by the piece and felt that his search was over. He believed that atonement for the wrongs that the Christian had done to underdeveloped peoples was in itself a justification for the missions. Schweitzer himself had written openly and often about the cruelty with which Western cultures had treated underdeveloped people, and how these practices had been justified by the Western intellectuals. Consider just how different Schweitzer's beliefs were to the "New Ethic" of the emerging eugenics and scientism:

> Our culture divides people into two classes: civilized men, a title bestowed on the persons who do the classifying; and others, who have only the human form, who may perish or go to the dogs for all the 'civilized men' care. ---- Oh, this 'noble' culture of ours! It speaks so piously of human dignity and human rights and then disregards this dignity and these rights of countless millions and treads them underfoot, only because they live overseas or because their skins are of different color or because they cannot help themselves. This culture does not know how hollow and miserable and full of glib talk it is. (Pgs. 76–80, "Albert Schweitzer: Essential Writings", James Brabazon, ed., Orbis Books, 2005)

In October 1905, Schweitzer made his intention to study medicine known to family and friends. He decided to enroll as a medical student at the beginning of the winter term and would be off to Africa once finished. At age 38, Schweitzer received his degree with a specialization in tropical medicine and surgery. This was an eight-year departure from his formal life in theology and music. He resigned from his academic posts, canceled long-term concert and lecture contracts and became totally dependent on a small band of friends for help. Together with his wife, Helene, Schweitzer started a program of fundraising to supply a hospital and underwrite expenses for its first two years. In 1912, armed with a medical degree, the Schweitzers made the commitment to work at their own expense in the Paris Missionary Society's mission at Lambaréné on the Ogooué River, in what is now Gabon. The couple set off to establish a hospital near an already existing mission post. The site was nearly 200 miles, or 14 days by raft upstream from the mouth of the Ogooué at Port Gentil. The hospital started out in a chicken coop and gradually expanded to treat thousands of patients.

When WWI broke out in the summer of 1914, Schweitzer and his wife, both Germans in a French colony, were put under supervision at Lambaréné by the French military. In 1917, the couple was taken to Bordeaux and interned in Garaison and then transferred to Saint-Rémy-de-Provence in March of 1918. The couple was freed on July 1918, and they returned to Alsace, where their daughter Rhena was born on January 14, 1919. They enjoyed several years together before Schweiter returned to Africa alone in 1927. Schweitzer would go back and forth from Europe to Africa between 1929 and 1937 and continued working there throughout World War II. Schweitzer continued to oversee the hospital until his death at the age of 90. He and his wife are buried on the hospital grounds.

Schweitzer's mirror image, and once devoted follower, Karl Brandt, would return to consider the choice he had made while awaiting his death sentence at Landsberg prison. The deep contrast between Albert Schweitzer and Adolf Hitler was not lost on Ulf Schmidt, Brandt's biographer. Schmidt characterizes Karl Brandt as a once devoted follower of Schweitzer who had made the choice to follow the path of Alfred Hoche and Adolf Hitler:

> Schweitzer and Hitler were the two most influential figures in Brandt's life. They were his two role models, his two mirrors', according to one of Brandt's fellow students. (Pg. 46, "Karl Brandt: Medicine and Power in the Third Reich", Ulf Schmidt, Bloomsbury Academic, 2007)

Ulf Schmidt recounts how Brandt would try to invoke his early devotion to Schweitzer as a way to evidence his humanitarian ethics:

> During the period of my studies I had already made contact with a doctor known not only in Germany, but beyond the borders of this country, Albert Schweitzer. And I intended, trained as a surgeon, to assist him with his medical work in Lambarene, in the French Congo; when, in 1932, I was ready, it was no longer possible to carry out this plan, because it was required that I should serve in the French army, which probably would have meant having to adopt French citizenship. (Pg. 44, "Karl Brandt: Medicine and Power in the Third Reich", Ulf Schmidt, Bloomsbury Academic, 2007)

Ironically, Alfred Schweitzer was forced to make this choice as well and chose to become a French citizen so he could continue his humanitarian work. What Karl Brandt failed to explain to the Nuremberg court was that he had heard Adolf Hitler speak in 1926 at a party rally in Weimar, had his nationalistic emotions peaked to the point where French citizenship would have been an abhorrent thought, and had joined the National Socialist party by 1932 when this decision was allegedly taken. [373] This was a daily topic of conversation between Karl Brandt and his cellmate at Landsberg, Rudolf Boeckh, the son of a priest whom himself had participated in the deportation of mental patients as part of the euthanasia

---

[373] Pg. 47 - "Karl Brandt: Medicine and Power in the Third Reich", Ulf Schmidt, Bloomsbury Academic, 2007.

program. [374] Karl Brandt maintained to the day of his death that his conscience was clear and that the euthanasia program was a legitimate medical endeavor. Brandt would do his best to play the part of the "good Nazi" which had successfully and fraudulently saved his best friend, Albert Speer, from the fate of execution. If Brandt had actually followed Schweitzer with the devotion he proclaimed, then the deep antagonism between the ideals of "will-to-live" and the notion of "life unworthy of living" could not have been lost to him:

> The question which haunts men and women today is whether life is worth living. Perhaps each of us has had the experience of talking with a friend one day, finding that person bright, happy, apparently in the full joy of life; and then the next day we find that he has taken his own life! Stoicism has brought us to this point, by driving out the fear of death; for, by inference it suggests that we are free to choose whether to live or not. But if we entertain such a possibility, we do so by ignoring the melody of the will-to-live, which compels us to face the mystery, the value, the high trust committed to us in life. We may not understand it, but we begin to appreciate its great value. Therefore, when we find those who relinquish life, while we may not condemn them, we do pity them for having ceased to be in possession of themselves. Ultimately, the issue is not whether we do or do not fear death. The real issue is that of reverence for life. (Pgs. 180-194, "The Ethical Mysticism of Albert Schweitzer", Henry B. Clark, Beacon Press, 1962)

Historians have omitted German scientists and doctors such as Rudolf Virchow, Alexander Von Humboldt, and Alfred Schweitzer from the historical equation. They position figures like Ernst Rüdin, Alfred Ploetz and Wilhelm Schallmayer as the balance to the rabid anti-Semites like Rosenberg and Hitler, claiming that their science was not explicitly anti-Semitic and therefore not complicit in the crimes of The Holocaust. This excuse is used, by extension, to exonerate Fabian Socialists the likes of H.G. Wells, Francis Galton, Leonard Darwin, and Julian Huxley, and as a consequence, to distance other scientists the likes of the American eugenicists such as G.M. Goethe, Harry H. Laughlin, and Charles B. Davenport. The true balance is that humanitarian Germans like Humboldt, Schweitzer, and Virchow are at the opposing side of the scale. To buy into the notion that there was such a thing as a "good eugenicist" is to buy into the Speer-Brandt fabrication that a "good Nazi" could engage in mass murder but be innocent because they did not spew anti-Semitic rhetoric. To accept this line of thinking is to credulously believe the fabrications Karl Brandt made at the Nuremberg Doctors' Trial.

---

[374] Pg. 395 – "Karl Brandt: Medicine and Power in the Third Reich", Ulf Schmidt, Bloomsbury Academic, 2007.

Sec. 7 - FRANCIS GALTON'S "KANTSAYWHERE":

Sir Francis Galton, Charles Darwin's cousin and father of eugenics, died in January of 1911. Galton was a prolific writer and produced more than 340 papers and books. Galton devised the first weather map as well as several meteorological concepts. He devised a method for classifying fingerprints that proved useful in forensic science. He was a gifted statistician who created the concept of correlation and regression toward the mean. Galton applied his statistical methods to the study of human differences and inheritance of intelligence, and as a result, created the science of eugenics. He also coined the phrase "nature versus nurture," which inevitably became the central argument of those, like Galton, who argued that heredity was more important than environment. Even though his cousin incorporated Galton's eugenics into his Theory of Evolution, Galton remains in his famous cousin's shadow, likely because of the political implications of tracing back the consequences of eugenics to Charles Darwin.

Galton's fictional work, "Kantsaywhere," provides a clue as to this uncomfortable link, and makes it clear that from the onset even Galton's closest friends and followers were aware of the disturbing implications of subjecting humanity to Galton's eugenics. Galton's family certainly thought that "Kantsaywhere" should not be published. Galton's protégé, Karl Pearson, documents in his "Life and Letters of Francis Galton" that the first he heard of the work was when he was approached by Galton's niece and asked, with a "secretive" tone, to persuade Galton not to publish it as they were not comfortable with its contents. [375] Pearson includes in "Life and Letters" a copy of a March 27, 1911, letter from this niece, who claims to have destroyed her copy of "Kantsaywhere," but felt that if anything remained, Karl Pearson should be allowed to see before all of it was destroyed. [376] This niece was likely the Mrs. Lucy Amy Lethbridge, who Galton originally wrote to in order to personally instruct her that "Kantsaywhere must be smothered or suppressed" in a December 28, 1910, letter, just prior to Galton's death. [377] It is thus that any surviving portions of "Kantsaywhere" were published in Pearson's 1930 biography, "Life, Letters and Labours of Francis Galton by Karl Pearson." Pearson documents in "Life and Letters" that Galton was extremely busy promoting eugenics, and that "Kantsaywhere" was an attempt to reach those that had not taken note of his science. [378] According to Pearson, Galton felt there was a portion of the scientific community he had not convinced, and that a fictional glimpse of what a eugenic state may look like may help persuade them. However, the publisher outright rejected "Kantsaywhere," and it is likely that Galton's family helped dissuade him. After all, the only reason we even know of "Kantsaywhere" is because Galton's favorite niece became squeamish after destroying most of "Kantsaywhere," but decided to show the remaining pages to Pearson.

The fact that Karl Pearson went against the explicit dictates of Galton and the

---

[375] Pg. 411 - "Life, Letters and Labours of Francis Galton by Karl Pearson", Cambridge Univ. Press, 1930.
[376] Pg. 413 – Ibid.
[377] Pg. 412 – Ibid.
[378] Pg. 412 – Ibid.

executors of his estate says as much about Pearson as it does about Galton's fictional utopia. Karl Pearson, born Carl Pearson, was a brilliant statistician like his mentor. He had studied in Germany at the University of Heidelberg, where his name was first misspelled, but Carl decided to stay Karl reportedly because of his love of Germany and likely as a tribute to his socialist views. Some of Pearson's historians dispute this, but Karl proved to be a *prima donna* early and often enough to substantiate this alleged vanity. Pearson lived in personal controversy, namely with people that would otherwise be his supporters. This book has previously touched on and will further delve into the various temper tantrums Pearson threw over the subject of Mendel's work. It goes much further than that. He presented his resignation to "Biometrika," the journal he had co-founded along with Francis Galton, at least once because others disagreed with him. Even Leonard Darwin felt compelled to distance himself from Pearson and the Galton Committee after Pearson published his disdain for Leonard Darwin's views without first giving his colleague the courtesy of fleshing out their differences in private. Darwin replied that he had gone up against more "worthy adversaries" and subsequently resigned from the Galton Committee a few years after. We touched upon Pearson's spat with Davenport. Pearson had similar public disputes with R.A. Fisher and Hugo John Buchanan-Wollaston, both of which devolved into a prolonged back-and-forth in the journal "Nature." Thus, the fact that Pearson went against the explicit directives of Galton's estate must be considered in light of Pearson's zealotry and personal politics.

Karl Pearson was a well-known socialist, and as a Marxist and a eugenicist, Pearson was obsessed with the Marxist concept of "surplus population." He expended much ink into determining what many other fellow travelers, namely Margaret Sanger, termed "optimum population" in economic and political thought. In an article titled "The Moral Basis of Socialism," published in his 1888 book, Karl Pearson explains exactly how indispensable population control was to the cause of socialism:

> It is this "limit to efficient population" which is the duty of the statesman to discover, and to maintain, as far as possible, at each period of social growth. Removal of population, prohibition of immigration, and, if necessary, limitation of the number of births, are the means whereby the limit to efficient population may be approximately conserved. --- These are the questions which form the population problem, and demand our consideration. The Socialist of the marketplace, who ignores them, places himself outside the field of useful discussion. We must recognize the problem; and, when carefully investigated, it will be found to offer one of the strongest arguments in favour of Socialism with which I am acquainted. We may even say that Socialism is the logical outcome of the law of Malthus. (Pg. 319, "The Ethic of Freethought: And Other Addresses and Essays", Karl Pearson, Adam & Charles Black, 1901)

The murderous acts of numerous socialist dictators, namely Vladimir Lenin and Joseph Stalin, confirm that the desire to rid the collectivized body of "excess population" was an enduring concept in socialist states. This also goes a long way to confirm Adolf Hitler's socialist credentials. Francis Galton clearly believed that only a system of government that placed the welfare of the "society" over the interests of the "individual" would be able to erect the types of intrusive social controls which were indispensable in order to make a eugenic state feasible. This is a running theme which Galton emphasized in his socialist utopia:

> In Kantsaywhere they think much more of the race than of the individual, ---- A person is therefore more important as a probable progenitor of many others more or less like to him in constitution than as a mere individual. (Francis Galton, "Kantsaywhere", as appears in Pgs. 416-424, "Life, Letters and Labours of Francis Galton by Karl Pearson", Cambridge Univ. Press, 1930)

Karl Pearson knew equally well that it was only through the tight controls that a state-run on eugenic principles would maintain population growth at its "optimum" level and prevent "surplus population." Socialists traditionally think of the economy as a given amount of wealth to be evenly distributed. A growing population is clearly a threat to an economy where the focus is redistribution instead of growth. The growth of wealth implies profit, and profit implies "capitalism": a term considered profane by the Progressive and Fabian faithful. If profits and economic growth are to be disallowed, then population growth must be curtailed, prevented, and controlled, even at the expense of individual liberty. Pearson said explicitly so: "I think it is sufficiently clear that the limitation of population in the capitalistic organization of Society will hardly be attempted, and, if attempted, would not be successful." [379] In retrospect, he provided a good explanation as to why eugenics only got so far in the United States and Britain but excelled in National Socialism.

Francis Galton had provided a specific recipe for a eugenic state when he translated abstract eugenics into precise state policies in "Kantsaywhere." This was not a blueprint that Karl Pearson would simply throw into a fire, as the Galton estate required upon his death. The socialist scheme necessary for the functioning of "Kantsaywhere" must have been too attractive for Karl. He must have salivated at the 75 percent tax-rate that Galton envisioned the inhabitants of "Kantsaywhere" paying for the upkeep of their society:

> The inhabitants submitted as cheerfully to as heavy a rate in support of the College, as we do for the support of our Fleet, namely three quarters of £1 per head of the population. -- and could easily be persuaded to contribute more, if it were really needed. (Francis Galton, "Kantsaywhere", as appears in Pgs. 416-424, "Life, Letters and Labours of Francis Galton by Karl Pearson", Cambridge Univ. Press, 1930)

This necessity for an elevated tax rate becomes clear when one understands that "Kantsaywhere" is a "cradle-to-grave" socialist utopia, which provides for just about everything its inhabitants need in housing and education, but does so only in

---

[379] Pg. 321 - "The Ethic of Freethought: And Other Addresses and Essays", Karl Pearson, Adam & Charles Black, 1901.

proportion to the racial worth of the inhabitants:
> The College was to grant diplomas for heritable gifts, physical and mental, to encourage the early marriages of highly diplomaed parents by the offer of appropriate awards of various social and material advantages to relieve the cost of nurturing their children, to keep a minute register of results, and to discuss those results from time to time. (Francis Galton, "Kantsaywhere", as appears in Pgs. 416-424, "Life, Letters and Labours of Francis Galton by Karl Pearson", Cambridge Univ. Press, 1930)

To comprehend eugenics, one must understand it as a planned society. Galton regarded it as nothing less than an all-encompassing "religion," where all of society was organized around eugenic principles. So it was so in "Kantsaywhere":
> Their superstition certainly succeeds, even as it is, in giving a unity of endeavour and a seriousness of action to the whole population. They have no fear of death. Their funerals are not dismal functions as with us, but are made into occasions for short appreciative speeches dwelling lovingly on the life-work of the deceased. (Francis Galton, "Kantsaywhere", as appears in Pgs. 416-424, "Life, Letters and Labours of Francis Galton by Karl Pearson", Cambridge Univ. Press, 1930)

A eugenic society is a technocratic society. It elevates the doctor to that formerly occupied by the clergy and monarchy. The planner, the overseer, the doctor, the judges, and the scientists are put in a position of power to orchestrate, plan and design the society by micro-managing down to the individual copulation between two potential mates. Thus was the case of the "The Trustees" in "Kantsaywhere":
> The Trustees of the College are the sole proprietors of almost all the territory of Kantsaywhere, and they exercise a corresponding influence over the whole population. Their moral ascendancy is paramount. (Francis Galton, "Kantsaywhere", as appears in Pgs. 416-424, "Life, Letters and Labours of Francis Galton by Karl Pearson", Cambridge Univ. Press, 1930)

A common eugenic theme resonates: One crucial aspect of a eugenically organized society is that the doctor stops being responsible for the needs of the individual patient. The Hippocratic Oath is tossed in the garbage and is replaced with an oath to make all medical decisions on the basis of what is appropriate and convenient to society. If the individual patient's needs conflicted with the population's "germ plasm," then the choice for the eugenic doctor has already been made; the individual subordinates to the priorities of the collective. If the individual needed to be segregated, sterilized, or euthanized for the good of society, then the doctor's choice was clear: the doctor in a eugenically organized society was responsible to the social body, and not the individual:
> Labour Colonies are established where the very inferior are segregated under conditions that are not onerous, except that they must work hard and live in celibacy. (Francis Galton, "Kantsaywhere", as appears in Pgs. 416-424, "Life, Letters and Labours of Francis Galton by Karl Pearson", Cambridge, 1930)

Every aspect of the state became orchestrated by a central planning body, and this central planning body had the power to enforce their vision without regard to the wants or needs of the individual. Without that power, a eugenic society is simply not possible as the choice of self-preservation by individuals that have been decreed to be "unfit" could never be allowed to infect the collectivized body:

> An important Committee of this Council is charged with the care of those who fail to pass the Poll examination in Eugenics. Such persons are undesirable as individuals, and dangerous to the community, owing to the practical certainty that they will propagate their kind if unchecked. They are subjected to surveillance and annoyance if they refuse to emigrate. Considerable facilities are afforded to tempt them to go, and agents of the College who are settled in the nearer towns to which they are most likely to drift, are prepared to take charge of them on their arrival. Their passage out is paid, small sums are granted to them at first, on the condition of their never returning to Kantsaywhere. They must renounce in writing all its privileges before being allowed the cost of deportation. (Francis Galton, "Kantsaywhere", as appears in Pgs. 416-424, "Life, Letters and Labours of Francis Galton by Karl Pearson", Cambridge Univ. Press, 1930)

A utopia based on a racial ethic is by necessity obsessed with heredity and inheritable traits, good and bad. Race and heredity become the business of the state, and thus going against the racial mandates become crimes against the state: "the propagation of children by the Unfit is looked upon by the inhabitants of Kantsaywhere as a crime to the State." Society in Galton's "Kantsaywhere" was exclusionary by necessity, as threats to the racial health of the society by outsiders and immigrants had to be controlled just as strictly as the lives of its citizens:

> The difficulty must again be discussed here, relating to the introduction of unfit immigrants. Municipal laws have been enacted, that are quite as severe as those in America and elsewhere, to exclude impecunious immigrants, but they are enacted here for the purpose of excluding the immigration of the constitutionally unfit into Kantsaywhere. (Francis Galton, "Kantsaywhere", as appears in Pgs. 416-424, "Life, Letters and Labours of Francis Galton by Karl Pearson", Cambridge Univ. Press, 1930)

Every newcomer, whether visitor or settler underwent a physical entrance examination. Whoever passed the test received a "P.G. Passport." (P.G. = passed genetics) Every newborn member also had to submit themselves to similar tests. The solemnly celebrated "honorable examination" before the vaunted "Eugenic College of Kantsaywhere" was the central event of every citizen's life:

> The refusal to grant a Pass certificate is equivalent to an assertion that the person is unfit to have any offspring at all. By a second-class certificate that permission is granted, but with reservations. (Francis Galton, "Kantsaywhere", as appears in Pgs. 416-424, "Life, Letters and Labours of Francis Galton by Karl Pearson", Cambridge Univ. Press, 1930)

As much energy was expended at keeping the "Unfit" from contributing to Galton's socialist utopia as there was towards promoting racial health:

> A Bureau was charged with looking after the unclassed parents and their offspring, and much was done to make the lot of the unclassed as pleasant as might be, so long as they propagated no children. If they did do so kindness was changed into sharp severity. (Francis Galton, "Kantsaywhere", Pgs. 416-424, "Life, Letters and Labours of Francis Galton by Karl Pearson", Cambridge Univ. Press, 1930)

This is where the artificially positive taste to Galton's work, when communicated in the abstract, begins to reveal its totalitarian reality. The level of intrusion and control inevitably result in the kind of society humanity has come to deem repulsive:

> The restriction placed by public sentiment and, in extreme cases, by penalty, on the number of offspring that a couple may propagate in Kantsaywhere, is based on that of their joint marks. (F. Galton, "Kantsaywhere", as appears in Pgs. 416-424, "Life, Letters and Labours of Francis Galton by Karl Pearson", Cambridge Univ. Press, 1930)

In Galton's utopia, the breeding practices of humanity otherwise used on livestock became the mindset of human mate selection. It was the criterion of the breeder, the overseer, the state which is the ultimate determining factor:

> Persons may fall in love in Kantsaywhere as they do in England, on grounds more or less unaccountable to others, but it is felt here that the best girls and the best men should have frequent opportunities of becoming friends and the earliest chance of falling in love with one another. (Francis Galton, "Kantsaywhere", as appears in Pgs. 416-424, "Life, Letters and Labours of Francis Galton by Karl Pearson", Cambridge Univ. Press, 1930)

The individual human, for all eternity, has taken whatever steps they deem necessary to attain the mate of their choosing. The various rituals are countless. This is an individualistic and largely selfish process, in comparison to what Galton intended eugenics to be. Human mating is a highly personal process, and even cultures that practice pre-arranged mating do so for the benefit of the immediate family. Eugenics is the mirror opposite of this. Eugenics denies any individuality and strives to impose a social criterion on the various mating in a society. It subordinates the individual and the family to the perceived priorities of the society and actively curtails individual rights to accomplish its goals, mostly which are far-reaching and for the benefit of generations still not living. The decisions that go into the mating process are not those of the individual, or even of the family members, but of the technician, the doctor, the scientist, or "The College" as Galton put it, by ensuring that those that meet high eugenic marks after being tested and measured were mated together. As it is in modern-day socialist dogma, the resulting children were regarded as the property of the state as much as they were of their natural parents:

> The offspring of such marriages are reckoned foster children of the College during their childhood, and they and their 'College parents' are helped in many important ways. (Francis Galton, "Kantsaywhere", as appears in Pgs. 416-424, "Life, Letters and Labours of Francis Galton by Karl Pearson", Cambridge Univ. Press, 1930)

One can hardly be surprised that "Kantsaywhere," like its other utopian counterparts, employed city planning as a method central to the control and planned balancing act of the scheme. "Kantsaywhere" was a garden city, as were the ones designed by contemporary architects such as Frank Lloyd Wright and Le Corbusier, but with the eugenic priorities as the prevailing law, as in Adolf Hitler's plans for a "eugenic state." Like National Socialism and as it was in almost all other eugenic socialist societies proposed by the likes of Galton, the culture of "Kantsaywhere" was a back-to-nature and provincial cult:

> A country life is considered to be so highly conducive to the health and size of families that a large part of the wealth of Kantsaywhere is gladly allotted to its encouragement. (Francis Galton, "Kantsaywhere", as appears in Pgs. 416-424, "Life, Letters and Labours of Francis Galton by Karl Pearson", Cambridge Univ. Press, 1930)

Incidentally, one of the many tests conducted on individuals in "Kantsaywhere" was measuring the proportions of the body, muscular strength, fitness, speed, reflexes, and eye-sight. The "natural" was an aesthetic attribute. Therefore, the aesthetic portion of the test asked the candidate to pose in athletic or sculptural poses, as well as testing the candidates' talents in literature, art and overall intelligence. Karl Pearson could not have been oblivious to similar practices by eugenic minded "biometricians" inside of Hitler's Germany:

> I should say that they lay much stress on the aesthetic side of things at Kantsaywhere. 'Grace and Thoroughness' is a motto carved over one of the houses for girls in the College -- A loutish boy and an awkward girl hardly exist in the place. -- Musical speech and clear but refined pronunciation are thought highly of. (Francis Galton, "Kantsaywhere", as appears in Pgs. 416-424, "Life, Letters and Labours of Francis Galton by Karl Pearson", Cambridge Univ. Press, 1930)

History should allow people like Galton a long enough life to view the fruits of their labor. It would have been only fair for Francis Galton to be forced to listen to a speech by Adolf Hitler, or to answer to an International tribunal as Karl Brandt did:

> They look confidently forward to a coming time when Kantsaywhere shall have evolved **a superior race of men**. (emphasis mine, Francis Galton, "Kantsaywhere", as appears in Pgs. 416-424, "Life, Letters and Labours of Francis Galton by Karl Pearson", Cambridge Univ. Press, 1930)

The sentiments and parallels between Francis Galton's eugenic state and that which would later be erected by the German National Socialists under Hitler are but the logical outcome of Galton's eugenic policies. William H. Tucker, author of "The Science and Politics of Racial Research" documents further parallels:

> A number of scientists on both sides of the Atlantic had long concluded that the Jews were "parasites." The revered Galton had written that they were "specialized for a parasitic existence." His protégé, the eminent statistician Karl Pearson, who praised Hitler's racial policies, had warned England that the inferior Jewish immigrants, "hastening to profit from the higher civilization of an improved humanity," might well develop into a "parasitic race." (Pgs. 125-126, "Science and Politics of Racial Research", Univ. of Illinois Press, 1996)

The German National Socialists reciprocated the praise for the British scientist who switched his name from Carl to Karl in admiration of all things German. A December 1932 article in the journal "Nature" documents that Eugen Fischer and Erwin Baur, of the *Berlin Gesellschaft fur Anthropologie, Ethnologie und Urgeschichte* honored Pearson with the Rudolf Virchow medal:

> The award is made in recognition of Prof. Pearson's conspicuous services for the advancement of the study of human biology, and especially his pioneer work in the field of biometrics and his contributions to the study of eugenics, in which he has carried on and extended the work of the late Francis Galton. (nature.com, Pg. 838, "Nature," Vol. 130, Dec. 3, 1932)

In conveying the announcement of the award, Eugen Fischer recalled the fact that up to the present, Pearson was the only person outside of Central Europe to receive the award and "acknowledged" their "great indebtedness" to Pearson's work. This is no small matter when one realizes that Eugen Fischer and Erwin Baur are two of the three authors of the infamous 1921 book, *"Menschliche Erblichkeitslehre und Rassenhygiene,"* most commonly referred to as the "Baur-Fischer-Lenz" book which had been personally hand-delivered to Adolf Hitler while he was serving time in Landsberg prison. Recall that Fischer and Baur were also prominent leaders of the Kaiser-Wilhelm Institute which provided the scientific support for Hitler's policies and processed the "tests" conducted by the doctors in the death camps.

Galton's family and his publisher knew there was something unappealing about the implications of eugenics once its social policies were clearly mapped out in "Kantsaywhere." Their opinions must have pressed heavily upon Galton, as Galton concluded shortly after being rejected by the publisher that:

> Kantsaywhere must be smothered or be suppressed. It has been an amusement and has cleared my thoughts to write it. So now let it go to "Wont-say-where." (Francis Galton, "Kantsaywhere", as appears in Pgs. 416-424, "Life, Letters and Labours of Francis Galton by Karl Pearson", Cambridge Univ. Press, 1930)

The late nineteenth century saw a flowering of utopian fiction. Edwin Abbott's "Flatland," published in 1884, depicted an imaginary society of geometrical figures where social status was determined by the number or types of angles. In 1890,

William Morris published "News from Nowhere," which took the reader into a future London populated by socialist artisans. Edward Bulwer-Lytton's "The Coming Race" of 1871, introduced the Vril-ya, a race of superhuman beings living in cities built within a vast subterranean cave system. Most notably was Edward Bellamy's "Looking Backwards" published in 1887, which introduced the readers of the era to the mixing of concepts of "nationalism" and "socialism," and the centrally planned and eugenic Boston of the year 2000. Karl Pearson documents in "Life and Letters of Francis Galton" that Galton was reading Thomas More's "Utopia," Plato's "Republic," Butler's "Erewhon," and Harrington's "Oceana" while writing "Kantsaywhere." [380]

"Kantsaywhere" paved the way for a legion of followers like Harry H. Laughlin and H.G. Wells who continued Galton's work by authoring their own utopian schemes. Laughlin and Wells were working toward the same aim but from opposite directions. Wells primarily wrote eugenic novels about futuristic utopias, and in his spare time was involved with the various international eugenic societies which sought to implement his dreams. Laughlin wrote the model eugenic laws for the benefit of, or under contract by legislatures and judicial bodies which were put into practice towards a eugenic end. Laughlin dedicated his free time to writing futuristic utopian proposals for one-world governments like those imagined by H.G. Wells. This enduring relationship between eugenic utopians and their works of fiction can hardly be regarded as a coincidence. Three things must happen in order to implement a eugenic state:

- The individual must become subservient to the society to make the eugenic quality of the society the governing principle.
- The society must become a centrally planned society where the governing elite has the power to sift those deemed "fit" from those considered "unfit."
- This central governing body is given the power to segregate, punish, and suppress unwanted elements. Without this power of enforcement, the eugenic utopia inevitably fails.

In short, eugenic aspirations necessitate a "total state" solution. Those that seek to shape humanity to their liking, as if sculptors manipulating clay, must have total power, lest the wishes of the "unfit" are allowed to sabotage the eugenic goals of the society. The "total state" of dreams and imagination, the "ideal state" solutions that propose a government powerful enough to provide and enforce a "cradle-to-grave" solution, ultimately became the horrid social phenomenon we now refer to as "totalitarianism."

---

[380] Pg. 411 - "Life, Letters and Labours of Francis Galton by Karl Pearson", Cambridge Univ. Press, 1930.

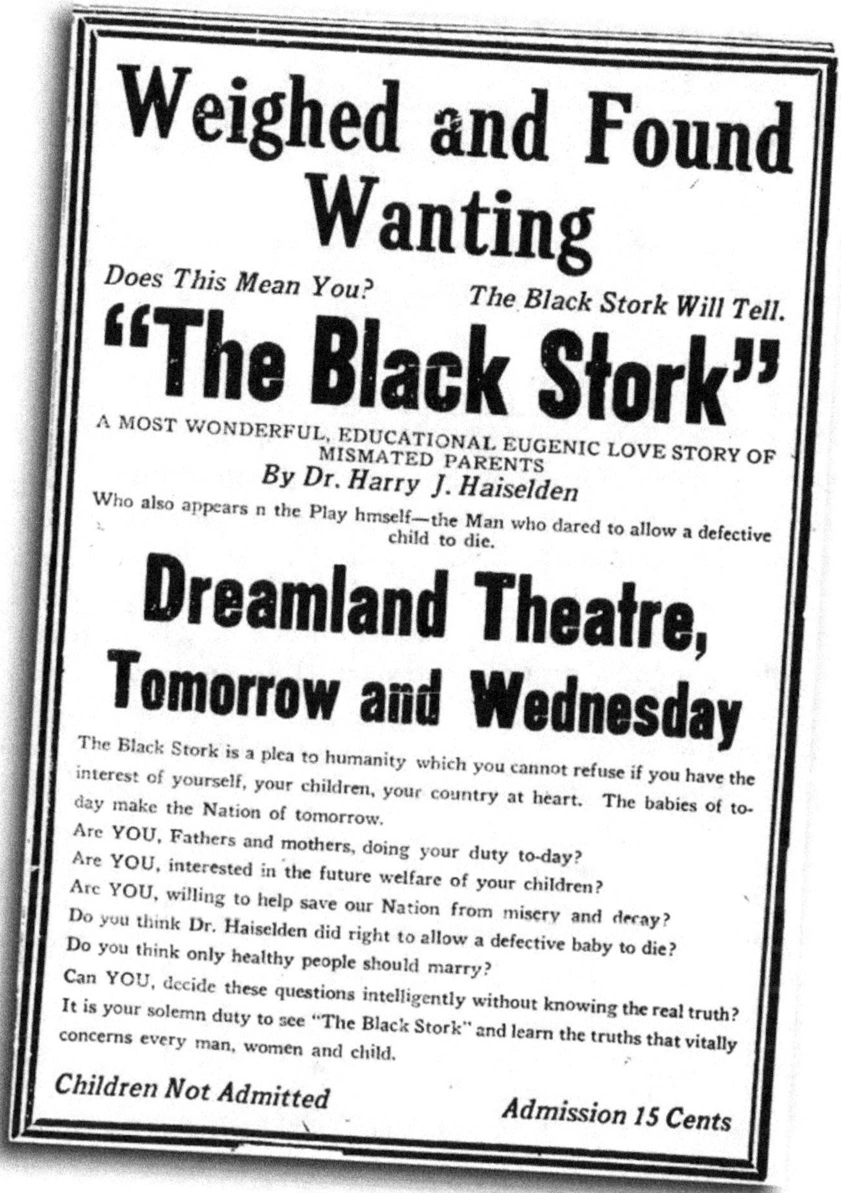

FIGURE 9: Advertisement for "The Black Stork" movie. Note that it is billed as a "eugenic" story.

Chap. 8: 1910 to 1906

AMERICAN FRONT: African-American boxer Jack Johnson defeats Anglo-American boxer James J. Jeffries. The results of the heavyweight match spark race riots across the United States. • **SCIENCE & TECHNOLOGY:** The first Victor Victrola, a phonographic record player, is manufactured. – SOS becomes an international distress signal. – HMS Dreadnought, the first all-big-gun warship, is commissioned. A 40,000-year-old Neanderthal boy skeleton is found at Le Moustier in southwest France. The United States Army Signal Corp Division purchases the world's first military airplane, a Wright Military Flyer, from the Wright Brothers. Geronimo The first air mail airplane flight takes place between Dayton, Ohio and Columbus, Ohio. • **EUROPEAN FRONT:** Karl Lueger retires as mayor of Vienna. • **LIFE:** Red Cloud, Sioux warrior dies. Alfred Dreyfus is exonerated. He is reinstated in the French Army on July 21. – Mahatma Gandhi coins the term Satyagraha to characterize the Non-Violence movement in South Africa. Bugsy Siegel, American gangster is born. – Adolf Eichmann, German war criminal is born. – Mount Vesuvius erupts and devastates Naples.

Sec. I – TOWARDS A COLLECTIVE GUILT???

On his 75th birthday, November 25, 1910, Andrew Carnegie announced the establishment of an endowment with a gift of $10 million. The resulting Carnegie Endowment for International Peace became a foreign-policy think tank based in Washington, D.C. Andrew Carnegie, like other leading internationalists of his day, believed that war could be eliminated by stronger international laws and organizations. "I am drawn more to this cause than to any," he wrote in 1907. The Carnegie Foundation had been in operation since 1908, and Nicholas Murray Butler was instrumental in persuading Andrew Carnegie to provide the initial $10 million funding towards that end. They corresponded through 1909, and subsequently, Carnegie's single largest charitable commitment was his creation of the Carnegie Endowment for International Peace.

Butler was an American philosopher, diplomat, and educator obsessed with the prospect of using influential charities like the Rockefeller and Carnegie foundations to significantly influence the Federal government. He was up to the task. Butler was also a recipient of the Nobel Peace Prize. He became so well-known and respected that The New York Times printed his Christmas greeting to the nation every year. In 1887, he co-founded and became president of the New York School for the Training of Teachers, which later affiliated with Columbia University. From 1890 to 1891, Butler was also a lecturer at Johns Hopkins University. In 1901, Butler became acting president of Columbia University, and in 1902 formally became president. Butler was president of Columbia University for 43 years, the longest tenure in the university's history, retiring in 1945. Among the many dignitaries in attendance at his investiture was President Theodore Roosevelt.

Butler also aroused controversy. Like many American intellectuals in the 1920s, he was an early admirer of Italian fascist Benito Mussolini and worked to forge cultural relations between Columbia University and Italian educational institutions. Butler also forged links with universities in Hitler's Germany. In 1933, Butler invited Hans Luther, the German ambassador to the United States, to speak at Columbia in defense of Hitler's policies and National Socialism. Butler rejected student appeals to cancel the invitation, calling the request "illiberal" and citing the need for academic freedom:

The request was made by the Columbia Social Problems Club, which contended:

"Inviting the Nazi envoy to lecture on the foreign policy of his government and giving him an official reception means not only failing in our duty to oppose the Nazi onslaught, but signifies, if not open endorsement of the Nazi actions, at least placing their principles on the same level with other viewpoints." (nytimes.com, "Columbia U. President Butler refuses to bar Nazi Envoy; Stresses need for Academic Freedom", New York Times, Pg. 6, November 20, 1933 – NYT Archives 1933)

In the wake of student protests, Butler retorted that Luther represented "the government of a friendly people," and that students who criticized the Luther invitation were nothing more than "ill-mannered children." Butler insisted that "academic relationships have no political implications." More than one thousand students and faculty, including Nobel Laureate Harold Urey and world-renowned anthropologist Franz Boas, signed a petition opposing Columbia's participation in Heidelberg. The student newspaper, The Spectator, also opposed the exchange between the institutions, and students staged a "Mock Heidelberg Festival" on campus, complete with mock book burning. [381] None of this swayed Butler.

Clearly, Butler was not squeamish about Nazism. Incidentally, Butler was friends with and shared views with Theodore Roosevelt on white supremacy and racial integration. Roosevelt and Butler differed about annexing Hawaii, but both agreed upon the inferiority of the native Hawaiians. Roosevelt felt they were ripe for an old-fashioned conquering, while Butler felt that the Hawaiians were simply not up to racial muster to be included in the United States public. TIME Magazine covered Butler's comments on December 22, 1947, in an article titled "TERRITORIES: Knock on the Door." Butler opposed statehood for the then territory of Hawaii, arguing that "in population, in language, and in economic life (Hawaii) is distinctly a foreign land. ... (Its people) are not and could not be members of the United States of America in any true sense."

Consider the implications. This was the person in charge of two institutions that are key to the subject matter of this book: He was president of Columbia University and the Carnegie Foundation. Columbia University produced some of the key figures that were instrumental for the eugenics movement for both the United States and Europe leading up to the Holocaust, and the Carnegie Foundation provided the funding for the major eugenic groups in the United States and in Germany. Without the academic and financial support, it is doubtful eugenics could have grown beyond the idea of cranks and radicals.

Associate Professor Stephen Norwood of University of Oklahoma is the author of the book "The Third Reich in the Ivory Tower." In it, Norwood documents the academic community's support for Hitler in the 1930s and a pattern of cooperation with Hitler's Germany:

↠ More than twenty US colleges and universities took part in the 1936 Heidelberg event.

---

[381] wymanInstitute.org, "Columbia Invites Hitler to Campus", David S. Wyman, Institute for Holocaust Studies, Sept. 20, 2007.

- Harvard hosted a visit by Hitler's foreign press spokesman, Ernst "Putzi" Hanfstaengl.
- American University chancellor Joseph Gray visited and praised Hitler's Germany.
- The dean at the M.I.T., Harold Lobdell showed support for the permission given to dock Hitler's warships in Boston's harbor by personally tearing down the protest posters put up as a reaction to their presence.
- M.I.T. participated in a 1937 celebration at the National Socialist bastion, the University of Göttingen, Germany.
- Yale, Princeton, and others continued student exchanges with Hitler's Germany into the late 1930s.

Eugenics and its most violent incarnations were able to feign scientific legitimacy precisely because of the high praise some of the most respected institutions around the world gave it. Adolf Hitler's Third Reich was a direct beneficiary of the high regard these institutions had for eugenic causes. Butler held the purse that funded these universities and institutions. In 1904, the Carnegie Institution established the laboratory complex at Cold Spring Harbor on Long Island, where Harry H. Laughlin and Charles Davenport managed their eugenics campaign. From Cold Spring Harbor, eugenics advocates agitated in the legislatures of America, as well as the nation's social service agencies and associations. Edwin Black, an author of several books on The Holocaust, posted a paper online that states this point in no uncertain terms:

> Eugenics would have been so much bizarre parlor talk had it not been for extensive financing by corporate philanthropies, specifically the Carnegie Institution, the Rockefeller Foundation and the Harriman railroad fortune. They were all in league with some of America's most respected scientists hailing from such prestigious universities as Stamford, Yale, Harvard, and Princeton. These academicians espoused race theory and race science, and then faked and twisted data to serve eugenics' racist aims. (Edwin Black, "The Horrifying American Roots of Nazi Eugenics", Sept. 2003 – Available at researchgate.net)

Consider the web of inconvenient relationships when the *alma maters* of the elite and powerful became entangled in the most reviled "crimes" in human history. The Nuremberg Trials failed outright to document the cozy relationship between American, British, and German eugenics. Arguably, this was because of the influence the very powerful and politically connected enjoyed. "Collective Guilt," as such, was then and remains largely a measure of political affiliation, not evidence or culpability.

Sec. 2 - EUGEN FISCHER'S "REHOBOTH BASTARDS":

Eugen Fischer was a German professor of medicine, anthropology, and eugenics. He became the director of the Kaiser Wilhelm Institute of Anthropology, Human Heredity, and Eugenics during the Third Reich, and was appointed rector of the Frederick William University of Berlin by Adolf Hitler in 1933. The Rockefeller Foundation supported both the Kaiser Wilhelm Institute of Psychiatry and the Kaiser Wilhelm Institute of Anthropology, Human Heredity and Eugenics. The Rockefeller Foundation partially funded the construction of the Institute and helped keep the Institute afloat during the Depression, and Fischer coordinated his work with fellow International Federation of Eugenics Organizations members during this era.

Fischer had been recommended for the directorship of the Kaiser Wilhelm Institute by Erwin Baur, whom Fischer had co-authored the infamous "Baur-Fischer-Lenz" book. Baur, Fischer, and Lenz had all started working together in Freiburg, where students and teachers alike cultivated a "racially aware" pursuit of the sciences. Alfred Ploetz approached Eugen Fischer while he was at Freiburg, whom at Ploetz's urging established a local Racial Hygiene Society chapter, whom Fischer would frequently announce in the lectures he gave to his students. [382]

In 1908 Fischer traveled to German South-West Africa to conduct field research. He studied the "Rehoboth bastards," offspring of German fathers and African women in Rehoboth, present-day Namibia. It is interesting to juxtapose and compare the justifications for socialist eugenics and the conquests of the colonial period. Both are propagandized as actions in the benefit of those that inevitably become its victims. Germans attempted to portray themselves as "civilizing agents" in what is now known as the "Herero Incident." That is, their mission was to modernize the natives along the lines of white European Christian culture. [383] The "civilizing" rationale was needed to justify the establishment of an authoritarian structure and military presence as the natives relentlessly resisted what the Germans attested to be beneficial for the Africans. The peak of the massacres that for many epitomized the evil of German colonization, was the slaughter of the Herero peoples in the war of 1904-1907. For more than twenty years, the Herero had attempted to live peacefully with the Germans. The Germans ratcheted up their aggressions against the Herero, raping women, stealing property, and lynching those who protested. The population of the Herero dropped from 80,000 to 15,000 by the time all was said and done. The remaining 15,000 were put into concentration camps. [384]

The phrase "concentration camp" was first used by the Spaniards in the colonization of Cuba, and then adopted by the British during the Boer War. The Germans, with their inferiority complex regarding colonization, were eager to prove their might and willingness to use the same brutal tactics as the British and

---

[382] Pg. 143 - "Health, Race and German Politics Between National Unification and Nazism, 1870-1945", Paul Weindling, Cambridge Univ. Press, 1993.
[383] Pg. 43 – Ibid.
[384] Pg. 43 – Ibid.

Spaniards. [385] Of note is that many of the women in the concentration camps were forced into becoming sex slaves. The resulting children would become the test subjects for Eugen Fischer's racial studies. The mixed-race children would be subjected to racial tests of all kinds, such as head and body measurements, and eye and hair examinations. These studies became the prime scientific justification for the Nuremberg marriage restriction laws. Note Fischer's observation:

> Without exception, each European people that has assimilated the blood of inferior races has paid for this absorption of inferior elements by intellectual, spiritual, and cultural decline. (Pg. 45, "Hitler's Black Victims: The Historical Experiences of Afro-Germans, European Blacks, Africans, and African Americans in the Nazi Era Victims", Clarence Lusane, Taylor & Francis, 2002)

This was the underlying assumption of eugenics as a science intended to protect the needs of society. Its Darwinian roots were front and center:

> So accord them just the measure of protection they may require as a race which is inferior to us, in order to continue their existence: nothing more, and only as long as they are of use to us. Otherwise survival of the fittest, i.e., to my mind, in this case, extinction. This point of view sounds almost brutally egotistic, but whoever thinks through thoroughly the notion of race, can not arrive at a different conclusion. (Pg. 45, "Hitler's Black Victims: The Historical Experiences of Afro-Germans, European Blacks, Africans, and African Americans in the Nazi Era Victims", Clarence Lusane, Taylor & Francis, 2002)

Historians have come to categorize this Herero massacre as the trial run for The Holocaust due to its parallels and similarities. Aside from the use of "concentration camps," the Germans also conducted medical experiments including sterilization and injections of smallpox, typhus, and tuberculosis. The observation is justified, as the scientists and anthropologists who studied the skulls and racial characteristics in the African colonies ultimately became the leading racial anthropologists for the Third Reich. [386] This is precisely the case with Eugen Fischer. Fischer was at the lead of the crimes against the Herero. Fischer's recommendations were followed, and by 1912 interracial marriage was prohibited throughout the German colonies. Fischer resumed his "bastard studies" at the end of World War I and continued through the beginning of the Third Reich. Fischer also collaborated with Charles Davenport on this project. The work was formally completed in 1913 as "The Rehoboth Bastards and the Problem of Miscegenation among Humans" in the form of a field study intended to study the interbreeding between the races. While some historians claim that Fischer's work was a legitimate anthropological study, Fischer's direct application reveals otherwise. It is difficult to see how something deemed a "crime against humanity" can still be explained away as scientifically legitimate work. Fischer truly was pioneering the type of crimes Mengele would later be identified with. In the years of 1937-1938, Fischer and his

---

[385] Pg. 45 – "Hitler's Black Victims: The Historical Experiences of Afro-Germans, European Blacks, Africans, and African Americans in the Nazi Era Victims", Clarence Lusane, Taylor & Francis, 2002.
[386] Pg. 45 - Ibid.

colleagues analyzed 600 children in Hitler's Germany descending from French-African soldiers who occupied Western areas of Germany after World War I. Verschuer recommended sterilization as a remedy in 1927, and following Francis Galton's eugenic findings, claimed there was a biological basis for class structure; he condemned democracy as a "quantitative rather than a qualitative social system, which posed undue financial burdens on the natural elite." [387] All these children were subjected to sterilization during the Nazi era.

More to the point, Eugen Fischer's own words in his study of the "Bastards" evidence that he was in the business of "sterilization" and "extermination" decades prior to the Third Reich, at a time when Adolf Hitler was nothing but an aspiring artist. Fischer was named the head of the Kaiser Wilhelm Institute in 1927, when Hitler was barely emerging from Landsberg prison, and when Hitler's political future was still largely in question. Fischer worked with Otmar Freiherr von Verschuer at the Kaiser-Wilhelm Institute at this time. Verschuer oversaw the Department of Human Genetics, where he conducted research on 700 pairs of twins testing for the inheritance of mental qualities, namely the common eugenic assumptions about criminality as an inborn trait. As this book previously documents, Verschuer was the man in charge of the infamous Dr. Mengele's activities, thus Verschuer's work with twins must be considered as part of Mengele's horrid experiments on twins. In 1935, after Hitler took power, Verschuer and Fischer continued to work at the Institute, but Verschuer shifted his primary attention to the Frankfurt Institute for Genetic Biology and Racial Hygiene, leading the sterilization effort in the city of Frankfurt. In 1942, Verschuer succeeded Fischer as Director of the Kaiser-Wilhelm Institute and continued his twin studies. Two of Verschuer's most well-known assistants were Karin Magnussen and Josef Mengele. Case in point, Karin Magnussen studied eyes from twins at Auschwitz harvested for her by Mengele at Auschwitz. [388]

On March 27-28, 1941, Verschuer attended the Frankfurt Institute for the Investigation of the Jewish Question that ultimately resulted in the implementation of the Final Solution. He was also the director of the Hadamar Clinic and oversaw its participation in the T4 Euthanasia program. At the close of the war, Verschuer hid or destroyed evidence of the complicity of the Kaiser-Wilhelm Institute or kept records hidden at his family home. However, it must be remembered that members of the Allied prosecution at Nuremberg were keenly aware of these relationships. More precisely, it would be impossible to believe that the once member of the Kaiser Wilhelm Institute, Leo Alexander, was unaware of Verschuer's leadership role.

Eugen Fischer is the subject of historical ambivalence, where many have questioned his culpability in the atrocities of the Third Reich. Many have painted Fischer as the victim of professional coercion under Hitler's reign and questioned whether he was one of the rabid anti-Semites. This skin-deep characterization of what it meant to be a National Socialist misunderstands what "racism" meant for

---

[387] Pg. 437 - "Health, Race and German Politics Between National Unification and Nazism, 1870-1945", Paul Weindling, Oxford Univ. Press, 1998.

[388] Pg. 3 – "Eyes from Auschwitz. A lesson in National Socialist racial delusion and medical research. The case of Dr. Karin Magnussen", Hans Hesse, plain text, Essen 2001.

Adolf Hitler. Hitler learned about "scientific racism" from the likes of Eugen Fischer and not the other way around. This is where the 1999 commission by the Max-Planck institute clarifies, after half a century of stonewalling. One of the reasons for the change of name from Kaiser-Wilhelm to Max-Planck was to avoid the uncomfortable relationship between German science and Hitler's policies. Doris Kaufmann, one of the authors of the 1999 study *"Geschichte Der Kaiser-Wilhelm-Gesellschaft,"* documents that it was the Allied prosecution at Nuremberg which initially adopted and tacitly collaborated with the efforts of Third Reich scientists desperately trying to distance themselves from the crimes of The Holocaust:

> [T]he authorities considered that further investigation of hospitals and universities was undesirable, ... [because] if undertaken on a large scale it might result in necessary removal from German medicine of large number of highly qualified men at a time when their services are most needed. (Pg. 642, *"Geschichte Der Kaiser-Wilhelm-Gesellschaft"*, Wallstein verlag, 1999)

Leo Alexander clearly knew just how arbitrary this artificial line of demarcation truly was. The prosecutors released and exonerated doctors and scientists they knew to be culpable, and thus took that first decisive step in creating the myth of the coerced and victimized doctor under Hitler. They did so either in an attempt to maintain some semblance of order in the catastrophic conditions of post-war Germany, as Doris Kaufmann alludes, or to leave the ties between American doctors and institutions unexplored, as the case of Ernst Rüdin and Eugen Fischer exemplify. Fischer not only corresponded and collaborated regularly with the Cold Spring Harbor office that had been created with Rockefeller and Carnegie money, but the Rockefeller Foundation had given the money in 1927 to construct the wing of the Kaiser-Wilhelm Institute where Fischer's work would be developed. Like Rüdin, Fischer had personal contacts with Margaret Sanger, who personally invited Fischer to visit the United States and her home in 1930. Eugen Fischer and co-author Erwin Baur had attended Sanger's 1927 symposium on world population held in Geneva. As this book documents, Sanger would later establish the "Negro Project," where "birth control" was used as a eugenic measure to reduce the African-American population, much like Fischer had begun to propose with his Rhineland Bastard studies.

Sec. 3 - "HARD" VS. "SOFT" SCIENCE:

"Science commits suicide when it adopts a creed."
Herbert Spencer

Godfrey Harold "G. H." Hardy was a prominent English mathematician, known for his achievements in number theory and mathematical analysis. He shares credit for the Hardy-Weinberg Principle of 1908, which provided hard mathematical proof against the claims of the eugenicists. The principle was thus known as Hardy's Law in the English-speaking world until 1943 when Curt Stern pointed out that it had first been formulated independently in 1908 by the German physician Wilhelm Weinberg. By 1908, the equilibrium model developed by Godfrey N. Hardy and Wilhelm Weinberg disproved the claim that degenerate families were increasing the societal load of dysgenic genes. The Hardy-Weinberg equation also showed that sterilization of affected individuals would never appreciably reduce the percentage of mental defectives in humanity. At the same time, George Shull, at the Cold Spring Harbor Station for Experimental Evolution, showed that hybrid corn plants were more vigorous than pure-bred ones. Together, these findings refuted the notion that racial purity offered any biological advantage or that race-mixing destroys "good" racial types.

Consider the timing and weight of these scientific findings. The work by Hardy and Weinberg was hardly isolated or too obscure to have been noticed by the eugenic-minded scientific community. These principles were used to identify the various blood groups in humans; Felix Bernstein, working with funding from the Rockefeller Institute, used the principle to further refine the work of Karl Landsteiner.[389] In other words, there is no way the scientists behind eugenics could claim ignorance of its implications to the science of heredity.

Sober minded sceintists did ultimately take down the eugenics movement. On October 25th, 1938, the leadership of the Eugenics Research Association called a "special meeting" to change its name to "Association for Research in Human Heredity." As previously discussed in this book, a review panel convened by the Carnegie Institution in 1935 concluded that the majority of work sponsored by the Eugenics Record Office was without scientific merit and recommended a halt to its lobbying for eugenic social programs, such as sterilization and immigration restriction. They concluded that human genetics research should steer clear of eugenics in light of events transpiring in Germany.[390] A specifically damaging letter of June 3rd, 1935, by the man appointed by the Carnegie Institution to audit Cold Spring Harbor, Professor L.C. Dunn of Columbia University had to have been of some weight in the matter. The letter from Dunn to the Carnegie Institution directly questions whether the work that had been done at the Cold Spring Harbor facility was politically biased or fact-based:

---

[389] Pg. 119 – "Eugenics, Human Genetics and Human Failings: The Eugenics Society, its sources and its critics in Britain", Pauline M.H. Mazumdar, Routledge, 1992.

[390] Pg. 199 - "In the Name of Eugenics: Genetics and the Uses of Human Heredity", Daniel J. Kevles, Harvard Univ. Press, 1995.

In this connection I think it is open to question whether it is wise to continue such a record office under the patronage of a research institution as a "Eugenics Record Office." "Eugenics" has come to mean an effort to foster a program of social improvement rather than an effort to discover facts." (eugenicsarchive.org, Item ID:1092 – 1096, "L.C. Dunn letter to President Merriam, about eugenics in the U. S. and in Germany", multiple pages, Cold Spring Harbor Lab.)

The review panel was, in essence, calling for less politicized and a purer science; just the kind of science G.H. Hardy aspired to, and what his principle pointed the way to. This had to be the influence of Dunn's letter at play. Dunn closed his letter by informing Merriam that he viewed the methodology practiced at the Cold Spring Harbor facility as mirroring those practiced in National Socialist Germany and that neither was intent on finding scientific fact, but were rather the hollow exercises of those intent on limiting scientific and individual liberty:

> I have just observed in Germany some of the consequences of reversing this order as between program and discovery. The incomplete knowledge of today, much of it based on a theory of the state which has been influenced by the racial, class and religious prejudices of the group in power, has been embalmed in law, and the avenues to improvement in the techniques of improving the population have been completely closed. Although some progress may be made in reducing the proportion of those elements which are undesirable to the regime, the cost appears to be tremendous. The geneological record offices have become powerful agencies of the state, and medical judgments even when possible, appear to be subservient to political purposes. Apart from the injustices in individual cases, and the loss of personal liberty, the solution of the whole eugenic problem by fiat eliminates any rational solution by free competition of ideas and evidence. Scientific progress in general seems to have a very dark future." (eugenicsarchive.org, Item No.: 1092 – 1096, Cold Spring Harbor Lab.)

The 1935 letter from L.C. Dunn was copied to Harry H. Laughlin, and it suggested closing the Cold Spring Harbor facility and focusing any future efforts on a pure science-based research on "human heredity." It seems that Laughlin likely tried to insert himself into the changing directions of the Carnegie Institution by submitting proposals that adopted Dunn's suggestion that the focus of "eugenics" be dropped and "human heredity" and "genetics" be adopted. Correspondence in 1938 from Laughlin to the heads of the Carnegie Institution entitled "Proposed Clinic of Human Heredity" was part of his negotiations according to the correspondence in the archives. [391]

Laughlin's attempts to remain relevant and employed failed, as in 1939 Vannevar Bush, the president of the Carnegie Institution asked Laughlin to follow his mentor Davenport into retirement. Thus, in nothing more than the quiet internal politics and deliberations of an institution, the doors were shut on one of the most influential laboratories in 20th Century history. Charles B. Davenport and Harry H.

---

[391] Item ID# 1795–1804 - eugenicsarchive.org, Cold Spring Harbor Lab, DNA Learning Center.

Laughlin had significantly altered the course of history by cloaking themselves in the supposed objectivity of science and using their credentials to enact sterilization laws in 30 of the States in the Union, influence the creation of major immigration acts in the United States Congress, provide expert testimony for landmark cases before the US Supreme Court, and then turn over the benefit of their experience to the National Socialist government under Adolf Hitler.

More to the point, all this quiet political maneuvering transpired several decades after the Hardy-Weinberg Principle had provided hard evidence against the viability of eugenics. Why did it take science so long to do an about-face on eugenics? The scientific community didn't dispute the validity of the principle, they just seemed to refuse to believe that their previously held convictions that "defectives" should not reproduce were mistaken. After all, it had been no one less than Charles Darwin to propose that humanity could benefit from the animal breeder's. Commendable as Professor L.C. Dunn's frankness may have been, his recommendations were done quietly and behind the scenes. In the decades between when the scientific community was provided the Hardy-Weinberg Principle and the end of World War II, there were but a handful of insufficient efforts to speak up and contest eugenics. All but a handful of papers questioned the science, and less pointed to its violation of medical ethics.

In fact, the comparably pitiful handful of pages dedicated to questioning the validity of eugenics pales in comparison to the mountains of work, mostly authored by scientists or medical doctors, and mostly containing the "racialist" views we otherwise ascribe to incompetents such as Adolf Hitler. A "racialist" outlook was not just common; it was implicit and explicit to the consensus in the movement. The eugenics movement began with Charles Darwin proposing that evidence of evolution lay in the differences among the "races of the world," and with his estimation that British Anglo-Saxon Protestants were at the pinnacle of evolution, and the colored races were closer to apes than to man. Both Francis Galton and Charles Darwin intended for the Theory of Evolution to be interpreted as potentially working backward, where individuals or "races" could "degenerate," or de-evolve into a throwback, an atavism, where entire "races" could revert back to something closer to apes than a man through sexual selection. Eugenics simply would not exist without this fear for "degeneration," and in turn, the fear of "degeneration" would not exist without blind faith in Charles Darwin. Thus, countering or reversing the political influence of the likes of Darwin was no small task.

Devout Darwinists will equivocate that Agassiz, Spencer, and Nott had established a "racialist" science before Charles, and they would be right. However, it is equally true Darwinism was intentionally billed as a monumental turning point in history by its proponents from the onset, and that derision and ridicule were beset on anyone that dare doubt by its propagandists, namely Thomas H. Huxley. This was as true then, as it was leading up to The Holocaust. This is the reason so few scientists questioned eugenics even when science had disproven its basic foundations with the advent of the Hardy-Weinberg Principle in 1908. The careers of Francis Galton and Leonard Darwin would have been inconsequential, and the eugenics movement impotent if it wasn't for the politics that Darwinists peddled from the onset. This was the stated purpose of the X-Club after all, a topic this book will touch on later. The truth is that Francis, Leonard, and the eugenics movement purchased legitimacy and respectability with Charles Darwin's reputation.

Historians should stop regarding Hitler's "Mein Kampf" as original in any way, shape or form. It is no wonder so few people read it, as "Mein Kampf" was a sloppy plagiarism of disparate sources to the point of being an incoherent composition. The appalling realization isn't that "Mein Kampf" was singularly racist but rather that "Mein Kampf" reads exactly like the multitude of scientific journals and books that preceded it by decades, and that these supposedly legitimate works of science were just as viciously racist.

The notion that the eugenics movement could be cleanly divided into "positive" and "negative" eugenics is but another highly questionable affair as well, for there is no clear line of demarcation that can be drawn. It is more accurate to say that eugenicists recognized that there was more than one way to skin a cat, and mate choice was but one option next to segregation, sterilization, and outright elimination. A sculptor is a sculptor whether he detracts from marble or adds with clay. Anyone that has done an honest audit of the various eugenic books and articles quickly comes to terms with the scope and nature of the movement. Mainstream and leading eugenicists from around the world discussed dispensing with the "lower" 10 percent to 15 percent of the population for several generations. Thus, it is difficult to believe that scientists around the world didn't suspect that Hitler's National Socialists were carrying out precisely what they promised, especially when reports of the concentration camps started surfacing in the press. Legislators in the United States and Britain had spent a significant amount of time debating eugenic immigration and sterilization laws. The Poor Laws and various Mental Deficiency Acts in Britain as well as the major immigration bills and sterilization laws in the United States were all eugenic through and through and debated on a "racialist" polemic. Thus, it is hard to believe that the various generations of legislators, judges, and lawyers from that generation were genuinely surprised at what was transpiring in National Socialist Germany. Or more to the point, they did not recognize the overlaps and parallels between the racism of the German eugenicists and their American counterparts.

These observations should by no means be construed as an attack on science. To the contrary, this is intended to be high praise for those that practice "pure science," and which rightfully place science above the political fray that Darwinists are too often caught up in. The truth is that the Hardy-Weinberg Principle was pure science and thus lacked the propaganda megaphone that was integral to the eugenics movement. Francis Galton was not a scientist, and Harry H. Laughlin was not a lawyer. Yet, Galton passed off his amateurish work as scientific because he was Charles' cousin and Harry H. Laughlin passed himself off as an expert legislator to the US Congress because of his Ivy League credentials. The Hardy-Weinberg Principle shares its mundane and mind-numbing scientific nature with Gregor Mendel's work. Hardy was a pure mathematician and held applied mathematics in some contempt. He just happened to play cricket with the geneticist Reginald

Punnett, who, in turn, introduced the challenge of the mathematical problem to him after failing to counter the arguments of a fellow geneticist. Hardy thus became the somewhat unwitting founder of a branch of applied mathematics, which in turn disproved almost a century of work by eugenic-minded biologists. His affection for pure science is Hardy's intended legacy, and the best example one can use to defend true science against the intrusions of politicized scientists. Hardy was enamored by the purity of his science and not likely to engage in a debate about the validity of eugenics as the basis for society or government. Hardy preferred his work to be considered pure mathematics, perhaps because of his detestation of war and the military uses to which mathematics had been applied. He made several statements similar to that in his 1940 book "A Mathematician's Apology":

> I have never done anything 'useful'. No discovery of mine has made, or is likely to make, directly or indirectly, for good or ill, the least difference to the amenity of the world. (Pg. 83, G.H. Hardy, "A Mathematician's Apology", The University Press, 1940)

This is where the peculiar nature of Gregor Mendel's story gains further relevance. Gregor Mendel was a member of the clergy but was conducting "pure science" while the secular scientists, who used their work as a pulpit, gained the respect and recognition Mendel never saw during his lifetime. This is why historians don't wonder if the work of Gregor Mendel and Alfred Russell Wallace lead to the Holocaust. The reason is that none of them peddled the politics or propaganda that Thomas H. Huxley, Charles Lyell, Francis Galton, or Charles Darwin traded in. Darwinists made Darwinism a political issue, and thus set up Charles Darwin to be held responsible for the consequences of those political views. A long line of political stunts beginning with T.H. Huxley's X-Club on through the "Savage Debate," the Black Stork, and the Monkey Trial controversies were overly contentious, divisive, and fully manufactured outrage designed to make a scientific debate a socio-political one. These bully tactics persisted just long enough to help eugenics flourish with minimum criticism from the one profession that is built upon a healthy application of skepticism: SCIENCE.

Sec. 4 - ADOLF HITLER'S "IDEAL STATE":

A lot of paper and ink has been wasted psycho-analyzing Adolf Hitler. Much of it is well-intended in its search for some clue as to what pathological illness lay inside the mind of a madman. Most of it is centered around Hitler's youth, namely his years in Vienna. This book evidences that Hitler was hardly original in any of the elements of National Socialism that led up to and created The Holocaust. Hitler was just the political impetus for the long-held aspirations of many scientists, doctors, philosophers, political thinkers, and jurists before him. What is important to the subject matter of this book is analyzing the grander question of what type of personality is attracted to fashioning themselves "masters" and the making of "slaves." What type of personality finds self-worth in controlling the most intimate details of the lives of others, and more precisely, in controlling and administering the lives of total strangers? Conversely, what kind of person willingly surrenders control over the most intimate aspects of their lives to others? George Orwell was right; Hitler is but one of various others in a long line of "utopians," namely like H.G. Wells. The personality peculiarities of the "screaming defective" are important only as they fit the patterns and practices of the type. [392]

Adolf Hitler had from very early youth displayed a desire to control those around him. Hitler's teacher, Dr. Huemer, claimed that the young Adolf demanded the "unconditional subordination from his schoolmates." [393] This fact was verified by August Kubizek, Hitler's roommate in Vienna. Hitler moved to Vienna in 1906 and lived with Kubizek for more than three years. In his memoirs, Kubizek recalls the ranting and ravings of the young aspiring artist, which were by Kubizek's admission one-sided diatribes where the young Hitler lectured, and his friend was supposed to submit silently and approvingly. Reading Kubizek's memoirs leads one to an inescapable conclusion: that the young Hitler was the stereotypical antisocial, starving artist, whose philosophical influences were Schopenhauer and Nietzsche. [394] Predictably, as is typically the case with discontented artistic youth, the obtuse and pronounced socio-political criticism was the subject of his venting and lecturing:

> He was at odds with the world. Wherever he looked, he saw injustice, hate and enmity. Nothing was free from his criticism; nothing found favour in his eyes. (Pg. 153, "The Young Hitler I Knew: The Memoirs of Hitler's Childhood Friend", 1955)

Of note is how Kubizek describes the political diatribes that the young Adolf engaged in whenever Hitler communicated the opinionated views of a young, artist-activist youth:

> These speeches, usually delivered somewhere in the open, seemed to be like a volcano erupting. It was a though something quite apart from him was bursting out of him. Such rapture I had only witnessed so far in the theater, when an actor had to express some violent emotions, and at first, confronted by such eruptions, I could only stand gaping and passive, forgetting to applaud. But soon I realized that this was not play-acting. No, this was not acting, not exaggeration, this was really felt, and I saw that he was in dead earnest. Again and again I was filled with astonishment at how fluently he expressed himself, how vividly he managed to convey his feelings, how easily the words flowed from his mouth when he was completely carried away by his own emotions. Not what he said impressed me first, but how he said it. This to me was something new,

---

[392] "Wells, Hitler and the World State", George Orwell, Horizon, London, Aug. 1941.
[393] Pg. 11 – "Hitler's Vienna: A Dictator's Apprenticeship", Brigitte Hamann, Oxford Univ. Press, 1999.
[394] Pg. 183 – Ibid.

magnificent. I had never imagined that a man could produce such an effect with mere words. All he wanted from me, however, was one thing – agreement. (Pgs. 13–14, "The Young Hitler I Knew: The Memoirs of Hitler's Childhood Friend", 1955)

In fact, August Kubizek describes a surprising aspect of Hitler's youthful convictions. Hitler was, as are the stereotypical activist youths of past and present, a self-proclaimed "pacifist":

When I knew Adolf Hitler, he was utterly averse to "anything to do with war or soldiers.". . . The idea of compulsory military service could infuriate him. No, he would never let himself be forced into being a soldier. (Pgs. 77-78, "The Young Hitler I Knew: The Memoirs of Hitler's Childhood Friend", 1955)

Then again:
One night he spoke of the aeroplane of the Wright brothers. He quoted from a newspaper that these famous aviators had built a small, comparatively lightweight gun into their aircraft and had made experiments in the effect that shooting form the air would likely to have. Adolf, who was a pronounced pacifist, was outraged. As soon as a new invention is made, he said, it is immediately put into the service of war. (Pg. 245, "The Young Hitler I Knew: The Memoirs of Hitler's Childhood Friend", 1955)

True to the starving artist stereotype, the young Adolf Hitler also displayed a pronounced anti-religious sentiment and conviction:

As long as I knew Adolf Hitler I never remember his going to church. ... In conclusion, I would describe Hitler's attitude towards the church at the time as follows: he was by no means indifferent to the church, but the church could give him nothing. (Pgs. 80 – 81, "The Young Hitler I Knew: The Memoirs of Hitler's Childhood Friend", 1955)

August Kubizek's memoirs are cautiously considered and quoted herein, as many historians distrust the work of Hitler's cohorts or friends. This author views the memoirs of Kubizek, Speer, and Hanfstaengl as evidentiary testimony by firsthand witnesses to a crime. As is the case with any crime, the disparate witnesses are questionably reliable. They are, however, first-hand witnesses to a crime, and should be treated as such.

Kubizek describes a young artist who read tirelessly, wrote poems in a journal, and had no ambitions about money, only artistic and cultural accomplishment. [395] Kubizek documents how the young Hitler predictably had it out for the land-owning class, and how his lectures often ended in a "furious attack" on the "real estate speculators and the exploiting landlords." Kubizek explains how these diatribes against the land-owning class were part of the often discussed topic of city-planning

---

[395] Pgs. 92-93 - "The Young Hitler I Knew: The Memoirs of Hitler's Childhood Friend", August Kubizek, Houghton Mifflin, 1955.

by the young aspiring architect, and how in these lectures, Hitler would often convey how "private speculation in land would be forbidden." [396] Kubizek also documents how the young, starving artist-architect, had very well-developed socio-political ideals:

> Adolf was radically opposed to alcohol as he was to nicotine. ---- In any case, he found for this new Vienna a solution which was as radical as it was bold: a popular drink! ---- the firm Franck, who manufactured a coffee substitute. . . which cost only one heller a glass. Adolf liked this drink so much that he mentioned it again and again. If one could provide every household, he said, with this cheap and wholesome beverage, or with similar nonalcoholic drinks, one could do without the inns. When I remonstrated that the Viennese, from my knowledge of them, would be most unlikely to give up their wine, he replied brusquely, "You won't be asked!" as much as to say in other words "Nor will the Viennese either." ---- But he did not find a substitute for tobacco as a companion to his "People's Drink". (Pgs. 170 – 171, "The Young Hitler I Knew: The Memoirs of Hitler's Childhood Friend", 1955)

Kubizek describes how the young Adolf rolled all these problems into one all-encompassing solution: "The Ideal State." Everything, according to the young Adolf, could and would be solved "in the Storm of the Revolution":

> Another ever recurring expression was the "German Ideal State," which, together with the conception of the "Reich," was the dominating factor in his thinking. This "Ideal State" was in its basic principles, both national and social, social above all in respect to the poverty of the masses of the working class. More and more thoroughly, Adolf worked on the idea of a state which would give its to the social requirements of our times. (Pg. 172, "The Young Hitler I Knew: The Memoirs of Hitler's Childhood Friend", 1955)

Even the young architect's dreams were related to the "Social Reform" the young Adolf envisioned coming about through a "Revolution" and the erection of an "Ideal State":

> I asked Adolf, occasionally, what connection there was between the remote problems which we encountered during our visits to Parliament and his professional preparation. He would answer, "You can build only when you have first created the political conditions for it." (Pg. 181, "The Young Hitler I Knew: The Memoirs of Hitler's Childhood Friend", 1955)

Even music and art would be absorbed into the jurisdiction of the "Ideal State" and become an integral part of the "Social Reform" the young Adolf envisioned, a conviction that would be proven true by Joseph Goebbels's various propaganda efforts and the Exhibition of German Art:

> Even purely artistic experiences, like listening to a concert, which others accepted passively, roused his active interests and became problems of universal concern,

---

[396] Pgs. 167-169 – "The Young Hitler I Knew: The Memoirs of Hitler's Childhood Friend", August Kubizek, Houghton Mifflin, 1955.

for nothing was allowed to remain unimportant in the "Ideal State" of his dreams. (Pg. 206, "The Young Hitler I Knew: The Memoirs of Hitler's Childhood Friend", 1955)

Interestingly enough, even the most personal of affairs, sexuality and interpersonal relationships, were to be within the jurisdiction of the "Ideal State," though not yet by eugenic measures, but incidentally through the political schemes typical of socialism:

> When he used to describe to me in vivid terms the necessity of early marriage, which alone was capable of ensuring the future of the people; when he used to set forth for my benefits measures for increasing the number of children per family, measures which later were actually put into practice; when he expounded to me the connection between healthy housing and a healthy family life and described how, in his Ideal State, the problems of love, of sexual relations, of marriage, of family, of children would be solved. (Pg. 230, "The Young Hitler I Knew: The Memoirs of Hitler's Childhood Friend", 1955)

According to the young Adolf, his "Ideal State" would obviously eradicate social inequality, as any good socialist utopia aspires to accomplish:

> Of course, in the Ideal State there was no longer any Sink of Iniquity. With these words Adolf described the prostitution which was then rife in Vienna. - All this filled Adolf with boundless rage. But for this spreading prostitution he blamed not only those actually practicing it, but those responsible for the prevailing social and economic conditions. A "Monument to the Shame of our Times," he called prostitution. (Pgs. 234–235, "The Young Hitler I Knew: The Memoirs of Hitler's Childhood Friend", 1955)

All these convictions, with the exception of Hitler's youthful pacifism, were enshrined into law by the Adolf Hitler's National Socialist state. Hitler had been a utopian socialist from a very young age and persisted in his convictions to the day he died. Ironically enough, his friend Kubizek attributed Adolf's hard-headed obtuseness with inbreeding in the Hitler family:

> The most outstanding trait in my friend's character was, as I had experienced myself, the unparalleled consistency in everything that he said and did. There was in his nature something firm, inflexible, immovable, obstinately rigid, which manifested itself in his profound seriousness and was at the bottom of all his other characteristics. Adolf simply could not change his mind or his nature. Everything that lay in these rigid precincts of his being remained unaltered for ever. (Pg. 35, "The Young Hitler I Knew: The Memoirs of Hitler's Childhood Friend", 1955)

In fact, August Kubizek likely documented a horrific aspect of the older Adolf Hitler he probably did not intend to allude to. Kubizek, in retelling the story of young Adolf's enduring obsession for a young woman from Linz, recalls that Hitler would have them both commit suicide together, an altogether creepy revelation knowing the fate that would ultimately befall Eva Braun, along with all the other Hitler women that attempted or committed suicide:

> Adolf contemplated suicide seriously. He would jump into the river from the Danube bridge, he told me, and then it would be over and done with. But Stefanie would have to die with him – he insisted on that. (Pg. 64, "The Young Hitler I Knew: The Memoirs of Hitler's Childhood Friend", 1955)

The above observation isn't intended as a sidebar. Hitler's relationships with women point to a lust for control, which likely resulted in more than one of their suicides. This should hardly be a surprising aspect of a utopian socialist. Above all, what the young and old Hitler evidence is the "*libido dominandi*" inherent in socialist utopians. "*Libido dominandi*" is the term coined by St. Augustine, and it translates into "passion for domination." This certainly describes not just Hitler, but the other utopian socialists that aspired to control and regulate all aspects of their fellow humans. Gorman Beauchamp aptly describes this aspect of the "sadism" in "socialist utopias" by pointing out that totalitarian regimes "arise not so much because it is man's nature to be a slave as because they find effective ways of converting men into slaves." [397] Beauchamp quotes Bruno Bettelheim as he describes the mechanism "the inescapable power of the totalitarian regime rests exactly on its ability to reach into even the most minute and private life activities of the individual." [398] Likewise, Erich Fromm argues that the servile personality that willingly accepts a master is essentially masochistic, defining masochism as not merely a sexual but a social phenomenon. Fromm opines on the allure through which these regimes "convert men into slaves":

> The masochistic person…is saved from making decisions, saved from the final responsibility for the fate of his self, and thereby saved from the doubt of what decisions to make. He is also saved from the doubt of what the meaning of his life is or who "he" is. These questions are answered by the relationship to the power to which he has attached himself. The meaning of his life and the identity of his self are determined by the greater whole into which the self has submerged. (Pg. 173, "Escape from Freedom", Erich Fromm, Rinehart, Inc., 1941)

Erich Fromm's observations as to the application of "altruistic" undertones in collectivist and socialist societies certainly coincide with the same observations made by the famous individualist, Ayn Rand:

> The different forms which the masochistic strivings assume have one aim: to get rid of the individual self, to lose oneself; in other words, to get rid of the burden of freedom. ("The Legend of the Grand Inquisitor: The Utopian as Sadist", Gorman Beauchamp, Humanitas, Vol. XX, Nos. 1 and 2, 2007)

But if masochism describes the psychology of the ruled in totalitarian societies,

---

[397] Pgs. 126-151 - Gorman Beauchamp, "The Legend of the Grand Inquisitor: The Utopian as Sadist" Humanitas, Vol. XX, Nos. 1 and 2, 2007.
[398] Pg. 145 – Ibid. – Citing Bruno Bettelheim, "The Informed Heart: Autonomy in a Mass Age, Avon,1971, Pgs. 97-107.

what explains the psychology of the rulers? Fromm's answer is "sadism." Totalitarian rulers are sadists, in the sociological, not purely sexual sense. [399] Fromm expands on this observation:

> Not the infliction of pain per se, but the "wish for power," Fromm suggests, "is the most significant expression of sadism," which "appears frequently under the guise of love. The rule over another person, if one can claim that to rule over him is for the person's own sake, frequently appears as an expression of love, but the essential factor is the enjoyment of domination." Indeed, the sadist may give his victim "everything — everything except one thing: the right to be free and independent." The "love" that the benevolent sadist displays, that is, depends entirely on his ability to dominate; if this power ceases, so does his "love." ---- The sadistic person needs his object just as much as the masochistic needs his. . . In both cases the integrity of the individual self is lost." Therefore, Fromm concludes perceptively, "in a psychological sense, the lust for power is not rooted in strength but in weakness. It is the expression of the inability of the individual self to stand alone and live. (Pg. 148, "The Legend of the Grand Inquisitor: The Utopian as Sadist", Humanitas, Vol. XX, Nos. 1 and 2, 2007)

The observation that "utopias" are made up of masochist "slaves" and sadist "masters" can easily describe what transpired in Germany under Adolf Hitler. In 1943, the American Office of Strategic Services (OSS) received "A Psychological Analysis of Adolf Hitler: His Life and Legend," written by Walter C. Langer with assistance from other leading psychoanalysts, in an effort to help the Allies understand the dictator. The OSS report states that Hitler was "impotent" and had "possibly even a homosexual streak in him." The OSS was not off the mark. Hitler's personal valets and housekeepers reported that despite their best efforts, they were never able to find any proof or evidence that Eva Braun and Adolf Hitler had sexual relations. Eva Braun had her own adjoining bedroom, but no markings were ever left on the bedsheets, clothing, or undergarments carefully inspected by the nosy housekeepers. Nor were they able to detect, despite their best efforts, any excursions or encounters between the chancellor and his female companion. Poignantly enough, the fact that four of the six women Hitler had relationships with committed suicide points to an unnatural kind of relationship.

More to the point, Hitler claimed no such "impotence" when it came to his relationship with the German people. Hitler claimed to give himself fully to the German people and sacrifice of himself for their behalf. Without his position of Führer, he was nothing more than a social ingrate, and Hitler was keenly aware of this fact as this had been his pitiful reality until German socialists and nationalists took note of his oratory skills. Hitler needed to be Führer as much as his devotees needed him for their own self-worth. Case in point, Hitler often claimed that he had never married because he was "married to the German people." [400] This is only supported by the factoid claiming that Hitler confessed reaching orgasm at the peak

---

[399] Pg. 147 - "The Legend of the Grand Inquisitor: The Utopian as Sadist", Gorman Beauchamp, Humanitas, Vol. XX, Nos. 1 and 2, 2007.
[400] "Adolf and Eva", Dorothy Gallagher, New York Times, Nov. 16, 2011.

of his speeches to his doctors. [401] Thus, it can easily be argued that Adolf Hitler gleaned more physical satisfaction from his ability to make the German public enact the unspeakable than he did from any physical contact with his female companions.

Of note is that Hitler demanded that all possibility for Germany to live on past his demise be eradicated. What has come to be known as Hitler's "Nero Decree" of March 19, 1945, was the explicit "scorched earth" order from Hitler to Albert Speer. It may as well have been an order for Germany to commit suicide by his side, as did Eva Braun. In this sense, Hitler's relationship with the German people fits the "Utopian as Sadist" analysis proposed by Gorman Beauchamp. The Germans who willingly subjected themselves to National Socialism were nothing more than Hitler's masochistic mistress. This aspect of the chancellor was also perceived by the Office of Strategic Services:

> He is firmly convinced that the furious pace and the epochal age in which he lived and moved (he really is convinced that he is the motivating force and the moulder of that age) will terminate soon after his death, swinging the world by nature and inclination into a long span of digestive process marked by a sort of quiet inactivity.

Langer quotes Howard K. Smith:
I was convinced that of all the millions on whom the Hitler Myth had fastened itself, the most carried away was Adolph Hitler, himself. ("A Psychological Analysis of Adolf Hitler: His Life and Legend", Walter C. Langer and Henry A. Murray, OSS, 1943)

The 1934 book "The Revolutionary Ideas of the Marquis De Sade," by Geoffrey Gorer, documents the utopia crafted by the father of all sadists, the Marquis himself. The work and the life of the infamous Marquis are a testament to the sadism inherent in both fictional and actual utopias. In 1788, the Marquis de Sade crafted a story about the utopian city of Tamoe. De Sade's Tamoe was set upon an "unknown island" and its planned garden city was an essential part of its utopian scheme:

> …it was town-planned, consisting of circular boulevards set with uniform two-storey houses surrounded by gardens. When he reached the king's house he was astounded to notice that except for its slightly larger size it was no different from any other; there were no guards and no parade of any sort; people entered freely. (Pg. 156, "The Revolutionary Ideas of the Marquis de Sade", Geoffrey Gorer, Wishart & Company, 1934)

Predictably enough, the utopian Tamoe was the byproduct of disdain for "private property, class distinctions, religion," and most importantly, traditional morality. De Sade's fictional King Zamè had once traveled to Europe with the explicit mandate from his father to gather knowledge, much as the "Merchants of Light" of Francis Bacon's imagination. Europe had frightened him, and Tamoe had

---

[401] "The Life and Times of Adolf Hitler", Joshua Hehe, Medium Mag., Dec. 18, 2017.

been designed specifically to avoid becoming like Europe:
> He found the greatest causes of European misery in four things — private property, class distinctions, religion and family life. He therefore proceeded to abolish or transform these institutions. Absolutely all property was made over to the State. Under certain conditions people had the usufruct of property, provided that they developed it properly, during their life-time; on death it reverted automatically to the State. The State controlled all manufactures. Since everybody was working for the State, directly or indirectly, and since all had equal wealth — or rather commodities and comfort — class distinctions were abolished. (Pg. 157, "The Revolutionary Ideas of the Marquis de Sade", Geoffrey Gorer, Wishart & Company, 1934)

The parallels persist. As was the case with Edward Bellamy's industrial army, the citizenry of Tamoe was organized into an "industrial army" of centrally planned labor:
> Outstanding civic virtue was rewarded by military titles — which are meaningless but flatter the holder. — People with irremediable anti-social characters were exiled. — Only crimes which harm society were taken any notice of. — If people neglected their land they were moved to uncultivated ground where greater effort was required for the same result; if they showed improvement their original home was given back to them. (Pg. 159, "The Revolutionary Ideas of the Marquis de Sade", Geoffrey Gorer, Wishart & Company, 1934)

The King's home was just one way to demonstrate his egalitarian standing among all citizens of Tomoe. The dietary choices and plain lifestyle are noteworthy as well:
> He had nothing which the poorest of his subjects hadn't got. Like them he was a vegetarian and water drinker, not from motives of religion, but of diet and humanity. (Pg. 161, "The Revolutionary Ideas of the Marquis de Sade", Geoffrey Gorer, Wishart & Company, 1934)

True to the secularist and anti-clerical aspects of the typical utopian proposal, de Sade's fictional government had strict controls over the minds and hearts of its citizens. Religion was banished, other than the worship of Nature:
> All priests were banished and religion reduced to a vague theistic Nature worship, of a voluntary nature. There were not temples and no vested interest in religion. There were also no professional lawyers and discussion of theology or laws punished as one of the gravest anti-social crimes. There was no money and commerce was restricted to exchange within the island. (Pg. 160, "The Revolutionary Ideas of the Marquis de Sade", Geoffrey Gorer, Wishart & Company, 1934)

As was the case in Adolf Hitler's National Socialist utopia, art had a specific propaganda function, and public consumption of art that deviated from the message, or that was art for art's sake, was explicitly forbidden:

All luxury arts were forbidden. Painting, music, dancing, the theater were encouraged but were only developed by amateurs. All the art was inclined to furnish moral propaganda. (Pg. 160, "The Revolutionary Ideas of the Marquis de Sade", Geoffrey Gorer, Wishart & Company, 1934)

More to the point, population control was integral to the scheme. "Celibacy" was considered to be "anti-social" in a society that punished persistent "anti-social" behavior by exile. "Divorce was granted at the request of either party," but "nobody was allowed more than two divorces." [402] The unmarried and divorced "had smaller houses and less land." The children of the marriage were put into a State school as soon "as soon as they were weaned" where the parents could visit, but the children were not allowed to leave. [403] De Sade had very specific ideas about "optimum population" and according to Geoffrey Gorer, "reaches conclusions very similar to those put forward by Malthus three years later in his Essay of Population." Gorer quotes de Sade, who was against the preservation of malformed or diseased children:

> Any child who is born without the necessary qualities which will allow him to become one day a useful citizen has no right to life and the best thing to do is to deprive him of it the moment he gets it. (Pg. 152, "The Revolutionary Ideas of the Marquis de Sade", Geoffrey Gorer, Wishart & Company, 1934)

Gorer documents that de Sade was a participating member of the French Revolution, as well as one of its causes. However, it is interesting to note that when the "senseless butcheries of the Terror" occurred, de Sade distanced himself from his fellow revolutionaries. The most striking and telling incident is that because of the Revolution, de Sade was named "president of the bench" in the court that by coincidence tried the very aristocrats that had placed him in a prison cell for decades, the President and Madame de Montreuil, de Sade's former in-laws. "With magnanimity worthy of his heroine Justine, he voted against their execution." [404] This, of course, landed de Sade in jail again, as his fellow revolutionaries punished "moderantism." Gorer documents that de Sade was staunchly against violence that lacked justification, rhyme, or reason. He was against the death penalty from "his earliest works onward":

> The law is false when it merely punishes, detestable when its only object is to destroy the criminal without teaching him, to frighten without improving him, and to commit an infamy as great as the original one without gaining anything from it. -- Is murder a crime or not? If it is not, why punish it? If it is, why punish it by a similar crime?" (Pgs. 146-148, "The Revolutionary Ideas of the Marquis de Sade", Geoffrey Gorer, Wishart & Company, 1934)

All of de Sade's magnanimity and disdain for senseless violence poses an interesting juxtaposition between the two most infamous sadists of all time; Adolf Hitler and the Marquis de Sade. Clearly the Marquis de Sade's "sadism" was not to

---

[402] Pg. 159 - "The Revolutionary Ideas of the Marquis de Sade", Geoffrey Gorer, Wishart & Company, 1934.
[403] Pg. 157 – Ibid.
[404] Pg. 57 – Ibid.

be found in a pseudo-sexual lust for blood or carnage, but in a deeper and more sophisticated type of sadism: His insatiable appetite to make others do unspeakable acts, acts they would not have played part in without de Sade's persuasion. The perverse side of de Sade, which ultimately enshrined his name as the very essence of "sadism," was his "passion for domination," his *"Libido Dominandi,"* his pleasure in working up lesser intellects and weaker souls into a frenzy orchestrated by himself. This is a type of sadism that runs deeper than a fleeting lust of a purely physical and sexual nature. It is a lust of the kind that satisfies hungrier entities nearer to Mephistopheles, Machiavelli, and maybe Lucifer himself. It is a lust to possess, control, and direct even the most intimate and personal aspects of another human being. We make the assumption that 'money' is the 'root of all evil,' but seldom make the connection that money is just another tool or implement in the sadist's dungeon; money is an implement of control. What is the root of all greed? Control; a lust for control, a "Libido Dominandi." How does a sadistic lust for control blossom as fundamentally evil? Any insulation that discards empathy and shields the sadist from the consequences of the domination of others is at its essence evil; no different than the emotional shield the Nietzschean Nazis erected when they deemed "compassion" to be "weakness." The desire to control the most intimate aspects of humanity, namely the reproductive rights of others is sadism at its worst; when it comes to eugenics, it is sadistic dominance masqueraded as a science.

As de Sade's magnanimity proved, the sadist's lust was only satisfied for him if the participants willingly submitted themselves to control by a master. Thus, as Erich Fromm proposes, the indispensable ingredient to "sadism" is the willing participation of the "masochist." Gorer provides an exchange between characters in de Sade's "Juliette," and points to the astounding modernity of the book, which was written in the eighteenth century, but which spoke to the realities of Hitler's Germany or Stalin's USSR: "Tyranny, which first frightens sovereigns, or rather those that govern them, ends almost always in providing them with pleasures." [405]

If we are to believe Erich Fromm, then the fact that the father of "sadism" created a "socialist utopia" is much more than just a coincidence. The "Ideal State" crafted by the Marquis de Sade was an overt exercise in his "sadism," as was the "Ideal State" of Hitler's creation. Gorer provides some insight into de Sade's powers of persuasion, which in turn inform us about Adolf Hitler's talent with oratory:

> De Sade clearly foresaw the revolution that was approaching, even prophesying it in some of his writings. It is even tempting to say that he caused it. In June of 1789 he tried to escape by forcing his way through the sentries but was prevented. Thereupon he had the idea of inciting the people against the Bastille, which he did by scattering from his windows notes describing the bad treatment the prisoners were receiving; on July 2 he improvised a loudspeaker from a tube and a funnel and called on the populace to rescue the prisoners who were having their throats cut. A crowd was gathered by this device and the governor of the prison thought sufficiently seriously of the danger to write: "If Monsieur de Sade is not removed to-night from the Bastille I cannot be answerable to the King for

---

[405] Pg. 97 – "The Revolutionary Ideas of the Marquis de Sade", Geoffrey Gorer, Wishart & Company, 1934.

the safety of the building." On July 3 he was therefore transferred to the asylum of Charenton. Eleven days later the ancient and almost empty fortress of the Bastille was stormed by the mob, whose anger against it had been so inexplicably roused. (Pg. 53, "The Revolutionary Ideas of the Marquis de Sade", Wishart & Company, 1934)

By their own accounts, "socialist utopias" require a "unity of purpose" and a "solidarity" among the masses, and the "purpose" under which all "unify" is the prerogative of the benevolent leadership and the elite. "Solidarity" in this sense is nothing more than "submission," to the extent to which these socialist schemes intrude into the very personal aspects of the lives of the people, be it marriage, reproduction, or parenting decisions. To willingly surrender these very personal aspects of an individual's life to the will of a "master" is, in essence, to surrender one's individuality. The phraseology of the socialists evidences this aspect of surrender of individual autonomy. The people are de-personalized by becoming known as the "masses," a phrase that a government concerned with the upholding of individual rights would otherwise refrain from using.

Geoffrey Gorer reminds us of that often cited Vladimir Lenin maxim that you "keep the people in ignorance and superstition. . .because you fear them if they are enlightened; you drug them with opium. . . so that they shall not realize the way you oppress them." [406] As this book documents, Lenin's "opium" could easily be Aldous Huxley's "soma," as both were utilized to keep the "masses" in a complacent stupor. The famous author, George Orwell picked up on this "sadistic" aspect of "utopian" governments and how they are at odds with the ideal of individual autonomy or sovereignty. Orwell's "Nineteen Eighty-Four" depicts Oceania as a collectivist society held together, not by force, but by propaganda and persuasion. "Nineteen Eighty-Four's" entire storyline is a play on the relationship between the "masses" and their "sadistic" master, who insists on actively monitoring the minds and hearts of his subjects through technology. "Big Brother" has a monitor in the bedrooms of every subject, and opinions are formed through the "Ministry of Truth." Oceania holds control over the sexual relationships of its subjects and punishes behavior it deems to be antagonistic to the solidarity of the social body. "Nineteen Eighty-Four" culminates in the "sadistic" reformation of its protagonist, as he is coerced to submit, acknowledging basic facts he knows to be false, such as how many fingers the inquisitor is actually holding up, as opposed to how many fingers were actually held up. As with other "socialist" and "collectivist" utopias, the suffering is insufficient to quench the desires of the benevolent and self-sacrificing master. Nothing but the complete submission to the will of the "sadist" satisfies the lust implicit in being a "master." In this way, socialism was from its inception, a submission of the masochistic masses to the will of the sadistic elite. The calls for "solidarity" by the altruistic leaders are now, and have always been demands for "submission" from those desiring to fully surrender themselves, no different than the textbook "masochist" beg for direction from their "masters."

---

[406] Pg. 122 - "The Revolutionary Ideas of the Marquis de Sade", Geoffrey Gorer, Wishart & Company, 1934.

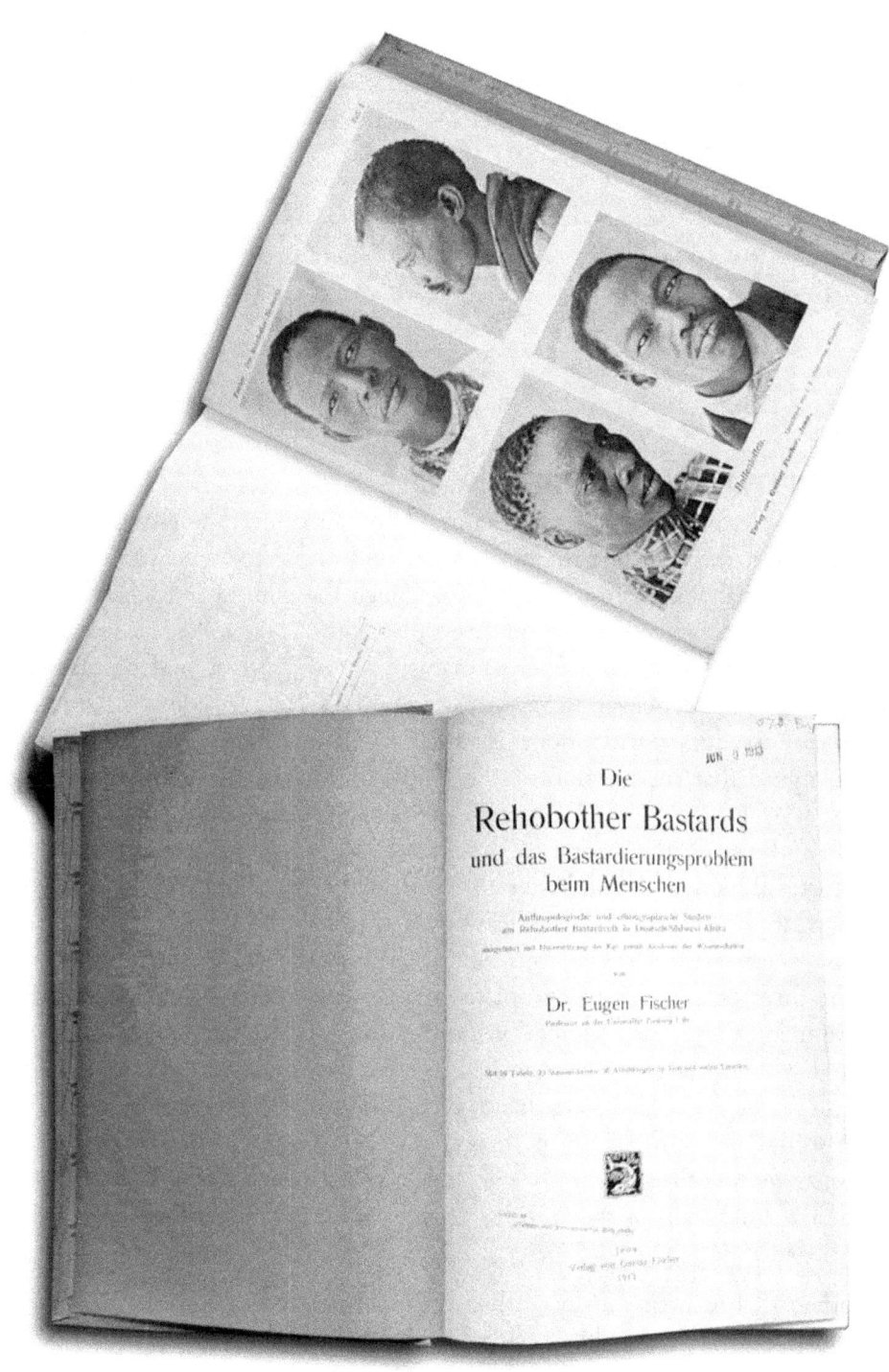

FIGURE 10: Charles B. Davenport's and Harry H. Laughlin's copy of Eugen Fischer's *"Rehobother Bastards."* This copy was part of the Eugenics Records Office library and is part of the Cold Spring Harbor library collection today.

Chap. 9: 1905 to 1901

NEW WORLD: THE US STOCK MARKET CRASHES. – US VICE PRESIDENT THEODORE ROOSEVELT FAMOUS PHRASE, "SPEAK SOFTLY AND CARRY A BIG STICK." – AMERICAN ANARCHIST LEON CZOLGOSZ SHOOTS US PRESIDENT WILLIAM MCKINLEY AT THE PAN-AMERICAN EXPOSITION. MCKINLEY DIES 8 DAYS LATER. – THEODORE ROOSEVELT SUCCEEDS WILLIAM MCKINLEY AS PRESIDENT OF THE UNITED STATES. **SCIENCE & TECHNOLOGY:** ALBERT EINSTEIN PUBLISHES HIS PAPER ON A HEURISTIC VIEWPOINT CONCERNING THE PRODUCTION AND TRANSFORMATION OF LIGHT, IN WHICH HE EXPLAINS THE PHOTOELECTRIC EFFECT USING THE NOTION OF LIGHT QUANTA. – ALBERT EINSTEIN SUBMITS HIS DOCTORAL DISSERTATION ON THE MOTION OF SMALL PARTICLES..., IN WHICH HE EXPLAINS BROWNIAN MOTION. IN THE COURSE OF THE YEAR, EINSTEIN PUBLISHES 4 PAPERS, FORMULATES THE THEORY OF SPECIAL RELATIVITY AND EXPLAINS THE PHOTOELECTRIC EFFECT BY QUANTIZATION. 1905 IS REGARDED AS HIS "MIRACLE YEAR." – ALBERT EINSTEIN PUBLISHES THE ARTICLE ON THE ELECTRODYNAMICS OF MOVING BODIES WHERE HE REVEALS HIS THEORY OF SPECIAL RELATIVITY. - THE WRIGHT BROTHERS' THIRD AEROPLANE (WRIGHT FLYER III) STAYS IN THE AIR FOR 39 MINUTES WITH WILBUR PILOTING. **LIFE**: DR. SEUSS, AMERICAN CHILDREN'S AUTHOR IS BORN. – REINHARD HEYDRICH, GERMAN NAZI OFFICIAL IS BORN. – SALVADOR DALÍ, SPANISH ARTIST IS BORN. ALOIS HITLER, AUSTRIAN CIVIL SERVANT, FATHER OF ADOLF HITLER DIES – JOHN DILLINGER, AMERICAN BANK ROBBER, GEORGE ORWELL, ENGLISH AUTHOR, AND HERBERT SPENCER, ENGLISH PHILOSOPHER, WERE BORN. WALT DISNEY, AMERICAN ANIMATOR AND FILM PRODUCER IS BORN.

Sec. I - "IN THAT HOUR IT BEGAN. . .":

Adolf Hitler has been quoted as stating that "one cannot understand National Socialism, if one does not understand Wagner," and who is to argue with the central figure of National Socialism as to just how much the composer Richard Wagner influenced the creation of the National Socialist state?

In Wagner, we find Hitler's vegetarianism, anti-Semitism, and his insatiable appetite for the drama of war. In Wagner, we also find Hitler's sadistic need to have total control over his creation, down to the last detail, and every last player. It can easily be argued that the erection of the National Socialist state and its dramatic bloodlust was, in fact, a large Wagnerian production, with Adolf Hitler being the designer of the stage, the costumes, the underlying concept, the storyline, and its protagonist, soliloquies and all. After all, Adolf Hitler was the man responsible for the design of the swastika, its application to the flag, the standards, the various uniforms, as well as the various props such as the cars, the armaments, and the stage set in the form of the various city plans he worked on with Albert Speer. Hitler commissioned extravagant presentations in the form of the Nuremberg Rallies and insisted that all their glory be captured as an art form by Leni Riefenstahl in "Triumph of the Will." Hitler was his own tragic figure and protagonist, who wrote his own soliloquies in the form of the extravagantly presented political rallies and speeches, as would otherwise be found in the Wagnerian opera of "Rienzi." Hitler's childhood friend recalls as much in the chapter from his memoirs titled "In That Hour it Began. . .":

> Hitherto I had been convinced that my friend wanted to become an artist, a painter, or perhaps an architect. Now this was no longer the case. Now he aspired to something higher, which I could not yet fully grasp. It rather surprised me, as I thought that the vocation of the artist was for him the highest, most desirable goal. But now he was talking of a *mandate* which, one day, he would receive from the people, to lead them out of servitude to the heights of freedom. – It was an unknown youth who spoke to me in that strange hour. He spoke of a special mission which one day would be entrusted to him, and I, his only listener,

could hardly understand what he meant. Many years had to pass before I realized the significance of this enraptured hour for my friend. (Pg. 100, "The Young Hitler I Knew: The Memoirs of Hitler's Childhood Friend", August Kubizek, Houghton Mifflin Company, 1955)

Kubizek's memoirs must be read with a bit of skepticism, as any first-hand account of a gargantuan catastrophe must be treated as a police officer takes into account the point-of-view of all eyewitnesses. That said, there is no sensible reason to doubt some of Kubizek's accounts, as they do nothing to exonerate Kubizek, Nazism, or Hitler. Several of Kubizek's recollections support accepted Hitler profiles, and more importantly, coincide with known aspects of Hitler's views and policies. Thus, Kubizek's recollections must be weighed as any witness accounts would be when observation aligns with occurrence.

With that in mind, the "hour" August Kubizek was referring to in the above quote was November 1905, after he and the young Adolf attended the playing of Wagner's "Rienzi" in Linz, a moment which the older Hitler would refer to time and time again. Kubizek described it as "the most impressive hour I ever lived through with my friend." [407] In "Rienzi," we find the tragic political figure, his monumental rise, and his dramatic and catastrophic downfall. Kubizek recalls that "never before and never again have I heard Adolf Hitler speak as he did in that hour," and thus conveys:

> Usually, after an artistic experience that had moved him, he would start talking straight away, sharply criticizing the performance, but after Rienzi he remained quiet a long while. This surprised me, and I asked him what he thought of it. He threw me a strange, almost hostile glance. "Shut up!" he said brusquely. ---- He looked almost sinister, and paler than ever. (Pg. 99, "The Young Hitler I Knew: The Memoirs of Hitler's Childhood Friend", August Kubizek, Houghton Mifflin Company, 1955)

The overpowering ending to Rienzi was full of roaring shouts of "Rienzi, Heil! Heil, people's tribune!" [408] It is thus easy to understand why National Socialist propaganda posed Hitler as a Reinzi reincarnate. This is likely why the overture in "Rienzi" became the anthem to which the many Nuremberg party conventions would be introduced.

Wagner and Hitler were both incredibly attentive to the venue in which their message was delivered. Wagner works were performed in a specially designed opera house; the "*Bayreuth Festspielhaus*," or "Festival Theatre," was designed and built by Wagner himself in 1871. Like Hitler after him, Wagner relied on inventions where current technology did not satisfy the immediate artistic needs. The innovations included darkening the auditorium during performances and placing the orchestra in a pit out of view of the audience. According to Albert Speer, even as the leader

---

[407] Pg. 98 - "The Young Hitler I Knew: The Memoirs of Hitler's Childhood Friend", August Kubizek, Houghton Mifflin, 1955.
[408] Pg. 24 – "Hitler's Vienna: A Dictator's Apprenticeship", Brigitte Hamann, Oxford, 1999.

of the Reich, Hitler still sketched stage-design concepts for Wagner operas and suggested them to his favorite stage manager, Benno von Arendt. Hitler would brag to dinner guests how he "sat over them for three weeks, night after night," despite his full appointment calendar as Chancellor. [409] Many of these architectural and design concepts made their way into the various Nuremberg party rallies. While the famously theatric "domes of light" or "cathedral of light" were Speer's design, the sea of red flags, the marching up towards the main stage to music by Wagner as darkness set, largely originated from Hitler's devotion to Wagnerian melodrama. [410]

Wagner was also an extremely prolific political pundit, authoring hundreds of books, poems, and articles throughout his life, many of a distinctly political nature. His writings covered a wide range of topics, including politics, philosophy, and detailed analyses of his own operas. Wagner's most infamous text was his *"Das Judenthum in der Musik"* or "Jewishness in Music," which he published in 1850. The work was a diatribe directed against Jewish composers in general and Giacomo Meyerbeer in particular. Needless to say, Hitler found inspiration for his anti-Semitism in Wagner, as the "Exhibition of Degenerate Art" would later evidence:

> …with all our speaking and writing in favour of the Jews' emancipation, we always felt instinctively repelled by any actual, operative contact with them. (Pg. 302, "Richard Wagner and the Jews", Milton E. Brener, McFarland, 2011)

Wagner argued that because Jews had no connection to the German spirit, Jewish musicians were only capable of producing shallow and artificial music. They therefore composed music to achieve popularity and, thereby, financial success, as opposed to creating genuine works of art: "Our whole European art and civilization. . . have remained to the Jew a foreign tongue." Wagner continues:

> …their racial difference prevented them from partaking in and contributing to European culture. They were unable to compose music because they lacked passion and were singularly devoted to the lure of money. In short, their alienness from the Volk community prevented them from producing truly original works of art. (Pg. 49, "Defenders of the Race: Jewish Doctors and Race Science in Fin-de-siècle Europe", John M. Efron, Yale Univ. Press, 1994)

Wagner republished his anti-Semitic pamphlet under his own name in 1869, with an extended introduction, leading to several public protests at the first performances of *Die Meistersinger*. He repeated similar views in later articles, such as "What is German?" Like Wagner, Hitler regarded his anti-Semitism to be nothing like the low-brow brand of "vulgar" anti-Semitism, and as with all other things Hitler, the influence from the composer became central to Hitler's ethos. Hitler's vegetarianism was but one way to mimic and pay homage to his idol. Wagner's political writings were Hitler's bible, and the pomposity of his style influenced Hitler whose education was, to say the least, incomplete. It was precisely in Richard Wagner that Hitler found the "granite foundations" for his views of the world. For

---

[409] Pg. 67 - "Hitler's Vienna: A Dictator's Apprenticeship", Brigitte Hamann, Oxford Univ. Press, 1999.
[410] Pg. 68 – Ibid.

example, in 1880, Wagner wrote at length about the benefits of vegetarianism, some of which can be found in "The Highest Motive for Vegetarianism" which is part of Wagner's essays from "Religion and Art." Note the similarities in radical thought:

> In an 1881 essay, Wagner had claimed that the human race had become contaminated and impure through racial mixing and the eating of animal flesh; a new kind of socialism was needed to purify Germany of these twin evils, calling upon "true and hearty fellowship with the vegetarians, the protectors of animals, and the friends of temperance" to save the German people from Jewish aggression. Wagner claimed that abstaining from a fleshy diet would allow a human moral redemption – possibly even for the Jews. (Pg. 136, "Nazi War on Cancer", Robert Proctor, Princeton Univ. Press, 2000)

Hitler claimed he was vegetarian due to his devotion to Richard Wagner: "I don't touch meat largely because of what Wagner says on the subject." [411] Wagner apparently made various attempts to be a consistent vegetarian in his daily life but was not fully consistent as has been documented about Hitler as well. Cosima Wagner's diary entry recalls that Wagner struggled "with an oath he has sworn not to eat meat, but only vegetables." Nietzsche was another distinct influence on Hitler, and it is by no coincidence that Nietzsche was also a vegetarian. [412] This is confirmed by the personal correspondence of Nietzsche's sister, Elizabeth. [413]

The commonalities persist. The Theosophists, which was a faith that appealed to eugenicists like Margaret Sanger and Helen Keller, thought the composer was one of them. "Richard Wagner and the English," by Theosophist Anne Dzamba Sessa claims that "all the sacred books of the East are there" in Wagner's library. She claims that Wagner expressed Buddhist views when corresponding with fellow composers and that Wagner told the infamous racist, Joseph Arthur Comte de Gobineau, that he was a Buddhist at heart. She quotes eugenicist Havelock Ellis as interpreting the "subtle mysticism . . . streaming over every bar of the music" and the occult influence in Wagner's music. The Madame of Theosophy herself, Helene P. Blavatsky, recognized Wagner as one of her own. [414] Consider this observation by a contemporary art critic attempting to understand the artistic impulses and inspiration of the famous German painter Max Beckmann:

> A lot of Theosophical theology dovetailed with Nazi mysticism. Many Theosophists, for example, believed that Richard Wagner was "the last of the initiates." Italian Futurism, grounded in Theosophy, was a precursor to Mussolini, and the return to nature and the reification of female fecundity characteristic of the Nazi volk were also elements of Theosophy. (artnet.com, "Deciphering Beckmann", Charlie Finch, July 17, 2003)

Why are Wagner's and Nietzsche's dietary habits of importance in a study of

---

[411] Pg. 136 - "Nazi War on Cancer", Robert Proctor, Princeton Univ. Press, 2000.
[412] ivu.org - "History of Vegetarianism - Friedrich Wilhelm Nietzsche", International Vegetarian Union – citing Cosima Wagner, Sept. 19, 1869.
[413] Ibid – citing "The Nietzsche-Wagner Correspondence", Pg. 45, "Experiences during the Winter of 1870", 1922.
[414] Pgs. 131-133 - "Lucifer: A Theosophical Magazine", Sept. 1887 – Feb. 1888.

the ideology that led to The Holocaust? In part, Hitler's and Wagner's vegetarianism is of historical importance as it evidences the influences they had in common. More importantly, both pivotal figures confused personal preference with political compulsion. The confusion of personal preference and political compulsion is central to any conversation about sadistically intrusive governmental controls. Hitler would seek out approval from Wagner's family and would make pilgrimages to Wagner festivals and the Wagner family home. Hitler invited his childhood friend August Kubizek to one of these gatherings 33 years after that pivotal experience that night of 1905 in Linz:

> In 1939, shortly before war broke out, when I, for the first time visited Bayreuth as the guest of the Reichs Chancellor, ... after a few words I sensed that he vividly recalled that hour and had retained all its details in his memory. He was visibly pleased that my account confirmed his own recollections. I was also present when Adolf Hitler retold this sequel to the performance of Rienzi in Linz to Frau Wagner, at whose home we were both guests. Thus, my own memory was doubly confirmed. The words with which Hitler concluded his story to Frau Wagner are also unforgettable for me. He said solemnly, **"In that hour it began."** (emphasis mine, Pg. 101, "The Young Hitler I Knew: The Memoirs of Hitler's Childhood Friend", August Kubizek, Houghton Mifflin, 1955)

Sec. 2 - FROM "MITTGART" TO "LEBENSRAUM":

Willibald Hentschel Varuna was a German agrarian, a *völkisch* writer, and political activist. His name was derived from the Hindu god of heaven. Hentschel studied for his doctorate under Ernst Haeckel at the University of Jena, and Hentschel was a devoted disciple of Haeckel that extrapolated Haeckel's Monism to its logical conclusion: a eugenic utopia that would start over by explicitly excluding the traditional religions and all the other "degenerating" influences that Monists deemed a danger to the Nordic race. In 1904, he published the book *"Mittgart"* in which he outlined a scheme to send 1000 ethnically pure women and 100 men picked for their military and athletic prowess to large country estates to procreate. Their children would then leave the estates at the age of 16 with the aim of traveling Germany and renewing the German racial stock. In *"Mittgart"* we find the early beginnings of the alternative lifestyle and philosophy that would later fuel both the German eugenic and utopian socialist movements, which in turn would become the basis for National Socialism. The eugenic thinking of the movement, along with its insistence to expand Germany for its allegedly superior racial stock, would become the basis of Hitler's "*Lebensraum*" expansionist policy. More so, the movement was a rebellion against the effects of capitalism and industrialization. Desperation for a radical social and cultural restructuring waivered created the hopes of an ever-improving economic progression as the filth, high-mortality, and social upheavals associated with urbanization and industrialization. These anxieties found expression in movements of international socialism, imperialism, anti-Semitism, and *Lebensreform*. [415] Willibald Hentschel further argued that in time the countryside would be the only place were pure Germans would be found. The colony was meant to actively accomplish the goal of cleansing Germans from the effects of "Semitism," while the cities would become segregated ghettos for the biologically unfit. [416]

Many other communes sprung up in Europe in the 1880s, and most were driven by a back-to-nature health movement coupled with some form of eugenic or socialist organization. Among them were the vegetarian colony, *Heimgarten*, founded in 1892, and *Eden* in 1893. They shared in common this devotion to a "natural" thinning of humanity's weaker elements as an organizing principle. They were organized along eugenic means, "without pity for the weak and for individual preference." [417] The movement was also integral to the "Garden City" movement, which eugenicists such as Alfred Ploetz were involved in. The utopian organization *Bund deutscher Bondenreformer,* for example, was a garden city and housing political organization that was among the most influential lobbying groups dedicated to urban renewal.

Hentschel founded the *Mittgart-Bund* to publicize his ideas and began preparations for the actual colony, which would be in Lower Saxony. The colony did not survive World War I. Hentschel's utopian socialist proposal attracted criticism not only from conservatives as an attack on the traditional family unit as well as from eugenic-minded propagandists who at this point in history were desperately trying to establish the legitimacy and seriousness of their scientific proposals. However, Mittgart did not depart history without first influencing some key figures. Alfred Ploetz was privately sympathetic but publicly critical of the polygamist nature of the experiment. Ploetz was not sold on the abstention from technology, and that the "progress of man could not be achieved by going back to an idealized culture of the past." [418] The German eugenicist, Wilhelm Schallmayer, called the program a "harmless private breeding enterprise in favor of the Nordic race." [419]

After World War I, Hentschel revised his idea, calling instead for migration of ethnic Germans into the east of the country to displace the Poles living there. Hentschel called for these Germans to be "*Artamanen*," a word he coined from *art* and *manen*, a Middle High German term meaning 'agriculture man' and indicating his desire for a retreat from urban life to an idyllic rural past. Hentschel's

---

[415] Pgs. 61-62 - "Health, Race and German Politics Between National Unification and Nazism, 1870-1945", Paul Weindling, Oxford Univ. Press, 1998.
[416] Pg. 152 - "Scientific Origins of National Socialism", Daniel Gasman, Transaction Publishers, 2007.
[417] Pg. 80 - "Health, Race and German Politics Between National Unification and Nazism, 1870-1945", Paul Weindling, Cambridge Univ. Press, 1993.
[418] Pg. 179 - "Nineteen Eighty-Four: Science Between Utopia and Dystopia" Everett Mendelsohn and Helga Nowotny, Springer Netherlands,1984.
[419] Pg. 179 – Ibid.

Artamanenbund was later absorbed into the National Socialist *Reichsnährstand* or Reich Agriculture Corporation under Walter Darré in 1933. [420] The organization was intended to promote the peasant warrior values; a core concept of what Adolf Hitler would understand *völkisch* to be. For Hentschel, racial mixing, contact with foreigners, industrialization, commercialization, urbanization, democracy, and the consumption of alcohol were all symptoms of German culture being "Semitized":

> For him, Semitism stood not for a particular race (although Jews were its modern agents) but for an ethnic principle of moral and cultural degeneration that had corrupted the ancient Israelites and now threatened the Germanic race. According to Hentschel, ancient Greek and Roman civilizations had collapsed because they had been unable to mobilize effective anti-Semitic movements. Only a strong countermovement could prevent the triumph of Semitism all over the world. The urgent task for Germans was to overcome the Semitism within themselves, and racial hygiene was the means to this end. (Pg. 297, "Antisemitism: A Historical Encyclopedia of Prejudice and Persecution", Richard S. Levy, ABC-CLIO, Vol. I, 2005)

Along with the polygamist nature of the Artaman League, Hentschel supported early versions of women's liberation and feminist movements that sought to remove the stigma of unmarried mothers and argued that the emancipation of women was a prerequisite for the natural health of the mother and their children. To this end, the Artaman League associated itself with the *Bund für Mutterschutz*, or in English, the League for the Protection of Mothers:

> Hentschel proposed to settle mothers on his estates. These contacts and plans for utopian mother colonies arouse from a distinctive blend of *völkisch* racism and feminism. The aims of the League were: "to protect motherhood in all its forms, as the mother was the source of the *Volkskraft*"; the "improvement of the race and of national welfare by breeding the healthy"; to establish rural settlements as an antidote to urban degeneration; and to secure paternal responsibility for offspring. The statutes declared in favor of racial hygiene so that the sick should not be a burden on the healthy and consume national strength and wealth. It was a mistake to take the sick and "weak elements" into municipal maternity homes. Instead mothers should re-populate the countryside. (Pg. 253, "Health, Race and German Politics Between National Unification and Nazism, 1870-1945", Paul Weindling, Oxford Univ. Press, 1998)

The policies of Hentschel's communes would later be echoed by the Hitler Youth and "*Lebensborn*" movements. "*Lebensborn*" was the controversial breeding program conducted by Heinrich Himmler, which broke all taboos in order to increase the Aryan population, including the kidnapping of infants in occupied Scandinavian countries and allowing Himmler's young SS officers to both rape and have extra-marital affairs:

> He wanted blond, blue-eyed children to receive military training in bucolic

---

[420] Pg. 297, "Antisemitism: A Historical Encyclopedia of Prejudice and Persecution", Richard S. Levy, ABC-CLIO, Vol. I, 2005.

settings without any book-learning until the age of sixteen. Hentschel despised business and modern industry. He promoted alternative lifestyles which included organic farming, deep green ecology, vegetarianism, nudism, and, homeopathy. The colonies' schools banned money to avoid commerce's corrupting influence. Hentschel hated lawyers. Therefore, if conflicts arose "litigants" had to settle matters through duels or boxing matches. (Pg. 397, "The Surreal Reich", Joseph Howard Tyson, iUniverse, 2010)

Hentschel joined the National Socialist Party on August 1st, 1929 but did not actively participate. However, Hentschel's ideas about eugenics and "blood and soil" were significantly influential on the Party ideology. The *Kommandant* of Auschwitz, Rudolf Höss, was one of the many future leaders of National Socialism who had at one point been a member of the Artaman League. [421] Among Hentschel's other admirers were Erich Ludendorff and Adolf Hitler. [422] Inspiring in Hitler a methodology for indoctrinating youth was certainly a weighty contribution to 20th Century history. Hitler made it clear time and time again that the future of National Socialism was in the success of its appeal to the youth, and thus the Hitler Youth was one of his first creations as leader of the party. During this time, Gustav Lenk founded another youth group named Greater German Youth Movement. On July 3, 1926, a two-day Nazi rally began and was attended by the youth group members. On Sunday, July 4, Gruber's Greater German Youth Movement was renamed as the *Hitler Jugend, Bund der Deutschen Arbeiterjugend* and thus the *Hitler Jugend* or Hitler Youth was born. Kurt Gruber was then officially proclaimed as its first leader, and the activities echoed those of Hentschel's policies:

> Just about every task, no matter how big or small, was turned into an individual, team, or unit competition. Activities for boys included games of hide and seek called 'Trapper and Indian,' and war games in which the boys formed platoons, put on red or blue armbands, then were supposed to hunt down the enemy and rip off the other color arm bands. This often resulted in fistfights and outright brawls between platoons. Younger, weaker boys got pummeled while platoon leaders stood by or even encouraged the fighting. Ripped shirts, along with scrapes and bruises were common during these field exercises, which were intended to toughen them up. (militaryhistoryonline.com, "Rulers of the World: The Hitler Youth", Walter S. Zapotoczny, Sept. 5, 2005)

Much of the school day was outdoors per Adolf Hitler's orders, as he did not want his youth to be a book-smart youth, but a youth that knew how to work in the fields, grow their own food and be proficient in paramilitary and survivalist activities. This curriculum was designed to create a "violently active, dominating, brutal youth...indifferent to pain, without weakness and tenderness." [423] The Hitler Youth

---

[421] Pg. 308 - "Health, Race and German Politics Between National Unification and Nazism, 1870-1945", Paul Weindling, Cambridge Univ. Press, 1993.
[422] Pgs. 239-243 - "Willibald Hentschel", Gregory Pelger, Handbook of the Volkish Sciences. People - Institutions - Research Programs – Foundations, Compiled by Matthias von Berg, Ed. V, 2008.
[423] militaryhistoryonline.com, "Rulers of the World: The Hitler Youth", Sept. 5, 2005.

would eventually replace the traditional elementary and secondary school system and become the venue for educating German youth. Students emerging from the elite Adolf Hitler Schools were in superb physical condition and devoted to Nazi ideology to a degree that was never achieved with the elder German public.

The youth wing of the Artaman League was fully incorporated into the Hitler Youth by the Third Reich in 1934. [424] This was no small measure, as by 1939 the Hitler Youth numbered as high as 8.8 million youths, necessitating a gargantuan infrastructure with 14 regional offices. To put this into context, Hentschel's vision inspired the creation of the Artaman League youth movement, whose members included future Third Reich leaders no less influential than the likes of Heinrich Himmler and Richard Walther Darré. Himmler reinterpreted the lessons he learned from Hentschel into various ones. The organic garden Himmler installed in the concentration camps he oversaw certainly were carryovers from Hentschel's back-to-nature inspiration. The Artaman vision would survive through Himmler who, throughout his time as *Reichsführer-SS*, retained his early dreams of a racially pure peasantry. Himmler was also close to his fellow member Rudolf Höss and would later advance him in the *Schutzstaffel* due in part to their history in the Artaman League. While overshadowed by the Final Solution, Himmler's *"Lebensborn"* project, the sexual component to National Socialism's eugenic policies, has to be one of the most bizarre and controversial aspects of the Third Reich. Beyond the dry eugenic ideology lay Himmler's belief that the "vitality" of the nation, namely his racially pure SS officers, could be regenerated by efforts such as the *"Lebensborn"* Project. According to the Jewish Virtual Library website, *"Lebensborn"* translates to "wellspring of life" or "fountain of life." *"Lebensborn"* was no afterthought either. Himmler founded the *"Lebensborn"* project on December 12, 1935, the same year the Nuremberg Laws outlawed intermarriage with Jews. This was no coincidence, as *"Lebensborn"* was integral to the Reich's eugenic goals.

Himmler's project was meant to resolve one of the concerns German eugenicists had fostered for nearly half a century. For decades, Germany's birthrate was decreasing. Himmler's goal was to reverse the decline and increase the "Aryan" population of Germany to 120 million and to provide the future leaders of a National Socialist "Aryan" nation. The project provided young girls who were deemed "racially pure" the possibility to give birth to a child in secret. This was accomplished by practicing what would otherwise be labeled "free love." Racially pure adolescents were encouraged to engage in pre-marital sex with out-of-wedlock pregnancies as the goal. The atmosphere was set as what can only be described as a *völkisch* summer camp where the youths would mingle, and even though boys would bunk in separate buildings than the girls, the girls were specifically instructed to leave the windows open at night, so the boys could climb in after dark. The resulting children would be turned over to an organization within Himmler's SS, which took charge of the child's education and adoption. Of course, both mother and father needed to pass a "racial purity" test. Blond hair and blue eyes were preferred, and

---

[424] Pg. 17 - "The Hitler Youth, 1922-45: An Illustrated History", Jean-Denis LePage, MacFarland, 2009.

family lineage had to be traced back at least three generations. During the ten years of the program's existence, at least 7,500 children were born in Germany and 10,000 in Norway. It was considered so basic to the eugenic philosophy of the National Socialist state that as the Allies closed on German territory the *"Lebensborn"* facilities were moved to the area in Bavaria where a final stronghold was planned. In fact, when Himmler addressed the Expert Advisory Panel on Population and Racial Policy, he qualified his project as such:

> I have come to the following conclusion: all the moral views we've had up till now that say, "All right, but not before marriage," are not going to get us anywhere. (Pg. 369, "Heinrich Himmler: A Life", Peter Longerich, OUP Oxford, 2012)

This was Heinrich Himmler leveraging the power he had amassed under Hitler, and ready to jettison any pretense to middle-class traditional Christian values that had been touted to ascend to power. Himmler wanted not only to accept illegitimate births but to promote them, as an integral part of a population strategy. Himmler's own writings about the sexual and marital policy of the SS clarify this. SS policy clarifies the extent to which, for reasons based on population policy, Himmler condemned the hostile attitude towards sexuality by the Church. Himmler's SS was to assume the role of avant-garde as far as population policy was concerned, by absolutely rejecting the Church's teaching on sexual morality, but as was typical of extreme eugenic policy under Adolf Hitler, this was to happen only after the beginning of the war. Hitler, as a fellow admirer of Hentschel, approved of Himmler's projects:

> I shall vigorously resist any legal or strong moral restriction on relationships between men and young women. In this I am certainly not alone, but am acting with the Führer's approval, for I have had repeated conversations with him about this subject. (Pg. 370, "Heinrich Himmler: A Life", Peter Longerich, OUP Oxford, 2012)

The *"Lebensborn"* project was financed by a tax on the SS ranks, with those with no children paying the highest penalty. Furthermore, Himmler was explicit about how the eugenic-minded policies of the state were to be practiced at the individual level, insisting that SS men take a close look at the "sisters, brothers, and parents" of any potential bride and "practice racial awareness." The SS officer was encouraged to have girlfriends of "low character" to enjoy a full sexual life, as Himmler believed those with liberated sexuality made the best soldiers. However, they were explicitly forbidden from marrying such girls, and Himmler wrote exactly what he expected his SS men to do if these relationships got too serious:

> I shall not marry you because I cannot justify doing so. How he makes the girl accept that is his business – but SS men must never behave in a way that is not decent but must rather be open and say: I'm sorry, I can't marry you as there have been too many serious illnesses in your family. (Pg. 373, "Heinrich Himmler: A Life", Peter Longerich, OUP Oxford, 2012)

There was certainly a sort of eugenic eroticism at play in the *"Lebensborn"* project, and the consequences and complications of unplanned for progeny persist to this day. [425] The tangled mess that Himmler's experiment left behind had enduring repercussions. The *"Lebensborn"* children who tried to uncover their past have come up against a "collective conspiracy of silence." Much of the lingering secrecy is largely due to the sultry aura that has always surrounded the *"Lebensborn"* project, which was from its onset been criticized as an "SS brothel."

Sec. 3- MEIN BÜCHER:

The popular history of the Third Reich is told with film reels, and one of the most famous film clips of the era is of the book burning. For right or for wrong, this image has created the impression that the leaders of the Third Reich and Adolf Hitler were anti-intellectual. This is a dangerous myth that belittles our enemies at the expense of knowing their true nature. Adolf Hitler was a devoted reader. One could question his choice of subjects but not his love of books. The history of this man, of this monster, is diametrically opposed to that of the thuggish simpleton we want to paint the National Socialists to be. Hitler was an avid reader, and his books were his life from the earliest days as a struggling artist on to the day he committed suicide in his bunker. He made sure to always have his books with him.

Hitler was also an avid reader of political newspapers while living in the poor houses of Vienna. Hitler's childhood friend, Kubizek, documents in his memoirs that Hitler had the slovenly habit of staying up late into the night reading and re-reading books and waking up late the next day. Both Kubizek and Brigitte Hamann attest to Hitler's capacity to rant endlessly about political or cultural issues. Hitler had always been a sponge for political topics and was particularly talented at regurgitating whatever he absorbed in endless rants, which in turn, seemed to cement the ideas in Hitler's mind.

"Books, books, always books!" August Kubizek once wrote. "I just can't imagine Adolf without books. He had them piled up around him at home. He always had a book with him wherever he went." Kubizek, Hitler's only real friend in his teenage years, recalled after the war that Hitler had been registered with three libraries in Linz, where he attended school, and had passed endless days in the baroque splendor of the Hofbibliothek, the former court library of the Hapsburgs, during his time in Vienna. *"Bücher waren seine Welt,"* Kubizek wrote: "Books were his world." (theatlantic.com, Timothy W. Ryback, "Hitler's Forgotten Library: The Man, His Books, and His Search for God", May 2003)

---

[425] "Children of the Lebensborn: The Search for Identity in Selected Literary Texts of the Berlin Republic", Karina Berger, Focus on German Studies, Issue #15.

Two of the books that heavily influenced Hitler while in prison were Henry Ford's autobiography, "My Life and Work," and his anti-Semitic tome "The International Jew." Both had been best sellers in Germany and largely responsible for informing Hitler's Jewish-Bolshevik conspiracy theories. The other works that would significantly influence the path that National Socialism would embark upon after Hitler's release from Landsberg prison were scientific tracts on the topic of eugenics and the race laws in the United States, Britain, and Germany, which Lehmann provided for him. Hitler read a lot while imprisoned in Landsberg and while writing "Mein Kampf." Most of what he read dealt with German history and political philosophy, but his publisher J.F. Lehmann made sure Hitler was thoroughly educated in the "science" of eugenics and euthanasia.

Books were central to the Hitler phenomenon, thus introspection into his reading habits is in order. Timothy W. Ryback is the director of the Salzburg Seminar and the author of the 1999 book "The Last Survivor: Legacies of Dachau," and more importantly, the book "Hitler's Forgotten Library." Timothy W. Ryback's article, "Hitler's Forgotten Library" is based on an unimpeachable premise: "You can tell a lot about a person from what he reads":

> Hans Frank, Hitler's personal lawyer and the "governor" of Nazi-occupied Poland, recalled before his 1946 execution at Nuremberg that Hitler carried a copy of Schopenhauer's The World as Will and Representation with him throughout World War I. During his incarceration after the failed 1923 Munich putsch, Hitler was regularly supplied with reading materials by friends and associates. He once referred to his time in Landsberg Prison as his "university paid for by the state." (theatlantic.com, Timothy W. Ryback, "Hitler's Forgotten Library: The Man, His Books, and His Search for God", May 2003)

Ryback takes it one step further. He conducted his analysis of Hitler's reading list on the basis of usage. Ryback paid close attention to the page marks, underlining and comments left by Hitler on the pages of the books he read and made note of those that appeared to have never been opened.

Beyond that, one can consult the cacophony of "Mein Kampf" for clues as to Hitler's influences. "Mein Kampf" remains a somewhat faithful testament to the occultist origins of the party, namely its origins in the Thule Society, which J.F. Lehmann belonged to, but more importantly Dietrich Eckart, the man who handpicked Hitler and was first to recognize his potential. Embark on any research that touches on the occult origins of Hitler's National Socialism, and you will arrive at conspiracy theory nirvana. It is at this juncture that the conspiracy theorists reach a drooling state of ecstasy as every angle of Hitler's occult origins is explored. However, some avenues of historical research are sometimes inescapable. These are just some of the more basic and dry historical facts connecting National Socialism and "the occult." The conspiracy theories take these facts in a direction that sounds more like fiction, but the fiction turns into fact when unimpeachable sources corroborate the facts. There is one fact that cannot be ignored: Adolf Hitler dedicated "Mein Kampf" to Dietrich Eckart. If that wasn't enough to remind us of the link between Hitler and German occultism, he also named the *Waldbühne* arena near the Olympic Stadium in Berlin as the "*Dietrich-Eckart-Bühne*" when it was opened for the 1936 Summer Olympics. The 1936 Summer Olympics were immensely important to Hitler, and his way of delivering his propaganda message to the rest of the world. Clearly, Eckart remains an important piece of the Hitler puzzle, and the Hitler-Eckart relationship was based upon philosophical foundations. Eckart schooled Hitler like J.F. Lehmann later would.

Dietrich Eckart was a German journalist and politician. Like Hitler, Eckart was born into a Catholic family and lost both his faith and his father early on in his life. Eckart was heavily influenced by the *Völkisch* writings by the author Jörg Lanz von Liebenfels. It was Liebenfels that introduced Eckart to Buddhist doctrine and Madame Blavatsky, the leader of the Theosophy movement that Margaret Sanger and Helen Keller also admired. After World War I, Eckart edited the anti-Semitic periodical "*Auf gut Deutsch*," or "In plain German," published along with Alfred Rosenberg and Gottfried Feder. A fierce critic of the German Revolution and the Weimar Republic, he vehemently opposed the Treaty of Versailles and was a proponent of the so-called "stab-in-the-back" legend which became the infamous rallying cry of those Jewish-Marxist conspiracy theorists that were, as Hitler later embellished, bitterly opposed to Versailles. Eckart met Adolf Hitler during a speech he gave before party members in 1919. Eckart's Thule Society believed in the coming of a "German Messiah" who would redeem Germany after its defeat in World War I. Eckart introduced his fellow Thule Society member, Rosenberg, to Hitler. Incidentally, Rosenberg was the editor of the *Münchener Beobachter*, a party newspaper, originally owned by the Thule Society. It was in the *Münchener Beobachter*, that Rosenberg published the "Protocols of the Elders of Zion."

None of this should be regarded as a side-note or a telling of trivia. When the New German Workers Party was folded into the National Socialist German Workers Party, the forty original members were also members of the *Thule Gessellschaft*. The English translation of "Mein Kampf" has an interesting quotation it attributes to Dietrich Eckart:

> We need a fellow at the head who can stand the sound of a machine gun. The rabble need to get fear into their pants. We can't use an officer, because people don't respect them anymore. The best would be a worker who knows how to talk… He doesn't need much brains, politics is the stupidest business in the world, and every market woman in Munich knows more than the people in Weimar. I'd rather have a vain monkey who can give the Reds a juicy answer, and doesn't run away when people begin swinging table legs, than a dozen learned professors. He must be a bachelor, then we'll get the women. (Pg. 48, "The American Axis: Henry Ford, Charles Lindbergh, and the Rise of the Third Reich", Max Wallace, Macmillan, 2003)

All of these factoids help us understand that the occultist aspect to National Socialism was poured into its foundations and that it was the books and newspapers of the German occultists that filled Hitler's mind where formal education was otherwise lacking. The insurance policy taken out on Hitler's book collection is revealing. In October 1934, the Gladbacher Fire Insurance Company insured Hitler's six-room apartment on the *Prinzregentenplatz*, in downtown Munich. In the letter of agreement accompanying the policy, Hitler valued his book collection, said to consist of 6,000 volumes, at 150,000 marks. The books represented half the value of the entire policy. The other half represented his art holdings. Ryback documents contemporary accounts:

> Herbert Döhring, who managed the Berghof from 1936 to 1943, told me that the library could accommodate no more than 500 or 600 volumes. "He reserved this space for the books he really cared about," says Döhring, who helped Hitler to sort the books. "He used to have me send the rest to a storage facility in Munich or to the new Reich Chancellery in Berlin." For his official Berlin residence Hitler had his architect, Albert Speer, design a vast library that occupied the entire west wing. "Inventory records of the Reich Chancellery that we found at the Hoover Institution at Stanford suggest that by the early 1940s Hitler was receiving as many as four thousand books annually," Daniel Mattern told me. In Munich, Gassert and Mattern also discovered architectural sketches for a library annex to the Berghof that was intended to accommodate more than 60,000 volumes. "This was a man with a lot of books," Mattern says. (theatlantic.com, Timothy W. Ryback, "Hitler's Forgotten Library: The Man, His Books, and His Search for God", May 2003)

So what happened to this formidable book collection? Timothy Ryback documents the handful of surviving sources of information in Hitler's beloved book collection. The books Hitler kept at his Reich Chancellery office were inventoried by the US armed forces that captured it, and this inventory is currently held by the Hoover Institute at Stanford University. The US Army's Twenty-first Counterintelligence Corps drafted a report on May 1945 of the contents of the bunker below the Berghof complex once they reached the "Eagle's Nest." Hans Beilhack then described what was found in a salt mine near Berchtesgaden in a Munich newspaper of 1946. The Library of Congress memorandum, dated January 9, 1952, details the "Hitler Library" after it arrived in the United States, but before it was accessioned into its rare book collection. The memorandum was written by Arnold Jacobius.

Timothy Ryback relies on the 1942 book "This Is the Enemy" by Frederick Oechsner but otherwise accuses its author of making "sensational claims." History proves he is not as flighty as Ryback would paint him to be, and Fred Oechsner's story is worth a side-track in order to shed light on this topic. What is left of Frederick Oechsner papers are currently held at the Louisiana Research Collection at Tulane University. The Tulane website provides important information about Oechsner. Oechsner worked for several newspapers as a foreign correspondent and a chief consultant in several US embassies during his lifetime. Most importantly, between 1942 and 1945, he worked for the Office of Strategic Services, Supreme Headquarters Allied Expeditionary Force and special assistant to Ambassador

Robert D. Murphy, who was Political Advisor to General Eisenhower. From 1947 to 1952, Oechsner was Special Assistant to Assistant Secretary of State for Public Affairs, and Director of the Office of International Information and Cultural Affairs. The Orlando Sentinel's obituary for Oechsner pays respect to him as the man "who interviewed Adolf Hitler and advised Dwight D. Eisenhower during 35 years as a journalist." Oechsner interviewed Hitler four times before the United States entered the war and later taken hostage along with other journalists once the US entered the war. [426] The 1959 book by Hugh Baillie tells the firsthand account of just how close Oechsner got to Hitler. In fact, Fred Oechsner was also one of the first to report that Hitler's mental health was deteriorating. The Western Star newspaper published an article in March 1943 reporting on how Hitler had gone missing from the public eye for months under the excuse that he was at the front with his soldiers. The article made some pretty bold claims, which we now know to be true:

> There are several stories which I heard from the lips of a man who has closely watched Hitler's career from its earliest beginning. The man is Fred Oechsner, a former colleague of mine. – Long before anybody else took Hitler seriously, Oechsner wrote to me: "This man is some day going to be the bull in Europe's china shop." Oechsner, who is now in Washington, told me that the following story which he also repeats in his excellent book, "This Is the Enemy." -- It is his opinion that Hitler is an outstanding example of a half-trained, half-educated person with a phenomenal talent for absorbing and co-ordinating information and detail gleaned from other sources." (Baukhage, "Hitler in Mental Decline? Close Observers Say Yes", Western Star, March 19, 1943

TIME Magazine decided to quote excerpts from Oechsner's observations prior to the publishing of "This Is the Enemy." The article notes that Hitler:
> ... has undoubtedly read most of the 7,000 military books in his library. ---- In a book on diet, Vegetarian Hitler penciled this marginal note: "Cows were meant to give milk, oxen for drawing loads." ---- He is fascinated by astrology and spiritualism, has photographs of the stellar constellations at important moments of his life. ("GERMANY: Inside Hitler", TIME, June 22, 1942)

Furthermore, Oechsner's career with President Eisenhower, the elite OSS military intelligence service, and United Press would indicate that he was a serious man with all the credentials necessary for credible intelligence gathering and reporting. The fact that Oechsner actually sat down and interviewed Adolf Hitler on various occasions, aside from attending state diners that Hitler and all of the top National Socialists attended, qualifies him as a more reliable source than anyone analyzing Hitler from afar. The profile of Hitler provided by Oechsner is a goldmine for historians, as he had the perfect approach: He was both an agent and a journalist, who spoke German, and had a working relationship with all the higher-ups in the National Socialist government. His observations of Hitler are therefore more reliable

---

[426] orlandosentinel.com, "Frederick Oechsner, Writer and Diplomat", Orlando Sentinel, April 20, 1992.

than Timothy Ryback gives him credit for. Oechsner met Hitler on repeated occasions and was evidently able to acquaint himself intimately with the book collection: "I found that his personal library, which is divided between his residence in the Chancellery in Berlin and his country home on the Obersalzberg at Berchtesgaden, contains roughly 16,300 books." [427]

Thus, the 1,200 of Hitler's books currently held in the Library of Congress most likely represent less than 10 percent of the original collection. Timothy Ryback documents Oechsner's findings based on the notes and various markings left by Hitler in the pages of his books.

One book on Führertum – "leadership" - was presented to Hitler by the industrialist Fritz Thyssen, who had introduced him to some of Germany's leading businessmen at a decisive meeting in Düsseldorf in January of 1932. "To the Führer, Adolf Hitler, in memory of his presentation to the Düsseldorf Industrial Club," Thyssen wrote on the inside cover. Several books are inscribed to Hitler from Richard Wagner's youngest daughter, Eva, who had married Houston Stewart Chamberlain. Chamberlain was an anti-Semitic Englishman best known for his book The Foundations of the 19 Century, in which he advanced the thesis that Jesus was of Aryan rather than Semitic blood. Hitler read Chamberlain during his Vienna period, and had a brief audience with the aging anti-Semite at the Wagner estate shortly before being sent to Landsberg Prison.

CONTINUES...

In a French vegetarian cookbook with an inscription from its author, Maïa Charpentier, I encountered Monsieur Hitler végétarien. And I found hints of Hitler the future mass murderer in a 1932 technical treatise on chemical warfare that explores the varying qualities of poison gas, from chlorine to prussic acid (Blausäure). The latter was produced commercially as Zyklon B, which would be notorious for its use in the Nazi extermination camps. (theatlantic.com, Timothy W. Ryback, "Hitler's Forgotten Library: The Man, His Books, and His Search for God", May 2003)

Timothy Ryback then comes full circle back to the topic of the occult and its influence on Adolf Hitler. He noted that the OSS, which Oechsner was a part of, had commissioned a psychological profile on Hitler. Recall that in spring 1943, the US Office of Strategic Services, the forerunner to the CIA, commissioned Walter Langer to develop a "psychological profile." Langer clarified this was the first time the US government had attempted to psychoanalyze a world leader in order to determine "the things that make him tick." Over the course of eight months, assisted by three field researchers and advised by three other experts in psychology, Langer compiled more than a thousand typewritten, single-spaced pages of material on his "patient" including texts from speeches, excerpts from "Mein Kampf," interviews

---

[427] theatlantic.com, "Hitler's Forgotten Library: The Man, His Books, and His Search for God", Timothy W. Ryback, May 2003 – Citing Oeschner's "This Is the Enemy", 1942.

with former Hitler associates, and virtually every printed source available. Langer wrote:

> A survey of all the evidence forces us to conclude that Hitler believes himself destined to become an Immortal Hitler, chosen by God to be the New Deliverer of Germany and the Founder of a new social order for the world. He firmly believes this and is certain that in spite of all the trials and tribulations through which he must pass he will finally attain that goal. The one condition is that he follow the dictates of the inner voice that have guided and protected him in the past. (theatlantic.com, Timothy W. Ryback, "Hitler's Forgotten Library: The Man, His Books, and His Search for God", May 2003)

Experts and conspiracy theorists since have indulged pursuing every possible angle on Hitler's spiritual beliefs, going as far as proposing that Hitler was swayed by his alleged devotion to Catholicism as much or more than he was to his documented and verifiable devotion to the occult. Ian Kershaw argues that Hitler consciously constructed an image of himself as a messianic figure and eventually came to believe the very myth he had helped to fashion. "The more he succumbed to the allure of his own Führer cult and came to believe in his own myth, the more his judgment became impaired by faith in his own infallibility," Kershaw wrote in "The Hitler Myth." [428] Ryback contributes to this field of study:

> But believing in a messianic myth is not the same as believing in God. When I asked Kershaw in 2001 whether he thought Hitler actually believed in divine providence, he dismissed the notion. "I don't think that he had any real belief in a deity of any sort, only in himself as a 'man of destiny' who would bring about Germany's 'salvation,'" he declared. Gerhard Weinberg, who helped sort through the Hitler Library back in the 1950s, likewise dismisses the notion of Hitler as a religious believer, insisting that he was driven by the twin passions of Blut und Boden—racial purity and territorial expansion. "He didn't believe in anything but himself," Weinberg told me last summer. Most historians tend to agree." (theatlantic.com, Timothy W. Ryback, "Hitler's Forgotten Library: The Man, His Books, and His Search for God", May 2003)

Timothy Ryback further documents this aspect of Hitler by consulting the opinion provided by Hitler's personal secretary. The relationship between Hitler and Traudl Junge is well documented, and his relationship with her provides a more reliable source than that of National Socialist party elites, as Hitler kept a safe distance from them due to their constant political scheming.

> Traudl Junge, Hitler's former secretary, would not go so far as to say that Hitler believed in God, but she did believe that Hitler's repeated references to the divine were more than just for show. Junge—who died of cancer in February of last year—told me the previous summer that Hitler spoke of such things in private as well as in public. After two and a half years of daily contact with Hitler, she was convinced that he believed in some form of divine protection, especially after

---

[428] theatlantic.com, Timothy W. Ryback, "Hitler's Forgotten Library: The Man, His Books, and His Search for God", May 2003.

surviving a dramatic assassination attempt in 1944. "After the July 1944 attack," she told me, "I believe he felt himself to be an instrument of providence, and believed he had a mission to fulfill." (theatlantic.com, Timothy W. Ryback, "Hitler's Forgotten Library: The Man, His Books, and His Search for God", May 2003)

Timothy Ryback further clarifies:
For all the vitriol Hitler spewed upon Judaism, he came to hold Christianity in equal disdain. "Christianity is the worst thing that ever happened to mankind," he declared during an after-dinner rant in July of 1941. "Bolshevism is the illegitimate child of Christianity. Both are an outgrowth of the Jew." ---- Hitler was the classic apostate. He rebelled against the established theology in which he was born and bred, all the while seeking to fill the resulting spiritual void. As the Hitler Library suggests, he found no shortage of latter-day prophets peddling alternative theologies. Mathilde von Kemnitz, the wife of Erich Ludendorff, the venerated World War I general who joined Hitler in the Munich putsch, promoted a neo-Teutonic pagan cult that called for the destruction of churches and the creation of forest temples and places of sacrifice. (theatlantic.com, Timothy W. Ryback, "Hitler's Forgotten Library: The Man, His Books, and His Search for God", May 2003)

As with all the other topics covered in this book, the Western world, up until the 1990s, has only enjoyed half of the story of World War II as the other half had been hidden behind the "Iron Curtain." We must recall that the Soviet Army reached Hitler's bunker first. Mystery has surrounded what the Soviets took away from that bunker. By the time the Americans were allowed to view the bunker, the place had been already gutted by the Soviets. However, Colonel Albert Aronson was one of the Americans to be allowed into Hitler's bunker in May 1945. Here again, was a cache of occultism left behind in Hitler's private quarters. The remaining books left behind by the Russians were bequeathed to Aronson's nephews, who, in turn, donated them to Brown University in 1979. Today the eighty volumes are housed in the basement vault of Brown's rare-book collection at the John Hay Library. Timothy Ryback documents the contents of this part of Hitler's book collection, which must be weighed against the knowledge that anything that Stalin would have regarded as valuable would have been taken by the Soviets. They did take Eva Braun's underwear after all:

Brown's eighty Hitler books constitute a hodgepodge: picture books, art journals, an Italian libretto of Wagner's Walküre, a 1937 edition of Mein Kampf, and two editions of Alfred Rosenberg's The Myth of the 20 Century. The more than a dozen books on the occult include several devoted to Nordic runes, among them a 1922 history of the swastika, richly illustrated with nearly 500 diverse renderings. (theatlantic.com, Timothy W. Ryback, "Hitler's Forgotten Library: The Man, His Books, and His Search for God", May 2003)

Ryback reports that the collection provides "incontrovertible evidence on occultism, somnambulism, spiritualism." Ryback also offers his opinion as to what the contents of the book collection, as well as the various notes and underlining that Adolf Hitler left on the books he decided to take with him into his air-raid bunker, a telling decision by itself:

> Most scholars dismiss the notion that Hitler seriously entertained the ideas of these cults, but the marginalia in several of his books confirm at least an intellectual engagement in the substance of Weimar-era occultism. The Brown collection contains books by such figures as Adamant Rohm, a "magnetopathic doctor" from Wiesbaden; Carl Ludwig Schleich, a Berlin physician who pioneered the use of local anesthesia; and Joseph Anton Schneiderfranken, who wrote numerous books on reincarnation and otherworldly phenomena under the pseudonym Bô Yin Râ. ---- One of the most heavily marked books is Magic: History, Theory and Practice (1923), by Ernst Schertel. When I typed the author's name into one Internet search engine, I scored eight hits, including sites on Satanism, eroticism, sadomasochism, and flagellation. When I typed his name into Google, I scored twenty-six hits, including sites on parapsychology, astrology, and diverse sexual practices. According to a Web site for Germany's sadomasochistic community, Schertel wrote numerous books on flagellation and eroticism, and was "a central figure" in the German nudist movement of the 1920s and 1930s. ---- Hitler's copy of Magic bears a handwritten dedication from Schertel, scrawled on the title page in pencil. A 170-page softcover in large format, the book has been thoroughly read, and its margins scored repeatedly. I found a particularly thick pencil line beside the passage "He who does not carry demonic seeds within him will never give birth to a new world." (theatlantic.com, Timothy W. Ryback, "Hitler's Forgotten Library: The Man, His Books, and His Search for God", May 2003)

This takes us back to Eckart himself, and the influence he had on Hitler's mindset and occultist values. This man provided Hitler direction at a time when he was lost and destitute after World War I.

> One of the oldest volumes of literature still in the Hitler Library is a 1917 German edition of Peer Gynt, Henrik Ibsen's epic of a "Nordic Faust" who cuts a swath of human suffering --- on his way to becoming "emperor of the whole world." When challenged to account for his sundry trespasses, Gynt declares that he would rather burn in hell for excessive sins than simmer in obscurity with the rest of humanity. Edvard Grieg set this cruel play to beautiful music. Hitler's copy of Peer Gynt—handsomely illustrated by Otto Sager—bears a simple inscription by its German translator: "Intended for his dear friend Adolf Hitler. Dietrich Eckart. Munich, October 22, 1921." (theatlantic.com, Timothy W. Ryback, "Hitler's Forgotten Library: The Man, His Books, and His Search for God", May 2003)

Timothy Ryback also wrote "The Hitler Shrine" for The Atlantic Monthly on April 2005. In "The Hitler Shrine" Ryback gives account of the very close relationship between Dietrich Eckart and Adolf Hitler, with Eckart often receiving

Hitler in his underpants. Clearly, the relationship between Hitler and Eckart was more than can be claimed by his inner circle of National Socialism. The relationship preceded National Socialism and is clearly atypical for a leader who kept everyone at a formal arm's length, including the women in his life. Even Albert Speer was never at a comfort level where he would have received the Führer in his underpants. Thus, we circle round to Adolf Hitler's dedication of "Mein Kampf" to Eckart:

> And I want also to reckon among [Nazi heroes] that man, who, as one of the best, by words and by thoughts and finally by deeds, dedicated his life to the awakening of his, of our nation: Dietrich Eckart. ("How 'Catholic' Was the Early Nazi Movement? Religion, Race, and Culture in Munich, 1919-1924", Derek Hastings, Central European History, Vol. 36, No. 3, Pgs. 383-433, 2003)

The meaning and weight of the above statement cannot be regarded as equal to any other quote, as the dedication to a close friend in the Fuhrer's *magnum opus* is certainly to be taken to mean more than passing words or even a mention in a politically motivated stump speech. It would be historically disingenuous to weigh the value of the above statement in isolation. Context is everything. Eckart cannot be regarded as a distant mentor to Hitler, as the role of leader and mentor changed as the relationship evolved. Ryback recalls Eckart's closing words:

> After working with Hitler at an early Nazi Party event, Eckart began grooming him for political life. He bought Hitler his first trench coat, gave him instruction in public speaking, and introduced him to members of Munich society, often with the icebreaker "This is the man who will one day liberate Germany." Hitler once called Eckart the "polar star" of the Nazi movement, and dedicated the first volume of Mein Kampf to him. "Follow Hitler!" Eckart allegedly exhorted on his deathbed, in 1923. **"He will dance, but the music to which he dances was composed by me."** (emphasis mine, theatlantic.com, "Hitler's Forgotten Library: The Man, His Books, and His Search for God", Timothy W. Ryback, May 2003)

That last sentence by Eckart is crucial in the understanding where Hitler's occult influences lead. The full quote of Eckart's last words are as follows:

> Follow Hitler! He will dance, but it is I who have called the tune. I have initiated him into the 'Secret Doctrine,' opened his centers in vision and given him the means to communicate with the Powers. Do not mourn for me: I shall have influenced history more than any other German. (Pg. 16, Midstream, Theodor Herzl Foundation, Vol. 44, 1988)

Dietrich Eckart's "*Der Bolschevismus*" has another interesting quote: "To want to annihilate somebody with all one's might, and to meanwhile suspect that the act will lead to one's own downfall is, if you like, the tragedy of Lucifer." [429] This is where the unreal world of the occult touches on very real and very important world

---

[429] Pg. 120 - "Hitler's Library", Ambrus Miskolczy, Central European University Press, 2003.

of geopolitics and the aspirations of the like-minded individuals which directly or indirectly influenced the trajectory of history. The reference to the "Secret Doctrine" and "Lucifer" can only mean one thing in relation to Dietrich Eckart; the "Secret Doctrine" is the book written by the founder of Theosophy, Madame Blavatsky, and "Lucifer" was the name of her movement's magazine. This is where more likely than not Hitler's radical "racialism" took root and originated. Hitler allegedly kept a copy of Blavatsky's "The Secret Doctrine" by his bedside. Based on the reliable sources quoted above, this would hardly be farfetched, as Blavatsky's Theosophy was part of Dietrich Eckart's, Alfred Rosenberg's, Guido Von Liszt's, and Anton Drexler's intellectual repertoire. Bottom line is that Hitler surrounded himself with Madame Blavatsky's followers. All of this serves to prove that these sources brought to him, namely that of Edward Bellamy's "national socialism" through his strong links to Madame Blavatsky's Theosophy. The frequent statements that Blavatsky made about Bellamy in her books, lectures, and journals indicate the level to which her followers were committed to the movement:

> The organization of Society, depicted by Edward Bellamy, in his 'Looking Backward,' admirably represents the Theosophical idea of what should be the FIRST GREAT STEP towards the full Realization of Universal Brotherhood. ("Key to Theosophy," H.P. Blavatsky, Theosophical Publishing House, 1889)

> Have not you heard of the Nationalist clubs and party which have sprung up in America since the publication of Bellamy's book? They are now coming prominently to the front, and will do more and more as time goes on. Well, these clubs and this party were started in the first instance by Theosophists. One of the first, the Nationalist Club of Boston, Mass., has Theosophists for President and Secretary, and the majority of its executive belong to the T.S. In the constitution of all their clubs, and of the party they are forming, the influence of Theosophy and of the Society is plain, for they all take as their basis, their first and fundamental principle, the Brotherhood of Humanity as taught by Theosophy." ("Key to Theosophy," H.P. Blavatsky, Theosophical Publishing House, 1889)

Recall that "Lucifer" was the name of a journal published by Madame Blavatsky. The first edition was issued in September 1887 in London. The journal was first published by Blavatsky. From 1889 until Blavatsky's death in May 1891, Annie Besant, the famous British "Birth Control" activist, was a co-editor. Besant then published the journal until September 1895, when George Robert Stowe Mead became a co-editor. The journal was subsequently renamed to "The Theosophical Review." In the "Lucifer" journal, one can find references to Bellamy:

> Edward Bellamy's remarkable romance, "Looking Backward," has started in America a movement that bids fair to become of considerable importance. Men and women touched with "the enthusiasm of humanity," and feeling a sense of personal shame for the inhumanity of our present social system, have been fired by the beauty of the Socialist Utopia to make an effort towards bringing it about;

and they are gathering themselves into "Nationalist Clubs: to work for its realization.

CONTINUES...

The central idea of the movement, as expressed in the constitution of the Boston Nationalist Club, is "The nationalization of industry and the promotion of the Brotherhood of Humanity." The Boston Club has established The Nationalist as its organ, and starts its career with articles from the pens of Edward Bellamy himself.

CONTINUES...

In the opening number Edward Bellamy tells how he came to write "Looking Backward" starting with the idea of "a fairy tale of social felicity" and transmuting it into "the vehicle of a definite scheme of industrial organization." We notice with interest that three of the writers in this first issue belong to the Theosophical Brotherhood, a sign that the American brethren mean to work, as well as speak, for the Brotherhood of Humanity. We wish our young contemporary good speed. (Pg. 440, "Lucifer: A Theosophical Magazine", Vol. 4, March-Aug. 1889)

So, who was this woman? Helena Petrovna Blavatsky was a self-professed psychic and mystic. Of specific importance is that National Socialists found in her work the claim that humanity had descended from a series of seven "Root Races," with the "Aryan Race" as the fifth of the bunch. She described the Aryan race with the following words:

> The Aryan races, for instance, now varying from dark brown, almost black, red-brown-yellow, down to the whitest creamy colour, are yet all of one and the same stock -- the Fifth Root-Race -- and spring from one single progenitor, (...) who is said to have lived over 18,000,000 years ago, and also 850,000 years ago -- at the time of the sinking of the last remnants of the great continent of Atlantis. -- Blavatsky, (Pg. 249, "The Secret Doctrine, the Synthesis of Science, Religion and Philosophy: Anthropogenesis", Theosophical Publishing House, Vol. II, 1921)

Blavatsky used "Root Race" as a technical term to describe human evolution over the large time periods in her cosmology. However, she also claimed that there were modern non-Aryan peoples who were inferior to Aryans. She regularly contrasts "Aryan" with "Semitic" culture, to the detriment of the latter, asserting that Semitic peoples were an offshoot of Aryans who have become "degenerate in spirituality and perfected in materiality." She also claimed that some peoples were "semi-animal creatures." These atavisms included "the Tasmanians, a portion of the Australians and a mountain tribe in China." She characterized them as the National Socialist scientists would, as "semi-human stocks," and further included in this rung of her racial hierarchy the "wild men of Borneo, the Veddhas of Ceylon," and the "Negritos," and "Andaman Islanders." The Cambridge Centre for Western Esotericism agrees with the Hitler-Theosophy link, and points to "Mein Kampf":

> In Mein Kampf (1925) Adolf Hitler wrote: "All great cultures of the past perished only because the original creative race died out from blood poisoning." Hitler had become familiar with the concept of an endangered racial heritage through reading texts such as Human Heredity by the German eugenicists Baur, Fischer and Lenz (published 1921), and through his early influences during the wilderness years of his life in Vienna particularly the work of Ariosophist (Aryan occult wisdom) thinkers such as Guido von List and Jorg Lanz von Liebenfels." (ccwe.wordpress.com, "Face of the Devine: The Esoteric Roots of Physiognomic Photography," Dr. Christopher Webster, October 22, 2008)

The book "Antisemitism" was written by top scholars and offers worldwide coverage of the origins, forms, practitioners, and effects of anti-Semitism, leading to the Holocaust. Hannah Newman wrote the section on Blavatsky and had this to say about Theosophy's influence on the National Socialists:

> Blavatsky's influence ranged well beyond Thosophical circles and later contributed to Nazi ideology. One link was Baron Rudolf von Sebotendorf, a devoted Blavatsky fan and founder of the Thule Society (in 1918). The Munich-based organization borrowed heavily from The Secret Doctrine and counted several future Nazi leaders month its members or hangers-on. As early as 1920, Sebottendorf named the Jews as cosmic enemies to be "cleaned out" as a "final goal." Another link was Blavatsky disciple Karl Houshofer, whose "geopolitical" doctrines served the Nazis before and after 1933, and who some speculate may have introduced Hitler to The Secret Doctrine after their meeting in Landsberg Prison in 1924. However, yet another Blavatsky disciple, Dietrich Eckart, boasted that he had initiated Hitler into The Secret Doctrine. Hitler later dedicated Mein Kampf to Eckart. (Pg. 73, "Antisemitism: A Historical Encyclopedia of Prejudice and Persecution", Hannah Newmann, Vol. I, ABC-CLIO, 2005)

Likewise, Theosophy and eugenics were inseparably intertwined in the United States. Edward Bellamy and the leadership of the various "Nationalist Clubs" were Theosophists, and through Bellamy also eugenicists. A September 1913 article from the New York Times article documents how the two movements identified and intermingled into a single cause:

> New Aryan stock that is destined to produce a new Messiah and rule the world is developing on the Pacific Coast, according to prominent Theosophists gathered here to-day to attend the opening session of the twenty-seventh annual meeting of the American Section of the Theosophical Society. ("New Messiah Rising, Theosophists Say", NYT, Sept. 5, 1913)

This New York Times article goes on to quote the leadership of the movement, and the mix between Madame Blavatsky's Theosophy and the type of thinking so prevalent in the ranks of Nazism is unmistakable, if not chilling:

> This root race is the sixth sub-race of Aryan stock, and there are unmistakable signs that it has appeared on the Pacific Coast," said Max Wardall of Seattle. "It is a new physical type, and is the result of the gradual process of reincarnation, in our opinion. We believe this race is destined to rule the earth. Eugenics has played an important part in the development of the new type, which is taller, more athletic, and somewhat darker than the prevailing type. Its members have a finer nervous organization and a higher spiritual perception. – At the proper time we expect a Messiah to appear and direct the destinies of the new race, the same as Christ did centuries ago. ("New Messiah Rising, Theosophists Say", NYT, Sept. 5, 1913)

This is likely the bill of goods Dietrich Eckart sold a young Adolf Hitler. Hitler was the typical lanky and weakly social ingrate and outcast, willing to attach himself and extract validity and belonging from ideas that spit in the face of traditional European culture. Before Eckart, the young wandering and impoverished artist was an avid consumer of political writings and radical thinking. He spent those "missing years" in Vienna scratching out a meager existence by selling his watercolor art through various older mentors and associates he met while living at the homes.

Theosophy, like eugenics, was fluid and diverse in its iterations and applications to German *völkisch* thinking. It would be impossible to separate these two movements from the era as they were so prevalent and pervasive at the time.[430] The social circles that filled the ranks of Fabian Socialism, Theosophy, Aryan superiority, and thus eugenics were frequented by like-minded people. The movements shared readerships and memberships:

> Strange faiths, like the Nordic cults fostered by Wagner's Bayreuth, found some vocal backers; Huston Stewart Chamberlain, a transplanted Englishman who became Wagner's son-in-law, propagated the notion of an Aryan Jesus. The founder of Theosophy, Madame Blavatsky, dictatorial, omniscient, believable to those inclined to believe – W.B. Yeats was her most celebrated disciple – advertised her "secret doctrine" as nothing less than a synthesis of science, religion, and philosophy. Noteworthy in her grandiose claim was the inclusion of science, a wry tribute to the prestige of physicists and biologists. (Pg. 174, "Schnitzler's Century: The Making of Middle-class Culture, 1815-1914", Peter Gay, W. W. Norton & Company, 2002)

This was no different in cosmopolitan Munich or Vienna. Bottom line is that Aryan superiority, socialism, and eugenics were widespread movements. They attracted enthusiastic support from activist and reform-minded sectors of society. They looked for solutions to the catastrophes of the past, and they were easy prey for the soothsayers and false prophets. "Reform" was in the air, and none of it was rooted in the humanitarian or Judeo-Christian values of previous generations. In their view, the values inherited from the Enlightenment had failed them. By the time

---

[430] See Generally - "A Science for the Soul: Occultism and the Genesis of the German Modern" Corinna Treitel, 2004.

the National Socialist rolled into town, the representative style democracy in the United States was also seen as a failure due to the Great Depression. European radicals were willing to listen to just about anything and believe in just about anybody.

The influences on Adolf Hitler were many and varied. In Hitler's library, we find the foundation of the philosophy that J.F. Lehmann and Dietrich Eckart would construct in the mind of the young and poorly educated Adolf Hitler. One thing is for sure: The Brown Shirts and SS thugs have provided the illusion of what contemporarily would be called "street credibility" to an otherwise lanky and weakly artist-type that was Adolf Hitler. Hitler was far from being a physical presence and was better characterized as a know-it-all pseudo-intellectual loudmouth that was energized by radical ideas. He was intent on redesigning the world per the prescriptions of the various books he digested and regurgitated, and never came across an idea too radical to raise his suspicions or better judgment. To the contrary, Hitler disdained half-measures and moralistic calls for restraint or caution. The more radical the idea, the more he was enamored by it and the more he insisted on its implementation. His occultist views can best be explained in the context of his other views; Hitler was a sponge for any radical concepts that would replace traditional thought. It is doubtful that Hitler ever had a genuinely original idea.

August 12, 1939.

Prof. Dr. Ernst Rüdin, President,
Fourth International Congress for Eugenics,
Zimmstrasse 11,
Berlin W 62, Germany.

Dear Professor Rüdin,

We have just received announcement of the Fourth International Congress of Eugenics. Workers in this field in all of the countries of Pan America congratulate the International Committee on its selection of Rüdin as President, of Vienna for the site, and 1940 for the date. The whole setting presages a successful meeting.

In order to hold the advances thus far made in building the science of Eugenics and to plan the next steps in research and trial, it is necessary that a new congress assembles soon; that its business be to take stock of the world's knowledge of human heredity; to evaluate the technique of practical population-control; and to exchange experiences and plans among leaders in the biological betterment of mankind.

I am taking the pleasure in sending by today's parcel post to your laboratory, addressed to the President of the Fourth International Congress of Eugenics, a package of books and papers. These comprise some records of the past congresses and current studies on the subject of eugenics as a science and as a practical art.

Very faithfully yours,

Harry H. Laughlin
Secretary of the
Third International Congress of Eugenics.

FIGURE 11: CORRESPONDENCE BETWEEN HARRY H. LAUGHLIN AND ERNST RÜDIN DATED AUGUST 12, 1939, A YEAR AFTER KRISTALLNACHT, AND JUST DAYS FROM THE INVASION OF POLAND. *(HEREIN PUBLISHED AND PRINTED FOR THE FIRST TIME WITH PERMISSION OF THE SPECIAL COLLECTIONS DEPARTMENT AT TRUMAN UNIVERSITY. — BOX C-2-5:3 LAUGHLIN PAPERS)*

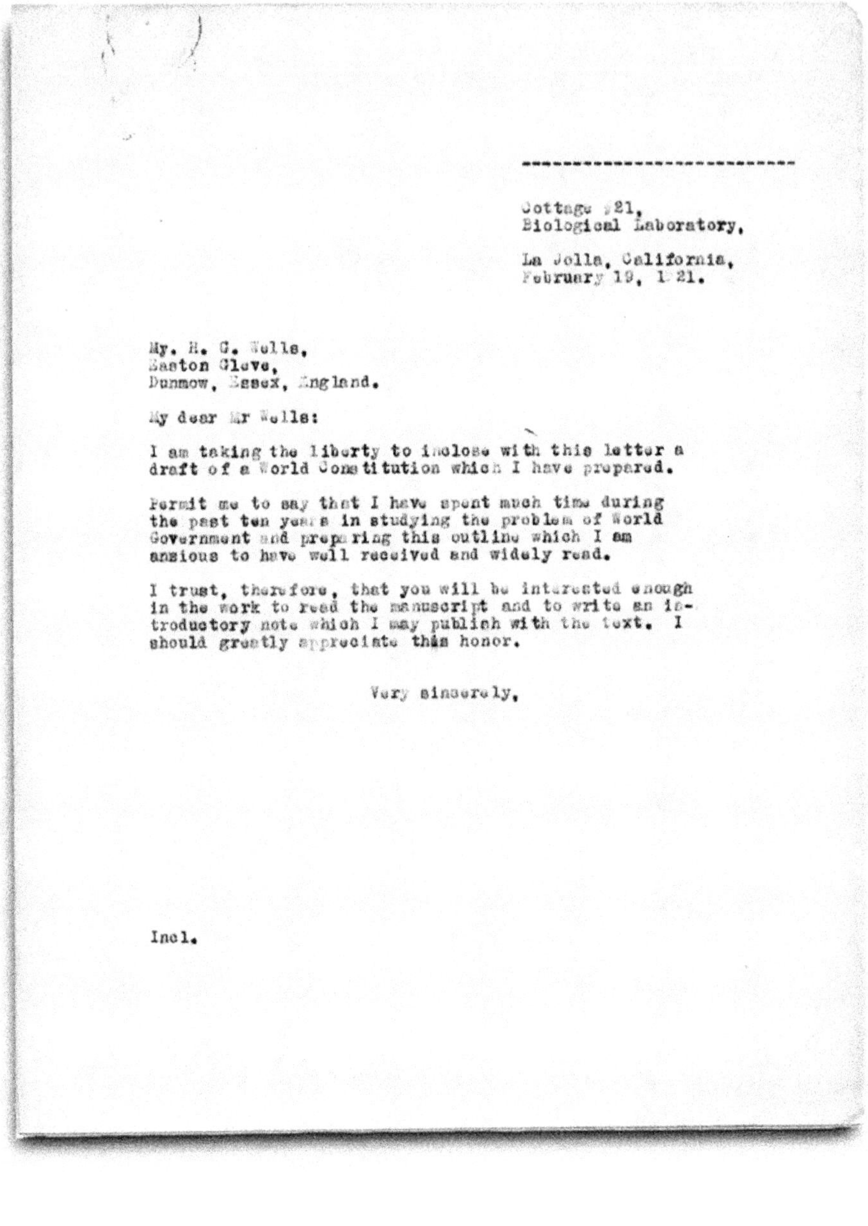

Cottage #21,
Biological Laboratory,
La Jolla, California,
February 19, 1921.

Mr. H. G. Wells,
Easton Glebe,
Dunmow, Essex, England.

My dear Mr Wells:

I am taking the liberty to inclose with this letter a draft of a World Constitution which I have prepared.

Permit me to say that I have spent much time during the past ten years in studying the problem of World Government and preparing this outline which I am anxious to have well received and widely read.

I trust, therefore, that you will be interested enough in the work to read the manuscript and to write an introductory note which I may publish with the text. I should greatly appreciate this honor.

Very sincerely,

Incl.

FIGURE 12: CORRESPONDENCE BETWEEN HARRY H. LAUGHLIN AND H.G. WELLS REGARDING LAUGHLIN'S ONE-WORLD EUGENIC GOVERNMENT PROPOSAL. *(HEREIN PUBLISHED AND PRINTED FOR THE FIRST TIME WITH PERMISSION OF THE SPECIAL COLLECTIONS DEPARTMENT AT TRUMAN UNIVERSITY. — BOX B-5-4B:11 LAUGHLIN PAPERS)*

Chap. 10: 1900

AMERICAN FRONT: CARRIE NATION BEGINS HER CRUSADE TO DEMOLISH SALOONS. **SCIENCE & TECHNOLOGY:** MAX PLANCK ANNOUNCES HIS DISCOVERY OF THE LAW OF BLACK BODY EMISSION, MARKING THE BIRTH OF QUANTUM PHYSICS. **LIFE:** FRIEDRICH NIETZSCHE, GERMAN PHILOSOPHER AND WRITER DIES. — HEINRICH HIMMLER, HEAD OF THE NATIONAL SOCIALIST SS, AND RUDOLF HÖSS, NATIONAL SOCIALIST OFFICIAL ARE BORN.

Sec. I - FROM GOOD PUPIL TO FAITHFUL APOSTLE:

For the past few decades, Darwinists have been hard at work, desperately trying to establish the view that Darwinism was "misapplied" by individuals that "misunderstood" him in the drafting of the policies that led to The Holocaust. This claim needs to be re-examined, as it does not stand up to scrutiny. Clearly, Darwin's sons had the benefit of knowing his father, and by Leonard's and Francis's accounts, their father supported the eugenics that they dedicated their lives to. Two of the people most responsible for creating the ideology that directly leads to The Holocaust, Francis Galton, and Ernst Haeckel, were not just endorsed by Charles Darwin, but their work was incorporated into Darwin's second book, "The Descent of Man." In addition, we know for a fact that many influential individuals had the benefit of either being educated directly by Charles Darwin, or if not Darwin, his most famed supporter and champion of Darwinism, T.H. Huxley. We know for a fact that two important members of the international eugenics movement, Henry Fairfield Osborn and H.G. Wells, both were students of T.H. Huxley. The Royal Society certainly thought Henry Fairfield Osborn to have been a good pupil of Darwin's as they honored him with their prestigious Darwin Medal. Beyond that, it must be remembered that both the Royal Society and the Linnaean Society believed Julian Huxley to understand his grandfather's work, as they awarded him the Darwin Medal as well as the Darwin-Wallace Medal. Lastly, all the most prominent eugenicists in the United States, Britain, and Germany understood their views to be founded in Darwin's theories and said so explicitly. These were the most lauded sons of Cambridge, Oxford, and the Ivy League institutions. Darwin's biological theory had very real ramifications for social theory from the onset and not simply an unfortunate afterthought to Holocaust history as Darwinists would have us believe:

> Adrian Desmond and James Moore in their 1991 biography, Darwin: The Life of a Tormented Evolutionist, make clear that natural selection was intended as more than a theory of life's origins. "'Social Darwinism' is often taken to be something extraneous, an ugly concretion added to the pure Darwinian corpus after the event, tarnishing Darwin's image," they write. "But his notebooks make plain that competition, free trade, imperialism, racial extermination, and sexual inequality were written into the equation from the start-Darwinism was invented to explain human society." (commonwealmagazine.org, "The Gentle Darwinians: What Darwin's Champions Won't Mention", Peter Quinn, Commonweal, Vol. CXXXIV, No. 5, March 9, 2007)

The political propagandizing of Darwin's theory was also part of its initial presentation. This is precisely what Hooker and Huxley wanted from Darwin, and the otherwise reserved Darwin happily rode their extensive propaganda efforts to eternal fame. Galton converted the theory into a proposal for governance, an all-encompassing creed to be followed like a "religion." Eugenics, in turn, is political at its core because Darwinism was political from the onset per the efforts of Hooker and Huxley. The utopian and statist politics cannot be separated from the eugenics, and eugenics, as conceived by Francis Galton and Leonard Darwin, cannot be separated from its Darwinian roots. One simply cannot accomplish what eugenics seeks to accomplish, to treat humanity like a breeder, without having the government take the position of the farmer, and the population taking the subordinate position of the livestock, precisely as Charles Darwin himself postulated in "Descent of Man." This is bequeathing the state with the position of "master" or "overseer" of the population. Thus, every word written in justification of eugenics is a proposal for the future, and a Darwinian one by necessity.

That said, there is one eugenicist, out of all these faithful students of Darwinism, who dedicated his entire life to translating Galton's and Darwin's work into a vision for a new world: H.G. Wells, who was taught Darwinism by T.H. Huxley and debated eugenics with Francis Galton himself. Wells would throughout his life extrapolate the gospel of eugenics into various different fictional utopias. It is also no coincidence that the height of H.G. Well's fame came at the turn-of-the-century. Published in 1901, his first non-fiction bestseller was "Anticipations of the Reaction of Mechanical and Scientific Progress Upon Human Life and Thought." The book anticipated what the world would be like in the year 2000. This was a persisting theme for Wells. His other works persist along the line of eugenic utopian thought: "Mankind in the Making" (1903), "A Modern Utopia" (1905), "Men Like Gods" (1923), "The Science of Life" (1930), and "The Work, Wealth and Happiness of Mankind" (1931)

The 1905 "A Modern Utopia" and the 1901 "Anticipations" were the most revealing of all of H.G. Wells' utopian visions. His Malthusian population theory together with the critical view of free-market capitalism combined to create what Wells called a "modern" vision of an ideal society, and most interestingly, a "New Republic." Wells acknowledges at the beginning of "Modern Utopia" that the book was neither a novel nor an essay. "A Modern Utopia" was the result of what Wells called "a peculiar method," one which he believed to be "the best way to a sort of lucid vagueness which has always been my intention in this matter." [431] This "lucid vagueness" is the ambiguity necessary to keep the reader believing in the viability of the utopian scheme. Wells knew that too much reality was detrimental to utopian schemes. Case in point, Edward Bellamy's "Looking Backward" had been significantly successful due to its "lucid vagueness," while the specificity and elaboration on actual policy proposals extrapolated in the sequel, "Equality," had by most accounts been the reason for its complete failure. Wells, like Bellamy, oscillated between specificity and vagueness, never allowing the reader to approach close

---

[431] Pg. xxxi – "A Modern Utopia", H.G. Wells, Chapman & Hall, Ld., 1905.

enough to their creation to reveal its true nature. Thus, it can be stated that both Bellamy and Wells peddled in platitudes, to maintain this "suspension of disbelief," this "lucid vagueness," for the reader to be enamored of the proposed future as if in a dream. This is certainly true when it came to depicting how otherwise harsh eugenic policy would be administered. Note the deceitfully romantic feel to this passage from chapter nine entitled "The Faith, Morals, and Public Policy of the New Republic":

> And the ethical system of these men of the New Republic, the ethical system which will dominate the world state, will be shaped primarily to favour the procreation of what is fine and efficient and beautiful in humanity beautiful and strong bodies, clear and powerful minds, and a growing body of knowledge and to check the procreation of base and servile types -- To do the latter is to do the former; the two things are inseparable. ---- In the new vision death is no inexplicable horror, no pointless terminal terror to the miseries of life, it is the end of all the pain of life, the end of the bitterness of failure, the merciful obliteration of weak and silly and pointless things. . . (onlineliterature.com, "Anticipations of the Reaction of Mechanical and Scientific Progress upon Human Life and Thought" – Original published by North American Review, June-Nov. 1901)

However idealistic the above passage may seem, its goals were explicit. The unavoidable description of the Fabian future is its intolerance to diversity, adversity, or change. Statist proposals are by their very nature static, vulnerable to the consequences of change. Utopias by definition cannot withstand change, as they assume to have arrived at perfection. They are perfectionist aspirations whose equilibrium can only be disturbed by the injection of a new technology, a different culture, a different art, a disproportion between male and female, a rise or fall in productivity, a rise or fall in population, or an element of the population which refuses to adhere to their predetermined lives. Utopias are fragile playthings of the mind of a single individual. They cannot withstand participatory collaboration or deliberation.

> Humanity has set out in the direction of a more complex and exacting organization, and until, by a foresight to me at least inconceivable, it can prevent the birth of just all the inadaptable, useless, or merely unnecessary creatures in each generation, there must needs continue to be, in greater or less amount, this individually futile struggle beneath the feet of race; somewhere and in some form there must still persist those essentials that now take shape as the slum, the prison, and the asylum. (onlineliterature.com, "Anticipations of the Reaction of Mechanical and Scientific Progress upon Human Life and Thought" – Original published by North American Review, June-Nov. 1901)

All this ethnic cleansing was to provide a pristine future. Like Laughlin's one-world government proposal, Wells' utopia is a one-world-state, using modern technologies to provide for a unified citizenry.

If the surmise of a developing New Republic a Republic that must ultimately become a World State of capable rational men, developing amidst the fading contours and colours of our existing nations and institutions be indeed no idle dream, but an attainable possibility in the future. (onlineliterature.com, "Anticipations of the Reaction of Mechanical and Scientific Progress upon Human Life and Thought" – Original published by North American Review, June-Nov. 1901)

True to his Fabian Socialist underpinning, Wells' 1905 "Modern Utopia" was a expression of global socialism, where all citizens were allegedly provided with the means to live, and where "individual liberty" is better characterized as "freedom" from having to earn a living, or as many socialist then and after would characterize it, free from the burdens of freedom. "Cradle-to-grave" governmental proposals arise from this utopian dogma. Take note of Section 4 of the chapter entitled "Failure in a Modern Utopia" which incidentally is posted online by Marxists.org:

> The modern Utopia will give a universal security indeed, and exercise the minimum of compulsions to toil, but it will offer some acutely desirable prizes. The aim of these devices, the minimum wage, the standard of life, provision for all the feeble and unemployed and so forth, is not to rob life of incentives but to change their nature, to make life not less energetic, but less panic-stricken and violent and base, to shift the incidence of the struggle for existence from our lower to our higher emotions, so to anticipate and neutralize the motives of the cowardly and bestial, that the ambitious and energetic imagination which is man's finest quality may become the incentive and determining factor in survival. (marxists.org, "A Modern Utopia", Originally published by the Fortnightly Review, Oct. 1904-April 1905)

However, H.G. Wells recognized the primary reason why the preceding utopian schemes were eugenic by their very nature. Wells was aware that to maintain the guarantee of providing all a minimum economic life, resources must not be depleted or strained by an ever-growing population. In other words, to redistribute wealth equally, the collective wealth cannot be depleted by a population that increases beyond the availability of commodities. As such, the one major restriction in Wells' "Modern Utopia" was a eugenic control:

> For a multitude of contemptible and silly creatures, fear-driven and helpless and useless, unhappy or hatefully happy in the midst of squalid dishonor, feeble, ugly, inefficient, born of unrestrained lusts, and increasing and multiplying through sheer incontinence and stupidity, the men of the New Republic will have little pity and less benevolence. To make life convenient for the breeding of such people will seem to them not the most virtuous and amiable thing in the world, as it is held to be now, but an exceedingly abominable proceeding. (onlineliterature.com, "Anticipations of the Reaction of Mechanical and Scientific Progress upon Human Life and Thought" – Original published by North American Review, June-Nov. 1901)

Therefore, in "A Modern Utopia," reproduction was strictly regulated, with the goal of sustaining an optimum population that was limited along racial lines:

> They will rout out and illuminate urban rookeries and all places where the base can drift to multiply; they will contrive a land legislation that will keep the black, or yellow, or mean-white squatter on the move -- No doubt the sentimentalist and all whose moral sense has been vigorously trained in the old school will find this rather a dreadful suggestion. (onlineliterature.com, "Anticipations of the Reaction of Mechanical and Scientific Progress upon Human Life and Thought" – Original published by North American Review, June-Nov. 1901)

Following the footsteps of Malthus, Darwin, and Galton, Wells had identified unchecked population growth as the greatest danger to the utopian society: "a State whose population continues to increase in obedience to unchecked instinct, can progress only from bad to worse." Wells was hardly squeamish about describing how the population would be checked. This book quotes Wells at length precisely so the reader can ascertain the true nature of the ideas which these authors committed to permanence, and as Orwell pointed out, how they are inescapably married to their actual application by the Nazis [432]:

> This thing, this **euthanasia of the weak and sensual**, is possible. On the principles that will probably animate the predominant classes of the new time, it will be permissible, and I have little or no doubt that in the future it will be planned and achieved. -- **In such matters the New Republic will entertain no superstition of *laisses faire.*** (emphasis mine, onlineliterature.com, "Anticipations of the Reaction of Mechanical and Scientific Progress upon Human Life and Thought" – Original published by North American Review, June-Nov. 1901)

One could easily take the above quote by H.G. Wells and ascribe them to "Mein Kampf" without raising any suspicions. That was the crux of Orwell's biting criticism of Wells in his 1941 op-ed. Of course, the mindset appropriate to institutionalized euthanasia as a population control scheme must go hand-in-hand with the policy, as it did with the Hitler Youth and the SS death squads in the Third Reich. Compassion and sentimentality have no place where a systematic eradication of significant portions of the population is necessary:

> The men of the New Republic will not be squeamish, either, in facing or inflicting death, because they will have a fuller sense of the possibilities of life than we possess. They will have an ideal that will make killing worth the while; like Abraham, they will have the faith to kill, and they will have no superstitions about death. -- People who cannot live happily and freely in the world without spoiling the lives of others are better out of it. That is a current sentiment even to-day, but the men of the New Republic will have the courage of their opinions. (emphasis mine, onlineliterature.com, "Anticipations of the Reaction of Mechanical and Scientific Progress upon Human Life and Thought" – Original published by North American Review, June-Nov. 1901)

---

[432] "Wells, Hitler and the World State", George Orwell, Horizon, Aug. 1941.

Clearly, religion and its morality can have no place in a society where the definition of "murder" must be altered to accommodate the state's population policy, as was the case in the utopian schemes of the Third Reich and the USSR:

> They will have no positive definition of God at all. They will certainly not indulge in "that something, not ourselves, that makes for righteousness" (not defined) or any defective claptrap of that sort. They will content themselves with denying the self-contradictory absurdities of an obstinately anthropomorphic theology. (Pg. 306, "Anticipations of the Reaction of Mechanical and Scientific Progress upon Human Life and Thought", Harper & Brothers ed., 1901)

Most poignantly, Wells understood precisely where his opinion on population came from. Wells was dedicated to a Malthusian world-view, as this was the world-view of his mentors and teachers T.H. Huxley, Francis Galton and Charles Darwin. Here is Wells' opinion on Malthus:

> Probably no more shattering book than the Essay on Population has ever been, or ever will be, written. It was aimed at the facile Liberalism of the Deists and Atheists of the eighteenth; it made as clear as daylight that all forms of social reconstruction, all dreams of earthly golden ages must be either futile or insincere or both, until the problems of human increase were manfully faced. (Pg. 312, "Anticipations of the Reaction of Mechanical and Scientific Progress upon Human Life and Thought", Harper & Brothers ed., 1901)

Wells portrays his utopia as a society without poverty, allegedly with free choice of occupation and interest. However, this notion of free will is revealed as false as Wells fully admits his utopian society was micromanaged by an elite group of "voluntary noblemen" called "samurai":

> It has become apparent that whole masses of human population are, as a whole, inferior in their claim upon the future, to other masses, that they cannot be given opportunities or trusted with power as the superior peoples are trusted, that their characteristic weaknesses are contagious and detrimental in the civilizing fabric, and that their range of incapacity tempts and demoralizes the strong ---- To give them equality is to sink to their level, to protect and cherish them is to be swamped in their fecundity. ---- Liberalism is a thing of the past, it is no longer a doctrine, but a faction. (Pg. 314, "Anticipations of the Reaction of Mechanical and Scientific Progress upon Human Life and Thought", Harper & Brothers ed., 1901)

Note the tone towards ethnic minorities and the lack of empathy for those he deems lesser; a recipe for totalitarian oppression, if not worse. Wells is honest in describing the reality of his proposal. Wells' words would have made Hitler proud, and very likely inspired him as did the works of other utopian socialists and eugenicists. Consider this passage. It predates Adolf Hitler's and Henry Ford's antipathy towards Judaism by decades:

> **And how will the New Republic treat the inferior races?** How will it deal with the black? How will it deal with the yellow man? How will it tackle that alleged

termite in the civilized woodwork, the Jew? **Certainly not as races at all.** It will aim to establish, and it will at last, though probably only after a second century has passed, establish a world-state with a common language and a common rule. All over the world its roads, its standards, its laws, and its apparatus of control will run. It will, I have said, make the multiplication of those who fall behind a certain standard of social efficiency unpleasant and difficult, and it will have cast aside any coddling laws to save adult men from themselves. ---- And the Jew also it will treat as any other man. It is said that the Jew is incurably a parasite on the apparatus of credit. If there are parasites on the apparatus of credit, that is a reason for the legislative cleaning of the apparatus of credit, but it is no reason for the special treatment of the Jew. If the Jew has a certain incurable tendency to social parasitism, and we make social parasitism impossible, we shall abolish the Jew, and if he has not, there is no need to abolish the Jew. ... And for the rest, those swarms of black, and brown, and dirty-white, and yellow people, who do not come into the new needs of efficiency? Well, the world is a world, not a charitable institution, and I take it they will have to go. (emphasis mine, Pg. 340, "Anticipations of the Reaction of Mechanical and Scientific Progress upon Human Life and Thought", Harper & Brothers ed., 1901)

Substantially similar population control policies appear in all utopian socialism, fictional or real, throughout the era, and were a core concept behind Fabian Socialism and American Progressivism. Their governing concepts faltered without this population policy, as their government structure assumed that wealth was a fixed figure, to be distributed, and at odds with the capitalistic endeavors necessary to grow wealth. To admit that wealth needed to grow to keep up with natural population increases, was to admit the necessity of capitalism. This is an admission no self-respecting Fabian Socialist or American Progressive would willingly make. All these political creeds were disgusted enough by the "chaos" and "competition" of capitalism to revile its uncontrolled growth, namely its boom-to-bust cycles. Either way, "growth" was not an option – only equitable distribution and redistribution of capital. If the proverbial economic pie could not grow to accommodate a larger population, then the population had to be held in check. The centrally planned society is significantly compromised by uncontrolled and unpredictable sexual activity. A population that is unpredictable cannot be planned for, and the pristine and "lucid" utopian vision collapses under the weight of uncertainty. Statist economic policy needed a static population. Thus, Eugenic population controls were consistently prevalent in the governmental schemes, fictional or real, as dreamed up by the eugenicists, Fabians, and Progressives. Therefore, it should come as no surprise that the most vaunted of Fabian Socialist economists, John Maynard Keynes, was an avid supporter and leading member of the international eugenics movement. It is also no surprise that all communal experiments in the United States, namely John Humphrey Noyes's Oneida Colony, employed strict eugenic population control measures that severely intruded in the most private of personal decisions one could imagine, down to the enforcement of male continence during the sexual act.

And for the rest, those swarms of black, and brown, and dirty white, and yellow people, who do not come into the new needs of efficiency? Well, the world is a world, not a charitable institution, and I take it they will have to go. The whole tenor and meaning of the world, as I see it, is that they have to go. So far as they fail to develop sane, vigorous, and distinctive personalities for the great world of the future, it is their portion to die out and disappear. (Pg. 342, "Anticipations of the Reaction of Mechanical and Scientific Progress upon Human Life and Thought", Harper & Brothers ed., 1901)

Leonard Darwin foresaw the day when "eugenics would become not only a grail, a substitute for religion, as Galton had hoped but a 'paramount duty' whose tenets would presumably become enforceable." [433] Discarding religion and giving an aristocratic elite power over the population similar to the power a farmer enjoys over his farm animals is arrogant, to say the least, and it takes a zealot not to see the hubris or inherent danger in these demands. Aside from eugenics, Leonard Darwin wrote and lectured extensively on strictly political subjects. He wrote two books on "Municipal Ownership" and "Municipal Trade," which read like proposals for a Marxist appropriation of the "means of production." Note the similarities to Wells:

To save the race, compulsion would be necessary in many cases, and where needed it must be fearlessly adopted. If by compulsion is meant the actual use of physical force, compulsion should only be employed to enforce imprisonment or segregation; the latter term meaning confinement in comfort. Compulsion is now permitted if applied to criminals, lunatics, and mental defectives; and this principle must be extended to all who, by having offspring, would seriously damage future generations. Pgs. 141–143, "Race Deterioration and Practical Politics", Leonard Darwin, Eugenics Review, Oct. 17, 1925)

Clearly, Leonard Darwin, like Wells, was not squeamish about the use of force towards racial hygiene. Like Wells, and Hitler after him, Leonard Darwin was a self-appointed micro-manager of humanity. He was a central planner through and through. The 1907 book "Municipal Ownership" by Leonard Darwin gives insight on where Leonard Darwin stands on *laissez-faire* economics and planned economies. Leonard Darwin, as can be expected from his utopian eugenic views, was a "planner." Just like Wells, Leonard believed there to be an aristocratic or scientific elite that had the right and/or ability to plan humanity. What he calls for in "Municipal Ownership" is in essence "control" by the state of a planned economy. What Leonard Darwin is describing by "Municipal Ownership" is what is in modern times known as "nationalization" of industry, and among the pros and cons in Leonard Darwin's analysis of where the benefit will land, or how the investment in nationalized industry will serve the socialistic ends of "distributed wealth":

This enquiry concerning private industry is a necessary preliminary to a study of municipal ownership; because, in cases where municipal ownership would now be an improvement on private industry, it would not necessarily be so if private

---

[433] Pg. 347 - "A Life of Sir Francis Galton", Nicholas Wright Gillham, Oxford Univ. Press, 2001.

industry were better controlled. (Pg. x, "Municipal Ownership: Four Lectures Delivered at Harvard University", E.P. Dutton, 1907)

Case in point, an 1861 letter from Karl Marx to Ferdinand Lassalle probably underscores the subject of this section best. In this letter, Karl Marx voiced his opinion that "Darwin's work is most important and suits my purpose in that it provides a basis in natural science for the historical class struggle." [434] Marx and Engels obviously recognized Darwinism for what it was: in the realm of politics, and not in any way, shape or form a "pure science." Likewise, George Bernard Shaw was quoted as saying: "The only fundamental and possible socialism is the socialisation of the selective breeding of man." [435] Shaw's proclamation along with Karl Marx's statement goes to the heart of the matter: eugenics simply isn't possible without a heavy-handed statist governmental policy. Eugenics and socialism are one and the same, too intertwined and interdependent to be divorced. As such, supporters of Marxist state planning often found the idea of a planned genetic future attractive.

"The Webbs supported eugenic planning just as fervently as town planning." Beatrice Webb declared eugenics to be "the most important question of all" while her husband remarked that "no eugenicist can be a laissez-faire individualist." (Pgs. 351-353, "Measuring the Mind: Education and Psychology in England 1860-1990", Alan Woodridge, British Journal of Educational Studies, Vol. 43, No. 3, Sep. 1995)

As the above passage alludes, the antithesis to these utopian schemes is *laissez-faire* capitalism and *laissez-faire* democracy, both of which were universally detested by the ranks of the eugenics movement. Unimpeded or undirected individual freedom implies freedom not to subscribe to the utopian vision, and unimpeded liberty implies the liberty to conduct one's life in a way that is contradictory to the utopian scheme. It is no wonder these Fabians and Progressives detested *laissez-faire* policies as they did. The sought-after perfection cannot stand much choice. If the population is free to question the planners and the elite in the direction of their centrally planned schemes, then people will likely choose to follow their own dreams, rather than to fall into line in order to accomplish someone else's elitist utopian vision. Freedom and liberty obviously imply chaos, at least as seen from the point of view of those utopian socialists whom demand order, "solidarity," and a "unity of purpose." Capitalism is the unavoidable consequence of *laissez-faire* economics, as there is no plan inherent to "capitalism." However much socialist pundits want to paint "capitalism" as a governmental structure, the fact remains that there is no such thing as a "capitalist" form of government. There is no such thing as a "capitalist manifesto." In fact, despite the vast amount of recommendations on how to succeed in "capitalist" ventures, there is no ideology beyond "buy low – sell high" to a

---

[434] marxists.catbull.com, "Marx-Engels Correspondence 1861-Marx To Ferdinand Lassalle, In Berlin", Source: MECW, Vol. 41, Pg. 245.
[435] newstatesman.com, "The Eugenics Movement Britain Wants to Forget," Victoria Brignell, 2010.

"capitalistic" worldview. "Capitalism" is simply what occurs when a population has unimpeded and undirected economic freedom. Capitalists transform dreams into products, and the dream to continue developing that product is made possible by profits; profits that are intended to perpetuate the individualistic aspirations of the proprietor, not the central planner.

Adam Smith is frequently called the father of modern economics. His best-known work is "An Inquiry into the Nature and Causes of the Wealth of Nations," which has been shortened by most people to "Wealth of Nations," first published in 1776. Smith wrote at the time of Mercantilism and an emergent middle class that was eager to break free from the traditional systems of the old aristocracy. The market system was maturing, and the new middle class benefited the most from it. There were many who advocated letting markets work free of government regulation, the most famous of which were the Physiocrats of France who invented the phrase "*laissez-faire*," or "let it be." This phrase has become almost synonymous with Smith's position on economic interventionism. He thought that the government should play a very limited role in regulating markets. Note the stark difference to the utopian schemes previously described:

- People are self-interested.
- People naturally trade as a means of getting what they want.
- In a "free" market, people will not exchange unless both gain.
- Self-interest will cause individuals to buy what they want and produce goods that others.
- Prices tell buyers and sellers the wants and needs of society.
- People will unintentionally meet society's needs as they pursue their self-interest without government intervention.

Smith laid the intellectual framework that explained the free-market, and which still holds true today. He is most often recognized for the expression "the invisible hand," which he used to demonstrate how self-interest guides the most efficient use of resources in a nation's economy, with public welfare coming as a by-product. Smith argued that state and personal efforts specifically dedicated to promoting social good are ineffectual compared to unbridled market forces. The date of publication for "Wealth of Nations" coincided with the American Revolution. America's Founding Fathers, particularly Alexander Hamilton, James Madison, and Benjamin Franklin, created a government structure meant to allow for the freedom prescribed by Adam Smith. Modern proponents of *laissez-faire* capitalism such as Ludwig Von Mises and Ayn Rand picked up on the observation of an "invisible hand" in a capitalistic society and provided their own proposals along their own lines of thinking. They called it a "harmony of interests." One of the basic tenets of Ludwig Von Mises' *laissez-faire* economics is "the harmony of rightly understood interests." [436] More to the point, Von Mises's approach is not a simply utilitarian one, but one rooted in humanistic goals and desires, where the "general well-being"

---

[436] "Von Mises on the Harmony of Interests" Henry Oliver, Jr., Ethics journal, Vol. 70, No. 4, July 1960.

achieved by prosperity allows for humanity to express itself. Herein lay the crux of this argument: *laissez-faire*, let it be, allows humanity to express itself without the reigns or restraints that eugenic central planners, the glorified herders of animals and men, would place on the populace.

These Libertarian ideals are expounded here as opposites help define the extremes of eugenic statism. Ludwig Von Mises delivered six lectures in Buenos Aires in 1959 on capitalism, socialism, interventionism, inflation, foreign investment, and politics. In "Economic Policy," Von Mises documents that it was this very doctrine of "the harmony of interests" that socialists opposed.[437] They spoke of an "irreconcilable conflict of interests." In the first chapter of the "Communist Manifesto," Marx and Engels claimed that there was an irreconcilable conflict between classes. Von Mises points out that the Manifesto could not illustrate any examples other than those drawn from the conditions of pre-capitalistic society to attack the doctrine of "harmony of interests." As this book documents, the "Manifesto" was written in the late 1840s, and neither Marx or Engels ever lived to witness the liberating aspects of *laissez-faire* economics as we enjoy today.

Ironically enough, H.G. Wells's futurist views were equally arcane. H.G. Wells often complained that the professional was the subordinate of the less technically or scientifically knowledgeable superior, what he calls the "irresponsible wealth" or the "charlatan governing class"; clearly, a view that failed to anticipate the barons of the "idea economy" in the digital age, a failure of Wells's short-sighted futurisms. Wells's views also coincide with the young Adolf Hitler. He saw no direction, no plan, no efficient decision making in *laissez-faire* economics and therefore dismissed these freedoms as a passing fad yet to crumble under the consequences of its own chaos:

> Politically modern Democracy takes the form of denying that any specific person or persons shall act as a matter of intrinsic right or capacity on behalf of the community as a whole. (Pg. 160, "Anticipations of the Reaction of Mechanical and Scientific Progress upon Human Life and Thought", Harper & Brothers ed., 1901)

This utopian balancing act described above is precisely what makes socialist micro-management the recipe for a society helplessly suspended in stasis. The individual elements are to obey and conform to their predetermined roles. Individual initiative becomes a potential danger rather than a creative force. As Wells' aptly points out, new developments create new opportunities and generate a new group interest to be contended with. The more successful the innovation, the more radical the change that ensues, and the more unpredictability there is in a newly formed and misunderstood sector of society. While any sensible and honest reading of the eugenic-utopian aspirations depicted by H.G. Wells will concede that they come uncomfortably close to the proclamations and deeds of Hitler's Third Reich, it is equally correct to point out that they mirror and originate with Darwin, Malthus, and Galton, as Wells himself understood his work to be. Wells, better than anyone, understood that he was not just their pupil, but their dedicated apostle. His world-

---

[437] "Economic Policy: Thoughts for Today and Tomorrow", Ludwig Von Mises, Ludwig von Mises Institute, 2006.

vision was their world-vision:
> Impinging on geological discovery, it awakened almost simultaneously in the minds of Darwin and Wallace, that train of thought that found expression and demonstration at last in the theory of natural selection. -- As that theory has been more and more thoroughly assimilated and understood by the general mind, it has destroyed, quietly but entirely, the belief in human equality which is implicit in all the "Liberalizing" movements of the world. (Pg. 313, "Anticipations of the Reaction of Mechanical and Scientific Progress upon Human Life and Thought", Harper & Brothers ed., 1901)

Wells was the archetypal socialist and eugenic utopian. He was a man made of books and unhindered communication, yet his utopian writings evidence that he was otherwise unable to recognize the forces at play until it was too late. It seems that George Orwell's August 1941 article in Horizon Magazine finally devastated and awoke the self-styled utopian to the consequences of his utopian socialism. Wells spent the early years of the war bitterly lampooning Hitler, only to have his respected colleague point out that Wells's utopian visions were alive in Hitler's technocratic, eugenic, and Spartan form of socialism. Orwell published "Wells, Hitler and the World State" in August of 1941, and it seems that Wells thereafter spent a significant amount of effort backpedaling on the subject of eugenics and individual rights. Recall the sinister nature of the quotes from Wells's various works, and compare them to these post-1941 quotes below:

> There are claptrap phrases about backward races and inferior peoples . . . There are no backward races. All over the earth babies start from scratch, full of distinctive and untried possibilities, which the New World will develop eagerly. (Pg. 79 – "H.G. Wells's Eugenic Thinking of the 1930s and 1940s", John S. Partington, Utopian Studies, Vol. 14, No. 1, 2003 - From "Man's Heritage", Radio broadcast 1944)

Wells even turned his back on his mentors, Charles Darwin, T.H. Huxley, and all of his Fabian Socialist colleagues that had been clamoring for a "directed evolution" by "selective breeding," proclaiming in 1944:

> There is no analogy between human breeding and the methods of animal breeders . . . We have to take everything we beget. Nor do we want a set type, we want a great variety of types." (Pg. 79 – "H.G. Wells's Eugenic Thinking of the 1930s and 1940s", John S. Partington, Utopian Studies, Vol. 14, No. 1, 2003)

Nor was the attack on the Darwin-Galton Fabians subtle. Consider the doctoral thesis that Wells penned in 1944:

> There he declared that **"Galton had the mental disposition of a Fascist and was all for fuehrers and duces"** Perhaps this is unfair on Galton as Wells was clearly influenced by his eugenic research. But it is equally clear that Wells, as an old man of 78, did not want to pass away with the taint of Galtonian eugenics upon him. The Second World War, and the eugenic experiments being revealed by

the liberation of the concentration camps and death camps of Central Europe, had poisoned the reputation of eugenics and apparently forced Wells, the erstwhile half-baked eugenicist, to reject it out of hand. (emphasis mine, Pg. 79 – "H.G. Wells's Eugenic Thinking of the 1930s and 1940s", John S. Partington, Utopian Studies, Vol. 14, No. 1, 2003 – From pg. 183, "Thesis", 1944)

"Parricide" indeed, as George Orwell had mused. Orwell understood the importance H.G. Wells had in the early 20th Century. Wells's influence on the vast swarm of planning-obsessed technocrats and utopians made Wells one of the rightful parents of the movement:

> If one looks through nearly any book that he has written in the last forty years one finds the same idea constantly recurring: the supposed antithesis between the man of science who is working towards a planned World State and the reactionary who is trying to restore a disorderly past. In novels, Utopias, essays, films, pamphlets, the antithesis crops up, always more or less the same. . . . I doubt whether anyone who was writing books between 1900 and 1920, at any rate in the English language, influenced the young so much. The minds of all of us, and therefore the physical world, would be perceptibly different if Wells had never existed. ("Wells, Hitler and the World State", George Orwell, Horizon London, August 1941 – Reprinted in "Critical Essays", 1946)

Alas, much of what Wells had "imagined and worked for" was "physically there in Nazi Germany. The order, the planning, the State encouragement of science, the steel, the concrete, the aeroplanes, are all there." [438] Wells had been given freedom of association and communication, and in return, dedicated his life to eradicating that open opportunity for others. Ironically, Wells exemplified the pathetic mistrust of technological change so common to utopians and collectivist planners. Wells may have loved airplanes, but he wanted strict "federal world control of the air." [439] Was Wells's need for control pathological? It certainly was typical of the Fabian type. Wells simply did not understand that entrepreneurship is at the core of innovation and that innovation needs freedom of unplanned association. This is not an observation made in the abstract. Interestingly enough, these contradictory forces of planned and unplanned progress played out in one of the most important events in world history. The greatest testament to *laissez-faire* capitalistic liberty is the success of the Wright Brothers. The Smithsonian Institution shunned the brothers as they were not part of the formally educated scientific elite that would have been logically picked to produce a flying machine. The Smithsonian Institution hired its own "expert," and based on the "merit" of his resume, funded this "expert's" venture into creating a flying machine. The Wrights were bicycle repairmen from some small and rural town. The brothers didn't possess the university degrees, or from the Smithsonian's perspective, the technical know-how necessary to produce a flying machine. To be fully truthful, the Wright Brothers were the capitalistic chaos that

---

[438] "Wells, Hitler and the World State", George Orwell, Horizon London, August 1941 – Reprinted in "Critical Essays", 1946.
[439] Ibid.

eugenic utopians like John Maynard Keynes, H.G. Wells, Harry H. Laughlin, and just about every Fabian Socialist and American Progressive derided. The Wright Brothers were simply not part of the planned progress according to the vaunted Smithsonian Institution or had the credentials to argue with the elite minds of this prestigious government-run and funded institution. The story of the Wright Brothers is also the greatest refutation to any aspirations of planning society of elite "samurai," as H.G. Wells proposed. The Wright Brothers used their "capital" as well as their personal motivation to produce what all the influence and political might of the Smithsonian Institution could not. Their story debunks any notion that a central planning body can guide and control the outcome of an economy by picking the winners, by picking the "samurai," by choosing who leads and who follows by applying logic and reason. In much the same way, it debunks the claim of the eugenicists that they can pick the biologically superior or inferior, the productive or the wasteful, or the deserving or undeserving of life. Clearly, the Wright Brothers were not candidates in the list of future leaders that their contemporary eugenicists hoped would lead society to prosperity. The brothers knew there was a high possibility of failure, yet they only seemed to thrive on failed experiments.

It is also one of the greatest ironies in history that the capitalist Wright brothers outdid the self-proclaimed futurist, H.G. Wells. The Wright brothers dreamed and engineered the future, while Wells only bloviated about it. In almost every way, the Wright Brothers put figures like H.G. Wells and John Maynard Keynes to shame. H.G. Wells specifically spent his entire life dreaming of, planning for, and designing the future. His futuristic visions, in retrospect, can only be regarded as impotent and flaccid in comparison to the efforts and vision of the Wright Brothers. The Wright Brother's flying machine did more to pull humanity into the future than any of H.G. Wells' utopian fictions ever could have. Wells only dreamed of modern travel. The Wright Brothers, largely because of the economic freedom afforded them by the American tradition of *laissez-faire* capitalism, made modern travel a reality.

Sec. 2 - WHERE WAS THE HOLOCAUST BY THE "FASCISTS"?

The terms "Left" and "Right" have become painfully useless in delineating political affiliations, and in retrospect, it is doubtful that they ever were useful. Historically speaking, they quickly fall apart when discussing political structures at a global level, as the definitions of "Left" and "Right" differ greatly when one crosses oceans or borders. The term "liberal" has long since been of no use as well, as it was usurped by the Fabian Socialists and American Progressives to represent policies that are historically the most intrusive to personal autonomy and individual "liberty." Most modern-day "liberals" are quite happy to surrender individual autonomy to the state in the pursuit of communal or utopian dreams. In turn, traditional "liberals," or "classical liberals," have distanced themselves by inventing the entirely new category of "libertarianism" to indicate the political values that used to be associated with the term "liberal" before collectivist and socialist forces usurped it. Even the term "conservative" is of little use when documenting world history, as one first has to address what precisely is being "conserved" by the different political groups around the world. The term "conservative" is of little use when describing political alliances between the United States and Britain, as the role of traditional aristocracies and monarchies becomes divisive and destructive to any theoretical grouping. Clearly, no red-blooded "conservative" in the United States wants anything to do with aristocracies or monarchies sanctioned by religious institutions, as it is precisely an animosity towards the British Crown and the corrupt ways of the bishops and magistrates that fueled the American Revolution and inspired the Founding Fathers to have such a vocal disdain for "titles of nobility."

The fog of war that clouded all political discussions during and in the wake of the Cold War has definitely warped any consistent definition of "right" and "left," "conservative" and "liberal." Most of this confusion is based on the alliances formed during World War II. Historians and political pundits are fixated with the Axis alliance between Hitler's National Socialism and the Fascism of Franco and Mussolini, thus lump them all together as "fascist" despite significant and tangible differences. The logic is obviously flawed and inconsistent as the political allegiance between the USSR and the United States was certainly not indicative of commonality in political philosophies. Ideologically speaking, Stalin certainly thought that he had more in common with Hitler, and their collusion certainly would have endured, if it were not for the fact that Hitler thought Stalin and all Eastern European Slavs to be useful only as slaves of the Aryans. Likewise, the differences between Mussolini's and Franco's "fascism" and Hitler's "Nationalized" form of "Socialism" are pronounced, and philosophically evidence a gulf not otherwise present between the governing philosophies of Hitler and Stalin.

First, neither Hitler or Stalin would ever have allowed the Catholic Church to maintain the power that it did in Spain and Italy. Secondly, the Catholic electorate or philosophical indifference on the part of Mussolini and Franco meant that neither of them ever showed an interest in either "race hygiene" or "eugenics" to the pervasive extent to which eugenics controlled anything and everything under National Socialism. Neither Mussolini's Italy nor Franco's Spain enacted genocidal policies central to their overall political scheme. To the contrary, eugenics as state policy otherwise appears more pronounced in "progressive" minded democracies, namely through Theodore Roosevelt or Winston Churchill, than they do in Fascist Spain or Italy.

There was a multiplicity of proposals for a "third way" to organize and govern, somewhere between democracy and communism as the 19th century turned into the 20th. Italian Fascism, German National Socialism, and Spanish National Syndicalism were the three regimes that historians typically ascribe to the broader label of "fascism." The proposals were varied in ideology and actual application, but through them ran a string which held the "national" as supreme over the individual, a belief that the experiment of democracy had failed, that a communal or social unity was the necessary spirit to forward the interests of the people and nation, and a departing with the "internationalist" taint of the Bolshevik communists and socialists. Their departure from the communists or socialists was due to the belief that their communal efforts extended only so far as their people or nation reached, and they had contempt for calls for a "one world government" or "international socialism." Other than a refusal to bow to Moscow, as the Bolsheviks would have wanted, their methods of governing were indistinguishable from those of Lenin, Stalin, or other International Socialists. More precisely, none of them would have fit "conservatism" in the political arena of the United States, as American "conservatism" has always sought to "conserve" the Founding Father's notion of "limited government" and *laissez-fair* democracy.

Other than their allegiance to Hitler's National Socialism, the only reason to cover National Syndicalism or Italian Fascism in this book is to underline just how irrelevant they were in respects to eugenics and The Holocaust, and thus help clarify for posterity, where these ideologies originate from and must be relegated to in the future. Neither the Spanish National Syndicalism nor the Italian Fascists ever enacted any type of national push to purge society from its undesired biological elements. Surely, they employed the use of internment camps for their police states, but these two states had no participation in the history of eugenic sterilization, segregation or euthanasia. In fact, whatever meager utterances there may have been inside of these regimes towards a eugenic movement is minuscule in comparison to those adopted in the United States, Britain, or the various Scandinavian countries, none of which are commonly associated with the ideologies of National Socialism. Before the reader gets too alarmed by this unpopular position, let it be known that this is also the position held by *Yad Vashem* in Israel and the National Holocaust Memorial in Washington, DC.

This is not to say that racism didn't exist in either Spain or Italy, and the fundamental distinctions are of historical importance: While this Hispanic author cannot speak for racism in Italy, he can say with confidence that Spain, and its Hispanic descendants, are among the most racist cultures. If a vulgar form of racism was requisite for genocide, then the Spaniards had plenty of it. Yet, "racialism" was not the central organizing theme for Franco as it was for Hitler.

Spaniard Fascism, or National Syndicalism, did, however, share with Hitler a pronounced disdain for *laissez-faire* or American style democracy. The Spanish Phalanx of the Assemblies of the National Syndicalist Offensive, known simply as the Falange, is the name of several political movements and parties dating to Spain of the 1930s. The word Falange means phalanx formation in Spanish. Members of the party were called Falangists, or in Spanish, *Falangistas*. The Syndicalism facet of the movement was a type of economic system proposed as a replacement for capitalism and an alternative to International Socialism. This was the governing philosophy as proposed by Ramiro Ledesma Ramos in his publication, "La Conquista del Estado," or "Conquest of the State." This publication was launched in 1931 and the first issue contained a manifesto for National Syndicalism. The original iterations of Falangism were similar to Italian fascism in certain respects. It shared its contempt for Internationalist Bolshevism as well as for *laissez-faire* democracy. It was inspired by Integralism and the Action Française. Integralism, or Integral nationalism, is an ideology according to which a nation is an organic unity. It places the nation or the state as an end and a moral good, rather than a means. The term "integralism" was coined by the French journalist Charles Maurras, whose conception of nationalism was illiberal and anti-internationalist. Keep in mind that the architects of Roosevelt's "New Deal" would equally proclaim that it was an alternative to unplanned capitalism and International Socialism.

The main figure in Spanish National Syndicalism was Francisco Paulino Hermenegildo Teódulo Franco y Bahamonde, otherwise known as Franco. Franco's reign outlived that of Hitler's and Mussolini's as he was the Spanish dictator, military general, and head of state from October 1936 until his death in November 1975. A fundamental difference between the Italian and Spanish Fascists from Hitler's National Socialism is that the Spanish and Italian Fascists were not secular movements and this was exemplified by the title Franco gave himself: Franco used the title *"Caudillo de España, por la gracia de Dios,"* meaning "Leader of Spain, by the grace of God," a title Hitler would have scoffed if not laughed at for himself.

Despite Spain's proven track record for violence and subjugation throughout the Conquest and Inquisition, what is of note is that there was no violent racial hygiene movement during Franco's reign. In this respect, Franco's reign recedes into irrelevance as far as The Holocaust and eugenics are concerned. This is not to say that Franco was not prone to violence. The opposite is true, as Franco ruled with an iron fist. However, none of the eugenic ideology one finds in Hitler's National Socialism is present or was ever enacted. There were no efforts to exterminate or sterilize millions to maintain the Spanish "race." There was no effort to cleanse or maintain the purity of the "germ-plasm" or the "racial stock" of the nation. There was no effort to control or limit reproduction, and this is primarily because the Spanish Fascists were not secularists and deferred to the Catholic Church to an extent that Hitler would never have. The generally accepted history of Franco and The Holocaust is the one portrayed by "The Holocaust Chronicle":

> Although Franco sympathized with the Axis powers, his political policies saved an estimated 17,000 Jews from death camps. ---- Franco frustrated the SS by declaring descendants of Sephardic Jews eligible for Spanish citizenship, and thus entitled to asylum in Spanish embassies. Spain consequently became a main avenue of escape for Europe's Jews. Some hoped to find asylum within the country, but most intended to embark from Spanish ports for sanctuary overseas. The fall of France in 1940 unleashed a flood of refugees seeking entry into Spain. Initially, the Spanish government willingly granted transit visas, but then authorities became more hesitant to open frontiers. Still, many refugees slipped across the northern border illegally, trekking over hazardous mountain routes. By the summer of 1942, Jewish aid organizations helped an estimated 7500 pass through Spain to continue their journeys. Spanish authorities worked to discourage refugees from remaining in the country, and established internment camps for those who did. When border crossings increased again in 1943,

refugees were permitted to live in Spanish cities. (Pg. 331, "The Holocaust Chronicle", Publications International, Ltd., April 2000)

To mark the importance of this shift in policy, where Franco changed from allowing Jews to not only pass through but remain in Spain, must be checked against what was transpiring in the United States at the time. As this book has documented, Cordell Hull, the Secretary of State under the Roosevelt Administration, made a repeated and concerted effort to keep Jews from arriving on American shores. The reader will recall that he did so by leveraging the Johnson-Reed Immigration Restriction Act of 1924. As a result, fewer than 30,000 Jews a year reached the United States, and many were turned away due to immigration policies enacted by the Progressives, which explicitly justified their efforts with the eugenic logic of controlling the "germ-plasm" and "racial integrity" of the United States.

As far as wartime alliances are concerned, the relationship between Germany and Spain must also be scrutinized. Franco may have helped Hitler prior to the war, but that willing cooperation changed after the outbreak of war. Hitler met with General Franco on the French border at Hendaye on October 23rd, 1940. At Hendaye, Franco refused to enter the war or even allow German troops to transit Spain to attack the British at Gibraltar. It is of note that Franco was able to stand firm largely because of a report by Admiral Canaris, the head of German Military Intelligence. The often reported and overemphasized pre-war relationship between Spain and Germany is, in fact, the relationship between Franco and Canaris. Canaris had worked with Franco during the Spanish Civil War and had a close personal relationship with the Spanish dictator. He told him privately that Hitler was now obsessed with Russia and would not risk any kind of diversion in Spain. Thus, Franco felt secure in his refusal to help Hitler during the war. Franco also refused to hand over Spanish or foreign Jews to the National Socialists. Franco did close the Spanish border in an act of solidarity with the Nazis but allowed Jews and others with Portuguese visas to transit Spain.

Wilhelm Franz Canaris was a German admiral, head of the Abwehr, the German military intelligence service, from 1935 to 1944, and secretly a member of the German Resistance. Canaris was deeply frustrated by a briefing from Hitler before the attack on Poland. During the briefing, he was informed about a series of exterminations that had been ordered and which Canaris was required to take notes on. These notes were sent to MI6, the British Intelligence agency. In September 1939, Canaris visited the front and witnessed examples of the war crimes committed by the infamous *SS-Einsatzgruppen*. He also received reports from Abwehr agents about many other incidents of mass murder throughout Poland. Canaris kept detailed records of these atrocities in his personal diary, which he entrusted to Werner Schrader, one of his subordinates and fellow resistance member. After 1942, Canaris visited Spain frequently and was probably in contact with British agents in Gibraltar. More to the point, Canaris intervened to save Jews from persecution by getting them to Spain. The most notable person Canaris assisted was the then Lubavitcher Rebbe in Warsaw, Rabbi Yosef Yitzchok Schneersohn. Canaris' involvement in the July 20th attempt on Hitler's life by the now-famous Lieutenant Colonel Claus Schenk Graf von Stauffenberg, a practicing German Catholic like many of the resistance, was his downfall and the reason for his assassination by the National Socialists.

Franco's assistance to Jewish refugees is one that must be treated with caution, as Franco is not necessarily the picture of humanitarian compassion. However, the facts cannot be ignored if one is to give an honest historical assessment of the Holocaust. A generally accepted estimate suggests that Spain helped save 20,000-35,000 Jews by letting refugees pass through the country. Another 5,000 Jews were saved by Spanish diplomats serving outside of Spain. Most of these, about 3,500, were Hungarian Jews. Diego Carcedo's book titled "A Spaniard in the Face of the Holocaust," describes how Spanish diplomat Angel Sanz Briz managed to save thousands of Hungarian Jews while he served as Spanish ambassador in Budapest, a series of humanitarian acts that would have been immeasurably harder to accomplish under Franco's dictatorship, if Franco had not concurred. Of note is that in 1991, Angel Sanz Briz was awarded the title of Righteous among Gentiles by *Yad Vashem*, the prestigious Holocaust studies institute.

As far as Spanish eugenics are concerned, Belén Jiménez-Alonso of the Department of Basic Psychology at in Madrid, Spain details the Spanish government's policy as stated in the official eugenic platform under "*Primeras Jornadas Eugénicas Españolas*" or "First Spanish Eugenic Days" (FSED) of 1933. [440] Jiménez-Alonso makes sure to qualify this movement as "Latin Eugenics" as distinguished from the "mainline eugenics" as practiced in the United States, Britain, Germany and Scandinavia of the same era. As this book documents, all the proponents of "eugenics" in the United States, England, Scandinavia, and Germany were devoted to disbelief in "environmental" factors, and wholeheartedly devoted to the notion that all social ills were the product of "heredity." As such, the "eugenics" described by Jiménez-Alonso is in stark contradiction to the science of "eugenics" as would have been defined by Francis Galton, Leonard Darwin, Harry H. Laughlin, Charles B. Davenport, Alfred Ploetz, Wilhelm Schallmayer, or any other prominent leaders of the international eugenics movement. Case in point: Jiménez-Alonso himself documents that this meager program in Spain capitulated to the "conservative" accusations that it was "pornographic" due to its intrusion into sexuality, a traditional sentiment that the likes of Himmler, Hitler, Göring, Rosenberg, and Goebbels would have ridiculed. Jiménez-Alonso documents governmental measures that call for "personal responsibility," the very antithesis to government-imposed, coerced and controlled sexual relations like the ones proposed by the "race betterment" and "racial hygiene" eugenicists.

This is not to say that the Spanish were wholly free of the philosophical zealotry typical to the intellectual elite of the era. There were Spanish intellectuals calling for campaigns as aggressive as the American eugenic sterilization campaigns and the German extermination campaigns. However, they were recognized for what

---

[440] "Eugenics, Sexual Pedagogy and Social Change: Constructing the Responsible Subject of Governmentality in the Spanish Second Republic", Belén Jiménez-Alonso, Elsevier, Vol. 39, Issue 2, June 2008.

they were and marginalized to the extremities. Jiménez-Alonso documents:
> ...the utopian proposal of Quintiliano Saldaña regarding 'racial responsibility' in order to illustrate that the exigency of a State that imposes constraints upon citizens, that is, one of the extremes of the compromise between civil rights and a State intervention, place him at the limits of acceptable intervention in liberal government. (Pgs. 177-272, "Eugenics, Sexual Pedagogy and Social Change: Constructing the Responsible Subject of Governmentality in the Spanish Second Republic", Belén Jiménez-Alonso, Elsevier, Vol. 39, Issue 2, June 2008)

Although he attributes the fundamental differences between "Latin Eugenics" and "mainline eugenics" to a difference between "positive" and "negative" eugenics, with all due respect to Jiménez-Alonso, the policies he documents belong neither to "positive," "negative" or "mainline eugenics" as defined by its proponents. The policies of the FSED are not the "religion" of "applied biology towards better human breeding" as would be described by Francis Galton, Charles Davenport, or Leonard Darwin. The FSED policies are not focused on the "racial quality" of generations of the future, but with the individual health of the present generation. The FSED doesn't even qualify as "birth control" and the pseudo-eugenic measures enacted by Margaret Sanger. As such, it cannot be categorized as "eugenics," as it would not be categorized this way by any of the leading proponents of "positive" or "negative" eugenics, or even its cousin, "Birth Control." The use of the term "eugenics" by the Spanish government in their FSED campaign is a misnomer, as they describe public assistance measures that are no different than the welfare programs of any other state that enacts sanitary or hygienic reforms. In fact, these measures would be described more as part of the sexual revolution in the U.S. and Britain. What Jiménez-Alonso describes is a victory for the individual over the zealotry of self-proclaimed conductors of society. If correct, then Spanish intellectuals in a "fascist" regime succeeded in defending the reproduction rights of the individual.

That the Spanish "conservatives" were more careful not to tread on individual rights than the intellectual and political leaders of the United States provides a lasting distinction to the fundamental difference between "fascism" and "conservatism." Even the subsequent Fascist government that deposed the Spanish "conservatives" found ways to respect human rights where the Progressive leadership of the contemporaneous United States failed. General Franco is hardly the archetype of humanitarian values. Yet, his regime was able to find balance with "individual rights," or more precisely "Constitutional Rights," which the contemporaneous American Progressives the likes of Supreme Court Justice Oliver Wendell Holmes, Jr. intentionally discarded. More to the point, Franco's regime found a way to respect human reproductive rights where the American "progressives" set out to use the power of the state to coerce tens of thousands of sterilizations. Franco's regime found a way to absorb thousands of Jewish immigrants escaping the Holocaust, while his contemporary Franklin Delano Roosevelt turned them away in equal numbers despite having greater resources and ability to provide assistance.

The same analysis must be made for the other "fascist" dictatorship in Italy. Italian Fascism, or in Italian, "*Fascismo,*" is the original manifestation of fascism. This ideology is associated with the National Fascist Party which under Benito Mussolini ruled the Kingdom of Italy from 1922 until 1943. Etymologically, "*Fascismo*" derives from the Italian "*fascio,*" or "league," which in turn is derived from the Latin "*fasces,*" or "bundles." These "bundles" were the ancient Roman Symbol of Authority, the idea being that thin sticks of lesser structural quality, bound together, create a solid structural whole. The imagery conveys the essence of strength through communal and social cooperation, hence the "corporative" term that European historians use to describe movements based on similar ideologies. Italian Fascism is the creation of Giovanni Gentile, whose 1932 "Doctrine of Fascism" became the party platform of Italian Fascism. Benito Mussolini usurped Gentile's work and published it under his name in 1933. Mussolini prefaced his version of the "Doctrine" with the following historical perspective:

> If the 19 century was the century of the individual (liberalism implies individualism) we are free to believe that this is the 'collective' century, and therefore the century of the State.

CONTINUES . . .

> The Fascist conception of the State is all-embracing; outside of it no human or spiritual values can exist, much less have value. Thus understood, Fascism is totalitarian, and the Fascist State—a synthesis and a unit inclusive of all values— interprets, develops, and potentiates the whole life of a people. (Pg. 14, "Doctrine of Fascism", Enciclopedia Italiana, 1932 – Translation by Chip Berlet, politicalresearch.org)

Clearly, the "conservatism" that historians allege to be Italian Fascism is at odds with the definition of "conservatism" that Americans would recognize. Mussolini often spoke of celebrating the burial of the "putrid corpse of liberty." [441] Mussolini obviously had no respect for the concepts of *laissez-faire* democracy, "limited government," or "separation of powers" as would be proclaimed by American style "conservatism."

This was so in Hitler's economic plan as well. Günther Reimann, the man who was an underground Communist revolutionary and expert economist, described in painful detail precisely how this type of economic and governmental structure functioned in National Socialist Germany in his 1939 book "The Vampire Economy." Reimann describes the disastrous results of National Socialism's "planned economy," where every transaction of goods or funds had to be approved and monitored by Hitler's bureaucrats. Hitler's "vampire" economy set the prices of goods exchanged between businesses as well as the prices of goods charged the

---

[441] Pg. 23 – "Fascism and Democracy in the Human Mind: A Bridge Between Mind and Society", Israel W. Charny, Univ. of Nebraska Press, 2006 - translated from a written statement of 1934.

consumer; clearly not an economic policy inspired by Adam Smith. Albert Speer documents the effects of this pervasive micro-management in his memoirs as well, only to recall the coerced investment in machinery and technology that a company in a free-market economy would never have entered into. In Hitler's National Socialism, every profit earned was forcefully redirected and reinvested to expand the economy towards the armament effort. Clearly, the domestic economic policy of the "corporate state" is hardly in line with even the most perverted definition of what "conservatism" meant. In the end, neither Mussolini nor Hitler were in any way, concerned about maximizing profits for either the "capitalist" businessmen or themselves.

Yet, as was the case with Franco, the one drastic difference between Mussolini's original *Fascismo* and Hitler's later adaptation is the absence of eugenics from its nationalistic program. This also must be attributed to the significant influence of the Catholic Church and The Vatican in Italy, both politically and religiously speaking, as was the case in Franco's Spain. Anyone and everyone concerned with the eugenic movement recognized the Catholic Church as its prime opponent. However, the testament of Italian Jews living in Mussolini's Italy during The Holocaust is the greatest evidence of the nonexistence of "eugenics" or "race hygiene" in Italian Fascist governmental policy. Jews in Italy enjoyed a relative amount of acceptance and assimilation for the era. Italian Jews were welcome, comfortable, and well-off in Italy. Unlike other Diaspora Jews, those in Italy saw no need for Zionism and felt it a betrayal of their adopted home:

> Because of their success in Italy and their full engagement in Italian society, Italian Jews were not as drawn to Zionism as some of their coreligionists in other European nations. One chronicler of the Jewish community in Rome noted, that there was little interest in Zionism. "Italian Jewry, or to be more precise the Italian Jews, considered themselves closed within the borders of the country they were living in, ecstatic at their own successes in politics, science, industry, the arts, journalism, and were well on their way towards the most complete assimilation, paving the way for the next generation to be completely absorbed and having their identity canceled." -- A member of one of Turin's leading Jewish families, Ettore Ovazza, publicly rejected an appeal to aid the Zionist movement. "I cannot as an Italian participate in a program of such extreme consequences, particularly now in this moment, when we have a greater duty to participate in the front lines of the reconstruction of our country. In few nations in the world does the Jew enjoy such consideration as in Italy. ... We do not believe that in order to feel intimately connected to our fellow Jews suffering unjust persecutions it is necessary to create a second fatherland." (acjna.org, "The Italian Holocaust: The Story of an Assimilated Jewish Community", Peter Egill Brownfeld, American Council for Judaism, Fall 2003)

When Mussolini and the Fascists seized power in Italy, the Italian Fascists had Jewish supporters and key members. The fact that Mussolini allowed Jews to hold office as in the Fascist government goes a long way to differentiate Mussolini from Hitler. There were even some Jews in the National Fascist Party, such as Ettore

Ovazza who in 1935 founded the Jewish Fascist paper "*La Nostra Bandiera*." In fact, the Fascists enacted the Falco Laws which abrogated article 8 of the Italian constitution guaranteeing religious freedom. Though Mussolini and the Roman Catholic Church were to quarrel in the 1930s, these were invariably minor squabbles and were quickly patched up. The most important of these quarrels occurred in July 1938, when Mussolini introduced the Charter of Race. Hitler used his influence in an attempt to get some eugenic measures passed by his allies. In 1938 Mussolini felt compelled to issue the Manifesto of Italian Racism and declared the Italians to be part of a "pure race." The Jews were excluded from the pure Italian race. Pope Pius XII sent a letter to Mussolini protesting the new laws, and it is a testament to the Italian population's traditional Christian morals that these laws had little if any effect in actual practice.

> Even within Italy itself, Mussolini's anti-Jewish legislation lacked the 'sharp edge' that characterized similar legislation around the continent. In 1938, for example, he gave the green light to a decree restricting Jewish involvement in certain professions. However, the decree was 'weighted-down' by so many loop-holes and exceptions (for war veterans, churchgoers, "essential" workers and even members of the Fascist party!) that enforcement became virtually impossible. Even with the war under way, according to noted Holocaust scholar Raul Hilberg, a "large segment" of the Jewish population in Italy remained "almost wholly unaffected" by the legislation. (Dissertation draft for the Dept. of Political Science, U.C., San Diego, Ethan J. Hollander, "Italian Fascism and the Jews: Brown? or Shades of Gray?", 2003 – E.J. Hollander is An Assistant Professor at Wabash College, IN, since 2008)

Ethan J. Hollander, like many historians of Italian Fascism, believes the anti-Semitic laws enacted by Mussolini were nothing but "lip service" to Hitler's ascendency to prominence, where Hitler was once the apprentice to Mussolini. Hollander offers Mussolini's personal appraisal of the laws as communicated by the dictator to his sister:

> The attitude with which the fascist regime enforced these policies reflected Mussolini's attitude in passing them. Responding to his sister's concerns about the anti-Jewish legislation, Mussolini called the laws "a showy but cheap token payment" to his Axis partners. (Dissertation draft for the Dept. of Political Science, U.C., San Diego, Ethan J. Hollander, "Italian Fascism and the Jews: Brown? or Shades of Gray?", 2003 – E.J. Hollander is An Assistant Professor at Wabash College, IN, since 2008)

Hollander proposes that while most Fascist movements shared ideologies that incorporated intense nationalism, bitter anti-Internationalism combined with militarist cults-of-personality, anti-Semitism was not common to movement. Hollander's views certainly gain further weight when one considers the even wider opposition Hitler's anti-Semitism received from the other Fascist dictator, Franco. In the view of Mussolini and many of his henchmen, the "Jewish Question" of so-called German "fascism" was, at best, a waste of time. Mussolini communicated his

disdain for National Socialism's racism in 1934 while speaking in Bari:
> "Thirty centuries of history allow us to look with supreme pity on certain doctrines which are preached beyond the Alps by the descendants of those who were illiterate when Rome had Caesar, Virgil and Augustus."---- "The Jews," on the other hand, Mussolini remarked a few years earlier, "have lived in Rome since the days of Kings [and] shall remain undisturbed." (Dissertation draft for the Dept. of Political Science, U.C., San Diego, Ethan J. Hollander, "Italian Fascism and the Jews: Brown? or Shades of Gray?", 2003 – E.J. Hollander is An Assistant Professor at Wabash College, IN, since 2008)

Mussolini was unable, in 1933, to convince Hitler that racism was unproductive, yet eventually decided that an alliance with Germany was highly desirable. Thus, Mussolini made the politically calculated move of introducing anti-Semitic legislation as a good-faith gesture towards the Italian-German alliance. As such, Mussolini's anti-Jewish attitude was the product political tactics and not ideology. Hollander calls for a contextualizing of Mussolini's scant racial policies to the more rabid cooperation of Hitler's occupied territories and the non-occupied surrounding countries:

> In occupied Yugoslavia, Greece and France, thousands upon thousands of Jews sought refuge from Nazi persecution by escaping into Italian zones of operation and, later, into Italy itself. That Mussolini took active steps to protect these Jews seems unlikely. But that he knew what was going on — and chose to ignore it — seems almost certain. ---- Mussolini's reluctance was not without its consequences. Over 80 percent of Italy's Jewish population survived the war. It is unnecessary to stress, I hope, that the murder of over 7,000 individual human beings constitutes yet another tragic chapter in the history of the Holocaust. But in comparison to the survival of Jews around occupied Europe (Norway: 54 percent; the Netherlands: 33 percent; Hungary: 22 percent; Romania: 57 percent), the result is noteworthy. (Dissertation draft for the Dept. of Political Science, U.C., San Diego, Ethan J. Hollander, "Italian Fascism and the Jews: Brown? or Shades of Gray?", 2003 – E.J. Hollander is An Assistant Professor at Wabash College, IN, since 2008)

Hollander rightfully appeals to reason in placing Mussolini in the context of his contemporaries, and asks that we not sensationalize or give Mussolini more credit than he deserves:

> Mussolini was a far cry from fanatics like Hitler who, even when the war was all but lost, devoted precious military resources to killing Jews. He was a far cry, even, from Stalin, who practiced mass-murder on a scale heretofore unknown. Calling Mussolini "one of the biggest villains of the 20s Century" is to make him far greater than he actually was. ---- The Holocaust was a product of antisemitism and not of fascism. **Claims that the two are necessarily connected are uninformed, usually sensationalist, and cannot be justified historically.** (emphasis mine, Dissertation draft for the Dept. of Political Science, U.C., San Diego, Ethan J. Hollander, "Italian Fascism and the Jews: Brown? or Shades of

Gray?", 2003 – E.J. Hollander is An Assistant Professor at Wabash College, IN, since 2008)

That said, the credit belongs to the Italian people. If "collective guilt" characterizes the behavior of the German population, then "collective righteousness" can be utilized to describe how the Italians behaved when coerced to cooperate in the "crimes against humanity." Italian people and its religious institutions helped shield the Italian Jewish community from the horrid fate that Eastern European Jews befell under National Socialism:

> Even once the anti-Semitic campaign had begun in earnest, there was little sympathy for the campaign to be found. A fascist party report from December 21, 1938, from Turin, probably the most anti-fascist city in Italy, states, "Uncertainty and discontent regarding the Jewish problem lingers on with almost everyone. No one identifies with the racial campaign as it has been conducted, and people are wondering, but not out of pietism, where it is going and what results are expected from the measures taken and those to come in the future. I have been informed of sermons given in some churches in town, sermons dealing exclusively with the racial problem, which is not viewed favorably by the Catholic Church. In Catholic circles the entire anti-Jewish policy is being criticized and such criticism, well known to the public, is creating solidarity with the Jews that surfaces everywhere. (acjna.org, "The Italian Holocaust: The Story of an Assimilated Jewish Community", Peter Egill Brownfeld, American Council for Judaism, Fall 2003)

On July 25, 1943, the fascist Grand Council voted Mussolini out of power. Marshal Pietro Badoglio took over. German influence in Italy was obviously put in peril by Mussolini's defeat, so Berlin sent German forces to occupy Italy. Italy became no different than Poland, Hungary, or Belgium under Hitler's grasp. However, the Germans quickly found that the Italian population would not cooperate with the Final Solution as the Hungarians had. The senior SS representative in Italy, Lieutenant-Colonel Knochen, wrote on February 12, 1943, "The best of harmony prevails between the Italian troops and the Jewish population." The Italian population had responded by protecting their Jewish neighbors:

> The Germans were particularly perturbed because the Italians not only protected Jews on their territory, but when they occupied parts of France, Greece, the Balkans, and elsewhere, they protected the local Jewish populations there also. On December 13, 1944 Josef Goebbels, Hitler's propaganda minister wrote in his diary, "The Italians are extremely lax in the treatment of the Jews. They protect the Italian Jews both in Tunis and in occupied France and will not permit their being drafted for work or compelled to wear the Star of David." (acjna.org, "The Italian Holocaust: The Story of an Assimilated Jewish Community", Peter Egill Brownfeld, American Council for Judaism, Fall 2003)

The strong dominance of the Catholic faith played an important role in the fate of the Italian Jews. It was instrumental at the neighborhood level:

There is no doubt that Catholic priests and parishes throughout Italy did a tremendous service in aiding the Jews. -- Italian historian Liliana Piciotto Fargion writes, "Certainly the extant documents give the impression of a Vatican policy merely concerned with not irritating the Germans, and that it was inclined towards a policy of non-intervention. On the other hand, it is fair to record that, in contrast to the official position taken by Vatican diplomacy, there were many high-ranking prelates and individual priests, as well as convents, who gave considerable assistance to the Jews in hiding, of which the pope must have been aware. -- In the town of Assisi, a rescue effort (made famous by the book and film "The Assissi Underground") took place. In Assisi, 300 Jews were saved by Father Rufino Niccacci. He dressed many of the Jews as nuns and monks, taught them Catholic rituals, and hid them in monasteries and parishioners' homes." (acjna.org, "The Italian Holocaust: The Story of an Assimilated Jewish Community", Peter Egill Brownfeld, American Council for Judaism, Fall 2003)

In fact, a cinematographic event that mirrored the movie "Schindler's List" was instrumental in protecting Jews in a similar fashion as Oskar Schindler had in the use of his factories in the occupied territories:

In 1943, the Vatican-run Catholic Cinematographic Center, commissioned one of Italy's greatest movie makers, Vittorio de Sica, to make "La Porta del Cielo" (The Gate of Heaven). The movie was shot inside the Basilica of St. Paul's and came under the protection of the Vatican. Hundreds of people worked on the film as extras. The Jewish extras were allowed to live within the Basilica. De Sica arranged to drag out the production to protect the Jews. De Sica's son Christian said, "Originally, filming was only supposed to last for a few weeks, but my father purposely extended it to six months until the Americans arrived in Rome. At the end, they were only pretending to be filming as they had run out of film." Sadly, De Sica's efforts were not enough. In February 1944 the Nazis stormed the area and arrested 60 people. (acjna.org, "The Italian Holocaust: The Story of an Assimilated Jewish Community", Peter Egill Brownfeld, American Council for Judaism, Fall 2003)

On September 26, 1943, the German occupation forces demanded 50 kilograms of gold from the Jews within 36 hours or 200 Jews would be deported to Germany or the Russian front. In the first few hours, only five kilograms were collected so Jewish leaders went to the Vatican for help. They were told that the Vatican would make up the difference. The word spread around Rome, and the response of the community proved the Vatican's offer to be unnecessary. A crowd of people gathered outside the synagogue to make contributions:

It seemed that the whole of Rome-eager to express its disgust with the German occupation-had risen up in defense of the Jews. Word of the ransom had spread quickly through the streets and brought Christians and Jews from all parts of the city to converge on the synagogue, carrying gold watches, earrings, pins, bracelets, cuff links, wedding rings, cigarette cases and coins." Those without gold brought cash with which gold was purchased on the black market. (Pg. 195, "Benevolence and Betrayal: Five Italian Jewish Families Under Fascism", Alexander Stille, Macmillan, 2003)

The Roman-Jewish literary critic Giacomo Debenedetti described the scene of Catholics entering the synagogue with their gifts:
> Cautiously, as if afraid of being refused, uncertain whether to offer gold to the rich Jews, some 'Aryans' presented themselves. They entered the hall adjacent to the synagogue full of embarrassment, not knowing if they should take off their hats or keep their heads covered, according to Jewish custom. Almost humbly, they asked if they could - well if it would be all right to...Unfortunately, they did not leave their names. (Pg. 84, "Days of Remembrance, April 18-25, 1993: Fifty Years Ago: Revolt Amid the Darkness: Planning Guide for Commemorative Programs", US Holocaust Memorial Museum, 1993)

The Jews managed to raise more than 50 kilograms in the required time, but this only delayed the Germans from acting against the Jews. On October 16, 1943, the Germans entered the ghetto and started to round up the Jews. The Gestapo command in Rome sent a report to headquarters in Berlin in which once again the absence of widespread Italian anti-Semitism was evident:
> All available forces of the [German] security and police forces put to use. -- As the German police were breaking into some homes, attempts to hide Jews in nearby apartments were observed, and it is believed that in many cases they were successful. (Pg. 366, "The Righteous: The Unsung Heroes of the Holocaust", Martin Gilbert, Henry Holt & Company, 2010)

An online article by the US National Holocaust Memorial Museum website provides their opinion of Fascist Italy's non-involvement in the Holocaust:
> Though they collaborated with Germany in many ways, including the promulgation of antisemitic legislation, neither Italy nor Hungary deported Jews until Germany directly occupied those countries. (ushmm.org, Article ID: 10005466, "Collaboration", US Holocaust Memorial Museum, Washington, D.C.)

The National Holocaust Memorial Museum comes to this conclusion by putting Italy's behavior into context, and by comparing what other countries did in similar situations:
> Lithuanians, Latvians, Estonians, Belorussians, and Ukrainians spontaneously formed groups which the German SS and police then purged and reorganized. From the beginning, members of these "partisan" or "self-defense" groups killed hundreds of Jews as well as real and perceived Communists. ---- The government of Vichy France cooperated with the Germans by enacting the Statut des Juifs (Jewish Law), which defined Jews by race and restricted their rights. -- Norwegian police and paramilitary formations assisted SS and German police units in the deportation of Jews to Auschwitz-Birkenau. ---- Likewise, local civilian and police authorities collaborated closely with the Germans in Belgium

and the Netherlands in rounding up and deporting Jews residing in those two countries. ---- The Ustasa government of Croatia built its own concentration camps. By the end of 1942, the Croat authorities had killed more than two-thirds of Croatia's Jews (around 25,000), many of them in the Jasenovac camp system. Croat police and Ustasa militia also killed between 320,000 and 340,000 ethnic Serbs, some of them in Jasenovac, but the majority in the villages in which they resided. Slovak officials deported nearly 80 percent of the Slovak Jewish population in cooperation with the Germans during 1942. (ushmm.org, Article ID: 10005466, "Collaboration", US Holocaust Memorial Museum, Washington, D.C.)

Put into the context of what was transpiring in countries under Hitler's influence, the efforts of the Spanish and the Italians to save their Jewish neighbors or help them escape Europe has never really been recognized by American academia. Historians and the mass media simplistically lump Fascist Italy and Spain together with Hitler's National Socialism. This is not to say that Fascism should be indemnified as benign. Franco and Mussolini were brutal dictators after all. However, this only serves as a measuring stick to the acts of their contemporaries. If Franco and Mussolini acted with a minimum amount of humanitarian values in facing The Holocaust, then what can be said about their contemporaries on the Allied side of the line? As we have seen, the Fascist dictator of Spain accommodated the tens of thousands of Jews Roosevelt's Administration turned away as Roosevelt chose to maintain the immigration laws passed by the eugenic-minded Progressives even after learning of the brutal realities facing European Jews. Too often we hear historians and political zealots alike defend the American Progressives and British Fabians the likes of Margaret Sanger, Theodore Roosevelt, Winston Churchill, and the countless number of Darwinist eugenicists by stating that their brand of racism was typical for the era. Franco and Mussolini were of this era as well, yet even these brutal dictators acted with more respect for the sanctity of human life at the time when others offered vocal support for Hitler's eugenic legislative efforts. This type of "scientific" racism was isolated to a well-organized and elitist group of zealots, and not at all a symptom of the era.

Sec. 3 - A CONSPICUOUS REVERSAL OF ROLES:

The US population according to the 1900 census was 76,212,168. The *fin de siècle* fears and anxieties were at their peak as the new millennium rolled around. The expression *fin-de-siècle* has connotations of decadence, which are seen as typical for the last years of a culturally vibrant period, *La Belle Époque*, and of anticipative excitement about, or despair about, the onslaught of change, which had increasingly accelerated since the Industrial Revolution. For some, it was a time of optimism that the quickly evolving science and technology would find a solution for all of humanity's problems. For others, the pace of change was incredibly intimidating and destabilizing.

More to the point, all the racially obsessed prophets of doom of the early 20th century pointed to the US Census 1900 and 1910 as proof that the country was being "overrun" by "inferior stocks." The peak year of European immigration was in 1907 when 1,285,349 persons entered the country. By 1910, 13.5 million immigrants were living in the United States out of a 92,228,496 total population. The eugenicists were concerned about the massive influx of Irish and Italian Catholics, Jews from Eastern Europe escaping the pogroms, and Slavs. On the other side of the country, the California population had experienced an influx of Oriental immigrants that had come to build the transcontinental railroad. They crowded into the cities and transplanted their customs. The history of Irish and Italian gangsters illustrates this point. While gangsters were robbing banks in Northeast and Midwest cities, gunslingers were robbing trains in the West. Immigrants became synonymous with the new industry of organized crime, at a level that had not been seen or experienced by the descendants of the primarily rural Puritans, Amish, Quakers or Shakers.

As far as the African-American population went, the facts the eugenic experts marketed to presidents and congressmen, were flat-out lies. It would be ridiculous to contend that the eugenic statisticians were mistaken, or that they had misinterpreted the numbers, considering the sizeable amount of time and energy they spent dissecting the Census. The reality is too obvious for all of them to have missed. The truth in the numbers is that the African-American population plummeted from 19.3% in 1790 to an all-time low of 9.7% between 1920 and 1930, precisely the time that these prophets of doom were making their strongest push for population control. In other words, the problem wasn't that the numbers of African-Americans were increasing, as the eugenic prophets of doom repeatedly complained. The problem was that they were increasing where these intellectual elites lived and increasing in conjunction with the influx of foreigners. This explains why the eugenicists of the Northeast were primarily preoccupied with the blacks, Italians, Irish, Jews, and Slavs, almost to the exclusion of any mention of the Chinese or Mexicans, and inversely, why the prominent California eugenicists were almost exclusively preoccupied with the Mexican and Chinese. Somewhere between 25 percent and 35 percent of the African-American population in the United States had migrated to the industrial cities in the North. At the same time, almost all the immigrant population came in through the Northeast or Southwest, exactly where the bastions of eugenic thought came to be.

When the Emancipation Proclamation was signed in 1863, less than 8 percent of the African American population lived in the North. In 1900, about 90 percent of blacks still lived in the Southern states. The Great Migration was the movement of 2 million blacks out of the Southern United States to the Midwest, Northeast, and West from 1910 to 1930. African Americans migrated to escape the lingering prejudices in the South, as well as to seek jobs in industrial cities. The Great Migration created the first large urban black communities in the North. It is conservatively estimated that 400,000 blacks left the South in 1916 through 1918 to take advantage of a labor shortage in the wake of the First World War. As a result, between 1910 and 1930, the African American population grew by about 40 percent in Northern states, mostly in the major cities. In 1910, the African-American population of Detroit was 6,000. By the start of the Great Depression in 1929, its African-American population had climbed to 120,000. In 1900, Chicago had a total population of 1,698,575. By 1920, the city had added more than 1 million residents. During the second wave of the Great Migration (1940–1960), the African-American population in Chicago grew from 278,000 to 813,000.

Populations increased so rapidly among both African-American migrants and new European immigrants that there were housing shortages in many major cities, and the newer groups crammed into the oldest, most rundown housing. Migrants often encountered residential discrimination, in which white homeowners and realtors prevented migrants from purchasing homes or renting apartments in white neighborhoods. In addition, when blacks moved into white neighborhoods, whites would often react violently toward their new neighbors, including mass riots in front of their new neighbors' homes, bombings, and even murder. Since African-American migrants retained many Southern cultural and linguistic traits, such cultural differences created a sense of "otherness" in terms of their reception by others who were living in the cities before them. Stereotypes ascribed to black people during this period and ensuing generations often derived from African-American migrants' rural cultural traditions, which were maintained in stark contrast to the urban environments in which the people resided. All these tendencies contributed to creating the "racial divide" in the North, which had not existed during the Civil War or Revolutionary War eras.

Competition for jobs and housing, combined with the era's fear for the effects of urbanization and industrialization fueled the fears that the US population was in danger of falling into perpetual "degeneration." "Degeneration," as the reader recognizes by now, was a term carried forth from the 19th Century into the 20 Century by the proponents of eugenics. It literally meant what the term implies; the fear that inferior genetic stocks would force the general population into a reverse evolution, backward into a state of primitiveness. If evolution was the mechanism by which species improved, then certainly it was also the avenue by which they could "degenerate" back towards a primitive state if inferior elements were introduced into the gene pool, or to use the eugenicist's term, "germ plasm." These were the forces that instigated segregation in the ex-abolitionist North. Segregation in the North was but one, of various other solutions for maintaining the "germ plasm" pure. At the time that the Jim Crow laws of the South were calling for separate bathrooms, separate water fountains, separate schools, and separated seating within the same bus, eugenicists were calling for a complete geographical "segregation" and institutionalization of the population of the "unfit." As such, the black population in the United States had gone from being looked down upon by the aristocratic Southern socialites to being unwanted by the Northern oligarchy. They went from being kept outside of the plantation house in the South to being prohibited from living in the suburban housing developments in the North. They escaped the Southern bigot only to fall prey to the Northern elitist. Evidence of this fact is that the grandchildren of prominent Northeastern abolitionists were the most influential eugenicists in the movement.

Charles Benedict Davenport, the kingpin of the International eugenics movement, was born in Stamford, Connecticut, to Amzi Benedict Davenport, an abolitionist and temperance man of puritan stock, who railed about abolition and temperance as deacon of the Plymouth congregation. An August 26th, 1894, obituary for Amzi in The New York Times states he was "a member of the Massachusetts Historical and Genealogical Societies, and was very proud of his ancestry, which he traced back over 800 years." Not surprisingly, much of the literature produced by the various organizations Davenport influenced was pathologically nostalgic about the "white race" that descended from the families of the original colonies.

Madison Grant's father, Gabriel Grant of New York, was a surgeon for the North's Union army during the Civil War. The New Jersey Civil War Heritage Association describes Grant as "native-born Protestant descendants of the original Dutch and English settlers" and as a member of the Second New Jersey Infantry. Just the title of Madison Grant's highly influential 1916 book, "The Passing of the Great Race," explains Grant's prejudices and motivations.

Supreme Court Justice Oliver Wendell Holmes, Jr., the man who would infamously proclaim that "three generations of imbeciles are enough," and thus legitimize compulsory sterilization in the United States, and Germany by extension, served in the Union Army's 20th Massachusetts Regiment during the Civil War. That he is remembered by legal scholars as the "champion of the common man" is laughable, to say the least, as his 1927 <u>Buck v. Bell</u> opinion was significantly influenced by his disdain for the allegedly "shiftless" and "uneducated" common people of the South. He was the son of the famous poet and Doctor Oliver Wendell Holmes, Sr. from Cambridge, Massachusetts. Both son and father were the products of Harvard University. The son's elitist and eugenic outlook was taught to him by the father, who famously declared that "moral idiocy is the greatest calamity a man can inherit," and sarcastically urged people to thus "choose good grandparents."

Henry Pratt Fairchild was the descendant of Cassius Fairchild, who enlisted in the Union Army becoming a colonel in the 16th Wisconsin Volunteer Infantry Regiment. His nephew, David Fairchild, the renowned botanist who started Fairchild Tropical Gardens in Coral Gables, Florida, married Alexander Graham Bell's daughter. Alexander Graham Bell was also known for his support of the eugenics movement.

Henry Farnham Perkins was one of a long line of prestigious presidents of the American Eugenics Society. His mother was Mary Judd Farnham, an 1863 graduate of Knox College. She attended the debates between Abraham Lincoln and Stephen

A. Douglas at Knox College on October 7, 1858. She was the president of the Vermont Chapter of the Woman's Christian Temperance Union and was active in her church and philanthropic work.

A Yale University study publicized in the Chicago Tribune article "US Eugenics Paralleled Nazi Germany," details the big-money individuals that financed the American eugenics movement. Without exception, they are all Northeastern and Southwestern elites. The Tribune merely added a few more names that had gone missing in the various books about eugenics. A close look and one sees a repeating pattern:

> Robert Garrett, whose family had amassed a fortune through banking in Maryland and the B&O railroad, helped finance the two critical International eugenics congresses. Born in Baltimore County, Maryland, Garrett came from a wealthy family and studied in Princeton University. The two International eugenics conferences were instrumental in achieving cooperation between German and American eugenicists, and it is through this cooperation that American eugenic legislation came to be the model for the infamous Nuremberg Laws. Here is Leonard Darwin's pronouncement at the 1912 conference: "As an agency making for progress, conscious selection must replace the blind forces of natural selection; and men must utilize all the knowledge acquired by studying the process of evolution in the past in order to promote moral and physical progress in the future. The nation which first takes this great work thoroughly in hand will surely not only win in all matters of international competition, but will be given a place of honour in the history of the world." ("US Eugenics Paralleled Nazi Germany", Chicago Tribune, Feb. 15, 2000 – citing Leonard Darwin, First Intl. Eugenics Congress, 1912)

The most infamous example of ex-Union abolition families turned eugenicist has to be Wickliffe Draper. The Pioneer Fund was founded by Draper following the 1936 Olympics when his namesake, Foy Draper, was edged out for Olympic glory by Jesse Owens. Wickliffe was the son of George Albert Draper, an American textile industrialist, and Wickliffe used his father's textile fortune to start the Pioneer Fund. They were the descendants of Ira Draper, a prosperous farmer from Weston, Massachusetts. Wickliffe's great-great-grandfather, James Draper, had landed in Boston in 1650 and was one of the first men in the American colonies to engage in the business of weaving and selling cloth. Civil War historians point out that Northern industrialists were complicit in the ills of slavery, as they profited from the financial boom created by Eli Whitney's invention. This is exactly where the Draper fortune was made; as a byproduct of Southern cotton that had been grown by slaves.

The families of Cleveland H. and Cleveland E. Dodge used some of the Phelps Dodge & Company copper mine fortune to support eugenics. They were the descendants and heirs of William Earle Dodge, Sr., a New York businessman, referred to as one of the "Merchant Princes" of Wall Street in the years leading up to the American Civil War. Dodge was born in Hartford, Connecticut, and was a noted abolitionist, a Native American rights activist, and served as the president of the National Temperance Society from 1865 to 1883. His son, Charles Cleveland Dodge, was one of the youngest brigadier generals in the Union Army during the Civil War at the age of twenty-one.

Andrew Preston, the founder of The Boston Fruit Company, funded the Pioneer Fund and the American Eugenics Society. United Fruit became the present-day Chiquita Brands International. The United Fruit Company was a US corporation that traded mainly in bananas grown on Third World plantations, and this history is notorious by itself. According to the "Massachusetts of Today: A Memorial of the State, Historical and Biographical" published for the 1893 World's Fair by the Massachusetts Board of Managers, Andrew Woodbury Preston was born in Beverly, Massachusetts, in June 29, 1846, to Benjamin and Sarah Lee Preston. "He is old New England stock, being descended from one of the three brothers who came from England and settled in Massachusetts early in the seventeenth century."

John H. Kellogg, who started the Kellogg's Cereal Company, was a founder of the Race Betterment Foundation along with Irving Fischer and Charles Benedict Davenport. Kellogg was an advocate of vegetarianism and is best known for the invention of the Corn Flakes breakfast cereal. He practiced medicine in Battle Creek, Michigan, where he ran a sanitarium using holistic methods, with a particular focus on nutrition, exercise, and enemas for the cure of any and all kinds of ailments. Kellogg was outspoken on his beliefs on race and segregation, although he himself adopted several black children. Kellogg was in favor of racial segregation and believed that immigrants and non-whites would damage the gene pool. He acted as a sort of mentor and advisor to Wickliffe Draper through his publications. Draper adopted Kellogg's recommendations and beliefs on subjects like racial segregation, anti-miscegenation laws, staunch anti-immigration attitudes and the lifestyle choice of total sexual abstinence as a life-long habit.

This is not to say that there weren't eugenicists from the Southern United States, and from descendants of the Confederacy. There were plenty, and many of the Southern States enthusiastically passed eugenic laws, namely North Carolina and Virginia. However, the names listed above are the ones that made the eugenics movement happen. The Nazi scientists from the respected European institutions like the Kaiser Wilhelm Institute didn't seek out the fringes or subordinate institutions of American science. The names listed in this book is the list of individuals that historians credit for the success of the movement, and namely for their relevance to The Holocaust.

The story was no different "across the pond," as the English would say. The entire Darwin-Wedgewood-Galton family descended from relatives committed to the abolitionist cause. The Wedgwood medallion was the most famous image of a black person in all 18-century art. Josiah Wedgwood, Britain's renowned potter and grandfather of Charles Darwin, was a man of conscience, deeply interested in the consequences of the American War of Independence and the French Revolution. His friendship with Thomas Clarkson, abolitionist campaigner and the first historian of the British abolition movement, aroused his interest in slavery. Wedgwood copied the original design by the Society for Effecting the Abolition of the Slave Trade as a cameo in black and white. The inscription "Am I Not a Man and a Brother?" became the catchphrase of British and American abolitionists. Medallions were sent in 1788 to Benjamin Franklin, who was then president of the Pennsylvania Abolition Society.

The descendants of the Darwin-Galton side of the family spent as much effort trying to segregate the population as its ancestors had tried to liberate it. This reversal of roles, from abolitionists to segregationists persisted through the family. The sons, grandsons, and granddaughters of Darwin and Galton would take up Galton's eugenics crusade, and find employment in the various hospitals, homes, organizations, and committees dedicated to eugenics. In fact, eugenics became a "family business" for the Darwin-Galton side of the family:

- Florence Henrietta Darwin was a Eugenics Society life fellow. She was Leonard Darwin's third wife and cousin of the writer Virginia Woolf, also a eugenicist. Woolf wrote in her diary: "On the tow path we met and had to pass a long line of imbeciles...They should certainly be killed."
- Francis Darwin was a Darwin Medalist 1912, and a member of the Cambridge Eugenics Society.
- Horace Darwin, Charles Darwin's son, was a member of the Cambridge Eugenics Society.
- Nora Darwin, Horace Darwin's daughter, edited of The Autobiography of Charles Darwin. She married one of Sir Thomas Barlow's sons. Sir Thomas Barlow himself attended the 1st International Eugenics Congress of 1912.
- His son, and husband to Nora, Sir Thomas Dalmahoy Barlow, was a Eugenics Society life fellow. Ruth Frances Darwin, Horace Darwin's other daughter was the Secretary of the Cambridge Association for the Care of the Feeble-Minded.

Women were not allowed to join the Cambridge Eugenics Society, so many notable Cambridge-affiliated ladies joined the Cambridge Association for the Care of the Feeble-Minded instead. For example, Florence Keynes, John Maynard Keynes's mother, Catherine Whetham, the wife of eugenicist William Dampier Whetham, Ruth Francis Darwin who married the famous eugenicist William Rees-Thomas, and Ida Darwin, Horace's wife, were all members of the Cambridge Association for the Care of the Feeble-Minded:

- Ida Darwin, Horace Darwin's wife, was chairman of the executive committee of the Cambridge Association for the Care of the Feeble-Minded.
- In 1910 the CACFM and the Cambridge Eugenics Society cooperated to pressure the government to pass a bill for the compulsory segregation of the "feeble-minded." The Ida Darwin Hospital was one result of this effort.
- Ruth Darwin was also on the Brock committee, which recommended

sterilization of the eugenically unfit. Leonard Darwin's daughter, Ruth Darwin, was on the 1931 Brock Committee as well.

- George Howard Darwin, Charles Darwin's son, was a Cambridge Eugenics Society member as well as being part of the Cambridge Association for the Care of the Feeble-Minded. Maud de Puy Darwin, George Howard Darwin's wife, was a Eugenics Society fellow 1925, and a life fellow of the Central Committee for Mental Welfare.
- Charles Galton Darwin, the grandson of Charles Darwin and son of George Howard Darwin, was Eugenics Society life fellow, vice-president in 1939, director in 1939, and president from 1953-1959.

According to the December 2004 newsletter published by the Galton Institute's website, Charles Galton Darwin was also an advisory editor Mankind Quarterly. The main article in the inaugural issue of Mankind Quarterly was part one of "World Population," by Charles Galton Darwin. Mankind Quarterly came under heavy criticism after the publication of the controversial eugenic book, "The Bell Curve," and rightfully so. The founders of the journal were Otmar Freiherr von Verschuer, Reginald Ruggles Gates, Corrado Gini, Robert Gayre, Henry Garrett, and Roger Pearson. Roger Pearson was Karl Pearson's brother and a vocal and avid supporter of Adolf Hitler.

If Charles Galton Darwin desired to avoid a connection between National Socialism and the Darwin name, his choice of employment as advising editor to Mankind Quarterly was surely strange. Of all the individuals involved in the publication of Mankind Quarterly, the most vicious was Otmar Freiherr von Verschuer. Verschuer was the German human biologist and eugenicist primarily concerned with researching heredity by studying biological twins. Verschuer's history has been documented by various historians. Verschuer was the director of the now infamous Kaiser Wilhelm Institute of Anthropology, Human Heredity, and Eugenics in Berlin and the Institute for Genetic Biology and Racial Hygiene. Verschuer received Heinrich Himmler's permission to work in Auschwitz from 1944 on. Verschuer became known to the world because of the reports of the Auschwitz victims to the Nuremberg Tribunal about his assistant Dr. Josef Mengele, the SS doctor known to the victims as the "Angel of Death." It was due to Verschuer's recommendation that Dr. Mengele got the "prestigious" position at Auschwitz to continue Verschuer's twin studies. If the intention was to avoid any connection between the Darwin-Galton family and the National Socialists, then working hand-in-hand with individuals directly complicit in the Auschwitz horrors is the last thing one would do. Clearly, Charles Galton Darwin accepted Verschuer's ugly past, as Mankind Quarterly has been a continuation of the eugenicist's work leading up to and through the Holocaust. Anyone doubting where Charles Galton Darwin's sentiments really lie need only read his 1952 book, "The Next Million Years," where he predicts a eugenic and Malthusian catastrophe. Charles Galton Darwin argues that voluntary birth control was insufficient to avoid a eugenic catastrophe. His support for the work of Mankind Quarterly should come as no surprise:

...the policy of paying most attention to the inferior types is the most inefficient way possible of achieving perfectibility of the human race... this preoccupation with the weaker members is part of the present menacing trend of political thought which insists on absolute equality.

CONTINUES . . .

[In] social democracy... the well-to-do are rather more likely than others to possess hereditary ability... but the more prosperous members of the community are not producing their share of the next generation... The whole thing is a catastrophe which it is now almost too late to prevent... (Pg. 145, "The Chief Sea Lion's Inheritance", Tom Blainey, Troubadour Publishing Ltd, 2011)

Thus, nepotism facilitated this reversal of roles from humanitarians to eugenicists. Marriage is a time-honored method of reinforcing the political relationships of scientific elites. "Many a budding scientist married a professor's daughter." This was especially true in the Darwin, Galton, Haeckel, Virchow, and Hertwig families. [442] Modern-day Darwinists will work themselves into a frenzy if anyone dares accuse Grandpa Charles of supporting the eugenics movement and its obvious link to the Holocaust. The Ben Stein documentary "EXPOSED" touched on this contentious subject, and in turn received much grief and criticism for it. If anything, Stein failed by not fully documenting the solid links between the Darwin family and the Holocaust, namely Leonard Darwin's public pronouncement that his father approved of the work of the eugenics movement. Recall that Leonard Darwin's 1926 book "The Need for Eugenic Reform" book is dedicated to the memory of his father, Charles, and that the dedication stated with confidence that he approved of his life's work in eugenics. Leonard Darwin again confirms this position in a letter to Karl Pearson dated January 14, 1914:

> I should chuck most of it but for a sense of duty and a belief that my Father would have liked me to do what little in me lies as regards Eugenics." (EUGENICS ARCHIVE, ITEM No.: 12049 -- Cold Spring Harbor Laboratory's -- DNA Learning Center -- Dolan DNA Learning Center, Harlem DNA Lab & DNA Learning Center West)

Darwinists aggressively advertise the family's connection to the abolition movement while they flat out deny any connection to eugenics. So, it begs to question: What do they know that Charles Darwin's own sons and nephews didn't? This is a classic case of selective recollection, where the events of 1860 are more vividly recalled than the more recent events of 1920. If there is no connection between Darwin and eugenics, then the remainder of the Darwin-Galton family didn't get the memo, as they have enthusiastically supported the cause for four to five generations since Francis Galton created the movement. If Historians are right

---

[442] Pg. 33 - "Health, Race and German Politics Between National Unification and Nazism, 1870-1945", Paul Weindling, Oxford Univ. Press, 1998.

in saying that the eugenics movement lost momentum because of the revelations of the Nuremberg Trials, then Darwin's progeny apparently didn't share in that collective revulsion, as they continued to actively promote eugenics decades after the end of World War II. The one exception in the Darwin-Galton-Wedgwood family, and a truly outstanding one, was Colonel Josiah Clement Wedgewood, or Josiah Wedgewood IV, who argued vigorously and brilliantly against eugenic legislation as the Member of Parliament. Historians have forgotten Wedgewood's valiant efforts, as clearly, remembering is a tacit recognition of the fact that it was the efforts of his Darwin-Galton family members he was fighting against.

Historians are typically content to find discernible patterns. The above pattern demonstrates a complete exclusivity in ownership of the eugenics movement by an elite group of families. The fact that these powerful families were at one point synonymous with humanitarianism and abolition is an aspect of eugenic history that has been overlooked, likely intentionally, as these are the names of individuals and institutions through which much political and academic legitimacy is derived to this day and age.

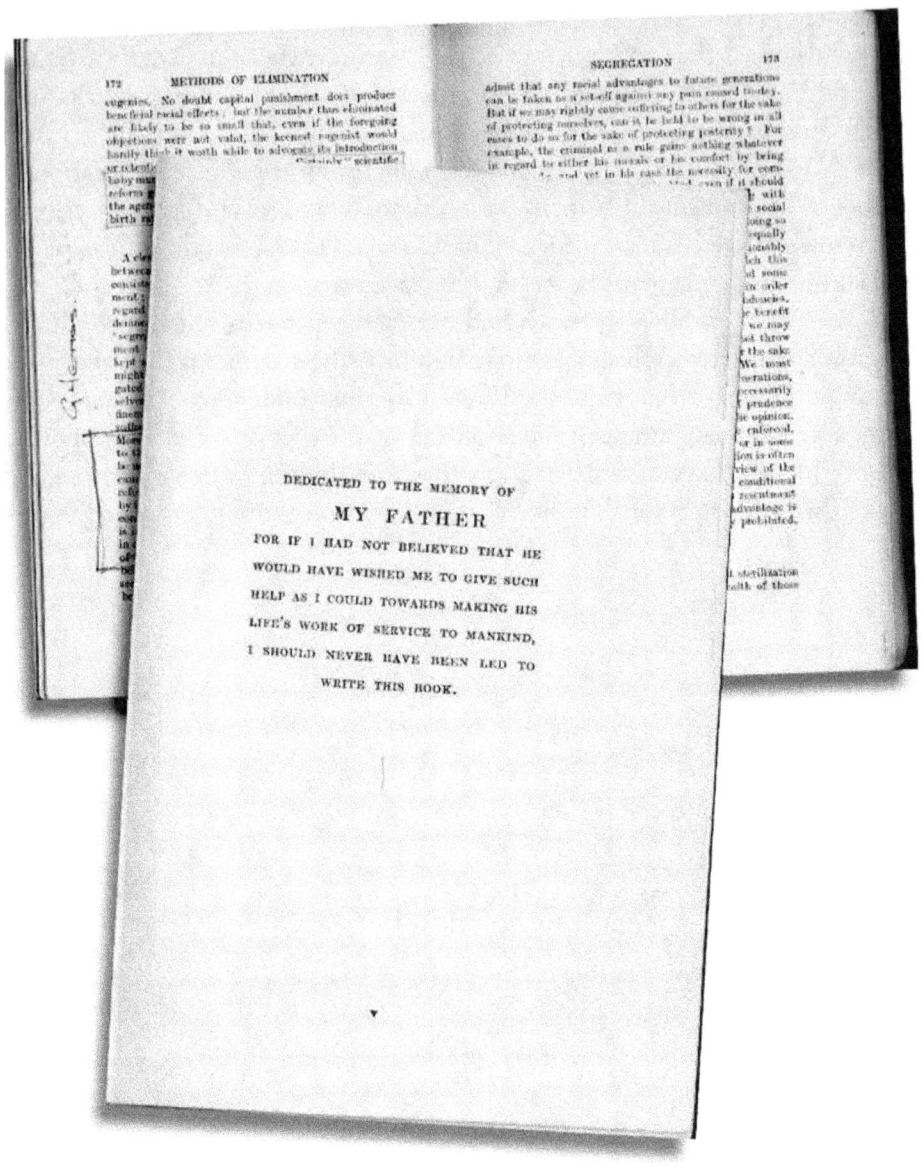

FIGURE 13: Scans from Leonard Darwin's book "The Need for Eugenic Reform", including the chapter titled "Methods of Elimination", and the dedication page. The dedication documents that Charles Darwin condoned and approved of his son's work on eugenics.

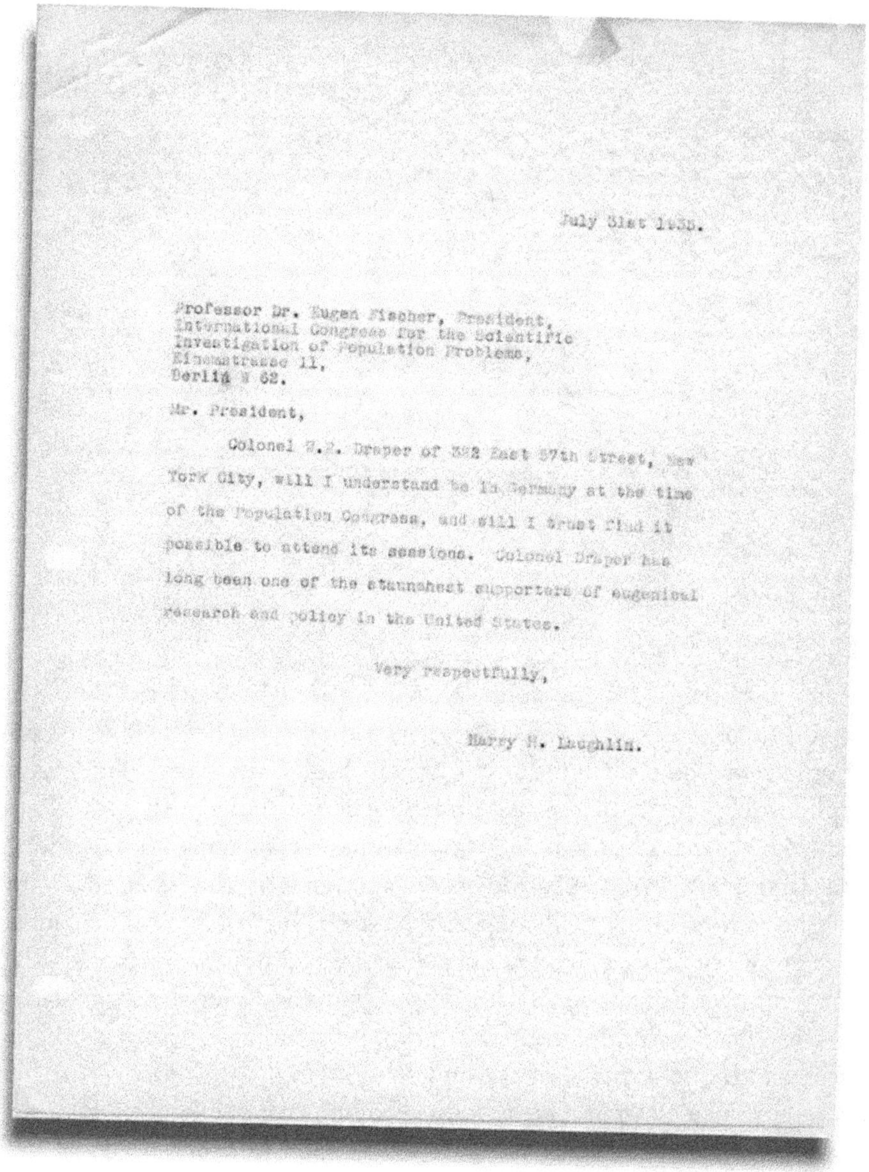

July 31st 1935.

Professor Dr. Eugen Fischer, President,
International Congress for the Scientific
Investigation of Population Problems,
Einemstrasse 11,
Berlin W 62.

Mr. President,

Colonel W.P. Draper of 322 East 57th Street, New York City, will I understand be in Germany at the time of the Population Congress, and will I trust find it possible to attend its sessions. Colonel Draper has long been one of the staunchest supporters of eugenical research and policy in the United States.

Very respectfully,

Harry H. Laughlin.

FIGURE 14: CORRESPONDENCE BETWEEN HARRY H. LAUGHLIN AND EUGEN FISCHER, ONE OF THE AUTHORS OF THE INFAMOUS "BAUR-FISCHER-LENZ" BOOK, DATED JULY 31, 1935. THE LETTER REQUESTS AN INVITATION FOR WICKLIFFE DRAPER TO ATTEND THE EUGENICS CONFERENCE ORGANIZED BY HITLER'S RACE SCIENTISTS. (HEREIN PUBLISHED AND PRINTED FOR THE FIRST TIME WITH PERMISSION OF THE SPECIAL COLLECTIONS DEPARTMENT AT TRUMAN UNIVERSITY. - BOX D-2-3:14, LAUGHLIN PAPERS)

Chap. 11: 1899 to 1895

AMERICAN FRONT: UTAH IS ADMITTED AS THE 45TH US STATE. - THE UNITED STATES ANNEXES THE HAWAIIAN ISLANDS. - JOHN D. ROCKEFELLER'S STANDARD OIL COMPANY CONTROLS 84 PERCENT OF THE USA'S OIL AND MOST AMERICAN PIPELINES. **EUROPEAN FRONT:** EMILE ZOLA PUBLISHES J'ACCUSE A LETTER ACCUSING THE FRENCH GOVERNMENT OF WRONGFULLY PLACING ALFRED DREYFUS IN JAIL **SCIENCE & TECHNOLOGY**: WALTER ARNOLD, OF EAST PECKHAM, KENT, ENGLAND, IS FINED 1 SHILLING FOR SPEEDING AT 8 MPH, THUS EXCEEDING THE CONTEMPORARY SPEED LIMIT OF 2 MPH. THE FIRST SPEEDING FINE. H.L. SMITH TAKES THE FIRST X-RAY PHOTOGRAPH. – THE FORD QUADRICYCLE, THE FIRST FORD VEHICLE EVER DEVELOPED THE WORD "COMPUTER", MEANING AN ELECTRONIC CALCULATION DEVICE, IS FIRST USED. ROBERT ALLISON OF PORT CARBON, PENNSYLVANIA, BECOMES THE FIRST PERSON TO BUY AN AMERICAN-BUILT AUTOMOBILE WHEN HE BUYS A WINTON AUTOMOBILE THAT HAD BEEN ADVERTISED IN SCIENTIFIC AMERICAN. - LEÓ SZILÁRD, HUNGARIAN-AMERICAN PHYSICIST IS BORN. EDWIN SEWELL BECOMES THE WORLD'S FIRST CAR DRIVER TO BE KILLED IN A CAR ACCIDENT. - BAYER CREATES ASPIRIN. - THE PAPERCLIP IS PATENTED. **LIFE:** AL CAPONE, AMERICAN GANGSTER IS BORN. – ERNEST HEMINGWAY IS BORN. - ALFRED HITCHCOCK IS BORN. CALEB BRADHAM NAMES HIS SOFT DRINK PEPSI-COLA. - ENZO FERRARI IS BORN. - M. C. ESCHER IS BORN. MARK TWAIN, RESPONDING TO RUMORS THAT HE IS DEAD, IS QUOTED BY THE NEW YORK JOURNAL AS SAYING, "THE REPORT OF MY DEATH WAS AN EXAGGERATION." – AMELIA EARHART, AMERICAN AVIATOR IS BORN – JOSEPH GOEBBELS, GERMAN NAZI PROPAGANDIST IS BORN. J. EDGAR HOOVER, AMERICAN FEDERAL BUREAU OF INVESTIGATION DIRECTOR IS BORN. – FREDERICK DOUGLASS, AMERICAN EX-SLAVE AND AUTHOR DIES. – THOMAS HENRY HUXLEY, ENGLISH EVOLUTIONARY BIOLOGIST KNOWN AS "DARWIN'S BULLDOG" DIES. – FRIEDRICH ENGELS, GERMAN COMMUNIST PHILOSOPHER DIES. – LOUIS PASTEUR, FRENCH MICROBIOLOGIST AND CHEMIST DIES.

Sec. I - THE *"ÜBER ETHIK"*:

Ayn Rand has been quoted as stating that if you can "identify the dominant philosophy of a society" that "you can predict its future." This book works its way backward from the outcome, in all the horror of The Holocaust, back to finding the "dominant philosophy" in the society that brought it about. In the process, this book has documented how traditional morality was intentionally discarded, and the dearly won freedoms and liberties of *laissez-faire* democracy intentionally reversed. In this sense, The Holocaust was fully predictable; the "New Ethic" of the era demanded no less of a radical outcome. In 1899, Auguste Forel had written an article titled *"Ueber Ethik"* in the 28th edition of the *"Zukunft"* journal. Forel was a socialist activist and a psychiatrist deeply invested in promoting biological progress of the desirable races, and the elimination of the undesired races and the unfit:

> Which races can be of service in the further evolution of mankind, and which are useless? And if the lowest races are useless, how can they be gradually extinguished? (Pg. 193, "Out of My Life and Work", G. Allen & Unwin Limited, 1937)

In 1905, Auguste Forel's book "The Sexual Question," discussed Darwinian sexual selection as the frame of thought necessary to justify infanticide and euthanasia. Forel called the malformed infants "little apes," echoing the predominant view that the malformed and handicapped were atavist throwbacks to earlier stages of evolution. More poignantly, Forel's 1908 published lecture titled "Life and Death" posed the question "Is life worth living?" referring to the mentally abnormal, the malformed, or hereditary criminals, all of which he claimed were "a plague for society."

Helene Stöker, the socialist-minded leader of the League for the Protection of Mothers, a similar organization to Margaret Sanger's Planned Parenthood, was another activist leveraging Darwin and Galton to promote a "new ethic" for society to be based on. Forel and Stöker were far from being alone. Nor can they be regarded as radicals if one inventories the political climate of many of their intellectual contemporaries who followed the logical path from Darwinism to Galton's eugenics and onward. As this book provides evidence for, most Darwinists concluded that society had to be turned on its head, and redesigned and remade to answer Forel's question about "which races" were to "further evolution" for mankind. Traditional morality had to be jettisoned, and the state remade to respond to the "laws of nature" as opposed to the "natural law" espoused by the Enlightenment.

Here, a full forty years prior to The Holocaust, were the core concepts of genocide and ethnic cleansing. The debate over exactly if, or how The Holocaust was the proximate result of Darwinian thought is bitterly contested. The Darwinists deny it vehemently, but the evidence is overwhelming. The same goes for Nietzsche's apologists. The obvious connections are denied, even if reason and logic are sacrificed in the process. In tracing our steps backward through time, we must begin at the most notorious of crime scenes: Auschwitz. There is too much written about the slogan that was hanging over the main gate, "Work Shall Set You Free," and too little written about the slogan hanging over the superintendent's desk: "Compassion is weakness." Yet, if one seeks an explanation as to how humans can engage in such horrid acts of brutality, one must first understand the psychological shield they wielded against empathy and sentimentality. The notion that humanitarian empathy was a sign of weakness was crucial for the advent of National Socialism under Hitler. It was crucial to the training of the SS, the Hitler Youth, and more importantly, the writing, enacting and enforcement of all the eugenic and euthanasia laws passed by the regime. This notion is at the core of the National Socialists capacity for, and more importantly, endurance in maintaining the pace of the horrid acts of brutality for decades on end. This is a significantly important phenomenon, historically speaking, as impromptu violence needs no explanation. It is part of the human condition. Mass violence is also part of the human condition. War is part of human history. Organized, mechanistic, and industrialized murder is something quite other. It is one of the aspects that makes The Holocaust such a perplexing occurrence, and thus requires deeper introspection.

Needless to say, much of this disdain for the Judeo-Christian morality of the Enlightenment Era is rightfully attributed to Nietzsche's influence on German culture. Nietzsche himself was the most famous product of an entire generation of intellectuals whom were bitterly entrenched in their efforts to replace traditional religious morality with a secular morality. Nowhere is the profound impact of Darwinism on culture and philosophy more apparent than with Friedrich Nietzsche:

> The possibility has been established for the production of a **Master Race**, the future "masters of the earth" . . . made to endure millennia ----- a higher kind of men who . . . employ democratic Europe as their most pliant and supple instrument for getting hold of the destinies of the earth. (emphasis mine, Pg. 112, "Nietzsche's Machiavellian Politics", Don Dombowsky, Springer, 2004)

Then again in other writings:
> ... not merely a **Master Race** whose sole task is to rule, but a race with its own sphere of life, with an excess of strength ... strong enough to have no need of the tyranny of the virtue imperative." (emphasis mine, Pg. 253, "The Parent as Citizen: A Democratic Dilemma", Brian Duff, Univ. of Minnesota Press, 2011)

Nietzsche's admirers claim that simply pointing to quotes about a "master race" is a superficial way to fault Nietzsche with The Holocaust, and they are right. However, they are wrong when one realizes the deep influence Nietzsche's disdain for compassion, pity, and whatever else he deemed the "slave" mentality had on a political culture which by necessity had to harden the hearts of its recruits. Ultimately, this is Nietzsche's contribution to National Socialism; the elevation of callousness to a virtue, or worse, a trait deemed a quality of the superior, the elite. One can summarize training of the SS and the Hitler Youth as a scholastic purging of compassion, sentimentality, or empathy:

> Pity thwarts the whole law of evolution, which is the law of natural selection. It preserves whatever is ripe for destruction; it fights on the side of those disinherited and condemned by life; by maintaining life in so many of the botched of all kinds, it gives life itself a gloomy and dubious aspect. (Pg. 47, "The AntiChrist", A.A. Knopf, 1920)

Richard Weikart's book "From Darwin to Hitler" clarifies how new cultural and economic concepts resulted from the Darwinian revolution. Weikart provides an onslaught of examples of how our moral ethic was transformed in the wake of Darwin. In fact, Weikart's book could easily be titled "From Nietzsche to Hitler" as it documents the change in ethics and morality that so exemplifies this transition. Weikart comments on this phenomenon:

> Before the advent of Darwinism in the mid-nineteenth century, there was no significant debate in Europe over the sanctity of life, which was entrenched in European thought and law (though, as with all ethical principles, not always followed in practice). Judeo-Christian ethics proscribed the killing of innocent human life, and the Christian churches explicitly forbade murder, infanticide, abortion, and even suicide. The ideology as "the right to life," which according to John Locke, was one of the supreme rights of every individual. Until the second half of the nineteenth century, and to a large extent even on into the 20th century, both the Christian churches and most anticlerical European liberals upheld the sanctity of human life. (Pg. 145, "From Darwin to Hitler: Evolutionary Ethics, Eugenics and Racism in Germany", Palgrave Macmillan US, 2004)

Darwin's "Origins of the Species" had clear ethical, moral and political implications. This certainly was clear to his followers, detractors and promoters alike. Darwin proved as much with the publication of "The Descent of Man" and with his "Autobiography," where he clearly proclaims that one must turn to instinct alone to determine between right and wrong when one no longer believes in God or the human soul. However, more important than Darwin's direct assertions about morality are the implications explicit in his work, namely "Descent" where he proposes the adoption of an animal breeder's outlook on human life in preventing the worst stocks from propagating. It is this aristocratic view; this "master-slave" mentality, which presupposes that one human can determine the worth of another, and thus deny him the "right to life" like a breeder would exterminate the worst strands of his stock. This was the greatest impetus for the rise of the "moral relativism" which justified segregation, sterilization, and extermination to do precisely what Darwin had proposed in "Descent." As Weikart states, "Darwinism was a matter of life and death, and no one understood this better than Darwin." [443] Adrian Desmond and James Moore, the famous Darwin biographers, state in their 1991 book "Darwin," that Darwinism "was always intended to explain human society." [444] Darwin's 1838 "M" notebook was filled with references to morality. [445] Thus, we can say with confidence that Darwinism was always intended to supplant traditional morality, long before Thomas H. Huxley leveraged Darwin's name for his own political causes. The path was certainly paved by Charles Darwin himself, as his theory set the ground rules for this "New Ethic."

Recall that the person responsible for popularizing the Darwinian ethic to Germany was the naturalist Ernst Haeckel. His scientific work morphed into his Monistic philosophy. "Origin" inspired Haeckel's work, and Charles Darwin, in turn, incorporated Haeckel's interpretations of evolutionary theory in "The Descent of Man." Haeckel's Monism, in line with Darwin's personal convictions, postulated that:

- Darwinism undermines the mind-body dualism and renders superfluous the idea of a soul.
- Darwinism implies determinism, as it explains human existence on the basis of inheritance via evolution.
- Darwinism implies moral relativism, as morality with the absence of a Creator is relevant only to the laws of evolution.
- Human behavior and thus moral character are largely determined as hereditary traits that result from the evolutionary struggle of a species.
- Natural selection begets group selection and defines the rules of group survival, thus the defining force in evolving human behavior.

Haeckel's 1904 "The Riddle of the Universe" and "The Wonders of Life" were among the most popular books in turn-of-the-century Germany. Haeckel was not alone. Bartholamäus von Carneri was the first German to write on the subject, albeit less recognized than Haeckel. Carneri, like Haeckel after him, saw in Darwin a coherent scientific worldview that did not rely on religious notions of morality.

The other figure critical to erecting this "New Ethic" by popularizing the

---

[443] www.touchtonemag.com, archives, "EUGENOCIDE: Darwinism & the Rise of German Eugenics", Richard Weikart.
[444] Pgs. Xxi, 243, 263, 269 – "Darwin", Adrian Desmond and James Moore, Penguin UK, 1991.
[445] See generally - "Metaphysics, Materialism, and the Evolution of Mind: Early Writings of Charles Darwin," Edited by Paul H. Barrett, Univ. of Chicago Press, 1974.

concept of "degeneration," was Max Nordau, the physician and one of the founders of Zionism. Nordau was a "totalitarian" in the sense that he extrapolated this "New Ethic" and applied it to anything and everything under the sun. Every aspect of humanity from art to politics was dissected by Nordau and labeled "degenerate" if Nordau believed it went contrary towards forwarding the species onwards and upwards in the evolutionary ladder. It is absolutely correct to state that Darwin "united" humanity into one species. It is also correct to state that Darwin supplanted the horizontal polygenic view which deemed different races as different species and placed all of humanity in a vertical and hierarchical evolutionary ladder where some races, as well as some elite individuals, were superior and more evolved than others. Specifically, Darwin placed white Protestant Britons at the top and blacks at the bottom. Nordau, in line with his Darwinian counterparts, took Darwin's stratification of humanity along with the jettisoning of religious metaphysics and thus formed a new conception of existence. Nordau states as much in his 1922 edition of "Morals and the Evolution of Man":

> Good and bad, derive not only their existence but their measure and their significance from the views of the community. They are therefore not absolute but variable; they are not an immutable standard amid the ever-changing conditions of humanity, a rule by which the value of the actions and aims of mortals are indisputably determined, but are subject to the laws of evolution in society and therefore in a constant state of flux." (Pg. 73, "Morals and the Evolution of Man", Funk & Wagnalls Company, 1922)

Earlier in 1883, Nordau had published "The Conventional Lies of Our Civilization" which further clarify his position on "law and morality":

> We believe that the evolution of the human species as well as all other species is perhaps only possible – and in any case is furthered – through natural selection, and that the struggle for existence shapes in its widest sense all of human history as well as the existence of the most obscure individual; and is the basis for all phenomena of politics as well as social life. That is our worldview. From this flows all our principles of life and our conception of law and morality. (Pg. 29, "From Darwin to Hitler: Evolutionary Ethics, Eugenics and Racism in Germany", Richard Weikart, Palgrave Macmillan US, 2004)

Eduard Oskar Schmidt, the professor of zoology at the University of Strasbourg during this era, was another to follow Darwin's trend of thought:

> If we contemplate the ethnology and anthropology of savages, not from the standpoint of philanthropists and missionaries, but as cool and sober naturalists, destruction in the struggle for existence as a consequence of their retardation (itself regulated by the universal conditions of development), is the natural course of things. (Pg. 191, "From Darwin to Hitler: Evolutionary Ethics, Eugenics and Racism in Germany", Richard Weikart, Palgrave Macmillan US, 2004)

Friedrich Jodl, the professor of ethical philosophy of the University of Vienna and editor of the "International Journal of Ethics," agreed with his Viennese and German contemporaries: "Morality, too, is a product of evolution, and is in a state of continual transformation." [446] Jodl would later confess that he hoped that the "International Journal of Ethics" would "become a stronghold in the struggle against the theological spirit." Jodl, like Thomas H. Huxley before him, saw Darwinism as a war against traditional morals and ethics. [447] Around the same time, another German biologist, Arnold Dodel, proclaimed in his 1904 work "*Aus Leban und Wissenschaft*" that the "new world view actually rests on the theory of evolution. On it we have to construct a new ethics." History would grant him his desires, as well as his demand that "all values" be reevaluated upon the basis of this "New Ethic." [448]

Oscar Peschel in his 1870 article titled "*Nekrolog der Tasmanier*" published in "*Das Ausland*" No.: 43 proposed a new way to see the displacement and eventual eradication of the Tasmanian as a moral positive; a popular sentiment later to be known as "Manifest Destiny" and touted by Theodore Roosevelt in his writings:

> Everything that we acknowledge as the right of the individual will have to yield to the urgent demands of human society, if it is not in accord with the latter. The decline of the Tasmanians therefore should be viewed as a geological or paleontological fate: the stronger variety supplants the weaker. This extinction is sad in itself, but sadder still is the knowledge, that in this world the physical order treads down the moral order with every confrontation. (Pg. 8, "From Darwin to Hitler: Evolutionary Ethics, Eugenics and Racism in Germany", Richard Weikart, Palgrave Macmillan US, 2004)

Peschel's view resonated with Friedrich Hellwald, whom in his 1875 book "The History of Culture in Its Natural Evolution" proposed that the massacre of the American Indians by the Spanish Conquistadors was "an inexpressible blessing," and categorized the American Indians as "beasts of prey," the status awarded to them in the Darwinian racial ladder:

> …science knows no "natural right." In nature only one right reigns, which is no right, the right of the stronger, violence. But violence is also the highest source of law, since without it legislation is unthinkable. …that just as in nature the struggle for existence is the moving principle of evolution and perfection, in that the weak are worn away and must make room for the strong, so also in world history the destruction of the weaker nations through the stronger is a postulate progress." (Pg. 169, "From Darwin to Hitler: Evolutionary Ethics, Eugenics and Racism in Germany", Richard Weikart, Palgrave Macmillan US, 2004 - *Culturgeschichte in ihrer natürlichen Entwicklung bis zur Gegenwart* – Pgs. 44-45)

This idea of "progress" resonated with Albert E. F. Schäffle, the professor of

---

[446] Pgs. 108-209 – "Moral Philosophy", Friedrich Jodl, 1895.
[447] Pg. 33 - "From Darwin to Hitler: Evolutionary Ethics, Eugenics and Racism in Germany", Richard Weikart, Palgrave Macmillan US, 2004.
[448] Pg. 43 – Ibid.

the University of Tübingen and later the University of Vienna, whom incidentally argued that the national economy should be organized in a form of state socialism that ensured that the race would predominate over individualistic greed; a pretty good summation of what Hitler believed National Socialism to be. Schäffle believed that the Darwinian struggle for existence implied a racialist based ethic, where the well-being of the race was the ultimate goal of a society pitted against other races. Likewise, Robby Kossmann, a German zoologist and medical professor wrote in his 1880 essay titled "The Importance of the Life of an Individual in the Darwinian World View":

> ...the Darwinian world view must look upon the present sentimental conception of the value of the life of a human individual as an overestimate completely hindering the progress of humanity. The human state also, like every animal community of individuals, must reach an even higher level of perfection, if the possibility exists in it, through the destruction of the less well endowed individual, for the more excellently endowed to win space for the expansion of tis progeny...The state only has an interest in preserving the more excellent life at the expense of the less excellent." (Pg. 78, "From Darwin to Hitler: Evolutionary Ethics, Eugenics and Racism in Germany", Richard Weikart, Palgrave Macmillan US, 2004)

A pattern is easily discernible here. Many German intellectuals were voicing a new social ethic that foreshadowed the coming Nazi regime. For example, in 1909 Max von Gruber, professor at the University of Munich gave a speech honoring Darwin's hundredth birthday, explaining how suffering and death, through Darwinian spectacles, fulfilled a higher purpose:

> The never-ceasing struggle is, according to him [Darwin], not useless. It constantly clears away the malformed, the weak, and the inferior among the generations and thus secures the future for the fit. Thus only through the inexorable extermination of the negative variants does it provide living space for the strong and its strong offspring, and it keeps the species healthy, strong, and able to live. (Pg. 74, "From Darwin to Hitler: Evolutionary Ethics, Eugenics and Racism in Germany", Palgrave Macmillan US, 2004)

The physician Eduard David, a Social Democratic member of the German parliament, explained the connections between Darwinism and eugenics:

> A strong counterbalance to the degenerative effect of this imbalance and atrophy of a people's organic condition is the rapid death of the damaged individual, as well as any of its weak progeny. This process of natural selection is frustrated through institutions of social assistance, which aim at preserving the life of damaged organisms, allowing them to reproduce and also preserving the lives of their progeny with inferior health. (Pg. 83, "From Darwin to Hitler: Evolutionary Ethics, Eugenics and Racism in Germany", Palgrave Macmillan US, 2004)

The above list is hardly comprehensive. You could fill various texts with the work of scientists from around the world who departed from pure scientific work and entered the political and philosophical arena with the intention of remaking man in Darwin's image. Like their eugenic descendants, the early Darwinists spent an inordinate amount of time and energy on non-scientific work, namely that of a political nature. "Pure science" was a casualty of this "New Ethic," or more precisely, the "New Ethic" jettisoned the notion that a scientist's work should not be value-ridden. The discarding of "scientific objectivity" was one of the precursors to "scientific prejudice" and certainly a precursor to the "scientific racism" that paved the way to The Holocaust.

As we know, J.F. Lehmann completed Hitler's eugenic education by bringing him the compiled works of the movement. However, Hitler's mind had already been primed with the musings of the evolutionary racists. These were the radical notions that filled Hitler's reading list, which he absorbed with untrained and uncritical acceptance, and in turn, regurgitated as if they were his own ideas. Joseph Adolf Lanz, or otherwise known as Lanz von Liebenfels was a very well-known Pan-German author in the many newspapers that Adolf Hitler devoured while living in Vienna. Most importantly, Lanz von Liebenfels wrote for "*Ostara*," which included mostly topics of a eugenic or Darwinian nature with article titles such as "Introduction to Racial Science," "Judging Character by the Shape of the Skull," "Moses as Darwinist," and "Master Ethics Based on Men's Rights." Lanz von Liebenfels characterized the new morality in these terms: "Everything that is good for the superior race is moral, and everything that is harmful, immoral." [449]

Lanz von Liebenfels was, in turn, a disciple of Guido von List, and all the Pan-German publications quoted List or published him on a regular basis. List divided mankind into groups, namely the Aryan "masters," whereas the rest were slaves, servants, or "herd people." Hitler's preference for List is evidenced by his favorite bookseller and List disciple, Elsa Schmidt-Falk. [450] Of importance to many historians has been the fact that List predicted the coming of a "strong man," an "invincible one," which Schmidt-Falk testified as an integral part of Hitler's conception of himself. Both List's and Schmidt-Falk's proclamations also evidence a belief in Madame Blavatsky's Theosophy. List clearly subscribed to the "New Ethic" of the era, as the preface to his 1898 book "The Invincible: Basics of a German Weltanschauung" stated:

> For centuries those in power, who were in charge of mankind's education, tried to hone down and ultimately erase the individual peoples' basic national characteristics so they could keep chasing after the total illusion of the leveling of all tribal differences; they were led by the horrible intention of starting to raise a uniform mankind. (Pg. 213, "Hitler's Vienna: A Dictator's Apprenticeship", Brigitte Hamann, Oxford Univ. Press, 2000)

Likewise, Arthur de Gobineau's infamous "Essay on the Inequality of the Human Races" was published around 1900 in German, and its message was clear:

---

[449] Pg. 218 - "Hitler's Vienna: A Dictator's Apprenticeship", Oxford Univ. Press, 1999 - As translated by Brigitte Hamann.
[450] Pg. 213 – Ibid.

the "white race" was superior and destined to bring order to the world. Houston Stewart Chamberlain, the Richard Wagner biographer that married into the Wagner family at the time that Hitler came to become intimate friends of the Wagners published "The Foundations of the Nineteenth Century." Chamberlin and the famous Pan-German, Georg Schönerer co-founded the Richard Wagner Association, and called for "selective breeding" according to Darwinist principles:

> Once you have recognized the miracles selection can achieve, how a race horse or a daschund or an "exuberant" chrysanthemum is gradually bred by carefully eliminating all inferior elements, then you will also recognize the efficiency of the same phenomenon in the human race. (Pg. 203, "Hitler's Vienna: A Dictator's Apprenticeship", Bridgette Hamann, Oxford Univ. Press, 2010)

The above notion was nothing more than recalling the "breeder" ethic integral to Charles Darwin's work, as further extrapolated by Francis Galton, Karl Pearson, and Leonard Darwin:

> We have forgotten to appreciate the value of breeding, in other words, of knowing that all noble species can be but the result of well-planned breeding with a strict selection of mates. The phrase about the equality of all men has clouded our brains. (Pg. 204, "Hitler's Vienna: A Dictator's Apprenticeship", Brigitte Hamann, Oxford Univ. Press, 2010 - Hamann quoting Schönerer in "Unadulterated German Words," 1908)

Naturally, voices in support of traditional ethics emerged. Josiah Wedgwood was not the only one of the era to have his head screwed on right, and "racism" was not common to all the era as the Darwin's and Nietzsche's apologists proclaim. H.G. Well's understanding of history and his social Darwinism came under fire from the English Catholic Hilaire Belloc. In a piece entitled Mr. Belloc Objects to "The Outline of History," and "Mr. Belloc Still Objects." See also G.K. Chesterton, "Eugenics and Other Evils: An Argument Against the Scientifically Organized State." Despite the opposition, this "New Ethic" was the *zeitgeist* of *fin-de-siècle* Europe, and to a large extent America. The *zeitgeist* was saturated with terminology such as "master race," the "unfit," "race of masters," the "masterly race," the "slave" and "degeneracy." All these intellectuals rejected the fundamental principle of legal equality, democracy, and traditional morality. This is the side of The Holocaust and Adolf Hitler that we struggle to understand and maybe even refuse to understand for fear that his shadow may cast upon Darwin and Nietzsche culpability we would not want to ascribe to them. However, we instantly recognize a distinctness about what transpired under Adolf Hitler that makes these murders different and apart from other mass murders we have otherwise termed "genocide." Hitler's Holocaust was not by any means the largest of mass murders. Stalin and Mao's mass murders eclipse Hitler's in sheer numbers by themselves. We can easily categorize the African slave trade and the Spanish Conquest in line with the "genocide" committed by these Communists. Yet, there is something that sets National Socialism's murder aside and apart from humanity's long history of "genocide." R.J. Rummel's proposal that we call all these mass murders by the state "democide," however compelling, misses the mark. We cannot categorize The Holocaust easily with the African slave trade or the murders by the Communists. This is how "a holocaust" under the German National Socialists became "The Holocaust," as there is an aspect of what the German National Socialists did that just doesn't allow our human sensibilities to place it in the same category. Richard Weikart is probably the most accurate depiction in labeling it "EUGENOCIDE," as the term is more precise in depicting the systematic, technological, and scientific aspects of the murders. Weikart used this term as the title of the article he wrote for Touchstone magazine in the July-August 2004 edition.

> One of the alluring features of Darwinism, it seems to me, is that it offers a secular answer to the problem of evil and death. Indeed, it was more than an answer—it gave Darwinists hope and inspiration that suffering and death would ultimately spawn progress. Darwin clearly viewed death and destruction as an engine of evolutionary progress, as we see in the penultimate sentence of On the Origin of Species: "Thus, from the war of nature, from famine and death, the most exalted object which we are capable of conceiving, namely, the production of the higher animals, directly follows." ---- The Darwinian idea of death as a natural engine of evolutionary progress represented a radical shift from the Christian conception of death as an unnatural, evil foe to be conquered. This shift would bring in its train a whole complex of ideas that would alter ways of thinking about killing and the "right to life." (Pg. 73, "From Darwin to Hitler: Evolutionary Ethics, Eugenics and Racism in Germany", Palgrave Macmillan, 2004)

Weikart aptly points out that Adolf Hitler was a devoted follower of this "New Ethic" that had taken root decades before Adolf had even been born. However much some historians want to box Hitler's National Socialism as a "conservative" or "right-wing" movement, Hitler's own words and legislative actions betray their efforts. Adolf Hitler was a devout Darwinist and eugenicist. His domestic policy is right in line with that of Edward Bellamy and Leonard Darwin's "nationalization" programs, informed by Keynesian economics through Hjalmar Horace Greeley Schacht, and in the genre of H.G. Wells' socialist utopias. Hitler's "ethic" was a eugenic one, and the entire National Socialist state was erected upon eugenic foundations. To be sure, if one charts the full history of the movement from 1848 to 1948, then one comes to the sober realization that The Holocaust is the ten-year zenith of a 100-year history of this "New Ethic." Hitler and the National Socialists are certainly the most insidious and most important part of the overall puzzle, but they are only 10 percent of a 100-year history. The momentum had been built up, and society had been transformed to accept the *"Über Ethik."* Adolf Hitler rode the apex of this wave to achieve unchecked power, as this was what was prescribed by so many intellectual and respected voices prior to him. He did what the intellectual elite had been clamoring for since science started dividing up humanity into "races" and devoting itself to a "racialist" understanding of human society. Hitler explained as much as he was amassing power in early on in 1923:

But we National Socialists stand here at an extreme position. We know only one people, for whom we fight, and that is our own. Perhaps we are inhumane! But if we save Germany, we have accomplished the greatest deed in the world. Perhaps we perpetrate injustice! But if we save Germany, we have abolished the greatest injustice of the world. Perhaps we are immoral! But if our people is saved, we have paved the way again for morality. (Pg. 28, "Hitler's Ethic: The Nazi Pursuit of Evolutionary Progress", Richard Weikart, Springer, 2009)

Hitler's unpublished 1928 manuscript provides further explanation of Hitler's ethic which is consistent with the "New Ethic" emerging from Darwinian and Galtonian circles:
> While nature only allows the few most healthy and resistant out of a large number of living organisms to survive in the struggle for life, people restrict the number of births and then try to keep alive what has been born, without consideration of its real value and its inner merit. Humaneness is therefore only the slave of weakness and thereby in truth the most cruel destroyer of human existence. (Pg. 93, "A Concise History of Euthanasia: Life, Death, God, and Medicine", Ian Dowbiggin, Rowman & Littlefield, 2007)

Yet, one need not rely on Adolf Hitler's unpublished works to make this point. His many speeches revisit this "*Über Ethik*" in one way or another. Hitler's "Mein Kampf" illustrated the same Darwinian and Nietzschean sentiment:
> If reproduction as such is limited and the number of births decreased, then the natural struggle for existence, which only allows the strongest and healthiest to survive, will be replaced by the obvious desire to save at any cost even the weakest and sickest; thereby a progeny is produced, which must become ever more miserable, the longer this mocking of nature and its will persists. . . . A stronger race will supplant the weaker, since the drive for life in its final form will decimate every ridiculous fetter of the so-called humanness of individuals, in order to make place for the humaneness of nature, which destroys the weak to make place for the strong. (Pgs. 113-114, "Jewish Tradition and the Challenge of Darwinism", translation by G. N. Cantor, Univ. of Chicago Press, 2006)

Hitler embellished how this new Darwinian ethic applied to National Socialism. More to the point, one could attribute this quote to any of the above-mentioned intellectuals and not commit an unjust portrayal of their views:
> …by no means believes in the equality of races, but recognizes along with their differences their higher or lower value, and through this knowledge feels obliged, according to the eternal will that rules this universe, to promote the victory of the better, the stronger, and to demand the submission of the worse and weaker. It embraces thereby in principle the aristocratic law of nature and believes in the validity of this law down to the last individual being. It recognizes not only the different value of races, but also the different value of individuals. . . But by no means can it approve of the right of an ethical idea existing, if this idea is a danger for the racial life of the bearer of a higher ethic. (Pg. 7, Richard Weikart, "From

Darwin to Hitler: Evolutionary Ethics, Eugenics and Racism in Germany", Palgrave Macmillan, 2004)

As such, neither "genocide" nor "ethnic cleansing" suffice to explain what happened in National Socialist Germany, as these concepts depict a single-minded effort to eliminate but one foreign element in society. Thinking that National Socialism's goals either begun or ended with the eradication of the Jews is an incomplete and insufficient depiction of history. We know that Hitler's and the National Socialist intention was for a "Thousand-Year Reich" and a perpetual "racial state." As this book documents, the effort to create and maintain a "pure" German people began with the eradication of handicapped Aryans:

> Believe you me, all of National Socialism wouldn't be worth a thing if it were limited to Germany and didn't finalize the rule of the superior race over the whole world for at least 1,000 to 2,000 years. (Pg. 132, *"Aufbau des deutschen Sozialismus: Mit einem Nachwort von Dr. Claus-Martin Wolfschlag, Vol. 3, Natur et Mythos"*, Otto Strasser, 2nd Ed., 1936, Reprinted By: Haag + Herchen, 2013 - Hitler to Otto Strasser)

Hitler's "racial state" was concocted in geological time, framed in the scope of Darwinian evolution. The concept of a "Thousand-Year Reich" is one of evolutionary scope, and proof of this is what Hitler planned if the German people proved to be lesser than the pinnacle of human evolution. This is evidenced by the "scorched earth" order he gave Albert Speer when Hitler deemed the war effort lost. Hitler's infamous "Nero Decree" of March 14th, 1945, would have destroyed all means of subsistence "within the Reich territory" if Speer had actually carried it out. Both Hitler and Speer knew that this would be the death of the German people. Historians agree that Hitler was not dissuaded by this observation as in his mind Germans had been proven unworthy of existence, evolutionarily speaking:

> If, however, the German people were to become weak one day, it wouldn't deserve anything but to be eradicated by a stronger people; in that case, Hitler said, one wouldn't be able to pity it either." – Goebbels recounting a February 1943 conversation with Hitler in the wake of Stalingrad debacle. (Pg. 235, "Hitler's Vienna: A Dictator's Apprenticeship", Brigitte Hamann, Oxford, 1999)

Thus, one would be justified to take Adolf Hitler at his word when he stated that he was not driven by "vulgar" racist views. To think that The Holocaust was only about the elimination of the Jews is to forget the hundreds of thousands of non-Jewish murders and downplay the scope and scale of the crime. It would forget the tens of thousands of innocents, "Aryan" infants, children, and adults murdered in the T4 Euthanasia Program. It would erroneously set aside Heinrich Himmler's Lebensborn program to breed a pure "master" race, or consequently, a "race of masters" bred for the specific task of world domination. No just and equitable criminal court would allow such evidence to fall by the wayside.

If one is to question how Adolf Hitler was able to convince the most educated and the most cultured nation of the time to engage in a sustained campaign of mass murder, torture and genocide, a significant part of the answer lay in the fact that much prior to Hitler, this "New Ethic" had taken root in an otherwise cosmopolitan and well-educated culture. To be more specific, this *"Über Ethik"* was a definitive prerequisite for what transpired under National Socialism, and it goes a long way to explain why Hitler was able to find so many "willing executioners." [451] Hitler didn't convince these "willing executioners" of discarding the traditional ethic that would otherwise have prevented them from participating in the atrocities. These "willing executioners" had jettisoned the traditional morality in following their idols, namely Nietzsche, Haeckel, and Darwin. It was not only intellectually fashionable, but amply acceptable to adopt such a hardened worldview, and the ranks of the National Socialists were perfectly conditioned to succumb to Hitler's "leadership principle" in accepting the task of carrying out his dastardly commands.

Both Eric Fromm and Ayn Rand are at least partially vindicated in pointing out that for every sadist, there is an ample supply of masochists. Ayn Rand is also correct that we should not be surprised at the outcome of this "New Ethic." We reap what we sow. The "Final Solution" is very much so the logical outcome of a 100-year-long campaign to remake man and morality:

> *You have destroyed all that which you held to be evil*
> *and achieved all that which you held to be good.*
> *Why, then, do you shrink in horror from the sight of the world around you?*
> *That world is not the product of your sins,*
> *it is the product and the image of your virtues.*
> *It is your moral ideal brought into reality in its full and final perfection.* [452]

Sec. 2 - WHERE WAS THE N.A.A.C.P. DURING THE EUGENICS ERA?

Daylanne K. English, Professor of African-American literature at Macalester College in St. Paul, Minnesota, wrote the 2004 book "Unnatural Selections: Eugenics in American Modernism and the Harlem Renaissance." The book weaves through the political and scientific perspectives of the literary elite, namely African-American artists which represented the cultural leadership which helped define African-American culture as it departed from the Reconstruction Era and into the turn-of-the-century. Despite its focus on a select number of individuals, Professor English's book is indispensable towards a greater understanding of the political and cultural movement that was eugenics. Professor English's book is singularly insightful in the "self-selection" process that permeated throughout the larger movement. She cuts through the air of arrogance inherent in the scientific claims of the era and

---

[451] Title of Daniel Goldhagen's 1996 book, which has now become a popular phrase to characterize the doctors and scientists of the Nazi regime.
[452] John Galt's soliloquy, "Atlas Shrugged," Ayn Rand.

points out that what all of these self-styled scientists were doing is proposing that society "unnaturally select" who would procreate and whom would not. These proposals were more often than not, exercises in what Professor English labels as "self-selection," where the ideal "fittest" were mirror images of the selector.

Professor English's work is also indispensable when one comes to the realization of just how important the American Civil War and Reconstruction eras were to the history of the eugenics movement. World history leading up to World War I and World War II cannot be suitably comprehended without coming to terms with the tectonic cultural shift of Emancipation. The American political experiment and Lincoln's work prohibited the African-American community from being marginalized or ignored as the black communities of the European colonies had been. The words of The Declaration of Independence, which President Lincoln followed as his bible, prohibited any other outcome. Liberia could not and would not be America's Australia, which the British had used to isolate the unwanted portions of society. The integration of the African-American community into American political and cultural life was an earth-shaking event which in turn birthed both positive and negative consequences.

Of all the cultural icons Professor English documents in "Unnatural Selections," none was more enigmatic or politically influential than W.E.B. Du Bois. William Edward Burghardt Du Bois was the African-American sociologist, historian, civil rights activist, Pan-Africanist, author, and co-founded the NAACP. The National Association for the Advancement of Colored People began publishing "Crisis" magazine under his leadership, and Du Bois was its primary editor, from 1910 to 1934. In stark contrast to Booker T. Washington, whom had been born into slavery, Du Bois was born in urban Massachusetts. Du Bois grew up in a tolerant community. After graduating from Harvard, where he was the first African American to earn a doctorate, he became a professor of history, sociology, and economics at Atlanta University. Du Bois rose to national prominence as the leader of the Niagara Movement, a group of African-American activists who wanted equal rights extended to the African-American community. This movement countered the work of Civil War era African-American leader, Booker T. Washington, who crafted a proposal called the "Atlanta Compromise" which provided that Southern blacks would submit to white political rule, while in return Southern whites guaranteed that blacks would receive basic educational and economic opportunities. Du Bois insisted on "equal" civil rights. Du Bois presented a paper titled "The Conservation of Races" while attending the Negro Academy in 1897. In this paper Du Bois rejected Frederick Douglass' plea for black Americans to integrate into white society, writing: "…we are Negroes, members of a vast historic race that from the very dawn of creation has slept, but half awakening in the dark forests of its African fatherland." [453] Du Bois paper evolved into a proposal that African-Americans could be "uplifted" to equal cultural prominence by an intellectual elite which he dubbed the "talented tenth." "Uplift" by the elite was central to Du Bois proposal, and "breeding" and

---

[453] Pg. 39 - "Race and Racism in Continental Philosophy", Robert Bernasconi/Sybol Cook, Indiana University Press, 2003.

"educating" to create this elite was an integral part of his proposal. Professor English documents:

> By the 1920s, Du Bois offered a kind of interracial reproductive solution to the problem of New Negro subjectivity in the modern United States, arguing in a Crisis editorial that the race must begin to "train and breed for brains, for efficiency, for beauty." (Pg. 16-17, "Unnatural Selections: Eugenics in American Modernism and the Harlem Renaissance", Univ. of North Carolina Press, 2004)

While one may be initially distrusting of a thesis that proposes that a civil rights icon may have been equally narcissistic as the eugenic-minded "self-selectors," the evidence provided by Professor English cannot be overlooked if an honest appraisal of the era is to be achieved. The "talented tenth" and the "New Negro" were the conceptual products of Du Bois's work. This work extended to much more than a passing comment or lingering idea. It was an integral part of his leadership and thus inseparable from his contribution to the relevant history. Furthermore, as this book evidences, this intermix between science and politics was hardly isolated to W.E.B. Du Bois. As Daniel Kevles, author of the book "In the Name of Eugenics" put it, "The left mixed its eugenics with the socialist reconstruction of society." [454]

The privileged urban life Du Bois had grown up in changed drastically during this time. These changes in the density and diversity of Northern urbanity likely inspired a reaction from Du Bois, as it had done in other like-minded white eugenicists of the era, all of which saw in the newly congested urbanity as one of the primary reasons for "degeneration." To recall, roughly 28 million immigrants came to the United States at the time that Southern blacks were escaping the failures of the Reconstruction South. Between 1890 and 1920, more than 1.2 million Southern blacks migrated to the Northern industrial metropolis, with at least 300,000 migrating in a single decade between 1910 and 1920. Professor English quotes Margaret Sanger's sentiments:

> I am glad to say that the US government has already taken certain steps to control the quality of our population through the drastic immigration laws... But while we close our gates to the so-called 'undesirables' from other countries, we make no attempt to discourage or cut down the rapid multiplication of the unfit and undesirable at home. (Pg. 40, "Unnatural Selections: Eugenics in American Modernism and the Harlem Renaissance", Univ. of North Carolina Press, 2004)

Margaret Sanger would attempt to solve the defects she saw in the internal "migratory" policy of the United States by creating the "Negro Project," which would intentionally curtail the reproduction of poor, urban, blacks through "birth control clinics." As this book documents, Sanger realized she needed the help of African-American leaders to successfully enact the "Negro Project." Sanger's clinic was directed by a 15-member advisory board consisting of African-American doctors, nurses, clergy, journalists, and social workers. Planned Parenthood

---

[454] Pg. 174 - "In the Name of Eugenics: Genetics and the Uses of Human Heredity", Univ. of California Press, 1995.

Federation of America's own publication, "The Truth about Margaret Sanger" admits as much. More to the point, Sanger's efforts were publicized in the African-American press and churches and received the approval and cooperation of W. E. B. Du Bois.

Du Bois elaborated on the scope of his eugenic work through his literature and activism. As Professor English documents, Du Bois's 1903 publication titled the "Talented Tenth" is replete with socio-biological terms such as "exceptional men" and elitist hierarchies where the "best of the race" are crowned the redeemers of the African-American community as they "guide the Mass away from the contamination and death of the Worst." [455] These terms and phrases clearly communicate that Du Bois regarded the "talented tenth" to be biologically superior to the "worst" of the "race." As Professor English explains, Du Bois's racial hierarchies identified a "self-selected" elite and in turn denigrated the undesirables as the "worst":

> While Du Bois's use of the term "Talented Tenth" is quite well known, few scholars cite his coinage of the term "submerged tenth" in The Philadelphia Negro, his groundbreaking sociological study. In The Philadelphia Negro, Du Bois divided the families of Philadelphia into "four grades," with "Grade 4" being the "lowest class of criminals, prostitutes and loafers; the 'submerged tenth'. The Philadelphia Negro, along with a number of later black and urban sociological studies, documented the apparently unregulated behaviors of migrant and working-class "Negroes" in American cities, as well as their potentially deleterious effects on the African American uplift project. The Philadelphia Negro's sometimes elitist interracial politics emerge out of Du Bois's anxious awareness of the influx of "untrained and poorly educated [Negro] countrymen, rushing from the hovels of the country. . . into the strange life of a great city" in tension with his reification of an already established urban Negro upper class. (Pg. 45, "Unnatural Selections: Eugenics in American Modernism and the Harlem Renaissance", Univ. of North Carolina Press, 2004)

Again, neither the "Talented Tenth" or the "Submerged Tenth" can be understood as passing comments or undeveloped concepts. Du Bois persisted on this track and dedicated a significant amount of time and effort to developing his eugenic ideas. Professor English documents that he touched on them again in "The Souls of Black Folk," where Du Bois applied the notion of a "lowest class" of African-Americans, explicitly identifying them as the post-Reconstruction rural South sharecroppers as the "submerged tenth," a term that echoes the disdain against rural cultures that mainline eugenicists displayed, and which came front and center in the deliberations of the 1927 <u>Buck v. Bell</u> Supreme Court case.

The NAACP's "Crisis" publication was also leveraged to propagandize Du Bois's eugenic vision in methods that hardly differed from Harry H. Laughlin's and Charles B. Davenport's work. Professor English documents that "Crisis" quite often depicted families and individuals as examples of Du Bois's "Talented Tenth." The

---

[455] Pg. 41 - "Unnatural Selections: Eugenics in American Modernism and the Harlem Renaissance", Daylanne K. English, Univ. of North Carolina Press, 2004.

October 1916 edition of "Crisis" hand-picked a teacher who was doing his part to prevent "race suicide," a term often used by the Anglo-American eugenicists and Nazis themselves. Professor English accurately states that the yearly "prize baby contests" published in the October 1919 edition of "Crisis" were the African-American equivalent to the "Fitter Family" contests that are now infamously related to the mainstream eugenics movement. [456] Professor English points to the June 1928 edition of "Crisis" as the most egregious, if not comical, example of Du Bois's eugenic experiments. Nearly the entire issue was dedicated to covering Yolande Du Bois's wedding, and Du Bois's efforts as editor poorly disguised his intent to frame his daughter's wedding as that of a "eugenic dynasty." [457] Professor English documents that the groom, a poet named Countèe Cullen, was the mate Du Bois personally hand-picked for his daughter. Professor English hardly disguises her comedic delight in the fact that this eugenic mating ended abruptly when Du Bois's prototypical male turned out to have deeper affections for his homosexual lover and lifetime companion, Harold Jackman. W.E.B. Du Bois had demonstrated his arrogance and ignorance when he later blamed the failure of the marital experiment on Yolande's sexual inexperience. [458]

W.E.B. Du Bois found himself at the crossroads and turning point of race relations in the United States. He was a direct product of the turn-of-the-century push away from antiquity and into the modernity that science and technology promised, and he saw the world as the rest of the intellectual elites of the Northeastern Ivy Leagues understood it. Providence or irony placed him in Hitler's Germany, allowing him to compare the eugenic racism the Germans subjected the Jewish community to the racism Du Bois saw in the American South. It is unlikely Du Bois recognized eugenics itself as inherently racist as upon visiting Germany, Du Bois "unbinding affection for the Germans" only allowed for an interpretation which deemed Hitler's treatment of the Jews was "legal," as opposed to the "unconstitutional" treatment of blacks in the United States. [459]

Du Bois's definitions of "legality" and "constitutionality" are clear indications of the overall movement's attitude towards collectivism and *laissez-faire* constitutionalism. Du Bois was swept up by the same elitist movement that accepted collectivism as an option to *laissez-faire* capitalism. Like his Anglo-American eugenicist counterparts, Du Bois saw in a racialist collectivism a solution to the social problems of the world around him. The "submerged tenth" was no freer to continue their simple lifestyle than were the "talented tenth" free to practice "breeding" that would entail "race suicide." Du Bois's daughter was one of the first victims of his zealotry. The black populace which never came to exist, the individuals we will never have the pleasure of knowing as a result of his collaboration with Margaret Sanger, are the enduring legacy of his eugenic views.

---

[456] Pg. 49 - "Unnatural Selections: Eugenics in American Modernism and the Harlem Renaissance", Daylanne K. English, Univ. of North Carolina Press, 2004.
[457] Pg. 55 – Ibid.
[458] Pg. 57 – Ibid.
[459] Pgs. 397-403, 467 - "W.E.B. Du Bois: Fight for Equality and the American Century (1919-1963)" David Levering Lewis, Henry Hold & Co., 2001.

Professor English's work helps us understand that comprehending the trajectory between a "race of masters" to a "master race" is not that of easy answers or commonplace cultural conceptions. Civil rights icons like W.E.B. Du Bois were equally liable to engage in the narcissistic "self-selecting" eugenic exercises, placing himself at the pinnacle of being and devaluing those he claimed to protect. Du Bois is a singularly tantalizing example as history placed him at the cross-roads and providence provided him an opportunity to contemplate the American and German crisis. Professor English's work also forces us to break away from the facile and commonplace conception of racism and sheds light on the fact that the eugenics drive to eradicate the "unfit" was in many ways of whites against whites and blacks against blacks.

Sec. 3 - WILHELM SCHALLMAYER'S COLLECTIVIST UTOPIAS:

Wilhelm Schallmayer was born in Mindelheim, Southern Germany, in 1857. He first started to study philosophy and law at the University of Leipzig, but later changed to medicine and finished his studies with his MD thesis at the University of Munich in 1886. Schallmayer is best known as the winner of the award-winning essay for the Krupp competition titled "Heredity and Selection in the Life-Process of Nations." The essay was published in 1903 as part of the winning prize, and together with Alfred Ploetz's early work, Schallmayer and Ploetz became the fathers of German eugenics.

Wilhelm Schallmayer, like the majority of eugenicists of his era, was a utopian socialist who subscribed to a pronounced reformist and revolutionary political ethic. Schallmayer, like Ploetz, was an early proponent of European unification, a pacifist, and a devoted follower of Ernst Haeckel, and thus a Monist:

> The eugenicists, Forel, Ploetz, Schallmayer and Woltmann, were concerned to reconcile the contradictions between socialism and Darwinism. Their solutions removed some of the harsher aspects of class struggle and of the struggle for survival. In the social sphere, national unity was substituted for class struggle, and the biological instincts of altruism and mutual aid were emphasized. (Pg. 95, "Health, Race and German Politics Between National Unification and Nazism, 1870-1945", Paul Weindling, Oxford Univ. Press, 1998)

Socialism and communism informed Schallmayer's career in medicine. Schallmayer studied economics and collectivist political theories at the University of Leipzig, where "he found the works of Karl Marx and the German economist and social theorist Alfred Schaeffle especially interesting." [460] Thus, it can be said that

---
[460] Pg. 18 - "The Wellborn Science: Eugenics in Germany, France, Brazil, and Russia", Mark B. Adams, Oxford, 1990.

Schallmayer, like Ploetz, was a radical revolutionary first, and chose eugenics only as a means to achieving his ideal society:

> Schallmayer typified the attempt at formulating a collectivist social philosophy, and the expectation that medical science could solve social problems. Civil and economic categories were evaluated in biological terms. **Human life was not to be considered in terms of productive capacity, but as biological capital.** He suggested in 1891 that state socialism and social medicine could alter the meaning of marriage. The selection of partners ought not to be made by criteria of wealth but by intelligence and physique. (emphasis mine, Pg. 95, "Health, Race and German Politics Between National Unification and Nazism, 1870-1945", Paul Weindling, Oxford Univ. Press, 1998)

While historians of socialist sympathies may distance the socialist component of eugenics, an honest reading of Schallmayer's work clarifies that the goals of the eugenicists could only be accomplished by a state with total control over society; a sentiment shared by none other than Marx and Engels as this book will later document. Schallmayer explicitly pointed to the collectivist and socialist requirements for accomplishing his eugenic goals, going as far as specifically asking for the population to carry "health passports." It is by no coincidence that Wilhelm Schallmayer found inspiration in Edward Bellamy's "nationalized" brand of "socialism," as Schallmayer was directly or indirectly describing a eugenic utopian state. By now the reader should recognize the template:

> Schallmayer considered that the social implications of the use of hereditarian biology and medicine were collectivist solutions to social deviancy. His belief in doctors as medical officials, compulsory medical tribunals and health passports marked a positive attitude to the state that contrasted to the movements for deregulation of the mid nineteenth century. From about 1886 Schallmayer began work on a treatise on the problem of medicine and degeneration. He was inspired by Bellamy's utopian writings which depicted the doctor as the arbiter of social values. Schallmayer considered that the economic basis of medicine should be altered by appointing doctors as state officials. He proposed a system of health passports and of comprehensive registration of diseases. The experience of medical practice made him critical of the individualistic attitudes of doctors and psychiatrists. He condemned their concern for the welfare of individual patients, and their lack of regard for the social consequences of inherited psychiatric illnesses. (Pg. 86, "Health, Race and German Politics Between National Unification and Nazism, 1870-1945", Paul Weindling, Oxford Univ. Press, 1998)

Sheila Faith Weiss author and Schallmayer biographer documents that Schallmayer wanted to make Germany a kind of eugenic utopia as expressed by the physician character that plays the part of a tour guide to the traveling protagonist in Bellamy's "Looking Backward":

> It is indeed revealing that the utopian vision depicted in Edward Bellamy's Looking Backward so captured the attention and approval of Schallmayer.

Bellamy's future socialist society placed a premium on productivity, efficiency, and proper management of human resources.

CONTINUES . . .

As Schallmayer put it, such a society is a place where "the effectiveness of natural selection is not curtailed." Through a policy of rational selection Schallmayer sought to create the kind of meritocratic state envisioned by Bellamy. (Pg. 63, "Race Hygiene and National Efficiency: The Eugenics of Wilhelm Schallmayer", Univ. of California Press, 1987)

Sheila Faith Weiss also wrote the article titled "The Race Hygiene Movement in Germany," which documents just how much Schallmayer's work was founded upon Darwin's theory of "natural" and "sexual selection":
> Haeckel always stressed Darwin's selection principle as the most important engine of forward directed organic change: indeed, for Haeckel, Darwinism was synonymous with selection. Weismann, who came to reject the possibility of the inheritance of acquired characteristics through his work on heredity, afforded Darwin's principle of natural selection an even greater role in organic and social evolution than did the author of the Origin of the Species himself. (Pg. 198, "The Race Hygiene Movement in Germany", Osiris, 2 Series, Vol. 3, 1987)

Some historians overplay Schallmayer as a proponent of "positive eugenics" where voluntary participation in a "rational" selection of mating partners is portrayed as more benign than "negative eugenics." The harsher truth is that barely any eugenicist can be classified as belonging to either side of this fictional demarcation, as Schallmayer himself aspired to a eugenics policy enforced with the power of the state to actively sequester, segregate, and prevent the marriage or mating of people he considered "unfit." These policies can hardly be considered "voluntary." Sheila Faith Weiss, while allowing Schallmayer this courtesy, points to the obvious conundrum created by this position, a prejudice not unlike the "self-selection" described by Professor Daylanne K. English:
> He emphasized positive eugenics: convincing the "fitter" groups in society to increase their fertility rate. The question of course remained: Which groups were, biologically speaking, the "fittest"? Schallmayer assumed that biology would one day decide the question objectively. "In the meantime," he argued, "it would not be incorrect to view highly socially productive individuals, especially the better educated, as being, on the average, more biologically valuable." ---- The class bias implicit in Schallmayer's criteria could hardly be more blatant: his own social group, the *Bildungsbürgertum*, turns out to be the "fittest." Other eugenicists shared this orientation. (Pgs. 205-206, "The Race Hygiene Movement in Germany", Osiris, 2 Series, Vol. 3, 1987)

Schallmayer is important precisely because he was the most influential of a long line of eugenic masterminds to provide a polite and refined face to what was otherwise a brutal and uncompassionate science. He did so by distancing himself from the overt racists, namely Gobineau's Aryan racism. In 1910 Schallmayer famously attacked the followers of Gobineau for their naive Nordic racism in an edition of *"Verebung und Auslese."* In this sense, Schallmayer is the prototypical, if not stereotypical eugenicist that regarded his "self-selecting" prejudices as scientific. While historians have often painted Schallmayer as the kinder and gentler kind of German eugenicists, Schallmayer's attitude towards the needy is distinctly of the type that subscribed to a Nietzschean disdain for traditional sentimentalism and compassion. Schallmayer railed against doctors who pointed to the low statistical chances that the offspring of a mental defective may produce mentally challenged children:

> Schallmayer regarded such 'humane' views as too soft. He was convinced that most mental illness was inherited, and that psychiatry was culpable in allowing the sick back into society where they might marry. He argued for laws to prevent the mentally ill from marrying and having children who would inevitably pose problems in the future. His view that 'the mad are a burden to the state' was to be a eugenic rallying cry in future years. (Pg. 86, "Health, Race and German Politics Between National Unification and Nazism, 1870-1945", Paul Weindling, Oxford Univ. Press, 1998)

Thus, Wilhelm Schallmayer can be regarded as the root of the German movement that used statistics and doomsday scare tactics about the reproductive rate of the "unfit" drowning and ultimately bringing down German culture. Schallmayer is the father of this strain of German eugenics which would lead to infamous films such as *"Erbkrank,"* which served as key propaganda pieces for the Third Reich's eugenic policies. He was heavily influenced by the positivist psychology of Theodule Ribot, who argued that not just disease, but a propensity for crime were hereditary. In turn, Ribot and his disciple Schallmayer were admirers of the British eugenicists and philosophers, including Spencer, Darwin, Haeckel and namely, Galton. [461] As such, Schallmayer's state-enforced eugenics were no less benign than those that Galton proposed in his Kantsaywhere utopian novel. As with Laughlin and Galton, the politics came first, and the coerced eugenics were justified by social, economic, and political grieving. Schallmayer like Galton proposed the creation of medical genealogies, health passports, and marriage restrictions. Like Galton, Laughlin, H.G. Wells, and all the utopian eugenicists after him, Schallmayer promoted the scientist and the doctor to elite overseer positions in the plantation that was his eugenic utopia. [462] He certainly regarded the population as a herd to be culled and mated; as this Darwinian "selectionist" outlook along with his experience working with "mental defectives" meant that Schallmayer simply didn't believe in the ability of

---

[461] Pg. 85 - "Health, Race and German Politics Between National Unification and Nazism, 1870-1945", Paul Weindling, Oxford Univ. Press, 1998. – See also Pg. 19, "The Wellborn Science: Eugenics in Germany, France, Brazil, and Russia", Mark B. Adams, Oxford Univ. Press, 1990.

[462] Pg. 19 - "The Wellborn Science: Eugenics in Germany, France, Brazil, and Russia", Mark B. Adams, Oxford Univ. Press, 1990.

therapeutic medicine to heal the "defectives." [463]

How was this proponent of "respectable" and "scientific" racism brought to the forefront? In 1897 negotiations began for a substantial prize on social applications of Darwin's "Theory of Evolution." The wealthy industrialist Alfred Krupp, the son of the munitions magnate, had a keen interest in this aspect of science, and eugenicists cemented the relationship between Krupp and Ernst Haeckel to make this contest a reality. Krupp set aside 30,000 marks for a contest to answer the question: "What can we learn from the theory of evolution about internal political development and state legislation?" [464] However, those managing Krupp's competition were sensitive to the public perceptions that the contest was the idea of Ernst Haeckel, whom himself had been the focus of various well-publicized controversies about Darwinism's application to society. The competition was given the name of the "Jena Prize Competition," and it was suggested that Haeckel should not be utilized to publicize the competition. The competition was to be judged by two different panels. The first panel was made up of Heinrich Ernst Ziegler, the zoologist, Johannes Conrad, the economist, and Dietrich Schäfer, the historian. A committee made of Haeckel, Conrad and the paleontologist Eberhard Fraas was to settle any disparities and deadlocks that may have arisen in the first panel. The top eight award-winning manuscripts would be published individually and as a part of a series titled *"Natur und Staat: Beiträge zur naturwissenschaftlichen Gesellschaftslehre,"* which translates to "Nature and State: Contributions Toward a Scientific Study of Society." Fritz Krupp and the judges wanted to use the competition to demonstrate that Darwin's theory neither "possessed the state-damaging character attributed to it by its opponents" nor in any way "destroyed morals." Their goal was to demonstrate that Darwinism could be the groundwork for a "New Ethic" founded on "a scientific-sociological basis." [465]

There were sixty entries, of which forty-four came from Germany, eight from Austria, four from Switzerland, two from Russia, and two from the United States. The first prize was awarded to Schallmayer's 381-page "*Vererbung und Auslese im Lebenslauf der Völker,*" which translates to "Heredity and Selection in the Life-Process of Nations." He received 10,000 marks on March 7, 1903. Heinrich Ernst Ziegler, one of the panelists, praised Schallmayer's works a "hygienic-sociological" approach to the question. [466] Schallmayer argued in his paper that while the 19th century had treated Darwin's evolutionary hypothesis on a purely theoretical basis, "the 20th century is called upon to apply the theory of descent to everyday life." Schallmayer devoted nearly 25 percent of the book's contents to Darwin and Weismann, stressing the importance of "selection" in the "hereditary process," and gave dire apocalyptic predictions for nations that ignored the "management" of its

---

[463] Pg. 19 – "The Wellborn Science: Eugenics in Germany, France, Brazil, and Russia", Mark B. Adams, Oxford Univ. Press, 1990.
[464] Pg. 69 – "Race Hygiene and National Efficiency: The Eugenics of Wilhelm Schallmayer", Sheila Faith Weiss, Univ. of Cal. Press, 1987.
[465] Pg. 20 – "The Wellborn Science: Eugenics in Germany, France, Brazil, and Russia", Mark B. Adams, Oxford, 1990.
[466] Pg. 20 – Ibid.

"human resources." [467]

Posterity must note that there were plenty of voices of caution warning against the obtuse paternalism in Schallmayer's proposal. Ferdinand Tönnies publicly unleashed upon the premise of the Schallmayer's Krupp Prize entry. Ferdinand Tönnies had never had any sympathy for the Nietzsche cult, namely his demands for "compulsory controls on marriage." Tönnies compared Schallmayer to Galton, voicing doubts over Galton's claim over the inheritance of mental qualities or the soundness of his analogies between biological and social organisms. Of specific importance to the theme of this book is that Tönnies accused Schallmayer and Galton of being "utopian." [468] Psychologists Alfred Vierkandt joined Tönnies attack and defended the traditional view of the social sciences. Vierkandt's review, "An Invasion of the Humanities by the Natural Sciences?" accurately prophesized that creating the foundation for society upon Weismann's and Schallmayer's crude biological reductionism was a precarious and dangerous road to take. [469]

Schallmayer's "national biology" would indeed be at least partially responsible for Hitler's "national socialism," or as Hitler's deputies would later put it, National Socialism would be "applied biology." [470] Schallmayer's theoretical "courts," "health passports," and doctors as the arbiters of social worth would prove to be prophetic. Darwin's theory, largely because of Schallmayer, became the basis for the "state policies" as Schallmayer and Ploetz recommended, and which Karl Brandt employed in the murderous T4 Euthanasia program. Fritz Lenz, one of the co-authors of the infamous "Baur-Fischer-Lenz" book, called Schallmayer's work "a masterpiece in German eugenics." [471] Schallmayer's book was also the original inspiration for the Third Reich's war on "race poisons." Schallmayer's winning Krupp publication pointed to alcoholism as "a main source, probably the main source of progressive degeneration phenomena of our time." [472] Thus, the link between Schallmayer and the eugenics of the Third Reich is clear and unambiguous, only further underscoring that the deepest roots of Nazism's ideological tree did not originate in pedestrian level bigotry or prejudices. It is no coincidence that in 1904, following the success of the Krupp competition, Ploetz founded the *"Archiv für Rassen-und Gesellschafts-Biologie,"* the first journal totally dedicated to the cause of eugenics in the world. [473] Prior to the Krupp competition, Ploetz and Schallmayer were "lone prophets in their eugenics crusade" in Germany. [474] The idea of eugenics began to coalesce into a movement in Germany in 1903, the years immediately following the publication of *"Vererbung und Auslese."* [475]

---

[467] Pg. 21 – "The Wellborn Science: Eugenics in Germany, France, Brazil, and Russia", Mark B. Adams, Oxford, 1990.
[468] Pgs. 121-122 - "Health, Race and German Politics Between National Unification and Nazism, 1870-1945", Paul Weindling, Oxford Univ. Press, 1998
[469] Pg. 122 – "Health, Race and German Politics Between National Unification and Nazism, 1870-1945", Paul Weindling, Oxford Univ. Press, 1998
[470] Pg. 123 – Ibid.
[471] Pg. 1295 - *"Münchener Medizinische Wochenschrift"*, Fritz Lenz, Vol. 66, 1919.
[472] Pg. 154 – "On the Imminent Physical Degeneration of Civilized Humanity and the Nationalization of the Medical Profession", Wilhelm Schallmayer, Berlin; Neuwied: Heuser, 1891.
[473] Pg. 22 - "The Wellborn Science: Eugenics in Germany, France, Brazil, and Russia", Mark B. Adams, Oxford, 1990.
[474] Pg. 21 – Ibid.
[475] Pg. 21 – Ibid.

The truth is that Schallmayer was the cookie-cutter mold for scientists working under Hitler's regime. Schallmayer was outspoken against having his science influenced by mythology about "Aryan" or "Nordic" races, which were largely the product of Germanic folklore. He warned against having eugenics being guided by anti-Semitic bigotry or Nordic mysticism. Historians, namely Sheila Faith Weiss, have written about Schallmayer as being free from the "racism" that permeated all of the work of most of his eugenic colleagues just as they have about Rüdin and Osborn. While the observations are technically correct, they generalize and oversimplify as to what constitutes being a "racist." Jews, blacks, Hispanics, and orientals can be just as "racist" as any Anglo, without ever having to believe in Nordic mysticism or subscribe to anti-Semitic views. To understand what makes a "racist," we must understand the roots of the term back to its original "racialist," or more precisely, a person who ranks, quantifies, and values the diverse people of the human race based on their ethnic background. Racial hierarchies that rank and value the different permutations of humanity from "superior" to "inferior" are by definition "racist," whether the vantage point is taken from a scientific estimation or a cultural preference. Scientists who believe that a preferred "race" can be deteriorated or polluted by "selecting" the wrong ethnicity as a mate is by definition "racist." By this definition, Wilhelm Schallmayer was most definitely a racist as he was a devoted "selectionist" that subscribed to Darwin's and Haeckel's racial hierarchies.

The reason Schallmayer should be deemed as dangerous is that he is the source of the smokescreen and excuse, intentional or not, that was used by the defendants at the Nuremberg Trials. Both Albert Speer and Karl Brandt painted themselves as the "good Nazis" by explaining that they were not the vulgar bigots that could be found among the ranks of the Brown Shirts, or even like Hitler, Rosenberg, or Himmler. In this sense, Brandt and Speer were right; they were much more polite and refined than the fire-breathing bigots among the ranks of the National Socialists. They would not resort to racial slurs or indulge in racial propaganda. Albert Speer kept a tidy and polite demeanor while millions upon millions were murdered in the work camps he oversaw, and he politely and quietly took the possessions of murdered or expatriated Jews. Karl Brandt, who was best friends with Albert Speer, and who had a chance in jail to confer with Speer prior to the trials, was also a polite and patient professional. If we believe Brandt's version of the events, he was only connected to the "good euthanasia," regardless if the very doctors and medical machinery employed in his "good" Euthanasia Programme were used in the murder of hundreds of thousands of "unfit" Germans, as well as the murder millions upon millions of Jews and Gypsies. If Brandt and Speer are guilty, then so is Schallmayer, and to a much greater extent as he qualifies as one of the masterminds behind the murders.

Schallmayer's brand of polite eugenics continues to provide a cover, a myth, a veneer of scientific legitimacy to the "science" of allegedly "rationally" practiced "selection," where those deemed anti-social or unfit for society are first "subordinated," then "segregated," and ultimately "eliminated." This is the polite eugenics that Darwin's son, Leonard, propagandized through the International

Eugenics society he organized. This was a polite but brutal "selectionism" based upon a not-so-subtle elitism. Wilhelm Schallmayer said it plainly: "evolution leads undeniably to the demand for the continued development of ethics in the sense of evolutionary ethics." [476]

It is this myth of "civilized" eugenics which was used by the Allied prosecution at the Nuremberg Doctors' Trial to create an imaginary line between the extermination camps and the universities that ordered Mengele's experiments. One was artificially deemed as professional and benign, and the other as militant and complicit, even though there was no evidence to justify such a demarcation. To the contrary, the evidence pointed to the fact that there was no "good euthanasia," and that the professional research and educational aspect of German eugenics was inseparably and undeniably entangled in the crimes of The Holocaust. This is the origin of the myth which allowed the kingpins of German eugenics to walk free while their subordinates paid the price. It is this myth that still clouds our understanding of exactly what conspired to get the most cultured and educated nation of the era to commit the most horrific crimes at an unprecedented scale.

Sec. 4 - "SEPARATE BUT EQUAL":

Plessy v. Ferguson, 163 US 537 (1896) is a landmark US Supreme Court decision in the history of jurisprudence in the United States, upholding the constitutionality of state laws requiring racial segregation in private businesses, under the doctrine of "separate but equal." The decision was handed down by a vote of 7 to 1 with the majority opinion written by Justice Henry Billings Brown and the dissent written by Justice John Marshall Harlan. In 1890, the State of Louisiana passed a law that required separate accommodations for blacks and whites on railroads, namely separate railway cars. This was the "separate but equal" legal concept that the Supreme Court ultimately endorsed. As the following quote indicates, even when it came to the segregation down racial lines, the position of those defending the law was that it did not invoke racism:

> Laws permitting, and even requiring, their separation, in places where they are liable to be brought into contact, do not necessarily imply the inferiority of either race to the other, and have been generally, if not universally, recognized as within the competency of the state legislatures in the exercise of their police power. The most common instance of this is connected with the establishment of separate schools for white and colored children, which have been held to be a valid exercise of the legislative power even by courts of states where the political rights of the colored race have been longest and most earnestly enforced. (Pg. 974,

---

[476] "Darwinism & the Culture of Death," Anne Barbeau Gardiner, New Oxford Book Review, June 2006.

"American Constitutional Law: Essays, Cases, and Comparative Notes", Rowman & Littlefield Publishers, Vol. I, 2010 – Quoting Plessy)

Homer Plessy's ordeal was instigated and orchestrated in order to file a "test case." Homer Plessy was part of a group called the Free People of Color in New Orleans. The group was dedicated to repealing the offensive and repressive law, and they eventually persuaded Homer Plessy to challenge it. The choice of Plessy was an interesting one, as Plessy also exemplified the "one-drop rule," which drew a stark line down a eugenic-inspired racial view. Anyone found to have been tainted by a "single drop" of biological inheritance deemed to be inferior was considered to belong to the "colored people." Plessy was born a free man and was an "octoroon," which was the term for someone of seven-eighths Caucasian descent and one-eighth African descent. From the Supreme Court's opinion:

> The petition for the writ of prohibition averred that petitioner was seven-eights Caucasian and one-eighth African blood; that the mixture of colored blood was not discernible in him; and that he was entitled to every right, privilege, and immunity secured to citizens of the United States of the white race; and that, upon such theory, he took possession of a vacant seat in a coach where passengers of the white race were accommodated, and was ordered by the conductor to vacate [163 US 537, 542] said coach, and take a seat in another, assigned to persons of the colored race, and, having refused to comply with such demand, he was forcibly ejected, with the aid of a police officer, and imprisoned in the parish jail to answer a charge of having violated the above act. (law.cornell.edu, Plessy v. Ferguson (163 US 537), Argued: April 18, 1896, Decided: May 18, 1896 – Legal Information Institute, Cornell Law)

There was another eugenic side to the Plessy incident that has not commanded the focus of historians: One must put Plessy into the context of the timeline of US history to fully understand the Plessy case. Historians and political pundits alike take the all too facile approach of considering Plessy part of a series of insults and injuries on colored people that had occurred uninterrupted from the onset of the creation of the United States. This view is false and uninformed. To understand Plessy, one must first understand that the case happened in the wake of the Civil War. The North had won and now ruled over the South with an iron fist. The North imposed Reconstruction Era legislation over Southern cities with the harshness as that of an occupying and conquering army. The animosities between North and South lingered as the wounds were fresh and unhealed when Homer Plessy decided to challenge the Louisiana law, and the US Supreme Court was still viewed as the tool of the occupying Union force. Put into context, one must first understand that Plessy took place within recent memory of Abraham Lincoln emancipating the African-American population, and a very bitter, bloody, and destructive Civil War had been won to impose "equal opportunity." Plessy, in this context, was a swing of the pendulum back towards the incendiary events that led to the Civil War. Plessy was a u-turn by the Union's Supreme Court back to the line of thinking that it had condoned with the Dred Scott decision, which had helped precipitate the war in the first place. Plessy was a very large step backward, which created a formidable obstacle that would take half a century to overcome. The US Supreme Court had the duty, if not the opportunity, to vindicate everything that was won in the Civil War. The legal path and legislative justification had been clearly laid out before the Supreme Court by President Abraham Lincoln and the hundreds of thousands who gave their lives for the cause. That the US Supreme Court decided to go in the complete opposite direction is of critical importance.

On June 7, 1892, Plessy boarded a car of the East Louisiana Railroad that was designated for use by white patrons only. The railroad company had been informed already as to Plessy's racial lineage, and after Plessy had taken a seat in the whites-only railway car, he was asked to vacate it and sit instead in the blacks-only car. Plessy refused and was arrested immediately. Plessy was convicted and begun to scale the ladder up to the Supreme Court.

In his State court battle, Homer Adolph Plessy v. The State of Louisiana, Plessy argued that the state law requiring East Louisiana Railroad to segregate trains had denied him his rights under the Thirteenth and Fourteenth Amendments of the US Constitution. However, the judge presiding over his case, John Howard Ferguson, ruled that Louisiana had the right to regulate railroad companies as long as they operated within state boundaries. Plessy sought a writ of prohibition. Homer Plessy accurately raised civil rights issues from the onset, but when the case finally reached the Supreme Court the court did not find a difference in quality between the whites-only and blacks-only railway cars, thus providing the justification for the otherwise factually dubious statement of "separate but equal."

The Supreme Court's logic is suspect. The Plessy opinion fully recognizes that the courts had deemed the practice of putting different races in different boxcars in a rail to be a violation of civil rights. The Supreme Court engaged in the dubious and almost childish rationalization that separating the races within the same boxcar was a substantially different prospect and legal question:

> No question arises under this section as to the power of the state to separate in different compartments interstate [163 US 537, 548] passengers, or affect, in any manner, the privileges and rights of such passengers. All that we can consider is whether the state has the power to require that railroad trains within her limits shall have separate accommodations for the two races. (Pg. 101, Scott J. Hammond/ Kevin R. Hardwick/Howard L. Lubert, "Classics of American Political and Constitutional Thought: Reconstruction to the Present", Hackett, 2007)

First of all, an honest survey of the reality of the situation would have quickly revealed that the amenities were far from "equal." However, Justice Brown's opinion made the facile and questionable assumption that those that deemed blacks to be inferior would actually give them "equal" accommodations. If the observation seems laughable to us now, it should have been even more so to those who lived within the bitter racial divides of the era:

> We consider the underlying fallacy of the plaintiff's argument to consist in the

assumption that the enforced separation of the two races stamps the colored race with a badge of inferiority. If this be so, it is not by reason of anything found in the act, but solely because the colored race chooses to put that construction upon it. (Pg. 102, Scott J. Hammond/ Kevin R. Hardwick/Howard Leslie Lubert, "Classics of American Political and Constitutional Thought: Reconstruction to the Present", Hackett Publishing, 2007 – Quoting Plessy)

Of note is the fact that this Supreme Court was made up of Northerners. The only Southern Justices in this session of the Supreme Court was Justice Dough White and Justice Harlan, which ironically had been pro-Union during the Civil War. Even as Justice Harlan's dissenting opinion called for a "color-blind" constitution, his "racialist" views betrayed the eugenic taint of the elite. The dissent Harlan wrote highlighted the fact that the Chinese, a race he viewed as inferior, could still ride with whites:

There is a race so different from our own that we do not permit those belonging to it to become citizens of the United States. Persons belonging to it are, with few exceptions, absolutely excluded from our country. I allude to the Chinese race. (Pg. 106, Scott J. Hammond/ Kevin R. Hardwick/Howard Leslie Lubert, "Classics of American Political and Constitutional Thought: Reconstruction to the Present", Hackett Publishing, 2007 – Quoting Plessy)

Put into the timeline of US history, Harlan's dissent reveals how a still dominant Union North was beginning to show its "racialist" character. Here was the reversal of roles discussed in previous chapters. The Northeastern abolitionists had emancipated the African American population. This was also the generation of Northeastern elites that commenced the drive towards Prohibition and Progressivism. This was the Northeastern generation that vigorously followed Edward Bellamy and a dream of a socialist utopia. This was the Northeastern population that adopted Charles Darwin's "science" as gospel and rejected the values of the Founding Fathers as antiquated dogma. This was a generation inspired by Darwin, Galton, Morel, and home-grown Ivy League "scientific racialists" like Theodore Roosevelt. Therefore, <u>Plessy v. Ferguson</u> cannot be understood without first understanding this historical context. Comprehending this political context is understanding that the decision delivered in Plessy did not have to be so. It was a decision influenced by the racial tensions in the North as much as it was about the Segregated South.

Justice Brown, who wrote the majority opinion for Plessy, was the typical Northeastern elitist. He grew up in a New England merchant family. He graduated from Yale in 1856 and received basic legal training at Yale and at Harvard. Brown hired a substitute to take his place in the Union Army during the Civil War and served as US Attorney General. Ironically, the author of the dissenting opinion, Justice John Marshall Harlan, was a Southerner from Kentucky. Justice John Marshall Harlan, who vocally decried the excesses of the Ku Klux Klan, wrote a scathing dissent in which he prophetically predicted the court's decision would be seen in the same negative light as the Dred Scott v. Sandford decision the US Supreme Court made in 1857. Harlan was proven right, yet his observation evidences the arrogance of the Supreme Court Justices: a brutal Civil War had been fought and a President murdered between the Dred Scott and Plessy decisions. These decisions did not happen in a vacuum, although, that is the impression we get from Justice Harlan's statement. The Plessy decision should not be regarded as the moral equivalent to the Dred Scott decision. It is decidedly worse for its arrogant ambivalence to the vast amount of sacrifices it ignores. Only an elitist view from atop the ivory tower of the Supreme Court could produce such a detached sense for historical context and reality.

Mark S. Weiner, the author of "Americans Without Law," is also of the opinion that cases like Plessy v. Ferguson cannot be understood out of context. Plessy needs to be considered with a slew of cases of the judicial era which also depart from tradition and engage in what author Weiner calls a "judicial racialism" which cover the Supreme Court's attitude towards American Indians, Puerto Ricans, Philippines, Hawaiians, and other peoples who came under the "protection" of an expansionist United States. Weiner's primary thesis is that racial minorities in the 19th and early 20th centuries were kept outside of our nation's civic boundaries by law, in particular by "a culturally potent and institutionally productive language of law." [477] Weiner relies on the work of German anthropologist Franz Boas, who was a leading contributor to scholarship on culture during this era. Weiner argues that Boas' transformation of the idea of culture, which Boas used as a proxy for racialist thinking, is illuminated by juridical racialism, in particular by "encouraging new rubrics for thinking about the nature of race in relation to the concept of law – rubrics ... that were absorbed into the law itself." [478] Weiner thoroughly analyzes a series of Supreme Court decisions, and some congressional statutes, and argues that judicial reasoning reflects leading intellectual thinking of the day, namely leading "racialists" of the day such as Senator Henry Cabot Lodge and Madison Grant. Thus "judicial racism" was the product of "scientific racism," and it would persist on being so on through the 1927 Buck v. Bell decision.

Weiner further observes: "In his work in Congress ... Lodge consistently spoke in the language of Teutonic juridical racialism, his political concerns deeply driven by its worldview." [479] Lodge's worldview was reflected in various judicial opinions and writings of the period, which Weiner classifies into two camps – "judicial traditionalists," like Justice John Marshall Harlan who believed that the Constitution follows the flag, and "judicial modernists" like Justices Edward White and Henry Billings Brown, who believed that Congress intended these ethnicities to live outside of the constitutional protections established for whites. Billing's bio certainly supports this view. Justice Henry Billings Brown was an active member of the American Social Science Association. As such, Justice Brown gleaned much of his judicial opinion from the work of the science that was in-vogue during this era:

---

[477] Pg. 1 - "Americans Without Law: The Racial Boundaries of Citizenship", Mark S. Weiner, NYU Press, 2006.
[478] Pg. 15 – Ibid.
[479] Pg. 64 – Ibid.

Brown was a man of many parts. He had been active in the American Social Science Association and, by all accounts, **took a keen interest in the major intellectual trends of the day.** He was familiar, therefore, with the thinking of Yale professor William Graham Sumner, regarded as one of the fathers of American sociology. The language setting forth his basic assumption constitute a virtual restatement of Sumner's basic proposition. In Brown's words: "Legislation is powerless to eradicate racial instincts or to abolish distinction based upon physical differences, and the attempt to do so can only result in accentuating the difficulties of the present situation... If one race be inferior to the other socially, the Constitution of the United States cannot put them upon the same plane." (emphasis mine, Pg. 148, "The Shifting Wind: The Supreme Court and Civil Rights from Reconstruction to Brown", John R. Howard, SUNY Press, 1999)

Plessy legitimized the move towards segregation and provided an impetus for further racially-minded laws. Legislative achievements won during the Reconstruction were erased through means of the "separate but equal" doctrine. More specifically, Plessy v. Ferguson guaranteed the state's right to implement racially separate institutions requiring them only to be of "equal" quality; ironically, one of the main contentions of the Southern Confederates claimed "State's rights" in their support for their pro-slavery laws. Supreme Court Justice John Harlan made this very prediction in his dissenting opinion:

> ...we shall enter upon an era of constitutional law, when the rights of freedom and American citizenship cannot receive from the nation that efficient protection which heretofore was unhesitatingly accorded to slavery and the rights of the master. (Pg. 647, "American Constitutional Law: Essays, Cases, and Comparative Notes", Rowman & Littlefield Publishers, Vol. 2, 2010)

As the untangling of interrelationships is the *modus operandi* of this book, it is of importance to mention that, according to Robert Proctor, the German eugenicists were obsessed with American Jim Crow laws like the one Plessy v. Ferguson upheld. Proctor says as much in the chapter he contributed to Arthur L. Caplan's symposium on bioethics and The Holocaust:

> Nazi physicians on more than one occasion argued that German racial policies were relatively liberal compared with the way blacks were treated in the US. Evidence for this was usually taken from the fact that in several southern states, a person with 1/32 black ancestry was legally black, whereas if someone was 1/8 Jewish in Germany (and for many purposes, ¼ Jewish), that person was legally Aryan. Nazi physicians spent a great deal of time discussing American miscegenation legislation; German medical journals reproduced charts showing the states in which blacks could or could not marry whites, could or could not vote, and so forth. ---- In 1939, Germany's leading racial hygiene journal reported that the University of Missouri had refused to admit black students. The same year, the journal reported the recent refusal of the American Medical Association to admit black physicians to its membership. German physicians

only recently (in 1938) barred Jews from practicing medicine (except on other Jews); racial theorists were thereby able to argue that Germany was not alone in its efforts to preserve racial purity. (Pg. 33-34, Chap.: Nazi Biomedical Policies, "When Medicine Went Mad: Bioethics and the Holocaust", Humana Press, 1992)

At least one other historian agrees with Proctor. Ben S. Austin, an author for the online journal, the Jewish Virtual Library, makes a direct link between <u>Plessy v. Ferguson</u> and the National Socialist's Nuremberg Laws:

> The Congress of the National Socialist Workers' Party (NAZI) convened in Nuremburg, Germany on September 10, 1935. Among the many items of business on the Nazi agenda was the passage of a series of laws designed (a) to clarify the requirements of citizenship in the Third Reich, (b) to assure the purity of German blood and German honor and (b) to clarify the position of Jews in the Reich. These three laws, passed on September 15, 1935, and the numerous auxiliary laws which followed them are called the Nuremberg Laws. --- Please take special note of the similarity between these laws and the Jim Crow Laws which were passed in the United States following the Compromise of 1877, upheld by the US Supreme Court in Plessy vs Ferguson (1896) and remained in effect until the court reversed the "separate but equal" doctrine in Brown vs the Board of Education of Topeka (1954). It is clear that Hitler used the Jim Crow segregation statutes as his model for defining Jews in the Third Reich. (Article no longer posted as of July 2018)

More to the point, the "Baur-Fischer-Lenz" book points to the fact that the legitimatization of Jim Crow anti-miscegenation laws was a catalyst for the "race hygiene" movement that started long before Adolf Hitler. In fact, Fischer's work started with those of African descent. As this book documents, Fischer authored "The Rehoboth Bastards and the Problem of Miscegenation among Humans," the book which decried the racial mixing of Africans and Germans that inevitably resulted from Germany's African colonies. Fischer concluded in his study that the colored races did not deserve the same legal protections as whites. Fischer would collaborate with major American eugenicists on his miscegenation studies, including Charles Davenport from Cold Springs Harbor:

> We still do not know a great deal about the mingling of the races [Rassenmischung]. But we certainly do know this: Without exception, every European nation [Volk] that has accepted the blood of inferior races – and only romantics can deny that Negroes, Hottentots, and many others are inferior – has paid for its acceptance of inferior elements with spiritual and cultural degeneration. – Consequently, one should grant them the amount of protection that an inferior race confronting us requires to survive, no more and no less and only for so long as they are of use to us. (As quoted in pg. 11, "The Origins of Nazi Genocide: From Euthanasia to the Final Solution," Henry Friedlander, Univ. of North Carolina Press, 1997)

Since this book peddles on historical juxtapositions, it is permissible to document that the most surreal of the Third Reich's anti-black laws was the prohibition of Jazz. Its performance was seen as a cultural pollutant. This is ironic, as many historians of the Jazz genre regard the upholding of the "separate but equal" laws in Homer Plessy's New Orleans as the legislative measure that helped create Jazz. The law forced classically trained musicians of mostly white background but deemed black per the "one-drop-rule," to have to resort to performing only with African-American Gospel musicians; a mixture which would produce the iconic soul of the Jazz virtuoso. [480]

Sec. 5 - FROM "COMMUNISME" TO "RASSENHYGIENE":

In 1933 Wilhelm Frick conscripted Fritz Lenz, Ernst Rüdin, Hans F.K. Günther, and Alfred Ploetz to write the Third Reich's racial laws as an "expert advisory committee for population and racial policy." The immediate results were the 1933 and 1935 Nuremberg Laws. Historians marvel at the dizzying pace by which volumes upon volumes of new laws were passed in the early days of the Hitler regime. The truth is that the eugenic zealots had them ready and waiting, courtesy of their American friends. Equally true is that Hitler's eugenic utopia had been planned and dreamed about by prominent European activists for decades prior, and that the blueprint for Hitler's eugenic Eden had been hashed and rehashed by the social planners and experts long before him.

Hitler personally appointed Ploetz to a professorship in appreciation for a lifetime of work on eugenics in 1936. As such, Hitler, and the rest of Germany for that matter considered Ploetz as the founding father of the "race-based state." Ploetz first proposed the theory of racial hygiene in his "*Grundlinien einer Rassenhygiene*" or "Racial Hygiene Basics" in 1895 in his book "The Efficiency of our Race and the Protection of the Weak." The eugenic aspects of this racially structured policy proposal would include the systematic measuring by examination of the moral and intellectual capacity of citizens to decide on marriage, reproductive rights, and social position. Per Ploetz, disabled children would be aborted, and the sick and the weak would be "eliminated."

Ploetz himself was the product of the emerging "New Ethic." The aptly titled book, "The Vertigo Years" by Philipp Blom, diagnoses the psychological forces at play during this time in Europe. In this short span of time, between the death of Queen Victoria and the outbreak of WWI, a new world order was being ushered into being, triggering the wide anxieties over the quickening pace of change. The

---

[480] See generally: PBS documentary "Jazz", Ken Burns and Geoffrey Ward, Jan. 2001.

forced transformation on a public already teetering on the precipice of social anxieties set the stage for the following disastrous decades:

> With supreme Prussian application, he wrote in his 1895 work "The Excellence of Our Race and the Protection of the Weak" that procreation must not be left to "some accident, an hour of inebriation, but regulated according to fundamental principles established by science." If such dutiful copulation resulted in a malformed child, "the college of doctors ... will give it a kind of death with a small dose of morphine." ---- The founder and tireless propagator of the German Society for Race Hygiene, Ploetz was by no means more extreme than other writers, all of whom published successful books and articles. "We do not approve of any false humanity," wrote the avowedly racist eugenicist Theodor Fritsch. "Whoever seeks to preserve the degenerate and depraved, limits space for the healthy and strong, suppresses the life of the whole community, multiplies the sorrows and burdens of existence and helps rob happiness and sunshine from life. Where human power cannot triumph over sorrow, there we honour death as a friend and redeemer." Fostering the strong would get nowhere without killing the weak, it was believed, and here Nietzsche was used to give ammunition to those who wanted to kill to be kind: "even the most careful selection of the best can accomplish nothing, if it is not linked with a merciless elimination of the worst people . . . Zarathustra preaches: Do not spare your neighbor! . . . Therefore this means becoming hard against those who are below average and in them to overcome one's own sympathy." (Pg. 314, "The Vertigo Years: Europe, 1900-1914", Basic Books, 2010)

Ploetz was born in Swinemünde, Germany and he grew up and attended school in Breslau, as part of this generation caught up in turn-of-the-century hysteria. Ploetz studied political economy in Breslau where he began his friendship with Carl Hauptmann, brother of the famous author Gerhart Hauptmann, together with which Ploetz founded a secret racialist youth society in 1879. Recall that Carl Hauptmann was a student of Ernst Haeckel, and Gerhart Hauptmann and Ploetz attended some of his lectures. It is thus that Ploetz's penchant for eugenic utopias sprouted from these social connections. The group developed a plan for founding a colony in one of the pacific states and named itself the "Pacific association." Unsurprisingly, their utopian Pacific community would be a "friendly, socialist and maybe also pan-Germanic basis."

Ploetz had a wide-ranging intellect that related philosophy and social sciences to an obsession with heredity and race: "Science was to weld socialism and nationalism into a coherent ideology of biological social reform and be the weapon in the struggle to regenerate the race." [481] One could have predicted the popularity of the Nazi creed with that one sentence alone. While the youthful oath of blood brotherhood was an adolescent escapade, behind it lay an enthusiasm for nature and a significant transition in German nationalism.

Racial ardour was fueled by a youthful fascination with Darwinism and the

---

[481] Pg. 64 – "Health, Race and German Politics Between National Unification and Nazism, 1870-1945", Paul Weindling, Oxford Univ. Press, 1998.

idealization of German national culture. Between 1870 and 1914 many adolescent renegades read Haeckel and reveled in the adventures of natural history collecting. Enthusiasm for natural history went with a fascination for 'primitive' racial prowess as in adventure stories glorifying German history. Favorite books were tales by the Breslau historian and writer, Felix Dahn, about Nordic warriors – the theatrical *Kampf um Rom* of 1867 and Odins Trost combining Germanic myths of a struggle of Teutons and Jews with ideas of harmony with nature and the universe. This nationalistic culture reflected the disappointed hopes of 'Gross-Deutsche' idealists hoping to incorporate Austria into Bismarck's Germany. (Pg. 64, "Health, Race and German Politics Between National Unification and Nazism, 1870-1945", Oxford Univ. Press, 1998)

Paul Weindling's "Health, Race, and German Politics" provides a tour through this peculiarly similar timeline of Ploetz's life, and the intellectual groundswell that prepared the German public for what would be later required of them by the National Socialist power structure. Schools became a nationalist flashpoint and demands for colonies expressed the social insecurities of an economically hard-pressed middle class that also found outlets in the movements for *"Lebensreform,"* and anti-Semitism. These various currents of disenchantment sought to dislodge the dominance of the aristocratic-Junker ruling elite, undo the economic individualism of classical liberalism, and enlarge the scope for nationalist and centralist activities. A select group of activist youth sought to address these commonplace political gripes fueled primarily with the obsession of preventing racial degeneration. They formed the League to Reinvigorate the Race in 1879. Their aim was to unite all Germans in a world state, and unsurprisingly, a utopian colony. They swore a midnight oath of blood brotherhood at an oak outside Breslau, their Silesian hometown. [482]

Recall that *"Lebensreform,"* or in English "life reform," was one of the activist movements which sprung up in the 1880s in Germany and Switzerland. The movement propagated a back-to-nature lifestyle, emphasizing among others health food, raw food, organic food, nudism, sexual liberation, alternative medicine, and religious reform along with abstention from alcohol, tobacco, drugs, and vaccines. Some prominent members such as Rudolf Steiner intertwined Madame Blavatsky's Theosophy into their reformist views as an alternative to traditional Christianity. The movement's most zealous followers were those that were awakened by Haeckel's mystical naturalism and the conviction that "natural selection" had "degenerative" implications:

> Moral and political remedies were not enough: it was necessary to purify the cultural and scientific structures that had been so debased by industrialization. Biology and health were central to the reformist strategy. There was revulsion from liberal economic progress and civic freedoms as having produced 'the social problem' to which liberal individualism offered no solutions. Convictions grew

---

[482] Pg. 64 - "Health, Race and German Politics Between National Unification and Nazism, 1870-1945", Paul Weindling, Oxford Univ. Press, 1998.

that industrial society required collective institutions for guaranteeing the physical basis of existence through adequate diet, housing, and health care. (Pg. 62, "Health, Race and German Politics Between National Unification and Nazism, 1870-1945", Oxford Univ. Press, 1998)

The movement coincided with the pinnacle of utopian socialism, as fueled by the eugenic-minded followers of Edward Bellamy. Thus, German eugenics in the form of "racial hygiene" became much broader than just a proposal for "selective breeding" of hereditary traits, but a campaign against the potential "racial poisons" that were perceived as threatening the hereditary pool such as alcohol, meat, and tobacco. The movement demanded a transformation of lifestyle, namely the rejection of capitalism's consumerism. [483]

According to the Encyclopedia Britannica definition for "nudism," the first known nudist club, *Freilichtpark* or "Free Light Park," appeared about 1903 near Hamburg. The movement was part of the *Lebensreform* movement and was bolstered by Richard Ungewitter's 1906 book *"Die Nacktheit,"* which translates to "Nakedness." The book went through several printings, and as early as 1907, Ungewitter followed up with a pamphlet called "Nudity and Culture." The following observation depicts the erotic admixture between naturalist and Nazi movements, which would later merge under Heinrich Himmler:

> Ungewitter also affixed mystic Aryan and temperance features to the simple *Nacktkultur* philosophy: nudism, abstinence from alcohol and tobacco, and vegetarian diets were the means by which the German race would regenerate itself and ultimately prevail over its neighbors and the diabolical Jews, who were intent on injecting putrefying agents into the nation's blood and soil. (Pgs. 138-139, "Voluptuous Panic: The Erotic World of Weimar Berlin", Mel Gordon, Expanded Edition, Feral House, 2008)

In 1923, Richard Ungewitter voiced a commitment to "racial hygiene" as an integral part of the "reform" of the German people. While this view instigated many defections among his followers, Ungewitter had voiced such sentiments in works much prior to 1923. His 1910 book "Nudity and Culture" clearly stipulated that the "culture of nudity" was created by him so that the "selection" of mates depended upon the ability of a German woman to be able to appreciate the "naked Germanic man." Nudity would enable German women to "select" the "Strong and Healthy mates" and thus prevent the "weaklings" from "reproducing." [484] Furthermore, Ungewitter built upon these views by publishing "Degeneration of the Race: A Wake-up Call at the Eleventh Hour" in 1934 and had written explicitly anti-Semitic tracts entitled *"Rassenverschlechterung durch Juda"* as early as 1919. In other words, racialism had always been an inseparable part of the movement.

Furthermore, this "nudist" reform movement was hardly a forgotten precursor,

---

[483] Pg. 62 - "Health, Race and German Politics Between National Unification and Nazism, 1870-1945", Paul Weindling, Oxford Univ. Press, 1998.
[484] Pg. 130 – "Nudity and Culture", Richard Ungewitter, 1910.

but rather a concept wholly integral to Hitler's Nazism. The pedestrian concept of the prudish and conservative "Nazi" is wholly a product of current political mores redefining history. Spiegel Online published a book review titled "Naked Nazis" which reviews the extent to which the Third Reich worshipped the naked human body. The article documents how a popular book in Hitler's Germany, Hans Surén's "*Mensch und Sonne*," or "Humans and Sun," was an artistic compendium of nude photographs that included lyrical praise of the male member, instructions for yoga-like exercises, and even naked skiing:

> The SS magazine *Das Schwarze Korps* (The Black Corps), advertized for Surén's book, even giving it an entire page in a pre-Christmas issue. In it they say: "We want a strong and joyful affirmation of body awareness, because we need it to build a strong and self-confident race." Nudity was seen partly as a means of encouraging the "health of the race." And if that also happened to serve the voyeuristic desires of readers, that was accepted. (speigel.de, "Naked Nazis: Book Reveals Extent of Third Reich Body Worship", Hilmar Schmundt, Spiegel, June 16, 2011)

The article documents that, far from being censored by the supposedly prude Nazis, Hans Surén was named the special agent for physical education as part of the celebrations for the 1936 Olympics. Along with Leni Riefenstahl, Surén and other German artists conveyed the importance of physical fitness to eugenic breeding. Their depictions of the human body were racially charged propaganda pieces intended to forward the regime's eugenic ideology. Furthermore, any honest appraisal of the content of Hitler's infamous 1937 *Grosse deutsche Kunstausstellung*, or "Great German Art Exhibition," held at the House of German Art attests to the overt eroticism and outright worship of muscular "Aryan" women and men in both sculpture and painting. Hitler's ideal of the racially superior "Aryan" had very concrete aesthetic expression, and it was an ideal that was integral to the *völkisch* back-to-nature aspect of the regime. The wholesome peasantry was an aesthetic ideal as much as it was a political or economic aspiration that was deeply rooted in Germany's *Lebensreform* movement and Hitler's adoration for classical Greece. This brings us back to Alfred Ploetz and the radical inspiration for his eugenics and the roots of coercive "total state" social hygiene solutions. Ploetz had moved his studies to Breslau out of his sense of a mission to solve the nation's social problems, and where he could find like-minded radicals. He and his activist brethren studied socialist writings on population growth, namely, Karl Kautsky's writings. On November 1st, 1883 they established a utopian society called *Pacific*. The name was an homage to Charles Fourier's socialist utopia, *Democracie Pacifique*. [485] Pacific would also be a back-to-nature commune, as Ploetz and his collegiate friends were part of the *"Lebensreform"* movement. They dressed in woolen clothing by the doctor and zoologist, Gustav Jaeger. The attire was supposed to express the "Darwinian" conviction that a man was a mammal, and that man should wear

---

[485] Pg. 67 - "Health, Race and German Politics Between National Unification and Nazism, 1870-1945", Paul Weindling, Oxford Univ. Press, 1998.

clothing made from mammalian fibers. [486] The group included Ferdinand Simon, the later advocate of the German temperance movement and husband to the German socialist, August Bebel, and Wolfgang Heine, who would become the socialist Prussian Minister of the Interior. These political radicals hoped that art, science and more importantly, centrally planned social organization could be given legitimacy by establishing their basis in laws derived from nature. At Breslau the Ploetz circle formed the nucleus of a student society of Darwinian enthusiasts. Wilhelm Breitenbach wrote an enthusiastic letter to Darwin, and Haeckel and Eduard Strasburger became honorary members. The students understood that evolutionary biology offered a path to scientific socialism. [487] While some would argue that Ploetz's radical circle was harkening towards what today may be called a "holistic" outlook, it is their devotion to "state-enforced" health measures that cross the line from life-style choice to militant nationalism, or more precisely, the belief in what Hitler would later call the "total state," or what we now call "totalitarianism":

> They cultivated the Platonist philosopher, Rudolf Eucken, who developed a philosophy of the **totality of 'Life'**, and popularized idealism as an antidote to the technical and economic culture of the Reich. The group – explored the ideas on human perfectibility of utopian writers such as Plato, Thomas More, Tommaso Campanella and Robert Owen. (emphasis mine, Pg. 68, "Health, Race and German Politics Between National Unification and Nazism, 1870-1945", Paul Weindling, Oxford Univ. Press, 1998)

The group agreed to pay Ploetz's way to the United States specifically to study the various American communal experiments. Ploetz traveled to Chicago in 1884 and decided to join the Icarians in the Adams County, Iowa settlement. The Icarians were one of many utopian communes that sprung up in the wide-open vastness of the United States. Originally a French utopian movement, their leader Étienne Cabet led his followers to America where they established a group of socialist communes during the period from 1848 through 1898. Cabet had been introduced to the ideas of Sir Thomas More, the author of "Utopia" and Robert Owen, one of the other founders of utopian colonies in the United States. Cabet began to advocate a collectivist social movement, for which he invented the term "*communisme*." Upon his return, Cabet published "*Voyage en Icarie*," or in English "The Voyage to Icaria," a narrative blueprint of a communist Utopia. Cabet's book was tremendously popular; notoriety that Cabet leveraged to persuade fifteen hundred followers to depart to the United States in 1848 and settle near Fort Worth, Texas. In 1852, the Icarians purchased land in Adams County, Iowa, to form a new permanent settlement, and began a colony there until 1860, when the colony went bankrupt. Many members moved to a new site in Iowa where the colony persisted until an internal disagreement in 1870 between the "*vieux icariens*" and the "*jeunes icariens*" over women's suffrage. The disagreement instigated a split, and the "*jeunes icariens*"

---

[486] Pg. 66 – "Health, Race and German Politics Between National Unification and Nazism, 1870-1945", Paul Weindling, Oxford Univ. Press, 1998.
[487] Pg. 67 – Ibid.

created yet another colony separated by about a mile on the same property. Ironically, all these collectivist movements that obsessed with overpopulation were always able to find more vacant land away from civilization. This was true of the communes then, as it was for the communes that cropped up because of the 1970s hippies.

In between all this mess, Ploetz was supposed to study the commune and report back to his friends who were interested in creating similar a venture back in Germany. The Icarian experience was specifically instrumental in Ploetz's development as a "total state" eugenicist, as Ploetz would later regard "race hygiene" not as compartmentalized as an aspect of science, but as the underlying and controlling concept of society. Ploetz came away from the United States with a conviction that society needed to be rationally planned and its every aspect consciously designed. For the Icarians, the remedy for any societal problem would be a better social and political organization. The society was free in the sense that you were free to join and free to leave. However, once a member you were compelled to subject yourself to its principles entirely. Like most communes of this period, Icaria's labor was divided by sex. Women took care of the domestic chores, whereas men were assigned to be mill or shop workers, farmers, or laundry washers. Children were also given work assignments. Work was highly regimented and monitored by supervisors. Yet, Ploetz came away more radical than the Icarians, feeling that the failure of the utopian colonies in the Americas was proportional to the amount of individual freedom they allowed. The dissolution convinced Ploetz that collectivist idealism was not enough. He drew up a "Constitution of the Freeland Society" which mapped out a form of collectivism upon racial principles. According to Ploetz, racial purity and a healthy citizenry had to be maintained for such a society to survive, and thus had to be mandated. [488] Ploetz would cite Friedrich Nietzsche's "Also Sprach Zarathustra" in his first treatise on racial hygiene, invoking Nietzsche's aphorism on the evolution from the species to a super-species, and on the degenerative and dysgenic effects of self-interest, individualism, and egoism. [489]

When Ploetz returned to study medicine in Zurich, he added temperance and prohibition to his radical views. This is how Ploetz first met Rüdin, the other father of National Socialist eugenics. Rüdin was also a young utopian delving in temperance and socialism. Rüdin and his friends had established an abstinence association, *Humanitas*. Ploetz and Rüdin were kindred spirits, equally influenced by Bebel, Forel, Bung, and Edward Bellamy's utopian novels. [490] In turn, Ploetz convinced his old friends Lux, Simon, and Carl and Gerhardt Hauptman to take a vow of abstinence, as Rüdin's friends. Together, this group of like-minded youth founded the International Association to Combat Alcohol Consumption. The group, like the long string of others founded by Ploetz, was strictly secular and looking to distance itself from the Christian anti-alcohol movements. Their abstinence from alcohol was justified by racial motives and was the beginning of

---

[488] Pg. 69 – "Health, Race and German Politics Between National Unification and Nazism, 1870-1945", Paul Weindling, Oxford Univ. Press, 1998.
[489] Pg. 69 – Ibid.
[490] Pg. 72 – Ibid.

"racial hygiene's" strong stance against "racial poisons."

All of this utopian dreaming was a lifelong pattern for Ploetz. Ploetz would spend a considerable portion of his life organizing groups around his utopian socialist aspirations throughout his life. Ploetz fell back on his radical roots in the upheaval following the First World War. Recall that Ploetz created the secret society, the Nordic Ring, or the *Ring der Norda*, in 1907 and then reconstituted it in 1910 as the *Nordischer Ring*. The Nordic Ring was expanded the following year into an athletic club and renamed *Bogenklub München*, or the Munich Archery Club. Ploetz clarified that the goals of the organization had not changed and that the archery club was "more than a sports club"; it was "a shoot from which a true program of eugenics would grow." [491] In the revolutionary aftermath of WWI, this Archery Club was again reconstituted into the *Deutscher Wider-Bund*, or German Widar Association, the aim of which was still "*die Pflege deutschen Menschentums*," the fostering of the German human type.

In 1890 Ploetz became a doctor and married Ernst Rüdin's sister Pauline. The marriage had been born out of a devotion to utopianism, and this is very likely the reason why the couple returned to the United States to settle in Springfield, Massachusetts, where the couple opened a medical practice and bred chickens. The choice of Springfield, Massachusetts was an odd one, to say the least. Ploetz's choice can be explained by his devotion to Edward Bellamy. Massachusetts was the home and locale of Edward Bellamy's "Looking Backward," and the cause of many reformist clubs like the ones created by Ploetz. Ploetz used his time in the United States to cement his theories on race and begin writing the books he became famous for. Ploetz also nourished new friendships with the anarchists and socialists and joined the Springfield Socialist Party. It is thus that Ploetz surrounded himself by a people in Springfield equally committed to utopian socialism and temperance. Bellamy, in turn, had been an admirer of Galton's 1873 work on "stirpiculture," a term which Galton replaced with "eugenics" in 1883. Ploetz saw in the Bellamy-Galton combination a "scientific" formula to his utopian designs. Many German socialists had been inspired by the Bellamy-Galton formula for a classless world community, or in German, "*Volksgemeinscchaft*." Bellamy and Galton together provided a methodology for utopian designs upon Darwinian evolutionary terms. Ploetz saw in them the mechanisms, the template for a "biological utopia from elements of state socialism, sanitary reform, and Darwinism. Scientific positivism was to be linked with collectivist social philosophies." [492] In Bellamy's novel was everything Ploetz aspired to: eugenics, a naturalist and green approach to city planning, and socialist solidarity, thus Ploetz immersed himself in the socialism and progressivism emerging from movements like Bellamy's "Nationalist Clubs."

Ploetz's experience in the United States reveals more than just the roots of the movement in Germany. Ploetz, like Schallmayer and Rüdin, were the cookie-cutter molds for all eugenicists that would follow, if not core Nazi dogma itself. Ploetz

---

[491] Pg. 71 - "Brownshirt Princess: A Study of the Nazi Conscience", Lionel Gossman, Open Book Publishers, 2009.
[492] Pg. 76 - "Health, Race and German Politics Between National Unification and Nazism, 1870-1945", Paul Weindling, Oxford Univ. Press, 1998.

illustrated just what he absorbed from race relations in the United States during the afternoon of October 21, 1910, at the first meeting in Frankfurt of the German Sociological Society. The contentious debate was over the paper presented by Ploetz on "The Concepts of Race and Society." The famous debate between Max Weber and Alfred Ploetz began with Ploetz making the typical eugenic argument that cultures could "degenerate" and that once great nations committed "suicide," or more specifically "race suicide," by not tending to breeding stock. Weber confronted Ploetz for polluting his science with racial considerations:

> **DR. PLOETZ:** "The ancient Greeks were referred to here. But wouldn't it be much better if contemporary Greece were inhabited by the ancient Greeks and not by those who live there today, or at least if it were inhabited by people who behaved like the ancient Greeks!
> **MAX WEBER:** They wouldn't have that culture!
> **DR. PLOETZ:** All right, another culture! If only the people had the same brains...
> **MAX WEBER:** Perhaps they still do have them!
> **DR. PLOETZ:** But they do not accomplish the same things as the ancient Greeks. Surely it wouldn't be a pity if the race today possessed the same qualities that had shaped the upper stratum at that time. One doesn't usually wish that a people shouldn't continue because it has had a lustrous period. Why shouldn't they continue? I would wish the same thing for our German nation (as Professor Schulze-Gavernitz already said). No one can wish more warmly than I that our German nation should have a glorious future, but one that endures-not one that is cut off like the Greeks. (Pg. 309, "Max Weber, Dr. Alfred Ploetz, and W.E.B. Du Bois: Max Weber on Race and Society II", Sociological Analysis, Vol. 34, No.4, Pgs. 308-312, Winter 1973)

Incidentally, the conversation then turns to what Dr. Ploetz observed in the race relations in the United States, with Ploetz defending his views by specifically pointing out that it was the American elite, the educated, and the upper echelon of American society which segregated the African-American population, and thus their opinion should be taken as the opinion of scientifically minded and logical people. More specifically, Ploetz points to the "Yankee," clearly referring to the American North:

> **DR. PLOETZ:** I also wish to say a few words on the question of the Negro. I have lived in the United States four years, and as a doctor I have treated Negroes and whites and have spoken a great deal with educated and uneducated Americans about their antipathy towards the Negro. I can say that it is not so much because of the odor although in the summer it is very penetrating and, for example, in the hotels the Negroes are compelled to wash themselves from head to foot.
> **MAX WEBER:** Others do it by themselves! (Merriment from the audience)
> **DR. PLOETZ:** Only the higher, not the lower strata who don't think of it. But that is not the basic reason. The point is that the Yankee, including the better inhabitants-in this matter the leading social class sets the standard-the Yankee

hesitates to have social relationships with Negroes because he feels himself compromised by uninhibited morals, the more defective intelligence, and the more foolish behavior on the average of the Negro. He feels himself compromised just as whenever a man from our upper classes lets himself be seen, not with a poor, but with a foolish and dumb man. This is one of the basic reasons indicated by them. Negroes are now becoming doctors, by thousands there are now Negro doctors. But just try one such doctor; place yourself under his treatment and see the kind of examination he gives, and the type of diagnosis, and how he behaves! This is more or less a caricature in order to express the matter sharply.

MAX WEBER: You know that they exclude Negroes from the universities! And naturally they (the Negroes) only had their own universities in the beginning.

DR. PLOETZ: That must compel reflection-that even the scholars have shut them out from the universities. There must be a reason for this. Max Weber: With deference to the protest of their white students-quite obviously!

DR. PLOETZ: No, I must defend the college students. For it is not only the colleges, not only the universities, they are excluded from many other institutions. It is because of their intellectual and moral inferiority. (Pgs. 311-312, "Max Weber, Dr. Alfred Ploetz, and W.E.B. Du Bois: Max Weber on Race and Society II", Sociological Analysis, Vol. 34, No.4, Pgs. 308-312, Winter 1973)

Ironically, Weber turned to the example of W.E.B. DuBois to defend African-Americans from Ploetz's racism. Max Weber had briefly met W.E.B. DuBois, but apparently his brief meeting did not interlude into Du Bois's own views on eugenics. As we know from Daylanne K. English's research for her book "Unnatural Selections," Du Bois shared beliefs in a biologically superior "talented tenth," "race suicide," and the rest of the typical dogmas which elitist eugenicists espoused. More specifically, Ploetz himself was making references to the "strata" even within whites, as Du Bois himself had repeatedly separated American blacks into the "top tenth" and the "submerged tenth".

After returning from the United States, Ploetz digested this Bellamy-Galton-Darwin-Marx admix and regurgitated and reformulated it into his 1895 book entitled "The Fitness of our Race and the Protection of the Weak" or *"Die Tüchtigkeit unserer Rasse und der Schutz der Schwachen."* This contribution to the prevailing radicalism and zealotry in German science was a timely one. A belief in fixes to the environment had collapsed under the influence of Darwin; the medical community of the 1870's was convinced that the born defective and socially deviant were incurable regardless of improvement in living conditions, and worse, a danger to the gene pool.

The fact that Ploetz, the father of "race hygiene" and German eugenics, was a utopian socialist with a conviction that society needed to be planned and designed had long-reaching impact, considering that the one politician that would take up his cause was Adolf Hitler. In Ploetz, Hitler found a template for a hyper-centralized society, hardened by its contempt towards the individualist and traditional mores.

Ploetz also shared an affinity for city planning with Hitler. The idea of selective human breeding, propagated by Galton, Ploetz, and others, appeared in one of Ebenezer Howard's diagrams of utopian schemes, namely the one of 1898. The leading German eugenicists were members of the boards of the German garden cities organization which directly lobbied for city planning as an integral part of "race hygiene" measures, and it is no coincidence that many of the members of the Ploetz fraternity were also part of the parallel garden city organizations. The author Wilhelm Bolsche acted as a middleman between the eugenicists and garden city movement. He was also a German biographer of both Darwin and Ernst Haeckel. As such, Bolsche was one of the most widely read writers of the German activist and reform social circles leading up to WWI. Bolsche acted on his convictions as well. The author backed up his writings with activism as a member of the Friedenshagen Group and the New Community, or *Friedenshagener Kreis* and *Neue Gemeinschaft*. Incidentally, the New Community was the first German commune in 1901; formed in Schlachtensee, a town near Berlin. Bolsche was one of the first members in Ploetz's German Society for Eugenics, or in German, *Deutsche Gesellschaft fur Rassenhygiene*, along with Ernst Haeckel and Gerhart Hauptmann. [493]

In the context of these proto-Nazi convictions, Ploetz's racism against Jews was too pronounced to ignore. His contribution to National Socialist eugenics was too important. Ploetz resigned his position as political editor of the magazine "*Welt am Montag*" because the other two editors were Jews, and also became uneasy upon discovering that one of the benefactors of his journal, the "*Archiv für Rassen – und Gesellschaftsbiologie*" was Jewish. This is where Ploetz's "racial hierarchies" became a topic of historical importance. When in 1904, Ploetz had also founded the periodical "*Archiv für Rassen-und Gesellschaftsbiologie*" with Fritz Lenz, Ploetz proudly announced its creation to one of his idols, Ernst Haeckel, stating that the "*Archiv*" was founded as a campaigning force on the side of Darwinism. Of note is that contributors to the first volume of the "*Archiv*" included intellectuals that would later become important to the National Socialist ideals, namely Friedrich Ratzel, the geographer to whom the infamous idea of "*Lebensraum*" expansionist policy is attributed to. Ernst Haeckel is attributed for giving Ploetz the idea of starting the "*Archiv*" and Ploetz frequently used Haeckel's notoriety and fame to market the journal. Ploetz was a frequent visitor to Jena, to participate in Ernst Haeckel's Monist League, as was Wilhelm Schallmayer. The "Racial Hygiene Society" was the product of Ploetz's networking with Haeckel, Rüdin, and Ziegler. The society was formed by them in Berlin between April and June 1905, and Ploetz became chief editor of the "*Deutsche Gesellschaft für Rassenhygiene,*" or the "German Association of Eugenics" in 1905.

Ploetz died at the age of 79 in 1940, at the peak of National Socialism. Otmar von Verschuer, the director of the Kaiser-Wilhelm Institute which oversaw Mengele's "twin studies," wrote a book to commemorate Ploetz. On page 71 of the book titled "Alfred Ploetz," Verschuer praised his "inner sympathy and enthusiasm with the

---

[493] Pg. 303 - Wolfgang Voigt, "Garden City as Eugenic Utopia", Planning Perspectives, No. 4, Pgs. 295-312, 1989.

National Socialist Movement." Ernst Rüdin also wrote in honor of his good friend and brother-in-law. On page 474 of the ARGB paper titled "Honor of Prof. Dr. Alfred Ploetz," Rüdin praised Ploetz as a man "by his meritorious services has helped to set up our Nazi ideology."

All of this is of historical importance because the German radical youth at the *fin de siecle* largely predicted the type of government they would espouse once that generation came to power. Clearly, these radicals had no interest in traditional or conservative governance. Why have the radical environmentalist roots of Nazism been forgotten or overlooked? Why have historians been reluctant to delve into the common roots shared by the 1960s environmentalism and naturalist movements and Hitler's National Socialist core ideology? These are either politicized or poorly researched views, which fail to understand just how pervasive the nature and health aspect of National Socialism truly was. Organic farming ultimately found its expression though Heinrich Himmler's gardens at Dachau, as well as through the Third Reich's vast health campaigns against unnatural ingredients and food dyes. Vegetarianism was propagandized by Adolf Hitler himself. Naturalism, in general, found its expression in the "blood and soil" and back-to-nature concepts so integral to National Socialism. Abstinence from alcohol and tobacco had an entire government program by the Third Reich dedicated to preventing its "racial stock" from consuming "racial poisons." What began as reform movement evolved into the authoritarian compulsion to adopt the health habits originally proposed by the early *Lebensreform* movement. Much as it happens today, the "collectivist" observations of a nationalized healthcare system incite many to proclaim that an individual's personal choices ultimately affect the economic bottom line, and thus the society as a whole. Unfortunately, the histories of the two movements are too entangled to separate without risking outright censorship of historical facts. This is precisely what has happened. Proponents of these movements go to great lengths to fabricate an illusory distance that is not truthful. Case in point, some of the most prominent practitioners of *Lebensreform* such as Bill Pester, Benedict Lust, and Arnold Ehret immigrated to California and directly influenced the hippie movement later.

FIGURE 15: Various eugenic periodicals distributed in the United States and Europe, including "Eugenical News," "Biometrika," and "The Eugenics Review." - Author's personal collection.

Chap. 12: 1894 to 1890

NEW WORLD: ELLIS ISLAND BEGINS ACCOMMODATING IMMIGRANTS TO THE UNITED STATES. PANIC OF 1893: A CRASH ON THE NEW YORK STOCK EXCHANGE STARTS A DEPRESSION. PULLMAN STRIKE: THREE THOUSAND PULLMAN PALACE CAR COMPANY WORKERS GO ON A "WILDCAT" (WITHOUT UNION APPROVAL) STRIKE IN ILLINOIS. **SCIENCE & TECHNOLOGY:** THOMAS A. EDISON FINISHES CONSTRUCTION OF THE FIRST MOTION PICTURE STUDIO. – RUDOLF DIESEL RECEIVES A PATENT FOR THE DIESEL ENGINE. THE US SUPREME COURT LEGALLY DECLARES THE TOMATO TO BE A VEGETABLE. **OLD WORLD:** GANDHI COMMITS HIS FIRST ACT OF CIVIL DISOBEDIENCE. **LIFE:** FOR THE FIRST TIME, COCA-COLA IS SOLD IN BOTTLES. – RUDOLF HESS IS BORN. – ALDOUS HUXLEY, ENGLISH AUTHOR AND FUTURIST IS BORN. HERMANN GÖRING IS BORN. - ALFRED ROSENBERG IS BORN. - THE FIRST PENALTY KICK IS AWARDED IN A FOOTBALL MATCH. - ERWIN ROMMEL, GERMAN FIELD MARSHAL BETTER KNOWN AS "THE DESSERT FOX" IS BORN. – P. T. BARNUM, AMERICAN SHOWMAN AND INSPIRATION TO MANY GENERATIONS OF AMERICAN POLITICIANS IS BORN. – MIRZA GHULAM AHMAD CLAIMS TO BE THE PROMISED MESSIAH, THE SECOND COMING OF JESUS. HO CHI MINH, PRIME MINISTER OF NORTH VIETNAM IS BORN.

Sec. I - FASHIONING THE NOOSE THEY WILL HANG YOU BY:

As far as can be ascertained, it was Sir John Herschel in a lecture before the Royal Society of London, on March 14, 1839, who made the word "photography" known to the world. The word photography is based on the Greek (*photos*) "light" and (*graphé*) "representation by means of lines" or "drawing," together meaning "drawing with light." Half a century later, in 1884, George Eastman developed the technology of film to replace photographic plates, leading to the technology used by film cameras. Then, moving pictures came along when in 1895 the Lumière Domitor camera was invented by Charles Moisson, the chief mechanic of the Lumière works at Lyon. These technologies changed how people viewed and conceived of their world, no less drastically than the change that came with Galileo's discovery that the Earth revolved around the Sun. These inventions completely changed the way humanity viewed and understood time and space, and in turn, radically altered humanity's perspective of its place in the universe. The cultural and political reactions to the art movements that followed must be understood in the context of just how radical these changes indeed were. For the purposes of this book, the National Socialist "Exhibition of Degenerate Art" cannot be understood outside of this context. Understanding the earth-shaking nature of the changes allows an understanding of why those most violently opposed to it reacted in such a visceral fashion.

With instantaneous exposure, photography enabled the ability to record a moment in time. No longer did photographers have to ask their subjects to pose for the long exposures. Life could be captured, and the moment frozen in time. Moving pictures, in turn, captured the high-speed movement of the newly industrialized world. They collapsed space and time, as the moviemaker could take the viewer from the deep desert sands to the vastness of the ocean, and to the peak of a mountaintop with quick editing. While this experience may seem natural to us, it was ground shaking at a time when the majority of the population simply did not travel further than a couple of miles beyond their homes. This altered reality, in turn, influenced the arts, namely through movements like Analytic Cubism. Cubism is a style of painting Picasso developed along with Georges Braque. Braque's paintings of 1908–

1913 mimicked moving pictures via a simultaneous perspective. Braque was representing the aesthetic of a mobile mind, with instantly and rapidly changing perspectives. The "simultaneous" perspective is the term artists use to communicate an artistic attempt to collage and collapse together various views of the same object or scenery in one depiction. The result is a simplification down to the planes and geometrical shapes as they recede back into the various vanishing points of the various perspectives. Cubism is literally a play on time and space, and a direct product of photography and moving pictures affecting the traditional art world. For all eternity, painters had tried to accurately depict the details of a subject. Classical painters were largely graded by their ability to depict reality and express realism with an unreal medium. Art historians point to the Renaissance for its mastering of perspective, and thus enabling painters to depict a vision the way the human eye experiences it. Then someone gave photographers the ability to capture the world with instant exposure. Photographers were then able to capture with one click of the shutter what it took painters weeks or months to reproduce with oil paints. The effect on the art of the era was a liberating one. Painters were slapped out of centuries of the doldrums of trying to be technically proficient, instead of creative in expression. Painters now were freed to not just depict the reality that they saw, but the reality that they felt, or even imagined. They were free to depict ideas and concepts on canvas, without having the anchor of technical realism holding them to professional expectations. Instead of capturing a single moment, artists could now attempt at capturing motion, the motion of the marvelous machines of their boyhood dreams; locomotives, steamships, and airplanes. All of this came to fruition at the turn-of-the-century, along with rapid industrialization. The *fin de siecle* rattled artists and demanded that they feel different and look at the world with new eyes, and technology gave them the waking slap they needed to see the emerging new world. This drastic change of pace, artistic and real, garnered the ire of circles that feared the pace of modern industrial living. As we know, the *fin de siecle* was dominated by a fear of "degeneracy," and "degeneracy" in the arts was diagnosed as reflecting the "criminality," "alcoholism," and "idiocy" of the times.

Ironically enough, the one person in history responsible for popularizing the concept of cultural "degeneracy" was Jewish. Max Nordau, like Leo Alexander after him, would unwittingly and unknowingly help fashion the noose which European Jewry would ultimately be hung by. Max Nordau's controversial book "*Entartung*," was published in Europe in 1892, and released in English as "Degeneration" in 1895. Incidentally, Nordau dedicates the book to Cesare Lombroso, who was also of the Jewish faith, and titled the book after the term originally coined by Lombroso. Nordau's "Degeneration" was intended as a scientific diagnosis of European culture, using its artistic cultural products as proof of various medical diagnoses including but not limited to symbolism, spiritualism, egomania, mysticism, and diabolism. Nordau prophesized the coming of a human catastrophe of unprecedented proportions, with "degeneration" as its cause. Place this into context: The uproar Nordau helped create at the turn-of-the-century can only be compared to current fears of Global Warming. Note that Nordau pinned fault upon industrial modernity,

as had all other eugenicists:
> Parallel with the growth of large towns is the increase in the number of the degenerate of all kinds – criminals, lunatics, and the 'higher degenerates' of Magnan. (Pg. 36, "Degeneration", D. Appleton & Co., 1892/1895)

Max Nordau was already a man of international fame when he wrote his infamous book, and this fame was only redoubled by "Degeneration." Nordau was born Simon Maximilian Suedfeld, and ironically enough, the co-founder of the World Zionist Organization. He was a philosopher, writer, orator, and practicing physician. As the son of a rabbi, Nordau received a traditional Jewish education and remained an observant Jew until his eighteenth year, when he became a militant naturalist and Darwinist. Nordau achieved fame as a thinker and social critic with the 1884 publication and subsequent banning of "The Conventional Lies of Our Civilization." The book sharply criticized what Nordau defined as "the religious lie," the corruption and oppression of monarchical and aristocratic regimes, the deceptions of political and economic establishments, and the hypocritical adherence to outworn sexual mores.

Nordau's "Degeneration" is of historical importance primarily because it made eugenics popular beyond that of the scientific elite. Nordau went much further to connect eugenic fears of "degeneration" to cultural fears of change at precisely the time when these fears were at their peak, during the turn-of-the-century apocalyptic fervor. Modernity had not only visibly transformed the cities through technology, but technology, namely photography, had forever changed the aspirations of artists. The artistic results of these new artistic directions were not received well by cultural critics such as Nordau, who saw all the "degenerative" aspects of the era embodied in the new art forms:
> In the civilized world there obviously prevails a twilight mood which finds expression, among other ways, in all sorts of odd aesthetic fashions. All these new tendencies, realism or naturalism, 'decadentism,' neo-mysticism, and their sub-varieties, are manifestations of degeneration and hysteria, and identical with the mental stigmata which the observations of clinicians have unquestionably established as belonging to these. But both degeneration and hysteria are the consequences of the excessive organic wear and tear suffered by the nations through the immense demands on their activity, and through the rank growth of large towns. (Pg. 43, "Degeneration", D. Appleton & Co., 1892/1895)

Of importance is to realize that Nordau and his fellow eugenicists were not engaging in cultural or artistic criticism but proposing that "degeneration" be treated like an epidemic and a disease, which by their estimation, would otherwise conspire to overthrow Western civilization. The book "Degeneration" was very much a way of proving that Darwin's "evolution" was working backward, and that the "feeblemindedness," "alcoholism," and "pauperism" scientists were pointing to were evidence of humanity de-evolving and retrogressing into savagery:
> In any case, it is an evidence of diseased and debilitated brain-activity, if consciousness relinquishes the advantages of the differentiated perceptions of

phenomena, and carelessly confounds the reports conveyed by the particular senses. It is a retrogression to the very beginning of organic development. It is a descent from the height of human perfection to the low level of the mollusk. To raise the combination, transposition and confusion of the perceptions of sound and sight to the rank of a principle of art, to see futurity in this principle, is to designate as progress the return from the consciousness of man to that of the oyster. (Pg. 142, "Degeneration", D. Appleton & Co., 1892/1895)

Thus, one cannot overemphasize how Nordau's international fame helped fuel the fire under the *fin-de-siecle* apocalyptic psychosis. "Degeneracy" would be the rallying cry of reformists and revolutionaries up on through The Holocaust and was a mania that ended only because of Hitler. Hitler himself would make "degeneracy" a central theme of two of his most significant propaganda efforts; first with Leni Riefenstahl's "Triumph of the Will" and the 1937 Exhibit of Degenerate Art thereafter:

> We must create the New Man so that our race will not succumb to the phenomenon of **degeneration so typical of modern times.** (emphasis mine, Adolf Hitler - At the 1935 Party Assembly in Nuremberg, documented by "Triumph of the Will")

Case in point, Adolf Hitler regarded the "degenerate" art as evidence that cultural and biological evolution was shifting distinctly away from the "pure Aryan," and specifically towards the "degenerate" and lesser evolved Jew. For Adolf Hitler, "modern" art was Jewish art, and the specific modern artists of Jewish and non-Jewish faiths were targeted as if they were Rabbis or cultural leaders. In fact, "Degenerate Art" is the direct translation of the German term *"Entartete Kunst"* used by Hitler for art that didn't fit his definition of good German art. By 1937, some 16,000 artworks had been removed from museums and galleries in Germany. These pieces were brought together again in an exhibition mocking modern art, comprised of 650 confiscated works by about 112 artists, opened in Munich on July 19, 1937, and then toured Germany, Austria, and Poland. More than 3 million people saw the exhibition. It was one of the most important propaganda efforts by the Third Reich, as it did much to clarify the cultural direction for the "total state," which sought to micro-manage every aspect of society, especially its cultural heritage. Hitler was very precise as to what art would and would not be part of German culture from 1937 onwards. Here is a relevant portion of Hitler's inaugural speech at the German Art Exhibition on 18 July 1937:

> Cubism, Dadaism, Futurism, Impressionism, etc., have nothing to do with our German people. For these concepts are neither old nor modern, but are only artifactitious stammerings of men to whom God has denied the grace of a truly artistic talent, and in its place has awarded them the gift of jabbering or deception. (Pg. 49, "Artists of World War II", Barbara McCloskey, Greenwood Publishing Group, 2005)

Thus, the social and cultural ailment that Max Nordau had framed as necessitating the importance and urgency given to an impending catastrophe became precisely what Hitler's National Socialism set out to correct with its heavy-handed censorship and cultural controls. National Socialism set out to cleanse Germany of demented *avant-garde*, to eradicate the influence of "race toxins" that harmed the German "germ-plasm," and they embarked on a grand campaign to reverse the ills of industrialization by enacting compulsory laws and grand programs to make for eugenically and culturally "cleansed" cities and workplaces. Hitler said as much in "Mein Kampf":

> ...social activity must never and on no account be directed toward philanthropic flim flam, but rather toward the elimination of the basic deficiencies in the organization of our economic and cultural life that must – or at all events can – lead to the **degeneration of the individual.** (emphasis mine, Pg. 147, "Hitler's Vienna: A Dictator's Apprenticeship", Oxford Univ. Press, 1999)

What Max Nordau denigrated in his books, the National Socialists disparaged in art expositions that juxtaposed the medical photographs of malformed humans next to the contorted depictions of the human figure by modern artists. To them, the link between the "degenerate" malformed humans and the intentional contortion of the human figure in modern art was inescapable proof of "degeneracy" infecting the otherwise pure German culture. It was the "atavism" of the more primitive cultures infecting the Aryan and Teutonic society.

> In all these districts there is a marked absence of any serious resistance, even by the so-called intellectual classes, against this Jewish **contagion**. And the simple reason is that the intellectual classes are themselves physically **degenerate**, not through privation but through education. (emphasis mine, Pg. 188, "Mein Kampf: English Edition", MVR, 2015)

Hitler perfectly comprehended the trajectory of art history and alluded to it. Hitler, as an artist himself, held the resulting "modernism" with deep disdain. Ironically, these passages out of "Mein Kampf" seem only as further evidence of Hitler's plagiarism. Only this time he seems to plagiarize Nordau:

> At the turn of the last century a new element began to make its appearance in our world. It was an element which had been hitherto absolutely unknown and foreign to us. In former times there had certainly been offences against good taste; but these were mostly departures from the orthodox canons of art, and posterity could recognize a certain historical value in them. But the new products showed signs, not only of artistic aberration but of spiritual degeneration. Here, in the cultural sphere, the signs of the coming collapse first became manifest. – The Bolshevization of art is the only cultural form of life and the only spiritual manifestation of which Bolshevism is capable. – Anyone to whom this statement may appear strange need only take a glance at those lucky States which have become Bolshevized and, to his horror, he will there recognize those morbid monstrosities which have been produced by insane and degenerate people. All those artistic aberrations which are classified under the names of cubism and dadism, since the opening of the present century, are manifestations of art which

have come to be officially recognized by the State itself. This phenomenon made its appearance even during the short-lived period of the Soviet Republic in Bavaria. At that time one might easily have recognized how all the officials posters, propagandist pictures and newspapers, etc., showed signs not only of political but also of cultural decadence. (Pg. 191, "Mein Kampf: English Edition", MVR, 2015)

Nordau's reach was hardly secluded to the visual arts. His criticism truly was "totalitarian" in scope and reach. Nordau criticized the works of other writers as if he were diagnosing his opponents as patients suffering from the ailment of "degeneracy." Nordau went as far as diagnosing images of other authors and pointing to their physical features in support of his observation that their work was not only "degenerate," but that the artists and authors themselves were atavistic throwbacks to some earlier form of evolution:

> If we look at the portrait of the poet, by Eugene Carriere, of which a photograph serves as frontispiece in the Select Poems of Verlaine, and still more at that by M. Aman-Jean, exhibited in the Champs de Mars Salon in 1892, we instantly remark the great asymmetry of the head, which Lombroso has pointed out among degenerates, and the Mongolian physiognomy indicated by the projecting cheek-bones, obliquely placed eyes, and thin beard, which the same investigator looks upon as signs of degeneration. (Pgs. 119-120, "Degeneration", D. Appleton & Co., 1892/1895)

Sadly enough, Nordau's work reads astonishingly similar to the preposterous claims of National Socialist propaganda criticizing Jewish and Bolshevik art. The justifications for the 1937 Exhibit of Degenerate Art read astonishingly similar to Nordau's work. It is in this way that Max Nordau would help fashion the noose that would later be used on his European Jewish community, namely its greatest artists and authors:

> The Symbolists, so far as they are honestly degenerate and imbecile, can think only in a mystical, i.e., in a confused way. The unknown is to them more powerful than the known; the activity of the organic nerves preponderates over that of the cerebral cortex; their emotions overrule their ideas. When persons of this kind have poetic and artistic instincts, they naturally want to give expression to their own mental state. (Pg. 118, "Degeneration", D. Appleton & Co., 1892/1895)

Nordau's impact should not be downplayed. An entire genre of literature developed around Nordau's "Degeneration," which in turn fueled the fires of eugenics. Linda L. Maik has documented the impact that "Degeneration" had as far away as the United States. Maik documents that "Degeneration" just "may have been the most controversial international best-seller of the 1890s." [494] The English translation had been published in America in 1895. "This 566-page indictment of

---

[494] Pgs. 607-623, "Nordau's Degeneration: The American Controversy", Linda L. Maik, Journal of the History of Ideas, Vol. 50, No. 4, Oct. - Dec. 1989.

Europe's *fin-de-siecle* art, music, literature, and philosophy offered its readers Nordau's diagnosis" of the arts in the 1890s:

> Nordau claimed that pressures of society produced artists who exhibited the same degenerative characteristics as criminals. His meld of social science, medical science, and aesthetics led to a literary brouhaha seldom seen before or since his time. (Pgs. 607–623, "Nordau's Degeneration: The American Controversy", Linda L. Maik, Journal of the History of Ideas, Vol. 50, No. 4, Oct. - Dec. 1989)

Where Maik's analysis falls short is in depicting the immense impact "Degeneration" had decades after its publication. This cannot be measured by the number of editions, translations, or reviews as a typical book. The influence of "Degeneration" can only be understood once one comprehends that this became the underlying concept of every eugenically inspired movement from Nordau on through to the Nuremberg Trials. Maik is correct in stating that Nordau was "one of the last to attempt to integrate ideas that would soon diverge," and that "the arts, science, and morality were intertwined in the nineteenth century." [495] Whether this separation occurred as the scientific and industrial revolutions grew too big for one discipline to handle, or as a general change of approach towards specialization, Nordau's approach must be understood as a criticism for all of society, as industrial society failed to live up to Nordau's views on what constituted a civilized existence.

> Degenerates are not always criminals, prostitutes, anarchists, and pronounced lunatics; they are often authors and artists," he asserted. He continued in the following Ruskin-esque vein: "This phenomenon is not to be disregarded. Books and works of art exercise a powerful suggestion on the masses. It is from these productions that an age derives its ideals of morality and beauty. If they are absurd and anti-social, they exert a disturbing and corrupting influence on the views of a whole generation.... Then Nordau introduced his critical contribution, the application of scientific principles, specifically Lombroso's theory of criminal degeneration, to aesthetic criticism. (Pgs. 607-623, "Nordau's Degeneration: The American Controversy", Linda L. Maik, Journal of the History of Ideas, Vol. 50, No. 4, Oct. - Dec. 1989)

Nordau's book is just painful to read due to its over-the-top pessimistic view of humanity. Nordau's critics compared his arrogance to a palpable and unavoidable stench in a small room. As Maik documents, even Lombroso, Nordau's idol, cited Nordau's "audacity, intrepid even to insolence." [496] Lombroso also accused Nordau of excess in condemning novels, being prudish and chaste. Lombroso, however, also gave his disciple tacit praise in his 1895 Century Magazine review of Nordau's "Degeneration" by qualifying Nordau's diagnosis of humanity as having "put his finger on our most open wound...." Others were not as diplomatic. Edward E. Hale, Jr. of The Dial's review of "Degeneration" was less generous and picked apart only

---

[495] Pgs. 607–623 –"Nordau's Degeneration: The American Controversy", Linda L. Maik, Journal of the History of Ideas, Vol. 50, No. 4, Oct. - Dec. 1989.
[496] Pgs. 607–623 – Ibid.

the scientific premises Nordau used to support the book, and then declined to discuss the book's basic thesis, saying it should be reviewed "by a specialist in brain diseases." Anti-Semitism also resurfaced because of Nordau's and Lombroso's Jewish faith, and Nordau's heavily insulting style, some openly calling him a "quick-witted Jew."

Linda L. Maik finalizes her paper by stating that "In the hindsight of almost one hundred years, the failures of 'Degeneration' are glaring. Nordau's reactionary, almost desperate, use of mid-century rationality to eradicate late-century irrationality failed." [497] Clearly, this view can only stand if one were to pull the book out of historical context and comment on it as if it stood in a sealed vacuum of one of a multitude of indistinguishable art critiques. "Success" would be a difficult term to use for a work that found its greatest support in Hitler's House of Degenerate Art, which arguably can be said to have been the literal and physical expression of Nordau's thesis. It is the allegedly "degenerate" influence of modernism, impressionism, and abstract art and architecture that Hitler put on display across the street from the classic and patriotic German art Hitler considered to be "sane," "hygienic" and not suffering from the "atavism" that Nordau took pains to expose. The House of Degenerate Art and all the anti-modernist propaganda that the National Socialists distributed were in agreement, knowingly or unknowingly, with Nordau's "Degeneration" on a point-by-point, issue-by-issue, case-by-case basis. Interestingly enough, the only points of disagreement were on Richard Wagner and Nietzsche, whom Nordau hated, and Hitler adored and idolized.

We can speak of the utopian works of literature in this context. Utopias are by their very nature, static visions. They go to great lengths to eschew the effects of time and changing circumstances. They assume an ability to enforce the vision of the creator upon what would otherwise be a world of constant change. A statist-utopia is thus a static existence. The disturbing effects should be obvious, but the allure is as powerful as a narcotic. The paralyzing effect that results from trying to live another person's vision is the resulting reality of utopian societies. It is the reverse of creating a two-dimensional oil painting of a three-dimensional world; it flattens life and freezes the vantage point to a single perspective. It halts all individual initiative or diversity by effectively enforcing a halt on humanity. The history of the Soviet Union proves this point. The century of Soviet rule wasted the lives of generations for the sake of a utopian vision. Upon the fall of the USSR, the liberated Russians emerged on a world that had passed them by, with their cars, telephones, art, and conspicuous lack of modern computing evidencing the cultural stasis that had been Bolshevism.

This is the difference between taking hold of an artistic vision and having an artistic vision take hold of you; between having a vision and being had by a vision. This was the conundrum at the turn of the century of art representing reality, and life representing art. Dr. Alexis Carrel, the French eugenicists that supported the National Socialist Vichy occupation government, spoke about the National

---

[497] Pgs. 607-623 - "Nordau's Degeneration: The American Controversy", Linda L. Maik, Journal of the History of Ideas, Vol. 50, No. 4, Oct. - Dec. 1989.

Socialist's project of social engineering in the terms of being a sculptor, and nothing could be a more accurate depiction of Adolf the artist:

> To progress again, man must remake himself. And he cannot remake himself without suffering. For he is both the marble and the sculptor. In order to uncover his true visage, he must shatter his own substance with heavy blows of his hammer. (Intro., "Man, The Unknown", Hamilton, 1938)

Sec. 2 - THOMAS HENRY HUXLEY'S *"PROLEGOMENA"*:

Thomas H. Huxley wrote "Evidence of Man's Place in Nature" in 1863, where he first attempted to apply evolutionary theory to mankind. Yet, the most curious, perplexing, and unexplored addition to this topic came in 1894 with "Prolegomena." Huxley, widely known as Darwin's Bulldog, is one of the prime reasons as to why Alfred Russel Wallace, Gregor Mendel, and even the Erasmus Darwin didn't receive due credit for developing a theory of how life evolves in nature. At the very least it can be said that they were not canonized like Charles Darwin was by his zealous followers. Huxley made it his life's goal to make sure that Darwinian evolution replaced not just traditional religion, but all competing theories as well. It was the fight that Thomas H. Huxley wanted, and he made sure the "Origin of the Species" was received as such, thus pulling Darwin, willing or unwilling, out of the confines of science and placing him front and center in the political arena:

> I finished your book yesterday.. . .As for your doctrines I am prepared to go to the Stake if requisite. . .I trust you will not allow yourself to be in any way disgusted or annoyed by the considerable abuse & misrepresentation which unless I greatly mistake is in store for you. . . I am sharpening up my claws and beak in readiness. (darwinproject.ac.uk, Darwin Correspondence Project, Univ. of Cambridge, Letter No.: 2544, T. H. Huxley to Charles Darwin, November 23, 1859, re: Origin of Species)

If one wonders if Charles Darwin's work belongs in such a contentious political arena, it is instrumental to note that Charles Darwin himself took no steps to stop Huxley's enduring efforts to politicize and polarize in his name. This silence speaks volumes of Darwin's personal political posture. Darwin may have stayed above the fray, but this did not mean he was not politically motivated. This eternal argument, which Thomas H. Huxley is mostly responsible for igniting, served to encourage and forward the Theory of Evolution into a political polemic about the human condition. Darwin warned his audience that "light will be thrown on the origin of Man" in "Origin." [498] In the meantime, Thomas Henry Huxley did more than

---

[498] Pg. 424 – "On the Origin of Species by Means of Natural Selection: Or, The Preservation of Favored Races in the Struggle of Life", Charles Darwin, Appleton, 1864.

anyone else to advance Darwinism's acceptance among scientists and the public alike, and Darwin's cousin and son took the argument the route of basing an entire "religion" and proposal for government based upon the Theory of Evolution.

There was more than one interpretation to be gleaned from nature's processes. Herbert Spencer argued for non-intervention on the ways of nature. Spencer's "Social Darwinism" is the non-interventionist revelation based upon the Theory of Evolution. It asks that humanity let the strongest survive and take no actions to intrude on the evolution of humanity by either helping or disturbing the "struggle." "Social Darwinism" was thus used to justify great successes and great suffering. Eugenics is the mirror opposite of this non-interventionist attitude. Eugenics is the extreme of intervention, assuming control over the most basic of human functions specifically to control the direction of evolution, and explicitly to take the results away from the chance that exists in nature. This is precisely the concept that is addressed by T.H. Huxley's 1894 "Prolegomena": intervention vs. non-intervention.

Huxley's "Evidence on Man's Place in Nature" was originally published five years after Darwin's "Origin of Species." It was one of the first attempts to apply evolution explicitly to humans. Huxley had gained notoriety in defending and advancing Darwin's Theory of Evolution, namely in the famous 1860 debate with Bishop Samuel Wilberforce at the Oxford Union. The Bishop defended the Bible against what he perceived to be a Godless science. It was the first amongst a long line of debates and deliberations on the "ape origins" of man. Huxley famously retorted by stating he was not ashamed to claim an ape as his ancestor in this debate. As a result, T.H. Huxley became known for deploying a biting wit and sarcasm. This is what makes the tone of "Prolegomena" so important and noteworthy: its lack of the biting sarcasm and wit. Clearly, something was amiss when Huxley penned "Prolegomena".

"Prolegomena" was added by Thomas Huxley to the published version of the Romanes lecture in which he presented "Ethics and Evolution" in 1894. Historians have documented Huxley's discontent with Herbert Spencer's idea of "survival of the fittest." Yet, at the opposing side of non-intervention, he found his idol's close family members entrenched firmly on the side of intervention. The tone of "Prolegomena" makes it amply clear that Huxley is neither content with intervention or non-intervention into human evolution. One can easily argue that Huxley added "Prolegomena" to his famous works as an expression of discontent with either extreme. "Prolegomena" uses the juxtaposition of a tended vs an untended garden to weigh the pros and cons of intervention. Most notably, it does so in a gentle, equivocating voice of parable. Thus, the man who took great joy in terrorizing those that were afraid of the implications of Darwinian evolution, postponed the political offensive and injected abstract storytelling with the gentleness of a parent reading for children at bedtime. Obviously, this topic was a house made of glass for Huxley, as Darwin's son, Leonard Darwin, and Darwin's cousin, Francis Galton, were actively proposing a society along the premises of extreme intervention into human evolution, a position he clearly doubted, and thus posed a political conundrum to those close to Darwin's heart.

This was no small consideration for Huxley. Darwin's historians have aptly noted how Darwin's immediate family heavily influenced and haunted his political decisions to publish "Origin." Even the sheepish and gentle Darwin also warned, prophetically so, about checking humanity's sense of "sentimentality" and "compassion" in some effort to intervene with human evolution. Huxley was apparently equally disturbed by science following the morality that Galton desired for his eugenic "religion," as he was with succumbing to traditional ethics: "Science commits suicide when it adopts a creed." [499]

"Prolegomena" expounds upon the amount of commitment that is necessary to manipulate human evolution, as does a gardener in order to maintain the manicured illusion of a walled-in and unnatural garden. The maintenance of this intentionally unnatural landscape requires constant intervention against the thoughtless forces of evolution, which Huxley calls "the cosmic process":

> The garden is in the same position as every other work of man's art; it is a result of the cosmic process working through and by human energy and intelligence; and, as is the case with every other artificial thing set up in the state of nature, the influences of the latter, are constantly tending to break it down and destroy it. (archive.org, T.H. Huxley, "Evolution and Ethics: Prolegomena, 1825-1895", 1894)

In this way, Huxley communicates that the evolutionary process is entirely natural, but human societies are entirely artificial. Huxley provides a cautious warning to his close friends, that one which embarks upon erecting a eugenic state had better be prepared to "weed the garden" for all eternity. Huxley also recognized that unnatural selection was at odds with human compassion:

> Since law and morals are restraints upon the struggle for existence between men in society, the ethical process is in opposition to the principle of the cosmic process, and tends to the suppression of the qualities best fitted for success in that struggle. (archive.org, T.H. Huxley, "Evolution and Ethics: Prolegomena, 1825-1895", 1894)

The moral struggle, which Huxley terms "the ethical process," will forever be at odds with the needs of survival in nature, thus the choices of traits to breed for, the decisions to be made by the overseeing "gardener," the eugenicist, would become an unending struggle according to Huxley:

> That which lies before the human race is a constant struggle to maintain and improve, in opposition to the State of Nature, the State of Art of an organized polity. (archive.org, T.H. Huxley, "Evolution and Ethics: Prolegomena, 1825-1895", 1894)

Huxley identifies the human qualities which served us so well in a primitive past and which threaten us so much in a social present. Interestingly enough, H.G. Wells

---

[499] Pg. 191 - "Models-Based Science Teaching: Understanding and Using Mental Models", Steven Gilbert, NSTA Press, 2011 - Quoting Herbert Spencer, "The Factors of Organic Evolution", April-May 1886.

lifted this passage and utilized it in his apocalyptic novel of eugenical experimentation gone wrong, "The Island of Dr. Moreau":

> For his successful progress, throughout the savage state, man has been largely indebted to those qualities which he shares with the ape and the tiger; his exceptional physical organization; his cunning, his sociability, his curiosity, and his imitativeness; his ruthless and ferocious destructiveness when his anger is roused by opposition. But, in proportion as men have passed from anarchy to social organization, and in proportion as civilization has grown in worth, these deeply ingrained serviceable qualities have become defects. (Pg. 51, T.H. Huxley, "Collected Essays", Cambridge Univ. Press, 2011 - Pg. 221, H.G. Wells, "The Island of Dr. Moreau", Broadview Press, 2009)

Huxley recognized that "fittest" is a term relative to the environment that an organism may find itself in, and not subject to absolute morality:

> There is another fallacy which appears to me to pervade the so-called "ethics of evolution." It is the notion that because, on the whole, animals and plants have advanced in perfection of organization by means of the struggle for existence and the consequent "survival of the fittest;" therefore men in society, men as ethical beings, must look to the same process to help them towards perfection. I suspect that this fallacy has arisen out of the unfortunate ambiguity of the phrase "survival of the fittest." "Fittest" has a connotation of "best;" and about "best" there hangs a moral flavour. In cosmic nature, however, what is "fittest" depends upon the conditions. (Pg. 80, T.H. Huxley, "Collected Essays", Cambridge Univ. Press, 2011)

Huxley argued that the conditions in which humanity first flourished have changed with the growth of civilization. Thus, he contended that we needed to alter our perception of what constitutes survivalist values and drop the harsh "gladiator" mentality:

> In place of ruthless self-assertion it demands self-restraint; in place of thrusting aside, or treading down, all competitors, it requires that the individual shall not merely respect, but shall help his fellows; its influence is directed, not so much to the survival of the fittest, as to the fitting of as many as possible to survive. It repudiates the gladiatorial theory of existence. (Pg. 82, T.H. Huxley, "Collected Essays", Cambridge Univ. Press, 2011)

Huxley uses the term "horticultural process," as practiced by his imaginary gardener to communicate the prejudice that those making the unnatural selections in directing human evolution will impose upon the outcome:

> The gardener, on the other hand, restricts multiplication; provides that each plant shall have sufficient space and nourishment; protects from frost and drought; and, in every other way, attempts to modify the conditions, in such a manner as to bring about the survival of those forms which most nearly approach the standard of the useful or the beautiful, **which he has in his mind**. (emphasis mine, Pg. 14, T.H. Huxley, "Collected Essays", Cambridge Univ. Press, 2011)

Huxley reminds his eugenic fellows that the one process they do not control is the state of nature, and that this is the ultimate controlling factor in the plight of humanity, and that changes will come which affect the theoretical "garden" regardless of the efforts or wishes of its overseers:

> If the fruits and the tubers, the foliage and the flowers thus obtained, reach, or sufficiently approach, that ideal, there is no reason why the status quo attained should not be indefinitely prolonged. So long as the state of nature remains approximately the same, so long will the energy and intelligence which created the garden suffice to maintain it. However, the limits within which this mastery of man over nature can be maintained are narrow. If the conditions of the cretaceous epoch returned, I fear the most skillful of gardeners would have to give up the cultivation of apples and gooseberries; while, if those of the glacial period once again obtained, open asparagus beds would be superfluous, and the training of fruit trees against the most favourable of mouth walls, a waste of time and trouble. (archive.org, T.H. Huxley, "Evolution and Ethics: Prolegomena, 1825-1895", 1894)

And herein lies just one of the ways in which these eugenic utopias are doomed to fail. The eugenic utopia is still subject to the tantrums of the universe, and its eternal onslaught of change. Thus, the stasis and control that the imaginary "gardener" may desire are ultimately subject to the whims of nature. Huxley underscores his point by expanding the point-of-view of the gardener to the point of view of an omniscient creature, greater than man, yet tending to man as the gardener had tended to his small plot. Huxley argues that even the omniscient and god-like "administrative authority" would still contend with having to subjugate nature:

> Let us now imagine that some administrative authority, as far superior in power and intelligence to men, as men are to their cattle, is set over the colony, charged to deal with its human elements in such a manner as to assure the victory of the settlement over the antagonistic influences of the state of nature in which it is set down. He would proceed in the same fashion as that in which the gardener dealt with his garden. In the first place, he would, as far as possible, put a stop to the influence of external competition by thoroughly extirpating and excluding the native rivals, whether men, beasts, or plants. And our administrator would select his human agents, with a view to his ideal of a successful colony, just as the gardener selects his plants with a view to his ideal of useful or beautiful products. (archive.org, T.H. Huxley, "Evolution and Ethics: Prolegomena, 1825-1895", 1894)

The omniscient "administrative authority" would still have to impose an artificial existence that ultimately worked against and was detrimental to the natural process in order to create the desired "earthly paradise" which protected man from the uncertainty of nature:

> Thus the administrator might look to the establishment of an earthly paradise, a

true garden of Eden, in which all things should work together towards the well-being of the gardeners: within which the cosmic process, the coarse struggle for existence of the state of nature, should be abolished; in which that state should be replaced by a state of art; where every plant and every lower animal should be adapted to human wants, and would perish if human supervision and protection were withdrawn; where men themselves should have been selected, with a view to their efficiency as organs for the performance of the functions of a perfected society. And this ideal polity would have been brought about, not by gradually adjusting the men to the conditions around them, but by creating artificial conditions for them; not by allowing the free play of the struggle for existence, but by excluding that struggle; and by substituting selection directed towards the administrator's ideal for the selection it exercises. (archive.org, T.H. Huxley, "Evolution and Ethics: Prolegomena, 1825-1895", 1894)

This is where Thomas H. Huxley proved smarter than Leonard Darwin, Francis Galton, H.G. Wells, Margaret Sanger, and all those Ivy League educated biologists who foolishly pursued this eugenic Eden for their entire lives. It is as if Huxley was watching them, bemused like an owner of a dog watches as the dog chases its tail, not knowing whether to put a stop to the foolishness or sit back and enjoy the show. Huxley knew that this utopian existence, this "earthly paradise," was but an illusion as the proverbial "serpent" in any eugenic "Eden" is the constant flux in the population; the desired stasis is an impossibility:

But the Eden would have its serpent, and a very subtle beast too. Man shares with the rest of the living world the mighty instinct of reproduction and its consequence, the tendency to multiply with great rapidity. The better the measures of the administrator achieved their object, the more completely the destructive agencies of the state of nature were defeated, the less would that multiplication be checked. (archive.org, T.H. Huxley, "Evolution and Ethics: Prolegomena, 1825-1895", 1894)

Huxley proposes that this "administrator" may even have to succumb to unleashing the realities of nature to contend with the uncontrollable variables:

When the colony reached the limit of possible expansion, the surplus population must be disposed of somehow; or the fierce struggle for existence must recommence and destroy that peace, which is the fundamental condition of the maintenance of the state of art against the state of nature.

CONTINUES...

Supposing the administrator to be guided by purely scientific considerations, he would, like the gardener, meet this most serious difficulty by systematic extirpation, or exclusion, of the superfluous. The hopelessly diseased, the infirm aged, the weak or deformed in body or in mind, the excess of infants born, would be put away, as the gardener pulls up defective and superfluous plants, or the breeder destroys undesirable cattle. Only the strong and the healthy, carefully matched, with a view to the progeny best adapted to the purposes of the administrator, would be permitted to perpetuate their kind. (archive.org, T.H. Huxley, "Evolution and Ethics: Prolegomena, 1825-1895", 1894)

Here was Thomas Henry Huxley, the most zealous of Darwinists, gently prodding his eugenic counterparts. Amusingly enough, Huxley, the devoted Darwinist, even seems to taunt and tempt a reaction from his mentor, the pigeon breeder, Charles Darwin:

> I have other **reasons for fearing that this logical ideal of evolutionary regimentation—this pigeon-fanciers' polity—is unattainable.** In the absence of any such a severely scientific administrator as we have been dreaming of, human society is kept together by bonds of such a singular character, that the attempt to perfect society after his fashion would run serious risk of loosening them. (emphasis mine, Pg. 47, T.H. Huxley, "Evolution and Ethics, 1893-1943", Pilot Press, 1947)

Huxley ends "Prolegomena" with a polite conclusion clearly meant, not for the non-interventionist "Social Darwinists," but for the interventionists, the utopian socialists. Huxley knew precisely who this group of eugenicists was. It was a group that included Charles Darwin's cousin and son. Huxley's choice of speaking in parables about the viability of eugenics is very likely an insight into the inner politics of the group. Yet, his conclusion is clear as to where Huxley stood on Galton's proposal:

> I have briefly described the nature of the only radical cure, known to me, for the disease which would thus threaten the existence of the colony; and, however regretfully, I have been obliged to **admit that this rigorously scientific method of applying the principles of evolution to human society hardly comes within the region of practical politics; not for want of will on the part of a great many people; but because, for one reason, there is no hope that mere human beings will ever possess enough intelligence to select the fittest.** (emphasis mine, archive.org, T.H. Huxley, "Evolution and Ethics: Prolegomena, 1825-1895", 1894)

Paul White's book, "Thomas Huxley," documents that Huxley continued to work over the question of ethics and evolution to the end of his life, and that this work is reflected in a paper he never finished titled "Civil History and Natural History." In it, Huxley concludes that there were no ethical principles to evolution. It is replete with the concepts of Spencer's "Social Darwinism":

> The so-called "Ethics of Evolution" rests upon the supposition that social progress like natural historical progress is dependent on the struggle for existence. Therefore it insists that outside the charmed circle of "natural rights" the struggle for existence shall have full play **– so long as nobody directly interferes with anybody he not only may but ought to get all he can and keep all he gets…** (emphasis mine, Pg. 167, "Thomas Huxley: Making the Man of Science", Cambridge Univ. Press, 2003)

In "Civil History and Natural History" Huxley makes it clear that he believes that all struggle would come to a halt once "cradle-to-grave" care was established by a socialist utopian scheme:

> The first great step towards progress in the Civil History world is the establishment of security of life and property for all, without reference to their adaptability or indeed to anything else than the fact that they are some human being. Consequently when that state has been reached – the struggle for existence of the Natural History world is at an end. (Pg. 167, "Thomas Huxley: Making the Man of Science", Cambridge Univ. Press, 2003)

Consider the implication of the above paragraph. Here was Darwin's most formidable general stating in no uncertain terms that the Darwin-Galton followers were wrong, and furthermore, that no eugenic state should be implemented, but a welfare state which provided for all regardless of social stature or societal value. The precarious dividing lines persisted down the family lines. Thomas H. Huxley's grandson, Aldous Huxley, the novelist who wrote the dystopian novel "Brave New World," well understood the principles his grandfather extrapolated in "Prolegomena," and continued his grandfather's work of warning humanity of the hubris of eugenics, the hubris of pretending man can ever "select the fittest." His brother Julian did not inherit his grandfather's wisdom. As we know, Julian Huxley was a prominent member of the British Eugenics Society and was still proposing eugenic solutions in the immediate aftermath of The Holocaust.

Sec. 3- HARVARD'S CHARLES B. DAVENPORT:

Charles Benedict Davenport, the undisputed leader of the eugenics movement in the United States was born in Stamford, Connecticut. The son of a Northern abolitionist, Amzi Benedict Davenport, Charles attended Harvard University, earning a Ph.D. in biology in 1892 and married Gertrude Crotty, a zoology graduate, in 1894. Davenport completed his undergraduate degree in 1889, and he worked that year at the biological station at Woods Hole, Massachusetts. He continued at Harvard toward the Ph.D., winning the Thayer Scholarship in 1890 and 1891. He received his doctorate in 1892. Davenport then traveled to England to meet Galton and Pearson in 1897 and became an early convert to eugenics. The product of his new-found faith was his 1899 "Statistical Methods with Special Reference to Biological Variation." According to his friend and fellow biologist Oscar Riddle, this was the first book to bring Karl Pearson's Galtonian statistical eugenics to American academia. [500]

---

[500] Pg. 118 - "Legacy of Malthus: The Social Costs of the New Scientific Racism", Allan Chase, 1975.

Davenport was appointed the director of the summer school of the Brooklyn Institute of Arts and Sciences Biological Laboratory at Cold Spring Harbor, New York, in the spring of 1898. The creation of the Eugenics Records Office at Cold Spring Harbor serves to pinpoint who was Davenport's inspiration. The ERO was the product of the networking and collaboration between Charles B. Davenport and his British counterparts, Leonard Darwin, Francis Galton, and Karl Pearson. Andrew Carnegie had been inspired by Herbert Spencer's interest in acquired characters and written to Francis Darwin in 1900 indicating his interest in financially supporting such an effort. [501] The Carnegie Institution was subsequently founded in 1902, and Charles Davenport began campaigning for the Carnegie Institute to invest additional funds for a department of eugenics at Cold Spring Harbor. The surviving correspondence between Charles Davenport and Francis Galton has preserved for posterity this critical exchange. The October 14, 1902 letter from Davenport to Galton requesting a reference for his proposal for the Station for Experimental Evolution illustrates how the Darwin-Galton reputation was leveraged to commence a formal and structured eugenics movement in the United States:

> Dear Mr. Galton: Word has just reached me that it is possible that some action may be taken by the Carnegie Institution at a Board meeting in November in relation to my application for the Establishment of a station for the Experimental study of Evolution at Cold Spring Harbor, Long Island. The Board would be glad of any testimony relative to (1) the importance of such a station, (2) my qualifications as possible director and (3) the suitability of the locality. Of the last point of course you cannot speak but I feel that it would be a great help to the cause if you could find time to write a short letter concerning the importance of the station proposed [illegible] any thing concerning my equipment for the position that you may care to hazard. The establishment of the station is a thing I have much at heart and for which I am ready to sacrifice a great deal. Trusting that you will not feel my request too bold, I remain, Sincerely yours, Chas. B. Davenport. (dnalc.org, Item Id: 12000, "Charles Davenport letter to Francis Galton, requesting a reference for his proposal for the Station for Experimental Evolution", DNA Learning Center, Cold Spring Harbor Lab.)

In 1904, the Carnegie Institution established the Cold Spring Harbor laboratory, making Davenport its director in 1905. The following year the name was changed to the Department of Experimental Evolution, a name revealing of the Darwinian influence at play. Again, the personal correspondence documents how important the trans-Atlantic relationships were to this crucial step towards American eugenics. An Oct. 26, 1910 letter illustrates this relationship:

> My dear Galton: So you see the seed sown by you is still sprouting in distant countries. And there is great interest in Eugenics in America, I can assure you. We have a plot of ground of 80 acres, near New York City, a house with a fire proof addition for our records. We have a superintendent, a stenographer, and

---

[501] Pg. 225 - "Treasure Your Exceptions: The Science and Life of William Bateson", Alan G. Cock and Donald R. Forsdyke, Springer Science & Business Media, 2008.

two helpers besides to train field workers. These are all associated with the Station for Experimental Evolution, which supplies Experimental Evidence of the methods of heredity. ---- I want to tell you how much I have enjoyed reading your autobiography. You have quite put yourself into it; and that makes it much more valuable than any "Life" by another hand. It would please you to realize how universal is the recognition in this Country, of your position as the founder of the science of Eugenics. And, I think, as the years go by, humanity will more and more appreciate its debt to you. In this country we have run "Charity" mad. Now, a revulsion of feeling is coming about, and people are turning to your teaching. With best wishes for continued strength and health & expression of my [illegible - professional?] esteem, Yours faithfully, Chas B. Davenport. (dnalc.org, Item Id: 12000, "Charles Davenport letter to Francis Galton, about opening the Eugenics Record Office and the debt to him as founder of eugenics", DNA Learning Center, Cold Spring Harbor Lab.)

The surviving correspondence at the Eugenics Records Office demonstrates the extent to which there was collaboration across national borders to create a widespread and world-wide eugenics movement. These scientists were as meticulous in creating lists and cataloging information like their German counterparts. All the important players were kept in the loop, despite the oceans that separated them. As explained earlier, the relationships were leveraged when it came time to rescue German science from the aftermath of WWI. A November 11th, 1922, letter from Charles Davenport to Leonard Darwin illustrates how this team helped rebuild the destitute eugenics movement after the devastation and disruption caused by World War I:

> Dear Major Darwin: Thank you for your kind letter of November first. I am arranging to have two copies of the sterilization book sent to you. I gathered from contact with geneticists and eugenicists in Austria and Germany that so far from eugenics not being recognized by scientific societies that the German Government is about the only one that has asked and secured the cooperation of leading scientific men (certainly members of leading scientific societies) to cooperate with the Government by constituting a committee to which should be referred all legislation of eugenical import. Apart from the international society of Dr. Alfred Ploetz in Munich, the liveliest society dealing with eugenical matters is the Deutsche Geselschaft fur Vererbungswissenschaft of which Dr. H. Hachtsheim, Landwitach, Hochschule zu Berlin, Invalidenstrasse 42, Berlin, H.4, is secretary. With kind regards to Mrs. Darwin, as well as yourself, Sincerely yours, Chas. B. Davenport, Director." (dnalc.org, Item Id: 10435, "Charles Davenport letter to Leonard Darwin about German government interest in eugenics", DNA Learning Center, Cold Spring Harbor Lab.)

In order to contextualize this November 11, 1922 letter, one must remember that the infamous 1933 Nuremberg Laws were a verbatim translation of the "Model Eugenical Sterilization Law" written by Davenport's protégé, Harry Laughlin, and utilized to pass sterilization laws in dozens of States in the Union. This is why historically speaking, we should no longer differentiate between German and American eugenicists. They are more accurately categorized as a monolithic movement. Davenport responded to Professor Soren Hanson from Copenhagen, Denmark on October 14, 1925, again evidencing the cooperation across oceans and borders:

> Thank you for your frankness in sending me a copy of your letter to Major Darwin concerning my proposal in the matter of immigration. My proposal illustrates the difficulty in making applied eugenics and international matter. I should prefer to confine the international aspects of eugenics pretty well to investigations into human heredity, human biology in general and anthropology. On the appropriateness of an international exchange of such studies I am sure no one would have a difference of opinion. – But, alas, for the criminalistic and the degenerates, since it seems to be impracticable to put them all on ships and keep them traveling back and forth on the Atlantic Ocean through the rest of their lives, I see no way out but to prevent breeding them. (dnalc.org, Item Id: 10438, "Charles Davenport response to Soren Hanson about eugenics", DNA Learning Center, Cold Spring Harbor Lab.)

This is how the international eugenics movement was birthed. It would find form in the International Federation of Eugenics Organizations. Davenport founded the IFEO in 1925, with Eugen Fischer as chairman of the Commission on Bastardization and Miscegenation in 1927. Charles B. Davenport was able to position himself to work with so many key historical figures the likes of the Darwin-Galton family because of his Harvard credentials. While Francis Galton and Leonard Darwin leveraged Charles Darwin's fame to position themselves professionally, Davenport used Harvard's fame to raise himself to their level. This is exemplified by the reach and access Davenport had with America's famous families, namely the Roosevelt family. The "C.B. Davenport Papers" held at the American Philosophical Society contains a January 3, 1913, letter from President Theodore Roosevelt to Davenport evidencing this observation:

> My dear Mr. Davenport: I am greatly interested in the two memoirs you have sent me. They are very instructive, and, from the standpoint of our country, very ominous. You say that these people are not themselves responsible, that it is "society" that is responsible. I agree with you if you mean, as I suppose you do, that society has no business to permit degenerates to reproduce their kind. It is really extraordinary that our people refuse to apply to human beings such elementary knowledge as every successful farmer is obliged to apply to his own stock breeding. Any group of farmers who permitted their best stock not to breed, and let all the increase come from the worst stock, would be treated as fit inmates for an asylum. Yet we fail to understand that such conduct is rational compared to the conduct of a nation which permits unlimited breeding from the worst stocks, physically and morally, while it encourages or connives at the cold selfishness or the twisted sentimentality as a result of which the men and women ought to marry, and if married have large families, remain celibates or have no children or only one or two. Some day we will realize that the prime duty the

inescapable duty of the good citizen of the right type is to leave his or her blood behind him in the world; and that we have no business to permit the perpetuation of citizens of the wrong type. [type obscured] Faithfully yours, [signed] Theodore Roosevelt – (American Philosophical Society, Image #1242 – dnalc.org, Item Id.: 11219, "T. Roosevelt letter to C. Davenport about 'degenerates reproducing'", DNA Learning Center, Cold Spring Harbor Lab.)

The fact that both Charles Davenport and Theodore Roosevelt were both interested in eugenics is no coincidence. They were both products of Harvard, and in turn, Harvard protégés like Charles Davenport perpetuated the eugenics creed for several generations at Harvard. In fact, it is impossible to write the history of eugenics without continually stumbling upon the work of Harvard graduates and professors. It is impossible to disentangle Harvard from the history of eugenics. More specifically, it is impossible to imagine a eugenics movement without Charles Davenport, Madison Grant, Henry Fairfield Osborn, and Lothrop Stoddard.

Like many Harvard students before and after him, the young Theodore came under the influence of Harvard professor Nathaniel Southgate Shaler. Shaler was an American paleontologist and geologist who wrote extensively on the theological and scientific implications of the Theory of Evolution. Shaler, in turn, had studied under Louis Agassiz at Harvard College and would go on to become a Harvard fixture in his own right, as lecturer and professor of paleontology for two decades and as professor of geology for nearly two more. Shaler was also an apologist for slavery and an outspoken believer in the superiority of the Anglo-Saxon race. In his later career, Shaler continued to support Agassiz's polygenism, a theory of human origins that was often used to support racial discrimination. Shaler served as Harvard's Dean of Sciences and was considered one of the university's most popular teachers. Shaler exemplified Northern racism, as, despite his clear prejudice against the black populations, Shaler also served as a Union officer in the American Civil War, ironically fighting for the equality of African-Americans. Shaler's own words evidence that his views did not change even after the Civil War, despite all that President Lincoln spoke and wrote on the subject. The Atlantic Monthly published a controversial article in November 1884. The article was titled "The Negro Problem," and was published along with the dissenting and supporting views as side notes. In "The Negro Problem," Shaler claimed:

> ... this trial of the African as an American citizen is the most wonderful social endeavor that has ever been made by our own or any other race. If it succeeds, even in the faintest approach to a fair measure; if these men, bred in immemorial savagery and slavery, can blossom out into self-upholding citizens, fit to stand alone in the battle with the world, then indeed we must confess that human nature is a thing apart from the laws of inheritance, ---- that man is more of a miracle in the world than we deemed him to be. (Pgs. 696-709, N.S. Shaler, "The Negro Problem", Atlantic Monthly, Vol. 0054, Issue 325, Nov. 1884 – Available at theatlantic.com)

Shaler, like the pro-slavery demagogues of the Civil War era, looked to the examples of emancipated blacks in Haiti and Jamaica as evidence that blacks were not fit for self-government, and thus not fit to be citizens of a country based on the premise of self-government:

> The forecast of the unprejudiced observer was exceedingly unfavorable. Every experiment of freeing blacks on this continent has in the end resulted in even worse conditions than slavery brought to them. The trial in Hayti, where freemen of the third generation from slaves possess the land to the exclusion of all whites, has been utterly disastrous to the best interest of the negro. ---- There is now in Hayti a government that is but a succession of petty plundering despotisms, a tillage that cannot make headway against the constant encroachments of the tropical forests, a people that is without a single trace of promise except that of extinction through the diseases of sloth and vice. ---- In Jamaica the history, though briefer, is almost equally ominous. The emancipation of the negro was peaceable, and was not attended, as in Hayti, by the murder or expulsion of the whites. Yet that garden land of the tropics, that land which our ancestors hoped to see the Britain of the South, has been settling down toward barbarism, and there is nothing left but the grip of the British rule to keep it from falling to the state of the sister isle. (Pgs. 696-709, N.S. Shaler, "The Negro Problem", Atlantic Monthly, Vol. 0054, Issue 325, Nov. 1884 – Available at theatlantic.com)

Shaler, like many Northern abolitionists, blamed Southern slaveholders for causing the problem of bringing foreign elements into the American gene pool. Shaler's thinking was in line with abolitionist thinking that produced the country of Liberia as the first solution of eugenic segregation:

> I am not deploring the freeing of these Africans of America: that was the least of evils. These people were here in such numbers that any effort for their deportation was futile. It was their presence here that was the evil, and for this none of the men of our century are responsible. – The burden lies on the souls of our dull, greedy ancestors of the seventeenth and eighteenth centuries, who were too stupid to see or too careless to consider anything but immediate gains. There can be no sort of doubt that, judged by the light of all experience, these people are a danger to America greater and more insuperable than any of those that menace the other great civilized states of the world. (Pgs. 696-709, N.S. Shaler, "The Negro Problem", Atlantic Monthly, Vol. 0054, Issue 325, Nov. 1884 – Available at theatlantic.com)

Shaler, as did many Northern elitists, regarded the emancipated population as a eugenic problem threatening the "Teutonic" and "Aryan" bloodlines:

> The real dangers that this African blood brings to our state lie deeper than the labor problem. ---- I have now set forth the fear that must come upon any one who will see what a wonderful thing our modern Teutonic society is; how slowly it has won its treasures, and at what a price of vigilance and toil it must keep them; and therefore how dangerous it must be to have a large part of the state separated in motives from the people who have brought it into existence. ----

> The African question is a very serious matter, I should like to propose the following statement of the prime nature of the dangers, and the means whereby they may be minimized, if not avoided. ---- First, I hold it to be clear that the inherited qualities of the negroes to a great degree unfit them to carry the burden of our own civilization; that their present Americanized shape is due in large part to the strong control to which they have been subjected since the enslavement of their blood; that there will naturally be a strong tendency, for many generations to come, for them to revert to their ancestral conditions. ---- Next, I hold it to be almost equally clear that they cannot as a race, for many generations, be brought to the level of our own people. (Pgs. 696-709, N.S. Shaler, "The Negro Problem", Atlantic Monthly, Vol. 0054, Issue 325, Nov. 1884 – Available at theatlantic.com)

According to the 1910 book "Theodore Roosevelt as an Undergraduate," by Donald Wilhelm, the young Theodore was more than the usual student at one of Shaler's lectures. He was his prodigy. Much of Shaler's views on race relations became gospel for Roosevelt and remained with him through his years as President of the United States. The line drawn between Agassiz, Shaler, Davenport, and Theodore Roosevelt is crucial to the understanding of the American Eugenics Society, and the deep impact it had on society. Theodore Roosevelt's experience was similar to that of Davenport's. The students that Shaler taught at Harvard would all rally around Darwinism, and the "scientific" theories that supported its ranking of the races as explained in Darwin's "Descent of Man." Edward Laurens Mark, Hersey professor of anatomy and director of Harvard's zoological laboratory until his retirement in 1921, was one of the professors that caused the transition for Harvard students to accept Darwinism. Marks was one of the directors of the zoology department at Harvard. According to Wilhelm, young Theodore took the course titled "Natural History III – Zoology" taught by professor E.L. Marks in his junior year at Harvard. Theodore Roosevelt and E.L. Marks had an amiable relationship. [502] This is of note, as the students of E.L. Marks comprise a list of the top eugenicists in history, including Herbert Spencer Jennings, Robert M. Yerkes, and most notably Charles Benedict Davenport. [503]

These men shared a commonality of upbringing and social status. Shaler and Roosevelt bonded in a common ancestry. Both were distinct "Unionists" supporting the cause of the North, but with family ties to the Confederacy and its aristocratic way of Southern life:

> With wealth and influence his father supported the national government with all his might; his mother sympathized with her two brothers, one serving the Confederacy abroad, the other destined to give the command that made the last gun flicker at the approaching Kearsarge from the battered side of the Alabama. (Thomas G. Dyer, "Theodore Roosevelt and the Idea of Race", Louisiana State University Press, 1980)

---

[502] "Harvard System", Eli Chernin, BMJ, Vol. 97, Oct. 22, 1988.
[503] Lefalophodon, An Informal History of Evolutionary Biology Web Site.

There were only 800 students at Harvard at the time Roosevelt and Davenport attended. Thus, it was a close-knit community of social clubs and memberships as any other Ivy League of the day. The young Roosevelt was a member of the Phi Beta Kappa honorary society and Alpha Delta Phi along with Oliver Wendell Holmes. Donald Wilhelm describes the very close relationship and bond that grew between the young Roosevelt and Shaler:

> Roosevelt was "soon a member of the Natural History Society, flourishing under the presidency of that remarkable man, Professor Nathaniel Southgate Shaler. In the absence of Professor Shaler, Roosevelt himself presided, for he was elected undergraduate vice-president in his junior year. As a boy he was intensely interested in natural history and his constant enthusiasm was one of the causes of Professor Shaler showing such a distinct fondness for him. (Pg. 13, Donald Wilhelm, "Theodore Roosevelt as an Undergraduate", John W. Luce and Company, 1910)

Wilhelm's book tells an interesting story about the later eugenicist's attitude towards testing, ranking, and placement:

> The weakling and the coward are out of place in a strong and free community. In a republic like ours the governing class is composed of the strong men who take the trouble to do the work of government; and if you are too timid or too fastidious or too careless to do your part in this work, the you forfeit your right to be considered one of the governing and you become one of the governed. (Theodore Roosevelt, "An Address Delivered at the Harvard Union" - Pg. 84, Donald Wilhelm, "Theodore Roosevelt as an Undergraduate", John W. Luce and Company, 1910)

Why are all these relationships important? World history would simply not be the same if Davenport and the veritable battalion of Ivy League eugenicists were removed from the historical timeline. Without this Ivy League prestige, the eugenics movement in the United States would likely not have the impetus or reputation it enjoyed. All those books, scientific journals, laws, all of the policies, all of those crucial eugenic organizations, were the product of the American Ivy Leaguers and their equivalent British institutions. More to the point, these Ivy Leaguers controlled the content and the staff of the leading institutions and scientific journals. As we have seen, they also controlled the legislators. One simply has to go down the line of presidents for the American Eugenic Society, the Human Betterment Foundation, the Pioneer Fund, and the Immigration Restriction League to see how they are, almost without exception, all Ivy Leaguers.

- Charles Benedict Davenport – Harvard (Kingpin of American eugenics).
- Oliver Wendell Holmes, Jr. – Harvard (1927 Buck v. Bell opinion author)
- Lothrop Stoddard – Harvard (Nazi Eugenic court collaborator)
- Earnest A. Hooton – Harvard Professor
- Lawrence Lowell – President of Harvard (Immigration Restriction

League)
- Prescott Hall – Harvard (Immigration Restriction League)
- Theodore Roosevelt – Harvard, Colombia Law.
- Wickliffe Preston Draper – Harvard (Founder of the Pioneer Fund)
- Clarence Cook Little – Harvard (American Eugenics Society President)
- Harry L. Shapiro – Harvard (American Eugenics Society President)
- Dr. Katzen-Ellenbogen – Harvard (Buchenwald collaborator)
- Robert DeCourcey Ward – Harvard (Immigration Restriction League)
- E.L. Marks (Harvard zoology)
- Herbert Spencer Jennings - Harvard
- Robert M. Yerkes - Harvard (Eugenics intelligence testing)
- Dudley Sargent – Harvard (Inspired Dr. Haiselden's eugenic infanticide)
- John B. Trevor – Harvard (Political impetus behind anti-immigration lobby)

The above list is much more than a theoretical or academic exercise. It is, as explained, the list of personalities that commanded the eugenics movement with real-world consequences. Journalist Welling Savo concurs:

> Harvard was a brain trust of eugenic thought. In 1926, at least nine members of the Eugenics Society's advisory council were also on the Harvard faculty, and many more were affiliated with Harvard as students and researchers. The society's vice president, Charles Davenport, was a Harvard-trained biologist who also founded the Eugenics Records Office, which kept tabs on people's genetic backgrounds. Like Hooton, Davenport believed that increased charity, philanthropy, and medical advances had interfered with the natural survival of the fittest. Two of Davenport's Harvard associates, Robert DeCourcey Ward and Prescott Hall, spearheaded something called the Immigration Restriction League; they, along with other eugenicists, were instrumental in persuading Congress to curtail the influx of "inferior immigrants" by imposing literacy tests and other restrictions. (Pg.128, Welling Savo, "The Master Race", Boston Magazine, Vol. 40, No. 12, Dec. 2002)

Harvard wasn't alone either. Many of the other Ivy League schools offered eugenics courses and produced the remainder of the key figures in the movement. It is certainly telling that the top 20 to 30 people responsible for such inhuman behavior are exclusively the product of only five schools, the Ivy League schools, and its non-Ivy equals, such as Johns Hopkins and Stanford. Here is the list from Harvard's Ivy League rival, Yale:

- Irving Fischer – Yale (Galton Society)
- Madison Grant – Yale University, Colombia Law School
- Henry Pratt Fairchild – Yale (American Eugenics Society President)
- Henry F. Perkins – Yale (American Eugenics Society President)
- Ellsworth Huntington – Yale Professor (Am. Eugenics Society President)

- ⇢ Pres. William Howard Taft – Law Professor. (Life Extension Institute)
- ⇢ William Graham Sumner – Professor

From proud institutions of the State of California:
- ⇢ William Shockley – Cal. Tech, PhD from MIT, Stanford Professor. (Pioneer Fund)
- ⇢ Arthur Rober Jensen – Cal. Berkley, PhD from Columbia. (Pioneer Fund)
- ⇢ Samuel Jackson Holmes – Cal. Berkley (Human Betterment Foundation)
- ⇢ Paul Popenoe – Stanford (Human Betterment Foundation)
- ⇢ David Star Jordan – Stanford (Human Betterment Foundation)
- ⇢ Charles M. Goethe – Cal. State, Sacramento (E.R.O. of Northern California)

From the remaining member schools of the Ivy League:
- ⇢ John D. Rockefeller, Jr. – Brown.
- ⇢ Henry Crampton – Colombia (American Eugenics Society founder)
- ⇢ Maurice Bigelow – Colombia (American Eugenics Society President)
- ⇢ Henry Fairfield Osborn – Princeton University, Colombia Professor.
- ⇢ Marion S. Norton (Olden) – Princeton (Eugenic court collaborator)
- ⇢ Harry H. Laughlin - Princeton
- ⇢ Woodrow Wilson – Princeton President

The list could continue for several pages. However, listed are the individuals who had a significant effect on the eugenics movement leading up to World War II, and more importantly, held the keys to success for the young and aspiring scientists. Richard Hernstein and Charles Murray, the authors of the infamous 1994 book "The Bell Curve" for example, graduated from and/or were employed by Harvard. Many of these turn-of-the-century elites were members of more than one of the key organizations. They also crossed over to organizations such as the World Wildlife Fund, the Sierra Club, and Planned Parenthood. Recall that the Immigration Restriction League, which was primarily responsible for the 1924 Immigration Restriction Act, was founded by five Harvard graduates. Dr. J. Ewing Mears, the surgeon who helped pioneer the involuntary sterilization procedures so valued by Harry H. Laughlin and Charles Benedict Davenport, left Harvard an endowment of $60,000 for Harvard's eugenic program. Harvard rejected the donation, most likely because the Harvard trustees were offended by the limiting conditions, that Harvard teach eugenics only according to Mears' criterion. The Harvard newspaper covered the university's refusal of the funds in a May 1927 article. It quotes Arthur Brisbane, the famous newspaperman that worked for both Hearst and Pulitzer, as well as being a Harvard alumnus:

> Eugenics at present is more guesswork than science. Ninety per cent of the alumni will approve the action of the Harvard trusties. If in John Harvard's day somebody had offered a legacy to develop the possibility of getting power out

of boiling water, or harnessing lightning, they would have rejected it with general approval. Fifty years ago if anyone had offered Harvard $1,000,000 for the study of flying he would have been told, 'You must not make this great university ridiculous.' Eugenics in days to come will be the greatest, most important of all sciences. (thecrimson.com, "Jumping at Conclusions", Harvard Crimson, May 28, 1927)

To underscore the above claim that these Ivy League eugenicists held the keys to success within the scientific community for several generations, Davenport was president or vice president of ten of the 64 societies in which he was a member and was on the editorial boards of eight scientific journals. Davenport also contributed substantially to the emerging sciences of evolutionary biology, and he was one of the most prominent proponents of the adoption of mathematical and statistical methods by biologists. That, of course, is the polite way of saying that he measured noses and craniums like his Nazi counterparts. From 1900 until his death in 1944, Davenport was one of the best known and most influential scientists in the world. As one of his colleagues, Oscar Riddle, argued, "Davenport was unquestionably one of the leaders of biology in his generation; and his generation was one in which biology made phenomenal advances." [504] These are respectable credentials which illustrate the source of the political influence wielded by the "grand wizards" of "scientific racism."

Oscar Riddle is mentioned here because Riddle worked at Cold Spring Harbor alongside Davenport and Laughlin. Riddle's career provides a glimpse into the movement. In his time, Riddle was one of the top biologists in the United States. Riddle was a devout atheist and held the conviction that religion posed a serious threat to scientific advancements. He garnered national attention for a speech debunking religious superstition in 1936. He is also quoted in the "NAS Biographical Memoir" of Charles Benedict Davenport. In it Riddle defines the eugenics creed is as follows:

- ↠ I believe in striving to raise the human race to the highest plane of social organization, of cooperative work and of effective endeavor.
- ↠ I believe that I am the trustee of the germ plasm that I carry; that this has been passed on to me through thousands of generations before me; and that I betray the trust if (that germ plasm being good) I so act as to jeopardize it, with its excellent possibilities, or, from motives of personal convenience, to unduly limit offspring.
- ↠ I believe that, having made our choice in marriage carefully, we, the married pair, should seek to have 4 to 6 children in order that our carefully selected germ plasm shall be reproduced in adequate degree and that this preferred stock shall not be swamped by that less carefully selected.
- ↠ I believe in such a selection of immigrants as shall not tend to adulterate our national germ plasm with socially unfit traits.

---

[504] "Zoology of the Twentieth Century: Charles Davenport's Prediction for Biology", Mark Largent, American Philosophical Society Library Bulliten, Jan. 2002. – Sourced from Academia.edu.

⇢ I believe in repressing my instincts when to follow them would injure the next generation.

The first point evidences that neither Davenport nor his eugenic brethren were political "conservatives," as some historians of the eugenics movement have claimed. In fact, it should be obvious that Davenport clearly did not believe in any form of *laissez-faire* policy. Davenport's political beliefs fall right in line with Julian Huxley's socialist agenda as written into "The Eugenic Manifesto." The first point clearly places him within the bounds of Fabian Socialism, Progressivism, or within Edward Bellamy's brand of "nationalistic" form of "socialism." Davenport knew well that to accomplish his eugenic dreams the autonomy or liberty of the individual had to be subordinated to that the society, and his 1910 booklet "Eugenics" states as much:

> Governments spend scores of thousands of dollars and establish rigid inspections to prevent the spread of the coitus disease of the horse but the Spirochete parasite that cause the corresponding disease in man and entails endless misery on hundreds of thousands of innocent children may be disseminated by anybody, and is being disseminated by scores of thousands of persons in this country, unchecked, under the protection of the "personal liberty" flag. (Pg. 4, "Eugenics: The Science of Human Improvement by Better Breeding", JAMA, April 23, 1910)

One must comprehend that the difference in prestige between the Ivy Leagues and a common state university was much more pronounced in those days. These elites were in a position to maneuver the sciences to the direction of their liking, as was clearly done by Charles B. Davenport. The Ivy Leagues received the bulk of the grant money. Their alumni were the heads of hospitals as well as the heads of prominent medical and scientific journals. They had the ability to frame the argument and suppress dissenting voices. They had the political and personal connections to the higher positions in government. More importantly, they had the ear of scientists and legislatures at home and abroad. To be more specific, the German race scientists were simply not in touch with the town bigots from the various Southern towns that the KKK flourished in. The race hygienists in Europe were in active contact with American scientists through the American Eugenics Society, the Human Betterment Foundation, and the Immigration Restriction League, all of which were the product of the North-Eastern Ivy League elites. The comparison between Northern and Southern types of racism is not intended to diminish the horrors of the thousands of lynchings between the Reconstruction Era and World War II, but rather to understand the nature of two distinct and separate threats. To borrow a phrase from the present-day militant environmentalists, the Southern bigot "acted locally," while the elitist eugenicists "thought globally."

Lynchings in the South were, by and large, very personal local affairs, with many of the earlier victims being white. [505] There occurred as little as 50 and as much as

---

[505] "The Negro Holocaust: Lynching and Race Riots in the United States 1880-1950," Robert A. Gibson, Yale course curriculum posted in the Yale website.

230 lynchings per year in the United States for a total of 4,730 between 1882 and 1951. [506] Eugenicists thought in much more "industrial" terms; they thought in percentages of the population. Leon F. Whitney thought that no less than 10 percent of the entire population needed to be eradicated from the gene pool. The Ivy Leaguers were just a bit more civilized in their communication than their KKK counterparts. They used charts and scientific journals to forward their racist demands. The KKK held theatrical midnight rallies where they burnt crosses and wore white costumes. The Ivy Leaguers had Senate Hearings and scientific symposiums and wore tailored suits and white lab coats.

Nevertheless, both the KKK and the Ivy League eugenicists shared the same target, or as the KKK would say, "the spics, the niggers, the Jews, and the Papists." The Ivy League scientists merely added the "epileptic, the feeble-minded, the syphilitic, the imbecile, the moron, the mongolic, the drunkard, and the criminal" to that list, and then proceeded to incorporate the list into legislation so judges and justices like Oliver Wendell Holmes, Jr. could conduct their manhunts under the veil of respectable legality. This is an important distinction to those that are looking for answers for the "industrial" magnitude and scope of the Holocaust; the "Nazis" did not bother with a handful of lynchings per village. They enacted a governmental policy that enlisted nurses, doctors, scientists, lawyers and judges after literally copying the American eugenic legislation verbatim to eradicate entire percentages of the population from the gene pool.

Clearly, the *modus operandi* of the vulgar bigot is dramatically different in nature and scope from that of the "scientific racist," which sprung from the laboratories and lecture halls of biology departments in the top intellectual institutions in the world. The resulting scope of their crimes would also prove to be dramatically different. There were approximately 4,700 total lynchings in the United States due to the vulgar bigots. The body count from "scientific racism" extends into the many millions.

---

[506] "The Negro Holocaust: Lynching and Race Riots in the United States 1880-1950," Robert A. Gibson, Yale course curriculum posted in the Yale website.

Chap. 13: 1889 to 1885

SCIENCE & TECHNOLOGY: KARL BENZ UNVEILS THE BENZ PATENT MOTORWAGEN. THE NATIONAL GEOGRAPHIC SOCIETY IS FOUNDED. EDWIN HUBBLE, AMERICAN ASTRONOMER IS BORN. – THE FIRST LONG DISTANCE ELECTRIC POWER TRANSMISSION LINE IN THE UNITED STATES IS COMPLETED, RUNNING 14 MILES BETWEEN A GENERATOR AT WILLAMETTE FALLS AND DOWNTOWN PORTLAND, OREGON. GEORGE EASTMAN REGISTERS THE TRADEMARK KODAK AND RECEIVES A PATENT FOR HIS CAMERA. **LIFE:** VINCENT VAN GOGH PAINTS STARRY NIGHT – THE FIRST ISSUE OF THE WALL STREET JOURNAL IS PUBLISHED. JOSEPH P. KENNEDY, SR., AMERICAN POLITICIAN AND FATHER OF PRESIDENT JOHN F. KENNEDY IS BORN. – DURING A BOUT OF MENTAL ILLNESS, DUTCH PAINTER VINCENT VAN GOGH INFAMOUSLY CUTS OFF THE LOWER PART OF HIS OWN LEFT EAR. GERMAN ARCHITECT LUDWIG MIES VAN DER ROHE IS BORN. GEORGE PATTON, AMERICAN GENERAL IS BORN. – ULYSSES S. GRANT, AMERICAN CIVIL WAR GENERAL AND THE 18 PRESIDENT OF THE UNITED STATES DIES. •

Sec. I - GIVING BIRTH TO THE 20th CENTURY:

This book documents how criminal activity at the turn-of-the-century significantly influenced eugenic legislation in the United States. Criminal behavior was one of the symptoms of industrialized urbanity that inspired radical reformist movements. The "criminal mind," according to Lombroso, was evidence of "degeneration" and by extrapolation, evidence of an atavistic regression back to primitive humanity. It is informative to re-examine some of the most recognizable historical figures within this context. Jack the Ripper is the name given to the most infamous serial killer in history. If the "Dear Boss" letter delivered to the Scotland Yard that September of 1888 can be trusted as being written by The Ripper, then he should also be regarded as a prophet of the history to follow:

One day men will look back and say I gave birth to the 20 Century.
(Allegedly from Jack the Ripper, "Dear Boss" letter, Sept. 1888)

The Ripper terrorized the Whitechapel district on the east side of London in 1888. The murders were experienced in the collective conscience as part of the wider problem of urbanization and industrialization. Every social ill was attributed to urbanity and industrialization, namely due to the strenuous and unhygienic living conditions it created. Irish immigrants swelled the populations of England's major cities, including the East End of London, where the Whitechapel district lay. From 1882, Jewish refugees from Eastern Europe and Tsarist Russia moved into the same area, and this only helped fuel the xenophobia typically aimed at Eastern European immigrants. In October 1888, London's Metropolitan Police Service estimated that there were 1200 prostitutes and about 62 brothels in Whitechapel. Racism, crime, and real deprivation fed public perceptions that Whitechapel was a notorious den of degeneracy.

In 1888, perceptions of a "degenerate" population were strengthened when a series of vicious and grotesque murders attributed to "Jack the Ripper" received unprecedented coverage in the media. The "canonical five" are widely believed to be the work of the Ripper. Most experts point to deep throat slashes, abdominal and genital-area mutilation, removal of internal organs, and progressive facial mutilations as the distinctive features of Jack the Ripper's modus operandi. Ripper historian,

Philip Sugden pointed to the fact that contemporaries were baffled by the lack of conventional motive. The murders didn't seem to be instigated by money, jealousy, or revenge. So, in search for a logical explanation, anthropology became part of the speculation. [507] Here is where the Ripper's story merges with the history of eugenics. The Ripper was feared as either a cultural or biological "atavism," or a throwback to some lesser evolved form of humanity. Sugden proceeds to report some specifically relevant reactions from the contemporary British press:

> It is so impossible to account . . . for these revolting acts of blood, commented one, that the mind turns as it were instinctively to some theory of occult force, and the myths of the Dark Ages rise before the imagination. Ghouls, vampires, bloodsuckers, and all the ghastly array of fables which have been accumulated throughout the course of centuries take form, and seize hold of the excited fancy. (lightnovelgate.com, Chap.: A Century of Final Solutions, "The Complete History of Jack the Ripper", Philip Sugden, Carroll & Graf, 1994. – citing Southern Guardian, January 5th, 1889)

Precisely, the murders were seen as the proximate cause from a "degenerate" society resulting from industrialization, urbanization, and immigration:

> Suppose we catch the Whitechapel murderer, can we not, before handing him over to the executioner or the authorities at Bradmoor, make a really decent effort to discover his antecedents, and his parentage, to trace back every step of his career, every hereditary instinct, every acquired taste every moral slip, every mental idiosyncrasy? Surely the time has come for such an effort as this. We are face to face with some mysterious and awful product of modern civilization. (lightnovelgate.com, Chap.: A Century of Final Solutions, "The Complete History of Jack the Ripper", Philip Sugden, Carroll & Graf, 1994. – citing Southern Guardian, January 5th, 1889)

The Ripper, like the "paupers" and "criminal types," was the animalistic, and more precisely "atavistic," throwback to a more primitive existence brought to the urban centers in unhealthy numbers by modern trains and ships. According to David Wilson, Professor of Criminology at Birmingham University, this was also the case with England's first serial killer, Mary Ann Cotton:

> In a previous, agricultural era, Mary Ann Cotton's activities would have been watched, reported upon and controlled by her neighbors and their informal surveillance. Only in the age of water power and steam were people free to leave their agricultural past behind them and shift restlessly from one settlement to another. In so doing, they could become whoever and whatever they wanted to be – even a serial killer. (dailymail.co.uk, "Britain's First Serial Killer", David Wilson, The Daily Mail, Feb. 5, 2012)

In 1873, Mary Ann Cotton was arrested, tried and hanged for the murder of the seven-year-old Charles Edward Cotton. The so-called Black Widow killer who

---

[507] lightnovelgate.com, "The Complete History of Jack the Ripper", Philip Sugden, Carroll & Graf, 1994. – See Generally Chptr: A Century of Final Solutions.

posed as a wife, widow, mother, friend, and nurse to murder perhaps as many as 21 victims is now largely forgotten. Two decades before Jack the Ripper, Mary Ann Cotton had already become a killing machine, likely murdering as many as eight of her own children, seven stepchildren, her mother, three husbands, a lover, and an inconvenient friend. She would live off her new husbands, start a family, then poison them with arsenic. Mary Ann Cotton was understood by the authorities and the emerging profession of criminology as a product of the "shiftlessness" attributed to "degenerates" of the era, always in transition from her childhood onward.

Back in the United States, there was also a lesser-known urban serial killer during this era. The American "ripper" known as H.H. Holmes outdid his mentor and was one of the first documented American serial killers. H.H. Holmes made Jack the Ripper look like a petty crook. The case was notorious in its time and received wide publicity through a series of articles in William Randolph Hearst's newspapers as Holmes chose to hunt tourists during the Chicago World's Fair. The Columbian Exposition, also known as The Chicago World's Fair, was held to celebrate the 400 anniversary of Christopher Columbus's arrival in the New World. Interestingly enough, the pristine neoclassical cityscape design of the fair was a direct, but hopeful, rebuttal to the grimy reality that was turn-of-the-century urbanity. The fair's layout was a historic event as Tesla and George Westinghouse introduced visitors to AC power by using it to illuminate the Exposition. The lighted city was meant to convey the futuristic and optimism of rescuing urbanity from the darkness it had acquired from the soot and ever-increasing density.

H.H. Holmes had other architectural plans in mind for the fair. Holmes opened a hotel that he had designed and built specifically with murder in mind. The building was a maze of hidden rooms, vaults, and shafts designed to allow Holmes to corner, murder, and subsequently dismember his victims, meanwhile appearing like any other building in the cityscape. Holmes took an unknown number of his victims from the 1893 Chicago World's Fair, which was less than two miles away from his "World's Fair" hotel. While he confessed to 27 murders, of which nine were confirmed, his actual body count could be as high as 250.

All this debauchery and violence had a direct influence on eugenics. By the 1840s, Whitechapel and its enclaves had already devolved into a seemingly insurmountable problem of poverty and overcrowding. Whitechapel Road and the small dark streets branching from it that contained the greatest suffering, filth, and danger. In 1902, the American author Jack London, looking to write a counterpart to Jacob Riis's seminal book "How the Other Half Lives," dressed in ragged clothes and took up residence in the typical home which Whitechapel residents had to endure. He documented his experiences in "The People of the Abyss." Jack London was a socialist and thought it tantalizing to explore and document the living conditions offered by the city that had invented modern capitalism. The juxtaposition of the poverty, homelessness, exploitive work conditions, prostitution, and infant mortality of Whitechapel made it a focal point for leftist reformers and revolutionaries.

Jack London was not the only one to leverage Whitechapel's destitute situation as a political launchpad. Eugenicists like George Bernard Shaw's Fabian Society met regularly in Whitechapel. Vladimir Ilyich Lenin, who boarded and led rallies in Whitechapel during his exile from Russia, used the stark contrast between British aristocracy and Whitechapel poverty to provide the grim imagery of class-struggle. As such, many criminologists of the era were the most ardent supporters of the eugenics movement. It is by no coincidence that socialists, namely the members of the Fabian Society, which would champion scientific proposals at curing the social ills found in urban centers like Whitechapel and American cities like New York and Chicago. Eugenicists became Fabian Socialists and Fabian Socialists supported the eugenics movement precisely because of its promise to control and eradicate the problems found in city centers like Whitechapel. This is also the reason why the fictional utopias are also city planning proposals, namely the works of H.G. Wells and Edward Bellamy. Much like the design of the Chicago World's Fair, the European garden city movement, which united so many socialists, city planners, and eugenicists was a reaction and a counterproposal aimed at alleviating the realities of the newly industrialized urbanity.

Sec. 2 - BELLAMY'S "LOOKING BACKWARD" IS PUBLISHED:

"Looking Backward: 2000-1887" was the utopian novel by Edward Bellamy which kicked off the "third-way" socio-economic revolution that was meant to offer an option to the extremes of International Communism and *laissez-faire* capitalism. The book tells the story of Julian West, a young Bostonian who, towards the end of the 19th century, falls into a deep, hypnosis-induced sleep and wakes up 113 years later. He finds himself in Boston in the year 2000. During his deep sleep, the United States has been transformed into a socialist utopia where cooperation and solidarity, instead of capitalistic competition, have become the organizing principle of society. Everything in Bellamy's Boston of the year 2000 was sacrificed for the good of the society, and this subordination of the individual to the social body was done willingly as the society had, according to Bellamy, "evolved" a sense of solidarity through eugenic means.

"Looking Backward" cannot be regarded as any other book. It was the third-largest bestseller of its time, after "Uncle Tom's Cabin" and "Ben-Hur." It influenced a formidable number of intellectuals and appears by title in many of the major Marxist writings of the day. Three American intellectuals, Charles Beard, John Dewey, and Edward Weeks, interviewed separately in 1944, proclaimed Edward Bellamy's "Looking Backwards" second only to Marx's *Das Kapital* as the most influential book of modern times. [508] Alfred Kelly, the author of "The Descent of

---

[508] Pg. 157 - "An Underground History of American Education", John Taylor Gatto, Oxford Village Press, 2000. – Sourced through archive.org.

Darwin," concluded that "Looking Backward" was "probably the best-loved novel among working people" after conducting a study of sociological surveys, statistical reports, and questionnaires distributed to workers taking evening courses. "Translated as *Im Jahre 2000*, the novel appeared in serial form in many socialist newspapers." [509] In fact, "Looking Backwards" had a vast amount of influence on early Russian revolutionaries:

> Kautsky was quick to see that Bellamy's evolutionary vision in effect lifted the burden of struggle from the proletariat. In his review of *Looking Backward* for *Die Nue Zeit* he took Bellamy to task for his totally un-Marxist view of history. Where was the all-important class struggle? He asked. Yet Kautsky recommended the book highly because its entertaining view of a noncapitalist future would stimulate the working-class reader to further study. (Pg. 133, "The Descent of Darwin: The Popularization of Darwinism in Germany, 1860-1914", Univ. of North Carolina, 1947)

Historians rightfully place "Looking Backward" in the history of "totalitarianism." Sylvia Bowman's book, "Edward Bellamy Abroad," helps to prove that Bellamy's Nationalist dogma was the ideological precursor of "authoritarian socialists" in America and Europe. Bowman's book is a survey of Bellamy's impact outside of the United States which, despite the intentions of Bowman, clearly maps out the case that Bellamy's book was the inspiration for a "number of individuals and movements that can with accuracy be regarded as the forerunners of the fascists." [510] Carl J. Guarneri confirms the dramatic effect on collectivist and socialist politics outside of the United States:

> Russian economist claimed in 1906 that Looking Backward had provided "more effective propaganda of the ideas of socialism among the broad masses than any other book during the past thirty years" (M.I. Tugan-Baranovsky, qtd. in Nikojulin 72). Certainly some of the Italian readers of the 1913 edition of Looking Backward felt this way. "Comrade Bellamy," one wrote in the book's margins, "I cannot tell you how impressed I was when I read your book.... I think that if socialism were practiced in the manner you propose, it might bring about a golden age.... Hurray for Socialism!" ("An American Utopia and Its Global Audiences: Transnational Perspectives on Edward Bellamy's Looking Backward", Carl J. Guarneri, Before the American Studies Association of Turkey, Ankara, November 1, 2006, Utopian Studies, Vol. 19, No. 2, 2008, pp. 147-187)

Professor Guarneri claims to have written his work due to the total lack of analysis of the book's impact on the international public. He claims that very few, if any, of Bellamy's critics or supporters analyze just how important the book was outside of the United States. Guarneri also believes that if Columbia University

---

[509] Pg. 133 - "The Descent of Darwin: The Popularization of Darwinism in Germany, 1860-1914", Alfred Kelly, Univ. of North Carolina, 1947.
[510] Pg. 137, "Authoritarian Socialism in America: Edward Bellamy & the Nationalist Movement", Arthur Lipow, Univ. of California Press, 1982.

inquiry would have been conducted in 1935 Germany, the intellectuals of that country would have also credited "Looking Backwards" as one of the most influential political books of the era:

> While Looking Backward took its final shape as "a romance of the ideal nation," Bellamy intended it as "a romance of an ideal world" (Bellamy Speaks 200) -- In 1935, when they were asked to name the ten most influential books worldwide of the previous fifty years, the philosopher John Dewey and historian Charles Beard placed Looking Backward second only to Marx's Das Kapital. (Sadler 553) If an analogous survey were taken in Britain or Germany, the results would probably have been similar. ("An American Utopia and Its Global Audiences: Transnational Perspectives on Edward Bellamy's Looking Backward", Carl J. Guarneri, Before the American Studies Association of Turkey, Ankara, November 1, 2006, Utopian Studies, Vol. 19, No. 2, 2008, pp. 147-187)

Guarneri also points to the fact that by Bellamy's and Hitler's time, the "socialists" of the world had grown disillusioned with the small utopian projects, such as Oneida Colony or the Icarian commune Alfred Ploetz had temporarily been part of. As documented earlier, Ploetz certainly felt that the Icarians were not radical enough for his goals. Karl Marx voiced a similar disillusionment with petty and small projects. Guarneri goes on to document the various ways in which Bellamy's "Looking Backward" influenced European thinkers. He documents Europe's fascination with adopting the model of an industrialized American workforce, and without naming the obvious link to "Fordism" or "Taylorism," or without touching upon the deep influence Henry Ford had on Adolf Hitler. Bellamy sought to employ the same processes of mechanization and centralization that capitalists were deploying but in the service of the collective. Bellamy described this approach in the appendix to "Looking Backward" as a "forecast, in accordance with the principles of evolution, of the next stage in the industrial and social development of humanity." [511]

Guarneri should be commended for supplementing the history of Edward Bellamy with an International perspective. However, his study suffers from the same deficiencies as the Bellamy historians he criticizes. It is unknown if Guarneri simply misses the obvious commonalities between Bellamy's "national" form of "socialism and Hitler's "National Socialism," or if he is twisting logic into a pretzel to avoid a juxtaposition that is understandably uncomfortable for Bellamy admirers. This is best evidenced by Guarneri's description of Bellamy's "collective magic trick" in the support of the "capitalist class" in the fictional future. This is the same basis by which contemporary socialists contend that Hitler's policies were "far-right" or "ultra-conservative" in nature. Historians for decades have pointed to Hitler's cooperation with Germany's industrial capitalists in his ascension to power as proof

---

[511] Pgs. 336-337 - "An American Utopia and Its Global Audiences: Transnational Perspectives on Edward Bellamy's Looking Backward", Carl J. Guarneri, Before the American Studies Association of Turkey, Ankara, November 1, 2006, Utopian Studies, Vol. 19, No. 2, 2008, pp. 147-187.

that Hitler's "National Socialism" belonging to the "far-right" instead of "socialism." Guarneri further documents that the French critics of "Looking Backward" complained of the "corporate" structure that Bellamy proposed for an entire society. This, too, is a commonality with Hitler's Germany. French critics found that Bellamy had "corrupted socialism" with "Fordism" by stressing mechanical efficiency and material abundance. [512] This political maneuver was predicted by Bellamy, the scion of the political left:

> In Bellamy's collective magic trick, the gigantic corporate trusts become the public's "Great Trust" when the people stage a nonviolent coup, taking over 11 consolidated business and capital and organizing them as an enormous public operation. Because the change was seen as rational and in everyone's interest, it was not opposed by the capitalists or the result of class warfare, but arrived peacefully when all groups rallied to the "National Party." ("An American Utopia and Its Global Audiences: Transnational Perspectives on Edward Bellamy's Looking Backward", Carl J. Guarneri, Before the American Studies Association of Turkey, Ankara, November 1, 2006, Utopian Studies, Vol. 19, No. 2, 2008, pp. 147-187)

However much historians want to ignore the Bellamy-Hitler link, it was Bellamy's intention that his fictional utopia received credit for the "Great Change" he prophesized as occurring in the hearts and minds of his imagined populous. Bellamy prophesized that the origins of such a "Great Change" would be his fictional citizenry's "religion of solidarity." Bellamy himself prophetically predicted the effects of the Great Depression on the German public in "Looking Backward" when he states that "the intoxicating effect of hope on minds long accustomed to despair" is what gave such wide acceptance to the 'Great Change.'" The British Theosophist Annie Besant certainly credited Bellamy for Fabian collectivism. In their eyes, both Theosophy and Bellamy's Nationalism were "religions of solidarity." [513]

This fundamental "change" was intended to be a physical one as well as mental and emotional. Many historians have detected strains of nostalgic anti-urbanism in Bellamy's "village utopian," yet they fail to make the link to the utopian aspirations that Hitler and his fascination with the German countryside and "*völkisch*" elements. Hitler's "blood and soil" ideal was both political and aesthetic. Guarneri discusses a similar strain in Bellamy's urban planning:

> A similar convergence took place between Bellamy's blueprint and new developments in urban planning. Although Looking Backward provided few details about urban design in 2000, Bellamy's generalized conception of the new Boston as a composite of country and city life inspired Ebenezer Howard, founder of the Garden City movement in England. Howard was "fairly carried away" by Looking Backward and arranged for a British edition to be published. Howard developed his plan for a British Nationalist colony into Garden Cities

---

[512] Pgs. 336-337 - "An American Utopia and Its Global Audiences: Transnational Perspectives on Edward Bellamy's Looking Backward", Carl J. Guarneri, Before the American Studies Association of Turkey, Ankara, November 1, 2006, Utopian Studies, Vol. 19, No. 2 (2008), pp. 147-187 (41 pages).
[513] Ibid.

of Tomorrow (1898), a treatise that brought him fame and influence on both sides of the Atlantic." ("An American Utopia and Its Global Audiences: Transnational Perspectives on Edward Bellamy's Looking Backward", Carl J. Guarneri, Before the American Studies Association of Turkey, Ankara, November 1, 2006, Utopian Studies, Vol. 19, No. 2, 2008, pp. 147-187)

None of these similarities between Hitler's and Bellamy's *"völkisch"* movements can be said to be superficial. Bellamy's vision was much like Hitler's "nationalist" movement. Bellamy appealed to the middle class and the professional class by "leaving Victorian conventions of gender and family untouched." Bellamy's book appalled cultural radicals like William Morris for this very reason. [514] The Bellamyte version of "nationalist socialists" also shared with their later German counterparts a socialist and collectivist base. The ranks of the Socialist Party of America (SPA) was centered in regions where Bellamytes resided, like Boston and California. Among them was Job Harriman, Eugene V. Debs's vice-presidential running mate. The 700,000 strong Utopian Society of America advocated a literal version of Bellamy's vision: "an end to private ownership, the establishment of a priceless, profitless system …and the creation of a great cooperative commonwealth." [515]

Guarneri, like many other academics, attempts the conceptual tightrope walk of Cold War polemics. Guarneri spends much ink on trying to explain why Bellamy's "Nationalism" should be interpreted as "international" socialism. To his credit, Guarneri provides quotes where Bellamy alludes to such a distinction. However, this is nothing more than the all too typical "party line" politics identified with the International Socialist movement. All of the regimes that have identified themselves as "international communists" or "international socialists" have engaged in this double-talk, as all of these regimes have also gratuitously leveraged "nationalism" to engender mass support. This is true from the USSR to Cuba, and onto China and North Korea. All these regimes, without exception, have at one time or another engaged in flagrant chest-pounding "nationalistic" appeals to the masses in times of both war and peace, to either inspire war-militarism or a peacetime "industrial army."

Yet, the most important commonality between the fictional world portrayed in "Looking Backward" and Hitler's actual Germany is the eugenic mission. This cements "Looking Backward" firmly in the ranks of eugenic utopias. The author of "The Descent of Darwin," Alfred Kelly, documents that Bellamy's allegedly superior spirit of cooperation and solidarity had come about by Darwinian principles of evolution. According to Bellamy's postscript, his predictions were based upon "the principles of evolution"; an "evolution" from a "bad Darwinian" society to a "good Darwinian" society though a eugenic "refinement of the race." [516] The best example of this recurring theme is with the Fabian Socialists. Not only did Fabians like John

---

[514] Pgs. 336-337 -"An American Utopia and Its Global Audiences: Transnational Perspectives on Edward Bellamy's Looking Backward", Carl J. Guarneri, Before the American Studies Association of Turkey, Ankara, November 1, 2006, Utopian Studies, Vol. 19, No. 2 (2008), pp. 147-187 (41 pages).

[515] Ibid.

[516] Pg. 133, "The Descent of Darwin: The Popularization of Darwinism in Germany, 1860-1914", Alfred Kelly, Univ. of North Carolina, 1947.

Maynard Keynes draw up the actual "blueprint" for a "centrally planned" society, but Keynes, H.G. Wells, and other Fabians together with Bellamy were ardent supporters of eugenics. Carl J. Guarneri provides an opinion on the matter:

> In England, Bellamy's influence became entwined with Fabianism, which shared his professional-class detachment and his evolutionary socialist agenda. H.G. Wells, whose utopias owed a strong debt to Bellamy, recommended Looking Backward to George Bernard Shaw, who eventually adopted Bellamy's commitment to strict economic equality. According to the historian R. C. K. Ensor, the trajectory of nearly all British socialist propagandists of the 1890s was to move from Henry George's land 32 reform program to Bellamy's state socialism. ("An American Utopia and Its Global Audiences: Transnational Perspectives on Edward Bellamy's Looking Backward," Before the American Studies Association of Turkey, Ankara, November 1, 2006)

That said, the best way to understand Bellamy's eugenic convictions is to read his own words. Bellamy's eugenic beliefs are described in the conversation between his protagonist, Julian West and the character named Dr. Leete:

> It means that for the first time in human history the principle of sexual selection, with its tendency to preserve and transmit the better types of the race, and let the inferior types drop out, has unhindered operation. The necessities of poverty, the need of having a home, no longer tempt women to accept as the fathers of their children men whom they neither can love nor respect. Wealth and rank no longer divert attention from personal qualities. Gold no longer 'gilds the straitened forehead of the fool.' The gifts of person, mind, and disposition; beauty, wit, eloquence, kindness, generosity, geniality, courage, are sure of transmission to posterity. Every generation is sifted through a little finer mesh than the last. The attributes that human nature admires are preserved, those that repel it are left behind. There are, of course, a great many women who with love must mingle admiration, and seek to wed greatly, but these not the less obey the same law, for to wed greatly now is not to marry men of fortune or title, but those who have risen above their fellows by the solidity of brilliance of their services to humanity. These form nowadays the only aristocracy with which alliance is distinction. (Pg. 161, Chap: 25, "Looking Backward", Edward Bellamy, Houghton Mifflin, 1929)

The Dr. Leete character continues on to describe the racial superiority of the inhabitants of the future and ascribes this superiority to the textbook eugenic goal of purifying the race within three generations through drastic eugenic measures. Of specific importance to the doctor was the stamping out of "individual" concerns of past eras, and subordinating them to the good of society, again a textbook eugenic view adopted by the German National Socialists and Fabian Socialists alike:

> You were speaking, a day or two ago, of the physical superiority of our people to your contemporaries. Perhaps more important than any of the causes I mentioned then as tending to race purification has been the effect of untrammeled sexual selection upon the quality of two or three successive

generations. I believe that when you have made a fuller study of our people you will find in them not only a physical, but a mental and moral improvement. It would be strange if it were not so, for not only is one of the great laws of nature now freely working out the salvation of the race, but a profound moral sentiment has come to its support. Individualism, which in your day was the animating idea of society, not only was fatal to any vital sentiment of brotherhood and common interest among living men, but equally to any realization of the responsibility of the living for the generation to follow. To-day this sense of responsibility, practically unrecognized in all previous ages, has become one of the great ethical ideas of the race, reinforcing, with an intense conviction of duty, the natural impulse to seek in marriage the best and noblest of the other sex. The result is, that not all the encouragements and incentives of every sort which have provided to develop industry, talent, genius, excellence of whatever kind, are comparable in their effect on our young men with the fact that our women sit aloft as judges of the race and reserve themselves to reward the winners. Of all the whips, and spurs, and baits, and prizes, there is none like the thought of the radiant faces which the laggards will find averted. (Pg. 96, Edward Bellamy, "Looking Backward: 2000-1887, With extra chapter", William Reeves, 1895)

Even more telling is Bellamy's overt derision against having "sentimental" considerations stand as an obstacle to the nation's eugenic goals, thus making his eugenic vision no different than those of H.G. Wells, Leonard Darwin, Julian Huxley, or more importantly, the Nietzschean vision of Hoche and Binding. In his society, the eugenically unsuccessful are relegated to celibacy, and the woman's "evil sort of courage" in discarding them from the gene-pool is applauded.

Celibates nowadays are almost invariably men who have failed to acquit themselves creditably in the work of life. The woman must be a courageous one, with a very evil sort of courage, too, whom pity for one of these unfortunates should lead to defy the opinion of her generation – for otherwise she is free – so far as to accept him for a husband. I should add that, more exacting and difficult to resist than any other element in that opinion, she would find the sentiment of her own sex. Our women have risen to the full height of their responsibility as the wardens of the world to come, to whose keeping the keys of the future are confided. Their feeling of duty in this respect amounts to a sense of religious consecration. It is a cult in which they educate their daughters from childhood. (Pg. 96, Edward Bellamy, "Looking Backward: 2000-1887, With extra chapter", William Reeves, 1895)

The protagonist, Julian West, even goes home with a romantic novel given to him by the character Dr. Leete, "concerning the modern view of parental responsibility." Here was Bellamy's fictional proposal for films like "The Black Stork" and *"Erbkrank."* Here was Edward Bellamy's proposal for the weeding out of "lives unworthy of living."

It is important to note that "Looking Backward," as it was with any other eugenic utopia, inspired as many copies as it did antagonistic responses. Arthur Bird's

1899s "Looking Forward," William Morris's 1890s "News from Nowhere," and S.F. Sharapov's 1902s "Fifty Years Later" was among many direct responses that offered alternative visions of the future. Richard Michaelis' 1890s "Looking Further Forward" and Ernst Mueller's 1891 *"Ein Rueckblick aus dem Jahre 2037 auf das Jahr 2000"* were anti-utopian fictions that aimed to show the impossibility or danger of Bellamy's plan. Patterns persist as the utopian fixation becomes stereotypical, dogmatic, and altogether predictable. In this way, the revolting and jarring aspects of Bellamy's "Looking Backward" inspired dystopian works from sober-minded authors, just like the ones Aldous Huxley and George Orwell wrote in response to H.G. Wells and his comrades.

Sec. 3 - "FORGOTTEN FATHERLAND":

Ben Macintyre rediscovered the story of Nietzsche's sister and the utopian colony she created in Paraguay. "Forgotten Fatherland" tells Macintyre's personal adventure to find this long-lost utopian gem within the deepest parts of South America. Macintyre's account goes full circle to underscore the crucial role this utopian vision played in the creation of the Nietzsche mythos, and later, Hitler's utopian vision. By popularizing her brother's work and propagandizing her utopian venture, Elizabeth Nietzsche returned home to become a mentor and an icon to Germans intent on redefining and recreating their Fatherland. Macintyre claims that Elizabeth Nietzsche made her brother famous at the same time insuring he would be forever infamous for her connivance to associate him with Hitler's National Socialism.

Elizabeth Nietzsche is now universally disliked as if she were some turn of the century Yoko Ono. There has been a lot written on just how much Elizabeth intervened or polluted her brother's work with her own injections and editions. Macintyre reminds us of her greatest personal accomplishment and call to fame: the catastrophic failure of the utopian colony named "New Germany," which was built for the stated purpose of escaping the European Germany that had been corrupted by "Jewish influence," and recreating a sanctuary for those of pure Aryan blood in the deepest reaches of the New World. Macintyre documents that despite how well known and important as Elisabeth Nietzsche was to National Socialist mythos, "New Germany" is now forgotten. It no longer appears in the maps of the area, and the Paraguayan authorities have become oblivious to the fact it ever existed. Macintyre had to consult Elisabeth Nietzsche's 1891 book, "Bernhard Förster's Colony New Germany in Paraguay" just to figure out where New Germany was located on the map. Though a well-publicized failure, her attempt helped catapult her and her brother to the status of cultural icons for the generation of Germans that would later create the National Socialist racial utopia. Elizabeth's utopian community was a reflection and realization of the radical beliefs of that generation, birthed out of anti-Semitism, vegetarianism, and a racial nationalism. [517] Macintyre acutely identifies Elisabeth Nietzsche's Paraguay adventure as an early exercise in Hitler's *"Lebensraum,"* though fifty years prior to his coming to power, and three years prior to him being born. Hitler was born on April 20, 1889. Elisabeth Nietzsche and Bernhard Förster began their journey down the South American river on March 15th, 1886. Yet, their intentions and the outcome were consistent with Hitler's subsequent attempts at an Aryan utopia and consistent with the other utopian experiments conducted in the secluded vastness of the New World:

> Every one of the German men and women who now loaded their few possessions onto oxcarts, the great-wheeled *carretas*, and moved with painful slowness along the quay had been selected on the basis of their genetic purity, their Aryan racial characteristics. Most were from Saxony, victims of an economic crisis in Germany that had left much of the peasantry landless and nearly destitute; but many also shared the Försters' ideal of a community cleansed of Jewish influence, of the taint of Jewish capitalism. It was the Jews, they all agreed, who had forced them out of the Fatherland. Förster spoke of Germany as a "stepfatherland," a place where honest German virtues were being blighted, where culture was at the mercy of Zion. (Pg. 3, "Forgotten Fatherland: The search for Elisabeth Nietzsche", Macmillan, 1992)

To further contextualize "New Germany," we must note that Elisabeth Nietzsche and her brother were the product of the first generation to wholeheartedly adopt Charles Darwin's theories. This was the generation that turned the corner from controversy to accepted science. In Germany, the highly respected scientist Ernst Haeckel was one of the first of many to take Darwinism and extrapolate it to its logical outcome. Haeckel, like Francis Galton, saw in Darwinism the basis of a society based on the secular values derived from science. Francis Galton took Darwinism and created the "religion" of eugenics. Ernst Haeckel took Darwinism and created Monism, a movement that was in part religious philosophy and part science. Both were creations so entangled with their nationalism, anti-clericalism, and a "racialist" outlook that it is unlikely that either Galton or Haeckel knew where their prejudice began and their science ended. Unsurprisingly then, the history of Elisabeth Nietzsche's "New Germany" parallels that of the many other Darwinian-utopian experiments throughout history. More precisely, "New Germany" parallels Hitler's National Socialism and the majority of utopian proposals:

- The project was a return to nature, and incorporated vegetarianism and holistic living.
- The project was born of the fear of "degeneration," both cultural and physical.
- Preserving racial purity was seen as a way of counteracting the "degeneration."

---

[517] Pg. xv - "Forgotten Fatherland: The search for Elisabeth Nietzsche", Ben Macintyre, Macmillan, 1992.

- The culprit of cultural and physical "degeneration" was pinpointed to the immigrant.
- Capitalism was deemed to be a symptom or contributor to that "degeneration."
- Population control was integral to the project.
- Individuals deemed "unfit" to contribute to the utopian vision were excluded, segregated, or eliminated.
- Strict obedience in the wisdom of the "master" was necessary to accomplish the vision.
- Social hierarchies were based upon racialist or physical criterion.
- Society was to be scientifically engineered.
- Centrally planned and controlled economies, or in the smaller scales, economics controlled by the "master" or visionary.
- The project was an exercise in self-aggrandizement and megalomania.
- The project relied on propaganda to sell an image to the public which the reality did not justify.
- The foreseeable economic woes of the project forced compromises to the utopian vision.

It comes as no surprise then that Bernhard Förster, the father figure of the commune, also shared with Hitler a devoted passion for all things Richard Wagner, namely his vegetarianism and his anti-Semitism. Another similarity is that "New Germany" and Hitler's National Socialism both ended with one or both of its patriarchs or matriarchs committing suicide in the theatrical fashion of Wagnerian flavor. Once it was clear that "New Germany" had been an abject failure and personal destruction could not be avoided, Bernhard Förster poisoned himself, just like Hitler, Göring, and Goebbels after him. In fact, like Hitler and Eva Braun, the matriarch and patriarch of "New Germany" would not intend to survive the failure of their project. Bernhard Förster was quoted by Dr. Jaensch, a German doctor residing in Paraguay at the time, that "he and his wife would simply take poison if the colonial project failed." [518] The "master," or rather Fuhrer, had also shown the vile of poison to at least one of the colonists.

However, the end of "New Germany" proved to be the beginning of Friedrich Nietzsche's notoriety. Elisabeth did not share in Bernhard's penchant for the theatrical and did not take her own life in Wagnerian fashion. Elisabeth returned to Germany to continue propagandizing "New Germany" at the same time usurping power over her brother's estate to position herself as the icon that she ultimately became. Elisabeth martyred her fallen husband by playing into the xenophobia that had bought them notoriety in the first place:

> Oh you anti-Semites, is that your loyalty, your courage, shamefully to abandon one of your most ideal leaders?. . . Anti-Semitism has above all a positive aspect: the urge to deepen and ennoble the true German characteristics; it is motivated

---

[518] Pg. 143 - "Forgotten Fatherland: The search for Elisabeth Nietzsche", Ben Macintyre, Macmillan, 1992.

by the urge to create or renew institutions which strengthen true Germanness in an idealistic or economic sense and protect it from foreign influences... What is my husband fighting for here and now? Is it not true Germanness? And the goal? Is it not to create a new German place as a substitute for the old?... Let anti-Semitism prove through action, here in Nueva Germania, that it aims to create something in the true German tradition. (Pg. 137–138, "Forgotten Fatherland: The search for Elisabeth Nietzsche", Macmillan, 1992)

Elisabeth would dedicate the rest of her life to publicizing their work. Much of her motivation was her economic need, and her needs overlapped with the power her devotees in the new National Socialist government acquired. Much of her collaboration and pandering in the National Socialist political campaign was in exchange for political favors in the form of extended copyrights for the literary work in her brother's estate, and further aggrandizement of the Nietzsche myth by the National Socialist state. As such, the construction of memorials and museums were part of the propaganda exchange between Elisabeth Nietzsche and the National Socialist movement.

It must be noted that all of this was done against her brother's clearly expressed wishes. Friedrich had made it painfully clear, while he still had control over his mind and voice, that he wanted absolutely nothing to do with his sister's anti-Semitic colony or any of his brother-in-law's anti-Semitic propaganda. Elisabeth had tried tapping Friedrich for money to support her "New Germany" and Friedrich had at all times turned her down by clearly expressing his disapproval. Macintyre quotes Friedrich Nietzsche:

> My position is financially insecure, and yours has not been proven. But above all our wishes and our interests do not coincide insofar as your project is an anti-Semitic one. If Dr. Förster's project succeeds, then I will be happy on your behalf and as far as I can, I will ignore the fact that it is the triumph of a movement which I reject. If it fails I shall rejoice in the death of an anti-Semitic project. (Pg. 128, "Forgotten Fatherland: The search for Elisabeth Nietzsche", Macmillan, 1992)

Much has been written in an attempt to surgically separate Friedrich Nietzsche from the movements Elisabeth Nietzsche made him an integral part of. Typically, either the Nietzsche following misunderstands the true nature of National Socialism and bases its assumptions on pedestrian generalities of its history, or those that understand National Socialism misunderstand Friedrich Nietzsche. Neither of these views actually matter as the historically accurate realization is that Friedrich's work would never have been known to the extent that it is today if it were not for Elisabeth's tireless efforts to create the mythos surrounding it. Much of that need burning inside of Elisabeth Nietzsche was born out of personal ambitions intertwined with the "New Germany" project. These efforts cannot be separated from the propaganda exchanges made between Elisabeth Nietzsche and Hitler's National Socialist government.

Furthermore, as this book evidences, Friedrich Nietzsche did not need to condone anti-Semitism in order to deeply influence National Socialism. No one can deny the anti-clerical aspect of Nietzsche's work, which was explicitly intended to engender a "New Ethic" and discard traditional morality. The underlying current throughout this aspect of Nietzsche's work is his disdain for sentimentalism, and this would be his most significant contribution to National Socialism. Surely one could spend volumes debating if Nietzsche's "superman" or "overman" was the inspiration for National Socialism's eugenic program to elevate the Aryan breeding stock. However, it is the derision Nietzsche showers on the Judeo-Christian mores of compassion and sentimentalism that made him an indispensable tool for the National Socialists. It is the complicity of great minds, Nietzsche included, that sustains that one question about The Holocaust alive: <u>How do you convince the most highly educated and cultured people of the era to engage in mass murder?</u> The answer is clear if one is open to the uncomfortable political and cultural implications: You can conscript the most educated as your "willing executioners" if you appeal to their intellect and vanity, as asking them to act like a mob cannot be sustained for the decade that National Socialism endured. Mobs murder in smaller scales even when highly organized as the KKK was. In order to systematically eradicate millions upon millions of innocent women and children National Socialism needed the calculated and methodical aspects of science and technology, and more importantly, sanction from ideological icons of high stature, precisely like Nietzsche.

Lately much has been written to portray The Holocaust as a haphazard undertaking. Certainly, these mass-murderers encountered their share of obstacles. This only serves to prove this point. One must realize that it required a methodical persistence, dedication, and ingenuity to overcome the obstacles natural to the disposal of millions upon millions of cadavers. It is this persistence and organization of resources that must be sustained. Sustaining nearly a decade of brutality is made possible by making the project a scientifically respectable and ideologically justified effort. Alas, the commander in charge of Auschwitz hung a plaque above his desk that stated that "Compassion was weakness," and this plaque goes a long way to explain what happened. Hitler Youth and the SS troops were trained to see "compassion" as "weakness," and death camp staff was hand-picked upon the ability to discard with traditional compassion and Christian sentimentality. The success and failure of The Holocaust thus hinged on the ability to discard traditional values, namely in the overturning of the traditional medical ethics otherwise enshrined in the Hippocratic Oath. Even the age-old secular value of promising to "do no harm" to the individual patient had to be overturned and discarded for the medical and scientific community to offer the collaboration Hitler's government found indispensable to their cause. All of Hitler's "willing executioners" were part of the upper echelons of the most educated and culturally sophisticated country of the era. That these elite sectors of humanity were able to act with such methodical brutality and dedication evidence the philosophical foundation of National Socialism.

Thus, it is impossible, if not laughable to try to pry Nietzsche from The Holocaust. Nietzsche was being dragged into the debate surrounding eugenics even prior to The Holocaust, even though he was not anti-Semitic or even a supporter of Darwin:

> In Britain, the members of Francis Galton's Eugenics Society also included a number of Nietzscheans, such as Maximilian Mügge (who characterized Nietzsche as "the pioneer of eugenics") and Havelock Ellis. Mügge, in an article titled "Eugenics and the Superman," which appeared in the Eugenics Review, placed a racist construction on Nietzsche's concept of the will to power. Eugenicists characteristically insisted on reading Darwinism into Nietzsche's thought in spite of Nietzsche's profound mistrust of Charles Darwin. (Pgs. 85-86, "Historical Dictionary of Nietzscheanism", Carol Diethe, Scarecrow Press, 2007)

Macintyre, the author of "Forgotten Fatherland," is part of the camp that disagrees that National Socialism can be attributed to Nietzsche, but provides a tantalizing quote from Nietzsche himself on these matters:

> I know my fate. One day there will be associated with my name the recollection of something frightful, of a crisis like no other before on earth, of the profoundest collision of conscience, of a decision evoked against everything that until then had been believed in, demanded, sanctified. I am not a man. I am dynamite. (Frontmatter of "Forgotten Fatherland" - quoting Nietzsche, "Ecce Homo", Chap.: Why I am Destiny)

Chap. 14: 1884 to 1880

EUROPEAN FRONT: THE MARRIED WOMEN'S PROPERTY ACT 1882 IN BRITAIN ENABLES WOMEN TO BUY, OWN AND SELL PROPERTY AND TO KEEP THEIR OWN EARNINGS. **SCIENCE & TECHNOLOGY**: MEXICAN GENERAL MANUEL MONDRAGÓN CREATES THE MONDRAGÓN RIFLE THE WORLD'S FIRST AUTOMATIC RIFLE. LIFE: HARRY S. TRUMAN, 33 PRESIDENT OF THE UNITED STATES IS BORN. – ELEANOR ROOSEVELT, FIRST LADY OF THE UNITED STATES IS BORN. – GREGOR MENDEL, CZECH GENETICIST WHO STARTED A EUGENIC AND GENETIC REVOLUTION DIES. ANTONI GAUDÍ BEGINS TO BUILD THE SAGRADA FAMÍLIA CATHEDRAL. - **LIFE** MAGAZINE IS FOUNDED. – JOHN MAYNARD KEYNES, ENGLISH ECONOMIST, EUGENICIST, AND SOCIALIST IS BORN. – LOTHROP STODDARD, AMERICAN EUGENICIST AND RACIST IS BORN. – ANGELA HITLER, AUSTRIAN ELDER HALF-SISTER OF ADOLF HITLER IS BORN. – THE GERMAN COMPOSER RICHARD WAGNER DIES OF A HEART ATTACK IN VENICE, ITALY. ALOIS HITLER, JR., AUSTRIAN ELDER HALF-BROTHER OF ADOLF HITLER IS BORN. – FRANKLIN DELANO ROOSEVELT, 32 PRESIDENT OF THE UNITED STATES IS BORN. – RALPH WALDO EMERSON, AMERICAN PHILOSOPHER AND WRITER DIES. – STANDARD OIL OF NEW JERSEY IS ESTABLISHED. PABLO PICASSO, SPANISH PAINTER IS BORN. – FYODOR DOSTOEVSKY, RUSSIAN NOVELIST DIES. - HELEN KELLER, AMERICAN SPOKESWOMAN FOR THE DEAF AND BLIND IS BORN. - RICHARD STRAUSS' FIRST MAJOR WORK, A SYMPHONY IN D MINOR, IS PREMIERED.

Sec. I - PACE V. ALABAMA:

Pace v. Alabama was a case in which the US Supreme Court affirmed that Alabama's anti-miscegenation statute was constitutional. "Miscegenation" was defined as marriage, cohabitation and sexual relations between whites and "negroes" by Alabama's statute, Ala. code 4189. After the Civil War, the reconstituted Alabama legislature had passed an anti-miscegenation measure in 1866, which made interracial marriage and interracial sex a felony that resulted in a prison sentence of two to seven years. The plaintiff, Tony Pace, an African-American man, and Mary Cox, a white woman, were residents of the state of Alabama, who had been arrested in 1881 because of their sexual relationship. They were sentenced to two-years imprisonment, charged with "adultery or fornication," not with marriage or attempted marriage, as interracial marriage simply would not have been possible in Alabama at the time.

Both Pace and Cox appealed their conviction. They both claimed the anti-miscegenation statute violated the U.S. Constitution. On appeal, the Alabama Supreme Court affirmed their conviction, ruling that the statute did not violate the equal protection clause of the Fourteenth Amendment because it did not constitute discrimination for or against either race to prohibit interracial sexual relations. While focusing on the crime of "adultery or fornication" and not mentioning the state statute's prohibition of interracial marriage directly, the court did go on to condemn all sexual relations between whites and blacks on a eugenic basis:

> The evil tendency of the crime [of adultery or fornication] is greater when committed between persons of the two races ... Its result may be the amalgamation of the two races, producing a mongrel population and a degraded civilization, the prevention of which is dictated by a sound policy affecting the highest interests of society and government. (Pace & Cox v. State, 69 Ala 231, 233 - 1882)

Pace's attorney, John Tompkins, appealed the ruling to the US Supreme Court. Apart from the passing of the Fourteenth Amendment, there was little case law to serve as precedent at the federal level at this moment in time. Thus, the Supreme Court based its decision to uphold the penalties and punishments against Pace and Cox upon the premise that the penalties and punishments had been "equal" for both the white and black persons, thus not in violation of the "equal protection" clause:

> The counsel is undoubtedly correct in his view of the purpose of the clause of the amendment in question, that it was to prevent hostile and discriminating state legislation against any person or class of persons. Equality of protection under the laws implies not only accessibility by each one, whatever his race, on the same terms with others to the courts of the country for the security of his person and property, but that in the administration of criminal justice he shall not be subjected, for the same offense, to any greater or different punishment. Such was the view of congress in the re-enactment of the civil-rights act, after the adoption of the amendment. -- The one prescribes, generally, a punishment for an offense committed between persons of different sexes; the other prescribes a punishment for an offense which can only be committed where the two sexes are of different races. There is in neither section any discrimination against either race. Section 4184 equally includes the offense when the persons of the two sexes are both white and when they are both black. Section 4189 applies the same punishment to both offenders, the white and the black. (Pace & Cox v. State, 69 Ala 231, 233 - 1882)

The United States Supreme Court overturned Pace v. Alabama in 1967, in Loving v. Virginia, and in the 1964 case of McLaughlin v. Florida. Loving v. Virginia, 388 US 1 (1967) was a landmark civil rights case in which the US Supreme Court, in a unanimous decision, declared Virginia's anti-miscegenation statute, the Racial Integrity Act of 1924, unconstitutional, thereby overturning Pace v. Alabama (1883) and ending all race based legal restrictions on marriage in the United States. The plaintiffs, Mildred Loving and Richard Perry Loving were residents of the Commonwealth of Virginia who had been married in June 1958 in the District of Columbia, having left Virginia to evade the Racial Integrity Act. Upon their return to Virginia, they were charged with a violation of the ban. They were found sleeping in their bed by a group of police officers who had invaded their home in the hopes of finding them in the act of sex. In their defense, Mrs. Loving had pointed to a marriage certificate on the wall in their bedroom. Ironically, this marriage certificate became the evidence the police needed for a criminal charge, as it proved they were in fact married. Specifically, they were charged under Section 20-58 of the Virginia Code, which prohibited interracial couples from being married out of state and then returning to Virginia, as well Section 20-59, which classified "miscegenation" as a felony, punishable by a prison sentence of between one and five years. On January 6, 1959, the Loving couple pled guilty and was sentenced to one year in prison, with the sentence suspended for 25 years on condition that the couple moved out of the State. The lower court judge, Leon M. Bazile, justified his opinion by attempting an interpretation, not of law, but of God's intentions:

> Almighty God created the races white, black, yellow, malay and red, and he placed them on separate continents. And but for the interference with his

arrangement there would be no cause for such marriages. The fact that he separated the races shows that he did not intend for the races to mix. (Pg. 7, Werner Sollors, "Interracialism: Black-White Intermarriage in American History, Literature, and Law", Oxford Univ. Press, 2000)

The Loving couple moved to the District of Columbia, and on November 6, 1963, the American Civil Liberties Union filed a motion on their behalf in the state trial court to vacate the judgment and set aside the sentence on the grounds that the violated statutes ran counter to the Fourteenth Amendment. This set in motion a series of lawsuits that ultimately reached the Supreme Court. The US Supreme Court overturned the convictions in a unanimous decision, dismissing the Commonwealth of Virginia's argument that a law forbidding both white and black persons from marrying persons of another race, and providing identical penalties to white and black violators, could not be construed as racially discriminatory. The court ruled that Virginia's anti-miscegenation statute violated both the Due Process Clause and the Equal Protection Clause of the Fourteenth Amendment. In its decision, the court wrote:

> Marriage is one of the "basic civil rights of man," fundamental to our very existence and survival.... To deny this fundamental freedom on so unsupportable a basis as the racial classifications embodied in these statutes, classifications so directly subversive of the principle of equality at the heart of the Fourteenth Amendment, is surely to deprive all the State's citizens of liberty without due process of law. The Fourteenth Amendment requires that the freedom of choice to marry not be restricted by invidious racial discrimination. Under our Constitution, the freedom to marry, or not marry, a person of another race resides with the individual and cannot be infringed by the State. (Loving v. Virginia, 388 US 1 (1967)

The Supreme Court concluded that anti-miscegenation laws were inherently discriminatory and had been enacted to perpetuate white supremacy:

> There is patently no legitimate overriding purpose independent of invidious racial discrimination which justifies this classification. The fact that Virginia prohibits only interracial marriages involving white persons demonstrates that the racial classifications must stand on their own justification, as measures designed to maintain White Supremacy. (Loving v. Virginia, 388 US 1 (1967)

The respect for the right to contract or marry can hardly be said to be revelations of the late 1960s. The question should not be why the court that presided over Loving v. Virginia saw fit to respect these traditional concepts. The more pressing question is why, a century earlier in Pace v. Alabama, it had chosen to ignore them. The reason why the State of Alabama enacted such a law in the immediate aftermath of the Civil War is self-explanatory. They simply could not conceive of a world where past masters comingled on equal terms with the population that just days prior had been their slaves. It is no revelation that the pro-slavery forces saw individuals of African descent as inferior. The reasons why Vice-

President turned President Andrew Johnson turned away from Abraham Lincoln's policies have been well documented. The real question, which has not been satisfactorily addressed, is why the US Supreme Court of the 1880s forced the country to take a 180-degree turn from the costly gains of the Civil War and uphold the bigoted views of pro-slavery bigots. This is where the real and lasting damage was inflicted. The activism of the ex-Confederate sympathizers was to be expected, in fact, anticipated. The role that the US Supreme Court played in making racial hierarchies lawful was not the role that the Union's high court was expected to play. The reality is that the Pace v. Alabama opinion was hardly an aberration. This Supreme Court, being appointed mostly by Abraham Lincoln and Ulysses S. Grant, time and time again fell on the wrong side of history. It delivered a score of opinions that all but emasculated and voided the Civil Rights Amendments and statutes passed as the result of the Civil War. It did so again in Cumming v. Richmond County Board of Education, 175 US 528 (1899); in that instance, Justice Harlan, wrote an opinion that condoned the State of Georgia's failure to provide a high school for "colored" children as it did for white children. Justice Harlan, in palpable duplicity, argued against his own logic in other similar opinions, that "unequal" accommodations did not violate the Fourteenth Amendment.

The contradictory nature and myopic logic of the decisions delivered by the same set of Justices naturally leaves one doubting their intentions and perceiving an agenda. The fact that a different generation of Justices delivered equally dubious opinions leaves one doubting the institution as a whole. In 1927, the same year as the infamous Buck v. Bell opinion, the court ruled in Lum v. Rice, 275 US 78 (1927) that a child of Chinese descent could not attend the "white" school in her district because she was not considered "white" by their standards. What precisely were these racial standards? What were the legally binding racial hierarchies and definitions?

The answers to these questions can be found in the logic of two other opinions of the same decade. The US Supreme Court first in Ozawa v. United State, 260 US 178 (1922) and then in United States v. Thind, 261 US 204 (1923) delved into the question of racial definitions and demarcations. In Ozawa, the court held that "a person of the Japanese race" is not a "white person" and therefore was not eligible for citizenship in the United States. In Thind, the court similarly barred an individual of naturalized citizenship as he was a "high caste Hindu of full Indian blood." The court fully admitted not using a "scientific" definition of "white" or "Caucasian," but rather a "popular" understanding of the term. As we have seen, this same set of Justices condemned Carrie Buck to forced sterilization largely on the basis that she belonged to an undesirable and unwanted group of "poor, Southern, whites." Thus, the most accurate appraisal of this recurring racial selection process comes from Professor Daylanne K. English, who observed in her book "Unnatural Selections" that these "elitists" were practicing "self-selection."

As we know, the consequences of the Supreme Court's decisions upholding racial divisions were not limited to the United States. We know for a fact that eugenic studies of these court cases reached Adolf Hitler through the book written by Fritz Lenz, Erwin Baur, and Eugen Fischer. Recall that their book on miscegenation,

"*Menschliche Erblichkeitslehre und Rassenhygiene*" was personally taken to Hitler by J.F. Lehmann. Both Stefan Kühl of "The Nazi Connection" and Dr. Devra Davis of "The Secret History of the War on Cancer" felt this Hitler quote was important:
> I have studied with interest the **laws of several** American **states** concerning prevention of reproduction by people whose progeny would, in all probability, be of no value or be injurious to the racial stock. (emphasis mine, Davis - Pg. 52 / Kühl – Pg. 37)

Dr. Davis goes on to record that Hitler's unpublished book, "*Zweiter Buch*" (Second Book) which was to follow "Mein Kampf" in 1928 further declares Hitler's admiration for the anti-miscegenation laws in the United States:
> He contended that America was a dynamic, "racially successful" society that practiced eugenics and segregation and kept out "racially degenerate" immigrants from eastern and southern Europe. Hitler believed that the majority of Americans were true "Aryans" who felt, as he did, keenly threatened by a Jewish plutocracy. (Pg. 53, "The Secret History of the War on Cancer", Basic Books, 2009)

Eugen Fischer's 1913 book "The Rehoboth Bastards and the Problem of Miscegenation among Humans" delved deeply into understanding American anti-miscegenation laws as a basis for Fischer's proposals to prohibit black-white interracial offspring resulting from German African colonies, and Fischer's work would reach Hitler in the form of the infamous "Baur-Fischer-Lenz" book which dutifully cataloged and explained American, British, and Scandinavian eugenic laws. Clearly, the anti-miscegenation laws of the individual States did not address immigration into the United States, as this is purely the jurisdiction of the Federal law. Thus, Hitler's reference to keeping out "immigrants from eastern and southern Europe" can only be attributed to Harry H. Laughlin, Madison Grant, and Charles Davenport. Hitler was clearly referring to their work in passing Federal immigration restriction laws such as the Immigration Restriction Act in 1924, for which Harry H. Laughlin served as an expert for Congress prior to its passing. Hitler's reference to the "laws of several American states" is clearly a reference to the eugenic laws implemented by the 30 States detailed in the "Baur-Fischer-Lenz" book, or more precisely, Harry Laughlin's 1914 "Legal Aspects of Sterilization" and the 1922 "Eugenical Sterilization," which Fritz Lenz and Ernst Rüdin personally requested copies of. It also alludes to the various books by Paul Popenoe and Ezra Gosney on sterilizations in California. We know this because these are the publications J.F. Lehmann brought to Hitler's jail cell while he was researching and writing "Mein Kampf."

In retrospect, one can logically arrive at the conclusion that anti-miscegenation laws of the individual States would never have amounted to much, and definitely not gained the recognition by zealots half a world away, if the United States Supreme Court would not have sanctioned them. This is after all the stated reason the US Supreme Court exists: to protect the rights of the citizens against the unlawful encroachment of government, namely the abuses of power by State governments. This is the purpose of the Fourteenth Amendment, to check and balance against the State government's violations of the Bill of Rights and the Declaration of Independence. Clearly, the historical justification, legal precedent, and the laws at the Federal level existed at the time of opinions like Pace v. Alabama. No new Amendments were passed between Pace v. Alabama in 1883 and Loving v. Virginia in 1967. The US Supreme Court of 1967 was armed with the same statutes, same Amendments to the Constitution, and the same Bill of Rights and Declaration of Independence as it was in 1883. Yet, the results were drastically different and diametrically opposed to the earlier decisions. The disparity is disheartening. Hence, the impact of the US Supreme Court's clout when analyzed by foreigners cannot be overstated. Stefan Kühl documents the influence American racial laws on the creation of Hitler's National Socialist State:

> Nazi propagandists reacted to American criticism by arguing that ethnic minorities in the United States were treated in a similar way as were Jews in Germany. According to the Nazi view, large parts of the American public were critical of discrimination against the Jews, but did not apply the same standards to all forms of ethnic racism, particularly in regard to blacks. (Pg. 98, "The Nazi Connection: Eugenics, American Racism, and German National Socialism", Oxford Univ. Press, 1994)

Stefan Kühl also points to the 1939 "*Nationalsozialistiche Partei Korrespondenz*" article titled "Double Standard in the US." The article pointed to the fact that Americans thought of themselves as the country of freedom with the self-imposed task of defending humankind from the "race mania" of the National Socialist state at a time when lynching in the United States was at its peak. The anti-lynching laws were provided as an example of the American "double-standard." Stefan Kühl adds that the *"Berliner Börsenzeitung"* pointed out that Jews in Germany were not being "lynched." The article went on to state:

> The Nigger would well be surprised that the white American becomes outraged at the elimination of Jews from German universities, while they do not even consider the exclusion of Negroes from many American universities. (Pg. 99, "The Nazi Connection: Eugenics, American Racism, and German National Socialism", Oxford Univ. Press, 1994)

Case in point, the *"Preussiche Zeitung"* newspaper claimed in 1937 that in thirty states marriage between blacks and whites was forbidden. The *"Preussiche Zeitung"* also reported on American segregation laws and the frequency of lynching, a racial crime the *"Zeitung"* proudly stated did not occur in Germany. This is not an observation that escaped prominent African-Americans. We know that W.E.B. DuBois made the distinction between the racial laws in Hitler's Germany being lawful and the laws in the United States being unconstitutional. [519] We also know

---

[519] Pg. 197 – Notes to Ch. One, "Unnatural Selections: Eugenics in American Modernism and the Harlem Renaissance", Daylanne K. English, Univ. of North Carolina Press, 2004.

that the accomplished Olympic athlete, Jesse Owens, also felt he was treated more favorably by the Germans during the 1936 Olympic Games than he was home in the United States.

As difficult as it may be to agree with these observations, there is a reason why Jesse Owens and W.E.B. DuBois made such controversial observations. There was a fundamental difference between the "racism" of the lynch mob and the "scientific racism" of The Holocaust. While one may be able to draw comparisons between the intimidation that the Brown Shirts brought upon the daily lives of German Jews with the intimidation of the lynch mobs, the truth is that Hitler's National Socialists looked to prestigious educational institutions such as Harvard, Yale, Stanford and the research labs funded by the Rockefellers and the Carnegies for the information necessary to erect their eugenic state. They utilized legislation that had been seasoned in the Supreme Courts of 30 of the States and then in the US Supreme Court. Theirs was a "scientific racism" which was inspired by no less than Francis Galton, Ernst Haeckel, Thomas Huxley, H.G. Wells, George Bernard Shaw, Charles Darwin and his son Leonard Darwin.

The facile and commonplace conclusion is that the United States is a racist country. It is quite decidedly not. There was an equal or greater amount of resistance to the Supreme Court opinions between 1846 and 1946 as there was support. A brutal Civil War resulted from the opposing views, and an entire Nation suffered the consequences of a Civil War for the benefit of a minority slave population, which at the point amounted to not much more than 10 percent of its total population. The subsequent failure of some powerful Americans to follow the lead of the Founding Fathers does not in any way detract from the concepts consecrated in the Declaration of Independence or the US Constitution. Furthermore, it should not escape historians that those Americans complicit with Hitler's scientists and legislators can be pinpointed, separated, and identified. This group of people did not represent the greater population, and much of their elitist-racism was focused on eradicating every-day Americans whose only crime was being poor or lacking a formal education. However, in the end, the surest proof of just how "tolerant" the American people are is evidenced in the reaction of the Germans at the end of the war: the ex-Nazis did a mad dash towards the American front and decidedly away from the French or Soviet forces in an effort to reach the captors most likely to treat them humanely.

Sec. 2 - WEISMANN'S "GERM-PLASM":

Friedrich Leopold August Weismann coined the term "germ-plasm," which would be regurgitated by both eugenic propagandists and serious scientists alike for ages after him in support of both illegitimate and legitimate scientific efforts. The term would be used interchangeably with "gene pool" or "purity of blood" concepts by eugenicists. Scientifically speaking, "germ plasm" or polar plasm is a zone found in the cytoplasm of the egg cells of some organisms. More precisely, identifying the role of the polar plasm proved the "inherited" theory of human evolution, as opposed to the theory "acquired traits" that had competed in scientific circles. Weismann's first rejection of the inheritance of acquired traits was in a lecture in 1883, titled "On inheritance." ("*Über die Vererbung*") Elof Axel Carlson, author of "The Unfit" documents the pivotal importance of Weismann's work:

> Weismann, like Darwin, did not know the source of variations on which natural selection acted. Weismann, however, severely damaged the belief in the inheritance of any form of acquired characteristics. The shift among scientists was dramatic; before the 1870s almost all scientists believed Lamarckism, in some form, must be correct. By the mid-1880s serious doubts were expressed that this could be so, and after Weismann's analysis, adherents of Lamarckism dwindled year by year as the 19th century entered its waning years. Natural selection worked, with or without a Lamarckian mechanism for the origin of variations. The variations themselves were real. A parallel debate on the social significance of heredity was quite different in its outcome. Lamarckism implied the potential reversibility of undesirable traits; Weismann's theory of the germ plasm with refutation of Lamarckism created a pessimism in which those saddled with defective heredities were doomed to live less adaptive lives and to be stigmatized as possessing defective germ plasm. (Pg. 153, "The Unfit: A History of a Bad Idea", Cold Spring Harbor Press, 2001)

More to the point, making Lamarckism go out of fashion had significant, if not severe, social implications. Without Weismann, the eugenic-minded scientists had a significantly weaker argument in support of their calls for segregation, sterilization and euthanasia. In essence, Weismann dissuaded an entire generation of scientists from taking any environmental causes for allegedly hereditary defects seriously. By defeating Lamarck's "acquired characteristics," Weismann took the focus away from environmental causes for any defects, social or biological. This is of incredible importance in the history of eugenics as it made sterilization, segregation and euthanasia seem like the only viable options to rid humanity of the defects that were thus perceived to occur only because of defective genes, as opposed to being open to the possibility that the victims of such defects may have developed said defects from their interaction with the environment. Clearly, if environmental causes, such as poor nutrition, poor sanitary conditions, and other symptoms of poverty were attributed as the culprits, then extreme solutions such as sterilization would not have been given the consideration they were ultimately given.

The 1936 book commissioned by the Carnegie Foundation which was used to discontinue their support of the Cold Spring Harbor facility, "Eugenic Sterilization," makes direct reference to this portion of medical history:

> Moreover, it is clearly becoming apparent that geneticists and biologists, generally speaking, are retreating from the position in which they were placed by a whole-hearted acceptance of Weismannism. The reaction against Lamarck was extreme. It became quite the biological fashion to deny the environment any

place in the constitution of man, despite the obvious fact that nowhere in the world is there a germplasm which is not continually being bombarded, penetrated, and continuously molded by the environment. (Pg. 71, Abraham Myerson, "Eugenic Sterilization: A Reorientation of the Problem", American Neurological Association, Committee for the Investigation of Eugenical Sterilization, Macmillan, 1936)

The best example of this scientific and medical conundrum would have to be the disease of "pellagra," which was touted as a hereditary defect by Harvard eugenicist Charles B. Davenport for decades after lesser-known scientists had proven that "pellagra" was nothing more than the consequences of poverty. The story of "pellagra" has gone down in history as one of the biggest blunders, or more precisely, frauds of medical history. More specifically, it is the story of science turning its gaze away from environmental factors and focusing too much on hereditary origins for ailments it sought to cure. Allan Chase documents that in 1902, two previously unknown Americans, Charles Wardel Stiles and Irving C. Norwood, combined their talents to deliver a body blow to the claims of the international eugenics movement. Stiles was a parasitologist with the US Department of Agriculture and the son of a Methodist minister. Stiles had graduated from Wesleyan University in Connecticut and then set off to Europe to study medical zoology at the Collège de France, the University of Berlin, the University of Leipzig, and the Pasteur Institute. It is at this time that Stiles became interested in studying the hookworm, which had been discovered in 1789 in Germany. Note Allan Chase's characterization of Stiles:

> As the child of a family that took seriously the same Christian ethics despised by people like Madison Grant, Stiles was impressed as much by the social as by the medical challenges of hookworm disease. (Pgs. 193-194, "Legacy of Malthus: The Social Costs of the New Scientific Racism", Allan Chase, 1975)

Stiles would prove that much of the laziness attributed to poor Southern whites and blacks, and poor people, in general, was the proximate cause of hookworm invading the body and causing a thinning of the blood. The thinned blood, in turn, provided poor nourishment for the brain and the muscles. Stiles was ignored until December 1902, when Stiles presented a paper on hookworm disease at the Pan-American Sanitary Conference in Washington, D.C. The reporter that covered the conference for the "The New York Sun" was Irving C. Norwood. Allan Chase quotes Stiles recollection of Norwood's article:

> . . . reported the address with the headline that the "Germ of Laziness" had been discovered. This press story was published throughout the world, causing amusement in some circles and indignation in some quarters. My interpretation is that this newspaper reporter contributed an exceedingly valuable piece of work in disseminating knowledge concerning hookworm disease. The "Germ of Laziness" became common information. It would have taken scientific authors years of hard work to direct as much attention to this subject as Mr. Norwood did through his use of the expression "Germ of Laziness." (Pgs. 197-198, "Legacy of Malthus: The Social Costs of the New Scientific Racism", 1975)

Stiles was being modest or diplomatic. In hindsight, the reason he had such an uphill battle in changing opinions was that he was unknown in the scientific community, and to make matters worse, he was challenging the *a priori* notions of the Ivy League scientific elite, namely that of Charles B. Davenport. Stiles was challenging the eugenic notion that the less productive members of society were so because of heredity, instead of the living conditions. "Pellagra," otherwise known as miner's disease, brickmaker's disease, coolie's disease, and Negro slave's disease had been attributed to poor heredity by the international eugenics movement; and per their estimations, no cure was possible. The truth of the matter is that "pellagra" was caused not by deficient heredity, but by the lack of modern plumbing, toilets, the lack of footwear, and most importantly, the lack of sufficient food to compensate for the nutrients stolen by the parasites. "Pellagra" was decidedly not a disease of poor heredity. It was in fact, a disease of the conditions of poverty which prevailed mainly in the economically depressed American South.

Yet, it was not the public that needed convincing. It was the medical community, and this community's bread was buttered by the institutions that controlled the journals and the grants. Years after Stiles had provided incontrovertible evidence, Dr. Edward Jenner Wood, the chairman of the Pellagra Commission of the North Carolina State Board of Health still claimed that "the cause of pellagra is still unknown, and, indeed, at the present time there is more uncertainty about the whole matter than ever before." [520] Clearly, Dr. Wood did not know of or care for the work of Dr. Charles Wardel Stiles.

Allan Chase reports that in 1914, even with the backing of the US Public Health Service's Joseph Goldberger, Stiles still faced the formidable task of upending Charles B. Davenport's hold on the American scientific community. As Chase reports, Goldberger was more than technically trained to take on the challenge. He was also a victim. Not only had he been born poor but had the bad luck of contracting various parasites while conducting his research. Goldberger had contracted three of the diseases he was investigating, including yellow fever, dengue fever, and typhus. He was one of five children from a poor Jewish immigrant family from New York's Lower East Side. This gave him insight into the fraudulent medical accusations being laid by the Ivy League physicians on people from poor economic backgrounds. Furthermore, Goldberger was astute enough to go outside of the medical community, and cross-reference his findings with economic statistics. He hired Edgar Sydenstricker of the Public Health Service to prove the correlation between economics and the contracting of the disease. Yet, this was not enough for Goldberger. Goldberger, his wife, and his research associates proceeded to inject blood from an infected victim, to swallow pills made of a carrier's intestinal discharge, and even swallow pills containing pieces of the scales from the skin rashes common to the illness. None of them contracted "Pellagra," but Goldberger did not stop there. Goldberger conclusively proved that Pellagra was a disease of poverty by

---

[520] Pg. 202 - "Treatise on Pellagra for the General Practitioner", Dr. Edward Jenner Wood, State Board of Health, North Carolina, Pellagra Commission, 1912.

proving that the disease could be caused by making his test subjects live on a high-carbohydrate, high-fat, no-protein diet designed to simulate the typical diet of the world's poor.

Notably, Goldberger's success caused the two men in charge of the Pellagra Commission to quit and to admit that Goldberg was right. Unfortunately, the man that would take over the Pellagra Commission was none other than Charles B. Davenport. Between 1914, the year Goldberger had disproven Davenport, and 1928, the deaths attributed to Pellagra multiplied eightfold, from 847 to 6,523 per year. [521] This was a testament to Davenport's Ivy League reputation. In 1916, with full knowledge of the reasons why his predecessors at the Pellagra Commission had quit, Charles B. Davenport published his eugenic-minded report on Pellagra in the "Archives of Internal Medicine." Allan Chase documents that a significant portion of the medical and scientific community was happy with Davenport's findings and thought of Pellagra in eugenic terms as late as 1933. Allan Chase reports that Charles B. Davenport reprinted his report in Bulletin No. 16 of the Eugenics Records Office and that this final report of the Pellagra Commission "is now a collector's item, particularly among those fascinated by great American frauds." Allan Chase explains:

> with the issuance of the Davenport-doctored final report of the Thomson Pellagra Commission, the more backward (if educated) segments of the greater society now had a very official report - over 400 pages long, with mathematical, genetical, and all-so-very-scientific tables and figures, signed by government physicians such as Garrison and Siler as well as by the man billed in the Sunday newspaper supplements as America's greatest biologist, C.B. Davenport. (Pg. 221, "Legacy of Malthus: The Social Costs of the New Scientific Racism", Alfred Knopf, 1975)

---

[521] Pg. 212 - "Legacy of Malthus: The Social Costs of the New Scientific Racism", Allan Chase, Alfred Knopf, 1975.

Chap. 15: 1879 to 1875

AMERICAN FRONT: Crazy Horse of the Oglala Sioux surrenders. — American President Rutherford B. Hayes signs a bill allowing female attorneys to argue cases before the Supreme Court of the United States. **SCIENCE & TECHNOLOGY:** Alexander Graham Bell is granted a patent for an invention he calls the telephone. — Nikolaus Otto files his patent for the four-stroke cycle internal combustion engine. Thomas Edison announces his invention of the phonograph. · Emile Berliner invents the microphone. **LIFE:** In Utica, New York, Frank Woolworth opens the first of many of 5 and 10-cent Woolworth stores. · Albert Einstein is born. Upton Sinclair, American writer is born. — Joseph Stalin is born. — Louis Chevrolet, Swiss-born race driver and automobile builder is born. · Heinz Tomato Ketchup introduced. · Adolphus Busch's brewery first markets Budweiser. D. W. Griffith, American film director of the controversial film The Birth of a Nation is born. — Ferdinand Porsche is born. — The first organized indoor game of ice hockey is played in Montreal, Canada.

Sec. I – FROM "STIRPICULTURE" TO "EUGENICS":

The Oneida Community, a religious commune founded by John Humphrey Noyes in 1848 in Oneida, New York, disintegrated into disarray and dissent, and finally came to its conclusion in 1879. Oneida was a "planned community," thus, it had no choice but to address the question of population to insure the equitable distribution of life's necessities. It was a collectivist venture that practiced Complex Marriage, Male Continence, Mutual Criticism, and Ascending Fellowship. "Complex marriage" was the first way of micro-managing the population of the commune, and this effort began with the colony in 1846. "Stirpiculture" was the resulting strategy for planning human capital of this community, which aimed at "perfectionism." The program was introduced in 1869, the same year Francis Galton published "Hereditary Genius." Like the later "race hygiene" by Alfred Ploetz and Galton's "eugenics," stirpiculture was a selective breeding program designed to systematically improve the biological capital of the community. Pierrepont B. Noyes was one of John Humphrey Noyes's various eugenically engineered children. Pierrepoint counted 62 different experiments similar to his father's:

> Communism was once rife in the US, but not the sort preached by Earl Browder and William Zebulon Foster. A religious, not a political belief, communism was attempted in 62 U. S. communities during the 19 Century, from Massachusetts' Brook Farm to Indiana's New Harmony. ---- Strangest of U. S. social experiments, these communist groups are now vaguely remembered as something between a co-operative and a free-love colony. Most successful, most notorious of all communist experiments was the Oneida Community, scene of the "world's one great experiment in human eugenics." The subject of many a historical sidelight, Oneida Community last week filled the background of an auto biography written by one of its "eugenic" descendants, whose father, John Humphrey Noyes, founded and led the Community for more than 30 years in the light of "scientific propagation and true Christian Communism." (time.com, "Books: Stirpiculture", TIME Mag., March 22, 1937)

John H. Noyes was born in September 1811 and educated at Dartmouth, Andover, and Yale. Graduating from Yale Theological Seminary in 1833, the redheaded, fanatic Noyes was caught up in the Perfectionist movement and joined a "Free Church" in New Haven. He was asked to leave the church when he declared himself "sinless" in 1834. Noyes gradually gained a position of authority in the Perfectionist movement, and he began to attract followers who located at Putney, Vermont. They signed a contract of partnership and formed the Putney Corporation. Noyes and his followers believed that the self-perfection they each sought was a four-stage process. First, one achieved spiritual perfection, which was followed by an intellectual perfection, then one strove toward moral and, finally, physical perfection. Noyes hoped to develop a Perfectionist group that would achieve these four stages of development successfully. However, complex marriage and male continence were not welcome in Putney, Vermont, and Noyes and his followers were expelled. This is why they ultimately migrated to Oneida, New York, where the infamous collectivist colony was established.

One of the allegedly "scientific" aspects of "complex marriage" was the practice of "*coitus reservatus*," or male continence. Male continence was essential to the colony's aspirations to control the time and place of birth. By controlling pregnancy, the colony could control the female members to freely practice a sexual communism. Here is Hilda Herrick Noyes, M.D. and George Wallingford Noyes, A.B., presumably John H. Noyes offspring, quoting him at the Second International Congress of Eugenics, where all the leading eugenicists would have heard her speak or read the official publication of the speeches:

> Male continence not only relieves us of undesirable propagation but opens the way for scientific propagation. We are not opposed to procreation . . . but we are in favor of intelligent, well-ordered procreation. The time will come when scientific combination will be freely and successfully applied to human generation. The common objection to Male Contience is that it is unnatural and unauthorized by the example of the lower animals. But cooking, wearing clothes, living in houses are unnatural in the same sense. In a higher sense I believe it is natural for rational beings by invention and discovery to improve nature. Until men and women by moral cultures elevate their sexual life above that of the brutes they are living in unnatural degradation. (Pg. 374, "Scientific Papers of the Second International Congress of Eugenics: Held at American Museum of Natural History, New York, September 22-28, 1921", Williams & Williams, 1923 - quoting John H. Noyes)

Complex marriage was started under strict regulations. The women were free to reject all suitors, and the sexual encounter was normally made through a third party whose function it was to record all such encounters for the preservation of community records. Child-rearing "took a village" in Oneida as well. The children were removed from the influence of their parents and placed under the care of the community members. The childcare program was the community's way of indoctrinating the children in the Perfectionist philosophy. Toys were owned by the community not the individual children, for example. In the twenty-three years from 1846 to 1869, there were only 44 births, with eight of these births to women who were pregnant prior to joining the community, five births which were sanctioned by the group, and the remaining 31 births were due to accidental conceptions in a population of approximately 200 adults. Unplanned births were a mortal sin to those obsessed with planned societies, so changes to the overall strategy inevitably followed. Stirpiculture or "scientific propagation" was not just a second step towards controlling reproduction in the commune; it was an attempt at breeding a new race. Noyes was attempting to produce a physical and moral improvement to the human race by explicitly prohibiting the breeding of "inferior" individuals, and by endorsing the propagation of children form the best individuals the community offered. The community unanimously voted to adopt the policy of Stirpiculture, and Noyes, of course, was anointed as the arbiter of "inferior" and "superior." Fifty-three women signed pledges dedicating themselves to the project. The pledge stipulated:

- That we do not belong to ourselves in any respect, but that we do belong first to God, and second to Mr. Noyes as God's true representative.
- That we have no rights or personal feelings in regard to child bearing which shall in the least degree oppose or embarrass him in his choice of scientific combinations.
- That we will put aside all envy, childishness and self-seeking, and rejoice with those who are chosen candidates; that we will, if necessary, become martyrs to science, and cheerfully resign all desire to become mothers, if for any reason Mr. Noyes deem us unfit material for propagation. Above all, we offer ourselves "living sacrifices" to God and true Communism.

In retrospect, the "furthering of liberty" was just a pretty phrase in the sleight-of-hand trick used to convince the credulous to forfeit all their liberties. Thirty-eight of the men of the community signed a similar document declaring their willingness to participate in the experiment. All the potential pairings were reviewed by Noyes and the stirpicultural committee, which existed for fifteen months beginning in 1875 before any individuals were allowed to have children. 51 applications were submitted, nine were rejected as "unfit" and 42 were accepted by him and the committee. There was a 12 to 13-year difference between the older males and younger females, which sometimes turned out to be uncle-to-niece parings. The documentation of the selection process was destroyed, but we know from other records that the selections were first based on the spiritual development of the parents, and later when the committee was formed, the physical and mental development of the parents played an important role. George Wallingford Noyes had compiled a journal of the Oneida colony. In it is the leadership's description of "stirpiculture" as a Darwinian experiment:

> We are studying Darwin and the Bible on stirpiculture; we intend to build the final wing of our Mansion house next summer, and give it to the children with the best equipment that science can furnish for their training; the Community has so far perfected the discipline of its affections that it is ready, as with one heart, for a faithful trial of the experiment of rational breeding." -- The resulting experiment in stirpiculture, or "eugenics" as it would now be called, extended

from 1869 to 1879 inclusive, a period of eleven years. (library.syr.edu, Chap.: Stirpiculture, "Life of John Humphrey Noyes", George Wallingford Noyes, Oneida Community Collection, Syracuse Univ., Vol. V, 1864-1878)

So, where did John H. Noyes get his inspiration for such radical ideas? Noyes was allegedly concerned for the common man, and thus he studied the writings of Robert Owen, the Scottish industrialist who was to leave Scotland and to open a more equitable society in the United States. He also read the doctrines of the French socialist Charles Fourier being heralded in the New York Tribune. Then came the economic depression of 1837, and Noyes turned to the communal economic doctrines which formed the basis of the Shakers and of Brook Farm, the latter of which had just been organized outside of Boston at West Roxbury. He became convinced that socialism without religion was impossible. Socialism combined with a religious devotion to perfectionism, however, could become invincible; an observation well in line with Galton's eugenic creed.

All Community members were expected to work, each according to his or her abilities. Women tended to do much of the domestic duties. Although more skilled jobs tended to remain with one person, Community members rotated through the more menial jobs, working in the house, the fields, or the various industries. Ironically enough, Oneida would become the most enduring of all the utopian colonies in the United States due to its success with free-market capitalism, namely the production and sale of the flatware of the Oneida name. As the Community thrived, it began to hire employees, and ultimately became a major employer in the area.

Each member of the Community had all his/her needs looked after: clothing and bedding supplies were furnished as needed, and each member eventually received pin money to spend. Since men and women worked together, this arrangement also forwarded the finding of new sexual partners. Those who shirked work were given "Mutual Criticism" and denied sexual partners. For the benefit and the edification of the residents, Noyes offered spiritual counseling and held discourses as to the meaning of life and the ways to improve it. The achievement of moral perfection, he stressed, was a beginning, not an end:

> We are opposed to excessive, and of course, oppressive procreation, which is almost universal. We are opposed to random procreation, which is unavoidable in the marriage system. But we are in favor of intelligent well-ordered procreation. The physiologists say that the race cannot be raised from ruin until propagation is made a matter of science; but they point out no way of making it so. Procreation is controlled and reduced to a science in the case of valuable domestic brutes; but marriage and fashion forbid any such system among human beings. We believe the time will come when involuntary and random propagation will cease, and when scientific combination will be applied to human generation as freely and successfully as it is to that of other animals. (Pgs. 55-66, "John Humphrey Noyes and the Stirpiculture Experiment," Philip R. Wyatt, Journal of the History of Medicine and Allied Sciences, Vol. 31, No. 1, January 1976)

This 1849 statement by Noyes came within a year of Marx and Engels 1848 "Communist Manifesto." Marx and Engels were well aware of the predecessors they had in the communes that had cropped up in the American countryside, and they wrote about their successes and failures. Mostly, they attempted to distance themselves from the overwhelming failure that these communal experiments came to represent during their time. "Utopian socialists" is the term Marx and Engels used to describe their predecessors, Noyes, Fourier, Saint-Simon, Owen, and others which had tried and failed at the various communal experiments. Marx and Engels officially distanced themselves from these failures in Chapter 3 of the "Communist Manifesto," and later wrote on what they deride as "vulgar socialism." Clearly, these experiments were present upon the minds of their contemporaries, and any proposal for a new socialist scheme had to address the failures of their predecessors and explain how they would be different. The topic must have been a lingering one for the duo, as Engels felt compelled to address it again and again, specifically in 1880 with an essay by Engels dedicated to the subject titled "Socialism: Utopian and Scientific." The following excerpts are from Chapter I, "The Development of Utopian Socialism":

> Then came the three great Utopians: Saint-Simon, to whom the middle-class movement, side by side with the proletarian, still had a certain significance; Fourier; and Owen, who in the country where capitalist production was most developed, and under the influence of the antagonisms begotten of this, worked out his proposals for the removal of class distinction systematically and in direct relation to French materialism. ---- One thing is common to all three. Not one of them appears as a representative of the interests of that proletariat which historical development had, in the meantime, produced. Like the French philosophers, they do not claim to emancipate a particular class to begin with, but all humanity at once. Like them, they wish to bring in the kingdom of reason and eternal justice, but this kingdom, as they see it, is as far as Heaven from Earth, from that of the French philosophers. (Pg. 5, "Socialism: Utopian and Scientific", S. Sonnenschein, 1892)

And referring to Saint-Simon, Fourier, and Owen, Engels states:
> In a word, compared with the splendid promises of the philosophers, the social and political institutions born of the "triumph of reason" were bitterly disappointing caricatures. ... This historical situation also dominated the founders of Socialism. To the crude conditions of capitalistic production and the crude class conditions correspond crude theories. The solution of the social problems, which as yet lay hidden in undeveloped economic conditions, the Utopians attempted to evolve out of the human brain. Society presented nothing but wrongs; to remove these was the task of reason. It was necessary, then, to discover a new and more perfect system of social order and to impose this upon society from without by propaganda, and, wherever it was possible, by the example of model experiments. These new social systems were foredoomed as Utopian; the more completely they were worked out in detail, the more they could not avoid drifting off into pure phantasies.

CONTINUES...

These facts once established, we need not dwell a moment longer upon this side of the question, now wholly belonging to the past. We can leave it to the literary small fry to solemnly quibble over these phantasies, which today only make us smile, and to crow over the superiority of their own bald reasoning, as compared with such "insanity." For ourselves, we delight in the stupendously grand thoughts and germs of thought that everywhere break out through their phantastic covering, and to which these Philistines are blind. (Pgs. 10-12, "Socialism: Utopian and Scientific", S. Sonnenschein, 1892)

From Chapter 3, "Critical Utopian Socialism and Communism":
The Socialist and Communist systems properly so called, those of Saint-Simon, Fourier, Owen and others, spring into existence in the early undeveloped period, described above, of the struggle between proletariat and bourgeoisie. ... Therefore, although the originators of these systems were, in many respects, revolutionary, their disciples have, in every case, formed mere reactionary sects. They hold fast by the original views of their masters, in opposition to the progressive historical development of the proletariat. They, therefore, endeavor, and that consistently, to deaden the class struggle and to reconcile the class antagonisms. They still dream of experimental realization of their social Utopias, a founding isolated phalansteries, of establishing "Home Colonies," of setting up a "Little Icaria" ---- duodecimo editions of the New Jerusalem -- and to realize all these castles in the air, they're compelled to appeal to the feelings and purses of the bourgeois. By degrees they sink into the category of the reactionary conservative Socialists depicted above, differing from these only by more systematic pedantry, and by their fanatical superstitious belief in the miraculous effects of their social science. (Pg, 59, Ch. 3, "Manifesto of the Communist Party", C.H. Kerr, 1906)

Marx and Engels both straddle an ill-defined line between "scientific socialism" and "utopian socialism," as naturally there was no real demarcation between their ideas and their predecessors to justify this demarcation. Noyes especially considered his efforts to be "scientific," and enshrined his "science" with the term "Stirpiculture" in an effort to repackage the science of heredity in human breeding. We now have the luxury of looking back and comparing Marxist endeavors to those of the "vulgar socialists," and the failures of the vast numbers of communist experiments at the commune level are frightening mirrors of the grander and more catastrophic failures of the nation-wide communal experiments. The communal experiments fared no better by awarding themselves a capital "C" in their definition; nor were they any more or less scientific, disciplined or rigorous. Maybe, the best criticism of utopian schemes came from Founding Father, Samuel Adams, decades prior to Marx and Engels:
The utopian schemes of leveling and a community of goods, are as visionary and

impractical as those which vest all property in the crown. These ideas are arbitrary, despotic, and, in our government unconstitutional. ("The life and public service of Samuel Adams", William V. Wells, Brown & Company, Vol. 3, 1865 – quoting Samuel Adams)

Gradually, by 1878 disillusion was setting in within the Oneida commune. The members were losing confidence in the aging Noyes. The idea of the imminent Millennium faded, and thus their position within it as the advance guard for Jesus also faded. College education of some of the young, along with reading and traveling was undermining the religious underpinnings of the community. The sexual controls were breaking down. Naturally, sexual partners wanted to make their own choices instead of going through the Elders of the Community. Outside forces came into play as well. In the 1870s, Anthony Comstock got Congress to ban any mention of birth control, the very laws that would be the focus of Margaret Sanger's efforts and legal justification for jailing her. This ban struck at the basic practice of controlling births, which Noyes had always advocated publicly. Then in 1878, John Meers, a Presbyterian minister and a teacher at Hamilton College, along with some other clergy, took a public stand against Oneida and accused Noyes of running a "concubine." On June 23, 1879, in the face of arrest and a lawsuit, Noyes fled to Canada under the cover of night. With Noyes' departure, his opponents within the commune now demanded constitutional government with elections, the abolition of the "Ascendancy of Fellowship," the hierarchal structure in which decisions were made by the Elders, including sexual privileges, and the end to all sexual controls in favor of freedom of sexual privileges. In exile on the Canadian side of Niagara Falls, Noyes proposed ending "Complex Marriage," thereby permitting legal marriages. Complex Marriage came to an end at 10 a.m. on August 28, 1879. Feminine dresses began to appear, women's hair grew longer, and Mutual Criticism died.

One prominent eugenicist who decided to publish using John Humphrey Noyes's term "Stirpiculture" was M.L. Holbrook. Holbrook's book "Homo-Culture," herein quoted, was the reprint of the 1897 book previously titled "Stirpiculture." Conspicuously enough, Holbrook titled his book using the term used by Noyes, and never uses the word "eugenics" within the text, and only mentions Galton a handful of times in his "Homo-Culture" reprint of "Stirpiculture." M.L. Holbrook was a member of prestigious associations, and much like Leonard Darwin, had significant influence over his contemporaries. According to his New York Times obituary, Martin Luther (M.L.) Holbrook was a member of the very exclusive organization, the Twilight Club, whose members included Mark Twain, Calvin Coolidge, and many other prominent figures of the time. A quick online search will reveal that M.L. Holbrook and Herbert Spencer collaborated in at least two publications regarding the rearing of children. Holbrook, like Adolf Hitler after him, was inspired by early Greek practices of infanticide and eugenics as his inspiration:

> Stirpiculture in this extended sense was not unknown to the ancients, both in theory and in practice. As to the former, the most noted example is that of Plato,

who, in his "Republic," proposed certain arrangements as to marriage and the bringing up of children which he thought would improve the race, and hence be beneficial to the State. The State was to Plato all in all, and he considered that it should form one great family. This idea could not be carried into effect, however, so long as independent families existed, and therefore those arrangements had for one of their chief aims the abolition of what we regard as family life. This Plato thought was the best for the State, and the advantage which was supposed to accrue to it by the absence of separate families is expressed in a marginal note, which says: "There will be no private interests among them, and therefore no lawsuits or trials for assault or violence to elders." (Pg. 10)

Plato's Restrictions on Parentage: The children of the inferior class were not to be reared, "if the flock is to be maintained in first-class condition." This infanticide would matter little to the parents, as they had no control over their coming together, nor concern with the rearing of their offspring. (Pg. 11)

As to the rearing of them, we need only say that the children allowed to live were to be placed in the custody of guardians, to be appointed by the State from among the most worthy of either sex, who were to bring them up in accordance with the principles of virtue. (Pg. 12)

CONTINUES ...

Making Children the Property of the State: The principles which were embodied in the scheme proposed by Plato, in his "Republic," to bring about an improvement in the race are mainly two: First, restriction on the formation of procreative unions; second, infanticide. The breaking up of private or separate families necessarily resulted from the operation of his "marriage" regulations, and was intended to emphasize the idea which Plato, like Lycurgus, insisted on, that the children belonged to the State. (Pg. 22, "Homo-culture: Or, The Improvement of Offspring Through Wiser Generation", M.L. Holbrook, 1897)

Interestingly enough, Holbrook cites Darwin and not Galton, as the modern origin of the notion that the human race could be improved by "selective" and "rational" breeding, and furthermore, that selective breeding had immediate aesthetic implications of improving the race:

> That sexual selection has actually resulted in modification of human physical structure, Darwin thinks can be shown by reference to the ancient Persians, whose type was greatly improved by intermarriage with the beautiful Georgian and Circassian women. He refers to several similar cases, and particularly to the Jollofs of West Africa, whose handsome appearance is said to be due to their retaining for wives only their most beautiful slaves, the others being sold. (Pg. 31)

CONTINUES ...

The investigations of Darwin as to the operation of sexual selection had reference chiefly to the modification of physical characters. He did not altogether lose sight, however, of its possible influence in affecting for the better the mental characteristics of the race. He concludes his enquiry by the remark that "Man might by selection do something, not only for the bodily constitution and frame of his offspring, but for their intellectual and moral qualities. Both sexes ought to refrain from marriage if they are in any marked degree inferior in body or mind; but such hopes are Utopian, and will never be even partially realized until the laws of inheritance are thoroughly known. Every one does good service who aids towards this end. (Pg. 33, "Homo-culture: Or, The Improvement of Offspring Through Wiser Generation", M.L. Holbrook, 1897)

Here again, Holbrook recognizes Darwin as the intellect who looked upon human charity with disdain and as an obstacle for any eugenic aspiration:

There seems an antagonism between nature's methods of bettering the physical condition of the race and the efforts of man himself, acting under the guidance of his moral feelings, to prevent the action of natural law. Mr. Darwin recognized this, and referred to it in his great work, "The Descent of Man," where he says: "With savages, the weak in body and mind are soon eliminated, and those that survive commonly exhibit a vigorous state of health. We civilized men, on the other hand, do our utmost to check the process of elimination. We build asylums for the imbeciles, the maimed and the sick; we institute poor laws; and our medical men exert their utmost skill to save the life of every one to the last moment." (Pg. 142)

CONTINUES ...

"There is," says he, "reason to believe that vaccination has preserved thousands who from a weak constitution would have succumbed to smallpox. Thus the weak members of civilized communities propagate their kind. No one who has attended to the breeding of domestic animals will doubt but this must be highly injurious to the human race. Excepting in the case of man himself hardly any one is so ignorant as to allow his worst animals to breed." (Pg. 143, "Homo-culture: Or, The Improvement of Offspring Through Wiser Generation", M.L. Holbrook, 1897)

Of note is that Holbrook recognized John Humphrey Noyes as the first to experiment with selective and rational breeding, as opposed to Galton:

An Experiment in Stirpiculture: Noyes was the founder of a religious sect, the members of which, owing to their desire for freedom from sin, were called Perfectionists. Holiness was the first principle of their creed, and Noyes thought to transmit that condition from one generation to another by a process of stirpiculture. To overcome the "selfishness" of monogamic marriage he devised a "system of regulated promiscuity, beginning at earliest puberty, and by a method of his own invention he separated the amative from the propagative functions." (Pg. 37, "Homo-culture: Or, The Improvement of Offspring Through Wiser Generation", M.L. Holbrook, 1897)

Therefore, Holbrook cited Galton as making suggestions towards an ideology already in practice. Interestingly enough, Holbrook notes that Galton's proposals were too close to "socialism" to be broadly accepted:

> **Human Selection:** Under the head of human selection Galton and Wallace have made some interesting and valuable suggestions for improving the health and quality of man. Mr. Galton proposed a system of marks for family health, intellect and morals, and those members of families having the highest number were to be encouraged to marry early by state endowments sufficient to enable them to make a good start in life, early marriages being favorable to large families. It was a bold suggestion, savoring too strongly of socialism or state control of marriage to suit many of us. (Pg. 135, "Homo-culture: Or, The Improvement of Offspring Through Wiser Generation", M.L. Holbrook, 1897)

Through all this, the comical irony is that the one element that kept the Oneida community afloat were its capitalistic ventures, despite the fact that one of its most famous members was Leon Czolgosz, better known as President William McKinley's assassin and Communist agitator. The silverware they made at Oneida is also its surviving legacy. The Oneida Community eventually became the giant silverware company Oneida Limited. From a 100% communist enterprise, where even clothing was not personally owned, the Community became a joint-stock company fueled by profit, marketing, and conspicuous consumption of luxury items. Oneida Limited enjoyed its capitalist success on through to this century. H.G. Wells was another famous visitor there in 1906, and aptly observed: "It was difficult to borrow a hammer."

Sec. 2 - "HUMAN ZOOS" – EVOLUTION ON DISPLAY:

"Human zoos," sometimes called "negro villages," were 19th and 20th Century exhibits of humans, typically in their alleged natural or primitive state. The displays often emphasized the cultural differences between those of European descent and non-European peoples. These ethnographic zoos were intended as educational exhibitions, often the part of actual zoos, museums, and most famously, World Fairs. The fact that these zoos gained significant popularity in the 1870s reveals the "educational" message they intended to communicate. "Human zoos" thrived in the golden age of Darwinism, and they purported to display the lesser evolved "savages" in contrast to allegedly higher evolved descendants of European civilizations. For enhanced effect, the displays would often be exhibited physically next to laudatory displays of Western technology and culture. They juxtaposed "positive" vs "negative," "acceptable" vs "unacceptable," much in the same way Hitler's Degenerate Art Exhibit would decades later. More to the point, these exhibitions were presented as "scientific" in their educational worth, and not just as entertainment.

Human zoos could be found in Paris, Hamburg, Antwerp, Barcelona, London, Milan, New York, and Warsaw, with 200,000 to 300,000 visitors attending each exhibition. In Germany, Carl Hagenbeck, a merchant in wild animals and future entrepreneur of many European zoos, decided to exhibit Samoan and Sami people as "purely natural" populations in 1874. In 1876, he sent a collaborator to the Egyptian Sudan to bring back some wild beasts and "Nubians." This "Nubian Exhibit" was very successful in Europe and toured Paris, London, and Berlin. He also dispatched an agent to Labrador to secure several *"Esquimaux,"* or Eskimos and Innuits from Hopedale, and they were exhibited in his Hamburg Tierpark between 1877 and 1912.

In France, approximately thirty ethnological exhibitions along the lines of human zoos were presented at the *"Jardin zoologique d'acclimatation."* Its director, Geoffroy de Saint-Hilaire organized various ethnological spectacles that presented Africans and Inuit. Both the 1878 and the 1889 Parisian World's Fair presented a "Negro Village." The 1889 World's Fair displayed 400 indigenous people as the major attraction. In conspicuous juxtaposition were Alexander Graham Bell's telephone and Thomas Edison's phonograph.

Of course, the Americans were no different. In 1906, the Harvard eugenicist extraordinaire, Madison Grant, head of the New York Zoological Society and the Immigration Restriction League, had Congolese pygmy Ota Benga put on display at the Bronx Zoo alongside apes and other animals. Ota Benga was a 103-pound, 4-feet 11-inch African Pigmy that was brought from the Kasai River, Congo Free State, South Central Africa. Madison Grant, who was also the head of the American Zoological Society, decided that Otto belonged in a cage as an exhibit. At the behest of Grant, the zoo director William Hornaday placed Ota Benga in a cage with the chimpanzees, then with an orangutan named Dohong, and labeled him "The Missing Link," suggesting that, in evolutionary terms, Africans like Ota Benga were closer to apes than were Europeans. A New York Times story of September 18, 1906 documents the opening of the "Monkey Exhibit":

> [New Yorkers] made for the monkey house to see the star attraction in the park – the wild man from Africa. They chased him about the grounds all day, howling, leering and yelling. Some of them poked him in the ribs, others tripped him up, all laughed at him. (Pg. 28, "Booker T. Washington and the Struggle against White Supremacy: The Southern Educational Tours, 1908–1912", David H. Jackson, Springer, 2008)

As such, "Human Zoos" were a booming industry in the age of scientific racism which was fueled by Darwinism. Otto Benga, very literally, helped blur the line between the exhibitor and the exhibited, yet one must ask oneself just exactly where this demarcation falls in today's world. One has to question where anthropologists cross the line in that questionable zone between the "Human Zoos" and arguing that native villages should be preserved and kept safe from modernization as if they were nothing more than the clan of Jane Goodall's apes. Where is the benevolence of deciding that entire groups of human beings should be deprived of both the dangers and benefits of modernity just so their primitive, and precarious way of life can be preserved for posterity? We degrade ourselves by drawing such artificial lines between humans and humans. When one engages in "othering" fellow humans in the name of science, one falls in line with the likes of Francis Galton and Madison Grant. This is the artificial line that was drawn by turn-of-the-century Darwinists who otherwise hypocritically claimed that man was just another animal in nature but placed themselves on the other side of the cage that housed Otto Benga.

However, the most notorious example of human beings exhibited in this fashion was that of Saartjie Baartman of the Namaqua, often referred to as the 'Hottentot Venus'. Baartman initially exhibited in a small show in England, just as John Merrick, the "Elephant Man" had been in Whitechapel, England. Sadiah Qureshi tells the story of Saartjie ("little Sara" in Dutch) in her article "Displaying Sara Baartman, the 'Hottentot Venus'." [522] Sadiah Qureshi's article was principally written as the result of the very public and international controversy which ultimately involved Nelson Mandela. However, it is instrumental in narrating the story of Sara Baartman in the context of her time, and the wider implications of her plight.

No record of Baartman's real name exists. Baartman was brought to Liverpool, England in 1810 by Alexander Dunlop, the surgeon of an African ship and exporter of museum specimens from the Cape. Baartman went on display in the Piccadilly neighborhood in London. Members of the public were invited to view the "Hottentot Venus" for two shillings. Baartman was advertised as possessing the "kind of shape which is most admired among her countrymen." The show took place upon "a stage two feet high, along which she was led by her keeper, and exhibited like a wild beast; being obliged to walk, stand, or sit as he ordered." [523] As Qureshi aptly points out, the fact that iron bars were missing did not diminish the central theme that Baartman was no more than a "caged beast."

Ethnological exhibitions such as the "Hottentot Venus" not only invoked the conceit of imperial superiority but served to blur the demarcation between "caged beast" and human individuality. Naturally, they were also sources of political controversy. Qureshi explains that controversy was a part of Baartman's history from the onset. In fact, it can be argued that one of the first shots in the battle between abolitionists and pro-slavery forces was fired in the name of Sara Baartman. Baartman's exhibition aroused intense public interest when abolitionists objected to her display on humanitarian grounds. In December of 1810, the Morning Chronicle, an abolitionist newspaper in England, published an article denouncing the men who profited from Baartman's exhibition. The Morning Chronicle stated that "It was contrary to every principle of morality and good order" to allow the

---

[522] "Displaying Sara Baartman, the 'Hottentot Venus'", Sadiah Qureshi, SAGE Journals, History of Science, Vol 42, Issue 2, 2004.
[523] web.mit.edu – "Bring back the Hottentot Venus", Race Science in Media, June 15, 1995.

show, as it connected "offence to public decency, with that most horrid of all situations, Slavery." A very public legal battle ensued, which likely lead to the sharp decline in attendance. Even though the court found in favor of the owners of the show, Baartman's exhibition occurred at precisely the moment when the abolitionist issue was gathering strength in England.

Qureshi opines that the declining revenue in England ultimately resulted in Baartman ending up at the hands of Frédéric Cuvier in France, and as the subject of the scientific eugenic elite. In the spring of 1815, Baartman spent three days at the *Jardin des Plantes* under the observation of various professors of the *Muséum d'Histoire Naturelle*. Here she posed nude for the images that appeared in the first volume of Étienne Geoffroy Saint-Hilaire's and Cuvier's now-iconic "*Histoire Naturelle des Mammifères.*" Again, these were the efforts of the scientific elite, and not necessarily the exploits of circus exhibitioners such as those of P.T. Barnum. Cuvier was highly regarded in France as the founder of geology and the leading intellect of the nation. The images of Baartman are prominently displayed in the opening pages of Cuvier's book and serves as the only images of a human in the extensively illustrated tome. The remainder of the book depicts a vast variety of mammals, including numerous species of apes and monkeys. Quereshi opines that Baartman's poses are disturbingly similar to the other mammalian specimens in the volume.

In December 1815, Baartman died from an illness Georges Cuvier diagnosed as "*une maladie inflammatoire et eruptive.*" Her death posed a problem for Cuvier and the other zoologists in the Paris museum. It meant an end to her availability as a specimen unless they intervened. Geoffroy Saint-Hilaire appealed to the authorities on behalf of the *Muséum d'Histoire Naturelle* to retain the corpse on the grounds that it was a singular specimen of humanity and therefore of special scientific interest. The appeal was approved, and the body taken to the *Muséum* where Cuvier conducted the autopsy and triumphantly published a detailed account of Baartman's anatomy. Cuvier's report reveals his belief that she represented an inferior human form. Cuvier's extended discussion of Baartman's facial features confirmed his political and scientific convictions. True to his devotion to eugenic craniometry, Cuvier also included his observations of a live Baartman in his report and relates her supposedly rapid and unexpected movements to those of a monkey. He justified this categorization by pointing to the features of her cranium. According to Cuvier, her ears were small and weakly formed, as those of an orangutan. He further opined that she frequently jutted her lip outwards like a simian. Cuvier claimed that Baartman's skull resembled a monkey's more than any other he has examined. Cuvier held other beliefs common to the eugenicists that would follow him. He believed environmental influences on evolution were minimal, that anatomical and cranial measurement differentiated the human races, and that physical and mental differences between the races were an indication of racial worth. His decision to categorize her as a *Boschimanne*, rather than *Hottentote*, further suggests that for Cuvier, Baartman was as close as possible to an ape, and not a full-fledged member of the human race. Qureshi summarizes the phenomenon:

Throughout the history of colonial occupation at the Cape, many representations of indigenous peoples have been used to facilitate their subjugation. Wildness and savagery characterized depictions of the Khoikhoi during the seventeenth century, quickly establishing them as the 'link' between ape and human in nature's great hierarchy. -- Flora, fauna and people were all commodities to be collected. The agricultural relevance of botanical knowledge fueled nationalist interest in plants, whilst animals caged in menageries provided the public with entertainment and evidence of imperial success. (Pgs. 233-257, "Displaying Sara Baartman, the 'Hottentot Venus'", SAGE Journal, Vol. 42, Issue 2, June 1, 2004)

Georges Cuvier's work influenced several generations of 'scientists' that were all too eager to categorize humanity with racial hierarchies. He was a Protestant and a believer that all men descended from the biblical Adam. Curvier believed there were three distinct races: the Caucasian, Mongolian, and Ethiopian. He claimed Adam and Eve were Caucasian and the origins of mankind and the other two races originated by survivors escaping in different directions after the catastrophe the Bible described as leveling Earth 5,000 years prior. The Mongolian and Ethiopian races were the descendants of survivors henceforth living in complete isolation from each other. He wrote his opinion about the superiority of Caucasians in page 71 of his 1798 "*Tableau Elementaire de L'histoire Naturelle des Animaux,*" translated here:

> The white race, with oval face, straight hair and nose, to which the civilised people of Europe belong and which appear to us the most beautiful of all, is also superior to others by its genius, courage and activity. (Pg. 96)

Regarding those of African descent, Cuvier wrote:
> The Negro race... is marked by black complexion, crisped of woolly hair, compressed cranium and a flat nose. The projection of the lower parts of the face, and the thick lips, evidently approximate it to the monkey tribe: the hordes of which it consists have always remained in the most complete state of barbarism. (Pg. 94, "African Intimacies: Race, Homosexuality, And Globalization", Neville Wallace Hoad, Univ. of Minnesota Press, 2007)

According to Clifton C. Crais and Pamela Scully, Cuvier's writings, were "particularly influential to Charles Darwin as he began elaborating his theory of evolution," and his prior understanding of the Hottentot shaped Darwin's ideas on human diversity and sexuality." [524] Prior to her death, Cuvier had pleaded with both Henri de Blainville and Baartman to allow an examination of her *tablier*, with de Blainville even offering her money; but she refused and took great care to preserve her modesty. Cuvier only succeeded when her cadaver lay before him. His meticulous description of the *tablier*, including its length, thickness, and appearance folded and unfolded, takes up a long passage that is graphic and violating.

---

[524] Page 144-145, "Sara Baartman and the Hottentot Venus: A Ghost Story and a Biography", Clifton C. Crais and Pamela Scully, Princeton Univ. Press, 2010.

Cuvier was not alone in his quasi-pornographic pursuits. Many 'scientists' contemporary to Cuvier bemoaned the difficulty of persuading the Khoikhoi to expose themselves for their studies. François Le Vaillant, known for his images of Khoikhoi women, documented the lengths to which he pleaded with Khoikhoi woman to reveal themselves to him. Le Vaillant's images frequently present Khoikhoi women reclining and revealing themselves enough to reveal breasts and parted legs exposing the labia. As late as 1911, a frustrated Dorothy Bleek complained of the Khoisan that: "It is exceedingly difficult to get photos of the natives without their clothes on." [525] William Somerville was another gentleman traveler in the quest for unusually pronounced female genitals. Between 1799 and 1802, William Somerville was stationed in Africa as a garrison-surgeon. He took advantage of his position as a doctor to conduct his voyeuristic studies. Somerville described these observations in a paper which he deposited at the Royal Society in 1806 and later published in 1816:

> It is but justice to the modesty of the Hottentots to say that I have constantly found as many difficulties in the part of the women to submit to the exposure parts which a closer inspection required, as in all probability would have occurred in persuading an equal number of females of any other description to undergo examination. (Pg. 238, "William Somerville's Narrative of His Journeys to the Eastsern Frontier and to Kattakoe 1779-1802", William Somerville, Van Riebeeck Society, 1979)

The touring of Africa to survey its inhabitants was also a prominent pastime for those British gentlemen-scientists like Francis Galton, and in the case of "gentlemen" like Francis Galton, the study was far from detached or "gentlemanly." Galton engaged in what by any current standard would be considered more pornographic than scientific, literally finding fascination with the African female's allegedly larger than normal buttocks, genital area, and breasts. As such, Francis Galton was one of those gentlemen travelers braving the distant African landscape to intimately catalog the naked native bodies. Observing a Khoikhoi woman in the distance, Galton writes:

> I profess to be a scientific man, and was exceedingly anxious to obtain accurate measurements of her shape; but there was a difficulty ... I did not know a word of Hottentot ... I therefore felt in a dilemma as I gazed at her form, that gift of bounteous nature to this favoured race which no mantua-maker, with all her crinoline and stuffing, can do otherwise than humbly imitate. The object of my admiration stood under a tree, and was turning herself about to all of the compass, as ladies who wish to be admired usually do. (Pg. 243, "The Natural History of Man Being an Account of the Manners and Customs of the Uncivilized Races of Men", Rev. J. G. Wood, Routledge, Vol. I, 1868 – Quoting Galton)

---

[525] "Displaying Sara Baartman, the 'Hottentot Venus'", Sadiah Qureshi, SAGE Journals, History of Science, Vol 42, Issue 2, 2004.

The skinning, dissecting, and preservation of human bodies in the name of science was but one of the disturbing features of the treatment of the African people in the nineteenth century. Sadiah Qureshi reports that many Khoikhoi women were preserved via taxidermy as were the animals captured in the European African excursions of the time. Their skins were stripped and stuffed to preserve them as specimens. As such, the exhibit of Sara Baartman's skeleton and plaster cast greeted any visitor passing case 33 at the *Musée de l'Homme* up until the late 1970s, when feminists began to protest her display. Efforts by Nelson Mandela finally achieved her repatriation and burial in her native land in April 2002.

Such disheartening episodes in the history of science help us understand the origins of the "rank order hierarchies" that were core to the eugenic creed. [526] This scientific zeitgeist found expression in decade after decade of world exhibitions. By 1933, the idea that human groups could be ranked along an evolutionary scale had become part of popular culture. Like its predecessor, the Century of Progress Exposition of 1933 sought to naturalize this hierarchy by juxtaposing displays of "primitive" peoples alongside ones that demonstrated the purported superiority of the white American elite. Thus, for example, the fair organizers erected a quaint "Indian Village" in the looming shadow of the General Motors Tower, a modernist temple dedicated to the ascendant American auto industry. The real Native Americans who inhabited the ersatz tepees of the Indian Village served as reminders of an earlier way of life that had been rendered obsolete by the steam engine, the automobile, and other advances produced by white American civilization. Now vanquished and domesticated on reservations, Native Americans were seen largely as harmless or even ennobled, more deserving of pity than of fear.

None of this was considered unusual or outside of the general message of the fair. The most enduring memory from the fair was the Futurama exhibit for General Motors by the famous designer, Norman Bel Geddes. The grand exhibit is popularly remembered as the "World of Tomorrow," and it was explicitly intended to portray a eugenic and sanitized industrial future. Bel Geddes was a devoted apostle of the eugenic creed. [527] In retrospect, Bel Geddes incorporated every aspect which would have been important to a eugenic art exhibit by the Nazis: a juxtaposition of the eugenic and dysgenic, superior and inferior races, efficiency, hygiene, high-technology, eugenically stylized male and female nudes, fast-paced modern transportation, and even a dash of Madame Blavatsky's Theosophy, which Bel Geddes also fully subscribed to. [528] In fact, Bel Geddes was a devotee of Ernst Haeckel and endeavored to have Haeckel's theories inform his designs. In 20/20 hindsight, the Futurama could easily have served as the template for Hitler's Degenerate Art and German Art exhibits, or a Leni Riefenstahl production:

> In two exhibits that for undocumented reasons were never produced, Gnome Village and the South Sea Island, Bel Geddes would have placed his evolutionary

---

[526] Pgs. 105-128 - "The Misuse of Biological Hierarchies: The American Eugenics Movement, 1900-1940," Garland E. Allen, History and Philosophy of the Life Sciences 5, no. 2, 1983.
[527] Pgs. 193-245 – "The Futurama Recontextualized: Norman Bel Geddes's Eugenic 'World of Tomorrow'", Christina Cogdell, American Quarterly, Vol. 52, No. 2, June 2000.
[528] Pg. 216 – Ibid.

inferiors on display: dwarfs as representatives of the degenerate and disabled "Lilliputioan race," and beautiful female "primitives" ostensibly available to the Fair-going men. The Crystal Lassies continued this theme but placed a nude white female center-stage as a four-dimensional representation of the evolution of consciousness for the viewer's enlightenment. Bel Geddes completed the progression with the Futurama, which literally embodied the conception and birth of an Anglo-American male's vision of Progress. All four of these exhibits share both a common linkage in the evolutionary hierarchy and common structural similarities that Bel Geddes used almost formulaically to control the experience of the visitor. (Pg. 209, "The Futurama Recontextualized: Norman Bel Geddes's Eugenic 'World of Tomorrow'", Christina Cogdell, American Quarterly, Vol. 52, No. 2, June 2000)

It is worth noting, to expand on one of the running themes of this book, that Bel Geddes expressed his utopian vision with the same "lucid vagueness" utilized by H.G. Wells and Edward Bellamy in their utopian novels. The allusion to the "fourth-dimension" and the "Spic and Span Town" eugenic juxtaposition could just as easily be described as non-participatory walk-through versions of Bellamy's imagined America of the year 2000. Bel Geddes understood the value of "strategically blurring" of the vision in order to "manipulate his audience into accepting his vision of the future and to help them overlook the disturbing social realities present in his exhibits." [529] The audience was ushered through with an automated conveyor, never allowed to ponder, as with deeper introspection or participation the exhibit would be revealed as a sinister Stepford Wife dystopia.

Elsewhere at the fair, the juxtapositions continued to be extrapolated and displayed in the prominently located Hall of Science building, where a real-life atavistic "tribe" and supposedly far more dangerous group of "degenerates" was being put on display by the heads of the eugenics movement. The exhibition was the work product of Harry H. Laughlin and the Cold Spring Harbor eugenics team headed up by Charles B. Davenport. The "tribe" the eugenicists displayed with photographs and family pedigrees was the "Tribe of Ishmael." According to the exhibition, these modern-day "savages" were:

> A Degenerate Family ... which, despite opportunities, never developed a normal life. Shiftless, begging, wanderers, sound enough in body, their hereditary equipment lacked the basic qualities of intelligence and character on which opportunity could work. (Pg. 90, Christina Cogdell, "Eugenic Design: Streamlining America in the 1930s", Univ. of Pennsylvania Press, 2010)

The marriage of terms like "savage" and "degenerate" strike at the core of eugenics. Just as the Indian Village stood next to the General Motors Tower, thereby highlighting the gulf between them, the eugenicists had erected a display devoted to "A Superior Family: The Roosevelt Family-Stock" on panels adjoining those dedicated to the Ishmaels, a family line of alleged rural "degenerates." At the head

---

[529] Pg. 223 – "The Futurama Recontextualized: Norman Bel Geddes's Eugenic 'World of Tomorrow'", Christina Cogdell, American Quarterly, Vol. 52, No. 2, June 2000.

of the Roosevelt family tree stood Jonathan Edwards, the famous Puritan theologian. Official-looking portraits of Theodore Roosevelt and Franklin Delano Roosevelt framed the genealogical tree, along with photographs of lesser-known members of the clan and the legend "Pedigree showing the distribution of inborn qualities in a family which produced two presidents of the United States." Harry H. Laughlin had worked tirelessly with members of the Roosevelt family to compile the lauded family tree that would be displayed alongside those of "degenerate" family trees. The message of the world's fair eugenics exhibition was crystal clear: if the Roosevelt's were America's best family, the rural-poor "Ishmaels" and the "Jukes" were its worst.

Sec. 3 – THE "SAVAGE DEBATE":

The Scopes Monkey Trial has been touted as an event of singular historical importance. Yet, Americans were almost 50 years behind Europe in playing out this debate of landmark ridiculousness. In September of 1877, the very prominent scientists Rudolf Virchow and Ernst Haeckel had a very public and very contentious debate along the same lines as the Scopes trial. Like the Scopes Trial, the debate between Haeckel and Virchow was whether evolutionary ideas should be taught in the state-schools of Germany. Haeckel was in favor, whereas Virchow argued that evolution was too hypothetical and socially dangerous for student curricula. In many ways similar to the Scopes Trial, the two sides of the argument were very much two sides of the same coin. Both Haeckel and Virchow were Progressive-minded scientists who were openly antagonistic towards traditional religion.

Rudolph Virchow was the German doctor, anthropologist, pathologist, prehistorian, biologist and politician, known for his advancement of public health. Popularly recognized as "the father of modern pathology," Virchow is credited with multiple important discoveries. Virchow's most widely known scientific contribution is his cell theory. He is cited as the first to recognize leukemia cells. Virchow is also known for elucidating the mechanism of pulmonary thromboembolism, coining the term "embolism" and "thrombosis." Furthermore, Virchow founded the medical fields of cellular pathology and comparative pathology, the methodology of comparing the diseases common to humans and animals. Virchow also developed a standard method of autopsy procedures. Beyond that, Virchow was also an impassioned advocate for social and political reform. Virchow entered the political scene by siding with the democrats in the 1848 revolution in Germany and becoming an outspoken enemy of the German government. In 1859, he became a member of the Municipal Council of Berlin. Virchow was elected to the Prussian Diet in 1862, as the leader of the Progressive Party. He was a member of the Reichstag from 1880 to 1893 where he worked to improve the health care conditions for the Berlin citizens.

More poignantly, Virchow cooperated with Bismarck in the *Kulturkampf*, the anti-clerical campaign against the Catholic Church which General Ludendorff later identified with. It was, in fact, Rudolf Virchow as the Progressive deputy in the Prussian legislature who coined the term "*Kulturkampf*" to describe the liberation of public life from sectarian impositions. Priests and bishops who resisted the *Kulturkampf* were arrested or removed from their positions. By the height of anti-Catholic legislation, half of the Prussian bishops were in prison or in exile, a quarter of the parishes had no priest, half the monks and nuns had left Prussia, a third of the monasteries and convents were closed, 1800 parish priests were imprisoned or exiled, and thousands of laypeople were imprisoned for helping the priests. As such, Virchow could hardly be considered part of any conservative movement. Like the Progressive populist, William Jennings Bryan, which historians to this day wrongly categorize as defending the "conservative" views at the Scopes' Trial, Virchow would find himself defending a conservative point-of-view in the European version of the Monkey Trial.

The whole German controversy, as it would later play out in the United States, was triggered by the punishment of a teacher for his teaching of Darwinism. The teacher in the German controversy was Heinrich Ludwig Hermann Müller, a botanist who provided important evidence for Darwin's theory of evolution. Müller was an early investigator of coevolution. Coevolution is the change of a biological object triggered by the change of a related object. For example, the coevolution of different species includes the evolution of a host species and its parasites. Müller was the author in 1873 of "*Die Befruchtung der Blumen durch Insekten*," a book translated at the suggestion of Darwin in 1883. Müller and Darwin corresponded frequently, amounting to 36 letters between the two, and Darwin cited him extensively in "The Descent of Man." Müller was also a biology teacher at the *Realschule* in the Westphalian city of Lippstadt, where his teachings became the subject of an article written by newspaper "*Westfälischer Merkur*" in 1876. The pro-Darwinist journal "*Kosmos*" would respond in kind. The controversy would incite an investigation by the authorities and libel suits by Müller against several newspapers, as well as the street-level battles for the high and mighty like Haeckel and Virchow to quibble about:

> The courts found no evidence that Müller was an enemy of Christianity... It is difficult to say whether Müller's classes really were an indirect threat to religion. Müller claimed he was always very careful to separate theories and personal opinions from firmly established scientific facts. One of his former students recalled that the classes were always exciting and that no one was misled or encouraged to question religion. (Pg. 62, "The Descent of Darwin: The Popularization of Darwinism in Germany, 1860-1914", Univ. of North Carolina, 1947)

In actuality, Müller had resolved the argument to the satisfaction of the oversight authorities in 1876, but as the real crux of the argument was political, the contentiousness persisted beyond an incident that otherwise had amounted to nothing more than a meeting between a teacher and his employer. Unfortunately, the courts were slow, and Müller's legal battle did not come to a resolution until 1879. In the meantime, Ernst Haeckel, like the ACLU and Mencken after, took the opportunity to propagandize the debate to a national level. Haeckel reacted by "leading a series of ferocious debates at the *Naturforscher Versammlungen* in 1877, 1882 and 1886." [530] At the Fiftieth Congress of the Association of German Scientists and Physicians in Munich, Haeckel's speech asserted with his usual brashness that the Theory of Evolution was incontrovertibly true and brushed off any calls for experimental or evidentiary proof in support of the "theory" as a sign of ignorance. Even more uncomfortable was Haeckel's insistence that Darwinism not only taught but that it become the underlying theme of the entire curriculum, with his views of the "unity of nature" as the controlling concept for the entire work-day of the students. Haeckel wanted Christianity taught, but only to characterize it as dogma. The audience must have been offended as they refrained from the usual polite applause at the end of Haeckel's performance. Haeckel's old mentor, Rudolf Virchow, countered four days later with an address titled "The Freedom of Science in the Modern State." Virchow argued that Darwinism was a yet unproven hypothesis, thus its inclusion in the school curriculum could damage the reputation of science. Virchow believed schools should only teach accepted knowledge, not in vogue theories as children did not possess the maturity of judgment necessary to distinguish between hypothesis and knowledge. [531]

As would be the case in the Americas, the debate had political implications far beyond that of the content of school curriculums. It marked a crossroads in German science and medicine, not to mention the accepted morality and ethics of an entire people. The disagreement created an enduring rift between mentor and apprentice that would echo persistently as Germans and Austrians debated the proper role of science while their countrymen deliberated over the allure of authoritarian collectivism and the freedoms of *laissez-faire* policies:

> Whereas Virchow was a critic of Bismarck and remained individualistic and anti-hierarchical in his politics and science, Haeckel glorified the German Reich as highly evolved. He argued that evolutionary theory should be the basis of education in the newly united nation. Indeed, he went further and suggested that the study of cellular organisms proved the existence of a natural religion based on duty, division of labour and the subordination of egoism to the social whole. (Pg. 43, "Health, Race and German Politics Between National Unification and Nazism, 1870-1945", Oxford Univ. Press, 1998)

Exactly how important was this now forgotten episode in history? If one wants to pinpoint exactly where German society took a turn towards a totalitarian form of nationalism, the most logical point is what Paul Weindling characterizes as this "savage debate." Virchow represented the altruistic and humanistic German, whose

---

[530] Pg. 43 - "Health, Race and German Politics Between National Unification and Nazism, 1870-1945", Paul Weindling, Oxford Univ. Press, 1998.

[531] Pg. 58 - "The Descent of Darwin: The Popularization of Darwinism in Germany, 1860-1914", Univ. of North Carolina, 1947.

tradition included world-renowned scientists such as Alexander Von Humboldt and Albert Schweitzer. Ernst Haeckel led a generation of German and Austrian doctors and scientists who intentionally devalued the individual and subordinated the autonomous human to the needs of the "race" and the "nation." Historically speaking, this is a debate that was decidedly won by Haeckel, as the generation of scientists of the turn-of-the-century which exerted their influence during World War I and World War II were overwhelmingly followers of Haeckel. Haeckel's Monism would guide these doctors and scientists down the path towards The Holocaust:

> After his dispute with Virchow, he wrote to his friend, the poet Hermann Allmers, of the need to continue 'propaganda' for the evolutionary world view. Haeckel despised the piety and compromises with the churches of the successive Prussian ministers. When judged from his biological vantage point, it appeared that government, education and justice remained in a state of barbarism. (Pg. 45, "Health, Race and German Politics Between National Unification and Nazism, 1870-1945", Oxford Univ. Press, 1998)

However, Virchow was Haeckel's mentor, and thus Virchow was able to landsome good rhetorical punches. Virchow ridiculed Haeckel's reliance on his "ape-man skulls," correctly dismissing them as mischaracterized as "missing links," a fact would come back to haunt Haeckel's career. Most poignantly, Virchow revealed the dangers of a radically politicized science:

> Now imagine for a moment how the theory of evolution looks today in the mind of a socialist. Yes, gentlemen, that may appear funny to some, but it's very serious; and I hope that the theory of evolution will not bring to us all the horrors which similar theories have actually wrought in a neighboring country. After all, if pursued logically, this theory has an unusually ominous side; and I hope it hasn't escaped you that socialism is in close sympathy with it. We must be clear about this. (Pg. 59, "The Descent of Darwin: The Popularization of Darwinism in Germany, 1860-1914", Univ. of North Carolina, 1947)

In this respect, history has vindicated Virchow. The forgotten casualty of Ernst Haeckel's zealotry is the very humane history of German and Austrian scientists and doctors that came prior to this rift. Prior to this distinct change in ethic and morality, German and Austrian scientists represented the best in humanity. Yet, largely due to Haeckel, the enduring image is that of the sadistic German doctor, instead of the humanistic Alexander Von Humboldt or Albert Schweitzer. This new generation of doctors and scientists would openly express disdain and disrespect for traditional values and espouse Haeckel's slogan of "fearless advance" in science as the means of realizing radical political aims. [532] It was no longer their duty to care for and protect the weak, but rather to eradicate them and treat them as an infection on the society as a whole. Nowhere was this *"Über Ethik"* more pronounced than in those scientists, which adopted Haeckel's Monism as the blueprint for "eugenics"

---

[532] Pg. 125 - "Health, Race and German Politics Between National Unification and Nazism, 1870-1945", Paul Weindling, Cambridge Univ. Press, 1993.

and "race hygiene":

> The reaction against the liberal medicine of Virchow and Pettenkofer was expressed by an attack on individualism. Ploetz dealt with the distinctions between "individual hygiene", "social hygiene" and "racial hygiene". He saw a fundamental conflict between individual hygiene as opposed to racial or social hygiene. For individual hygiene conflicted with the racial priorities of the elimination of undesirable characteristics. Racial and social hygiene thus had to counter the harmful effects of individualism. (Pg. 131, "Health, Race and German Politics Between National Unification and Nazism, 1870-1945", Oxford Univ. Press, 1998)

The fact that Virchow's son, Hans Virchow, joined Alfred Ploetz's Racial Hygiene Society, exemplifies the shift from a humanistic and individualistic approach to the collectivized racial biology. [533] The adoption of the "race hygiene" paradigm was an all-encompassing dedication which married socialism, social hygiene, and Aryan ideologies because of the racial hierarchies developed as a consequence of Darwin's "civilized" and "savage" classification of the races:

> Haeckel subordinated history to a cosmic law of cause and evolution that stretched from inorganic nature to human culture. He saw anthropology as a branch of zoology, and psychology was an off-shoot of physiology. To understand psychology, it was necessary to make comparisons with "lower" forms of intellectual life: "children, the mentally defective, the mentally ill, and lower human races – and their mental life must be compared with that of the highest animals…" He proclaimed a new science of "comparative animal psychology." This would explain the origins of all state and social formations: "the differences between the highest and lowest humans were greater than those between the lowest humans and the highest animals." (Pg. 55, "Health, Race and German Politics Between National Unification and Nazism, 1870-1945", Oxford Univ. Press, 1998)

Consider the historical importance of anthropomorphizing all medical ailments. Virchow saw the variations in humanity as pathological variations, as opposed to the racial hierarchies that Darwinism implied. As this book documents, this is an important distinction, which was the dividing line between scientists and doctors that discarded traditional ethics and those that upheld them, like Virchow. Virchow visited the Caucasus in 1881 and 1894, and concluded that it was not the cradle of the white race, if any such racial distinctions existed at all:

> Virchow rejected the notion of "higher" and "lower" races. None of the living races was lower than another. Race was "hereditary variation". Virchow thought it unlikely that racial types were permanent. He condemned the view that pathological variations such as microcephaly were atavistic reversions. While regarding certain races as "pathological" variations from the parent type, the crucial distinction between peoples was cultural. Virchow distinguished between

---

[533] Pg. 135 – "Health, Race and German Politics Between National Unification and Nazism, 1870-1945", Paul Weindling, Cambridge Univ. Press, 1993.

Naturvölker and *Kulturevölker*. Rather than the search for a single "missing link" between ape and man as demanded by such Darwinians as Haeckel, it was necessary to scour the earth for human remains and cultural artifacts to show the immense potential for human variation. (Pg. 55, "Health, Race and German Politics Between National Unification and Nazism, 1870-1945", Oxford Univ. Press, 1998)

This is a crucial distinction for anyone who would like to defend evolution without defending Darwinism. Many scientists of the era believed that science could explain the phenomenon of heredity and biological diversity. It was specifically Darwin, Haeckel, and Galton who believed that there was a hierarchy of races. [534] Darwinists since the "Savage Debate," the Scopes' Trial, and the creation of the X-Club have tried to frame Darwinism as synonymous with science itself, claiming that arguing against Darwin is arguing against science. Clearly, the history of Rudolf Virchow, Gregor Mendel, Alfred Russel Wallace, and even Erasmus Darwin would contest that claim.

What was the ingredient that radicalized scientists from Haeckel onwards? It was Darwinism. Virchow after all, was the professor, and Haeckel his student. Without Darwin's support, Haeckel had allure but was subservient to Virchow's reputation. History must recognize that Charles Darwin bolstered Haeckel's standing in the scientific community by incorporating Haeckel's racist theories into "The Descent of Man." Historians have been too easy on Charles Darwin, claiming he was the victim of having his science misrepresented and misused. This is at best a partial view of the total history, which ignores the fact that Ernst Haeckel's rabid and disgusting form of "scientific racism" was well developed and published by the time Charles Darwin published "The Descent of Man." Furthermore, this must be judged in the light that a reputable scientist like Rudolf Virchow had warned the world of Haeckel's excesses, and others had proven that Haeckel's work was intentionally fudged and thus fraudulent.

Virchow would remain cautious about endorsing Darwinism's, its "unbridled popularization." [535] To the end of his life Virchow insisted that scientific questions would be answered on their own terms. Virchow pointed to the inherent danger of jumping to the conclusion that Darwinism held the key to all questions about human civilization. The Holocaust would ultimately prove him right. History must recognize that while not all "race hygienists" were anti-Semitic, every single one of them was a devoted and radicalized Darwinist.

---

[534] Pgs. 105-128 - "The Misuse of Biological Hierarchies: The American Eugenics Movement, 1900-1940," Garland E. Allen, History and Philosophy of the Life Sciences 5, no. 2, 1983.

[535] See Generally: "The Descent of Darwin: The Popularization of Darwinism in Germany, 1860-1914", Univ. of North Carolina, 1947.

Sec. 4 – FROM "ATAVISM" TO "DEGENERATION":

Cesare Lombroso, born Ezechia Marco Lombroso was an Italian criminologist and founder of the Italian School of Positivist Criminology. Lombroso rejected the established Classical School, which held that crime was a characteristic trait of human nature, rather looking at criminality as an inherited trait specific to individuals that were "born criminal," and which could be identified by physical defects. Lombroso saw criminality as a birth defect which revealed in the criminal as having reverted back to savagery, or in the term used by Lombroso as an "atavism" that was literally a product of evolution working in reverse. By now the reader recognizes the importance of this conception; the terms "degenerate" and "atavism" would be used interchangeably to communicate a diagnosis that evolution had worked in reverse through heredity, or more precisely, poor mate selection.

Lombroso was born in Verona on 6 November 1835 to a wealthy Jewish family. He studied literature, linguistics, and archeology at the universities of Padua, Vienna, and Paris, but changed his plans and became an army surgeon in 1859. In 1866 he was appointed visiting lecturer at Pavia, and later took charge of the insane asylum at Pesaro in 1871. He became a professor of forensic medicine and hygiene at Turin in 1878. That year he wrote his most important and influential work, *"L'uomo delinquent,"* which went through five editions in Italian and was published in various European languages. However, it was not until 1900 that his work was published in English, at which point, his work was significantly influential with British and American eugenicists who agreed that behavioral traits were both inherited and a sign of "degeneration." Like the eugenicists that followed, Lombroso's general theory of atavism suggested that criminals can be distinguished from non-criminals by multiple physical anomalies. Lombroso postulated that behavioral maladies were closely tied to and correlated to physical deformities. He postulated that criminals demonstrated physical features reminiscent of apes, lower primates, and early man. As such, the behavior of these biological "throwbacks" could only be expected to run contrary to the rules and expectations of modern civilized society.

Lombroso spent years amassing physiological data through a series of postmortem examinations and anthropometric studies of criminals, the insane, and normal individuals. Through these studies of the criminal's physical attributes, Lombroso became convinced that the "born criminal" could be anatomically identified by such items as a sloping forehead, ears of unusual size, asymmetry of the face, excessive length of arms, asymmetry of the cranium, and other "physical stigmata." Lombroso's research methods were clinical and statistical, with precise details of skull dimension and other measurements. Lombroso also maintained that criminals had less sensibility to pain and touch; more acute sight, as well as a lack of moral sense, namely an absence of remorse. Lombroso believed that "born criminals," or otherwise stated as the "criminal type" displayed more vanity, impulsiveness, vindictiveness, and cruelty. Besides the "born criminal" Lombroso also described "criminaloids," or the occasional criminals, criminals by passion, moral imbeciles, and criminal epileptics. More importantly, they condemned any affiliated individual as incurable and irredeemable.

This is the point in this backward timeline where a seemingly innocuous idea ignites from spark to flame. Lombroso's ideological heir would be Karl Pearson, the founder of the eugenic journal "Biometrika." Lombroso, like Galton after him, engaged in similar studies of geniuses and gifted individuals. Lombroso postulated that artistic genius was a form of hereditary insanity. To support this assertion, he began assembling a large collection of "psychiatric art." Note the pattern in practice; Lombroso's methodology hardly differed from Max Nordau's. Of specific importance is that this claim to the ability to identify the criminal was the reason why Harry H. Laughlin's benefactor, Judge Harry Olson, funded the publication of his "Model Eugenical Law" which was extrapolated along with various expert opinions from famous jurists in the 494 page "Eugenical Sterilization in the United States." [536] This was the pattern in practice which played out in the United States, Britain, Germany, Canada, and various Scandinavian nations:

- Scientific theory is propagandized into socio-political mainstream thought.
- Journals, organizations, and institutions are formed to bolster the new found branch of science.
- Accepted scientific dogma is proposed as legal concepts by the experts.
- Expert analysis is distilled into legal concepts by sympathetic jurists.
- Legislators leverage the reputations and academic titles of the expert jurists and scientists in order to claim a higher ground to any opposition in the parliaments and legislatures.
- Theories once relegated to the fringes become governmental infrastructures and the subject-matter of political platforms.

As this book has evidenced in previous chapters, this certainly was what transpired in the case of eugenic sterilization, eugenic immigration controls, and eugenic euthanasia and abortion in the United States, Britain, Germany, Canada and the various Scandinavian nations that enacted such laws. Lombroso's history fits the pattern: Lombroso's pivotal book was translated into English by the eugenicist Havelock Ellis. In turn, Ellis' circle of friends included Fabian Socialist, George Bernard Shaw, and other progressive thinkers, specifically Margaret Sanger. Ellis formally entered the discussion over eugenics with his 1912 book "The Task of Social Hygiene" which he used to vocally support "the science and art of Good Breeding in the human race:"

> Eventually, it seems evident, a general system, whether private or public, whereby all personal facts, biological and mental, normal and morbid, are duly and systematically registered, must become inevitable if we are to have a real guide as to those persons who are most fit, or most unfit to carry on the race. Unless they are full and frank such records are useless. (Pg. 200, "The Task of Social Hygiene", Houghton Mifflin Co. 1912)

---

[536] See Chptr. "1922 – Model Eugenical Law" in "H.H. Laughlin: American Progressive, American Scientist, Nazi Collaborator" by this author.

As a contemporary progressive thinker, Ellis supported eugenics and served as president of the Galton Institute and as vice-president to the Eugenics Education Society. As such, Ellis would not condemn the Third Reich's eugenic legislation, as from his view they had scientific justification. However much Ellis would have liked to distance eugenics from racism, the work he translated for Lombroso did much to cement Darwinism's postulate of humans as "naked apes." "Atavisms" and "degenerates" would be seen as proof of Darwin's "Theory of Evolution." Without ever having to utter a racial slur, the implications were clear; breed with a race lower in the ranks of evolution, per Mr. Darwin himself, and the consequences would be a lowering of the biological quality of your offspring. Lombroso's observations, as we have seen, had a distinct effect on both cultural and scientific minds. Ironically, the skull measurements Lombroso used to define "criminality" and "atavistic" features were eventually used by his students to measure evolutionary purity, namely by German scientists to classify Jews as biologically inferior. The sloping foreheads, the elongated arms, the larger ears, and the characteristics of the nose would become indications of rank in evolutionary terms, namely those that Hitler's henchmen attributed to the Jewish type, or *"Judentypen."* Lombroso, like his devotee Nordau, helped fashion the noose from which his fellow Jews would be hung from.

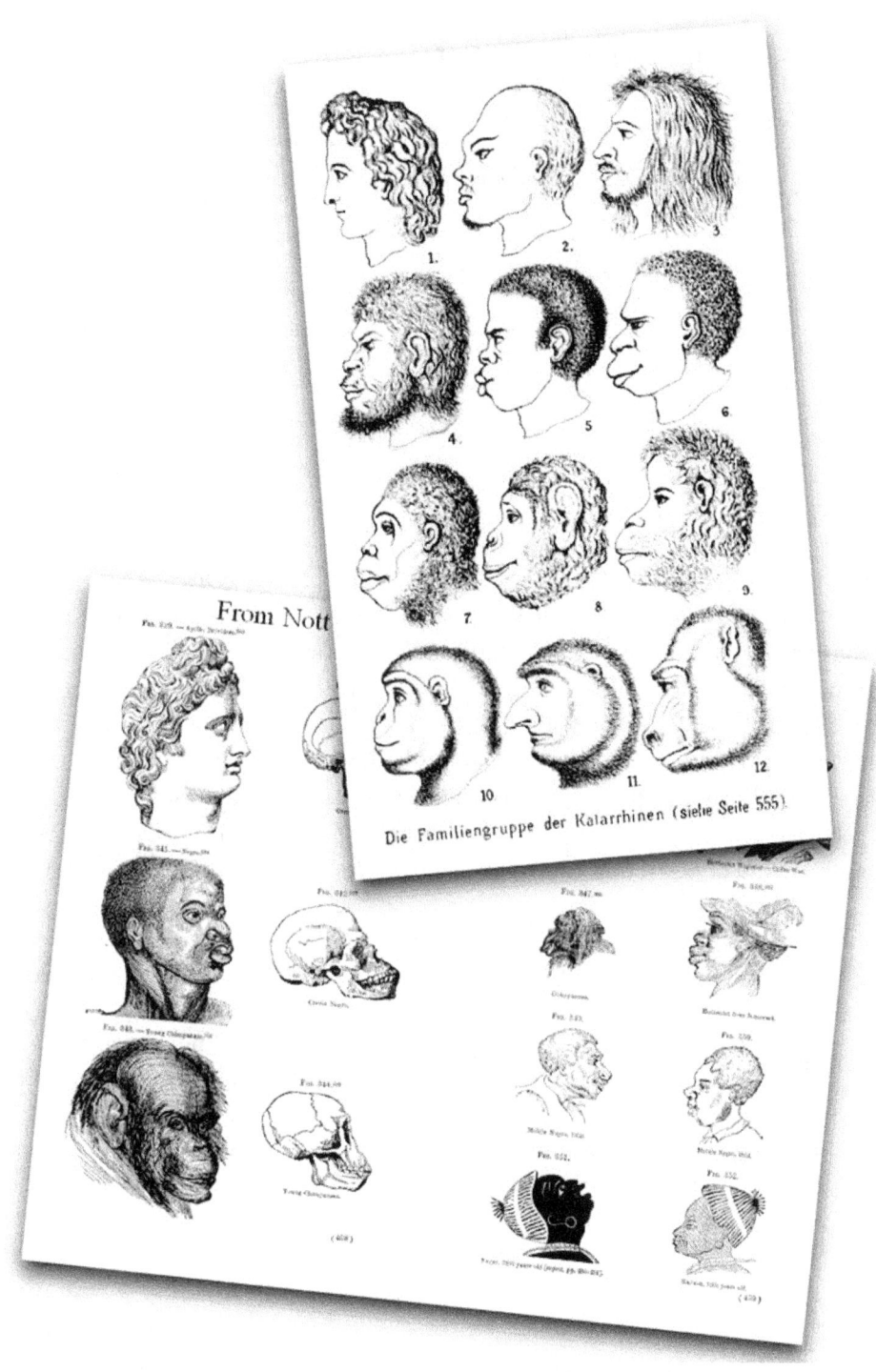

FIGURE 16: ETHNOGRAPHIC IMAGES FROM THE VARIOUS BOOKS BY ERNST HAECKEL OR HIS AMERICAN COUNTERPARTS, JOSIAH NOTT AND GEORGE GLIDDON. THE WORK OF THESE FAMOUS BIOLOGISTS INFORMED THE EUGENICS MOVEMENT ON HOW BIOLOGY VIEWED THE HUMAN RACE.

Chap. 16: 1874 to 1870

AMERICAN FRONT: A POLITICAL CARTOON FOR THE FIRST TIME SYMBOLIZES THE UNITED STATES DEMOCRATIC PARTY WITH A DONKEY. – VIRGINIA REJOINS THE UNION THE WOMAN'S TEMPERANCE LEAGUE IS ORGANIZED BY ELIZA DANIEL STEWART. GEORGIA BECOMES THE LAST FORMER CONFEDERATE STATE TO BE READMITTED TO THE UNION, AND THE C.S.A. IS DISSOLVED. **EUROPEAN FRONT:** GERMAN TROOPS LEAVE FRANCE UPON COMPLETION OF PAYMENT OF INDEMNITY FOR THE FRANCO-PRUSSIAN WAR. – ROME BECOMES THE CAPITAL OF UNIFIED ITALY. - LEAGUE OF THE THREE EMPERORS IS CREATED. IT LINKS THE CONSERVATIVE MONARCHS OF AUSTRIA-HUNGARY, GERMANY AND RUSSIA IN AN ALLIANCE AGAINST RADICAL MOVEMENTS. **SCIENCE & TECHNOLOGY:** ANTONIO GARCÍA CUBAS MAKES FIRST SCHOLARLY DESCRIPTION OF THE RUINS OF THE TOLTEC CAPITAL IN TULA, HIDALGO, MEXICO. **LIFE:**. – LEVI STRAUSS AND JACOB DAVIS RECEIVE A US PATENT FOR BLUE JEANS WITH COPPER RIVETS. THE PRICE IS $13.50 PER DOZEN. – JOHN D. ROCKEFELLER, JR., AMERICAN ENTREPRENEUR IS BORN. – ERNST RÜDIN, SWISS PSYCHIATRIST, GENETICIST, AND EUGENICIST IS BORN. – WINSTON CHURCHILL IS BORN. - LEVI STRAUSS AND JACOB DAVIS RECEIVED UNITED STATES PATENT# 139121 FOR USING COPPER RIVETS TO STRENGTHEN THE POCKETS OF DENIM WORK PANTS. – THE HEINEKEN BREWERY IS FOUNDED IN AMSTERDAM, THE NETHERLANDS. ROSA LUXEMBURG, GERMAN SOCIALIST POLITICIAN IS BORN. – ORVILLE WRIGHT, AMERICAN AVIATION PIONEER, CO-INVENTOR OF THE AIRPLANE IS BORN. VLADIMIR LENIN, RUSSIAN REVOLUTIONARY AND FIRST PREMIER OF THE SOVIET UNION IS BORN. - CHARLES DICKENS, BRITISH NOVELIST DIES. – ROBERT E. LEE, CONFEDERATE CIVIL WAR GENERAL DIES. - CONSTRUCTION OF THE BROOKLYN BRIDGE BEGINS.

Sec. I - FROM RESERVATION TO CONCENTRATION CAMP:

The 1870s were a decade when the solution of segregating unwanted people flourished in both the United States and Britain. In England, James Greenwood, author of the 1869 book "The Seven Curses of London" singled out "paupers, professional thieves, professional beggars, fallen women, inebriates, gambles, and mismanaged charity" as the problems to be dealt with. Greenwood estimated that the 100,000 pauper children swarming the streets of London were the offspring of "felons, cripples, and idiots." The chapter titled "The Best Remedy" in Greenwood's book arrived at a solution, using British colonies as a form of reservation:

> All other remedies considered, we come back to that which is cheapest, most lasting, and in every way the best—emigration. ---- This, of course, as applying to unwilling and undeserved pauperism. These are the sufferers that our colonies are waiting to receive with open arms. They don't want tramps and vagrants. They won't have them, well knowing the plague such vermin would be in a land whose fatness runs to waste. But what they are willing to receive, gladly and hospitably, are men and women, healthy, and of a mind to work honestly for a liberal wage. New Zealand has room for ten thousand such; so has Australia and Canada. (gutenberg.org, Chap.: XXIV, "The Seven Curses of London", Fields, Osgood, & Company, 1869)

Around the same time, the United States established its first Native American reservation. Both the African American and Native American communities in the United States had suffered great hardships since the dawn of the Republic. After the Civil War, however, conditions radically changed. The slaves were freed while the remaining tribes of Native Americans were herded into reservations. In stark contrast, the segregation of the American Indian occurred just when the African American was gaining essential freedoms for the first time. Native Americans were not even considered American citizens at the time of Reconstruction, as the 14th Amendment that gave blacks their citizenship, excluded Native Americans. In the years immediately following the Civil War, blacks, due to a strong Republican influence in the Federal and state governments, were far better off economically, politically, and socially than their Native American counterparts. While the Indians lost their land because of the ever-moving drive westward, blacks gained suffrage and equality under the law. In fact, many escaped slaves or emancipated blacks went to the newly opened lands of the West to live as cowboys and farmhands.

Post-bellum America was also the setting for the final and total defeat of the Indians at the hands of expansionist American policy. With the threat of disunion posed by the Confederacy removed, the United States was once again able to continue its inexorable march to the Pacific Ocean. Standing in the way of total continental domination were Native Americans living in the Great Plains. These last remaining tribes would become the targets of what can only be described as a hunting expedition by the Union Army.

These are the entangled histories of the emancipated blacks, the Native Americans, and eugenical legislation. These entangled histories share in common the consequences of arrogance and elitism. One of the most inexplicable aspects of United States history is that the same Union Army which emancipated the African American slave was used to forcefully capture, subjugate, and segregate the Native American. The same army that was used to liberate African American men, women, and children from being held against their will in the Southern plantation, was used to literally hunt down, capture, and segregate the men, women, and children of Native American descent to corral them into reservations. Ironically, or insultingly enough, both acts were justified by a high-browed empathy with the well-being of both people allegedly in mind.

In late 1875, Sioux and Cheyenne defiantly left their reservations, outraged over the continued intrusions of whites into their sacred lands in the Black Hills. The Battle of Little Big Horn, otherwise known as "Custer's Last Stand," was a direct result of the various Indian Appropriation Acts passed by Congress. A considerable number of acts were passed under the same name throughout the 19th and early 20th centuries, but the most notable landmark acts consist of the 1851 Indian Appropriations Act and the 1871 Indian Appropriations Act. The 1851 Indian Appropriations Act allocated funds to move western tribes onto reservations. Reservations were allegedly both protected and enclosed by the US government. According to the Federal government at that time, reservations were created to protect the Native Americans from the growing encroachment of whites moving westward. Any honest retrospect recognizes that the tribes like the Sioux or the Cheyenne only needed protection from the US Government itself, and not from small groups of white settlers.

The laws passed also evidence the arrogance and air of superiority rampant during this era. The 1871 Indian Appropriations Act ended the practice of treating Native American tribes as sovereign nations by declaring that all Native Americans be treated as unassociated individuals and legally designated "wards" of the federal government. The 1871 Act was directly intended to dismantle the tribal structure of Native Americans. Under the Act, the US government embarked on a policy of corralling the Native American population into *"rancherias,"* where food and care from the Federal government could be distributed to each individual Native American in exchange for staying out of the way of expansion and within the boundaries of the reservations. The Act contradicted and violated centuries of treaties signed between 1607 to 1776, which dealt with the Native Americans as "independent nations" within the geographic boundaries of the British colonies. At least 175 treaties had been signed with the British and colonial governments. After the American Revolution, the United States Federal government replaced the British and colonial governments and between 1778 to 1868 at least 371 treaties were ratified between the Federal government which treated the Native American tribes as "independent nations" and specifically stipulated that the new American government would not interject itself to govern over individual Native Americans.

The welfare state imposed by these 1871 Acts clearly was intrusive. It is of note that "wards of the state" is a status otherwise reserved for orphans or the disabled. Needless to say, the Sioux nor the Cheyenne were anything but defenseless. These were some of the greatest warriors to walk the earth. They had won battles against the US Army before, and they would not be easily corralled and kept like animals in a reservation. The Sioux and Cheyenne gathered in Montana with the great warrior Sitting Bull to fight for their lands. The US Army dispatched Lt. Colonel George Custer and the Seventh Cavalry to force the large Native American army back to the reservations. On June 25, 1876, Custer and the 7 Cavalry fought perhaps the biggest alliance of Native Americans that had ever collaborated.

Custer has not been treated kindly by historians, but for whatever it is worth, Custer held a strong opinion on the constitutionality and morality of how the US government treated the Native Americans. Custer leveraged the fame he amassed as a Civil War general and published a book two years prior to his historic death. The book was titled "My Life on the Plains." Custer's opinion was that Congress was influenced by corrupt motives when making decisions about its policy towards the Native Americans. More importantly, it was an early, but enlightening indictment of the corruption that ensues when massive government infrastructures engage in the business of being "masters" to "wards of the state":

> The army as a unit, and from motives of peace and justice, favors giving this control to the Secretary of War. Opposed to this view is a large, powerful, and at times unscrupulous party, many of whose strongest adherents are dependent upon the fraudulent practices and profits of which the Indian is the victim for the acquirement of dishonest wealth practices and profits which only exist so long as the Indian Bureau is under the supervision of the Interior Department. (Pg. 113, "My Life on the Plains: Personal Experiences with Indians", Sheldon, 1875)

"My Life on the Plains" was published well into Custer's fame, as his fame originated by his boldness in the Civil War, thus Custer's estimation of Congress and the various governmental agencies dealing with the Native Americans was written knowing that his reputation as an officer loyal to the Union was at stake.

History since has painted Custer as a brash and arrogant S.O.B. This may be so, and certainly his willingness to follow orders of a questionable morality qualify this observation. However, questioning orders may not be a redeeming character trait in an officer, thus Custer fought bravely for the Union despite he was pro-slavery, and then went into battle to segregate into reservations a people he certainly thought were being victimized by the heavy hand of the US government.

Most revealing is the fact that Custer outright accused the Union, and namely Congress, of enacting a policy under the hypocritical excuse of caring for the Native Americans, but which was in actuality intended to personally enrich those in charge of distributing the goods intended to care for the "wards." That this had been the Union he had fought and put his life on the line for should not go unnoticed by history:

> It seems almost incredible that a policy which is claimed and represented to be based on sympathy for the red man and a desire to secure to him his rights, is shaped in reality and manipulated behind the scenes with the distinct and sole object of reaping a rich harvest by plundering both the Government and the Indians. (Pg. 114, "My Life on the Plains", Sheldon, 1875)

Custer documents in his book that the Native Americans sarcastically referred to the US government as the "Great Father" for caring for them as "wards of the state," but leaves no doubt what motivations were precisely behind the "Great Father's" supposed "benevolence":

> To do away with the vast army of agents, traders, and civilian employees which is a necessary appendage of the civilian policy, would be to deprive many members of Congress of a vast deal of patronage which they now enjoy. There are few, if any, more comfortable or desirable places of disposing of a friend who has rendered valuable political service or electioneering aid, than to secure for him the appointment of Indian agent. The salary of an agent is comparatively small. Men without means, however, eagerly accept the position; and in a few years, at furthest, they almost invariably retire in wealth. Who ever heard of a retired Indian agent or trader in limited circumstances? Plow do they realize fortunes upon so small a salary? In the disposition of the annuities provided for the Indians by the Government, the agent is usually the distributing medium. Between himself and the Indian there is no system of accountability, no vouchers given or received, no books kept, in fact no record except the statement which the agent chooses to forward to his superintendent. (Pg. 114, "My Life on the Plains: Personal Experiences with Indians", Sheldon, 1875)

As far as the legitimacy of the political decisions made by the Union, Custer was right, even though his public derision towards the Congress has since been lost to history due to the infamy of his defeat. Posterity has lost sight of how the relevant laws of this era bundled the Native Americans, African Americans, and Oriental immigrants as protectorates of the "White Man's Burden." The Civil Rights Bill of April 9th, 1866 declared all emancipated African Americans born in the United States to be citizens of the United States, and by extension to enjoy equal protection under the law. Ironically enough, the same Union that declared emancipated blacks to enjoy such rights as inalienable to their person per the Declaration of Independence, also deemed Native Americans to be devoid of such individual autonomy as "wards of the state." The history of these two victimized people becomes important to the subject of this book when one realizes that the concept of "segregation" was a by-product of the Western "territories." US Government policy towards Native Americans was significantly influenced by the January 1874 case of Ward vs. Flood. The California Supreme Court in Ward vs. Flood upheld that colored children need not be accepted for attendance at a white school in order to meet the "equality under the law" prescribed by the Civil War amendments. Ward vs. Flood dealt with an April 4th, 1870 California law which contained the following provisions:

> Section 56. – **The education of children of African descent, and Indian children, shall be provided for in separate schools**. Upon the written application of at least ten such children to any Board of Trustees, or Board of Education, a separate school shall be established for the education of such children; and the education of a less number may be provided for by the Trustees, in separate schools, or in any other manner. (emphasis mine)

This judicial hurdle proved to be all-important. The California Supreme Court upheld the 1870 law which provided for separate schooling for white and colored children. In turn, this decision formed the bedrock of the "separate-but-equal" doctrine which that US Supreme Court adopted in the infamous case of Plessy v. Ferguson in 1896. Plessy v. Ferguson would not be overruled until the Supreme Court's Brown v. Board of Education of Topeka, Kansas decision of 1954. More importantly, the California Supreme Court's Ward vs. Flood not only set the legal precedent for school segregation but set the tone for policies of "Segregation" in general which would resonate on through to the eugenics era. The application of this legal precedent was certainly a sizeable step towards eugenic legislation that would follow.

In 1879, the government set up the Carlisle Indian School. This first off-reservation military-style boarding school for Indians was established in Pennsylvania. The school employees created a model curriculum, disciplinary regime, and educational strategy designed to "kill the Indian and save the child." [537] This was followed by the 1891 Indian Education Act. This Congressional Act authorized the Commissioner of Indian Affairs "to make and enforce by proper means" rules and regulations to ensure that Indian children attended schools designed and administered by non-Indians. In 1893 the Indian Education Act was expanded by making school attendance for Indian children compulsory and authorized the BIA to withhold rations and government annuities to parents who did not send their children to school. To put this into context, projects like the Carlisle Indian School simply don't happen if the governing elite respect the parent-child relationship, and

---

[537] Pg. 112 – "Fighting Colonialism with Hegemonic Culture: Native American Appropriation of Indian Stereotypes", Maureen Trudelle Schwarz, SUNY Press, 2013.

the cultural and religious choices which the parent passes on to the child. They certainly would not have happened if the US Government had honored the many treaties that respected the autonomy of the Native American nations. Those governing elite which created the Carlisle Indian School embarked upon a campaign of cultural annihilation by explicitly destroying any cultural identity in the Native American children under their jurisdiction.

The intent to eradicate the Native American culture is also evidenced by subsequent acts of the Federal government. In 1880 the US Congress decreed "Civilization Regulations" which created a series of "crimes" that could only be committed by Native Americans practicing their cultural norms. The practices of medicine men, ceremonies like the Sun Dance, leaving the reservation without permission, were all outlawed. In 1883 the Courts of Indian Offenses were established, and the Secretary of the Interior established a dedicated court system to uphold the 1880 Civilization Regulations to eliminate "heathenish practices" among the Indians. Two major court decisions made the Federal government's paternalism clear. The 1886 decision of the United States v. Kagama in the US Supreme Court came about when the two Native Americans on the Hoopa Valley Reservation in northern California killed another Indian on the reservation. In the years prior, these would have been crimes for the "independent nation" or the "tribe" to contend with, as they did not involve anyone outside of the tribe. If the law had been enforced and applied as it was with white citizens, these crimes would have been the jurisdiction of the State unless the crimes reached across State lines. The Federal government had no business intruding. However, the Native Americans were prosecuted and found guilty by the Federal government upholding the Major Crimes Act of 1885, which made a list of crimes committed inside of the "reservations" the jurisdiction of the Federal government. The Native Americans rightfully argued that Congress did not have the constitutional authority to pass the Major Crimes Act. The US Supreme Court, however, upheld the full and absolute power of the Congress to pass the Major Crimes Act and of the power of the Federal government, not the state or tribal governments, exclusive powers to deal with tribes. The US Supreme Court's opinion reeks of paternalism:

> **These Indian tribes are the wards of the nation.** They are communities dependent on the United States - dependent largely for their daily food; dependent for their political rights. They owe no allegiance to the states, and receive from them no protection. Because of the local ill feeling, the people of the states where they are found are often their deadliest enemies. From their very weakness and helplessness, so largely due to the course of dealing of the federal government with them, and the treaties in which it has been promised, there arises the duty of protection, and with it the power. (emphasis mine, United States v. Kagama, 118 US 375 (1886)

The second case was United States v. Sandoval. The Court upheld the application of Federal liquor-control law to the New Mexico Pueblos, even though Pueblo lands had never been designated by the Federal government as reservation land, and thus did not have the legislative mandate to preside over tribal issues as it did for Native Americans in actual "reservations." Again, the US Supreme Court ruled that an unbroken line of Federal legislative, executive and judicial actions had:

> ...attributed to the United States as a **superior and civilized nation the power and duty of exercising a fostering care and protection over all dependent Indian** communities within its borders... (emphasis mine, United States v. Sandoval, 231 US 28 (1913)

These are the words of the highest court in the United States of America applying the logic of white-supremacy and more poignantly, the justification that the slave-masters of the South had used to justify their "peculiar institution." It must be noted that the logic employed by the US Supreme Court is not the logic Thomas Jefferson employed in the Declaration, but a "racialist" logic which ranks races hierarchically, as would Darwin, Huxley, and the race-based biologists and anthropologists of the era. The Court was clearly not shy about using terms such as "superior," "dependent," or "civilized" to establish the relationship between the Federal government and the Native American population.

For decades scholars interested in the history of segregation have frequently drawn comparisons between the United States and South Africa. This is not a new phenomenon. In the late nineteenth and early 20th century, some of the most respected political theoreticians looked to connections between the American South and southern Africa. Early in the 20th century, for example, after traveling in the American South, the South African based state segregationist Maurice Evans felt encouraged to voice the similarities he saw. Maurice Evans's "Black and White in South East Africa" was the "first thoroughgoing and broadly disseminated theory of segregation." [538] It enjoyed a wide circulation and frequently cited in political debates. Evans was strongly influenced by the American South, which he had closely studied and written about in his "Black and White in the Southern States." Evans believed in segregation as better to the alternative of allowing whites to completely displace the conquered race, or to allow it to racially mix and thus "degenerate." Evans was known for his three principles for governing of the native races:

- The white man must govern.
- The Parliament elected by the white man must realize that while it is their duty to decide upon the line of policy to be adopted, they must delegate a large measure of power to those especially qualified, and must refrain from undue interference.
- The main line of policy must be the separation of the races as far as possible, our aim being to prevent race deterioration, to preserve race integrity, and to give both opportunity to build up and develop their race life. (Pg. 151, "Segregation and Apartheid in Twentieth Century South Africa", Psychology Press, 1995)

---

[538] Pg. 150 - "Segregation and Apartheid in Twentieth Century South Africa", William Beinart and Saul Dubow, Psychology Press, 1995.

Evans's principles are a display of the "paternalism and trusteeship" components of the ideology which segregation was an integral part of. More specifically, segregation is subordination. Explicit in the logic of "reservations" and "segregation" is the view that one race is subordinate and lesser than the other. Of note is the inverse, which decries a governmental relationship where a specific group is deemed as the "masters." This view coincided with the scientific view that mixing the races is a cause of "degeneration," where the "superior" race can recede backward in the racial hierarchy by mixing with races that are, as Darwin and Lombroso explained, closer to apes than to the white man. Explicit in all anti-miscegenation and segregation laws was fear in what the scientists of the era termed "atavisms," which was the result of "degeneration" or the march of evolution turned backward. This was the reasoning behind separation and segregation of the races, and the benevolent "pity" towards the "inferior" race was integral to the logic of all eugenic-minded legislation. Henry H. Goddard, the author of the infamous 1912 study, "Kalikak Family: A Study in the Heredity of Feeble-Mindedness," worked to begin a program of segregation of adults and children whose alleged bad inheritance supposedly needed to be kept out of the wider gene pool. Richard L. Dugdale's 1874 study, "The Jukes: A Study in Crime, Pauperism, Disease, and Heredity," and Arthur Estabrook's revisit of Dugdale's work, "The Jukes in 1915" both called for "eugenic segregation" and/or "sterilization." Note Madison Grant regurgitating language that would later be utilized by National Socialist legislative bodies:

> Whether we like to admit it or not, the result of the mixture of the two races, in the long run, gives us a race reverting to the more ancient, generalized and lower type. The cross between a white man and an Indian is an Indian… and **the cross between any of the three European races and Jew is a Jew**. (emphasis mine, Pg. 112, "Race, Racism, and Science: Social Impact and Interaction", John P. Jackson and Nadine M. Weidman, Rutgers Univ. Press, 2005)

The solution which Madison Grant proposed for this "atavistic" reversion to the "lower type" was to "eliminate the worst by segregation or sterilization." Thus, the logic and language of segregation for eugenic goals can be traced to all prominent eugenicists, as quotes from later generations of prominent eugenicists like Margaret Sanger and Leonard Darwin evidence:

> Apply a stern and rigid policy of **sterilization and segregation** to that grade of population whose progeny is already tainted or whose inheritance is such that objectionable traits may be transmitted to offspring. (emphasis mine, Pg. 106, Margaret Sanger, "A Plan For Peace," Birth Control Review, April 1932)

Darwin's son, Leonard, like Margaret Sanger and the rest of the eugenics movement on up to German legislators during the Third Reich, frame the question of segregating a portion of the public as a safety and health measure. This was the hypocrisy General Custer had pointed out in his now-forgotten book. These eugenic zealots were well aware of the civil rights implications of their proposals. Leonard Darwin recognized the civil rights argument against segregation, but fell on the side

of sacrificing civil rights for the alleged health of the overall society:
> Moreover, any interference with liberty must remain open to the objection that it creates a precedent which might be unwisely followed in other directions. But segregation cannot be at once condemned on these grounds; for all reforms do both god and harm, and all must be judged by the way in which the balance turns. We may, however, conclude that on account of these objections segregation is in fact only likely to be enforced when it is demanded in order to safeguard the public, or when the racial defects of those confined are very glaring. (Pg. 172, "The Need for Eugenic Reform", Leonard Darwin, D. Appleton & Co., 1926)

Of note is that Leonard and his father Charles came from a family of radical abolitionists, and Leonard's view on slavery was adopted verbatim from what his father wrote on the subject:
> We consider slavery immoral because of its demoralizing effect on the slave-owner. (Pg. 258, "The Need for Eugenic Reform", D. Appleton & Co., 1926)

Clearly, Leonard Darwin's morality fell on the side of "pity" and short of "empathy." Any notion that the reason slavery is harmful is because of its effects on the slave-owner is clearly a supremacist point-of-view. Leonard Darwin may have displayed "pity" for those unfortunate victims of the eugenic segregation policies he and his colleagues lobbied for, but it certainly cannot be claimed that Leonard Darwin felt empathy for those that they would sequester into segregated encampments. He certainly did not see them as equals, deserving of equal rights to "life, liberty, and the pursuit of happiness." This sentiment is apparent in the paternalism of the US Supreme Court's dealings with the Native American population. All these movements, the segregation of African Americans, the segregation of Native Americans into reservations, and the eugenic segregation and sterilizations were couched in the language of "pity" and concern for the safety and well-being of the "inferior" and "dependent" types. Those looking to history for lessons may look to the entangled and shared history of these movements, as well as to the words of the author of the Declaration of Independence. A letter from Thomas Jefferson to Thomas Cooper, dated November 29, 1802, illustrate his distrust of government pretending to be the people's caretaker:
> If we can but prevent the government from wasting the labours of the people, under the pretence of taking care of them, they must become happy. (loc.gov, The Thomas Jefferson Papers Series I - General Correspondence - 1651-1827)

Historians often refer to these "wars" between the Native American tribes and the Union as "forced relocations." This is a misnomer, to put it lightly, as we know that the orders given to US Army officers like George Armstrong Custer explicitly called for the natives to be forced back into reservations and to ensure that they stay segregated. "Forced relocation" may have been a necessary part of the overall history, but the underlying intent was forced "segregation." In retrospect, it is fair to state that the Great Sioux War was no war by the conventional sense. The US Army was utilized to capture, subdue, and corral men, women, and children into permanent encampments we now call "reservations." The only thing that kept these military campaigns from being outright hunting escapades was the fact that some select tribes, namely the Sioux and the Cheyenne, were too skilled at war to be categorized as easy prey. Once proud warriors were reduced to "wards of the state," dependent on the Federal government for their daily subsistence. The Antiquities Act of 1906 is instrumental in illustrating this point. Passed by Progressive-minded Theodore Roosevelt, this Act deemed Native American artifacts, including the remains of their buried ancestors, the property of the US Government. Historians can consult Martin Luther King, Jr. to find their moral compass:

> Any law that uplifts the human personality is just. Any law that degrades the human personality is unjust. All segregation statutes are unjust because segregation distorts the soul and damages the personality. It gives the segregator a false sense of superiority and the segregated a false sense of inferiority. (Pg. 162, "The Liberatory Thought of Martin Luther King Jr.: Critical Essays on the Philosopher King", Robert E. Birt, Lexington Books, 2012)

This was the US Government's policy until 1917, as a tangential result of World War I, when the United States extended the right of citizenship to those "native" to the land. When the US entered WWI, about 17,000 Native Americans served in the armed forces. Some Native Americans, however, specifically resisted the draft because they were not citizens and did not have the right to vote on the matter, or because they felt it would be an infringement of their tribal sovereignty. In 1919, Native American veterans of the war were granted citizenship. However, it is not until 1924 with the Indian Citizenship Act when this citizenship came with voting rights.

Sec. 2 - FROM "SCIENTISM," TO "RACIALISM," TO "RACISM":

When Charles Darwin came up with his "Theory of Evolution" the available fossil evidence indicated that the Earth was much older than originally thought. However, this fossil evidence worked against Darwin when extrapolating and extending his "Theory" to include humanity, as no ancestral human fossil evidence had been found by 1859 when Charles Darwin's "Origin of the Species" was first published. Darwin described the lack of fossils evidencing the transitioning from simian to human as "the most obvious and gravest objection which can be urged against my theory."[539] There simply was no fossil evidence supporting human evolution, and this may be part of the reason why Darwin chose not to include

---

[539] Pg. 292 – "On the Origin of Species by Means of Natural Selection, or the Preservation of Favoured Races in the Struggle for Life", Charles Darwin, John Murray, 1859.

humanity in his 1860 publication of "The Origin of the Species." Yet, one forgotten fact regarding the history of Darwin's work is that the term "missing link" which is so commonly bandied about in order to argue for or against Darwin was a term that preceded Darwin's publication of the "Origin of the Species" by many years. "Origin of the Species" was published on November 24, 1859. The Online Etymology Dictionary by the historian Douglas Harper gives credit to Charles Lyell for the first use of the term "missing link" in 1851. The term was first used in a scientific context by Lyell in the third edition of his 1851 book "Elements of Geology" where Lyell used it to point out the missing parts of the geological column that would be necessary to prove that species evolved over time. Also, the observation that species evolve over time was an idea already accepted through Lamarckism and Darwin's grandfather, Erasmus. Darwin explains so in the introduction to "Descent" by praising Lamarck and Haeckel as proponents of the same concept, and by opining that his book otherwise contained "hardly any original facts in regard to man." [540] However, it is important to note that the term "missing link" did not gain its weighty scientific and political connotations until after Darwin's publication of "Origin," when Lyell used it again on page xi of his 1863 book "Geological Evidences of the Antiquity of Man." In this context, historians must take note that it was Lyell which brought T.H. Huxley to Darwin's service, intent on instigating the political debate that later ensued upon the publication of "Origin of the Species." Lyell wrote that it remained a profound mystery how the huge gulf between man and beast could be bridged. But it was Darwin's work that imbued this term with the political and scientific impetus that made it the basis for the archeological quest and veritable Holy Grail of science.

The fossils necessary as evidence for the mechanisms of evolution remained absent in the ten years between the publication of Darwin's "Origin" in 1860 and "Descent" in 1871. As such, Darwin's theory of "sexual selection," as the mechanism by which "natural selection" progresses, remained largely the product of deductive reasoning and Darwin's observation skills. Yet, it must be clearly understood that Charles Darwin did not embark on proposing a half-finished theory. Darwin intended to present a complete and all-encompassing theory, which included humanity. Darwin did provide for a "missing link" to close the gaping hole between humanity as a lower form of animal life and the human species in its evolved form; Charles Darwin proposed that the "higher apes" were the earlier forms, and Africans and Aborigine "savages" the transition between "apes" and the highly evolved White Anglo Saxon Englishman. Darwin explicitly states this several times in "Descent of Man":

> The sole object of this work is to consider, firstly, whether man, like every other species, is descended from some pre-existing form; secondly, the manner of his development; and thirdly, the value of the differences between the so-called races of man. (Pg. xx, "The Descent of Man, and Selection in Relation to Sex", D. Appleton, 1872)

---

[540] Pgs. xx-xxi - "The Descent of Man, and Selection in Relation to Sex", Charles Darwin, D. Appleton, 1872.

Darwin's stated reasons for the publication of "Descent" is of specific importance in the history of "racialism," as it was through him that this perceived "differences between the so-called races of man" was "valued" by Darwin's followers. Darwin continues along this train of thought in the introduction to "Descent of Man":

> Nor shall I have occasion to do more than to allude to the amount of difference between man and the anthropomorphous apes: for Prof. Huxley, in the opinion of most competent judges, has conclusively shown that in every visible character man differs less from the higher apes than these do from the lower members of the same order of Primates. (Pg. xx, "The Descent of Man, and Selection in Relation to Sex", D. Appleton, 1872)

Recall that Darwin bolstered his arguments in "Descent of Man" by extensively citing Ernst Haeckel. Between "Origin of Species" and "Descent of Man," the idea of "lower animals" representing earlier stages in evolution had been popularized by Ernst Haeckel. Haeckel's pedigree illustrations of vertebrates morphing from one evolutionary step to another in a sort of evolutionary sequence not only served to popularize Darwinism in Germany but to inform Charles Darwin's own work on the subsequent publication of "Descent." Darwin fully deferred to Haeckel in the introduction to "Descent," acknowledging Haeckel's extrapolations as the source of many of the theories in "Descent":

> This last naturalist, beside his great work, *Generelle Morphologie* (1866), has recently (1868, with a second edit. in 1870) published his *Natürliche Schöpfungsgeschichte*, in which he fully discusses the genealogy of man. If this work had appeared before my essay had been written, I should probably never have completed it. (Pgs. xx – xxi, "The Descent of Man, and Selection in Relation to Sex", D. Appleton, 1872)

The other major advancement in science which allowed Darwin to move forward and beyond the self-imposed limitations of "Origin" is Francis Galton's work on eugenics and "Stirpiculture." As was the case with Ernst Haeckel's interpretation of Darwinism returning to inform Darwin, Francis Galton's work with eugenics was also used by Darwin as the foundation of the concepts contained within "Descent." While many historians place Galton and Haeckel as following and even misinterpreting Darwinism, any honest reading of Darwin's "Descent" proves that in actuality, that pivotal book was the product of a four- or five-way conversation between Darwin, Galton, Lyell, and Haeckel. Darwin may have started the conversation with the 1860 publication of "Origins," but Darwin fully relied on Galton, Huxley, and Haeckel in order to formulate the concepts Darwin published in "Descent" in 1871. Galton had incorporated Darwin's findings with Morel's and Lombroso's theory of "Degeneracy" to describe how the human species would either "progress" or "regress" as a consequence of Darwin's "sexual selection." Together with Haeckel and Huxley, Darwin had "aped" man. With "Descent," Darwin finally answered the question of how his "Theory of Evolution" applied to mankind, and his answer incorporated Haeckel's and Galton's eugenic logic into the "Theory."

None of these developments can be said to be the product of empirical science. Darwin was limited to the confines of comparative anthropology since there were no fossils from which to provide empirical evidence. Comparative anthropology, to begin with, is a highly subjective science whose findings are inescapably a reflection of the observer, and in Darwin's case, the 19th Century aristocrat's prejudices and elitism are palpable in his work. This aspect of the work is only exposed as that much more elitist considering how much Darwin relied on Galton's "Hereditary Genius," which is about as elitist as British aristocracy can get, as well as Ernst Haeckel's work, which is about as white supremacist as one can imagine. From Darwin's aristocratic vantage point, the "savages" he encountered in his voyages seemed to him "lesser evolved." While the subjective observation of technical advancements may be valid, what made Darwin's observations historically important is that he regarded these "coloured races" to be also biologically less evolved "missing links." Haeckel and Galton concurred, and thus "The Descent of Man" is imbued with characterizations of biological theories that are replete with subjective observation.

More to the point, Darwin could not, or would not, consider that humans were equal biologically speaking. Darwin knew this egalitarian view was contrary to the Theory of Evolution, as he chose to define it. Humanity could not be regarded as one monolithic and homogeneous group biologically speaking as this worked against Darwin's view that humanity was in a constant state of flux or biological transition because of "sexual selection." To consider all of humanity as being "created equal" would undermine his "Theory." Therefore, Darwin did not express evolution as the consequence of a value-free biological diversity. Darwin broke humanity down into different stages of evolution, from lesser to greater. Darwin explicitly categorized Africans and Aborigines as closer to "apes" than they were to whites to illustrate his understanding of how evolution occurred. Thus, it can be stated with some certainty that Charles Darwin himself never sought out an archeological "missing link." The "savages" in Darwin's work literally became his "missing link" providing the transition from a pre-human anthropoid to its pinnacle, white European aristocrats:

> The break between man and his nearest allies will then be wider, for it will intervene between man in a more civilised state, as we may hope, even than the Caucasian, and some ape as low as a baboon, instead of as now between the negro or Australian and the gorilla. (Pgs. 200-201, "The Descent of Man, and Selection in Relation to Sex", D. Appleton, 1872)

This was the vile racism of Ernst Haeckel's work endorsed and incorporated into Darwinism as an integral and inalienable part of the Theory. Darwin, by adopting and endorsing Haeckel, had "aped" entire portions of humanity and provided scientific legitimacy to T.H. Huxley's condescending notion that the "coloured races" were a type of "monkey," "ape," or "chimp." Historians explain this away by describing Darwin's actions as "uniting" humanity into a single family, as opposed to the "polygenic" theories which regarded the different races as if they were different species. This is technically true. Darwin did "unite" humanity in stark contrast to the "polygenic" theories of Nott and Gliddon. In hindsight, it is difficult to see how Darwin's "aping" of non-whites is something to be applauded.

A relatively recent academic paper tries to grapple with the controversial topic of "scientific racism" and its relationship to Darwin. The paper by Jonathan Marks points out that the "polygenesis" argument by the Americans pro-slavery scientists, Nott and Gliddon, was a static view of humanity that explained the diversity in humankind by claiming that the different races were actually different species. It did so, by pointing to the lack of change that could be discerned by analyzing the depictions of African man in archeological findings:

> In their famous publication, Types of Mankind (1854), Nott and Gliddon, quoted with approval the definition of ethnology as provided by the editor of London Ethnology, Luke Burke, 'as a science which investigates the mental and physical differences of mankind' (p. 49). – It was not historical or climatic explanations to which Nott and Gliddon appealed in order to account for physical and cultural differences, but the innate fixity invested in the racialized body. It was precisely because the body was perceived as 'natural' and thus ahistorical - outside the influences and variables of time - that it was accorded the privilege of 'evidence' in establishing the mental and moral attributes of diverse races. Indeed, heralded as proof of the fixity of races (and hence, by inference, their separate origins), the evidence that polygenists proffered pointed to the fact that ancient Egyptian paintings revealed the blackness of Africans as far back as three thousand years thereby discrediting the temporality of climatic explanations as articulated by their opponents. "The races, as far as history carries us, are now the same as they were in the earliest antiquity." (Crawford, 1861, p. 358). (Pgs. 35-50, J. Marks, Chap.: 3, "The Scientific and Cultural Meaning of the Odious Ape-Human Comparison", The Nature of Difference: Science, Society and Human Biology, 1st Ed., Taylor & Francis Group, 2006)

In postulating that racial diversity existed as proof of a constantly transitory evolutionary phenomenon, Darwin both argued for "common descent" for all of humanity as well as its inherent inequality. Inevitably this was the birth of "scientific racism." The inequality of Darwin's postulate was inescapably integral to a theory of constant modification through sexual choices amongst a spectrum of "fitness":

> To assert man's common unity was to explain away the differences, the diversity of human cultures and physiological forms. Once this fundamental proposition was denied, once the polygenists defended the theory of multiple human times, race as an irreversible, timeless category of differentiation was born. With it was modern racism. (Pgs. 35-50, J. Marks, Chap.: 3, "The Scientific and Cultural Meaning of the Odious Ape-Human Comparison", The Nature of Difference: Science, Society and Human Biology, 1st Ed., Taylor & Francis Group, 2006)

As Jonathan Marks points out, Charles Lyell, Charles Darwin, and Thomas H. Huxley were all abolitionists, monogenists, and evolutionists. Jonathan Marks quotes Darwin's close friend Charles Lyell in his 1873 "The Antiquity of Man," explicit in his "aping" of those of African descent by stating: "The average Negro skull differs from that of the European ... in all which points an approach is made to the simian type."[541] Josiah Nott and George Gliddon, on the other hand, were polygenist, pro-slavery, and creationists. Yet, the "odious ape-human comparison" explicitly described in Darwinian evolution can hardly be said to be any more or any less de-humanizing than Nott and Gliddon's zoomorphisms. Consider the 1865 essay by Thomas H. Huxley:

> It may be quite true that some negroes are better than some white men; but no rational man, cognizant of the facts, believes that the average negro is the equal, still less the superior, of the average white man. ---- The highest places in the hierarchy of civilization will assuredly *not* be within the reach of our dusky cousins. (Pgs. 17-18, T.H. Huxley, "Emancipation: Black and White, In Man's Place in Nature, and Other Anthropological Essays", Macmillan, 1865)

Huxley was the first academic to come out openly and loudly proclaim humanity's ape-like ancestry. The similarity of people to apes was the cornerstone of his 1863 "Man's Place in Nature," the slim tome that shot Thomas H. Huxley to fame. He unsheathed his claws in Darwin's defense and did his best work in propagandizing. He pushed evolution into inflammatory areas. His talks on our gorilla cousins caused a storm. Marks comments on the political effects of Huxley's writings:

> In other words, the position of black people, subordinate to whites ---- more apelike, more bestial, intermediate between European and ape ---- was largely unaffected by the Darwinian revolution, which readily appropriated the familiar imagery of pre-Darwinian racial thought. **The nonwhite races embodied in connection between Europeans and the apes.** The invocation of primates as a tool for dehumanizing outsiders ---- most infamously, the Irish and the Africans ---- was simply transferred to an evolutionary discourse and thereby **given exaggerated validity as science; prerevolutionary images associating apes and "lesser races" were now simply vested with the authority of Darwinism."** (emphasis mine, Pgs. 35-50, J. Marks, Chap.: 3, "The Scientific and Cultural Meaning of the Odious Ape-Human Comparison", The Nature of Difference: Science, Society and Human Biology, 1st Ed., Taylor & Francis Group, 2006)

Jonathan Marks concludes his "odious ape-human" analysis by stating that evolutionary thought can be "benign," and that it was the interpretation of those who followed or surrounded Darwin that perverted it in ways that were not necessary. In correspondence with this author, Mr. Marks admits that Darwinian evolutionary theory would fall apart, or otherwise could not dispense with the hierarchical ranking from "fittest" to "unfit." Darwin's evolution through "sexual selection" implied a selection between "lesser" and "greater" as the impetus of the evolutionary progress and regress. Darwin did not propose a simple diversity that was divorced from the prejudices he wrote into the Theory. It is precisely this aspect

---

[541] Pgs. 35-50, J. Marks, Chap.: 3, "The Scientific and Cultural Meaning of the Odious Ape-Human Comparison", The Nature of Difference: Science, Society and Human Biology, 1st Ed., Taylor & Francis Group, 2006.

of Darwinism that precludes Darwinian evolution from ever being "benign." It is this very ranking of "fit" and "unfit" which is at the core of eugenics and "racialist" theories, namely that of "degeneracy." "Degeneracy" is a real phenomenon only to those that believe in the value-laden concepts of "progression" and "regression," and this concept is of value only to those that "self-select" themselves as the pinnacle of progress. It is thus fully incorrect to state that Darwin didn't participate in this ranking of "fit" and "unfit" humans. Eugenics was fully incorporated into Darwin's "Descent of Man." As such, entire sections of "Descent" read exactly like the mainline eugenics and "race hygiene" of Francis Galton, Charles Davenport, Alfred Ploetz, Leonard Darwin, and Karl Pearson:

> With savages, the weak in body or mind are soon eliminated; and those that survive commonly exhibit a vigorous state of health. We civilised men, on the other hand, do our utmost to check the process of elimination; we build asylums for the imbecile, the maimed, and the sick; we institute poor-laws; and our medical men exert their utmost skill to save the life of every one to the last moment. There is reason to believe that vaccination has preserved thousands, who from a weak constitution would formerly have succumbed to small-pox. Thus the weak members of civilised societies propagate their kind. No one who has attended to the breeding of domestic animals will doubt that this must be highly injurious to the race of man. It is surprising how soon a want of care, or care wrongly directed, leads to the degeneration of a domestic race; but excepting in the case of man himself, hardly any one is so ignorant as to allow his worst animals to breed. (Pg. 180)

CONTINUES...

> The aid which we feel impelled to give to the helpless is mainly an incidental result of the instinct of sympathy, which was originally acquired as part of the social instincts, but subsequently rendered, in the manner previously indicated, more tender and more widely diffused. Nor could we check our sympathy, even at the urging of hard reason, without deterioration in the noblest part of our nature. The surgeon may harden himself whilst performing an operation, for he knows that he is acting for the good of his patient; but if we were intentionally to neglect the weak and helpless, it could only be for a contingent benefit, with an overwhelming present evil. We must therefore bear the undoubtedly bad effects of the weak surviving and propagating their kind; but there appears to be at least one check in steady action, namely that the weaker and inferior members of society do not marry so freely as the sound; and this check might be indefinitely increased by the weak in body or mind refraining from marriage, though this is more to be hoped for than expected. (Pg. 181, "The Descent of Man, and Selection in Relation to Sex", D. Appleton, 1872)

Furthermore, Charles Darwin did not stay within the boundaries of biology or anthropology. Darwin fully participated in extrapolating the political implications and applications of his Theory. Darwin painted outside the lines of science, and the socio-political dogmas extrapolated by Charles Darwin were adopted and regurgitated by several generations of eugenicists. As previously evidenced, Darwin's observations on vaccination and the dysgenic effects of war would resonate on through Leonard Darwin, David Starr Jordan, Leon Whitney, and later, Adolf Hitler; all of which made nearly identical proclamations:

> In every country in which a large standing army is kept up, the finest young men are taken by the conscription or are enlisted. They are thus exposed to early death during war, are often tempted into vice, and are prevented from marrying during the prime of life. On the other hand the shorter and feebler men, with poor constitutions, are left at home, and consequently have a much better chance of marrying and propagating their kind. (Pgs. 161-162, "The Descent of Man, and Selection in Relation to Sex", D. Appleton, 1872)

"The Descent of Man" persists on the themes that would be standard for eugenic-minded tracts, and as Darwin explained, he may have not published if Haeckel had published before him. This would have been wise, as the eugenic themes in "Descent" would become well-weathered clichés of the movement. Quoting and drawing from Galton's "Hereditary Genius," Darwin enlightens the reader as to how evolution can work backward as "degeneration" that destroys entire nations:

> It has been urged by several writers, that as high intellectual powers are advantageous to a nation, the old Greeks, who stood some grades higher in intellect than any race that has ever existed, ought, if the power of natural selection were real, to have risen still higher in the scale, increased in number, and stocked the whole of Europe. Here we have the tacit assumption, so often made with respect to corporeal structures, that there is some innate tendency toward continued development in mind and body. But development of all kinds depends on many concurrent favorable circumstances. Natural selection acts only tentatively. Individuals and races may have acquired certain indisputable advantages, and yet have perished from failing in other characters. (Pg. 117, "The Descent of Man, and Selection in Relation to Sex", D. Appleton, 1872)

Thus, it is correct to state that Darwin not just endorsed, but fully incorporated Galton's eugenics into his theory of "natural selection," namely the premise that personality traits, positive and negative, were inherited:

> During this same period the Holy Inquisition selected with extreme care the freest and boldest men in order to burn or imprison them. In Spain alone some of the best men—those who doubted and questioned, and without doubting there can be no progress—were eliminated during three centuries at the rate of a thousand a year.

CONTINUES...

There is apparently much truth in the belief that the wonderful progress of the United States, as well as the character of the people, are the results of natural selection: for the more energetic, restless, and courageous men from all parts of

Europe have emigrated during the last ten or twelve generations to that great country, and have there succeeded best. (Pg. 118, "The Descent of Man, and Selection in Relation to Sex", D. Appleton, 1872)

Darwin explicitly noted that with his theory "progress is no invariable rule." Darwin believed the "sexual selection" could work in reverse, towards negative effects, and that man could sink into "indolence" as a result. This was Darwin's way of expressing the dogma of "degeneracy," or more precisely, that this concept so central to militant eugenicists originated with Charles Darwin:

> It even appears from what we see, for instance, in parts of South America, that a people which may be called civilized, such as the Spanish settlers, is liable to become indolent and to retrograde, when the conditions of life are very easy. (Pg. 119, "The Descent of Man, and Selection in Relation to Sex", D. Appleton, 1872)

This conception of humanity resonated far beyond scientific circles. One only needs to read Margaret Sanger's 1920 "Woman and the New Race" to understand that Sanger and her colleagues had adopted an orthodox understanding of Darwinism:

> The lower down in the scale of human development we go to the less sexual control we find. It is said that the aboriginal Australian, the lowest known species of the human family, **just a step higher than the chimpanzee in brain** development, has so little sexual control that police authority alone prevents him from obtaining sexual satisfaction on the streets." (emphasis mine, nyu.edu, Margaret Sanger, "What Every Girl Should Know," The Public Writings and Speeches of Margaret Sanger, 1920)

These were the "scientific" concepts that were leveraged to draft all the laws used to exclude, segregate, and ultimately eliminate large swaths of humanity. Without this ranking from "unfit" to "fit," the determinations and lines of demarcation made for sterilization, segregation, and extermination made no logical sense. It is this "scientific" ranking, given "exaggerated validity," as Marks would state, which were at the core of American immigration and sterilization policies, which were later translated into the German National Socialist sterilization and extermination laws. It is this "odious ape-human comparison" which forever changed the trajectory of Darwinism and placed it on the path where "racialism" would ultimately become "racism," and where "race theory" would inevitably be transformed into "eugenic theories." It's these "rank-order hierarchies" which were the indispensable main ingredient to "scientific racism." [542] Jonathan Marks concludes that Darwin's "Descent of Man" suffers the fate of an unconvincing sequel to "Origins of the Species" and that it served only to legitimize the socio-

---

[542] "The Misuse of Biological Hierarchies: The American Eugenics Movement, 1900-1940", Garland E. Allen, History and Philosophy of the Life Sciences, Vol. 5, No. 2, 1983, pp. 105-128.

political concepts of the era:

> What is not controversial is the fact that Darwin himself was heavily influenced by the anthropology of his time. It is for this very reason that Descent of Man (1871) has been criticized as a largely unoriginal work reiterating many of the social Darwinist theories that were in their turn, further elaborated upon, expanded and legitimated with the theoretical possibilities natural selection opened up. (Pgs. 35-50, J. Marks, Chap.: 3, "The Scientific and Cultural Meaning of the Odious Ape-Human Comparison", The Nature of Difference: Science, Society and Human Biology, 1st Ed., Taylor & Francis Group, 2006)

Jonathan Marks underestimates or underplays Darwin's fame. Here, Darwin may well have indulged in incorporating questionable theories in "Descent," but it is his doing that lifted these theories from their marginal status. His "Origin of the Species" had catapulted Darwin to the top of his profession and enduring adulation. Thus, by endorsing and incorporating Haeckel's and Galton's work into a necessary aspect of the "Theory," Darwin literally legitimized racial hierarchies as "scientific." Etymology, the technical term for word history, helps illustrate that what we now regard as "scientific racism" was born out of Darwin's work in his 1871 book "The Descent of Man." The etymology of "racism" and "racialism" clarifies that while the term "race" is much older than Darwinism, the consecration of the concept into the realm of science is dated to precisely the publication date of "Descent." The Online Etymology Dictionary documents this aspect of history:

> **RACIST:** 1932 as a noun, 1938 as an adjective, from *race* (n.2); *racism* is first attested 1936 (from Fr. *racisme*, 1935), originally in the context of Nazi theories. But they replaced earlier words, **racialism (1871)** and *racialist* (1917), both often used early 20c. in a British or South African context.

> **RACE:** "people of common descent," c.1500, from M.Fr. *razza* "race, breed, lineage," possibly from It. *razza*, of unknown origin (cf. Sp., Port. raza). ---- "group of people with common occupation" (c.1500), and "generation" (c.1560). Meaning "tribe, nation, or people regarded as of common stock" is from c.1600. Modern meaning of "one of the great divisions of mankind based on physical peculiarities" is from 1774 (though even among anthropologists there never has been an accepted classification of these). ---- Klein suggests these derive from Arabic *ra's* "head, beginning, origin" (cf. Heb. rosh). O.E. *þeode* meant both "race" and "language;" as a verb, *geþeodan*, it meant "to unite, to join." Race-riot attested from 1889, Amer.Eng. – (www.etymonline.com)

Harper Collins online dictionary provides a definition of "race," "racialism," and "racist" that is consistent with the Online Etymology Dictionary:

> **racism or racialism** -- Origin: 1905–10; racial + -ism -- the belief that races have distinctive cultural characteristics determined by hereditary factors and that this endows some races with an intrinsic superiority over others. (dictionary.com, Harper Collins)

Allan Chase, author of "The Legacy of Malthus" also consulted the etymology section to understand the origins of the term "racism":

> **Racism** – which according to Webster is "the program or practice of racial discrimination, segregation, persecution, and domination, based on racialism," which in turn is defined as "the doctrine or feeling of racial differences or antagonisms, especially with reference to supposed racial superiority, inferiority, or purity. (Pg. 72, "Legacy of Malthus: The Social Costs of the New Scientific Racism", 1975)

A March 13th, 2007 article asked John Simpson, editor of the "Oxford English Dictionary Online" if the terms "racialism" and "racism" meant the same thing:

> Yes, says John Simpson. ---- They didn't start out that way, but they are now considered one in the same. Racialism and racialist are older terms, dating from the early 20 Century. When the words were first used in the early 1900s, they loosely referred to semi-anthropological theories about biological differences among races. It was a way that people tried to legitimize racist beliefs and practices, but over the years scientists rejected such theories. (March 13, 2007, "BBC News")

An October 1939 issue of "The Crisis" journal distributed by the NAACP offers an example of how the term was used prior to The Holocaust, and as insight as to how African Americans witnessed and regarded German racism:

> A party charged with an offense replies, not by denying the charge, but by making a similar charge against the accuser. Such an argument is employed by the Schwartze Korps, organ of the German secret police and Hitler's Elite Guard, in urging the segregation of Jews in "Jim Crow" cars on German railroads, including Jews of American citizenship. "This solution," states the Schwartze Korps, "follows a documented democratic example. For the world's freest country, where even presidents denounce the devilish invention of race consciousness, does not permit its State citizens with equal rights but a darker hue to sit, much less sleep, next to a white person, even if the white is only a sewage worker and the black a world boxing champion or other national hero. The colored people will be relentlessly driven by an equally colored conductor into their own rolling kraal. The obvious answer to the *tu quoque* argument is that "two wrongs do not make one right." But we are not here concerned with answering the argument. In view of the other measures taken by the Nazis against the Jews, this measure, if put into effect, would be a mere pin prick, but, as Americans, we admit to smarting under this thrust of the Nazis. Their defense is no defense, but their accusation is a valid indictment. Racialism is wrong whether it be an Aryan racialism directed against Jews or a white racialism directed against Negroes. (N.A.A.C.P., "The Crisis," Oct. 1939)

The book "Theories of Race and Racism," by Les Back and John Solomos documents the scientific origins of the concepts of "racialist" views:

Several common features indicate that racialism belongs to the spiritual family of scientism. Indeed, we have seen how the latter is characterized by its affirmation of an integral determinism ---- Scientism is also characterized by its demand that science formulate society's goals and indicate legitimate means for attaining them. One might call racialism the tip of the scientistic iceberg. (Pg. 67, "Theories of Race and Racism: A Reader", Routledge, 2001)

More to the point, Les Back and John Solomos document that the "racialism" inherent to "scientism" originates from the scientific desire to create empirical hierarchies and categories, a concept crystallized by Garland E. Allen:

The desire for scientism, exemplified in the valorization of systematic categorization based on empiricism, inevitably produces some instances which refuse to be contained by the conceptual boundaries established. In these cases either the lines of demarcation have to be reordered or the exceptions denied, and this is why stereotypes are protean rather than stable. (Pg. 269, "Theories of Race and Racism: A Reader", Routledge, 2001)

You would be hard-pressed to find someone more knowledgeable about eugenics than Garland E. Allen. His summation of the use of "rank-order hierarchies" in biology to rank humanity is on point. Here is Professor Allen on what he terms "rank-order" and "value-judgment" hierarchies:

One of the persistent problems of evolutionary theory in the past has been the influence which rank-order hierarchical thinking has maintained in viewing and constructing natural relationships (taxonomic or phylogenetic) among organisms. The great chain of being or scala naturae represents what is essentially a rank-order hierarchy in which those groups higher up in the scale are viewed as better (more perfect, more complex, or nearer the divine) than those lower down. (Pg. 106 – "The Misuse of Biological Hierarchies: The American Eugenics Movement, 1900 – 1940", History and Philosophy of the Life Sciences, Vol. 5, No. 2, 1983, Pgs. 105-128)

Garland Allen clarifies that rank-order hierarchies are not mere classificatory devices in the way they were utilized by evolutionary scientists; they tend to emerge from the context of the social preferences, the "self-selection" as Daylanne English would put it, on the part of the those crafting the rank-order. As Garland Allen points out, the "chief feature of rank-order hierarchies is that they are based on value-judgments in which higher levels, or categories, are invested with more value than lower-level categories." [543] Every single eugenicist, starting really with Charles Darwin, applied what Madison Grant would later call the "ethnic pyramid." [544] As Garland Allen points out, The Holocaust was simply not possible without this ideological foundation:

In Germany, under the Nazis, eugenic ideology was carried to its logical end,

---

[543] Pg. 106 – "The Misuse of Biological Hierarchies: The American Eugenics Movement, 1900 – 1940", Garland E. Allen, History and Philosophy of the Life Sciences, Vol. 5, No. 2, 1983, Pgs. 105-128.
[544] Pg. 117 – Ibid.

with lower categories in the hierarchy of racial value being decimated. Racial purity became the by-word of the holocaust. It is not stretching the pint too much, I think, to argue that without the prevalence of eugenic thinking, without the confusion of rank-ordered hierarchies, the holocaust could never have been mounted to the level that it was. (Pg. 127 – "The Misuse of Biological Hierarchies: The American Eugenics Movement, 1900 – 1940", History and Philosophy of the Life Sciences, Vol. 5, No. 2, 1983, Pgs. 105-128)

Les Back and John Solomos excuse Darwin by subscribing to the opinion that Darwin "cut the ground from under the feet of the topologists." [545] They base this on an opinion that "Darwin himself said, that great as is the physical unlikeness of the various races of men their likenesses are greater, and upon this rests the whole scientific doctrine of Human Brotherhood." [546] Yet, Darwin himself undermines this argument by breaking humanity up into stratified levels of evolution, and literally resigning Africans and Aborigines to the lower strata of humanity. Darwin legitimized "rank-order hierarchies," and the term "racialist" subsequently became a respectable way of describing this scientific approach. Furthermore, it is of note to point out that Les Back and John Solomos document the "racialist" justifications of Hitler's Third Reich as being rooted in Darwin and Galton by quoting Alfred Rosenberg, Hitler's leading racial theorist:

> …whole cultural life for decades has been more or less under the influence of biological thinking, as it was begun particularly around the middle of the last century, by the teachings of Darwin, Mendel and Galton and afterwards has been advanced by the studies of Ploetz, Schallmayer, Correns, de Vries, Tschermak, Baur, Rüdin, Fischer, Lenz and others. . . It was recognized that the natural laws discovered for plants and animals ought also to be valid for man. . . (Pg. 219, "Theories of Race and Racism: A Reader", Routledge, 2001)

Thus, it can be said that the Nazi scientists were interpreting Darwinian theory precisely to the logical extrapolation provided by Charles Darwin and his close-knit group of disciples. Without these racial, and by Darwin's implication, evolutionary hierarchies within the human species, "The Descent of Man" was a useless waste of ink, and Charles Darwin knew it. Darwin's "Theory" as it applied to man was inescapably elitists and racist, per Darwin's own definition. A belief in "progression" and "degeneration" implies a belief in hierarchy and direction. It is linear thinking at its worst. In 20/20 hindsight, Darwinism is inescapably pinned down by antiquated, if not comical, notions of aristocracy.

Nor can it be said that these racial assumptions were necessary or inevitable. Jonathan Marks is admirably and courageously correct in saying so. We need only look to Mendel to debunk that notion. Mendel proved that the mechanisms of heredity need not adopt any hierarchical notions and need only chart the changes that come with infinite combinations of broad biological diversity. Darwin and his

---

[545] Pg. 57 - "Theories of Race and Racism: A Reader", Les Back and John Solomos, Routledge, 2001.
[546] Pg. 219 – Ibid.

disciples did the exact opposite. The Darwinian clique was explicit in claiming that British Anglo-Saxon Whites were at the pinnacle of that hierarchy and that all of evolution points in the direction of Anglo-Saxon whiteness. This was an embarrassingly linear paradigm; implying direction in what is, in reality, a non-linear process. Darwin evidences his own Victorian beliefs in "progression" and "regression" by loading his theory with value-laden prejudices. It is no coincidence that eugenic-minded elitists, starting with Francis Galton, began abusing science by claiming that "natural aristocracies" were a legitimate scientific proposal.

Darwin could not see past his social status, as there were plenty of contemporary indicators to suggest that the "coloured races" were not biologically less evolved. Harriet Tubman, Fredrick Douglas, Sojourner Truth, and Nat Turner upended the notion that cultural backwardness was an indicator of lesser evolved biology. If Charles Darwin was as interested in the cause of the African slave as some modern historians would like to claim, he certainly had plenty of examples to draw from which clearly evidenced that a lesser technological evolution was not in any way indicative of biological worth. Human history persists to provide proof against the views Darwin enshrined into "The Descent of Man." While Darwin didn't have the benefit of pre- and post-World War II Japan, it certainly stands as proof of just how a culturally antiquated people can become more advanced and prosperous than even Darwin's beloved England. The 20th century has provided a series of anthropological experiments by splitting North and South Korea, North and South Vietnam, and East and West Germany to prove that biology and heredity have very little to do with cultural evolution, as Darwin's clique postulated.

Let it be clear what this author's intentions are: This is an argument for the type of empirical science practiced in Mendel's pea experiments and the Hardy-Weinberg principle, and against the political time bomb that Darwinism was intended to be from the onset. Darwin's apologists insist that he was practicing "pure science." This is an insult to our intelligence, as comparative anthropology has never been considered "pure" by scientists. Comparative anthropology is inevitably polluted by the prejudices of the observer, and significantly handicapped by the personal knowledge set of the anthropologist that practices it. Furthermore, it is hardly a secret that T.H. Huxley, Charles Lyell, and Ernst Haeckel were drastically politicizing influences on Charles Darwin. Huxley and Lyell pushed Darwin into a fistfight with traditional Christianity, and Haeckel took advantage of this to propose his own religion of Monism. From its onset, Darwinism was intended to instigate and to drive a wedge in society to weaken traditional Christianity's dominance and to free up science from the limitations Christianity put on it. While one can surely make an argument for the positive aspect of freeing science, it is just as correct to state that Darwinism also ushered in a 100-year period when science literally dedicated itself to the "religion" that Francis Galton proposed eugenics should be. There were real consequences for these bully tactics, one of which was the silencing or downplaying of viable competing scientific voices, namely that of Mendel's purer and more empirical approach and methodology.

Sec. 3 – FROM "AQUIRED" TO "UNIT" CHARCTERISTICS:

Historians of the eugenics movement attribute much of its faults and deficiencies to a poor understanding of heredity. They point to the oversimplification of the mechanisms through which hereditary traits are passed from one generation to another as the misunderstanding that led scientists to believe that they could eradicate what are, in reality, complex behavioral traits or physical traits that are the compounded result of a combination of factors. It is true that eugenicists simplified genetic inheritance to a one-to-one relationship, where each defect was regarded as a singular trait that could be bred out of the species, thus by forbidding those with an undesirable trait from having children, the undesirable trait would cease to be passed on. This was the eugenic understanding of heredity. As we have seen, alcoholism, prostitution, and pauperism were among the behavioral traits they sought to eradicate. Cancer, Down's Syndrome, and physical deformities were among the physical traits Nazis targeted with the weapon of eugenic breeding. It is through this 20/20 hindsight, that it is easy to brush off the eugenics movement as a "pseudo-science," as many scientists would like to do, by pointing to their oversimplification of the mechanisms of heredity. However, the truth is that eugenics rose out of a general confusion on the matters, largely attributable to Charles Darwin.

Historically speaking, early efforts stand as proof that the public was ready for a theory of evolution that departed from the literal reading of the Bible, much prior to Darwin, as Spencer's and Chambers's work evidence. This also goes a long way to disprove that Darwinism was necessary to dislodge science from the hold of the Church. Lamarck recognized that the problem of environmental influences was bound with the problem of heredity as far back as 1800. Lamarck recognized half a century prior to Darwin that there can be no evolution to more complex forms unless there were variations from generation to generation. His *Systeme des Animaux sand Vertebres* introduced his theory of a "path," or what would later be called evolution. However, Lamarck postulated that life originated by spontaneous generation and degraded and multiplied to different variations. It is also fair to state that Lamarck's theory was based more on philosophic principles than on a fully formed science of anthropology. Lamarck was followed by Robert Chambers, who in 1844 published the best-selling "Vestiges of the Natural History of Creation" anonymously, as he was afraid to associate his name with the work. The work was not well received academically as it attributed creation to God. However, like Darwin after him, Chambers rejected the Biblical timeline for the age of the earth by pointing to the fossil evidence, an important step that Lyell and Darwin would later propose as integral to the Theory of Evolution. Chambers' book went through 11 editions and sold over 25,000 copies, in comparison to the 1,700 copies of "Origin of the Species" that Darwin originally sold. There is also the work of Herbert Spencer, who was the first to correlate physical or behavioral characteristics to heredity in his 1863 "Principles of Biology." Spencer is also credited for coining the term "evolution" to describe, not Darwin's, but Lamarck's development hypothesis. Beyond that, Spencer is also credited for coining the term "survival of the fittest" in

1852, a full six years before Darwin published his theory.

Ironically enough, the first true attempt to explain heredity through the scientific method, as opposed to observation and deduction, was done by the Catholic friar Johann Gregor Mendel. Mendel conducted his famous experiments with crossbreeding peas in 1865. He was Darwin's contemporary but unfortunately was completely unknown as he worked in isolation, out of a monastery, and was not a recognized member of the scientific community. Mendel was easy to ignore, as he lectured on his findings only twice and did not have the formidable political propaganda popularizing his contributions like T.H. Huxley, Charles Lyell, Joseph Dalton Hooker, and Ernst Haeckel provided for Darwin. Although 150 copies of Mendel's paper were sent to major libraries around the world, the world didn't take notice until the turn-of-the-century. Interestingly enough, even though Mendel was a Catholic friar, he never used his science to bloviate about philosophy or theology. Mendel never bloviated or painted outside the lines as Darwin did. Mendel's paper stays focused on the topic and never attempts to extrapolate sociological arguments or political theories. Mendel's work spanned a mere 20-plus pages, as opposed to thousands of pages penned by Darwin, and at no point did Mendel prostitute his work for political causes for or against the role of the Church or the existence of God. Mendel's findings stood as scientific data produced by the scientific method, without the pompous bloviating about how his work applied or did not apply to political or philosophical discourse.

The February 27, 2009 article titled "Why didn't Darwin discover Mendel's laws?" written by Charlotte Webber reviews an article by the same title published by Jonathan C. Howard in the "Journal of Biology." The article doesn't answer why Darwin ignored or chose to dismiss the work that Mendel sent to him. Instead, it asks why Darwin failed where Mendel succeeded, despite being contemporaries. Charlotte Webber points out that "Mendel solved the logic of inheritance in his monastery garden with no more technology than Darwin had in his garden at Down House," and asks: "why couldn't Darwin have done it too?" Webber concludes that "Mendel had a good understanding of biology, but his understanding of physics, statistics and probability theory were far superior to Darwin's." Jonathan C. Howard believes Darwin's background, influences, and research focus gave him a viewpoint that prevented him from interpreting the evidence that was all around him, even in his own work:

> "Quantitative variation was at the heart of Darwin's evolution, and quantitative variation is the last place where clean Mendelian inheritance can be seen," says Howard. "Darwin boxed himself in, unable to see the laws of inheritance in continuous variation, unable to see the real importance of discontinuous variation where the laws of inheritance could be discerned". ("Why Didn't Darwin Discover Mendel's Laws?", Jonathan C. Howard, Journal of Biology, BioMed Central, Feb. 24, 2009)

To be fair to Charles Darwin, if the biographical work on his family relationships is to be trusted, Darwin was horrified, if not paralyzed, by the implications of evolution and "degeneration." Charles had married his first cousin, Emma Wedgwood, and was knowledgeable enough about breeding to know of the ill-effects of breeding animals that come from too close relations. It appears as if Darwin felt that he was personally paying for violating these dictates of animal breeding as his daughter Annie died at a young age of 10. Many Darwin biographers speculate that Darwin's relationship with Emma was the reason for the reluctance to publish, citing Emma's devout Christian values and Darwin's increasing atheism as one of various theories. Some speculate that Charles Darwin shied away from publishing his discoveries for decades after he claimed to have made them due to the psychological impact of Annie's death. There may be some truth to this as Darwin apparently couldn't bring himself to attend his child's funeral. Some attribute this absence to Darwin's increasing atheism; others to the increasing realization that the hereditary consequences of having children with his first cousin implied. [547] Charles Darwin's family was a good example of his own theory about plant hybridization: that inbreeding could negatively affect the health and number of resulting offspring. Darwin authored three botanical books all of which demonstrated that cross-fertilization was much more beneficial than self-fertilization for maintaining robust and plentiful plant species.

Studies have inquired into the inbreeding in Darwin's family tree. The scientists at Ohio State University traced the genealogy of the Darwin and Wedgwood families back four generations. As we know, Emma Wedgewood, was Darwin's first cousin. Darwin's mother and grandfather also were Wedgwoods, and his mother's parents were third cousins. Emma's and Charles's marriage produced 10 children, three of whom died before age 10, and three of the six surviving children with long-term marriages did not produce any offspring. Darwin's third child, Mary Eleanor, lived for only 23 days and died in 1842 of an unknown cause. Annie, his first daughter, and second child, died in 1851, and his last child, Charles Waring, died at 18 months of scarlet fever in 1858.

Whatever the justification for Darwin's reluctance to publish or inability to produce the work of the scientific rigor and empiricism that Mendel demonstrated, it is important to note that Charles Darwin only marginally attempted to explain the mechanism of heredity in his 1860 "Origin of the Species." Darwin first tried his hand at a scientific explanation as to the hereditary mechanisms of evolution in 1868 with his "Variations of Animals and Plants under Domestication." The title is telling, as what Darwin was doing was extrapolating his experience as a livestock breeder towards something more akin to eugenics. Elof Axel Carlson quotes Darwin describing his idea as the "provisional hypothesis of pangenesis," which was an expansion of the ideas briefly touched upon in the first chapter of "Origin of the Species":

> It is universally admitted that the cells or units of the body increase by self-division or proliferation, retaining the same nature, and that they ultimately become converted into the various tissues and substances of the body. But besides

---

[547] phys.org - "Study: Darwin Was Right to Worry that Marriage to His Cousin Affected His Offspring", Emily Caldwell, Research News, May 3, 2010.

this are dispersed throughout the whole system; that these, when supplied with proper nutriment, multiplied by self–division, and are ultimately developed into units like those from which they were originally derived. These granules may be called **gemmules**. They are collected from all parts of the system to constitute the sexual elements, and their development in the next generation forms a new being; but they are likewise capable to transmission in a dormant state to future generations and may then be developed. (emphasis mine, Pg. 143, "The Unfit: A History of a Bad Idea", Elof Axel Carlson, Cold Spring Harbor Laboratory Press, 2001)

Darwin's cousin, Galton, took again to tinkering with his cousin's theories. Galton decided to test Darwin's "pangenesis" and "gemmules" by transfusing blood among different varieties of rabbits. In one experiment he tied two rabbits together so that their carotid arteries could be surgically crossed, each pouring blood of the other strain into their circulation. No combination or experiment in swapping the blood of different variations of rabbits produced a crossing of characteristics. Thus, in 1871, Galton submitted his findings to the "Proceedings of the Royal Society" stating:

> The conclusion from this large series of experiments is not to be avoided, that the doctrine of **Pangenesis, pure and simple, as I have interpreted it, is incorrect**. (emphasis mine, Pg. 146, "The Unfit: A History of a Bad Idea", Elof Axel Carlson, Cold Spring Harbor Laboratory Press, 2001)

Elof Axel Carlson documents that Charles Darwin was "appalled" and proceeded to defend himself by publishing a rebuttal in the journal "Nature." Carlson describes the rebuttal as Darwin "lamely" defending his idea by stating that he never claimed that "gemmules" were transferred through the circulating blood. More telling of the politics of Darwinism is the fact that despite knowing to be correct, Francis Galton, a 50-year-old man by this time, caved in and backpedaled with a combination of laudatory praise and parable. Elof Axel Carlson recalls the embarrassing episode:

> In the story he imagined himself and Darwin to be early ancestors of man. Galton "heard his trusted leader utter a cry, not particularly well articulated, but to my ears more like that of a hyena than any other animal." The animal cry was a warning that Galton interpreted as a hyena in the bush. He carefully searched his surroundings but found no such hyena but there was a threatening leopard instead. "I am given to understand for the first time that my leader's cry had no reference to a hyena down in the plain, but a leopard up in the trees; his throat had been a little out of order ---- Well, my labor has not been in vain; it is something to have established the fact that there are no hyenas in the plain, and I think I see my way to a good position for la look out for leopards among the branches of the trees. **In meantime, Vive Pangenesis.** (emphasis mine, Pg. 148, "The Unfit: A History of a Bad Idea", Cold Spring Harbor Laboratory Press, 2001)

Poor Francis! Francis, after all, was riding Darwin's coattails to fame. Being slapped down by his mentor obviously hurt a man that was desperately seeking to follow his cousin into scientific respectability. Galton's side of the family made its fortune from banking and armaments sales. Galton's father had always shown off young Francis as a child protégée, but Francis proved to be less than the phenomenon that his father touted. After a lackluster try at mathematics, Francis tried his hand at a medical career but did not complete his medical studies. Instead, he inherited a fortune when his father died and decided to become a "gentleman scientist." In Galton's defense, he did contribute to science by identifying the practical use of fingerprints. However, one could make a strong argument that Galton's repackaging of other people's ideas as "eugenics" would not have had the impact that it did without the benefit of having his cousin's name associated with it. Recall that Francis was repackaging Noyes' "Stirpiculture" and other similar theories by less palpable and less socially acceptable sources. The close family ties between the Galton-Darwin-Wedgwood family greatly bolstered Galton's career, and subsequently, Leonard Darwin provided further impetus by joining the effort as the head of the International eugenics movement.

Academia has been unreasonably kind to Francis Galton. By comparison, historians have been highly respectful of this "gentleman scientist" while dismissing Lamarck for not having formal credentials. They have subordinated Mendel to Darwin for working in isolation as a Catholic friar instead of as a professional scientist. The same prejudice went into choosing between Alfred Russel Wallace and Darwin. It is also easily arguable that academia has actively shielded Francis Galton from culpability in the crimes of The Holocaust because Galton's work only leads back to Darwin. Darwin is championed by historians as providing scientific proof of a "common descent" between blacks and whites in an era when other scientists were claiming blacks to be a different species, namely Louis Agassiz. While Lamarckism and Darwinism were hotly debated, Gregor Mendel was forgotten for decades. To his credit, Gregor Mendel never fell back on nepotism or politicking to promote his science. In September 2006, the Chicago Tribune covered the Chicago's Field Museum exhibit on Mendel. Kevin Felheim, the manager of the museum's Pritzker Laboratory for Molecular Systematics and Evolution is of the opinion that:

We would not have evolutionary biology today if we did not have Mendel's discoveries. His ideas still apply to the research work we do today. (articles.chicagotribune.com, "Field Celebrates Genetic Pioneer: Augustinian Friar was Discovering the Secret of Genetic Inheritance in 1850s, While Darwin was Publishing his Theory", William Mullen, Sept. 12, 2006)

Consider Felheim's exclusion of the Darwin name in this bold claim of how "evolutionary" biology could not exist without Mendel. The truth is that despite Galton's cowardly capitulation and gratuitous butt-kissing, Galton was right. Case in point, there are no modern geneticists that cite Darwin's "gemmules" or "pangenesis" as the mechanisms of heredity. However, "Mendelian trait" is a term used daily by today's scientists. This is certainly more than what can be said about

Darwin's theory of "pangenesis." How much of the endless bloviating in Darwin's two tomes is still utilized by scientists on a day-by-day basis? This is a question that would gain the vicious ire of the modern-day Darwinists, but it is an honest question that originates with the actual reading of Darwin's two voluminous books. These books are filled with conjecture and allegory to a nauseating level that would only engender ridicule if a similar work was published as "science" today. The same accusation cannot be made of Mendel's work. Mendel's work is as respectable today as it was when it was first published. Alas, this is a problem with a politicized science filled with Darwinists that have never read Darwin's books, Marxists that have never read Marx, and Malthusians that have never read Malthus.

The Chicago Tribune article also documented a fact that is not reported enough by historians. It is only just and proper that history record that one of those 150 copies of Mendel's paper went to Charles Darwin:

> The local scientific society in Brno published his results in 1866, and Mendel paid for 40 copies of the paper to be printed and sent to leading European research centers and scientists, including Darwin. ---- 20-century archivists eventually found some of those copies in libraries, never opened, including one in Darwin's library. (articles.chicagotribune.com, William Mullen, "Field Celebrates Genetic Pioneer: Augustinian Friar was Discovering the Secret of Genetic Inheritance in 1850s, While Darwin was Publishing his Theory", Sept. 12, 2006)

Even stranger is the very popular notion that attempts to morph Mendel and Darwin into one. Mende's personal correspondence evidence that he would have been vehemently opposed to a characterization of his work supporting Darwin's. Mendel's theory was "obviously constructed to deny all Darwin's ideas about heredity and thus his theory of descent with modification." [548] This morphing of Mendel and Darwin is a very recent development, as it differs from the original interpretation of their relationship:

> In 1902, [Gustave Niessl] suggested that it was believed in the 1860s that Mendel's work was in *competition* with, as opposed to *complementary* to, that of Darwin and Wallace. (emphasis his, Pg. 209, "Mendel's Opposition to Evolution and to Darwin", B.E. Bishop, The Journal of Heredity, 1996:87-3)

This is an important distinction to make; to understand that Mendel's understanding of how genetics worked was in opposition to Darwin's. Historians of the eugenics movement often characterize eugenics as a "pseudo-science" precisely because of its simplistic approach to genetics, describing the character or physical traits as having a one-to-one relationship. Similarly, simplistic descriptions of the biological mechanisms at work in heredity appear more than once in Darwin's work. Darwin's 1877 book "The Different Forms of Flowers on Plants of the Same Species" details breeding experiments involving a well-defined "unit" character. Darwin's "gemmules" are strikingly like the "unit characters" which eugenicists used

---

[548] Pg. 205 – "Mendel's Opposition to Evolution and to Darwin", B.E. Bishop, The Journal of Heredity, 1996:87(3)

as the foundation of their claims, and for which eugenics earned the label of "pseudo-science." Darwin allegedly chose not to experiment likely because Darwin believed "that the rules of inheritance were too complex and not ready for definitive analysis." [549] This may be so, but the drive to explain heredity through Darwinian spectacles persisted. It was a simplistic belief in a "unit character" as the mechanism of inheritance which eugenicists clung to from Galton on through. That they were also devout Darwinists only helps support the observation that much of their erroneous analysis is rooted in their blind faith and an all too accurate understanding of Darwin's "Theory".

---

[549] sciencedaily.com - "Why Didn't Darwin Discover Mendel's Laws?", Journal of Biology, March 2009.

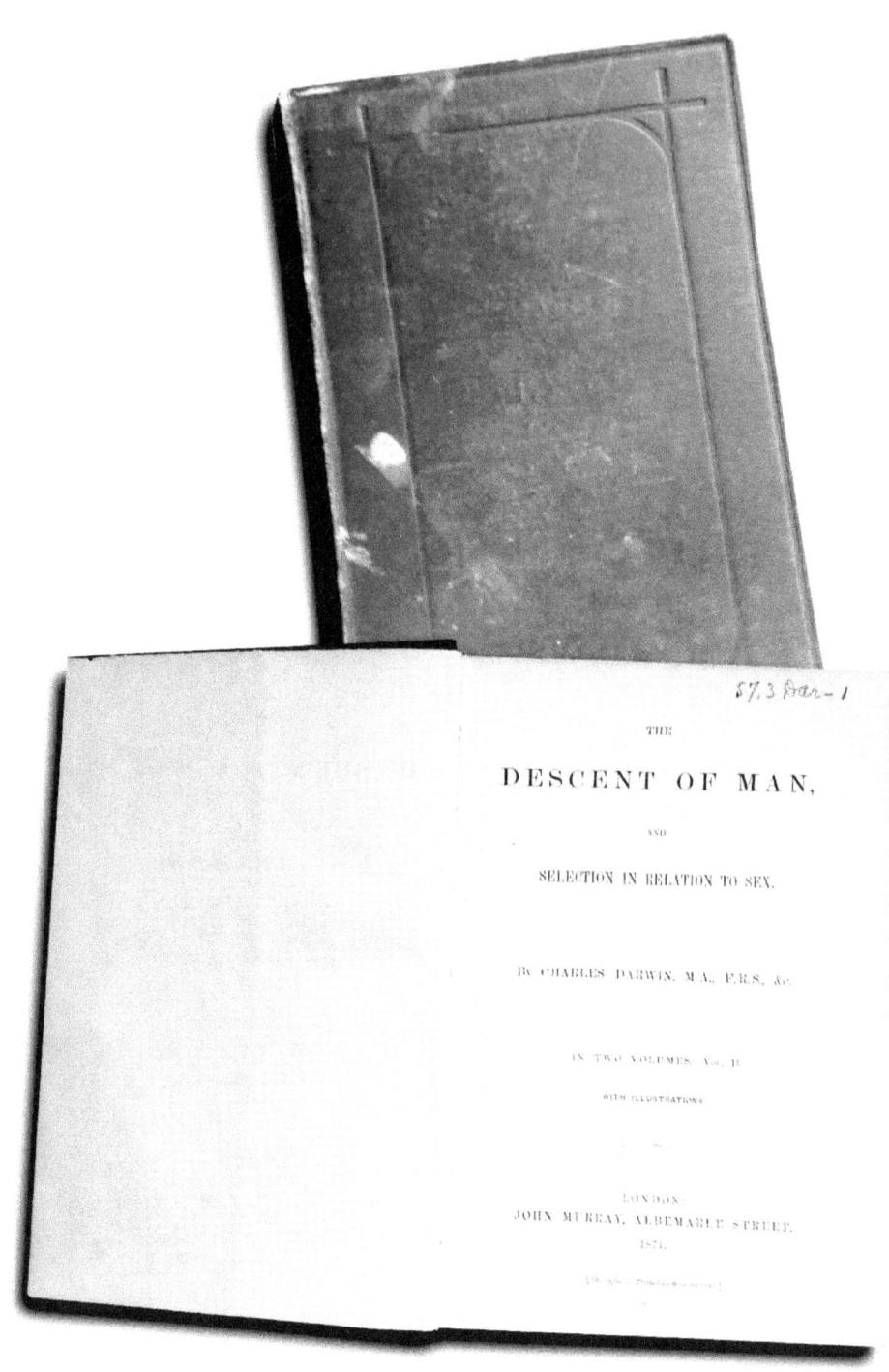

FIGURE 17: Charles B. Davenport's and Harry H. Laughlin's copy of Darwin's "Descent of Man." This copy was part of the Eugenics Records Office library, and is now part of the library collection at Cold Spring Harbor Laboratory in New York.

Chap. 17: 1869 to 1865

SCIENCE & TECHNOLOGY: The Transcontinental Railroad is completed in Promontory, Utah. –The first issue of the scientific journal Nature is published. – In Egypt, the Suez Canal, linking the Mediterranean Sea with the Red Sea, is inaugurated. - Dmitri Mendeleev makes periodic table. - Friedrich Miescher discovers deoxyribonucleic acid (DNA) in the pus of discarded surgical bandages. **AMERICAN FRONT:** African-American men are granted the right to vote in the District of Columbia. – Nebraska is admitted as the 37 US state. – Alaska is purchased for $7.2 million from Alexander II of Russia, about 2 cent/acre ($4.19/km²), by United States Secretary of State William H. Seward. Woman's suffrage: In New York, Susan B. Anthony and Elizabeth Cady Stanton form the National Woman's Suffrage Association. –**EUROPEAN FRONT:** August Bebel and Wilhelm Liebknecht found the Social Democratic Workers' Party of Germany. **LIFE:** The first game of American Football between two American colleges is played. - American outlaw Jesse James commits his first confirmed bank robbery in Gallatin, Missouri. W. E. B. Du Bois, American civil rights leader is born. – Maxim Gorky, Russian author is born. Frank Lloyd Wright, American architect and visionary is born. – Marie Curie, Polish-born scientist, recipient of the Nobel Prize in Chemistry and Physics is born. - Wilbur Wright is born. Lewis Carroll publishes Alice's Adventures in Wonderland. - Erich Ludendorff, German general is born. - P. T. Barnum - The Humbugs of the World - Karl Marx - Value, Price and Profit

Sec. I - INHERITED LEGITIMACY:

Galton's career can be divided into two parts. During the first, Galton was engaged in African exploration, travel writing, geography, and meteorology; though the voyeuristic quality to much of this earlier work probably slots Galton as an early precursor to Hugh Heffner. The second part began after he read "Origin of Species." As we know, "Origin" convinced Galton that humanity could be improved through selective breeding. Galton's first published his opinion that humanity could benefit from an organized and systematized procreation in 1865 in "Hereditary Talent and Character":

> The power of man over animal life, in producing whatever varieties of form he pleases, is enormously great. It would seem as though the physical structure of future generations was almost as plastic as clay, under the control of the breeder's will. It is my desire to show more pointedly than - so far as I am aware - has been attempted before, that mental qualities are equally under control. - In investigating the hereditary transmission of talent, we must ever bear in mind our ignorance of the laws which govern the inheritance even of physical features. We know to, a certainty that the latter exist, though we do not thoroughly understand their action. The breeders of our domestic animals have discovered many rules by experience, and act upon them to a nicety. But we have not advanced, even to this limited extent, in respect to the human race. (Pg. 157, "Hereditary Talent and Character", Macmillan's Magazine, Vol. 12, Pgs. 157-166, Macmillan and Company, 1865)

Galton's own words prove that from the onset the science of eugenics aimed at controlling personality traits in human beings through selective breeding, and not just the prevention of diseases as medicine ought to be. Galton was from the onset in the business of building a "master race" of superhumans. Galton's insistence that he was the first to contemplate human breeding would turn out to be a dubious claim which British newspapers would call Galton to task on. British newspapers recalled how Victoria Woodhull's lectures on eugenics were publicly condemned as inappropriate and would question Galton's claim of original thinking. Galton's first article also evidences that Galton either ignored or was not aware of the fact that this type of human breeding experiment had already been speculated upon by less reputable minds:

> As no experiment of this description has ever been made, I cannot appeal to its success. I can only say that the general resemblances in mental qualities between parents and offspring, in man and brute, are every whit as near as the resemblance of their physical features; and I must leave the existence of actual laws in the former case to be a matter of inference from the analogy of the latter. (Pg. 158, "Hereditary Talent and Character", Macmillan's Magazine, Vol. 12, Pgs. 157-166, Macmillan and Company, 1865)

Galton was talented with statistics, and his article describes the method and sources from which he amassed evidence of "hereditary talent." Mostly, Galton relied on "dictionaries" of famous people, and it should have been no surprise that his conclusion was an elitist one as his source of data was a text which cataloged European aristocracies and class distinctions. It is clear that Galton himself looked with suspicion upon the accomplishments of the "commoners." One only needs to look to his view of the "commoners" that escaped British rule:

> The North American people has been bred from the most restless and combative class of Europe. Whenever, during the last ten or twelve generations, a political or religious party has suffered defeat, its prominent members, whether they were the best, or only the noisiest, have been apt to emigrate to America, as a refuge from persecution. Men fled to America for conscience' [sic] sake, and for that of unappreciated patriotism. Every scheming knave, and every brutal ruffian, who feared the arm of the law, also turned his eyes in the same direction. (Pg. 325, "Hereditary Talent and Character", Macmillan's Magazine, Vol. 12, Pgs. 157-166, Macmillan and Company, 1865)

By contrast, Francis Galton's "scientific" estimation of the qualities of "Englishmen" seems far more generous than those he attributes to others:

> Narrow thoughts of self by no means absorb the minds of ordinary men; they occupy a secondary position in the thoughts of the more noble and generous of our race. A large part of an Englishman's life is devoted to others or to the furtherance of general ideas, and not to directly personal ends. (Pg. 324, "Hereditary Talent and Character", Macmillan's Magazine, Vol. 12, Pgs. 157-166, Macmillan and Company, 1865)

Even the rapists and murderers among the Englishmen were admired by Francis Galton. Galton admired how they allegedly behaved with "decorum and propriety" even after brutally murdering innocent little girls:

> Moral monsters are born among Englishmen, even at the present day; and, when they are betrayed by their acts, the law puts them out of the way, by the prison or the gallows, and so prevents them from continuing their breed. Townley, the murderer, is an instance in point. He behaved with decorum and propriety; he was perfectly well-conducted to the gaol officials, and he corresponded with his mother in a style that was certainly flippant, but was not generally considered to

be insane. (Pg. 324, "Hereditary Talent and Character", Macmillan's Magazine, Vol. 12, Pgs. 157-166, Macmillan and Company, 1865)

Galton's book was first published in 1869 between Darwin's "Origins" and "Descent" books. The second edition, with an additional preface, was released in 1892 with minimal to no corrections. Galton continued with his original observation on how Darwin's "natural selection" could be harnessed for human breeding by engaging in "rational" or "scientific" form of "selection," namely in his 1874 "English Men of Science," his 1883 "Human Faculty," and his 1889 "Natural Inheritance." While some would apologize for Galton with the false claim that Galton's work was free of the racism of the German eugenicists that would follow. This claim quickly falls apart. The truth is that Galton's work was imbued with racially charged observations from the onset:

> . . . a race of sane men may be formed who shall be as much superior mentally and morally to the modern European, as the modern European is to the lowest of the Negro races. (Pg. x, "Hereditary Genius: An Inquiry Into its Laws and Consequences", Macmillan & Co., 1869)

These were the premises that Charles Darwin deemed to be valid enough as a "science" as he both cited Galton's "Hereditary Genius" as a major source and incorporated Galton's logic into his own in publishing "The Descent of Man." Note the content Darwin saw fit to incorporate into his science:

> Or it may prove that the Negroes, one and all, will fail as completely under the new conditions as they have failed under the old ones, to submit to the needs of a superior civilization to their own; in this case their races, numerous and prolific as they are, will in course of time be supplanted and replaced by their betters. (Pg. xxvi, "Hereditary Genius: An Inquiry Into its Laws and Consequences", Macmillan & Co., 1869)

Not only did Charles Darwin accept these unconfirmed and unsubstantiated subjective observations as "science," but it should be pointed out that Charles Darwin never gave the kind of praise and attention to the writings of his various abolitionist family members, or even the various "negro" literary sources that so frequently appeared in the abolitionist publications. Charles Darwin, the man that Darwinist apologists claim sympathized with the cause of the African man, not only ignored the work of prominent ex-slaves but instead championed the work of Galton and Haeckel, two of the most racist men in human history. Note the above and below passages. Is this observation fit for the legacy of a "gentle abolitionist"?

> Fourthly, the number among the negroes of those whom we should call half-witted men, is very large. Every book alluding to negro servants in America is full of instances. I was myself much impressed by this fact during my travels in Africa. The mistakes the negroes made in their own matters, were so childish, stupid, and simpleton-like. (Pg. 339, "Hereditary Genius: An Inquiry Into its Laws and Consequences", Macmillan & Co., 1869)

Historians must take note of the fact that Galton's prejudices were hardly personal in nature. To the contrary, they were an integral part of his attempt at a dispassionate "science":
> In short, classes E and F of the negro may roughly be considered as the equivalent of our C and D—a result which again points to the conclusion, that the average intellectual standard of the negro race is some two grades below our own. (Pg. 338, "Hereditary Genius: An Inquiry Into its Laws and Consequences", Macmillan & Co., 1869)

All of this must be put into the context of the timeline of scientific discovery. Posterity must gauge exactly how justified Francis Galton's obsession with systematized and choreographed fornication truly was. While Francis Galton was busy pondering if people like him should be put in charge of other individual's bedtime activities, Friedrich Miescher was discovering deoxyribonucleic acid, more commonly known as DNA. Miescher's work paved the way for the identification of DNA as the carrier of inheritance while Darwin and Galton were postulating the existence of "gemmules" and "unit characters" in Darwin's "Pangenesis." More so, it is ironic that the more significant work in the science of inherited characteristics was done by an individual that would certainly be excluded from participating in the sciences in Francis Galton's eugenic utopia, "Kantsaywhere." Friedrich Miescher had a partial hearing impairment, and thus was precisely the type of human Galton's eugenics sought to eradicate from the human gene pool. Note also that Miescher's discovery was that of a chemical structure, not a figment of some philosophical fancy contrived by imagination. Miescher's was true scientific discovery through experimentation and inspection.

In this same decade between the publishing of "Origin of the Species" and "The Descent of Man," Dmitri Mendeleev created the first version of the periodic table of elements. Using the table, Mendeleev predicted the properties of elements yet to be discovered. In this same decade, Louis Pasteur and Robert Koch established the germ theory of disease, which explained away many of the debilitating ailments which Galton and his followers attributed as inherited birth defects. Gregor Mendel published his laws of inheritance in this decade as well, taking an empirical, as opposed to subjective, approach to genetics. The Transatlantic telegraph cable was successfully completed, allowing transatlantic telegraph communication for the first time, and English botanist Richard Spruce completed a 15-year expedition to the Andes and Amazon Basin during which he has collected more than 30,000 plant specimens. Allan Chase, the author of "The Legacy of Malthus," puts Galton into context:
> Even in terms of available nineteenth-century knowledge of natural selection and social medicine, this was an extraordinary exhibition of intellectual and moral bankruptcy. Only a cruel and thoroughly prejudiced ignoramus in British medical history could have, as late as 1873, written that in the new urban slums Nature selects only the least fit to survive the infectious and other deficiency diseases of poverty. As any first-year medical student could have told Galton,

between the passage of the Registration (of medical statistics) Act of 1836 and the Public Health Act of 1848 – which established England's first General Board of Health – England had long since begun its generations of world leadership in the creation of productive programs for the prevention of contagious and deficiency diseases associated with the new industrialized urban environments. (Pg. 102, "Legacy of Malthus: The Social Costs of the New Scientific Racism", 1975)

However, the unfortunate truth is that Galton's and Darwin's family was inbred in more ways than one. Their nepotism and self-centered political posturing prevented them from seeing very far outside their cliques or bubble. Galton quoted Darwin, and Darwin quoted Galton, Haeckel quoted Darwin, Darwin quoted Haeckel, and so the veil of scientific legitimacy grew by mutual adulation. This trend only grew exponentially as Galton and Darwin acquired devoted zealots as their scientific disciples. The trend continued as the American eugenicists would cite their European counterparts, and the European eugenicists would point to the American eugenic accomplishments as validation of their claims.

Most poignantly, the work that was published by Galton and Darwin was severely at odds with the work their family members were conducting as part of the abolitionist movement. Galton's and Darwin's work is a long way away from the slogan "Am I not a Man and a Brother?" which Darwin's own grandfather, Josiah Wedgwood, popularized by producing thousands upon thousands of medallions with the slogan. More precisely, through his grandfather, Charles Darwin had direct access to Thomas Clarkson. Thomas Clarkson was an English abolitionist and a leading campaigner against the slave trade in the British Empire. He helped found The Society for Effecting the Abolition of the Slave Trade and helped achieve passage of the Slave Trade Act of 1807, which ended British trade in slaves, and indispensable to the abolition of slavery worldwide. Clarkson was first attracted to the abolitionist cause when he participated in a competition while at Cambridge in 1785. Clarkson entered a Latin essay. The topic of the essay, set by university vice-chancellor Peter Peckard, was *"Anne liceat invitos in servitutem dare,"* or in English, "Is it lawful to enslave the unconsenting?" Clarkson read everything he could on the subject, including the works of Anthony Benezet, a Quaker abolitionist. After winning the prize, Clarkson had the essay translated so that it could gain a wider audience. In 1789 Clarkson also published "An Essay on the Slave Trade," and in 1788, Clarkson published his "Essay on the Impolicy of the African Slave Trade." Together, these works provided a firm basis for William Wilberforce's first abolitionist speech in the House of Commons on 12 May 1789, and its twelve propositions, which ultimately led to the abolition of slavery in the UK. Clarkson cites recognized intellects throughout history in support of his egalitarian views. It is quoted here for the purposes of comparison to Galton's and Darwin's words:

> Seneca, who saw many of the slaves in question, "What is a knight, or a libertine, or a slave? Are they not names, assumed either from injury or ambition?" Or, shall I say with him on another occasion, "Let us consider that he, whom we call

our slave, is born in the same manner as ourselves; that he enjoys the same sky, with all its heavenly luminaries; that he breathes, that he lives, in the same manner as ourselves, and, in the same manner, that he expires". (Pg. 14, "An Essay on the Slavery and Commerce of the Human Species, Particularly the African", J. Phillips & George-Yard, 1785)

Interestingly, Clarkson utilized Galtonian logic and recounted the various "geniuses" that have existed over the ages as proof against the inferiority of the "coloured slave":

> How then shall I begin? Shall I enumerate the many instances of fidelity, patience, or valour, that are recorded of the servile race? Shall I enumerate the many important services, that they rendered both to the individuals and the community, under whom they lived? Here would be a second source, from whence I could collect sufficient materials to shew, that there is no inferiority in their nature. But I decline to use them. I shall content myself with some few instances, that relate to the genius only: I shall mention the names of those of a servile condition, whose writings, having escaped the wreck of time, and having been handed down even to the present age, are now to be seen, as so many living monuments, that neither Grecian, nor Roman genius, was superior to their own. The first, whom I shall mention here, is the famous Aesop. (Pg. 14, "An Essay on the Slavery and Commerce of the Human Species, Particularly the African", J. Phillips & George-Yard, 1785)

Clarkson's citing of Aesop is more than relevant, as it is clearly the mirror image of the logic utilized by Galton in "Hereditary Genius." Aesop was recognized as "genius" by Aristotle, Herodotus, and Plutarch. An ancient literary work called "The Aesop Romance" describes Aesop as a strikingly ugly slave, who by his cleverness acquires freedom and becomes an adviser to kings and city-states. In the Middle Ages, Aesop is written about as a black Ethiopian. Clarkson continues:

> To these truly ingenious, and philosophical works of Aesop, I shall add those of his imitator Phoedrus, which in purity and elegance of Style, are inferior to none. I shall add also the Lyrick Poetry of Aleman, which is no servile composition; the sublime Morals of Epictetus, and the incomparable comedies of Terence. — Thus then does it appear, that the excuse which was uniformly started in defence of the treatment of slaves, had no foundation in whatever either in truth or justice. The instances that I have mentioned above, are sufficient to shew, that there was no inferiority, either in their nature, or their understandings: and at the same time that they refute the principles of the ancients, they afford a valuable lesson to those, who have been accustomed to form too precipitate a judgment on the abilities of men: for, alas! How often has secret anguish depressed the spirits of those, whom they have frequently censured, from their gloomy and dejected appearance! And how often, on the other hand, has their judgment resulted from their own vanity and pride? (Pgs. 15-16, "An Essay on the Slavery and Commerce of the Human Species, Particularly the African", J. Phillips & George-Yard, 1785)

One could easily argue that Thomas Clarkson's employed a much more rigorous approach than that of Francis Galton, who echoed the words of those that supported slavery and intentionally denigrated the Africans. Galton sat at home and simply took the writings of pro-slavery authors and self-aggrandizing catalogs of European aristocracy at face value. By comparison, Clarkson spent two years traveling around England gathering evidence. He interviewed 20,000 sailors during his research. All in all, Thomas Clarkson rode by horseback some 35,000 miles for evidence. He also enlisted the help of Alexander Falconbridge and James Arnold, two ship's surgeons whom he met in Liverpool. They had been on many voyages aboard slave ships and were able to recount their experiences in detail for publication.

Case in point, these were the writings that were immediately available to both Francis Galton and Charles Darwin because of the close relationship between Thomas Clarkson and their family. Even without the close family ties, this work was so important to contemporary British politics, that it is correct to state that Darwin's and Galton's departure from its humanistic nature is a departure from the traditions that they were born into. Like their German and American counterparts, Darwin and Galton were going in the opposite direction from an earlier humanitarian trend. It is telling that Francis Galton published his "McMillan's" article anonymously and that he desisted in working further on the concept of human breeding for a decade or so after the publication of "Hereditary Genius." It is even more telling that Galton could not stomach the eugenic world he imagined in "Kantsaywhere," and thus instructed that it never be published. Galton sensed the vulgarity in his proposals and knew them to be contrary to the prevailing humanitarian thinking that had carried over to his generation from the Enlightenment. Darwin's own doubts in the publishing of "Origin" has been thoroughly documented. Darwin's and Galton's pessimism were at odds with the faith in humanity so clearly expressed by their abolitionist family members and the abolitionist friends of the family. It is unjust to characterize them otherwise; that is, unjust to the humanitarian ancestors of Charles and Francis.

Sec. 2 - THE ESSENCE OF ZEALOTRY:

Known as 'Darwin's Bulldog on the Continent' and 'the Huxley of Germany', Ernst Heinrich Philipp August Haeckel is known as the scientist who perpetrated a fraud upon fraud to promote the Theory of Evolution. Haeckel's enthusiasm for the Theory of Evolution led him to fraudulently manufacture 'evidence' to prove Darwin's views. Despite his enduring fame and adulation by the most fervent support of Darwin, the history of Ernst Haeckel has brought nothing but shame and disgrace to the sciences. Ernst Haeckel is the textbook fraudster who organizes and falsifies the evidence to fit his claims. Despite being exposed by other scientists, Haeckel's enduring strategy was to insult and personally attack those that disagreed with the fabrications he presented as gospel, a practice that was adopted by his observant disciples.

What makes Haeckel's fraudulent claims criminal in a very real sense is that they were actively used to destroy the lives of those he disagreed with, and to bolster and justify movements that would literally murder under the assumption that Haeckel was a prophet of a world-view, a new religion, and a "New Ethic" based on scientifically proven facts. As is otherwise documented in this book, Ernst Haeckel went far beyond trying to prove Darwin's "Theory of Evolution." Ernst Haeckel set out not just to use science to debunk traditional religion as many supporters of Darwin had set out to do. Ernst Haeckel set out to create an entire religion around Darwinism, destroy anything that was at odds with his gospel, and create an entire society based on his world view. Daniel Gasman, author of "The Scientific Origins of National Socialism" explains:

> Haeckel's Monoism advocated a fundamental and radical departure from the established intellectual and moral traditions of humanistic and rational science, drawing upon alternative heretical and non-Christian traditions of thought that stressed, among other things, the absence of a personal God, the meaninglessness of existence, the essential amorality of the cosmos, and opposition to linear, progressive conceptions of history. His general assumption that the monotheistic God was dead, that mankind was divided into separate and eternally divergent biological races, that the transcendental religions were rooted in anti-scientific superstition, and that morality was historically relative were ideas that came to be accepted among many of the educated and semi-educated classes of Europe as irrefutable truths that were sanctioned by the most up-to-date science. (Pg. xiv, "Scientific Origins of National Socialism", Transaction Publishers, 2007)

It was Haeckel, not Hitler, which was the first German to vehemently propose that Darwinism and its Theory of Evolution must become "practical politics" and he called for a state that guided its principles as "applied biology," much in the same way that Francis Galton believed that eugenics needed to be more than a science, but a "religion" whose principles guided all aspects of government. Keep in mind that "applied biology" was also phraseology prominent Nazis used to define their political movement. All of these prominent Nazis adored Haeckel, and it was Haeckel that popularized the idea that politics had to be understood as "applied biology," an idea that would become one of the cardinal principles of National Socialism. [550]

As Daniel Gasman points out, Haeckel's influence on Hitler's National Socialists is not debatable. Haeckel was admired by Ernst Rüdin, Alfred Ploetz, and

---

[550] Pg. xv - "The Scientific Origins of National Socialism", Daniel Gasman, Transaction Publishers, 2007.

the other key eugenicists that implemented the infamous Nuremberg Laws. Haeckel himself fully subscribed to the myths of "Aryan" superiority popularized by proponents of Theosophy and other occultist replacements for traditional religion. Haeckel's words could easily fit within the pages of "Mein Kampf."

> There can be but one answer in the present advanced stage of natural and human history: No. The fate of those branches of the human family, those nations and races which struggle for existence and progress for thousands of years, is determined by the same **"eternal laws of iron"** as the history of the whole organic world which has people the earth for millions of years. (emphasis mine, Pg. xxii, "Scientific Origins of National Socialism", Transaction Publishers, 2007)

Hitler would paraphrase this concept in "Mein Kampf":
And the end will be that such a people will some day be deprived of its existence on this earth; for man can defy the **eternal laws** of the will to conservation for a certain time, but sooner or later vengeance comes. A stronger race will drive out the weak. (emphasis mine, Pg. 132, "Mein Kampf", Adolf Hitler, Houghton Mifflin, 1971)

That said, many historians, including Daniel Gasman, confuse Haeckel's derision for International Socialism as proof of his conservative values, even though Gasman himself goes to great lengths to explain how Haeckel desired more than anything to eradicate any trace of traditional religion or egalitarian values. This is an incoherent, thus unsupportable view. This is the same confusion that places Adolf Hitler as a man of the right. This is a superficial analysis which is a left-over from the Cold War polarization. Haeckel, like Hitler, detested the values of *laissez-faire* economics, traditional religion, and parliamentary democracy. Daniel Gasman is more accurate when he points out that Haeckel was a "German romantic nationalist," but as we have seen, Haeckel's and Hitler's "nationalism" was a racial one far departed from the traditional "God and country" type of patriotism generally ascribed to conservatism:

> The Germans, Haeckel and his followers contended, must either accept a new philosophy based on evolution and science and unite with the forces of nature, or cease, through weakness and deterioration, to exist as a nation. (Pg. 31, "Scientific Origins of National Socialism", Transaction Publishers, 2007)

Haeckel is that point of demarcation between the lauded German scientist like Virchow and Schweizer and the stereotypical sadistic German scientist. Haeckle's racial hierarchies made his "science" aggressive towards humans:

> In organizing their new cultural revolution the Monists came out in opposition to all ideas, religious or secular, which expressed the essential equality of mankind. They argued that men, as primarily biological creatures, were naturally divided into separate, racially determined species. It was their belief that the varied races of mankind were endowed with differing hereditary characteristics not only of color, but also more importantly of intelligence, and that external physical characteristics were a sign of innate intellectual and moral capacity. For

Haeckel, for example, 'woolly-haired' Negroes were 'incapable of a true inner culture and of a higher mental development', and he noted that 'no woolly-haired nation has ever had an important "history." Rather, the making of a real history had to be attributed to the white races, and even more specifically to the Germanic ones. In fact, it was only among the white Germanic races that one could find those individuals who possess a 'symmetry of all parts, and that equal development, which we call the type of perfect human beauty. (Pg. 39, "Scientific Origins of National Socialism", Transaction Publishers, 2007)

It is equally ridiculous for Haeckel's apologists to paint him as a martyr of science, occupying an undeserved place next to Galileo, as Haeckel's Monism was not just contentious towards traditional Christianity; it was also violently aggressive towards the secular ideals. Haeckel's work is also an affront to the scientific method. Responsible historians should clearly depict the various frauds Haeckel perpetrated, as it is incorrect to persist upon the claim that Haeckel was a "martyr" upon realization of the fact that he was a proven snake-oil-salesman. Haeckel was the first person to draw an evolutionary 'family tree' for mankind, and this first tree turned out to be suspect itself. Haeckel's "anthropods" illustration in the German edition of his 1868 book, "The History of Creation" is the graphic depiction of Darwin's racialist evolutionary hierarchy, with the ape slowly morphing into an "Aryan," passing through the Aborigine and African intermediaries depicted as being more ape-like than their Caucasian counterparts. This chart was wholly pulled from Haeckel's imagination, and not at all from any discovery process of an empirical nature.

Haeckel, like Darwin before him, set out to explain the "origins" of life on Earth, and not just how species evolved. In order to fill the gap between inorganic matter and the first signs of life, Haeckel invented a series of minute protoplasmic organisms which he called "Monera." This was decades after Louis Pasteur had already disproven the idea of spontaneous generation. Yet, Haeckel still believed that proteins had super-evolutionary capacities. Haeckel insisted that his "Monera" was proof for the existence of the type of life forms that Pasteur had already disproven. In 1868, a prestigious German scientific journal published 73 pages of Haeckel's speculations, with more than 30 drawings of these imaginary "Monera." The Darwinian mutual-adulation strategy was utilized to give clearly specious scientific claims an air of respectability. Right on key, Thomas H. Huxley reported finding something that fitted Haeckel's descriptions in mud samples that had been dredged from the bottom of the North Atlantic and preserved in alcohol. Huxley named them "*Bathybius haeckelii*" in order to credit Haeckel. Unfortunately for T.H. Huxley and Ernst Haeckel, a chemist aboard an expeditionary ship in 1875 by the name of John Murray, discovered that these alleged protoplasm specimens were nothing more than amorphous gypsum, precipitated out of sea-water by alcohol. Murray published his findings in "Preliminary Report on the Scientific Results of the Voyage of HMS Challenger," which he had written for the Royal Society of London. Haeckel, as he typically would, refused the findings of other scientists. Yet,

Haeckel had nothing but fanciful renderings while other scientists had empirical findings. In fact, all of this was very likely a deliberate deceit, since Haeckel was an expert on marine organisms; and even published books on marine life. Needless to say, Haeckel had enough experience with actual marine life to know better.

The second and most damaging instance where Haeckel was exposed as massaging the evidence is the highly publicized incident involving the "Java Man," where Haeckel claimed one of his devoted disciples had found the "missing link." Haeckel believed that the only major difference between man and the ape was that men could speak, and apes could not. He, therefore, postulated a missing link which he called "*Pithecanthropus alalus*," or speechless ape-man, and had the artist, Gabriel Max, draw what the creature of Haeckel's imagination may look like if ever found. Haeckel's disciple, Eugene Dubois, set out to find the creature of Haeckel's imagination. Dubois claimed to find precisely this creature in a rock stratum known as the Trinil layer, named after a nearby village in central Java. Dubois wrote to his mentor describing the animal that Haeckel had described for his painter. Haeckel responded by publicly crediting his disciple with the finding of the "missing link," stating his congratulations as: "From the inventor of Pithecanthropus to his happy discoverer!" Dubois initially thought his discovery was the bones of a chimpanzee, despite the fact that there was no evidence of chimps or any of their ancestors living in Asia. It is not until after corresponding with Haeckel that Dubois triumphantly declared them to be the "missing link." [551] What ultimately became known as "Java Man," or the first claim to the finding of Darwin's "missing link," was immediately ridiculed by contemporary scientists as the skullcap and the femur from two different organisms. Dr. Rudolf Virchow, who had been studying skulls for much longer than Haeckel or Dubois, proclaimed that the skull belonged to an ape and that the femur in question was fully human. Dubois became increasingly "annoyed," "combative," and "defensive" as the opinions in the scientific community mounted against him to the point where Dubois became a recluse and refused to share the evidence of his findings with colleagues for quite some time. [552] It was not until the 1920s when Aleš Hrdlička convinced Dubois to make the fossil evidence of "Java Man" available again that the truth finally saw the light of day. The scientific community of the 1920s arrived at the same conclusion they had in 1895, that at best "Java Man" was an early human ancestor and not the "missing link" as originally claimed. Most modern scientists today agree that the femur and skull cap are from two different animals, vindicating the more sober and trustable analysis by Virchow.

In other words, in these first two instances, Haeckel had succeeded in embarrassing both his follower, Dubois, and his colleague T.H. Huxley with his overreaching and politicizing of science. Haeckel was also a source of embarrassment for his teacher and mentor, Rudolf Virchow. Virchow was but one of many scientists scathing in their criticism of Haeckel's overreaching claims that Dubois's findings were the "missing link." Haeckel had gone as far as assigning a zoological name to

---

[551] Pg. 84 - "A Million Years of Man: the Story of Human Development as a Part of Nature", Richard Carrington, New American Library, 1963.
[552] Pg 67 - "Human Evolution: A Guide to the Debates", Brian Regal, ABC-CLIO, 2004.

the imagined "speechless ape." For Haeckel to have given a zoological name to a creature that no one had proved to exist was for Virchow a great mockery of science. As we have seen, Virchow would also have to shield his beloved science from the consequences of Haeckel's irresponsible claims in the "Savage Debate" of 1877, the controversy over the teaching of Darwinism in German schools.

But Haeckel's long history of prostituting science didn't end there. Haeckel's illustrations of an embryo displaying signs of Darwinian evolution through its development was yet another instance where Haeckel's work was proven to be fraudulent. The first illustrations appeared in the "*Natürliche Schöpfungsgeschichte*," or in English the 1868 "Natural History of Creation," the next in the specifically embryological "*Anthropogenie*" of 1874, which managed six German editions by 1910 and was translated as "The Evolution of Man." Even the 2006 pro-Haeckel article by author Nick Hopwood from the Max Planck Institute makes a very long argument in order to finally admit that Haeckel's illustrations were fraudulent if claimed as science and not art: "This sharp practice was swiftly corrected and eventually admitted." [553]

Historians today treat Haeckel as a "romantic," which manipulated the factual evidence to convey ideas or theory. Yet, it was the scientific community that was most appalled by Haeckel's 'artistry.' Haeckel's racist drawings of brains, skulls, faces, of humans and primates, have been dismissed by anthropologists for over 50 years. Yet, one can find disturbing parallels between Haeckel's view of humanity and those incorporated into the "Theory of Evolution" by Charles Darwin in his "Descent of Man." So, what can be said of Darwin's reliance on this 'artist'? Note the absolute reliance on the "rank-order" and value-laden Darwinian hierarchies:

> …the lower races—such as the Veddahs or Australian Negroes—are psychologically nearer to the mammals—apes and dogs—than to the civilised European. We must, therefore, assign a totally different value to their lives … Their only interest are food and reproduction … many of the higher animals, especially monogamous mammals and birds, have reached a higher stage than the lower savages. (Pg. 406, "The Wonders of Life," Ernst Haeckel, Watts & Co., 1904)

Curiously enough, Wilhelm His, the man who would incidentally be a professor for Karl Brandt, the primary defendant at the Nuremberg Doctors' Trials, is the scientist credited for pointing out the gravity of the exaggerations and falsifications of the illustrations. In his 1874 book entitled "*Unserer Körperform und das physiologische Problem ihrer Ensthung,*" Wilhelm His exposed the claims made in the first edition of Haeckel's "*natürliche Schöpfungsgeschichte*":

> …wishing to show the likeness of embryos of different species, gives on page 242 figures of the egg, one hundred times magnified, of man, the ape and dog; and on page 248 also three figures of the embryo of the dog, of the chick and of the turtle. He points out quite amusingly certain features of the resemblance in

---

[553] Pgs. 260-301 - "Pictures of Evolution and Charges of Fraud: Ernst Haeckel's Embryological Illustrations", Nick Hopwood, The History of Science Society, 2006.

the three figures of these two series. -- there is absolutely identical arrangement in the eggs of the man and of the ape. – In short to make the pretended similarity as striking as possible, Haeckel used in two instances the same figure and gave it three different names. (Pg. 93, "The Beginnings of Science: Biologically and Psychologically Considered", Edward John and Komorowski Menge, Badger, 1918)

The fraud was initially pointed out by Professor Rütimeyer in *Archiv für Anthropologie*, Bd. III, s. 301. Professor His remarks that one would expect a retraction and excuse for the mistake; but none was forthcoming:

> Instead of this Haeckel in the preface of his later editions heaped heavy insults on Professor Rütimeyer, equally untrue in their substance as dishonorable in their form' (p. 169). He however saw fit to omit the duplicates. – In short, what purported to be copies of figures by leading authorities and respectable men were falsifications made to show a similarity which does not exist between the embryos of a man and dog. (Pg. 93, "The Beginnings of Science: Biologically and Psychologically Considered", Edward John and Komorowski Menge, Badger, 1918)

Haeckel finally admitted to the charges concerning the embryo illustrations in a January 9, 1909 letter to *"Münchener Allegemeine Zeitung,"* a weekly internationally distributed journal. This brings us back to Charles Darwin's uncritical acceptance and subsequent incorporation of Haeckel's "science." Charles Darwin was clearly astute enough to know the difference between wishful thinking and empirical discovery. Yet, Darwin paid homage to Haeckel in the introduction of "The Descent of Man," despite the fact Haeckel had been fully exposed by the time Darwin penned changes to his 1877 edition of "Descent of Man":

> The conclusion that man is the codescendant with other species ... is not in any degree new ... maintained by several eminent naturalists and philosophers ... especially by Häckel ... besides his great work "Generelle Morphologie" (1866), has recently (1868, with a second edition in 1870) published his "Natürliche Schöpfungsgeschichte," in which he fully discusses the genealogy of man. If this work had appeared before my essay had been written, I should probably never have completed it. Almost all the conclusions at which I have arrived I find confirmed by this naturalist, whose knowledge on many points is much fuller than mine. (Pg.19, intro., "The Descent of Man, and Selection in Relation to Sex", D. Appleton, 1872)

This is where Darwin's silence becomes too much to ignore. Clearly, Darwin knew enough about Haeckel's work to understand the extremely radical nature of Haeckel's politicking. Yet, even the 1876 edition of "Origin" stated that:

> Professor Häckel ... brought his great knowledge and abilities to bear on what he calls phylogeny, or the lines of descent of all organic beings. In drawing up the several series he trusts chiefly to embryological characters. (Pg. 384, "Origin of the Species," Darwin)

This was the case from the onset. Darwin was equally silent when T.H. Huxley used his work as a battering ram, and as this book documents, Charles Darwin was definitely aware of what his cousin Francis Galton was converting his work into. This is where the apologist claims that Darwin's followers misinterpreted and misused Darwin's science for destructive political causes rings hollow. Even though Darwin was clearly aware of the highly questionable goals his work was being used to legitimize, Darwin never lifted a finger to protest, and if Leonard Darwin can be trusted, he wholeheartedly agreed and supported the direction his work was being channeled to.

Ideas have consequences, especially when you frame them in apocalyptic terms and mount an all-out campaign to upend society. All this fraudulent activity is put into historical context by the direct relationship Haeckel had with the men that helped Hitler create the "racial state" that was the Third Reich. Haeckel's disdain for human life he considered "unworthy" or "unequal" translated directly into a belief in systematic and institutionalized euthanasia, and it is of note that he framed it much in the way that National Socialists would decades after him. Haeckel predated Hitler regarding the Spartan view of nature above nurture:

> Among the Spartans all newly born children were subject to a careful examination and selection. All those that were weak, sickly, or affected with any bodily infirmity, were killed. Only the perfectly healthy and strong children were allowed to live, and they alone afterwards propagated the race. (Pg. 91, "Scientific Origins of National Socialism", Transaction Publishers, 2007)

Characteristic of this "New Ethic," the Monist League and its enthusiastic disciples had "no absolute ethics." Those that adhered to Haeckel's all-encompassing views insisted that "objective good and evil in nature were nowhere to be found." [554] Haeckel and his followers would insist that this meant that "compassion" and "sentimentality" was reserved for the brethren of the Fatherland. As Daniel Gasman explains, this was the core "socialist" aspect of "solidarity" and "unity of purpose" which the Monist's, and the National Socialists thereafter adhered to:

> In opposition to unfettered individual freedom, Monism they wrote, wished to awaken a "healthy drive for socialization." It desired to cultivate an "insight" into the "mutual dependence of the individual and the community." Evolution, it was asserted, demonstrated that everywhere the individual must be placed by an "inborn drive" at the "disposal of the species." Conversely, the survival of the individual was of no importance. Life itself was only of relative value and depended solely upon the usefulness of the individual organism to its own species and to the evolution of life in general. No individual was of unique value in himself and no individual could appeal to a system of absolute ethics which guaranteed the preservation and the sanctity of life. (Pg. 48, "Scientific Origins of National Socialism", Transaction Publishers, 2007)

---

[554] Pg. 48 - "Scientific Origins of National Socialism", Daniel Gasman, Transaction Publishers, 2007.

The relationship between Haeckel and Hitler can in no way, shape, or form be considered speculative. Haeckel helped organize and judge the 1903 Krupp Prize which asked scientists to correlate Darwinism and socio-economic policy by asking: "What do we learn from the principles of biological evolution in regard to domestic political developments and legislation of states?" The result was Wilhelm Schallmayer's eugenic essay to be widely publicized in Germany; one of the "scientific" justifications for eugenic policy thereafter. Furthermore, most German scientists that were involved in such measures considered the work of Haeckel and his followers as their initial inspiration and guidance in the eugenics that ultimately paved the way for the Third Reich's euthanasia and eugenic policies. Haeckel himself was hardly ambivalent about his position on the sanctity of life. He explicitly said so in a letter to his devout Christian father in 1864:

> I share essentially your view of life, dear father, only I value human life and humans themselves much less than you. . . The individual with his personal existence appears to me only a temporary member in this large chain, as a rapidly vanishing vapor. . . Personal individual existence appears to me so horribly miserable, petty, and worthless, that I see it as intended for nothing but destruction. (As quoted by Richard Weikart, Pg. 76, "From Darwin to Hitler")

Haeckel himself advocated the destruction of abnormal newborns and invalids. He referred to this as "an act of kindness." Note that almost identical paragraphs are found in Hitler's "Mein Kampf," speeches, and propaganda films, namely *"Erbkrank"*:

> Hundreds of thousands of incurables—lunatics, lepers, people with cancer, etc., are artificially kept alive in our modern communities, and their sufferings are carefully prolonged, without the slightest profit to themselves or the general body ... If the total population of Europe is put at three hundred and ninety to found hundred millions, we have at least two million lunatics among them, and of these more than two hundred thousand are incurable. What an enormous mass of suffering these figures indicate for the invalids themselves, what a vast amount of trouble and sorrow for their families, and what a huge private and public expenditure! How much of this pain and expense could be spared if people could make up their minds to free the incurable from their indescribable torments by a dose of morphia! (Pg. 122, "The Wonders of Life," Ernst Haeckel, Watts & Co., 1904)

A quick survey of how Haeckel influenced the scientists directly linked to the Third Reich's eugenic euthanasia policies illustrates just how decisive Haeckel's influence was towards the perpetrating of the crimes of The Holocaust. This list, of course, would be much more extensive if not limited to the most obvious disciples of Haeckel in the creation of the National Socialist state. A more thorough survey would serve only to reveal the pervasiveness of Monist influence on National Socialist ideology and mythology:

ALFRED PLOETZ: The father of "race hygiene," the underlying principle of all that was National Socialism. Alfred Ploetz and his co-utopian pioneer, Carl Hauptmann attended his lectures. Hauptmann was his student. Ploetz dedicated the first issue of the infamous journal *"Archiv für Rassen – und Gesellschaftsbiologie"* to Haeckel.

FRITZ LENZ: The co-author of the infamous Baur-Fischer-Lenz book, which Hitler copied his eugenic policies for the writing of "Mein Kampf," was a fellow founder of the journal dedicated to Haeckel *"Archiv für Rassen – und Gesellschaftsbiologie,"* along with Alfred Ploetz.

WILHELM SCHALLMAYER: Was a prominent member of Haeckel's Monist League who on Haeckel's eightieth birthday thanked him for directing him onto the path of racial and eugenic analysis. It was Haeckel, according to Schallmayer, who taught them to aim for "the improvement of racial, social, and cultural conditions" by the practical implementation of the doctrine of evolution. [555]

ALFRED ROSENBERG: The fire-breathing propagandist of the Third Reich's race theories wrote in his memoirs of his "intellectual debt" to Haeckel. Rosenberg attended the *Realgymnasium* in Reval, who according to Rosenberg, was "completely based on the spirit of the scientific positiveness of the nineteenth century." Rosenberg's anti-Christian world view was founded upon his dedication to Monism. [556]

J.F. LEHMANN: The enthusiastic publisher of the infamous Baur-Fischer-Lenz book that inspired Hitler's "Mein Kampf" devoted an entire issue to Haeckel in *"Der Biologe"* in February of 1934. The issue praised Haeckel as a pioneer in the development of National Socialism. [557]

ALFRED HOCHE: Alfred Hoche, who co-authored with Karl Binding the infamous book titled, "Permitting the Destruction of Unworthy Life," which translated the ethics of Haeckel and Nietzsche into eugenic law, was a student of Haeckel's. [558]

FRIEDERICH NIETZSCHE: Nietzsche's "understanding of the life sciences" was directly influenced by Haeckel and one of his followers, Wilhelm Roux. [559]

Proof that Hitler's National Socialists were, in fact, devout "socialists" lay in the common admiration of Haeckel with the Bolsheviks. The Soviet system was even more eager to accept the Haeckel's "solid foundation" for nihilistic materialism. Vladimir Lenin adored Haeckel. Trofim Lysenko, who caused disastrous agricultural practices contributing to famines in the Soviet Union was also an admirer of Haeckel. As such, Haeckel's contribution to the brutality of the 20th century can hardly be exaggerated. Edward John and Komorowski Menge put Haeckel's undue influence on his followers into perspective:

> He (i.e. Haeckel) writes in so forcible and positive and determined a fashion from the vantage-ground of scientific knowledge, that he exerts an undue

---

[555] Pg. 92 - "Scientific Origins of National Socialism", Daniel Gasman, Transaction Publishers, 2007.
[556] Pg. 172 – Ibid.
[557] Pg. 171 – Ibid.
[558] osservatoreromano.va, "If Life is 'Unworthy of Being Lived'", L'Osservatore Romano, June 12, 2012.
[559] Pg. 150, Christian Emden, "Nietzsche On Language, Consciousness, And the Body", Univ. of Illinois Press, 2010.

influence on the uncultured among his readers, and causes them to fancy that only benighted fools or credulous dupes can really disagree with the historical criticisms, the speculative opinions, and philosophical; or perhaps unphilosophical, conjectures thus powerfully set forth. (Pg. 93, "The Beginnings of Science," Edward John and Komorowski Menge, Badger, 1918 - Quoting Sir Oliver Lodge, F.R.S., "Life and Matter")

The above passage is no passing observation. Haeckel's work was used as a batterinhg ram to communicate "racialist" theories to the general public. Haeckel's oversimplifications and racially charged science is what German "racialists" adopted as their gospel:

Men of the street and even of the schools, who have achieved popularity, tell us that science has explained everything, that science can do nearly anything. But the men acknowledged *as the great scientists* condemn all such statements and insist that those who make them are not scientists at all but mere workmen using the materials some one else has formed, and then not even using these materials justly. (emphasis theirs, Pg. 90, "The Beginnings of Science: Biologically and Psychologically Considered", Edward John and Komorowski Menge, Badger, 1918)

The story of how humanity descended to the brutality of The Holocaust cannot be told without accounting for Haeckel. Even his supporters eventually came to understand the consequences of using science as a battering ram:

This is so true that Professor Huxley, considered by any number of men as one of the great men of science, has gone on record as saying that he regrets that the term "applied science" was ever invented. (Pg. 88, "The Beginnings of Science: Biologically and Psychologically Considered", Edward John and Komorowski Menge, Badger, 1918)

Ernst Haeckel obviously gained a lot of enemies in the Christian community, and those animosities endure to this day as Haeckel's disciples persist in utilizing evidence known to be falsified to support philosophical and scientific claims against traditional religious values. That is neither here nor there as this is typical in the long history of contentiousness between the faithful and the devotees of science. Zealots will be zealots. However, it is critical to understand that the most biting criticism towards Haeckel didn't come from the Church but from the top ranks of the scientific community itself. Haeckel was accused of forgery or unbridled exaggeration by the international scientific community not once, not twice, but at least three or four times. Haeckel's work is an insult to science. The fact that Darwin never saw fit to check his use of Haeckel makes Darwin's "Descent of Man" equally suspect.

FIGURE 18: Lothrop Stoddard's "The Rising Tide of Color: The Threat Against White World Supremacy" is one of various 'racialist' books by famous American authors that directly influenced Adolf Hitler and the German eugenics movement.

Chap. 18: 1864 to 1860

AMERICAN FRONT: THE TINY CONFEDERATE SUBMARINE HUNLEY TORPEDOES THE USS HOUSATONIC, BECOMING THE FIRST SUBMARINE TO SINK AN ENEMY SHIP. – MONTANA IS ORGANIZED AS A UNITED STATES TERRITORY OUT OF PARTS OF WASHINGTON TERRITORY AND DAKOTA TERRITORY. **EUROPEAN FRONT:** FIRST INTERNATIONAL OF SOCIALISTS: THE INTERNATIONAL WORKING MEN'S ASSOCIATION IS FOUNDED. – THE INTERNATIONAL WORKINGMEN'S ASSOCIATION WAS FOUNDED IN LONDON. **LIFE:** SYLLABUS ERRORUM: POPE PIUS IX CONDEMNS THEOLOGICAL LIBERALISM AS AN ERROR AND CLAIMS FOR THE SUPREMACY OF ROMAN CATHOLIC CHURCH AUTHORITY OVER THE CIVIL SOCIETY. HE ALSO CONDEMNS RATIONALISM, SOCIALISM, COMMUNISM, SECRET SOCIETIES, BIBLE SOCIETIES, LIBERAL CLERICAL ASSOCIATIONS HENRY FORD, AMERICAN AUTOMOBILE MANUFACTURER AND INDUSTRIALIST IS BORN. - ALEXANDRE CABANEL PAINTS THE BIRTH OF VENUS

Sec. I - MAKING THE "THEORY" THE ONLY THEORY:

The X Club was a dining club of nine men who supported the theories of natural selection and academic liberalism in late 19-century England. Their main goal was to reform the Royal Society around a Darwinian perspective. After Charles Darwin's "On the Origin of Species" was published in 1859, the men began working together to aid the cause for naturalism and natural history. T.H. Huxley was the impetus. Huxley organized the first meeting of November 3, 1864. The club met in London once a month from November 1864 until March 1893, and its members were made up of the scientific elite, including George Busk, Edward Frankland, Thomas Archer Hirst, Joseph Dalton Hooker, John Lubbock, Herbert Spencer, William Spottiswoode, and John Tyndall, united by a "devotion to science, pure and free, untrammeled by religious dogmas." [560] However, in retrospect, the Club was created for anything but academic liberalism, as its history proves.

Of historical importance is that the group was accused of having too much power in shaping the scientific landscape of London in the 1870s and 1880s. Samuel Wilberforce and other Anglicans took their campaign to the British Association for the Advancement of Science, aiming to overthrow Huxley's "dangerous clique." Although the first attack came from the Anglicans like Wilberforce, this was hardly the most heated or most important debate. Subsequent criticism came from within the scientific community, and it is that episode in history which evidences that academic freedom was hardly the intent of the X Club.

Case in point, the rift began to emerge within the scientific community, not over theology, but over race theory. The Anthropological Society of London was created in 1863 by James Hunt. It had been modeled after Paul Broca's anthropological society in Paris, with "anthropology" denoting an emphasis on human physical characteristics. Pierre Paul Broca was a French physician, surgeon, anatomist, and anthropologist best known for his research on the frontal lobe of the human brain that is responsible for articulated language. Broca's work was the first anatomical proof of the localization of brain function and contributed to the development of physical anthropology, and in one way or another, help advance the eugenic science of anthropometry. James Hunt was a speech therapist in London, England. Originally, Hunt had been a member and honorary secretary of his

---

[560] physicstoday.scitation.org – "The X Club", Charles Day, Commentary & Review, Aug. 4, 2011 – Quoting Thomas Archer Hirst.

subsequent rival Ethnological Society of London. However, many members of this society disliked his attacks on humanitarian and missionary societies as well as on the anti-slavery movement. So, with the help of the explorer Richard Burton he set up the Anthropological Society of London, becoming its first president.

The resulting battle between the societies was a scandal within the scientific community, and the documentation reveals the political alliances of both groups. Hunt's paper "The Negro's Place in Nature" was greeted with boos and hisses when read at a British Association meeting in 1863 because of its defense of slavery. Burton's and Hunt's Society was created out of a scientific belief in "polygenism." Thus, the Anthropological Society, consistent with their "polygenic" views, supported the Confederate South in the American Civil War, arguing that the African slaves were a species of a separate creation from Anglo-Saxon whites, and genetically unsuited to freedom. Hunt established the Anthropological Review as the organ of the society and by 1867 the Society had reached 500 members. The society had an American Confederate agent helping to fund the council, and the Anthropological Society also sided with Edward Eyre, the governor of the then British colony of Jamaica, when the ruthlessly suppressed the slave uprising in 1866. [561]

While historians have leveraged the dispute between the Anthropological and Ethnological societies to make Darwinism the champion of abolition, a more sober and precise accounting reveals that neither of the members of either society considered the African their equal. Both Societies, namely the Ethnological Society's Huxley and Darwin, vocally proposed that Africans were closer to apes than to white men, a position that can hardly be said to be egalitarian or beneficial to the cause of abolition. Furthermore, modern proponents of the Ethnological Society have prolonged the X Club's political posturing, claiming that the Darwinian society was defending science against the influence of religion. This makes no logical sense considering that the Anthropological Society's "polygenesis" was blasphemous even by the loosest understanding of Christianity. Arguably, the Ethnological society's "common descent" theory was more consistent with the Biblical account of Adam and Eve than was "polygenesis." The Bible accounts for a single creation from Adam & Eve onwards. The "polygenical" view of creation by the Confederates of the Christian faith warped Biblical accounts by inventing "pre-Adam" humans.

Furthermore, it must be remembered that among the membership of the X Club were the founders of the eugenics movement. Eugenics was a consequence of Darwinian "monogenesis," which subscribed to the scientific view that all of humanity originated from the same creation. The "polygenic" view subscribed to a view that blacks and whites were different creations, and adherents to this view typically believe that a matting of blacks and whites would produce unfertile and barren offspring, much like a mule. In fact, the racist term "mulatto," used to describe the offspring of a black and white person, is a "polygenic" term referring directly to the barren offspring of a horse and donkey mating. The Online

---

[561] Pg. 54 - "New History of Anthropology", Henrika Kuklick, John Wiley & Sons, 2009.

Etymology Dictionary provides the history of the term:
> *mulatto* (n.) 1590s, "offspring of a European and a black African," from Sp. or Port. mulato "of mixed breed," lit. "young mule," from mulo "mule," from L. mulus (fem. mula) "mule" (see mule (1))

Adrian Desmond and James Richard Moore, the Darwinist authors of the famous book, "Darwin's Sacred Cause" document how important the "hybrid fertility" was to the debates that included Louis Agassiz, Darwin, and the infamous pro-slavery Josiah Nott and George Gliddon:
> Morton joined an already heated dispute. The further he shifted Nott's way in 'favour of the doctrine of primeval diversities among men', the more necessary it became to follow up Nott's study of hybridity. After all, the mulatto, though a hybrid, was clearly fertile (even if only, as many Southerners believed, to a limited extent). So it became crucial to prove that animals too could casually hybridize. Morton had to discredit that old resilient definition of a species, which included its inability to produce fertile hybrids. (Pg. 201, "Darwin's Sacred Cause: How a Hatred of Slavery Shaped Darwin's Views on Human Evolution", Houghton Mifflin Harcourt, 2009)

In hindsight, neither the view of the Anthropological Society or the X Club can be regarded as representative of "humanitarian" views of either their era or later. The views of both the Anthropological Society and the X Club's Ethnological Society were unquestionably racially charged, and both prostituted the abolition issue for their purposes. One thing must be noted though. The "polygenesis" view was myopic and largely confined to the political polarization resulting from the American Civil War. It was simplistic in the sense that it limited itself to dealing mostly with the relationships between African blacks and European whites. The view persisted in the aftermath of the American Civil War as part of the polemic tied to the Reconstruction Era but died thereafter. Only the furthest extremes of white supremacy today believe that blacks and whites are a different species. While some neo-Nazis still hold this view, they are a statistically insignificant minority even among neo-Nazis, and very far departed from being the mainstream "polygenists" emerging from Louis Agassiz's Harvard University. On the other hand, the X Club's Darwinian view can be said to be more sophisticated in its political perspective, and of a broader and geopolitical nature as it obsessed over all the "races." As such, it was an immensely more dangerous and volatile view than the views of the "polygenic" simpletons. Darwinian racial hierarchy, with European whites at the pinnacle of human evolution and Aborigines and Africans closer to apes than to whites, tied the Darwin's theory of "sexual selection" and Morel's theory of "degeneracy" to fabricate the fear that sexual relations between European whites and any other race would inevitably result in a biological retrogression. As a proximate result, every "race" perceived to be lesser evolved than European whites would be seen as a danger to Western culture as the fears of "degeneration" grew to become part of the *zeitgeist*. More precisely, Eastern European Jews, the Chinese, the

Hispanic, and every other racial gradation would be regarded as a biological detriment if incorporated into Western society's "selection" of "sexual" partners; thus, the eugenically motivated laws that followed.

While belief in "polygenesis" dissipated along with the divide created by the American Civil War, Darwinism's inherent "racialist" nature remains unaddressed as its devoted followers work tirelessly to prohibit any discourse that would counter their politics. As such, the enduring legacy of the X Club was its tactics. The members of the X Club and the Ethnological Society actively used their influence to limit the contributions the Anthropological Society made to the British Association for the Advancement of Science. The battle waged by the X Club was waged as the vulgar partisan politics unbecoming of the sciences. They sought to censor by political and economic influence, instead of allowing the facts and the science to weed out erroneous theories through intellectual debate. Much of this subterfuge was accomplished by nominating its members to offices of major societies, as well as the blocking of pension and medal claims for those that were seen as the enemies of the society. The proof is in the pudding: Between the time of its inception in 1864 and its termination in 1893, the X Club and its members gained prominence over the British scientific community. Between 1870 and 1878, Hooker, Spottiswoode, and Huxley held office in the Royal Society simultaneously, and between 1873 and 1885, they consecutively held the presidency of the Royal Society. Spottiswoode was treasurer of the Society between 1870 and 1878 and Huxley was elected Senior Secretary in 1872. Frankland and Hirst were also of importance to the Society, as they had previously held the position of Foreign Secretary between 1895 and 1899, and the latter served on the Council three times between 1864 and 1882. Five members of the X Club held the presidency of the British Association for the Advancement of Science between 1868 and 1881. Hirst was elected president of the London Mathematical Society between 1872 and 1874 while Busk served as Examiner and eventually President of the Royal College of Surgeons. Frankland also served as President of the Chemical Society between 1871 and 1873.

Not surprisingly, during this time, the members of the X-Club began to win awards within the British scientific community. Among the nine, three received the Copley Medal, namely the inordinate amount of influence its members had in the nomination of Charles Darwin for the medal in 1864. Five members received the Royal Medal, two received Darwin Medals, one received the Rumford Medal, one received the Lyell Medal, and one received the Wollaston Medal. A shameless eighteen honorary degrees were handed out among the nine members. Two of the members were knighted, one served as Privy Councillor, one as Justice of the Peace, three as Corresponding Members, and one a Foreign Associate of the French Academy of Sciences.

As the members of the Club continued to gain prominence and outsiders marginalized, other scientists, namely Richard Owen, accused the group of having too much influence in shaping the British scientific landscape. Considering the exclusionary tactics of the Club, it is understandable why this scientist became the political enemy of the X Club. He was intentionally framed as Charles Darwin's creationist whipping boy despite the fact that he was Britain's leading biologist in the mid-nineteenth century, who well before the Origin of the Species advocated an evolutionary theory as the origin of species. Owen's sin was that his version of evolution was a non-Darwinian evolutionary theory at the time when Darwin was being placed upon a pedestal by his propagandizing and politicking minions. [562] In other words, Richard Owen approached his inquiries in a scientific manner, using scientific terms, just neither more or less the product of "hard science" than Charles Darwin's work. The methodology and resulting assumptions had nothing to do with an orthodox reading of Biblical creation as many historians claim. They simply disagreed with Darwin:

> Owen represented "biology without Darwin" in more than one sense. The two great naturalists differed above all about the nature of organic evolution. They held opposing views on the origin of life from lifeless matter (Owen postulated multiple spontaneous "emergences"; Darwin kept the issue at arm's length), on the mechanism of species development (Owen stressed an inner, "genetic" cause, Darwin external, natural selection), on the pattern of evolution through geologic time (Owen saw in it a structural logic, Darwin the haphazardness of contingency), and on "man'd place in nature" (Owen stressed the unity of humanity and its distance from the apes: the Darwinians constructed close racialist links between "lower humans." and "higher apes") (Pg. xi, "Richard Owen: Biology Without Darwin", Nicolaas A. Rupke, Univ. of Chicago Press, 1994)

Much can be questioned about the scientific validity of Richard Owen's work. None of it can be said to be the product of Christian theology as his postulates are not part of the belief system described in Christianity's Bible. There is nothing in the Holy Bible that describes creation as "nomogeny," "physiochemical conditions," "protogenal jelly-specks," or "organic crystallization." Owen advocated "nomogeny," a coming into existence caused by natural law, not the hand of a divine creator. He speculated in "Anatomy of Vertebrates" that life originated as the result of physicochemical conditions that produced "organic crystallisation." [563] Thus, the accusations that Richard Owen was a "creationist" can only said to have been politically charged mischaracterizations intended to undermine confidence in what was a scientific postulate, correct or incorrect as they may have been. It was a comical and shameful assertion for the X Club members to make.

As this book has documented, much of the so-called "debate" between "theology" and "science" were in actuality two sides of the same coin arguing against each other. This was the case in the infamous Scope's Monkey Trial, as well as the debates between Virchow and Haeckel. In none of these instances was an orthodox Christianity represented, thus none of them were truly a legitimate struggle against traditional Christianity as they are characterized. They invoke the actual plight of

---

[562] Pg. xi - "Richard Owen: Biology Without Darwin", Nicolaas A. Rupke, Univ. of Chicago Press, 1994.
[563] Pg. Pg. 173 – Ibid.

actual victims of theology, namely Galileo, in an erroneous and fraudulent manner. No one was arguing for a Biblical Adam and Eve in any of these so-called debates between "theology" and "pure science." There was no Holy Inquisition or trials before the clergy for these false martyrs of modern science. This is not to say that arguing Biblical accounts of creation against Darwinian Evolution is a desirable or even worthwhile debate. It is just to say that more often than not what is presented as history is nothing more than political propaganda. Most of the time, these debates were arguments within the political circle that included only like-minded Progressives and Fabians, atheists and occultists, socialists and communists.

Was the X Club too powerful? The answer may lie in the history of Charles Darwin's friend, and co-discoverer of the theory of evolution, Alfred Russel Wallace. The fact that Darwin is credited to the exclusion of his contemporaries and predecessors is a testament to the power leveraged by the X Club. Alfred Russel Wallace was important to the sciences for various reasons. First, he co-discovered natural selection and prompted Darwin to finally rush his "Origin of Species" to press. Second, Wallace is perhaps one of the modern world's greatest scientific explorers. When Wallace returned from his eight-year exploration of Southeast Asia and the Malay Archipelago he wrote "The Malay Archipelago" in 1869, regarded by "The Dictionary of Scientific Biography" as "one of the finest scientific travel books ever written." The third reason for Wallace's importance is his work in biogeography. His 1876 "Geographical Distribution of Animals" is regarded as one of the seminal works of science. The fact that a scientist like Wallace is not remembered like Darwin, despite having scooped Charles, is a testament to the political power of the X Club. The reasons are complex but largely related to the complete and sweeping dominance of Darwinian evolution. From the very beginning, when the theory of natural selection was unveiled to the scientific community at the Linnaean Society on July 1, 1858, the entire program was engineered by Darwin's colleagues and close friends, Joseph Hooker and Charles Lyell, to give their friend priority. When "Origin" was published a little over a year later modern evolutionary theory literally became Darwin's theory, despite the many other iterations of evolutionary theory that existed prior to Darwin. Darwin's allies sought to solidify the "Theory" by managing its every promotional and public aspect so as to gain paradigmatic status for it within the scientific community. Huxley composed the X Club to facilitate this goal. Huxley's skillful management of the X Club and the political power it amassed ensured the success of Darwinism. Even Wallace collaborated in resigning himself to obscurity. Wallace had no recourse but to concede defeat and subsequently use "Darwinism" to describe his own theory. Today, when Wallace is mentioned at all, it is only with respect to awarding Darwin credit for the work that Wallace beat Darwin to publishing.

Furthermore, by forgetting that Wallace beat Darwin to the punch, the evangelical atheists are allowed to devalue any scientific hypothesis that is not as materialistic or reductionist as the militant atheists would like science to be. Any theory that is not materialistic and reductionist is discredited even though the "discovery" which Charles Darwin shares with Wallace is originally not an atheistic proposal. For better or for worse, correct or incorrect, the only honest history is that Wallace's theory was that of an "intelligent" evolution with purposive design. This fact is seldom if ever mentioned when giving Wallace a share of the credit that is mostly given to Darwin, and this by itself is a disservice to a factual understanding of world history. The X Club can be said to have accomplished their stated goal beyond their expectations as, politically speaking. This is an erroneous and unduly forced limitation on scientific inquiry. Case in point, the much more lucid empirical work by Mendel was lost to science while the field obsessed with Darwin.

It is at this juncture that we must recall exactly who Mendel was, and why his work did not receive the attention that Darwin's did. Gregor Johann Mendel is known as the "father of modern genetics." Mendel was a cleric. Inspired by Frank Unger, Mendel decided to stay on at the monastery and use his time to carry out practical experiments in biology. We are told that the bishop in charge allegedly disallowed the monks to teach biology, but Mendel's personal correspondence reveals that several monks assisted Mendel with his experiments. [564] Between 1856 and 1863 Mendel cultivated and tested some 29,000 pea plants. The extended study resulted in Mendel postulating the Law of Segregation and the Law of Independent Assortment, which later became known as Mendel's Laws of Inheritance. Mendel published his "Experiments on Plant Hybridization" and read it at two meetings of the Natural History Society of Brünn in Moravia in 1865. It was received favorably and generated reports in several local newspapers. Later, in 1866, Mendel published his work on heredity in the Journal of the Brno Natural History Society. It fell flat. It had absolutely no impact. The complex and detailed work he had produced was not understood and his total lack of clout in the scientific community helped only to ensure that his work would remain unrecognized. If Mendel had been a professional scientist, instead of a cleric, his work may not have gone unnoticed. His work was understood as theories concerning hybridization rather than inheritance, which was what the scientific community was swarming over at the time. Because of the unfortunate circumstances, Mendel was cited only three times over the next three decades.

It is one of the great and unrecognized ironies that so many of the scientific-minded, central-planning, eugenic-utopians would later be debunked largely due to the rediscovery of Mendel's work. Nothing about Mendel's grand contributions to history were planned, foreseen, or even anticipated. Mendel's life is a testament to humanity's ability to progress in non-linear and unplanned directions. It was not until the early 20th Century that the importance of his ideas was realized. Mendel touched minds he never suspected, and which existed several generations down the trajectory of history. In turn, those future scientific minds found valuable scientific work where they least expected it, from the grounds of a religious institution.

Those 20th Century scientists quickly replicated Mendel's results. Biologists flocked to the theory and the science of genetics was born. Without all the avenues being open to any and all who wished to inquire, it is doubtful that Mendel's work

---

[564] Pg. 206 – "Mendel's Opposition to Evolution and to Darwin", B.E. Bishop, Journal of Heredity, 1996:87.

would have resurfaced to have the profound impact it did on modern science. All that was required is that men be free to investigate and inquire for Mendel's humble work to become relevant decades after his death. Mendel's work would most likely have remained ignored if left to the devices of overseeing elite, who voiced a severe animosity to science being conducted by the Church. Would the X Club have permitted Mendel to outshine Darwin? The evidence weighs strongly against that. The elite ignored his work during his lifetime, and it is not until science rediscovered a more egalitarian spirit that Mendel's work was picked up and utilized without regard for who had created it.

As we have seen, Darwin's disciples created eugenics, and Mendelism evolved into modern genetics. Based on the evidence presented in this book, it would be easy to argue that the bully tactics employed by the Darwinists delayed the modern science of genetics. This was the proximate cause of their aggressive tactics towards any competing theories. Those eugenicists did their best to block any scientific work that threatened to uproot their dogma, and the geneticists worked aside from and with little respect for what the eugenicists did. In the case of Karl Pearson, this specifically meant actively excluding any scientists who adopted Mendel's work from the journals or associations he controlled. In the case of Davenport's pellagra, this meant that a working cure was ignored for generations.

More importantly, Mendel provided for science a non-hierarchical and non-racialist view of the laws of heredity. Mendel summarized in less than 30 pages a clear, systematic, and empirical description of what Darwin bloviated in thousands of pages injecting personal observation, conjecture, and anecdote. Darwin's evolution was value-laden, linear in thinking, and polluted by his Victorian conceptions of "progress," thus his theory implied that evolution had not just a racial hierarchy, but a direction towards an allegedly more perfect or "evolved" human. Mendelism implies only a pattern or a mechanism by which new iterations arise out of diversity. Even though Mendel was a priest, his science implies no grand "origin," hierarchy, or direction. Case in point, you have to delve into his personal correspondence to discern that Mendel undertook his experiments in "opposition to" and not "complementary to" Darwin's work, as mainstream historians would otherwise have us believe. [565] It is doubtful that Mendel would approve of the fact that modern science morphs his work and smashes it like clay into general support for Darwin.

Historians do not like to indulge in hypothetical scenarios. Yet, it is hardly unfair to point out that stifling intellectual diversity never leads humanity down the right path. This is exactly what the X Club was meant to do, and precisely what it accomplished. One can only speculate what history may have been like if there was more scientific diversity, right, wrong, leading up to and through the turn-of-the-century. In shielding Darwinism from criticism, its devoted follower also defended the eugenic component that Charles Darwin incorporated into "The Descent of Man." With eugenics incorporated into "Theory of Evolution" by Darwin himself,

---

[565] Pg. 209 – "Mendel's Opposition to Evolution and to Darwin", B.E. Bishop, Journal of Heredity, 1996:87.

the fraudulent claims made by Galton and Haeckel received an undue acceptance and protection from a powerful group of scientific elites set on thwarting any challenges to the creed. All of those fabricated spectacles, from the temper tantrums of the X Club on through the "test cases" of the Scopes' Monkey Trial, the "Savage Debate," and <u>Buck v Bell</u> helped fan the flames of the academic intolerance which ultimately helped the eugenic masterminds exert control over the field of science during all those critical decades leading up to The Holocaust. One thing is fairly certain: the eugenics movement gained popularity and political acceptance proportionally to Darwinism's political gains. Eugenics could only have gone as far as Darwin's reputation pulled it. The inevitable consequence of removing all of Darwin's enemies and providing artificial notoriety and manufactured political acceptance is that the eugenics movement was pulled up to prominence that it would never have enjoyed otherwise. Eugenics would have stayed the movement by cranks and small utopian experiments like those proposed by Victoria Woodhull and practiced by John Humphrey Noyes.

Sec. 2 - MARX ON DARWINISM & EUGENIC SUBORDINATION:

Karl Marx made his anti-slavery convictions known, well, by publishing them, as opposed to Charles Darwin, who kept them private. Incidentally, Marx also had very distinct opinions about Darwin. Since contemporary socialists have gone to great lengths to marry secular socialism with Darwinism, it may be of importance to shed light on precisely how Karl Marx felt about his contemporary, Charles Darwin. Author Ronald E. Meek provides a thorough account of Marx and Engels's view on population control in his 1971 book, "Marx and Engels on the Population Bomb." Meek provides ample quotations to accurately depict the duo's views on Darwinism and how the work of the famous biologist was relevant to their socialist or collectivist movements:

> ...Herr Lange (*Ueber die Arbeiterfrage*, etc., 2. ed.) sings my praises loudly, but with the object of making himself important. Herr Lange, you see, has made a great discovery. The whole of history can be brought under a single great natural law. This natural law is the phrase (in this application Darwin's expression becomes nothing but a phrase) "the struggle for existence," and the content of this phrase is the Malthusian law of population or, rather, overpopulation. So, instead of analyzing the struggle for existence as represented historically in varying and definite forms of society, all that has to be done is to translate every concrete struggle into the phrase, "struggle for existence," and this phrase itself into the Malthusian population fantasy. One must admit that this is a very

impressive method — for swaggering, sham-scientific, bombastic ignorance and intellectual laziness. - From Marx's letter to Kugelmann of June 27, 1870. (Pg. 196, "Marx and Engels on the Population Bomb: Selections from the Writings of Marx and Engels Dealing with the Theories of Thomas Robert Malthus", Ramparts Press, 1971)

It is no secret that Darwin relied heavily on Malthus, and Marx and Engels were keen on this aspect of Darwin's work. Malthus, in turn, was a British Parson who was equally obsessed with "the perfectibility of society" as were his radical American contemporaries who ventured to the "New World" to establish their perfectly balanced "planned communities." Meeks provides a quote from Malthus' "Essay":

> This natural inequality of the two powers of population, and of production in the earth, and that great law of our nature which must constantly keep their effects equal, form the great difficulty that to me appears insurmountable in the way to the perfectibility of society. (Pg. 5, "Marx and Engels on the Population Bomb: Selections from the Writings of Marx and Engels Dealing with the Theories of Thomas Robert Malthus", Ramparts Press, 1971)

Thus, herein lays the hold of Malthusian population control that defines "left-of-center" theory hundreds of years after Malthus was proven wrong by the Agricultural Revolution, and into the "sham-scientific" claims of contemporary Global Warming fanatics that have now married Marx and Malthus. Ironically, Marx did not hesitate to call Malthus's book a "plagiarism from beginning to end," a "libel on the human race," and "nothing but a sensational pamphlet." [566] In "Capital" Marx bites at Malthus by stating that the "whole of his population theory is a shameless plagiarism" stolen from John Stuart Mill. [567] Marx's criticism only got harsher in "Theories of Surplus Value," vol. 3, 1861-1863:

> Malthus's work, The Measure of Value, ect. -- is **a very model of intellectual imbecility**, winding its way casuistically through its own inner confusion. (emphasis mine, Pg. 155, "Marx and Engels on the Population Bomb: Selections from the Writings of Marx and Engels Dealing with the Theories of Thomas Robert Malthus", Ronald E. Meek, Ramparts Press, 1971 — Citing "Theories of Surplus Value," Vol. 3, 1861-1863)

If the reader reminds me of Malthus, whose "Essay on Population" appeared in 1798, I remind him that this work in its first form is nothing more than a **schoolboyish, superficial plagiary of De Foe, Sir James Steuart, Townsend, Franklin, Wallace, etc., and does not contain a single sentence thought out by himself.** (emphasis mine, Pg. 88, "Marx and Engels on the Population Bomb: Selections from the Writings of Marx and Engels Dealing with the Theories of Thomas Robert Malthus", Ramparts Press, 1971 — citing Marx's "Capital")

---

[566] Pg. 18 - "Marx and Engels on the Population Bomb: Selections from the Writings of Marx and Engels Dealing with the Theories of Thomas Robert Malthus", Ronalsd E. Meek, Ramparts Press, 1971 — citing "Marx and Engels, Selected Correspondence", Pg. 170.
[567] Pg. 25 — Ibid.

Marx's and Engels' views on Malthus are quoted here at length in order to establish Marx's view of Darwin. Clearly, Marx considered Malthus' work to be scientific fraud, cooked and prepared for political purposes of the "English State Church," instead of the honesty expected from science:

> "Parson" Malthus does not sacrifice the exclusive interests to production, but does his best to sacrifice the demands of production to the exclusive interests of the existing ruling classes or sections of them, and to this end **he falsifies his scientific conclusions.** That is his scientific meanness, his sin against science, quite apart from his **shameless and mechanical plagiarism.** Malthus's scientific conclusions are considerate when the ruling classes in general and the reactionary elements among these ruling classes in particular are concerned; that is, **he falsifies science on behalf of these interests.** His conclusions are, however, inconsiderate where the oppressed classes are concerned. And it is not only that he is inconsiderate. He affects inconsiderateness, takes a cynical pleasure in this role, and **exaggerates the conclusions** – insofar as they are directed against those living in poverty – to an even greater extent than could be scientifically justified from his own point of view. (written 1861 – 1863) (Pg. 136-137, "Marx and Engels on the Population Bomb: Selections from the Writings of Marx and Engels Dealing with the Theories of Thomas Robert Malthus", Ramparts Press, 1971 - citing Marx's "Theories of Surplus Value", Vol. 2)

Marx and Engels were right. Parson Malthus was so incorrect he should have been long forgotten. Unfortunately, as Marx and Engels point out, Malthus lives through Darwin. They thought that Darwin's work relied too heavily on a work they considered to be deceitful, political, and a work of plagiarism. Interestingly enough, Marx criticizes Darwin for not being able to see beyond the prejudices of the society he was born to, an opinion this author clearly shares:

> …As regards Darwin, whom I have looked at again, it amuses me that he says he applies the "Malthusian" theory also to plants and animals, as if Malthus's whole point did not consist in the fact that his theory is applied not to plants and animals, but only to human beings – in geometrical progression – as opposed to plants and animals. It is remarkable that Darwin recognizes among brutes and plants his English society with its division of labor, competition, opening up of new markets, "inventions," and Malthusian "struggle for existence." It is Hobbes's *belum omnium contra omnes*, and it is reminiscent of Hegel in the *Phenomenology*, where bourgeois society figures as "spiritual animal kingdom," while the Darwin the animal kingdom figures as bourgeois society." From Marx's letter to Engels of June 18, 1862 (Pg. 195, "Marx and Engels on the Population Bomb: Selections from the Writings of Marx and Engels Dealing with the Theories of Thomas Robert Malthus", Ramparts Press, 1971)

I too was struck, the very first time I read Darwin, with the remarkable likeness between his account of plant and animal life and the Malthusian theory. From Engels' letter of Lange of March 29, 1865 (Pg. 85, "Marx and Engels on the

Population Bomb: Selections from the Writings of Marx and Engels Dealing with the Theories of Thomas Robert Malthus", Ramparts Press, 1971)

Engels rightly points out that prior to Darwin, the same scientists and theoreticians were marveling, not at the "struggle for existence," but at the wonderful balance of nature:

> Before Darwin, the very people – who now see nothing but *struggle* for existence everywhere were stressing precisely the *cooperation* in organic nature – how the vegetable kingdom supplies the animal kingdom with oxygen and foodstuffs while the animal kingdom in turn supplies the vegetable kingdom with carbonic acid and manures… (Pg. 197, "Marx and Engels on the Population Bomb: Selections from the Writings of Marx and Engels Dealing with the Theories of Thomas Robert Malthus", Ramparts Press, 1971)

Without the Malthusian checks and balances in nature, as described by Darwin, the competition for subsistence and existence as pruning tools to guide the evolution would not happen. Malthus had to be revisited and legitimized, or Darwin's "theory" would otherwise fall apart like a house of cards. Malthus had been proved wrong by the time that Darwin had written his theory, and Marx and Engels knew it. Marx and Engels knew Malthus had falsified the evidence to justify his politics. Yet, the need to legitimize Malthus only grew more persistent as the Darwinian revolution became a cultural revolution which later begot several political revolutions. As Meeks points out, John Maynard Keynes and the Progressive movement greatly admired Malthus, and the "third-way" movements that adopted Bellamy's "nationalization" and Keynesian economics thus were married to Malthusian theory. Here is Keynes' assessment of Malthus':

> If only Malthus, instead of Ricardo, had been the parent stem from which nineteenth-century economics proceeded, what a much wiser and richer place the world would be today! (Pg. 43, "Marx and Engels on the Population Bomb: Selections from the Writings of Marx and Engels Dealing with the Theories of Thomas Robert Malthus", Ramparts Press, 1971)

Both Marx and Engels recognized how cruel Malthusian-based economics truly was. Engels says as much in no uncertain terms in his 1845 "Condition of the Working Class in England in 1844." Note how Engels gleans a distinctly eugenic foundation to Malthus' theories:

> Malthus declares in plain English that the right to live, a right previously asserted in favor of every man in the world, is nonsense. He quotes the words of a poet, that the poor man comes to the feast of Nature and finds no cover laid for him, and adds that "she bids him begone," for he did not before his birth ask of society whether or not he is welcome. This is now the pet theory of all genuine English bourgeois, and very naturally, since it is the most specious excuse for them, and has, moreover, a good deal of truth in it under existing conditions. If, then, the problem is not to make the "surplus population" useful, to transform it into available population, but merely to let it starve to death in the least

objectionable way and to prevent its having too many children, this, of course, is simple enough, provided the surplus population perceives its own superfluousness and takes kindly to starvation. (Pg. 71, "Marx and Engels on the Population Bomb: Selections from the Writings of Marx and Engels Dealing with the Theories of Thomas Robert Malthus", Ramparts Press, 1971)

Marx and Engels exposed Darwin as uncritically adopting Malthusian theory. Darwin had advanced Malthus and stretched his theory beyond where the evidence permitted. With Darwin's popularity, the blind application of Malthus' work to political-economic theory went much further than Malthus ever dreamed of. Consider Engels' *"Anti-Dühring"* of 1878:

> The main reproach leveled against Darwin is that he transferred the Malthusian population theory from economics into natural science, that he never got beyond the ideas of an animal breeder, and that in his theory of the struggle for existence he pursued **unscientific semi-poetry**, and that the whole of Darwinism, after deducting what had been borrowed from Lamarck, **is a piece of brutality directed against humanity.** (emphasis mine, Pg. 203, "Marx and Engels on the Population Bomb: Selections from the Writings of Marx and Engels Dealing with the Theories of Thomas Robert Malthus", Ramparts Press, 1971)

A pattern is indeed discernible, and Engels's analysis should not be regarded as speculative. Engels and Marx were right. Darwin himself had admitted that his theory of "Natural Selection" was wholeheartedly derived from Malthus, and history has unfortunately proven that Darwin's uncritical incorporation of such inhumane ideals as resulting in "brutality directed against humanity."

> Darwin acknowledged that his natural selection "is the doctrine of Malthus applied with manifold force to the whole animal and vegetable kingdoms; for in this case there can be no artificial increase of food, and no prudential restraint from marriage. (Pg. 8, Daniel P. Todes, "Darwin without Malthus: The Struggle for Existence in Russian Evolutionary Thought", Oxford Univ. Press, 1989)

Engels took exception to Darwin's flaccid explanation:
> Now Darwin would not dream of saying that the origin of the idea of the struggle for existence is to be found in Malthus. He only says that his theory of the struggle for existence is the theory of Malthus applied to the animal and plant world as a whole. However great the blunder made by Darwin in accepting so naively and without reflection the Malthusian theory, nevertheless anyone can see at the first glance that no Malthusian spectacles are required in order to perceive the struggle for existence in Nature – who was it that gave the most definite impulse to work in this direction? No other than Darwin. (Pgs. 205-205, "Marx and Engels on the Population Bomb: Selections from the Writings of Marx and Engels Dealing with the Theories of Thomas Robert Malthus", Ramparts Press, 1971)

More importantly, Engels recognized that a "controlled" and "planned" economy was the only economic and political system that could enact the controls over the growth of population that the Malthusians demanded:

> There is, of course, the abstract possibility that the number of people will become so great that limits will have to be set to their increase. But if at some stage communists society finds itself obliged to regulate the production of human beings, just as it has already come to regulate the production of things, it will be precisely this society, and this society alone, which can carry this out without difficulty. - From Engels' letter to Kautsky of February 1st, 1881 (Pg. 119, "Marx and Engels on the Population Bomb: Selections from the Writings of Marx and Engels Dealing with the Theories of Thomas Robert Malthus", Ramparts Press, 1971)

Engels is absolutely correct: "Control" is indispensable for eugenics. Absolute political control and eugenics are two sides of the same coin. One cannot exist without the other. All planned economies, whether the works of futuristic fictions or actual collectivist governments, necessitate a eugenic program. "Control" is the key to maintaining the fragile stasis that planned economies so desperately try to balance. "Control" is indispensable in the effort to shield society from the violent upheavals in economic history. "Control" over every last detail of human life is vital in order to engineer the outcome of economic life, and ensure that equal results, as opposed to "equal opportunity" is achieved. This is the idea that firebrand pro-slavery advocate, George Fitzhugh would popularize; that to control one must first enslave. [568]

There are several formidable threats to being able to guarantee "equal results" for all of society, and "excess population" or uncontrolled population is one of the largest threats to the effort of an engineered outcome. One simply cannot plan for an economic future with the population growing out of its planned boundaries. Likewise, one simply cannot afford to have unproductive elements in one's "industrial army," or what the Bolsheviks would call "useless eaters." Mr. Engels was absolutely correct that it is only an all-encompassing, all-knowing, and all-powerful government, with power over the life and death of individual citizens, which can successfully enact a eugenic program. The goals of eugenics simply cannot be achieved without the totalitarian power to segregate, confiscate, incarcerate, and exterminate without fear of push-back from those elements of the population that are being manipulated. Absolute power which incites absolute fear in the population is a necessary ingredient for a eugenic program.

The pattern of bolstering progressive ideals upon succeeding generations of devoted Malthusians can be said to be this trajectory of "scientific racism" from 1848 to 1948. Darwin had relied heavily on Malthus, even though the Agricultural Revolution had already proved Malthus wrong by the time Malthus published his infamous work. Incidentally, Darwin also relied heavily on Ernst Haeckel, even though reputable scientists like Rudolf Virchow had proven beyond a shadow of a doubt that Haeckel had falsified and exaggerated several of his most important

---

[568] See Generally – "Cannibals All!: Or, Slaves Without Masters", George Fitzhugh, A. Morris, 1857.

claims. Galton, in turn, relied heavily on Darwinism in proposing his eugenic theory, even though his proposals for "rational" human breeding had proven to be catastrophes when tried in the various socialist utopias in the United States, and ridiculed when these activists spoke of them in England. Leonard Darwin and Charles B. Davenport advanced eugenics after Galton even though the Hardy-Weinberg Principle had disproven the core concept of dysgenic heredity permanently altering the trajectory of human evolution. Keynes had relied heavily on Malthus and Darwin for his economic theory and even persisted in popularizing central planning despite the catastrophic failures of such schemes in the first decade of Bolshevik Russia. Even though it was obvious that all these people were peddling failed doctrines, several generations of the Huxley, Darwin, and Galton families redoubled their efforts towards having Darwinism replace traditional religion, and their political counterparts worked equally zealously to make Keynes the replacement for the emerging *laissez-faire* democracy.

The scientists and doctors who carried out the crimes of The Holocaust defended their actions as being based on the work of reputable scientists, and the economic planners behind the Third Reich relied heavily on Keynes. Hitler's economic minister, Dr. Hjalmar Horace Greeley Schacht, who incidentally was named after the socialist-abolitionist Horace Greeley, would implement much of what Keynes proposed. Scientists and doctors like Mengele, Rüdin, Ploetz, and Verschuer were devoted Darwinists and, as proven in previous pages, relied heavily on the work of American and British Darwinists such as Leonard Darwin, Francis Galton, Charles B. Davenport, Madison Grant, Henry Fairfield Osborn, and Harry H. Laughlin. These scientists and economists were the infamous "men in white coats" who first educated Adolf Hitler with the dogmas of the international eugenic community. It was the "men in white coats" who wrote the laws and developed the techniques that would be used in these camps. It was the "men in white coats" that pulled the handles which released the gasses in the extermination camps. It is the ideological heirs to these "men in white coats" who continue to rename and repackage this scientific propaganda, this failed theory, this horrid mistake, and fraudulent falsification popularly known as "eugenics."

FIGURE 19: Eugenic-Health propaganda distributed by the National Socialists. Note the emphasis on the cost comparison of maintaining a healthy German family to that of an "unfit" or "feebleminded" person.

Chap. 19: 1859 to 1848

SCIENCE & TECHNOLOGY: Louis Pasteur begins studying fermentation. A telegraph cable is laid beneath the English Channel. - Rifling technique to manufacturing of firearms first employed. - Railroads begin to supplant waterways as the primary means of transporting goods. - Henry Bessemer patents the Bessemer process. **AMERICAN FRONT:** California is admitted as the 31st US State. The Kansas–Nebraska Act is signed into law. Congressman Preston Brooks of South Carolina beats Senator Charles Sumner with a cane. Edwin Drake drills the first oil well in the United States near Titusville, Pennsylvania. – Oregon becomes the 33 State. - The largest Slave Auction in history, dubbed as 'The Weeping Time'. - The Washington Monument is established. – The 2-day Women's Rights Convention opens in Seneca Falls, New York. - Thomas Garret is apprehended after leading 2700 slaves to freedom on the Underground Railroad. **EUROPEAN FRONT:** Feudalism and serfdom abolished in Ottoman Empire. Edison, American inventor is born – Alexander Graham Bell, Scottish-born inventor is born – Karl Bayer, Austrian chemist is born – Joseph Pulitzer, newspaper magnate is born. - Frederick William IV emperor of the new German national state. **LIFE:** Vincent van Gogh, Dutch painter is born. – The New York Times is founded. – The Reuters news service is founded. – Richard Wagner's opera Lohengrin premieres. - A Tale of Two Cities by Charles Dickens is published. - Big Ben rings for the first time in London. - Billy the Kid, American outlaw is born. - Woodrow Wilson is born. - Sigmund Freud, Austrian psychiatrist is born. – Nikola Tesla, Serbian inventor is born. – John Quincy Adams, 6 President of the United States dies.

Sec. I - FROM A "MASTER RACE" TO A "RACE OF MASTERS":

Slavery was in every respect a counter-revolution to the Revolution of the Founding Fathers. The pro-slavery position was a counter-revolution that explicitly sought to disprove the founding concepts that "all men are created equal" and thus "equal before the law," with "equal rights to life, liberty, and the pursuit of happiness." This counter-revolution was started by the grandsons of the Founding Fathers. One can argue that the United States swerved in this direction after Founding Fathers like John Adams and Thomas Jefferson were no longer around, and when their own sons, such as John Quincy Adams, had passed the torch to a generation that took power beyond the overwhelming shadow of the Founding Fathers. It would have been difficult, if not impossible, to argue against the founding concepts prior to that.

Southern proponents of slavery absolutely relied on the notion that Africans were not their "brothers," and that they were a subordinate people not in any way "created equal." This is where the lawyer George Fitzhugh stepped in and cited Aristotle's hierarchy of society based upon the hierarchy of the family, with paternal leaders and subordinate children and slaves. This is where the concept of a "race of masters" or a "master race" originated, in reestablishing the concept of a right to rule over others as an inherited trait. Fitzhugh states as much in his most famous work, "Cannibals All! or Slaves Without Masters":

> Whilst we hold that all government is a matter of fource, we yet think the governing class should be numerous enough to understand, and so situated as to represent fairly, all interests. The Greek and Roman masters were thus situated; so were the old Barons of England, and so are the white citizens of the South. If not all masters, like Greek and Roman citizens, they all belong to the **master race**, have exclusive rights and privileges of citizenship, and interest not to see this right of citizenship extended, disturbed, and rendered worthless and contemptible. (emphasis mine, Pgs. 245-246, "Cannibals All! Or, Slaves Without Masters", A. Morris, 1857)

Another pro-slavery intellectual to write about a "race of masters" was the lawyer George S. Sawyer in his 1858 book, "Southern Institute." Sawyer shares with Fitzhugh the idea of a natural aristocracy, born to rule by their racial attributes, a not-so-dissimilar concept as the kings and queens of antiquity proclaimed to be ordained by God. Note how similar the words and concepts are to those famous British biologists and anthropologists:

> Hitherto we have been unable to make any distinction between the intellectual capacity, mental and moral characteristics of the race of masters and slaves in any age or nation; but have proceeded upon the hypothesis that they were both of the same type of mankind, and equal in those particulars. And we find the truth of this supposition strikingly illustrated in the subsequent history of those nations from which, anciently, slaves were principally obtained. These nations have all, except Africa, risen to supremacy in letters, science, arts, and arms over the nations that once held their sons in bondage. (Pg. 147, "Southern Institute; or, An Inquiry into the Origin and Early Prevalence of Slavery and the Slave-Trade", 1858)

Sawyer is of historical importance because he helped Confederate political icons like John Calhoun approach the debate in the form of a legal argument. Sawyer echoed Calhoun in the sentiment and idea that black inferiority could be upheld based on their tacit consent to slavery: "the social, moral and political history of the negro race bears strong testimony against them; it furnishes the most undeniable proof of their mental inferiority." [569] Similar sentiments were being voiced around the world. Intellectuals began to seriously question the Enlightenment's "equality" within "humanity," and they leveraged anthropology and archeology to do so.

Joseph Ernest Renan was a French expert of Middle East ancient languages and civilizations, philosopher, and writer. He is best known for his influential historical works on early Christianity and political theories, especially concerning nationalism and national identity. In his 1850 "*La Reforme*" Renan expressed his belief that political policy should take into account supposed racial differences between the "race of masters" and the "tillers of soil":

> The regeneration of the inferior or **degenerate races** by the **superior races** is part of the providential order of things for humanity. ---- Nature has made a race of workers, the Chinese race, who have wonderful manual dexterity and almost no sense of honor...A race of tillers of the soil, the Negro; treat him with kindness and humanity, and all will be as it should; **a race of masters and soldiers, the European race**. Reduce this noble race to working in the ergastulum like Negros and Chinese, and they rebel... But the life at which our workers rebel would make a Chinese or a fellah happy, as they are not military creatures in the least. (emphasis mine, Ernest Renan, "*La Reforme intellectuelle et morale*" – Translation by Chris Miller, "War on Terror: The Oxford Amnesty Lectures", Oxford Univ. Press, 2009)

Even the Unitarian minister Theodore Parker, whose words and quotations

---

[569] Pg. 212 - "From Slavery to Freedom: A History of African Americans", John H. Franklin and Alfred A. Moss, Jr., Knopf, 1974.

would later inspire speeches by Abraham Lincoln and Martin Luther King, Jr., and be recognized as a leader of the abolitionist movement expressed such sentiments. Theodore Parker decrees "Caucasians" as being the "master of other races":

> "The Caucasian differs from all other races: he is humane, he is civilized, and progresses. He conquers with his head as well as with his hand ... The Caucasian has been often **master of the other races** – never their slave. (emphasis mine, Pg. 181, "Race and Manifest Destiny: The Origins of American Racial Anglo-Saxonism", Reginald Horsman, Harvard Univ. Press, 1981)

As such, history must record that the concept of a "race of masters" or a "master race" flowered in the United States as part of the antebellum polemic. The Oxford English Dictionary credits William J. Grayson with having first used the phrase "master race," even though Joseph Ernest Renan's use of "race of masters" predated Grayson's use by five years. William John Grayson was a US Representative from South Carolina. Grayson received a classical education and devoted himself to the law and practiced in Beaufort, South Carolina. He was a member of the state legislature and served in Congress from 1833 to 1837. In politics he was conservative and on the whole, opposed to disunion, but never took a stance antagonistic to the institution of slavery. By all accounts, he was a man of culture, a poet. His 1855 poem "The Hireling and the Slave," utilized the now infamous term:

> *For these great ends hath Heaven's supreme command*
> *Brought the black savage from his native land,*
> *Trains for each purpose his barbarian mind,*
> *By slavery tamed, enlightened, and refined;*
> *Instructs him, from a **master-race**, to draw*
> *Wise modes of polity and forms of law,*
> *Imbues his soul with faith, his heart with love,*
> *Shapes all his life by dictates from above.*
> (emphasis mine)

Grayson, like Fitzhugh, defended slavery on a socio-economic basis, where the benefit of being taken care of is expounded as a greater way of life than confronting the burdens of liberty and freedom. Like Fitzhugh, he went on to compare the suffering of whites for hire, the "hirelings," as employees burdened with liberty in the rapidly industrialized economy to the suffering of the enslaved population:

> If, in consequence of the evils incident to hireling labor – because there are severe, heartless, grinding employers, and miserable, starving hirelings, it were proposed to abolish hireling labor, it would be quite as just and logical as the argument to abolish slavery because there are sufferings among slave, and hard hearts among masters. The cruelty or suffering is no more a necessary part of the one system than of the other. (Pg. vi, "The Hireling and the Slave", J. Russell, 1854)

Grayson touched on the theme which would define the transition from the 19th to the 20th century. He defined slavery as the duty of the elite to take care of the weak from "cradle-to-grave," lest they free them to suffer in their liberation without anyone to provide them food and shelter. This is a concept that the famous Marxist historian, Erich Fromm, would later regard as the core concept behind Bolshevik collectivism and National Socialism's promise to relieve its subjects from the "burdens of freedom":

> Slavery is that system of labor which exchanges subsistence for work, which secures a life-maintenance from the master to the slave, and gives a life-labor from the slave to the master. The slave is an apprentice for life, and owes his labor to his master; the master owes support, during life, to the slave. Slavery is the Negro system of labor. He is lazy and improvident. Slavery makes all work, and it insures homes, food, and clothing for all. It permits no idleness, and it provides for sickness, infancy, and old age. It allows no tramping or skulking, and it knows no pauperism. (Pg. vii, "The Hireling and the Slave", J. Russell, 1854)

Grayson framed the benevolence of slavery around the notion that there was no such thing as a slave for "whom nobody cares or provides." In this, he was right, albeit in a detestable way. The slaves, after all, were regarded as "property," and valued property as the predominantly agricultural economy was in deep debt to Northern bankers with their slaves as collateral:

> If slavery is subject to abuses, it has its advantages also. It establishes more permanent, and therefore, kinder relations between capital and labor. It removes what Stuart Mill calls "the widening and imbittering feud between the class of labor and the class of capital." It draws the relation closer between master and servant. It is not an engagement for days or weeks, but for life. There is no such thing with slavery as a laborer from whom nobody cares or provides. The most wretched feature in hireling labor is the isolated, miserable creature who has no home, no work, no food, and in whom no one is particularly interested. This is seen among hirelings only. (Pgs. vii-viii, "The Hireling and the Slave", J. Russell, 1854)

Grayson's preface explains his political position in prose, and the poem presents them in verse. The theme in prose and verse are similar, maintaining the topics of a "cradle-to-grave" benefit to the slave as being more humane than casting the "hireling," or wage-laborer, to fend with the harsh realities of industrialized capitalism with no guarantees of housing or sustenance. Interestingly enough, this "cradle-to-grave" concept is one that survives in collectivist, Fabian, and Progressive political platforms. Curiously enough, the famous political pundit, Milton Friedman gives Edward Bellamy credit for coining the phrase in "Looking Backward." [570] While attributing such a politically consequential concept to a Progressive icon such as Bellamy is tantalizing, it is comical what the actual history reveals; that "cradle-to-grave," the proud Progressive concept is the product of a slave-owner's racialist desire to subjugate non-whites to enslavement as a consequence of dependence:

---

[570] Pg. 93 – "Free to Choose: A Personal Statement", Milton Friedman / Rose Friedman, Harcourt, 1980.

> *How small the choice, **from cradle to the grave**,*
> *Between the lot of the hireling, help, or slave!*
> *To each alike applies the stern decree*
> *That man shall labor; whether bond or free,*
> (Pg. 22, "The Hireling and the Slave", J. Russell, 1854)

Grayson's poem "The Hireling and the Slave," touched on all of these themes, and it seems as if Rudyard Kipling, the author of the infamous 1899 poem "The White Man's Burden" was answering Grayson verse for verse. Kipling would talk of the dangers of "famine" on that portion of the population that was cast aside, while Grayson spoke of the "mocking" of "freedom" when one finds oneself cast into these desperate circumstances:

> *The manumitted serfs of Europe find*
> *Unchanged this sad estate of all mankind;*
> *What blessing to the churl has freedom proved,*
> *What want supplied, what task or toil removed?*
> *Hard work and scanty wages still their lot,*
> *In youth o'erlabored, and in age forgot,*
> *The mocking boon of freedom they deplore,*
> *In wants and labors never before.*
> *Free but in name – the slaves of endless toil,*
> (Pg. 22, "The Hireling and the Slave", J. Russell, 1854)

Kipling's poem toyed with the conscience of the imperialists of the era, daring them quite literally to "search" their "manhood" and question what the "judgment" of their "peers" will be in taking account for the suffering caused by capitalistic exploitation. Grayson, by contrast, asked those abolitionists to question the "philanthropy" in the consequences of freeing a people allegedly unprepared for liberty:

> *There, unconcerned, the philanthropic eye*
> *Beholds each phase of human misery;*
> *Sees the worn child compelled in mines to slave*
> *Through narrow seams of coal, a living grave,*
> *Driven from the breezy hill, the sunny glade,*
> *By ruthless hearts, the drudge of labor made,*
> *Unknown the boyish sport, the hours of play,*
> *Stripped of the common boon, the light of day,*
> *Harnessed like brutes, like brutes to tug, and strain,*
> *And drag, on hands and knees, the loaded wain:*
> (Pg. 24, "The Hireling and the Slave", J. Russell, 1854)

Grayson's poem paints Southern slavery as the "repose" and "sanctuary" protecting the Africans from being prayed on by those that would abuse them in a world of seafaring commerce and conquest. Grayson pokes at the ugly reality that the slave-trade was assisted by African's themselves participated, "kidnapped by brothers" and "by fathers sold," and thus depicted the Southern institution literally as the benevolent "white man's burden" intervening as protective "masters" by "God's command" to "tame and elevate the Negro mind." Grayson conceded that it was not an enviable situation for the "Negro," but the best that could be offered to him until the "utopian" dreams of the abolitionist become practicable. He maintained that the system of slavery was much more benevolent than the option the abolitionists proposed:

> *And yet the master's lighter rule insures*
> *More order than the sternest code secures:*
> *No mobs of factious workmen gather here,*
> *No strikes we dread, no lawless riots fear;*
> (Pg. 45, "The Hireling and the Slave", J. Russell, 1854)

It is this "escape" from the "burdens of freedom," and towards a "cradle-to-grave" paternalism, which socialists would later base their own counter-revolution upon. These notions were at extreme odds with the founding concepts of the United States. The Declaration of Independence and Constitution were clearly understood and upheld by the first justices of the US Supreme Court. This aspect of "equality before the law" was expressed by a US Supreme Court still operating within the shadow of the Founding Fathers. The case of <u>Chisholm v. Georgia</u> eloquently preserves the mentality of the Founding Generation:

> Concerning the prerogative of Kings, and concerning the sovereignty of States, much has been said and written; but little has been said and written concerning a subject much more dignified and important, the majesty of the people. – To the Constitution of the United States the term SOVEREIGN, is totally unknown. There is but one place where it could have been used with propriety. – MAN, fearfully and wonderfully made, is the workmanship of his all perfect CREATOR: a State; useful and valuable as the contrivance is, is the inferior contrivance of man; and from his native dignity derives all its acquired importance.

CONTINUES...

> ...the sovereignties in Europe, and particularly in England, exist on feudal principles. That system considers the Prince as the sovereign, and the people as his subjects; it regards his person as the object of allegiance, and excludes the idea of his being on an equal footing with a subject, either in a Court of Justice or elsewhere.

CONTINUES...

> ...The Same feudal ideas run through all their jurisprudence, and constantly remind us of the distinction between the Prince and the subject. No such ideas obtain here; at the Revolution, the sovereignty devolved on the people; and they

are truly the sovereigns of the country, but they are sovereigns without subjects and have none to govern but themselves; the citizens of America are equal as fellow citizens, and as joint tenants in the sovereignty. --- Sovereignty is the right to govern; a nation or State-sovereign is the person or person in whom that resides. In Europe the sovereignty is generally ascribed to the Prince; here it rests with the people; there, the sovereign actually administers the Government; here, never in a single instance; our Governors are the agents of the people, and at most stand in the same relation to their sovereign, in which regents in Europe stand to their sovereigns.
(Chisholm v. Georgia, 2 US 419 (US Supreme Court 1793)

Historians of the American Revolution concede that it was an unfinished struggle; that the Founding Generation had postponed the issue of slavery in order to push forward a united front during the Revolutionary War. The proximate result of this postponement was that the generations immediately following the American Revolution could not, or would not, legitimize this "feudalism" of "masters" and "subjects" while the significant costs of achieving these liberties were still prominent upon their minds. The pro-slavery counter-revolution would try to reinstate these very antagonistic ideals of "Prince and subject" and "feudal sovereignties." The pro-slavery counter-revolution had to wait to emerge from the shadow of the Founding Fathers and first contend with the significant legal hurdles left behind by the Founding Fathers. The Founding Fathers left an uphill battle for the forces of slavery by writing in what Abraham Lincoln would later call "covert language" into the law of the land, making the survival of the institution of slavery a legal minefield for the South. [571] If any of the Founding documents or treaties had recognized the concept of a "slave" as "property" then abolitionists would not have had a legal leg to stand on. This was the core of legal scholar Abraham Lincoln's message when he was just a candidate; a message the Southern slave owner knew to be a clear and present danger. Concepts such as the "race of masters" or a "master race" had to be contrived in order to wage the formidable intellectual and legal battle against the "covert language" enshrined in the founding documents. If 20th Century intellectuals such as Erich Fromm are correct, then this counter-revolution persists to this day. We are still trying to shed the "burdens of freedom" in exchange for secular feudalism.

---

[571] For more on this subject, see also: "THE 3/5ths CLAUSE: The "Covert Language" of the Founding Fathers", A.E. Samaan, www.academia.edu, Feb. 2014.

Sec. 2 - DE-EVOLUTION, DEGENERATION, AND LIBERATION:

Seventy-two years after the American Revolutionaries signed the Declaration of Independence, Europe, and a sizeable chunk of the world, looked upon their own governments and demanded change. The Revolutions of 1848, known in some countries as the "Spring of Nations," "Springtime of the Peoples" or the "Year of Revolution," were a series of political upheavals. This period of revolution was the only Europe-wide collapse of traditional authority up to this date, but within a year reactionary forces had won out, and the revolutions collapsed. This revolutionary wave began in France in February and immediately spread to most of Europe and parts of Latin America. Over 50 countries were affected, even though there was no cooperation among the revolutionaries in different countries.

The world seemed entangled in fits of union and disunion, all of which questioned the political relationships of antiquity and tinkered with the revolutionary concepts of individual liberty. The ideological pendulum swung in both directions. After the defeat of the Prussians by Napoleon at the battle of Jena in 1806, the prevailing consensus was that the battle was lost because the Prussian soldiers were thinking for themselves instead of following orders. The product of this self-criticism was the "Addresses to the German Nation" by Prussian philosopher Johann Gottlieb Fichte. "Addresses to the German Nation" promoted the idea that the state was the instrument necessary to acquire social and moral progress for the German-Speaking people. Fichte taught at the University of Berlin from 1810 to his death in 1814. His 1807 "Address to The German Nation" is considered a work European "altruism," a sacrifice of the self for the sake of society, and adopted by various Progressive and Socialist thinkers after him:

> ...the noble-minded man will be active and effective, and will sacrifice himself for his people. Life merely as such, the mere continuance of changing existence, has in any case never had any value for him, he has wished for it only as the source of what is permanent. But this permanence is promised to him only by the continuous and independent existence of his nation. In order to save his nation he must be ready even to die that it may live, and that he may live in it the only life for which he has ever wished. (Pgs. 136-138 / 143-145, Johann Gottlieb Fichte, "Addresses to the German Nation", trans. R. F. Jones & G. H. Turnbull, Chicago: Univ. of Chicago Press, 1922)

Fitche talked of the early struggles of the Germanic tribes against the onslaught of the overpowering Romans, and defined "freedom" as the freedom to continue in the ways of the "race" and the "nation":

> ...Freedom to them meant just this: remaining Germans and continuing to settle their own affairs, independently and in accordance with the original spirit of their race, going on with their development in accordance with the same spirit, and propagating this independence in their posterity. All those blessings which the Romans offered them meant slavery to them because then they would have to become something that was not German, they would have to become half-Roman. They assumed as a matter of course that every man would rather die than become half a Roman, and that a true German could only want to live in

order to be, and to remain, just a German and to bring up his children as Germans. (Pgs. 136-138 / 143-145, Johann Gottlieb Fichte, "Addresses to the German Nation", trans. R. F. Jones & G. H. Turnbull, Chicago: Univ. of Chicago Press, 1922)

The psychological effects of disunion on the German-Speaking people cannot be overstated, and disingenuous politicians such as Adolf Hitler were able to push their finger into this never-healing wound. Napoleon had divided the German-Speaking geography into smaller states, and French policy thereafter sought a divided Germany for one justification or another. The Pan-German dream of unification drove the Anschluss that united Germany and Austria into one German nation, and Hitler's drive to consolidate the pockets of German-Speaking populations in Eastern Europe was justified under these terms. Towards the end of World War II, millions died needlessly, as the war was prolonged as Hitler and Goebbels were able to remind the German public of the consequences of being split up as they had been various times in their history. The Morgenthau Plan, having been written by a Jewish member of President Roosevelt's cabinet, gave Goebbels the justification to instill fear of an "iron curtain" descending upon them. Winston Churchill later picked up on Goebbels' prediction and quoted him in the speech that wrongfully attributed the term "iron curtain" to Churchill.

Adolf Hitler considered his German National Socialist movement to be a continuation and fruition of what had begun in 1848. Hitler "diligently studied" the revolution of 1848. [572] The revolutionary spirit sparked in Germany on March 13th, 1848 in Hitler's beloved Vienna, and became a long-standing theme for Hitler, as he had been a Pan-German since his schoolboy days in Linz. Hitler attributed his version of "nationalism" to his history teacher in the Technical School he attended in Linz, "Herr Doktor Leopold Pötsch":

> I am still touched when I think of the grey-haired man, the fire of whose words sometimes made us forget the present and, as though by magic, transported us into the past, and out of the mist of time transformed the dry historical facts into vivid reality. There we sat, wildly enthusiastic, sometimes moved to tears. (Pg. 51, "The Young Hitler I Knew: The Memoirs of Hitler's Childhood Friend", 1955)

The above quote is from August Kubizek. Kubizek opines that Dr. Pötsch was more than just a teacher. Dr. Pötsch also served on the town council and was a leader of the Nationalist Party. Kubizek testifies to Pötsch being the reason why Hitler from a very young age identified with Germany, despite being Austrian:

> I believe that the absolute love for everything that was German which Pötsch combined with his aversion to the Hapsburg Monarchy was the decisive revelation for the young Hitler. This fervent devotion to the German people gave him a firm foundation for the rest of his life. Adolf Hitler remained grateful to his old history teacher throughout his life, indeed his attachment to school and

---

572 Pg. 111 - "Hitler's Vienna: A Dictator's Apprenticeship", Brigitte Hamann, Oxford Univ. Press, 1999.

teacher grew with the passing of the years. In 1938 Hitler came to Klagenfurt and met Pötsch again. He spent more than an hour in a room alone with the frail old man. When he left the room he said to those accompanying him, "You cannot imagine how much I owe to that old man." (Pg. 52, "The Young Hitler I Knew: The Memoirs of Hitler's Childhood Friend", 1955)

Note the above; Hitler had always been opposed to the monarchy. Opposition to the monarchy was a revolutionary idea in an era that considered monarchists as conservatives. Kubizek also describes how Hitler's entire world view, from his architectural and artistic aspirations to his political views, starting at the very young age of 16, was entirely molded upon a Nationalist world view:

> Yet one word, which regularly cropped up in his discourse, always struck me: the "Reich." With this word he used to wind up his long outpourings. Whenever he had talked himself into a blind alley and was at a loss how to continue, he would say categorically: "This problem will be solved by the Reich"; if I asked, for instance, who would finance all these gigantic building projects which he sketched on his drawing board, his brief answer was "The Reich." Even trivialities were left to the care of the "Reich." – Even the care for the blind, or the protection of animals belonged, in his opinion, to the jurisdiction of the "Reich!" The word "Reich" is used in Austria for the territory of Germany; its inhabitants are called Reich's Germans. But my friend's use of the term, meant more than merely the German State, though he carefully avoided any more exact definition. For to him the word was simply a portmanteau expression, which comprised everything that was politically important to him - and that was a lot. (Pg. 75, "The Young Hitler I Knew: The Memoirs of Hitler's Childhood Friend", August Kubizek, Houghton Mifflin, 1955)

As with all "nationalism" that attempts at defining the union, the definition of "otherness" is implicit. Defining the "nation" implies defining what doesn't belong, what must be discarded, and as many of these 1848 wars and revolutions proved, what must be broken from and cordoned off in this exercise of disunion:

> With the same fanaticism with which he loved the German people, and this "Reich," did he reject everything foreign. He had no desire to know other countries. That longing for distant lands so typical of all open-minded young people was utterly alien to him – even the artist's classical enthusiasm for Italy. There was only one place for his plans and ideas – the Reich. His violent nationalism, which was unequivocally directed against the Hapsburg Monarchy, showed all the particular predispositions of his character, especially the iron consistency with which he struck to everything he had once accepted as correct. The Nationalist ideology became his political creed and formed an unalterable element of his nature. No failure or setback would change him. He remained till his death what he had been at sixteen – a Nationalist. (Pgs. 75 – 76, "The Young Hitler I Knew: The Memoirs of Hitler's Childhood Friend", August Kubizek, Houghton Mifflin, 1955)

The aura of "nationalism" persisted on through the decades, well into the time when Hitler lived in Vienna and was witness to the frequent uprisings in support of the various nationalist movements. He delighted in the drama the leaders of these various movements displayed in the Vienna Parliament, evidence that these revolutions were not a settled issue. The causes that sparked the revolutions in 1848 were alive and well after the turn-of-the-century. August Kubizek recalls that the "spirit of nationalism" dominated the Linz Technical School long after the Revolutions of 1848. Students and teachers alike were opposed to the traditional institutions of the monarchy. Kubizek quotes Hitler:

> Money was collected for Sudmark and Schulverein, one's sentiments were manifested by wearing cornflowers and black-red-gold colours, we used "Heil" as a greeting and sang "Deutschland über Alles" instead of the Hapsburg Imperial Hymn. All this in spite of warnings and punishment. (Pg. 73, "The Young Hitler I Knew: The Memoirs of Hitler's Childhood Friend", 1955)

The Revolution of 1848 failed in their attempt to unify the German-speaking states into a single nation because the Frankfurt Assembly was unable to take any definitive action toward unification and thus degenerated into a mere debating society. The democratic and liberal forces in Germany of 1848 were confronted with the need to build a nation-state and a constitutional state at once, which overstrained them. The German Revolution of 1848 thus failed where the American Revolution of 1776 succeeded in taking disparate States and uniting them into a single union while maintaining their independence and freedom. This is what the American Founding Fathers called *"Imperium in Imperio."* The Latin phrasewas used frequently by the Founding Generation to communicate the idea of "divided sovereignty," as all of them regarded their "country" to be what we now call a "State." For example, John Adams's regarded his "country" to be "Massachusetts." As such, the American Revolution in 1776 issued its Declaration of Independence drafted by the "Representatives" of the "united States," with the "u" in "united" not being capitalized, and declared "these Colonies" to be "Free and Independent States." James Madison further clarified the specificity of this text in Federalist 39, when he stated that the act of establishing the Constitution was "not as individuals composing one entire nation, but as composing the distinct and independent States to which they respectively belong." Madison, thus explained, that the creation of the "United States" under the Constitution was "not a *national*, but a *federal* act." This is why the grammar of the US Constitution refers to the States in the plural. For example, in Article 3, Section 2, the jurisdiction of the Federal courts is said to include cases arising under "the Laws of the United States, and treaties made . . .under ***their*** Authority." (emphasis mine)

Thus, in America, a union was created of disparate cultures and economies, albeit with the advantage of having one common language. Clearly, the lingering disparities would erupt again in 1860 when the differences became intolerable between the cultures of the industrialized North and the aristocratic South, and the Founding Fathers predicted this. They knew their Revolution was an unfinished one, namely because of the lingering issue of slavery. The unfinished business of the American Revolution of 1776 erupted again in the American Civil War, much in the same sense as the unfinished business of the Revolutions of 1848 thus resurfaced in World War I. The difference lay in that the American Revolutionaries were successful in dispelling the British monarchy and erecting a form of government where independence was successfully preserved without compromising the integrity of the Union. The Pan-German Revolutionaries not only failed in shaking the antiquated monarchy but as a consequence that monarchy persisted in pretending its existence could serve as a bonding agent for disparate ethnicities. The only truth in the monarch's arrogance was in the fact of its military superiority over the revolutionaries. Insurgents quickly lost in street fighting to King Ferdinand's troops. Ferdinand was restored to power in Vienna, but the tensions remained; Vienna became the "Babel" of lingering cultural tensions that Hitler so despised. Case in point, Hitler declared in a speech in Frankfurt that "fate had blessed him": "We can now consider the work for which our ancestors fought and bled ninety years ago to be accomplished." [573]

This book has documented how eugenics formed a sort of counter-revolution to the American Revolution, looking to reverse its egalitarian value system of individual rights and the autonomy of local communities and its citizens from the zealous aspirations of the ruling elite. The American Revolution eschewed the notion of a natural elite, either as the pretenses of the monarchy they had just claimed emancipation from, or in the form of any single individual who would "amass power" in the "same hands." From its onset, eugenicists had a pronounced disdain for egalitarian values and *laissez-faire* democracy starting with Francis Galton. Galton spoke of democracy in the January 1873 article in "Fraser's Magazine" titled "Hereditary Improvement":

> But it goes farther than this, for it asserts that men are of equal value as social units, equally capable of voting, and the rest. This feeling is undeniably wrong, and cannot last. (Pg. 85, "Legacy of Malthus: The Social Costs of the New Scientific Racism", Allan Chase, Alfred A. Knopf, 1977)

As is documented by this book, this derision towards *"laissez-faire"* democracy was shared by German, American, and British eugenicists alike, likely without exception. Frederick Henry Osborn, the Princeton graduate and founding member of several eugenic organizations, whom the American Philosophical Society considered to have been "the respectable face of eugenic research in the post-war period" said:

> The true spirit of American democracy that all men are born with equal rights and duties has been confused with the political sophistry that all men are borne with equal character and ability to govern themselves and others, and with the educational sophistry that education and environment will offset the handicap of heredity. – The right of the state to safeguard the character and integrity of the race or races on which its future depends is, to my mind, as incontestable as

---

[573] Pg. 111 - "Hitler's Vienna: A Dictator's Apprenticeship", Brigitte Hamann, Oxford Univ. Press, 1999.

the right of the state to safeguard the health and morals of its people. (Pg. 278, "Legacy of Malthus: The Social Costs of the New Scientific Racism", Allan Chase, Alfred A. Knopf, 1977)

More to the point, this disdain for egalitarian values, namely when they are spread across a diversity of ethnicities, became the cause behind the immigration reform of the eugenicists. The congressional report that repealed and replaced the Immigration Restriction Act of 1924 quotes Harry H. Laughlin's views on *laissez-faire* democracy:

> We in this country have been so imbued with the idea of democracy, or the equality of all men, that we have left out of consideration the matter of blood or natural inborn hereditary mental and moral differences. No man who breeds pedigreed plants and animals can afford to neglect this thing. (Pgs. 1853-1854, 82nd Congress, "Hearings before the President's Commission on Immigration and Naturalization", US Gov. Printing Office, Sept. 30 and Oct. 29, 1952 – Available at catalog.hathitrust.org, No.: 100671453)

This book amply documents the equal amount of disdain which Adolf Hitler felt towards the concepts of *laissez-faire* democracy and individual liberty, especially when it came to apply or deny those rights to the non-Aryan German citizenry. This book documents his thoughts on the matter, so posterity can understand precisely how the ideals of "sacrifice," "unity of purpose" and "altruism" played in the submerging of the individual under the prerogative of society. These were the forces that caused such tumultuous eruptions towards union or disunion in 1848, and which in turn generated divisions in society that engendered distinct ideas of who belonged and who was to be excluded. As we have seen, the criterion for exclusion was couched in notions of cultural "degeneration," a concept that too has roots in the revolutions of the era. This was the case in various of the 1848 revolutions, namely in France. In France, the revolution of 1848 became known as the February Revolution. The street demonstrations of workers and artisans in Paris, France, on February 22-24, 1848, which resulted in the forced abdication of King Louis Philippe of France and his departure from France to live in Britain.

The Revolutions of 1848 also had an unintended effect on eugenic history as they served to promote August Morel. Bénédict Augustin Morel was a French physician born in Vienna, Austria. He was a heavily influential figure in the field of psychiatry, as well as in popular culture, during the mid-19 century, but his influence grew as a proximate result of the changes in power due to the 1848 revolutions. It can easily be argued that he was the first to postulate that species would evolve according to the selection of mates. The only difference between Morel and Darwin is that Morel's "degeneration" focused on the negative possibility that mate selection may cause progeny to systematically regress to a more primitive type, while Darwin's theory focused mostly on the forward movement of the process. Whether this process is regarded as positive or negative evolution, forwards or backward is immaterial to the fact that the process of genetic mutation by mate selection was postulated and documented by Morel. That said, Darwin directly addressed the possibility that evolution could have a "degenerative" and "atavistic" effect, as without recognizing this, his theory simply would not make logical sense. Clearly, if mate selection could not influence the process of evolution backward, then it certainly could not move it forward. Daniel Pick, author of "Faces of Degeneration" points to this aspect of Darwinism. Darwinism, as Pick puts it, was "explicitly progressivist":

> There is now a significant and rapidly growing body of work on the politics of Darwinism. Evolutionary theory, it has been made plain, must be understood historically; we can trace in Darwin's metaphors and narrative patterns, wider Victorian social concerns and fears. Darwinism was undoubtedly social, inextricably enmeshed in the language, politics, culture of a past. (Pg. 6, "Faces of Degeneration: A European Disorder, C.1848-1918", Cambridge Univ. Press, 1989)

Daniel Pick also explains that "progress was the religion of the nineteenth century, just as Catholicism was of the Middle Ages," and thus, we understand the desire for Darwin's generation to prefer the theory which explained how society and humanity moved forward. Although Morel's work was an equally valid exposition of the Theory of Evolution, the negative tone of Morel's work relegated it to the morbid fears of his generation, more likely to fill the pages of gothic novels such as Dracula and Frankenstein than to be adopted as the replacement for the Holy Bible, as T.H. Huxley vigorously lobbied Darwinism to become.

Morel was looking for the causes of mental illness in the process of human heredity. Morel, influenced by various pre-Darwinian theories of evolution, saw mental deficiency as a process of mental deterioration. Between 1843 to 1845, Morel traveled in the Netherlands, Switzerland, Germany, and Italy, in particular to study their lunatic asylums. Morel's theory of hereditary "degeneration" was in turn inspired by Johann Friedrich Blumenbach. Blumenbach's 1776 essay titled "The Degeneration of Races" divided humankind into five principal varieties: Caucasian, Mongolian, Ethiopian, American, and Malay. Although Blumenbach's "degeneration" theory postulated racial variances, Blumenbach himself adamantly and persistently argued against an interpretation of his theory as a criticism on the inherent abilities of non-Caucasian races. Blumenbach personally regarded the Caucasian as the "better and preferable" variety, and Ethiopian and Mongolian types as diverging from the original Caucasian Adam and Eve. Blumenbach's regarded the variations, in skin pigmentation for example, as the results of the exposure to the tropical sun, as in the case of African skin color, and the blisteringly cold wind as in the case of Eskimo skin pigmentation. Morel's "degeneration" differed from Blumenbach's in that Morel described the process as a consequence of heredity and the selection of mates, and not just environmental influences. In 1848 Morel was appointed the director of the lunatic asylum Asile d'Aliénés de Maréville at Nancy of Maréville. It is at Maréville asylum he studied the mentally retarded, searching their family histories and beginning to postulate that mental defects were a product of mating and heredity. It is at Maréville that Morel's theory of "degeneration" coalesced into a theory of evolutionary and biological deterioration.

More to the point, the years between 1846 and 1850 were critical, as it is while Morel worked in the asylums that Morel's writings on "cretinism" began to influence the scientific world around him. Daniel Pick points first to Morel's 1846 *Pathologie Mentale* and then to his work with the Archbishop of Chambery in the 1850s. Morel concluded that some "cretins," or drastically deformed and deficient patients, were suffering from a fixed and being beyond the reach of cure by either medical means or improvement in the environment. The Archbishop pointed to environmental factors, and the debate only pushed Morel further to the conclusion that the origin was biological and hereditary. The Archbishop vehemently argued against Morel's insistence that these "cretins" needed to be segregated in order to protect society, and rather pointed to the need to protect the patients from the environment. Morel saw "racial degeneration" as the consequence of the uncontrolled reproduction of "degenerates," which by this time, included mental deficiencies grouped in with the physical birth defects.

Daniel Pick also points to the years between 1848 and 1850 as critical in the shift towards eugenics, as the Revolution of 1848 created political opportunities for Morel. Morel's friend, Buchez, would become president of the National Assembly, and it is through this political relationship that Morel's appointment at Maréville was possible. Morel's reputation grew to one of the most respected Parisian medical authorities, and his progressive views were in vogue. More importantly, the pessimism of Morel's theory seemed to resonate with the views of French liberals whom at the time could not consider progress as inevitable, as the fruits of 1789 and 1830 proved otherwise:

> In the wake of 1848 there was an extraordinary flurry of historical interpretation and re-orientation. Certainly to many contemporaries the vicissitudes of revolution seemed to call into question the very terms of liberal progressivism. Pessimism began to colonize liberalism in increasingly powerful and sustained ways. "Pessimism", wrote Charles de Remusat in 1860, "has made great progress in recent times". Many Frenchmen, he added, who thirty or forty years earlier had been full of hope and enthusiasm for the principles of the Revolution had now come to the conclusion that modern democracy was no more than "turbulent decadence." (Pgs. 56-57, "Faces of Degeneration: A European Disorder, C.1848-1918", Cambridge Univ. Press, 1989)

Thus, the first full analysis of the adverse effect of modernity, or the slackening of natural selection on the genetic quality of the population, was made by Morel in the 1850s. Morel perceived that child mortality rates were declining in France, largely because of improvements in public health, but the inescapable thought in Morel's mind was that this implied that many children who previously would have died were now surviving. It is at this time in French history that the population of Paris practically doubled, and as a consequence the filth and squalor of the poor became a poignant issue to be contended with. As Daniel Pick argues:

The era of the July monarchy was the era of laissez-faire ideology and, in opposition, of the rise of socialism and social Catholicism as movements committed to the systematic intervention of the state for the improvement of social conditions. It is against this reality and this set of competing ideologies, it has been suggested, that Morel proselytized on behalf of a medical profession committed to the prevention of the social conditions of degeneration and aloof from political squabble. (Pg. 53, "Faces of Degeneration: A European Disorder, C.1848-1918", Cambridge Univ. Press, 1989)

Morel concluded that the increased survival rate and reproduction of the less fit must, in turn, result in deterioration in the overall quality of the population. He identified the characteristics for which this was taking place as *"physique"* (health), *"intellectuelle"* (intelligence) and *"morale"* (moral character). Morel's postulates were the same linear thinking of "progression" and "regression," albeit more pessimistic in their emphasis on "degeneration" as opposed to Darwin's "evolution." Morel's "degeneration" clearly defined the physical implications of genetic deterioration as an effect of the process of mate "selection" and survival in the given environment, precisely what Darwin laid claim to with his theory of sexual selection. Morel published *"Traité des dégénérescences physiques, intellectuelles et morales de l'espèce humaine et des causes qui produisent ces variétés maladives"* in 1857, in which he explains the nature, causes, and indications of human "degeneration." This was years before "Origin of the Species," which was published in 1859, depending on whether the credit is given upon the date of discovery or the date of publication.

Morel believed that the above characteristics were transmitted in families from parents to children, through both genetic and environmental processes. Arguably as a proximate result of the rapid urbanization and the ensuing squalor, Morel came to believe that there was a genetic class of criminals, prostitutes, and paupers, a segment of society that was later to become known as the underclass, and that these groups had higher fertility than the rest of the population; yet another concept central to eugenics. The "degenerative" possibilities of evolution were clearly on the mind of Francis Galton when he came up with the science of eugenics, and clearly influential upon Charles Darwin when he incorporated Galton's eugenics into his "Descent of Man" in 1871. However, once placed in timeline format, it is easy to see that all of the pieces which Charles Darwin ultimately coalesced between "Origin of the Species" and "Descent of Man" were already in place by the 1850s. Erasmus Darwin had provided Charles with a vision of nature transmuting by mate selection. Charles Lyell had provided Darwin with the concepts of Geographical Time and "missing links." Morel had described the scientific mechanism of the theory, only working the logic backward.

In the Americas, ideology would swing the pendulum backward in the wake of the humanitarian gains of the Revolutionary War. George Gliddon's 800-page "Types of Mankind" was published in 1854, and it provided fuel to the scientific fire under the pro-slavery and anti-miscegenation politics. Darwin's "Origin of the Species" helped discredit much of what was claimed by Gliddon. However, it also provided justification and substantial impetus for the fears of evolution operating in reverse because of amalgamation with those races considered by Darwinists to be closer to apes than to the white man. This concept of hereditary degeneration was at the core of all the anti-miscegenation laws, and the fears of the consequences of racial amalgamation before and after the American Civil War. To be precise, the term "degeneration" itself can be found in the Lincoln debates with Douglas, where marriage between blacks and whites was a topic of both candidate's speeches:

> These statistics show that slavery is the greatest source of amalgamation; and next to it, not the elevation, but the **degeneration** of the free blacks. Yet Judge Douglas dreads the slightest restraints on the spread of slavery, and the slightest human recognition of the negro, as **tending horribly to amalgamation.** (emphasis mine, Pg. 114, "Lincoln & Darwin: Shared Visions of Race, Science, and Religion", James Lander, SIU Press, 2010)

While it has been in vogue for historians to point to the influence of the churches in support of the "ownership" of slaves, it must be noted that the *miscegenation* component to the pro-slavery argument was inescapably an argument that was waged in the arena of science. The 1860 book "Cotton is King, and Pro-Slavery Arguments" reprinted Dr. Samuel A. Cartwright's 1857 "Natural History of the Prognathous Species of Mankind." Samuel A. Cartwright had been trained in medicine by the famous doctor and signer of the Declaration of Independence, Benjamin Rush. In "Natural History" Cartwright claims:

> ...not that the negro is a brute, or half man and half brute, but a genuine human being, anatomically constructed, about the head and face, more like the monkey tribes and the lower order of animals than any other species of man. (Pg. 707, "Cotton is King, and Pro-slavery Arguments: Comprising the Writings of Hammond, Harper, Christy, Stringfellow, Hodge, Bledsoe, and Cartwright, on this Important Subject", Elliot, E.N., Negro Universities Press, 1860)

It was upon this observation that Cartwright, the Confederate physician claimed that the different skin colors among the "coloreds" was itself a product of "degeneration":

> Blackness is a characteristic of the prognathous species of the genus home, but all the varieties of all the prognathous species are not equally black. Nor are the individuals of the same family or variety equally so. The lighter shades of color, when not derived from admixture with Mongolian or Caucasian blood, indicate **degeneration** in the prognathous species. The Hottentots, Bushmen and aborigines of Australia are inferior in mind and body to the typical African and Guinea and the Niger. (emphasis mine, Pgs. 708-709, "Cotton is King, and Pro-slavery Arguments: Comprising the Writings of Hammond, Harper, Christy, Stringfellow, Hodge, Bledsoe, and Cartwright, on this Important Subject", Elliot, E.N., Negro Universities Press, 1860)

While the religious component to the pro-slavery argument died with the Civil War, the scientific component behind the anti-miscegenation argument only gained force and legitimacy in the elite institution of both North and South as it rode the wave of Darwinism. In the 1880s the criminologist Cesare Lombroso believed he found evidence of degeneration by studying the corpses of criminals. The mixture of Galton's eugenics and Morel's "degeneration" came full circle to be applied to humanity's psyche by Max Nordau's 1892 book "Degeneration," which by itself was a significant influence on culture and science. "Degeneration" had far-reaching implications on through to the eugenic theories that motivated Hitler's racial policies. It was a frequent theme in Hitler's speeches and a recurring and prominent topic throughout "Mein Kampf":

> In North America the Teutonic element, which has kept its racial stock pure and did not mix it with any other racial stock, has come to dominate the American Continent and will remain master of it as long as that element does not fall a victim to the habit of **adulterating its blood**. In short, the **results of miscegenation** are always the following: (a) The level of the superior race becomes lowered; (b) **Physical and mental degeneration** sets in, thus leading slowly but steadily towards a progressive drying up of the vital sap. (Pg. 212, "Mein Kampf", Marco Roberto Translation – Accessed via googlebooks.com)

The catastrophic fears which eugenicists of the Third Reich communicated in the propaganda films like *"Erbkrank"* were literally the fear of having their Nordic stock "degenerate" due to intermarrying with Africans, gypsies, and Jews. The praise Adolf Hitler gives the United States in the above quote is for the eugenic laws written by the American elites documented in this book. "Degeneration" is the underlying concept stringing this 100-year arc of time between William Grayson's "race of masters" and Adolf Hitler's "master race." Yet, as this book demonstrates, Darwinism was the impetus behind this 100-year trajectory between Bénédict Augustin Morel's theory of "degeneration" and The Holocaust. For better or for worse, the more Thomas H. Huxley and his followers succeeded in supplanting religion with Darwinism, the more Darwinism gave impetus to the theories of "degeneration" and its proximate eugenics. The fears of amalgamation and miscegenation simply did not die with the other outdated concepts behind slavery as the Darwinists insured that the science of eugenics endured into the modern era.

As such, "degeneration" was the foundation for this *"Über Ethik"* that transformed over 100 years of history between 1848 and 1948. Yet, the driving ideological forces at play in that span of time persist to this day. War is incidental to ideology, and the arc of the times arguably points to further misery. We may just prove Aldous Huxley, Erich Fromm, and George Fitzhugh right. The enticement to "escape from freedom," to surrender our individual autonomy for some servile existence in the hubris of some elusive utopian scheme is the probable outcome that we have not shaken. We have an abundance of slaves looking for "masters," and plenty of sadists looking to glean pleasure from controlling the most intimate details of the lives of others. We have failed to heed to the lessons of history.

Much has been made of the fact that Abraham Lincoln and Charles Darwin were born on the same day. This fact would seem more like a coincidence if it were a singular occurrence. John Adams and Thomas Jefferson perished on July 4, 1826, exactly 50 years to the day of the signing of the Declaration of Independence they had drafted together with Benjamin Franklin. Thomas Jefferson looked back on his life's work and considered that the words he had enshrined in The Declaration of Independence were now being proven by science. He clearly did not anticipate the prominence of Charles Darwin and his cousin Francis Galton while reminiscing on the fiftieth anniversary of the Declaration of Independence:

> The general spread of the light of science has already laid open to every view that the palpable truth, that the mass of mankind has not been born with saddles on their backs, nor a favored few booted and spurred, ready to ride them legitimately, by the Grace of God. (loc.gov, "Thomas Jefferson to Roger Weightman", June 24, 1826)

Fifty years earlier, on June 11, 1776, Congress had appointed a "Committee of Five," consisting of John Adams, Benjamin Franklin, Thomas Jefferson, Robert R. Livingston, and Roger Sherman, to draft a declaration to claim independence from Britain. Adams and Franklin decided that Jefferson's writing style was most suited. Jefferson wrote the Declaration of Independence while in Philadelphia, and presented this early draft to Adams and Franklin:

> We hold these truths to be sacred & undeniable; that all men are created equal & independant, that **from that equal creation they derive rights inherent & inalienable**, among which are the preservation of life, & liberty, & the pursuit of happiness. (emphasis mine, loc.gov, Thomas Jefferson, "Jefferson's 'original Rough draught' of the Declaration of Independence", Declaring Independence: Drafting the Documents, June 1776,)

This author finds this first working draft of the Declaration supportive to the central concepts of this book. The use of the words "from that equal creation" hint towards the widely debated meaning of the final draft's "created equal." This original wording alludes to the act of creation, as opposed to the results of it. Jefferson meant to convey that we were all products of the same miracle of creation, which thus endows each and every one of us with equal rights. No legitimate Jefferson or Constitutional historians take that phrase to have been written to convey that all men 'are equal' in mind, body, or spirit. This was unimportant for the task at hand and irrelevant to Jefferson's ideology. Rather, it was equality of status before the law that Jefferson was concerned with. Jefferson was writing still as 'a Royal subject,' thus, the writing of the Declaration was an act of high treason. He was given the task of writing a declaration of emancipation from an individual considered to be his better by birthright, his monarch, his "master." Through his words, Jefferson placed all humanity on the same level, regardless of birthright. Jefferson's 1787 letter to David Hartley underscores this point: "I have no fear that the result of our experiment will be that men may be trusted to govern themselves without a master." President Abraham Lincoln's impetus sourced from his admiration for the words enshrined in the Declaration of Independence. History proved Lincoln's to be correct, and it is through Lincoln, not Darwin, as some historians may claim, which the dignity of the human survives as a moral compass:

> I have a dream that one day this nation will rise up and live out the true meaning of its creed: "we hold these truths to be self-evident, that all men are created equal". (Martin Luther King, Jr., "I Have a Dream", Speech delivered Aug. 28, 1963, Lincoln Memorial, Wash. D.C.)

The subsequent 100 years between the Revolutions of 1848 and the Nuremberg Trials would be the years where the concept of Liberty was most challenged and tested. Arguably so, the challenge still stands. There is a significant portion of mankind which still believes that most men need a master, a ruler, an overseer to preside over them:

> Sometimes it is said that man cannot be trusted with the government of himself. Can he, then, be trusted with the government of others? Or have we found angels in the form of kings to govern him? Let history answer this question. (Pgs. 148-152, Thomas Jefferson, First Inaugural Address, "The Papers of Thomas Jefferson: Feb. 17 to April 30, 1801", Princeton Univ. Press, Vol. 33, 2006)

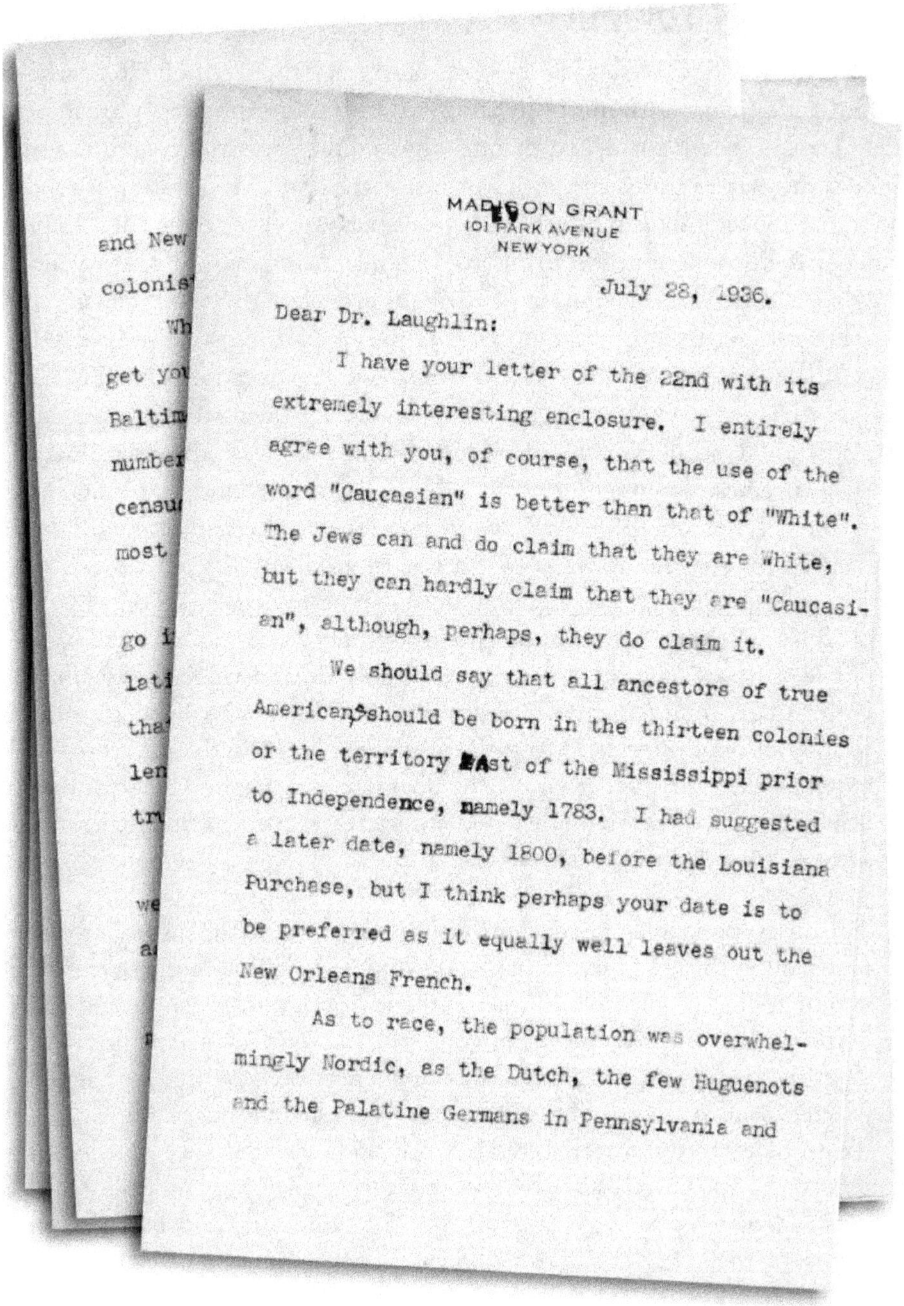

MADISON GRANT
101 PARK AVENUE
NEW YORK

July 28, 1936.

Dear Dr. Laughlin:

I have your letter of the 22nd with its extremely interesting enclosure. I entirely agree with you, of course, that the use of the word "Caucasian" is better than that of "White". The Jews can and do claim that they are White, but they can hardly claim that they are "Caucasian", although, perhaps, they do claim it.

We should say that all ancestors of true Americans should be born in the thirteen colonies or the territory East of the Mississippi prior to Independence, namely 1783. I had suggested a later date, namely 1800, before the Louisiana Purchase, but I think perhaps your date is to be preferred as it equally well leaves out the New Orleans French.

As to race, the population was overwhelmingly Nordic, as the Dutch, the few Huguenots and the Palatine Germans in Pennsylvania and

FIGURE 20: CORRESPONDENCE FROM MADISON GRANT TO HARRY H. LAUGHLIN DISCUSSING CHANGING THE USE OF THE TERM "WHITE" FOR "CAUCASIAN", AS "JEWS" WOULD NOT BE ABLE TO CLAIM TO BE "CAUCASIAN". THE COLLABORATION BETWEEN GRANT AND LAUGHLIN WAS INSTRUMENTAL TO THE PASSING OF THE JOHNSON-REED IMMIGRATION RESTRICTION ACT, WHICH KEPT JEWISH REFUGEES FROM REACHING US SHORES DURING THE HOLOCAUST. (HEREIN PUBLISHED AND PRINTED FOR THE FIRST TIME WITH PERMISSION OF THE SPECIAL COLLECTIONS DEPARTMENT AT TRUMAN UNIVERSITY. — BOX: D-5-4:10 — LAUGHLIN PAPERS)

Past is Prologue

This book was written upon the observation that the seeds of Holocaust denial take root and prosper with misinformation. Clarity and transparency are imperative, as they leave no room for denial theories that would deprive the victim's justice or rob the living of a future. Generations of historians have enthusiastically gone about their craft knowing full well that 'he who owns the past, owns the future.' Improperly documented history, or more precisely, fraudulent versions of history not only deprive the victims due recognition of their suffering but also rob the living of a fair chance at a future free from the dangers of repeating past injustices. The 2001 book, "The Unfit: A History of a Bad Idea," by Elof Axel Carlson was printed by the Cold Spring Harbor Press, likely in an act of repentance for the institution's eugenic past. The reader will recall that Cold Spring Harbor became the epicenter of the American eugenics movement under Charles B. Davenport and Harry H. Laughlin. Quoted here at length, Elof A. Carlson provides a powerful admonition to the historians of the eugenics movement and The Holocaust:

> <u>A great deal of the literature on the eugenics movement is based on a myth</u>. The myth is comforting because it pits the forces of evil and power (bigotry, racism, privileged classes) against the forces of innocence and vulnerability (the poor, the retarded, the insane, the downtrodden). Seen in this light, eugenics is a weapon of oppression used to maintain the wealthy and the influential and to minimize the harm done by those who do not contribute to society, who demand help from society, or who inflict guilt, crime, social burdens, and higher taxes on society's most successful benefactors.
>
> <u>The myth is wrong and dangerous</u>. It is wrong because the history of the unfit presented in this book has shown a much more complex development of ideas leading to the eugenics movement and the Holocaust. It is dangerous because it overlooks the numerous people of good will, many with outstanding credentials as social reformers, whose contributions became distorted or applied in mischievous ways. More difficult for us to understand is how caring people who did so much for humanity were able to include ideas that we now look on as inhumane. It is not easy for me to acknowledge that liberals, socialists, outstanding physicians, social workers, philanthropists, and brilliant scholars (some of them Jewish) were as much a contributing force to the eugenics movement and what led to its perversion in the Holocaust as were the mean-spirited, psychopathic, selfish, ignorant, and bigoted enthusiasts of the movement. (Pgs. 351-352, "The Unfit," emphasis mine)

Elof A. Carlson goes on to state that eugenics is a "movement of neither of the political left or the political right." He is completely correct that the history of eugenics is based on a myth. However, this myth and this misinformation runs deeper than Mr. Carlson depicts in his admonition, likely since his study in "The Unfit" limits itself to the scientific community outside of National Socialist Germany and largely before its time. The net was cast wider in the research that inspired this book.

We know precisely who were the men behind this international eugenics movement precisely because they were as meticulous in record-keeping as their German counterparts. Their political preferences are a matter of historical fact; thus, we can define in quite certain terms the political taint that was common to this international group of scientists, lawyers, and doctors. Casting broad culpability to all of Germany, all of Britain or all the United States is wrong morally, ethically, and historically because we know exactly who these men were.

Beyond that, Mr. Carlson may be incorrect that the intentions of allegedly "well-meaning" scientists, which would do away with a significant portion of the population for the sake of the environment or a utopian scheme, are not as callous as those that would carry out the deed of eradicating that portion of the population. This is, after all, one of those lingering questions about The Holocaust: where were all the men of sober mind and compassion? The answer, as it continues to this present day, is that these elite, the men of sober minds, the intellectuals, the political leaders, and namely the judges and justices of the highest courts, were precisely the ones to propose that a significant portion of humanity be eradicated for some allegedly worthy cause. As was the case with the turn-of-the-century eugenic fears of "racial degeneration," the most brutal schemes came cloaked in the legitimacy of science. The science then, as it is now, was portrayed as irrefutable and as sufficient justification for the most radical of socio-economic proposals.

We must also remember that this notion of the scientist acting in good faith was the defense strategy by Karl Brandt at the Nuremberg Doctors' Trial. Brandt tried to paint himself as the "good Nazi," as his friend Albert Speer had successfully done in his own trial. Neither Brandt nor Speer was lying when they claimed that they did not partake in the overt anti-Semitism and racial slurs as had Hitler, Rosenberg, and Goebbels. Yet, Speer and Brandt alike were instrumental in the murder, torture, and mutilation of millions upon millions of victims, and were arguably more directly involved in the actual act of murder than were Rosenberg, Goebbels, or even Hitler himself. This is the excuse modern scientists give for the likes of Alfred Ploetz and Wilhelm Schallmayer. Any claim that their allegedly pure eugenics should not be confused with the racially motivated eugenics of National Socialism serves only to insult the memory of their victims.

Karl Brandt's defense strategy is preserved in the extensive documentation printed by the US Government after the Nuremberg Trials. The US Government Printing Office published the full document set of the various trials held at Nuremberg. The volumes titled "The Medical Case," which refers to the Doctors' Trial is documented to contain 11,538 in mimeographed court proceedings by itself, and 901 exhibits. Paul Lombardo, the author that dissected the fraudulent nature of the US Supreme Court Case of Buck v. Bell in "Three Generations No Imbeciles" reiterates the defendant's strategy at the Doctors' Trial:

> Brandt's attorney introduced documents quoting extensively from eugenics literature. He cited Harry Laughlin's 1914 proposal calling for the sterilization of fifteen million Americans and also quoted a translation of the Buck opinion from a German text on eugenics. – Other Nuremberg defendants also cited Buck,

and a translation of the Holmes opinion appeared again as a defense example in the exhibit "Race Protection Laws of Other Countries. (Pg. 239, "Three Generations No Imbeciles: Eugenics, the Supreme Court, and Buck v. Bell", JHU Press, 2008)

More poignantly, Paul Lombardo hints at the likely reason why captured Germans, namely Ernst Rüdin, were let go:

Targeted as a potential defendant at Nuremberg by Leo Alexander, Rüdin was arrested in 1945. But he cited the widespread sterilization program in the United States and his collaboration with Americans as evidence that his involvement in the German domestic program was entirely legal. (Pg. 238, "Three Generations No Imbeciles: Eugenics, the Supreme Court, and Buck v. Bell", JHU Press, 2008)

There is a significant difference between Rüdin and Brandt; Rüdin was the architect and mastermind, and Brandt was carrying out the orders based on the laws and science delineated by the likes of Ernst Rüdin, Alfred Ploetz, Wilhelm Schallmayer, Karl Binding, Alfred Hoche, Fritz Lenz, and Erwin Baur. Brandt, like Mengele after him, would be hung for carrying out the plans of these masterminds, most of which were allowed to walk free and live their lives with their reputations intact. Some, as this book has documented, kept collaborating and closely working with the American institutions that assisted them prior to World War II. That Rüdin was allowed to walk while Brandt was hung is likely a showing of just how much Rüdin would be able to embarrass the Allied prosecution with his extensive knowledge of American and British eugenics.

Case in point, the terms "eugenics" or "racial hygiene" are mentioned only once in the official transcripts of the Nuremberg Doctors' Trial, and then only by a third party called to the stand. This book documents how entangled were American and British "eugenics" with the "racial hygiene" policies enacted by the Third Reich. Yet, nowhere does the Allied prosecution allow the mentioning of any of these extensive relationships. By the time the Nuremberg Trials came around, the United States Congress had investigated all American businessmen that conducted business with the enemy. Furthermore, the US State Department had, through their connections with various Latin American governments, dragged any people of German descent or connection into concentration camps in Texas. Nearly 5,000 innocent Latin Americans had their lives destroyed, and property confiscated, only to be imprisoned with what later turned out to be only 150 to 175 legitimate Nazi conspirators. Many of these were German Jews that had restarted their lives again in Latin America, which then found themselves imprisoned in Texas next to actual Nazis, and mostly on the basis of innuendo and conjecture. [574] As historians have aptly documented, the US Government showed very little leniency or caution when dealing with Japanese Americans when they corralled all of them, regardless of evidence or actual

---

[574] See Generally – "Nazis and Good Neighbors: The United States Campaign Against the Germans of Latin America in World War II", Max Paul Friedman, Cambridge Univ. Press, 2003.

complicity, into concentration camps of their own.

In other words, the American government was willing to act on the slightest of connections with Nazi Germany or Imperial Japan and ruin the lives of many thousands in a process based on nothing more than a rumor. Yet, the ample amount of connections between American scientists and Hitler's henchmen went completely undocumented and untouched. These scientific and legislative masterminds behind the Third Reich's murderous policies were on the most part allowed to go on with their lives, never having to answer for the outcome of the policies and ideas they provided Hitler. The definition of complicity provided by the Allied prosecution at Nuremberg is useful in determining who should have been brought forth. Count #1 is for the "Common Design or Conspiracy." The measure and definition of "common design" as stated by Telford Taylor in the indictment is:

> …acting in concert with each other and with others, unlawfully, willfully, and knowingly were principals in, accessories to, ordered, abetted, took a consenting part in, and were connected with plans and enterprises involving the commission of war crimes and crimes against humanity. (Pg. 10, "Trials of War Criminals Before the Nuremberg Military Tribunals Under Control Council Law No. 10", US Gov. Printing Office, Vol. I, Oct. 1946 – April 1949)

Furthermore, the final judgment given by the Nuremberg Doctors' Trial extrapolates who was considered to be part of "common design" and "conspiracy":

> …Any person **without regard to nationality** or the capacity in which he acted is deemed to have committed a crime as defined in this Article, if he (a) was a principal or (b) was an accessory to the commission of any such crime or ordered or abetted the same or (c) took a consenting part therein or (d) was connected with plans or enterprises involving its commission or (e) was a member of any organization or group connected with the commission of any such crime * * *. (emphasis mine, Pg. 173, "Trials of War Criminals Before the Nuremberg Military Tribunals Under Control Council Law No. 10", US Gov. Printing Office, Vol. II, Oct. 1946 – April 1949)

This definition of "common design and conspiracy" was broad enough to encompass those that drafted the laws and developed the scientific ideals that supported Hitler's racial laws. The definition is broad enough to include any non-Germans who may have aided and abetted, or as the definition provides "without regard to nationality" had been "connected with plans" which lead up to The Holocaust.

Even more disheartening is the fact that the Doctors' Trial made the murder of millions a secondary issue by focusing on the medical experiments, which by comparison had claimed only several hundred victims. Horrific as these experiments may have been, their nature only serves to underscore the relationship between the civilian and military scientists working in the extermination camps. More to the point, the charges of "Crimes against Humanity," which were unmistakably of a "eugenic" nature, were never defined as being conducted for "eugenic" reasons. Count #2 for "War Crimes" defines "Sterilization Experiments" as medical experiments deemed to be of a criminal nature. One would naturally expect that the "sterilization experiment" part of the indictment would make some reference to "eugenic" sterilization, namely, to clearly define the motive and intent behind the crime as any criminal trial seeks to accomplish. Yet, this critical portion of the indictment, which should strive to define the "crime" as thoroughly as possible, fails to mention any "eugenic" motives:

> From about March 1941 to about January 1945 sterilization experiments were conducted at the Auschwitz and Ravensbrueck concentration camps, and other places. The purpose of the experiments was to develop a method of sterilization which would be suitable for sterilizing millions of people with a minimum of time and effort. These experiments were conducted by means of X-ray, surgery, and various drugs. Thousands of victims were sterilized and thereby suffered great mental and physical anguish. The defendants Karl Brandt, Gebhardt, Rudolf Brandt, Mrogowsky, Poppendick, Brack, Pokorny, and Oberheuser are charged with special responsibility for and participation in these crimes. (Pg. 13, "Trials of War Criminals Before the Nuremberg Military Tribunals Under Control Council Law No. 10", US Gov. Printing Office, Vol. I, Oct. 1946 – April 1949)

Telford Taylor's opening statement itself makes immediate mention in the opening sentence that the "murders, tortures, and other atrocities" were "committed in the name of medical science," but fails to mention precisely what "science" this was. Taylor even makes an important distinction; the trial was very much so a "murder trial." As is the case with any murder trial, proving for and leaving no doubt as to motive and intent is paramount. This is the universally accepted and critical difference between "murder" and involuntary "manslaughter." "Manslaughter" is the unfortunate deprivation of life due to accident or negligence, but to prove "murder" you must prove intent. West's legal dictionary makes the following distinctions:

> The unlawful killing of a human being without any deliberation, which may be involuntary, in the commission of a lawful act without due caution and circumspection. ---- The essential distinction between the two offenses is that malice aforethought must be present for murder, whereas it must be absent for manslaughter. Manslaughter is not as serious a crime as murder. (West's Legal Dictionary)

Karl Brandt and his defense lawyer understood this basic and fundamental notion of trials for the crime of murder. Karl Brandt made sure to point this out in his final plea as read and presented by his defense counsel Dr. Seratius:

> I should like to point out that no indictment for negligence has been brought in, and that the concept of crime against humanity committed by negligence cannot exist. (Pg. 132, "Trials of War Criminals Before the Nuremberg Military Tribunals Under Control Council Law No. 10", US Gov. Printing Office, Vol. II, Oct. 1946 – April 1949)

Thus, to embark on the grandest and most significant murder trial of all history without clearly and thoroughly defining precisely the motive or intent, namely that medical or scientific justification, is to defraud the court of the vital information needed in order to act with the competence and legitimacy expected of any court of law. This was, after all, not just the explicit reason for holding the trial, but the self-imposed goal as documented by the prosecution:

> It is our deep obligation to all peoples of the world to show why and how these things happened. It is incumbent upon us to set forth with conspicuous clarity the ideas and motives which moved these defendants to treat their fellow men as less than beasts. The perverse thoughts and distorted concepts which brought about these savageries are not dead. They cannot be killed by force of arms. They must not become a spreading cancer in the breast of humanity. They must be cut out and exposed, for the reason so well stated by Mr. Justice Jackson in this courtroom a year ago. (Pg. 28, "Trials of War Criminals Before the Nuremberg Military Tribunals Under Control Council Law No. 10", US Gov. Printing Office, Vol. I, Oct. 1946 – April 1949)

Telford Taylor then proceeds to quote Justice Jackson's memorable pronouncement from the main Nuremberg Trial:

> The wrongs which we seek to condemn and punish have been so calculated, so malignant, and so devastating, that civilization cannot tolerate their being ignored because it cannot survive their being repeated. (Pg. 28, "Trials of War Criminals Before the Nuremberg Military Tribunals Under Control Council Law No. 10", US Gov. Printing Office, Vol. I, Oct. 1946 – April 1949)

Taylor makes it a point to mention that of the 28 defendants before him, all but 3 were not doctors, and more importantly, Taylor points out that their actions were the "inevitable result of the sinister doctrines which they espoused." [575] More poignantly, Telford Taylor makes it clear that "wherever those doctrines may emerge and prevail, the same terrible consequences will follow." [576] Yet, again, the Allied prosecution makes these sweeping and poignant observations without naming "those sinister doctrines" by its internationally accepted terminology, as the standard of "conspicuous clarity" would demand. This same glaring omission persists throughout the documents, even when describing "euthanasia" and "sterilization" in medical detail.

Even worse is that the indictment goes into the detail of documenting that body parts were being harvested for research and scientific use. The experts hired by the Allied prosecution, namely Leo Alexander, had full knowledge that these body parts were headed to the institutions whose stated purpose was the specialized science of "eugenics." In fact, the documents go into detail describing the harvesting of skeletons for "racial" reasons, again without ever mentioning the terms "eugenics" or "racial hygiene." The segment describing the "Jewish Skeleton Collection" states in part:

---

[575] Pg. 29 - "Trials of War Criminals Before the Nuremberg Military Tribunals Under Control Council Law No. 10", US Gov. Printing Office, Vol. I, Oct. 1946 – April 1949.
[576] Pg. 29 – Ibid.

Having arrived at the laboratory, the comparison tests and anatomical research on the skull, as well as determination of the race membership of pathological features of the skull form, the form and size of the brain, etc., can proceed. The basis of these studies will be the photos, measurements, and other data supplied on the head, and finally the tests of the skull itself. (Pg. 54, "Trials of War Criminals Before the Nuremberg Military Tribunals Under Control Council Law No. 10", US Gov. Printing Office, Vol. I, Oct. 1946 – April 1949)

The tribunal then revisited and slightly revised its description of how and why these body parts were harvested, again dancing around the description of the anthropometric measurements so famously known to be part of the science of eugenics, but never mentioning the science by name:
> One hundred twelve Jews were selected for the purpose of completing a skeleton collection for the Reich University of Strasbourg. Their photographs and anthropological measurements were taken. Then they were killed. Thereafter, comparison tests, anatomical research, studies regarding race, pathological features of the body, form and size of the brain, and other tests were made. The bodies were sent to Strasbourg and defleshed. (Pg. 179, "Trials of War Criminals Before the Nuremberg Military Tribunals Under Control Council Law No. 10", US Gov. Printing Office, Vol. II, Oct. 1946 – April 1949)

Furthermore, the defense invited an attack, or at least an investigation, into the complicity of the civilian doctors and scientists. Karl Brandt defended the right of the State to make such critical decisions that compromised the integrity and autonomy of the individual, and by extension brought the efforts of the civilian institutions into the fold:
> What prevents the state from ordering killing in the sphere of euthanasia too? The answer is that there is no motive which might justify an action of this kind. The economic motive of eliminating "useless eaters" is certainly not sufficient for such measures. Such a motive was never upheld by the defendant Karl Brandt; it was apparently mentioned by others as an accompanying contingency and later taken up by counter propaganda. The defendant Karl Brandt considered the motive of pity for the patient to be the decisive one. This motive is tacitly accepted for euthanasia on the deathbed, and doctors in all countries increasingly acknowledge it. (Pg. 135, "Trials of War Criminals Before the Nuremberg Military Tribunals Under Control Council Law No. 10", US Gov. Printing Office, Vol. II, Oct. 1946 – April 1949)

Brandt had defended himself by holding up the various eugenic books, scientific publications, and namely the legislation used within the United States to justify this very intrusion into the rights of the individual. It is of note that in justifying his own practices, Karl Brandt uses the very same logic that US Supreme Court Justice, Oliver Wendell Holmes, Jr., wrote into the opinion he delivered in the 1927 Buck v. Bell case:
> There may be people who realize that the community has the right to ask them

for a sacrifice. Their feeling of justice may tell them that insistence on humanity has its limits. If humanity means the appeal to the strong not to forget the weak in the abundance of might and wealth, the weak should also make their contribution when all be in need. (Pg. 128, "Trials of War Criminals Before the Nuremberg Military Tribunals Under Control Council Law No. 10", US Gov. Printing Office, Vol. II, Oct. 1946 – April 1949)

Even more revealing are the numbers of those identified as victims of the allegedly unlawful experimentation for the purposes of waging war. Telford Taylor counts them off in the Opening Statement of the Prosecution:
They were 200 Jews in good physical condition, 50 gypsies, 500 tubercular Poles, or 1,000 Russians. The victims of these crimes are numbered among the anonymous millions who met death at the hands of the Nazis and whose fate is a hideous blot on the page of modern history. (Pg. 27, "Trials of War Criminals Before the Nuremberg Military Tribunals Under Control Council Law No. 10", US Gov. Printing Office, Vol. I, Oct. 1946 – April 1949)

Taylor summarizes by saying "or 1,000 Russians," as they were not the addition to, but the approximate total amount of victims; a number that by any reasonable measure paled in importance considering the purpose of these unprecedented trials were for the murder of millions. Put more plainly, the Allies erected an unprecedented post-war legal structure specifically to document for all posterity crimes of an unprecedented nature. Yet, the entire Doctors' Trial was geared around the scientific experimentation, with the murder of millions falling into the distant background. To further complicate the issue, medical experimentation on humans was admittedly within the prerogative of the various nations to erect laws and safety measures. Experimentation was not murder, and as clarified, even accidental death resulting from human experimentation does not fall within the universal distinction of what murder entailed. However horrific these experiments of a military taint may have been, they paled in comparison to the millions upon millions murdered, tortured, or mutilated by these same doctors in the name of "racial hygiene" and "eugenics." Inflating the importance of the experimentation inevitably belittled, or worse, clouded the issue for posterity. More precisely, it made Holocaust history ripe for the many Holocaust denial conspiracy theories that followed.

As documented in the introductory chapters of this book, the Allied prosecution could not even claim innocence in the contentious issue of human medical experimentation. Both the United States and Britain had a significant record of morally and legally questionable experimentation on human subjects, and all the experts and leaders of the Allied prosecution knew it. Even worse, the Allied prosecution knew that the expert they hired to whitewash American medicine, Dr. Ivy, did so by committing fraud upon the court.

Furthermore, the opening statements, indictments, and final judgment of the main Nuremberg Trial, which brought leaders like Göring and Speer to account, practiced the same evasiveness and sleight-of-hand as the Doctors' Trial. Nowhere is the central role of "eugenics" or "racial hygiene" clarified. Instead, prosecutor Jackson and the Allied legal team used term "thanatology" for his opening statement of December 9, 1946, a term never used by the criminals to refer to the their "science," or much less to describe the nature of the "intent" behind the murders they so carefully planned:

> Crimes Committed in the Guise of Scientific Research - Mankind has not heretofore felt the need of a word to denominate the science of how most rapidly to kill prisoners and subjugated people in large numbers. This case and these defendants have created this gruesome question for the lexicographer. For the moment, we will christen this macabre science **"thanatology,"** the science of producing death. The thanatological knowledge, derived in part from these experiments, supplied the techniques for genocide, a policy of the Third Reich exemplified in the "euthanasia" program and in the widespread slaughter of Jews, gypsies, Poles and Russians. This policy of mass extermination could not have been so effectively carried out without the active participation of German medical scientists. (ushmm.org, "Trials of War Criminals Before the Nuremberg Military Tribunals Under Control Council Law No. 10", US Gov. Printing Office, Oct. 1946 – April 1949 – Citing Telford Taylor's Opening Statement in the Main Trial)

Paul Lombardo provides a clue in his book that may help explain such a curious omission of "eugenics" from the language of the Doctors' Trial, and its substitution by Justice Jackson with the term "thanatology." The US Supreme Court was given the chance to reverse the 1927 case of Buck v. Bell in 1942, just a few years prior to the Doctors' Trial in the Skinner v. Oklahoma case, but despite the immediate evidence coming from Hitler's Germany and the mounting dissenting voices in the scientific community, the Supreme Court upheld the Buck decision. Robert Jackson, the lead prosecutor for the Allies at Nuremberg was one of the nine Supreme Court Justices for the Skinner case:

> Jackson pointed to the Buck case as the more precise us of eugenic criteria, writing, "This Court has sustained such an experiment with respect to an imbecile, a person with definite and observable characteristics, where the condition had persisted through three generations and afforded grounds for the belief that it was transmissible and would continue to manifest itself in generations to come." By directly referencing the alleged facts in Buck, Jackson, like Douglas, endorsed that decision's eugenic logic. (Pg. 232, "Three Generations No Imbeciles: Eugenics, the Supreme Court, and Buck v. Bell", JHU Press, 2008)

No honest person that reads the eugenic literature that leads up to both the Skinner and Buck cases can deny the overwhelming commonalities and parallels between American eugenics and the Third Reich policies. In obscuring the direct connection, people like Justice Jackson set the table for the various Holocaust denial conspiracy theories. Matters are painted in an even darker light when one realizes that one of the judges working under Justice Jackson at Nuremberg would serve after the war as a director for the infamous Pioneer Fund, the foundation created by H.H. Laughlin and Wickliffe Draper. Judge John M. Woolsey, Jr.'s story follows the pattern of Ivy League educated conservationists. [577]

Recall the case of Dr. Olga Lang, the Chief Research Analyst at Nuremberg that requested Telford Taylor's help in getting her book on Nazi eugenics published. The outline for her book, "Master Race and Genocide" at the Telford Taylor Papers at Columbia University more accurately describe Nazi eugenics than all the work of the presentations and statements made by the American Prosecution at Nuremberg. She was trained in Russian Demographic Methodology and had traveled with her famous husband, Karl Wittfogel to China to conduct detailed studies of the region. [578] She had been a journalist and correspondent for the Soviet Trade Union Newspaper. In other words, she had the background to digest and fully understand all the evidence she helped prepare for Cases #1 and Case #8 of the Subsequent Trials. She had access to all the evidence available as she worked out of the 7771 Document Center in Berlin. Her outline depicts Nazi eugenics with more clarity than even the majority of Holocaust literature existing 75 years thereafter. Here were all the components discussed in the preceding pages: Nietzsche, Race Hygiene, Nordicism, euthanasia of "useless eaters," prohibition of mixed marriages, "Blood and Soil," stud farm methods, Himmler's breeding experiments, cultural extermination, and kidnapping of Nordic children all neatly presented and explained. None other than Dr. Rafael Lemkin, the man famous for coining the term and definition of "genocide" had recommended that her project be funded and completed. [579] The Institute of European Affairs at Colombia University had pledged their help. [580] More to the point, as Telford Taylor would tell the Rockefeller Foundation, her proposal perfectly fit the requirements for the charter of the Carnegie Endowment for International Peace. [581] Telford Taylor also presented the project to James T. Shotwell at the Carnegie Endowment for International Peace, only to "round out the case of Miss Olga Lang" with Shotwell before communicating their denial to Dr. Lang. They denied her supposedly because it did not fit the charter of the Carnegie Endowment for the Peace. Telford Taylor knew this not to be true as he pinpointed the applicable paragraph and page of the charter. [582] But alas, Shotwell was one of the founders of UNESCO along with Julian Huxley. The denial is certainly strange and raises more questions than it answers, but Olga Lang is not being written about here because of having her book project denied. She is being written about here because her scant pages make more sense and paint a much clearer picture of Nazi eugenics than the lawyers and judges she was assisting were able to provide for the Nuremberg Tribunal and all posterity for that matter. Is it possible that a legal assistant had a better understanding of the

---

[577] piooneerfund.org/Founders.html Founders and Former Directors.
[578] "Chinese Family and Society", Dr. Olga Lang, Yale Univ. Press, 1946.
[579] BOX 46 – Folder No. 5-3-2-11 – Telford Taylor Papers, Columbia Univ., Rare Book & Manuscript Library, Call No.: MS#1647, Letter from Olga Lang to Telford Taylor, March 15th, 1949.
[580] Ibid.
[581] Ibid.
[582] Ibid.

"crimes against humanity" than America's select team of lawyers and judges?

Can it be that Olga Lang understood the core concepts behind eugenics better than the lauded Supreme Court Justice Jackson? No honest person, who reads the vast amount of "racial hygiene" or "eugenic" literature written by or consumed by the German scientists and legislators can claim, as Jackson did, that "mankind has not heretofore felt the need of a word to denominate the science." Posterity must finally treat this characterization as a falsehood, if not an outright lie and fabrication. It is precisely by making the acts of these scientists otherworldly and nondescript that the opportunity for conjecture and denial is made ripe for the endless stream of Holocaust denial theories. These "crimes against humanity" were fully explainable in terms that made historical sense, and which explained why so many Germans signed up and collaborated with them. These ideas were in vogue for nearly a century prior to Adolf Hitler. These ideals were provided with a patina of legitimacy and intellectual worth by figures no less adulated than Nietzsche, Malthus, and Darwin. Thus, the leadership of the Third Reich could claim the high ground in requesting that the population participate in erecting the eugenic utopia that had been the dream of like-minded individuals for nearly a century prior. Hitler appealed to the vanity of the professional class in Germany. Hitler appealed to a German sense of intellectual and scientific superiority in asking his people to make these long-held utopian dreams a reality. This is how you convince the land of "poets and thinkers" to commit mass murder; you appeal to their intellectual vanity.

It is infuriating to realize that those punished at Nuremberg, including Karl Brandt, were nothing but foot soldiers in comparison to the scientific and legal masterminds behind the Third Reich's murderous policies. Joseph Mengele was conducting the research other scientists ordered, namely the scientist at the Rockefeller funded Kaiser-Wilhelm Institute. The "Jewish Skeleton Collection" the prosecution referred to was ordered by scientists that were never made to answer for their "collaboration" or "connection" as delineated by the "Common Design or Conspiracy" proclamation. As this book documents, one of the architects of the Third Reich's murderous policies, Ernst Rüdin, was captured and let go. Rüdin lived until 1952. His brother-in-law, Alfred Ploetz, died in 1940, but it is not until very recently that history has begun to correct the record on just how instrumental Ploetz was in setting the table, figuratively speaking, for The Holocaust. Eugen Fischer, one of the authors of the "Baur-Fischer-Lenz' book which was directly used by Adolf Hitler to define the eugenic policies delineated in "Mein Kampf" lived until 1967, never having to answer for his "connections" or "complicity." Erwin Baur died in 1933, but the other co-author Fritz Lenz lived until 1976, also never having to answer to posterity for the policies he instigated. Otmar Freiherr von Verschuer, the head of the Kaiser-Wilhelm Institute and man in charge of Joseph Mengele, lived until 1969 despite having documented ties to Himmler as the person authorizing the work that Mengele conducted for him, namely the human experiments that were supposedly at issue. In 1951, Verschuer was awarded the prestigious professorship of human genetics at the University of Münster, where he established one of the largest centers of genetics research in West Germany. Hans Harmsen lived until

1982 and enjoyed notoriety and fame as one of the founders of International Planned Parenthood.

More to the point, Eugen Fischer's connection has gone undocumented as his work on the babies of black and white parents he conducted with Charles B. Davenport lead directly back to Davenport's history as a Harvard educated, and Rockefeller and Carnegie funded scientist. Ernst Rüdin's work inescapably connects back to Margaret Sanger and more importantly, to the International Federation of Eugenic Organizations that directly implicates C.M. Goethe, Leon Whitney, Karl Pearson, and most significantly Leonard Darwin. Exposing the connection between Madison Grant and Harry H. Laughlin to J.F. Lehmann serves only to document their devotion to Darwinism. Following this trail of crumbs culminates on the realization that the prodigal sons of Harvard, Yale, Stanford, and other vaunted institutions were deeply committed to the cause of sterilizing the young boys and girls we now refer to as "The Greatest Generation." Exposing Ploetz serves only to reveal his devotion to the American icon, Edward Bellamy, and by extension, reveal just how thoroughly "socialist" and "collectivist" Hitler's Nazism really was. Understanding how integral the work of the Darwinist zealot, Haeckel was to the masterminds of the Third Reich's eugenic policies brings Darwin's inexplicable acceptance of Haeckel's fraudulent claims to the forefront. Karl Binding and Alfred Hoche both died prior to the end of World War II, but their extensive ties to Nietzsche and the extent to which Nietzsche influenced their euthanasia policies has gone sufficiently undocumented that Nietzsche's apologists can fraudulently claim that he had no influence on the outcome of The Holocaust. The political tangles and inconvenient connections overflow the limits of this single book.

Doris Kaufmann wrote in her 2000 book, *"Geschichte Der Kaiser-Wilhelm-Gesellschaft"* that the Allied prosecutors were well aware of just how extensive and deeply-entrenched in German science and medicine were the "eugenic" and "racial hygiene" policies of the Third Reich:

> [T]he authorities considered that further investigation of hospitals and universities was undesirable, ... [because] if undertaken on a large scale it might result in necessary removal from German medicine of large number of highly qualified men at a time when their services are most needed. (Pg. 642, *"Geschichte Der Kaiser-Wilhelm-Gesellschaft"*, Max Planck Society, 2000)

Yet, can it honestly be said that Germany would not have survived without a dozen or so fewer Nazis? Scientists like Rüdin, Verschuer, and Harmsen were hardly indispensable and were not providing a service that the immediate needs of post-war chaos demanded. They were not doctors, as were the type that was needed in the post-war chaos. They were researchers and writers, and more specifically, the carriers, those "merchants of light," and propagators of the "perverse thoughts and distorted concepts" which the Allied prosecution identified as being the proximate cause and instigator of the "savageries." Doris Kaufmann explains:

> Publicizing German medical atrocities could undermine wholesale public confidence in clinical science." To avoid the appearance that the entire medical

community could no longer be trusted, the Nuremberg Medical Trial political appointees." ... presented medical researchers as having been 'perverted' by the manipulative control of the SS and as poisoned by Nazism..." and instead [missing verb] that "the human experiments were so ill-conceived as not to be worthy of the status of science..." (Pg. 638, *"Geschichte Der Kaiser-Wilhelm-Gesellschaft"*, Max Planck Society, 2000)

There is an alternative way of interpreting the above statement. By exonerating medical researchers, the Nuremberg prosecution created the myth that the motives behind the murder were a mystery, and furthermore the myth that "medicine went mad"; a myth that has left a vacuum for a conspiracy theorist to fill. Some may even claim that revisiting this epoch is to engage in revisionist history. This would be disingenuous. One cannot call it a revisionist history when the very institutes where these historically important crimes originated openly admit culpability. One cannot call it revisionist history when the various international organizations which collaborated leave stacks of documents that properly characterize the movement's true history. Case in point, Doris Kaufmann was part of the team commissioned by the Max Planck Institute to investigate into its past, from before it changed its name from the Kaiser Wilhelm to Max Planck to disassociate the institute's previous collaboration with the Nazi regime. With the approval of the administrative council and the senate of the Max Planck Society the Presidential Commission was established by the society's president in 1997. The commission was headed by two historians, neither of which were members of the Max Planck Society: Prof. Dr. Reinhard Rürup of the Technical University of Berlin and Prof. Dr. Dr. h.c. Wolfgang Schieder of the University of Cologne. The commission announced its purpose with the following statement:

> The occasion of the Max Planck Society's 50th anniversary constituted the background for the foundation of an independent commission investigating the history of the Kaiser Wilhelm Society under National Socialism. The Kaiser Wilhelm Society's past as the predecessor organisation and especially its connections to the NS-Regime are regarded as an integral part of the Max Planck Society's past as well. The relation of the Kaiser Wilhelm Society to the NS-Regime, the scientific and political conduct of its representatives and scientists during the period of National Socialism, and finally the consequences of this conduct for the Max Planck Society are to be investigated and eventually published as completely as possible, without any constraints or institutional bias. For this reason independent historians were entrusted with the direction of the commission and the guidance of its work, while external historians of science were engaged for leading and implementing the research program itself. The five-year research program of the Presidential Commission "History of the Kaiser Wilhelm Society in the National Socialist Era" started with an international Conference in March 1999 reviewing current research and giving interpretive perspectives on the History of Science in National Socialism. (mpiwg-berlin.mpg.de, "Presidential Commission 'History of the Kaiser Wilhelm Society in the National Socialist Era'", Max Planck Society)

If Doris Kaufmann's research and interpretation of history are reliable, and there is no reason to doubt it, then this erroneous notion of science having been "perverted," this costly and fraudulent myth, was in large part the fabrication of the Allied prosecution at Nuremberg. The Allied prosecution's intentional omission of the integral nature of "eugenics" and "racial hygiene" is a tacit admission by omission. That the men in charge of post-war policy, namely Secretary of State Cordell Hull, Prime Minister Winston Churchill, and a formidable presence of Rockefeller men were the decisive political powers behind the Nuremberg Trials only makes this 'admission by omission' that much more suspect. This "perversion of science" story has been the excuse that has shielded American and British scientists and legislators from their own complicity.

For us, for posterity, it is the lie that has allowed the "science" behind the crimes to persist to this day in disparate legislative and scientific efforts. Cocksure contemporary scientists clamor to reduce the world's population by significant percentages, justifying their demands with claims that are at best, equally as questionable as the science of eugenics was entering the 20th Century. We embark the 21st Century with politicians and political lobbyists committed to submerging the individual under the State's prerogative in some ill-informed and misguided attempt to again "socialize" and "nationalize" medicine. The scientific technology and the means to "cleanse" humanity of undesirable hereditary traits have only grown more formidable as we submerge our rights as individuals under the prerogative of a self-proclaimed elite. A significant portion of the population has been convinced that they need to be saved from the consequences of their freedom. Propaganda has allowed these elites to convince formidable swaths of the electorate to grow disdainful of the legislative documents that were put in place precisely to protect us from the zealotry of a handful of misguided or powerful few. We embark on the 21st Century with ethics all the more stunted and our legal protections more compromised and debilitated. We embark upon this precarious path, fully convinced that the past has receded into history, and confident that The Holocaust won't repeat itself as it was the fault of a single madman, long since dead and vanquished.

"The future is the present projected.
Our notions of the future have something of that
significance which Freud attributes to our dreams. And
not our notions of the future only:
our notions of the past as well.
For if prophecy is an expression of our
contemporary fears and wishes,
so too, to a very great extent, is history."

~ Aldous Huxley ~

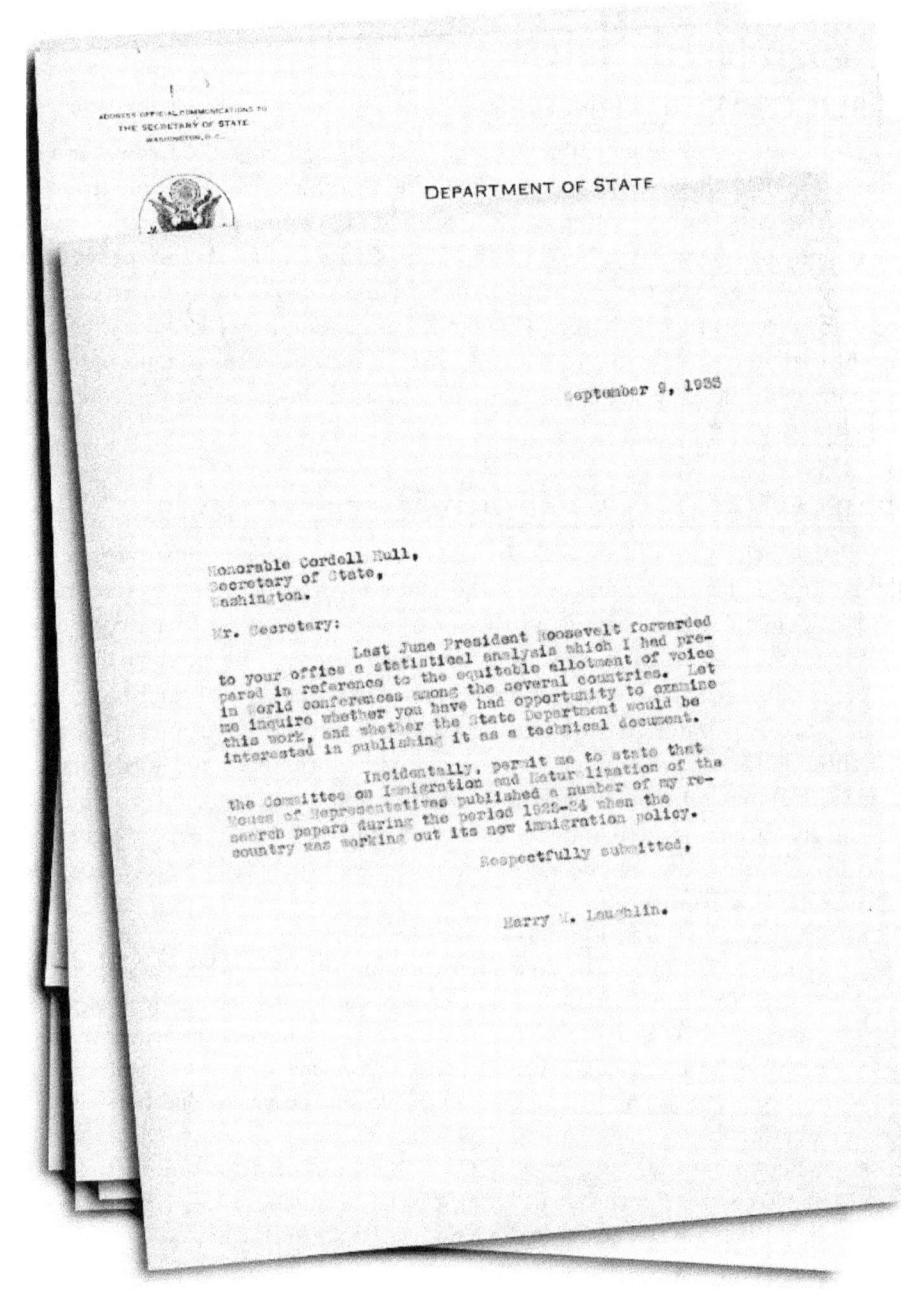

FIGURE 21: CORRESPONDENCE BETWEEN HARRY H. LAUGHLIN AND SECRETARY OF STATE, CORDELL HULL DISCUSSING LAUGHLIN'S PLAN FOR A ONE-WORLD GOVERNMENT. (HEREIN PUBLISHED AND PRINTED FOR THE FIRST TIME WITH THE PERMISSION OF THE SPECIAL COLLECTIONS DEPARTMENT AT TRUMAN UNIVERSITY. — BOX: D-2-1:1 — LAUGHLIN PAPERS)

Bibliography & Notes:

BIBLIOGRAPHICAL NOTES:

What was once scarcely accessible to the general public through the archives and journals, are becoming available to everyone online. The clear majority of people that will come across this book will do so through search engines as opposed to libraries, journals, or even a physical copy of the book itself. More often than not, the researcher of the 21st Century will see only the page that results from a Google Books query, and not have ready or even manageable access to the index or citation pages at the end of a physical copy of the book. It is for this reason that I have documented sources in-line or in footnotes, so they appear on the same page. The democratization of core knowledge weighs heavy in the scales.

PRIMARY SOURCES – ARCHIVAL COLLECTIONS:

There has been a lot of conjecture written about the eugenics movement, its political affiliations, and its intentions despite the hard evidence left behind by the masterminds and kingpins of the movement in the form of personal and official correspondence. That is where speculation ends, and the truth begins. The personal papers of the American eugenics movement can be found in these archives. Researchers will find that even if one perpetrator destroyed their correspondence, there are copies in the collections of those either in the sending or receiving end of the back-and-forth that spanned educational institutions, professional organizations, nations, and continents. Even seemingly inconsequential musings, scribbles, and newspaper clippings help paint a picture of the mindset of the eugenicist against which all other speculation about the movement must be weighed.

- Truman State University, MO – Pickler Memorial Library – Manuscript Collections – Special Collections – Harry Hamilton Laughlin. – Aside from being Davenport's protégé, Laughlin functioned as the clearinghouse for the international eugenics movement. His papers are seldom, if ever, visited goldmine of correspondence between the American, German, British, and Scandinavian eugenic leadership.
- American Philosophical Society, PA – Genetics and Eugenics Collection. – This archive holds the American Eugenics Society records and correspondence.
- California Institute of Technology, CA – Archives – Register of the E. S. Gosney Papers and Records of The Human Betterment Foundation, 1880-1945. – E.S. Gosney's foundation was second only to Cold Spring Harbor and the Kaiser-Wilhelm Institute in importance as a hub of eugenic research.
- Image Archive on the American Eugenics Movement, DNA Learning Center, Cold Spring Harbor Laboratory, Cold Spring Harbor, NY. – Sourced through: dnalc.org – eugenicsarchive.org
- Cold Spring Harbor Laboratory Library, Cold Spring Harbor, NY. – The archival section holds Charles B. Davenport's book and journal collection. The contents of this collection are telling by itself.
- Carnegie Institution of Washington, D.C. – Eugenics Records Office Files – Archived Records. – I was told by the archivist that I was one of very few, if not the only one, to ever request these files. However, Prof. Garland Allen, later informed me that he did scour through this collection. This collection is key in understanding the various projects entrusted to Cold Spring Harbor by the famous institution, as well as how the famous heads of the institution, namely Vannevar Bush interacted with figures

- such as Laughlin and Davenport.
  - Columbia University, NY – Rare Book & Manuscripts, Butler Library - Telford Taylor Papers. – Taylor was a pivotal figure for the American prosecution during the Nuremberg Trials. His papers are indispensable.
  - United States National Archives, Washington D.C. – The Military & Military Engagements / WWII (1941-1945) / Records About the Holocaust and War Crimes.
  - University of Iowa – Libraries, Special Collections & Publications - Charles F. Wennerstrum Papers. – Justice Wennerstrum was one of the judges to preside over the Nuremberg Trials. His perspective is of interest as he felt strongly that the format and rules of the Trials betrayed American jurisprudence.
  - United States Library of Congress, Washington D.C. – Manuscript Division – Robert H. Jackson Papers. – Justice Jackson served as Chief Prosecutor for the American legal team at Nuremberg.
  - The Margaret Sanger Papers Project, nyu.edu,
  - Chicago Tribune Archives, chicagotribune.newspapers.com - The Chicago Tribune seemed to cover the inner workings of Hitler's Germany with clarity and thoroughness that is present in no other media of the era.
  - New York Times Article Archive, archive.nytimes.com.

PERSONAL CONVERSATIONS AS PRIMARY SOURCES:

A single conversation can forever change your perspective. There are several scholars and friends who provided encouragement and a vital perspective necessary to mature this book into its final form. Two of these individuals are worth special mention:

- Ken Gemes of Birkbeck University of London is a recognized expert on Nietzsche. Nietzsche cannot be avoided if one wants to write a thorough history of eugenics leading up to The Holocaust. Professor Gemes was generous enough to sit down with me on several occasions and converse about Nietzsche.
- Garland Allen of Washington University of St. Louis is one of the first academics to take on the American eugenics movement. His papers remain the most formidable sources of information on the subject. He is now retired but was kind enough to provide me with much valued guidance.
- Professor Jonathan Marks from the University of North Carolina was kind enough to answer my questions on the "ape-human" issue of evolutionary biology.
- Paul Lombardo is a Regents' Professor and Bobby Lee Cook Professor of Law in the Center for Law Health and Society at Georgia State University. He has continually provided clarity on the issue of eugenics cases before the U.S Supreme Court, namely Buck v. Bell.
- Stefan Kühl is a Professor of Sociology at the Faculty of Sociology of the University of Bielefeld. He has on many occasions been kind enough to answer questions and provided direction.

LEGAL AUTHORITIES:

"American Constitutional Law: Essays, Cases, and Comparative Notes", Rowman & Littlefield Publishers, Vol. 2, 2010.

Buck v. Bell, 274 US 200, 47 S. Ct. 584, 71 L. Ed. 1000 - Supreme Court, 1927

Buck v. Bell, 143 Va. 310, 130 SE 516 - Va: Supreme Court, 1925

Chisholm v. Georgia, 2 US 419, 1 L. Ed. 440, 1 S. Ct. 16 - Supreme Court, 1793

Cumming v. Richmond County Bd. of Ed., 175 US 528, 20 S. Ct. 197, 44 L. Ed. 262 - Supreme Court, 1899

Dred Scott v. Sandford, 60 US 393, 15 L. Ed. 691, 15 L. Ed. 2d 691 - Supreme Court, 1857

Everett v. Truman, 1948, 334 U.S. 824, 68 S.Ct. 1081.

"Federalist 39", James Madison, The Conformity of the Plan to Republican Principles, Jan. 16, 1788.
Gong Lum v. Rice, 275 US 78, 48 S. Ct. 91, 72 L. Ed. 172 - Supreme Court, 1927
In the Matter of the Sterilization of Gloria Cavitt, 157 N.W.2d 171 (1968). 182 Neb. 712.
Jacobson v. Massachusetts, 197 US 11, 25 S. Ct. 358, 49 L. Ed. 643 - Supreme Court, 1905
Loving v. Virginia, 388 US 1, 87 S. Ct. 1817, 18 L. Ed. 2d 1010 - Supreme Court, 1967
McLaughlin v. Florida, 379 US 184, 85 S. Ct. 283, 13 L. Ed. 2d 222 - Supreme Court, 1964
Ozawa v. United States, 260 US 178, 43 S. Ct. 65, 67 L. Ed. 199 - Supreme Court, 1922
Pace v. Alabama, 106 US 583, 1 S. Ct. 637, 27 L. Ed. 207 - Supreme Court, 1883
Pace & Cox v. State, 69 Ala 231, 233 - 1882
Plessy v. Ferguson, 163 US 537, 16 S. Ct. 1138, 41 L. Ed. 256 - Supreme Court, 1896
Poe v. Lynchburg Training School and Hospital, 518 F. Supp. 789 - Dist. Court, WD Virginia, 1981
Roe v. Wade, 410 US 113, 93 S. Ct. 705, 35 L. Ed. 2d 147 - Supreme Court, 1973
Schechter Poultry Corp. v. United States, 295 U.S. 495 (1935)
Skinner v. Oklahoma ex rel. Williamson, 316 US 535, 62 S. Ct. 1110, 86 L. Ed. 1655 - Supreme Court, 1942
United States v. Thind, 261 US 204, 43 S. Ct. 338, 67 L. Ed. 616 - Supreme Court, 1923

GENERAL BIBLIOGRAPHY:

Adams, Mark B. - "The Wellborn Science: Eugenics in Germany, France, Brazil, and Russia", Oxford, 1990.
Allan, Garland E. – "The Misuse of Biological Hierarchies: The American Eugenics Movement, 1900-1940", History and Philosophy of the Life Sciences, Vol. 5, No. 2 (1983), pp. 105-128.
 - "Flaws in Eugenics Research: Social Origins of Eugenics", eugenicsarchive.org, March 2, 2004.
 - "Hugo De Vries and the Reception of the 'Mutation Theory'", Journal of the History of Biology, Vol. 2, No. 1, Explanation in Biology, Spring, 1969, Pgs. 55-87.
 — "Rewriting Mental Testing History: The View from the American Psychologist", Sage Race Relations Abstracts 11 #2 (May 1986), with Steven A. Gelb, Andrew Futterman, and Barry A. Mehler, Sourced From: ferris.edu
Alliance for Human Research Protection - "1933: American donates $1,000,000 to Kaiser-Wilhelm; 400,000 Germans to be sterilized", Sourced From: ahrp.org.
American Eugenics Society – "Eugenical News", Volume No. 7, No. 11, Nov. 1922.
 – "Organized Eugenics", Jan. 1931.
American Neurological Association – "Eugenic Sterilization: A Reorientation of the Problem", American Neurological Association, Committee for the Investigation of Eugenical Sterilization", Macmillan, 1936.
Anthony, Susan B. - "The Trailblazing Documentation on Women's Enfranchisement in USA, Great Britain & Other Parts of the World", History of Women's Suffrage Trilogy, Ida H. Harper, Google ebook.
Armstrong, John A. – "Ideology, Politics, and Government in the Soviet Union", Praeger, 1978.
avalon.law.yale.edu – "Nazi Conspiracy and Aggression: Vol. IV, Doc., No. 1708-PS", Yale Law School, The Avalon Project.

~ B ~

Back, Les and Solomos, John – "Theories of Race and Racism: A Reader", Routledge, 2001.
Baker, Robert and McCullough, Laurence – "Medical Ethics' Appropriation of Moral Philosophy: The Case of the Sympathetic and the Unsympathetic Physician", Kennedy Institute of Ethics Journal, March 2007.
Baldwin, Roger - "A New Slavery: Forced Labor: The Communist Betrayal of Human Rights," 1953.
Barker, Michael - "The Life and Controversies of Henry Fairfield Osborn: Part I of II", swans.com, Feb. 13, 2010.
Baron, Lawrence – "The Holocaust and American Public Memory, 1945-1960", Holocaust and Genocide Studies, Vol. 17, Issue 1, Jan. 1, 2003.
Barrett, Paul H - "Metaphysics, Materialism, and the Evolution of Mind: Early Writings of Charles Darwin," Edited by Univ. of Chicago Press, 1974.
Baur, Erwin and Fischer, Eugen and Lenz, Fritz - "Human Heredity," English version: Eden & Ceder Paul, 1931.
Baumslag, Naomi – "Murderous Medicine: Nazi Doctors, Human Experimentation, and Typhus", Praeger, 2005.
Beauchamp, Gorman - "The Legend of the Grand Inquisitor: The Utopian as Sadist" Humanitas, Vol. XX, Nos. 1 and 2, 2007.
Beckner, Chrisanne - "Darkness on the Edge of Campus: University's Philanthropic 'Godfather' Was Mad About Eugenics", Sacramento News and Review, Feb. 19, 2004– Now posted at newsreview.com

Beinart, William and Dubow, Saul - "Segregation and Apartheid in Twentieth Century South Africa", Psychology Press, 1995.
Bellamy, Edward - "Equality", Cosimo, Inc. Printing, 2008.
— "Looking Backward: 2000-1887", Houghton Mifflin, 1929.
— "Looking Backward: 2000-1887 – With Extra Chapter", William Reeves, 1895.
Bellamy, Marion - "Edward Bellamy Today: A Lecture", Peerage Press, 1936.
Benedict, Burton and Lowie, Robert H. – "The Anthropology of World's Fairs: San Francisco's Panama Pacific International Exposition of 1915", Museum of Anthropology, Scholar Press, 1983.
Benedict, Susan and Shields, Linda – "Nurses and Midwives in Nazi Germany: The 'Euthanasia Programs'", Routledge, 2014.
Berger, Karina - "Children of the Lebensborn: The Search for Identity in Selected Literary Texts of the Berlin Republic", Focus on German Studies, Issue #15.
Bergman, Ph.D., Jerry - "Human-Ape Hybridization: A Failed Attempt to Prove Darwinism", Acts and Facts, Vol. 38, 2009.
Bernard, Larry - "Historian Examines US Ethics in Nuremberg Medical Trial Tactics", Cornell Chronicle, Sept. 17, 2006.
Bernasconi, Robert and Cook, Sybol - "Race and Racism in Continental Philosophy", Indiana University Press, 2003.
Birt, Robert E. – "The Liberatory Thought of Martin Luther King, Jr.: Critical Essays on the Philosopher King", Lexington Books, 2012.
Bishop, B.E. – "Mendel's Opposition to Evolution and to Darwin", The Journal of Heredity, 1996:87(3)
Binding, Karl and Hoche, Alfred – "The Release of the Destruction of Life Devoid of Value, Its Measure and Its Form", Felix Meiner in Leipzig, 1920, Translation by Robert I. Sassone, 1975.
Black, Edwin - "The Story of the New Jersey Doctor Who Helped Kill Prisoners at Buchenwald in the Name of Eugenics", waragainsttheweak.com, Nov. 10, 2003.
— "The Horrifying American Roots of Nazi Eugenics", Sept. 2003, Sourced From: researchgate.net
Blainey, Tom – "The Chief Sea Lion's Inheritance", Troubadour Publishing, Ltd., 2011.
Blavatsky, Helene Petrova – "Key to Theosophy", Theosophical Publishing House, 1889.
— "The Secret Doctrine, the Synthesis of Science, religion and Philosophy: Anthropogenesis", Theosophical Publishing House, Vol. II, 1921.
Blom, Philipp – "The Vertigo Years: Europe, 1900-1914", Basic Books, 2000.
Bollmann, Jacqueline - "The Influence of Eugenics on the Social Welfare Legislation of Britain and Denmark in 1913 and 1929", 2009.
Brabazon, James – "Albert Schweitzer: Essential Writings", Orbis Books, 2005.
Bradshaw, David - "BOOKS / Planning for a Brave New World", January 23, 1994, Sourced From: independent.co.uk
Brener, Milton E. – "Richard Wagner and the Jews", McFarland, 2011.
Brignell, Victoria - "The Eugenics Movement Britain Wants to Forget," 2010, Sourced From: newstatesman.com
Broberg, Gunnar and Roll-Hansen, Nils– "Eugenics and the Welfare State: Norway, Sweden, Denmark, and Finland", Michigan St. Univ. Press, 1996.
Brownfeld, Peter Egill – "The Italian Holocaust: The Story of an Assimilated Jewish Community", American Council for Judaism, Fall 2003, Sourced From: acjna.org
Browning, Christopher R. and Matthäus, Jürgen - "The Origins of The Final Solution: The Evolution of Nazi Jewish Policy, September 1939-March 1942", Random House, 2004.
Brownlow, Kevin - "Hollywood", Thames Television documentary. – Book version: "Hollywood: The Pioneers", Knopf, 1979.
Buckley, Cara - "Fleeing Hitler and Meeting a Reluctant Miss Liberty", New York Times, July 8, 2007.
Buckley, Stephen - "Human Weeds", St. Petersburg Times, Nov. 11, 2001.
Burleigh, Michael - "Death and Deliverance: 'Euthanasia' in Germany, C.1900 to 1945", CUP Archive, Oct. 27, 1994.
Burns, Ken and Ward, Geoffrey - "Jazz", PBS documentary, Jan. 2001.

~ C ~

Cahier, Michael – "The Artistic Ambitions of Prometheus: with the tastes of an autodidactic petit-bourgeois", defunct personal website of Cahier.
Caldwell, Emily - "Study: Darwin Was Right to Worry that Marriage to His Cousin Affected His Offspring", phys.org Research News, May 3, 2010.
Calney, Mark - "D. W. Griffith and 'The Birth of a Monster' How the Confederacy Revived the KKK and Created Hollywood", The American Almanac, January 11, 1993.
Cantor, G.N. – "Jewish Tradition and the Challenge of Darwinism", Univ. of Chicago Press, 2006.
Caplan, Arthur L. - "When Medicine Went Mad: Bioethics and the Holocaust", Humana Press, 1992

Carlson, Elof Axel - "Herman J. Muller: A Biographical Memoir", nasonline.org, 2009.
Carlson, Elof Axel - "The Unfit: A History of a Bad Idea", Cold Spring Harbor Laboratory Press, 2001.
– "Biographical Memoir Hermann Joseph Muller. 1890-1967", Biographical Memoirs, National Academies Press, Vol. 91, Nov. 2009.
Carrington, Richard - "A Million Years of Man: The Story of Human Development as a Part of Nature", New American Library, 1963.
Charny, Israel W. – "Fascism and Democracy in the Human Mind: A Bridge Between Mind and Society", Univ. of Nebraska Press, 2006 - translated from a written statement of 1934.
Chase, Allan - "Legacy of Malthus: The Social Costs of the New Scientific Racism", 1975.
Chernin, Eli - "Harvard System", BMJ, Vol. 97, Oct. 22, 1988.
Chicago Tribune – "US Eugenics Paralleled Nazi Germany", Feb. 15th, 2000.
Childs, Donald J. – "Modernism and Eugenics: Woolf, Eliot, Yeats, and the Culture of Degeneration", Cambridge Univ. Press, 2001.
Christianson, Scott - "The Last Gasp: The Rise and Fall of the American Gas Chamber", Univ. of Cal. Press, 2010.
Clark, Henry B. – "The Ethical Mysticism of Albert Schweitzer", Beacon Press, 1962.
Clarkson, Thomas – "An Essay on the Slavery and Commerce of the Human Species, Particularly the African", J. Phillips & George-Yard, 1785.
Cock, Alan G. and Forsdyke, Donald R. - "Treasure Your Exceptions: The Science and Life of William Bateson", Springer Science & Business Media, 2008.
Cogdell, Christina – "The Futurama Recontextualized: Norman Bel Geddes's Eugenic 'World of Tomorrow'", American Quarterly, Vol. 52, No. 2, June 2000.
– "Eugenic Design: Streamlining America in the 1930s", Univ. of Pennsylvania Press, 2010.
Cook, David Paul - "Darwinism, War, and History: The Debate over the Biology of War from the 'Origin of species' to the First World War", Cambridge Univ. Press, 1994.
Council of Foreign Relations – Review of Henry Krieger's *"Das Rassenrecht in Den Veringten Staaten"*, Foreign Affairs, July 1937.
Crais, Clifton C. and Scully, Pamela - "Sara Baartman and the Hottentot Venus: A Ghost Story and a Biography", Princeton Univ. Press, 2010.
Crabbe, P. – "Implementing Ecological Integrity: Restoring Regional and Global Environmental and Human Health", Scientific Affairs Division of NATO", Conference Proceedings, June 2000.
Custer, George, Lt. Colonel – "My Life on the Plains: Personal Experiences with Indians", Sheldon, 1875.

~ D ~

Darrow, Clarence - "The Eugenics Cult", The American Mercury, V8, No. 30, June 1926.
– "The Darrow-Kennedy Debate", Garrick Theater, Maclaskey & Maclaskey Court Reporters, John F. Higgins Printers, March 23, 1919.
Darwin, Charles – "On the Origin of Species by Means of Natural Selection: Or, The Preservation of Favored Races in the Struggle of Life", Appleton, 1864.
- "The Descent of Man, and Selection in Relation to Sex", D. Appleton, 1872.
Darwin, Francis - "Galton Lecture", Eugenics Education Society, Eugenics Review, Feb. 16th, 1914.
Darwin, Leonard - "The Need for Eugenic Reform", D. Appleton & Co., 1926.
– "Striving for National Fitness: Eugenics in Australia, 1910s to the 1930s", Doctoral Thesis, 1996.
– "Modern Eugenics and Human Behavior", Metropolitan Publishing Co., 1900, Sourced From: archive.org.
– "Municipal Ownership: Four Lectures Delivered at Harvard University, 1907", E.P. Dutton, 1907.
– "Race Deterioration and Practical Politics", Eugenics Review, Oct. 17th, 1925.
Davenport, Charles B. – "Eugenics: The science of Human Improvement by Better Breeding", JAMA, April 23rd, 1910.
Davis, Devra – "The Secret History of the War on Cancer", Basic Books, 2009.
Dearborn Independent – "The International Jew", Dearborn Publishing Co., 1920-1922, From archive.org.
Desmond, Adrian and Moore, James – "Darwin", Penguin UK, 1991.
– "Darwin's Sacred Cause: How a Hatred of Slavery Shaped Darwin's Views on Human Evolution", Houghton Mifflin Harcourt, 2009.
Dewey, John – "The Later Works of John Dewey, 1925-1953: Essays, Reviews, Miscellany, and a Common Faith 1933-1934", SIU Press, 2008.
Diethe, Carol – "Historical Dictionary of Nietzscheanism", Scarecrow Press, 2007.
Dietrich, Donald J. – "Catholic Eugenics in Germany, 1920-1945: Hermann Muckermann, S.J. and Joseph Mayer", Journal of Church and State, Vol. 34, No. 3, Summer 1992, Pgs. 575-600.
Douglas, Donald M. - "The Evangelist's Apprenticeship: Hitler's Effectiveness as a Public Speaker, 1919-1921", Wichita State University Bulletin, Feb. 1974.
Dombowsky, Dom – "Nietzsche's Machiavellian Politics", Springer, 2004.

Dowbiggin, Ian - "A Merciful End: The Euthanasia Movement in Modern America", Oxford Univ. Press, 2003.
– "A Concise History of Euthanasia: Life, Death, God, and Medicine", Rowman & Littlefield, 2007.
Duff, Brian – "The Parent as Citizen: A Democratic Dilemma", Univ. of Minnesota Press, 2011.
Dyer, Thomas G. – "Theodore Roosevelt and the Idea of Race", Louisiana State Univ. Press, 1980.

~ E ~

Efron, John M. – "Defenders of the Race: Jewish Doctors and Race Science in Fin-de-siecle Europe", Yale Univ. Press, 1994.
Elliot, E.N. – "Cotton is King, and Pro-slavery Arguments: Comprising the Writings of Hammond, Harper, Christy, Stringfellow, Hodge, Bledsoe, and Cartwright, on this Important Subject", Negro Universities Press, 1860.
Ellis, Havelock - "Nationalisation of Health", T. Fisher Unwin, 1892.
- "Sex in Relation to Society: Studies in The Psychology of Sex", Volume 6, 1937, reprinted by Butterworth-Heinemann, 2013.
Emden, Christian - "Nietzsche On Language, Consciousness, And the Body", Univ. of Illinois Press, 2010.
Enciclopedia Italiana – "Doctrine of Fascism", 1932, Translation by Chip Berlet, Sourced From: politicalresearch.org
Engels, Friedrich – "Socialism: Utopian and Scientific", S. Sonnenschein, 1892.
English, Daylanne K. – "Unnatural Selections: Eugenics in American Modernism and the Harlem Renaissance", Univ. of North Carolina Press, 2004.
Engs, Ruth – "Clean Living Movements: American Cycles of Health Reform", Greenwood Publishing Company, 2001.
Etkind, Alexander - "Beyond Eugenics: the forgotten scandal of hybridizing humans and apes", Studies in History and Philosophy of Biological and Biomedical Sciences, Vol. 39, Issue 2, June 2008.
Evans, Richard J. - "The Coming of the Third Reich", Penguin, 2004.
- "The Third Reich in Power", Penguin, 2006.
Evans, Suzanne E. and Dee, Ivan R. – "Forgotten Crimes: The Holocaust and People with Disabilities", 2004.1 Pg. 27 – Ibid.

~ F ~

Fichte, Jonathan Gottlieb – "Addresses to the German Nation", Translated by R.F. Jones & G.H. Turnbull, Chicago Univ. Press, 1922.
Fijalkow, Yankel - "Hygiene, Population Sciences and Population Policy: a Totalitarian Menace?" Contemporary European History, Vol. 8, No. 3.
Finch, Charlie – "Deciphering Beckmann", Art Net, July 17th, 2003, Sourced From: artnet.com
Fitzhugh, George – "Cannibals All!: Or, Slaves Without Masters", A. Morris, 1857.
Flynn, John T. – "The Roosevelt Myth", Devin-Adair Company, 1944.
Forel, Auguste – "Out of My Life and Work", G. Allen & Unwin Limited, 1937.
Frankfurter Zeitung – "Hitler's Testimony Before the Court for High Treason from Frankfurter Zeitung", Sept. 26, 1931, Translated by the Office of U.S. Chief of Counsel, Nuremberg, Translated Nov. 1945, Doc. No.: 2152-PS. Sourced From: lawcollections.library.cornell.edu
Franklin, John H. and Moss, Jr., Alfred A. - "From Slavery to Freedom: A History of African Americans", Knopf, 1974.
Friedlander, Henry – "The Origins of Nazi Genocide: From Euthanasia to the Final Solution", Univ of North Carolina Press, Nov. 9, 2000.
Friedman, Max Paul – "Nazis and Good Neighbors", Cambridge Univ. Press, 2003.
Friedman, Milton and Friedman, Rose – "Free to Choose: A Personal Statement", Harcourt, 1980.
Fromm, Erich – "Escape from Freedom", Rinehart, Inc., 1941.

~ G ~

Gallagher, Dorothy - "Adolf and Eva", New York Times, Nov. 16, 2011.
Galton, Francis – "Hereditary Talent and Character", Macmillan's Magazine, Vol. 12, 1865.
– "Hereditary Genius: An Inquiry Into its Laws and Consequences", Macmillan & Co., 1869.
Gardiner, Anne Barbeau - "Darwinism & the Culture of Death," New Oxford Book Review, June 2006.
Gasman, Daniel - "Scientific Origins of National Socialism", Transaction Publishers, 2007.
Gatto, John Taylor - "An Underground History of American Education", Oxford Village Press, 2000. – Sourced through archive.org.
Geary, Dick – "Who Voted for the Nazis? Electoral History of the National Socialist German Workers Party", History Today, October 1998.
Gerdtz, Joan - "Disability and Euthanasia: The Case of Helen Keller and the Bollinger Baby", Life and Learning, No. XVI, Pgs. 491-500, 2006.
Ghallager, Maggie - "The Human Betterment League", National Review, December 12, 2011.
Gibson, Robert A. - "The Negro Holocaust: Lynching and Race Riots in the United States 1880-1950," Yale

course curriculum posted in the Yale website.
Gilbert, Steven - "Models-Based Science Teaching: Understanding and Using Mental Models", NSTA Press, 2011 - Quoting Herbert Spencer, "The Factors of Organic Evolution", April-May 1886.
Gilbert, James – "Redeeming Culture: American Religion in an Age of Science", Univ. of Chicago Press, 2008.
Gilbert, Martin – "The Righteous: The Unsung Heroes of the Holocaust", Henry Holt & Co., 2010.
Giles, Eugene - "Two faces of earnest A. Hooton", Volume 149, Issue S55 Supplement: Yearbook of Physical Anthropology, 2012.
Gillham, Nicholas Wright - "A Life of Sir Francis Galton", Oxford Univ. Press, 2001.
Gillis, Anna Maria – "From News Wire to Newsweekly: 75 Years of Science Service", Science News, March 1st, 1997.
Goodrich, Peter and Valverde, Mariana – "Nietzsche and Legal Theory: Half-Written Laws", Routledge, Aug 21, 2013.
Goebbels, Joseph – "Diary of Joseph Goebbels", Sourced From: holocaustresearchproject.org
Goethe, C.M. – "Sierra Cabin . . . From a Skyscraper: A Tale from the Sierran Piedmont", 1943.
– "Seeking to Serve", Keystone Press, 1949.
Gorer, Geoffrey - "The Revolutionary Ideas of the Marquis de Sade", Wishart & Company, 1934.
Gordon, Mel – "Voluptuous Panic: The Erotic World of Weimar Berlin", Expanded Edition, Feral House, 2008.
Gossman, Lionel - "Brownshirt Princess: A Study of the Nazi Conscience", Open Book Publishers, 2009.
Grant, Madison – "The Passing of the Great Race or the Racial Basis for European History", Charles Scribner's Sons, 1916.
Grayson, William J. – "The Hireling and the Slave", J. Russell, 1854.
Gregory, William K. – "Biographical Memoir of Henry Fairfield Osborn, 1857-1935", Vol. XIX, Third Memoir, National Academy of Sciences, 1937.
Greenwood, James – "The Seven Curses of London", Fields, Osgood & Company, 1869.
Grossmann, Atina - "Reforming Sex: The German Movement for Birth Control and Abortion Reform", Oxford Univ. Press, 1995.
Guarneri, Carl J. "An American Utopia and Its Global Audiences: Transnational Perspectives on Edward Bellamy's Looking Backward", Before the American Studies Association of Turkey, Ankara, November 1st, 2006, Utopian Studies, Vol. 19, No. 2, 2008, pp. 147-187.
Gunn, James E. – "The Road to Science Fiction: From Wells to Heinlein", Scarecrow Press, 2002.

~ H ~

Haeckel, Ernst – "The Wonders of Life", Watts & Co., 1904.
Hacohen, Malachi Haim - "Karl Popper: The Formative Years, 1902-1945," Cambridge Univ. Press, 2002.
Hamann, Brigitte – "Hitler's Vienna: A Dictator's Apprenticeship", Oxford Univ. Press, 1999 – Translated by Thomas Thorton.
Hammond, Scott J. and Hardwick, Kevin R. and Lubett, Howard L. – "Classics of American Political and Constitutional Thought: Reconstruction to the Present", Hackett, 2007.
Handlin, Oscar - "Hearings Before the Presidential Commission on Immigration and Naturalization – Appendix: Special Studies Memorandum by Oscar Handlin – I. Basic Assumptions of the National-Origins Quota", 82nd Congress, 2nd Session, 1952.
Hanfstaengl, Ernst – "Hitler: The Memoir of the Nazi Insider Who Turned Against the Fuhrer", Arcade Pub., 2011.
Hardy, G.H. – "A Mathematician's Apology", The University Press, 1940.
Harkness, Jon M. - "Nuremberg and Wartime Experiments on US Prisoners", Ph.D., JAMA, Nov. 27, 1996 – Written for the 50th anniversary of the Nuremberg Doctors' Trial.
Hastings, Derek – "How 'Catholic' Ws the Early Nazi Movement? Religion, Race, and Culture in Munich, 1919-1924", Central European History, Vol. 36, No. 3, Pgs. 383-433, 2003.
Harvard Crimson – "Jumping to Conclusions", May 28th, 1927, Sourced From: thecrimson.com
Hehe, Joshua - "The Life and Times of Adolf Hitler", Medium Mag., Dec. 18, 2017.
Heinsohn, Gunnar - "What Makes the Holocaust a Uniquely Unique Genocide?", Journal of Genocide Research, 2000, 2(3), 411–430.
Heinz, Heinz A. – "Hitler: Personal Recollections: Memoirs of Hitler From Those Who Knew Him", Pen and Sword, 2014.
Hesse, Hans – "Eyes from Auschwitz. A lesson in National Socialist racial delusion and medical research. The case of Dr. Karin Magnussen", plain text, Essen 2001.
Hitler, Adolf – "Mein Kampf", James Murphy translation, gutenberg.net.au
– "Mein Kampf", Marco Roberto Translation, Sourced From: googlebooks.com
Hirobe, Izumi - "Japanese Pride, American Prejudice: Modifying the Exclusion Clause of the 1924 Immigration Act," Stanford Univ. Press, 2001.
History News Network - "The Horrifying American Roots of Nazi Eugenics", George Mason Univ., Nov. 25,

2003.
Hoad, Neville Wallace – "African Intimacies: Race, Homosexuality, and Globalization", Univ. of Minnesota Press, 2007.
Hochman, Elaine S. - "Architects of Fortune: Mies Van Der Rohe and the Third Reich", Fromm International Pub. Corp., 1989.
Holbrook, M.L. – "Homo-culture: Or, The Improvement of Offspring Through Wiser Generation", M.L. Holbrook, 1897.
Holmes, Oliver Wendell "Natural Law", Harvard Law Review, Volume 32, 1918.
Holocaust Chronicle, The – "The Holocaust Chronicle", Publications International, Ltd., April 200.
Hollander, E.J. – "Italian Fascism and the Jews: Brown? Or Shades of Gray?", Dissertation draft for the Dept. of Political Science, U.C., San Diego.
Hopwood, Nick - "Pictures of Evolution and Charges of Fraud: Ernst Haeckel's Embryological Illustrations", The History of Science Society, 2006.
Horsman, Reginald – "Race and Manifest Destiny: The Origins of American Racial Anglo-Saxonism", Harvard Univ. Press, 1981.
Howard, John C. – "Why Didn't Darwin Discover Mendel's Laws?", Journal of Biology, Biomed Central, Feb. 24th, 2009.
Howard, John R. – "The Shifting Wind: The Supreme Court and Civil Rights from Reconstruction to Brown", SUNY Press, 1999.
Hunter, George William – "A Civic Biology: Presented in Problems", American Book Co., 1914.
Huxley, Aldous - "Ends and Means: An Inquiry into the Nature of Ideals", Routledge, Sep. 2017.
Huxley, Julian – "UNESCO Its Purpose & Philosophy: A Preparatory Commission of UNESCO", Cat. No. 6817, unesco.org.
– "UNESCO and its Programme: The Race Question", 1950, unesdoc.unesco.org.
– "The Eugenics Manifesto", published as "Social Biology and Population Improvement", Nature, No. 144, Sept. 16, 1939, Pgs. 521-522.
– "Eugenics and Society", The Galton Lecture given to the Eugenics Society, Eugenics Review, Vol. 28:1/13, Doc. ID 11751, dnalc.org.
Huxley, T.H. – "Evolution and Ethics and Other Essays", D. Appleton, 1894, Sourced From: archive.org
– "Emancipation: Black and White, In Man's Place in Nature, and Other Anthropological Essays", Macmillan, 1865.

~ I ~

Ibrahim, Sami Daoud - Book Review for: "Man the Unknown", Harper Brothers 1935 edition.
International Vegetarian Union - "History of Vegetarianism - Friedrich Wilhelm Nietzsche", ivu.org citing Cosima Wagner, Sept. 19th, 1869.

~ J ~

Jackson, David H. – "Booker T. Washington and the Struggle against White Supremacy: The Southern Educational Tours, 1908-1912", Springer, 2008.
Jackson, John P. and Weidman, Nadine M. – "Race, Racism, and Science: Social Impact and Interaction", Rutgers Univ. Press, 2005.
Jefferson, Thomas – "Jefferson's First Inaugural Address: The Papers of Thomas Jefferson: Feb. 17 to April 30, 1801", Princeton Univ. Press, Vol. 33, 2006.
– "Jefferson's 'original Rough draught' of the Declaration of Independence", Declaring Independence: Drafting the Documents, June 1776, Sourced From: loc.gov
– "Thomas Jefferson to Roger Weightman", June 24th, 1826, Sourced From: loc.gov
– "The Thomas Jefferson Papers Series 1. General Correspondence. 1651-1827.
jewishvirtuallibrary.org - "Göring Commission to Heydrich".
– Report to the Secretary on the Acquiescence of this Government in the Murder of the Jews", Henry Morgenthau Jr., and Randolph Paul, January 13th, 1944.
Jiménez-Alonso, Belén - "Eugenics, Sexual Pedagogy and Social Change: Constructing the Responsible Subject of Governmentality in the Spanish Second Republic", Elsevier, Vol. 39, Issue 2, June 2008.
Jodl, Friedrich – *"Geschichte der Ethik in der Neueren Philosophie"*, Harvard, 1895.
Johnson, Albert R. - "The Birth of Bioethics", Oxford University Press; 1st edition (1998), 2003.
Jordan, David Starr and Jordan, Harvey Ernest - "War's aftermath; a preliminary study of the eugenics of war as illustrated by the civil war of the United States and the late wars in the Balkans", Houghton Mifflin, 1914.
Journal of Church and State, - "Catholic Eugenics in Germany, 1920-1945: Hermann Muckermann, S.J. and Joseph Mayer," "Catholic Eugenics", Vol. 34, No. 3 (SUMMER 1992), pp. 575-600.

~ K ~

Kaufmann, Doris – *"Geschichte Dr Kaiser-Wilhelm-Gesellschaft im Nationalsozialismus. Bestandsaufnahme* und Perspektiven der Forschung. 2 Bde, Göttingen", Wallstein, 2000.

Keiper, Caitrin - "Brave New World at 75", Number 16, Spring 2007.

Keller, Helen - "How I Became a Socialist", New York Call, Nov. 3rd, 1912.

Kelly, Alfred - "The Descent of Darwin: The Popularization of Darwinism in Germany, 1860-1914", Univ. of North Carolina, 1947.

Kemperink, M.G. – "Visualizing Utopia", WHS Roenhorst Peeters Publishers, 2007.

Kennedy, Foster – "The Problem of Social Control of the Congenital Defective: Education, Sterilization, Euthanasia", American Journal of Psychiatry, July 1942, Vol. 99, Pgs. 13-16.

Kershaw, Ian – "The Hitler Myth", Oxford, reissued 2001.

Kevles, Daniel J. - "In the Name of Eugenics: Genetics and the Uses of Human Heredity", Harvard Univ. Press, 1995.

King, Jr., Martin Luther – "Main in a Revolutionary World", Sermon at the United Church of Christ, Chicago, July 6th, 1965.

– "I Have a Dream", Speech at the Lincoln Memorial, Washington D.C., Aug. 28th, 1963.

Koenigsberg, Richard A. – "Hitler's Ideology: Embodied Metaphor, Fantasy and History", IAP, Dec. 1, 2007.

Krannawitter Thomas L. and Palm, Daniel C. - "A Nation Under God?: The ACLU and Religion in American Politics", Rowman & Littlefield, 2005.

Kubizek, August - "The Young Hitler I Knew: The Memoirs of Hitler's Childhood Friend", 1955.

Kühl, Stefan - "The Nazi Connection: Eugenics, American Racism, and German National Socialism", Oxford, 1994.

Kuklick, Henrika - "New History of Anthropology", John Wiley & Sons, 2009.

~ L ~

Lander, James – "Lincoln & Darwin: Shared Visions of Race, Science, and Religion", SIU Press, 2010.

Langbein, Hermann - "People in Auschwitz", Published with The US Holocaust Memorial Museum, Univ. of North Carolina Press, 2004.

Langer, Walter C. and Murray, Henry A. – "A Psychological Analysis of Adolf Hitler: His Life and Legend", For the United States Office of Strategic Services, 1943.

Laqueur, Walter and Breitman, Richard – "Breaking the Silence", Simon & Schuster, Mar 1st, 1987.

Largent, Mark - "Zoology of the Twentieth Century: Charles Davenport's Prediction for Biology", American Philosophical Society Library Bulletin, Jan. 2002. – Sourced from Academia.edu.

Laughlin, Harry - "Analysis of America's Melting Pot Hearings Before the Committee on Immigration and Naturalization House of Representatives" Sixty-Seventh Congress, Third Session of Nov. 21st, 1922, (Serial 7-C Washington Government Printing Office 1923)

– "Eugenical Sterilization in the United States", Psychopathic Laboratory of the Municipal Court of Chicago, Dec. 1922.

Lefalophodon, An Informal History of Evolutionary Biology Web Site.

Lehmann, Peter - "Progressive Psychiatry: Publisher J. F. Lehmann as Promoter of Social Psychiatry under Fascism", Changes: An International Journal of Psychology and Psychotherapy, Vol. 12, No. 1, 1994, translation by Peter Stastny.

Lenz, Fritz - *"Münchener Medizinische Wochenschrift"*, Vol. 66, 1919.

Lemkin, Raphael – "Axis Rule in Occupied Europe: Laws of Occupation, Analysis of Government, Proposals for Rederess", The Lawbook Exchange, Ltd., 2005.

LePage, Jean-Denis - "The Hitler Youth, 1922-45: An Illustrated History", MacFarland, 2009.

Levy, Richard S. - "Antisemitism: A Historical Encyclopedia of Prejudice and Persecution", ABC-CLIO, Vol. 1, 2005.

Lewis, David Levering - "W.E.B. Du Bois: Fight for Equality and the American Century (1919-1963)" Henry Hold & Co., 2001.

Lifton, Robert Jay – "The Nazi Doctors: Medical Killing and the Psychology of Genocide", Basic Books, 1986.

Lilla, Mark – "The Reckless Mind: Intellectuals in Politics", Review Books, 2006.

Lipow, Arthur - "Authoritarian Socialism in America: Edward Bellamy & the Nationalist Movement", Univ. of California Press, 1982.

Lissner, Scott L. – "The Holocaust Began with People with Disabilities", 2009, incl.ca.

Littell's Living Age – "Heil Lincoln!", March-August 1936.

Lombardo, Paul - "Pioneer's Big Lie", Albany Law Review, Vol. 66. No. 4, Summer 2003.

- "Three Generations No Imbeciles: Eugenics, the Supreme Court, and Buck v. Bell", JHU Press, 2008.

Lombroso, Cesare – "The Task of Social Hygiene", Houghton Mifflin Co., 1912, Translated by Havelock Ellis.

Longerich, Peter – "Heinrich Himmler: A Life", OUP Oxford, 2012.

Lucifer: A Theosophical Magazine - "Lucifer: A Theosophical Magazine", Sept. 1887 – Feb. 1888.

Luhrssen, David - "Hammer of the Gods: The Thule Society and the Birth of Nazism," Potomac Books, Inc.,

2012.

Lusane, Clarence - "Hitler's Black Victims: The Historical Experiences of Afro-Germans, European Blacks, Africans, and African Americans in the Nazi Era Victims", Taylor & Francis, 2002.

~ M ~

Macintyre, Ben - "Forgotten Fatherland: The search for Elisabeth Nietzsche", Macmillan, 1992.

Maienschein, Jane and Ruse, Michael – "Biology and the Foundation of Ethics", Cambridge Univ. Press, 1999. – Citing "Will to Power", IV, 862 and IV, 1055.

Maik, Linda L. - "Nordau's Degeneration: The American Controversy", Journal of the History of Ideas, Vol. 50, No. 4, Oct. - Dec. 1989.

MANAS - "Great Reformers: Edward Bellamy", Vol. II, No. 33, Aug. 17th, 1949.

Marrus, Michael R. - "The Origins of the Holocaust", Walter de Gruyter, Jan. 1989.

Marks, Jonathan – "The Scientific and Cultural Meaning of the Odious Ape-Human Comparison", The Nature of Differences: Science, Society and Human Biology, 1st Ed., Taylor & Francis Group, 2006.

Marx, Karl and Engels, Friedrich – "Manifesto of the Communist Party", C.H. Kerr, 1906.

marxists.catbull.com, "Marx-Engels Correspondence 1861-Marx To Ferdinand Lassalle, In Berlin", Source: MECW, Vol. 41, Pg. 245.

Max Planck Society – "Presidential Commission 'History of the Kaiser Wilhelm Society in the National Socialist Era", Sourced From: mpiwg-berlin.mpg.de

Mazumdar, Pauline M.H. – "Eugenics, Human Genetics and Human Failings: The Eugenics Society, its sources and its critics in Britain", Routledge, 1992.

McElroy, Wendy - "Freedom, Feminism, and the State", Independent Institute, Jan. 1, 1991 – Citing Alan P. Grimes, "The Puritan Ethic and Woman Suffrage", Oxford University Press, 1967.

McWhorter, Ladelle - "Racism and Sexual Oppression in Anglo-America: A Genealogy", Indiana Univ. Press, 2009.

Medoff, Rafael – "The Jews Should Keep Quiet: Franklin D. Roosevelt, Rabbi Stephen S. Wise, and the Holocaust", Univ. of Nebraska Press, 2019.

Meek, Ronalsd E. - "Marx and Engels on the Population Bomb: Selections from the Writings of Marx and Engels Dealing with the Theories of Thomas Robert Malthus", Ramparts Press, 1971 – citing "Marx and Engels, Selected Correspondence", Pg. 170.

Mehler, Barry A. - "Rewriting Mental Testing History: The View from the American Psychologist," Steven A. Gelb, Garland E. Allen, Andrew Futterman, and Sage Race Relations Abstracts 11 #2, May 1986 - Posted in the online archives of Ferris University's Institute for the Study of Academic Racism.

Mendelsohn, Everett and Nowotny, Helga - "Nineteen Eighty-Four: Science Between Utopia and Dystopia" Springer Netherlands,1984.

Menge, Edward J. – "The Beginnings of Science: Biologically and Psychologically Considered", The Gorham Press, 1918.

McCloskey, Barbara – "Artists of World War II", Greenwood Publishing Group, 2005.

Michaud, Eric – The Cult of Art in Nazi Germany", Stanford Univ. Press, 2004.

Michels, John – "Science", The Science Press, New Series Vol. XL, July-Dec. 1914.

militaryhistoryonline.com, "Rulers of the World: The Hitler Youth", Sept. 5th, 2005.

Miller, Chris – "War on Terror: The Oxford Amnesty Lectures", Oxford Univ. Press, 2009.

Miller, Timothy - "The Quest for Utopia in 20 Century America. Volume I: 1900-1960", Syracuse Univ. Press, 1998.

Mindrum, Michael R. - "Time for another revolution? The Flexner Report in Historic Context, Reflections on our Profession", Coronary Artery Disease Journal, 2006 Ed.

Miskolczy, Ambrus - "Hitler's Library", Central European University Press, 2003.

mit.edu – "Bring back the Hottentot Venus", Race Science in Media, June 15th, 1995.

Mitgang, Herber – "Lindbergh Said to Regret Misconceptions over Jews", April 20th, 1980.

Montagu, Basil – "The Works of Francis Bacon, Lord Chancellor of England: With a Life of the Author", Carey and Hart, Vol. 1, 1844.

Moore, Randy - "Evolution in the Courtroom: A Reference Guide", ABC-CLIO, 2002.

Morgan, Ted - "Reds: McCarthyism in 20th Century America," Random House, 2003.

Morrison, David – "Heroes, Antiheroes, and the Holocaust: American Jewry and Historical Choice", Geffen, 1995.

Morning Post of London – "War and Racial Progress", July 2nd, 1915.

Mostert, Mark – "Useless Easters: Disability as Genocidal Marker in Nazi Germany", The journal of Special Education, Vol. 36, Issue 3, Nov. 1st, 2002.

Mullen, William – "Field Celebrates Genetic Pioneer: Augustinian Friar was Discovering the Secret of Genetic Inheritance in 1850s, While Darwin was Publishing his Theory", Chicago Tribune, Sept. 12th, 2006, Sourced From: articles.chicagotribune.com

Mulvey, Paul - "Political Life of Josiah C. Wedgwood: Land, Liberty and Empire, 1872-1943", Boydell &

Brewer, 2010.

Myerson, Abraham - "Eugenic Sterilization: A Reorientation of the Problem", American Neurological Association, Committee for the Investigation of Eugenical Sterilization", Macmillan, 1936.

~ N ~

NAACP – "The Crisis", Oc. 1939.

Naler, Gary D. - "The Curse of 1920", Self-Publish, 1994.

National Jewish Monthly, The – "Niemoller Speaks!", May 1941 – From history.ucsb.edu, Prof. Harold Marcuse.

National Magazine, - "The National League of Medical Freedom: Its Aim and Its Contention", Vol. 39, April-Sept. 1912.

Nevins, Michael – "A Tale of Two Villages: Vineland and Skillman, Nj", iUniverse, 2009.

Nevins, Michael - "Abraham Flexner: A Flawed American Icon," iUniverse, 2010.

New Republic, The - "Physicians' juries for defective babies", Helen Keller, December 18th, 1915, pp. 173-74.

New York Times, The - "Collaborators in a Quest for Human Perfection", M.D. Abigail Zuger, Aug. 28th, 2007.
- "To Save Our Institutions: The Object of a Powerful League Recently Formed", May 16th, 1890.
– "In 1938, The World Knew", Nov. 9th, 1988
- "JURY OF SURGEONS STUDIES BABE'S CASE; Holds Second Examination and Finds More Defects in Chicago Child", Nov. 19th, 1915.
– "Medical Freedom", May 18th, 1910. – "Babes of the Future: Major Leonard Darwin Tells True Purposes of Eugenics", Dec. 21st, 1912. – "Colombia U. President Butler Refuses to Bar Nazi Envoy: Stresses Need for Academic Freedom", Nov. 20th, 1933.
– "New Messiah Rising, Theosophists Say", Sept. 5th, 1913.

Newman, Hannah – "Antisemitism: A Historical Encyclopedia of Prejudice and Persecution", Vol. I, ABC-CLIO, 2005.

Newton, Michael – "White Robes and Burning Crosses: A History of the Ku Klux Klan from 1866", McFarland, 2014.

Nicol, Caitrin - "Brave New World at 75", The New Atlantis, Spring 2007.

Nietzsche, Friedrich – "Genealogy of Morals", Translation by Horace B. Samuel, M.A., Boni & Liveright, 1921.
– "The Genealogy of Morals", Courier Corp., 2012.
– "The Will to Power", Penguin UK, Jan 26th, 2017.
– "The AntiChrist", A.A. Knopf, 1920.

nobelprize.org, Nomination Database, Nomenee: Alfred Ploetz, Number: 29-1.

Nordau, Max – "Morals and the Evolution of Man", Funk & Wagnalls Company, 1922.
– "Degeneration", D. Appleton & Co. 1892/1895.

North, Michael – "The Greek Oath", National Library of Medicine, 2002, Sourced From: nlm.nih.gov.

Noyes, George Wallingford – "Life of John Humphrey Noyes", Oneida Community Collection, Syracuse Univ., Vol. V, 1864-1878, Sourced From: library.syr.edu

Noyes, Hilda Herrick – "Hilda Herrick Noyes, M.D. and George Wallingford Noyes, Address, Scientific Papers of the Second International Congress of Eugenics: Held at American Museum of Natural History, New York, Sept. 22-28, 1921", Williams & Williams, 1923.

Nugel, Bernfried and Meckier, Jerome – "Aldous Huxley Annual", *LIT Verlag Münster*, Dec. 28th, 2009.

Numbers, Ronald L. - "The Creationists: From Scientific Creationism to Intelligent Design," Univ. of Ca., 2006.

nuremberg.law.harvard.edu – "Opening Statement for the United States of America", Dec. 9th, 1946, HLSL Item No.: 565.

~ O ~

O'Keefe, J. Theodore – "Veteran American Journalist Provides Valuable Inside Look at Third Reich Germany", Journal of Historical Review, Vol. 19, No. 2, 2000.

Oliver, Jr., Henry "Von Mises on the Harmony of Interests" Ethics Journal, Vol. 70, No. 4, July 1960.

orlandosentinel.com, "Frederick Oechsner, Writer and Diplomat", Orlando Sentinel, April 20th, 1992.

Orwell, George - "Wells, Hitler and the World State", Horizon Mag., Aug. 1941, Sourced from www.Orwell.ru
– Reprinted in "Critical Essays", George Orwell, Secker & Warburg, 1946.

osservatoreromano.va, "If Life is 'Unworthy of Being Lived'", L'Osservatore Romano, June 12th, 2012.

Overy, Richard - "Interrogations: The Nazi Elite in Allied Hands, 1945", Allen Lane, 2001.

~ P ~

Padfield, Peter – "Himmler: Reichsführer-SS", MacMillan, 1990.

Pain, Stephanie - "Blasts from the past: The Soviet ape-man scandal", New Scientist online, Aug. 23, 2008.

Partington, John S. – "H.G. Wells's Eugenic Thinking of the 1930s and 1940s", Utopian Studies, Vol. 14,

No. 1, 2003.
Patterson, Martha H. - "The American New Woman Revisited," Rutgers Univ. Press, 2008.
Paulson, Eric - "Biohistory", Occidental Quarterly Online Journal, May 26th, 2010.
Pearson, Karl - "Life, Letters and Labours of Francis Galton by Karl Pearson", Cambridge Univ. Press, 1930.
— "The Ethic of Freethought: And Other Addresses and Essays", Adam & Charles Black, 1901.
Pelger, Gregory - "Willibald Hentschel", Handbook of the Volkish Sciences. People - Institutions - Research Programs – Foundations, Compiled by Matthias von Berg, Ed. V, 2008.
Pernick, Martin S. - "The Black Stork: Eugenics and the Death of "Defective" Babies in American Medicine and Motion Pictures since 1915", Oxford Univ. Press, 1996.
Phalen, William J. - "American Evangelical Protestantism and European Immigrants, 1800-1924", McFarland, 2011.
Pick, Daniel – "Faces of Degeneration: A European Disorder, C. 1848-1918", Cambridge Univ. Press, 1989.
physicstoday.scitation.org – "The X Club", Charles Day, Commentary & Review, Aug. 4th, 2011 – Quoting Thomas Archer Hirst.
Popenoe, Paul – "The German Sterilization Law", Journal of Heredity, Doc. ID 12208, dnalc.org.
Proctor, Robert - "Nazi Medical Ethics: Ordinary Doctors?", Military Medical Ethics, Vol. 2, 2003, Pg. 410
— "Nazi War on Cancer", Princeton Univ. Press, 2000.
— "Racial Hygiene: Medicine under the Nazis", Harvard Univ. Press, 1988.
Pugliese, Joseph – "Biometrics: Bodies, Technologies, Biopolitics", Routledge, Dec. 6, 2012.

~ Q ~

Quinn, Peter – "The Gentle Darwinians: What Darwin's Champions Won't Mention", Commonweal, Vol. CXXXIV, No. 5, March 9th, 2007, Sourced From: commonwealmagazine.org
Qureshi, Sadiah "Displaying Sara Baartman, the 'Hottentot Venus'", SAGE Journals, History of Science, Vol 42, Issue 2, 2004.

~ R ~

Radinitzky, Gerard - "NOTAS: On the Marxist's Rejection of the Distinction Between Pure and Applied Science, and its Consequences for Marxist Science Policy", Revista Portuguesa de Filosofía, T. 41, Fasc. I (Jan. - Mar. 1985), Pgs. 95-99.
Rafter, Nicole - "Earnest A. Hooton and the Biological Tradition in American Criminology", Journal Criminology, Vol. 42, Issue 3 of 4, Aug. 2004.
Raico, Ralph - "Rethinking Churchill - Churchill and the New Liberalism", Mises.org, Nov. 14th, 2008.
Ratu, Sikeli Neil - "Anti-Semitism and American Refugee Immigration Policy during the Holocaust: A Reassessment", Dissertation for the University of Sydney, 2006.
Rauschning, Hermann - "The Revolution of Nihilism, Warning to the West", Translated by E. W. Dickes, Longmans-Green, 1939. – "Hitler Speaks: A Series of Political Conversations with Adolf Hitler on his Real Aims", Thornton Butterworth, Ltd., 1939.
Reggiani, Andres Horacio – "God's Eugenicst: Alexis Carrel and the Sociobiology of Decline", Berghahn Books, 2007.
reason.org – "The Never-Ending Business of Centralizations", Dec. 22nd, 2010.
Regal, Brian - "Human Evolution: A Guide to the Debates", ABC-CLIO, 2004.
Reynolds, Dave – "Davis Apologizes for 20,000 Sterilized", Inclusion Daily Express, March 12th, 2003, mn.gov
Royal Institute of International Affairs in England - "Speeches of Adolf Hitler: April 1922-August 1939", Oxford Univ. Press,1942.
Roosevelt, Theodore – "The Great Adventure: Present-Day Studies in American Nationalism", Essay #7: Lincoln and Free Speech, theodorerroosevelt.org.
Rupke, Nicolaas A. - "Richard Owen: Biology Without Darwin", Univ. of Chicago Press, 1994.
Ryback, Timothy W. - "Hitler's Forgotten Library: The Man, His Books, and His Search for God", theatlantic.com, May 2003.

~ S ~

Saeed, Tarik – "What is Wrong with Black People \\\ White People?", Feb. 20th, 2013, google.com ebook.
Sanger, Margaret - "The Pivot of Civilization", Brentano's Publishers, 1922.
— "An Autobiography", Dover Publications, 1971.
— "The Autobiography of Margaret Sanger", Dover Pub., 1938.
— "Birth Control and Racial Betterment", Birth Control Review, Feb 1919, Library of Congress Microfilm 131:0099B.
— "A Plan for Peace", Birth Control Review, April 1932. – "What Every Girl Should Know", The Public Writings and Speeches of Margaret Sanger, 1920, Sourced From: nyu.edu
Santaniello, Weaver – "Nietzsche, God, and the Jews: His Critique of Judeo-Christianity in Relation to the Nazi Myth", SUNY Press, 2012.
Savo, Welling - "The Master Race", Boston Mag., May 15th, 2006.

Schallmayer, Wilhelm – "On the Imminent Physical Degeneration of Civilized Humanity and the Nationalization of the Medical Profession", Berlin; Neuwied: Heuser, 1891.

Schleiermacher, Sabdste - "Racial Hygiene and Deliberate Parenthood: Two Sides of Demographer Hans Harmsen's Population Policy", Reproductive and Genetic Engineering: Journal of International Feminist Analysis, 1990;3(3):201-10, quoting Pg. 21, Pro Familia Magazin, Kaupen-Haas, Pg. 41, 1984.

Schlesinger, Jr., Arthur Meier - "The Politics of Upheaval: 1935-1936, the Age of Roosevelt", Volume III, Houghton Mifflin Books, 2003.

– "The Coming of the New Deal, 1933-1935", Houghton Mifflin Harcourt, 2003.

Schmidt, Ulf – "History and Theory of Human Experimentation: The Declaration of Helsinki and Modern Medical Ethics", and Andreas Frewer, Steiner, 2007.

- "Justice at Nuremberg: Leo Alexander and the Nazi Doctors' Trial", Palgrave Macmillan UK, 2004.

- "Karl Brandt: Medicine and Power in the Third Reich", Bloomsbury Academic, 2007.

Schmuhl, Hans-Walter - "The Kaiser Wilhelm Institute for Anthropology, Human heredity and Eugenics, 1927-1945" Boston Studies in the Philosophy of Science, Vol. 259, 2008.

Schmundt, Hilmar – "Naked Nazis: Book Reveals Extent of Third Reich Body Worship", Speigel, June 16th, 2011, Sourced From: speigel.de

Schoenl, William and Peck, Danielle - "Advertising Eugenics: Charles M. Goethe's Campaign to Improve the Race", Endeavour Journal, Vol.34 No.2.

Schreiber, Bernhard – "The Men Behind Hitler: A German Warning to the World", From toolan.com

Schwarz, Maureen Trudelle – "Fighting Colonialism with Hegemonic Culture: Native American Appropriation of Indian Stereotypes", SUNY Press, 2013.

sciencedaily.com - "Why Didn't Darwin Discover Mendel's Laws?", Journal of Biology, March 2009.

Scientific Temperance Journal, - "Hitler's Attitude toward Alcohol", Spring 1933.

Seidl, Daniella - *"Zwischen Himmel Und Hölle-Das Kommando 'Plantage' Des Konzentrationslagers Dachau"* or in English, "Between Heaven and Hell: The Command 'Plantation' at the Dachau Concentration Camp", 2009.

Shaler, N.S. – "The Negro Problem", Atlantic Monthly, Vol. 0054, Issue 325, Nov. 1884.

Shirer, William L. – "The Rise and Fall of the Third Reich", Secker & Warburg, London; 1960.

Shlaes, Amity - "The Forgotten Man: A New History of the Great Depression", Harper Collins, 2007.

Shuster, Dr. Evelyne - "Fifty Years Later", New England Journal of Medicine, Nov. 13th, 1997.

Silberman, Steve - "NeuroTribes: The Legacy of Autism and the Future of Neurodiversity", Penguin, 2016.

Snyderman, Mark and Herrnstein, Richard J. - "Intelligence Tests and the Immigration Act of 1924," American Psychologist, No.: 38, Sept. 1983.

Sociological Analysis, – "Max Weber, Dr. Alfred Ploetz, and W.E.B. DuBois: Max Weber on Race and Society II", Vol. 34, No. 4, Winter 1973, Pgs. 308-312.

Solomos, John and Black, Les - "Theories of Race and Racism: A Reader", Routledge, 2001.

Somerville, William – "William Somerville's Narrative of His Journeys to the Eastern Frontier and Kattakoe, 1779-1802", Van Riebeeck Society, 1979.

Speer, Albert - "Inside the Third Reich: Memoirs of Albert Speer", Avon, 1971.

Spiro, Jonathan Peter - Defending the Master Race: Conservation, Eugenics, and the Legacy of Madison Grant", UPNE, 2009.

Spotts, Frederic - "Hitler and the Power of Aesthetics," Overlook Press, 2018.

Stein, S.D. – "Live Unworthy of Life and other Medical Killing Programmes", Jan. 29th, 2007, Sourced From: archive.org

Steinweis, Alan E. - "Art, Ideology, & Economics in Nazi Germany", Univ. of North Carolina Press, 1993.

Steigmann-Gall, Richard – "The Holy Reich: Nazi Conceptions of Christianity, 1919-1945", Cambridge Univ. Press, 2003.

Stern, Dr. Alexandra Minna - "Sterilized in the Name of Public Health: Race, Immigration, and Reproductive Control in Modern California", American Journal of Public Health, V.95(7), July 2005.

Stille, Alexander – "Benevolence and Betrayal: Five Italian Jewish Families Under Fascism", Macmillan, 2003.

Stoddard, Lothrop - "Into the Darkness: Nazi Germany Today", Duell, Sloan, & Pearce, Inc., 1940.

Stölz, Christoph – "Nazi Sculptures at World Cup Venue Spark Protest", *Deutsche Welle*, June 2nd, 2006.

Strasser, Otto - *"Aufbau des deutschen Sozialismus: Mit einem Nachwort von Dr. Claus-Martin Wolfschlag, Vol. 3, Natur et Mythos",* 2nd Ed., 1936, Reprinted By: Haag + Herchen, 2013.

Stulman, Tova - "The Holocaust in the Movies", Jewish Press review of "Imaginary Witness", Jan. 9th, 2008.

Sugden, Philip - "The Complete History of Jack the Ripper", lightnovelgate.com, Carroll & Graf, 1994.

Szaz, Thomas S. – "The Theology of Medicine: The Political-philosophical Foundations of Medical Ethics", Syracuse Univ. Press, 1988.

~ T ~

Taylor, Milton W. – "Viruses and Man: A History of Interactions", Springer, July 21st, 2014.

theguardian.com – "The Churchill You Didn't Know", Nov. 27th, 2007.

theyeshivaworld.com - "Tonight – 80th Yartzheit: Kristallnacht – the Night of Broken Glass", posted 24 October 2018.
thetimes.co.uk – "German Organic Gardening Guru Alwin Seifert Took Tips from Dachau Experiments", Article No.: 6831453, 2009.
TIME Mag. – "Praise for Nazis", Sept. 9th, 1935.
- "Adolf Hitler: Man of the Year, 1938", Jan. 2nd, 1939.
- Mar. 22nd, 1937 editorial on Joseph Goebbels.
- "British Commonwealth of Nations: Young Darwin", May 3rd, 1926.
- "GERMANY: Inside Hitler", June 22nd, 1942.
- "Books: Stirpiculture", March 22nd, 1937.
Times of London – "A Black Day for Germany", Nov. 11, 1938.
Tischauser, Leslie Vincent - "The Changing Nature of Racial and Ethnic Conflict in United States History: 1492 To the Present", University Press of America, 2002.
Treitel, Corinna - "A Science for the Soul: Occultism and the Genesis of the German Modern" 2004.
Trombley, Stephen – "The Right to Reproduce: A History of Coercive Sterilization", Weidenfeld and Nicolson, 1988.
trumanlibrary.org – 97. Radio Report to the American People on the Potsdam Conference, President Harry Truman.
Tyson, Joseph Howard – "The Surreal Reich", iUniverse, 2010.

~ U ~

Ungewitter, Richard – "Nudity and Culture", 1910.
United Methodist Church – "An Apology for Support of Eugenics", Petition 81175-C2-R9999, March, 30th, 2008.
United States Gov. Printing Office, - "Trials of War Criminals Before the Nuremberg Military Tribunals Under Control Council Law No. 10", Vol. I, Oct. 1946 – April 1949.
– "Hearings Before the President's Commission on Immigration and Naturalization", 82nd Congress, Sept. 30th to Oct. 29th, Sourced From: catalog.hathitrust.org, No.: 100671453.
– "Nazi Conspiracy and Aggression", Vol. III, Doc.: 615-PS, 1946.
United States Holocaust Memorial – "Collaboration", Article ID: 10005466, Sourced From: ushmm.org
– "Days of Remembrance, April 18-25, 1993: Fifty Years Ago: Revolt Amid the Darkness: Planning Guide for Commemorative Programs", 1993.
United States Office of Strategic Services - "Nuremberg Trials: The Holocaust: Selected Documents in Eighteen Volumes", Vol. 11: The Wannsee Protocol, Translation by John Mendelsohn for the 1944 Report on Auschwitz by the OSS, New York: Garland, 1982.
- "Office of Strategic Services, Adolf Hitler Source Book & Psychological Profile", Available at nizkor.org.
Univ. of Chicago Library - "Guide to the American Civil Liberties Union Illinois Division Records 1920-1982", Historical Note, 2013.
Usher, Sean – "Aldous Huxley to George Orwell: My Dystopia is Better Than Yours", Jan./Feb. 2017 – From Usher's book "Letters of Note", Vol. 2, 2016.

~ V ~

Voigt, Wolfgang - "Garden City as Eugenic Utopia", Planning Perspectives, No. 4, Pgs. 295-312, 1989.
Von Kuehnelt-Leddihn, Erik - "Leftism Revisited: From de Sade and Marx to Hitler and Pol Pot", Regnery Gateway, 1990.
Von Mises, Ludwig - "Economic Policy: Thoughts for Today and Tomorrow", Mises Institute, 2006.
Von Verschuer, Otmar Freiherr *"Geschichte Der Kaiser-Wilhelm-Gesellschaft im Nationalsozialismus. Bestandsaufnahme und Perspektiven der Forschung. 2 Bde, Göttingen"* Wallstein, 2000, ISBN 3-89244-423-4, Translation provided by enacademic.com.

~ W ~

Wallace, Max – "The American Axis: Henry Ford, Charles Lindbergh, and the Rise of the Third Reich", Macmillan, 2003.
Wallace, Mike – "Interview with Aldous Huxley", Mike Wallace Papers: 1956-1963, Univ. of Michigan, Bentley Historical Archive, Call No.: 85472 Aa 2.
Watson, Bruce - "Sacco and Vanzetti: The Men, the Murders, and the Judgment of Mankind", Penguin, 2008.
Warsch, Sean – "A 'holocaust' Becomes 'The Holocaust'", Jewish Magazine, Oct. 2006, jewishmag.com.
Weber, Matthias M. - "Ernst Rüdin, 1874-1952: A German Psychiatrist and Geneticist", American Journal of Medical Genetics (Neuropsychiatric Genetics) 67 (1996): 343–346.
Webster, Dr. Christopher – "Face of the Devine: The Esoteric Roots of Physiognomic Photography", Oct. 22nd, 2008, Sourced From: ccwe.wordpress.com
Weikart, Richard - "EUGENOCIDE: Darwinism & the Rise of German Eugenics", touchtonemag.com.
- "From Darwin to Hitler: Evolutionary Ethics, Eugenics and Racism in Germany", Palgrave Macmillan

US, 2004.
- "Hitler's Ethic: The Nazi Pursuit of Evolutionary Progress", Springer, 2009.

Weindling, Paul - "Health, Race and German Politics Between National Unification and Nazism, 1870-1945", Cambridge Univ. Press, 1993.
- "The Nazi Doctors and the Nuremberg Code: Human Rights in Human Experimentation", Oxford Univ. Press, 1992.

Weiner, Mark S. - "Americans Without Law: The Racial Boundaries of Citizenship", NYU Press, 2006.

Weiss, Sheila Faith – "Race Hygiene and National Efficiency: The Eugenics of Wilhelm Schallmayer", Univ. of Cal. Press, 1987.
- "The Race Hygiene Movement in Germany", Osiris, 2 Series, Vol. 3, 1987.

Weissmann, Karlheinz – "The Epoch of National Socialism", The Journal of Libertarian Studies, Fall 1996.

Wells, H.G. – "A Modern Utopia", Chapman & Hall, Ld., 1905.
- "Science of Life", Doubleday, Doran, Inc., 1931.
- "New Worlds of Old", A. Constable & Co., 1908.
- "Anticipations of the Reaction of Mechanical and Scientific Progress upon Human Life and Thought", North American Review, June-Nov. 1901, Sourced From: onlineliterature.com

Wells, William V. – "The Life and Public Service of Samuel Adams", Brown & Company, Vol. 3, 1865.

Western Star, The – "Hitler in Mental Decline? Close Observers Say Yes", March 19th, 1943.

Whitney, Leon – "The Case for Sterilization", Frederick A. Stokes Company, 1934. - archive.org
- "Unpublished Autobiography 1971", American Philosophical Society, American Eugenics Society Papers, Vol. 1, 50 pgs., Mss.B.W613b.

Willhelm, Donald – "Theodore Roosevelt as an Undergraduate", John W. Luce and Co., 1910.

Wilson, David – "Britain's First Serial Killer", The Daily Mail, Feb. 5th, 2012, Sourced From: dailymail.co.uk

Wiskemann, Elizabeth - "The Testament of Adolf Hitler: The Hitler – Bormann Documents, February-April 1945", Cassell, 1961.

Witkowski, Jan A. - "Davenport's Dream: 21st Century Reflections on Heredity and Eugenics", CSHL Press, 2008.

Wood, Dr. Edward Jenner - "Treatise on Pellagra for the General Practitioner", State Board of Health, North Carolina, Pellagra Commission, 1912.

Wood, J.G. - "The Natural History of Man Being an Account of the Manners and Customs of the Uncivilized Races of Men", Routledge, Vol. 1, 1868.

Woodridge, Alan – "Measuring the Mind: Education and Psychology in England 1860-1990", British Journal of Educational Studies, Vol. 43, No. 3, Sept. 1995.

Wyatt, Philip R. – "John Humphrey Noyes and the Stirpiculture Experiment", Journal of the History of Medicine and Allied Sciences, Vol. 31, No. 1, Jan. 1976.

Wyman, David S. - "Columbia Invites Hitler to Campus", wymanInstitute.org, Institute for Holocaust Studies, Sept. 20, 2007.

Wyndham, Diana H. - "Striving for National Fitness: Eugenics in Australia, 1910s to the 1930s", ses.library.usyd.edu.au, Doctoral Thesis, 1996.

~ Z ~

Zapotoczny, Walter S. – "Rulers of the World: The Hitler Youth", Sept. 5th, 2005, Sourced From: militaryhistoryonline.com

Index:

25-Point Programme (Nazi), 216, 220
A Civic Biology, 292, 360
Abolition, 221, 222, 285, 310, 355, 531, 532, 533, 536, 537, 645, 646, 701, 716, 717
ACLU (American Civil Liberties Union), 359, 360, 361, 362, 658
Aldous Huxley, 11, 89, 90, 92, 126, 208, 209, 211, 212, 214, 215, 261, 418, 584, 599, 622, 748
Alexander, Leo, 14, 16, 18, 19, 24, 30, 31, 111, 121, 122, 127, 228, 230, 355, 373, 374, 455, 456, 585, 754, 757
Allen, Garland E., 4, 349, 686
American Birth Control, 65, 81, 94
American Homogeneity, 303, 305
American Museum of Natural History, 63, 205, 382, 640
American Neurological Association, 72, 105, 127, 128, 129, 130, 131, 423, 636
Anti-Semite, 289, 489
Anti-Semitic, 102, 151, 283, 285, 289, 345, 354, 355, 356, 359, 367, 368, 401, 439, 476, 480, 485, 486, 489, 523, 524, 525, 563, 574, 625, 627, 661
Appalachian Appendectomies, 105, 234
Applied Biology (Concept), 69, 121, 520, 562, 704
Applied Eugenics (Concept), 29, 602
Aryan, 30, 31, 45, 77, 78, 85, 100, 113, 114, 115, 117, 119, 123, 166, 169, 171, 173, 182, 183, 205, 230, 271, 273, 277, 320, 323, 325, 327, 336, 355, 371, 420, 480, 482, 489, 495, 496, 497, 547, 551, 560, 563, 569, 574, 575, 587, 588, 604, 622, 623, 626, 660, 685, 705, 706, 743
Atavism, 256, 408, 459, 588, 591, 613, 662
Auschwitz, 12, 13, 41, 51, 68, 69, 70, 72, 76, 87, 111, 228, 231, 318, 338, 348, 352, 355, 455, 481, 527, 535, 541, 626, 756, 776
Baby Knauer, 103, 403, 410
Baur, Erwin, 129, 244, 290, 317, 318, 319, 320, 329, 330, 343, 356, 359, 366, 369, 371, 384, 447, 453, 456, 496, 562, 570, 631, 632, 687, 712, 754, 762
Baur-Fischer-Lenz (book), 317, 318, 319, 329, 330, 343, 356, 359, 366, 371, 384, 447, 453, 562, 570, 632, 712, 762
Beer Hall Putsch, 26, 193, 194, 197, 198, 297, 298, 300, 317, 369
Bell Curve (Book), 43, 535, 608
Bellamy, Edward, 117, 126, 135, 136, 137, 138, 140, 141, 143, 144, 145, 146, 190, 191, 214, 256, 271, 272, 274, 275, 279, 291, 307, 310, 324, 357, 364, 378, 406, 414, 448, 469, 494, 495, 496, 502, 549, 558, 567, 574, 578, 610, 615, 616, 617, 618, 728, 763, 776

Bellamy, Francis, 135
Bellamy, Marion, 137, 271
Binding, Karl, 343, 345, 346, 355, 404, 712, 754, 763
Binding-Hoche (Book), 345, 353
Biohistorian, 385
Biohistory, 383
Birth Control, 60, 62, 65, 85, 94, 95, 97, 98, 226, 332, 333, 334, 335, 340, 360, 494, 520, 673
Birth of a Nation (Film), 375, 639
Black Stork (film), 360, 403, 404, 405, 406, 407, 409, 410, 411, 621
Blavatsky (Madame), 235, 336, 406, 486, 494, 496, 497, 547, 573
Bloch, Edward, 169
Boas, Franz, 384
Brandt, Karl, 23, 30, 72, 76, 103, 106, 107, 108, 109, 110, 111, 165, 199, 230, 231, 233, 260, 326, 330, 352, 353, 356, 358, 435, 436, 438, 439, 446, 562, 563, 708, 753, 754, 756, 758, 762
Brave New World, 92, 93, 126, 208, 209, 210, 211, 212, 214, 215, 261, 418, 599
British Eugenics Society, 11, 58, 61, 62, 66, 225, 265, 599
Bronx Zoo, 380, 382, 649
Buchenwald, 38, 44, 45, 86, 607
Buck v. Bell, 1927, 55, 61, 83, 152, 153, 237, 239, 240, 241, 242, 244, 248, 249, 293, 320, 418, 432, 433, 531, 555, 568, 606, 631, 753, 758, 760
Buck, Carrie, 238, 242, 248, 249, 293, 432, 433, 631
Bush, Vannevar, 126, 458
Cal State Sacramento, 64, 85, 393
California, 16, 60, 62, 63, 64, 76, 134, 147, 150, 155, 226, 335, 359, 380, 387, 388, 389, 391, 392, 393, 529, 554, 559, 582, 608, 616, 619, 670, 671, 731
Cannibals All, 731
Capitalism, 69, 141, 156, 168, 174, 202, 271, 272, 278, 321, 322, 323, 324, 327, 335, 369, 442, 479, 502, 507, 509, 510, 511, 514, 516, 517, 556, 574, 614, 615, 623, 642, 734
Caplan, Arthur L., 15, 23, 169, 170, 569
Carlson, Elof Axel, 24, 92, 236, 635, 691, 692, 752
Carnegie Institution of Wash. D.C., 45, 120, 123, 125, 126, 132, 296, 305, 382, 423, 452, 457, 458, 600
Carrel, Alexis, 145, 147, 150, 591
Case for Sterilization (Book), 152, 153, 154, 158, 159, 160, 161, 162, 163, 167
Casti Connubii, 86, 160, 199, 201
Catholic Church, 102, 111, 130, 160, 195, 197, 198, 199, 201, 236, 280, 351, 515, 517, 522, 523, 525, 657, 715
Caucasian, 196, 205, 308, 565, 631, 652, 678, 706, 733, 744, 747
Central Planning, 135, 143, 209, 220,

783

247, 340, 392, 444, 514, 729
CHASE, ALLAN, 153, 156, 301, 636, 637, 638, 685, 700, 772
CHRISTIAN PROSS, 8, 41, 165
CHURCHILL, WINSTON, 22, 26, 27, 33, 43, 59, 76, 100, 284, 285, 291, 427, 515, 528, 666, 739, 765
CITY PLANNING, 116, 117, 388, 446, 578, 581, 615
CIVIL RIGHTS, 20, 140, 375, 569, 631, 669
CIVIL WAR, 96, 276, 313, 355, 363, 364, 376, 426, 518, 530, 531, 532, 553, 565, 567, 603, 612, 628, 630, 634, 666, 668, 716, 717, 718, 742, 747
COLD SPRING HARBOR, 24, 34, 45, 58, 59, 60, 66, 85, 89, 92, 120, 124, 126, 132, 152, 204, 236, 265, 292, 296, 307, 310, 318, 412, 423, 424, 425, 452, 456, 457, 458, 536, 600, 601, 602, 603, 609, 635, 655, 692, 752
COLD WAR, 8, 25, 40, 41, 42, 103, 191, 219, 324, 515, 619, 705
COLOMBIA UNIV., 229, 607, 608
COMMITTEE ON THE NEGRO, 17, 253
COMMUNIST INTERNATIONAL, 223, 343
COMMUNIST MANIFESTO, 511, 643, 644
COMPASSION, 149, 160, 198, 260, 286, 287, 288, 345, 346, 348, 405, 436, 519, 542, 560, 594, 626, 710, 753
COMPASSION IS WEAKNESS (CONCEPT), 338, 541
COMPULSORY STERILIZATION, 64, 127, 151, 240, 244, 246, 247, 339, 531
CONGRESSIONAL REPORT (1952 REPEAL), 303, 304, 305
CONQUEST OF A CONTINENT (BOOK), 384
CONSERVATISM, 21, 41, 139, 173, 219, 231, 232, 276, 280, 285, 323, 351, 376, 377, 378, 399, 515, 519, 549, 575, 582, 617, 644, 657, 666, 705, 733
CONSPIRACY, 19, 23, 25, 36, 39, 140, 275, 277, 281, 334, 346, 366, 370, 484, 485, 486, 490, 755, 759, 760, 764 (SEE ALSO: NUREMBERG TRIALS)
COUNCIL OF FOREIGN RELATIONS, 124, 365, 374
COUNCIL ON FOREIGN RELATIONS, 124
COVERT LANGUAGE, 737
CRIMES AGAINST HUMANITY, 8, 12, 14, 22, 23, 43, 44, 72, 162, 229, 242, 340, 755, 762
DACHAU, 19, 111, 178, 179, 200, 485, 582
DARROW, CLARENCE, 139, 140, 294, 295, 360, 405
DARWIN, CHARLES, 54, 58, 61, 156, 208, 253, 254, 256, 264, 265, 285, 287, 296, 316, 330, 334, 355, 357, 359, 377, 379, 382, 383, 386, 389, 407, 408, 410, 422, 426, 430, 434, 435, 440, 459, 460, 461, 501, 502, 506, 512, 533, 534, 535, 536, 543, 548, 567, 592, 593, 598, 602, 623, 627, 634, 647, 652, 661, 675, 676, 677, 678, 679, 686, 687, 688, 689, 690, 691, 692, 694, 699, 701, 703, 708, 709, 710, 715, 718, 719, 720, 722, 723, 746, 748, 749
DARWIN, ERASMUS, 592, 661, 746
DARWIN, FRANCIS, 156, 316, 422, 423, 434, 435, 534, 600
DARWIN, LEONARD, 57, 58, 59, 60, 90, 91, 98, 105, 109, 143, 149, 152, 157, 161, 172, 173, 225, 233, 256, 257, 258, 259, 260, 261, 262, 263, 264, 265, 266, 274, 283, 286, 291, 296, 309, 313, 315, 330, 357, 359, 370, 379, 386, 407, 420, 426, 427, 428, 429, 430, 435, 439, 441, 459, 502, 508, 519, 520, 532, 534, 535, 536, 548, 549, 593, 597, 600, 601, 602, 621, 634, 645, 673, 674, 681, 682, 693, 710, 729, 763
DARWIN'S BULLDOG, 11, 386, 540, 592, 703
DARWINISM, 136, 249, 254, 271, 272, 273, 276, 294, 334, 338, 381, 383, 386, 401, 402, 406, 459, 461, 501, 502, 509, 541, 542, 543, 545, 546, 548, 549, 550, 557, 559, 561, 564, 572, 578, 593, 605, 616, 619, 623, 627, 648, 649, 657, 658, 659, 660, 661, 664, 677, 678, 680, 681, 683, 684, 687, 688, 689, 692, 693, 704, 708, 711, 716, 718, 720, 722, 723, 727, 729, 744, 748, 763
DAVENPORT, CHARLES B., 17, 34, 49, 58, 59, 60, 62, 63, 95, 98, 105, 121, 123, 127, 152, 161, 163, 195, 204, 205, 207, 226, 229, 233, 264, 265, 283, 286, 290, 292, 293, 301, 304, 309, 318, 320, 330, 332, 333, 334, 335, 347, 359, 381, 384, 387, 388, 389, 405, 409, 412, 413, 421, 422, 423, 425, 428, 435, 439, 441, 452, 453, 454, 458, 519, 520, 531, 533, 555, 570, 599, 600, 601, 602, 603, 605, 606, 607, 608, 609, 610, 632, 636, 637, 638, 655, 681, 722, 729, 752, 763
D-DAY, 53, 54
DECLARATION OF INDEPENDENCE, 190, 254, 311, 377, 416, 418, 553, 633, 634, 670, 672, 674, 736, 738, 741, 747, 749
DEGENERATE ART, 112
DEGENERATION, 108, 155, 158, 171, 173, 182, 205, 256, 261, 355, 401, 406, 411, 459, 480, 530, 544, 554, 558, 562, 570, 573, 585, 586, 587, 588, 589, 590, 612, 623, 624, 662, 673, 681, 682, 687, 691, 717, 743, 744, 745, 746, 747, 748, 753
DESCENT OF MAN (BOOK), 128, 253, 265, 357, 379, 434, 501, 502, 542, 543, 593, 605, 647, 657, 661, 676, 677, 678, 681, 682, 683, 684, 687, 688, 699, 700, 708, 709, 713, 722, 746
DOCTOR'S TRIAL, 25, 30, 31, 32, 35, 36, 55, 63, 65, 71
DRAPER, WICKLIFFE, 19, 120, 121, 152, 309, 364, 384, 532, 533
DUBOIS, W.E.B., 707
DUE PROCESS, 152, 227, 237, 238, 241, 242, 244, 245, 630
DULLES, JOHN FOSTER, 34, 35, 374
DUNN, L.C., 125, 126, 457, 458, 459
DUTY TO BE HEALTHY (CONCEPT), 164, 165, 167
EASTABROOK, ARTHUR, 61
ECKART, DIETRICH, 368, 371, 485, 486, 492, 493, 494, 496, 497
EISENHOWER, DWIGHT D., 15, 34, 38, 39, 43, 44, 46, 55, 488
ELLIS, HAVELOCK, 60, 73, 272, 334, 336, 419, 477, 627, 663
ENABLING ACT, 66, 186, 194, 201, 225

ENGELS, FRIEDRICH, 147, 224, 363, 509, 511, 540, 558, 643, 644, 723, 724, 725, 726, 727, 728
ENGLISH, DAYLANNE K., 98, 552, 580, 631, 686
ERBKRANK (FILM), 91, 120, 130, 158, 172, 262, 332, 385, 387, 407, 409, 410, 560, 621, 748
EUGENIC COURTS, 18, 20, 82, 83, 87, 238, 244 (SEE ALSO: HEREDITARY HEALTH COURTS)
EUGENICAL STERILIZATION (BOOK), 30, 49, 66, 82, 83, 105, 109, 120, 128, 129, 130, 131, 152, 153, 225, 226, 237, 244, 245, 246, 247, 248, 264, 318, 343, 356, 359, 601, 636
EUGENICS MANIFESTO, 88, 89, 90, 91
EUGENICS RECORD OFFICE, 34, 158, 226, 303, 388, 414, 457, 458
EUGENICS RESEARCH ASSOCIATION, 45, 85, 99, 100, 120, 304, 457
EUGENOCIDE, 254, 549
EUTHANASIA, 12, 15, 18, 29, 30, 31, 70, 72, 73, 79, 80, 103, 104, 106, 107, 108, 109, 110, 111, 145, 148, 153, 154, 199, 233, 253, 283, 309, 343, 344, 345, 350, 351, 352, 353, 354, 355, 356, 357, 358, 360, 403, 404, 406, 409, 410, 418, 420, 421, 428, 435, 436, 438, 439, 485, 505, 516, 540, 541, 564, 635, 710, 711, 757, 758, 760, 763
EVOLUTIONARY HIERARCHY, 12, 26, 55, 70, 167, 223, 225, 253, 254, 340, 400, 414, 496, 652, 654, 655, 661, 673, 680, 686, 687, 688, 706, 717, 722, 731
EXHIBITION OF DEGENERATE ART, 113, 476, 584
FABIAN SOCIALISM, 61, 85, 134, 136, 148, 192, 208, 213, 215, 256, 272, 274, 285, 291, 307, 315, 334, 405, 420, 427, 428, 429, 439, 442, 497, 503, 504, 507, 512, 513, 514, 610, 615, 618, 619, 620, 663, 734
FASCISM, 70, 101, 102, 103, 134, 135, 136, 191, 212, 220, 279, 367, 368, 369, 515, 516, 521, 523, 524, 527, 528
FASCIST, 57, 103, 284, 308, 515, 520, 521, 522, 523, 527, 528
FEEBLEMINDED, 64, 103, 155, 157, 158, 233, 246, 284, 288, 293, 296, 304, 318, 408, 430, 431, 432, 433, 504, 534, 611
FINAL SOLUTION, 51, 52, 72, 76, 78, 79, 80, 119, 230, 329, 330, 338, 455, 482, 525, 552, 570
FIN-DE-SIECLÉ, 254, 587, 590
FISCHER, EUGEN, 71, 81, 83, 105, 108, 120, 129, 152, 231, 290, 309, 317, 318, 319, 320, 329, 330, 334, 343, 356, 359, 366, 369, 371, 384, 405, 409, 447, 453, 454, 455, 456, 496, 533, 562, 570, 602, 607, 631, 632, 687, 712, 762, 763
FITZHUGH, GEORGE, 728, 733, 748
FLEXNER REPORT, 34, 372, 373
FLEXNER, ABRAHAM, 372
FORD, HENRY, 116, 151, 209, 277, 278, 280, 281, 282, 283, 284, 291, 318, 319, 327, 357, 359, 412, 485, 617, 715
FORDISM, 137, 617
FOUNDING FATHERS, 131, 142, 143, 160, 191, 224, 311, 315, 377, 378, 416, 418, 510, 515, 567, 634, 731, 736, 737, 741
FRANCO, 70, 279, 515, 516, 517, 518, 519, 520, 522, 523, 528, 666
FRICK, WILHELM, 66, 81, 225, 571
FROM DARWIN TO HITLER (BOOK), 254, 255, 256, 265, 434, 542, 544, 545, 546, 549, 551, 711
FROMM, ERICH, 183, 466, 471, 734, 737, 748
FÜHRERPRINZIP, 187, 219, 223, 224, 269
GALTON SOCIETY, 334, 384, 607
GAMBLE, CLARENCE, 65, 94
GARDEN CITY, 117, 118, 479, 581, 618
GASMAN, DANIEL, 400, 401, 402, 479, 704, 705, 710, 712
GENEALOGY OF MORALS (BOOK), 346, 347
GENETIC HEALTH COURTS, 152
GENOCIDE, 8, 28, 29, 31, 33, 43, 79, 286, 287, 288, 328, 387, 516, 548, 551, 552, 760
GOEBBELS, JOSEF, 112, 113, 525
GOETHE, C.M., 58, 60, 64, 85, 91, 123, 126, 159, 163, 195, 196, 283, 308, 309, 310, 315, 380, 384, 385, 393, 763
GOOD NAZI (CONCEPT), 109, 171, 356, 439, 753 (SEE ALSO: SPEER, ALBERT)
GÖRING, HERMANN, 27, 77, 217, 276, 584
GRANT, MADISON, 48, 49, 81, 123, 163, 195, 196, 290, 301, 302, 303, 304, 307, 309, 310, 311, 315, 333, 375, 376, 377, 378, 380, 381, 382, 383, 384, 385, 387, 422, 531, 568, 603, 607, 632, 636, 649, 650, 673, 686, 729, 763
GREAT DEPRESSION, 18, 57, 66, 97, 134, 144, 181, 185, 339, 498, 530, 618
GREATEST GENERATION, 40, 53, 55, 162, 315, 359, 431, 763
GREELEY, HORACE, 549, 729
GREEN REPORT, 16
GRIFFITH, D.W., 375, 376, 639
GÜNTHER, HANS, 83
HAECKEL, ERNST, 107, 108, 199, 253, 255, 256, 265, 290, 373, 400, 401, 402, 403, 406, 410, 435, 478, 501, 536, 543, 552, 557, 559, 560, 561, 563, 572, 573, 576, 581, 623, 634, 654, 656, 657, 658, 659, 660, 661, 676, 677, 678, 682, 684, 688, 690, 699, 703, 704, 705, 706, 707, 708, 709, 710, 711, 712, 713, 719, 723, 728, 763
HAISELDEN, HARRY J., 360, 403, 404, 405, 408, 409, 410, 411, 412, 413, 417, 418
HAMANN, BRIGITTE, 270, 289, 398, 399, 400, 547, 548, 551
HANDLIN, OSCAR, 49, 303
HANFSTAENGL, ERNST, 197, 202, 204, 275, 276, 297, 299, 300, 319
HARDY-WINEBERG PRINCIPLE, 457, 459, 460
HARMSEN, HANS, 99, 230, 339, 340, 762
HARVARD, 34, 44, 59, 62, 63, 64, 85, 86, 127, 130, 132, 183, 205, 229, 237, 249, 253, 274, 276, 285, 291, 297, 301, 319, 329, 334, 359, 360, 361, 372, 403, 452, 531, 553, 567, 599, 602, 603, 605, 606, 607, 608, 634, 636, 649, 717, 763
HEALTH RACE AND GERMAN POLITICS (BOOK), 367, 369, 371, 372, 373, 380,

411, 453, 455, 479, 480, 481, 536, 557, 558, 560, 562, 572, 573, 574, 575, 576, 577, 578, 658, 659, 660, 661
HEIDELBERG UNIVERSITY, 48
HEREDITARY GENIUS, 156, 318, 357, 434, 639, 678, 682, 699, 702, 703
HEREDITARY HEALTH COURTS, 82, 227 (SEE ALSO: EUGENIC COURTS)
HEYDRICH, REINHARD, 76, 77, 474
HIMMLER, HEINRICH, 81, 171, 178, 220, 263, 337, 480, 482, 483, 501, 535, 551, 582
HIPPOCRATIC OATH, 25, 73, 108, 165, 345, 348, 350, 409, 443, 626
HITLER YOUTH, 174, 260, 288, 345, 480, 481, 505, 541, 542, 626
HOCHE, ALFRED, 343, 346, 353, 355, 356, 359, 404, 435, 438, 712, 754, 763
HOCHMAN, ELAINE S., 115, 119, 170, 182, 183, 184, 185, 203
HOOTON, EARNEST, 17, 261, 384
HOTTENTOT VENUS, 650
HOUSE COMMITTEE ON IMMIGRATION, 48, 49, 162, 302, 303, 304, 305, 382
HUDLOW, RAYMOND, 53, 54, 55, 56, 155
HULL, CORDELL, 47, 48, 49, 50, 51, 52, 81, 301, 316, 382, 518, 765
HUMAN BETTERMENT FOUNDATION, 60, 62, 65, 85, 86, 95, 152, 391, 393, 606, 608, 610
HUMAN EXPERIMENTATION, 14, 15, 16, 33, 68, 72, 759
HUXLEY, ALDOUS, 208, 210, 214, 215, 472, 766
HUXLEY, JULIAN, 11, 12, 13, 33, 48, 60, 73, 88, 90, 91, 92, 93, 109, 126, 199, 208, 209, 214, 215, 258, 261, 283, 310, 330, 334, 356, 380, 386, 439, 501, 599, 610, 621
HUXLEY, T.H., 126, 208, 309, 386, 402, 501, 502, 506, 512, 593, 594, 595, 596, 597, 598, 676, 680, 688, 690, 706, 707, 710, 715, 744
ICARIANS, 576, 577, 617
IDEAL STATE (CONCEPT), 224, 329, 448, 464, 465, 471, 472
IMAGINARY WITNESS (FILM), 39, 42
IMMIGRATION AND NATIONALITY ACT OF 1952, 301, 302
IMMIGRATION COMMISSION. SEE CONGRESSIONAL REPORT
IMMIGRATION RESTRICTION ACT, 21, 48, 51, 81, 123, 195, 301, 308, 309, 376, 382, 518, 608
IMMIGRATION RESTRICTION LEAGUE, 49, 301, 302, 304, 307, 606, 607, 608, 610, 649
INALIENABLE RIGHTS, 131
INDIVIDUAL LIBERTY, 314
INSTRUMENT FOR THE COMMON GOVERNMENT, 310, 312, 314
INTERNATIONAL EUGENICS CONGRESS, 90, 427, 532, 534
INTERNATIONAL FEDERATION OF EUGENIC ORGANIZATIONS, 59, 60, 225, 763
INTERNATIONAL JEW, 277, 278, 281, 282, 283, 319, 326, 327, 329, 485
INTERNATIONAL SOCIALISM, 224, 279, 370, 516, 705
INTO THE DARKNESS (BOOK), 81
IRON CURTAIN, 5, 7, 8, 25, 27, 41, 491

IVANOV, ILYA, 250
IVY LEAGUE, 94, 301, 329, 332, 334, 375, 376, 382, 387, 567, 597, 606, 607, 608, 609, 610, 611, 637
IVY, ANDREW, 16
IVY, ANDREW C., 14, 17, 374
JACKSON, ROBERT, 27, 760
JACOBSON V. MASSACHUSETTS, 238, 239, 240
JENNINGS BRYAN, WILLIAM, 294, 295, 360, 657
JESUIT, 198
JIM CROW, 530, 569, 570, 685
JOHNSON, ALBERT, 301, 304, 305
JUKES, 130, 318, 656, 673
JURISDICTION, 25, 26, 47, 164, 178, 242, 245, 248, 340, 464, 465, 632, 671, 740, 741
KAISER WILHELM INSTITUTE, 18, 24, 34, 69, 71, 130, 166, 199, 225, 227, 228, 252, 373, 453, 455, 535, 764
KANTSAYWHERE, 126, 309, 440, 442, 443, 444, 445, 446, 447, 448, 560, 700, 703
KATZEN-ELLENBOGEN, EDWIN, 44, 45, 86, 607
KAUFMANN, DORIS, 227, 228, 456, 763, 764, 765
KELLER, HELEN, 63, 285, 335, 336, 360, 405, 406, 409, 412, 477, 486, 628
KENNEDY, FOSTER, 72, 73
KEYNES, JOHN MAYNARD, 60, 61, 285, 334, 417, 428, 434, 507, 514, 534, 620, 628
KING, MARTIN LUTHER, JR., 98, 217, 331, 675, 733, 750
KRISTALLNACHT, 49, 50, 53, 67, 100, 101, 150, 389
KU KLUX KLAN, 78, 94, 268, 340, 375, 376, 567
KUBIZEK, AUGUST, 275, 277, 290, 398, 462, 463, 465, 475, 478, 484, 741
KÜHL, STEFAN, 59, 60, 82, 86, 87, 122, 163, 381, 384, 633
KULTURKAMPF, 197, 657
LAISSEZ-FAIRE, 102, 134, 143, 164, 173, 376, 378, 419, 508, 509, 510, 511, 513, 514, 516, 521, 540, 556, 610, 615, 658, 705, 742, 743, 746
LAND OF POETS AND THINKERS (CONCEPT), 8, 38, 182
LANDSBERG, 193, 268, 283, 286, 297, 299, 300, 317, 319, 326, 329, 343, 371, 438, 447, 455, 485, 489, 496
LAUGHLIN, HARRY H., 4, 19, 34, 48, 49, 58, 59, 60, 61, 66, 67, 77, 81, 82, 83, 89, 105, 109, 120, 121, 123, 125, 126, 127, 129, 132, 141, 151, 152, 153, 157, 158, 159, 161, 163, 164, 195, 196, 225, 226, 227, 237, 238, 244, 245, 247, 248, 264, 265, 283, 286, 290, 292, 296, 302, 304, 305, 306, 307, 308, 309, 310, 311, 312, 313, 314, 315, 316, 318, 320, 330, 333, 334, 343, 344, 347, 356, 358, 359, 363, 376, 382, 384, 385, 387, 388, 389, 390, 391, 412, 428, 432, 439, 448, 452, 458, 459, 460, 503, 514, 519, 555, 560, 601, 608, 609, 632, 655, 656, 729, 743, 752, 753, 763
LEAGUE OF NATIONS, 11, 28, 134, 145, 343
LEBENSBORN, 69, 263, 480, 482, 483, 484, 551

LEBENSRAUM, 77, 110, 235, 269, 401, 479, 581, 623
LEBENSREFORM, 117, 171, 234, 255, 479, 573, 574, 575, 582
LEGACY OF MALTHUS (BOOK), 153, 157, 301, 302, 315, 435, 599, 636, 638, 685, 701, 742, 743
LEHMANN, J.F., 106, 276, 284, 319, 366, 369, 370, 371, 380, 381, 485, 632, 763
LEMKIN, RAPHAEL, 28
LENIN, VLADIMIR, 40, 78, 223, 235, 250, 268, 286, 441, 472, 516, 615, 666, 712
LENZ, FRITZ, 66, 70, 81, 83, 105, 129, 290, 317, 318, 319, 320, 329, 330, 343, 366, 369, 371, 372, 380, 381, 384, 453, 496, 562, 570, 571, 581, 631, 632, 687, 754, 762
LIFE UNWORTHY OF LIFE, 30, 256, 344, 352, 353, 439
LINCOLN, ABRAHAM, 76, 122, 123, 268, 269, 276, 396, 531, 553, 565, 566, 603, 631, 733, 737, 747, 748, 749, 750
LINDBERG, CHARLES, 21
LINDBERGH, CHARLES, 11, 150, 151, 486
LIVES NOT WORTH LIVING (CONCEPT), 72
LOMBARDO, PAUL, 125, 229, 248, 320, 433, 753, 754, 760
LOOKING BACKWARD (BOOK), 135, 136, 139, 143, 146, 190, 191, 214, 272, 357, 494, 495, 502, 558, 578, 615, 616, 617, 618, 619, 620, 621, 622, 734
LUDENDORFF, 197, 198, 297, 481, 491, 657, 697
LYELL, CHARLES, 676, 679, 688, 690, 720
MADAGASCAR PLAN, 77
MALTHUS, 153, 441, 470, 505, 511, 685, 700, 724, 725, 726, 727, 728, 772
MAN OF THE YEAR (TIME), 100
MANKIND QUARTERLY (PUB.), 43, 535
MARQUIS DE SADE, 468
MARX, KARL, 136, 143, 147, 190, 224, 270, 272, 278, 331, 363, 509, 511, 557, 558, 580, 615, 617, 643, 644, 694, 697, 723, 724, 725, 726, 727, 728
MASTER RACE (CONCEPT), 7, 31, 93, 150, 170, 217, 225, 260, 263, 286, 345, 346, 349, 389, 391, 425, 542, 548, 557, 697, 731, 733, 737, 748
MAX-PLANCK INSTITUTE, 229, 456
MEGALOMANIA, 118, 624
MEIN KAMPF (BOOK), 26, 66, 88, 106, 113, 114, 136, 169, 182, 244, 268, 269, 277, 278, 279, 280, 283, 284, 285, 286, 287, 288, 290, 291, 299, 309, 319, 326, 330, 343, 356, 359, 366, 370, 460, 485, 486, 489, 491, 493, 496, 505, 550, 588, 589, 632, 705, 711, 712, 748, 762
MEN LIKE GODS (BOOK), 208, 214, 502
MENDEL, GREGOR, 128, 318, 421, 422, 423, 424, 425, 460, 461, 592, 628, 661, 687, 688, 690, 691, 693, 694, 700, 721, 722
MENGELE, JOSEF, 23, 34, 68, 69, 71, 228, 229, 373, 454, 564, 581, 729, 754, 762
MENTAL DEFICIENCY ACT, 22, 225, 258, 266, 285, 426, 432, 434
MENTAL TESTING, 303
MERCHANTS OF LIGHT, 57, 68
MERCY KILLING, 30, 72, 79

MERRIAM, JOHN C., 59, 125, 380, 382, 384, 458
METHODIST, 197, 361, 376, 636
MEYERSON, ABRAHAM, 127
MISCEGENATION, 317, 533, 569, 570, 628, 629, 630, 631, 632, 673, 746, 747, 748
MISSING LINK, 252, 661, 676, 678, 707
MODEL EUGENIC LAW, 49, 152, 237, 244, 247, 264, 318, *SEE* MODEL LAW
MODEL LAW, 30, 66, 225, 244, 247, 248
MONIST, 557, 581, 710, 711, 712
MONKEY TRIAL (SCOPES), 291, 294, 360, 361, 365, 405, 656, 719
MORGENTHAU, HENRY JR., 46, 48, 50, 51, 52, 53, 739
MUSSOLINI, 70, 102, 191, 202, 268, 279, 284, 298, 317, 450, 477, 515, 517, 521, 522, 523, 524, 525, 528
MYERSON, ABRAHAM, 127, 129, 636
NAACP, 98, 375, 553, 555, 685
NATIONAL ACADEMY OF SCIENCES, 16, 88, 385
NATIONAL ORIGINS ACT, 301
NATIONAL RESEARCH COUNCIL, 16, 17, 253, 374
NATIONALIST CLUBS, 136, 406, 495, 496, 578
NATIVE AMERICANS, 55, 248, 408, 654, 666, 667, 668, 669, 671, 672, 674, 675
NATURAL SELECTION, 11, 91, 107, 260, 287, 501, 512, 532, 542, 544, 546, 559, 573, 635, 676, 682, 684, 699, 700, 715, 719, 720, 727, 745
NAZI CONNECTION (BOOK), 59, 61, 82, 83, 86, 87, 110, 120, 121, 122, 125, 152, 163, 213, 244, 317, 381, 384, 385, 632, 633
NAZI WAR ON CANCER (BOOK), 78, 79, 164, 165, 166, 168, 169, 170, 171, 173, 174, 175, 176, 177, 178, 179, 477
NEED FOR EUGENIC REFORM (BOOK), 173, 256, 257, 258, 259, 260, 261, 262, 263, 264, 265, 357, 536, 674
NEGATIVE LIBERTIES, 191, 192
NEGRO PROJECT, 94, 97, 98, 100, 331, 456, 554
NEW ARYAN MAN, 78, 113, 117
NEW DEAL, 134, 135, 137, 138, 139, 140, 142, 207, 233, 285, 291, 517
NEW ETHIC (CONCEPT), 429, 543, 547, 548, 549, 550, 552, 659, 710
NEW JERSEY, 44, 45, 86, 121, 139, 285, 382, 531, 628
NEW YORK TIMES, 52, 88, 142, 251, 364, 405, 408, 413, 425, 427, 450, 451, 496, 531, 645
NIEMÖLLER, FRIEDRICH GUSTAV EMIL MARTIN, 84, 102, 200, 201
NIETZSCHE, FRIEDRICH, 93, 286, 290, 319, 337, 338, 340, 345, 346, 347, 348, 349, 350, 351, 352, 353, 354, 355, 357, 359, 435, 462, 477, 501, 541, 542, 548, 552, 562, 572, 577, 591, 622, 623, 624, 625, 626, 627, 712, 762, 763
NOBEL PRIZE, 67, 145, 150, 410, 426, 435, 697
NORDAU, MAX, 171, 357, 544, 585, 586, 587, 588, 589, 748
NORDIC, 83, 108, 122, 123, 182, 183, 196, 205, 234, 269, 275, 277, 302, 367,

372, 380, 381, 389, 478, 479, 491, 492, 497, 560, 563, 573, 578, 748
NORTH CAROLINA, 28, 65, 98, 117, 180, 181, 182, 184, 185, 186, 348, 376, 415, 554, 555, 556, 616, 619, 633, 637, 657, 658, 659, 661
NORWAY, 232, 233, 309, 483, 524
NOYES, JOHN HUMPHREY, 507, 639, 640, 641, 642, 643, 644, 645, 647, 693, 723
NUREMBERG CODE, 8, 9, 14, 16, 30, 165, 339, 420
NUREMBERG LAWS, 69, 120, 121, 145, 227, 318, 482, 532, 570, 571, 601, 705
NUREMBERG TRIBUNAL, 103, 227, 229, 356, 535
O'KEEFE, THEODORE J., 81, 82
ONEIDA, 507, 617, 639, 640, 641, 642, 645, 648
ORGANIC GARDEN, 178, 482
ORWELL, GEORGE, 11, 89, 90, 210, 212, 260, 261, 472, 474, 622
OVERMAN, 286, 347, 626
OVERY, RICHARD, 26, 27
PALMER RAIDS, 362
PASSING OF THE GREAT RACE (BOOK), 63, 163, 301, 302, 375, 376, 377, 378, 379, 380, 381, 383, 384, 531
PAUL, RANDOLPH, 46, 47
PEARL, RAYMOND, 60, 157, 334, 384, 405, 425
PELLAGRA, 636, 637, 638
PERNICK, MARTIN S., 121, 403, 404, 407, 408, 409, 410, 412, 413, 417, 418
PIONEER FUND, 19, 120, 384, 532, 533, 606, 607, 608
PIVOT OF CIVILIZATION (BOOK), 85, 96, 97, 331, 332, 333, 334, 335, 337, 338, 340
PLANNED PARENTHOOD, 11, 60, 62, 94, 98, 99, 230, 240, 331, 339, 340, 406, 540, 554, 608, 763
PLATO, 67, 146, 209, 349, 353, 354, 448, 576, 645, 646
PLEDGE OF ALLEGIANCE, 135
PLESSY V. FERGUSON, 564, 567, 568, 569, 570, 670
PLOETZ, ALFRED, 58, 59, 66, 67, 105, 106, 109, 118, 225, 235, 244, 265, 290, 309, 310, 315, 320, 329, 330, 358, 368, 369, 370, 371, 372, 380, 381, 406, 410, 411, 439, 453, 479, 519, 557, 558, 562, 571, 572, 573, 575, 576, 577, 578, 579, 580, 581, 582, 601, 617, 639, 660, 681, 687, 704, 712, 729, 753, 754, 762, 763
POE V. LYNCHBURG, 241, 242, 247
POLYGENESIS, 679, 716, 717, 718
POPENOE, PAUL, 61
POPULATION CONTROL, 48, 63, 86, 99, 315, 393, 441, 470, 505, 507, 723, 724
PRECAUTIONARY PRINCIPLE, 172
PRINCETON, 60, 78, 79, 86, 130, 147, 164, 165, 166, 168, 169, 170, 171, 173, 174, 175, 176, 177, 178, 179, 285, 307, 382, 452, 477, 532, 608, 652, 742, 750
PRO FAMILIA (ORG.), 99, 339, 340
PROCTOR, ROBERT, 21, 71, 164, 165, 166, 168, 170, 171, 173, 174, 176, 177, 179, 477, 569
PROHIBITION, 134, 168, 259, 343, 417

PROLEGOMENA, 126, 309, 593, 594, 596, 597, 598, 599
PROSS, CHRISTIAN, 8, 9, 339, 421
PROTOCOLS OF ZION (BOOK), 327
QUOTAS, 50, 51, 302, 303
RABBI WISE, STEPHEN SAMUEL, 51, 52
RACIAL HYGIENE, 23, 33, 34, 48, 59, 66, 70, 71, 106, 118, 149, 166, 167, 168, 169, 173, 175, 199, 225, 226, 231, 265, 276, 310, 315, 318, 340, 367, 370, 376, 436, 480, 508, 519, 569, 571, 574, 577, 578, 660, 754, 757, 759, 760, 762, 763, 765
RACIAL POISONS, 259
RACIAL STATE, 29, 48, 66, 67, 69, 78, 81, 85, 217, 227, 331, 551, 710
RACIALIST, 81, 269, 273, 302, 336, 381, 382, 384, 385, 389, 390, 407, 459, 460, 546, 549, 556, 563, 567, 568, 623, 624, 672, 681, 684, 685, 687, 706, 713, 718, 719, 734
RAND, AYN, 466, 510, 540, 552
RASSENHYGIENE, 66, 317, 447, 571, 581, 632
RAUSCHNING, HERMANN, 218, 219
REHOBOTHER BASTARDS, 318
REICHSTAG, 66, 118, 186, 192, 193, 194, 200, 201, 270, 298, 656
REIGNER, GERHARDT, 51
REVOLUTIONS OF 1848, 302, 397, 400, 738, 742, 750
ROCKEFELLER, 18, 34, 45, 49, 60, 66, 92, 121, 124, 125, 127, 147, 229, 230, 241, 283, 362, 364, 365, 371, 372, 373, 374, 412, 450, 452, 453, 456, 457, 540, 608, 666, 762, 763, 765
ROE V. WADE, 64, 240, 241
ROOSEVELT, THEODORE, 137, 269, 276, 285, 301, 376, 380, 382, 414, 417, 451, 474, 515, 528, 545, 567, 602, 603, 605, 606, 607, 656, 675
ROSENBERG, ALFRED, 109, 110, 183, 184, 188, 197, 198, 199, 384, 439, 486, 491, 494, 519, 563, 584, 687, 712, 753
ROYAL SOCIETY, 382, 385, 386, 501, 584, 653, 692, 706, 715, 718
RÜDIN, ERNST, 109
RUMMEL, R.J., 548
RYBACK, TIMOTHY W., 485
SANGER, MARGARET, 58, 60, 63, 65, 85, 94, 97, 98, 100, 124, 160, 226, 230, 286, 331, 333, 334, 335, 336, 337, 338, 339, 340, 360, 361, 362, 363, 406, 441, 456, 477, 486, 520, 528, 540, 554, 555, 556, 597, 673, 683, 763
SCANDINAVIA, 23, 226, 232, 233, 234, 235, 264, 277, 286, 519
SCHALLMAYER, WILHELM, 310, 330, 439, 479, 519, 557, 558, 560, 563, 564, 574, 581, 711, 753, 754
SCHECHTER POULTRY CORP. V. UNITED STATES, 140
SCHLEIERMACHER, SABSTE, 99
SCHMIDT, ULF, 14, 31, 109, 110, 438
SCHWEITZER, ALBERT, 435, 436, 437, 438, 659
SCIENTIFIC RACISM, 147, 284, 380, 456, 547, 568, 609, 611, 634, 661, 679, 684, 728
SCOPES' MONKEY TRIAL, 293, 360, 378, 657

SELF-SELECTION (CONCEPT), 552, 559, 631
SHUTESBURY, 162, 163, 433
<u>SKINNER V. OKLAHOMA</u>, 55, 240, 760
SLAVERY, 136, 212, 314, 321, 355, 361, 532, 533, 553, 569, 603, 604, 630, 631, 650, 669, 674, 679, 680, 701, 703, 716, 717, 723, 728, 731, 732, 733, 734, 735, 736, 737, 738, 742, 746, 747, 748
SOCIAL BODY, 187, 245, 344, 419, 443, 444, 472, 615
SOCIAL DARWINISM, 225, 270, 501, 593, 598
SPANISH INQUISITION, 39, 69, 87, 517, 682, 720
SPEECHES OF ADOLF HITLER (BOOK), 142, 186, 187, 188, 189, 192, 321, 322, 323, 324, 325, 326, 327, 328
SPEER, ALBERT, 109, 115, 118, 171, 174, 175, 176, 183, 207, 290, 326, 356, 439, 468, 474, 475, 487, 493, 522, 551, 563, 753
STALIN, 22, 26, 40, 41, 42, 76, 78, 88, 91, 101, 102, 161, 191, 213, 223, 224, 249, 250, 252, 286, 441, 471, 491, 515, 516, 524, 548, 639
STANFORD UNIV., 61, 63, 64, 130, 132, 148, 229, 291, 292, 301, 313, 330, 359, 387, 388, 389, 394, 487, 607, 608, 634, 763
STARK, HANS, 338, 348
STATE DEPARTMENT, UNITED STATES, 46, 47, 48, 49, 50, 51, 52, 53, 754
STODDARD, LOTHROP, 60, 61, 81, 82, 83, 84, 85, 87, 96, 98, 109, 159, 227, 228, 334, 380, 603, 606, 628
STRENGTH THROUGH JOY, 116
SUBSEQUENT NUREMBERG TRIALS, 27
SUPREME COURT - UNITED STATES, 14, 17, 20, 22, 27, 29, 34, 36, 49, 54, 55, 61, 64, 82, 83, 132, 139, 140, 141, 142, 149, 152, 229, 237, 238, 239, 240, 241, 244, 245, 248, 249, 293, 320, 332, 362, 418, 432, 434, 459, 520, 531, 555, 564, 565, 566, 568, 569, 570, 584, 628, 629, 630, 631,632, 634, 639, 670, 671, 672, 674, 736, 753, 758, 760
T4 EUTHANASIA, 29, 69, 72, 76, 79, 80, 244, 329, 352, 355, 356, 418, 420, 435, 455, 551, 562
TALENTED TENTH, 553, 554, 555, 556, 580
TAYLOR, TELFORD, 16, 17, 21, 27, 755, 756, 757, 759
THANATOLOGY, 31, 32, 33, 760
THEORY OF EVOLUTION, 255, 265, 377, 386, 423, 435, 440, 459, 561, 592, 593, 603, 658, 664, 675, 677, 678, 689, 703, 704, 708, 722, 744
THEOSOPHY, 235, 335, 336, 337, 406, 477, 486, 494, 496, 497, 547, 573, 618, 705
THIRD WAY (POLITICAL), 134, 137, 191, 324, 331, 515, 726
THREE-PANEL COURTS, 20, 83, 98, 152, 153, 227, 238, 243, 244, 358 (SEE ALSO: EUGENIC COURTS)
THULE SOCIETY, 368, 369, 402, 485, 486, 496
TIME MAGAZINE, 100, 101, 102, 114, 256, 257, 451

TOTAL STATE (CONCEPT), 118, 164
TRIUMPH OF THE WILL, (FILM), 144, 145, 174, 207, 474, 587
TRUMAN UNIVERSITY, 59, 126, 163, 195, 196, 308, 310, 311, 312, 313, 314, 334
TUSKEGEE EXPERIMENTS, 15
TVA (TENN. VALLEY AUTHORITY), 135, 138, 143
U.S. CONSTITUTION, 134, 160, 190, 237, 311, 315, 343, 418, 566, 628, 634, 741
UNESCO, 11, 12, 13, 33, 48, 88, 92, 208, 310
UNITED NATIONS, 11, 12, 13, 25, 47
UNITED STATES CONGRESS, 34, 306, 343, 459, 754
UNITY OF PURPOSE, 80, 108, 189, 192, 217, 400, 472, 509, 710, 743
USELESS EATERS (CONCEPT), 30, 76, 80, 174, 256, 352, 728, 758
USSR, 5, 8, 11, 21, 25, 27, 41, 89, 224, 277, 471, 506, 515, 619
UTOPIA, 117, 118, 138, 191, 208, 209, 214, 283, 448, 479, 494, 502, 504, 576, 581, 597, 616, 617, 618, 619, 620
VAMPIRE ECONOMY, 220, 521
VAN DER ROHE, MIES, 115, 182, 184, 203, 207
VEGETARIANISM, 175, 176, 177, 469, 477, 479, 489, 574
VIENNA, 67, 71, 116, 119, 168, 216, 270, 272, 289, 370, 398, 399, 400, 450, 461, 464, 465, 484, 489, 496, 497, 544, 546, 547, 662, 742, 743
VIRCHOW, RUDOLF, 252, 345, 435, 439, 447, 536, 656, 657, 658, 659, 660, 661, 707, 708, 719, 728
VIRCHOW, RUDOLPH, 656
VOLKSWAGEN, 116, 117, 279
VON HUMBOLDT, ALEXANDER, 435, 439, 659
VON VERSCHUER, OTMAR, 70, 581
VORSORGEPRINZIP, 172, 173
WAGNER, RICHARD, 177, 181, 474, 476, 477, 489, 548, 591, 624, 628
WALLACE, ALFRED RUSSEL, 592, 661, 693, 720
WANNSEE CONFERENCE, 72, 76, 77, 78, 79, 330
WAR CRIMES TRIBUNAL, 27
WEDGEWOOD, JOSIAH, 428, 429, 533, 534, 537, 691
WEDGWOOD, JOSIAH, 426, 428, 429, 430, 432, 433, 434, 533, 548, 701
WEIKART, RICHARD, 254, 255, 265, 434, 542, 549, 711
WEINDLING, PAUL, 370, 371, 411, 479, 573, 658
WEISS, SHEILA FAITH, 558, 559, 563
WELFARE STATE, 61, 233, 599, 668
WELLS, H.G., 21, 60, 67, 73, 85, 89, 117, 126, 160, 208, 209, 210, 211, 214, 215, 283, 286, 290, 291, 309, 315, 316, 332, 334, 347, 378, 385, 386, 405, 420, 427, 439, 448, 462, 501, 502, 503, 504, 505, 511, 512, 513, 514, 549, 560, 594, 595, 597, 615, 620, 621, 622, 634, 648, 655
WENDELL HOLMES, JR., OLIVER, 153, 237, 238, 249, 428, 432, 433, 520, 531, 606, 611, 758
WHEN MEDICINE WENT MAD (BOOK), 15, 21, 23, 33, 34, 69, 70, 71, 105, 169, 170,

570
WHITE MAN'S BURDEN, 735
WHITE SUPREMACY, 451, 630
WILL TO POWER (BOOK), 346, 347, 348, 349, 351, 357

WORLD WILDLIFE FUND, 11, 89, 608
YALE, 19, 132, 222, 229, 285, 291, 301, 307, 329, 334, 383, 417, 452, 476, 532, 567, 569, 607, 610, 611, 634, 639, 763